ABRAHAM LINCO

Abraham Lincoln

A Life

VOLUME TWO

Michael Burlingame

The Johns Hopkins University Press
Baltimore

Johns Hopkins Paperback edition, 2013
9 8 7 6 5 4 3 2 1

The Johns Hopkins University Press
2715 North Charles Street
Baltimore, Maryland 21218-4363
www.press.jhu.edu

The Library of Congress has cataloged the hardcover edition of this book as follows:

Burlingame, Michael, 1941–
  Abraham Lincoln : a life / Michael Burlingame.
    p. cm.
  Includes bibliographical references and index.
  ISBN-13: 978-0-8018-8993-6 (hardcover: alk. paper)
  ISBN-10: 0-8018-8993-6 (hardcover: alk. paper)
    1. Lincoln, Abraham, 1809–1865.   2. Presidents—United States—
  Biography.   I. Title
  E457.B95   2008
  973.7092—dc22
  [B]   2007052919

A catalog record for this book is available from the British Library.

ISBN-13: 978-1-4214-1058-6
ISBN-10: 1-4214-1058-3

Special discounts are available for bulk purchases of this book. For more information,
please contact Special Sales at 410-516-6936 or specialsales@press.jhu.edu.

The Johns Hopkins University Press uses environmentally friendly book
materials, including recycled text paper that is composed of at least 30 percent
post-consumer waste, whenever possible.

For Lewis E. Lehrman, Lincolnian extraordinaire

CONTENTS

Illustrations follow pages 270 and 558

ABRAHAM LINCOLN

"The Man Does Not Live Who Is More Devoted to Peace Than I Am, But It May Be Necessary to Put the Foot Down Firmly"
From Springfield to Washington
(February 11–22, 1861)

The ever-obliging Lincoln agreed to undertake a taxing, circuitous, 1,900-mile train journey from Springfield to Washington in order to accommodate Republican friends in various states where they wanted him to speak. There were obvious drawbacks: the trip would be tiring, he would be exposed to potential assassins, and such a journey would not suit Lincoln's taste for simplicity and aversion to any form of pomp. More-over, though he would have to speak often, he could say little, for he wished to post-pone until the inauguration any mention of his policy regarding the swiftly evolving secession crisis. Because the journey would be indirect—Indianapolis, Cincinnati, Columbus, and Pittsburgh, then a detour through Cleveland, Buffalo, Albany, New York, Trenton, Philadelphia, and Harrisburg—it would consume twelve days. To demonstrate his indifference to assassination threats, Lincoln would have preferred a more direct route than the roundabout one finally selected. (John W. Garrett, presi-dent of the Baltimore and Ohio Railroad, said that Lincoln "abandoned the idea of coming to Washington via Wheeling [Virginia], in consequence of certain alleged threats of violence from parties in Virginia and Maryland.")[1]

These considerations did not deter Lincoln, for he believed that official invita-tions from state legislatures could not be ignored. John Hay, perhaps reflecting Lin-coln's thoughts, offered another reason for his decision: "The progress of the President elect cannot but be fortunate in its influence upon the tone of public feeling in the Union. The devotion which men in general feel for their government is a rather vague and shadowy emotion. This will be intensified, and will receive form and coloring, by personal interviews of the people themselves with their constitutional head."[2] The trip would also divert attention from the secession crisis and might enhance Lincoln's legitimacy if huge crowds turned out to welcome him. "It is important to allow full scope to the enthusiasm of the people just now," Salmon P. Chase told Lincoln upon learning of his proposed itinerary.[3]

Other concerns doubtless influenced Lincoln as he pondered whether to take a long, slow journey to the nation's capital. In selecting a cabinet, he told Thurlow

Weed, he "had been much embarrassed" by "his want of acquaintance with the prominent men of the day."[4] The train trip would allow him to consult with Republican leaders outside Illinois about patronage and policy matters. Moreover, he might inspire the people he addressed in Indiana, Ohio, Pennsylvania, New Jersey, and New York with the same kind of confidence that he had generated among juries and voters in the Prairie State. Lincoln understood that those who elected him were eager to see what he looked like, and he was willing to satisfy their curiosity.

Originally, Lincoln had intended to have his wife and younger sons join him in New York for only the final leg of the trip. He evidently wanted to spare them the fatigue of the longer journey. On February 9, he changed plans because General Scott advised that his wife's "absence from the train might be regarded as proceeding from an apprehension of danger to the President."[5] This must have pleased Mary Lincoln, who was eager to accompany her husband. At the last minute, however, the plan was again altered, for reasons that are not entirely clear, and Mrs. Lincoln was not aboard when the train left Springfield. (She joined it at Indianapolis the next day.)

En route from the Illinois capital to the U.S. capital, Lincoln ended months of public silence with a flurry of speeches foreshadowing his eagerly awaited inaugural address. But as his train zigged and zagged its way eastward over the tracks of two dozen different railroads, his rhetoric seemed to zig and zag between confrontation and conciliation. Was he a hawk or a dove? Some days he seemed to be the former, other days the latter.

The Trip Begins

The train consisted of three ordinary coaches and a baggage car; Lincoln occupied the rear car. The entourage included his eldest son, Robert, and his two secretaries (John G. Nicolay and John Hay), as well as journalists, political allies, and friends. For protection, a military escort was arranged, but to avoid a bellicose appearance, some of its members joined the party later. Among those guarding the president-elect were army officers who volunteered for that duty while on leave, including Colonel Edwin V. Sumner, Captain John Pope, Captain William B. Hazen, Major David Hunter, and Captain George Whitfield Hazzard. Assisting them were James M. Burgess, whom the governor of Wisconsin detailed to Springfield as a bodyguard; Thomas Mather, adjutant general of Illinois; Ward Hill Lamon, Lincoln's burly colleague at the bar and close personal friend; and Elmer E. Ellsworth, a young militia leader who had achieved national renown and was a surrogate son to Lincoln. The president-elect denied the necessity for such an escort, insisting that "there was no danger whatsoever."[6] He wanted to avoid appearing as though he traveled under guard.

In charge of travel arrangements was William S. Wood, a one-time jeweler and hotel manager who came to Springfield in January 1861 at the suggestion of Seward, Weed, and their friend Erastus Corning, a railroad manager, prominent New York Democrat, and relative of Wood. Seward claimed that Wood had had vast experience with railroads, had organized long excursions, and knew many railroad officials. Wood was handsome, self-important, and condescending. On the trip he paid close attention "to the whims and caprices of Mrs. Lincoln."[7] (She could be difficult on trains. Returning from a shopping trip to New York earlier that winter, she used free passes on each leg of the journey. In Buffalo, she found herself without a pass for one stretch and indignantly protested when she was asked to pay. Her son Robert appealed to the superintendent of that company: "the old woman is in the cars raising h—l about her passes—I wish you would go and attend to her!")[8]

As the train rolled eastward on the morning of February 11, Lincoln took a pencil and on a large pad wrote out a speech that he was to deliver in Indianapolis later that day. As he filled the sheets, his secretaries took them and made copies. John Hay reported that "[s]omething of the gloom of parting with neighbors and friends, bidding farewell to the community in the midst of which he has lived for a quarter of a century," seemed to affect him. "He was abstracted, sad, thoughtful, and spent much of his time in the private car appropriated to his use."[9] Lifting his spirits briefly were large crowds cheering him vociferously as the train passed through hamlets like Cerro Gordo, Sadorous, and Iresdale. At Decatur, thousands had gathered to pay him honor. When he descended from the train, they insisted on shaking his hand, embracing him, and showering him with blessings. At the second stop (in Tolono), the crowd badgered him into giving a speech, which amounted to little more than a polite acknowledgment of their warm welcome. Their response was as intensely wild as if he had read them his inaugural address. The brakeman on the train found it "soul stirring to see these white whiskered old fellows, many of whom had known Lincoln in his humbler days, join in the cheering."[10]

And so it went for the next twelve days. As Nicolay recalled, it "is hard for anyone who has not had the chance of personal observation to realize the mingled excitement and apprehension, elation and fatigue which Mr. Lincoln and his suite underwent, almost without intermission for the period of nearly two weeks during this memorable trip."[11] Hay recollected that there "was something of religious fervor in the welcome everywhere extended to him, and the thronging crowds that came out under the harsh skies to bid him God-speed."[12] Repeatedly Lincoln ascribed such enthusiasm to the office he would soon occupy and to the nation he would lead rather than to himself personally. If the crowds were impressed, Henry Villard was not. "Lincoln always had an embarrassed air" on such occasions and he resembled "a country clodhopper appearing in fashionable society, and was nearly always stiff and unhappy in his off-hand remarks," Villard wrote.[13]

At each stop, enthusiastic committees greeted Lincoln on behalf of legislatures, governors, Wide Awakes, workingmen's clubs, and many other organizations, each one anxious to shake hands, deliver speeches, extend invitations, and exchange stories. Lincoln's friends, concerned for his safety and comfort, grew alarmed when he submitted himself to the mercy of these well-meaning but often inept committeemen. The resulting confusion was dangerous, as Nicolay remembered: amid "the push and crush of these dense throngs of people, in this rushing of trains, clanging of bells, booming of guns, shouting and huzzas of individuals and crowds, it was difficult to instantly determine which call was the more important or more proper, and a false start might not only bring on an irretrievable waste of time and a derangement of official programmes and processions, but a false step even might bring danger to life or limb under wheels of locomotives or carriages." The impatient committees would occasionally "tumble pell-mell into a car and almost drag Mr. Lincoln out before the train had even stopped, and habitually, after stoppage, before the proper police or military guards could be stationed about a depot or stopping place to secure necessary space and order for a comfortable open path to the waiting carriages." For a while Lincoln "could not resist the popular importunings," for his "sympathy with and for the people made him shrink, not as a matter of reasoning but apparently upon some constitutional impulse, from any objection to or protest against the over eagerness and over officiousness of these first greetings." Only "after some days of experience and several incidents of discomfort" did he conquer that impulse, "but having mastered it he kept it for the remainder of the journey under perfect control, and would remain seated in his car until he received the notice agreed upon that preparations outside had been deliberately completed."[14]

Mary Lincoln also found the committees a trial. Halfway through the trip, Captain Hazzard, part of the military escort, reported that "Mr. & Mrs. Lincoln are worried almost out of their lives by visiters of both sexes. Every village sends a reception committee of twenty or thirty, and some of them bring their wives, so that not only are all the seats in the cars taken but the pass way is filled with people standing. Neither the President nor his wife have one moment's respite and they are evidently tired of it."[15] The Lincolns enjoyed little privacy outside their sleeping area, for people came and went at will.

At Lafayette, Indiana, Lincoln offended some listeners with his impromptu remark that "we are bound together, I trust[,] in Christianity, civilization, and patriotism."[16] Rabbi Isaac Mayer Wise of Cincinnati took umbrage: "We do not believe there is a German infidel, American eccentric, spiritual rapper or atheist in the northern states who did not vote for Mr. Lincoln. Let us see how much benefit he will derive from their Christianity."[17]

Hard-Line Speech in Indianapolis

That evening at Indianapolis, where a thirty-four-gun salute and thousands of vehemently hurrahing Hoosiers greeted him, Lincoln pleased stiff-backed opponents of appeasement with a startling preview of his inaugural address. He began his remarks, delivered from the balcony of the Bates House to an audience of 20,000, by analyzing the words "coercion" and "invasion." "Would the marching of an army into South Carolina, for instance, without the consent of her people, and in hostility against them, be coercion or invasion?" he asked. (Although he did not mention it, Lincoln may well have been thinking of George Washington's dispatch of 12,000 troops to crush the Pennsylvania Whiskey Rebellion in 1794.) Yes, he conceded, "it would be invasion, and it would be coercion too, if the people of that country were forced to submit." At the same time, if the federal government "simply insists upon holding its own forts, or retaking those forts which belong to it,—[cheers,]—or the enforcement of the laws of the United States in the collection of duties upon foreign importations,—[renewed cheers,]—or even the withdrawal of the mails from those portions of the country where the mails themselves are habitually violated; would any or all of these things be coercion? Do the lovers of the Union contend that they will resist coercion or invasion of any State, understanding that any or all of these would be coercing or invading a State? If they do, then it occurs to me that the means for the preservation of the Union they so greatly love, in their own estimation, is of a very thin and airy character. [Applause.]" If they became ill, "they would consider the little pills of the homoeopathist as already too large for them to swallow." They regarded the Union not "like a regular marriage at all, but only as a sort of free-love arrangement,—[laughter,]—to be maintained on what that sect calls passional attraction. [Continued laughter.]" (A Southern paper sarcastically queried, "Is not this a chaste and elevated comparison? Is it not on a level with the dignity of the subject?"[18] In later years, Lincoln might have likened secession to a no-fault divorce.)

Lincoln then asked: "By what principle of original right is it that one-fiftieth or one-ninetieth of a great nation, by calling themselves a State, have the right to break up and ruin that nation as a matter of original principle? Now, I ask the question—I am not deciding anything—[laughter,]—and with the request that you will think somewhat upon that subject and decide for yourselves, if you choose, when you get ready,—where is the mysterious, original right, from principle, for a certain district of country with inhabitants, by merely being called a State, to play tyrant over all its own citizens, and deny the authority of everything greater than itself. [Laughter.] I say I am deciding nothing, but simply giving something for you to reflect upon."[19]

This hard-line speech, though couched in mild terms, thrilled the crowd, which shouted: "That's the talk!" and "We've got a President now!" John Hay reported that Lincoln's delivery was as impressive as the substance of his remarks. His voice was "clear" and "sonorous," and his "colloquial" style "singularly effective." There was, Hay said, "something inspiring in the individual presence of the man. His manners are simple almost to naiveté; he has always a friendly, sometime a jocose word for those who approach him; but beneath all this, the resolute, determined character of the man is apparent."[20]

The Northern press carried Lincoln's address, which Congress and the public regarded as a sign that he would resist secession. According to Henry Villard, the speech was "of the greatest significance, although it deals more in intimations than in definite assertions."[21] In Cincinnati, the speech "created an immense sensation," for it was "looked upon as a decided coercion pronunciamento" and a "declaration of war against the South."[22] William L. Hodge, a Louisianan who would be appointed assistant secretary of the treasury months later, reported that Lincoln's "foolish," "uncalled for," and "unfortunate" Indianapolis speech was "doing vast mischief" in Washington, where the president-elect's best friends deprecated it. It was, Hodge claimed, having a "very unfortunate" effect on the Peace Conference and Unionists in Virginia.[23]

Southern senators and congressmen, indignant at the Indianapolis speech, threatened to block all legislation, including the means to pay the government's expenses. Many of their constituents inferred that Lincoln would dispatch troops to enforce the law. Southern newspapers criticized the "reckless boldness" of the speech, which "breathed of war" and amounted to "sporting with fire-balls in a powder magazine."[24]

The New Orleans *Crescent* belittled Lincoln's use of rhetorical questions: "Mr. Lincoln betrays an utter inability to rise to the dignity of his subject. He resorts to the indirect and unsatisfactory and undignified expedient of *asking questions* of the populace before him, instead of coming out like a man, and saying flatly what he means. Too timid to express boldly his sentiments, he resorts to the roundabout way of putting interrogatories, thereby suggesting what he would not declare openly—and then, for fear of its being considered too great a committal, reminding the people that they must recollect he was only asking questions, not expressing opinions!"[25]

Northern papers, in contrast, defended Lincoln's position as the only one that duty permitted. "Other ground than this the President elect could not take, if he would regard his oath 'to preserve, protect and defend the Constitution,' unless he were to regard it as in fact the rope of sand which another construction has seemed to make it," observed the Boston *Daily Advertiser*.[26] The New York *Tribune* hailed Lincoln's speech as a welcome indication of his resolve to insist that if concessions were to be offered, the South had to make them. Should Lincoln's implied insistence on collecting the revenues and retaking federal facilities lead to war, so be it, declared the New York *Evening Post:* "if war comes, it must be made by the South; but let the South understand, when it does come, that eighty years of enterprise, of accumulation and of progress in all the arts of warfare have not been lost upon the North."[27] The New York *Herald,* however, condemned the speech for exhibiting "the obstinacy of an intractable partisan" and proclaiming "a line of policy adverse to union and to peace, and eminently adapted, not only to enlarge, strengthen and consolidate the new Southern republic, but to destroy the hopes of law and order of the North in a wasting civil war."[28] *Frank Leslie's Illustrated Newspaper* worried that some passages were "capable of a terrible misconstruction."[29] Seward's friends, surprised by the belligerent tone of the Indianapolis address, sent a telegram asking if it were genuine. Thurlow Weed left Washington immediately after reading Lincoln's remarks, and Cassius M. Clay warned that "Lincoln will have to modify his Indiana speech so as to hold onto the status quo—a blow struck to regain lost forts will unite the South."[30] Lincoln had evidently intended to give this speech to the Indiana Legislature on the following day, but that event was canceled.

The fatigue caused by a reception the night before may have been responsible for the change in plans; there the president-elect's "coolness under the terrific infliction of several thousand hand-shakings" prompted Hay to remark that "he unites to the courage of Andrew Jackson the insensibility to physical suffering which is usually assigned to bronze statues." The young assistant secretary judged that "the rack, the thumb screw, King James's boot, the cap of silence, with all the other dark and recondite paraphernalia of torture, become instruments of cheerful and enlivening pastime, beside the ferocious grip and the demoniac wrench of the muscular citizen of the West." Lincoln's prankish son Robert made matters worse by standing outside the hotel and guiding dozens of mischievous lads to shake the hand of his unsuspecting father. Because the ordeal almost prostrated Lincoln, his advisors resolved to keep future receptions short.

Things did not go smoothly at the Indiana capital. Like many other committees in charge of arrangements, Indianapolitans proved imperfect. Outsiders appropriated the carriages designated for the presidential party, compelling most of the entourage, clutching their luggage, struggle through the crowds to the Bates House. Hay found that the hotel's "halls, passages, and rooms have been congested with turbulent congregations of men, all of whom had too many elbows, too much curiosity, and a perfectly gushing desire to shake hands with somebody—the President, if possible; if not, somebody who had shaken hands with him."[31] Chaos reigned in the dining room, where Lincoln had to sit twenty minutes before being served. Waiters mishandled orders, spilled sugar down patrons' backs, and brought biscuits to those ordering ham and pickles to those requesting tea. The mayhem amused Lincoln.

The president-elect was emphatically not amused when his son misplaced a carpetbag containing the only copies of his inaugural address. Robert, not yet 18 years old, had accepted an invitation by fellow adolescents to see the city's sights, and carelessly left the precious bag with a hotel desk clerk. When asked about the location of the valise, Robert replied to his father in a tone of "bored and injured virtue." A "look of stupefaction" came over Lincoln's face as he heard what the lad had done, "and visions of that Inaugural in all the next morning's newspapers floated through his imagination," according to Nicolay. "Without a word he opened the door of his room, forced his way through the crowded corridor down to the office, where, with a single stride of his long legs, he swung himself across the clerk's counter, behind which a small mountain of carpetbags of all colors had accumulated." With a little key, the president-elect began opening all the black bags, much to the surprised amusement of onlookers. Eventually, he discovered his own carpetbag, which he took charge of thereafter. Ward Hill Lamon testified that he "had never seen Mr. Lincoln so much annoyed, so much perplexed, and for the time so angry." He added that Lincoln "seldom manifested a spirit of anger toward his children—this was the nearest approach to it I had ever witnessed."[32]

Conciliatory Speeches in Cincinnati

The next morning, Mrs. Lincoln arrived in Indianapolis a few moments before the presidential train departed for Cincinnati. En route to the Queen City she impressed one observer unfavorably. As a gentleman with a newspaper passed by her, she asked: "Is that a Cincinnati paper you have in your hand?" When assured that it was, she queried: "Does it say anything about us?" Taken aback by her self-importance, he was reminded of "an honest Dutchman, who had unexpectedly been elevated to the position of major of the militia. When the result of the election was known, his children wanted to know if they would now all be majors. 'No, you fools,' indignantly replied the mother, 'none but your daddie and me.'"[33] Lincoln's gloom lifted this day, the fifty-second anniversary of his birth. "He has shaken off the despondency which was noticed during the first day's journey," John Hay informed readers of the New York *World*. As the president-elect prepared to leave Indianapolis, some Illinois friends bade him farewell and returned home. Among them were Jesse K. Dubois and Ebenezer Peck, who embraced him vigorously, clipped a lock of hair as a souvenir, and urged him "to behave himself like a good boy in the White House."[34] Illinois Democrats satirically recommended that the hair be preserved as a state treasure. As the train sped along at 30 miles per hour, huge crowds at each station greeted the president-elect with wild cheering. At one stop, Lincoln indulged his well-wishers with some brief remarks in which he took his customary modesty to extreme lengths. "You call upon me for a speech," he told the residents of Lawrenceburg, Indiana. "I have been selected to fill an important office for a brief period, and am now, in your eyes, invested with an influence which will soon pass away; but should my administration prove to be a very wicked one, or what is more probable, a very foolish one, if you, the PEOPLE, are but true to yourselves and to the Constitution, there is but little harm I can do, thank God!"[35]

Approaching Cincinnati in midafternoon, the train was forced to halt by a crowd so large that it spilled onto the tracks. Police had to clear the way into the depot. As Lincoln proceeded to his hotel—a ride in an open carriage lasting two and a half hours—he was hailed by more than 50,000 people lining the streets. A future president, Rutherford B. Hayes, reported that there "was a lack of comfort in the arrangements, but the simplicity, the homely character of all was in keeping with the nobility of this typical American."[36] Another witness described a source of that discomfort: Lincoln was "standing erect with uncovered head, and steadying himself by holding on to a board fastened to the front part of the vehicle. A more uncomfortable ride than this, over the bouldered streets of Cincinnati, cannot well be imagined. Perhaps a journey over the broken roads of Eastern Russia, in a tarantass [a low-slung, horse-drawn carriage informally known as a "liver-massaging device"], would secure to the traveller as great a degree of discomfort. Mr. Lincoln bore it with characteristic patience."[37] Hay noticed that all windows were thronged, "every balcony glittered with bright colors and fluttered with handkerchiefs; the sidewalks were packed; even the ledges and cornices of the houses swarmed with intrepid lookers-on." There "were flags everywhere where there were not patriots; and patriots everywhere there were not flags."[38] Adorning hotels and other buildings were large signs with such hawkish mottos as "The Union Must and Shall Be Preserved," "Welcome to the President of Thirty-Four States," "The Time Has Come When Demagogues Must Go Under," and "The Security of a Republic Is in the Maintenance of the Laws."[39] As the carriage slowly proceeded, a heavy-set German sitting atop a gigantic beer barrel hoisted his stein of lager and shouted to the president-elect: "*God be with you. Enforce the laws and save our country. Here's your health.*"[40]

From the balcony of his hotel, Lincoln gave a much less confrontational speech than the one he had delivered at Indianapolis. (Indeed, for most of the trip he toned down his rhetoric, perhaps because of the unfavorable press response to his remarks at the Indiana capital.) He quoted the conciliatory words he had addressed to Kentuckians when he spoke at Cincinnati two years earlier: "When we do, as we say, beat you [in an election], you perhaps want to know what we will do with you. I will tell you, so far as I am authorized to speak for the opposition, what we mean to do with you. We mean to treat you, as near as we possibly can, as Washington, Jefferson, and Madison treated you. We mean to leave you alone, and in no way to interfere with your institution; to abide by all and every compromise of the constitution, and, in a word, coming back to the original proposition, to treat you, so far as degenerated men (if we have degenerated) may, according to the examples of those noble fathers—Washington, Jefferson and Madison. We mean to remember that you are as good as we; that there is no difference between us, other than the difference of circumstances. We mean to recognize, and bear in mind always, that you have as good hearts in your bosoms as other people, or as we claim to have, and treat you accordingly." He declared that "in my new position, I see no occasion, and feel no inclination, to retract a word of this."[41]

These conciliatory remarks pleased compromise enthusiasts. "Every word is so carefully selected with direct reference to the affairs of Government that their soothing, quieting influence cannot fail to be felt," predicted an Indiana woman.[42] The Philadelphia *Pennsylvanian* approved of the "different tone" of this speech compared with his Indianapolis address, although the paper thought he was rather condescending toward Kentuckians.[43] To a local rabbi, Lincoln seemed like "a country squire for the first time in the city" who would "look queer in the white house, with his primitive manner."[44]

That evening Lincoln dodged an opportunity to address the secession crisis when he received a serenade from more than 2,000 German workingmen who urged him to stand by his antislavery principles: "We trust, that you, the self-reliant because self made man, will uphold the Constitution and the laws against secret treachery and avowed treason."[45] Instead of replying directly to those remarks, Lincoln dwelt on immigration, homestead laws, and the American dream. He began by explaining why he would avoid talking about the subject that was on everyone's mind: "I deem it my duty—a duty which I owe to my constituents—to you, gentlemen, that I should wait until the last moment, for a development of the present national difficulties, before I express myself decidedly what course I shall pursue. I hope, then, not to be false to anything that you have to expect of me." Such reticence contrasted sharply with the spirit of his Indianapolis speech.

Lincoln then waxed philosophical, endorsing the cardinal principle of the utilitarian Jeremy Bentham: "I hold that while man exists, it is his duty to improve not only his own condition, but to assist in ameliorating mankind; and therefore, without entering upon the details of the question, I will simply say, that I am for those means which will give the greatest good to the greatest number." Turning to a subject that he seldom treated, he praised homestead legislation, to which the German delegation had alluded in its address: "in so far as the Government lands can be disposed of, I am in favor of cutting up the wild lands into parcels, so that every poor man may have a home." He spoke about his vision of the just society and the role of immigrants in it: "In regard to the Germans and foreigners, I esteem them no better than other people, nor any worse. [Cries of good.] It is not my nature, when I see a people borne down by the weight of their shackles—the oppression of tyranny—to make their life more bitter by heaping upon them greater burdens; but rather would I do all in my power to raise the yoke, than to add anything that would tend to crush them. Inasmuch as our country is extensive and new, and the countries of Europe are densely populated, if there are any abroad who desire to make this the land of their adoption, it is not in my heart to throw aught in their way, to prevent them from coming to the United States."[46]

The evening reception in Cincinnati was an ordeal. For forty-five minutes Lincoln shook hand after hand until he finally excused himself. On the whole, the event in the Queen City was a success. Rutherford B. Hayes told a relative that the "impression he made was good. He undoubtedly is shrewd, able, and possesses strength in reserve." Prophetically Hayes added, "This will be tested soon."[47]

Unfortunate Speech in Columbus

On February 13, the train proceeded to Columbus, where Lincoln was scheduled to address the state legislature. Although quite tired and feeling somewhat ill, he conversed freely with other passengers. Speaking of the demands that the South made on the North, he was reminded of a squabble between his two younger sons. "One of them had a toy that the other wanted and demanded it in terms emphatic and boisterous. At length he was told to let his brother have it in order to quiet him. 'No, sir,' was the sturdy response, 'I must have it to quiet myself.'"[48] Because Lincoln was a bit hoarse from speaking outdoors so often, his friends tried to keep him from further unnecessary oratory, but he could not resist saying a few words at stops along the way. In Xenia, a large crowd, including many blacks, greeted him with especially intense enthusiasm. After his remarks, he found it difficult to return to the train as the crowd pressed forward to touch his hand.

Upon arriving at the Ohio capital, Lincoln found it jammed with people swarming in from the countryside. At the depot, many thousands boisterously welcomed the train with loud huzzahs. Hay invited his New York readers to imagine "a quiet inland city of the second class suddenly transformed into your own bustling, jostling Broadway, with—and here the comparison fails—smiling faces and holiday attire, stores and dwellings gaily decorated, the pavements neither muddy nor dusty, the atmosphere balmy as spring, music falling upon the ear and military display greeting the eye."[49] The local Republican paper noted that Lincoln's manner "told how deeply he was affected by the enthusiasm of the people."[50] At the statehouse, the legislature's solemn reception of the president-elect so moved him that he was, according to one observer, "hardly able to do himself justice in his reply to the address of the President of the Senate; but the earnestness and conscientiousness that plainly shone on his face effected more with the audience than words could."[51] The words Lincoln chose were unfortunate. He clumsily tried to play down the seriousness of the crisis: "there is nothing going wrong. It is a consoling circumstance that when we look out there is nothing that really hurts anybody. We entertain different views upon political questions, but nobody is suffering anything."[52]

Critics jumped on these remarks. An indignant New York congressman asked rhetorically: "Have not our forts and vessels been seized, our arsenals invaded, and our mints robbed, by men and States in arms?"[53] The president-elect was "a fool" for uttering "sheer nonsense," wrote a Philadelphian; "everybody about here is 'hurt,' and 'suffering,' and everything is 'wrong' in the eyes of everyone except these robber republicans, who have ruined the country and now pretend that all is right, when 6 states are forming an independent government."[54] Conservative newspapers scolded Lincoln for betraying "a most lamentable degree of ignorance touching the revolutionary evils of the day." How, they asked, could he possibly ignore the "sweeping bankruptcy of our merchants, the stoppage of our manufactories, the universal stagnation of trade, and the tens of thousands of poor laboring people thrown out of employment by the unrest of the times"?[55] Not all journals were so harsh. The Philadelphia *Press* charitably speculated that Lincoln must have been thinking of the rural West rather than the urban East. Some interpreted the president-elect's remarks as a stiff-back declaration. Journalist Henry M. Smith reported that Lincoln "left the inference very strong on the minds of his hearers that there was nothing to compromise—as the North had done no wrong to any man or section, and proposed doing nothing worse than maintaining the Union, upholding the Constitution and executing the laws."[56] At least one Columbus resident who did not view the speech that way told Lincoln, "you've got to give them rebels a hotter shot than that before they're licked."[57]

At the reception afterward, an immense crowd streamed into the recently completed state capitol from three directions. Among his well-wishers was a gentleman holding aloft a baby, which Lincoln kissed. When the infant's mother asked the president-elect to name him, he smiled and said: "Abraham is too big for such a wee atom of humanity. I will name him Lincoln." He kissed the babe again and returned it to its mother, who replied: "*We* will add the Abraham, for *he* saved his people." The crowd cheered lustily.[58]

Lax security arrangements imperiled Lincoln's safety. The rotunda area was bisected by two wide aisles, perpendicular to each other, one of which was designated to channel callers toward the president and then away from him to the exit on the opposite side of the building; the other aisle was to be closed. The guards shutting off the transverse aisle were inadequate and allowed people to enter through three doors, with only one exit provided. As Nicolay recalled, "before anyone was well aware of the occurrence there was a concentric jam of the crowd toward the President-elect which threatened to crush him and those about him." Luckily, the exceptionally strong Ward Hill Lamon planted himself in front of Lincoln and stemmed the tide long enough for his friend to seek shelter behind a pilaster. There, overcome by heat, Lincoln stopped shaking hands and instead simply bowed to the people as they passed by. Hay remarked that if "royalty was ever more effectually pushed about, punctured with elbows, shouted at, and gazed at, than the President elect on this occasion, why then—royalty is greatly to be pitied; and if royalty ever took it all with half the grace Mr. Lincoln did, why—royalty must be very good natured." When informed that the electoral votes had been counted in Congress and he was declared duly elected, Lincoln with palpable gratitude and relief remarked emotionally: "'Tis well."[59]

One of the many observers of this scene, the future president James A. Garfield, had mixed feelings about the Lincolns. "In some respects I was disappointed in Lincoln," he wrote, "but in most he surpasses expectation. He has raised a pair of whiskers, but notwithstanding all their beautifying effects he is distressingly homely. But through all his awkward homeliness there is a look of transparent, genuine goodness, which at once reaches your heart, and makes you trust and love him. His visits are having a fine effect on the country. He has the tone and bearing of a fearless, firm man." Garfield detected in Lincoln "no touch of affectation" and called him "frank—direct—and thoroughly honest." The president-elect's "remarkable good sense—simple and condensed style of expression—and evident marks of indomitable will—give me great hopes for the country. . . . After the long dreary period of Buchanan's weakness and cowardly imbecility, the people will hail a strong and vigorous leader." Garfield depicted Mary Lincoln as a "stocky, sallow, pugnosed plain lady" with "much of the primitiveness of western life. He stands higher on the whole in my estimation than ever. She considerably lower."[60] Lincoln's host in Columbus, Governor William Dennison, thought that he seemed "worn out from the fatigues of his journey."[61]

Embarassing Speech in Pittsburgh

On Valentine's Day, as the presidential party headed toward Pittsburgh, torrents of rain fell, inspiring hope in Lincoln that he might not have to address crowds along the way. He "stated that he had determined to make, for the rest of the trip, as few speeches as possible, thus avoiding much fatigue."[62] To Ward Hill Lamon, he complained that "he had done much hard work in his life, but to make speeches day after day, with the object of speaking and saying nothing, was the hardest work he ever had done. 'I wish,' said he, 'that this thing were through with, and I could find peace and quiet somewhere.'"[63]

Despite the bad weather, huge crowds turned out at the stopping points and insisted on a speech. On more than one occasion, he told an anecdote by way of an apology for not complying. He knew of a man, he said, who had a good chance of winning his party's nomination for a county office. He rented a horse to canvass extensively throughout the county. On the morning of the party convention, he mounted the nag and headed toward the county seat, but even though he applied the whip and spurs energetically, his horse made such slow progress that by the time he arrived, the convention had adjourned and he had lost the nomination. Upon returning the nag to its owner, the man asked him what such a horse was good for. "Why, a good horse for a funeral, I guess!" came the reply. "No, my friend," said the would-be candidate, "never hire that horse out for a funeral." "Why not?" "Because if that horse pulls the hearse, the Judgment Day will come before the corpse gets to the graveyard!" So, said Lincoln, that was just his case, for "if he stopped at every station to make a stump speech he would not arrive at Washington until the inauguration was over."[64]

Lincoln devised another clever stratagem for handling crowd demands for a speech. He stayed inside the train until the conductor announced its imminent departure, at which point Lincoln emerged onto the platform of the car and bowed to his well-wishers as the locomotive pulled out of the station. When a committee from Steubenville, where a half-hour stop was scheduled, asked him to speak, he replied jocularly that he felt like an old rooster belonging to a peripatetic Illinois farmer who tied up his fowls before making each of his many moves. Whenever the farmer began loading furniture into his wagon, the rooster would fling himself down on his back and cross his legs, ready to be tied up. Emulating that rooster, Lincoln said he would accommodate the committee by giving an address.

To the crowd of 20,000, including not only Buckeyes but also Virginians who had crossed the ice-choked Ohio River, he offered a preview of an argument he would spell out more fully in his inaugural address: "Though the people have made me by electing me, the instrument to carry out the wishes expressed in the address, I greatly fear that I shall not be the repository of the ability to do so. Indeed I know I shall not, more than in purpose, unless sustained by the great body of the people, and by the Divine Power, without whose aid we can do nothing. We everywhere express devotion to the Constitution. I believe there is no difference in this respect, whether on this or on the other side of this majestic stream [the Ohio River]. I understand that on the other side, among our dissatisfied brethren, they are satisfied with the Constitution of the United States, if they can have their rights under the Constitution. The question is, as to what the Constitution means—'What are their rights under the Constitution?' That is all. To decide that, who shall be the judge? Can you think of any other, than the voice of the people? If the majority does not control, the minority must—would that be right? Would that be just or generous? Assuredly not! Though the majority may be wrong, and I will not undertake to say that they were not wrong in electing me, yet we must adhere to the principle that the majority shall rule. By your Constitution you have another chance in four years. No great harm can be done by us in that time—in that time there can be nobody hurt. If anything goes wrong, however, and you find you have made a mistake, elect a better man next time. There are plenty of them."[65]

A Democrat in the audience found Lincoln's delivery "rather quizzical" and thought that while his face indicated "good humor" and "fine social qualities," it lacked "the higher order of intellectual developments, so necessary for the position he is called to occupy." He considered the president-elect's remarks noncommittal, containing little "either to approve or disapprove, unless we are much gratified or dissatisfied with the 'day of small things.'"[66]

At Rochester, Pennsylvania, a member of the crowd shouted out, "What will you do with the secessionists?" Lincoln replied evasively, "My friend, that is a matter which I have under very grave consideration."[67]

Thanks to the delay caused by a freight train accident, Lincoln arrived two hours late in Pittsburgh. Nicolay told his fiancée that "we hardly expected to find a soul at the depot. It was a vain illusion. The depot and grounds were literally jammed full of people." Confusion reigned, for the presidential party's carriages had been stationed so close to the tracks that the horses took fright as the locomotive approached with its bell clanging and its steam whistle screaming. In the resulting near-stampede, Lincoln had to locate the carriage meant for him. His entourage, fearing for his safety, struggled to help him amid the panicky horses and the shouting committeemen, spectators, and drivers. Mercifully, no one was hurt. "We finally got Mr. Lincoln into a carriage," Nicolay reported, "but having accomplished that, it looked for a while as if we would never get the carriage out of the crowd that was pushing and pulling and yelling all around us."[68]

When Lincoln finally reached the hotel, another crowd awaited him. Standing on a chair in the lobby, he made brief remarks to his unusually good-natured well-wishers. He thanked them for supporting the Republican cause in the election: "By a mere accident, and not through any merit of mine, it happened that I was the representative of that cause, and I acknowledge with all sincerity the high honor you have conferred on me. ['Three cheers for Honest Abe,' and a voice saying, 'It was no accident that elected you, but your own merits, and the worth of the cause.'] I thank you, my fellow citizen, for your kind remark, and trust that I feel a becoming sense of the responsibility resting upon me. ['We know you do.'] I could not help thinking, my friends, as I traveled in the rain through your crowded streets, on my way here, that if all those people were in favor of the Union, it can certainly be in no great danger—it will be preserved. [A voice—'We are all Union men.' Another voice—'That's so.' A third voice—'No compromise.' A fourth—'Three cheers for the Union.'] But I am talking too long, longer than I ought. ['Oh, no! go on; split another rail.' Laughter.] You know that it has not been my custom, since I started on the route to Washington, to make long speeches; I am rather inclined to silence, ['That's right'] and whether that be wise or not, it is at least more unusual now-a-days to find a man who can hold his tongue than to find one who cannot. [Laughter, and a voice—'No railery Abe.']" He promised to speak to them more fully in the morning.[69]

One of Lincoln's principal aims in that address on February 15, delivered to 5,000 people standing beneath a sea of umbrellas, was to assure Pennsylvanians of his soundness on the tariff issue. But before dealing with that controversial topic, he explained his reluctance to discuss the secession crisis: "It is naturally expected that I should say something upon this subject, but to touch upon it at all would involve an elaborate discussion of a great many questions and circumstances, would require more time than I can at present command, and would perhaps unnecessarily commit me upon matters which have not yet fully developed themselves. [Immense cheering, and cries of 'good!' 'that's right!'] The condition of the country, fellow-citizens, is an extraordinary one, and fills the mind of every patriot with anxiety and solicitude. My intention is to give this subject all the consideration which I possibly can before I speak fully and definitely in regard to it—so that, when I do speak, I may be as nearly right as possible."

As he had done in Columbus, Lincoln played down the dangers of the secession movement: "there is really no crisis except an artificial one! What is there now to warrant the condition of affairs presented by our friends 'over the river?' Take even their own view of the questions involved, and there is nothing to justify the course which they are pursuing. I repeat it, then—there is no crisis, excepting such a one as may be gotten up at any time by designing politicians. My advice, then, under such circumstances, is to keep cool. If the great American people will only keep their temper, on both sides of the line, the troubles will come to an end, and the question which now distracts the country will be settled just as surely as all other difficulties of like character which have originated in this government have been adjusted. Let the people on both sides keep their self-possession, and just as other clouds have cleared away in due time, so will this, and this great nation shall continue to prosper as heretofore."

Somewhat lamely Lincoln addressed the tariff issue, which, he admitted, he did not fully comprehend: "I must confess that I do not understand this subject in all its multiform bearings, but I promise you that I will give it my closest attention." He was equally lame in his admission of ignorance regarding the pending Morrill Tariff: "The tariff bill now before Congress may or may not pass at the present session. I confess I do not understand the precise provisions of this bill, and I do not know whether it can be passed by the present Congress or not." He promised to abide by the rather vague protectionist plank of the Republican platform, which he had Nicolay read to the crowd. "We should do neither more nor less than we gave the people reason to believe we would, when they gave us their votes," he said. Reverting to arguments he had made sixteen years earlier, Lincoln stressed the wastefulness of transporting goods across the Atlantic when those goods could be produced domestically at roughly the same cost. He endorsed the old Whig proposition that the executive should defer to the legislature and suggested that he would carry out whatever tariff policy Congress adopted.[70] Later in the journey, he would declare that these remarks "were rather carefully worded. I took pains that they should be so."[71]

Ignoring his protectionist statement, the New York *World* praised Lincoln's explanation of his silence on secession as "the wise utterance of a statesman who realizes the full weight of his responsibility to the nation for the preservation of its government; who feels bound to deliberate before he acts; who will not stultify himself by unnecessary committals to a line of proceeding with a new state of facts or the arguments of his constitutional advisers might prove to be unwise; and who is too self-contained to assume the part of President before he is invested with the office."[72] The New York *Tribune* took heart from his statement that "[w]e should do neither more nor less than we gave the people reason to believe we would, when they gave us their votes," interpreting that as a pledge to carry out the Chicago Platform plank on slavery expansion.[73]

With good reason, Henry Villard judged this speech the "least creditable performance" of the trip, calling it "nothing but crude, ignorant twaddle, without point or meaning." It "proved him to be the veriest novice in economic matters" and strengthened Villard's "doubts as to his capacity for the high office he was to fill."[74] His view was shared by Democratic papers, which called the speech "a lamentable though brief rigmarole of confusion and contradiction" that showed "an ignorance so gross that school-boys might laugh at him." The Pittsburgh *Post* remarked that although the Morrill tariff bill had been under consideration by Congress for three sessions, Lincoln "does not seem to be thoroughly informed on it—any more than he is upon the geography of Pittsburgh, when he speaks of the South as 'across the river.'"[75] The Springfield, Massachusetts, *Republican* was more charitable, finding it "not strange that Mr. Lincoln should have been somewhat puzzled" by the tariff plank of the Republican platform, for "it was built diplomatically, to satisfy both protectionists and free traders, and is capable of a great variety of interpretations."[76] In Washington, some Republicans speculated that "if Mr. Lincoln endorses the Chicago platform in toto, as he intimated in his Pittsburg[h] remarks, he and Mr. Seward must be at issue."[77]

Detour to Cleveland

The train pulled out at 10 A.M., zigging westward toward the next stop, Cleveland. When it halted briefly on the outskirts of Pittsburgh, hundreds of railway workers cheered the president-elect so lustily that he was quite touched. En route to the Forest City, Lincoln and his family rested quietly in their car. Afflicted with a bad cold, the president-elect said little and spent most of his time perusing newspapers and silently reflecting. The quiet was broken at Ravenna, where well-wishers fired a celebratory cannon so near the train that a window shattered, covering Mrs. Lincoln with shards of glass and frightening her badly. The sentiments expressed by the crowds grew more hawkish as the train proceeded through western Pennsylvania and the Western Reserve of Ohio.

At Ashtabula, after listening to the president-elect's brief remarks, the crowd demanded to see Mrs. Lincoln. Her husband "said he didn't believe he could induce her to come out. In fact he could say that he never succeeded very well in getting her to do anything she didn't want to do."[78]

In Cleveland, despite snow, rain, and mud, 30,000 people lined the two-mile stretch of Euclid Avenue connecting the depot with the city center. They rushed hither and thither trying to catch a glimpse of Lincoln. The superabundance of flags prompted one newspaperman to marvel that a "Vesuvian eruption of Stars and Stripes in the immediate vicinity could not have more completely covered the buildings."[79] Judge David Davis reported that "the appointments were the finest & the displays of enthusiasm as great as anywhere." He was especially impressed with the mansions along what he termed the "the handsomest street, I ever saw."[80] Nicolay informed his fiancée that "for the first time we found the crowd tolerably well controlled by the police and military, and got through without any jam, though there was again a great crowd at the hotel." In general, the arrangements proved better than those at any previous stop.[81] Standing in a carriage, Lincoln bowed and waved his hat in acknowledgment of the crowd's cheers.

From the balcony of the Weddell House, the president-elect assured his audience of 10,000 that the secession furor "is altogether an artificial crisis. In all parts of the nation there are differences of opinion and politics. There are differences of opinion even here. You did not all vote for the person who now addresses you. What is happening now will not hurt those who are farther away from here. Have they not all their rights now as they ever have had? Do they not have their fugitive slaves returned now as ever? Have they not the same constitution that they have lived under for seventy odd years? Have they not a position as citizens of this common country, and have we any power to change that position? (Cries of 'No.') What then is the matter with them? Why all this excitement? Why all these complaints? As I said before, this crisis is all artificial. It has no foundation in facts. It was not argued up, as the saying is, and cannot, therefore, be argued down. Let it alone and it will go down of itself (Laughter)." He apologized for cutting short his remarks, pleading a sore throat as justification.[82]

At a reception that evening, Congressman Albert Gallatin Riddle noted that while Lincoln seemed totally unselfconscious around males, "he was constrained and ill at ease, surrounded, as he several times was, by well-dressed ladies."[83] He gave his weary arms and hands a rest by having the guests simply file past him at a safe distance. That tactic was soon abandoned, however. Nicolay remembered that the "experiment was tried two or three times but always with unsatisfactory results. To the curious individuals who were passing it seemed a performance and created an impression, ranging from the feeling on the one hand that they were assisting at an animal show, to that on the other, that they were engaged in a grotesque ceremony of mock adulation." In Lincoln "it produced a consciousness not only of being on exhibition, but as if he were separated by an abyss from those with whom as fellow-citizens and constituents it was more than ever an imperative duty to be brought into closer relations and sympathy." Thus "the crowd could only pass by him, either with a meaningless smirk or an open-mouthed stare; no talk either of earnestness or pleasantry was possible. This was infinitely worse than the utmost fatigue, and Mr. Lincoln returned to the old custom where a cordial grasp of the hand and a fitting word formed an instantaneous circuit of personal communion."[84] His awkward appearance when bowing amused one observer, who said it could not "be caricatured. . . . His chin rises—his body breaks in two at the hips—there is a bend of the knees at a queer angle."[85]

A local Democratic paper called Lincoln "a clever man" and "a well disposed gentleman," but thought him "not equal to the present emergency." It feared that his "triumphal procession to the Capital will prove a funeral procession to his reputation." He had won praise for his campaign against Douglas two years earlier, but the Lincoln of 1861 failed to live up to the promise of 1858: "The Douglas Lincoln was certainly a better speaker than President Lincoln and a much smarter man in every respect."[86]

Calamitous Reception in Buffalo

Leaving Cleveland on the morning of February 16, the presidential cavalcade hugged the shore of Lake Erie en route to Buffalo. Lincoln, still fatigued from the exertion of the previous day, was subdued. Because of hoarseness, he spoke less than he had earlier on the trip. At Girard, to everyone's surprise, Horace Greeley boarded, mistakenly thinking it was the regular train. Nicolay marched him into the presidential car, where he greeted the Lincolns. Embarrassed by his blunder, the eccentric editor detrained at the next station, Erie. There, at a lunch break, the city magistrates urged Lincoln to try some of their wine. "I have lived fifty years without the use of any liquors, and I do not wish to change my habits now," he replied.[87] A resident of Erie thought the president-elect "has been materially improved, in appearance, by the growth of whiskers, and though somewhat hoarse, and suffering slightly from fatigue, seemed to be in good health and spirits."[88] He "excused himself from speaking at any length." A local journalist detected in the president-elect's eyes "a blending of gravity and goodness" which "wins confidence and affection, and satisfies one of his fitness for the great office." His smile conveyed "much evident sincerity" and his bow "real courtesy."[89]

At Westfield, New York, Lincoln asked if there were a little girl in the audience who had written him in October suggesting that he grow a beard. (Earlier, his friend Gurdon Hubbard had told Lincoln that such a change would lend him dignity.) Eleven-year-old Grace Bedell had resented schoolmates' hostile comments about the candidate's appearance. Responding to those slurs and to the unflattering poster image of Lincoln that her father had brought home, she wrote the candidate: "I have got 4 brother's and part of them will vote for you any way and if you will let your whiskers grow I will try and get the rest of them to vote for you[.] [Y]ou would look a great deal better for your face is so thin. All the ladies like whiskers and they would tease their husband's to vote for you and then you would be President. My father is a going to vote for you and if I was a man I would vote for you to but I will try and get every one to vote for you that I can."

Lincoln, who was glad to receive letters having nothing to do with politics or patronage, asked in reply: "As to the whiskers, having never worn any, do you not think people would call it a piece of silly affection if I were to begin it now?"[90] But he took her advice anyway, and by February it was reported that "a vigorous growth of comely whiskers has entirely changed his facial appearance. The improvement is remarkable. The gaunt, hollow cheeks, and long, lank jawbone are so enveloped as to give fullness and rotundity to the entire face."[91] A young woman in Springfield concurred, writing that the "whiskers are a great improvement." (Years later a dissenting artist contended that "no man who ever understood the singular form & character of Lincoln's chin & lower jaws would dream of covering them.")[92]

In response to his query at Westfield, a young boy shouted: "there she is, Mr. Lincum," pointing out Grace Bedell, a comely, black-eyed, blushing girl. Her elderly father led her to the train, where Lincoln gave her a kiss and said: "You see, I let these whiskers grow for you, Grace."[93] His gesture confused the youngster, who thought only of returning home to her mother.

At Dunkirk, Lincoln electrified the crowd of 12,000 with a brief, stirring declaration. On a platform adorned with a flagstaff, he concluded his remarks simply: "Standing as I do, with my hand upon this staff, and under the folds of the American flag, I ask you to stand by me so long as I stand by it."[94] John Hay found it "impossible to describe the applause and the acclamation with which this Jacksonian peroration was greeted. The arches of the depot echoed and re-echoed with the ring of countless cheers. Men swung their hats wildly, women waved their handkerchiefs, and, as the train moved on, the crowd, animated by a common impulse, followed, as if they intended to keep it company to the next station. Inside the cars the enthusiasm created by the conclusion of the speech was scarcely less than the outside assemblage had exhibited. The company evinced a general disposition to intone hurrahs and sing patriotic songs out of tune."[95]

On the afternoon of February 16, the presidential party encountered chaos at Buffalo, where 75,000 people welcomed it. As the train pulled into the station, the wildly cheering crowd tried to compress itself to catch a glimpse of the president-elect. A company of soldiers, with heroic effort, cleared a path for Lincoln, who was greeted briefly by ex-President Millard Fillmore. No sooner had the former and future presidents made their way to a carriage than the frenzied crowd surged toward them, sweeping aside soldiers protecting the honored visitor. In the crush, some men fainted and others were badly injured, including an elderly gentleman whose ribs were broken, and Major David Hunter, who suffered a dislocated collarbone. Only with aggressive, persistent elbowing were Nicolay and the rest of the entourage able to reach their coaches. The president-elect, Hay reported, "narrowly escaped unpleasant personal contact with the crowd. An intrepid body-guard, composed partly of soldiers and partly of members of his suite, succeeded, however, in protecting him from maceration, but only at the expense of incurring themselves a pressure to which the hug of Barnum's grizzly bear would have been a tender and fraternal embrace."[96] Not surprisingly, Lincoln's companions insisted that he refuse to subject himself to such dangerous receptions unless he was assured that he would receive better protection.

Things were not much better at the hotel, where, Nicolay complained, "all was confusion—the committee not only did nothing but didn't know and didn't seem to care what to do. We took the matter into our own hands and finally arranged pretty much everything."[97] The mayor welcomed Lincoln with a little speech, to which he responded with sentiments he had expressed many times earlier. Understandably, his voice was starting to show signs of wear; during some passages he could scarcely be heard. With customary modesty, Lincoln insisted that "I am unwilling, on any occasion, that I should be so meanly thought of, as to have it supposed for a moment that I regard these demonstrations as tendered to me personally. They should be tendered to no individual man. They are tendered to the country, to the institutions of the country, and to the perpetuity of the [liberties of the] country for which these institutions were made and created." Employing a firmer tone than he had used earlier, he urged the crowd to "[s]tand up to your sober convictions of right, to your obligations to the Constitution, act in accordance with those sober convictions, and the clouds which now arise on the horizon will be dispelled, and we shall have a bright and glorious future; and when this generation has passed away, tens of thousands will inhabit this country where only thousands inhabit [it] now."[98] In Washington this speech was regarded as the best he had given so far on his journey.

Reaction to the Speeches

Lincoln's earlier addresses had disappointed many in the nation's capital. Benjamin Brown French, who would serve as chief marshal at Lincoln's inaugural, told his brother that "[w]e all like . . . old Abe but wish he would leave off making little speeches. He has not the gift of language, though he may have of western gab."[99] The Washington correspondent of the Democratic Cincinnati *Enquirer* reported that "Lincoln's harangues are received very unfavorably," and Republicans "are restive under the charge of having elected an ignoramus for a president." They "now see their leader's weakness, and are striving to cover it up by all the means in their power."[100] Another Washington correspondent of a Democratic paper alleged that the "mortification of the republicans at Mr. Lincoln's recent speeches increases with every fresh emanation from the presidential tripod."[101] Yet another averred that Lincoln "has fallen immensely in the estimation of even his own party," for his speeches "are regarded as failures."[102]

Even some Republicans condemned "his declarations as unnecessarily irritating and impolitic."[103] One disenchanted Republican was Charles Francis Adams, who told a friend that Lincoln's "speeches have fallen like a wet blanket here. They put to flight all notions of greatness. But he may yet prove true and honest and energetic, which will cover a multitude of minor deficiencies."[104] In his diary, Adams lamented that "in this lottery we may have drawn a blank," for the speeches "betray a person unconscious of his own position as well as of the nature of the contest around him. Good natured, kindly, honest, but frivolous and uncertain. . . . I confess I am gloomy about him. His beginning is inauspicious. It indicates the absence of the heroic qualities which he most needs." On February 19, Adams told his family that "ten days before, the whole game was in Seward's hands; but now it was surrendered again to the chapter of accidents. The difficulty was wholly owing to Lincoln's folly in not consulting with his official advisers, but saying whatever came into his head. Thus he was dividing his party deplorably—destroying the chance of union in action. Seward's position had thus been made lamentable; for, with his strength exhausted, he was surrounded by opponents, friends and foes; and here now was Lincoln, without consultation or understanding with Seward, and with no apparent regard for the policy indicated by him, showing an ignorance as complete as lamentable of the position of public affairs, fomenting dissensions and jealousies already too formidable." Presciently, Adams speculated that war would break out within two months.[105]

Another Republican congressman, Samuel R. Curtis of Iowa, deplored Lincoln's journey as "unfortunately prolonged" and "foolishly performed." Curtis especially regretted that the president-elect "made light of grave questions."[106] He did, however, praise the Indianapolis speech as "judicious," even though he would have preferred that Lincoln wait till March 4 before making any policy pronouncements.[107] An Indiana Democrat, Representative William S. Holman, thought that the president-elect's "speeches, & even willingness to receive the triumphal receptions along the line of his journey in the present perils of his country, argues forcably against his possessing the qualities necessary for the crisis."[108]

The unsuccessful vice-presidential candidate of the Constitutional Union Party, Edward Everett, judged that Lincoln's speeches "have been of the most ordinary kind, destitute of every thing not merely of felicity & grace, but of common pertinence. He is evidently a person of very inferior cast of character, wholly unequal to the crisis."[109] A wag quipped that Lincoln's best speech "was that in which he said he had '*nothing to say.*'"[110] The editor of the Springfield, Massachusetts, *Republican* called Lincoln a "simple Susan" and speculated that "the men who fought a week at Chicago to nominate him have probably got their labor for their pains."[111] John Bigelow wryly observed that the president-elect's "forensic performances have not raised the standard of American oratory materially" and that he "does not yet begin to apprehend the difficulties of his position."[112] Lincoln's undignified manner offended a Rhode Island Republican, who complained that it was "with unfeigned mortification I have read his jokes & the accounts of his kissing young women. Imagine Washington on a journey to the Federal Capital, joking, kissing women. When the Queen of England on her throne, in dignified terms expresses her solicitude for our welfare at this critical and anomalous period, Mr. Lincoln sees no danger & is reported to have said 'No one is hurt,' and jokes, & kisses the women."[113]

The Philadelphia *Public Ledger* deplored Lincoln's "flippancy," while the *Argus* of that city remarked that he "dispatches the most serious subjects with a joke, and asserts, with a smile, that the present crisis is purely 'artificial.' The tariff and other kindred subjects, which should be familiar to every one aspiring to statesmanship, he acknowledges he does not understand. No definite plan of action seems to have been matured for his administration, but everything is to be left to chance. The humiliating spectacle is thus presented of the President elect of this great confederacy indulging in the merest clap-trap of the politician, thanking the people for voting for him, flattering their local pride, and appealing to their sectional animosities." The Washington correspondent of the New York *Express* noted that the "tone of levity and frivolity, which characterizes the speeches of Mr. Lincoln, causes the hearts of our citizens to sink within them. They perceive already that he is not the man for the crisis."[114]

Even some admirers of Lincoln's speeches believed he should not have delivered them. The president-elect, wrote George Templeton Strong, "has said some things that are sound and creditable," but "I should have been better pleased with him had he held his tongue altogether."[115] The New York *World* protested that even though Lincoln's speeches had been "wise," the journey "after the manner of princes and conquerors, is in bad taste," as well as "useless," "undignified," and "foolish." He should have remained silent until March 4.[116]

Some regretted that Lincoln's itinerary did not include the Upper South, for it was believed that a personal appearance there could relieve anxieties about his policies. But in fact, many residents of the Border States were taken aback by Lincoln's seeming belligerence and unfounded optimism. In Baltimore, criticism of Lincoln's journey was common. Newspapers there decried the "mortifying spectacle" he was making of himself with speeches that were "contradictory and frivolous in substance and delivered in a style that is painfully wanting in the dignity that should belong to the President elect when discussing topics upon which the existence of the Republic depends."[117] The *Sun* scornfully observed that there "is that about his speechification which, if it were not for the gravity of the occasion would be ludicrous to the destruction of buttons. Indeed, we heard his Columbus speech read yesterday amidst irresistible bursts of laughter."[118] Baltimore's literary lion, John Pendleton Kennedy, exclaimed: "Those speeches of his by the way side!—what awful promises of a President!"[119] In western Virginia, a leading Unionist lamented that "Mr. Lincoln, by his speeches in the North, has done us vast harm. If he will not be guided by Mr. Seward but puts himself in the hands of Chase and the ultra republicans, nothing can save the cause of the Union in the South."[120] A Kentuckian scorned the president-elect's "puerile and narrow minded, heartless speeches" and the "debased populace, who are cheering him on in his Union-dooming policy."[121] Melodramatically, the Louisville *Democrat* complained that as "the nation is writhing and groaning in its terrible agony, Mr. Lincoln smiles and jests. While in the very depths of its tribulation and despair, it stretches out its bleeding arms to him for words of hope and assurance, he offers them his cant and his slang, and perpetrates his shallow and disgusting witticisms."[122]

Norman B. Judd, who was part of Lincoln's entourage, disagreed with such criticism. Writing from Buffalo, he reported that "the demonstrations at all points have been very imposing, and whatever doubts may have existed as to the expediency of this kind of journey . . . would be entirely dispelled if the doubters could see what I have seen and whatever opinion may be formed by persons only reading about Mr. L's [passage?] I can say that it has been effective in the extreme." The "excursion will do an immense Service politically," he predicted.[123] James A. Garfield also thought the "tour is having a very fine effect in strengthening the hopes of the union men—and the back-bones of 'Emasculates.'"[124] By the same token, Lincoln's speeches convinced residents of the Lower South that they now had to deal with no weak-willed clone of James Buchanan but rather a firm leader resolved to maintain the Union. They assumed his policies would lead to war, which they confidently assumed they would win.

Lincoln was gaining the affection as well as the respect of many auditors. "Each of the million men whom he meets will have deeper interest in his success, for having seen him, and heard him," predicted the *Ohio State Journal*.[125] O. H. Dutton of the New York *Tribune* noted that Lincoln's power lay "not in his presence or in his speech, but in the honesty and gloriously refreshing sincerity of the Man. In him there is no guile; but he has not the weakness which is often the characteristic of what the Yankees call cleverness. Look at his mouth, and, while you will see nothing dogmatic or overbearing there, you will know that he to whom it belongs is not to be trifled with, and that any trust committed to his keeping will be guarded with unflinching honor. His passage through the country has been like the return of grateful sunshine after a cloudy Winter's day. The people breathe more freely, and hope revives in all hearts."[126] While acknowledging that the president-elect did not seem to be a particularly gifted extemporaneous speaker, the Springfield, Massachusetts, *Republican* praised his "distrust of his own capacity for the important position he is about to take, his confidence in the divine guidance and protection, his fraternal and conciliatory spirit towards all parties and all sections, and his firm adherence to essential principles." Although his addresses contained clichés about upholding the Constitution and enforcing the laws, the *Republican* noted that "from a man of trusted sincerity and integrity even these common-places have had significance and power, and have increased the general confidence that the government has fallen into safe hands at the great crisis in its history."[127] Thurlow Weed's Albany *Evening Journal* aptly observed that it "is no easy matter to talk so much and to do so little harm in talking. . . . Very few men have the faculty to say nothing, and fewer still to speak at all under circumstances like those which surround Mr. Lincoln, without doing mischief."[128] The Providence *Journal* declared that the president-elect's speeches were "fully justifying the confidence which has been placed in him."[129] A Washington correspondent for a Republican paper reported that Lincoln's utterances "exercised a most salutary influence among the Republicans, both in and out of Congress."[130]

Tiring though it was, the journey also had a salutary effect on Lincoln's spirits, which rose dramatically. The "encouragement he has received, [and] the hearty support he has been promised, have more than counterbalanced the fatigues of the way," noted a reporter traveling with the president-elect.[131]

The presidential party spent a quiet Sunday in Buffalo, where Lincoln seemed tired but in good spirits. He and his companions were glad for the much-needed respite. Lincoln had shaken hands for two hours at a reception Saturday night. O. H. Dutton explained why the president-elect was especially tired after such an ordeal: "It is absolutely impossible for Mr. Lincoln to be a formalist in anything. If he makes a speech, he must say what he thinks; and when he shakes hands, he does it with a hearty will, in which his entire body joins. The consequence is that he is more weary after receiving a hundred people than some public men we could all name after being shaken by a thousand."[132] With ex-President Millard Fillmore, he attended church services presided over by Father John Beason, a noted American Indian preacher. Afterward Fillmore hosted Lincoln and his wife for lunch. The couple spent the rest of that cold, damp day quietly at their hotel.

Awkward Arrangements in Albany

In order to depart for Albany at 5:45 A.M., the entourage arose at 4 o'clock on Monday, February 18. It was a "grey, cold, dull winter morning, with snow on the ground," Nicolay recollected. The "spectral dawn outside, and gloom and ominous shadows dimly penetrated by a few feeble lamp-rays inside the depot" gave "an air of unreality to the muffled or flitting forms." Adding to the spooky effect were "the clanging and hissing sounds that came back in hollow echoes from walls and arches."[133] Hay, who deeply resented having to awake so early, called down maledictions on the organizer of the trip, William S. Wood. The young secretary summarized the journey across the Empire State in three words—"crowds, cannon, and cheers"—and painted a composite picture of the day's images: "Such crowds—surging through long arches, cursing the military and blessing Old Abe; swinging hats, banners, handkerchiefs, and every possible variety of festival bunting, and standing with open mouths as the train, relentlessly punctual, moved away. The history of one is the history of all; depots in waves, as if the multitudinous seas had been let loose, and its billows transformed into patriots, clinging along roofs and balconies and pillars, fringing long embankments, swarming upon adjacent trains of motionless cars, shouting, bellowing, shrieking, howling, all were boisterous; all bubbling with patriotism. The enthusiasm for the President was spontaneous and universal; and when we reached Albany, everybody present congratulated himself that he had been a witness of one of the most memorable of triumphal processions which this or any other country has ever witnessed."[134]

En route, Lincoln and his companions discussed a widely publicized squabble between Governor E. D. Morgan and the New York State Legislature over arrangements for the cavalcade's visit to Albany. The governor sought to be Lincoln's host exclusively, but the legislature wanted him to be more accessible to everyone. Both the press and the presidential entourage found such bickering "undignified and absurd."[135] At Buffalo, a persistent Morgan staffer had importuned Lincoln to stay and dine at the governor's house; the president-elect agreed to do so because he understood that no other arrangements had been made. A while later, at Utica, members of the New York state special legislative committee on arrangements boarded the train and urged Lincoln not to spend all his time at the governor's mansion but to attend a public reception at the Delavan House hotel. When told that arrangements were already settled in keeping with Morgan's request, Lincoln ordered that the governor be informed that he would spend some time at the hotel reception. To a representative of the governor who protested that Morgan "would be very angry at this change," Lincoln replied simply: "I can't help it."[136] He accommodated both parties by first dining at the governor's and then attending the reception at the hotel.

Rested after his Sabbath in Buffalo, though still suffering from hoarseness and a sore chest, Lincoln was pleased by the support pledged to him en route to Albany. His wife was not pleased, however, with his appearance. He had been wearing a battered, dust-covered hat, a threadbare overcoat, and trousers that failed to reach his unshined shoes. Mrs. Lincoln ordered William H. Johnson, the black servant accompanying them, to fetch the president-elect's new hat and coat, which improved his appearance markedly. (A journalist described Johnson as "a likely mulatto" who was "a very useful member of the party" and whose "untiring vigilance" as "he took care of the Presidential party is entitled to high credit.")[137] The journalist Joseph Howard, Jr., reported that "Mr. Lincoln seemed physically better than at any time since leaving Springfield. The new hat and coat produce an effect that is very perceptible, and at the same time beneficial, though it is very doubtful if the wearer of them knows or cares anything about it."[138] Meanwhile, as the train sped through a snowstorm past Batavia, Rochester, Utica, Syracuse, and Schenectady, the recently resigned senator from Mississippi, Jefferson Davis, was being inaugurated as provisional president of the Confederate States of America in Montgomery, the capital of both Alabama and the newly proclaimed nation.

Lincoln's party reached the capital of New York in the afternoon amid great confusion. Because the police and the military were late in arriving, the large crowd surged unimpeded against the cars. After the tardy soldiers finally cleared a path to the speaker's platform, Lincoln and the mayor emerged to faint cheering. The pushy crowd at first did not recognize the weary, bewhiskered gentleman who scarcely resembled the hearty, clean-shaven candidate depicted in popular prints. On the platform, Lincoln listened to the mayor's welcoming speech and responded to it briefly. As he proceeded to the capitol, the public showed less enthusiasm than Westerners had displayed. Standing before Governor Morgan, he appeared pale and careworn. The local Democratic paper remarked that the president-elect "does not look as if he had the bodily vigor to stand the pressure upon him. He evidently has not the superiority of nature which compels respect and commands isolation, even amid crowds. Rude hands jostled him and his underlings commanded him; and all about him the struggle was who was to control him."[139]

In the chamber of the New York Assembly, Lincoln took his customary self-deprecation to unusual lengths, expressing gratitude to the legislature for its invitation: "It is with feelings of great diffidence, and I may say with feelings of awe, perhaps greater than I have recently experienced, that I meet you here in this place. The history of this great State, the renown of those great men who have stood here, and spoke here, and been heard here, all crowd around my fancy, and incline me to shrink from any attempt to address you. . . . It is true that while I hold myself without mock modesty, the humblest of all individuals that have ever been elevated to the Presidency, I have a more difficult task to perform than any one of them."[140]

After dining with Governor Morgan, Lincoln attended the reception at the Delavan House, where 1,000 people shook his hand. According to a legislator in attendance, "Mrs. Lincoln, although nearly forty [actually forty-two], was dressed like a girl of eighteen with little loops over her shoulders, her arms bare. She wore white kid gloves, and outside of her gloves she wore every ring she possessed. One of the ladies on the Reception Committee on meeting her asked if she didn't find life much gayer in the East. And Mrs. Lincoln 'sizing her up' coolly replied 'Oh no, we have always been used to this.'"[141] Henry Villard judged that the "whole reception has been a sort of failure—a miserable botch, characterized by snobbery throughout. The only part that passed off in any decent manner was the proceedings in the House. The whole affair has opened up developments and heart burnings that will make hereafter a bitter fight in the republican party."[142]

The time spent in Albany, though disagreeable, had not been wasted. A journalist covering that city reported that "the impression made upon the masses here by the appearance and demeanor of the President elect has been unexpectedly favorable. So much has been said in disparagement of the personal appearance of Mr. Lincoln that imagination had depicted him with ogre-like lineaments; but, his face having been much improved by the beard, . . . he is found, on actual inspection, to be a perfectly presentable man, and in his frank and open features the people read at once the sure indications of a kind, generous and truthful nature."[143] One favorably impressed Albany clergyman said of Lincoln: "I think ninety five percent more of him, than before I saw him. . . . He will put his foot down pretty firmly in time. . . . I like Mr. Linco[l]n much. He is in the hearts of the people who have seen him more than any other man."[144] A Massachusetts man who traveled to Albany said Lincoln "looked 100 per cent better than I was led to suppose from any picture etc I had seen."[145] At the next stop (Troy), an abolitionist in the audience confided to his diary that "Mr. Lincoln is a better looking man than his portraits represent him."[146]

In Albany, Thurlow Weed took charge of arranging a place for the Lincolns to stay in Washington prior to the inauguration. He was acting on behalf of Seward, who had invited the president-elect to lodge with him. Lincoln, at the prompting of his wife, who disliked Seward intensely, wrote to Illinois Congressman Elihu B. Washburne on February 15: "I have decided to stop at a public, rather than a private house, when I reach Washington; and Mrs. L. objects to the National [Hotel] on account of the sickness four years ago." (In 1857, at that hostelry president-elect Buchanan, along with several other guests, had taken gravely ill.) "With this to guide you, please call to your assistance all our Republican members from Illinois, and select and engage quarters for us."[147] The following day, he telegraphed Seward about the changed plans. On February 19, Weed informed Willard's Hotel that the president-elect and his aides would be staying there. But that very day Washburne, after consulting with Trumbull and his fellow Republican congressmen from Illinois, had rented a furnished house for the Lincolns. (According to a journalist, the public "is much divided as to the choice of a hotel or private house for his temporary stay. The former is so manifestly in accordance with propriety, and the accepted usage of his predecessors, that there ought to be no hesitation concerning it.")[148] The following day,

Lord Thurlow read a press account of Washburne's arrangements and informed Willard's of the fact. Lincoln supposed that Washburne, who did not receive the president-elect's letter till late on February 18, had chosen Willard's. On February 21, Weed and Ward Hill Lamon explained to Willard's that the presidential entourage would be their guests as of February 23. Simultaneously, Lamon informed Washburne that "Mr. Lincoln desires me to say to you that Mrs Lincoln objects to going to a private house. It is decided to go 'Willards Hotel[.]' It will be explained to you on our arrival."[149]

The hotel management, understandably confused by the flurry of contradictory messages, asked Colonel E. V. Sumner to specify in writing what was desired. When told of this switch in plans, Lincoln said: "I fear, it will give mortal offense to our friends, but I think the arrangement a good one. I can readily see that many other well-meant plans will 'gang aglee,' but I am sorry. The truth is, I suppose I am now public property; and a public inn is the place where people can have access to me."[150] When the party arrived in the capital, a wealthy merchant, William E. Dodge, hurriedly vacated an elegant suite at Willard's to make way for the Lincolns. The rest of the presidential entourage, however, had to settle for what Nicolay deemed "sorry accommodations."[151] The confusion stemmed from Washburne's misreading of Lincoln's letter and the president-elect's delay in deciding on the kind of accommodations he wanted.

Reception in New York

Lincoln was relieved to depart Albany. As the train rolled toward New York City, he was so tired and feeling so poorly that he took little interest in political discussions. Upon reaching the town of Hudson, he was surprised and gratified by the special new car put at his disposal. It featured the latest heating and ventilating technology, plush carpets, luxurious ottomans and sofas, elegant upholstery, national flags suspended at each end, and star-spangled coverings for the walls and ceiling. He spoke at several stops, including Poughkeepsie, where he addressed a crowd of 10,000: "It is with your aid, as the people, that I think we shall be able to preserve—not the country, for the country will preserve itself, (cheers), but the institutions of the country—(great cheering); those institutions which have made us free, intelligent and happy—the most free, the most intelligent and the happiest people on the globe. (Tremendous applause.) I see that some, at least, of you are of those who believe that an election being decided against them is no reason why they should sink the ship. ("Hurrah.") I believe with you, I believe in sticking to it, and carrying it through; and, if defeated at one election, I believe in taking the chances next time. (Great laughter and applause.)" He did not think that the voters "have chosen the best man to conduct our affairs, now—I am sure they did not—but acting honestly and sincerely, and with your aid, I think we shall be able to get through the storm."[152]

Stephen R. Fiske, who replaced Henry Villard as the New York *Herald*'s correspondent covering the president-elect's journey, was struck by the unpretentious quality of Lincoln and his wife, whom he described as "common sense, home-like folks, unused to the glitter and gutter of society. Towering above all, with his face and forehead furrowed by a thousand wrinkles, his hair unkempt, his new whiskers look-ing as if not yet naturalized, his clothing illy arranged, Mr. Lincoln sat towards the rear of the saloon car." Despite his unprepossessing appearance, the president-elect was obviously, Fiske said, "a man of immense power and force of character and natu-ral talent. He seems so sincere, so conscientious, so earnest, so simple hearted, that one cannot help liking him, and esteeming any disparagement of his abilities or de-sire to do right as a personal insult."[153]

Arriving in Manhattan, Lincoln was glad to find 1,300 police efficiently control-ling the crowds (the largest of the entire journey) along the streets connecting the train station and the Astor House. "Such a crowd as greeted his arrival I have never seen," wrote an observer. "A distance of probably six miles, on the route from the De-pot to the Hotel, the streets were positively jammed with human beings, of all sizes, sexes, and colors."[154] During the ride, Lincoln occasionally stood to acknowledge cheers, but for the most part he remained seated, manifestly drained by the rigors of the trip. Despite appearing pallid and sorely burdened by his grave responsibilities, he seemed to one journalist "firm, self-possessed, and . . . equal to the stupendous task before him."[155] George William Curtis noted that "he looked at the people with a weary, melancholy air, as if he felt already the heavy burden of his duty."[156]

Accounts of the public's reaction varied. Some sources reported that onlookers, who were mostly men, cheered him cordially but not enthusiastically. But one woman who observed the procession recorded in her diary that there was "great enthusiasm," and another wrote that Lincoln "was obliged to ride with his hat off, so continual was the cheering and waving of handkerchiefs."[157] At the Astor House, Walt Whitman observed Lincoln descend from his carriage. The poet was impressed with the president-elect's "perfect composure and coolness—his unusual and uncouth height, his dress of complete black, stovepipe hat push'd back on the head, dark-brown com-plexion, seam'd and wrinkled yet canny-looking face, black, bushy head of hair, dis-proportionately long neck, and his hands held behind as he stood observing the people."[158] During a reception Lincoln met the superintendent of police, John A. Kennedy, whom he greeted warmly: "I am happy to express my thanks and acknowl-edgements to you, Sir, for the admirable arrangements for the preservation of order. I can assure you that they were much appreciated." When Kennedy replied that he was merely doing his duty, Lincoln said: "Yes; but a man should be thanked for doing his duty right well."[159]

Importuned by the crowd outside, Lincoln stepped to the balcony and made his customary nonspeech, during which he betrayed no signs of hoarseness and seemed remarkably self-possessed. When complimented on his brief statement, he replied: "There was not much harm in it at any rate."[160] The Lincolns dined with Hannibal Hamlin and his wife, who were also en route to Washington. When oysters on the half-shell were served, the president-elect regarded them with some puzzlement and said ingenuously, "Well, I don't know that I can manage these things, but I guess I can learn."[161]

After dinner Lincoln consulted with leading politicians and businessmen. When queried about his plans to deal with secession, he said he never crossed a river until he reached it. Weed and others eager to placate the South were "much crosser than bears" at Lincoln's unwillingness to endorse a compromise.[162] Disappointed by his interview with the president-elect, Weed told Seward: "The conversation was confined to a single point, in relation to which I have no reason to suppose that he listened with profit. . . . My solicitude in reference to the Country is not diminished."[163]

Next morning, Lincoln breakfasted with the wealthy merchant Moses Grinnell and twenty-nine other business leaders, who urged the appointment of Cameron as secretary of the treasury. The stock market rose because the president-elect hobnobbed with conservative Wall Streeters rather than with Radicals. Grinnell hoped the breakfast "may do some good; at all events, I kept him from having the Greel[e]y clique around him."[164]

Further raising the hopes of compromisers was Lincoln's response to the official welcome extended by Mayor Fernando Wood, who wished to appease the secessionists and had openly called for New York to follow their lead and declare itself a "free city." A member of the presidential entourage was struck by the contrast between the two men: Lincoln, "tall, gaunt and rugged, with angular, rough-hewn features, but a kindly expression, unpolished in manner and ungraceful in speech, but evidently sincere and genuine," little resembled Wood, "erect and agile, with a perfectly smooth face, easy graceful manners and fine address, but with a countenance as devoid of any indication of his thoughts and as free from the least sign of impulse or genuineness of any kind."[165] At 11 A.M., Lincoln visited City Hall, where Wood, with customary blandness, delivered a jeremiad about the woeful condition of business in the city: "All her material interests are paralyzed. Her commercial greatness is endangered. She is the child of the American Union. She has grown up under its maternal care, and been fostered by its paternal bounty; and we fear that if the Union dies, the present supremacy of New-York may perish with it. To you, therefore, . . . we look for a restoration of fraternal relations between the States—only to be accomplished by peaceful and conciliatory means."[166]

Observers murmured disapproval of Wood's rudeness, but Lincoln took no offense. Seemingly preoccupied, he listened to these remarks with a dreamy look in his eye, smiled pleasantly when Wood finished, drew himself up to his full height, and responded in a voice weakened by a cold. His reply was unscripted, for upon arriving in New York, he admitted, apropos of his scheduled meeting with the mayor: "I haven't any speech ready. I shall have to say just what comes into my head at the time."[167] What came into his head were these remarks: "In reference to the difficulties that confront us at this time, and of which your Honor thought fit to speak so becomingly, and so justly, as I suppose, I can only say that I fully concur with the sentiments expressed by the Mayor. In my devotion to the Union, I hope I am behind no man in the Union. . . . There is nothing that can ever bring me willingly to consent to the destruction of this Union, under which not only the commercial City of New-York, but the whole country has acquired its greatness, unless it would be that thing for which the Union itself was made. I understand a ship to be made for the carrying and preservation of the cargo, and so long as the ship can be saved, with the cargo, it should never be abandoned. This Union likewise should never be abandoned unless it fails and the possibility of its preservation shall cease to exist, without throwing passengers and cargo overboard. So long, then, as it is possible that the prosperity and liberties of this people can be preserved in the Union, it shall be my purpose at all times to preserve it."[168]

When the doors opened to admit the public, they tumbled in pell-mell, reminding onlookers of the onrush of a breached reservoir, the tapping of a beer barrel, or the popping of a champagne cork. As these well-wishers pressed toward him, Lincoln tossed off a characteristic pun: "They are members of the Press." After shaking thousands of hands, he backed away and merely bowed to the multitude as it passed by. He made an exception for women, explaining that "their hands don't hurt me," and for veterans of the War of 1812. He shook 2,000 hands and bowed 2,600 times in two hours. When a gentleman suggested that he might be unanimously reelected, Lincoln replied: "I think when the clouds look as dark as they do now, one term might satisfy any man." Said another: "I must shake hands with you, because they say I look like you," prompting Lincoln to quip: "I take it that that settles that you are a good looking man." Upon leaving City Hall, Lincoln reportedly told the mayor "that, without intending any disparagement of others, he considered his (Mr. Wood's) speech the most appropriate and statesmanlike yet made on a like occasion, and that he (Mr. Lincoln) indorsed every word of it." Among political leaders of the city, this well-publicized comment was viewed as one of his most meaningful statements, for in conjunction with his formal reply to the mayor, it indicated that the president-elect might support compromise.[169] Lincoln seemed to be further distancing himself from his tough Indianapolis speech.

When one of the mayor's staff suggested to Lincoln that he might don a mask and participate incognito in the party scene of Verdi's *Un Ballo in Maschera*, then playing in town, the president-elect replied: "No, I thank you. The papers say I wear a mask already."[170] That evening he attended a performance of the opera, ironically the only one in the standard repertoire about the assassination of an American political leader. Arriving after the overture had begun, he quietly slipped into his seat unnoticed by the crowd. As the music proceeded, however, his presence was detected, and all eyes turned from the stage to his box, where he sat stroking his freshly grown whiskers. At the end of the opening act, the large audience cheered him lustily, shouting his name, waving hats and handkerchiefs. Calm and collected, he rose, bowed, and "gave one the idea of power, stern, rugged and uncompromising; but still there was in the smile something gentle, benevolent and kindly, giving the assurance that justice would be tempered with mercy, and that stern principle would be leavened with that wisdom which springs from a knowledge of the human heart and a sympathy with human weakness."[171] When the curtain rose on act two, the cast and chorus interpolated a spirited rendition of the Star Spangled Banner, at the close of which a huge American flag descended from the flies, touching off a frenzy of patriotic enthusiasm. Lincoln was deeply moved.

Back at the Astor House, he was treated to more music by Verdi when a band serenaded him with selections from *Nabucco* and *Il Trovatore*. Too fatigued and unwell to respond, Lincoln asked Hannibal Hamlin, who had joined him that afternoon, to do the honors. Adding to the decibel level at the Astor House was a clutch of men who stood in the hallway near Lincoln's room bellowing throughout the night. In the morning he appeared quite tired, saying "he had slept scarcely at all."[172]

In New York, Lincoln impressed some leading Democrats, among them an alderman and a judge. The former "said he had seen Lincoln & liked the man, said he was much better looking & a finer man than he expected to see; and that he kept aloof from old politicians here & seemed to have a mind of his own." The latter remarked that the president-elect "has an eye that shows power of mind & will & he thinks he will carry us safely."[173] At the other end of the political spectrum, an abolitionist minister deemed Lincoln "a clever man, & *not so bad* looking as they say." He "is not stiff; has a pleasant face, is amiable & *determined*," and should "deliver our country from the thral[l]dom of imbecility, knavery & slavery."[174]

Some men in the Astor House discussed the president-elect: "We have now a President who will show that he is at the head of a Government, not a political committee."

"He isn't a handsome man, but he don't look weak."

"If his backbone is strong as his arm, we shall have someone to rely on."[175]

A guest at another leading hotel was less enthusiastic. Lincoln "is making an ass of himself," he told a friend. It was "disgusting, and exceedingly humiliating . . . that we have become so degenerate, as to forward an obscure *ignoramus* like the President Elect—to the highest position in the known world."[176]

Resuming the Hard-line Stance

On February 21, the presidential party crossed the Hudson River into New Jersey, where Lincoln dashed the hopes of soft-liners who had found encouragement in his previous day's remarks to Mayor Wood. En route to Trenton, he appeared moody as he sat silent amid the elegant surroundings of his special car. In Newark, he took note of the effigy of a black-bearded man with a whip in his hand hanging from a beam and bearing a label, "The Doom of Traitors."[177]

At the state capitol, Lincoln addressed the General Assembly, emphasizing a theme he had hinted at in his Indianapolis speech ten days earlier. Speaking in a soft, conversational voice, he said: "I shall do all that may be in my power to promote a peaceful settlement of all our difficulties. The man does not live who is more devoted to peace than I am. [Cheers.] None who would do more to preserve it. But it may be necessary to put the foot down firmly." John Hay reported that while delivering that last sentence, "with great deliberation and with a subdued intensity of tone," he "lifted his foot lightly, and pressed it with a quick, but not violent, gesture upon the floor." Another observer noted that as he delivered that line, "his shoulders seemed to straighten, and his eye to kindle." Hay wrote that he "evidently meant it. The hall rang long and loud with acclamations. It was some minutes before Mr. Lincoln was able to proceed."[178] George Alfred Townsend recalled that in "the shouts and cheers and yells and shrieks," one "could hear not only the resolution of battle, but the belief that there was now going to be a fight. The South had bluffed so long" that the Republicans were finally "resolved on a war, and did not mean to waste any time about taking up the gage of battle."[179] When the cheering died down, Lincoln "bent forward, and with a smile and manner that is both inimitable and indescribable," asked the legislators, "if I do my duty, and do right, you will sustain me, will you not?"[180] Hay noted that there "was a peculiar naiveté in his manner and voice, which produced a strange effect upon the audience. It was hushed for a moment to a silence which was like that of the dead. I have never seen an assemblage more thoroughly captivated and entranced by a speaker than were his listeners."[181]

These bold remarks seemed to clash with the more moderate tone Lincoln had adopted since his Indianapolis address. The reception at Trenton and the reaction to his appearances over the past few days evidently convinced him that the North favored the hard-line policy that he himself preferred.

Before the New Jersey State Senate, Lincoln reminisced about his youth: "away back in my childhood, the earliest days of my being able to read, I got hold of a small book, such a one as few of the younger members have ever seen, 'Weems' Life of Washington.' I remember all the accounts there given of the battle fields and struggles for the liberties of the country, and none fixed themselves upon my imagination so deeply as the struggle here at Trenton, New-Jersey. The crossing of the river; the contest with the Hessians; the great hardships endured at that time, all fixed themselves on my memory more than any single revolutionary event; and you all know, for you have all been boys, how these early impressions last longer than any others. I recollect thinking then, boy even though I was, that there must have been something more than common that those men struggled for. I am exceedingly anxious that that thing which they struggled for; that something even more than National Independence; that something that held out a great promise to all the people of the world to all time to come; I am exceedingly anxious that this Union, the Constitution, and the liberties of the people shall be perpetuated in accordance with the original idea for which that struggle was made, and I shall be most happy indeed if I shall be an humble instrument in the hands of the Almighty, and of this, his almost chosen people, for perpetuating the object of that great struggle."[182]

As he prepared to leave the capitol, Lincoln was mobbed and "set upon as if by a pack of good natured bears, pawed, caressed, punched, jostled, crushed, cheered, and placed in imminent danger of leaving the chamber of the assembly in his shirt sleeves, and unceremoniously at that." After lunching at a collation (referred to as a "cold collision" by one New Jersey legislator), the entourage left for Philadelphia, where it arrived at 4 P.M. to find a crowd of 100,000 exuberant people braving the extreme cold and disregarding the threat of a snowstorm. Upon detraining, Lincoln and his party quickly became caught up in great confusion, for the local committee, like so many of its counterparts in other cities, proved inept, bustling about aimlessly. Chaos prevailed as the party tried to enter the waiting carriages. Poor Lincoln, sitting in an open barouche, had to shiver for over half an hour as the flustered committeemen yanked his traveling companions from vehicles to which they had not been assigned. At the Continental Hotel, he reiterated his earlier remarks about the artificiality of the crisis, though he carefully added that "I do not mean to say that this artificial panic has not done harm."[183]

The Possibility of Assassination

That night, after the customary reception, which exhausted him, Lincoln received alarming news that assassins planned to kill him as he passed through Baltimore on February 23. The bearer of this warning, a well-known Chicago detective and friend of Norman B. Judd, Allan Pinkerton, had been hired by the head of the Philadelphia, Wilmington, and Baltimore Railroad, Samuel M. Felton, to investigate rumors that his line would be sabotaged as Lincoln's train rolled along its tracks to Washington. Felton and others had been alerted by an unnamed Baltimorean that a group in the Monumental City planned to set fire to a bridge as Lincoln's train approached it, then attack the cars and kill the president-elect. Earlier, Felton had received similar warnings from the prominent social reformer, Dorothea Dix.

Baltimore was known as "Mobtown" for its bloody history of political violence. In the fall of 1856, as Know-Nothing clubs battled their Democratic opponents, 14 people were killed and 300 injured. Thereafter the two leading clubs—the Blood Tubs and the Plug Uglies—maintained the tradition of partisan mayhem in that "murder-haunted town," as Oliver Wendell Holmes called it.[184] When President-elect Buchanan passed through it en route to his inauguration in 1857, thugs insulted him.

While in Baltimore with some of his agents, Pinkerton inadvertently learned of serious plots to assassinate the president-elect while he was changing trains. The entourage was scheduled to arrive at the depot of the Philadelphia, Wilmington, and Baltimore line and depart from the depot of the Baltimore and Ohio Railroad, over a mile distant. As the party made its way between the two stations, conspirators planned to create a disturbance drawing off the police and then, as a crowd surged around the carriages, kill Lincoln. On February 12, Pinkerton wrote Judd, informing him of the danger and recommending a change in Lincoln's itinerary. In Philadelphia, Judd met with Pinkerton and Felton, who laid out the substantial evidence they had accumulated about the Baltimore plot.

Convinced by their presentation, Judd summoned Lincoln to hear Pinkerton's case. The president-elect, according to Pinkerton, "listened very attentively, but did not say a word, nor did his countenance . . . show any emotion. He appeared thoughtful and serious, but decidedly firm."[185] He inquired about details of the plot and asked Pinkerton for his opinion. The detective said he anticipated that a deadly assault would be made and cited several reasons for so thinking: the murderous expressions of reckless men who were prepared to sacrifice their lives to kill a supposed tyrant; the disloyalty of police superintendent George P. Kane; and the dangers presented by large crowds (such as the one in Buffalo that injured Major Hunter, or the one in Columbus that nearly crushed the president-elect). Lincoln remained silent for a while. When Judd and Pinkerton urged him to take the train to Washington that very night, the president-elect insisted that he must fulfill his obligation to raise a flag over Independence Hall the next morning and then address the Pennsylvania State Legislature in Harrisburg.

Later that night, William Henry Seward's son Frederick reported a similar tale to Lincoln. General Winfield Scott had learned from the newly appointed inspector general of the District of Columbia, Colonel Charles P. Stone, that conspirators planned to assassinate the president-elect as he passed through Baltimore. Stone's informant was a New York detective, David S. Bookstaver, who had been snooping about Baltimore for three weeks. On the morning of February 21, as Lincoln left New York, Bookstaver told Stone "that there is serious danger of violence to and the assassination of Mr Lincoln in his passage through that city should the time of that passage be known. He states that there are banded rowdies holding secret meetings, and that he has heard threats of mobbing and violence, and has himself heard men declare that if Mr Lincoln was to be assassinated they would like to be the men. He states further that it is only within the past few days that he has considered there was any danger, but now he deems it imminent. He deems the danger one which the authorities & people in Baltimore cannot guard against. All risk might be easily avoided by a change in the travelling arrangements which would bring Mr Lincoln & a portion of his party through Baltimore by a night train without previous notice."[186]

General Scott reported this information to Seward, who wrote Lincoln urging him to change his travel plans. When the senator's son handed him that letter, Lincoln inquired about the sources of Stone's information, explaining that there "were stories or rumours some time ago, before I left home, about people who were intending to do me a mischief. I never attached much importance to them—never wanted to believe any such thing. So I never would do anything about them, in the way of taking precautions and the like." But Stone's warning, based on sources different from Pinkerton's, convinced Lincoln to take the threat seriously.[187]

The president-elect received other such warnings, most notably from Captain George W. Hazzard, who was part of his military escort. In an undated memorandum, probably composed on board the train, Hazzard, who had spent several years in Baltimore, recommended that Lincoln avoid passing through that city as originally scheduled. He alleged that Police Chief Kane lacked integrity and had not controlled the city's notoriously violent gangs; that the police would not provide adequate protection; that several thugs in Baltimore would gladly sacrifice their own lives "for having stabbed a 'black republican president'"; and that Baltimore's leading citizens and newspapers favored secession. To support his argument, Hazzard cited "the violent assaults made, in the presence of the whole police force commanded by Marshal Kane *in person*, on the republican procession in that city last summer" and "the murder of one policeman by a rowdy, for attempting to arrest another rowdy for an assault—and the shooting of a second policeman by a couple of assassins while standing at his own fireside for swearing to the identity of the individual who had killed the first policeman." To avoid danger, Hazzard urged Lincoln to bypass Baltimore altogether or to slip through the town incognito.[188] (None of the reminiscences of people involved in this affair refers to Hazzard's memo, but it seems unlikely that it would have been ignored.)

On December 30, a man from Boston sojourning in Baltimore had warned Lincoln that "it will be madness for you to attempt to reach Washington at any time," for the citizens of Baltimore were such rabid secessionists that they had threatened his own life for merely suggesting that the president-elect was a gentleman.[189] An anonymous woman similarly wrote Lincoln that she had been assured "that there existed in Baltimore, a league of ten persons, who had sworn that you should never pass through that city alive."[190] Ominously, the city fathers planned no official greeting or reception for the president-elect, nor did the governor or the legislature do so. All these warning signs made it seem prudent to heed the advice of Pinkerton, Felton, Seward, Judd, Hazzard, et al. and avoid passing through Baltimore as originally planned. Judd warned Lincoln that "the proofs that have now been laid before you cannot be published" lest they compromise Pinkerton's agents. "If you follow the course suggested—of proceeding to Washington to-night—you will necessarily be subjected to the scoffs and sneers of your enemies, and the disapproval of your friends, who cannot be made to believe in the existence of so desperate a plot."

Lincoln replied firmly: "I've Known Pinkerton for years and have Known and tested his truthfulness and sagacity and my judgement co-incides with yours." Authorizing Pinkerton to make all necessary arrangements, he agreed to return to Philadelphia that evening and take the late train to Washington surreptitiously. Cool and calm, Lincoln predicted that he would face no danger once he reached Washington.[191] (But in fact, he did receive death threats after his arrival at the capital, and Judd asked Felton to continue investigating rumors of assassination plots.) Later, Lincoln explained to Congressman Isaac N. Arnold: "I did not then, nor do I now, believe I should have been assassinated, had I gone through Baltimore, as first contemplated; but I thought it wise to run no risk, where no risk was necessary."[192]

On February 24, Police Chief Kane retroactively confirmed the wisdom of the itinerary change, saying: "There would have been a riot if Mr. Lincoln had crossed the city according to the original program. The Plugs on the one hand were determined on giving him a rousing reception, and the Tubs (a democratic organization) were equally determined to prevent the Plugs from giving the president elect any reception at all. The feeling was so violent between these two parties that a fight would certainly have attended Lincoln's passage through the city. . . . when blood has once been shed, they are not controllable. In the row, Mr. Lincoln would have been grossly insulted and probably killed."[193] The Baltimore correspondent of the New Orleans *Picayune* reached the same conclusion. Others believed that an attack was planned on the Republicans greeting the train rather than on its passengers. Subsequent events justified Kane's alarm, for in April, secessionists in Mobtown burned bridges, rioted, and committed murder as they executed plans hatched in January by some of the men accused of conspiring against the president-elect.

Speeches in Pennsylvania

At sunrise on February 22, Lincoln stood before Independence Hall, where he was to hoist a new American flag containing thirty-four stars. (Kansas had been admitted to the Union a few weeks earlier.) Clearly, the warnings of Pinkerton and the others were on his mind, for in an impromptu address inside the historic building he alluded to assassination as well as to the Declaration of Independence: "all the political sentiments

I entertain have been drawn, so far as I have been able to draw them, from the sentiments which originated, and were given to the world from this hall in which we stand. I have never had a feeling politically that did not spring from the sentiments embodied in the Declaration of Independence. (Great cheering.) I have often pondered over the dangers which were incurred by the men who assembled here and adopted that Declaration of Independence—I have pondered over the toils that were endured by the officers and soldiers of the army, who achieved that Independence. (Applause.) I have often inquired of myself, what great principle or idea it was that kept this Confederacy so long together. It was not the mere matter of the separation of the colonies from the mother land; but something in that Declaration giving liberty, not alone to the people of this country, but hope to the world for all future time. (Great applause.) It was that which gave promise that in due time the weights should be lifted from the shoulders of all men, and that all should have an equal chance. (Cheers.) This is the sentiment embodied in that Declaration of Independence. Now, my friends, can this country be saved upon that basis? If it can, I will consider myself one of the happiest men in the world if I can help to save it. If it can't be saved upon that principle, it will be truly awful. But, if this country cannot be saved without giving up that principle—I was about to say I would rather be assassinated on this spot than to surrender it. (Applause.)"

Lincoln assured the crowd that he sought to avoid war, but insisted that if the South attacked federal facilities, his administration would retaliate: "Now, in my view of the present aspect of affairs, there is no need of bloodshed and war. There is no necessity for it. I am not in favor of such a course, and I may say in advance, there will be no blood shed unless it be forced upon the Government. The Government will not use force unless force is used against it. (Prolonged applause and cries of 'That's the proper sentiment.')" Lincoln closed his brief remarks with another allusion to his possible death: "I have said nothing but what I am willing to live by, and, in the pleasure of Almighty God, die by."[194]

Outside, before a vast assemblage braving the winter chill, Lincoln removed his coat and firmly tugged the halyards, sending a large flag up the pole to unfurl and float majestically in the breeze as the newly risen sun illuminated it. Enhancing the patriotic tableau, a band played the national anthem and the militia fired a salute. The crowd of 30,000 cheered wildly, reminding one observer "of some of the storied shouts which rang among the Scottish hills, in the days of clans and clansmen."[195] A newspaperman who had been with the presidential party all along wrote that at "no time has so popular an incident occurred during the trip. All things combined to make it not only impressively grand, but emphatically popular."[196] A local Democratic paper scorned Lincoln's talk of "an equal chance" as a disguised plea for the emancipation and enfranchisement of blacks, and called the president-elect "obscure, rude, ignorant, vulgar and boorish."[197] According to Samuel Francis Du Pont, commandant of the Philadelphia Navy Yard, Lincoln "made a very favorable impression" in the City of Brotherly Love. "Younger and much finer looking than his portraits," the president-elect, according to Du Pont, was a "pleasurable surprise—tall and gaunt like Clay and without the latter's grace, he is still very pleasing and evidently self-reliant and far above the crowd who composed his suite."[198]

At 8:30 A.M., Lincoln departed for Harrisburg; en route, Judd spelled out the details of the altered itinerary: in the evening, Lincoln would return to Philadelphia on a special train, board the 10:50 P.M. regular train for Washington, accompanied only by Lamon, Pinkerton, and one of Pinkerton's agents; they would arrive in the nation's capital at 6 A.M.; telegraph wires from Harrisburg would be cut. In the Pennsylvania capital, Lincoln discussed the plan with a few members of the entourage, emphasizing the need for secrecy. Yet he insisted that his wife be informed, for, he said, "otherwise she would be very much excited at his absence."[199] He was right.

When told of the changed plans, Mrs. Lincoln "became very unmanageable," according to Alexander K. McClure, who observed the scene. She demanded that she be allowed to accompany her husband on the new route and, McClure recalled, "spoke publicly about it in disregard of the earnest appeals to her for silence. Prompt action was required in such an emergency, and several of us simply hustled her into her room with Col. Sumner and Norman Judd . . . and locked the door on the outside. The men with her explained what was to be done and forced her to silence as she could not get out of the door." McClure "thought Mrs. Lincoln was simply a hopeless fool and was so disgusted with her conduct that evening" that he never spoke to her again.[200] The trip to Harrisburg that morning was ominous. "All along the route from Philadelphia," John Hay reported, "receptions seemed more the result of curiosity than enthusiasm. Even at Harrisburg, not one man in a hundred cheered. The crowds everywhere were uniformly rough, unruly, and ill bred." Lincoln "was so unwell he could hardly be persuaded to show himself." At the state capital, the "arrangements were unprecedentedly bad; some of the suite and party were unaccommodated with rooms; several in one bed, and others had no rooms at all. The crowd, and the fatiguing ceremonies of the day, and the annoyances and vexation at the badly conducted hotel, proved too much for the patience of the party, who vented their disgust loudly. The committee-men did nothing, and were in every one's way."[201]

Also ominous were Lincoln's remarks in response to a welcoming speech by Governor Andrew G. Curtin. Alluding to a review he had witnessed earlier in the day, the president-elect declared: "While I have been proud to see to-day the finest military array, I think, that I have ever seen, allow me to say in regard to those men that they give hope of what may be done when war is inevitable." He did not say *if* war was inevitable, but *when* it was inevitable. To offset the apparent belligerence of this remark, he expressed the hope that no blood would be shed. He took pains in his later address to the state legislature to underscore his peaceable intentions.[202] Even more ominously, a man on the street asked Lincoln: "How soon are you going to send us down South?" He replied "that there would be no occasion for such a course, but that he was glad to see that there was one ready to act, if the cause of his country should demand him. At this a number cried out, 'we will all go, if you want us.'"[203]

Entering Washington

At the hotel that afternoon, Lincoln had Judd summon Curtin and the most prominent members of the entourage, saying: "I reckon they will laugh at us, Judd, but you had better get them together." When they were assembled, the president-elect told them: "I have thought over this matter considerably since I went over the ground with Pinkerton last night. The appearance of Mr. Frederick Seward, with warning from another source, confirms my belief in Mr. Pinkerton's statement. Unless there are some other reasons, besides fear of ridicule, I am disposed to carry out Judd's plan."[204] Colonel Sumner, who "almost wept with anger," exclaimed: "That proceeding will be a d–d piece of cowardice." Indignantly, he added, "I'll get a Squad of cavalry Sir, cut our way to Washington Sir." Judd replied, "Probably before that day comes, the inauguration day will have passed." The president-elect named the flamboyant Lamon to be his sole bodyguard on the trip, for in the East, Lamon—unlike Hunter and Sumner—was little known; as a native Virginian, he had a Southern accent; he was 6 feet 2 inches tall, muscular, courageous, devoted to Lincoln, and armed with a pair of revolvers, two derringers, brass knuckles, and a huge bowie knife. Sumner protested that he had undertaken to escort Lincoln all the way to Washington, but Judd managed to distract the colonel long enough so that Lamon and Lincoln could depart by themselves, much to Sumner's displeasure. They boarded the special train around 7 P.M., at which time all telegraph lines from Harrisburg were severed.

At 10 o'clock, Lamon and Lincoln, accompanied by two railroad officials, reached West Philadelphia, where they were met by Pinkerton and another railroad executive. The men rode about in a carriage to kill time before the 10:50 departure of the regularly scheduled train to Washington. When it pulled into the station, Lincoln, stooping over to disguise his great height, climbed aboard through the sleeping car's rear door, accompanied by Lamon and Pinkerton. The president-elect, who was described to the conductor as an invalid, promptly entered his berth and drew the curtains. During the ride to Baltimore, Lincoln told a joke sotto voce, but otherwise the three men remained silent. At 3:30 A.M., they reached Baltimore, where horses dragged the car one mile to the Washington Branch depot.

After a long layover, they departed for Washington, arriving at 6 A.M. As Lincoln and his two companions strode through the depot, E. B. Washburne, who had been alerted by Frederick Seward, emerged from behind a huge pillar, saying: "Abe you can't play that on me." With an elbow, Pinkerton jabbed the congressman and, as the detective raised his fist, Lincoln exclaimed: "Don't strike him Allan, don't strike him—that is my friend Washburne.—don't you recognize him?" (Washburne reported to his wife that Lincoln "is very well considering how much he has been jaded and worn down." Years later he recalled that the president-elect resembled "a well-to-do farmer from one of the back towns of Jo Daviess County coming to Washington to see the city, take out his land warrant and get the patent for his farm.")[205]

All four men took a hack to Willard's Hotel. Two minutes after their arrival they were met by Seward, who had overslept and was thus unable to greet the party at the station. (He had been slated to meet and accompany Lincoln to his hotel; Washburne was originally assigned to perform the same office for Mrs. Lincoln in a separate carriage.) The senator, out of breath, said he "had in his possession conclusive evidence showing that there was a large organization in Baltimore to prevent the passage of Mr. Lincoln through that City and he felt confident that Mr. Lincoln could not have come through in any other manner without blood-shed: that this knowledge was what induced him after consultation with General Scott to send his son to Philadelphia to meet Mr. Lincoln with these letters and to urge a change of route; that this change would doubtless create quite a 'Furore', but that he (Seward) would defend it, and endorse it, and that had Mr. Lincoln not taken this step—Genl. Scott was so plainly convinced of the danger to Mr. Lincoln that in all probability he would have sent United States Troops to Baltimore to-day to receive and escort the President Elect." Pinkerton protested that his sources reported no such grandiose threat. Explaining that he was tired, Lincoln repaired to his room.[206]

Shortly after notifying Judd and others that Lincoln had arrived safely, Pinkerton encountered the excited Lamon, who wanted to telegraph the Chicago *Journal* an account of the trip and his role in it. Pinkerton urged him to do nothing without Lincoln's approval and stressed the importance of shaping the story favorably. Later, Pinkerton wrote that Lamon "was determined to make a 'Splurge' and have his name figure largely in it" and that he "talked so foolishly that I lost patience with him and set him down in my own mind as a brainless egotistical fool."[207]

Seward's prediction about a "furore" was accurate. Newspaper descriptions of the "undignified and ridiculous flight by night" proved most embarrassing.[208] Joseph Howard, Jr., of the New York *Times* wrote a highly colored account, describing Lincoln's garb as a cowardly disguise: "He wore a Scotch plaid cap and a very long military cloak, so that he was entirely unrecognizable."[209] In fact, the president-elect had on an old overcoat and a new soft wool hat that he had been given in New York. (Three years later, Howard was jailed for forging a presidential proclamation that appeared in two New York papers.) The "fact that the President elect has sneaked & skulked into the Federal Capitol as if he were an absconding felon, has occasioned the most profound mortification among the Republicans here," New Hampshire Senator John P. Hale reported from Washington.[210] Iowa Congressman Samuel R. Curtis found it "humiliating to have a President smuggled into the capital by night."[211]

Curtis's colleague Henry L. Dawes recalled that Howard's story touched off "a sudden and painful revulsion of feeling" toward Lincoln, "which waited for neither reason nor explanation." The "outcry came near being 'away with him, crucify him.' 'He had sneaked into Washington,' 'he was a coward,' 'the man afraid to come through Baltimore was unfit to be president,' 'Frightened at his own shadow.'" Those "and worse epithets" greeted the president-elect.[212] "These are not times for a high public officer to play the woman," sneered some Philadelphians, who predicted that his "flight was a disgrace from which he can never recover."[213] Caricaturists ridiculed Lincoln mercilessly. George Templeton Strong rightly feared that "this surreptitious nocturnal dodging or sneaking of the President-elect into his capital city, under cloud of night, will be used to damage his moral position and throw ridicule on his Administration."[214] One journalist claimed that the night journey had ruined "the reputation Mr. Lincoln enjoyed for Jackson-like firmness and boldness that the people were anxious once again to see in an occupant of the Presidency."[215] An Indiana Republican leader opined that Lincoln "was in the hands of cowardly men" and that "the Republican cause has thereby been greatly damaged." The president-elect "had better died in the transit" than ignominiously sneaking through Baltimore.[216] The New York *World* expressed disbelief that "a man of his bold and open bearing, who has hewn his way with strength of arm, and will, and force of character to his present high position, would blench at the first show of danger, and of his own choice, travel by night into the capitol."[217]

Republican newsmen who had been accompanying Lincoln called his change in plans "cowardly" and unfavorably compared his action to that of the South Carolinians: "They say nothing can excuse or justify such conduct. . . . Ill-advised, injudicious, indeed every epithet is showered upon the movement." Worthington G. Snethen, a leading Baltimore Republican and a member of the disappointed welcoming committee, complained that "this was a shameful way to treat men who had risked their lives to vote for Lincoln, and that it would have been perfectly safe for Lincoln to have walked through the city."[218] In Michigan, the Republican governor expressed indignation: "I am ashamed when I think of what derision it will be received in the South. If Lincoln don't take the reins vigorously in his own hands smite these villains 'hip & thigh' then the concern is not worth running any longer."[219] The *Illinois State Register* scolded Lincoln: "the dignity of his station, and regard for the character of the country, should have forbidden that he should sneak to the nation's capital incog., like a refugee from justice."[220] Elsewhere in Illinois people had "a deep feeling of shame, mortification, sorrow & indignation."[221] Southern papers denounced Lincoln "as a coward, a more than coward, because of his sending his wife and family over a railroad and in a train in which he was afraid to travel himself."[222]

Some Republicans defended Lincoln's action. The Cincinnati *Gazette* speculated that if he had been killed, "civil war would have broken out immediately, for an enraged North would have blamed the South for the crime and taken swift revenge." If Seward, Scott, Pinkerton, Judd, and the others had entertained any doubts about Lincoln's safety, "it was their imperative duty to urge upon him to forego the Baltimore reception."[223] An Indiana Republican thought Lincoln had shown "true courage," for if he had ignored the warnings and been attacked, "he would have been, in some degree, responsible for any acts of violence, outrage, or bloodshed" in Baltimore.[224] "Who does not remember," asked editor John W. Forney in the course of justifying Lincoln's action, "only a few years ago, when, in broad daylight, some of these fiends in human shape murdered or wounded, or struck down, in the streets, a number of the most respected and influential citizens?"[225] The Baltimore *American* called Lincoln's action "a simple and practical avoidance of what might have been an occasion of disorder and of mortification to all interested in the preservation of the good name of our city."[226]

Lincoln may have overreacted to a threat that was perhaps exaggerated, but given the bloody history of Baltimore mobs and the fatal attack they were to make on Union troops passing through that city on April 19, his decision seems to have been a reasonable precaution, especially since the warnings came from independent sources. Yet Lincoln came to rue that decision, telling friends that he considered it one of the worst mistakes he ever made. His embarrassment at appearing weak and fearful may have disposed him in the momentous coming weeks to avoid steps that might deepen that unfortunate impression.

"I Am Now Going to Be Master"
Inauguration
(February 23–March 4, 1861)

The nation's capital, with its 75,000 inhabitants, was little more impressive in 1861 than it had been when Lincoln first set foot there thirteen years earlier. "As in 1800 and 1850, so in 1860, the same rude colony was camped in the same forest, with the same unfinished Greek temples for workrooms, and sloughs for roads," according to Henry Adams.[1] It was traversed by a noisome canal, which was little more than a malarial open sewer. Henry Villard described the town as "a great straggling encampment of brick and mortar, spread over an infinite deal of space, and diversified with half a dozen government palaces, all in a highly aggravating and inconvenient state of incompleteness." Society was "shifting, unreliable, and vagabondish to the last degree," and it was "always full of cormorants, speculators, and adventurers." Its hotels were "vast caravansaries of noise and rush," its markets extremely expensive, its newspapers insubstantial, and its hot, humid climate "among the worst in the world."[2]

Lincoln's arrival cheered up the town, which had been in despair as the South girded for war and the Buchanan administration dithered. The influential journalist John W. Forney noticed "more joyous faces this Sabbath morning than I have met in years. The friends of the Union, on the streets and in the hotels, are full of buoyant hope, and the enemies of the Union are correspondingly cast down." The president-elect's appearance among them, "like the return of Napoleon to Paris from Elba, has effected a magical change in the opinions of politicians, and the anticipations of the local population."[3] Yet people were unsure what the president-elect's policy would be, for his speeches en route to the capital had oscillated between hard-line and conciliatory approaches to secession.

Dealing with the Washington Peace Conference

Fatigued from the long trip, Lincoln relaxed before breakfasting with Seward, who at 11 A.M. escorted him to the White House. His visit surprised President Buchanan. After a brief chat with the lame-duck chief executive, Lincoln was introduced to the members of his cabinet. On the way back to Willard's, he called on General Scott briefly. That afternoon, the president-elect was, as Iowa Senator James Harlan recalled, "overwhelmed with callers. The room in which he stood, the corridors and halls and stairs leading to it, were crowded full of people, each one, apparently, intent on obtaining an opportunity to say a few words to him *privately*."[4] On March 2, John Hay reported that his boss "sits all day in his parlor at Willard's, receiving moist delegations of bores. That he is not before this torn in pieces, like Actaeon, is due to the vigor of his constitution, and the imperturbability of his temperament."[5]

On the evening of February 23, Mary Lincoln and the rest of the presidential entourage reached Washington. In Baltimore, an unruly mob had greeted them with three loud cheers for Jefferson Davis and three groans for Lincoln. As the party detrained in the Monumental City, the crowd surged back and forth with such force that it drove people off the platform and trampled them. Roughneck boys and men, not content merely to knock the hats off of leading Republicans, surrounded Mrs. Lincoln's car, insulting her rudely. Captain John Pope overheard many ugly expressions and observed several menacing faces amid the crowd, which he thought "consisted precisely of the people capable of [committing an] outrage."[6]

Nonetheless, at lunch Mrs. Lincoln told her hosts "that she felt at home in Baltimore, and being a Kentuckian, was sometimes too conservative for some of Mr. Lincoln's friends."[7] She added that "her husband was determined to pursue a conservative course."[8] With "much indignation" she denounced Lincoln's advisors and said that she had recommended that he "not depart from the route which he had first intended to take."[9] In Washington she continued to proclaim her conservative views.

That night, after dining with Seward, Lincoln held an informal reception for members of the Washington Peace Conference. Lucius E. Chittenden, a delegate from Vermont, admired Lincoln's great aplomb in dealing with a group that included some political opponents. "The manner in which he adjusted his conversation to representatives of different sections and opinions was striking," Chittenden recalled. "He could not have appeared more natural or unstudied in his manner if he had been entertaining a company of neighbors in his Western home."[10] Lincoln impressed them with his uncanny memory. As he was introduced to the delegates by their last names, he recalled most of their first names and middle initials. To several he mentioned their family histories. Betraying no anxiety, he conversed with them warmly, candidly, and with animation. He paid special attention to Southern delegates, particularly the Virginia Unionist William C. Rives, a former senator and minister to France. The diminutive, venerable Rives told his son that when he was presented to Lincoln, the president-elect "took me cordially by the hand—said he had imagined I was at least six foot high, as he always formed an idea of every person he had heard much of. On my remarking to him . . . that I felt myself to be a small man in his presence—he said aloud, so that all the company heard him, 'you are any how a giant in intellect.' I bowed & retired. This piece of Western free & easy compliment passed off among his admirers for first rate Parisian cleverness & tact." Some Southern delegates took umbrage at Lincoln's words, calling him a "boor" and a "cross-roads lawyer." To Rives, Lincoln appeared "to be good natured & well-intentioned, but utterly unimpressed with the gravity of the crisis & the magnitude of his duties." He "seems to think of nothing but jokes & stories. I fear, therefore, we are to expect but little from his influence with the Convention."[11]

When introduced to the unusually tall Alexander W. Doniphan of Missouri, the president-elect asked: "Is this Doniphan, who made that splendid march across the Plains, and swept the swift Camanchee before him?" The general modestly acknowledged that he was that man. "Then you come up to the standard of my expectations," said Lincoln.[12] Recalling their days in Congress together, Lincoln told Reverdy Johnson of Maryland, "I had to bid you good-bye just at the time when our intimacy had ripened to a point for me to tell you my stories."[13]

Asked if he backed the plan that the Peace conferees seemed likely to adopt—James Guthrie's report urging restoration of the Missouri Compromise line, along with half a dozen less controversial measures—Lincoln allegedly "said he had not thoroughly examined it, and was not therefore prepared to give an opinion. If there was no surrender of principle in it[,] it would be acceptable to him."[14] (Unlike the Crittenden Compromise, Gutherie's proposal stipulated that no new territory could be acquired without the approval of a majority of both the Slave and the Free States.) Although this statement seemed to indicate that Lincoln would support compromise measures, Massachusetts delegate John Z. Goodrich reported after a brief conversation with him that "I cannot doubt he is firm & desires no compromise."[15] Most callers were unable to tell which way the discreet president-elect leaned. "Everybody here seems to look to Lincoln & Lincoln says 'delighted to see you &c &c', but no one gets his tongue & everyone has his ear," reported a fellow guest at Willard's.[16]

One who did get Lincoln's tongue was the New York merchant William E. Dodge, who expressed fears that "the whole nation shall be plunged into bankruptcy" and that "grass shall grow in the streets of our commercial cities." Lincoln sternly replied that he would carry out his oath of office to defend the Constitution: "It must be so respected, obeyed, enforced, and defended, let the grass grow where it may." In a more conciliatory tone he added, "If it depends upon me, the grass will not grow anywhere except in the fields and the meadows."[17]

The Peace Conference seemed unable to reach a consensus; on February 26, it voted down Guthrie's report. The following day, however, after the Illinois delegation reversed itself—perhaps at Lincoln's instigation—that report was approved, cheering up friends of conciliation. "Every one seemed to breathe easier and freer than before," wrote a former Ohio congressman. Southern Unionists "were especially joyous and reanimated, not because they had obtained all they had desired, but because they believed the recommendations of the convention would effectually arrest the tide of secession in their states if they were favorably received by Congress."[18] Lincoln's Illinois friend William H. L. Wallace, who had come to the capital to angle for a government job, told his wife that the outcome of the conference "gives great satisfaction to all conservative men of all parties. Indeed the crisis seemed so threatening that most good men forgot party & only regarded the safety of the country." Governor Thomas Hicks of Maryland informed Wallace "that if the conference adjourned without doing anything, . . . he should immediately call the Legislature of his state together & the state would at once secede." Similarly, John Bell confided that Tennessee would probably have pulled out of the Union if the Conference had fizzled.[19]

Lincoln may have persuaded his fellow Illinoisans serving as delegates at the Peace Conference to change their minds. One member of the Prairie State delegation, John M. Palmer, recalled that the president-elect "advised us to deal as liberally as possible with the subject of slavery." (Palmer voted for the Guthrie report with some reluctance.)[20] Moreover, the motion to reconsider was made by Lincoln's former law partner, good friend, mentor, and political ally, Stephen T. Logan. On February 25, John W. Forney reported that Palmer and Logan "have been closeted with him [Lincoln] since his arrival here."[21] The "reconsideration was attributed to the interference of Mr. Lincoln or of his recognized friends," a Massachusetts delegate recalled.[22]

On February 26, the Conference adjourned earlier than planned, evidently so that its members could meet with the president-elect. Governor Hicks warned Lincoln that if the delegates failed to approve a compromise proposal, Maryland would promptly secede. That night, Stephen A. Douglas begged Lincoln to consult with the Illinois commissioners and thereby save the Union. The senator warned that if the Conference failed to agree on a compromise plan, the Upper South and Border States might well secede. He "reminded Mr. Lincoln that he had children as well as Mr. Douglas, and implored him, 'in God's name, to act the patriot, and to save to our children a country to live in.'" Lincoln "listened respectfully and kindly, and assured Mr. Douglas that his mind was engrossed with the great theme which they had been discussing, and expressed his gratification at the interview."[23] The president-elect then met with Illinois's delegates, who the next day voted for Guthrie's report.

That same night several other commissioners (including Rives and George W. Summers of Virginia, Guthrie and Charles S. Morehead of Kentucky, and Doniphan) also urged the president-elect to support a compromise. Lincoln reminded Rives of Aesop's fable about a lion who fell in love with a beautiful damsel, "and how the lion who desired to pay his addresses, solicited permission from the bride's father, and how the father consented, but with the advice that as the lion's teeth were sharp and the claws long, and not at all handsome, he advised the King of Beasts to pull out the one and cut off the other, which being done, the good father easily knocked the lion in the head. So when we have surrendered Fort Sumter, South Carolina will do this with us." When Rives and others insisted that Sumter "could not be relieved without the loss of thousands of lives, and to hold it was but a barren honor," Lincoln replied with a dramatic proposal to solve the Sumter crisis: "You, gentlemen, are members of the Convention. Go to Richmond. Pass a resolution that Virginia will not in any event secede, and I may then agree with you in the fact a State any day is worth more than a fort!"[24] Morehead recorded that in response to Rives's comment about Virginia seceding if coercive measures were taken, Lincoln jumped up and exclaimed: "Mr. Rives! Mr. Rives! if Virginia will stay in, I will withdraw the troops from Fort Sumter."[25] (Months later, the president, referring to this conversation, "talked about Secession Compromise and other such. He spoke of a committee of Southern Pseudo Unionists coming to him before Inauguration for guarantees &c. He promised to evacuate Sumter if they would break up their Convention, without any row or non-sense. They demurred.")[26] This was not the last time Lincoln would make that offer.

The following day, just after the Guthrie scheme won approval with the help of Illinois's commissioners, Lincoln told Washington city leaders "that though the plan of settlement adopted by the Peace Convention was not the one he would have suggested, he regarded it as very fortunate for the country that its labors had thus eventuated harmoniously."[27] Some stiff-back Republicans who held Lincoln responsible for passage of the Guthrie plan loudly denounced the Conference's action and threatened "to give their faithless choice for the Presidency the slip."[28] The only senate Republican who endorsed submitting the Peace Conference plan (a constitutional amendment with seven sections) to the states was Lincoln's close friend Edward D. Baker. No hard evidence suggests that the Oregon senator took that stand at Lincoln's urging, but he may well have done so. Despite Baker's support, the Guthrie proposal went nowhere in Congress.

Threatening to go somewhere was a force bill, which Lincoln helped scuttle. Introduced by Ohio Congressman Benjamin Stanton, that measure authorized the president to call up the militia to suppress an insurrection against the U.S. government and take other military steps. After heated debate, in which Southern Unionists anathematized it, the bill was scheduled to come before the House for a vote on March 1. That day, Representative Alexander R. Boteler of Virginia, fearing that his state would secede immediately upon the passage of such legislation, called on the president-elect, who greeted him warmly: "I'm really glad you have come, and wish that more of you Southern gentlemen would call and see me, as these are times when there should be a full, fair, and frank interchange of sentiment and suggestion among all who have the good of the country at heart." Boteler asked if Lincoln would help defeat the pending force bill. "Of course," came the reply, "I am extremely anxious to see these sectional troubles settled peaceably and satisfactorily to all concerned. To accomplish that, I am willing to make almost any sacrifice, and to do anything in reason consistent with my sense of duty. . . . I'll see what can be done about the bill you speak of. I think it can be stopped, and that I may promise you it will be." When Boteler requested permission to inform his colleagues of this pledge, Lincoln told him: "By no means, for that would make trouble. The question would at once be asked, what right I had to interfere with the legislation of this Congress. Whatever is to be done in the matter, must be done quietly."[29]

It is not certain that Lincoln took steps to derail the force bill, but he probably did so; that very night the House adjourned before voting on the measure, thus killing it. (Evidently, it was thought that the Militia Act of 1795 authorized the president to summon troops for suppressing an insurrection.) His good friend and political confidant Elihu B. Washburne led the move to adjourn. Southern Unionists, convinced that Lincoln would not have the power—and lacked the inclination—to use force against the seceded states, were cheered temporarily. Six weeks later they would feel differently. Whatever he may have done about the force bill, Lincoln definitely helped defeat Ohio Congressman John A. Bingham's bill providing for the offshore collection of import duties.

Lincoln met congressmen and senators on February 25, when Seward escorted him to the Capitol. The New Yorker's face glowed with obvious delight as he introduced the president-elect to everyone; Seward was like a child showing off a new plaything. In the House, Representatives immediately swarmed around Lincoln and received warm, cordial handshakes. Among the less enthusiastic congressmen greeting him was Massachusetts Republican Henry L. Dawes, who had pictured the incoming chief executive in his mind's eye as a kind of deity. "Never did [a] god come tumbling down more suddenly and completely than did mine," Dawes remembered, "as the unkempt, ill-formed, loose-jointed, and disproportioned figure of Mr. Lincoln appeared at the door. Weary, anxious, struggling to be cheerful under a burden of trouble he must keep to himself, with thoughts far off or deep hidden, he was presented to the representatives of the nation over which he was to be placed as chief magistrate."[30] Lincoln towered over the congressmen, resembling "a lighthouse surrounded by waves."[31] As Seward busily urged Democrats to allow themselves to be introduced to Lincoln, he encountered resistance; ominously, only a few accepted the invitation. Virginia Senator James M. Mason, scowling contemptuously, was among those who rebuffed Seward's appeal. In the House, about a dozen Southern Representatives ostentatiously remained seated when the president-elect entered the chamber. Roger A. Pryor of Virginia tried to look like a giant but managed only to resemble a "malicious schoolboy."[32]

Some Southerners found Lincoln even more disillusioning than did Dawes. Alexander W. Doniphan of Missouri thought it was "very humiliating for an American to know that the present & future destiny of his country is wholly in the hands of one man, & that such a man as Lincoln—a man of no intelligence—no enlargement of views—as ridicously vain and fantastic as a country boy with his first red Morocco hat—easily flattered into a belief that he is King Canute & can say to the waves of revolution, 'Thus far shalt thou come and no farther.'"[33]

Like some bipedal, oversized border collie, Seward shepherded Lincoln around Washington, while simultaneously stepping up his efforts to influence the president-elect's policy decisions and appointments. The Illinoisan's speeches en route to Washington caused the senator to remark that the prospect of having to educate Lincoln made him "more depressed than he had been previously during the whole Winter."[34] That education was pursued earnestly in the hectic days of late February and early March, when Lincoln grew ever more conciliatory.

Toning Down the Inaugural Address

Lincoln proved a willing pupil under Seward's tutelage, submitting his inaugural address to him for comment. Before arriving in Washington, Lincoln had shown it to Carl Schurz, who approved of its hard-line tone, and to Orville H. Browning, who did not. Browning thought the following passage too bellicose: "All the power at my disposal will be used to *reclaim* the public property and places which have fallen; to hold, occupy and possess these, and all other property and places belonging to the government, and to collect the duties on imports; but beyond what may be necessary for these objects, there will be no invasion of any State." Browning suggested that it

read: "All the power at my disposal will be used to hold, occupy and possess the property and places belonging to the government, and to collect the duties on imports &c"
and recommended "omitting the declaration of the purpose of reclamation, which
will be construed into a threat, or menace, and will be irritating even in the border
states." Browning conceded that in principle the original draft was justified, but argued cogently that in "any conflict which may ensue between the government and the
seceding States, it is very important that the traitors shall be the aggressors, and that
they be kept constantly and palpably in the wrong. The first attempt that is made to
furnish supplies or reinforcements to Sumter will induce aggression by South Carolina, and then the government will stand justified, before the entire country, in repelling that aggression, and retaking the forts. And so it will be everywhere, and all the
places now occupied by traitors can be recaptured without affording them additional
material with which to inflame the public mind by representing your inaugural as
containing an irritating threat."[35] Others echoed Browning's advice, which Lincoln
took, thus making his most important change to that document.

In Washington, Seward suggested many more alterations. Like Browning, he
tried to modify the address's belligerent tone. Boastfully, he told Lincoln, "I . . . have
devoted myself singly to the study of the case here, with advantages of access and free
communication with all parties of all sections. . . . Only the soothing words which I
have spoken have saved us and carried us along thus far. Every loyal man, and indeed
I think every disloyal man in the South will tell you this."[36] The modest Lincoln may
well have recoiled at this display of raw egotism, but he took the advice of his
secretary-of-state-designate to omit any allusion to the Chicago platform, which
could be interpreted as too partisan; to call secession ordinances "revolutionary"
rather than "treasonable"; and to soften the discussion of reclaiming government
property and references to exercising power.

More striking was Seward's recommendation about the conclusion of the address,
which in its original form posed a bellicose challenge to the secessionists: "In your
hands, my dissatisfied fellow countrymen, and not in mine, is the momentous issue of
civil war. The government will not assail you, unless you first assail it. You can have no
conflict, without being yourselves the aggressors. You have no oath registered in
Heaven to destroy the government, while I shall have the most solemn one to 'preserve,
protect and defend' it. With you, and not with me, is the solemn question of 'Shall it be
peace, or a sword?'" Lincoln took Seward's advice to drop the phrase "unless you first
assail it" and to replace the ominous final sentence with a lyrical appeal to sectional
fraternity. The senator proposed the following language, which called to mind James
Madison's 14th Federalist Paper: "I close. We are not we must not be aliens or enemies
but fellow countrymen and brethren. Although passion has strained our bonds of affection too hardly they must not, I am sure they will not be broken. The mystic chords
which proceeding from so many battle fields and so many patriot graves pass through
all the hearts and all the hearths in this broad continent of ours will yet again harmonize in their ancient music when breathed upon by the guardian angel of the nation."
(This was a variation on passages from Seward's senate speech of February 29, 1860,
when he sought to burnish his credentials as a Moderate.)

Like a rhetorical alchemist, Lincoln transformed those leaden words into a golden prose-poem: "I am loth to close. We are not enemies, but friends. We must not be enemies. Though passion may have strained, it must not break our bonds of affection. The mystic chords of memory, stretching from every battlefield, and patriot grave, to every living heart and hearthstone, all over this broad land, will yet swell the chorus of the Union, when again touched, as surely they will be, by the better angels of our nature." (The term "better Angel" occurs in Dickens's *David Copperfield*.)[37]

Lincoln did not take all of Seward's suggestions. Although he softened the passage dealing with seized federal installations by striking out the phrase "to reclaim public property and places which have fallen"—that was Browning's advice as well as Seward's—he did say: "The power confided to me, will be used to hold, occupy, and possess the property, and places belonging to the government, and to collect the duties and imposts; but beyond what may be necessary for these objects, there will be no invasion—no using of force against, or among the people anywhere." This was tougher than Seward's proposed language.[38]

The revised passage about holding federal property and collecting revenues did not sit well with Stephen T. Logan, to whom Lincoln read the address shortly before inauguration day. "I told him that the southern people would regard that language as a threat and the result would be war," Logan recalled. Lincoln demurred: "It is not necessary for me to say to you that I have great respect for your opinion, but the statements you think should be modified were carefully considered by me and the probable consequences as far as I can anticipate them."[39]

Among the most conciliatory portions of the address was one that struck the keynote, emphasizing the tentative nature of Lincoln's policy declarations: "So far as possible, the people everywhere shall have that sense of perfect security which is most favorable to calm thought and reflection. The course here indicated will be followed, unless current events, and experience, shall show a modification, or change, to be proper; and in every case and exigency, my best discretion will be exercised, according to circumstances actually existing, and with a view and a hope of a peaceful solution of the national troubles, and the restoration of fraternal sympathies and affections." (The second sentence represented a considerable expansion of the original draft, which merely said: "This course will be pursued until current experience shall show a modification or change to be proper.")

At the last minute, Lincoln added a paragraph dealing with the Adams-Corwin-Seward amendment to the Constitution guaranteeing slavery in the states where it already existed. On February 27, the House had defeated that measure, but the following day, when seven more Republicans supported it, the amendment obtained the requisite two-thirds majority. At 4 A.M. of Inauguration Day, March 4, this Thirteenth Amendment squeaked through the senate with a bare two-thirds majority (24–12). On the night of March 3, Lincoln may have gone to the Capitol and lobbied in favor of the measure without knowing its precise details. It read: "No amendment shall ever be made to the Constitution which will authorize or give to Congress the power to abolish or interfere, within any State, with the domestic institutions thereof, including that of persons held to labor or service by the laws of said State." Henry Adams claimed that it required "some careful manipulation, as well as the direct influence of the new President," to obtain passage.[40] In addition, Lyman Trumbull and Seward had a few days earlier introduced a resolution, probably with Lincoln's approval, urging states to issue a call for a national constitutional convention.

In preliminary drafts of his inaugural address, Lincoln had expressed no enthusiasm for changes to the Constitution. In his final revision, he alluded to the freshly-passed amendment and also endorsed Trumbull and Seward's suggestion that a national convention be held to consider other alterations to the document: "I can not be ignorant of the fact that many worthy, and patriotic citizens are desirous of having the national constitution amended. While I make no recommendation of amendments, I fully recognize the rightful authority of the people over the whole subject, to be exercised in either of the modes prescribed in the instrument itself; and I should, under existing circumstances, favor, rather than oppose, a fair oppertunity being afforded the people to act upon it. I will venture to add that, to me, the Convention mode seems preferable, in that it allows amendments to originate with the people themselves, instead of only permitting them to take, or reject, propositions, originated by others, not especially chosen for the purpose, and which might not be precisely such, as they would wish to either accept or refuse. I understand a proposed amendment to the constitution which amendment, however, I have not seen, has passed Congress, to the effect that the federal government, shall never interfere with the domestic institutions of the States, including that of persons held to service. To avoid misconstruction of what I have said, I depart from my purpose not to speak of particular amendments, so far as to say that, holding such a provision to now be implied Constitutional law, I have no objection to it's being made express, and irrevocable."

Those two concessions were, as journalist James Shepherd Pike observed, "as much as the Republicans can grant without entering upon the backing-down policy."[41] Ten months later, when Congressman John A. Bingham mentioned this last-minute insertion, Lincoln said: "It is extraordinary that I should have made such statements in my Inaugural. Are you not mistaken about this?" To Bingham it seemed as if the president "felt that the proposed Amendment had not been correctly reported to him, and that some one had blundered. He reproached no one, nor did he intimate how or by whose agency this passage came to be in the Inaugural Address."[42] Seward was probably Lincoln's (mis)informant.

Lincoln's willingness to support such an amendment was yet another indication of his desire to show that he was not inflexible (except with regard to slavery expansion and secession). He probably thought an unamendable amendment was a contradiction in terms as well as unconstitutional, and that the amendment (as he virtually stated in the inaugural) was a tautology, reaffirming what was already guaranteed in the Constitution. In all likelihood, he regarded his support of the amendment as little more than a sop to the Sewardites and to public opinion in the Upper South and Border States. He doubtless thought that the amendment had little chance of being adopted by three-quarters of the states.

On March 3, Seward offhandedly told dinner guests: "Lincoln that day had shown to him his inaugural address, and had consulted with him in regard to it."

The senator remarked "that while it would satisfy the whole country, it more than covered all his [Seward's] heresies." He added that the address showed Lincoln's "curious vein of sentiment," which the senator called "his most valuable mental attribute."[43] Two days earlier, Lincoln read a draft of the inaugural to the other men who had accepted cabinet positions. Reportedly, he also submitted that document to the scrutiny of Senators Trumbull, Wade, and Fessenden, as well as to Norman B. Judd. On March 3, William H. Bailhache of the Springfield *Illinois State Journal*, who came to Washington to help prepare copies of the inaugural, wrote his wife that the "original draft has been modified every day to suit the views of the different members of the Cabinet. The amendments are principally verbal & consist of softening some of the words & elaborating more at length some of the ideas contained in the original draft."[44]

Though not as conciliatory as Seward and Stephen T. Logan would have liked, Lincoln's address was tough but not bellicose. He would not try to repossess forts, customhouses, post offices, courthouses, and other federal facilities, nor would he permit the seizure of any more, such as Fort Sumter in Charleston harbor and Fort Pickens off Pensacola. As for collecting revenues, it was possible to do so aboard ships stationed outside Southern ports. Lincoln did not allude to this offshore option in his address, but in the following weeks he explored that solution as an alternative to having customs officials enforce the law onshore.

Lincoln's pledge to enforce the laws was softened by his declaration that "Where hostility to the United States, in any interior locality, shall be so great and so universal, as to prevent competent resident citizens from holding the Federal offices, there will be no attempt to force obnoxious strangers among the people for that object. While the strict legal right may exist in the government to enforce the exercise of these offices, the attempt to do so would be so irritating, and so nearly impracticable with all, that I deem it better to forego, for the time, the uses of such offices." (Why he specified "interior localities" and thus seemed to exempt coastal areas is a mystery.) Lincoln here referred to the ten states where he had received no votes at all. In a similar gesture of forbearance, he said that the "mails, unless repelled, will continue to be furnished in all parts of the Union."

The passage about "obnoxious strangers" reminded one observer of the instructions given by Shakespeare's Dogberry (in *Much Ado About Nothing*) to a watchman: "You shall comprehend all vagrom men; you are to bid any man stand, in the Prince's name."

"How if 'a will not stand?"

"Why, then, take no note of him, but let him go, and presently call the rest of the watch together, and thank God you are rid of a knave."[45]

In dealing with the Fugitive Slave Act, Lincoln was also conciliatory. The statute was constitutional and should be enforced, though he suggested that it might be amended to provide accused runaways greater due process: "in any law upon this subject, ought not all the safeguards of liberty known in civilized and humane jurisprudence to be introduced, so that a free man be not, in any case, surrendered as a slave? And might it not be well, at the same time, to provide by law for the enforcement of that clause in the Constitution which guarranties that 'The citizens of each State shall be entitled to all previleges and immunities of citizens in the several States'?"

Also conciliatory was Lincoln's reiteration of his oft-stated pledge not to interfere with slavery in the states where it already existed and his failure to stress the inflammatory issue of slavery in the territories. Alluding indirectly to the Dred Scott decision, Lincoln reiterated arguments he had made four years earlier in response to the Supreme Court's controversial ruling: "I do not forget the position assumed by some, that constitutional questions are to be decided by the Supreme Court; nor do I deny that such decisions must be binding in any case, upon the parties to a suit, as to the object of that suit, while they are also entitled to a very high respect and consideration, in all paralel cases, by all other departments of the government. And while it is obviously possible that such decision may be erroneous in any given case, still the evil effect following it, being limited to that particular case, with the chance that it may be over-ruled, and never become a precedent for other cases, can better be borne than could the evils of a different practice. At the same time the candid citizen must confess, that if the policy of the government, upon vital questions, affecting the whole people, is to be irrevocably fixed by decisions of the Supreme Court, the instant they are made, in ordinary litigation between parties, in personal actions, the people will have ceased, to be their own rulers, having, to that extent, practically resigned their government, into the hands of that eminent tribunal. Nor is there, in this view, any assault upon the Court, or the judges. It is a duty, from which they may not shrink, to decide cases properly brought before them; and it is no fault of theirs, if others seek to turn their decisions to political purposes."

Although Lincoln had clearly followed Seward's advice and softened the hard-line approach taken in early drafts of his inaugural, he emphatically rejected the doctrine of secession. "I hold that in contemplation of universal law, and of the Constitution, the Union of these States is perpetual." Hence no state, "upon its own mere motion," could legally secede. "I therefore consider that, in view of the constitution and the laws, the Union is unbroken; and, to the extent of my ability, I shall take care, as the constitution itself expressly enjoins upon me, that the laws of the Union be faithfully executed in all the states. Doing this I deem to be only a simple duty on my part; and I shall perform it, so far as practicable, unless my rightful masters, the American people, shall withhold the requisite means, or, in some authoritative manner, direct the contrary. I trust this will not be regarded as a menace, but only as the declared purpose of the Union that it will constitutionally defend, and maintain itself. In doing this there needs to be no bloodshed or violence; and there shall be none, unless it be forced upon the national authority."

Denying the state-compact theory espoused by secessionists, Lincoln maintained with some questionable logic that the Union was older than the states, but that was immaterial, for he argued plausibly that if two or more parties enter into a contract, it can be rescinded only if all of them agree. Moreover, the central point was not what the states were *before* they ratified the Constitution but what they became *after* doing so. The states may have been sovereign and independent before-hand but clearly they were no longer so afterwards. Quite pertinently, Lincoln cited the Constitution's supremacy clause and the preamble's reference to forming "a more perfect union," more perfect than the one established by the Articles of Con-federation and Perpetual Union. Curiously, he did not point to Article IV, section 3 of the Constitution, which stipulates that "no new State shall be formed or erected within the Jurisdiction of any other State; nor any State be formed by the Junction of two or more States, or Parts of States, without the Consent of the Legislatures of the States concerned as well as of the Congress." By inference, it seems logical to conclude that the Framers did not authorize the secession of a state without the permission of all the other states. Lincoln's constitutional arguments, echoing those put forth by James Madison during the Nullification Crisis thirty years ear-lier, were sound. He was part of a nationalist tradition expounded by Madison, Alexander Hamilton, John Marshall, Daniel Webster, Joseph Story, James Wilson, and others.

Lincoln offered practical as well as constitutional and historical objections to secession. If states were allowed to withdraw whenever they felt so inclined, chaos would result, leading to anarchy or tyranny: "Plainly, the central idea of secession, is the essence of anarchy. A majority, held in restraint by constitutional checks, and limitations, and always changing easily, with deliberate changes of popular opinions and sentiments, is the only true sovereign of a free people. Whoever re-jects it, does, of necessity, fly to anarchy or to despotism. Unanimity is impossible; the rule of a minority, as a permanent arrangement, is wholly inadmissable; so that, rejecting the majority principle, anarchy, or despotism in some form, is all that is left."

Lincoln pointed out the obvious economic, geographic, and political drawbacks to secession. "Physically speaking, we cannot separate. We cannot remove our re-spective sections from each other, nor build an impassable wall between them. A husband and wife may be divorced, and go out of the presence, and beyond the reach of each other; but the different parts of our country cannot do this. They cannot but remain face to face; and intercourse, either amicable or hostile, must continue be-tween them. Is it possible then to make that intercourse more advantageous, or more satisfactory, after separation than before? Can aliens make treaties easier than friends can make laws? Can treaties be more faithfully enforced between aliens, than laws can among friends? Suppose you go to war, you cannot fight always; and when, after much loss on both sides, and no gain on either, you cease fighting, the identical old questions, as to terms of intercourse, are again upon you." (Lincoln privately ridi-culed secession as a doctrine based on the premise that "the big tub ought to go into the little one.")[46]

Lincoln was following the advice he had given to Pennsylvania Governor Andrew G. Curtin, who had asked him how to couch his inaugural. The president-elect recommended that Curtin make clear "without passion, threat, or appearance of boasting, but nevertheless, with firmness, the purpose of yourself, and your State to maintain the Union at all hazzards."[47]

Completing the Cabinet

While trying to wean Lincoln away from his hard-line positions and rhetoric, Seward also lobbied intently for pro-compromise cabinet aspirants. Five of the seven posts had yet to be filled, including the office of secretary of the treasury. The struggle over that important position raged for days, with hard-liners supporting Salmon P. Chase and soft-liners, led by Seward and Weed, favoring Simon Cameron. Chase reportedly had Lincoln "by the throat and clings with the tenacity of a bull dog to his claim—against an amount of opposition wholly unprecedented."[48]

That the Pennsylvania boss would have a seat in the cabinet had been virtually settled during Lincoln's February 21 stopover in Philadelphia, where he met with James Milliken, a leading industrialist, and several other Cameron supporters. Milliken said that he was authorized to speak for McClure, Curtin, and other opponents of the Chief; that they had withdrawn their objections to Cameron and now supported his candidacy; and that the leading iron and coal men of the Keystone State desired his appointment. Lincoln replied "that it relieved him greatly" but that "he was not . . . prepared to decide the matter and would not until he should reach Washington. That, it had been suggested, it would perhaps be proper and desirable to retain some of the present cabinet officers, for a short time at least, if they would consent to remain." He referred specifically to the strong Unionists Joseph Holt, Edwin M. Stanton, and John A. Dix, who had stiffened Buchanan's backbone.[49]

Why the anti-Cameron forces capitulated is a mystery. According to one account, Cameron, acting on the president-elect's willingness to appoint any Pennsylvanian that the state's party leaders could agree upon, disingenuously offered to step aside in favor of Thaddeus Stevens if McClure, Curtin, and his other critics would withdraw their charges against him. When those critics complied, Cameron double-crossed them by using a letter from McClure to convince Lincoln that Pennsylvania Republicans were united behind the Chief. (Although he asserted that he was "very friendly" toward Stevens, Lincoln told a Pennsylvanian that at age 67, the congressman was too old. That seems implausible, for Stevens was the same age as Attorney-General-Designate Edward Bates. Lincoln considered the Great Commoner too radical rather than too ancient.)[50] Milliken paved the way for Cameron's victory by assuring McClure and Curtin that their faction would receive a fair share of the patronage. David Davis helped Cameron's cause by promising to read to Lincoln a list of reasons that Samuel A. Purviance, the attorney general of Pennsylvania, had drawn up for appointing Cameron treasury secretary.

In addition, some Pennsylvanians feared that if they could not settle on one of their own, their state's seat in the cabinet might be given to a New Jersey leader like William L. Dayton. Not all Pennsylvanians regarded Dayton unfavorably. Congressman John Covode told Lincoln: "I am satisfied that what I said to you about Dayton being a man that would suit Penna was right."[51] Robert McKnight, another Pennsylvania Representative, offered similar advice: "I firmly believe that the selection of Judge Dayton of N. Jersey would be more acceptable to the people of Penna" than

Cameron.[52] Some colleagues in the House echoed McKnight and Covode, and Governor Curtin reported that "there is a large sentiment in [favor of] Dayton for a place in the cabinet & I concur with it." The Jerseyman "would be very acceptable in this state."[53]

Other Pennsylvania Republicans demurred. "We want no New Jersey statesman for Pennsylvania," declared Thaddeus Stevens.[54] Cameron said he would just as soon "have an enemy at home as in N Jersey & did not want Dayton to be appointed."[55]

In Washington, opponents of Cameron besieged Lincoln. On February 26, John Hay reported that if the president-elect "was in any respect an object of sympathy while on his travels, he is certainly doubly so now. He has exchanged the minor tribulations of hand-shaking and speech-making for the graver woes which attach to the martyr toasted between two fires. The conservatives have chiefly had the presidential ear since the unexpected arrival last Saturday morning. Last night a deputation of the straight-outs had an interview with him, their rumored object being to defeat the appointment of Gen. Cameron to the cabinet."[56]

That visit may have been the one during which Thaddeus Stevens and several other members of Congress protested against Cameron, whom Stevens called "a man destitute of honor and honesty," one who would "make whatever department he may occupy a den of thieves."[57]

The president-elect asked the Great Commoner, "You don't mean to say that Cameron would steal?"

"No, I don't think he would steal a red-hot stove."

When Lincoln repeated this quip to Cameron, the Chief was so incensed that he refused to speak to Stevens.

The Lancaster congressman asked why Lincoln had repeated his hostile remark to Cameron. "I thought that it was a good joke, and I didn't think it would make him mad," replied the president-elect.

"Well, he is very mad and made me promise to retract. I will now do so. I believe I told you that I didn't think he would steal a red-hot stove. I now take that back."[58]

On February 28 and March 1, Lincoln met with Cameron, who later recalled that "he asked me what I wanted—told him I didn't want anything. He might take the offices and keep them. I spoke pretty sharp. He offered to make me Atty. Genl. or give me the Interior. I told him I was no lawyer; I didn't want anything if he couldn't give me what he had offered [in Springfield, namely, the portfolio of either the Treasury or the War Department]."[59] Since Lincoln had already decided to name Chase secretary of the treasury, he gave Cameron the War Department post.

As it turned out, the Cameron appointment was, as Horace White put it, "the most colossal blunder of Lincoln's public life."[60] If Pennsylvania Republicans had been able to unite on anyone else, or if the Chief's opponents had not caved in, or if McClure had submitted documents proving Cameron's lack of integrity, or if Cameron had come from a less important state, or if he had not been a candidate for president at the Chicago Convention, or if David Davis and Leonard Swett had not led the Pennsylvanians at that convention to believe that they would have a place in the cabinet, Lincoln might have avoided naming a man "whose very name stinks in the nostrils of the people for his corruption" (in Lincoln's own words).[61] Lincoln told his friend James C. Conkling that, though he was personally opposed to appointing Cameron because of his unsavory reputation, he had received a petition signed by many members of the Pennsylvania State Legislature, whose opinion he could not safely ignore: "It is highly important that the influence of so large and powerful a State as Pennsylvania should be on the side of the Government, and I must waive my private feelings for the public good."[62]

Cameron's selection pleased Seward, who had lobbied for him so hard that Montgomery Blair concluded that "Cameron was brought into the cabinet by Seward."[63] But that was not enough for the New York senator, who also wanted as colleagues former Whigs like Charles Francis Adams, Caleb B. Smith, and Henry Winter Davis, all soft-liners on secession. Lincoln did name Smith as secretary of the interior in preference to the 36-year-old Schuyler Colfax, explaining to the latter that "I had partly made up my mind in favor of Mr. Smith—not conclusively of course—before your name was mentioned in that connection. When you were brought forward I said 'Colfax is a young man—is already in position—is running a brilliant career, and is sure of a bright future in any event.' 'With Smith, it is now or never.'"[64] (In time, Lincoln came to regard Colfax as "a little intriguer,—plausible, aspiring beyond his capacity, and not trustworthy.")[65] Smith, who unlike Colfax aggressively campaigned for the job, proved to be a mediocre secretary, but Indiana had been promised a seat in the cabinet and no other Hoosier commanded so much home support.

Seward was not pleased with the remaining choices of former Democrats Gideon Welles for secretary of the navy, Montgomery Blair as postmaster general, and most especially Salmon P. Chase as treasury secretary. Lincoln favored Blair in part because of the influence of his family, especially his father, Francis P. Blair, Sr. The president-elect read that old man his inaugural address and asked for suggestions. Lincoln explained that "it was necessary to have Southern men & men of Democratic antecedents" and that Montgomery Blair "fulfilled both requirements."[66] Leading Maryland Republicans like Governor Thomas Hicks assured Lincoln that Henry Winter Davis was unacceptable to Union men in his state.

Welles, a newspaper editor and leader of the Connecticut Republican Party, proved to be a good choice, though his appearance made him the object of ridicule. Charles A. Dana recalled that the navy secretary "was a curious-looking man: he wore a wig which was parted in the middle, the hair falling down on each side; and it was from his peculiar appearance, I have always thought, that the idea that he was an old fogy originated." Massachusetts Governor John A. Andrew called him "that old Mormon deacon." To the public he was "Father Welles," and Lincoln referred to him as "Grandfather Welles." Undeniably, there was a "fossiliferous" quality to Welles, which prompted the New York *Herald* to deem him a "fossil almost from the Silurian period." Lincoln liked to tell a joke about Welles: "when asked to personate the grandmother of a dying sailor," the navy secretary begged off, saying "that he was busy examining the model of Noah's ark." But, Dana noted, Welles "was a very wise, strong man. There was nothing decorative about him; there was no noise in the street when he went along; but he understood his duty, and did it efficiently, continually, and unvaryingly."[67] He was familiar with the Navy Department, in which he had served as chief of the bureau of provisions and clothing during the Mexican War.

Montgomery Blair, who acquired a reputation as "the meanest man in the whole government," was "awkward, shy, homely and repellent," according to journalist Noah Brooks.[68] Another newspaperman, William Howard Russell of the London *Times*, was more charitable, describing the postmaster general as a leader of great influence and determination. "He is a tall, lean man, with a hard, Scotch, practical looking head," which served as "an anvil for ideas to be hammered on. His eyes are small and deeply set, and have a rat-like expression; and he speaks with caution, as though he weighed every word before he uttered it."[69] (To placate Henry Winter Davis, Lincoln gave him control of the Maryland patronage.)

In deciding between Cameron and Chase for the Treasury Department, Lincoln polled Republican senators, who favored the latter. Southerners regarded Chase's appointment as "a declaration of war" against their region.[70] They and Northern Conservatives lobbied furiously against the Ohioan. On February 24, Lincoln told John Z. Goodrich that "personally he preferred Chase for the Treasury Department to any other man—but added that he was very much embarrassed by the strong opposition to him by certain politicians in Ohio, Wade included."[71] Horace Greeley—who had been pressuring Lincoln to reject Cameron and to appoint Schuyler Colfax, Thaddeus Stevens, and Chase—was jubilant. After the cabinet choices were announced, the *Tribune* editor crowed to a friend: "we did, by desperate fighting, succeed in getting four honest and capable men into the Cabinet—by a fight that you never saw equaled in intensity and duration. Gov. Chase, the ablest Republican living, who (so Gen. Dix said) was almost indispensable to the Treasury, got it at last." Mrs. Lincoln evidently opposed the Ohioan, for Greeley said that Chase's appointment was obtained "by the determined [pluck?] and clear-headed sagacity of Old Abe himself, powerfully backed by Hamlin, who is a jewel. All the Kitchen Cabinet, including the female President, were dead against him, while the 'Border States' swore they would go out if he were put it in."[72] According to a close friend of Mrs. Lincoln, her "hostility to Mr. Chase was very bitter. She claimed that he was a selfish politician instead of a true patriot, and warned Mr. Lincoln not to trust him too far."[73]

The long struggle over the cabinet, which annoyed and depressed Lincoln, culminated on the night of March 2, when in an agitated voice he told his numerous callers, including Sewardites ferociously resisting the appointment of Chase and Blair, "it is evident that some one must take the responsibility of these appointments, and I will do it. My Cabinet is completed. The positions are not all definitely assigned, and will not be until I announce them privately to the gentlemen whom I have selected as my Constitutional advisers."[74] To Marylanders protesting against Blair, Lincoln was equally emphatic: "I have weighed the matter—I have been pulled this way and that way—I have poised the scales, and it is my province to determine, and I am now going to be master."[75] When Hannibal Hamlin bluntly asked him "whether the Administration was going to be 'a Seward or a Lincoln Administration,'" the president-elect emphatically answered that it would be the latter.[76] For good reason a journalist concluded that "Lincoln is found to possess a will of his own. He is as firm as a rock when he once thinks he is right."[77]

When some senators urged him to dump Seward, Lincoln expressed resentment against "the assumption which such a protest implies that he [Lincoln] will be unduly under the influence of any individual among his advisers."[78] Greeley, who was in Washington to lobby against the Seward-Weed faction, reported on February 28 that the president-elect "is honest as the sun, and means to be true and faithful; but he is in the web of very cunning spiders and cannot work out if he would," thus giving the "compromisers full swing."[79] But Seward himself hardly felt that he had mastered the president-elect. To be sure, he acknowledged that Lincoln was "very cordial and kind toward me—simple, natural, and agreeable." Among other things, the president-elect said: "One part of the business, Governor Seward, I think I shall leave almost entirely in your hands; that is, the dealing with those foreign nations and their governments."[80] Still, the New Yorker was not entirely happy with his attempts to move Lincoln toward compromise. When asked if "things were right at head quarters," Seward promptly answered: "No, they were not wrong, but scarcely quite right."[81]

In fact, Seward was so furious at Lincoln's choices that he threatened to renege on his agreement to join the cabinet. He complained "that he had not been consulted as was usual in the formation of the Cabinet, that he understood Chase had been assigned to the Treasury, that there were differences between himself and Chase which rendered it impossible for them to act in harmony, that the Cabinet ought, as General Jackson said, to be a unit. Under these circumstances and with his conviction of duty and what was due to himself, he must insist on the excluding of Mr. Chase if he, Seward, remained." The president-elect "expressed his surprise after all that had taken place and with the great trouble on his hands, that he should be met with such a demand on this late day." He asked Seward to think the matter over.[82] The next day, Seward formalized his refusal in a letter: "Circumstances which have occurred since I expressed to you in December last my willingness to accept the office of Secretary of State seem to me to render it my duty to ask leave to withdraw that consent. Tendering to you my best wishes for the success of your administration with my sincere and grateful acknowledgements of all your acts of kindness and confidence, towards me I remain, very respectfully."[83]

Seward overplayed his hand. Perhaps he had gotten a swelled head from his success in persuading Lincoln to soften his hard-line stance. It had been an impressive achievement. Before leaving Springfield, the president-elect had expressed a willingness to accept the Seward-Adams-Corwin New Mexico Compromise. Since arriving in Washington, he had approved the Guthrie plan passed by the Peace Conference; he had perhaps even maneuvered behind the scenes to have that plan adopted; he may have helped defeat a force bill; he definitely helped squelch a bill authorizing the offshore collection of custom duties; he had asked Seward's advice in drafting his inaugural address and had followed most of his suggestions; at Browning's urging he had omitted from that address the threat to repossess federal property in the seceding states; and he had appointed Cameron, a leading advocate of compromise, to the cabinet.

Lincoln also made conciliatory public remarks, including a statement on February 27 to Mayor James G. Berret of Washington. Addressing slaveholders in general as well as the mayor, Lincoln said: "I think very much of the ill feeling that has existed and still exists between the people of the section from whence I came and the people here, is owing to a misunderstanding between each other which unhappily prevails. I therefore avail myself of this opportunity to assure you, Mr. Mayor, and all the gentlemen present, that I have not now, and never have had, any other than as kindly feelings towards you as to the people of my own section. I have not now, and never have had, any disposition to treat you in any respect otherwise than as my own neighbors. I have not now any purpose to withhold from you any of the benefits of the constitution, under any circumstances, that I would not feel myself constrained to withhold from my own neighbors; and I hope, in a word, when we shall become better acquainted—and I say it with great confidence—we shall like each other the more."[84] Just why Lincoln became more conciliatory in the week before his inauguration is not entirely clear, but Seward's counsel surely played an important role in effecting that transformation. In addition, the president-elect became more aware of the depth of secessionist feeling in the Upper South and Border States, where Unionism was more conditional than he had understood when he was in Springfield.

Realizing that Seward meant to dominate him the way he had dominated President Zachary Taylor, Lincoln decided to call the senator's bluff by letting it be known that he might appoint someone else to head the State Department and name the New Yorker minister to Great Britain. Rumors spread quickly, including speculation that Chase was to be dropped. When Norman B. Judd heard that Henry Winter Davis rather than Montgomery Blair would become postmaster general, he asked Lincoln about this alteration in the reported cabinet slate. "Judd," came the reply, which clearly referred to Seward, "I told a man at eleven o'clock last night that if this slate broke again it would break at the head [i.e., Seward would have to go]."[85] The man he took into his confidence was George G. Fogg, to whom Lincoln said: "We must give up both Seward and Chase, I reckon; and I have drawn up here a list of the cabinet, leaving them both out." The new slate included William L. Dayton as secretary of state, John C. Frémont as secretary of war, and a New York opponent of Seward as secretary of the treasury. "I am sending this to Mr. Weed," Lincoln remarked.[86] To Seward he sent a different message, written as he was leaving the hotel to deliver his inaugural address: "Your note of the 2nd. inst. asking to withdraw your acceptance of my invitation to take charge of the State Department, was duly received. It is the subject of most painful solicitude with me; and I feel constrained to beg that you will countermand the withdrawal. The public interest, I think, demands that you should; and my personal feelings are deeply inlisted in the same direction. Please consider, and answer by 9 o'clock, A.M. to-morrow."[87]

Seward, aware that he had lost his gamble, capitulated. After conferring with the president on the night of March 4, he withdrew his resignation. Lincoln gave him "to understand that whatever others might say or do, they two would not disagree but were friends."[88] To his wife, Seward explained that Lincoln was "determined that he will have a compound Cabinet; and that it shall be peaceful, and even permanent. I was at one time on the point of refusing—nay, I did refuse, for a time to hazard myself in the experiment. But a distracted country appeared before me; and I withdrew from that position. I believe I can endure as much as any one; and may be that I can endure enough to make the experiment successful. At all events I did not dare to go home, or to England, and leave the country to chance."[89] Though defeated on this opening trick, Seward had not yet learned that Lincoln meant to control his own administration. In time, that lesson would sink in, but only after he issued another dramatic challenge to the president's authority.

Lincoln had to call Chase's bluff as well as Seward's. Assuming that the Ohioan would accept the treasury portfolio, he had not consulted him about the matter since arriving in Washington. On March 6, when the names of all cabinet members were submitted to the senate, the hypersensitive Chase explained to Lincoln his reluctance to accept the post. As Chase later recalled, the president "referred to the embarrassment my declination would occasion him," leading Chase to promise that he would reconsider. After Lincoln had Frank Blair sound out Congressman John Sherman about becoming treasury secretary, and rumors had spread that Chase would be named minister to England, Ohioans opposed to Chase reversed course and urged Lincoln to name him. Finally, Chase yielded.

Lincoln's "compound cabinet" did not please all Republicans. Charles Francis Adams called it a "motley mixture, containing one statesman, one politician, two jobbers, one intriguer, and two respectable old gentlemen."[90] The sardonic Thaddeus Stevens said it consisted "of an assortment of rivals whom the President appointed from courtesy, one stump-speaker from Indiana, and two representatives of the Blair family."[91] Actually, Lincoln chose his four competitors for the presidential nomination not as an act of courtesy but to strengthen his administration by having the most prominent leaders of the party's factions as well as the most important regions represented. He was especially concerned about the Border States, where the cabinet seemed acceptably "moderate and conciliatory in complexion."[92]

Lincoln was careful to balance the cabinet with former Whigs and former Democrats. When Weed protested that there were four of the latter and only three of the former, Lincoln replied that he had been a Whig and would be attending cabinet meetings. (He might also have pointed out that Cameron had hardly been a dyed-in-the-wool Democrat. The New York *Herald* satirically—and aptly—labeled him a "Democratic Know Nothing Republican Conservative.")[93]

Former Congressman David K. Cartter of Ohio asked Lincoln: "Do you not think the elements of the Cabinet are too strong and in some respects too conflicting?"

He replied: "It may be so, but I think they will neutralize each other."[94]

Inauguration Day

On the cloudy morning of March 4, Lincoln rose at 5 A.M. and, after eating breakfast and conferring with Seward, put the finishing touches on the address, which his son Robert read aloud to him. Until 11 A.M., he consulted with various other callers, including Bates, Welles, Cameron, Trumbull, David Davis, and Illinois state senator Thomas Marshall.

At dawn, crowds began gathering at the Capitol, where the senate was about to take a three-hour break after its all-night session. Two thousand volunteer soldiers, organized by Colonel Charles P. Stone acting on General Scott's orders, deployed to their posts; 653 regular troops, summoned from distant forts, together with the marines based at the navy yard, supplemented their ranks. Sharpshooters clambered to the roofs of the taller buildings fronting Pennsylvania Avenue, along which police took up positions. Cavalry patrolled the side streets. Plainclothes detectives circulated among the crowd with instructions to arrest for "disorderly conduct" anyone speaking disrespectfully of the new president. The sound of fife and drum filled the air. Flags and banners fluttered in the chill wind. Rumors of bloody doings were bruited about, though the heavy military presence made it unlikely that anyone would disturb the day's ceremony. Colorfully attired marshals assembled, ready to lead the procession. Gradually, the streets became choked with humanity, eagerly awaiting the appearance of the president-elect. Good humor, decorum, order, and enthusiasm prevailed among the people who turned out to witness the event. The Washington *National Intelligencer* called it "in some respects the most brilliant and imposing pageant ever witnessed in this Capital."[95] Ominously, however, the parade lacked the customary civic groups and political clubs, a sure sign that many Washingtonians did not sympathize with the new president or his party.

A handsome open barouche bore President Buchanan, looking rather feeble, to Willard's Hotel, where Lincoln climbed aboard, taking a seat beside the Old Public Functionary. The president-elect's bearing was "calm, easy, bland, self-possessed, yet grave and sedate."[96] Accompanying them were Lincoln's good friend, Oregon Senator Edward D. Baker, and Maryland Senator James A. Pearce. As the carriage, surrounded by a double row of cavalry and led by sappers and miners from West Point, rolled over the dusty cobblestones of Pennsylvania Avenue, cheers rang out from the dense crowd lining the sidewalks. The troops escorting the presidential carriage made it difficult for the 40,000 spectators to catch a glimpse of its occupants. To some observers, the troops seemed like guards conveying prisoners to their execution. In response to the sociable and animated observations made by Lincoln, who seemed calm and oblivious to the excited crowd, the anxiety-ridden, nerve-wracked Buchanan had little to say and gave the impression that he would have preferred to be elsewhere. Unable to engage Buchanan in conversation, Lincoln then stared at the floor of the carriage absently.

Arriving at the Capitol at 1:15 P.M., Lincoln and Buchanan descended from their carriage. The weary, sad-faced, white-haired incumbent aroused pity, for he seemed friendless and abandoned. By contrast, the black-haired, younger Lincoln, though looking somewhat awkward, radiated confidence and energy. The party repaired to the President's Room, where they shed the dust of Pennsylvania Avenue.

As Lincoln and Buchanan chatted amicably, John Hay eavesdropped on their conversation with "boyish wonder and credulity to see what momentous counsels were to come from that gray and weather-beaten head." Though Hay assumed that each "word must have its value at such an instant," that was not the case. "I think you will find the water of the right-hand well at the White-House better than that at the left," said Buchanan, who "went on with many intimate details of the kitchen and pantry." The president-elect "listened with that weary, introverted look of his, not answering." The following day, when Hay mentioned this colloquy, Lincoln "admitted he had not heard a word of it."[97]

Arm-in-arm the two presidents entered the senate chamber, where diplomats, congressmen, senators, military officers, state governors, justices of the Supreme Court, cabinet members, and other officials had foregathered. Preternaturally calm and impassive, Lincoln sat still, heedless of the gaze that all onlookers directed at him. The nervous, discouraged, and tired Buchanan, on the other hand, fidgeted and sighed gently. After the swearing in of Vice President Hamlin, the assembled dignitaries proceeded to a temporary platform erected over the steps of the east facade of the Capitol. That building was undergoing a major expension that had begun nearly a decade earlier. Above the ramshackle scaffolding loomed the skeletal, half-finished, new cast-iron dome, flanked by a crane. Before it stood thousands of cheering spectators of all ages and both sexes, coming from near and far, some from neighboring Pennsylvania, others from the distant Pacific coast. Many trekked in from the Midwest and Border States. The clouds which had seemed so threatening that morning had lifted, giving way to bright sunshine.

In his famously sonorous voice, Senator Baker announced: "Fellow Citizens: I introduce to you Abraham Lincoln, the President elect of the United States of America." Charles Francis Adams thought Baker undignified, speaking "just as if about to make a speech from the stump."[98]

Before rising to speak, Lincoln sought a place to put his hat. Observing his awkwardness, Stephen A. Douglas (according to an Ohio congressman who witnessed the proceedings) "gallantly took the vexatious article and held it during the entire reading of the Inaugural."[99] Lincoln then stood up, calm, cool, and self-possessed. The crowd cheered, but not vociferously.

After surveying the vast assemblage, Lincoln began deliberately and solemnly reading his address, which lasted thirty-five minutes. He seemed very much at ease and cheerful as he recited the carefully prepared text in a clear, high, firm voice that carried to the outer edge of the vast crowd. A Douglas Democrat reported that each sentence "fell like a sledge hammer driving in the bolts which unite our states."[100] Lincoln's voice faltered only in the final paragraph, whose reference to "the better angels of our nature" brought tears to many eyes. He delivered that peroration feelingly.

"What an audience!" exclaimed Republican leader John Z. Goodrich of Massachusetts. "How attentive!"[101] It often applauded, especially when Lincoln alluded to the Union. After his pronouncement that "I hold, that in contemplation of universal law, and of the Constitution, the Union of these States is perpetual," the lusty cheering went on and on. An exceptionally vigorous shout of approval greeted his pledge to "take care, as the constitution itself expressly enjoins upon me, that the laws of the Union be faithfully executed in all the states." The loudest demonstration occurred when he said to secessionists, "You have no oath registered in Heaven to destroy the government, while I shall have the most solemn one to 'preserve, protect and defend' it." This passage received several rounds of cheering, as did his firm statement that the "power confided to me, will be used to hold, occupy, and possess the property, and places belonging to the government, and to collect the duties and imposts." In addition to cheers, the crowd interjected shouts of "Good," "That's right," "We'll stand by you," "Thank God, daylight appears at last," and "That is the doctrine." On the platform, Douglas made *sotto voce* comments: "Good!" "that's so," "no coercion," and "good again." At the conclusion, the crowd waved hats and manifested its joy with thunderous applause.[102] Grenville M. Dodge of Iowa told his wife: "Old Abe delivered the greatest speech of the age. The 'Sermon on the Mount' only excels it. It is backbone all over."[103]

As the ancient, shriveled, parchment-faced Chief Justice Roger B. Taney, who resembled a "galvanized corpse," rose to administer the oath of office, he appeared very agitated, evidently upset by the new president's remarks about the Supreme Court. After Lincoln swore to "faithfully execute the office of President" and to "preserve, protect, and defend the Constitution," he kissed the Bible. People in the crowd tossed hats into the air, wiped their eyes, and shouted till they grew hoarse. Lincoln shook hands with Taney and the other dignitaries on the platform and then rode with Buchanan back down Pennsylvania Avenue to the White House, where a public reception was held. There the ex-president shook his successor's hand, wished him luck, and returned to Pennsylvania to write a defense of his administration. Lincoln cordially received all well-wishers and kissed thirty-four young girls, representing each state of the Union.

During the inaugural ceremony, Thurlow Weed left early and passed by Winfield Scott, stationed near the Capitol beside an artillery battery. The anxious general asked how the ceremony was going. "It is a success," answered Weed. "God be praised! God in his goodness be praised!" exclaimed Old Fuss and Feathers. The two men then embraced like a pair of joyful school-boys.[104]

The retiring president, who during the delivery of the inaugural "looked the very picture of a forlorn, wretched, careworn, conscience-sore, decrepit old man," seemed unenthusiastic.[105] Yet that afternoon, in conversation with friends, he called the address "high-toned, patriotic, conservative," and "very able."[106] (In fact, many passages in it closely resembled language Buchanan had employed in his annual message to Congress the previous December.)

Douglas was also positive about Lincoln's speech, which he termed "very dignified," and predicted that "it would do much to restore harmony to the country."[107] Lincoln, said the senator, "does not mean coercion; he says nothing about retaking the forts or Federal property—he's all right." The president "deals in generalities—he don't commit himself—and that is doubtless wise," and "the tone is very kind and conciliatory."[108] In the senate, Douglas described the inaugural as "a peace-offering rather than a war message" and said that Lincoln deserved "the thanks of all conservative men."[109] According to Edwin M. Stanton, "Lincoln & the family at the White House, are represented to be greatly elated at Douglas joining in defence of the new administration. It is said to be the chief topic of conversation with visitors at the Executive Mansion."[110]

That evening at the inaugural ball, held in a specially constructed pavilion accommodating 2,500 guests, Mrs. Lincoln entered on the arm of Senator Douglas, which some regarded as an indication that the Little Giant and the Rail-splitter had "buried the hatchet." Relieved to be safely installed, and drained by the ordeal of preparing and delivering his momentous address, the new president appeared tired. One woman blurted out: "Old Abe, as I live, is tipsy. Look at that funny smile."[111] After fifteen minutes of exchanging pleasantries in the receiving line, Lincoln remarked: "This hand-shaking is harder work than rail-splitting." But when the journalist Gail Hamilton offered to spare him the necessity of shaking her hand, he exclaimed: "Ah! Your hand doesn't hurt me."[112] (Lincoln's handshake as well as his hand could hurt; an English reporter told his readers that it "was so hard and so earnest, as to have reduced my own hand nearly to the consistency of pulp.")[113] Charles Francis Adams noted that the Lincolns "came in quite late. They are evidently wanting in all the arts to grace their position. He is simple, awkward and hearty. She is more artificial and pretentious."[114] One commentator wrote that the dignified First Lady "seems to feel her station is as high as that of any of the Queens of the earth."[115] An attendee recalled that it "at once became obvious to all that Mrs. Lincoln would never shine as a hostess in Washington society. She lacked presence, spontaneity, and all the magnetic and intellectual qualities which made Dolley Madison so popular."[116] When a correspondent of the New York *Herald* asked the president if he had any message to convey to that paper's editor, James Gordon Bennett, Lincoln replied: "Yes, you may tell him that Thurlow Weed has found out that Seward was not nominated at Chicago!"[117] The president stayed for only thirty minutes; his wife remained for another two hours.

Public Reaction to the Inaugural

People throughout the country eagerly read and discussed the inaugural. On Broadway, New Yorkers walking along with their noses buried in newspapers collided with each other. There speculation about the inaugural led to heated exchanges among impatient men waiting outside newspaper offices.

> "I'll bet he sticks just as firm as firm as a rock," predicted one.
> "Well, he won't," rejoined another.
> "Old Abe's the Shanghai chicken that'll not be afeared to fight."
> "Go long with you, he's as innocent as a sucking babe."
> "Fifty to a hundred dollars, he says coercion."
> "I take you; where's your money?"
> "Put it up; put it up; I'll hold stakes."
> "No you won't."[118]

One influential resident of the Empire State opined that the "tone of the Inaugural has caused some Republicans to be 'born again.' Our party seems now united."[119]

Baltimoreans nearly came to blows in their eagerness to obtain copies of the inaugural. In Charleston, anxious crowds surrounded newspaper bulletin boards where telegrams were posted. Richmond secessionists danced with joy, confident that Lincoln's address would strengthen their hand. Their counterparts in Nashville lustily crowed over the imminent prospect of war. In Montgomery, Alabama, Confederate leaders eagerly read the text as it came in over the telegraph. Vice-President Alexander H. Stephens exclaimed, "the man is a fool!" while Robert Toombs grumbled and Jefferson Davis clenched his teeth and remained silent.[120]

Northerners received the address positively. Benjamin Brown French, a New Hampshire native whom Lincoln was to appoint commissioner of public buildings, wrote that it "is conciliatory—peaceable—but firm in its tone, and is exactly what we, Union men, want."[121] Another admirer said it "breathes kindness & conciliation, but no dishonorable submission."[122] Others rejoiced that "we have a firm, vigorous, but temperate administration at this critical hour."[123] In Washington, Vermont Congressman Justin Morrill noted that the inaugural was acknowledged "by all to be a paper of extraordinary ability, and, handling difficult topics, one of extraordinary tact."[124] Weed's Albany *Evening Journal* thought Lincoln's address foreshadowed "the conciliatory spirit which will govern his administration, and presents solid ground upon which to base the hope that, ere long, the dark war clouds which hang over the Republic will be dispersed by the rising sun of fraternal fellowship and peace."[125] Iowa Congressman Samuel R. Curtis speculated that the inaugural would "cause reflection to supplant the excitement and fury that now seems to carry everything before it" and thus help to "arrest the revolution."[126] The New York *Tribune* rejoiced that "the Federal Government is still in existence, with a Man at the head of it," one "who will bring order out of seeming chaos, reason out of folly, safety out of danger."[127] Henry J. Raymond of the New York *Times* praised the inaugural's "intellectual and moral vigor" and "profound sincerity." It would have been impossible for Lincoln, said the *Times*, "to go further towards the conciliation of all discontented interests of the Confederacy" without "virtually abdicating the Presidency."[128] The Boston *Atlas and Bee* judged that the "language of conciliation—not compromise—is very freely and strongly used in the last half of the address, while the obligation to obey the expressed will of the people, as provided by law, is as distinctly announced." The only objection "can be possibly made to it, it is in too great a lenience to the revolutionists."[129]

Although most Northerners liked the substance of the inaugural, Lincoln's "rhetorical infelicities" did not suit everyone.[130] The Jersey City *American Standard* deplored it as "involved, coarse, colloquial, devoid of ease and grace, and bristling with obscurities and outrages against the simplest rules of syntax."[131] Others found Lincoln's prose "exceedingly plain, not to say hard-favored."[132] A virulently partisan Ohio Democrat, Congressman Clement L. Vallandigham, suggested that Seward had composed the inaugural, which he asserted was "not written in the direct and straightforward language . . . expected from the plain, blunt, honest man of the North-west." Vallandigham detected in the speech "the forked tongue and crooked counsel of the New York politician, leaving thirty millions of people in doubt whether it meant peace or war."[133]

The discriminating New York attorney George Templeton Strong was more favorably impressed, calling "the absence of fine writing and spread-eagle-ism" a "good sign." Though he objected to Lincoln's treatment of the powers of the Supreme Court and his moral condemnation of slavery, Strong praised the inaugural for being "unlike any message or state paper of any class that has appeared in my time, to my knowledge. It is characterized by strong individuality and the absence of conventionalism of thought or diction. It doesn't run in the ruts of Public Documents, number one to number ten million and one, but seems to introduce one to *a man* and to dispose one to like him." Strong recorded that "Southronizers [i.e., pro-Southern Northerners] approved and applauded it as pacific and likely to prevent collision. Maybe so, but I think there's a clank of metal in it."[134]

Many others heard that same clank, including the editors of the New York *Daily News,* who said that despite the address's "courteous, considerate, and even conciliatory tone," there "is still left a sting."[135] On Wall Street, a broker observed that he and his colleagues were "afraid there is too much fight in it," and consequently "the *market* is feverish."[136] *Frank Leslie's Illustrated Newspaper* remarked that the address's "words of peace and good-will seem to be traced by the bayonet point, by a mailed hand, and overtopping the figure of Mercy frowns the shadow of Force."[137] Varying the metaphor, Charles Sumner likened the inaugural to a "hand of iron in [a] velvet glove."[138]

Many feared the consequences of Lincoln's pledge to hold the forts and to collect the revenues. "Either measure will result in Civil War which I am compelled to look upon as almost certain," Edward Everett speculated presciently.[139] Most Southerners were of the same mind. The Richmond Whig and the Nashville *Union and American* both thought that sentence meant war. The Washington correspondent of the Charleston *Mercury* called it a "fiat of war" and grimly proclaimed that "the declaration of war has been spoken."[140] The editor of that journal warned that if Lincoln should attempt to carry out the policy implicit in that sentence, "there will be war—open, declared, positive war—with booming cannon and blood." He added dismissively: "If ignorance could add anything to folly, or insolence to brutality, the President of the Northern States of America has, in this address, achieved it. A more lamentable display of feeble inability to grasp the circumstances of this momentous emergency could scarcely have been exhibited." Scornfully the editor asked, "has this vain, ignorant, low fellow no counselors—nobody of any comprehension to control and direct him?"[141] The Washington *States and Union* denounced the inaugural as "a miserable shilly-shallying around Robin Hood's barn, meaningless and inexplicable."[142]

Political leaders of the Lower South echoed those views. Texas Senator Louis Wigfall declared that the "Inaugural means war," a "war to the knife and knife to the hilt."[143] Supreme Court Justice John A. Campbell of Alabama deemed it "a beastly thing," a "stump speech . . . wanting in statesmanship—of which he has none—and of dignity and decorum. I should call it an incendiary message—one calculated to set the country in a blaze. He is a conceited man—evidently he has been a great man in—Springfield, Illinois."[144] The Confederate Commissioners, several Southern members of Congress, and Lucius Quinton Washington "agreed that it was Lincoln's purpose at once to attempt the collection of the revenue, to re-enforce and hold Fort Sumter and Pickens, and to retake the other places. He is a man of will and firmness."[145] The readiness of warships in New York harbor convinced them that those plans would be implemented soon.

Some abolitionists disapproved of the inaugural, which they scorned as "double distilled conservatism" whose aim was to "gladden the hearts of 'doughfaces.'" The "Hour has come and gone," said Edmund Quincy, "but the Man was not sufficient for it. The speech was made with the face turned toward the South and with both knees bowed down before the idol it worships."[146] Frederick Douglass saw in the inaugural little hope "for the cause of our down-trodden and heart-broken countrymen [i.e., slaves]." The president "has avowed himself ready to catch them if they run away, to shoot them down if they rise against their oppressors, and to prohibit the Federal Government irrevocably from interfering for their deliverance."[147] Lydia Maria Child was willing to make "great allowance for the extreme difficulty of his position," but she nevertheless thought Lincoln "bowed down to the Slave Power to an *unnecessary* degree." The inaugural, she told John Greenleaf Whittier, "made *me* very doubtful of him."[148]

But other abolitionists thought that Lincoln "met the trying emergency with rare self possession and equanimity" and called his address "a very manly sensible document" that "must inspire the respect and confidence of all who are not blinded by jealousy or partizan zeal."[149] Elizur Wright deemed it "the most masterly piece of generalship which human history has yet to show," demonstrating "that the new President's heart is in the right place, and that, though far in advance of the average North, he knows how to make it follow him—solid."[150] Although Oliver Johnson deplored Lincoln's willingness to enforce the Fugitive Slave Act, he "was so exultant over the defeat of the compromise schemes in Congress and the failure of Weed and Seward in their efforts to exclude Chase from the Cabinet," that he "was predisposed to a favorable judgment of the Inaugural." He told a fellow antislavery militant that "when we consider what it *might* have been if Lincoln had fallen into Seward and Weed's trap, and when we compare it with former papers of the sort, we may well congratulate ourselves."[151]

Foreign press opinion was divided. The mighty London *Times* sneered at Lincoln's "childish" focus on constitutional issues while ignoring the political and practical reality of secession and suggested that he negotiate with the Confederate States.[152] *Punch* was more favorable, lauding the president's insistence that he could not allow such a dangerous precedent as secession to go unchallenged, lest seceders "go on seceding and subseceding, until at last every citizen will secede from every other citizen, and each individual will be a sovereign state in himself."[153] Across the English Channel, *La Patrie* in Paris criticized Lincoln's "irresolution."[154]

Some Northern Democrats were unimpressed. An Ohio legislator thought it contained "too much special pleading to satisfy any portion of the country." He sniffed that "I know many very *small politicians* who could get up as good an inaugural with two days labor—men who never dreamed of being statesman."[155] The ambiguity of the address left the public "at a loss to know what will be his line of policy in regard to the seceding states," commented the *Illinois State Register*.[156]

Such confusion was especially noticeable in the all-important Upper South and Border States. To many in that region the inaugural seemed bellicose. North Carolina

Senator Thomas Clingman warned that if the president "intends to use the power in his hands as he states in his inaugural, we must have war."[157] Such statements resonated with his constituents, who had narrowly rejected calls for a convention and were now reconsidering. Clingman's colleagues from Virginia were reportedly "most discouraged" by the thousands of onlookers at the inaugural ceremonies who were "prepared to sustain and defend the Union."[158] Representatives Henry C. Burnett and John W. Stevenson of Kentucky, along with Albert Rust of Arkansas, indignantly declared that "it smacks of coercion, compulsion, and blood."[159] Unionist delegates to the Virginia secession convention reported that the inaugural, which "came upon us like an earthquake, and threatened to overthrow all our conservative plans," had severely embarrassed them and weakened their position.[160] A resident of the Shenandoah Valley told Stephen A. Douglas that it was "almost dangerous for any one here even to suggest that the inaugeral is not a declaration of war."[161] The Baltimore *Sun* thought it "an exhibition of remorseless fanaticism and unprincipled partisanship," breathing "the spirit of mischief," assuming "despotic authority," and signaling a desire "to exercise that authority to any extent of war and bloodshed."[162]

Many in the Border States read it differently. Kentucky Congressmen Robert Mallory and Francis Bristow thought the address signified peace rather than war. Inspired by the inaugural, Representatives John Bouligny of Louisiana and Andrew J. Hamilton of Texas planned to return home "and battle for the flag and the Union."[163] In St. Louis, the *Missouri Democrat* called the inaugural "emphatically a peace message," and the *Missouri Republican* editorialized that "[s]o far as Missouri and the Border States are concerned, we have to say, that the positions assumed in the Inaugural . . . remove, to a great extent, the causes of the anxiety which have been felt by them, and do not furnish, in any sense, a justification for secession from the Union."[164]

Some Marylanders shared those views. A Baltimore correspondent said that the inaugural "is generally well spoken of, and hopes are freely entertained that it will have a good effect in restoring peace to the country. Maryland will unhesitatingly support the policy of Mr. Lincoln's inaugural, in preference to secession or disunion in any shape."[165] John Pendleton Kennedy liked the inaugural, with its "dignified and truthful" tone and "its spirit for the promotion of concord." To that literary son of Baltimore, it seemed "conciliatory and firm—promising peace, but breathing a purpose to resist aggression against the Government." He had "not the least doubt in the world" that the president "meant peace by it." Kennedy rejoiced that "Lincoln is beginning to perceive the realities of the case and is growing more and more conservative."[166] The Baltimore *American* deemed the inaugural "pacific" and asserted that "it furnishes no pretext for disunion."[167] The *Clipper* also maintained that the inaugural "means only peace and nothing but peace, as far as is possibly consistent with our national honor and the public welfare."[168]

In North Carolina, John A. Gilmer thought that Lincoln had given "most cheering assurances, enough to induce the whole South to wait for the sober second thought of the North."[169] A leading newspaper in the Tarheel State judged that the inaugural "is not unfriendly to the South" and that it "deprecates war and bloodshed, and pleads for the Union."[170] State Senator Jonathan Worth insisted that it "breathes peace to any candid mind."[171]

Some Tennessee papers detected peace rather than war in Lincoln's words. The Nashville *Republican Banner* commented that in light of his oath to enforce the laws, Lincoln had made a "mild and conservative address." The editors thought it conciliatory enough "to dispel all idea of 'coercion.'" Thus, "if civil war is to ensue, it will not be upon his responsibility."[172] The Knoxville *Whig* called the address "peace-loving and conservative in its recommendations."[173]

In the nation's capital, John C. Rives, the slaveowning editor of the Washington *Daily Globe,* tellingly asked critics of the inaugural "what position . . . the President of the United States could possibly take, other than that taken by President Lincoln, without a palpable, open violation of his inaugural oath, and an utter abnegation and abdication of all the powers of government?"[174] Border State congressmen like John S. Millson of Virginia, James M. Leach of North Carolina, and John S. Phelps of Missouri reportedly did "not endorse all the positions taken by Mr. Lincoln" but nevertheless praised "his decision and straightforwardness."[175] The Louisville *Democrat* sensibly observed that Lincoln "is powerless to extricate himself from the obligations of the Constitution. He cannot surrender the forts, if he desired; nor say, on the back of his oath to see that the laws are faithfully executed, that he will forbear their execution." Yet by including modifiers like "as far as practicable" and "unless the people will withhold the requisite means, or direct otherwise," he clearly created "a remonstrance against war."[176] In Alabama, the Mobile *Register* echoed that view, commenting that the tone of the inaugural "seems conciliatory, and upon the whole, rather more dignified—thanks, probably, to Mr. Seward—than recent emanations from the same source had led us to expect."[177]

The country shared the concern expressed by Maryland Congressman Henry Winter Davis, who admired Lincoln's inaugural but feared that he "will be another illustration of the wide difference between a writer & thinker & a man of action— between talking & administration. *If* he will *act* on his Inaugural his administration may yet be a great success."[178]

Lincoln could breathe a sigh of relief and look forward to a peaceable solution to the secession crisis. He had delivered a firm but conciliatory address that seemed likely to strengthen the hand of Southern Unionists. Now time could work its healing wonders. "Nothing valuable can be lost by taking time," he had said in his inaugural. Southerners would eventually realize that Lincoln was no wild-eyed abolitionist; the Upper South would probably remain in the Union; the Deep South would eventually come to understand that it was too small to survive as a viable nation and would therefore return to the fold. In May, Virginia voters would elect Unionists to Congress; in August, Tennessee, Kentucky and North Carolina would follow suit; in November, Maryland would do the same. The nation would be restored without bloodshed. Southern senators like Crittenden, Andrew Johnson, and Lazarus Powell of Kentucky declared "that the action of the past few days, with the Inauguration to-day, means peace and a settlement of all the National difficulties."[179] Johnson said that armed with the Thirteenth Amendment and the bills organizing the territorial governments in Dakota, Nevada, and Colorado with no provision regarding slavery, he could effectively prevail over secessionists in Tennessee.

On March 6 and 7, Congressmen Horace Maynard and Thomas A. R. Nelson of Tennessee asked Lincoln how his inaugural should be interpreted. He told them "that he was for peace, and would use every exertion in his power to maintain it; that he was then inclined to the opinion that it would be better to forego the collection of the revenue for a season, so as to allow the people of the seceding States time for reflection, and that regarding them as children of a common family, he was not disposed to take away their bread by withholding even their mail facilities. He expressed a strong hope that, after a little time is allowed for reflection, they will recede from the position they have taken."[180]

The day after the inauguration, Lincoln was shown a letter demolishing that rosy scenario. From Charleston, Major Robert Anderson wrote that his Fort Sumter garrison would run out of food within six weeks. The fort, sitting on an island in the harbor and ringed by hostile South Carolina batteries, must either be resupplied or surrendered. The former course would probably lead to war, the latter to "national destruction."[181] Lincoln had to choose between them.

21

"A Man So Busy Letting Rooms in One End of His House, That He Can't Stop to Put Out the Fire That Is Burning in the Other"

Distributing Patronage
(March–April 1861)

Lincoln's first six weeks in office taxed him so severely that in July he told his friend Orville H. Browning: "of all the trials I have had since I came here, none begin to compare with those I had between the inauguration and the fall of Fort Sumpter. They were so great that could I have anticipated them, I would not have believed it possible to survive them."[1] He had to make fateful decisions regarding war or peace while dealing with importunate office seekers. Two days after the inauguration, more than a thousand place hunters thronged the White House. Less than a month into his administration, the president told the editor of the New York *Times,* Henry J. Raymond, that "he wished he could get time to attend to the Southern question; he thought he knew what was wanted, and believed he could do something towards quieting the rising discontent; but the office-seekers demanded all his time. 'I am,' said he, 'like a man so busy in letting rooms in one end of his house, that he can't stop to put out the fire that is burning the other.'"[2] Four years later, Lincoln asked a senator plaintively: "Can't you and others start a public sentiment in favor of making no changes in offices except for good and sufficient cause? It seems as though the bare thought of going through again what I did the first year here, would *crush* me."[3] He said that he "was so badgered with applications for appointments that he thought sometimes that the only way that he could escape from them would be to take a rope and hang himself on one of the trees in the lawn south of the President[']s House."[4]

Lincoln devoted much time to patronage because he wished to unite his party and, by extension, the entire North. Judicious distribution of offices could cement the many Republican factions (former Whigs, Free Soilers, Know-Nothings, and anti-Nebraska Democrats) into a harmonious whole. Some thought it an unattainable goal, given the party's diversity. "It is morally impossible for any man, even of transcendent ability," said an Ohio editor, "to so distribute his patronage and shape the policy of his administration as to gratify and keep together such a heterogeneous compound of discordant materials as that of which the 'Republican' party is composed."[5]

As a participant in the 1849 patronage lottery, Lincoln had observed Zachary Taylor undermine his presidency by mishandling the distribution of offices. More recently, Presidents Franklin Pierce and James Buchanan had badly divided the Democratic Party not only with unwise policies regarding slavery but also with ill-advised use of the patronage power. The Buchanan administration had been warned by a Michigan senator who, while urging the selection of men "able and anxious to work for the redemption of the State," admonished that "these *little* matters in the way of the small appointments, if they go wrong, hurt us more than a wrong move on any question of the magnitude of a war with England, a great deal."[6] Unlike Pierce and Buchanan, Lincoln fully appreciated the significance of patronage, and through its wise distribution, he was able to keep Congress relatively happy and his party intact.

Lincoln faced challenges greater than his immediate predecessors had, for he must weed out disloyal civil servants as well as corrupt and incompetent ones. As Navy Secretary Gideon Welles noted, extensive "removals and appointments were not only expected, but absolutely necessary."[7] In his first week as president, Lincoln remarked "that all the departments are so penetrated with corruption, that a clean sweep will become necessary. This, however, will be the work of some months, too hasty removals being prejudicial to public business."[8] (He joked about the president whom he replaced. When one of his favorite journalists, Simon P. Hanscom, wrote that the Lincoln administration would be "a reign of *steel*," the pun-loving president asked: "Why not add that Buchanan's was the reign of *stealing*?")[9]

As Lincoln went about the Herculean effort of replacing 1,100 civil servants, an observer noted that "[a]ll parties are rapidly finding out that the President has a will of his own."[10] Unlike Buchanan and Pierce, he would not be dominated by strong-minded cabinet members or overbearing party leaders.

The Engulfing Tide of Office Seekers

The crush of brazen self-promoters applying for office was fierce. Seward, who regularly visited the White House, told his wife in mid-March that its "grounds, halls, stairways, closets, are filled with applicants, who render ingress and egress difficult." Lincoln, he added, "takes that business up, first, which is pressed upon him most. Solicitants for offices besiege him, and he, of course, finds his hands full for the present."[11] An economic slump helped swell the ranks of aspirants for even the worst-paying jobs. An Indiana congressman was sickened at the way Republicans were "fighting over offices worth one hundred to five hundred dollars."[12] If those clamoring for government posts "would bestow on some reputable calling the energy and toil they waste in securing a spoonful of Government pap," remarked *Frank Leslie's Illustrated Newspaper*, "they would die happier and wealthier men."[13]

On March 15, writing from the White House, John Hay told a friend that the "throng of office-seekers is something absolutely fearful. They come at daybreak and still are coming at midnight."[14] Hay's coadjutor, John G. Nicolay, was constantly hounded by supplicants who wanted "to see the President *for only five minutes*."[15] Assisting Nicolay and Hay was William O. Stoddard, serving as secretary to sign land patents, who recalled vividly the onslaught of office seekers: "such a swarm! Mingled with men of worth, energy, efficiency and highly meritorious political services, were the broken-down, used-up, bankrupt, creditless, worthless, the lame, the halt and the blind, from all the highways and byways of the North. To judge by the claims set forth, there were a thousand men at least upon whose individual labors and prowess had turned the fate of that eventful canvass [of 1860]. Men there were who had never been known to pay an honest debt in their lives, but who, nevertheless, 'expended their entire fortunes to secure Mr. Lincoln's election,' and who deemed it only fair that their immense expenditures should somehow be reimbursed from the overflowing coffers of Uncle Sam."[16]

One of those appealing to Lincoln's sense of gratitude, Hay recalled, "brought a good deal of evidence to prove that he was the man who originated his nomination. He attacked the great chief in the vestibule of the Executive Mansion, and walked with him to the War Department, impressing this view upon him." Waiting patiently while the president conducted his business, the aspirant "walked back to the White-House with him, clinching his argument with new and cogent facts. At the door the President turned, and, with that smile which was half sadness and half fun, he said: 'So you think you made me President?' 'Yes, Mr. President, under Providence, I think I did.' 'Well,' said Lincoln, opening the door and going in, 'it's a pretty mess you've got me into. But I forgive you.'"[17] (Another version of this story has Lincoln tell the supplicant, "I'll give you an office very quick if you will undo your work!")[18]

Lincoln rose early and spent at least twelve hours a day meeting with callers. The Cincinnati *Gazette* reported that he "is about the busiest person in Washington. He is working early and late. His time is taken up mostly with the ceaseless tide of office seekers constantly pouring in upon him. . . . His family only see him at dinner, he being compelled from fatigue to retire to his room as soon as he leaves his office." He "is besieged from morning till night in his ante-rooms, in his parlors, in his library, in his office, at his *matins,* at his breakfast, before and after dinner, and *all night,* until wearied and worn he goes to rest."[19] He allowed himself little time for meals, which he often left before his fellow diners finished eating. A frustrated office seeker observed that the president "is working himself down to a shadow in the vain struggle to consider every case himself."[20] At first, Lincoln planned to examine applications closely to keep patient merit from being eclipsed by the unworthy. Perhaps recalling his own experience in pursuing the commissionership of the General Land Office eleven years earlier, he told Carl Schurz in 1860: "Men like you, who have real merit and do the work, are always too proud to ask for anything; those who do nothing are always the most clamorous for office, and very often get it, because it is the only way to get rid of them. But if I am elected, they will find a tough customer to deal with, and you may depend upon it that I shall know how to distinguish deserving men from the drones."[21] Lincoln was "profoundly disgusted with the importunate herd of office beggars" and complained about being cooped up all day dealing with them.[22] He estimated disapprovingly that 30,000 office seekers flocked to Washington, but he quickly added that there were "some 30,000,000 who ask for no offices."[23] He predicted that "if this government is ever overthrown, utterly demoralized, it will come from this struggle and wriggle for office, a way to live without work; from which nature I am not free myself."[24] In July, shortly after the Union army's defeat at Bull Run, he asked an Illinois friend: "What do you think has annoyed me more than any one thing? . . . the fight over two post offices—one at our Bloomington, and the other at _____, in Pennsylvania."[25]

Some observers feared that Lincoln's health would be ruined by the unending demands of office seekers, who kept him confined to his office night and day. On March 13, he had to cut short his office hours to take a nap. Five days later, it was alleged that his time "is almost wholly engrossed in hearing applications for office. His order is, that all visitors shall be treated courteously and have a fair opportunity of communicating with him personally." Such a schedule "exposes him to harassing importunity, and seriously interferes with his own comfort and health."[26] A brief respite in mid-March afforded little relief, for as Lincoln noted, "when the flies commence leaving in the fall, the few remaining ones always begin to bite like the devil."[27] On March 24, it was reported that the "incessant calls upon the President are terrible. He is disturbed early in the morning and late in the night, and nothing but the persistent efforts of his friends induced him yesterday to issue an order to the effect that he would receive no visits, either of friendship or official, and yet he was intruded upon by some who ought to have commiserated his trouble."[28]

Many did commiserate. Lincoln's longtime friend Hawkins Taylor observed in late March that "Mr Lincoln is now more to be pitied than any man living; he is literally run down day and night."[29] Maine Senator William Pitt Fessenden wrote that the "poor President is having a hard time of it. He came here tall strong & vigorous, but has worked himself almost to death. The good fellow thinks it is his duty to see every body, and do every thing himself."[30] When Henry Villard expressed sympathy, Lincoln replied: "Yes, it was bad enough in Springfield, but it was child's play compared with the tussle here. I hardly have a chance to eat or sleep. I am fair game for everybody of that hungry lot."[31] But he empathized with many of them, saying: "They do not want much, and they get very little. Each one considers his business of great importance, and I must gratify them. I know how I would feel in their place."[32]

Others criticized Lincoln for wasting valuable time on patronage matters while the nation trembled on the brink of civil war. The New York *Times* declared: "Mr. Lincoln owes a higher duty to the country, to the world, to his own fame, than to fritter away the priceless opportunities of the Presidency in listening to the appeals of competing office-hunters, in whose eyes the loss of a thousand-dollar clerkship would be a catastrophe little inferior to the downfall of the Republic!"[33] On March 17, a leading Republican senator threatened that "if the administration did not soon commence devoting time to more momentous questions than the distribution of the spoils he would have to denounce it."[34] Senator James W. Nesmith of Oregon told his colleagues that "the Administration should have something else to think about. It is said that Nero fiddled while Rome was burning, and here are forty thousand office-seekers fiddling around the Administration for loaves and fishes, while the Government is being destroyed." If he were in the president's shoes, Nesmith declared, he "would turn the federal bayonets against the office seekers" and "drive them from the purlieus of this city."[35] Orville H. Browning urged Lincoln not to "permit your time to be consumed, and your energies exhausted by personal applications for office."[36]

White House Secretaries

To help manage the patronage crush, Lincoln had each caller screened by his sober, dignified, blunt chief personal secretary, John G. Nicolay, a 29-year-old German immigrant who did not hesitate to tell people his opinion of them. He was unflatteringly described as "the bulldog in the ante-room" with a disposition "sour and crusty;" as "very disagreeable and uncivil;" and as "a grim Cereberus of Teutonic descent" who had "a very unhappy time of it answering the impatient demands of the gathering, growing crowd of applicants which obstructs passage, hall and ante-room."[37] A more charitable portrait was drawn by the journalist John Russell Young, who said Nicolay "had the close, methodical, silent German way about him. Scrupulous, polite, calm, obliging, with the gift of hearing other people talk; coming and going about the Capitol like a shadow; with the soft, sad smile that seemed to come only from the eyes; prompt as lightning to take a hint or an idea; one upon whom a suggestion was never lost, and if it meant a personal service, sure of the prompt spontaneous return." All in all, Nicolay was a "man without excitements or emotions, . . . absorbed in the President, and seeing that the Executive business was well done."[38] One of his assistants, William O. Stoddard, called Nicolay a "fair French and German scholar, with some ability as a writer and much natural acuteness, he nevertheless—thanks to a dyspeptic tendency—had developed an artificial manner the reverse of 'popular,' and could say 'no' about as disagreeably as any man I ever knew." But, Stoddard pointed out, Nicolay served Lincoln well; his "chief qualification for the very important post he occupied, was his devotion to the President and his incorruptible honesty Lincoln-ward." The youthful German "measured all things and all men by their relations to the President, and was of incalculable service in fending off much that would have been unnecessary labor and exhaustion to his overworked patron." Stoddard thought that Lincoln "showed his good judgment of men when he put Mr. Nicolay where he is, with a kind and amount of authority which it is not easy to describe."[39] Though unprepossessing physically, the slender Nicolay struck the president of the Illinois Central Railroad as "a man of more ability than his appearance indicates."[40] Rather than placing the First Lady in charge of social arrangements, Lincoln chose Nicolay, who efficiently prepared seating charts, guest lists, menus, and the like for state dinners and other ceremonies.

Nicolay's principal assistant, John Hay, also helped breast the surging tide of office seekers, a task he found disagreeable. The relations between Hay and Lincoln resembled those between Alexander Hamilton and George Washington when the former served as the latter's principal aide. John Russell Young recalled that Hay "knew the social graces and amenities, and did much to make the atmosphere of the war[-]environed White House grateful, tempering unreasonable aspirations, giving to disappointed ambitions the soft answer which turneth away wrath, showing, as Hamilton did in similar offices, the tact and common sense which were to serve him as they served Hamilton in wider spheres of public duty."

(Hay's tactfulness was put to the test one day by a gentleman who insisted that he must see Lincoln immediately. "The President is engaged now," replied Hay. "What is your mission?" "Do you know who I am?" asked the caller. "No, I must confess I do not," said Hay. "I am the son of God," came the answer. "The President will be delighted to see you when you come again. And perhaps you will bring along a letter of introduction from your father," retorted the quick-witted secretary. Other lunatics also tried unsuccessfully to see the president.)[41]

Young, who often visited the White House during the Civil War, called Hay "brilliant" and "chivalrous," quite "independent, with opinions on most questions," which he expressed freely. At times sociable, Hay could also be "reserved" and aloof, "with just a shade of pride that did not make acquaintanceship spontaneous." Hay, Young said, combined "the genius for romance and politics as no one . . . since Disraeli," and judged that he was well "suited for his place in the President's family." Young depicted Hay as "a comely young man with [a] peach-blossom face," "exceedingly handsome—a slight, graceful, boyish figure—'girl in boy's clothes,' as I heard in a sniff from some angry politician." His youthful, "almost beardless, and almost boyish countenance did not seem to match with official responsibilities and the tumult of action in time of pressure, but he did what he had to do, was always graceful, composed, polite, and equal to the complexities of any situation which might arise." Hay's "old-fashioned speech" was "smooth, low-toned, quick in comprehension, sententious, reserved." People were "not quite sure whether it was the reserve of diffidence or aristocracy," Young remembered. The "high-bred, courteous" Hay was "not one with whom the breezy overflowing politician would be apt to take liberties." Young noticed "a touch of sadness in his temperament" and concluded that Hay "had the personal attractiveness as well as the youth of Byron" and "was what Byron might have been if grounded on good principles and with the wholesome discipline of home."[42]

Hay was an excellent conversationalist, as his friend Joseph Bucklin Bishop recalled: "He loved to talk, and his keen joy in it was so genuine and so obvious that it infected his listeners. He was as good a listener as he was a talker, never monopolizing the conversation. . . . He talked without the slightest sign of effort or premeditation, said his good things as if he owed their inspiration to the listener, and never exhibited a shadow of consciousness of his own brilliancy. His manner toward the conversation of others was the most winning form of compliment conceivable. Every person who spent a half-hour or more with him was sure to go away, not only charmed with Hay, but uncommonly well pleased with himself."[43] In early 1861, Frederick Augustus Mitchel, who attended Brown when Hay was a student there, encountered him at Willard's Hotel, casually leaning against a cigar stand; in response to Mitchel's congratulations on being named assistant presidential secretary, Hay replied: "Yes. I'm Keeper of the President's Conscience."[44]

Hay was not so much the conscience of the president as he was his surrogate son, far more like Lincoln in temperament and interests than was Robert Todd Lincoln. Hay's humor, intelligence, love of word play, fondness for literature, and devotion to his boss made him a source of comfort to the beleaguered president in the loneliness of the White House. Though twenty-nine years younger than Lincoln, Hay became as much a friend and confidant to the president as their age difference would allow. Congressman Galusha Grow, who served as Speaker of the House from 1861 to 1863, testified that "Lincoln was very much attached" to Hay "and often spoke to me in high terms of his ability and trustworthiness." Grow knew "of no person in whom the great President reposed more confidence and to whom he confided secrets of State as well as his own personal affairs with such great freedom."[45] Hay frequently wrote letters for Lincoln's signature; most of them were routine but one—the famous 1864 letter of condolence to the widow Bixby—achieved world renown.[46]

In 1881, when President-elect James A. Garfield invited Hay to serve another term as a White House secretary, he declined, explaining that "contact with the greed and selfishness of office-seekers and the bull-dozing Congressmen is unspeakably repulsive. The constant contact with envy, meanness, ignorance and the swinish selfishness which ignorance breeds needs a stronger heart and a more obedient nervous system than I can boast."[47] Much as Hay disliked the bulldozing lawmakers, he felt compassion for some of them. On March 6, he reported that congressmen "are waylaid, dogged, importuned, buttonholed, coaxed and threatened persistently, systematically, and without mercy, by day and by night."[48] A month after the election, an Indiana Representative wrote: "I wish there was an office for every deserving working Republican who desired it, but alas! there will not be one for every fifty, I fear."[49]

Hay also sympathized with some office seekers, who were, as he put it, "inspired by a strange mixture of enthusiasm and greed, pushed by motives which were perhaps at bottom selfish, but which had nevertheless a curious touch of that deep emotion which had stirred the heart of the nation in the late [1860] election." Amid "that dense crowd that swarmed in the staircases and the corridors, there were many well-to-do men who were seeking office to their own evident damage, simply because they wished to be a part, however humble, of a government which they had aided to put in power and to which they were sincerely devoted." Lincoln quickly found that he could not personally attend to most applicants. As Hay recalled, "the numbers were so great, the competition so keen, that they ceased for the moment to be regarded as individuals, drowned as they were in the general sea of solicitation. Few of them received office; when, after weeks of waiting one of them got access to the President, he was received with kindness by a tall melancholy-looking man, sitting at a desk with his back to a window which opened upon a fair view of the Potomac, who heard his story with a gentle patience, took his papers and referred them to one of the Departments, and that was all; the fatal pigeonholes devoured them."[50]

In late March, Nicolay persuaded his boss to limit business hours from 10 A.M. to 3 P.M.; soon thereafter he shortened them by two hours and eliminated Saturday visits.

Political Pressure and Unfortunate Appointments

Lincoln intended to call on his cabinet and Congress to help select applicants, but, as he told a friend, he "found to his Surprise, that members of his Cabinet, who were equally interested with himself, in the success of his administration, had been recommending parties to be appointed to responsible positions who were often physically, morally, and intellectually unfit for the place." Apparently, he added, "most of the Cabinet officers and members of Congress, had a list of appointments to be made, and many of them were such as ought not to be made, and they knew, and their importunities were urgent in proportion to the unfitness for the appointee."[51]

Congressmen, senators, and cabinet members were in fact less deeply concerned with the success of the administration than with their own short-term political gain. Adam Gurowski, an irascible, combative Polish nobleman and Radical abolitionist, noted in his diary that cabinet secretaries "have old party debts to pay, old sores to avenge or to heal, and all this by distributing offices." Through the use of patronage, "everybody is to serve his friends and his party, and to secure his political position. Some of the party leaders seem to me similar to children enjoying a long-expected and ardently wished-for toy. . . . They, the leaders, look to create engines for their own political security."[52] Gurowski was right. Patronage greased the wheels of political machines, and party service counted for more than honesty and competence when government jobs were being filled. Friendship or family ties with the powerful also weighed heavily in the balance.

Members of Congress could be touchy about their prerogatives in patronage matters. Galusha Grow of Pennsylvania angrily protested to Lincoln about the failure of his wife's brother to receive a judgeship. An onlooker was surprised when Grow spoke "impertinently" and "used threats." The president apologized and said that when making appointments he had forgotten about Grow's brother-in-law, who would get a place soon.[53] Charles Francis Adams somewhat mistakenly opined that the "difficulty with Mr Lincoln is that he has no conception of his situation. And having no system in his composition he has undertaken to manage the whole thing as if he knew all about it. The first evidence of this is to be found in his direct interference in the removal of Clerks in the Departments. The second is his nomination of persons suggested by domestic influence."[54]

A more accurate analysis of the administration's troubles appeared in the New York *Tribune*: the president and his cabinet "must alienate many by their distribution of the patronage; were they angels they could not fail to do this."[55] Lincoln felt bound to follow the well-established rule that Congress must be consulted about appointments. When the governor of Rhode Island protested against the administration's nominee for postmaster of Providence, Lincoln noted that both of the state's senators as well as two of its Representatives favored that candidate. "In these cases," he explained, "the Executive is obliged to be greatly dependent upon members of Congress; and while, under peculiar circumstances, a single member or two, may be occasionally over-ruled, I believe as strong a combination as the present never has been. I therefore beg you to be assured that if I follow the rule in this case, as it appears to me I must, it will be with pain and not with pleasure, that you are not obliged."[56]

Lincoln objected to some pestiferous lawmakers badgering him on behalf of their clamorous constituents. According to Stoddard, the president listened to office seekers and their congressional patrons "with a degree of patience and good temper truly astonishing. At times, however, even his equanimity gave way, and more than one public man finally lost the President's good will by his pertinacity in demanding provision for his personal satellites. Some Senators and Congressmen really distinguished themselves in this respect. I remember a saying of Mr. Lincoln's that comes in pretty well here: 'Poor _____, he is digging his political grave!'

"Why, how so, Mr. President? He has obtained more offices for his friends than any other man I know of," said Stoddard.

"That's just it; no man can stand so much of that sort of thing. You see, every man thinks he deserves a better office than the one he gets, and hates his 'big man' for not securing it, while for every man appointed there are five envious men unappointed, who never forgive him for their want of luck. So there's half a dozen enemies for each success. I like _____, and don't like to see him hurt himself in that way; I guess I won't give him any more."[57]

Not all members of Congress were so insensitive. When Ohio Senator John Sherman pressed him about some appointments, Lincoln slumped in his seat with a look of despair. This prompted Sherman to confess his shame at bothering him with such minor concerns and to promise that he would stop pestering him about them. The president's expression abruptly brightened, he sat upright, and his entire demeanor changed.

Cabinet secretaries engaged in fierce patronage battles. On March 26, Attorney General Bates reported that his colleagues "are squabbling around me . . . about the distribution of loaves & fishes."[58] Seward in particular aroused anger by meddling outside his department. Chase, too, poached on others' turf. Upset by the treasury secretary's attempt to dictate post office appointments, Samuel Galloway of Ohio warned that if Lincoln "permits his judgment to be swayed by the dictation of Chase he will soon draw upon himself universal contempt & condemnation. Chase has already alienated by his selfishness some of his warmest adherents in Ohio." In fact, Galloway asserted, "Chase is doomed and dead in Ohio."[59]

The treasury secretary protested both to Lincoln and to Seward that Ohio was not receiving its fair share of diplomatic appointments, which fell under the aegis of the State Department. Others protested that consulates were given disproportionally to Easterners and to ex-Whigs. (The president eventually ruled that the 262 diplomatic and consular posts should be distributed among the states based on their population.) Annoyed when Seward blocked the nomination of Chase's brother as a U.S. marshal in New York, the treasury secretary successfully appealed to Lincoln.

The intense battles between Chase and Seward reflected the antagonism between former Democrats and ex-Whigs. As journalist John W. Forney noted, the president would have to exercise unusual "tact and skill to prevent it [the cabinet] from exploding into ugly divisions."[60] Lincoln showed that he had what Forney thought necessary: exceptional tact and preternatural skill. Thurlow Weed, who worked hard on behalf of his own faction, was widely regarded as a master wire-puller, but Lincoln was shrewder. As the astute, Harvard-educated Daniel Wilder of Kansas noted, Weed "was not a fractional quarter section [160 acres] to Lincoln's township [23,040 acres]."[61] To Seward, the president explained his guiding principle: "In regard to the patronage, sought with so much eagerness and jealousy, I have prescribed for myself the maxim, 'Justice to all.' "[62] No one faction of the party was allowed to hog the best jobs.

An especially contentious struggle arose over the New York customhouse, whose leaders had a vast amount of patronage at their disposal and enjoyed munificent incomes. Members of the Horace Greeley faction, some of whom had worked for Lincoln's nomination at Chicago, urged the president to keep Seward from monopolizing the patronage. In the midst of their meeting with the president, a staff member interrupted with a message from the First Lady: "She wants you."

"Yes, yes," he said without making a move.

Soon thereafter the messenger returned and exclaimed: "I say, she wants you!"

Lincoln, though "evidently annoyed," paid no attention to this interruption. Instead he told his visitors: "One side shall not gobble up everything. Make out a list of places and men you want, and I will endeavor to apply the rule of give and take."[63]

Lincoln later said that Greeley and his allies demanded the top two posts in the customhouse and that they were "in favor of having the two big puddings on the same side of the board."[64] The puddings would be served up equitably on both sides of the board. Lincoln kept track of New York appointments in a little book, making sure to award "each faction more than it could get from any other source, yet never enough to satisfy its appetite," as Weed put it.[65]

A case in point was the battle over the collectorship of New York. "Whether Fort Sumpter shall be reinforced or surrendered, is less bruited than whether the strongholds of the New York custom house, post offices, &c., shall be surrendered to the 'irrepressibles,' or held on to by the 'conservatives,'" the Cincinnati *Commercial* reported in early March.[66] Seward and Weed fought to have Simeon Draper named collector of the port of New York, while their opponents championed the reserved, mild-mannered Hiram Barney, a prominent lawyer and a close friend and political ally of Chase. For years Lincoln had served as Barney's collecting agent in Springfield, and the two enjoyed a pleasant and mutually advantageous business relationship. Barney said that Lincoln "is as good as a brother to me."[67] Deferring to his treasury secretary, whose department had charge of customs collection, Lincoln selected Barney, who proved to be a disappointment. He was considered "an excellent man," but lacked popularity with the party as well as the merchants.[68] Weed protested in vain against Barney's selection, but he did manage to persuade Lincoln to give his faction other desirable places in the custom house despite Barney's reluctance to fire loyal, patriotic Democrats. Meanwhile, anti-Seward men complained that they received too few patronage plums.

In July, Lincoln moaned that the problem of choosing a surveyor of customs for New York "has given me more trouble than any since my election."[69] He finally selected Rufus Andrews, who was favored by the Greeley wing of the party. Lincoln rejoiced on those rare occasions when the squabbling factions in the Empire State could agree on an appointment. In May, he told Chase that one Christopher Adams "is magnificently recommended; but the great point in his favor is that Thurlow Weed and Horace Greeley join in recommending him. I suppose the like never happened before, and never will again; so that it is now or never."[70]

Lincoln knowingly made several questionable appointments. As Gideon Welles remarked, "some things were doubtless done, which, under other circumstances and left to himself he [Lincoln] would have ordered differently."[71] Charles Francis Adams thought that Lincoln, whom he called "a vulgar man, unfitted both by education and nature for the post of President," had been "quite obtuse" and hence had "made very bad selections for all branches of the service."[72] A conspicuous example of an unfortunate choice was the appointment of David P. Holloway as commissioner of patents. Holloway was a friend of Interior Secretary Caleb B. Smith. The senate committee investigating his nomination refused to report it out "on the ground of his presumed incompetence."[73] The main objection was his lack of any background in law or science. Nevertheless, Lincoln stood by Holloway, who beat out his chief competitor, an influential newspaperman, George G. Fogg of New Hampshire. Only by agreeing to give Fogg the Swiss mission was Lincoln able to win senate confirmation for Holloway. To George W. Julian, who denounced Holloway as "an incompetent and unworthy man," Lincoln replied: "There is much force in what you say, but, in the balancing of matters, I guess I shall have to appoint him."[74]

Some of Lincoln's more unfortunate choices were his personal friends, most notably Mark Delahay and Ward Hill Lamon. Lincoln's affection for the bibulous Delahay, whom Henry Villard described as "an empty-headed, self-puffing, vainglorious strut," was curious.[75] He may have felt sorry for the Kansas politico, who had little money and a large family, had been a law partner of Lincoln's close friend Edward D. Baker, had worked on an Illinois newspaper with a loyal ally of Lincoln, and was married to Louisiana Hanks, the daughter of one of Lincoln's cousins. Moreover, the president may have been trying to appease his old friend Jesse K. Dubois, who successfully urged Delahay's appointment as surveyor general of Kansas and Nebraska. When Lincoln later elevated Delahay to a judgeship, the appointment aroused strong opposition from Kansans who insisted that he had no qualifications for the bench. Jackson Grimshaw had been recommended by several of Lincoln's Illinois allies for that post and declared that it was "disgraceful to the President who knew Delahay and all his faults, but the disgrace will be greater if the Senate confirms him. He is no lawyer, could not try a case properly even in a Justice's Court, and has no character. Mr. Buchanan in his worst days never made so disgraceful an appointment to the bench."[76] A Kansan complained that there was "not a respectable lawyer in the State that is not absolutely shocked at the appointment."[77] When Congress launched an impeachment investigation, Delahay was revealed to be a corrupt drunkard whose behavior had disgraced the court. To avoid being removed on impeachment, he resigned.

Lamon's appointment as marshal of the District of Columbia was also highly controversial and created friction between Lincoln and Congress. "I went to Washington," Lamon recalled, "having been promised the consulship at Paris by Mr. Lincoln. But as soon as we realized how serious was the state of political affairs, [David] Davis, seconded by Lincoln himself, persuaded me to remain near the President's person to protect him from danger."[78] Lincoln probably felt pity for the financially straitened Lamon and gave him that remunerative post to help him out. Before nominating his one-time colleague at the bar, the president asked Republican leaders in Washington how they would react if he appointed an Illinois friend to serve as marshal, for he did not wish to name anyone objectionable to the city's residents. It was customary to select a Washingtonian for that post.

William P. Wood, a model-maker from Alexandria who was to become superintendent of the Old Capitol Prison during the Civil War, agreed to circulate a petition on behalf of Lamon. With some difficulty, Wood and his friends managed to obtain about 200 signatures. When he recommended that the assistant marshal, George W. Phillips, and all other members of the marshal's staff be fired for disloyalty, Lamon emphatically agreed to do so. Wood then helped raise money for Lamon's bond and did whatever else he could to facilitate his appointment. Wood, however, soon grew disenchanted with the Cavalier (as the Virginia-born Lamon was called), especially after he reneged on his pledge to fire Phillips and the others. Indignantly, Wood called at the White House four times to protest, only to be rebuffed. So in July he appealed to the senate, averring that "to enumerate in detail his [Lamon's] many violations of honor to his friends, would require too much space for this protest; suffice it to say, that instead of Republicans for his councillors and friends he has noted secessionists and villifyers of the present Administration; he attaches less importance to his word, than to the contents of a black bottle which he regards as his nerve regulator; he has almost entirely neglected his official duties as Marshal, leaving his deputy G. W. Phillips (the man whom he pledged his honor to remove) to perform the duties of Marshal; he has made himself obnoxious to the citizens of Washington by his deception falsehoods and dissipation." Some 2,500 such citizens signed a petition protesting against the appointment of a nonresident as marshal. Wood provided the senate with the names of several other Washingtonians who could confirm his story, including five of the dozen men who had recommended Lamon's appointment.[79] Benjamin Brown French testified that Lamon "did not attend [to] the duties *at all.*"[80]

Like Delahay, Lamon was investigated by a congressional committee, which in 1861 found him guilty of an "unwarranted and scandalous assumption of authority" in detaching a regiment from Missouri, bringing it east, and putting himself in charge of it as a brigadier general. For this misdeed, he was fined $20,000.[81] The following year Lamon again antagonized Congress, this time over the issue of fugitive slaves. As marshal of the District of Columbia, he was in charge of the Washington jail, unaffectionately known as the Blue Jug, where he held alleged runaways. Lamon was holding some of the fugitives belonging to disloyal masters for safekeeping until the war's end. During Lamon's tenure, overcrowding became a scandal at the Blue Jug, with the prison containing four times as many prisoners as it was designed to accommodate. Lamon collected 21¢ per day per prisoner, which yielded him a handsome profit. When outraged congressional Radicals tried to visit the jail, Lamon forbade them entrance.

One of those Radicals, James W. Grimes of Iowa, chairman of the Senate Committee on the District of Columbia, indignantly protested and took his case to Lincoln, who was too busy to receive him. The senate condemned Lamon's actions. Relations between Grimes and Lincoln became frosty thereafter, causing the president to lament in 1864 that in all his dealings with Congress "my greatest disappointment of all has been with Grimes. Before I came here [to Washington], I certainly expected to rely upon Grimes more than any other one man in the Senate. I like him very much. He is a great strong fellow. He is a valuable friend, a dangerous enemy. He carries too many guns not to be respected in any point of view. But he got wrong against me, I do not clearly know how, and has always been cool and almost hostile to me."[82] (On another occasion, Lincoln said he must appoint William F. Turner to an Arizona judgeship. "It is Grimes's man, and I must do something for Grimes. I have tried hard to please him from the start, but he complains, and I must satisfy him if possible.")[83] Horace White blamed the president's moral "obtuseness" in retaining Lamon in office for causing "the coolness that existed between Grimes & Lincoln."[84]

Other senators, including John P. Hale of New Hampshire and Henry Wilson of Massachusetts, were highly critical of the indiscreet, belligerent, quarrelsome Lamon, who virtually challenged Illinois Congressman Elihu B. Washburne to a duel. The Cavalier repeatedly clashed with General James S. Wadsworth, military governor of the District. In May 1862, a constituent warned Lyman Trumbull that "there is not one matter that has & still is *causing* so much reproach upon Pres. Lincoln, so much great shame to his sincere friends, as this Lamon business."[85] Lamon was widely scorned for singing "nigger-songs" and obscene madrigals, for having a weak intellect, and for lacking dignity.[86]

Despite numerous demands that he fire Lamon, Lincoln stood by his old friend, who served as an informal presidential bodyguard and companion not only on the train ride from Harrisburg to Washington but throughout the Civil War. Lincoln valued his humor, charm, high spirits, conviviality, and exceptional loyalty. Lincoln's fondness for Lamon persisted even though the Cavalier underwent a personality change soon after the election of 1860. According to David Davis, who knew whereof he spoke, Lamon then became full of himself. "I feel sorry for Hill Lamon," the judge wrote in January 1861, for "when he was in Bloomington with his negro boy, I made up my mind that his head was turned & that he would hereafter do no good—He makes himself ridiculous."[87] Four months later, Davis said "Hill Lamon is crazy. . . . I can[']t account for it & nobody else [can]."[88] An Illinois editor reported from Washington that "Lamon affects the great man here—rides up to the White House daily, & tries to be on the most familiar footing with the President. . . . His head is evidently turned by his prosperity."[89]

Another ethically suspect personal and political friend whom Lincoln favored was Edward D. Baker, the newly elected senator from Oregon. The ethnologist George Gibbs considered him "a very corrupt man."[90] As a law partner of Stephen T. Logan, Baker had mishandled clients' money. During the Civil War, he received substantial sums to raise a regiment; upon his death in October 1861, it was discovered that he had left $10,000 unaccounted for. His closest political adviser was the notoriously corrupt Andrew J. Butler, brother of Massachusetts politico Benjamin F. Butler.

Baker felt entitled to control all West Coast patronage because he was the only Republican senator from the Pacific Northwest. Prominent California Republicans,

led by James W. Simonton of the San Francisco *Bulletin,* businessman Leland Stanford (who would be elected governor later in 1861), and Joseph A. Nunes, resented
Baker's presumption and complained to Lincoln. On March 30, the antagonistic factions met at the White House to discuss offices in the Far West. Baker's opponents
were particularly upset that Democrat Robert J. Stevens, a son-in-law of the senator,
was being championed for superintendent of the San Francisco mint. When they
called at the Executive Mansion, they were surprised to discover Baker and his
henchman Butler there. The meeting began with Nunes delivering a temperate appeal, after which he handed the president a slate of suggested nominees for California
posts along with a mild remonstrance against Baker's interference. Simonton then
read a bitter attack on the Oregon senator, who, he said (perhaps alluding to Butler),
had "presented to the President, as a most substantial and respectable man, a person
whose antecedents and reputation Mr. Simonton denounced severely."[91] (In 1862, the
senate would unanimously reject the nomination of Butler to a captaincy in the
army.) Simonton characterized other men endorsed by Baker as gamblers and black-
guards.

Lincoln asked if he could keep the papers, including Simonton's remarks. The
editor said he would "like to make some emendations" to his manuscript. "Never
mind the emendations," replied Lincoln, "if it is mine, I want it as is." Then, "in a
withering tone of indignation," he said that Nunes's paper, "being *somewhat* respectful in its tone, I *think* I will keep; but this one," holding Simonton's text aloft, "I will
show you what I will do with it." He stepped to the fireplace and flung the offending
document into the flames.[92] Returning to his desk, Lincoln erupted in anger so vehemently that, as one observer put it, "everybody present quailed before it. His wrath
was simply terrible."[93] He declared: "I have known Colonel Baker longer and better
than any of you here, and these attacks upon him I know to be outrageous. I will
hear no more of them. If you wish to do so, present your recommendations for office,
and I will give them a respectful hearing, but no more of this kind of proceeding."[94]
Simonton "looked as though he had been struck by a thunderbolt, but finally recovered so far as to say, 'I have simply done my duty: I have nothing to expect from the
Executive, and in doing what I did, I merely meant to protect the interests of my
State.'"[95]

As the delegation left, one of Baker's friends threatened to shoot Simonton on the
spot. Soon the president called them back, but Simonton did not reappear. On being
told that the editor felt insulted, Lincoln sent a special messenger to fetch him, and
they reached an *entente cordiale,* though patronage matters were not settled then and
there. Later, the president explained that Simonton's paper "was an unjust attack
upon my dearest personal friend. . . . The delegation did not know what they were
talking about when they made him responsible, almost abusively, for what I had done,
or proposed to do. They told me that that was my paper, to do with as I liked. I could
not trust myself to reply in words: I was so angry."[96] It seems that Lincoln had implicitly promised Baker's daughter that her husband, Robert J. Stevens, would receive a
federal job, which he did win. (Two years later Stevens was unceremoniously removed
on charges of fraud.)

A similar fate befell Thomas J. Dryer, commissioner to the Hawaiian Islands and editor of the Portland *Oregonian*. Dryer, who claimed that he paid his good friend Baker several hundred dollars for his support in obtaining the commissionership, won that post despite allegations that he was "a vile, low, contemptible drunkard, unworthy to associate with honorable men."[97] In 1863, after much hesitation, Lincoln dismissed him in response to complaints from the Hawaiian government that he was a drunkard. Reportedly, Dryer was "rude, rough and repulsive to genteel society," and regularly flouted "all the proprieties of social life by a want of *savoir faire* or rather rough vulgarity or boorishness, which offends propriety, decency and conventional usage."[98]

Although Lincoln honored most of Baker's requests, the senator was disgusted when one of his opponents, William Rabe, was named postmaster at San Francisco. After the first round of patronage distribution ended, Baker mused: "Mr Lincoln has acted peculiarly, and although my very good friend . . . he has not done what . . . I would have expected, yet I am sure he has a real attachment to me."[99]

Lincoln's outburst against Simonton was regarded as "the first symptom of the much vaunted, but rather tardy Jacksonism of 'Old Abe.'"[100] (Other signs of the president's "latent Jacksonism" were manifesting themselves in late March as he dealt with the Fort Sumter dilemma.)

Illinois Appointees

Lincoln was especially vexed by patronage-hungry Illinoisans. Secretary of War Cameron complained that "the scramble is so great here, from all quarters, and especially *Illinois*, that we begin to despair."[101] John Hay misleadingly asserted that there "never was a President who so little as Lincoln admitted personal consideration in the distribution of places. He rarely gave a place to a friend—still more rarely because he *was* a friend." Lincoln "was entirely destitute of gratitude for political services rendered to himself."[102] Actually, the president did reward many of his Illinois friends, especially those who had helped him during his early days in the Prairie State. Uncle Jimmy Short, Lincoln's benefactor in New Salem, became agent for the Round Valley Indian reservation in California. Oliver G. Abell, son of a New Salem woman who acted as a surrogate mother to Lincoln, was appointed messenger in the General Land Office. Ethelbert P. Oliphant, who served with Lincoln in the Black Hawk War, became a judge in the Washington Territory. Lincoln's good friends and fellow clerks from New Salem days, William G. Greene and Charles Maltby, were named collectors of internal revenue.

Other Illinois friends of the president fared well at the patronage trough. Anson G. Henry was named surveyor general of the Washington Territory; Simeon Francis became a paymaster in the army; Allen Francis received a consulate in Canada; and Theodore Canisius served as consul in Vienna. Lincoln picked Archibald Williams as U.S. district attorney for Kansas. Samuel C. Parks served as associate justice of the Idaho Territory's Supreme Court. The pastor of Springfield's First Presbyterian Church, James Smith, whom Lincoln described as "an intimate personal friend of mine," represented U.S. interests as a consul in his native Scotland.[103] Jackson

Grimshaw became a collector of internal revenue and Gustave Koerner minister to Spain (after Carl Schurz resigned). For governor of the Washington Territory, Lincoln chose yet another Illinois friend, William Pickering, who had long served as a Whig member of the Illinois State Legislature. Lawrence Weldon was named district attorney for southern Illinois. Thomas J. Pickett became an agent of the Quartermaster's Department. William Jayne, Lincoln's personal physician and a brother-in-law of Lyman Trumbull, was appointed governor of the Dakota Territory. When Trumbull's brother Benjamin was made a land office receiver at Omaha, some Republicans howled in protest.

Yet other Prairie Staters won coveted places in the federal bureaucracy. Charles L. Wilson, editor of the Chicago *Journal,* was named secretary of the U.S. legation in London, despite the objections of the minister-designate to Great Britain, Charles Francis Adams. (According to a colleague in the legation, Wilson was "an ill-mannered bear," "slovenly in dress, deficient in good breeding, lazy in his habits," "vulgar, coarse, ill-natured, sulky, quarrelsome and disputatious.")[104] George M. Hanson of Coles County secured a post in the Northern Superintendency of California Indian reservations. Elias Wampole of Menard County went to Venezuela as a consul. (Lincoln had originally tried to give him a job in Philadelphia. When the director of the mint there balked, Lincoln told him: "You can do it for me, and you must." He did not.)[105] George W. Rives became a tax assessor. At Lincoln's request, William W. Danenhower, a Know-Nothing journalist, lawyer, and book dealer who had stumped for him in 1858 and 1860, was given a clerkship in the Treasury Department. David Davis helped procure the appointment of William Pitt Kellogg as chief justice of the Nebraska Territory.

When Elizabeth Ridgeway Corneau of Springfield, whom Lincoln called "a very highly valued friend," asked a place for her brother, the president tactfully wrote to the collector of customs in Philadelphia: "I do not *demand,* or *insist,* even, that you shall make any appointment in your office; but I would be much obliged."[106] He successfully urged the secretary of the senate to give a place to the son of Alexander Sympson of Carthage, "one of my best friends whom I have not, so far, been able to recognize in any substantial way."[107]

Illinois congressmen and senators objected to some of these appointments, which were made without their advice. Lyman Trumbull complained that Lincoln ignored most of the delegation's requests except for offices within the state and for minor posts outside it. "I see very little of Lincoln, & know little of his policy as to appointments or anything else," Trumbull reported in late March.[108] When Congressman William Kellogg sourly protested about the treatment of a friend, Lincoln found his ingratitude dismaying and in a memo composed around April 3, gave vent to his wounded feelings: "Mr. Kellogg does me great injustice to write in this strain. He has had more favors than any other Illinois member. . . . Is it really in his heart to add to my perplexities now?"[109]

Not all of Lincoln's Illinois friends succeeded in their quest for government positions. Usher Linder begged for any office but received none. Herndon was denied a patronage post because, Lincoln allegedly said, "he would be charged with paying the

debts of personal friendship with public patronage." (Herndon was offered a temporary assignment as a claims adjuster, which he declined.)[110] In May, when William W.
Orme lobbied on behalf of some Bloomington neighbors, Lincoln balked, saying
"that Illinois already had over 50 per cent of her share of appointments, and he did not
see how in the world he could give any more to her."[111]

Another Bloomington resident, David Davis, irritated the president with his patronage requests. The judge, said Lincoln, "has forced me to appoint Archy Williams
Judge in Kansas right off and Jno. Jones to a place in the State department: and I have
got a bushel of dispatches from Kansas wanting to know if I'm going to fill up *all* the
offices from Illinois." In naming Williams, Lincoln had not consulted with members
of the Illinois congressional delegation, who were understandably angry.[112] At Davis's
urging, Lincoln had also appointed Simon Cameron and Caleb B. Smith to the cabinet, and William P. Dole as commissioner of Indian affairs. Davis remained in
Washington for three weeks, returning home only when Lincoln announced that he
was suspending further appointments of Illinoisans. Before his departure, he told a
cousin that he was "shocked and mortified beyond expression" and that Lincoln
"lacks *will*—yields to pressure—& has been pressured by the radicals & mischievous
men," and that the administration would be "an utter failure."[113]

Other Illinois friends, including Governor Yates, were disappointed in Lincoln.
On March 7, Nicolay told Ozias M. Hatch, "Illinois is here in perfect hordes. You
may look out for a tremendous crop of soreheads."[114] Among the sorest of the soreheads was Jesse K. Dubois, who tried to win posts for both himself and his son-in-law,
James P. Luse, editor of the Lafayette, Indiana, *Journal*. "Uncle Jesse," said the president, "there is no reason why I don't want to appoint you, but there is one why I
can't,—you are from the town I live in myself."[115] As for Luse, Dubois insisted that he
be named superintendent of Indian affairs in Minnesota, but a resident of that state
won the position. "I am sorely disappointed in all my expectations from Washington,"
Dubois complained to the president. "I made only two or three requests of you. One
for the Northern Superintendency of Indian affairs for my Friend J. P. Luse. *My heart
was set* on this *application* for him, as in his appointment I could have transferd my
dying daughter from the Wabash Valley to the healthy climate of Minesotta and perhaps prolonged her life. I would not go to Washington as I did not wish to trouble
you, more than I could possibly help. *I did feel as though I had some claims for the favors
I asked for, but in all I have been disappointed*."[116] Lincoln replied that he was "as sorry
as you can be," but if he had appointed Luse "it would have been against the united,
earnest, and, I add, angry protest of the republican [congressional] delegation of Minnesota. . . . So far as I understand, it is unprecedented, [to] send an officer into a *state*
against the wishes of the members of congress of the State, and of the same party."[117]

When his other recommendations failed to yield results, Dubois wrote the president, bitterly observing that "I am *mortified* at *Luse's* Defeat. . . . I *am still so,* more
from the fact that I placed a too high an estimate on my *relations* with you, and did
not know my *position*. For I do know that I have insulted hundreds because I would
not importune you. I did suppose I had a right to a small share of the spoils, but let it
pass. It *is as painful to me* as it can be to you."[118] (The president did oblige Dubois by

giving offices to Mark W. Delahay and William Beck, both of whom proved embarrassments to the administration.) Four years later Dubois complained that "Lincoln is a singular man and I must Confess I never Knew him: he has for 30 years past just used me as a plaything to accomplish his own ends: but the moment he was elevated to his proud position he seemed all at once to have entirely changed his whole nature and become altogether a new being—Knows no one and the road to favor is always open to his Enemies whilst the door is hymetically sealed to his old friends."[119]

Dubois had a point: Lincoln often used patronage to attract new allies rather than reward old ones. When considering an appointment in Washington, Lincoln said "he thought it judicious to conciliate and draw in as much of the Democratic element as possible" and expressed a willingness to name a loyal Democrat as U.S. district attorney.[120] Leonard Swett sagaciously observed that the president "would always give more to his enemies than he would to his friends" because "he never had anything to spare, and in the close calculation of attaching the factions to him, he counted upon the abstract affection of his friends as an element to be offset against some gift with which he must appease his enemies. Hence, there was always some truth in the charge of his friends that he failed to reciprocate their devotion with his favors. The reason was that he had only just so much to give away—'He always had more horses than oats.'"[121] Varying the livestock metaphor, Lincoln rejected the appeal of one office seeker by observing that *there are too many hogs and too little fodder!*"[122]

Others felt as aggrieved as Dubois. Ward Hill Lamon complained that "Lincoln's weak point is, to cajole & pet his enemies and to allow his friends to be sacrificed and quietly look on and witness the success of his enemies at the expense and downfall of his friends."[123] In March, a frustrated office seeker from Iowa commented bitterly that senators "who never had a feeling of sympathy with Mr Lincoln" and "who fought his nomination to the last" were controlling patronage; "for a man to have been an original friend of Lincoln is now an objection to him with these men."[124]

Also feeling sore was David Davis, who was hurt because Lincoln gave him no office. In fact, the president had wanted to name him commissary-general of the army but did not pursue the idea after Winfield Scott objected to placing a civilian in that post. Davis was also miffed when Caleb B. Smith and Simon Cameron, both of whom he had championed for cabinet posts, ignored his recommendations for clerkships. Davis's good friend Leonard Swett also met with frustration in his quest for government jobs. He wished to serve as consul in Liverpool, a lucrative post, but he lost out to Thomas H. Dudley of New Jersey, whose case former Governor William A. Newell of the Garden State had forcefully pled. In reluctantly acceding to Newell's importunity, Lincoln said good-naturedly: "Well, Newell, I am like a farmer with a bundle of 'fodder' between two asses; and the wrong ass gets the fodder."[125] Swett was so hurt that he regretted applying for an office. Eventually, he proposed that if Davis were named to the U.S. Supreme Court, he would view that as reward enough for both of them. In 1862, Lincoln did nominate Davis to the high court, belatedly gratifying the two men who had been most instrumental in securing his nomination and election.

Joseph Knox, who had served as Lincoln's co-counsel in the Rock Island Bridge case, bitterly reminded the president of his "disregard of the request of *all* our Judges, backed up *by 130 members of our bar,* for my appt. to the office of U.S. Att'y for this District."[126] In 1862, when Lincoln nominated Isaac B. Curran, a Democrat of Springfield, for a consular post, the president's friends in the Illinois capital objected vehemently. "Our people feel disheartened, discouraged & disgraced and are ready to curse the administration and all that belong to it for its ill advised and outrageous appointments," Lincoln's friend James C. Conkling growled.[127] Springfield Republicans were especially upset by appointments in the quartermaster and commissary departments. Like Knox, Conkling lost his bid to become a U.S. district attorney and was convinced that Lincoln had betrayed him. "I almost adored him, for many years," Conkling said, "and spent my time and money freely for him, and did not know but that my feeling towards him were reciprocated, as least in a small degree, then to wake up to the consciousness of the fact that I was viewed by him with contempt—with disgust—as a bore to be shunned and avoided, was to me unaccountable and annoying."[128] In 1862, Horace White told William Butler he felt "the President, for whom we labored so hard two years ago, had now sacrificed you, & as many of his Illinois friends as possible."[129]

Lincoln's old friend Ebenezer Peck was chagrined when he failed to be named postmaster of Chicago. The editors of the Chicago *Tribune* wanted the job for one of their own, for they saw it as a way to expand the paper's influence. Many other newspaper proprietors coveted postmasterships for such practical reasons. The *Tribune* editors at first backed Joseph Medill but eventually settled on John Locke Scripps as their candidate. Lincoln, with divided loyalties, put off the decision until late March, when he gave his blessing to Scripps. The disappointed Peck wrote Lyman Trumbull that Lincoln "once said to me, that his greatest repugnance to politics was, that a man had occasion sometimes, to put his foot in the face of his best friend in order to lift himself a round higher on the ladder of ambition."[130] (Two years later Peck was appointed a judge of the U.S. Court of Claims.)

Other Midwestern Republicans were also indignant. William M. Dickson of Cincinnati believed he had been shabbily treated and sourly remarked that "no one can feel more personally aggrieved at Mr L than I do. Glad always to call upon me before his election, since then he has entirely forgotten me."[131] An Iowa congressman, angry at the failure of his candidate to win a land office job, concluded that Lincoln "has not as much Sagacity as I could wish. He is more of a joker than thinker."[132] Another Iowan noted with disgust that the "Goths and Vandals from the [Old] Northwest take things by storm."[133] Michigan Senator Zachariah Chandler told Lincoln that his state "has been utterly ignored in the distribution of offices by your administration[.] Illinois has rec'd eight times, Ohio seven, New York, Eleven & Maine three times as much as Michigan[.] Even Wisconsin has rec[eive]d more than three times as much in both honor & Emolument."[134]

Equally angry were Eastern Republicans who thought Lincoln was biased in favor of his own region. "Every thing in the way of office goes west," groused Maine Senator William P. Fessenden, who was besieged by clamorous job seekers and would-be contractors. "We shall hardly get the paring of a toe-nail in New England, and many people feel badly about it."[135] Fessenden's colleague, Henry Wilson of

Massachusetts, protested "against the appointment of so many Illinoisans and Indianans to important bureaus" in Washington.[136] Some New Yorkers felt the same way. One told Lincoln that the "partiality shone to a few of the western states have given great & just offence," for the "eastern & Northern public are not prepared to believe that all the virtue and talent is to be found in the west and therefore in the absence of proof of such facts very logically conclude it must be through the partiality of a western President."[137]

Trouble Saying "No" to Some (But Not All) Office Seekers

For all his shrewdness in distributing patronage, Lincoln found it difficult to resist applicants' tales of woe. "If I have one vice," he confessed, "and I can call it nothing else, it is not to be able to say no! Thank God for not making me a woman, but if He had, I suppose He would have made me just as ugly as He did, and no one would ever have tempted me. It was only the other day, a poor parson whom I knew some years ago in Joliet came to the White House with a sad story of his poverty and his large family—poor parsons seem always to have large families—and he wanted me to do something for him. I knew very well that I could do nothing for him, and yet I couldn't bear to tell him so, and so I said I would see what I could do. The very next day the man came back for the office which he said that I had promised him—which was not true, but he seemed really to believe it. Of course there was nothing left for me to do except to get him a place through one of the secretaries. But if I had done my duty, I should have said 'no' in the beginning."[138] California Senator John Conness complained that Lincoln had a "too kindly heart" and thus "would yield to the pressure for place."[139] In January 1861, Charles Henry Ray predicted that if Lincoln were to fail, "his dislike to say *no* to friends" would be the cause.[140]

Occasionally, Lincoln could avoid saying no and still turn aside importunate friends. When childhood chums William Jones and Nat Grigsby called in quest of jobs, the president skillfully finessed them before they could make their wishes known. He greeted them warmly and took them to the White House living quarters, where he introduced them to his wife: "Mary, here are two of my old Jonesboro friends who have journeyed all the way up here just to see their old friend. You know the office seekers are pestering the life out of me and I tell you it is a comfort to me to have these boys here especially when I know they do not come to bother me about some position or office. I must hurry back to the office and I want you to take good care of these boys till I can pull loose." Acting on this hint, Jones and Grigsby returned home without asking for anything.[141]

Lincoln was criticized not just for excessive tenderheartedness in distributing patronage but also for yielding too easily to pushy office seekers. One of them said "the practice seems to be with Lincoln that he yields to the man that bores [i.e., pesters] him the most."[142] Murat Halstead of the Cincinnati *Commercial*, who deemed the president a man "of no account," reported that he "yields not to merit or to the force with which an application is asked, but to importunity in the applicant."[143] Interior Secretary Smith agreed that in distributing patronage, the president "yields to the pressure brought to bear upon him."[144]

To avoid saying no, Lincoln sent many persistent job applicants to the Treasury Department and to the Arsenal with notes of introduction. So many would-be messengers, watchmen, and janitors armed with such notes descended on the treasury that George Harrington, assistant secretary of that department, protested. "Why, bless you," replied Lincoln, "did you suppose I expected you to appoint every one bringing you a note? Why, but for you and Genl Ramsey at the arsenal I should die. One week I send all such applicants to you and the next week to Genl Ramsey. I cannot refuse to see those needy people and I am forced to put them upon you and Ramsey. If I have a special desire for an appointment I will let you know." Lincoln's eyes twinkled as he made this confession.[145]

Sometimes in his desire to be accommodating, Lincoln inadvertently got himself into trouble with office seekers. In 1862, he explained to his Illinois friend George W. Rives, who sought work as a tax assessor: "I will not say unconditionally that I will appoint you, before the [internal revenue] law is passed, because I have been placed in an awkward position, heretofore, by promises made in advance, which I was urged to fulfill, but I think I know all about you, and can decide upon that readily when the time shall come for action."[146] Months earlier he observed that "he was glad that he had but four years to stay in Washington," for when he left Illinois, said he: "I was reputed an honest man, but here I hardly know what my friends do call me. I am beset by hundreds of men anxious for place, and in the hurry of the moment I sometimes give encouragement to people who in consequence charge me with a want of truth, if they do not receive the office for which they apply. It is much easier to please your neighbors and maintain a fair reputation in Springfield than in Washington!"[147]

If Lincoln had a hard time saying no to some office seekers, on occasion he could do so most emphatically. John Hay recalled sitting one day in the White House with the president "when a man who had been calling on him almost daily for weeks in pursuit of an office was shown in. He made his usual request, when Lincoln said: 'It is of no use, my friend. You had better go home. I am not going to give you that place.' At this the man became enraged, and in a very insolent tone exclaimed, 'Then, as I understand it, Mr. President, you refuse to do me justice.' At this, Lincoln's patience, which was as near the infinite as anything that I have ever known, gave way. He looked at the man steadily for a half-minute or more, then slowly began to lift his long figure from its slouching position in the chair. He rose without haste, went over to where the man was sitting, took him by the coat-collar, carried him bodily to the door, threw him in a heap outside, closed the door, and returned to his chair. The man picked himself up, opened the door, and cried, 'I want my papers!' Lincoln took a package of papers from the table, went to the door and threw them out, again closed it, and returned to his chair. He said not a word, then or afterward, about the incident."[148]

Massachusetts Congressman John B. Alley remembered a similar scene when two shameless office seekers accosted Lincoln on his way from the White House to the nearby War Department building. When their pestering became intolerable, the president, "evidently worn out by care and anxiety, turned upon them, and such an angry and terrific tirade, against those two incorrigible bores, I never before heard from the lips of mortal man."[149] One day on the street, when an office seeker boldly thrust a letter into the president's hand, he angrily snapped: "No, sir! I am not going to open shop here."[150] Lincoln also lost his temper at William Houston, brother of Texas Governor Sam Houston. In July, when Henry C. Whitney mentioned William Houston, the president "frowned like a bear and said—'don't bother me about Bill Houston[.] he has been here sitting on his a[s]s all summer, waiting for me to give him the best office I've got.'" Whitney suggested that perhaps Houston could have a minor clerkship, prompting an explosive response that seared itself into Whitney's memory: "'I hain't got it,' roared Lincoln with more impatience and disgust than I ever saw manifested by him." Whitney dropped the subject.[151]

Sometimes Lincoln replied to office seekers with gentle humor rather than anger. A Philadelphian who repeatedly boasted of his services to the party was told by the president: "I had in my pig sty a little bit of a pig, that made a terrible commotion—do you know why? Because the old sow had just one more little pig than she had teats, and the little porker that got no teat made a terrible squealing." Lincoln's caller took the hint and returned to Pennsylvania.[152] When a delegation asked Lincoln to name an ill friend of theirs as commissioner of the Hawaiian Islands, where the salubrious climate might improve his health, Lincoln replied: "I am sorry to say that there are eight other applicants for that place, and they are all sicker than your man."[153]

Dealing with Claims of Religion and Ethnicity

Trying to balance competing claims, Lincoln had to take into account religion as well as ideology, party antecedents, locality, and friendship. James Mitchell, a Methodist minister whom the president named to a post in the Interior Department, argued that since Methodists "aided largely to make Mr. Lincoln," they rightfully expected him "to meet the account to the full."[154] A parson in Alexandria felt that account was overdue. "We ask the govt. to recognize our people in bestowing patronage," he wrote, but the request went unheeded: "the treatment of our people by the Administration is an open, standing insult to the church. Episcopalians & Presbyterians have the government."[155] To redress that imbalance, prominent Methodists like Bishop Matthew Simpson of Evanston, Illinois, lobbied on behalf of their co-religionists for government jobs. For his fellow townsman, John Evans, Simpson obtained the governorship of the Colorado Territory. Professor J. W. Marshall, another Methodist worthy who solicited the bishop's aid, was appointed consul at Leeds. When Lincoln offered Simpson the chance to name the minister to Honduras, the bishop piously disclaimed any intention to dictate patronage decisions. But he did suggest that his friend, the Pennsylvania publisher Alexander W. Cummings, be given that post. In 1865, Simpson arranged to have Cummings appointed successor to Evans as governor of Colorado. That same year, Simpson succeeded in having another friend, James Harlan—a devout Methodist and a senator from Iowa—named secretary of the interior.

Later, Methodists railed against the "proscriptive Policy" that denied them their fair share of military patronage. "I cannot learn that we have a single voice in the Government, nor a prominent officer in the Army, notwithstanding we have furnished . . . more than fifty per cent of the entire Army," complained one D. H. Whitney. "Every Presbyterian and Episcopal Private is provided with some other position than that of carrying a gun."[156] In fact, Simpson was able to help Colonel Clinton B. Fisk win a general's stars. Dismayed by such sectarian lobbying, Lincoln declared "that he preferred the Episcopalians to every other sect, because they are equally indifferent to a man's religion and his politics."[157]

As he doled out patronage plums, Lincoln had to take into account ethnicity as well as religion. One particularly insistent group of office seekers, the German-Americans, gave him more trouble than most. "About one-third of the German population of the West are applicants for consulships," the New York *World* reported humorously.[158] Connecticut Republicans warned that they faced defeat in the April 1861 elections if German-Americans were not rewarded. Henry Villard wrote that native-born Republicans in the Midwest "openly acknowledge that their victory was, if not wholly, at least to a great extent, due to the large accessions they received in the most hotly contested sections from the German ranks."[159] Among those holding such a belief was Lincoln, who when distributing consulships and other foreign appointments asked Seward: "what about our German friends?"[160]

The secretary of state ignited an uproar by opposing the appointment of foreign-born citizens to diplomatic posts in Europe. "Next to Fort Sumter," said the Cincinnati *Commercial*, Seward's policy "excites the greatest interest."[161] At the center of the storm was Carl Schurz, the Prussian-born Wisconsin orator and indefatigable campaigner, who shamelessly lobbied for a first-class diplomatic appointment in Europe. "The celebrated Mr. Carl Schurz appears to be a difficult child for the Administration to baptize," as one journalist observed.[162] Lincoln had encouraged the young would-be diplomat, whom he liked and admired, but Seward, responding to pressure from the Catholic leadership of New York, raised objections. Other Republican leaders rightly considered Schurz "a very great egotist" whose demands were "impudent, in bad taste and selfish."[163] The secretary of state urged Schurz to accept a post in Latin America or a territorial governorship rather than a European mission. Schurz balked, insisting that he be named minister to Sardinia (i.e., Italy). He managed to persuade one competitor, Anson Burlingame, to withdraw from the field. When Schurz complained to Lincoln about Seward's opposition, the president told him: "I would have appointed you at once, but I deemed it my duty to consult my Secretary of State, with whom I should not like to quarrel right after the organization of the Cabinet. I appreciate your pride and I like it, and I shall be just to you." Schurz believed that his struggle for the Sardinian mission would force Lincoln to confront his domineering secretary of state. As time passed, Schurz viewed his case as part of the larger struggle Seward and his fellow compromisers were waging to control the administration.

When George Perkins Marsh of Vermont won the Sardinian post, Lincoln offered to appoint Schurz minister to Portugal, Brazil, Chile, or Peru. Schurz neither accepted nor rejected the proposed alternatives. "I gave him my mind without reserve," the disgruntled German wrote his wife. He told Lincoln "that he and the republicans had been heretofore supposed to have elected a President, and not a sub-Secretary of State" and "that two thirds of the republican Senators would be before long hostilely arrayed against the administration." On March 19, the New York *Herald* reported that the question of Schurz's appointment "seems to bother the administration more than anything else [except] the difficulty about Fort Sumter." That day the matter appeared to be resolved when Schurz agreed to accept the position as minister to Lisbon provided that its status would be elevated to a first-class mission (with a pay increase of $4,500). Seward, however, inexplicably refused to support that change.

On March 21, the president, secretary of state, and Schurz held a stormy meeting during which the young German refused to back down despite Seward's entreaties. "Lincoln grew quite pale, but I stood firm," Schurz told his wife. Though "fed up" with politics and Washington, Schurz felt obliged to stay because of "the possibility of breaking Seward's power over Lincoln, which would ruin the whole Administration." Schurz asserted that in "all things, including for example the Fort Sumter affair, Seward's fatal influence makes itself felt." With characteristic immodesty, he boasted: "I have done more than all the others to keep Lincoln on the right track." The president asked Montgomery Blair to act as an intermediary and persuade Schurz to accept the mission to Russia or Spain. Schurz agreed to the Spanish post, which had already been assigned to Cassius M. Clay. "Seward's hostility against me is so sharp and his influence over Lincoln is so great, that I am not sanguine enough to expect a favorable result," Schurz wrote. After mulling over the matter, Lincoln authorized Blair to ask Clay to give up the Spanish mission. To Schurz it seemed that "Lincoln has finally made up his mind to act independently." On March 28, the three-week struggle ended when Clay agreed to accept the mission to Russia rather than to Spain. The president thanked the Kentuckian, saying: "Clay, you have relieved me from great embarrassment."[164]

"So Seward's influence is conquered, and I am master of the battlefield," Schurz crowed. By stiffening Lincoln's backbone, he may have made it easier for the president to stand up to Seward when the Fort Sumter crisis reached a climax.[165] One strong critic of appeasing the South reported that it "is a matter of congratulation today *among Seward's opponents* that he has suffered the first serious defeat wh[ich] he has yet experienced in respect to any app[ointmen]t—in the instance of Schurz, against whom for a European Mission he had made an especial point."[166]

Although Seward opposed Schurz's appointment in part because of the young German-American's Radical antislavery views, several of the ministers sent abroad were staunch critics of the peculiar institution. In addition to Schurz, Marsh, and Clay, they included George G. Fogg (Switzerland), Norman B. Judd (Prussia), John Lothrop Motley (Austria), Rufus King (Papal States), Friedrich Hassaurek (Ecuador), Bradford R. Wood (Denmark), Anson Burlingame (China), and James Shepherd Pike (Holland). Many consuls were also militant opponents of slavery, among them Zebina Eastman (Bristol), Joshua R. Giddings (Montreal), John Bigelow (Paris), Thomas H. Dudley (Liverpool), Charles Dexter Cleveland (Cardiff), Thaddeus Hyatt (La Rochelle), Richard Hildreth (Trieste), Freeman H. Morse (London), and Hinton Rowan Helper (Buenos Aires). They helped educate their hosts about the fundamental issues of the Civil War. Radical antislavery leaders also won a large share of the three dozen posts in the western territories. The South reacted to these appointments indignantly, while Northern abolitionists applauded them.

In addition to Schurz, several other German-Americans won diplomatic assignments. In 1862, Koerner replaced Schurz at Madrid. (A delay in that appointment led Koerner to complain that Lincoln's "kindness to Mr. Schurz [which is really a very great weakness] had had a very *unkind* effect upon me." It was "very strange that a man whose true character he does not know at all, and who opposed him to the very last at Chicago, should be permitted to trifle with him and the Senate, and that I should be disgraced again, whom he does know, and who had ever stood by him. . . . If Lincoln prefers office-seekers and adversaries to old and tried friends very well.")[167] When Lincoln named Friedrich Hassaurek of Cincinnati as minister to Ecuador, whose capital, Quito, sits 9,000 feet above sea level, the witty Ohioan thanked the president "for appointing him to the highest place in his gift."[168] Charles N. Riotte of Texas represented the United States in Costa Rica. German-American consuls included Francis J. Klauser and George E. Wiss (the Netherlands), Henry Boernstein (Bremen), John P. Hatterscheidt (Moscow), George Schneider (Elsinore), and Charles L. Bernays (Zurich).

Other Diplomatic Appointments

One of Lincoln's first appointments was Norman B. Judd as minister to Berlin, a lucrative job. The president explained that although Judd was not his oldest friend, he was "so devoted and self-sacrificing a friend as to make the distinction of an early nomination to that mission a well due tribute."[169] When some Illinois associates objected to the selection of Judd, Lincoln replied: "It seems to me he has done more for the success of the party than any one man in the state, and he is certainly the best organizer we have."[170] To assist Judd, Herman Kreismann was named secretary of the legation. This irritated Seward, who complained about Lincoln's "utter absence of any acquaintance" with foreign affairs, "and as to men he was more blind and unsettled than as to measures." The nominations of Judd and Kreismann, he said, "were made without consultation, merely in fulfillment of a promise to give the former a Cabinet appointment, which he had been compelled to give up."[171] When a senator objected that Judd spoke no German or French, Stephen A. Douglas replied that Judd knew as much of those languages as the incumbent minister to Prussia.

The president filled other diplomatic and consular posts swiftly to counteract Confederate efforts at gaining recognition from European nations, some of which objected to the Republican high tariff. Henry S. Sanford of Connecticut, an experienced diplomat, was appointed quickly so that he could head off Rebel initiatives in London and Paris before settling into his post at Brussels. Fearing that the Confederacy would attack Mexico, Lincoln promptly appointed Thomas Corwin of Ohio as minister to that country in the hopes that he could negotiate a treaty guaranteeing its territorial integrity.

Some diplomatic appointees drew critical fire. Swiss-Americans objected to Charles L. Bernays, named consul at Zurich, because he was Jewish. (Jews were forbidden to reside in Switzerland.) George G. Fogg's displacement of Theodore S. Fay as minister to Switzerland dismayed an admirer, who said that even though Fogg "is a good fellow," he "is not fitted at all for a *diplomatic* position, and *Fay* sh[oul]d never have been superseded. He is the best informed man on European history & diplomacy and has the most valuable and intimate range of diplomatic social acquaintance of all the representatives of the U.S. abroad, & he is an anti-slavery man of long standing—from conviction."[172] Washington buzzed with criticism of many others for their lack of diplomatic experience and language skills and their membership in "the insolvent & the medium class."[173] Traditionally, diplomatic posts had been "the sewer through which flows the scum and refuse of the political puddle," said the New York *Tribune.* "A man not fit to stay at home is just the man to send abroad."[174] Among the more shameful emissaries representing the Great Republic were drunkards, smugglers, debauchees, and duelists. This was especially true of the consular service. Benjamin Moran, secretary of the U.S. legation in London, thought that "Mr. Lincoln's Consular appointments are the very worst yet made in my time."[175]

Decades after the Civil War, the former American consul in Rome, William James Stillman, echoed Moran's complaint. He wrote that "with the exception of Adams, at London, and Marsh, at Turin, we had hardly a representative abroad, either consular or diplomatic, who was a credit to the country. As the war continued, the importance of being respected in Europe became more evident, and a change took place; but the few men of respectable standing who were in foreign countries representing the United States of America were appointed on account of political pressure, and not on their merits."[176]

Lincoln admitted that political considerations played a role in foreign appointments. He chose Marsh minister to Sardinia and Anson Burlingame as minister to Austria, he said, "because of the intense pressure of their respective states, and their fitness also."[177] Marsh, who would achieve renown as a pioneering conservationist, was the uncle of Vermont Senator George F. Edmunds. It was widely believed that his experience as a diplomat, scholarly attainments, command of many European languages, and polished manners qualified him well for the post. When the Hapsburgs declared Burlingame, who had been defeated for reelection to Congress in 1860, *persona non grata* because of his support of Hungarian and Italian uprisings against Austrian rule, Lincoln sent him to China as U.S. minister plenipotentiary. The mercurial, egotistical, tempestuous James Watson Webb, a long-time friend of Seward and editor of the New York *Courier and Express,* lobbied hard for the post of minister to England but had to settle for Brazil, where he disgraced the diplomatic service by extorting a large sum from the local government. He had been offered the mission to Turkey, which he regarded insulting and wrote a churlish letter to Seward. When the secretary tried to show it to Lincoln, he declined to read it and evidently said some sharp things about Webb.

Webb was among the more unfortunate choices, but on the whole the diplomatic corps under Lincoln served creditably. As *The Nation* argued in 1867, Lincoln had put into office "the best set of foreign ministers we have had in many a day."[178] In addition to Adams and Marsh, others serving with honor included John Lothrop Motley in

Vienna, Sanford in Brussels, Schurz in Madrid, John Bigelow in Paris, Edward Joy Morris in Turkey, and Burlingame in China.

Although Adams was the most distinguished of that group, he was not Lincoln's first choice as minister to the Court of St. James; the president initially favored William L. Dayton, a political wheeler-dealer from New Jersey who had been the Republican vice presidential candidate in 1856. Seward and Chase persuaded Lincoln that Adams, son of one president and grandson of another, was better qualified than the Jerseyman. Adams uncharitably ascribed Lincoln's reluctance to appoint him to "that jealousy of Mr. Seward's influence that seems to pervade the narrow mind of the chief."[179] When Adams called at the White House to express his thanks, Lincoln replied: "Very kind of you to say so Mr Adams but you are not my choice you are Seward's man." He then turned to the secretary of state and said, "Well Seward I have settled the Chicago Post Office." Appalled by the president's seeming indifference to the importance of his high diplomatic office, Adams deprecated the "dull and inappreciative" Lincoln: "The impression which I have received is that the course of the President is drifting the country into war, by its want of decision. Every where at this place [Washington] is discouragement, not loud in words but in hopelessness of a favorable issue. For my part I see nothing but incompetency in the head. The man is not equal to the hour."[180]

Senator Charles Sumner, disappointed at not receiving the post that Adams won, resented both him and the president. To mollify Sumner, Lincoln allowed him *carte blanche* in awarding patronage to other Massachusetts Republicans. Three of the handful of first-class diplomatic posts went to residents of the Bay State: Adams, Burlingame, and Motley. This caused Midwesterners to complain that New Englanders had "every thing worth having—eleven chairmanships of committees in the Senate, a Vice-Presidency, a Cabinet office, the highest foreign mission, and two others of the first class, and a myriad of other lesser appointments."[181] When Sumner and Congressman John B. Alley urged the appointment of yet another Massachusetts resident as secretary of the London legation, the president rebuffed them. Tactfully, he agreed that their state could ably fill all the diplomatic and consular posts, adding "that he considered Massachusetts the banner State of the Union, and admired its institutions and people so much that he had sent his 'Bob' . . . to Harvard for an education." But, Lincoln explained, he had already appointed several Massachusetts citizens to diplomatic offices and that the man he had selected as secretary of the legation was from a swing state whose influential leaders he could not afford to alienate. Alley recalled that the president's reasoning, "together with his shrewd compliment to Massachusetts, restored our good humor." But, the president added, "I hope you will give me a little time before I hear from Massachusetts again." The congressman and Sumner found the explanation satisfactory.[182] Dayton became minister to France, a nation whose tongue he did not speak. In Paris he proved a capable but unexceptional diplomat.

Southern Appointments

Lincoln bolstered Southern Unionists by giving patronage to non-Republicans in the Upper South and Border States. To John A. Gilmer he explained that in Slave States with few Republicans, "I do not expect to inquire for the politics of the appointee, or whether he does or does not own slaves. I intend in that matter to accommodate the people in the several localities, if they themselves will allow me to accommodate them. In one word, I never have been, am not now, and probably never shall be in a mood of harassing the people either north or south."[183] To show that he was reaching out to Democrats and Constitutional Unionists, he cited the example of Louisville, where he appointed a John Bell supporter as postmaster rather than a Republican aspirant. Lincoln told a group of Baltimoreans who urged him to appoint only Republicans to office that "he was aware that the republicans who lived in Southern States were brave men, and fond of taking a tilt, but he doubted whether that would be the correct principle upon which he should settle the question, as to who should be Collector and Postmaster of Baltimore."[184] He authorized a friend to inform Maryland Governor Thomas H. Hicks, whose refusal to summon the legislature was widely regarded as a brave pro-Union stand, that "your recommendation will weigh *tons* for any appointments in Maryland."[185] Hicks told Seward that "[e]verything depends upon proper appointments to leading places in border States."[186] Maryland ex-Congressman Henry Winter Davis moaned that it was "disheartening to see Democrats whose only merit is that they served Buchanan" continue in office "when the active & young men of the Republican party are wholly thrust aside." Ominously he expressed the hope that in 1864 the Republicans would choose a president who "will weed out *all* democratic & old fogey influence from the Govt."[187] (In time, Davis would become a bitter enemy of the president.) Congressman James M. Ashley of Ohio expressed similar regrets.

Lincoln's policy sometimes backfired. In Washington, D.C., the fight over the local postmastership caused much trouble. The president wanted to name his friend from congressional days, Nathan Sargent, but felt constrained not to. (Sargent eventually won the post of commissioner of customs in Connecticut.) Lewis Clephane, former business manager of the antislavery *National Era* and secretary of the National Republican Association of Washington, was initially passed over in favor of an undeserving hack who had performed no services for the cause. Eventually, Clephane won that job, though his performance in it displeased the postmaster general. After acquiescing in Ward Hill Lamon's selection as marshal, Republicans in the District expected to receive the other posts. They were sorely disappointed when a resident of Maine became a naval officer in the customhouse and a New Yorker was named commissioner of public buildings. Other such appointments led Benjamin Brown French to lament that "Abraham seems to be inclined to ignore us Republicans [in Washington] on the ground that we are not popular!!"[188]

The president encouraged supporters of Kentuckian John J. Crittenden's candidacy for a seat on the Supreme Court. Upon assuming command of the State Department, Seward (evidently with Lincoln's approval) immediately requested Edwin M. Stanton to draw up papers nominating Crittenden to the high court. The secretary confidently predicted that Crittenden would be confirmed, but Radical Republicans, including Chase and Trumbull, objected so vehemently that the plan was scrapped. Lincoln stated "that he will not make any appointment which will be calculated to divide the Republicans in the Senate, as he desires to so act as to consolidate and strengthen the party."[189]

As he promised in his inaugural, Lincoln strove to appoint men to posts in the South who were unobjectionable to local residents. He urged his cabinet secretaries to make no removals on political grounds in that region, especially Virginia. When Montgomery Blair selected a postal agent for the Old Dominion who proved so unpopular that after his first run he was threatened with death should he return, Lincoln "expressed his regret that any obnoxious person was appointed mail agent on any mail route" in Virginia.[190] To one faction of Virginia Unionists who appealed for patronage, Lincoln "replied that he must pursue a cautious policy" and showed them a letter from Virginia Congressman Sherrard Clemens recommending that further action on Old Dominion appointments be postponed. To weaken Clemens's influence, John C. Underwood of another faction suggested that Lincoln be shown a letter in which Clemens described the president, after interviewing him, as "a cross between a sandhill crane and Andalusian Jackass," "vain, weak, puerile, hypocritical, without manners, without moral grace," an "abolitionist of the Lovejoy and Sumner type," "by all odds the weakest man who has ever been elected—worse than Taylor, and he was bad enough." When "he talks to you [he] punches you under your ribs. He swears equal to uncle Toby, and in every particular, morally and mentally, I have lost all respect for him." Clemens was shocked to discover that Lincoln "did not know what the Adams amendment was until I told him." The congressman predicted that "Virginia under his follies and puerilities, will secede."[191] To Clemens's embarrassment, his unflattering assessment of Lincoln appeared in the press.

As Lincoln dealt with patronage squabbles, the Fort Sumter crisis simmered ominously. He must choose among three options: should he reinforce the garrison, merely resupply it, or surrender it?

"You Can Have No Conflict Without Being Yourselves the Aggressors"
The Fort Sumter Crisis
(March–April 1861)

One of Lincoln's greatest challenges was taming his secretary of state. "I can't afford to let Seward take the first trick," he told Nicolay in early March.[1] While struggling with the Fort Sumter dilemma, Lincoln had to keep the wily New Yorker, who presumed he would serve as the Grand Vizier of the administration, from taking not just the first trick but the entire rubber. Seward hoped to dominate Lincoln just as he had dominated President Zachary Taylor. Charles Francis Adams, Jr., who knew and admired Seward, aptly described the Sage of Auburn's frame of mind as he settled into his new position as secretary of state: "He thought Lincoln a clown, a clod, and planned to steer him by . . . indirection, subtle maneuvering, astute wriggling and plotting, crooked paths. He would be Prime Minister; he would seize the reins from a nerveless President; keep Lincoln separated from other Cabinet officers—[hold] as few Cabinet meetings as possible; overawe and browbeat Welles and Cameron—get the War Navy and State [departments] really under his own control."[2]

Seward evidently wished the motto of the administration to be, "The King reigns, but does not govern."[3] He told a European diplomat that there "exists no great difference between an elected president of the United States and a hereditary monarch. The latter is called to the throne through the accident of birth, the former through the chances which make his election possible. The actual direction of public affairs belongs to the leader of the ruling party here just as in a hereditary principality."[4] The New Yorker considered himself, not Lincoln, the "leader of the ruling party." In his own eyes, he was a responsible, knowledgeable veteran statesman who must guide the naïve, inexperienced Illinoisan toward sensible appointments and policies. Unlike Lincoln, he did not believe that the new administration had to carry out the Republicans' Chicago platform. At a dinner given by Stephen A. Douglas in February 1861, Seward proposed a toast: "Away with all parties, all platforms, all previous committals, and whatever else will stand in the way of restoration of the American Union."[5] That same month, Seward told former Kentucky Governor Charles S. Morehead: "if this whole matter is not satisfactorily settled within sixty days after I am seated in the saddle, and hold the reins firmly in my hand, I will give you my head for a football."[6] Soon thereafter he crowed: "I have built up the Republican party; I have brought it to triumph; but its advent to power is accompanied by great difficulties & perils. I must save the party & save the Government in its hands. To do this, war must be averted; the negro question must be dropped; the 'irrepressible conflict' ignored; & a Union party, to embrace the border slave States inaugurated. I have already whipped [Virginia Senators James M.] Mason & [R. M. T.] Hunter in their own State. I must crush out [Jefferson] Davis, [Robert] Toombs & their colleagues in sedition in their respective States. Saving the border States to the Union by moderation & justice, the people of the Cotton States, unwillingly led into secession, will rebel against their leaders & reconstruction will follow."[7]

Charles Sumner, chairman of the Senate Foreign Relations Committee, warned Lincoln: "You must watch him [Seward] & overrule him!"[8] A prominent Indiana Republican feared that "Seward and his friends would create the impression that it was *his* administration! That will not do. The people must be made to understand from the start that Mr. Lincoln is the President in fact, as well as in name."[9] To control the meddlesome, headstrong, mercurial secretary of state was a Herculean task for the president, eight years Seward's junior and far less politically experienced. Seward naively thought that Southern disaffection could be overcome by clever intrigue, and he optimistically declared that the Deep South "will be unable to exist for long as a separate confederation and will return to the Union sooner or later."[10] He remarked insouciantly that "he & all his brothers & sisters seceded from home in early life but they all returned. So would the States."[11]

The Fateful Decision to Relieve Fort Sumter

The day after the inauguration, Lincoln was astounded not only by news that Major Anderson had a mere six weeks' worth of supplies, but also by a letter from General Scott stating that Anderson and his fellow officers believed that they must either surrender or be overrun. Scott recommended that the garrison be evacuated. The obese, vain, aged general was retreating from his hard-line position of October, when he had urged the reinforcement of forts throughout the South, including those in Charleston harbor. On March 3, he had written to Seward suggesting that it would be unwise, if not actually impossible, to subdue the South militarily and that it might be best for Lincoln either to endorse the Crittenden Compromise or else tell the Cotton States, "Wayward sisters, depart in peace!"[12]

Scott's unsettling about-face was effected by Seward, who exercised great influence over the general. All winter long the senator had assiduously cultivated him. Montgomery Blair thought that Scott had "fallen into Mr. [Charles Francis] Adams' error in regarding Mr. Seward as the head of the government, and for this reason surrendered his own better judgment to that of Mr. Seward."[13] On March 6, at Lincoln's request, Scott briefed Welles, Cameron, Seward, and other officials, who were dumbfounded when the general reiterated what he had written to the president. Welles and Cameron urged that the administration "take immediate and efficient measures to relieve and reinforce the garrison." Scott did not express an opinion but pointed out that an earlier attempt to provision the fort had failed. He added that since Major Anderson had shifted his base from Fort Moultrie to Fort Sumter, the South Carolinians had surrounded the latter with formidable batteries and were preparing an attack. Scott acknowledged, however, that the question was "one for naval authorities to decide."[14]

The following day, Lincoln again met with this small group for an informal discussion. Scott and his chief engineer, Joseph G. Totten, agreed that it would be impracticable to reinforce Sumter. Welles and his advisor, Captain Silas Stringham, insisted that the navy could do so. The skeptical Seward offered many suggestions and raised several questions, but no conclusions were reached.

On March 9, the full cabinet convened to hear some unsettling news. "I was astonished to be informed that Fort Sumter . . . *must* be evacuated," Bates confided to his diary.[15] That same day, Lincoln asked Scott how long Sumter could hold out, whether he could supply or reinforce the garrison within that time frame, and what additional means might be needed to accomplish that goal if present means were insufficient. He asked the general to put his answers in writing and to "exercise all possible vigilance for the maintenance of all the places within the military department of the United States; and to promptly call upon all the departments of the government for the means necessary to that end."[16] Incredibly, Scott ignored that directive. Instead, he simply replied that to save Sumter, he would need a large fleet, 25,000 more troops, and several months to train them. "As a practical military question," he said, "the time for succoring Fort Sumter, with any means at hand, had passed away nearly a month ago. Since then a surrender under assault, or from starvation, has been merely a question of time."[17] On March 11, Scott drafted an order instructing Anderson to evacuate the fort.

Lincoln gave serious thought to issuing that order but hesitated to do so. He may well have been tempted to accept Scott's advice. After all, the general spoke with great authority, and the president had no military background. Scott's letter criticized the Buchanan administration for allowing the South Carolinians to surround Fort Sumter with artillery, and Lincoln could plausibly blame the necessity for removing the garrison on his predecessor. But if Lincoln did so think, he did not so act. Instead he asserted his leadership against both Scott and Seward.

Based on leaks (probably from Seward), newspapers reported that the administration would remove the Sumter garrison. This speculation touched off a firestorm of indignant protest. In Illinois, that rumor cast a pall over Republicans, including Lincoln's good friend William Butler, who expostulated: "*death before disgrace*."[18] Another Republican leader in the Prairie State insisted that "it is of no use (however true it may be) to tell *us*, we *can not* keep or retake the public property at the South ('hold, occupy, and possess.') We can try. We can shed our *treasure* and *blood* in the defence and support of our principles and *lawful rights* as our Fathers did." Thousands who had voted for Lincoln in 1860 stood ready to "cheerfully shoulder their musket and hazard their *all* in *this world* in support of the principles for which we contended then. We have *compromised* and *truckled long* enough. War is bad. Civil war is worse, but if liberty and the right of the people to govern themselves was worth fighting for in the days of the Revolution, it is worth fighting for now."[19] The Radical abolitionist Parker Pillsbury scornfully remarked that "the abandonment of Fort Sumner [sic] goes to show that indeed we have no government at all."[20]

Montgomery Blair was so angry at the prospect of surrendering Fort Sumter that he prepared a letter of resignation. He described the cabinet discussions to his father, who, at the urging of some senators, called at the White House to stiffen Lincoln's backbone. The old man, with vivid memories of Andrew Jackson's forceful crushing of South Carolina nullifiers in 1832–1833, told Lincoln on March 12 "that the surrender of Fort Sumter, was virtually a surrender of the Union unless under irresistable force." He added that such a craven move would "lose his Administration irrevocably the public confidence—that submission to secession would be a recognition of its constitutionality." Blair condemned both Scott and Seward and warned that the president might be impeached if he followed their counsel. (Blair regretted his impetuosity, telling his son that same day: "I may have said things that were impertinent & I am sorry I ventured on the errand.")[21] Blair's views were held by many Northerners, including a Wall Street attorney who wrote that "one bold Jacksonian stroke of Lincoln would electrify the North & encourage the true friends of the country everywhere." But if "a part of the country is permitted to float off *he & all his assistants* in such a suicide will be damned to eternal infamy. We all have the most perfect confidence in *him*. We are willing to bear national disgrace & obloquy till he can turn out the traitors & fill the offices with true men. But no time must be frittered away."[22]

On March 13, at a caucus of Republican senators, it was proposed that they call on Lincoln to demand that Sumter be held. Ben Wade of Ohio said "he never much believed in total depravity, but in these apostate times he begins to think it is true, and that the Republican party will furnish a striking example of it, being likely to be damned before it is fairly born."[23] Although the caucus turned down the proposal, word of it leaked to the press and may have affected Lincoln's decision to resist the advice of Scott and Seward. At the end of the month, Lyman Trumbull introduced a resolution stating that it was the president's duty to enforce the law in the seceded states; this move was widely regarded as an attempt to intimidate Lincoln and compel him to resupply Sumter.

Montgomery Blair sought to convince the president that Sumter could be held despite the growing ring of South Carolina artillery surrounding it. On March 12, Blair summoned his brother-in-law, Gustavus V. Fox, a 34-year-old former naval officer who, in consultation with an expert on Charleston harbor, had devised a plan to relieve the fort. The previous month, that plan had won the endorsement of General Scott and other military men, but Buchanan refused to implement it lest he antagonize the newly formed Confederate government. Fox called for troops and supplies to be carried to the bar of Charleston harbor by a large commercial vessel, then transferred to light, fast tugboats that would convey them to the fort under cover of darkness and with the protection of an accompanying warship. The next day, Blair took the energetic, industrious, and self-assured Fox to the White House, where he outlined his scheme to the president.

Lincoln came to like and admire Fox, a cheerful, buoyant raconteur whose wife's sister was married to Montgomery Blair. Fox thus had a close personal connection to the administration and enjoyed an entrée to the White House, which he often visited. In August 1861 he became assistant secretary of the navy and in effect served as chief of naval operations, working smoothly with Navy Secretary Gideon Welles. Lincoln trusted Fox's judgment and often consulted him.

On the Ides of March, Fox briefed the cabinet. At that meeting, Generals Totten and Scott reiterated their objections. The president then asked all the secretaries to answer in writing a simple question: "Assuming it to be possible to now provision Fort-Sumpter, under all the circumstances, is it wise to attempt it?"[24] In a lengthy reply, Seward raised a number of objections: it would needlessly trigger a civil war, it was militarily impracticable, it would accomplish nothing worthwhile, and it would drive the Upper South and Border States into the Confederacy. In addition, he emphasized that the nation could never be made whole again, that a policy of conciliation should be pursued, and that Sumter was strategically unimportant. But he would insist that ships outside Southern ports collect import duties, even at the risk of provoking hostilities. Seward closed melodramatically, saying: "If this counsel seems to be impassive and even unpatriotic, I console myself by the reflection that it is such as Chatham gave to his country under circumstances not widely different."[25] (In 1775, William Pitt, Earl of Chatham, had urged the British government to be forbearing in its dealings with the American colonies, which were then on the verge of revolt.)

Attorney General Bates argued that provisioning the fort would be legal and physically possible, though imprudent. "It may indeed involve a point of honor or a point of pride, but I do not see any great national interest involved in the bare fact of holding the fort." He feared that if war resulted, it would seem to the world as if the North had provoked it and would lead to unimaginably horrid slave uprisings. He would, however, take a tough stand against any attempt to block the mouth of the Mississippi River and would make a show of resolve at the other forts remaining in Union hands, most notably Pickens in Florida.[26] Similarly, Welles argued that even though a relief expedition like the one being contemplated might work, the North could be compelled to fire the opening shot and thereby become guilty of shedding the first blood. Cameron said the administration should defer to those military men who denied the feasibility of resupplying the fort. Smith maintained that an expedition should be sent to Charleston only if it were able to bring overwhelming force to bear. While it was important to uphold the honor and authority of the government, there were other ways to achieve that end. Chase waffled, saying he would recommend provisioning the fort as long as it would not touch off a war, which the nation could ill afford. But such a war seemed to him unlikely. (According to Blair, Chase said: "Let the South go; it is not worth fighting for.")[27]

Montgomery Blair was the only cabinet secretary to favor the relief effort unconditionally. Secessionists were taking heart from Northern timidity and vacillation, he asserted; to continue an appeasement policy would only encourage them. To provision the fort, which was feasible in his view, would demoralize them and spark a Southern movement to reunite the country. (Indeed, many Southerners did doubt that the

North would fight. "You may slap a Yankee in the face and he'll go off and sue you but he won't fight!" said one.)[28]

While mulling over his options, Lincoln urged the cabinet to avoid offending the South. According to Welles, "he was disinclined to hasty action, and wished time for the Administration to get in working order and its policy to be understood."[29] Yet, despite advice from prominent military and civilian leaders, Lincoln hesitated to abandon Sumter. He knew that step would outrage the North, for as March dragged on, public opinion was growing ever more discontented with the president's "namby pamby course."[30] Former Assistant Secretary of the Treasury William L. Hodge told a New York banker that the administration "is losing precious time by their shilly shally policy which is as much a mystery to us here [in Washington] as it must be to you."[31] The president "must *act* soon, or forfeit his claim to our regard," declared young abolitionist Charles Russell Lowell.[32] Congressmen like Albert G. Porter of Indiana were starting to describe the president as "a timid indecisive man" who "lacks decision of character."[33] Lincoln's friends in Illinois were growing impatient with the administration's "do nothing policy."[34] Such a policy "is well enough *for awhile*, but it cannot answer much longer," observed an Ohio journalist on March 29.[35]

Edwin M. Stanton, who had served in Buchanan's cabinet as attorney general, was especially harsh in his criticism, complaining that there "is no settled principle or line of action—no token of any intelligent understanding by Lincoln, or the crew that govern him, of the state of the country, or the exigencies of the times. Bluster & Bravado alternate with timidity & despair—recklessness, and helplessness by turns rule the hour. What but disgrace & disaster can happen?" On March 19, he reported "that the administration not only have, as yet, no line of policy, but also believe that it *never can* have any—but will drift along, from day to day, without a compass."[36]

A western member of Congress asked Lincoln if the administration would collect import revenues in Southern ports.

"*If I can*," he replied.

"How about the forts? Will they be held?"

"If they can be."

"But, under existing laws, do you believe the revenues *can* be collected?"

Lincoln "confessed that he did not see how it could be done." His interlocutor left the White House dissatisfied.[37]

Even his good friend David Davis conceded that Lincoln "lacks *will*" and "yields to pressure."[38] The New York *Herald* called the administration "imbecile and weak."[39] The Washington *States and Union* scornfully demanded action: "We want Mr. Lincoln to show his hand; we want him to let us know decidedly and unequivocally what he means to do. These are pressing times; everything is going to the devil at a breakneck speed, which must, before long, precipitate his own government in hopeless bankruptcy. The people are clamoring for a policy."[40] On April 7, an Iowa Republican leader expressed fear that "our party and our country will go down together" if the administration did not adopt "a policy of some kind soon."[41]

In New England, where elections took place in the early spring, the public vigorously objected to appeasing the Confederacy. Pennsylvania Congressman John

Covode reported after stumping New Hampshire that the Democrats would have won there if he and other Republican campaigners had not assured voters that the Southern forts would be held and the revenue would be collected. Meanwhile, Midwestern voters defeated Republicans in municipal elections because of the administration's failure to confront the secessionists. A Cincinnati Republican told Lincoln that the party has "been beaten in our city election—the same in St. Louis—Cleveland—Rhode Island—Brooklyn—and lost two Members of Congress in Connecticut—all from the demoralization and discouraging effect produced by the apparent *inaction* and *temperizing* policy of the new Administration, and the *impression* that *Fort Pickens* was going to be given up also to the rebels!" He urged the president to "*Hold Fort Pickens*—re-enforce it to its full capacity."[42] A Connecticut Republican leader lamented that "the patriotic ardor of our friends . . . has been much dampened by the proposed withdrawal from Fort Sumpter, and the fear of a general back-down policy on the part of the Administration."[43]

With disgust, Benjamin Brown French complained that the "Administration seems to me to be playing 'shilly shally,' one day one way the next another way, & if this course is long persisted in all confidence will be lost, by every body, in Mr. Lincoln. I want him either way to say 'War' and let it come, or to back out honorably from Sumter & Pickens, & make the best of it. Not say, as he is now virtually saying, 'My Republican friends, you have elected me, & now you must lie quietly down, and permit the Courageous & Chivalric South to spit on you, & walk over you, & kick you, and do just as they d[am]n please with you.' This seems to be the policy *in acts,* if not in words."[44] Letters poured into the Capitol and White House insisting that if Sumter were abandoned, something else must be done to prove that the nation still had a government.

One obvious way to offset the evacuation of Sumter was to reinforce the only other major Deep South fort still in Union hands, Pickens off Pensacola, Florida. Bates had suggested that strategy privately, and some newspapers did so publicly. To make it possible to implement such a plan, Lincoln on March 5 verbally instructed Scott to hold Pickens and other Southern forts. A week later, when the president discovered that nothing had been done to carry out this order, he put it in writing. Two months earlier, Buchanan had sent reinforcements to Fort Pickens, but after dispatching them Old Buck agreed to an informal truce agreement whereby those troops would not be landed, and in return the Confederates would not attack the fort or emplace artillery threatening it. Thus matters stood when Lincoln was inaugurated. On March 12, in obedience to the new president's instructions, Scott ordered the two hundred troops aboard the U.S.S. *Brooklyn* to transfer to the fort, supplementing the eighty-one men already there.

To obtain more information before making up his mind, Lincoln took a number of steps, some of which were unconventional. For one, he asked the wife of an officer stationed at Fort Sumter, Abner Doubleday, if she would show him her husband's letters. In addition, he dispatched troubleshooters to Charleston, including Fox, who volunteered to visit that city and ascertain the feasibility of his plan after a consultation with Major Anderson. The president and General Scott approved his proposal, and on March 19 Fox left, telling his wife that "our Uncle Abe Lincoln has taken a high esteem for me."[45] Two days later Lincoln asked his Illinois friend Stephen A. Hurlbut, a bibulous native of Charleston who had studied law with the eminent South Carolina attorney and Unionist James L. Pettigru, to return to his hometown and sample public opinion. To accompany him as an informal bodyguard, the president dispatched Ward Hill Lamon, over Cameron's protest.

After three days spent interviewing many lawyers, merchants, working men, and transplanted Northerners, Hurlbut reported "that Separate Nationality is a fixed fact—that there is an unanimity of sentiment which is to my mind astonishing—that there is no attachment to the Union." He expressed serious doubt "that any policy which may be adopted by this Government will prevent the possibility of armed collision," and he was sure that "a ship known to contain *only provisions* for Sumter would be stopped & refused admittance." He did not predict that such a ship would be fired upon or that its dispatch would provoke an attack on Sumter. After hearing this assessment, Lincoln had Hurlbut repeat his findings to Seward, who continued to insist that Southern Unionists would thwart the secessionists. Hurlbut replied that Sumter "was commanded by batteries which had been erected without molestation," and "that it was the intention to reduce the fort at all hazards." He added that there "was no mistaking the entire unanimity and earnestness of the secession sentiment. There were hundreds of men delicately brought up, who never had done a day's work in their lives, yet who were out there on those islands throwing up entrenchments." After Hurlbut wrote up his report, Lincoln read it to the cabinet.[46]

That document clearly destroyed whatever hope Lincoln may have entertained that the Deep South would voluntarily return to the fold. Seward's faith in a peaceful reconstruction seemed more and more chimerical; war appeared to be the only means to restore the Union. Hurlbut's report may well have convinced Lincoln that since war was inevitable no matter what he did, it made sense to relieve Sumter and thus placate Northern hard-liners.

While Hurlbut was interviewing Charlestonians, Fox consulted with Anderson at Fort Sumter. Arriving in Charleston on March 21, he was allowed to visit the major, who predicted that his supplies would run out by April 15 and that any attempt to provision or reinforce the garrison would precipitate a war. It was too late, Anderson believed, and no relief vessels could slip past the South Carolina defenses. Fox did not argue the matter, but instead closely observed the fort and surrounding waters. What he saw convinced him that his plan would work, and he so informed Lincoln. When the president asked if a competent senior naval officer would endorse his proposal, Fox cited Captain Silas Stringham, who came to the White House and assured Lincoln and Scott that both he and Commodore Charles Stewart thought Fox's plan eminently practicable.

While the missions of Hurlbut and Fox yielded useful information, Lamon's provided harmful disinformation. The egotistical Cavalier misled South Carolina Governor Francis Pickens and Major Anderson by assuring them, without any authorization, that the Sumter garrison would soon be removed. He explained to the governor that his mission was to facilitate the evacuation of the fort. He also had a conversation with Anderson, after which he wrote Seward that he was *"satisfied of the policy and propriety of immediately evacuating Fort Sumpter."*[47] (Why Lamon reported to Seward is a mystery, since he was an old friend of Lincoln, who sent him on the mission.) Upon leaving town, Lamon told Governor Pickens he would return soon to help Anderson and his men withdraw. Apropos of this episode, Cameron later asked incredulously: "How came the President to have so much faith in Lamon?" It was a good question.[48]

More misleading still was Seward's conduct. In his frequent dealings with Upper South Unionists, he virtually assured them that Sumter would be evacuated. He did the same thing while acting as an intermediary between the administration and the three commissioners sent by the Confederate government to demand formal recognition from Lincoln (Martin J. Crawford, John Forsyth, and André B. Roman). Forbidden by Lincoln to receive those emissaries officially, Seward employed go-betweens to negotiate with them. At first, William M. Gwin, who had just finished a term as senator from California, played that role, but he grew suspicious of Seward, dropped out, and drafted a telegram to Jefferson Davis stating that the appointment of Chase to the cabinet meant war. Seward revised the text to read: "Notwithstanding Mr. Chase's appointment, the policy of the administration would be for peace, and the amicable settlement of all questions between the sections." Gwin sent the revised message to Montgomery and then departed Washington for the South, where he had grown up. Seward was thus communicating almost directly with the Confederate president without his own president's authorization.

For a brief time, R. M. T. Hunter of Virginia replaced Gwin as Seward's intermediary, but soon U.S. Supreme Court Justice John A. Campbell of Alabama assumed that function. On March 13, when the commissioners demanded that the Confederacy be acknowledged as an independent nation, Seward, fearing that a blunt refusal might precipitate war, desperately tried to stall them. (Actually, they were bluffing; the Confederacy needed time to get organized—especially to install more batteries around Charleston harbor—and they were playing for that time.) Two days later Seward told Justice Campbell that the administration was going to withdraw the Sumter garrison within a week, an act which would cause a political uproar in the North; if in addition to that concession Lincoln were to recognize the Confederacy directly or indirectly, his administration would be ruined. Moreover, the president would have to maintain the status quo at Fort Pickens in Florida. When Campbell asked what he could write to Jefferson Davis, Seward replied: "You may say to him that before that letter reaches him: (How far is it to Montgomery?)"

"Three days."

"You may say to him that before that letter reaches him, the telegraph will have informed him that Sumter will have been evacuated."

Based on his conversation with Seward, Campbell assured both Davis and the Confederate commissioners that he had "perfect confidence in the fact that Fort Sumter will be evacuated in the next five days." He sent a copy of this letter to Seward, who did not correct him. (Technically, Seward had made a prediction, not a pledge; but Campbell's language to the commissioners made it sound more like the latter than the former. If Seward thought Campbell's letter misrepresented him, he did not tell him so. Campbell had every reason to believe that Seward spoke for Lincoln.)

When five days passed and the Sumter garrison still remained in place, the commissioners asked Campbell for an explanation. The judge consulted Seward, who assured him that everything was all right and that he should come back tomorrow. When Campbell returned, the secretary "spoke of the prospect of maintaining the peace of the country as cheering. Spoke of [the] coercion proposition in the Senate with some ascerbity, and said in reference to the evacuation of Sumter that the resolution had been passed, and its execution committed to the President. That he did not know why it had not been executed. 'That Mr. L. was not a man who regarded the same things important that you or I would, and if he did happen to consider a thing important, it would not for that reason be more likely to command his attention. That there was nothing in the delay that affected the integrity of the promise or denoted any intention not to comply.'" Seward also reassured Campbell that the administration would not alter the situation at Fort Pickens. Campbell reported back to the commissioners that Sumter would be evacuated soon and that "no prejudicial movement to the South is contemplated as respects Fort Pickens."[49] (At that same time, Seward was telling William Howard Russell of the London *Times* that "nothing would be given up—nothing surrendered.")[50]

As Lincoln struggled with the Sumter dilemma, he concluded that if he removed its garrison, he could justify it as a matter of practical necessity while simultaneously asserting federal authority by reinforcing Fort Pickens. To take a hard line at Pickens would immunize him against charges that he had abandoned his inaugural pledge "to hold, occupy, and possess the property, and places belonging to the government." If, however, Pickens were not available as an offset to the surrender of Sumter, the evacuation of the Charleston fort would be tantamount to a formal recognition of the Confederacy's independence. As March drew to a close, Lincoln, in a discussion with three congressmen, "gave it to be understood, in unmistakable terms, that even though the evacuation of Fort Sumter should be determined upon, the other forts yet in possession of federal troops will be held to the last. He furthermore hinted rather more plainly at the intention of the government to blockade the southern ports, and collect the revenue with men-of-war."[51] He explained to Congress several weeks later that the reinforcement of Pickens "would be a clear indication of *policy*, and would better enable the country to accept the evacuation of Fort Sumter, as a military *necessity*."[52]

Lincoln was right about Northern public opinion regarding the forts. A leading Maine Republican, Neal Dow, wrote him that "the evacuation of Fort Sumpter will be fully approved by the entire body of Republicans in this State—and I doubt not in all the country. It is undoubtedly a Military *necessity*; and admits of no question as to its expediency. At first, the suggestion struck us unpleasantly, but when we learned the actual position of affairs, we saw that the measure is inevitable, and is a legacy of humiliation from the last administration, which cannot be declined. We hope no such necessity exists in the case of Fort Pickens."[53] A wealthy New York Republican

leader told Lincoln: "The public mind is fully prepared for the evacuation of Fort
Sumpter—as a military necessity entailed on the country by the late Administration—
the hopes once entertained of its being relieved are dead—& buried. It will be hazardous to revive them on an uncertainty. The relief of Fort Pickens & any other feasible
effort to hold what is tenable would in my opinion strengthen the Administration &
give courage to the Union men at the South."[54] Some "staunch Republicans" in Washington seemed reconciled to the abandonment of Sumter as long as it was "accompanied by the reinforcement of Fort Pickens, and a naval blockade of Southern ports to
collect the revenues of the Government."[55] Similar word came from Illinois.

The situation changed dramatically on March 28 at a White House state dinner,
where Lincoln at first seemed in good spirits.

Lincoln's mood changed abruptly when Scott recommended that Sumter *and*
Pickens be abandoned. Probably acting at the behest of Seward, the general said he
doubted "whether the voluntary evacuation of Fort Sumter alone would have a decisive effect upon the States now wavering between adherence to the Union and secession. It is known, indeed, that it would be charged to *necessity*, and the holding of Fort
Pickens would be adduced in support of that view. Our Southern friends, however,
are clear that the evacuation of both the forts would instantly soothe and give confidence to the eight remaining slaveholding States, and render their cordial adherence
to this Union perpetual."[56]

Scott's recommendation shocked Lincoln, who convened his cabinet the following day. "I never shall forget the President's excitement," Montgomery Blair wrote. In
an "agitated manner," Lincoln read Scott's letter "which he seemed just to have received." A "very oppressive silence" prevailed, which was only broken when Blair remarked: "Mr President you can now see, that General Scott, in advising the surrender
of Fort Sumter is playing the part of a politician, not of a general, for as no one pre-
tends that there is any military necessity for the surrender of Fort Pickens, which he
now says it is equally necessary to surrender, it is believed that he is governed by political reasons in both recommendations." As Blair recalled, "No answer could be
made to this point, and the President saw that he was being misled." (Fort Pickens,
unlike Sumter, was a mile and a half offshore and much harder for the Confederates
to attack than the Charleston installation. In addition, it was well supplied and protected by a Union fleet.) Lincoln's confidence in Scott was shaken, and from then on
the general's influence with the president waned. Seward's credibility also suffered
badly.

The thought then arose that Fort Sumter could perhaps be relieved after all;
maybe Montgomery Blair and Gustavus Fox were right, despite what Scott, Totten,
and the other army men had argued. But if Sumter were to be resupplied, it would
damage Lincoln's credibility in the South, where newspapers as well as the commissioners proclaimed that his administration would abandon the fort. Seward's
misleading words to the press and to the commissioners were to have deleterious consequences.

That night Lincoln did not sleep. The next day he confessed that he was "in the
dumps," and, according to Mary Lincoln, he "keeled over with [a] sick headache for

the first time in years."[57] At a noon cabinet meeting, the president took Bates's advice
and had each department head write out yet another opinion about Sumter. The
drama of the preceding night changed Welles's mind; he now recommended sending
both provisions and troops to Sumter and notifying South Carolina authorities of the
decision. "There is little probability that this will be permitted, if the opposing forces
can prevent it," Welles speculated, but "armed resistance to a peac[e]able attempt to
send provisions to one of our own forts will justify the government in using all the
power at its command, to reinforce the garrison and furnish the necessary supplies."
He also urged that "Fort Pickens and other places retained should be strengthened by
additional troops, and, if possible made impregnable. The Naval force in the gulf and
on the southern coast should be increased."[58]

Similarly, Chase abandoned his earlier position and expressed himself in favor "of
maintaining Fort Pickens and just as clearly in favor of provisioning Fort Sumter. If
that attempt be resisted by military force Fort Sumter should, in my judgment, be
reinforced."[59] Blair stated that he had "no confidence" in Scott's "judgment on the
questions of the day—His political views control his judg[men]t—& his course as
remarked on by the President shows that whilst no one will question his patriotism,
the results are the same as if he was in fact traitorous." Sumter "ought to be relieved
without reference to Pickens or any other possession—S[outh] C[arolina] is the head
& front of the rebellion & when that State is safely delivered from the authority of the
U S it will strike a blow ag[ain]st our authority from which it will take us years of
bloody strife to recover from."[60] Bates favored reinforcing Pickens but straddled the
Sumter issue: "As to fort Sumter—I think the time is come either to evacuate or relieve it."[61]

Seward had no allies except for Smith, who recommended the surrender of
Sumter but not Pickens. The secretary of the interior urged that the administration
"adopt the most vigorous measures for the defense of the other Forts, and if we have
the power I would blockade the Southern ports and enforce the collection of the revenue with all the powers of the Govt."[62] (Remarkably, Cameron was out of town.) So
three favored relieving Sumter, two opposed it, one waffled, and one was absent.

When the press reported that Pickens would be evacuated, Congress and the
public were outraged. As Republican lawmakers prepared to return home and face their
constituents, they called on Lincoln to inquire about his policy. Ben Wade exclaimed,
"Go on as you seem to be going. Give up fortress after fortress, *and Jeff Davis will
have you as prisoner of war in less than thirty days!*" In response, the president laughed.
When the collection of revenues at Southern ports was mentioned, Lincoln conceded
that he was, as he put it, "green as a gourd," and had turned the subject over "to his
attorney, Seward."[63]

The White House mailbag bulged with protests. "We (the people of the West)
have accepted the evacuation of Fort Sumter as a military necessity," a fellow Illinoisan wrote. "But you & your Cabinet cannot imagine our chagrin at the report of
the probable evacuation of Fort Pickins and that a portion of your Cabinet with the
Sec. of State at their head is in favour of peace and evacuation on almost any terms. It
has taken us all aback." This correspondent pled with the president: "in the name of

reason and consistency don[']t subject our country to another burning disgrace and shame in the shape of evacuating any of the Forts and defences without an effort to save them from that lawless rattlesnake crew."[64] An Ohio Republican who had served as a delegate to the Chicago Convention predicted that the "reinforcement of Fort Sumpter under existing circumstances, would secure to you an immortality of fame, which Washington might envy. The Surrender of Fort Pickens under any circumstances, will consign your name, and fame, to an ignominy, in comparison with which that of your immediate predecessor, will be tolerable, and [Benedict] Arnold[']s illustrious."[65]

In late March, when Lincoln received word that the U.S.S. *Brooklyn* had sailed from Pensacola to Key West for supplies, he wrongly assumed that she had taken with her the soldiers designated to reinforce Fort Pickens. In fact, those troops had been transferred to the U.S.S. *Sabine,* which remained on station at Pensacola. Unaware of this important datum, the president concluded that his March 12 order had "fizzled out."[66] Therefore, it was imperative to launch a new expedition to reinforce Pickens. In case that could not be effected before the Sumter garrison ran out of food, it was also essential to prepare a relief expedition for the Charleston fort. So on March 29 the president ordered Fox to make ready a squadron for the relief of Sumter but to enter into no binding agreements. This did not represent a point of no return, for Lincoln and Fox both knew that if relieving Sumter should become necessary in order to vindicate the power of the government, swift action was necessary. By mid-April, the garrison would be starved out; in order to get provisions to Charleston before then, an expedition would have to be organized immediately. If, however, it turned out that Scott's March 12 order to reinforce Pickens actually had been obeyed, or if the new Pickens expedition had reached Pensacola before the Sumter garrison exhausted its food supply, then Fox's mission could be scrubbed.

On the afternoon of March 29, Lincoln summoned Scott to the White House. In the course of their long conversation about the forts, the president said that *"Anderson had played us false"* and predicted that the administration "would be broken up unless a more decided policy was adopted, and if General Scott could not carry out his views, some other person might." He chided the Hero of Chapultepec for not promptly carrying out his directive of March 5 to reinforce Pickens.[67]

The president was not alone in suspecting Anderson's loyalty. In October 1860, Colonel E. D. Keyes, who had served with Anderson on Scott's staff for four years, confided to his journal that "if hatred and contempt for the people of the North and East, and especially the latter, and a boundless partiality for the South, are qualifications for a successor in command . . . [at Charleston], few better than Major Anderson can be found among my acquaintances in the army."[68] In late February, when Anderson notified Washington that he was running short of supplies and recommended against reinforcing the garrison, Joseph Holt wrote Lincoln a biting review of the major's inconsistency. Holt noted that in late December Anderson had claimed that he could hold out for a long time and that reinforcements could be sent at the government's leisure. The major then predicted that "we can command this Harbor as long *as our government wishes to keep it.*" In January, he continued forwarding optimistic reports, leading the War Department to postpone any attempt to send reinforcements or supplies but simultaneously to urge the major to notify it if any were needed. Although the major described the progress of the construction of batteries by the South Carolinians, he never indicated that he was endangered or felt the necessity for more supplies. The War Department understandably inferred from Anderson's reports that all was well.[69] In mid-March, the knowledgeable journalist D. W. Bartlett sensibly asked: "Was not Major Anderson perfectly aware six weeks ago that the batteries which were being erected at every commanding point in Charleston harbor would soon render a reinforcement impossible?" If so, "why did he not complain of the military works which were intended to compass his destruction and warn his Government in time?" Evidence was mounting, said Bartlett, "to show that Major Anderson has been playing a deep game for three months."[70] Lincoln found Anderson's volte-face so peculiar that he asked Holt if "any suspicion or doubt had ever arisen in his mind" about the major's loyalty. When Holt replied negatively, the president "expressed himself much gratified."[71]

Later, when hostilities seemed imminent, Anderson told General Lorenzo Thomas, "I frankly say that my heart is not in the war which I see is to be thus commenced."[72] He also informed Governor Pickens that "my sympathies are entirely with the South."[73] When Gustavus Fox spoke with Anderson on March 21, he became instantly aware of the major's pro-Southern views. Montgomery Blair thought it suspicious that Anderson had not dismantled the fort's flammable barracks and moved his men into the casemates as an attack grew ever more likely. (When the Confederates finally shelled the fort, the barracks were set afire by heated shot and explosive shells, which proved more efficacious than solid shot.) In May, John Hay confided to his diary that the "North has been strangely generous with that man [Anderson]. The red tape of military duty was all that bound his heart from its traitorous impulses."[74]

The ever-resourceful Seward, observing his plans crumble, frantically tried to salvage the situation. While maintaining his opposition to the relief of Sumter, he now recommended that Lincoln "at once and at every cost prepare for a war at Pensacola and Texas, to be taken however only as a consequence of maintaining the possession and authority of the United States."[75] (In Texas, the Unionist governor Sam Houston was resisting the secessionists, but when Lincoln offered to send troops, he declined.)

Seward Sabotages the Effort to Relieve Fort Sumter

Seward's sudden concern for Fort Pickens was puzzling, since he had previously shown little interest in that bastion; at the forefront of his mind on March 29 was the Sumter expedition. How could he explain to the Confederate commissioners and to Justice Campbell that his assurances about the evacuation of the Charleston fort were false? How could he maintain leadership in the administration, now that the president had overruled him, with the support of a plurality of the cabinet? How could he prevent the outbreak of civil war? One way was to sabotage the Sumter expedition by stripping it of its key component, the warship *Powhatan*, which was to transport howitzers, armed launches, and hundreds of troops. That vessel, it was understood, was the only one in the navy capable of carrying out the mission. Perhaps Lincoln could be persuaded to send it to Pensacola rather than Charleston. But Welles would probably want the *Powhatan* for the Sumter expedition. So the relief of Pickens must be undertaken without Welles's knowledge. But how? Seward could argue that the mission must be kept secret, lest word of it leak out and impel the Confederates to attack Pickens before ships arrived to protect it. (This possibility was not great, for several Union war vessels were already in the waters off Pensacola, and Confederate forces were too weak to seize the fort. The *Powhatan*'s presence was in fact unnecessary; it was not even needed to cover the transfer of troops from shipboard to the fort. As it turned out, that was done on April 12, five days before the *Powhatan* arrived at Pensacola.) Therefore, only Seward, the president, and officers in charge of the ships and troops should be informed. This highly irregular proceeding would certainly offend the secretaries of war and the navy, whom Seward regarded as ciphers. So the secretary of state, desperately seeking a way to preserve his honor, his leadership position, and the peace, scrambled to implement this devious scheme. He would also try to convince the president to let him take charge of the administration.

On March 29, Seward summoned his friend Captain Montgomery C. Meigs, an ambitious, vain, capable 45-year-old army engineer who was supervising the expansion of the Capitol and who had recently visited the forts at Pensacola, Key West, and Dry Tortugas, Florida. Alluding to the infirm, 75-year-old General Scott, Seward explained to Meigs "that he thought the President ought to see some of the younger officers, and not consult only with men who, if war broke out, could not mount a horse."[76] All along, Seward had been using Scott as his authority in arguing that Sumter should be abandoned. Now, with Scott discredited, the secretary needed some other military man to lend credibility to his strategizing. At the White House, Meigs confidently asserted that both Sumter and Pickens could be held. The danger in reinforcing the Florida fort was that Confederate vessels might intercept boats ferrying troops across Pensacola Bay. But, he said, if a swift warship were sent there immediately, it could protect those boats from Rebel attackers. (He thus supported Seward's new plan by implying that the *Powhatan* should go to Florida and thus become unavailable for the Sumter mission.) When Lincoln asked if Meigs would be willing to take command of forces in Florida, the captain protested that he could not give orders to his superiors stationed there. The president said he would investigate the matter and let him know soon if it might be possible to promote him quickly, as Seward suggested. Scott, however, overruled the secretary, and Meigs agreed to join the expedition as a subordinate.

Lincoln ordered that an expedition sail to Florida as soon as possible. The next morning when Seward informed Scott of the president's directive, the general exclaimed: "the great Frederick [of Prussia] used to say that 'when the King commands, nothing is impossible!' Sir, the President's orders shall be obeyed!"[77] Scott then consulted with his military secretary, Colonel E. D. Keyes, who argued that it would be extremely difficult to reinforce Fort Pickens. Scott directed him to share his thoughts with Seward. When the colonel pointed out the problems he had mentioned to Scott, Seward interrupted saying, "I don't care about the difficulties," and ordered him to fetch Meigs forthwith. Ten minutes later the captain and the colonel stood before Seward, who commanded them to devise a plan for reinforcing Pickens and present it at the White House no later than 3 P.M.

At the Executive Mansion, Meigs and Keyes read their proposals to Lincoln, who approved them despite his puzzlement at references to scarps, terreplains, barbettes, and the like. To command the ships involved, Meigs suggested a friend, Lieutenant David Dixon Porter, an ambitious, bold young officer who had distinguished himself seven years earlier on a mission to Cuba. "Gentlemen," the president directed, "see General Scott, and carry your plans into execution without delay." When they did so later that day, the general approved their scheme and wrote orders implementing it.[78]

Meanwhile, that same day, the Confederate commissioners called Justice Campbell's attention to a telegram from South Carolina Governor Pickens complaining that Lamon had failed to honor his promise to arrange for the evacuation of Sumter. Two days later, Seward told Campbell "that the President was concerned at the contents of the telegram. . . . that Colonel Lamon did not go to Charleston under any commission or authority from Mr. Lincoln, nor had he any power to pledge him by any promise or assurance; that Mr. Lincoln desired that Governor Pickens should be satisfied of this." Seward then handed the judge a note stating that "the President may desire to supply Fort Sumter, but will not undertake to do so without first giving notice to Governor Pickens." This represented a dramatic change from the secretary's earlier assurances to Campbell, who protested that if such a message were conveyed to Charleston, the authorities there would bombard Sumter immediately. Seward then consulted briefly with Lincoln and returned with a modified version of a message for the South Carolina governor: "I am satisfied the Government will not undertake to supply Fort Sumter without giving notice to Governor Pickens." This was still a far cry from what Campbell had been told previously. When the judge asked if Lincoln really intended to supply Sumter, Seward replied: "No, I think not, it is a very irksome thing to him to evacuate it. His ears are open to everyone, and they fill his head with schemes for its supply. I do not think that he will adopt any of them. There is no design to reinforce it."[79] Clearly, the secretary was deceiving the commissioners, unless he believed that he could sabotage the Sumter expedition and thereby thwart Lincoln.

On April 1, Porter and Seward reviewed the plans to reinforce Pickens. The lieutenant suggested that Lincoln, not the secretary of the navy, issue a direct order to ready the *Powhatan*. At a conference with Porter, Meigs, and Seward, Lincoln approved these arrangements, though he felt uneasy about bypassing normal channels and having his secretary of state in effect act as secretary of the navy.

"But what will Uncle Gideon say?" he asked.

"I will make it all right with Mr. Welles," Seward replied.

"This looks to me very much like the case of two fellows I once knew: one was a gambler, the other a preacher," said Lincoln. "They met in a stage, and the gambler induced the preacher to play poker, and the latter won all the gambler's money. 'It's all because we have mistaken our trades,' said the gambler; 'you ought to have been a gambler and I a preacher, and, by ginger, I intend to turn the tables on you next Sunday and preach in your church,' which he did." The formal order instructed Porter to sail the *Powhatan* into Pensacola harbor and cover the reinforcement of the fort. It was, as Meigs put it, "extracted" from the president, who may well have been confused about three different warships with Indian names beginning with the letter P (Powhatan, Pawnee, Pocohontas). While signing the various documents, Lincoln said: "Gentlemen, I don't know anything of your army and navy rules only don't let me burn my fingers."[80]

Because of the secrecy and haste involved, the plan quickly created a bureaucratic nightmare. The *Powhatan* was under the command of Captain Samuel Mercer, who received an order written by Porter and signed by Lincoln instructing him to turn the ship over to the lieutenant. On April 1, Welles, unaware of the Seward-Porter-Meigs-Lincoln scheme, ordered the *Powhatan* to be readied for duty as soon as possible. As if this were not sufficiently perplexing, another problem immediately arose: How was the Pickens expedition to be paid for? Congress had adjourned without appropriating money for such purposes. The only recourse was the secret-service fund of the State Department, which could be tapped with the approval of the president alone. So Lincoln authorized this unconventional funding arrangement, and Seward gave $10,000 to Meigs, who distributed it to both Porter and Keyes. The latter was responsible for hiring a steamer in New York and overseeing the preparation of the other ships.

Armed with his orders freshly signed by Lincoln, Porter left for New York on April 1. The next day the acting commandant of the Brooklyn Navy Yard, Andrew H. Foote, hesitated to let the lieutenant have the *Powhatan,* for the previous afternoon Welles's order assigning that vessel to Fox had arrived. Moreover, it was highly irregular for a mere lieutenant to replace a full captain in command of an important warship; it was even more irregular for such an order to be issued by the president and not the secretary of the navy. Foote suspected a rebel plot to steal the ship, for he knew that Porter was friendly with pro-Southern naval officers. Perhaps Porter himself was a traitor! After some cajoling, the lieutenant persuaded Foote to honor Lincoln's directive and to maintain secrecy. The *Powhatan* was ready to sail by April 6.

On April 1, Lincoln sent Welles copies of some of the documents he had that day approved, one of which seemed to undercut the secretary's authority. Indignantly, Welles called at the White House to protest. Lincoln, sensing his anger, asked: "What have I done wrong?" In addition to the orders regarding the Pickens expedition, he had signed instructions to Welles to send most of the navy to Mexico; to reassign his trusted assistant, Captain Stringham, to Pensacola; and to replace Stringham with Captain Samuel Barron. Welles explained to Lincoln that Barron's loyalty was suspect and that he could not work with such a man as his principal subordinate. (Barron soon thereafter joined the Confederate navy.) The restructuring of the department specified in Lincoln's directive would have put Barron virtually in charge of naval operations. Later, Welles wrote that there "is not in the archives and history of the Government a record of such mischievous maladministration . . . as this secret scheme."[81] By way of explanation, Lincoln said that Seward, "with two or three young men, had been there through the day, on a matter which Mr. Seward had much at heart; that he had yielded to the project of Mr. Seward, but as it had involved considerable detail and he had his hands full, and more too, he had left Mr. Seward to prepare the necessary papers. These papers he had signed, some without reading, trusting entirely to Mr. Seward, for he could not undertake to read all the papers presented to him; and if he could not trust the Secretary of State, whom could he rely upon in a public matter that concerned us all?" Lincoln "seemed disinclined to disclose or dwell on the project," but told Welles that "he never would have signed that paper had he been aware of its contents, much of which had no connection with Mr. Seward's scheme." The president countermanded the order reassigning Stringham and Barron, but he still did not fully inform Welles about the Pickens relief mission.[82]

On April 1, Lincoln was so badly indisposed that he declined to see visitors and complained that he was "nearly exhausted by the constant pressure on him."[83] Compounding that pressure, New York merchants and bankers lobbied him to have the Morrill Tariff repealed, arguing that it would ruin the country's finances. Lincoln expressed "apprehension that the treasury would soon be bankrupt" because the new tariff might not be enforceable in the South, and thus goods could be brought into southern ports duty-free and then transshipped north.[84] (He was, however, greatly pleased with the success of the first government loan under his administration, offered on April 2 and taken up at rates more favorable than the previous one.)

Four days later Seward and his son Frederick called on the navy secretary late at night with a telegram from Meigs and Porter asking for clarification of orders regarding the *Powhatan*, since confusion reigned at the Brooklyn Navy Yard. Seward demanded that Welles retract his order assigning that warship to Fox. Puzzled, Welles insisted that they consult the president immediately, even though the hour was late. En route to the White House, Seward "remarked that, old as he was, he had learned a lesson from this affair, and that was, he had better attend to his own business and confine his labors to his own Department." (In fact, the meddlesome Seward continued to poach on the domains of his cabinet colleagues, much to their annoyance.)

Around midnight they arrived at the Executive Mansion, where Lincoln was still up. Surprised by the telegram from Meigs and Porter, the president suggested that he may have misunderstood which vessel would serve as flagship for the Sumter squadron, confusing the *Pocahontas* with the *Powhatan*. (Fox's squadron consisted of the *Pawnee*, the *Pocahontas*, the *Powhatan*, and the *Harriet Lane*.) The navy secretary quickly retrieved documents from his office indicating that Lincoln had authorized the assignment of the *Powhatan* to Fox. To set things aright, Lincoln told Seward "that the Powhatan must be restored to Mercer—that on no account must the Sumter expedition fail." Seward said he "thought it was now too late to correct the mistake" and that "he considered the other project the most important, and asked whether that would not be injured if the Powhatan was now withdrawn." According to Welles, Lincoln "would not discuss the subject, but was peremptory—said there was not the pressing necessity in the other case. . . . As regarded Sumter, however, not a day was to be lost—that the orders of the Secretary of the Navy must be carried out." When

Seward opined that it might be too late to send a telegram to New York, Lincoln insisted that it be done nevertheless.[85]

Reluctantly, Seward obeyed, drafting a telegram to Porter ordering him to do as the president had instructed. Amazingly, it did not arrive until 3 P.M. the next day. Seward signed the message with his own name, not the president's. The frigate, which had already set sail, was overtaken and the message handed to Porter, who refused to obey it because it bore the signature of the secretary of state and he was operating on orders signed by the president. The headstrong Meigs approved Porter's action. Whether Seward deliberately sabotaged the change in plans by signing his own name rather than the president's is not known for certain, but it seems probable. He was trying to thwart the Sumter expedition, which he opposed fiercely. Calling Seward "that timid traitor" who "paralyzes every movement from abject fear," Fox accused him of "treachery" by "interfering with the other dep[artment]s as the last hope of preventing the reinforcing of Sumpter."[86] Gideon Welles always believed that "to save himself," Seward "detached the Powhatan from the expedition and sent her to Pensacola."[87] Without the *Powhatan*, Fox would probably not be able to carry out his orders.

On April 6, another Seward-inspired act threatening the Sumter expedition tends to confirm their suspicion. That day Seward's friend, James E. Harvey, the influential Washington correspondent of the Philadelphia *North American*, telegraphed a leading lawyer in South Carolina, Harvey's native state: "Positively determined not to withdraw Anderson. Supplies go immediately, supported by a naval force under Stringham if their landing be resisted. A Friend."[88] This dispatch reached the Palmetto State before the messenger sent by the president did. It may have induced the Confederates to attack Sumter while Fox's task force was still steaming toward Charleston. Seward was aware of this telegram and doubtless provided Harvey with the sensitive information. Soon thereafter, Seward had Harvey appointed minister to Portugal. Later, when the senate wanted to investigate Harvey's questionable conduct, the secretary of state blocked their plans. Seward brushed off the incident, saying that Harvey merely "thought he was in honor bound" to do what he did and that he should not be punished "for a piece of folly that did no harm & intended no disloyalty."[89]

Seward's conduct in this matter was sharply criticized by Charles Francis Adams, Jr., who found it hard to believe that "a man of Seward's experience, quickness of perception, and aptitude in the use of agents, did not know what he was about when he gave that information to Harvey. He was not a fool. . . . It was not, on his part, 'amazing carelessness.' It was a designed plan." Harvey's act was "a crime," for he was "just as much a spy within our lines as André was within the lines of Washington." The secretary of state "was using a spy within our lines to convey information to the enemy, in order to effect his own ulterior purposes,—to carry out at a critical moment a plan which had a distinct shape in his mind."[90] According to John Hay, the government had, in addition to the telegrams Harvey sent to South Carolina, "oral and written evidence of Harvey's complicity with the traitors. His most earnest defenders cannot rid him of the responsibility of so telegraphing the rebels that detection was for a time impossible. If his object was peace, he would have honorably used his own name."[91]

Lincoln apologized profusely to Welles, saying that "it was carelessness, heedlessness on his part—he ought to have been more careful and attentive," and that "we were all new in the administration; that he permitted himself, with the best intentions, to be drawn into an impropriety without sufficient examination and reflection." He assured the navy secretary that "he was confident no similar error would again occur." This willingness to "take upon himself the whole blame" was characteristic of Lincoln. As Welles put it, the president "never shunned any responsibility and often declared that he, and not his Cabinet, was in fault for errors imputed to them, when I sometimes thought otherwise."[92] Magnanimity was one of Lincoln's most extraordinary qualities, one that would serve him well over the coming years.

Welles also demonstrated magnanimity, for much as he resented Porter's conduct in the *Powhatan* fiasco, he, with Lincoln's approval, rapidly promoted the young officer in recognition of his obvious ability and talent. Porter, perhaps recalling those April days in 1861, wrote many years later that Lincoln "was not a demonstrative man, so no one will ever know, amid all the trials he underwent, how much he had to contend with and how often he was called upon to sacrifice his own opinions to those of others, who, he felt, did not know as much about matters at issue as he did himself. When he did surrender, it was always with a pleasant manner, winding up with a characteristic story."[93]

Seward's Offer to Take over the Administration

Meanwhile, Seward overplayed his hand once again. He had failed to learn from his earlier threatened withdrawal from the cabinet that Lincoln could not be intimidated. On April 1, he went even further, virtually offering to take over the administration. In a memorandum entitled "Some Thoughts for the President's Consideration," the frantic secretary of state rashly told Lincoln that the government, now four weeks old, had no foreign or domestic policy. The latter should be to "change the question before the public, from one upon Slavery, or about Slavery, for a question upon *Union* or *Disunion*." This could be achieved by shifting the country's focus from Sumter (which the public associated with the issue of slavery) to Pickens (associated in the public mind with the issue of union). Therefore, Sumter should be abandoned and Pickens reinforced. This rehash of his earlier policy recommendations probably did not surprise Lincoln.

The president was doubtless amazed, however, by Seward's foreign policy counsel. Alluding to recent events on the Caribbean island of Hispaniola, where Spain and France appeared to be maneuvering to reestablish colonial rule, the secretary urged Lincoln to "demand explanations" from those two European powers, "categorically at once." If they provided unsatisfactory answers, the president should "convene Congress, and declare war against them." On top of that eccentric suggestion, Seward hinted broadly that he would be glad to run the country: "whatever policy we adopt, there must be an energetic prosecution of it. . . . Either the President must do it himself, and be all the while active in it, or devolve it on some member of his Cabinet.

Once adopted, debates on it must end, and all agree, and abide." In case Lincoln did not catch his drift, Seward added: "It is not my special province; but I neither seek to evade, nor assume responsibility."[94]

Some commentators have argued that Seward did not mean what he said about declaring war in his memorandum. There is much evidence, however, suggesting that he was in earnest, especially about fighting Spain, which was a much weaker foe than either Britain or France. The idea of war with a European power was clearly in the air; Stephen A. Douglas was advised that "the only way under which we could or can possibly hope to save our union from destruction is to bring about a war with some foreign foe."[95]

The proposal to pick a fight was not a spur-of-the-moment impulse of Seward's; as early as December, he had told a meeting of New Englanders that if the country were invaded by France, England, or Austria, "all the hills of South Carolina would pour forth their population for the rescue of New York." The following month he made a similar statement to the German diplomat Rudolph Schleiden: "If the Lord would only give the United States an excuse for a war with England, France, or Spain, that would be the best means of reestablishing internal peace."[96] On another occasion he told Schleiden that "nothing would give so much pleasure as to see a European Power interfere in favour of South Carolina," for then he "should 'pitch into' the European Power, and South Carolina and the seceding States would soon join him in doing so."[97] At a dinner party on March 20, he had engaged in some saber-rattling at ministers from Great Britain, France, and Russia, demanding that they supply copies of instructions to their consuls in Southern ports. Lord Lyons, the British envoy, reported that Seward "went off into a defiance of Foreign Nations, in a style of braggadocio which was formerly not uncommon with him, but which I had not heard before from him since he had been in office. Finding he was getting more and more violent and noisy, and saying things which it would be more convenient for me not to have heard, I took a natural opportunity of turning, as host, to speak to some of the ladies in the room."[98] In January, Lyons reported that the New Yorker viewed British-American relations as "good material to make political capital of" and speculated that the incoming administration would be tempted "to endeavour to divert the public excitement to a foreign quarrel."[99] In later months, Seward's diplomacy was so bellicose that European leaders came to regard him as a dangerous arriviste. The Russian minister thought Seward so haughty and vain "that he would not listen to any advice," and Lyons said the secretary "has such unbounded confidence in his own sagacity and dexterity that nothing which can be said to him makes much impression."[100] According to Charles Sumner, Lyons and his French counterpart, Henri Mercier, "had both been so repelled by Seward's lofty tone with them, that they went to him as little as possible."[101]

In an attempt to calm Seward down, Lincoln responded gently but firmly to the secretary's bizarre April 1 memorandum, writing out a reply which he may have delivered orally. He assured Seward that the administration did indeed have a domestic policy, which he had spelled out in the inaugural: "to hold, occupy and possess the forts, and all other property and places belonging to the government, and to collect the duties on imports." Seward had approved that policy, and the two leaders were still in agreement except with regard to Fort Sumter. Lincoln denied that the relief of Pickens would be viewed as a pro-Union gesture while the relief of Sumter would be seen as a pro-abolitionist act; they both were attempts to uphold the government's integrity. The proposal to declare war on European powers he dismissed, saying that the "news received yesterday in regard to St. Domingo certainly brings in a new item within range of our foreign policy; but up to that time we have been preparing circulars and instructions to ministers and the like, all in perfect harmony, without a suggestion that we had no foreign policy." The president regarded Spain's actions in Santo Domingo as trivial. Seward's bid to assume responsibility for making and implementing policy Lincoln handled tactfully: "if this must be done, I must do it. When a general line of policy is adopted, I apprehend there is no danger of its being changed without good reason, or continuing to be a subject of unnecessary debate; still upon points arising in its progress, I wish, and I suppose I am entitled to have, the advice of all the Cabinet."[102]

Many would have reacted to Seward's haughty memo indignantly rather than magnanimously. Later in April, the president again demonstrated his forbearance toward Seward when informed by David Dudley Field that the secretary and his friends had not only opposed his nomination but also his election "until they found that he could be elected without them." Lincoln "replied that he knew that, but had forgiven them."[103]

Seward had originally planned to have his memorandum and Lincoln's response published in the New York *Times*. When the president rejected his proposal, the secretary of state inspired attacks on Lincoln in friendly journals. On April 3, the *Times* ran a blistering editorial, "Wanted—A Policy," containing the arguments in Seward's April 1 memo. Weed's Albany *Evening Journal* carried a similar piece.

Lincoln acknowledged his reliance on Seward's judgment about international affairs, though not in this instance. Soon after arriving in Washington, he had told Seward that "there is one part of my work that I shall have to leave largely to you. I shall have to depend upon you for taking care of these matters of foreign affairs, of which I know so little, and with which I reckon you are familiar."[104] When a caller offered advice on dealing with Great Britain, the president replied that "it does not so much signify what I think, you must persuade Seward to think as you do."[105] In June, Lincoln told Carl Schurz "that he deplored having given so little attention to foreign affairs and being so dependent upon other people's judgment, and that he felt the necessity of 'studying up' on the subject as much [as] his opportunities permitted him."[106] To the minister representing Bremen, Lincoln confessed: "I don't know anything about diplomacy. I will be very apt to make blunders."[107]

Ironically, in April it was Lincoln who had to keep the bellicose Seward from making a diplomatic blunder. It would not be the only time he would do so.

Lincoln's Offer to Swap Fort Sumter for Virginia

While the Sumter expedition was being mounted in early April, Seward continued trying to control events. There was still time, for the point of no return had not yet been reached. Neither the governor of South Carolina nor Major Anderson had been notified, and Fox's ships had not yet departed for Charleston. Perhaps something at the last minute might prevent the outbreak of war. To that end, Seward urged the president to summon the leader of Virginia's Unionists, George W. Summers, who was spearheading the fight against secession at the Richmond convention. On April 1, the secretary telegraphed Summers stating that Lincoln "desires your attendance at Washington as soon as convenient." Summers, sensing a plot to lure him away from the Old Dominion's capital on the eve of a crucial vote, was skeptical.[108] On April 3, a messenger arrived from Washington with instructions from Lincoln to tell Summers: "I want to see him at once, for there is no time to be lost; what is to be done must be done quickly. . . . If Mr. Summers cannot come himself, let him send some friend of his, some Union man in the convention in whom he has confidence and who can confer freely with me."[109] A caucus of Unionist leaders in Richmond decided that John B. Baldwin, one of the state's most devoted Union men, should meet with Lincoln in place of Summers. Baldwin left immediately for Washington.

Lincoln had established indirect contact with Baldwin through a mutual friend, Herring Chrisman, a Virginia-born attorney living in Abingdon, Illinois. In February, after Baldwin had been elected to the Virginia convention as one of its youngest delegates, he wrote to Chrisman "stating that the danger was great, and refusing to be responsible for the result in convention at all without an implicit declaration from Mr. Lincoln of a policy on which he could safely intrench giving him a *cart blanche*, without so much as a hint of what it should be." Chrisman showed this missive to Lincoln, who, after reading it, said: "Tell them I will execute the fugitive slave law better than it has ever been. I can do that. Tell them I will protect slavery in the States where it exists. I can do that. Tell them they shall have all the offices south of Mason & Dixon's line if they will take them. I will send nobody down there as long as they will execute the offices themselves."[110]

On April 4, as the Virginia convention was voting 89–45 against secession, Baldwin reported to Seward, who escorted him to the White House. There a much-disputed conversation took place, described in two contradictory accounts, one by Baldwin and the other by a friend of his, John Minor Botts, who spoke with Lincoln the following day. In 1866, Botts said the president had informed him that he had told Baldwin he would withdraw the Sumter garrison if Virginia would disband its convention. Botts recalled Lincoln saying: "I have always been an Old-line Henry-Clay Whig, and if you Southern people will let me alone, I will administer this government as nearly upon the principles that he would have administered it as it is possible for one man to follow in the path of another." Rhetorically he asked: "What do I want with war? I am no war man; I want peace more than any man in this country, and will make greater sacrifices to preserve it than any other man in the nation."[111] Earlier he had told a visitor from the Deep South, "There will be no blood shed during my Administration if I can prevent it."[112] But Baldwin testified that Lincoln showed little enthusiasm for compromise and made no offer to evacuate Sumter.

Lincoln may have deliberately misled Botts in describing his offer to Baldwin, but that seems out of character. Perhaps the president had intended to make the offer to

Baldwin but did not do so for some reason. Or Baldwin may have viewed Lincoln's offer as unimportant because it contained no assurance that his administration would not take action against the Lower South. Then again, Baldwin may have told less than the full truth in his postwar accounts of Lincoln's remarks. As a devoted Southern patriot who served in both the Confederate army and Congress, he could well have desired to make the president look belligerent instead of conciliatory and thus indirectly blame him for the outbreak of war. Or Baldwin may have believed that it was impossible to have the Virginia convention adjourn *sine die* at that point. It is impossible to say. The only thing resembling a contemporary report of Baldwin's account of his interview with Lincoln was written by the chairman of the convention's committee on federal relations, Robert Young Conrad. On April 6 he told his wife: "We hear directly from several gentlemen who have within one day or two called on Mr. Lincoln that he really does not know his own mind, is wavering in fact or (what is more likely) is unwilling to admit his weakness, for fear of being deserted by his party."[113]

Much evidence supports the conclusion that Lincoln did offer to remove the Sumter garrison if the Virginia convention would adjourn *sine die*. He said that he had *twice* proposed to abandon Sumter if Virginia would remain in the Union. In October 1861, while reminiscing about the secession crisis, the president mentioned the February meeting with William C. Rives during which he declared his willingness to swap Sumter for the Old Dominion. Then, said Lincoln, "he renewed the proposition to Summers but without any result." (In April, of course, he spoke not to Summers but to Baldwin, who was sent in Summers' place.) According to John Hay's diary account of this conversation, the "President was most anxious to prevent bloodshed."[114] On January 9, 1863, George Plumer Smith of Philadelphia wrote to Hay saying:

> A few days after the Convention at Richmond passed the ordinance of secession [on April 17], I accompanied a delegation from Western Virginia to Washington, to procure Arms for their defence at home.
>
> The President received us with much interest and kindness.
>
> During the interview, on my mentioning to him the fact that one of the Committee, Mr. [Campbell] Tarr, of Wellsburg—had been a member of the convention, Mr Lincoln spoke very freely of the attempts he had made to hold Virginia firm for the Union—and then, greatly to Mr Tarr's surprise mentioned, that amongst other influences, he had sent for Mr Baldwin, of Augusta Co. a member of the Convention, and had him in the White House with him alone—and told him, if they would pass resolutions of adherence to the Union, then adjourn and go home—he, the President, would take the responsibility, at the earliest proper time—to withdraw the troops from Fort Sumpter—and do all within the line of his duty to ward off collision.
>
> He then imposed strict silence upon us in regard to what he then had told us.
>
> Will you please now ask him whether what I state is correct, and whether he now cares about its becoming known.[115]

Hay replied: "I received your favor of yesterday this morning and at once laid the matter before the President. He directs me to state in reply that your statement is substantially correct, but that, for the present, he prefers that you would still withhold it from the public."[116]

Later, Smith gave a fuller version of this interview, which took place on May 1. Lincoln, according to Smith, said: "As soon as I began to get the hang of things here, I felt that, if I could hold on to old Virginia and through her, the Border States, we might yet escape . . . civil war—and, therefore, without consulting anyone but Mr Seward, had him write to Judge Summers to come here on important business, of which he, Mr Seward, would inform him on his arrival—but it must be kept a secret from the public. Knowing something of Judge Summers' timid character, we had requested that, if he could not come—he, or other Union men in the convention would choose a thorough Union man in his place, and they chose John B. Baldwin." Seward "met Baldwin at the Boat, took him to his own house—and later in the evening brought him over here." The two men spoke at length, with Lincoln urging his guest to do everything possible to save the Union. But, said the president, "I found him 'very fishy' on the matter." So Lincoln then proposed to remove the troops from Sumter if the Virginia convention adjourned *sine die*.[117]

Fellow members of the western Virginia delegation confirmed Smith and Tarr's recollections. In addition, Lincoln told several others, including Francis Pierpont, about his offer to Baldwin. According to Pierpont, Baldwin asked that both Forts Sumter and Pickens be abandoned. As the president had done with William C. Rives, he recounted Aesop's fable about the lion and the maiden. "It is enough to give up my teeth," Lincoln insisted, "but the claws I must reserve for my own use."[118] It is possible but unlikely that Lincoln deliberately misled these men or that he misremembered what had happened. In late April, Kentucky Senator Garrett Davis called on the president, who quite plainly told him that when Baldwin "came here from the Virginia convention he had made the proposition to Mr. Baldwin and his colleagues distinctly that if the Virginia convention would adjourn without doing anything he would withdraw the troops from Fort Sumter." Davis also told John B. Baldwin that Lincoln had informed him that Baldwin had received such an offer. Baldwin commented that "the high character of Mr. Davis satisfies me that what he says must be true & I am therefore brought to the conclusion that Mr. Lincoln has made such a statement."[119]

The day after Lincoln met with Baldwin, it was reported that the president told callers "he exhibited to the South, in his course, a peaceful disposition in every way." But there "was no disposition in the South evinced to do other than take advantage of his forbearance."[120] He believed that his administration's "good intentions have been misinterpreted, and the country, in the eyes of the world, is fast acquiring a reputation that it does not deserve."[121]

Three years later Gustavus Fox recalled that Lincoln had sent for a Unionist member of the Virginia convention "and assured him that if that convention would adjourn, instead of staying in session menacing the Gov't. that he would immediately direct Major Anderson to evacuate Fort Sumter." When that offer proved unavailing, the president on April 4 "sent for me and told me that the expedition [to relieve Sumter] might go forward."[122] That same day, Lincoln notified Anderson that a relief expedition was under way, but he did not inform Governor Pickens of this step, for that would represent the point of no return, and the president still wished to keep his options open as he awaited word from Florida. Two days later, he learned to his consternation that Scott's order of March 12—to have the troops aboard the *Brooklyn* transferred to Fort Pickens—had been refused by Navy Captain Henry A. Adams, in command of the Union squadron off Pensacola. Adams, who had three sons serving in the Confederate military, told Secretary Welles that he was unwilling to obey orders from an army officer—especially orders that would violate the truce which had been in effect since January—and requested further instructions.[123] (This was peculiar, for the Confederates had already broken the truce in early March by augmenting their forces at Pensacola.) Welles, in consultation with Lincoln, immediately dispatched Navy Lieutenant John L. Worden to Pensacola with orders directing Adams to carry out Scott's March 12 directive. Worden delivered the message on April 12, and the troops accordingly occupied Fort Pickens. There was insufficient time for the administration to learn this good news and call off Fox's mission. (On April 17, Porter's ships arrived at Pensacola and significantly reinforced Pickens, which remained in Union hands throughout the war.)

Lincoln must have felt exasperated beyond endurance. A month earlier, Major Anderson's message about his dwindling supplies had ruined Lincoln's original plan for dealing with secession. Now Captain Adams's refusal to obey orders wrecked his strategy for solving the Sumter dilemma. The president had hoped to follow the policy described in a New York *Tribune* editorial: "let them [the secessionists of the Deep South] severely alone—allow them to wear out the military ardor of their adherents in fruitless drillings and marches, and to exhaust the patience of their fellow-citizens by the amount and frequency of their pecuniary exactions—and the fabric of their power will melt away like fog in the beams of a morning sun. Only give them enough rope, and they will speedily fulfill their destiny—the People, even of South Carolina, rejecting their sway as intolerable, and returning to the mild and paternal guardianship of the Union."[124] Lincoln's faith in Southern Unionism remained strong. Ten weeks later he would tell Congress that it "may well be questioned whether there is, to-day, a majority of the legally qualified voters of any State, except perhaps South Carolina, in favor of disunion. There is much reason to believe that the Union men are the majority in many, if not in every other one, of the so-called seceded States. The contrary has not been demonstrated in any one of them. It is ventured to affirm this, even of Virginia and Tennessee."[125]

The Point of No Return

At 6 P.M. on April 6, hours after learning of Captain Adams's refusal to allow the reinforcement of Fort Pickens, Lincoln reluctantly sent the South Carolina governor word of Fox's expedition, stating that "an attempt will be made to supply Fort-Sumter with provisions only, and that, if such attempt be not resisted, no effort to throw in men, arms, or ammunition will be made, without further notice, or in case of an attack upon the Fort."[126] The last phrase meant that if the Confederates fired on Sumter, then an attempt would be made to reinforce it with men, arms, and supplies.

The next day elements of Fox's squadron left New York for Charleston. The die was finally cast, though as late as April 8 Fox still thought that the expedition might be called off.

When Lincoln issued the order to Fox and sent the fateful message to Governor Pickens, he did so after consulting only with Welles, Fox, and Montgomery Blair. (In 1862, Lincoln said "that when he determined to give the rebels at Charleston notice of his purpose, the entire cabinet was against him.")[127] Upon learning of this action later that evening, Seward expressed astonishment. "I want no more at this time of the Administration," he told George Harrington of the Treasury Department. "We are not yet in a position to go to war. While we have been quietly engaged in recalling as far and as fast as possible our scattered naval and military forces, the Rebels have been engaged in their preparation for an attack on Fort Sumpter, and the circumstances are such that any attempt on our part to bring on a conflict in Charleston Harbor . . . would meet with defeat and promptly arrest every effort of the loyal men" in the Upper South and Border States.[128]

Meanwhile, the Confederate commissioners were growing ever more alarmed as they read accounts of the fleet being outfitted in New York. On April 7, when Campbell relayed their concern to Seward, the secretary blandly reassured them: "Faith as to Sumter fully kept; wait and see." The commissioners inferred that the task force was bound for Pickens, since Seward pointedly made no mention of that fort. After the secretary of state formally turned down their renewed demand for recognition, they sent him a blistering letter and departed Washington.[129] Campbell also wrote Seward, declaring that the Confederate authorities felt themselves the victims of "systematic duplicity."[130] Since the secretary had repeatedly assured him that Sumter would be abandoned, his reaction was understandable.

Lincoln could not be sure that his decision would precipitate a war, though he had good reason to believe that it might. On January 9 the South Carolinians had fired on the *Star of the West* when it tried to relieve the fort, and on April 3 a small schooner flying the stars and stripes had been shelled as it attempted to enter Charleston harbor. But there was a remote chance that the Confederates would hesitate to fire on a ship conveying food to hungry men. Such restraint seemed unlikely, however, for if Confederate authorities allowed the fort to be supplied, they would be humiliated and Unionism in the Upper South and Border States would be bolstered. By announcing that he was sending food rather than troops, Lincoln had put his opponents on the horns of a dilemma; both options were unpalatable. As the Union fleet sailed south, a journalist reported it was "conceded on all sides that it was a most happy stroke of policy on the part of the Government to make first an attempt to relieve Major Anderson with provisions simply, as the refusal of the revolutionists to allow what must appear as a simple act of humanity, will not only fasten odium upon them in the eyes of the entire civilized world, but also greatly add to the moral strength of the true Government in the North, and to the Union sentiment in the Border Slave States."[131] In the apt words of Lincoln's private secretaries, when he "finally gave the order that the fleet should sail he was master of the situation; master of his Cabinet; master of the moral attitude and issues of the struggle; master of the public opinion which must arise out of the impending conflict; master if the rebels hesitated or repented, because they would thereby forfeit their prestige with the South; master if they persisted, for he would then command a united North."[132]

A Democratic newspaper in Ohio argued that by sending the fleet to Charleston, Lincoln was "shrewdly inviting the secessionists to open the ball," and a prominent New York Democrat, John L. O'Sullivan, saw "the cunning hand of the third rate village lawyer" at work. The president, Sullivan charged, had adroitly inveigled the South into firing the first shot in order to unite his party and to restore his sinking popularity.[133] Actually, Lincoln hoped to avoid, not provoke, bloodshed. If the Fort Pickens strategy had worked, he might have been able to do so; but it failed. By April 6, when the president sent his fateful message to the governor of South Carolina, he had exhausted every peaceful option short of acknowledging the legitimacy of secession or surrendering the basic principles of the Republican Party. He probably believed that war might well come as a result of the attempt to provision Fort Sumter, though he did not want war. From Hurlbut he learned that relief ships would be stopped, but that did not necessarily mean that Sumter would be shelled. And it was possible that the fort would not come under attack just because relief ships were heading its way. After all, the South Carolinians had not fired on Sumter when the *Star of the West* approached it. But if war were to come, Lincoln understandably wanted the blame for starting it to fall on the Confederates. As he announced to secessionists in his inaugural address, "In *your* hands, my dissatisfied fellow countrymen, and not in *mine,* is the momentous issue of civil war. The government will not assail *you,* unless you *first* assail *it.* You can have no conflict, without being yourselves the aggressors." It was widely believed in the North that "if the Southern Confederacy initiates a war for the simple reason that this government has seen fit to reinforce one of its garrisons, the entire responsibility of the conflict will rest with it."[134]

Lincoln may have shared Gustavus Fox's view that relieving Sumter was "the most important *peace* measure," for the fort's "weakness provokes an attack" and "more men & provisions &c. would prevent it & *perhaps* prevent entirely a civil war."[135] Even if war broke out, it might be brief and relatively bloodless.

As Porter and Fox began steaming southward on April 8, many Northerners took heart. A Connecticut Republican reported that "we all feel that Mr Lincoln has something of the Old Hickory about him. I hear on every hand. . . . 'Give the South (the rebels) a *good thrashing.*'"[136] A member of the Seventh New York National Guard urged the president to "[g]ive those South Carolina ruffians h–l and we will support you."[137] On April 11, when Lincoln asked John Minor Botts what remedy might cure secessionism, the Virginian replied: "Grape for the ranks and hemp for the leaders."[138]

Girding for War

If war did result from Lincoln's decision, he was assured of military assistance by Indiana Governor Oliver P. Morton, who proffered 6,000 militia to enforce the laws; by an agent of John A. Andrew, governor of Massachusetts, who pledged that 2,000 "picked troops ready for service" would be dispatched as soon as they were needed; by the governor of Rhode Island, who offered to defend Washington with "a Battery of light Artillery, 6 pr. Horses & men complete, and a force of 1000 men completely disciplined & equipped"; by a Kansan who proposed to raise 1,000 men to combat the secessionists; and by a patriotic New Yorker who wrote the president saying: "In the present crisis, and distracted state of the country, if your Honor wishes colored volunteers, you have only to signify by answering the above note at 70 E. 13 St. N.Y.C., with instructions, and the above will meet with prompt attention, whenever your honor wishes them."[139] General Scott recommended that ten companies of militia be recruited to protect the capital, and on April 11, the District of Columbia Militia was mustered into federal service.[140]

On the fateful sixth day of April, Lincoln met with the governors of Indiana, Maine, Illinois, Wisconsin, Michigan, and Ohio, who had been summoned to the capital by Horace Greeley to urge a hard line against secessionists. In addition, the president had invited Pennsylvania Governor Andrew G. Curtin to Washington, warning that the District seemed to be in danger of attack. To help gird for such a possibility, Lincoln wanted troops from the Keystone State available. He urged Curtin to persuade his legislature to reorganize the state's militia. The governor agreed to do so and promptly began drafting a message to the lawmakers in Harrisburg. On April 8, the president wrote him: "I think the necessity of being *ready* increases. Look to it."[141] Three days later, the legislators appropriated $500,000 for arming the militia. Lincoln asked several other governors to call up their militias and be prepared to defend the capital on a moment's notice. He predicted "that when the ball opened," Washington "will be the first [city] that will be attacked." He had been advised that he would have to take refuge elsewhere but insisted that he would remain in Washington "even if he had to be protected and surrounded by the military arm of the government."[142]

In the midst of all the excitement and anxiety, office seekers continued to pester Lincoln, who jocularly remarked on the morning of April 10 "that he would henceforth require all applicants to demonstrate their patriotism by serving three months at Forts Sumter and Pickens."[143] More soberly, he told a caller in the evening that soon it would become clear "whether the revolutionists dare to fire upon an unarmed vessel sent to the rescue of our starving soldiers." With a calm demeanor that contrasted sharply with the agitation around him, he "spoke very composedly" and seemed ready to abide by the consequences of his decision to provision Fort Sumter.[144] "I hope it may do some good," he told a congressman.[145]

The Confederate Decision to Inaugurate War

On April 10, Jefferson Davis and his cabinet had instructed the general in charge at Charleston, P. G. T. Beauregard, to insist upon the immediate surrender of Sumter; if Anderson declined, Beauregard was to reduce the fort. In authorizing the first shot, Davis rather than Lincoln seems to have been motivated by short-term political considerations. He desperately wanted the Upper South and Border States to join the Confederacy, and he could reasonably assume that once hostilities began, the eight Slave States that were not yet part of his government would join with the Deep South.

Other secessionists believed that to be the case. Former Congressman J. L. Pugh of Alabama explained in January, "I am oppressed by the apprehension that we are in great danger from the reconstructionists" (i.e., those who supported reunification of the country). Should the Republicans back the Crittenden Compromise, "the border states will present an unbroken front & my fear is we shall be overwhelmed." That threat would disappear once fighting broke out. "Now pardon me for suggesting that South Carolina has the power of putting us beyond the reach of reconstruction by taking Fort Sumter at any cost."[146] To a Charleston crowd, Virginia fire-eater Roger Pryor declared on April 10: "I assure you that just so certain as to-morrow's sun will rise upon us, just so certain will Virginia be a member of the Southern Confederation. We will put her in *if you but strike a blow*."[147] As the fleet sailed toward Charleston, the Indianapolis *Journal* editorialized that "the seceding States are determined to have war; because they believe a war will drive to their support the border slave States, and unite them all in a great Southern Confederacy. A policy of peace is to them a policy of destruction. It encourages the growth of a reactionary feeling. It takes out of the way all the pride and resentment which could keep the people from feeling the weight of taxation, and the distress of their isolated condition. It forces them to reason, and to look at the consequences of their conduct. A war buries all these considerations in the fury and glory of battle, and the parade and pomp of arms."[148] A Memphis newspaper anticipated that Davis might launch an attack "for the mere purpose of solidifying the revolution which has been precipitated" by "dragging into it the 'Border States.'"[149] Similarly, a correspondent for the New York *Times* speculated that "the necessity of excitement to sustain the secession movement may compel Mr. Davis either to assent to an open demonstration against the United States, or permit it to take place without opposition on his part."[150]

Six weeks after the fall of Sumter, Joseph Holt of Kentucky wrote that the Confederate leadership "sought the clash of arms and the effusion of blood as an instrumentality for impressing the Border States."[151] William Howard Russell of the London *Times* offered a similar analysis of the Confederate leaders: "When they thought that the time was ripe for exciting the border States and dragging them into it, they fired upon Fort Sumter."[152] Upon hearing of the bombardment, a leading Unionist member of the Virginia secession convention wondered if the South Carolinians "have really begun the war without necessity, in order to compel us to take part."[153]

While Davis wanted to maneuver the North into firing the first shot at Sumter, he was nonetheless willing to start the war at Fort Pickens. On February 3, he authorized the Confederate commander at Pensacola, his old friend Braxton Bragg, to bombard it, provided that he could capture it quickly. Ideally, Davis wrote, it would be advantageous to have the North fire the first shot, "but when we are ready to relieve our territory and jurisdiction of the presence of a foreign garrison that advantage is overbalanced by other considerations."[154] Davis did not identify those "other considerations," but one was doubtless the likelihood that Slave States north of the Confederacy would join it. (The war would probably have started at Fort Pickens if Bragg had felt more confident of his ability to carry it.)

The need to stoke secessionist fires was real. In Alabama, the editor of the Mobile *Mercury* warned that the Confederacy "is sinking into a fatal apathy, and the spirit and even the patriotism of the people is oozing out under this do-nothing policy. If something is not done pretty soon, decisive, either evacuation or expulsion [of the Sumter garrison], the whole country [i.e., the Confederacy] will become so disgusted with the sham of southern independence that the first chance the people get at a popular election they will turn the whole movement topsy-turvy so bad that it never on earth can be righted again."[155] Another Alabamian, James G. Gilchrist, exclaimed to the Confederate secretary of war in mid-March: "Sir, unless you sprinkle blood in the face of the people of Alabama they will be back in the old Union in less than ten days!"[156]

On April 10, ex-Senator Louis Wigfall of Texas telegraphed Davis from Charleston urging that the Confederates "take Fort Sumter before we have to fight the fleet and the Fort. General Beauregard will not act without your order. Let me suggest to you to send the order to him to begin the attack as soon as he is ready. Virginia is excited by the preparations, and a bold stroke on our side will complete her purposes. Policy and prudence are urgent upon us to begin at once."[157]

Dissenting was Secretary of State Robert Toombs, who warned Davis against an attack on Sumter. He maintained that "at this time, it is suicide, murder, and will lose us every friend at the North. You will wantonly strike a hornet's nest which extends from mountains to ocean, and legions, now quiet, will swarm out and sting us to death. It is unnecessary; it puts us in the wrong; it is fatal." Firing on that fort, he said, "will inaugurate a civil war greater than any the world has yet seen."[158] (Confederate commissioners in Washington had warned Toombs that an attack on Sumter would make the South appear "guilty of the unnecessary shedding of blood, & it would tend to concentrate public opinion at the North in favor of their government.")[159] In early April, Davis received similar counsel from Richard Lathers, a South Carolinian then living in New York, who predicted that "Civil war for the destruction of the Union, will unite every man at the North, irrespective of party or affiliation, in support of his government and the flag of his country. If conciliation now fails to protect the Union, the coldest man of the North will lay aside enterprises and profitable industry, and will fill the armies in defense of the supremacy of the government and its laws."[160] Simon Bolivar Buckner of Kentucky made a similar prophecy to the governor of his state: "If the south should aggress it will unite public sentiment at the north against them and civil war will ensue."[161]

Ignoring such advice, Davis made his fateful decision of April 10, even though there was no practical military reason for shelling Sumter. As he himself had pointed out in January, the "little garrison in its present position presses on nothing but a point of pride."[162] The attack on Sumter proved to be a major blunder, for it outraged and unified the North while dampening pro-Confederate sympathy in the Border States. If those states (Maryland, Kentucky, Missouri, and Delaware) had made common cause with their Southern sisters, Davis's government might well have won the war. It is impossible to know exactly why the Confederate president made such a costly mistake. Because of Seward's "systematic duplicity" in dealing with the Confederate commissioners, and because of the numerous press reports indicating that

Sumter would be evacuated, Davis mistrusted the Lincoln administration and its declarations of peaceful intent. News that Northern warships were fitting out for unknown destinations probably intensified his suspicion. Davis may also have been motivated by pique and wounded pride; hypersensitive about his honor, he probably felt offended by Lincoln's failure to recognize his government. Instead of notifying the Confederate authorities (i.e., Davis) of his intention to resupply Sumter, Lincoln had alerted the governor of South Carolina.

More significant, perhaps, was Davis's evident misreading of public opinion in the Border States and the North. Lincoln has been criticized for underestimating the strength of Southern disunionism, but insofar as the Civil War resulted from a misunderstanding of popular sentiment, Davis was at least as culpable. If the Confederate leader had been more sensitive to the political climate in the Border States, he could have allowed Fort Sumter to be resupplied and waited for an occasion when slavery rather than Union was perceived to be the central issue dividing the sections.

On April 12, at 4:30 A.M., the attack began. After valiantly resisting for a day and a half, the Sumter garrison surrendered. Remarkably, though thousands of rounds were fired, no one was killed during the bombardment, which touched off the bloodiest war in American history.

Gustavus Fox's squadron, shorn of the *Powhatan*, arrived at Charleston too late to affect the outcome. As Fox transported the Sumter garrison to New York, he told Anderson "how anxious the Pres[t] was that they (S[outh] C[arolina]) should stand before the civilized world as having fired upon bread."[163] Alluding to this important point, Lincoln wrote Fox on May 1: "You and I both anticipated that the cause of the country would be advanced by making the attempt to provision Fort-Sumpter, even if it should fail; and it is no small consolation now to feel that our anticipation is justified by the result."[164] In a draft of his July 4 message to Congress, Lincoln summarized the reasoning behind his decision: "I believed . . . that to [withdraw the Sumter garrison] . . . would be utterly ruinous—that the *necessity* under which it was to be done, would not be fully understood—that, by many, it would be construed as a part of a *voluntary* policy—that, at home, it would discourage the friends of the Union, embolden it's foes, and go far to insure to the latter a recognition of independence abroad—that, in fact, it would be our national destruction consummated."[165]

Lincoln had not permitted Seward to take the first trick, nor had he let the Confederates corner him. It was a masterful exercise of leadership. In June, Seward told his wife, "Executive skill and vigor are rare qualities. The President is the best of us." (But the secretary of state also thought Lincoln needed "constant and assiduous cooperation." Seward provided advice to Lincoln in frequent conferences and regular late afternoon carriage rides.)[166] Later that year, he declared to a close friend "that of all the men he knew, there was no one in the United States so well fitted to carry the country safely through the struggles as Mr. Lincoln."[167] The following year he called Lincoln "wise and practical," and in 1863 he told guests at a dinner party that the president was "the best and wisest man he has ever known" and repeatedly "compared Mr. Lincoln's task to our Saviour's and Mr. Lincoln to the Lord."[168] Months later, Seward called Lincoln's decision to relieve Sumter "the central and crowning act of the Administration," the one "which determined . . . that Republican institutions were worth fighting for." It meant "the preservation of the Union and in that, the saving of popular government for the World."[169]

In March 1865, Lincoln succinctly analyzed the outbreak of hostilities: "Both parties deprecated war; but one of them would *make* war rather than let the nation survive; and the other would *accept* war rather than let it perish. And the war came."[170] Lincoln may have been willing to accept war because he believed, as he told Orville H. Browning in February 1861, "far less evil & bloodshed would result from an effort to maintain the Union and the Constitution, than from disruption and the formation of two confederacies[.]"[171]

23

"I Intend to Give Blows"
The Hundred Days
(April–July 1861)

"I have desired as sincerely as any man—I sometimes think more than any other man—that our present difficulties might be settled without the shedding of blood," Lincoln told a group of ersatz soldiers in late April. The "last hope of peace may not have passed away. But if I have to choose between the maintenance of the union of these states, and of the liberties of this nation, on the one hand, and the shedding of fraternal blood on the other, you need not be at a loss which course I shall take."[1] Little did he and most of his contemporaries realize how much fraternal blood would flow in order to save that Union and preserve those liberties; 620,000 soldiers and sailors (360,000 Union, 260,000 Confederate), including some of Lincoln's closest friends, would die over the next four years, equaling the number of deaths in all other American wars combined, from the Revolution through the Korean War. One of those who failed to realize how bloody the war would become was Edwin M. Stanton, who on April 8 told a fellow veteran of service in Buchanan's cabinet: "I do not think peaceful relations will continue much longer. Nor indeed do I think hostilities will be so great an evil as many apprehend. A round or two often serves to restore harmony."[2]

In the fourteen weeks following the bombardment of Sumter, Lincoln acted firmly to meet the emergency. The challenge was daunting, for as he himself put it, the war "began on very unequal terms between the parties. The insurgents had been preparing for it more than thirty years, while the government had taken no steps to resist them. The former had carefully considered all the means which could be turned to their account. It undoubtedly was a well pondered reliance with them that in their own unrestricted effort to destroy Union, constitution, and law, all together, the government would, in great degree, be restrained by the same constitution and law, from arresting their progress. Their sympathizers pervaded all departments of the government, and nearly all communities of the people."[3]

In that hectic time, Lincoln followed the advice he had offered twelve years earlier when he suggested that the newly installed president, Zachary Taylor, should announce: "by the Eternal, I take the responsibility."[4] Lincoln took decisive hold of the government. In his first hundred days in office, he raised and supplied an army, sent it into battle, held the Border States in the Union, helped thwart Confederate attempts to win European diplomatic recognition, declared a blockade, asserted leadership over his cabinet, dealt effectively with Congress, averted a potential crisis with Great Britain, and eloquently articulated the nature and purpose of the war. While pursuing these objectives, he demonstrated that he had the same "indomitable will" that he ascribed to Henry Clay. But as he pointed out in his eulogy on the Great Compromiser, "this quality often secures to its owner nothing better than a character for useless obstinacy."[5] Lincoln, however, proved forceful without being obstinate or autocratic, and in so doing, infused his own iron will into the North as it struggled to preserve what he would call "the last, best hope of earth."[6]

Calling Up the Militia, Summoning Congress

On the evening of Friday, April 12, word of the attack on Fort Sumter reached Washington, where Lincoln calmly remarked that "he did not expect it so soon," for he had anticipated that the secessionists would wait until the arrival of Gustavus Fox's fleet.[7] When a congressional delegation asked his reaction to the news, he replied laconically: "I do not like it."[8] That day Lincoln met twice with the future commissioner of public buildings, Benjamin Brown French, who told his son that the president "is as firm as a rock, & means to show the world that there is a United States of America left yet."[9]

The following day, Lincoln remained outwardly unperturbed as he inquired about reports from South Carolina, commented on their probable accuracy, signed routine documents, and received callers. When suspicion was voiced that Anderson had behaved traitorously, Lincoln denied it, insisting that the major "acted in accordance with instructions" and that the "supply vessels could not reach him, and he did right." The president was glad that the bombardment had killed no one, though he was puzzled that the fleet, which arrived while the attack was in progress, had taken no part in the fighting.[10]

That Saturday, more visitors than usual came to the White House, including a delegation from the Virginia convention who wished to learn about the president's Southern policy. One of them recalled having "a long & earnest conversation with Mr. Lincoln, in which I showed him how war might, honorably, be avoided, by evacuating Fort Sumpter & withdrawing the mails, & closing the custom-houses, in South Carolina, taking care to blockade the ports. S. C. would thus have nobody to fight, & being deprived of her commerce, & mail facilities, would soon seek to return to the Union."[11] Lincoln replied that he might stop the mails in the seceded states, but he would not invade them in an attempt to collect import duties. He added that he reserved the right to send troops "to relieve a fort upon a border of the country."[12]

On Sunday, April 14, after receiving word of Sumter's surrender, the president met with General Scott, Pennsylvania Governor Andrew G. Curtin, and Alexander K. McClure, chairman of the military committee of the Pennsylvania State Senate. When Scott insisted that Washington could not be captured by the Confederate army, which was then in South Carolina, Lincoln observed: "It does seem to me, general, that if I were Beauregard I would take Washington."

"Mr. President," said Scott, "the capital can't be taken, sir; it can't be taken."[13]

When Lincoln asked how Pennsylvania would respond to a proclamation calling up the militia, Curtin pledged to send 100,000 men within a week. The president said: "Give me your hand, Andy. Thank God for that reply." The governor promptly sent a telegram to agents in the Keystone State, which on April 18 dispatched the first militiamen to arrive at the capital.[14]

Later that day, Zenos Robbins, the attorney who had helped Lincoln obtain a patent in 1849, informed him that "all your friends hope that there will be no more blank cartridges, but a square, direct, and powerful exhibition of the strength of the Government."

"Are those your opinions?" asked the president.

"Yes, sir!"

"Then I suppose that you will be interested in the newspapers to-morrow!" The press on Monday would carry a proclamation summoning state militias to put down the rebellion.[15]

Drafting that proclamation consumed much of Lincoln's time on Sunday. As he and the cabinet worked on it, they faced a dilemma: prompt action must be taken, but could the army and navy be expanded, unappropriated money be spent, Southern ports be blockaded, and the writ of habeas corpus be suspended, all without congressional approval? Would it be wise to call Congress into session immediately? Would Washington, nestled between Virginia and Maryland—two Slave States that might well secede—be a safe place for senators and representatives to gather? In late March, one observer in the District of Columbia predicted "that the chances are that Virginia will go out *and take the capital with her;—that as matters stand the chances are that the next Congress of the U. S. will not meet in Washington.*"[16]

Lincoln had been resisting appeals by businessmen and New York newspapers to call a special session of Congress. They argued that legislation was needed authorizing the collection of revenues offshore and that the Morrill Tariff Act must be modified to help replenish depleted federal coffers. Lincoln hesitated in part because elections for U.S. Representatives had not taken place in several states, including Kentucky, Tennessee, and North Carolina, all of which were scheduled to choose congressmen in August; Virginia was to do so in May. (In that era, not all states held congressional elections in November of even-numbered years.) Some argued that a special session could not be held before those August elections. Eighty-one members of the House had yet to be chosen, including twenty-six from seceded states and forty-one from the Upper South and Border States (Virginia, Tennessee, Kentucky, and North Carolina.)

The president also feared that a reconvened Congress might again try to pass compromise measures permitting slavery to expand. In late March, he said "that Congress would be called together, if he felt certain it would grant the legislation needed [to authorize collection of import duties offshore], and would not set about other business which might embarrass the administration." According to a journalist, it was "supposed by this he meant to deprecate any further attempts to compromise with the South. What if the new Congress, called together to give the president full power to collect the revenues in the seceded states, were to omit that work, and take up the old compromise patch-work?"[17] The Republican majority in the House would be small, and if some of its members joined the Democrats to insist on compromising basic party principles, the result might be unfortunate. From the White House, William O. Stoddard reported that the prospect of a special session created fears "that some false prophet of peace, with a craven heart and a slippery tongue, will bring in specious proposals of some sort to distract our National Council, and impair the unity and energy of its actions."[18] In addition, congressmen themselves opposed an extra session, for they would receive no extra compensation above a travel allowance, and they dreaded the prospect of spending a miserably hot and humid summer in Washington. Moreover, according to rumor, Jefferson Davis had warned that he would regard the summoning of a special session of Congress as an act justifying war.

Lincoln and his cabinet also favored delaying a special session of Congress lest such a deliberative body prove unable to act decisively, and Seward opposed a special session because he feared Congress might unwisely tinker with the Morrill Tariff. Lincoln may well have suspected that Congress might also make some blunder that would drive loyal Slave States like Kentucky into the arms of the Confederacy. So it was decided that Congress would not convene until July 4, allowing enough time to determine if Washington would be a safe place to meet. It also meant that some emergency measures would have to be taken without prior congressional approval, measures that might be of questionable constitutionality. Some Democrats complained about the failure to have Congress meet before July 4. The president "has two months of absolute despotic control" protested the Washington *States and Union*.[19] Lincoln's failure to summon Congress immediately has been criticized, but it is difficult to fault his decision, given the uncertainty that prevailed immediately after the bombardment of Fort Sumter. He did ask the leaders of the finance committees to spend two weeks in Washington in advance of the opening of Congress.

The cabinet also considered the size of a militia force to call up. Some favored 50,000; Seward and others recommended double that number. Lincoln split the difference and decided to ask the states to provide 75,000 men for three months' service, in accordance with a provision of the Militia Act of 1795. Once that number was selected, action was swift: the president drafted a proclamation, Cameron calculated the quotas for each state, Nicolay had the document copied, and Seward readied it to distribute to the press in time for Monday's papers.

In discussions about the proclamation, some advisors suggested that the North had far more resolve and enterprise than the South. Lincoln cautioned them, saying: "We must not forget that the people of the seceded States, like those of the loyal ones, are American citizens, with essentially the same characteristics and powers. Exceptional advantages on one side are counterbalanced by exceptional advantages on the other. We must make up our minds that man for man the soldier from the South will be a match for the soldier from the North and *vice versa*."[20]

Indeed, the North's obvious advantages in economic strength and manpower were so largely offset by the South's advantages that the North could well have been considered the underdog at the outset of the war. The Confederates did not have to conquer the North to win; they merely had to fend it off. The military technology of the day favored the defense, not the offense. (With its grooved barrel, the rifle, which became the primary infantry and cavalry weapon on both sides, had much greater range and accuracy than the smoothbore musket, giving soldiers on the defensive a great advantage over their attackers.) The South's morale was exceptionally high, for it felt as if it were fighting for the principles of 1776. Moreover, Confederates sought to repel what they understandably considered an invasion. Because most battles would take place on Southern soil, the Rebels would know the terrain better and have more accurate sources of intelligence. In addition, European nations, dependent on Southern cotton, seemed likely to support the Confederacy. The South's military leaders, at least in the eastern theater, were superior to their Northern counterparts, while Southern enlisted men were more familiar with firearms, more accustomed to hard riding, and more used to outdoor life than were Yankees. The North lacked a sophisticated governmental apparatus for conducting such a huge enterprise as the Civil War; mobilizing its vast resources would pose a grave challenge to the small, creaky, antiquated bureaucratic structures then available. A similar lack of organizational sophistication marked the civilian sector. A greater challenge still was maintaining Northern unity. How could Kentucky slaveholders be kept in harness with Northern abolitionists? Prohibitionists in Maine with beer-loving Germans in the Midwest? Racial egalitarians in New England with racists in most other states? Free traders with protectionists? Former Whigs with former Democrats? If those elements did not all coalesce, the South would prevail despite its inferior numbers and economic muscle. (The Free States had 3,778,000 white males between the ages of 18 and 45, while the Slave States had only 1,116,000.)

The language of the proclamation reflected Lincoln's anger at prominent secessionists, whom he regarded as a small handful who had dragooned their neighbors into disunion. In a draft of that document, he spoke of their "[in]sults, and injuries already too long endured." (In the final version, he referred more temperately to "wrongs" rather than "insults and injuries.") Justifying the resort to arms, he emphasized a theme he would reiterate again and again, most memorably at Gettysburg in 1863: "I appeal to all loyal citizens to favor, facilitate, and aid this effort to maintain the honor, the integrity, and the existence of our National Union, and the perpetuity of popular government." This war was not merely one to preserve the Union but also to vindicate democracy. The mission of the troops, he explained, would "probably be to repossess the forts, places and property, which have been seized from the Union; and, in every event, the utmost care will be observed, consistently with the objects aforesaid, to avoid any devastation; any destruction of, or interference with, property, or any disturbance of peaceful citizens, in any part of the country."[21]

In thus describing the likely tasks that the troops would perform, Lincoln showed questionable judgment, for it confronted the Upper South and Border States with a dilemma: either they would have to make war against fellow Southerners, or they would have to join them in secession. In Baltimore, John Pendleton Kennedy accurately predicted that the proclamation "will fire up the whole South, as it implies invasion and coercion."[22] By indicating that the militia would be used not simply to defend Washington but also to retake the forts, the president committed a "wicked blunder," Kennedy protested. Half of the adult males in Maryland, he said, would have gladly rallied to protect the capital, but they would not consent to invade the South. "We are driven into extremities by a series of the most extraordinary blunders at Washington, which I think must convince everybody that there is no ability in the Administration to meet the crisis. They have literally forced the Border States out of the Union, and really seem to be utterly unconscious of the follies they have perpetrated."[23]

In Kentucky, some Unionists were "struck with mingled amazement and indignation" at a proclamation which they said "deserves the unqualified condemnation of every American citizen."[24] But the Bluegrass State would remain loyal; in North Carolina, Virginia, Arkansas, and Tennessee, however, the Unionist sentiment, which had been waxing, abruptly waned. Those states withdrew from the Union after their governors indignantly refused to provide any militia. (Lincoln chastised the governor of Tennessee, Isham Harris, for his "disrespectful and malicious language." When informed that Harris complained about the seizure of a boatload of weapons, Lincoln said quietly: "He be d—d.")[25] The Upper South and Border States might have resisted secession, at least temporarily, if Lincoln had announced that troops would be used solely to defend Washington. As it was, North Carolina Unionists felt betrayed. One of their leaders, Jonathan Worth, wondered how Lincoln could have failed to anticipate "that he was letting loose on us a torrent to which we could oppose no resistance. It may be said, theoretically, that this should not have been the effect. Statesmen should have common sense. All sensible men knew it would be the effect. . . . He could have adopted no policy so effectual to destroy the Union."[26] In neighboring Virginia, Unionist leader John Minor Botts called the proclamation "the most unfortunate state paper that ever issued from any Executive since the establishment of the government," and William C. Rives blamed "Mr. Lincoln's unlucky & ill-conceived proclamation" for causing Virginia's catastrophic decision to secede. "Before that, all the proceedings of the Convention indicated an earnest desire to maintain the Union," Rives asserted.[27] Lincoln's proclamation transformed the sectional conflict in Tennessee from "the negro question" to "a question of resistance to tyranny," according to Senator A. O. P. Nicholson.[28]

Lincoln soon regretted that he had not justified the militia call as a defensive measure. On April 21, he exclaimed to the mayor of Baltimore: "I am not a learned man!" and insisted "that his proclamation had not been correctly understood; that he had no intention of bringing on war, but that his purpose was to defend the capital, which was in danger of being bombarded from the heights across the Potomac."[29] Repeatedly, he "protested, on his honor, in the most solemn way, that the troops were meant exclusively to protect the Capital."[30] When a leading Maryland Unionist, Reverdy Johnson, warned that the people of his state and Virginia feared that troops headed for Washington would invade the South, Lincoln denied any such intent. On

April 24, he assured the former senator that "the sole purpose of bringing troops *here* is to defend this capital. . . . I have no purpose to *invade* Virginia, with them or any other troops, as I understand the word *invasion*." But Lincoln insisted that he must strike back if Virginia attacked Washington or allowed other Rebels to pass through her territory to do so. "Suppose Virginia erects, or permits to be erected, batteries on the opposite shore, to bombard the city, are we to stand still and see it done? In a word, if Virginia strikes us, are we not to strike back, and as effectively as we can? Again, are we not to hold Fort Monroe (for instance) if we can? I have no objection to declare a thousand times that I have no purpose to *invade* Virginia or any other State, but I do not mean to let them invade us without striking back."[31]

The proclamation's call for only 75,000 militia for three months' service also drew criticism. Before issuing that document, Lincoln consulted Stephen A. Douglas, who recommended that the number be increased to 200,000. The president had asked George Ashmun to arrange an interview with the Little Giant. When the former Massachusetts congressman called on the Illinois senator, Douglas initially balked, protesting that "Mr. Lincoln has dealt hardly with me, in removing some of my friends from office, and I don't know as he wants my advice or aid." But persistent cajoling by Ashmun and an appeal from Mrs. Douglas persuaded the Little Giant to capitulate, and, accompanied by Ashmun, he met with Lincoln for two hours. After the president read a draft of the proclamation, Douglas urged the reinforcement of Cairo, Fort Monroe, Harper's Ferry, and Washington itself, and also warned about the danger of having troops pass through Maryland. He suggested that soldiers be detoured around Baltimore and that Forts Monroe in Virginia and Old Point Comfort in Maryland be secured. After the interview, Douglas informed the press that while he "was unalterably opposed to the Administration on all its political issues, he was prepared to sustain the President in the exercise of all his constitutional functions to preserve the Union, and maintain the Government, and defend the Federal Capital." The two men spoke "of the present and future without reference to the past." Lincoln was "very much gratified with the interview," which had been friendly.[32]

Shortly thereafter, Douglas told a friend: "I've known Mr. Lincoln a longer time than you have, or than the country has; he will come out all right and we will all stand by him."[33] On the floor of the senate he defended the proclamation, and, acting the part of a true statesman as he had done in the final stages of the 1860 campaign, he took to the stump, denouncing secession and urging his followers to support the Union. Lincoln had encouraged him "to arouse the Egyptians [i.e., residents of southern Illinois]."[34] The Little Giant proceeded to Springfield, where, on April 25, he delivered an electrifying address to the General Assembly. Douglas's prestige among Northern Democrats helped cement their loyalty to the Union cause.

Some agreed with Douglas's contention that a call for 200,000 troops was more reasonable than 75,000. Others recommended 300,000, and Horace Greeley even proposed that 500,000 men be enlisted. But those numbers seemed unrealistic at a time when the regular army had only 17,000 men, Northern arsenals contained few weapons and little equipment, and the treasury was virtually empty. In addition, the

1795 statute authorizing the president to call out the militia specified that it could serve for only thirty days after the next session of Congress began.

But in general, the proclamation was enthusiastically received in the North, where the bombardment of Sumter triggered a passionate uprising. Rage at the secessionists swept through the Free States like a tornado. As Lincoln put it later, "the response of the country was most gratifying, surpassing, in unanimity and spirit, the most sanguine expectation."[35] For too long Southerners had played the bully; now Northerners would stand up for themselves and their rights. The South must confront the pent-up anger of patient men. People in Vermont, wrote a Brattleboro resident, "have felt for the last three months mortified, indignant, 'mad clear through' at the disgrace & shame inflicted on us & we now rejoice & are glad that the insults heaped on us are to be avenged, & our wounded honor vindicated."[36] From Wisconsin, Senator James R. Doolittle reported that if "an Angel from Heaven had issued a proclamation it could hardly have received a heartier response than the proclamation of the President."[37] On April 16, John Hay noted that there "is something splendid, yet terrible, about this roused anger of the North. It is stern, quiet, implacable, irresistible. On whomever it falls it will grind them to powder."[38] Mass meetings throughout the North testified to the deep devotion felt for the Union. Thousands flocked to join the army. Seward's fear of divisiveness within the North proved illusory. Like the United States after the Japanese attack on Pearl Harbor in 1941, the Free States rallied around the flag with virtual unanimity.

Anxiety: Awaiting the Arrival of Troops

Immediately after the fall of Fort Sumter, Northern anxiety mounted steadily as disaster followed disaster. On April 17, Virginia seceded; on April 18, federal troops abandoned Harper's Ferry at the northern entrance to the vital Shenandoah Valley, torching the armory as they left; and on April 20, Union forces set afire the Gosport Navy Yard in Norfolk before evacuating it.

Lincoln found it hard to credit reports that Virginia had left the Union so precipitously. On April 17, when he learned of the Old Dominion's secession, he "said he was not yet prepared to believe that one of the founders of the Union, and the mother of so many of its rulers, was yet ready to break down her own work and blast her own glorious history by this act of treason."[39] That night it was feared that Confederates would attack the city. Rumors abounded that the fierce Texas Ranger Ben McCulloch would lead such an assault (although he was then in Arkansas and would never come east of the Mississippi River before his death in battle the following year). The loyalty of the District's thirty companies of raw militia was suspect. Lincoln and other Washingtonians awaited the arrival of troops from the North with deep apprehension. "Never was a capital left in such a defenceless condition," complained one member of an informal military force hastily thrown together to protect Washington.[40] On April 20 a colleague confided to his diary: "A universal gloom and anxiety sits upon every countenance." The city was "rife with *treason*, and the streets full of traitors." Anxiously he asked: "when will reinforcements come? Will it be too late?"[41]

Henry Villard recalled the "impatience, gloom, and depression" that enveloped the capital as day after day reinforcements failed to materialize. "No one felt it more than the President," according to Villard. "I saw him repeatedly, and he fairly groaned at the inexplicable delay in the advent of help from the loyal States."[42] Illinois Congressman Philip B. Fouke, who visited the White House on the night of April 22, reported that Lincoln was "especially exercised at the critical condition of the federal capital."[43] The next day the president exclaimed in anguish, "Why don't they come! Why don't they come!"[44] On April 25, he asked a Connecticut visitor, who thought he looked badly depressed: "What *is* the North about? Do they know our condition?"[45]

Compounding Lincoln's woes was the resignation of approximately one-third of the officers in the army and navy. Especially disconcerting was the case of Colonel John B. Magruder, commander of the Washington garrison, who, on April 18, had told the president: "Sir, I was brought up and educated under the glorious old flag. I have lived under it and have fought under it, and, sir, with the help of God, I shall fight under it again and, if need be, shall die under it." Lincoln replied: "you are an officer of the army and a Southern gentleman, and incapable of any but honorable conduct." The president added that "independently of all other reasons he felt it to be a constitutional obligation binding upon his conscience to put down secession," even though "he bore testimony to the honor, good faith, and high character of the Southern people, whom he 'knew well.'" Three days thereafter, however, the colonel announced his intention of quitting the service to join the Confederacy. Lincoln said later that he could not remember "any single event of my administration that gave me so much pain or wounded me so deeply as the singular behavior of Colonel Magruder." To the president "it seemed the more wanton and cruel in him because he knew that I had implicit confidence in his integrity. The fact is, when I learned that he had gone over to the enemy and I had been so completely deceived in him, my confidence was shaken in everybody, and I hardly knew who to trust anymore."[46]

More significantly, Colonel Robert E. Lee of Virginia spurned an offer that Lincoln unofficially conveyed through Francis P. Blair, Sr., to command the Union army. "Mr Blair," said the country's most capable officer, "I look upon secession as anarchy—if I owned the four millions of slaves in the South I would sacrifice them all to the Union—but how can I draw my sword upon Virginia, my native State?"[47] On April 23, Lee accepted command of the military forces of the Old Dominion. (Generals Winfield Scott, George H. Thomas, Philip St. George Cooke, John W. Davidson, L. P. Graham, William Hays, and John Newton—Virginians all—did not follow Lee's example.)

In July, Lincoln told Congress that it was "worthy of note, that while in this, the government's hour of trial, large numbers of those in the Army and Navy, who have been favored with the offices, have resigned, and played false to the very hand which had pampered them, not one common soldier, or common sailor has deserted his flag. Great honor is due to those officers who remained true, despite the example of their treacherous associates; but the greatest honor, and most important fact of all is, the unanamous firmness of the common soldiers and common sailors. To the last man, they have successfully resisted the traitorous efforts of those, whose commands, but an hour before, they obeyed as absolute law. This is the patriotic instinct of plain people. They understand, without an argument, that destroying the government which was made by Washington, means no good to them."[48] (Actually, twenty-six enlisted men resigned to join the Confederacy.)

In the midst of all the uncertainty, General Scott drew up emergency plans to protect the capital. He designated the massive treasury building as a refuge for the president and his cabinet, who would take shelter in the basement while troops assembled at nearby Lafayette Square. In the meantime, to guard the White House, Old Fuss and Feathers assigned Major David Hunter, who called on two Republican leaders, Cassius M. Clay of Kentucky and Jim Lane of Kansas, to organize informal units. Clay, who was preparing to leave for Russia to take up his duties as minister to the czar's government, hastily assembled the "Clay Battalion," a rag-tag company of a few dozen senators, congressmen, clerks, mechanics, and salesmen. The vain, melodramatic Clay appeared at the Executive Mansion "with a sublimely unconscious air, three pistols and an Arkansas toothpick [Bowie knife] and looked like an admirable vignette to 25-cents-worth of yellow-covered romance," according to John Hay.[49]

Supplementing these men were the "Frontier Guards," hurriedly organized at Major Hunter's request by the cunning, ambitious, violence-prone Jim Lane, senator from Kansas. Consisting of about fifty men, the Guards on April 18 took up residence in the White House, where Hay observed them as they "filed into the famous East Room, clad in citizens' dress, but carrying very new, untarnished muskets, and following Lane, brandishing a sword of irreproachable brightness. Here ammunition-boxes were opened and cartridges dealt out; and after spending the evening in an exceedingly rudimentary squad drill, under the light of the gorgeous gas chandeliers, they disposed themselves in picturesque bivouac on the brilliant-patterned velvet carpet—perhaps the most luxurious cantonment which American soldiers have ever enjoyed."[50] A member of the Guard wrote home, describing how he and his colleagues "slept sweetly on the President's rich Brussels [carpet], with their arms stacked in martial line down the center of the hall, while two long rows of Kansas ex-Governors, Senators, Judges, Editors, Generals and Jayhawkers were dozing upon each side, and the sentinels made regular beats around them." Those guardians were instructed to admit to the East Room no one who failed to give the password. When Lincoln tried to enter the hall, a sentinel barked "that *he could not possibly come in!*"[51] To the amusement of the other guards, Lincoln beat a hasty retreat. When the unit was disbanded after a few days, the president said in thanking them that "language was incapable of expressing how great an obligation he and the people all over this country are under to this little patriotic band of men, for their timely services in preventing, as they undoubtedly did prevent, this capital from falling into the hands of the enemy."[52]

Relieving tension slightly was the arrival of five unarmed companies of Pennsylvania militiamen on April 18. Accompanied by Cameron and Seward, Lincoln visited them at the Capitol to extend hearty thanks for their promptitude. One soldier recalled that when they entered, "[p]rofound silence for a moment resulted, broken by the hand clapping and cheers of the tired volunteers." The militiaman was "impressed by the kindliness of his [Lincoln's] face and awkward hanging of his arms and legs, his apparent bashfulness in the presence of these first soldiers of the Republic, and with it all a grave, rather mournful bearing in his attitude." After observing the men, some of whom had been wounded while passing through Baltimore, the president said: "I did not come here to make a speech. The time for speech-making has gone by, and the time for action is at hand. I have come here to give the Washington Artillerists from the State of Pennsylvania a warm welcome to the city of Washington and to shake every officer and soldier by the hand, providing you will give me that privilege." As he grasped their hands, they felt awestruck.[53]

That same day, Lincoln met with the celebrated author Bayard Taylor, who found him "calm and collected" as "he spoke of the present crisis with that solemn, earnest composure, which is a sign of a soul not easily perturbed."[54] In the evening, when informed that some daredevil Virginia guerrillas planned to swoop into the city and either capture or assassinate him, the president merely grinned. Mary Lincoln, however, was not so nonchalant, and John Hay had to do "some very dexterous lying" to calm her fears.[55]

On April 19, the anniversary of the 1775 battle of Lexington where Massachusetts men were the first to be killed in the Revolutionary War, members of the Sixth Massachusetts regiment were the first to die in the Civil War when a mob attacked them as they passed through Baltimore. In February, a leading politician in that city had warned that if the Lincoln administration "shall dare to bring its Black Republican cohorts to the banks of the Susquehanna" in order to defend Washington, "that river shall run red with blood before the first man of them should cross it."[56] Shots were exchanged, killing four soldiers and wounding thirty-six of their comrades; in addition, twelve civilians were killed and scores injured. The North howled in outrage, causing residents of the Monumental City to dread possible retaliation. When two of Baltimore's leading citizens expressed fear that indignant Northerners might swarm into the Free State, Lincoln offered them reassurance: "Our people are easily influenced by reason. They have determined to prosecute this matter with energy but with the most temperate spirit. You are entirely safe from lawless invasion."[57]

Upon learning of the attack on the Massachusetts Sixth, Lincoln was quite astounded, for he said that Maryland Governor Thomas H. Hicks "had assured him, the day before, that the troops would have no trouble in passing through Baltimore, and that if they wanted any troops from Washington he (Gov. Hicks) would telegraph." When Hicks wired saying "Send no more troops," the president mistakenly assumed that the governor meant that he wanted no help from the administration and that Hicks would "take care and see that the troops passed safely."[58] In fact, on April 18, Governor Hicks and Baltimore Mayor George W. Brown had written Lincoln ambiguously: "send no troops here." They repeated that message in a telegram the next day.[59] They meant to say "send no troops *through* here."

When the Massachusetts Sixth arrived in Washington, Lincoln shook hands with every member of the regiment and warmly greeted its commander, Colonel Edward F. Jones: "Thank God, you have come; for if you had not Washington would have been in the hands of the rebels before morning. Your brave boys have saved the capital. God bless them."[60] Seeing their shabby uniforms, the president directed that the troops be issued regular army shirts and trousers.

After midnight, when a delegation from Baltimore arrived at the White House to make an appeal like Hicks's, Nicolay refused to wake the president but called on the secretary of war, who indicated no interest in complying with their request. The next morning Lincoln encountered the Baltimoreans as he was about to confer with General Scott, who urged that reinforcements be sent around rather than through Baltimore. Temperamentally disposed to believe everyone fair and sincere, Lincoln agreed to this compromise solution, thus satisfying the committee. Half in jest, he told them that "if I grant you this, you will come to-morrow demanding that no troops shall pass around."[61]

At the urging of Henry Winter Davis, Lincoln then wired Hicks and Brown, summoning them to Washington for a consultation. Around midnight a telegram arrived from Brown stating that Hicks was unavailable and asking if he should come alone. At 1 A.M., Nicolay woke Lincoln, who had his secretary reply to the mayor: "Come."[62]

On April 20, Lincoln also met with Maryland Congressmen Anthony Kennedy and J. Morrison Harris, who repeated the message of previous Baltimore callers. Impatiently, Lincoln declared: "My God, Mr. Harris, I don't know what to make of your people. You have sent me one committee already, and they seemed to be perfectly satisfied with what I said to them." When Harris insisted that no more troops pass through his state, the president answered: "My God, Sir, what am I to do? I had better go out and hang myself on the first tree I come to, than to give up the power of the Federal Government in this way. I don't want to go through your town, or near it, if I can help it; but we must have the troops here to relieve ourselves, or we shall die like rats in a heap."[63]

Sunday, April 21, was an especially anxious day at the White House. That morning, Brown and several of his fellow townsmen fulfilled Lincoln's prediction by earnestly insisting that no troops pass through their state at all! The president at first balked, asserting emphatically that the protection of Washington "was the sole object of concentrating troops there, and he protested that none of the troops brought through Maryland were intended for any purposes hostile to the State, or aggressive as against Southern States." The delegation left, reassured of Lincoln's desire to avoid further bloodshed in the Free State. But upon reaching the depot to return home, they heard that Pennsylvania reinforcements had arrived in Cockeysville, 14 miles north of Baltimore, throwing the Monumental City into a panic. Indignantly, the delegation returned to the White House to demand that those troops be called off. Fearing that renewed hostilities between militia and civilians might play into the hands of Maryland's secessionists, Lincoln emphatically stated that "he had no idea they [the Pennsylvania troops] would be there today, and, lest there should be the slightest suspicion of bad faith on his part in summoning the Mayor to Washington and allowing troops to march on the city during his absence, he desired that the troops should, if it were practicable, be sent back at once."[64]

This decision outraged many Unionists, including some cabinet members. At a meeting soon after the Baltimoreans departed, Gideon Welles indignantly stormed out, remarking that "if that was their policy *he* would have no responsibility in the matter."[65] With characteristic belligerence, Seward "said the treason of Hicks would not surprise him—that the Seventh [New York regiment] could cut their way through three thousand rioters—that Baltimore delenda est [i.e., must be destroyed]."[66] In Pennsylvania, former Kansas Governor Andrew Reeder observed that the "report made by the Mayor of Balt. of his interview with the Presdt I am sorry to say has excited a good deal of indignation and if he tells the truth, the bearing of the Presidt. was too weak and lowly for the commander in chief to use to the representative of rebels."[67] Henry Villard told his editors that Lincoln "shrinks from the responsibility of striking blows & is altogether of too lenient a disposition towards the rebels. I know this from my own conversations with him."[68] The New York *Tribune* scornfully called Lincoln's decision to have troops avoid Baltimore "the height of Quixotic scrupulosity," and the rival New York *Times* went so far as to suggest that the president be impeached.[69] The New York *Evening Post* denounced the administration's "fatal blunders" in failing to protect the capital and the Norfolk Navy Yard.[70] A part-owner of that paper, John Bigelow, called at the White House and detected in the president "a certain lack of sovereignty." To Bigelow, Lincoln seemed "utterly unconscious of the space which the President of the United States occupied that day in the history of the human race, and of the vast power for the exercise of which he had become personally responsible." Strengthening that impression was the president's "modest habit of disclaiming knowledge of affairs and familiarity with duties, and frequent avowals of ignorance."[71] On May 8, New York Senator Preston King declared that Lincoln was "weak and unequal not only to the present crisis but to the position he holds at anytime."[72] In Washington, the eminent ethnologist George Gibbs deemed the lack of confidence in the administration a "great calamity." The president "seems to be signally unfit for such an emergency, wanting both in foresight, and in decision, and meddling in details which don[']t belong to him."[73] Supporters of the administration "find themselves unable to justify its moderation," Hiram Barney lamented. "The instant reopening of the usual lines of communication between Philadelphia & Washington at whatever cost, would be hailed with great satisfaction," he predicted, while warning that *unless that is done the administration will be severely censured and its moral hold on the community will be lost.*[74]

On April 24, Barney and other leading New York Republicans dined with Vice-President Hamlin; they agreed "that Lincoln & his cabinet need more energy & resolution—that their brains are not yet evacuated of the idea that something is to be done by compromise & waiting—that it is almost impossible in that atmosphere (Southern & sectional) to get a clear impression of the strength of the Northern feeling—& that unless they act with more promptness & vigor, they will be compelled to give way to some semi-revolutionary outbreak of Northern pluck & determination—perhaps a military head."[75] Lincoln "is yielding & pliable—with hardly back-bone enough for the emergency" and "dreads expense & all that," complained Manton Marble of the New York *World*.[76] Others accused the administration of pinch-penny timidity. A Cincinnati Republican exclaimed "there is nothing for which the Administration has been so much censured here from the beginning as an apparent reluctance to prosecute the war with vigor because of considerations of finance!"[77]

Lincoln dismissed press critics, saying "we can afford to pass them by with the dying words of the Massachusetts statesman [Daniel Webster], 'we still live.' I am sure they don't worry me any, and I reckon they don't benefit the parties who write them."[78] Privately, he was less stoical, calling hostile articles "villainous" and intimating to Seward that the editor of the New York *Times,* Henry J. Raymond, should receive no government office. (Seward had been hoping to appoint Raymond consul at Paris, for the editor had grown weary of journalistic drudgery and was eager to serve overseas.) Months later, when asked if he had read an editorial in a certain New York newspaper, Lincoln replied: "No, I dare not open that paper. I'd like now and then to see its editorials, for the fun of the thing, but if I do I'm sure to get seduced into reading its Washington dispatches—and then *my sleep is gone for one night at least.*"[79]

To those protesting his decision to have troops detour around Baltimore, Lincoln explained that he had gone out of his way, "as an exhaustion of the means of conciliation & kindness," to accommodate the municipal authorities who assured him that they had insufficient power to assure the safety of Union troops passing through their city but could guarantee undisturbed passage elsewhere in Maryland. He added "that this was the last time he was going to interfere in matters of strictly military concernment" and that "he would leave them hereafter wholly to military men."[80] (Eventually, he would change his mind about relying entirely on such men.) He also argued that it had been imperative to maintain the good will of the Maryland authorities lest they hinder troop movements via the alternate route through Perryville and Annapolis.

On April 22, when yet another group from Baltimore called to demand that troops be forbidden to pass through their state and that the Confederacy be recognized, Lincoln lost his customary patience. With some asperity he scolded them: "You, gentlemen, come here to me and ask for peace on any terms, and yet have no word of condemnation for those who are making war on us. You express great horror of bloodshed, and yet would not lay a straw in the way of those who are organizing in Virginia and elsewhere to capture this city. The rebels attack Fort Sumter, and your citizens attack troops sent to the defense of the Government, and the lives and property in Washington, and yet you would have me break my oath and surrender the Government without a blow. There is no Washington in that—no Jackson in that—no manhood nor honor in that." Lincoln insisted that he had "no desire to invade the South; but I must have the troops, and mathematically the necessity exists that they should come through Maryland. They can't crawl under the earth, and they can't fly over it. Why, sir, those Carolinians are now crossing Virginia to come here to hang me, and what can I do?" He added that "he must run the machine as he found it." There would be no need for a clash as Union soldiers crossed Maryland: "Now, sir, if you won't hit me, I won't hit you!"

But if those troops were forcibly resisted, he declared, "*I will lay Baltimore in ashes.*" When told that 75,000 Marylanders would resist the passage of Union troops, he promptly and decidedly "replied that he presumed there was room enough on her soil to bury 75,000 men." As the delegation left, Lincoln remarked to one of its members: "You have heard of the Irishman who, when a fellow was cutting his throat with a blunt razor, complained that he haggled it. Now, if I can't have troops directly through Maryland, and must have them all the way round by water, or marched across out-of-the-way territory, I shall be haggled."[81] Some fastidious members of this delegation thought Lincoln lacked dignity. The Rev. Dr. Richard Fuller, who was both a large-scale slave owner and a prominent Baptist leader, snorted that "nothing is to be hoped" from the president because he "is wholly inaccessible to Christian appeals—& his egotism will forever prevent his comprehending what patriotism means."[82]

(Lincoln's anger at Baltimoreans persisted. In September 1861, when Mayor Brown was arrested for aiding the Confederates, a delegation from the Monumental City pleaded for his release. The president replied: "I believe, gentlemen, if we arrested Jeff. Davis, committees would wait upon me and represent him to be a Union man." He recounted a conversation he had had with Brown in the spring during which that official had shown sympathy for the Rebels. "I have not heard of any act of mayor Brown since, which would lead to the belief that he was in favor of supporting the Government to put down this rebellion."[83] Two years later, when he hesitated to pardon young William B. Compton, who had been condemned to death as a spy, he was asked whether he "would receive a delegation of the most influential citizens of Baltimore, with the Hon. Reverdy Johnson at their head, if they will come in person and present a petition on behalf of Mr. Compton?" Indignantly the president exclaimed: "No! I will not receive a delegation from Baltimore for any purpose. I have received many delegations from Baltimore, since I came into office, composed of its most prominent citizens. They have always come to gain some advantage for themselves, or for their city. They have always had some end of their own to reach, without regard to the interests of the government. But no delegation has ever come to me to express sympathy or to give me any aid in upholding the government and putting down the rebellion. No! I will receive no delegation from Baltimore.")[84]

When Governor Hicks of Maryland suggested that Lord Lyons, Great Britain's minister to the United States, be asked to mediate the dispute between the North and the South, Seward replied with a letter that may have been drafted by Lincoln. He explained that the troops would be used merely to defend Washington. Alluding to the War of 1812, he added that he "cannot but remember that there has been a time in the history of our country when a general of the American Union, with forces designed for the defense of its capital, was not unwelcome anywhere in the State of Maryland, and certainly not at Annapolis." Firmly he insisted that "no domestic contention whatever that may arise among the parties of this republic ought in any case to be referred to any foreign arbitrament, least of all to the arbitrament of a European monarchy."[85] Many Northerners found this response excessively timid and insisted that Marylanders had to be warned that they must either cooperate or be crushed. A

Hartford banker wanted to inform Seward that the letter "raised here one universal shout of execration." Such "damned . . . wishy washy stuff does not 'go down' with us, not by a great deal. Why didn't he say, 'We propose to go through Baltimore & will lay your infernal city in ashes if a gun is fired.' That's the kind of talk the people want & they will back it up."[86] New Yorkers were also indignant; one said the letter "absolutely disgusts everybody; it is begging, mean, and truckling, instead of being as it should have been, firm, decisive and imperative."[87]

Baltimore's reigning literary lion, John Pendleton Kennedy, accurately predicted that "this refusal of a right of transit will arouse the whole North."[88] Throughout the Free States, people declared that if troops could not pass through Baltimore, the "city and its name should be swept from the face of the earth."[89] In Ohio, a leading Methodist clergyman insisted that "Maryland must be kept open" even it meant that "we make it a graveyard."[90] Andrew H. Reeder predicted that if "Baltimore was laid in ashes the North would rejoice over it and laud the Spirit that dictated the act."[91] Thundered the Indianapolis *Journal*: "If any Governor or Mayor stands in the way, let him be extinguished. If any city or State offers to thwart or oppose the military operations of the Federal Government, let every gutter run with blood, and every foot of ground within the State be furrowed by cannon, if necessary to vindicate the supremacy of the constitution."[92]

On April 27, Lincoln explained to an old friend that "he could easily have destroyed Baltimore, but that it would have been visiting vengeance upon a large body of loyal citizens, who were the property-holders, for the sake of punishing the mob who had committed the outrage upon the Massachusetts troops, but which mob, as to property, had little or nothing to lose."[93]

Meanwhile, Washington had become isolated from the North. On April 20, Maryland officials ordered the destruction of railroad bridges on lines connecting the capital with Baltimore. Telegraph wires were cut, and mail service to the District ceased. Troops heading there, among them the Seventh New York and the First Rhode Island regiments, were held up for several days as they sought alternate routes. Later, the president remarked that a man "who strangles himself, for whatever motive, is not more unreasonable than were those citizens of Baltimore who, in a single night, destroyed the Baltimore and Ohio railroad, the Northern Pennsylvania railroad, and the railroad from Baltimore to Philadelphia."[94]

One day, while nervously awaiting the arrival of reinforcements, Lincoln thought he heard cannonfire in the distance, signaling what he believed was a Confederate attack. Nonplussed by his aides' insistence that they heard nothing, he walked over to the Arsenal, which he found unguarded, much to his surprise and dismay. All was quite still both there and along his route back to the White House. As he returned, he asked passersby if they had heard cannonading earlier. When they said that they had not, he assumed his imagination was playing tricks on him.

By April 24, gloom and doubt seemed to infect everyone in Washington. Despairing, Lincoln told some of the Massachusetts soldiers who had survived the Baltimore attack, "I don[']t believe there is any North. The Seventh [New York] Regiment is a myth. R[hode] Island is not known in our geography any longer. *You* are the only

Northern realities."[95] Seward anticipated that "[a]ll Virginia, and all Maryland are to be upon us in mass."[96] Washingtonians not only feared a Confederate assault but also worried that a minor episode could touch off rioting or panic among the anxious populace. The 2,000 troops in Washington afforded some comfort, but it was thought that the 3,000-man District Militia might prove disloyal. Hence, despite criticism, Lincoln refused to call it up. Hotels emptied as people fled to safety outside Washington, while those who remained began girding for a siege. The threat of famine arose as flour supplies dwindled. Luckily, the moon shone brightly night after night, discouraging local secessionists who otherwise might have risen up against the city's few defenders.

On April 25, the thick gloom that had blanketed the capital for more than a week suddenly lifted as the crack New York Seventh arrived to thunderous cheers. "If they had been delayed two days longer revolution would have broken out in our midst," a relieved Frontier Guardsman told his wife.[97] Lincoln and Seward greeted them at the navy yard and shook hands all around. One soldier recalled that the president showed a "serious and almost fatherly demeanor" as "he bent slightly in taking our hands . . . . Indeed one hand was not enough to express his feeling, and with his left he took each of us by the elbow and gave a hearty pressure." As the troops marched past the White House, Lincoln, who was described as "the happiest-looking man in town," reportedly "smiled all over" and enthusiastically complimented the soldiers. During the following weeks, he regularly visited their camp.[98]

Even more encouraging was word that several more regiments were on their way from Annapolis, having skirted Baltimore by a water route from Perryville on the Susquehanna River to the Maryland capital. Those units came pouring into Washington during the last week of April, ensuring the safety of the city. Lincoln's decision to have those reinforcements avoid Baltimore, despite severe criticism from many Republicans, helped prevent Maryland from seceding. As an abolitionist journal pointed out, if he had "done anything to arouse yet more the passions and to unite the energies of the Marylanders, such as the assertion of the perfect right of a free passage for troops through Baltimore and his determination to enforce it, Washington might have been taken and he made prisoner by a *coup de main* before help could arrive."[99]

Fearing that Maryland lawmakers would pass an ordinance of secession, Massachusetts General Benjamin F. Butler urged Lincoln "to bag the whole nest of traitorous Maryland Legislators and bring them in triumph" to Washington. The president rejected that advice, telling Winfield Scott on April 25: "The Maryland Legislature assembles to-morrow at An[n]apolis; and, not improbably, will take action to arm the people of that State against the United States. The question has been submitted to, and considered by me, whether it would not be justifiable, upon the ground of necessary defence, for you, as commander in Chief of the United States Army, to arrest, or disperse the members of that body. I think it would *not* be justifiable; nor, efficient for the desired object. First, they have a clearly legal right to assemble; and, we can not know in advance, that their action will not be lawful, and peaceful. And if we wait until they shall *have* acted, their arrest, or dispersion, will not lessen the effect of their action. Secondly, we *can* not permanently prevent their action. If we arrest them, we can not long hold them as prisoners; and when liberated, they will immediately re-assemble, and take their action. And, precisely the same if we simply disperse them. They will immediately re-assemble in some other place. I therefore conclude that it is only left to the commanding General to watch, and await their action, which, if it shall be to arm their people against the United States, he is to adopt the most prompt, and efficient means to counteract, even, if necessary, to the bombard-ment of their cities—and in the *extremest* necessity, the suspension of the writ of ha-beas corpus."[100]

At the last minute, the Maryland Legislature decided to convene in Frederick, a Unionist stronghold, instead of Annapolis. The secessionist tide, which had flowed so strongly in eastern Maryland, was now ebbing. Federal soldiers occupied strong posi-tions near Baltimore and the state capital. On May 9, troops once again began pass-ing through the Monumental City en route to Washington. Rather than calling for a secession convention, the General Assembly sent a deputation to Lincoln to learn what military action he planned in their state and to protest various measures taken by the administration. On May 4, he bluntly told them "that while the Government had no intention to retaliate for Baltimore outrages by force of arms, it had deter-mined upon measures to secure the unobstructed passage of troops through their State, and would carry them out at all hazards." He also assured them that "the public interest and not any spirit of revenge should actuate his measures."[101] Nine days later, General Butler marched a thousand troops by night into Baltimore and occupied Federal Hill, thus making sure the city would remain pacified. After the legislature adjourned on May 14, Governor Hicks complied with Lincoln's proclamation by issu-ing a call for four militia regiments. In mid-June, Unionist candidates won elections in sixteen of the state's twenty-one counties, signifying that less than two months after the Baltimore riots, loyalty to the Union had reasserted itself in Maryland.

As Lincoln struggled to nurture Unionism in Maryland, he was assisted by Gov-ernor Hicks, who during the secession winter had supported the formation of a border state nation as a buffer between North and South. Bucking strong pressure, Hicks refused to call a secession convention. In September, however, the Lincoln adminis-tration feared that the Maryland Legislature, scheduled to meet at Frederick, might yet adopt an ordinance of secession. It was rumored that disunionists planned a *coup de main,* joining forces with Virginia rebels. To counter that possibility, Lincoln and Seward arranged with Generals George B. McClellan, John A. Dix, and Nathaniel P. Banks to have pro-secession legislators detained before they could reach Frederick. This decision, carried out primarily by the detective Allan Pinkerton, led to the arrest of fourteen legislators and guaranteed that the state would remain in the Union. In November, the election of a pro-Union governor, Augustus Bradford, along with a lopsided Unionist majority in the legislature, sealed the state's loyalty.

Civil libertarians objected that the arrest of the Maryland legislators was unlaw-ful. In reply, Lincoln argued that the "public safety renders it necessary that the grounds of these arrests should at present be withheld, but at the proper time they will be made public. Of one thing the people of Maryland may rest assured, that no arrest has been made, or will be made, not based on substantial and unmistakable complicity with those in armed rebellion against the Government of the United States. In no case has an arrest been made on mere suspicion, or through personal or partisan animosities; but in all cases the Government is in possession of tangible and unmistakable evidence, which will, when made public, be satisfactory to every loyal citizen."[102]

Privately, General Dix acknowledged that in arresting the legislators, breaking up the Baltimore police department, and taking similar steps, he had acted "on the 'plea of necessity' alone." In November, he confided to a fellow New York Democratic leader that "I have not had the time to look into the Constitution since I came.—'Inter arma silent leges!' Alas that it should be so!" He had received no specific instructions from the administration, and if his action were to be judged "by the Constitution or the laws, I am afraid you will make me out to be a very poor democrat. But two assurances I can give—that Maryland shall not go out of the Union, and that I have done & shall do nothing tyrannically, wantonly or unnecessary to the fixed purpose I have had in view."[103] McClellan, who had authorized Dix to make arrests "even where there is want of positive proof of their guilt," lauded his action in dealing with the legislators.[104] Dix said he was "not sure as to the President, though I think he regards my policy as the true remedy for the special phase of the malady of secessionism, which existed on the Eastern shore of Maryland. Whether he will regard it as the proper treatment for other phases of the disease I do not know."[105]

Stretching the Constitution: Emergency Measures

In the immediate aftermath of the attack on Sumter, Lincoln took a few relatively small steps without congressional approval: a convoy was dispatched to escort ships bearing gold from California; over a dozen merchant vessels were bought or rented to protect the coast and enforce a blockade; three prominent New Yorkers were given $2 million to spend as they saw fit for national defense; other leading private citizens of the Empire State received authorization to raise troops and provide supplies; and two naval officers were empowered to arm civilian vessels and use them to patrol the Potomac River and Chesapeake Bay. In explaining these measures a year later, the president said that there "was no adequate and effective organization for the public defence. Congress had indefinitely adjourned. There was no time to convene them. It became necessary for me to choose whether, using only the existing means, agencies, and processes which Congress had provided, I should let the government fall at once into ruin, or whether, availing myself of the broader powers conferred by the Constitution in cases of insurrection, I would make an effort to save it with all its blessings for the present age and for posterity. . . . The several departments of the government at that time contained so large a number of disloyal persons that it would have been impossible to provide safely, through official agents only, for the performance of the duties thus confided to citizens favorably known for their ability, loyalty, and patriotism. . . . I believe that by these and other similar measures taken in that crisis, some of which were without any authority of law, the government was saved from overthrow."[106]

More serious extraconstitutional steps were also taken in the eleven weeks between Sumter's fall and the convening of Congress in July. Lincoln acted unilaterally
in the belief that his emergency measures would be endorsed retrospectively by the
House and senate and thus made constitutional. On April 19, he declared his intention to blockade ports in the seven seceded states; a week later he extended it to cover
Virginia and North Carolina. He justified this action as a response to the Confederacy's announcement on April 17 that it would issue letters of marque, authorizing
privateers to prey on Union shipping. In the momentous cabinet session of April 14, a
majority agreed with Gideon Welles, who maintained that a blockade was more appropriate for a war between two nations rather than for a rebellion. Better to simply
close the ports in the seceded states, argued the navy secretary, who understandably
feared that the Union fleet was too small and antiquated to enforce a blockade. Attorney General Bates believed that a blockade was "an act of war, which a nation cannot wage against itself" but that closing ports was an entirely different matter. Seward,
however, countered that closing Southern ports might provoke foreign nations to declare war. Lincoln at first sided with Welles, but after Seward privately explained his
position, the president changed his mind and told the cabinet the following day "that
we could not afford to have two wars on our hands at once" and therefore he would
declare a blockade.[107]

Seward was right, for the British government had warned that closing the ports
where the administration had no control would be tantamount to an illegal paper
blockade, which Her Majesty's government would not honor. In July, when Congress
did authorize the president to close Confederate ports, Lincoln hesitated to do so. In
response to Orville H. Browning's question, "if we were in any danger of becoming
involved in difficulties with foreign powers," the president, looking quite melancholy,
replied affirmatively, for Britain and France "were determined to have the cotton crop
as soon as it matured." The South's coastline "was so extensive that we could not
make the blockade of all the Ports effectual," and the British government "was now
assuming the ground that a nation had no right, whilst a portion of its citizens were
in revolt to close its ports or any of them against foreign Nations." Congress had just
enacted a law "authorizing him, in his discretion, to close our ports, but if he asserted
the right of closing such as we could not blockade, he had no doubt it would result in
foreign war, and that under the circumstances we had better increase the navy as fast
as we could and blockade such ports as our force would enable us to, and say nothing
about the rest."[108] In February 1862, the British did officially recognize the Union
blockade, despite Confederate protestations that it was ineffective and hence illegal.

Realizing that the 75,000 militiamen called up on April 15 would be insufficient,
Lincoln two weeks later ordered the expansion of the armed forces far beyond what
Congress had authorized. On May 3, an official proclamation specified that 42,034
volunteers would be recruited to serve three years; in addition, 22,714 soldiers were to
be added to the regular army and 18,000 sailors to the navy. Here Lincoln violated
the explicit provision of the Constitution empowering Congress to raise armies. On
July 1, Lincoln explained to Lyman Trumbull "that he did not know of any law to
authorize some things which he had done; but he thought there was a necessity for

them, & that to save the constitution & the laws generally, it might be better to do some illegal acts, rather than suffer all to be overthrown."[109]

Such boldness helped reassure some Northern doubters. On May 2, Henry W. Bellows, a prominent New York divine, noted that the "Cabinet is gaining *confidence in* the country & *from* the country every day," and predicted that "much hasty criticism" would soon be withdrawn. The president's stock was rising, for, though "not *great*," he was nevertheless "very honest & resolute." (Soon thereafter, Bellows spoke with the president and was less complimentary, finding him "a good, sensible, honest man," but "utterly devoid of dignity" and "*without that presence* that assures confidence in his adequacy to his trying position." He had a "sweet smile" and a "patient, slow, firm mind," though Bellows had his doubts about its "comprehensiveness.")[110]

Lincoln's most controversial act was authorizing General Scott to suspend the writ of habeas corpus, thus allowing the government to arrest and detain persons without charges. Seward recommended that step, but Lincoln at first demurred. When the secretary of state argued that "perdition was the sure penalty for further hesitation," however, the president acquiesced.[111] The initial suspension, limited to military lines between Washington and Philadelphia, was authorized on April 27. Two weeks later Lincoln suspended the writ in Florida. In early July, he authorized Scott to do the same along the military lines between Washington and New York. Responding to several arrests in Washington, he counseled restraint in using the power thus granted: "Unless the *necessity* for . . . arbitrary arrests is *manifest,* and *urgent,* I prefer that they should cease."[112]

In May, one John Merryman, a wealthy Marylander serving as a lieutenant in a pro-secession cavalry troop that had helped cut telegraph wires and burn bridges, was arrested for preparing men to serve in the Confederate army. He sued for his freedom, arguing that the suspension of the writ was illegal. Roger B. Taney, the octogenarian chief justice of the U.S. Supreme Court, heard the case in his role as a circuit court of appeals judge. (In that era, Supreme Court justices served on both the high court and the appeals bench.) Taney ruled that Lincoln had acted unconstitutionally, for, he argued, only Congress, not the president, was authorized to suspend the writ of habeas corpus. In a judicial stump speech, the Maryland slaveowner declared that if Lincoln were permitted to usurp that congressional power, "the people of the United States are no longer living under a government of law; but every citizen holds life, liberty and property at the will and pleasure of the army officer in whose military district he may happen to be found." Referring to the president, Taney added that it was "up to that high officer, in fulfillment of his constitutional obligation to 'take care that the laws be faithfully executed,' to determine what measures he will take to cause the civil process of the United States to be respected and enforced."[113] Lincoln ignored the order, and Merryman remained in prison for a few weeks.

Agreeing with Taney was former Maryland Congressman Henry Winter Davis, who declared that the proclamation suspending habeas corpus was "illegal in every line." He feared "there is an utter oblivion of constitutional restraints at Washington. Lincoln is open to good advice; it must be that he cannot get it. He actually did not know till I shewed him the law, that he was not obliged to call for troops through the Governors, but could send his order to *any* officer of the militia!!"[114]

On July 4, in a message to Congress, Lincoln responded to Taney's arguments. In a draft of that important document (far more personal than the final version submitted to the House and the senate), he clearly explained his rationale: "The whole of the laws which I was sworn to take care that they be faithfully executed, were being resisted, and failing to be executed, in nearly one third of the states. Must I have allowed them to finally fail of execution, even had it been perfectly clear that by the use of the means necessary to their execution, some single law, made in such extreme tenderness of the citizens liberty, that practically, it relieves more of the guilty, than the innocent, should, to a very limited extent, be violated? To state the question more directly, are all the laws, *but one,* to go unexecuted, and the government itself go to pieces, lest that one be violated? Even in such a case I should consider my official oath broken if I should allow the government to be overthrown, when I might think that disregarding the single law would tend to preserve it—But, in this case I was not, in my own judgment, driven to this ground—In my opinion I violated no law—The provision of the Constitution that 'The previlege of the writ of habeas corpus, shall not be suspended unless when, in cases of rebellion or invasion, the public safety may require it' is equivalent to a provision—is a provision—that such previlege may be suspended when, in cases of rebellion, or invasion, the public safety *does* require it. I decided that we have a case of rebellion, and that the public safety does require the qualified suspension of the previlege of the writ of habeas corpus, which I authorized to be made. Now it is insisted that Congress, and not the executive, is vested with this power—But the Constitution itself, is silent as to which, or who, is to exercise the power; and as the provision plainly was made for a dangerous emergency, I can not bring myself to believe that the framers of that instrument intended that in every case the danger should run it's course until Congress could be called together, the very assembling of which might be prevented, as was intended in this case, by the rebellion."[115]

Lincoln had a good argument, for Congress in that era was often out of session, and an invasion or rebellion might well take place during one of its long recesses, just as had occurred in April. Clearly, in the case of Maryland that spring, emergency conditions prevailed. Joel Parker, professor of constitutional law at Harvard, observed a few months later that if Taney's interpretation of the Constitution were adopted, "the judicial power may be made quite as effectual to overthrow the government in time of war as the suspension of the *habeas corpus,* by order of the President, in time of peace, could be to overthrow the liberties of the people,—somewhat more so, indeed, as the effect of the latter could be more readily and securely avoided."[116] The eminent Philadelphia attorney Horace Binney issued a pamphlet criticizing Taney's opinion for "a tone, not to say a ring, of disaffection to the President, and to the Northern and Western side of his house, which it is not comfortable to suppose in the person who fills the central seat of impersonal justice." He maintained that Congress could not on its own *suspend* the privilege of the writ but could only *authorize* its suspension by the executive branch.[117] In another widely circulated pamphlet, former U.S. Attorney General Reverdy Johnson refuted the arguments of his fellow Marylander, Taney.

Taney's reasoning was indeed flawed. He argued that since the provision regarding habeas corpus appears in the Constitution's first article, which deals with the powers of Congress, the legislative branch, not the executive, was empowered to suspend the writ. But he failed to note that the original draft of that article stated that the "privileges and benefit of the Writ of Habeas Corpus shall be enjoyed in this Government in the most expeditious and ample manner; and shall not be suspended by the Legislature except upon the most urgent and pressing occasions, and for a limited time not exceeding _____ months." Later Gouverneur Morris revised it to read as it did in the ratified version of the Constitution. By replacing the original language with Morris's substitute, the framers implicitly rejected the notion that Congress alone was authorized to suspend the privilege.[118]

In his July 4 message, Lincoln did not explore the subject further but promised to submit a lengthy opinion by the attorney general. On July 5, Bates provided him such a document, which was forwarded to Congress the following week. It maintained that "if we are at liberty to understand the phrase ['the suspension of the privilege of the writ of habeas corpus'] to mean that in case of a great and dangerous rebellion like the present the public safety requires the arrest and confinement of persons implicated in that rebellion, I . . . declare the opinion that the President has lawful power to suspend the privilege of person's arrested under such circumstances; for he is especially charged by the Constitution with the 'public safety,' and he is the sole judge of the emergency which requires his prompt action."[119]

In 1862, a federal circuit court ruled in *ex parte Field* that the Militia Act of 1795 (authorizing the president to summon troops for the suppression of rebels) implicitly empowered him to suspend habeas corpus. Half a century later, the Supreme Court in *Moyer vs. Peabody* indirectly upheld the circuit court's reasoning in the *Field* case. Thus, Lincoln acted constitutionally in suspending habeas corpus where insurrection was actually taking place and in the absence of Congressional action forbidding him to do so.

In August, Congress, by a near-unanimous vote, approved a resolution stating that "all the acts, proclamations and orders of the President . . . [after March 4, 1861] respecting the army and navy of the United States, and calling out or relating to the militia or volunteers from the States, are hereby approved in all respects legalized and made valid . . . as if they had been issued and done under the previous express authority and direction of the Congress of the United States."[120] Two years later, the Supreme Court upheld this unorthodox procedure in the *Prize Cases*, involving a plaintiff who argued that the blockade was illegal from the time Lincoln announced it until July, when Congress in effect declared war. Upholding the blockade and all other emergency measures taken by Lincoln in the first weeks of the war, a bare five-man majority of the court ruled in the administration's favor.

Despite his early foray into extraconstitutionality, Lincoln generally respected constitutional restraints. In fact, political opponents for the most part were allowed free rein to criticize the administration; the press was rarely censored, even when editors called for the president's assassination; elections were conducted freely and fairly, with some bending of the rules in Border States; courts remained open; and, with one exception, legislatures met unimpeded. When urged to confiscate Southern property in the North, Lincoln replied: "No, gentleman, never." To rejoinders that the Confederates seized Northern property, he said: "They can afford to do a wrong—I cannot."[121] Democrats, however, railed against what they called the "irresponsible despotism of Abraham Lincoln!"[122] It was to become a standard shibboleth in future political campaigns.

Keeping Kentucky in the Union

Lincoln worried a great deal about Kentucky. During the first year and a half of the war, his most important policies were largely shaped to keep that state loyal. "I think to lose Kentucky, is nearly the same as to lose the whole game," he told his friend Orville H. Browning. "Kentucky gone, we can not hold Missouri, nor, as I think, Maryland. These all against us, and the job on our hands is too large for us. We would as well consent to separation at once, including the surrender of this capitol."[123] He allegedly said that to win the war he "*wanted* God on his side, but he *must* have Kentucky."[124] His concern was understandable, for the Bluegrass State ranked ninth in the nation in terms of population, seventh in terms of farm value, and fifth in terms of livestock value. Her men, horses, mules, grain, fruit, hay, hemp, and flax would all be valuable assets to whichever side Kentucky favored. Geographically she occupied a crucial location; Northern armies would have to pass through her to get at Tennessee, Mississippi, and Alabama. From Kentucky, Southern troops could establish a formidable defensive barrier along the Ohio and even penetrate the Midwest.

To retain his native state in the Union, Lincoln exercised preternatural tact, especially in dealing with slavery. In late April, he assured Kentucky Senator Garrett Davis, a strong Unionist, that the administration's intentions were not aggressive. He said he had "determined, that, until the meeting of Congress [on July 4], he would make no attempt to retake the forts, &c." but "would leave the then existing state of things to be considered and acted upon by Congress, unless he should be constrained to depart from that purpose by the continued military operations of the seceded States." Alluding to slavery, he added that he "intended to make no attack, direct or indirect, upon the institutions or property of any State; but, on the contrary, would defend them to the full extent with which the Constitution and laws of Congress have vested in the President with the power. And that he did not intend to invade with an armed force, or make any military or naval movement against any State, unless she or her people should make it necessary by a formidable resistance of the authority and laws of the United States. That if Kentucky or her citizens should seize Newport, it would become his duty and he might attempt to retake it; but he contemplated no military operations that would make it necessary to move any troops over her territories—though he had the unquestioned right at all times to march the U.S. troops into and over any and every State." Lincoln assured Davis that "if Kentucky made no demonstration of force against the United States he would not molest her." Lincoln voiced regret that the Bluegrass State had spurned his call for troops and had "not acted up to the principle of her great statesmen" like Henry Clay and to the platform "for which she cast her vote in the late Presidential election, 'the Union, the Constitution, and the Enforcement of the Laws.'"[125] (John Bell had carried Kentucky in 1860.)

When urged to send troops into Kentucky to defend persecuted Unionists, Lincoln replied: "I am exceedingly anxious to protect the Union men, and have taken all proper measures to do so, as well in Kentucky as in Tennessee, but I am the head of a great nation, and must be governed by wide forethought, as far as possible. I will illustrate my position by the fable of the farmer who returned home and found that, while his two little children were asleep, a number of snakes has taken part possession of the bed. He could not strike the snakes without endangering his offspring, and, therefore, he had to stay his hand."[126] But, he added, "I do not want to act in a hurry about this matter; I don't want to hurt anybody in Kentucky, but I will get the serpent out of Tennessee."[127]

Soon after the firing on Fort Sumter, Kentucky's legislature and its governor, the pro-secession Beriah Magoffin, expressed a wish to have their state remain neutral, in effect becoming an American Switzerland. At the very least, Lincoln told former Congressman Warner L. Underwood of Kentucky, he hoped the state "would stand by the Government in the present difficulties, but if she would not do that, let her stand still and take no hostile part against it, and that no hostile step should tread her soil."[128] Sometimes Lincoln employed humor to deflate Kentuckians' pleas for neutrality. In July, he told Judge George Robertson of Lexington "that neutrality did not become any of the friends of the government,—that while the citizen enjoyed his rights and the protection of the laws, he must also recognize his obligations and his duties." He then had a friend relate a joke about the British minister to Prussia who tried to enlist the Germans to support Great Britain in its wars. Frederick the Great politely refused. Later, the monarch at a state dinner offered that diplomat some capon. "No, sir," came the reply, "I decline having anything to do with *neutral animals!*"[129]

Occasionally, Lincoln would be less gentle with Kentuckians. When a state senator protested against Union troops occupying Cairo, Illinois (across the Ohio River from the Blue Grass State), Lincoln had John Hay pen a sarcastic response: "The President directs me to say that the views so ably stated by you shall have due consideration: and to assure you that he would certainly never have ordered the movement of troops, complained of, had he known that Cairo was in your Senatorial district."[130]

To placate Kentuckians, Lincoln honored the state's neutrality, though he regarded it as unrealistic. On July 4, he stated in his message to Congress that within the Border States "there are those who favor a policy which they call 'armed neutrality:' that is, an arming of those States to prevent the Union forces passing one way, or the disunion, the other, over their soil. This would be disunion completed. Figuratively speaking, it would be the building of an impassable wall along the line of separation—and yet, not quite an impassable one; for, under the guise of neutrality, it would tie the hands of the Union men, and freely pass supplies from among them to the insurrectionists, which it could not do as an open enemy. At a stroke, it would take all the trouble off the hands of secession, except only what proceeds from the external blockade. It would do for the disunionists that which, of all things, they most desire—feed them well, and give them disunion without a struggle of their own. It recognizes no fidelity to the Constitution, no obligation to maintain the Union; and while very many who have favored it are, doubtless, loyal citizens, it is, nevertheless, treason in effect."[131] Kentucky Unionists protested mildly that Lincoln misunderstood the reasons their state favored neutrality.

A week after expressing his misgivings about "armed neutrality," Lincoln was visited by Simon Bolivar Buckner, head of the pro-Confederate Kentucky State Guard militia, who said during a cordial interview that his state was justified because Lincoln had "confessedly violated the constitution, and, therefore, had no right to call upon Kentucky to aid him in this violation; and that, even if his acts were justified, as he claimed, by necessity, the same cause, when it was a question of internal peace in Kentucky, would justify the attitude she had assumed." The president replied that while he considered it his duty to suppress the insurrection, he wished to do so "with the least possible disturbance, or annoyance to well disposed people anywhere. So far I have not sent an armed force into Kentucky; nor have I any present purpose to do so. I sincerely desire that no necessity for it may be presented; but I mean to say nothing which shall hereafter embarrass me in the performance of what may seem to be my duty." Buckner reported that Lincoln "succeeded in impressing upon me the belief, that, 'as long as there are roads around Kentucky,' to reach the rebellion, it was his purpose to leave her unmolested, not yielding her right to the position she occupied, but observing it as a matter of policy."[132] A few weeks later, Lincoln offered Buckner a generalship, which the West Pointer declined; soon thereafter he assumed that rank in the Confederate army.

Although he refrained from sending troops into the Bluegrass State, Lincoln recommended to a group of Southern Unionists that young men in that state must be organized to resist Governor Magoffin, whose views were unrepresentative of most Kentuckians. To facilitate such resistance, he established a military presence at Newport, under the command of Robert Anderson, who was empowered to recruit volunteer regiments from both Kentucky and western Virginia. That appointment was shrewd, for, as Joshua Speed told Lincoln, Anderson's "name & lineage will give us [Unionists] great strength."[133] (An ardent Unionist, Speed proved invaluable in the effort to keep his state loyal. To Joseph Holt he expressed a keen desire "that my most intimate friend Mr Lincoln, who I shall ever regard as one of the best & purest men I have ever known, should be the instrument in the hands of God for the reconstruction of this great republic.")[134] In July, the president authorized Navy Lieutenant William "Bull" Nelson, then on loan to the army, to enlist Kentuckians. Lincoln also arranged with Speed to smuggle weapons into the state, including 20,000 rifles, which became known as "Lincoln guns." General George B. McClellan, in charge of the Department of the Ohio, told the president that, according to leading Kentucky Unionists, "the effect [of distributing arms] has been extremely beneficial, not only in giving strength to the Union party & discouraging the secessionists, but that it has proved to the minds of all reasonable men that the

Genl Govt has confidence in their loyalty & entertains no intention of subjugating them."[135]

Lincoln also dispatched able officers to Kentucky to lead the state's Unionist military forces. One was Captain Richard W. Johnson, a West Point graduate and native of the state. When Johnson applied for leave from the regular army to join the Kentucky Volunteers, he was denied, for the War Department felt acutely the need for professional officers. Lincoln called on Adjutant General Lorenzo Thomas and said: "I would like to have a leave of absence granted to my Confederate friend, Captain Johnson, to enable him to accept the position of lieutenant-colonel of a Kentucky cavalry regiment."

"It cannot be done," replied Thomas.

"But," rejoined Lincoln, straightening up until he seemed twice his normal height, "I have not come over to discuss this question with you, General Thomas, but to order you to give the necessary instructions." Captain Johnson obtained his leave then and there.[136]

On June 20, Lincoln's delicate cultivation of Kentucky paid off when Unionists captured nine of the state's ten congressional seats. The loyal candidates received a total of 92,460 votes and their opponents 37,700. Seven weeks later Unionists scored another triumph, winning 103 of the 138 seats in the General Assembly. On the heels of that August 5 Unionist triumph, Lieutenant Nelson established Camp Dick Robinson between Louisville and Danville, a move prompting Governor Magoffin to complain that the state's neutrality had been violated. In response, Lincoln explained that "there is a military force in camp within Kentucky, acting by authority of the United States, which force is not very large, and is not now being augmented. I also believe that some arms have been furnished to this force by the United States. I also believe this force consists exclusively of Kentuckians, having their camp in the immediate vicinity of their own homes, and not assailing, or menacing, any of the good people of Kentucky. In all I have done in the premises, I have acted upon the urgent solicitation of many Kentuckians, and in accordance with what I believed, and still believe, to be the wish of a majority of all the Union-loving people of Kentucky." Therefore, he declined to remove the camp. In closing, Lincoln gently but firmly chided the governor: "I most cordially sympathize with your Excellency, in the wish to preserve the peace of my own native State, Kentucky; but it is with regret I search, and can not find, in your not very short letter, any declaration, or intimation, that you entertain any desire for the preservation of the Federal Union."[137]

Kentucky's neutrality abruptly ended on September 3, when the willful Confederate General Leonidas Polk rashly occupied Columbus on the Mississippi River, prompting Union troops under U. S. Grant to seize Paducah. Polk's action resembled the blunder South Carolinians had made by attacking Fort Sumter; just as their bombardment had solidified the North and reduced the chances that the Border States would secede, the Confederate invasion of Kentucky helped secure that state to the Union. The General Assembly demanded the withdrawal of Polk's troops but not Grant's.

Keeping Missouri in the Union

In his effort to keep Missouri from seceding, Lincoln faced severe obstacles. With approximately 1.2 million residents, it was the most populous state in the Trans-Mississippi West. Its proximity to Kansas, Kentucky, and southern Illinois made it strategically important, if not as vital as Maryland and the Blue Grass State. Governor Claiborne F. Jackson, a secessionist who had denounced the president's troop requisition as "illegal, unconstitutional, and revolutionary," plotted to seize the St. Louis arsenal and distribute its muskets, powder, and cartridges to Confederate volunteers.[138] Opposing him were two impetuous Unionists, Congressman Frank Blair and Captain Nathaniel Lyon. At the end of April, the president authorized Lyon to enroll 10,000 Missourians into the army and to declare martial law in St. Louis. This action was highly irregular, but General Scott endorsed it because the times were "revolutionary."[139] On May 10, the headstrong Lyon, acting without authorization from Washington, thwarted Jackson's plans by capturing the governor's pro-secessionist militia before it could aid the Confederacy.

Lyon's rash act did not sit well with Lincoln, who wished to tread cautiously in Missouri. In early May, he told Charles Gibson, a judge of the court of claims and a political ally of Attorney General Bates, that "if he was compelled to send men from one side of Missouri to the other[,] which he did not anticipate[,] he would rather send them around than through the State in order to avoid any trouble. No troops will be sent to Missouri from other States. In short everything tending to arouse the jealousy of the people will be avoided."[140]

The president's desire to maintain calm was not shared by the young duo of Lyon and Blair, who claimed that the lethargic and complacent General William S. Harney, commander of the Department of the West, was hampering them. On May 21, Harney reached an agreement with Confederate General Sterling Price, in effect committing the Lincoln administration to treat Missouri as neutral. This act alarmed St. Louis Unionists, who feared that it would only postpone a day of reckoning and thus allow the secessionists to gird for it.

But Harney's move did not stop the informal warfare being waged by pro-Confederate forces. Indignant at the continuing violence against Missouri Unionists, Lincoln heatedly instructed Harney to end it. "The professions of loyalty to the Union by the State authorities of Missouri are not to be relied upon," he had Adjutant General Lorenzo B. Thomas inform Harney. "They have already falsified their professions too often, and are too far committed to secession to be entitled to your confidence, and you can only be sure of their desisting from their wicked purposes when it is out of their power to prosecute them. You will therefore be unceasingly watchful of their movements, and not permit the clamors of their partizans and opponents of the wise measures already taken to prevent you from checking every movement against the government, however disguised under the pretended State authority. The authority of the United States is paramount, and whenever it is apparent that a movement, whether by color of State authority or not, is hostile, you will not hesitate to put it down."[141]

When Blair recommended that Harney be transferred, Lincoln authorized him to do so only if it seemed absolutely necessary. "We have a good deal of anxiety here about St. Louis," he told the congressman on May 18. While it was important to protect friends of the government, if Harney were removed precipitously it would cause harm, especially since he had already been relieved of command in April and reinstated shortly thereafter. "We better have him a *friend* than an *enemy*," Lincoln wrote. "It will dissatisfy a good many who otherwise would be quiet. More than all, we first relieved him, then restored him, & now if we relieve him again, the public will ask, 'why all this vacillation.'"[142] Ignoring this counsel, Blair on May 30 used his authority to replace Harney with Lyon. That young captain led his troops westward toward Jefferson City, where Governor Jackson and General Sterling Price had assembled a pro-Confederate militia. As Lyon approached, Jackson and Price retreated, leaving the state's capital in Union hands. In July, a new provisional government was formed, with the conservative Unionist Hamilton R. Gamble as its governor. He proclaimed Missouri loyal to the Union and won the acquiescence of much of the state as well as official recognition from the Lincoln administration. In August, regular Confederate forces won the battle of Wilson's Creek, where Lyon was killed. But in March 1862 at the battle of Pea Ridge, Arkansas, the Rebels were defeated; thereafter, armed resistance to federal authority in Missouri took the form of widespread guerrilla warfare and savage bushwhacking. Missouri remained in the Union throughout the war.

Protecting Unionists in Western Virginia

When Unionists in western Virginia, a region culturally and economically distinct from the eastern portion of the state, appealed to Lincoln for help, he complied promptly. Federal control of that area was important, for through it passed the main rail line connecting the eastern seaboard with the Midwest (the Baltimore and Ohio). In addition, it shielded eastern Ohio, western Pennsylvania, and eastern Kentucky. Unionists there planned to move the seat of government from Richmond west of the Alleghenies, or else cut themselves off from the eastern portion of the state and become a separate entity. On May 1, at Lincoln's invitation, a committee from Butler County called at the White House, where they asked for $100,000 and 5,000 rifles. Influential Republicans urged the president to honor the request. Edwin M. Stanton wrote a legal brief justifying the transfer of federal arms to private parties in Virginia and pledged all his personal assets as bond to guarantee that the weapons would be used properly. Cameron saw to it that they were dispatched to the trans-Appalachian Virginia loyalists. Massachusetts Governor John A. Andrew also provided some weaponry from his state's arsenal.

After Virginia voters ratified an ordinance of secession on May 23, more forceful measures were required. The following day, when Congressman John S. Carlile of Clarksburg demanded that troops be sent into the Kanawha and Monongahela valleys, Lincoln replied: "we will help you."[143] Indeed, Ohio and Indiana troops promptly crossed the Ohio River and marched toward Wheeling. In June, Unionists held a convention and formed "the Reorganized Government of Virginia," purporting to represent the entire Old Dominion, with Francis Pierpont as its governor. On June 25, Lincoln, through Cameron, said he that he "never supposed that a brave and free people, though surprised and unarmed, could long be subjugated by a class of political adventurers always adverse to them, and the fact that they have already rallied, reorganized their government, and checked the march of these invaders demonstrates how justly he appreciated them."[144] The following month Lincoln recognized the new government's legitimacy; he had worked behind the scenes to come up with this plan instead of granting the Unionists' wish to establish a new state, a move he considered premature. Eighteen months later, however, he did approve that proposal.

Discouraging European Recognition of the Confederacy

While laboring to retain the Border States, Lincoln did not lose sight of another danger: the possible intervention of European nations, especially Great Britain, on behalf of the Confederacy. Even before the fall of Sumter, the British and French governments warned that if the administration cut off trade with the South, their major supplier of cotton, they might well recognize Jefferson Davis's government. Such a step would enable the Rebels to negotiate military and commercial treaties, to gain access to European ports, and thus to win the war. The matter came up immediately after hostilities began. In response to Lincoln's April 19 and 27 declarations of intent to blockade Southern ports, Queen Victoria on May 13 issued a Proclamation of Neutrality, granting the Confederacy belligerent status (but not official recognition), entitling it to employ privateers and take prizes to British ports, to borrow money from Great Britain, to obtain weapons from her, and to have commerce raiders built in her shipyards.

This was a premature act, for British shipping was in no immediate danger; the North could not begin to enforce a blockade for many months, and few Southern vessels could effectively serve as privateers. Moreover, Lincoln had not proclaimed a blockade but merely announced his intention to establish one. Still, the president's declarations, indicating that a real war was underway between two belligerents, necessitated some response from maritime powers like Great Britain. Prime Minister Palmerston, eager to avoid entanglement in the American Civil War, reminded his cabinet that "[t]hey who in quarrels interpose will often get a bloody nose" and that "[i]f you would keep out of strife, step not 'twixt man and wife."[145] The way to "keep out of strife," it seemed to Palmerston, was to declare neutrality. Charles Francis Adams, who arrived in London the very day that the queen's proclamation appeared in the press, objected that the document was hasty and that it indicated partiality toward the Confederates, giving them hope that they might well be recognized as an independent nation. The outraged North shared his inaccurate interpretation of the neutrality proclamation. The misunderstanding helped sour diplomatic relations between the two countries.

Seward indignantly remonstrated with Lord Lyons not only about the proclamation but also the willingness of Foreign Secretary John Russell to meet informally with Confederate commissioners. Privately, the secretary of state cursed the British ministry: "God damn them, I'll give them hell. I'm no more afraid of them, than I am of Robert Toombs."[146] (This reaction seemed excessive, coming from a man who had met informally with Confederate commissioners two months earlier.) With equal truculence, Seward on May 21 penned such a bellicose a dispatch to Charles Francis Adams that Lincoln felt compelled to moderate it, lest it provoke a war. (Years earlier the impulsive Seward confessed: "I love to write what I think and feel as it comes up.")[147] According to the Russian minister to the United States, Seward continued to believe that "the Unionist party in the South is quite strong and awaits only the presence of federal troops to declare itself" and that a foreign war would induce the seceded states to return to the fold.[148]

Upon receiving Seward's intemperate draft, the president consulted with the chairman of the Senate Foreign Relations Committee, Charles Sumner, who was shocked at the secretary's recklessness. The senator urged Lincoln to "watch him and overrule him" and recommended that the dispatch be toned down.[149] Just as Seward had moderated Lincoln's inaugural, so Lincoln did the same for Seward's instructions. He also condensed the document, for he considered Seward's style "too verbose—too much like 'machine writing.'"[150] When Seward composed the dispatch, he had not yet learned of the queen's proclamation, but he did know about Russell's willingness to confer with Confederate envoys and that the British and French had agreed to act in concert when dealing with the American Civil War.

Lincoln softened Seward's language at several points:

"The President regrets" instead of "The President is surprised and grieved"
"Such intercourse would be none the less hurtful to us" instead of "Such intercourse would be none the less wrongful to us"
"No one of these proceedings will pass unnoticed by the United States" instead of "No one of these proceedings will be borne by the United States"
Most importantly, Lincoln recommended that the dispatch contain the following sentence: "This paper is for your own guidance only, and not be read, or shown to any one" instead of several belligerent sentences closing the letter.[151]

Seward took many but not all of Lincoln's suggestions, effectively defanging and declawing the original ultimatum. (Seward intended to have Adams submit the remonstrance to John Russell and then suspend diplomatic relations until the ministry ended contact of any kind with the Southern commissioners.) Even in its modified version, the document astounded Adams, who confided to his diary that the Lincoln administration appeared "almost ready to declare war with all the powers of Europe. . . . I scarcely know how to understand Mr Seward." It appeared to him "like throwing the game into the hands of the enemy."[152] If he had delivered the document to Russell, it would, Adams thought, have ended his mission. Henry Adams, the minister's son and secretary, thought the dispatch "so arrogant in tone and so extraordinary and unparalleled in its demands that it leaves no doubt in my mind that our Government wishes to face a war with all Europe. That is the inevitable result of any attempt to carry out the spirit or the letter of these directions, and such a war is regarded in the dispatch itself as the probable result." Seward's policy was "shallow madness." Young Adams was "shocked and horrified by supposing Seward, a man I've admired and respected beyond most men, guilty of what seems to me so wicked and criminal a course as this."[153] He would have been even more horrified if he had read Seward's original draft.

Minister Adams tactfully summarized the document to Lord Russell, who explained that he had seen the Confederate emissaries only twice and had no intention of holding a third interview. Thus did Lincoln, with the assistance of Sumner and Adams, help defuse what could have been a diplomatic crisis leading to war with Great Britain. In late June, Sumner rejoiced that Seward "has changed immensely during the last month, & is now mild & gentle."[154] Following this episode, Lincoln came to rely more and more on Sumner for advice regarding foreign affairs.

The relationship between the senator and the president was a curious one, for initially Lincoln impressed Sumner as undignified, socially inept, and uncultured. When they first met, the president suggested that they "measure backs," but Sumner declined, pompously stating that it was time "for uniting our fronts against the enemy and not our backs." Lincoln allegedly remarked later, "I have never had much to do with bishops where I live, but, do you know, Sumner is my idea of a bishop." Sumner told Carl Schurz that he found Lincoln a puzzle. According to Schurz, the senator "could hardly understand this Western product of American democracy." Sumner was able to detect "flashes of thought and bursts of illuminating expression" in Lincoln's conversation, but because the senator lacked a sense of humor, "he often lost Lincoln's keenest points" and had difficulty shaking the belief that such a "seemingly untutored child of nature" could meet the challenges he faced. But because the president seemed to him a deeply committed opponent of slavery, and since abolition was Sumner's main concern, he overcame his misgivings. Despite the widespread belief that two such different men would be unable to cooperate, they generally did so because they respected one another's sincerity.[155]

Preparing the Army to Fight

Thanks to Northern outrage at the bombardment of Fort Sumter and to the energetic leadership of some governors, raising an army proved easy; training, equipping, arming, feeding, and supplying it, however, did not. For decades, Congress and state governments had neglected the military so badly that the North had great difficulty mobilizing its vast resources swiftly. Compounding the problem was the general lack of organizational sophistication throughout the economy and society. The United States, still an immature country in many ways, had few men and institutions experienced in organizing large-scale enterprises of any kind. Nowhere was such backwardness more evident than in the War Department, with its aged and small staff, antiquated rules, and stifling bureaucracy. As men eagerly enlisted, their requests for weapons, uniforms, and equipment overwhelmed Cameron and his bureau chiefs. They responded to urgent appeals so slowly that a few governors (notably John A. Andrew of Massachusetts, Andrew G. Curtin of Pennsylvania, Edwin D. Morgan of New York, and Oliver P. Morton of Indiana) took matters into their own hands, purchasing necessary paraphernalia at home and abroad.

Governor Morton repeatedly clamored for weapons. Warning of a possible invasion of Kentucky from Tennessee, he requested heavy ordnance to guard Indiana along the Ohio River and predicted an attack on Louisville. In September, Lincoln told telegraph operators at the War Department, "Morton is a good fellow, but at times he is the skeerdest man I know of."[156] And so Lincoln wrote the Indiana governor explaining the delay in supplying weapons: "I wish you to believe of us (as we certainly believe of you) that we are doing the very best we can. You do not receive arms from us as fast as you need them; but it is because we have not near enough to meet all the pressing demands; and we are obliged to share around what we have, sending the larger share to the points which appear to need them most. We have great hope that our own supply will be ample before long, so that you and all others can have as many as you need. . . . As to Kentucky, you do not estimate that state as more important than I do; but I am compelled to watch all points. While I write this I am, if not in *range,* at least in *hearing* of cannon-shot, from an army of enemies more than a hundred thousand strong. I do not expect them to capture this city; but I *know* they would, if I were to send the men and arms from here, to defend Louisville, of which there is not a single hostile armed soldier within forty miles, nor any force known to be moving upon it from any distance."[157]

Cameron authorized his henchman Alexander Cummings, a journalist and political operator, to buy war material in New York. Unlike the governors, Cummings spent money foolishly, paying far too much for horses, pistols, muskets, and rifles. He also purchased uniforms and blankets made of shoddy, a form of material that dissolved in the rain and came apart in high winds, and shoes and boots that quickly wore out. Fraud marred Cummings's dealings, prompting Congress to investigate and denounce him.

Corrupt quartermasters also cheated the government. One of the more flagrant examples was Reuben B. Hatch, brother of Lincoln's close friend Ozias M. Hatch. Operating out of Cairo, Illinois, as an assistant quartermaster on Ulysses S. Grant's staff, Hatch bought coal and lumber and then submitted inflated bills for their purchase, pocketing the difference between what he actually paid and what he received from the government. In addition, he sold the government horses and mules that had been seized from the enemy. Another example was General Justus McKinstry, Frémont's willful quartermaster in St. Louis, who was court-martialed and cashiered for defrauding the government of hundreds of thousands of dollars.

In addition to the resourceful governors, other civilians did yeoman work in helping to offset the War Department's inadequacy. Among them were William M. Evarts, Richard Blatchford, and Moses Grinnell of New York, who together received $2 million in government funds to buy military supplies. From one area of American life with significant organizational savvy—railroad corporations—came Thomas A. Scott to assist the beleaguered Cameron. Assuming the post of assistant secretary of war, this vice-president of the Pennsylvania Railroad efficiently reformed procedures, got rid of deadwood, and dramatically improved the functioning of the department, especially its handling of railroads. Lincoln was highly complimentary of Scott's work. Aiding Scott was Edward S. Sanford, president of the American Telegraph Company, who performed equally well after taking charge of military telegraphs. In New York, leading citizens established the Union Defence Committee, which significantly helped to raise men and money for the war effort. Dorothea Dix, renowned champion of reform in the treatment of the insane, organized a capable nursing corps. Assisting her was the U.S. Sanitary Commission, a volunteer organization established to protect and promote the health of the army.

Some military men stepped forward to fill the vacuum created by the War Department's ineptitude. The elderly General John E. Wool seized the initiative without waiting for department approval. His meritorious efforts in procuring arms and ammunition came to a halt when Cameron, allegedly at the behest of corrupt contractors, ordered him to resume his routine duties. Also efficient was Montgomery C. Meigs, a West Pointer who became quartermaster general in mid-June over the objections of Cameron. Francis P. Blair, Sr., described Meigs as a soldier with "energy, industry, knowledge of the wants of an army" as well as "zeal in the course [that] our army is about to vindicate" and "probity, punctuality & strong common sense in dealing with men."[158] In urging his appointment, Lincoln told General Scott: "I have come to know Col. Meigs quite well for a short acquaintance, and, so far as I am capable of judging I do not know one who combines the qualities of masculine intellect, learning and experience of the right sort, and physical power of labor and endurance so well as he."[159] Scott agreed, praising Meigs for his "high genius, science, vigor & administrative capacities."[160]

Cameron was clearly not up to his job. A political wheeler-dealer, he reveled in distributing patronage and awarding contracts to allies; he devoted more attention to those congenial chores than readying the nation to fight. Meigs found him "weak and infirm of purpose."[161] In August, the ethnologist George Gibbs assembled an astounding number of charges against the war secretary: he found that Cameron failed to obtain vital information about troop strength and distribution; ignored credible warnings about treasonous officers; provided inadequate support for the troops who poured into Washington in the early weeks of the war; recruited and mustered in three-years men lackadaisically; unreasonably delayed supplying transportation, animals, weapons, medicine, and artillery to the troops; awarded contracts to inept family members and political cronies; ordered inadequate inspection of food and clothing; issued and then countermanded orders carelessly; and generally mismanaged his department. In short, Gibbs concluded, Cameron had "shown neither foresight nor energy. He has had no comprehensive plan, if he has any plan at all. He has not devoted himself to military duties, but to contracts which belonged properly to the regular departments. Neither in capacity nor in character is he fitted for his place."[162] By late summer, public opinion had soured on Cameron more because of his unsuitable appointments than his questionable contracts.

Lincoln also made some blunders as the mobilization effort got under way. He was partly distracted by ongoing patronage squabbles, with Seward and Cameron leading the way as they lobbied on behalf of friends. On April 13, when the slate of

Philadelphia appointments was announced, the president told a Pennsylvania congressman he was greatly relieved to get that chore out of the way and "hoped now to be able to devote his attention exclusively to the condition of the country."[163] But contentious New Yorkers gave him little rest. A month after the bombardment of Fort Sumter, Lincoln felt "as though several thousand pounds weight" had been removed by the appointment of a slate for the Empire State.[164]

No sooner had civilian patronage been distributed than a great clamor arose for military positions. Especially coveted were paymasterships, with the rank of major, good pay, and little danger of being killed. Once again Illinoisans descended in shoals. In early 1862, Lincoln told Orville H. Browning that their state "has already had more than her share," that "complaints are made about it," and "that he cannot appoint any more Pay Masters there." Browning advised one importunate constituent: "I do not know of any thing in the way of an office to dispose of and there are certainly fifty applicants for every one at the disposal of the Government. There are a good many applicants here from Illinois, who have been pressing their claims all winter, without success. I know of no more unpromising business at present than the pursuit of office."[165]

As he distributed military patronage, Lincoln exasperated the governors by allowing ambitious politicos to raise regiments independently and by accepting them into service while Cameron was turning away units recruited in accordance with state regulations. A case in point was Daniel Sickles, the wealthy New York ex-congressman who had achieved notoriety just before the war by murdering his wife's lover (the son of Francis Scott Key) and then escaping punishment on a plea of temporary insanity. After Sickles claimed that he had raised enough men to constitute a brigade, New York Governor Edwin D. Morgan refused to give such a controversial man a brigadier general's commission. (Thurlow Weed warned Lincoln that Sickles was close to high-ranking men of suspect loyalty.) When Sickles asked the president if he would tolerate those hindering his efforts, Lincoln replied: "I like that idea of United States Volunteers" rather than state militia. "But you see where it leads to. What will the governors say if I raise regiments without their having a hand in it?" Cameron endorsed Sickles's plan, and Lincoln went along, saying to the acquitted killer on May 16: "whatever are the obstacles thrown in your way, come to me, and I will remove them promptly. Should you stand in need of my assistance to hasten the organization of your brigade come to me again, and I will give or do whatever is required. I want your men, General, and you are the man to lead them. Go to the Secretary of War and get your instructions immediately."[166] At Lincoln's insistence, Sickles received his commission.

At that same time, Morgan was indignant at Cameron's reluctance to accept many regiments already mustered in. When the governor complained about the War Department's confusion, Lincoln replied: "The enthusiastic uprising of the people in our cause, is our great reliance; and we can not safely give it any check, even though it overflows, and runs in channels not laid down in any chart."[167] The president settled the matter by appointing Morgan a major general of volunteers and placing him in command of the Department of New York. In November, when Colonel William H.

Allen of the First New York Volunteers, who had been dismissed for insubordination, asked Lincoln to reinstate him, the president replied: "I cannot afford to enter into a controversy with the Governor of a State that I rely upon more than any other to assist in putting down this terrible rebellion, and you must say as much to General Wool, and tell him that I say he must fix it up with Governor Morgan."[168]

In matters military, Lincoln said he relied on General Scott, but the poor health and advanced years of that septuagenarian hero hardly fitted him to meet the challenge posed by a conflict far vaster than anything he had known during either the War of 1812 or the Mexican War. So Lincoln gradually began to depend more on his own judgment. In August 1861, to facilitate the enlistment of volunteers, he issued an order eliminating much red tape. Commenting on this step, a journalist remarked that the president "is daily growing up to the altitude of his position, and with every hour learns more and more to comprehend his duties and his responsibilities."[169] That summer the president acknowledged that his administration had "stumbled along" but thought that on the whole it had done so "in the right direction."[170]

Annual Message: Defining War Aims, Explaining Actions

As July 4 approached, Lincoln put the finishing touches on his message to Congress, one of his most significant and eloquent state papers. For weeks he had been considering carefully what he wanted to say. On May 7, John Hay noted that his boss "is engaged in constant thought upon his Message: It will be an exhaustive review of the questions of the hour & of the future."[171] And so it was. Later that month, the president said that he was so frequently interrupted by visitors that "he shall be fortunate if he gets time to finish the message before the 4th of July."[172] From mid-June until Congress assembled, he devoted virtually all his waking hours to the message and received no callers other than cabinet members or other high-ranking officials. He revised his first draft extensively, incorporating many suggestions offered by Seward. When, however, the public printer suggested that "sugar-coated" was too undignified a term for use in such a formal address, Lincoln replied: "No, let it stand; it is a word the people use; they will know what it means."[173] As he considered how much money and how many men to request, he consulted members of Congress and corresponded with governors. Before submitting the message, he went over it in detail with the cabinet and read it to Charles Sumner.

While solicitous of congressional opinion, Lincoln did not adhere to the Whig notion that the executive branch must defer to the legislature and merely carry out its wishes. Though he occasionally paid lip service to that doctrine, his actions belied his words. He was an assertive, if tactful, president, unafraid to use the powers of his office to achieve victory in the war and unwilling to be cowed by governors, generals, cabinet members, newspaper editors, congressmen, senators, or anyone else.

On Independence Day, Lincoln reviewed a military parade and introduced various cabinet members and generals to a huge crowd gathered before the White House. When asked to speak himself, he modestly declined, saying: "I appear at your call, not to make a speech. I have made a great many dry and dull ones. Now I must fall back and say that the dignity of my position does not permit me to expose myself any more. I can now take shelter and listen to others."[174] (A slightly different version of these remarks had him say: "I have made a great many poor speeches, and now feel relieved that my dignity does not permit me to be a public speaker.")[175] Such unassuming modesty pleased the public. A Missourian who observed the president receive callers detected in him "no airs of assumed or hereditary dignity, nor stiffness, nor carrying the importance of the Presidential office into every day acts. His reception of men is cordial and unaffected, and his manner devoid of any personal claim for respect from the office he holds." Even his appearance on the streets of Washington endeared Lincoln to the public. The "half jaunty air . . . of his hat, as he rides in his barouche, beside Mrs. Lincoln, of an evening, is consoling to the spectator, who instinctively feels that even if he can write State papers with original and trenchant ability, yet a man of easy manners and kind good nature is Mr. President."[176]

On July 5, Lincoln's message was read to Congress, as was the custom for such documents. (The same was true of his annual December messages, forerunners of what later became known as state of the union addresses.) His principal goal was to define the stakes of the war, a subject he had discussed with his personal secretaries. On May 7, when John Hay told him that many correspondents wished him to abolish slavery, he replied: "For my own part, I consider the central idea pervading this struggle is the necessity that is upon us, of proving that popular government is not an absurdity. We must settle this question now, whether in a free government the minority have the right to break up the government whenever they choose. If we fail it will go far to prove the incapability of the people to govern themselves." Alluding to slavery, he added: "There may be one consideration used in stay of such final judgment, but that is not for us to use in advance. That is, that there exists in our case, an instance of a vast and far reaching disturbing element, which the history of no other free nation will probably ever present. That however is not for us to say at present. Taking the government as we found it we will see if the majority can preserve it."[177] That same day, Lincoln addressed a letter to the regent captains of the tiny principality of San Marino, Italy, in which he said that the war "involves the question whether a Representative republic, extended and aggrandized so much as to be safe against foreign enemies can save itself from the dangers of domestic faction."[178] To Nicolay, the president offered a similar analysis.

Lincoln elaborated on this theme in his message to Congress. "Our popular government," he wrote, "has often been called an experiment. Two points in it, our people have already settled—the successful *establishing* and the successful *administering* of it. One still remains—it's successful *maintenance* against a formidable attempt to overthrow it. It is now for them to demonstrate to the world, that those who can fairly carry an election, can also suppress a rebellion; that ballots are the rightful, and peaceful, successors of bullets; and that when ballots have fairly, and constitutionally, decided, there can be no successful appeal, back to bullets; that there can be no successful appeal, except to ballots themselves, at succeeding elections. Such will be a great lesson of peace; teaching men that what they cannot take by an election, neither can they take it by a war; teaching all, the folly of being the beginners of a war."

Later in the message Lincoln foreshadowed the celebrated speech he would give at Gettysburg more than two years later: "And this issue embraces more than the fate of these United States. It presents to the whole family of man, the question, whether a Constitutional republic, or a democracy—a government of the people, by the same people—can, or cannot, maintain its territorial integrity against its own domestic foes. It presents the question, whether discontented individuals, too few in numbers to control administration, according to organic law, in any case, can always, upon the pretences made in this case, or on any other pretences, or arbitrarily, without any pretence, break up their government, and thus practically put an end to free government upon the earth. It forces us to ask: 'Is there, in all republics, this inherent, and fatal weakness?' 'Must a government, of necessity, be too *strong* for the liberties of its own people, or too *weak* to maintain its own existence?'"

In the most eloquent passage of the address, Lincoln called the war "essentially a People's contest." For Unionists, "it is a struggle for maintaining in the world, that form and substance of government, whose leading object is, to elevate the condition of men—to lift artificial weights from all shoulders; to clear the paths of laudable pursuit for all; to afford all, an unfettered start, and a fair chance, in the race of life. Yielding to partial and temporary departures, from necessity, this is the leading object of the government for whose existence we contend." These words had a special resonance coming from a man who had made his way up from frontier poverty and ignorance. The president's democratic faith in the people shone through his description of the army. There were, he said, "many single Regiments whose members, one and another, possess full practical knowledge of all the arts, sciences, professions, and whatever else, whether useful or elegant, is known in the world; and there is scarcely one, from which there could not be selected, a President, a Cabinet, a Congress, and perhaps a Court, abundantly competent to administer the government itself."

Lincoln recounted the events leading to war, explaining why he had decided to relieve Fort Sumter. Some have regarded his version of events skeptically, but in fact he gave an accurate report of his thoughts and actions during the administration's first six weeks. In one regard, the message was an extension of Lincoln's inaugural, for it refuted at great length the secessionists' "ingenious sophism" that "any State of the Union may, *consistently* with the national Constitution, and therefore *lawfully*, and *peacefully*, withdraw from the Union, without the consent of the Union, or of any other State. The little disguise that the supposed right is to be exercised only for just cause, themselves to be the sole judge of its justice, is too thin to merit any notice. With rebellion thus sugar-coated, they have been drugging the public mind of their section for more than thirty years; and, until at length, they have brought many good men to a willingness to take up arms against the government the day *after* some assemblage of men have enacted the farcical pretence of taking their State out of the Union, who could have been brought to no such thing the day *before*."

A dangerous precedent would be set if the public were to accept secession in 1861: "by allowing the seceders to go in peace, it is difficult to see what we can do, if others choose to go, or to extort terms upon which they will promise to remain." He pointed out that the Confederates recently adopted a constitution that failed to include the right of secession. "The principle itself," he wryly observed, "is one of disintegration, and upon which no government can possibly endure." Logically, he showed how the doctrine of secession could be used to justify expelling a state from the union against its will, clearly a flagrant violation of states rights: "If all the States, save one, should assert the power to *drive* that one out of the Union, it is presumed the whole class of seceder politicians would at once deny the power, and denounce the act as the greatest outrage upon State rights. But suppose that precisely the same act, instead of being called 'driving the one out,' should be called 'the seceding of the others from that one,' it would be exactly what the seceders claim to do; unless, indeed, they make the point, that the one, because it is a minority, may rightfully do what the others, because they are a majority, may not rightfully do."

Lincoln denied that a majority of voters in any Confederate state, except perhaps South Carolina, truly favored secession. He caustically alluded to the conduct of the authorities in Virginia: "The course taken in Virginia was the most remarkable—perhaps the most important. A convention, elected by the people of that State, to consider this very question of disrupting the Federal Union, was in session at the capital of Virginia when Fort Sumter fell. To this body the people had chosen a large majority of *professed* Union men. Almost immediately after the fall of Sumter, many members of that majority went over to the original disunion minority, and, with them, adopted an ordinance for withdrawing the State from the Union. Whether this change was wrought by their great approval of the assault upon Sumter, or their great resentment at the government's resistance to that assault, is not definitely known. Although they submitted the ordinance, for ratification, to a vote of the people, to be taken on a day then somewhat more than a month distant, the convention, and the Legislature, (which was also in session at the same time and place) with leading men of the State, not members of either, immediately commenced acting, as if the State were already out of the Union. They pushed military preparations vigorously forward all over the state."

Apologetically, Lincoln asked Congress to endorse retrospectively the emergency measures he had taken since the bombardment of Fort Sumter. "It was with the deepest regret that the Executive found the duty of employing the war-power, in defence of the government, forced upon him. He could but perform this duty, or surrender the existence of the government. No compromise, by public servants, could, in this case, be a cure; not that compromises are not often proper, but that no popular government can long survive a marked precedent, that those who carry an election, can only save the government from immediate destruction, by giving up the main point, upon which the people gave the election. The people themselves, and not their servants, can safely reverse their own deliberate decisions. As a private citizen, the Executive could not have consented that these institutions shall perish; much less could he, in betrayal of so vast, and so sacred a trust, as these free people had confided to him. He felt that he had no moral right to shrink; nor even to count the chances of his own life, in what might follow. In full view of his great responsibility, he has, so far, done what he has deemed his duty. You will now, according to your own judgment, perform yours."

To supplement what he had already done, Lincoln urged Congress to authorize the creation of a huge army and to appropriate enormous sums of money. He had concluded in the two months since his call for 42,000 volunteers that Confederate resistance would be more formidable than earlier anticipated. "It is now recommended that you give the legal means for making this contest a short, and a decisive one; that you place at the control of the government, for the work, at least four hundred thousand men, and four hundred millions of dollars. That number of men is about one tenth of those of proper ages within the regions where, apparently, *all* are willing to engage; and the sum is less than a twenty-third part of the money value owned by the men who seem ready to devote the whole. A debt of six hundred millions of dollars *now*, is a less sum per head, than was the debt of our revolution, when we came out of that struggle; and the money value in the country now, bears even a greater proportion to what it was *then*, than does the population. Surely each man has as strong a motive *now*, to *preserve* our liberties, as each had *then*, to *establish* them. A right result, at this time, will be worth more to the world, than ten times the men, and ten times the money. The evidence reaching us from the country, leaves no doubt, that the material for the work is abundant; and that it needs only the hand of legislation to give it legal sanction, and the hand of the Executive to give it practical shape and efficiency. One of the greatest perplexities of the government, is to avoid receiving troops faster than it can provide for them. In a word, the people will save their government, if the government itself, will do its part, only indifferently well."[179]

As the message was read in the House, its members paid profound attention and frequently expressed their approval, especially at the call for 400,000 troops, which elicited loud, irrepressible, unrestrained applause from the congressmen and the galleries. "Hurrah for Uncle Abe!" shouted one solider, to which another spectator burst out, "Bully for him!"[180] The speaker of the House shrilly called for order, but in vain. Another passage received a particularly favorable reception: "A right result, at this time, will be worth more to the world, than ten times the men, and ten times the money."[181] The audience also liked the allusion to the loyalty of enlisted men as opposed to officers. The president's analysis of the doctrine of secession, according to one report, "was so direct and ingenious and so saturated with traces of the President's peculiar quaintness of humor, as to provoke more than once a general buzz of satisfied approval."[182] Some Republican congressmen deemed it "very Lincolnish" with its "new ways of putting old questions," "full of strong sense and irony," "admirable for the times[,] the people & the occasion," and predicted that it would be "very popular."[183]

In the upper chamber, the message was listened to in silence as a clerk read it in a low monotone. Occasionally, one senator would whisper to another, "It's too long," or "What's the point of going into that?" The consensus among them was "that the argumentative and historical parts of the message were unnecessary, but, as a Senator observed, the people had a right to know the facts of the case as they appeared to the mind of the Executive in making such propositions, and that nothing should be taken for granted or supposed to be known to those who were so materially interested in the result."[184] At the mention of $400 million and 400,000 troops, pro-Southern senators like John C. Breckinridge of Kentucky and Trusten Polk of Missouri shifted nervously in their seats.

The document won widespread public approval. Henry Villard reported that among "the throng that daily now frequent the hotels and capitol, none is found (save the secession spies who abound here) who does not heartily endorse the patriotic message of the President."[185] The New York *Tribune* praised its brevity and directness: "It gushes out from the earnest heart of the author, and goes straight to the hearts of the patriotic millions. Utterly devoid of rhetorical embellishment and official reserve, its positions will be comprehended and its arguments appreciated by every rational mind."[186] The Providence *Journal* liked "its perfect plainness, its downright honesty, its unmistakable sincerity" and its "manly and straight-forward words."[187] Benjamin Brown French pronounced it "the best, considering all things, that was ever sent to Congress. It goes as straight as a rifle ball to the mark, & without the least flourish, tells the whole story of our troubles so that every man woman & child who can read it can understand."[188]

Men of letters heaped praise on Lincoln's message. George William Curtis, editor of *Harper's Weekly,* privately called it "the most truly American message ever delivered. Think upon what a millennial year we have fallen when the President of the United States declares officially that this government is founded upon the rights of man! Wonderfully acute, simple, sagacious, and of antique honesty! I can forgive the jokes and the big hands, and the inability to make bows. Some of us who doubted were wrong."[189] In his magazine, Curtis was more formal but no less laudatory: "While many Presidents of many parties would have endeavored to save the Government by force of arms, not all Presidents would so clearly comprehend or so simply state what the Government was that they were saving. This Government was founded upon the rights of man; and for the first time in long years the President recognizes that fact. Presidents' messages for many years have been labored defenses of an oligarchical and aristocratic administration of the Government. At length there is a people's President, in no mean sense; and the Government of the United States is restored to its original principles. It is not a matter of party, but of patriotic congratulation."[190]

The Philadelphia lawyer and essayist Sidney George Fisher called the message "simple, clear, positive," "marked throughout by evident sincerity & truth," "wholly free from egotism or desire to produce an effect," and "earnest & candid." It demonstrated "remarkable power of thought & argument. The reflections are eminently just and the right of secession is treated in a manner at once clear, comprehensive and original." Fisher considered Lincoln's style "not polished or graceful, but nervous, compact & clear, the utterance of strong convictions seeking expression." The entire document was "pervaded by good feeling and loyal catholic spirit. In this hour of its trial, the country seems to have found in Mr. Lincoln a great man. I should judge that he has a clear head, a good heart, a strong will and high moral sentiment. Should he prove equal to the promise given by his [inaugural] speech, his message [to Congress] and his conduct thus far, he will be an unspeakable blessing to the nation." Lincoln, thought Fisher, was "the best *man* we have had for President since Jno. Q. Adams, he is the man for this crisis, worth, in the strength of his mind and character & purity of purpose all the rest of the cabinet put together."[191]

In late June, after Lincoln read the address to John Lothrop Motley, the noted historian told his wife that it "impressed me very favourably. With the exception of a few expressions, it was not only highly commendable in spirit, but written with considerable untaught grace and power."[192] Motley found the president to be "a man of the most extraordinary conscientiousness. He seemed to have a window in his breast. There was something almost childlike in his absence of guile and affectation of any kind."[193]

Also laudatory was the New York *World*, which praised the message's "homely and honest simplicity." Its style appealed to the public's preference for "vigorous, everyday common sense, quaint expression and shrewd mother wit" instead of "the pomp of artificial rhetoric." The editors predicted that the message would "strengthen that confidence in Mr. Lincoln's honesty and robust common sense, which causes the sturdy masses to feel that he is a man to lean against in a great emergency."[194] The *Ohio State Journal* liked the message's "blunt directness—its clearness of statement, and unaffected every-day diction, which is familiar without being undignified."[195] *Frank Leslie's Illustrated Newspaper* found it "remarkable for its directness and simplicity, for its grasp of the whole subject which now agitates the country, and for its ability in meeting the various subterfuges upon which the Secession leaders have based their action."[196]

Not every reader regarded Lincoln's prose favorably. English papers declared that the president "writes like a half-educated lawyer," that he "thinks like a European sovereign," and that his style was "[h]omely in language and somewhat apologetic in tone."[197]

While the *Illinois State Journal* rejoiced to find "no 'niggerism' in it" (that is, no mention of slavery), Frederick Douglass regretted that omission. "Any one reading that document, with no previous knowledge of the United States, would never dream from any thing there written that we have a slaveholders war waged upon the Government," Douglass complained.[198] At the other end of the political spectrum, some Democrats objected that the "necessity of circumstances placed in extenuation of the President's guilt, is precisely the same plea put in by tyrants, despots, and usurpers of every age of the world."[199] Kentucky Senator Lazarus Powell denied that there was any necessity for extraconstitutional action, arguing that there "never was a king, potentate, or sovereign, when he was assuming powers that did not belong to him for the purpose of crushing the liberties of his people, who did not do it under the plea of necessity."[200] Echoing this charge, an Ohio Democrat complained that Lincoln "makes himself a perfect monarch. I would see him d[amne]d before I would by my official vote legalize his unconstitutional acts."[201] Other Democrats protested against Lincoln's statement that the government should lift "artificial weights" from the shoulders of all men, for that implied that the shackles of slaves ought to be struck off. The Southern press condemned the message as the work of an "old perjurer," a "Usurper," and a "vulgar savage who seems to be making desperate efforts to imitate the Neros and Caligulas of old."[202]

Some friendly newspapers legitimately objected that "there is too much of the lawyer about it," that "it is too much marked by its special pleadings," and that excessive attention was devoted to Virginia's actions and to the settled question of the constitutionality of secession.[203]

Congress in Session: Dealing with the Crisis

Missing from the new Congress that assembled on July 4 were members from the seceded states, with the notable exception of Tennessee Senator Andrew Johnson. Thus, the Republicans were able to dominate both chambers by substantial majorities (106–42 in the House, 31–14 in the senate). Their party was divided into Radicals, Moderates, and Conservatives, who in time would clash, but not at this special session. Congress agreed to deal with only military, financial, judicial, and naval matters and to postpone all other business till December. As Wisconsin Senator Timothy O. Howe put it, the "resolution seems to be universal to do nothing more than the special occasion demands & to do that speedily—to use few words & no palaver—to clothe the President with the utmost potentiality of this great people, and command him to see that the 'Republic receives no detriment.'"[204] Lyman Trumbull accurately predicted that "[m]en & money will be voted without stint."[205]

Also missing was Stephen A. Douglas, who had died on June 3 at the age of 48 after heroically exerting himself to rally Northern Democrats in support of the war effort. His pro-Union speeches in Illinois and elsewhere taxed his waning strength and helped bring on his premature demise, which created a vacuum in the leadership ranks of the Northern Democracy. That gap would eventually be filled by less enthusiastic supporters of the Union cause like New York Governor Horatio Seymour, Senators James A. Bayard of Delaware and Jesse D. Bright of Indiana, former governor Thomas H. Seymour of Connecticut, and three Ohio congressmen: Clement L. Vallandigham, Alexander Long, and Samuel S. ("Sunset") Cox. They and their allies made Lincoln's job far more difficult than it would have been if Douglas had lived. In the emergency summer session, however, Democrats agreed not to act as obstructionists.

Congress obliged Lincoln by retroactively approving all his emergency measures except the suspension of habeas corpus. (The House and senate waited until March 1863 to ratify that controversial step. Some Republicans hesitated to vote for such a bill lest they imply that the president had no power to suspend habeas corpus without congressional authorization.) Among the seventy-six statutes the lawmakers passed before adjournment on August 6 were acts authorizing the enlistment of 500,000 volunteers for three years as well as the expansion of both the regular army and the navy; providing military leaders with larger staffs; enlarging the War Department; and empowering the Treasury Department to borrow $250 million, which would supplement the money raised by increased import duties and taxes ($20 million of direct levies on the states and territories and an income tax).

Some members shared the uneasiness expressed by James W. Grimes of Iowa, who told a fellow Republican senator that "we are about to encourage precedents that will be very dangerous to the rights of the States & to the liberties of the people."

Grimes called Lincoln's decision to expand the regular army by ten regiments "the most extraordinary assumption of power than any President has attempted to exercise." With trepidation he asked: "Where is this thing to stop?"[206]

In late July, Congress overwhelmingly approved John J. Crittenden's resolution stating that the war "has been forced upon the country by the disunionists of the southern States" and was not being waged "in any spirit of oppression, or for any purpose of conquest or subjugation, or purpose of overthrowing or interfering with the rights or established institutions of those States." The aim of the war was "to defend and maintain the supremacy of the Constitution, and to preserve the Union with all the dignity, equality, and rights of the several States unimpaired." Although some interpreted the resolution as a declaration that slavery would not be affected by the war, in fact slavery was not mentioned in the text and no promise was made to safeguard all "established institutions." Abolition might be a by-product of hostilities even if it was not a war aim. On August 4, in the presence of Crittenden, Lincoln assured Kentucky Congressman Robert Mallory that "this war, so far as I have anything to do with it, is carried on on the idea that there is a Union sentiment in those States, which, set free from the control now held over it by the presence of the Confederate or rebel power, will be sufficient to replace those States in the Union."[207]

By a much narrower margin, Congress also passed a Confiscation Act, seizing property (including slaves) employed by Confederates in direct support of military operations. It did not fully liberate bondsmen, but did represent a step on the path to emancipation. Despite its limited nature, the law cheered some Radicals, including Thomas Wentworth Higginson, who said he was "satisfied that we are gravitating towards a bolder anti-slavery policy . . . The desideratum is to approach a policy of emancipation by stages so clear and irresistible as to retain for that end a united public sentiment."[208] Lincoln was less enthusiastic about the Confiscation Act. Believing that it might violate the Constitution's Fifth Amendment provision that "no person shall be held to answer for a capital, or otherwise infamous crime, unless on a presentment or indictment of a grand jury, except in cases arising in the land or naval, forces, or in the militia, when in actual service in time of war or public danger" as well as Article 3, Section 3 ("no attainder of treason shall work corruption of blood, or forfeiture, except during the life of the person attainted"), he hesitated to approve the legislation. Moreover, he believed it was premature and might be a mere empty threat that would alienate the Border States; he allegedly exclaimed that "it will lose us Kentucky!"[209] Lincoln was reluctant, however, to veto the bill for fear it might imply that the Rebels could, with impunity, employ their slaves in a military capacity. Ultimately he signed the statute after prominent senators urgently lobbied him, but he did little to enforce it.

The lawmakers also established a pair of special investigating committees. One, under the chairmanship of Wisconsin Congressman John F. Potter, looked into disloyalty among government employees. Many Southerners had been appointed to office during the previous two administrations, and legitimate concerns were raised about their devotion to the Union. Unfortunately, Potter's committee pursued its mission clumsily, violating due process in denouncing men who were fired as a result.

Charges were often falsely made by those who hungered for the jobs held by the accused. When told that a prospective appointee sympathized with the Confederacy, Lincoln replied that if office seekers thought they could obtain the presidency itself, they would "before night prove [him] the vilest secessionist in the country."[210] One evening two callers warned him that a cabal of government employees planned to communicate with the nearby Confederate army. Asked what should be done, they replied that the suspects ought to be fired. "Ah, gentlemen," Lincoln interrupted, "I see it is the same old, old coon; why could you not tell me at once you wanted an office, and save your own time as well as mine?"[211]

Another committee was set up under the leadership of New York Congressman Charles H. Van Wyck to scrutinize government contracts. Though it did uncover fraud, the committee was highly controversial. When it criticized Ward Hill Lamon, Simon Cameron, and Gideon Welles, among others, John Hay denounced it as "an absurd fiasco" employed "chiefly as an engine to ventilate personal animosities and prejudices existing in the minds of the incorruptible committeemen against better people."[212] Lincoln complained that its most active member, Henry L. Dawes of Massachusetts, had "done more to break down the administration than any other man in the country."[213] (In mid-January, Dawes publicly charged that "there had been more money stolen from the Treasury during the first year of Mr. Lincoln's administration than it had cost to carry on the whole government during the entire term of Mr. Buchanan's administration." This utterance, Dawes told his wife, created "the awfulest hubbub you ever saw." Even friends like Senator Henry Wilson were "down on it.")[214] Leading Radicals in Congress, including Charles Sumner, Thaddeus Stevens, and Henry Wilson, shared the president's dim view of Dawes and the contracts committee.

The committee may have embarrassed the administration, but it conscientiously investigated misfeasance and malfeasance in raising and equipping a 500,000-man army and navy. Secretary of the Navy Gideon Welles had unwisely authorized his brother-in-law, George D. Morgan, to purchase ships on a commission basis rather than for a flat fee. While ship brokers claimed that they could have done the job for $5,000, Morgan's 1861 commissions totaled over $70,000. Morgan committed no fraud, but the government had spent far too much for his services. In Boston, John Murray Forbes did for free what Morgan did for a 2.5 percent commission. In addition to receiving criticism for Morgan's contract, Welles was denounced as "a miracle of inefficiency" and was blamed for the loss of important vessels when Confederates seized the Norfolk shipyard.[215]

While the House defeated a motion condemning Welles, the lawmakers did censure Simon Cameron, whose incapacity, carelessness, and inefficiency significantly harmed the war effort. Cameron's personal secretary as well as Assistant Secretary of War Alexander Cummings thought that their boss was a failure and that the War Department was "in the most hideous disorganization which it will take years to right."[216]

Lincoln was widely denounced for keeping Welles and Cameron on. The country was "disgraced by the astounding frauds in the Army & Navy both" and "looks upon the authorities at Washington as corrupt as Buchanan's administration," according to Lincoln's friend William M. Dickson.[217] A New Yorker complained that the president's "retention and sanction of Cameron & Well[e]s & all their transactions already causes an apprehension that he is also *corrupt* or what is worse that *he is weak* & under the control of Jobbers & Contractors." Nothing could save Lincoln "but the manifestation of a Jackson courage to extricate himself from the corrupt & selfish men by which he is surrounded."[218] Another New Yorker informed Lincoln that "it is universally believed that Cameron is a thief—All men believe you, upright—but know you lack experience and fear you lack *nerve.*"[219] The *National Anti-Slavery Standard* lamented that the country had "a weak but honest President, and a Cabinet made up principally of fourth-rate men."[220] In Boston and New York, influential Republicans launched a campaign to replace Caleb B. Smith, Cameron, and Welles with Nathaniel P. Banks, John A. Dix, and Joseph Holt. Their efforts enjoyed the approval of Charles Eliot Norton, a Cambridge litterateur who thought that the "inefficiency of the President & the Cabinet are our greatest present danger." Rhetorically, Norton asked: "Must we be content with feebleness where strength is needed, with mean-[n]ess for magnanimity, and cowardice for courage?"[221]

War in Earnest: Early Skirmishes and Bull Run

As Congress debated, legislated, and investigated, the administration made and executed war plans. A week after Sumter fell, James A. Hamilton asked Lincoln if he proposed to launch an offensive soon. "I intend to *give* blows," he replied. "The only question at present is, whether I should first retake Fort Sumter or Harper's Ferry."[222] He authorized Hamilton to say publicly that the president "is determined to prosecute the war . . . with all the energy necessary to bring it to a successful termination. He will call for a large additional force, relying upon Providence and the loyalty of the people."[223] He described his strategy more fully to John Hay on April 25: "I intend at present, always leaving an opportunity for change of mind, to fill Fortress Monroe with men and stores: blockade the ports effectually: provide for the entire safety of the Capitol: keep them quietly employed in this way, and then go down to Charleston and pay her the little debt we are owing her."[224] Fort Monroe, at the mouth of the James River in Virginia, was quickly reinforced with 15,000 men. But Lincoln withheld military action against the Old Dominion until that state's electorate officially ratified the ordinance of secession, which it did on May 23 by a three-to-one margin. Even before that vote was taken, Virginians had been openly aiding the rebellion. As the president noted in his July 4 message to Congress, they had "seized the United States Armory at Harper's Ferry, and the Navy-yard at Gosport, near Norfolk. They received—perhaps invited—into their state, large bodies of troops, with their warlike appointments, from the so-called seceded States. They formally entered into a treaty of temporary alliance, and co-operation with the so-called 'Confederate States,' and sent members to their Congress at Montgomery. And, finally, they permitted the insurrectionary government to be transferred to their capital at Richmond. The people of Virginia have thus allowed this giant insurrection to make its nest within her borders; and this government has no choice left but to deal with it, *where* it finds it."[225]

As soon as Virginia officially seceded, Lincoln authorized a mission to secure Alexandria. When one of his favorite surrogate sons, Colonel Elmer E. Ellsworth, asked to serve in the vanguard of that expedition, the president "replied that the first movement on Southern soil was one of great delicacy. Much depended thereon. He desired to avoid all violence. The people of Virginia were not in a mass disloyal and he wanted nothing to occur that might incense them against the government, but rather wished to so conduct the movement that it would win them over."[226] On May 24, federal troops crossed the Potomac and occupied Alexandria without opposition, though Ellsworth took umbrage at a Confederate flag flying atop a hotel. (Visible from the White House, that banner had been an irritant to Lincoln and his cabinet. Two weeks earlier Chase said with great emphasis that "if I had my way yesterday that Flag wouldn't be there this morning.")[227] Impetuously, the young officer dashed into the offending hostelry, clambered up the stairs to the roof, and hauled down the secessionist flag. As he descended, Ellsworth encountered the hotel proprietor, who shot him dead. News of his murder shocked Northerners and devastated Lincoln, who mourned him as if had been his own son. Upon learning of Ellsworth's death, he burst into tears, telling some White House callers, "[e]xcuse me, but I cannot talk." After regaining his composure, he said: "I will make no apology, gentlemen, for my weakness; but I knew poor Ellsworth well, and held him in great regard. Just as you entered the room, Captain Fox left me, after giving me the painful details of Ellsworth's unfortunate death. The event was so unexpected, and the recital so touching, that it quite unmanned me. . . . Poor fellow! It was undoubtedly an act of rashness, but it only shows the heroic spirit that animates our soldiers, from high to low, in this righteous cause of ours. Yet who can restrain their grief to see them fall in such a way as this; not by the fortunes of war, but by the hand of an assassin."[228] According to an account written many years later, the tearful president also said: "so this is the beginning—murder! Ah, my friends, what shall the end of all this be?"[229] In reply to a congressman who found consolation in the fact that the U.S. flag now waved over the Alexandria hotel, Lincoln exclaimed with tears in his eyes: "Yes, but it was at a terrible cost!"[230] Ellsworth's body was taken to the navy yard, where the president and his wife for a long while looked tearfully upon the face of their dead friend. Finally, Lincoln asked rhetorically: "My boy! My boy! Was it necessary that this sacrifice should be made?"[231] The body was removed to the White House, where funeral services were held the following day.

The president had a strong paternal affection for Ellsworth, and in some ways their relationship resembled that of a medieval knight to his squire. John Hay remarked that "Lincoln loved him like a younger brother."[232] The president may have identified with Ellsworth, an ambitious, self-educated poor boy, too proud to accept favors, alienated from his father (who expected the son to support him financially), with a sensitive conscience, a paternal streak, and a wealth of compassion and generosity. In 1860, he had worked in the Lincoln–Herndon law office, ostensibly as a student, but he spent most of his time on the campaign trail stumping for the Republican ticket. Lincoln extended heartfelt sympathy to Ellsworth's parents. "In the untimely loss of your noble son," he wrote them on May 25, "our affliction here, is scarcely less than your own. So much of promised usefulness to one's country, and of bright hopes for one's self and friends, have rarely been so suddenly dashed, as in his fall. In size, in years, and in youthful appearance, a boy only, his power to command men, was surpassingly great. This power, combined with a fine intellect, an indomitable energy, and a taste altogether military, constituted in him, as seemed to me, the best natural talent, in that department, I ever knew. And yet he was singularly modest and deferential in social intercourse. My acquaintance with him began less than two years ago; yet through the latter half of the intervening period, it was as intimate as the disparity of our ages, and my engrossing engagements, would permit. To me, he appeared to have no indulgences or pastimes; and I never heard him utter a profane, or an intemperate word. What was conclusive of his good heart, he never forgot his parents. The honors he labored for so laudably, and, in the sad end, so gallantly gave his life, he meant for them, no less than for himself."[233]

Indignation at Ellsworth's murder helped swell the enlistment rolls. Though Lincoln had called for only 42,000 volunteers, by July 1 over 200,000 had joined up.

In addition to occupying Alexandria, federal troops seized Arlington Heights overlooking Washington, where Robert E. Lee's mansion was located. Attention then shifted to Harper's Ferry, where fewer than 10,000 Confederates under Confederate General Joseph E. Johnston had assembled. Sixty-nine-year-old Union General Robert Patterson, who had served as Winfield Scott's second-in-command during the Mexican War, was selected to lead an expedition against them. With a force of 17,000, Patterson approached the town in mid-June, causing Johnston to retreat to Winchester. When urged to pursue the Confederates, the indecisive, fearful Patterson, whose troops called him "Granny," balked.

Further west in Virginia, Union forces proved more aggressive. In early June, they routed Confederates at Phillipi in a skirmish that became known as "the Phillipi races." A month thereafter at Rich Mountain and Corrick's Ford, 12,000 troops under the leadership of George B. McClellan, Thomas A. Morris, and William S. Rosecrans defeated Confederate forces led by Robert S. Garnett, who on July 13 became the first general killed in the war. McClellan received most of the credit for these minor victories, though Rosecrans deserved much of it. Union successes boosted Northern morale and paved the way for western Virginia to break away from the Old Dominion and establish itself as a new state.

These small-scale engagements whetted the appetite of the Northern public, which wanted its legions to attack the Confederate capital. Remarking on the overwhelmingly positive Northern response to the president's April 15 proclamation, *Harper's Weekly* declared that with "such support, and such resources, if this war is not brought to a speedy close, and the supremacy of the Government asserted throughout the country, it will be the fault of Abraham Lincoln."[234] When the impatient New York *Times* suggested that the president be replaced, Lincoln "spoke amusedly" of the paper's editorial "and said that the Government had three things to do: defend Washington: Blockade the Ports: and retake Government property. All possible dispatch was to be used in these matters & it w[oul]d be well if the people would cordially assist in this work, before clamoring for more."[235] In early May, several Northern governors met at Cleveland and warned the administration that "there is a spirit evoked by this rebellion among the liberty-loving people of the country that is driving them to action, and if the Government will not permit them to act for it, they will act for themselves."[236] Cabinet members also chafed at the inaction. Montgomery Blair denounced "the dilatory policy of the Administration," and Chase lamented that Lincoln had pursued "the Micawber policy of waiting for something, to turn up."[237] Chase's friend Murat Halstead of the Cincinnati *Commercial* groused to former Ohio Congressman Timothy C. Day that "there could not be a more inefficient man President of the United States than A. Lincoln. He is of no earthly or possible account."[238] Day replied that "the generous uprising of our people in behalf of the Republic is being chilled by the fast spreading idea, that a good cause is in incompetent hands."[239]

Representative Henry L. Dawes reported that Congress was "intensely wrought up to a vigorous prosecution of the war," and members were growing "suspicious that rail-splitting is not the highest qualification for Chief Magistrate."[240] Senator Henry Wilson called at the White House with a delegation of Radicals and told the president, "we saved you from an attack by the secessionists, but you are menaced by an even greater danger from the North. One retrograde step or even a moment's hesitation and you will be lost."[241] The Republican congressional caucus narrowly defeated Lyman Trumbull's resolution demanding that the army seize Richmond before July 21. At that meeting, Ohio Senator Ben Wade "was loud, furious and impudent, denouncing everybody civil & military as incompetent or treacherous."[242]

The press was equally impatient. The New York *Times* exclaimed "Action! Action! is the watchword." An army of 25,000 should capture Richmond within sixty days![243] "We want war," cried the Indianapolis *Journal,* "swift and overwhelming. The more terrible the war is made, the shorter it will be, and the more humane the policy. Let not the President suppose that the loyal North desires the war cloud to be gently and gradually discharged of its electricity."[244] "Forward to Richmond! Forward to Richmond!" trumpeted Horace Greeley's influential New York *Tribune.* The Confederate Congress should be prevented from meeting in the Virginia capital on July 20 as planned, insisted the *Tribune.* "By that date the place must be held by the national army!"[245]

Vexed by Greeley's hectoring, Lincoln asked the *Tribune*'s Washington bureau chief: "What in the world is the matter with Uncle Horace? Why can't he restrain himself and wait a little?" When informed that Greeley did not write every editorial, the president replied: "Well, I don't suppose I have any right to complain; Uncle Horace agrees with me pretty often after all; I reckon he is with us at least four days out of seven."[246] On April 27, when his old friend George T. M. Davis, representing the New York Union Defence Committee, said that the rebellion should be crushed swiftly and energetically, the president calmly replied that Baltimore was under control, that General Scott was capably supervising military affairs, and that the committee should be more patient and not agitate for "any excess of action." He assured the New Yorkers that the administration was "determined to act with all the dispatch and decision" within its power, yet it "would at the same time as strenuously avoid everything like *a spirit of revenge toward the South*."[247]

Meanwhile, the general-in-chief had been formulating strategy without consulting the president. "Scott will not let us outsiders know anything of his plans," Lincoln observed on June 17.[248] But the previous month, Old Fuss and Feathers had outlined to McClellan a scheme that became known as the "Anaconda Plan." The Confederacy, he recommended, should be encircled and crushed through the combined effects of a stringent blockade and a "powerful movement down the Mississippi" by an 80,000-man army, whose goal would be to capture New Orleans; thus girdled, the rebellion could be squeezed to death. Before marching southward, troops should have at least four months' training. This strategy, based on Scott's experience in the Mexican War and on the writings of European military theorists, encountered what the general called "the impatience of our patriotic and loyal Union friends." Since it contemplated no forward movement in Virginia and relied heavily on an upsurge of Southern Unionism, it was considered too passive and unrealistic.[249] Scott described this approach to Indiana Congressman Schuyler Colfax, who thought it "grand, but too slow to suit our Western enthusiasm. He [Scott] gets up the most magnificent plans of a campaign I have ever seen—but he ignores *political* necessities—such as the need of instant occupation of Memphis &c, though he said he would try to accelerate the movement thus far if possible. He needs some dashing Young American to be by his side constantly . . . to mix in that 'forward march' as much as possible, which Americans so love to hear."[250] Senator William P. Fessenden believed that Scott was behind the times and should have seized Manassas in late May. Eager to avoid bloodshed if possible, Scott said: "If the objective of the war is the reconstruction of the Union, if our enemies of today are to become our compatriots, it is impolitic to alienate them unduly."[251]

Others, including Edward Bates and Montgomery Meigs, approved of Scott's caution. Meigs served informally as a military advisor to Seward, and when the secretary of state asked how the war should be conducted, he recommended "a policy defensive in the main, offensive only so far as to occupy the important positions in the border states." He warned against a premature thrust into the South, with inadequately trained and supplied troops, led by inexperienced officers. Meigs also thought that it might be necessary to foment a slave uprising.[252]

Scott incurred ridicule for his prudent advice, which may have been influenced by reverses in June. General Benjamin F. Butler dispatched seven regiments from Fortress Monroe to attack Confederate forces half as numerous at Big Bethel, Virginia. On June 10, the outnumbered Rebels drove back the Federals, killing fifty-three and losing only one. A week later at Vienna, Confederates ambushed a train, capturing it and the Ohio troops aboard. Count Adam Gurowski, a Polish refugee who worked in the State Department, sneered that the elderly, infirm Scott was "too inflated by conceit to give the glory of the active command to any other man" and that someone should create "a wheelbarrow in which Scott could take the field in person."[253] Others suggested that Old Fuss and Feathers was under the influence of a daughter who allegedly supported the secessionists. Many army officers doubted that Scott's policy was energetic enough and thought he wasted time in excessive preparation.

Agreeing with those officers, Lincoln rejected Scott's cautious advice, for he was growing impatient. Calculating that the 50,000 Union forces in northern Virginia should be able to defeat the 30,000 Confederates there, the president decided to authorize an offensive. Since many Union soldiers were ninety-day militiamen whose enlistments would soon expire, he understandably wished to have them fight before they were discharged. He may also have believed that to postpone an attack would dispirit the North and perhaps even lead to European recognition of the Confederacy. He was therefore enthusiastic about a plan drawn up at Scott's request by General Irvin McDowell, an abrasive, hypercritical, 42-year-old gourmand and West Pointer in charge of the Department of Northeastern Virginia. The general, whom Montgomery Meigs called a "good, brave, commonplace fat man," proposed an attack on Beauregard's forces concentrating near Manassas, an important rail junction some 30 miles southwest of Washington. When it was objected that the men needed more training, Lincoln replied that the enemy suffered from the same problem: "You are green, it is true; but they are green, also; you are all green alike."[254] Though that was an accurate statement, it was misleading, for Union forces would have to maneuver in the presence of an entrenched enemy, a much greater challenge than the one the Confederates would face.

On June 25, Lincoln convened a council of war with Scott, Meigs, and the cabinet at which the president voiced a strong desire to trap Confederate forces under Thomas J. Jackson at Harper's Ferry, but Scott thought it unfeasible. Four days later at a second council of war, McDowell's fundamentally sound plan was discussed at length, with Meigs countering Scott's vigorous objections. As Meigs recorded in his diary, "I said that I did not think we would ever end this war without beating the rebels; that they had come near us. We were . . . stronger than they, better prepared, our troops better contented, better clothed, better fed, better paid, better armed. That we had the most violent of the rebels near us; it was better to whip them here than to go far into an unhealthy country to fight them, and to fight far from our supplies, to spend our money among enemies instead of our friends. To make the fight in Virginia was cheaper and better as the case now stood. Let them come here to be beaten, and leave the Union men in time to be a majority at home."[255] It was agreed to endorse McDowell's plan, which appeared likely to succeed if Confederate forces under Joseph E. Johnston at Winchester did not join Beauregard. To prevent the two Rebel commands from uniting, Scott ordered Patterson to hold Johnston in check. On July 3, when Lincoln received a dispatch from Patterson reporting that his men had crossed the Potomac and caused the enemy to fall back, the president read it to callers who noted that he was "affable but evidently much preoccupied."[256]

After many delays, McDowell began lurching toward Manassas on July 16, over a week later than the date agreed upon at the council of war. In the oppressive midsummer heat, the raw troops poked along, taking four days to reach their destination, marching poorly. As they proceeded, Lincoln understandably grew anxious. A caller on July 19 was struck by his "wearied and worried appearance." During their conversation, the president's "eye-lids dropped repeatedly and he seemed like a person who had been watching with a sick friend and deprived of his wonted sleep."[257]

Beauregard, learning of McDowell's advance, appealed for help to Johnston, who easily slipped away from the cautious Patterson and hastened to reinforce his threatened colleague. Upon receiving word of this development, Lincoln asked Scott if it might be wise to postpone McDowell's attack until Patterson could join him; the general-in-chief thought that would not be necessary.

On the morning of Sunday, July 21, McDowell's troops splashed across Bull Run and so successfully drove the Confederate left that victory seemed imminent. At noon, John G. Nicolay reported from the White House that "everybody is in great suspense. General Scott talked confidently this morning of success, and very calmly and quietly went to church."[258] Every fifteen minutes or so, Lincoln received dispatches from a telegrapher near the battlefield—young Andrew Carnegie—describing what he was able to hear. Uneasy because those bulletins implied that Union forces were retreating, the president shortly after lunch called on Scott, who was napping. (The 300-pound veteran suffered from gout and dropsy, among other ailments, and would doze off at inopportune times.) Lincoln wakened him and offered a pessimistic interpretation of the dispatches, which Scott insisted were poor indicators of the battle's progress, for shifting winds, echoes, and the like so affected sounds that no conclusion could be drawn from them. The general-in-chief assured Lincoln that McDowell would prevail. Back at the War Department, the president joined Seward, who puffed confidently on a cigar, and Cameron, who forcefully expressed optimism. Lincoln, according to a telegraph operator, was "deeply impressed with the responsibilities of the occasion" and, exuding "quiet dignity," made only a few measured observations. He grew more hopeful when midafternoon dispatches suggested that the Confederates were falling back. Scott believed this report and predicted that Union forces would soon take Manassas. Somewhat reassured, the president left for his customary afternoon ride, visiting the navy yard, where he told its commander, John A. Dahlgren, that "that the armies were hotly engaged and the other side [was] getting the worst of it."[259]

At six o'clock, an excited, frightened-looking Seward rushed into the Executive Mansion and asked Nicolay in a hoarse voice: "Where is the President?"

"Gone to ride."

"Have you any late news?"

Nicolay read a fresh dispatch by Lieutenant G. H. Mendell, forwarded by the journalist Simon P. Hanscom: "General McDowell wishes all the troops that can be sent from Washington to come here without delay. He has ordered the reserve now here under Colonel Miles to advance to the bridge over Bull Run, on the Warrenton road, having driven the enemy before him."[260]

"Tell no one," enjoined Seward. "That is not so. The battle is lost. The telegraph says that McDowell is in full retreat, and calls on General Scott to save the Capitol. Find the President and tell him to come immediately to Gen. Scott[']s."[261] (In fact, late that afternoon, the last of the Confederate reinforcements arrived from Winchester and helped turn the tide. In pell-mell fashion, McDowell's men retreated ignominiously to Washington, causing one wag to write that the troops evidently thought "these are the times that try men soles.")[262]

Thirty minutes later Lincoln returned, absorbed the bad news with no outward sign of alarm, and promptly strode next door to the War Department. There he read a dispatch from a captain reporting "General McDowell's army in full retreat through Centreville. The day is lost. Save Washington and the remnants of this army. All available troops ought to be thrown forward in one body. General McDowell is doing all he can to cover the retreat. Colonel Miles is forming for that purpose. He was in reserve at Centreville. The routed troops will not reform."[263] Lincoln and his cabinet gathered in Scott's office to follow the latest developments. The captain's dismal report was soon confirmed by a telegram from McDowell stating that his men, "having thrown away their haversacks in the battle and left them behind," were "without food" and "have eaten nothing since breakfast. We are without artillery ammunition. The larger part of the men are a confused mob, entirely demoralized. It was the opinion of all the commanders that no stand could be made this side of the Potomac. We will, however, make the attempt at Fairfax Court-House."[264] Scott was so dumbfounded by conflicting reports of success and failure that he scarcely credited the latter. Immediately, all available troops were sent to McDowell's aid.

Lincoln remained at the War Department until after 2 A.M. Upon returning to the White House, he stayed up throughout the moonlit night, listening to reports from noncombatant eyewitnesses. There were many of them, for Washingtonians, including members of Congress, had flocked to Manassas to observe the fight. Fresh from the battlefield, E. B. Washburne found the president huddled with his cabinet and Scott. The congressman wrote that he had never seen "a more sober set of men."[265] Montgomery Meigs called at 3 A.M. and described at length what he had observed. When Lincoln's old friend and fellow member of the Long Nine in the Illinois Legislature, Robert L. Wilson, asked what sort of news the president had from the front, he replied "in a sharp, shrill voice, '*damned bad*.'" (This was the only time Wilson ever heard Lincoln use profanity.)[266]

The next morning, as a drizzling rain heightened the atmosphere of gloom pervading the capital, footsore, discouraged soldiers straggled into town "like lost sheep without a shepherd."[267] Luckily for the Union cause, the Confederates did not press their advantage and besiege Washington, which they could well have done.

Many were quick to blame the debacle on Lincoln, for it was widely believed that in response to popular pressure he had ordered Scott to attack against his better judgment. Although Lincoln did acknowledge that if Scott had been allowed to conduct the campaign as he wished, the defeat "would not have happened," he nevertheless took umbrage at the general's suggestion that he had been coerced to take the offensive prematurely.[268]

"Sir," the general exclaimed to the president on that rainy, melancholy day, "I am the greatest coward in America. I will prove it. I have fought this battle, sir, against my judgment; I think the President of the United States ought to remove me to-day for doing it; as God is my judge, after my superiors had determined to fight it, I did all in my power to make the Army efficient. I deserve removal because I did not stand up, when my army was not in a condition for fighting, and resist it to the last."

Lincoln responded: "Your conversation seems to imply that I forced you to fight this battle."

Scott denied any such implication, saying: "I have never served a President who has been kinder to me than you have been."[269]

In fact, Scott had been pressured to attack not only by Lincoln but also by cabinet members and by congressmen and senators who threatened to censure him.

In the wake of such a humiliating defeat, many condemned "the inexplicable folly of the Administration." To all and sundry, Maryland ex-Congressman Henry Winter Davis expatiated on the "unfitness for their high task" of the president and his cabinet.[270] An editor of the New York *World* decried "the lack of all that splendid boldness which [Andrew] Jackson would have shown" and expressed doubt that the war could be waged successfully because of the "waning confidence of the people in the energy of Lincoln or the honesty of his cabinet or their ability to master the crisis & organize victory."[271] The "whole responsibility, in the end, falls upon the President," editorialized the New York *Herald*, and the Chicago *Evening Journal* hoped that Lincoln "appreciates the grave fact that *he alone* is most responsible of all."[272] Edwin M. Stanton ascribed the "catastrophe" to the "imbecility of this Administration." He charged that "irretrievable misfortune and national disgrace never to be forgotten are to be added to the ruin of all peaceful pursuits and national bankruptcy, as the result of Lincoln's 'running the machine' for five months."[273] Even Lincoln's good friend Leonard Swett complained that the government did not "seem to [be] conducted with ability, and I am afraid new disasters await us."[274]

The cabinet came in for severe criticism. Lyman Trumbull declared that it had no "affirmative, positive action & business talent." Moreover, Trumbull told a colleague, the president, "though a most excellent & honest man, lacks these qualities."[275] "Everything seems to be in confusion," the senator thought, "& when this is so in the cabinet & at headquarters we must expect it also on the field of battle."[276] In the cabinet, Frederick Law Olmsted detected "the greatest conceivable dearth of administrative talent" and grumbled that though Lincoln was "an amiable, honest, good fellow," nevertheless he "has no element of dignity; no tact, not a spark of genius."[277] Israel D. Andrews of Maine denounced all the cabinet members for having no "administrative ability" and for failing to comprehend "the immensity of the crisis." He also reported that a leading Westerner had told Lincoln: "Unless you soon change this Cabinet the people will change you and it."[278]

Many others demanded a cabinet shake-up. At a series of Republican meetings in New York, bitter recriminations were voiced against the secretaries of state, war, and the navy as well as the attorney general. "Mr. Lincoln must be compelled to call about him men of middle age, enjoying the business confidence, the moral approval, [and] the patriotic reliance of the nation" and "throw overboard all mere politicians, office-seeker-&-holders, aspirants to his own chair," wrote the Rev. Dr. Henry W. Bellows, chairman of the U.S. Sanitary Commission.[279] More harshly, an upstate New York attorney called Cameron "a rascal," Welles an "imbecile," and Seward a blunderer, and concluded that "Lincoln, it is a general impression with us, is a failure."[280] A former congressman from Pennsylvania urged that Winfield Scott be put in Cameron's place and Edward Everett in Seward's. Echoing the views of many, Assistant Secretary of the Interior John Palmer Usher predicted that if Welles and Cameron were not swiftly replaced, the entire administration "will go together to perdition."[281] Chase also was criticized for having championed McDowell and for allegedly threatening before the battle to quit if more regiments were received. Greeley did not demand a cabinet change only because he feared it would be futile. "No President," he wrote, "could afford to have it said that a newspaper had forced him to give battle, and then turned out his Cabinet because he lost that battle."[282]

But Greeley's New York *Tribune* did not hesitate to attribute the "shipwreck of our grand and heroic army" to the administration, which owed an apology "to the humiliated and astounded country."[283] Greeley, who acknowledged that he "was all but insane" after the battle, privately urged Lincoln to surrender to the Confederacy.[284] "You are not considered a great man, and I am a hopelessly broken one," the mercurial editor observed patronizingly in a letter to the president. If the Confederacy "*cannot* be beaten—if our recent disaster's fatal—do not fear to sacrifice yourself to your country. If the Rebels are not to be beaten—if that is your judgment in view of all the light you can get—then every drop of blood henceforth shed in this quarrel will be wantonly, wickedly shed, and the guilt will rest heavily on the soul of every promoter of the crime."[285] (John Hay aptly called this missive a "most insane specimen of pusillanimity.")[286]

When a New Yorker asked Lincoln about all this clamor, he replied: "Tell your friends to make war on the enemy, and not on each other."[287] He advised a delegation urging the removal of Cameron and Welles that "while swimming the river it was no time to swap horses."[288] Similarly, he informed a group of Philadelphia leaders that he "doubted, and the public probably doubted, his ability to meet the public expectations in carrying on the Government; but they need have no doubt of his intention." His only complaint was against the press's "spirit of fault-finding" as sometimes "manifested against the Government." Instead of being impatient, "it was rather the duty of each in his own sphere well to do his duty, and have a reasonable confidence that every other department was doing theirs as well. We would thus be able to turn our guns upon a common enemy, instead of firing into each other."[289] From a committee urging the removal of Cameron, Lincoln requested specific examples of his misconduct. When none was forthcoming, he concluded that "they each had a good-sized axe to grind."[290]

Defenders of the administration protested that such attacks would undermine public confidence and prove "suicidal."[291] Some critics tempered their strictures. George William Curtis, who thought the "administration has been inadequate," acknowledged that the North had "undertaken to make war without in the least knowing how. . . . We have made a false start, and we have discovered it. It only remains to start afresh."[292]

Lincoln agreed with that sentiment. To be sure, the defeat profoundly affected him; with intense emotion he told John D. Defrees, "if Hell is [not] any worse than this, it has no terror for me."[293] But he did not wallow in self-pity or pessimistic gloom. The morning after the battle, he impatiently remarked: "There is nothing in this except the lives lost and the lives which must be lost to make it good." Commenting on this statement, John Hay wrote that there "was probably no one who regretted bloodshed and disaster more than he, and no one who estimated the consequences of defeat more lightly. He was often for a moment impatient at [the] loss of time, and yet he was not always sure that this was not a part of the necessary scheme."[294] Lincoln assured House Speaker Galusha Grow: "My boys are green at the fighting business, but wait till they get licked enough to raise their dander! Then the cry will be, 'On to Richmond' and 'no Stone-walls will stop them!'"[295] In early August, he told a despondent friend: "We were all too confident—too sure of an easy victory. We now understand the difficulties in the way, and shall surmount them."[296] To Richard W. Thompson, who had served with him in Congress, the president explained how the battle had come about. Thompson was struck by "the hopefulness of his nature and his confidence in the final result, which he expressed with the fixed determination to omit nothing and not to slacken his exertions in the work of saving the nation's life."[297]

Years later, Walt Whitman paid tribute to Lincoln's resilience: "If there were nothing else of Abraham Lincoln for history to stamp him with, it is enough to send him with his wreath to the memory of all future time, that he endured that hour, that day, bitterer than gall—indeed a crucifixion day—that it did not conquer him—that he unflinchingly stemm'd it, and resolv'd to lift himself and the Union out of it."[298]

Two days after the battle, Lincoln visited some troops in the field, accompanied by Seward, who had suggested the excursion. En route they encountered Colonel William T. Sherman, commander of a brigade that had taken 300 casualties in the fight. When the colonel asked if they intended to inspect his camps, Lincoln said: "Yes; we heard that you had got over the big scare, and we thought we would come over and see the 'boys.'" At Lincoln's invitation, Sherman joined them, and as they rode along, the colonel "discovered that Mr. Lincoln was full of feeling, and wanted to encourage" the troops. Sherman requested that he "please discourage all cheering, noise, or any sort of confusion," for they had had "enough of it before Bull Run to ruin any set of men," and that what they needed "were cool, thoughtful, hard-fighting soldiers—no more hurrahing, no more humbug." Lincoln good-naturedly took the suggestion.

Upon reaching one of the camps, Lincoln, according to Sherman, "made one of the neatest, best, and most feeling addresses I ever listened to, referring to our late disaster at Bull Run, the high duties that still devolved on us, and the brighter days yet to come. At one or two points the soldiers began to cheer, but he promptly checked them, saying: 'Don't cheer, boys. I confess I rather like it myself, but Colonel Sherman here says it is not military; and I guess we had better defer to his opinion.'" In concluding, "he explained that, as President, he was commander-in-chief; that he was resolved that the soldiers should have every thing that the law allowed; and he called on one and all to appeal to him personally in case they were wronged. The effect of this speech was excellent."

As they passed by more camps, the president complimented Sherman "for the order, cleanliness, and discipline, that he observed." Seward and Lincoln remarked "that it was the first bright moment they had experienced since the battle."

At Fort Corcoran, Lincoln repeated to the troops the talk he had given earlier, including his suggestion that they complain to him if "they were wronged." One officer availed himself of this invitation, saying: "Mr. President, I have a cause of grievance. This morning I went to speak to Colonel Sherman, and he threatened to shoot me."

Lincoln replied, "Threatened to shoot you?"

"Yes, sir, he threatened to shoot me."

The president fixed the complainant with his gaze and remarked in a loud stage-whisper: "Well, if I were you, and he threatened to shoot, I would not trust him, for I believe he would do it." The fellow turned around and slunk off to the accompaniment of laughter from the troops.

As the small party drove on, Sherman explained why he had threatened the officer. Lincoln remarked: "Of course I didn't know any thing about it, but I thought you knew your own business best." The colonel thanked him for that expression of confidence and observed that the president's remarks would help maintain discipline in the regiment.[299]

At another camp, a solider complained to the president that Sherman had treated the men badly, forcing them to vacate a cozy barn in the midst of a rainstorm. Lincoln replied: "Well, boys, I have a great deal of respect for Colonel Sherman, and if he turned you out of the barn I have no doubt it was for some good purpose; I presume he thought you would feel better if you went to work to forget your troubles."[300]

That same day, Lincoln sketched a new military plan, calling for swift implementation of the blockade; further drilling and instruction of troops at Fort Monroe; holding on to Baltimore "with a gentle, but firm, and certain hand;" bolstering Patterson's forces in the Shenandoah Valley; leaving troops in western Virginia under the command of McClellan; making Missouri more of a priority and encouraging Frémont to be more active there; reorganizing the forces that had retreated from Manassas; swiftly discharging the ninety-day enlistees who were unwilling to serve longer; and bringing forward the new volunteer forces rapidly and stationing them along the Potomac. Once these goals were reached, Union forces would advance on three fronts: (1) in Virginia, take Strasburg and Manassas Junction, (2) keep open lines from Washington to Manassas and from Harper's Ferry to Strasburg, and (3) then launch simultaneous campaigns against Memphis and East Tennessee.[301]

When a delegation urged him to concentrate on attacking the Confederates farther south, say at Mobile or New Orleans, Lincoln said he was reminded of an Illinois farm couple whose daughter "had been troubled all her life with a ringing sound in her head, and they had spent a good deal of money in their efforts to cure her, but without success. One day a stranger in that part of the country was passing, and the farmer's wife rushed out of the house and asked him if he was a doctor. He said yes. Then she told him what was the matter with her daughter and asked him if he could cure her. He replied that he could not get the disorder out of her system, but she might put a mustard plaster on her feet and draw the ringing from the top to the bottom."[302]

To carry out his grand strategy, Lincoln summoned George B. McClellan from western Virginia, where his successes, though minor, had cheered the North. Ten days before the battle at Bull Run, the president anxiously awaited news from McClellan, who was closing in on the Confederates at Rich Mountain. Throughout the night of July 11–12, Schuyler Hamilton, an aide of General Scott's, called repeatedly at the White House with news of the battle. Finally, around 4 A.M., he brought a telegram announcing a Union victory. Lincoln seemed vexed at being aroused, for he was wearing only a short red shirt which he felt compelled for modesty's sake to hold down with both hands. Since he could not read the telegram without indecorously letting go of his shirt, Hamilton turned his back and handed the document over his shoulder to the embarrassed Lincoln. When Hamilton assured him that much evidence corroborated the good news from Rich Mountain, the president said "with a happy rhythm in his voice, a ripple of merriment and satisfaction, 'Colonel, if you will come to me every night and every hour of every night, with just such telegrams as that, I will come out not only in my red shirt, but without any shirt at all. Tell General Scott so.'"[303]

Two days later, similar good news came from a follow-up engagement at Corrick's Ford. In his western Virginia campaign, McClellan and his men had killed or captured 700 Confederates while suffering only two dozen casualties. No other Union commander had achieved anything like this success, small-scale though it was, so McClellan seemed a natural choice to replace McDowell. Prominent officers, he said, "assured him that McClellan possessed a very high order of military talent," and, he added, "he did not think they could all be mistaken."[304]

Lincoln went out of his way to console McDowell, whom he called "a good and loyal, though very unfortunate" officer who had to "drive the locomotive as he found it." He told the general: "I have not lost a particle of confidence in you," to which the insouciant McDowell replied: "I don't see why you should, Mr. President." He was demoted to division commander, while Robert Patterson was replaced by Nathaniel P. Banks shortly after Bull Run.[305] When Patterson asked Lincoln for vindication, the president told him: "I have never found fault with or censured you; I have never been able to see that you could have done anything else than what you did do. Your hands were tied; you obeyed orders, and did your duty, and I am satisfied with your conduct." Patterson recalled that these words were "said with a manner so frank, so candid, and so manly, as to secure my respect, confidence, and good will. I expressed to the President my great gratification with, and tendered my sincere thanks for, his fairness towards me, and his courtesy in hearing my case, and giving me some five hours of his time." When Patterson requested a court-trial "in order to have a public approval of my conduct, and stop the abuse daily lavished upon me," Lincoln said (as the general recalled) that "he would cheerfully accede to any practicable measure to do me justice, but that I need not expect to escape abuse as long as I was of any importance or value to the community, adding that he received infinitely more abuse than I did, but he had ceased to regard it, and I must learn to do the same."[306] To placate the general, Lincoln promoted his son to brigadier over Cameron's strenuous objections.

On July 27, McClellan officially took command of the Division of the Potomac, raising high Northern hopes. His presence in Washington "seems to inspire all with new courage and energy," reported William O. Stoddard from the White House.[307] The Young Napoleon, as General McClellan was called, would redeem the shameful defeat at Bull Run, whip the demoralized army into shape, and soon bring the war to a victorious close. Or so it was thought.

24

Sitzkrieg
The Phony War
(August 1861–January 1862)

In the wake of the ignominious defeat at Bull Run, a prominent journalist spoke for many when he confided to a colleague, "I am feeling bad—very bad. The Manassas disaster broke me down in a measure, but I could get over this—could understand it, and extract something good from it, were it not that I am wanting in Confidence in the Administration," which "either does not comprehend the magnitude of this rebellion; or they don't know, or don't want to learn, how to put it down." It could not "be suppressed by kindness; that's clear—and yet Mr Lincoln seems to think it can." The Republican Party, he lamented, "has gone up—and I only hope that our country, through the imbecility or cowardice, or treachery of her rulers, may not follow. We want a firm and able Administration, with a great and determined National policy, vigorously executed." He feared that another Bull Run "blunder and all would be lost. The people now more than half disgusted would then be wholly demoralized."[1]

Lincoln shared that fear. In early December, Benjamin Brown French, the commissioner of public buildings, asked him why the army had made no serious advance since July. The president replied: "If I were *sure* of victory we would have one at once, but we cannot stand a defeat, & we must be certain of victory before we strike."[2] In September, when a Philadelphian expressed to Lincoln the hope that troops would soon march against Richmond and stated "that those who had subscribed money, &c., had a right to look for some such demonstration," Lincoln quietly gazed at him and asked: "Will you tell us the route to take to Richmond? We tried it at Manassas, and found it like Jordan."[3]

Equally convinced that no attack should be made until victory seemed certain was the commander Lincoln had placed in charge of the army, George B. McClellan. The general hesitated to commit his forces, which he had splendidly trained and equipped. For half a year the Civil War resembled what World War II in Europe would become during the fall and winter of 1939–1940: a *sitzkrieg* (sitting war) instead of a *blitzkrieg* (lightning war). While the North grew exasperated with McClellan,

the president bore with his timidity month after month after month. Lincoln's patience was legendary but, as McClellan would eventually discover, finite.

From August 1861 to March 1862, the press regularly reported "all quiet on the
Potomac." At first, it was a simple statement of fact; eventually, it came to express
derision for McClellan's inactivity. In September, Lincoln asked the telegraph operator at the War Department, "what news?" When the reply came: "Good news, because none," the president remarked: "Ah! my young friend, that rule don't always
hold good, for a fisherman don't consider it good luck when he can't get a bite."[4]
McClellan was getting no bites.

McClellan to the Rescue

The vain, arrogant, 34-year-old McClellan shared the Northern public's view that he
was a savior. Shortly after arriving in Washington, he told his wife: "I find myself in
a new & strange position here—Presdt, Cabinet, Genl Scott & all deferring to
me—by some strange operation of magic I seem to have become *the* power of the
land. I almost think that were I to win some small success now I could become Dictator or anything else that might please me—but nothing of that kind would please
me—*therefore* I *won't* be Dictator. Admirable self denial!" After visiting the senate,
which showered him with congratulations, he mused: "All tell me that I am held responsible for the fate of the Nation & that all its resources shall be placed at my disposal. It is an immense task that I have on my hands, but I believe I can accomplish
it." Boastfully he reported that in Richmond it was said "that there was only one man
they feared & that was McClellan." With unconscious irony he insisted that "I am *not*
spoiled by my unexpected & new position—I feel sure that God will give me the
strength & wisdom to preserve this great nation. . . . I feel that God has placed a great
work in my hands."[5]

The general's cockiness was understandable, for he had been a high-achieving
wunderkind, having finished second in the class of 1846 at West Point, served creditably in the Mexican War, led a prestigious commission to observe the Crimean War,
invented a saddle that became standard cavalry issue, and become the president of a
railroad after quitting the service in 1857. Shortly after the fall of Sumter, he had received command of Ohio's militia, attaining the rank of major general in the regular
army (second only to Scott) in May 1861 and commanding the sole Union force that
won victories in the early months of the Civil War. Failure was unknown to this
Young Napoleon, which was unfortunate, for he could have profited from that painful experience as Lincoln, U. S. Grant, and other successful leaders in the war had
done. Instead, his head swelled all too easily, and he developed a paradoxical amalgam of timidity and overconfidence. His chest also tended to swell, especially when
issuing proclamations to his troops like one dated May 25: "Soldiers! I have heard
that there was danger here. I have come to place myself at your head and to share it
with you."[6]

While Lincoln and his constituents rejoiced at the triumph of Union arms in western Virginia, in fact McClellan had exhibited qualities there that boded ill. He ungenerously took credit due others, unfairly chastised subordinates, showed indecisiveness at

key points, failed to follow up on his victories, made repeated promises that he did not honor, was tardy and irresolute on the battlefield, showed a lack of initiative, and tended to whine unjustly about insufficient support. McClellan had devised an admirable strategy, but its success owed far more to his brigadier generals than to himself. These many shortcomings were overlooked partly because he won and partly because he was a skillful self-promoter, writing vainglorious dispatches that exaggerated his accomplishments.

On August 2, McClellan complied with the president's request by submitting what he called "a carefully considered plan for conducting the war on a large scale" that would end hostilities "at one blow." With 273,000 troops in his own army and an unspecified number in others, he proposed to take Richmond (which had become the Confederate capital on May 21), New Orleans, Charleston, Savannah, Montgomery, Pensacola, and Mobile and thus "crush out this rebellion in its very heart." To his wife he predicted that he would "carry this thing on 'En grand' & crush the rebels in one campaign—I flatter myself that Beauregard has gained his last victory."[7] In its impracticality, this scheme resembled the "Kanawha plan" that McClellan, known as Little Mac, had months earlier submitted to General Scott, who rightly dismissed it as unfeasible. (That scheme envisioned 80,000 men marching from Ohio to Richmond, across two mountain ranges, with no rail or water lines to feed and supply such a force.)

If McClellan showed weakness as a strategist, he proved an exceptionally able organizer and administrator. In the late summer and throughout the fall, he industriously drilled, trained, supervised, and inspired the troops under his command, replacing unfit officers, and thus creating a disciplined, well-equipped army. He renamed his force, which had been called the Division of the Potomac, the Army of the Potomac (which included not only the Division of the Potomac but also the troops in the District of Columbia and those which Patterson had commanded in the Shenandoah Valley). His soldiers loved him, for he seemed to care deeply about their well-being, even if he did not live among them in camp but rather in a comfortable house near the Executive Mansion. His martial bearing and air of self-possession inspired respect. Henry W. Bellows of the U.S. Sanitary Commission, which was dedicated to promoting the welfare of soldiers, said in September that there "is an indefinable *air of success* about him and something of the 'man of destiny.'" One of his brigadiers in the western Virginia campaign wrote that McClellan was personally "very charming" and that "his manner of doing business impressed every one with the belief that he knew what he was about."[8]

McClellan enjoyed showing off his army at reviews, which Lincoln gladly attended, even when the temperature in Washington reached 100 degrees, causing many troops to pass out. At one review, as the multinational Thirty-ninth New York regiment, known as the "Garibaldi Guards," marched by the platform on which the president and other dignitaries stood, each soldier removed from his hatband a small bouquet or a sprig of evergreen, which they tossed toward Lincoln, creating "a perfect shower of leaves and flowers." Nicolay reported that this gesture "was unexpected and therefore strikingly novel and poetical."[9] Another observer, Samuel F. Du Pont, wrote his wife that his initial impression of the president was "that he was the ugliest man I had seen, for one looking so young. This wore off and he has a certain poise and air which are not unpleasant—if he had lived in the East, he might have been graceful."[10] Some soldiers, however, complained that Lincoln's demeanor at reviews was too informal, that he talked with colleagues instead of paying full attention to the passing troops. A journalist who observed him shake hands with members of a New York regiment wrote that "I have seen nearly all of our great men, from Jackson down, go through the 'pump-handle movement,' but there certainly never was a man who could do it with the celerity and *abandon* of President Lincoln. He goes it with both hands, and hand over hand, very much as a sailor would climb a rope. What is to the satisfaction of all is, that he gives a good honest, hearty shake, as if he meant it."[11]

The president often visited army camps ringing the capital. On September 10, he and McClellan toured fortifications and reviewed George A. McCall's division, whose ranks cheered the general heartily. "You have no idea how the men brighten up now, when I go among them," McClellan told his wife. "I can see every eye glisten. Yesterday they nearly pulled me to pieces in one regt. You never heard such yelling. I did not think the Presdt liked it much."[12] (Such enthusiasm was not always spontaneous; General William F. Smith ordered his men to hurrah whenever they saw McClellan.) On November 20, at what Nicolay called "the largest and most magnificent military review ever held on this continent," Lincoln and McClellan galloped for two hours inspecting 50,000 men, passing before and behind each regiment on the plain between Munson's Hill and Bailey's Cross Roads. Nicolay, who was among the entourage following the two leaders, reported that Lincoln "rode [as] erect and firm in his saddle as a practical trooper—he is more graceful in his saddle than anywhere else I have seen him."[13] A journalist concurred, noting that the "President looked well in the saddle—much better than he ever looked on any other public occasion. He is an excellent horseman, and grace, impossible as it may seem, becomes a Lincolnian attribute when the executive legs are spurred and stirruped."[14] One of McClellan's staff officers was less complimentary, noting that as the president rode along holding his hat in one hand, he resembled a blind beggar. A corporal saw Lincoln with "one hand [a]hold of the bridle, the other convulsively clutched in the mane of his horse which never relaxed its hold except for a moment to crowd his hat further down over his eyes. His long legs were well clasped around the body of his horse, his hair & coat tails horizontal. He looked as though he was determined to go through it if it killed him but would be most almighty glad when it was over."[15]

Rather than fighting the nearby Confederates, McClellan defiantly campaigned against Winfield Scott, whom he wished to supplant as general-in-chief of the army. This came as a shock to Scott, for McClellan had praised him extravagantly in July: "All that I know of war I have learned from you, & in all that I have done I have endeavored to conform to your manner of conducting a campaign, as I understand the history of your achievements. It is my ambition to merit your praise & never to deserve your censure."[16] (In fact, McClellan's strategy and tactics in the Civil War resembled those he had observed Scott employ during the Mexican War.) Three weeks later, McClellan wrote Scott a very different letter, haughtily expressing alarm that the 100,000 Confederate troops facing them (a gross overestimate) placed Washington in *"imminent danger"* and urging that his own command be enlarged. After consulting with Seward that same day, McClellan wrote his wife: "How does he think that I can save this country when stopped by Genl Scott—I do not know whether he is a *dotard* or a *traitor*! I can't tell which. He *cannot* or *will* not comprehend the condition in which we are placed & is entirely unequal to the emergency. If he cannot be taken out of my path I will not retain my position, but will resign & let the adm[instratio]n take care of itself." Scott "is a perfect imbecile" who "understands nothing, appreciates nothing & is ever in my way."[17] Ironically, he complained that Scott "is for inaction & the defensive."[18]

Scott, understandably offended by McClellan's presumptuous tone, denied that the capital was in danger and, feeling infirm and undermined by his subordinate officer, asked to be retired. The president tried to smooth things over by persuading McClellan to withdraw his letter and requesting the general-in-chief to retract his. Scott, however, refused, explaining that "it would be against the dignity of my years, to be filing daily complaints against an ambitious junior" who ignored him, defied him, and dealt with cabinet members without consulting him.[19] (By communicating directly with McClellan, Lincoln and Cameron had inadvertently helped weaken Scott's authority.) Scott did not, however, insist that his resignation be accepted.

Try as he may, Lincoln was unable to stop the feuding between the hypersensitive Scott and his contemptuous subordinate; they continued to squabble for the next three months. McClellan ignored Scott's requests for information about his command, bypassed him in dealing with the administration, and flouted his chief's orders. On September 27, an ugly flare-up occurred in Lincoln's presence. At Scott's office, the president, Welles, Cameron, Seward, and McClellan met to discuss the military situation. When no one else seemed to know how many Union troops were in and around the capital, Seward offered an exact count, much to the chagrin of Old Fuss and Feathers, who indignantly asked: "Am I, Mr. President, to apply to the Secretary of State for the necessary military information to discharge my duties?" As they left, Scott confronted McClellan, saying: "When I proposed that you should come here to aid, not supersede, me, you had my friendship and confidence. You still have my confidence."[20] Lincoln intervened, remarking kindly that "he could not afford to permit them to disagree."[21] Little Mac boasted to his wife that "I kept cool, looked him [Scott] square in the face, & *rather* think I got the advantage of him. . . . I said nothing, merely looked at him, & bowed assent."[22] The president explained that in managing his generals, "he tried to cultivate 'good temper'" and "not to let any of them get mad with him, nor gain much by getting mad with each other."[23]

In October, when three impatient Radical Republican senators—Benjamin F. Wade of Ohio, Zachariah Chandler of Michigan, and Lyman Trumbull of Illinois—urged McClellan to advance on the enemy, he replied that he could do nothing as long as Scott remained in charge. Chandler came away deeply dissatisfied with McClellan, who, he said, seemed "to be devoting himself to parades" rather than "cleaning the country of Rebels."[24] The president warned McClellan that, ill-informed though the senators might be, they and their constituents could not be ignored. "I have a notion to go out with you and stand or fall with the battle," Lincoln mused.[25]

Those senators (deemed "the Jacobin club" by John Hay) also implored Lincoln to remove Scott.[26] In fact, the president on October 18 had read to cabinet a draft of a tactful letter accepting Scott's resignation. The aged general had become too ill and was too unfamiliar with war of such vast scope to be effective.

Two weeks later, the general-in-chief renewed his request that he be placed on the retired list. On November 1, Lincoln agreed and, along with the cabinet, paid a visit to Scott, who was too weak to sit up. The president read him a statement as he lay on his couch: "The American people will hear with sadness and deep emotion that General Scott has withdrawn from the active control of the army, while the President and a unanimous Cabinet express their own and the nation's sympathy in his personal affliction and their profound sense of the important public services rendered by him to his country during his long and brilliant career, among which will ever be grate-fully distinguished his faithful devotion to the Constitution, the Union, and the Flag, when assailed by parricidal rebellion." Lincoln assured the general that his staff would be well taken care of.[27] The aged hero of Lundy's Lane wept as he listened to the president's words, replied graciously, and shook hands with his visitors as he bade them a sad farewell. Upon emerging from the room, Lincoln, too, had tears in his eyes.

That evening, the president called on McClellan, who rejoiced in his triumph over Scott. Old Fuss and Feathers had magnanimously recommended Little Mac as his successor. After hearing McClellan read his order concerning Scott's retirement, the president said: "I should be perfectly satisfied if I thought that this vast increase of responsibility would not embarrass you."

"It is a great relief, sir. I feel as if several tons were taken from my shoulders today. I am now in contact with you, and the Secretary. I am not embarrassed by interven-tion."

"Draw on me for all the sense I have, and all the information. In addition to your present command, the supreme command of the army will entail a vast labor upon you."

"I can do it all," McClellan replied quietly.[28]

Around that same time, Little Mac told the president: "I think we will succeed entirely if our friends will be patient, and not hurry us."

"I promise you, you shall have your own way," Lincoln said.[29]

With this change in high command, impatient Northerners expected action. Angry at the army's inertia, several senators, including Trumbull, Wade, and Chan-dler, called on Lincoln. According to a journalist, they "kindled a brisk fire around his crazy and spavined old legs." They wanted to know who was responsible for the army's failure to move. The president "assured them that now and henceforth McClellan should be in full command [of] the Army of the Potomac [which] is to act under his orders, he [is] to be responsible for [an] advance, and to be actually unfettered."[30] Trumbull warned the president "that if the federal army did not achieve a decided suc-cess before winter set in, it would be very difficult not only to raise a fresh loan in the money market, but [also] to get Congress to authorize a new loan."[31] Wade expressed doubt that "the people of the northern states care to pay forty millions a month simply to retain Maryland in the Union, for that seems to be about all the government is doing, or attempting to do." He cautioned "that Congress would not allow the Army of the Potomac to winter" in Washington and declared: "Something, Mr. President, must be done. War must be made on the secessionists, or we will make war on the Administration."[32]

Back in Illinois, William H. Herndon wondered what his partner was doing. "Does he suppose he can crush—squelch out this huge rebellion by pop guns filled with rose water?" he asked. "He ought to hang somebody and get up a name for will or decisiveness of character. Let him hang some child or woman, if he has not courage to hang a *man*."[33] Equally bloody-minded was a Detroit resident who called for "war to the knife and the knife to the hilt" and expressed astonishment that "the Government has managed to be so far behind the people."[34]

The quarrelsome Young Napoleon, who seldom got along with superiors, implied that Scott alone had hindered him, and now that Old Fuss and Feathers was out of the way, he could take the offensive. But in fact, McClellan complained about the president as much as he ever did about Scott. To his wife, he described Lincoln as "an idiot," "the original gorilla," a "baboon," and "'an old stick'—& pretty poor timber at that." He denounced "the cowardice of the Presdt" and declared that "I can never regard him with feeling other than those of thorough contempt—for his mind, heart & morality."[35]

McClellan manifested his contempt for Lincoln in deeds as well as words. Less than two weeks after his elevation to the supreme command, he returned home from a wedding to discover the president, John Hay, and Seward waiting for him. According to Hay, the general "without paying any particular attention to the porter who told him the President was waiting to see him, went up stairs, passing the door of the room where the President and Secretary of State were seated. They waited about half-an-hour, and sent once more a servant to tell the General they were there, and the answer cooly came that the General had gone to bed." As they returned to the White House, Hay bemoaned "this unparrallelled insolence of epaulettes," but Lincoln "seemed not to have noticed it specially, saying it was better at this time not to be making points of etiquette & personal dignity."[36]

This snub from McClellan was hardly an isolated example. A month earlier, the English journalist William Howard Russell noted in his diary: "Calling on the General [McClellan] the other night at his usual time of return, I was told by the orderly, who was closing the door, 'The General's gone to bed tired, and can see no one. He sent the same message to the President, who came inquiring after him ten minutes ago.'"[37] Around that same time, Lincoln called at the general's headquarters, only to be told that he was "lying down, very much fatigued."[38] On another occasion, McClellan did not stop eating his breakfast when the president called; Lincoln was kept waiting till the general finished his meal, much to the surprise of an observer. One day David D. Porter was astounded by McClellan's reaction when a conversation he was having with the general concerning the New Orleans campaign was interrupted by a servant announcing that Lincoln wished to see him.

"Let him wait," said McClellan. "I am busy."

"Oh," remarked Porter, "don't send such a message to the President, he is very much interested in this matter, and it is not respectful to keep him waiting. Remember that he is our Commander-in-chief."

"Well," said the general, "let the Commander-in-chief wait, he has no business to know what is going on." Porter accurately concluded that McClellan's days were numbered.[39]

In December 1861, Lincoln asked McClellan to speak with Colonel Rush Hawkins, but the general refused. When Hawkins complained to Secretary of the Interior Caleb B. Smith about Little Mac's unwillingness to honor a presidential request, Smith assured him that such behavior was common.

Several months later, Lincoln once again found McClellan unwilling to get out of bed to meet with him. The president called at the general's house one Sunday morning and asked to see him. Soon McClellan's chief of staff, General Randolph Marcy, "came down and with flushed face and confused manner said he was very sorry but McClellan was not yet up. A strange expression came over Lincoln's face, as he rose and said, 'Of course he's very busy now, and no doubt was laboring far into the night.' He departed hastily."[40] McClellan was equally rude when he failed to keep an appointment with the president, General Ormsby M. Mitchel, and Ohio Governor William Dennison. After a long wait, Lincoln said with customary magnanimity and forbearance: "Never mind; I will hold McClellan's horse if he will only bring us success."[41] William O. Stoddard recalled how mortified he was one day when he accompanied Lincoln to the home of McClellan, who kept the president waiting for an unconscionably long time.

In early 1862, McClellan stood up Lincoln and the entire cabinet. As the president told General Ambrose E. Burnside in February, Little Mac "is a good fellow and means well," but he "don't know so much about etiquette as I do. I asked him to come and meet the Cabinet in Consultation the other day and he promised to do so. I called them together at 12 and all came, but no McClellan. At 1/2 past 12 Seward got impatient and went away, and at one all were gone. At half-past one McClellan came, and when I asked him why he was not here, he said he forgot it."

This absentmindedness reminded Lincoln of one of his legal cases. "When I was practicing law in Illinois a bad fellow in our town was charged with moral delinquency or in other words rape. He was accused of having committed two outrages on the woman—one in the afternoon and the other next day; everybody believed him guilty and when he applied to me to defend him, I refused; but he pled so hard and assured me so positively that the woman was a willing party that I consented to defend him and took up his cause. My friends remonstrated; but I was so convinced of the man's innocence that I determined to go on. At the trial, the woman gave in [an?] excellent direct testimony. I saw its effect on the jury and that it must be overcome; & in the cross examination I led her off to other topics and then suddenly returned to the charge.

"'Did you sleep with your husband after the first outrage?'"

"She said 'Yes.'

"'Did you tell him about it?'

"'No—I forgot.'"[42]

Even when McClellan deigned to allow the president to consult with him, he would not say much. In mid-December, Lincoln visited the general's house, accompanied by the eminent historian George Bancroft, who described Little Mac unflatteringly: "Of all the silent, uncommunicative, reserved men, whom I ever met, the general stands among the first. He is one, who if he thinks deeply keeps his thoughts to himself."[43]

McClellan's contempt for the president was partially rooted in snobbery. The scion of an eminent Philadelphia family, McClellan viewed many people as his social inferiors, among them Lincoln. Years after the war, he wrote that the sixteenth president "was not a man of very strong character, & as he was destitute of refinement—certainly in no sense a gentleman—he was easily wrought upon by coarse associates whose style of conversation agreed so well with his own."[44] (Other well-bred Philadelphians agreed with McClellan's assessment. William M. Meredith, attorney general of Pennsylvania and former treasury secretary under President Taylor, complained after several interviews at the White House that Lincoln was "greatly wanting in dignity," too "familiar in his manners, eternally joking and jesting and fond of telling bawdy stories in gross language," and "deficient in force, knowledge & ability.")[45]

McClellan had contempt for other civilian leaders, including the cabinet, which he scorned as "a most dispicable set of men." Seward he called "a meddling, officious, incompetent little puppy." Welles was "weaker than the most garrulous old woman you were ever annoyed by." Bates was an "inoffensive old man."[46] When he kept Edwin M. Stanton (Cameron's replacement as head of the War Department) cooling his heels, much as he did Lincoln, the infuriated secretary said: "That will be the last time General McClellan will give either myself or the President the waiting snub."[47] Chase told Little Mac that he was tired of calling on him and being told the general was too busy to be disturbed.

McClellan also denounced Radicals in Congress for their ideology as well as their meddlesome ways. A partisan Democrat, he had little sympathy for the antislavery cause or for blacks. He confided that he had "a prejudice in favor of my own race" and that he could not "learn to like the odor of either Billy goats or niggers." Radicals insisting on immediate emancipation, he thought, "had only the negro in view" and "cared not for the results" of the war, "knew little or nothing of the subject to be dealt with, & merely wished to accomplish a political move for party profit, or from sentimental motives." He told his wife, "I will not fight for the abolitionists." Tactlessly, he made these views known to leading Radicals, including the influential Senator Charles Sumner, with whom he had an interview soon after arriving in Washington.[48]

When the Radicals clamored for action, McClellan appealed to a Democratic leader in New York: "Help me to dodge the nigger—we want nothing to do with him. *I* am fighting to preserve the integrity of the Union & the power of the Govt—on no other issue. . . . As far as you can, keep the papers & the politicians from running over me."[49]

All Quiet on the Potomac

The self-aggrandizing McClellan may have conquered Scott, but the Confederates in Virginia went virtually unmolested. At the end of September, when the enemy abandoned Munson's Hill (within sight of the Capitol), Unionists were mortified to learn that the artillery posted there, which had intimidated McClellan, turned out to be "Quaker guns"—logs painted to resemble cannon. Confederates laughed while Northerners fumed. McClellan lamely consoled himself with the thought that the enemy "can no longer say that they are flaunting their dirty little flag in my face."[50]

This humiliating revelation did not keep McClellan from exaggerating Confederate strength, a mistake that affected all his decisions. A month later he submitted to Cameron a report (drafted by Edwin M. Stanton) stating that "all the information we have from spies, prisoners, &c., agrees in showing that the enemy have a force on the Potomac not less than 150,000 strong, well drilled and equipped, ably commanded, and strongly entrenched. It is plain, therefore, that to insure success, or to render it reasonably certain, the active army should not number less than 150,000 efficient troops, with 400 guns, unless some material change occurs in the force in front of us." By his own peculiar accounting methods, his army was far smaller, and therefore he could not launch an offensive without significant reinforcements. If they were provided, he would attack no later than November 25.[51] McClellan privately admitted that the Army of the Potomac was probably "condemned to a winter of inactivity."[52]

In actual fact, McClellan had between 85,000 and 100,000 effectives, while Joseph E. Johnston at Centreville and Manassas had only 30,000 to 35,000. The Young Napoleon could have assaulted Johnston, or Confederate positions on the south bank of the Potomac, or Winchester, or Leesburg, or Norfolk, all of which were vulnerable to a force as large as the Army of the Potomac. There was no excuse for the inactivity, which demoralized the North and encouraged the Confederates, whose contemptuous leaders began to refer sarcastically to McClellan as "the redoubtable McC."[53]

McClellan's exaggeration of Confederate strength stemmed in part, but only in part, from faulty information supplied by Allan Pinkerton, the detective who had warned Lincoln about the Baltimore assassination plot in February 1861. Little Mac hired him as his chief of intelligence well after the general had grossly overestimated Confederate forces in August. McClellan's central problem was not so much bad intelligence but a case of paranoia, which led him not only to see enemies everywhere but also to quarrel with superiors, mistrust most people, indulge in extreme secrecy, judge others harshly, cling to preconceived notions in the face of overwhelming evidence discrediting them, and refuse to acknowledge his own faults. Compounding his paranoia was a streak of narcissism, predisposing him to envy, arrogance, grandiosity, vanity, and hypersensitivity to criticism.

Blunders in the East

Public pressure for action led to a humiliating fiasco on October 21 at Ball's Bluff, Virginia, 40 miles from the capital, where Union forces under General Charles P. Stone, acting on vague orders from McClellan, crossed the Potomac to conduct a reconnaissance in force. During the Union repulse, the president's close friend, Colonel Edward D. Baker, was killed, along with dozens of others. A few weeks earlier, when Baker predicted that he would die in battle, the president tried to get him to dismiss such thoughts. Awaiting reports from the front, Lincoln prophetically said of Baker, "I am afraid his impetuous daring will endanger his life," and when this fear proved justified, he was devastated.[54] Emerging from the telegraph office with his head bowed down in grief and his ashen face streaked with tears, he failed to return the salute of the sentinel guarding the door. That night, unable to sleep, he paced back and forth in profound sorrow. At the funeral, he wept uncontrollably. A member of Baker's regiment, who attended that service and described the battle to Lincoln, said that the "President thought as much of Baker as a Brother."[55] William O. Stoddard also noted that Lincoln "loved him like a brother, and mourned his untimely death bitterly."[56] While listening to Colonel Charles Devens narrate the sad tale of Baker's demise, Lincoln interrupted repeatedly to ask: "When will this terrible war be over? Is there no way of stopping this shedding of blood?"[57] George Gibbs reported that things "certainly look very blue" at the capital and that Lincoln was so sure that Baker had been needlessly sacrificed that he "made a fuss" about it until shown evidence that the colonel had disobeyed orders.[58] The president later deemed Baker's death the "keenest blow" he suffered in the entire war.[59]

Occurring three months to the day after Bull Run, the disaster at Ball's Bluff demoralized the North badly. "The effect of the *last* Battle is more depressing than all other reverses," Thurlow Weed observed. "I was beset by hundreds in N.Y. asking unanswerable questions."[60] The commissary general of the Empire State declared the administration "an utter and palpable failure" and concluded that Lincoln "is not fitted for an emergency like this."[61] To Edwin M. Stanton, the administration's prospects "have never appeared more dark & gloomy than now." In Washington, he wrote, "[m]urmurs of discontent are heard on all sides."[62]

Frémont in Missouri

October was an unusually bad month for Lincoln. In the East, Baker's death, the ignominy of Ball's Bluff, the unseemly intrigue of McClellan against Scott, and Little Mac's failure to do much with his large army all combined to depress the president's spirits. On October 7, Stoddard reported from the White House that for the past few weeks Lincoln "has been looking pale and careworn, as if the perpetual wear-and-tear of the load which presses upon him were becoming too much even for his iron frame and elastic mind."[63]

That load was becoming oppressive indeed, especially since innumerable callers gave Lincoln little peace. He said "the importunities of the office seekers trouble him more than the rebellion of the secessionists."[64] In mid-October, Stoddard observed that "[n]ot a day passes but appeals are made to the Executive for action, on his part, that would be all but impossible if he were an absolute monarch, and many honest people doubtless feel themselves aggrieved that the President does not exercise, in their behalf, prerogatives which any crowned head of Europe would hesitate to assume."[65] Others pestered him with advice so often that he declared "that those who have the responsibility of managing the war, know how to conduct it as well as outsiders, and that he prefers not to be troubled with their counsels."[66]

Lincoln was especially upset by developments in the West. He said that there everything "military & financial is in hopeless confusion." Chase despaired because the government was within eleven days of exhausting the money raised by recent loans, its credit was gone at St. Louis, Cincinnati, and Springfield, and Congress had to audit immense claims. Events in Missouri were particularly distressing. That state, Lincoln remarked, was "virtually seized" by the Confederates, and "instead of having a force ready to descend the Mississippi" from Missouri, "the probability is that the army of the West will be compelled to defend St. Louis."[67] In September, the impulsive, flamboyant, grandiose John C. Frémont, commander of forces there, had predicted that the Confederates would take St. Louis within a few weeks.

Moreover, Frémont was on the verge of rebelling. According to Norman B. Judd, the general had "concluded that the Union was definitely destroyed and that he should set up an independent Government as soon as he took Memphis and organized his army."[68] In August, one of his division commanders, John Pope, speculated that Lincoln "will do in a different manner what Jeff Davis is doing directly—I mean that by neglect, corruption, & outrage, the States of the West will be driven to join together & act without reference to the authority of Gen[eral] Gov[ernmen]t."[69]

In Missouri, Frémont's impetuosity, tactlessness, poor judgment, egomania, ethical insensitivity, and administrative and military incompetence unfitted him for his heavy responsibilities. As one of his supporters ruefully noted, the "defect in Frémont was that he was a dreamer. Impractical, visionary things went a long way with him. He was a poor judge of men and formed strange associations. He surrounded himself with foreigners, especially Hungarians, most of whom were adventurers and some of whom were swindlers."[70] He would not have received such an important post if the Blair family, which had been friendly with him and his wife, had not lobbied vigorously on his behalf. As head of the Department of the West (encompassing Illinois, Missouri, Iowa, Kansas, Minnesota, Arkansas, western Kentucky, and the territories of Nebraska, Colorado, and Dakota), his most pressing task was to thwart Confederate attempts to conquer Missouri. He was then to raise an army and move on Memphis, thus helping to secure the Mississippi River, a goal that General Scott had originally proposed and that Lincoln endorsed heartily.

Shortly after his belated arrival at St. Louis on July 25, Frémont had to decide whether to reinforce the threatened Union position at Cairo, Illinois, or Nathaniel Lyon's small army in southwest Missouri. When he sensibly chose the former course, the impulsive, willful Lyon recklessly hurled his men against a much larger Confederate army at Wilson's Creek on August 10 and suffered a predictable defeat in which he was killed. Coming a scant three weeks after Bull Run, this setback further demoralized the public. A prominent journalist declared that "since the death of Lyon all confidence is gone."[71] Making matters worse still, in September, Confederates captured the 3,500-man Union garrison at Lexington, Missouri. Thus, in his first two months at St. Louis, Frémont had lost almost half the state. Through General Scott,

Lincoln instructed the Pathfinder "to repair the disaster at Lexington without loss of time."[72]

Frémont's political blundering upset Lincoln more than his military ineptitude. On August 30, the Pathfinder issued a proclamation establishing martial law throughout Missouri, condemning to death civilians caught with weapons behind Union lines, and freeing the slaves and seizing the property of rebels. Before issuing this fateful decree, he had consulted his wife and a Quaker abolitionist but no one in the administration.

While the Northern press generally lauded the Pathfinder's emancipation edict, Kentuckians indignantly denounced it as "an abominable, atrocious, and infamous usurpation."[73] Joshua Speed, a devoted Unionist, told his good friend Lincoln that the proclamation "will hurt us in Ky—The war should be waged upon high points and no State law be interfered with—Our Constitution & law both prohibit the emancipation of slaves among us—even in small numbers—If a Military Commander can turn them loose by the thousand by mere proclamation—It will be a most difficult matter to get our people to submit to it. All of us who live in Slave states whether Union or loyal have great fear of insurrection—Will not such a proclamation read by the slaves incline them to assert their freedom? And the owner whether loyal or not & the whole community suffer? I think the proclamation [goes] directly against the spirit of the law." So upset that he could neither eat nor sleep, Speed predicted that Frémont's decree "will crush out every vestage of a union party in the state— . . . So fixed is public sentiment in this state against freeing negroes & allowing negroes to be emancipated & remain among us—That you had as well attack the freedom of worship in the north or the right of a parent to teach his child to read—as to wage war in a slave state on such a principle."[74] Any man who tried to buck the opposition to emancipation in Kentucky, Speed colorfully explained, "had as well attempt to ascend the falls of Niagara in a canoe as to meet it, brave it, or change it."[75]

Robert Anderson, military commander in Kentucky, also warned Lincoln that Frémont's proclamation "is producing most disastrous results in this State, and that it is the opinion of many of our wisest and soundest men that if this is not immediately disavowed, and annulled, Kentucky will be lost to the Union. I have already heard that on the reception of the news from Missouri, this morning, a company which was ready to be sworn into the service was disbanded."[76] Kentuckians seemed to agree with the English newspaper that termed Frémont's proclamation a call for "negro insurrection, servile war, outrages and horrors without number and without name."[77] Montgomery Blair skewered the Pathfinder, acidly remarking that "with Frémont's surroundings, the set of scoundrels who alone have control of him, this proclamation setting up the higher law was like a painted woman quoting Scripture."[78]

Even before he had heard from Speed and Anderson, Lincoln gently but firmly urged Frémont to rescind the emancipation order, which went beyond the Confiscation Act passed by Congress in early August, freeing only those slaves directly supporting Confederate military efforts. The president advised Frémont that "the liberating slaves of traiterous owners, will alarm our Southern Union friends, and turn them against us—perhaps ruin our rather fair prospect for Kentucky." Tactfully, "in a spirit of caution and not of censure," Lincoln asked the general to modify his order to conform to the new law; he should do so as if it were his own idea, not as a grudging capitulation to a superior's order. Lincoln also instructed the Pathfinder to execute no one without presidential approval.[79]

The quarrelsome Frémont, who was temperamentally reluctant to follow orders and predisposed to ignore others' feelings, rashly declined to modify his decree voluntarily. He argued that if "I were to retract [the proclamation] of my own accord it would imply that I myself thought it wrong and that I had acted without the reflection which the gravity of the point demanded. But I did not do so. I acted with full deliberation and upon the certain conviction that it was a measure right and necessary, and I think so still."[80] Frémont defiantly ordered thousands of copies of the original proclamation distributed after the president had demanded its modification.

Reluctantly, Lincoln complied with Frémont's request for a direct order, and thus ignited a firestorm of protest. The White House mailbag overflowed with letters denouncing the revocation. Pro-secession Missourians took heart. One Illinois observer reckoned that the president's action "gave more 'aid and comfort to the enemy' in that State than if he had made the rebel commander, Sterling Price, a present of fifty pieces of rifled cannon."[81] A New York friend of the Pathfinder told Lincoln that "if he did not sustain the proclamation, Hamlin would take his place and would sustain it."[82] A similar threat appeared in an Auburn, New York, newspaper: "If he [Lincoln] will not regard the rights and will of his constituents, . . . we shall not be long in availing ourselves of all constitutional means to *put one in his place who will do it.*"[83] Frederick Douglass condemned the "weakness, imbecility and absurdity" of the administration's action. "Many blunders have been committed by the Government at Washington," Douglass declared, "but this, we think, is the biggest of them all."[84] William Lloyd Garrison ridiculed Lincoln's "timid, depressing, suicidal" letter to Frémont.[85] The *National Anti-Slavery Standard* called the president's action "one of those blunders which are worse than crimes."[86] Asking a question that preyed on many people's minds, James Russell Lowell wanted to know: "How many times we are to save Kentucky and lose our self-respect?"[87] The poet thought "an ounce of Frémont is worth a pound of long Abraham. Mr. L. seems to have a theory of carrying on war without hurting the enemy. He is incapable, apparently, of understanding that they *ought* to be hurt."[88] A Quaker abolitionist declared: "Better lose Kentucky, than keep her, at such a price. She will cheat us, in the end, unless we do with her, as with Missouri & Maryland—teach her submission, by the bayonet."[89]

Senators joined the chorus of criticism. William P. Fessenden of Maine called Lincoln's letter "very foolish," a "most weak and unjustifiable concession to the Union men of the border States," and reported that his constituents "are all for the proclamation, and the President has lost ground amazingly."[90] Fessenden added that "the intense selfishness of the President & Cabinet" had "disgusted every body."[91] Benjamin F. Wade scouted Lincoln's action, sneering that the president's attitude toward slavery "could only have come of one, born of 'poor white trash' and educated in a slave State."[92] Similarly, Gerrit Smith declared that Lincoln was "sadly perverted by his pro-slavery training."[93] Charles Sumner denounced the president as "a dictator,

Imperator,—what you will; but how vain to have the power of a God if not to use it God-like."[94]

Another Massachusetts antislavery champion, Lydia Maria Child, condemned Lincoln for being "narrow-minded, short-sighted, and obstinate," and exclaimed: "O Lord! O Lord! How we *do* need a Cromwell!" She urged all opponents of slavery to sustain Frémont: "We ought never to forget that he was the *first* man to utter the word, which millions long to hear."[95] George Bancroft told his wife: "We suffer from the want of an organizing mind at the head of the government. We have a president without brains."[96] From Chicago, Joseph Medill wrote that Lincoln's "frightfully retrograde" order to Frémont "comes upon us like a killing June frost—which destroys the comming harvest" and "has cast a funeral gloom" not only over the Windy City but also over "the state and the intire west." Nothing that Buchanan ever did "received so universal censure." Alluding to the ninety-first Psalm, Medill lamented that the "loss [of] a battle can be repaired: but this letter acts as a pestilence that walketh at noon day."[97] Medill's newspaper alleged that "[n]o Sunday in our recollection has been so broken by general indignation and rage."[98] In Wisconsin, people were so angry that one resident told his congressman that it "is utterly impossible for you to conceive what a whirlwind of grief & indignation" Lincoln's letter "has aroused throughout the North West." There the president "today could not carry the vote of [a] single town." Not even Buchanan was so roundly execrated as Lincoln now was.[99] In Minnesota, the feminist-abolitionist Jane Grey Swisshelm condemned the president's "imbecility, or treachery."[100]

In Ohio, the president was accused of succumbing to pressure from "chicken-hearted politicians."[101] Some thought Lincoln resembled Mr. Feeble Mind and Mr. Ready-to-Halt in John Bunyan's *Pilgrim's Progress,* while Frémont seemed like Great Heart. Cincinnati Republicans were "in a state of great consternation and wrath." A judge there reported that "no word describes popular sentiment but 'fury.' I have heard men of sense, such as are called conservative, advocate the wildest steps, such as the impeachment of Mr. Lincoln, the formation of a party to carry on the war irrespective of the President & under Frémont, etc., etc."[102] Jacob Brinkerhoff reported that Lincoln's action "falls like lead upon the hearts of the people of Ohio."[103]

Conservative papers like the New York *Herald* dismissed Lincoln's critics as "nigger-worshippers who have endeavored to make the struggle that has commenced a crusade against Southern institutions, in which oceans of blood should be shed to gratify the malice and folly of the school of which Garrison, Greeley, Gerrit Smith, Wendell Phillips and others are the prominent representatives." Lincoln had "in his mild rebuke of Fremont" dealt "very tenderly" with the general. Those who "continue to glorify the imprudent proclamation of Fremont are counseling insubordination in its most dangerous form." The Buffalo *Courier* predicted that the president's action "will gain ten supporters for every one he loses by showing his resolute determination to stand by the Constitution and the Laws to the greatest possible extent."[104] Thomas Ewing expressed great relief, for he thought that if Lincoln had not swiftly forced a modification of the proclamation, "it would have lost us Kentucky and the war would be now raging on the banks of the Ohio."[105]

In fact, to allow Frémont's proclamation to stand would be to authorize every department commander to set policy without reference to popularly elected officials. Moreover, Lincoln was obliged by his oath of office to modify the Pathfinder's edict. The Springfield, Massachusetts, *Republican* sympathized with Frémont but found it "gratifying to know that we have a president who is as loyal to law—when that is made to meet an emergency—as he is ready to meet an emergency for which no law is provided. The president is right."[106] Rather than attacking Lincoln, *Frank Leslie's Illustrated Newspaper* criticized Congress for passing such a halfway measure as the Confiscation Act. Other Republican journals, without taking sides, condemned the dissension within the party's ranks that Frémont had stirred up.

On September 10, Frémont's headstrong wife, nèe Jessie Benton (daughter of the eminent Missouri Senator Thomas Hart Benton), called at the White House and administered a tongue-lashing to the president. An admirer likened her to a dangerous, mammoth ironclad warship, "a She-Merrimac, thoroughly sheathed, & carrying fire in the genuine Benton furnaces" and armed with "guns enough to be formidable to a whole Cabinet."[107] Lincoln later remembered that she "taxed me so violently with many things that I had to exercise all the awkward tact I have to avoid quarrelling with her. . . . She more than once intimated that if Gen Fremont should conclude to try conclusions with me he could set up for himself."[108] Lincoln told one congressman that Mrs. Frémont, after "opening her case with mild expostulation," departed "in anger flaunting her handkerchief before my face, and saying, 'Sir, the general will try titles with you. He is a man and I am his wife.'"[109] Two years later she would refer to Lincoln's "sly slimy nature."[110]

When Elizabeth Blair Lee chided Jessie Frémont for acting like Catherine the Great, she shot back: "Not Catherine but Josephine." Mrs. Lee replied, "you are too imperious for her." Mrs. Frémont warned that her husband would challenge Frank Blair to a duel.[111] Frank's father told her she was acting "in very bad taste" and urged her to return to her family in St. Louis. He loftily added that in Washington "we make men and unmake them." She snapped: "I have seen some men of *your* making, and if that is the best you can do, I would advise you to quit the business."[112]

On September 12, the president wrote Jessie Frémont insisting that he entertained no doubts about her husband's "honor or integrity" and protesting "against being understood as acting in any hostility towards him."[113] (Three decades later, Mrs. Frémont implausibly reported that Lincoln treated her rudely, failing to offer her a seat, and accepting the letter she handed him "with an expression that was not agreeable." After she defended her husband, the president allegedly replied in a "sneering tone" that she was "quite a female politician.")[114]

Of the many protests deluging Lincoln, one from his friend Orville H. Browning surprised him most. In April, the conservative Browning had uncharacteristically, urged the president "to march an army into the South, and proclaim freedom to the slaves."[115] Frémont's "proclamation had the unqualified approval of every true friend of the Government within my knowledge," said Browning, who had just been appointed senator from Illinois to complete the term of the recently deceased Stephen A. Douglas. "I do not know of an exception. Rebels and traitors, and all who sympathize with rebellion and treason, and who wish to see the government overthrown, would, of course, denounce it. Its influence was most salutary, and it was accomplishing much good. Its revocation disheartens our friends, and represses their ardor."[116]

In the president's view, Frémont had acted unconstitutionally. Patiently Lincoln explained to Browning that the general's "proclamation, as to confiscation of property, and the liberation of slaves, is *purely political*, and not within the range of *military* law, or necessity. If a commanding General finds a necessity to seize the farm of a private owner, for a pasture, an encampment, or a fortification, he has the right to do so, and to so hold it, as long as the necessity lasts; and this is within military law, because within military necessity. But to say the farm shall no longer belong to the owner, or his heirs forever; and this as well when the farm is not needed for military purposes as when it is, is purely political, without the savor of military law about it. And the same is true of slaves. If the General needs them, he can seize them, and use them; but when the need is past, it is not for him to fix their permanent future condition. That must be settled according to laws made by lawmakers, and not by military proclamations. The proclamation in the point in question, is simply 'dictatorship.' It assumes that the general may do *anything* he pleases—confiscate the lands and free the slaves of *loyal* people, as well as of disloyal ones. And going the whole figure I have no doubt would be more popular with some thoughtless people, than that which has been done! But I cannot assume this reckless position; nor allow others to assume it on my responsibility. You speak of it as being the only means of *saving* the government. On the contrary it is itself the surrender of the government. Can it be pretended that it is any longer the government of the U.S.—any government of Constitution and laws,—wherein a General, or a President, may make permanent rules of property by proclamation? I do not say Congress might not with propriety pass a law, on the point, just such as General Fremont proclaimed. I do not say I might not, as a member of Congress, vote for it. What I object to, is, that I as President, shall expressly or impliedly seize and exercise the permanent legislative functions of the government."

Wrong in principle, Frémont's proclamation was ruinous in practice. "No doubt the thing was popular in some quarters," Lincoln told Browning, "and would have been more so if it had been a general declaration of emancipation. The Kentucky Legislature would not budge till that proclamation was modified . . . . I was so assured, as to think it probable, that the very arms we had furnished Kentucky would be turned against us." The president hastened to add that Browning "must not understand I took my course on the proclamation *because* of Kentucky. I took the same ground in a private letter to General Fremont before I heard from Kentucky."[117]

To another defender of Frémont's proclamation Lincoln replied: "We didn't go into the war to put *down* Slavery, but to put the flag *back;* and to act differently at this moment, would, I have no doubt, not only weaken our cause, but smack of bad faith; for I never should have had votes enough to send me here, if the people had supposed I should try to use my power to upset Slavery. Why, the first thing you'd see, would be a mutiny in the army. No! We must wait until every other means has been exhausted. *This thunderbolt will keep.*"[118]

Lincoln's fear was justified, for the public was not yet ready for emancipation. As the *National Anti-Slavery Standard* acknowledged in September, if he were to announce his intention to free the slaves, "nearly one-half of the people of the loyal States would utterly refuse to aid in carrying on such a war, and at least one-third of the army would lay down its arms." The abolitionist journal's Washington correspondent warned that a "premature movement of this kind might simply pave the way for the rule of Jeff. Davis over the whole land."[119] Eventually, antislavery idealism in the North would grow dramatically, but in the summer of 1861 George William Curtis accurately observed that some opposition to the peculiar institution was rooted in "abstract philanthropy," some in "hatred of slaveholders," some in "jealousy for white labor," but "very little" in "a consciousness of wrong done and a wish to right it."[120]

Lincoln was dismayed to learn from Frank Blair that Frémont let out contracts carelessly, secluded himself in his expensive mansion-headquarters, busied himself with trivial matters, and refused to draw up action plans. Blair regretted his earlier support of Frémont and now urged his dismissal. After Lincoln received numerous similar complaints from leading Kentucky and Missouri Unionists, he dispatched Montgomery C. Meigs and Meigs's brother-in-law, Montgomery Blair, to St. Louis to investigate. On their way, they stopped in Chicago to hand David Hunter a letter from Lincoln, written at the suggestion of General Scott: "Gen. Fremont needs assistance which it is difficult to give him. He is losing the confidence of men near him, whose support any man in his position must have to be successful. His cardinal mistake is that he isolates himself, & allows nobody to see him; and by which he does not know what is going on in the very matter he is dealing with. He needs to have, by his side, a man of large experience. Will you not, for me, take that place? Your rank is one grade too high to be ordered to it; but will you not serve the country, and oblige me, by taking it voluntarily?"[121] The accommodating Hunter proceeded to St. Louis with the quartermaster general and the postmaster general.

After conferring with Frémont, Montgomery Blair recommended his removal, explaining that the Pathfinder seemed "stupified & almost unconscious, & is doing absolutely nothing. I find but one opinion prevailing among the Union men of the State (many of whom are here) & among the officers, & that is that Fremont is unequal to the task of organizing the defences of the State."[122] (Blair's sister heard from a member of the Pathfinder's staff that his "seclusion & torpor" resulted from "the fact of his being an opium eater.")[123] Meigs discovered that Frémont was "living in state with bodyguards sentinels" and "building fortifications about the City at extravagant cost. He has built more gun-boats than directed. He is buying tents of bad patterns . . . at prices fixed by himself—not by the purchasing officers. The impression among the regular officers is that he is incapable, and that he is looking not to the Country but to the Presidency; he is thought to be a man of no principle. The rebels are killing and ravaging the Union men throughout the state; great distress and alarm prevail; in St. Louis the leading people of the state complain that they cannot see him; he does not encourage them to form regiments of defence, but keeps his eye fixed upon Cairo and the expedition down the Mississippi, while he leaves the state unprotected. Some talk of his intending to set off—like Aaron Burr—for himself with an independent empire. He lives in great style in a fine house. . . . A general at-mosphere of distrust and suspicion pervades the place; none of the regular officers seemed to think him honest."[124] The Pathfinder ignored Hunter, whose military ex-pertise could have helped him.

Even Frémont's admirers were appalled at his conduct. One wrote from St. Louis "that he fears all is going wrong, that Fremont has surrounded himself with a set of corrupt broken-down speculators from California, and is playing the very devil with the public money—that he is almost inaccessible to the best men. On one occasion Gov. Gamble could not get access to him for a week."[125]

Egged on by his hyperambitious, headstrong wife, known as "General Jessie," Frémont committed a major blunder by arresting Frank Blair immediately after his brother Montgomery had departed St. Louis. Frank Blair had criticized the general's failure to send reinforcements to Lexington. The bitter, vindictive Frémont denounced Blair's "insidious & dishonorable efforts to bring my authority into contempt with the Govt & to undermine my influence as an officer."[126] This high-handed act created an uproar in the national press. When the St. Louis *Evening News* came to Blair's de-fense, Frémont made matters worse by suppressing it and jailing the editor.

On September 17, Thomas S. Ewing, who had served in the senate with Fré-mont, wrote Lincoln that the Pathfinder was "a man of imperfect military education & no military experience & habitually jealous of those who possess these qualifica-tions which he has not—Those who knew him in California represented him to me as having there assumed state & pomp & ceremony under circumstances and in a style calculated to provoke ridicule—and that he was withal arrogant & jealous of power, quite disposed to combine the Russian autocrat with the Turkish Sultan—The sooner you call him to Washington for the purpose of consultation & dispose of him in a quiet way, the better."[127] Elsewhere Ewing described Frémont as "a vain pompous blatherskite."[128]

On September 19, Lincoln had General Scott draft an order instructing Frémont to turn over his command and report to Washington immediately. At Seward's sug-gestion, however, the president did not send it. It was feared that the popularity of Frémont and his proclamation, along with the difficulty of finding an adequate re-placement, made his removal inadvisable at that time.

Lincoln ordered the release of Frank Blair, but when that choleric congressman threatened to bring charges against Frémont, the Pathfinder once again arrested him, only to have General Scott countermand his act. Lincoln's calm handling of the con-troversy pleased Frank Blair's sister Elizabeth. She hoped that the president's "cool way of doing things will . . . teach the Blairs a lesson not to rush on at things or people so violently."[129] But Lincoln was not always decorous in handling Frémont's champions. To a friend of the Pathfinder, Lincoln abruptly declared: "Sir, I believe General Fré-mont to be a thoroughly honest man, but he has unfortunately surrounded himself with some of the greatest scoundrels on this continent; you are one of them and the worst of them."[130]

The exasperated president was sorely tempted to dismiss Frémont but hesitated when Illinois Governor Richard Yates warned that "the army of the West would rebel."[131]

Finally, Lincoln sent Cameron and Adjutant General Lorenzo Thomas to Missouri with an order relieve the Pathfinder, but only if he were not about to fight a battle. The meddlesome Chase, who informally assumed many of the war secretary's responsibilities, urged Cameron to "bear in mind that we must have vigor, capacity and honesty. If F[rémont] has these qualities sustain him. If not let nothing prevent you from taking the bull by the horns. We have had enough dilly dallying, temporizing and disgraces."[132]

When Lincoln asked General Samuel R. Curtis, commanding in St. Louis, his opinion of Frémont, he replied that the Pathfinder "lacks the intelligence, the experience & the sagacity necessary to his command."[133] (Curtis told Lorenzo Thomas that Frémont was not only "unequal to the command of an army" but also "no more bound by law than by the winds.")[134] Lyman Trumbull visited St. Louis and reported to the White House that he had "found a most deplorable condition of things there."[135]

In October, Lincoln asked 77-year-old General John E. Wool, the second-highest-ranking officer in the army, to aid Frémont. When Wool demanded complete control of the Pathfinder's department, however, the president withdrew his request. Wool sourly remarked that the country did not have "a man at the helm of state capable of directing affairs of state at this important crisis." While he believed that Lincoln was honest and well-intentioned, the president's "limited knowledge necessarily subjects him to be the instrument of others."[136]

Upon receiving the dismissal order from Cameron, Frémont begged for a chance to prove himself in battle, for he had belatedly started to move against Confederate forces in western Missouri. Cameron agreed to withhold the order on the understanding that Frémont would attack the Rebels soon. Meanwhile, damaging reports about the general continued to pour into the White House. Adjutant General Thomas, after conferring with David Hunter and others, submitted a blistering report urging Frémont's removal. The president received similar comments from Elihu B. Washburne, David Hunter, Charles G. Halpine, Ward Hill Lamon, John A. Gurley, Charles Gibson, John G. Nicolay, Thurlow Weed, and Josiah M. Lucas.

On October 22, Lincoln told the cabinet that "it was now clear that Fremont was not fit for the command" and that "Hunter was better." Seward dissented, arguing that the Pathfinder was too popular with the army to dismiss. Chase and Cameron concurred, to the disgust of Bates, who urged Lincoln "to avoid the timorous and vacillating course that could but degrade the Adm[inistratio]n and make it weak and helpless—to assume the powers of his place and speak in the language of command." To leave Frémont in charge after Cameron had countermanded his orders, repudiated his contracts, denounced his contractors, suspended his officers, and halted construction of fortifications at St. Louis would convince the public that the administration feared him. Heatedly the attorney general protested against having his home state sacrificed. Despite this passionate appeal, Lincoln agreed to delay action. Bates said the president hung "in painful and mortifying doubt" and that his suffering was "evidently great."[137] (Bates conceded that he had "demanded the recall of Genl. Frémont, possibly with too much emphasis & too often repeated.")[138]

Helping to stay Lincoln's hand was pressure from Radical senators and congressmen, who warned him that if he removed Frémont, "you displease millions of western men, but if you feel it to be your duty to do it, go ahead, but remember one thing—the western people will insist that the same rule be as rigidly applied to incompetent generals in this vicinity. It will never do to remove Fremont for incompetency and retain generals here whose names we can mention if they are also open to the same charge!"[139] Other Radicals, notably the editors of the Chicago *Tribune*, had grown disenchanted with the Pathfinder and said so publicly.

On October 24, Lincoln finally issued an order dismissing Frémont. Nine days later it was handed to the Pathfinder, who reluctantly turned over his command to Hunter. Lincoln suggested to the new commander of the Department of the West that he abandon the pursuit of the rebel commander, Sterling Price, pull back to Rolla and Sedalia, regroup his forces, guard the railroads, suppress local uprisings, and drive off invaders. Hopefully, he predicted that before spring arrived, "the people of Missouri will be in no favorable mood to renew, for next year, the troubles which have so much afflicted, and impoverished them during this."[140]

In 1863, Lincoln offered postmortems on Frémont's hundred-day career in Missouri: "I thought well of Fremont," he told John Hay. "Even now I think well of his impulses. I only think he is the prey of wicked and designing men and I think he has absolutely no military capacity."[141] To a group of abolitionists, he said: "I have great respect for General Fremont and his abilities, but the fact is that the pioneer in any movement is not generally the best man to carry that movement to a successful issue." A case in point was Moses, who "began the emancipation of the Jews, but didn't take Israel to the Promised Land after all. He had to make way for Joshua to complete the work. It looks as if the first reformer of a thing has to meet such a hard opposition and gets so battered and bespattered, that afterwards, when people find they have to accept his reform, they will accept it more easily from another man."[142]

Nicolay was less charitable in his assessment of Frémont, judging that the "d—d fool has completely frittered away the fairest opportunity a man of small experience ever had to make his name immortal."[143] Edward Bates was equally emphatic, declaring that the Pathfinder "has done more damage to our cause than half a dozen of the ablest generals of the enemy can do."[144]

Frémont's dismissal touched off an explosion of anger. The editor of the Cincinnati *Gazette*, Richard Smith, warned Chase that "the West is threatened with a revolution" because the "public consider that Frémont has been made a martyr." Even "sober citizens" were so enraged that they burned the president in effigy and yanked his portrait from their walls and trampled it underfoot. Rhetorically Smith asked: "Is it not time for the President to stop and consider, whether, as this is a government of the people, it is not unsafe to disregard and override public sentiment, as has been done in the case of Gen'l Fremont?" The Pathfinder, Smith explained, "is to the West what Napoleon was to France" while Lincoln "has lost the confidence of the people."[145]

Missouri Germans protested vehemently, as did militant opponents of slavery throughout the North. Protest meetings were held in New York, Cincinnati, and other cities. German troops in Frémont's army practically mutinied, swearing that they had joined up only because they wished to serve under the Pathfinder. At

Washington, opinion was reported to be "very much against the removal of Fremont just as he was about to give battle to the enemy. Much sympathy is expressed for the removed general, and indignation at the vacillation of President Lincoln. The simple truth is, Mr. Lincoln has been wavering about Fremont for six weeks, and had not the courage to remove him at the proper time, before he left St. Louis. He finally got his courage to the sticking point just as he was ready to fight, and had driven the rebels out of Missouri. Yet General Stone, after the Leesburg blunder, is untouched."[146] A Republican paper in Ohio patronizingly declared that Lincoln's "best friends and most intimate associates will hardly claim for him praise for any higher attribute than the absence of bad intentions."[147] Radicals interpreted Frémont's dismissal as yet another sign that the administration was soft on slavery. "Where are you, that you let the hounds run down your friend Fremont?" Thaddeus Stevens asked Simon Stevens.[148] Publicly, William Lloyd Garrison speculated that Lincoln's action would harm "the cause of the government, by depressing the moral sentiment and popular enthusiasm inspired by General Fremont's proclamation."[149] Privately, Garrison wrote that though the president was 6 feet, 4 inches tall, "he is only a dwarf in mind."[150] Parker Pillsbury was so disgusted with Lincoln's administration, which he deemed "the *wickedest* we have ever had," that he rejoiced "in defeat and disaster rather than in victory, because I do not believe the North is in any condition to improve any great success which may attend its arms."[151]

When Indiana Congressman George W. Julian insisted that Frémont be given another command, Lincoln replied that he could not do so without removing some other general. Julian's request reminded the president of a young man whose father urged him to take a wife. "Whose wife shall I take?" queried the son.[152] Lincoln told a St. Louis businessman that he did not "feel unkindly towards Fremont, but will never give him an independent command." The president would have appointed the Pathfinder minister to Russia "if he had treated him even civilly."[153] When the abolitionist Moncure D. Conway called at the White House to protest, Lincoln explained that "Frémont is in a hurry. Slavery is going downhill. We may be better able to do something towards emancipation by and by than now." Conway responded: "our fathers compromised with slavery because they said it was going downhill; hence, war to-day. Slavery is the commissary of the southern army."[154] In response to the public uproar, some cabinet members who had recommended Frémont's ouster expressed second thoughts. Mildly irritated, Lincoln complained that those men "now wished to escape the responsibility of it."[155]

Some Republican leaders, however, cheered Lincoln's decision. Henry Winter Davis, who eventually became a prominent Radical critic of the administration, applauded it and condemned "the abolition onslaught in Congress—which assails the *Prest.* for *leniency* in the war—& looks to a subjugation of the rebellious states—a freeing of *all* the negroes—& holding the country merely by military power governed by the U.S. under Territorial forms!!"[156] Even a few critics who deplored Frémont's dismissal admitted that his appointment had been a blunder.

In December, Lincoln once again had to deal with an inflammatory proclamation issued by an abolitionist general. On December 4, John W. Phelps, a Vermont

Radical commanding federal troops at Ship Island, Mississippi, amazed the president by announcing to the "loyal people of the Southwest" that Slave States were "under the highest obligations of honor and morality to abolish slavery." As soon they did so, "our Southern brethren . . . would begin to emerge from a hateful delirium" and "their days [would] become happy and their nights peaceable and free from alarm."[157] Indignant at the general's presumption in ignoring the administration's policy regarding slavery, Lincoln was tempted to dismiss Phelps, but rather than doing so, he simply ignored the proclamation. Phelps's unit was soon folded into Benjamin F. Butler's command, leaving the Vermont firebrand without the authority to issue similar documents. When Phelps resigned to protest Butler's foot-dragging on the recruitment of black troops, Lincoln did not intervene.

Naval Victories

Amid the gloomy aftermath of Bull Run, the navy provided the only bright spot for the North. In August, with the help of troops under Ben Butler, the navy seized control of Hatteras Inlet on North Carolina's Outer Banks. The small-scale operation, which deprived the Confederates of a privateer haven, required only seven ships. But minor though it was, this victory just after McDowell's humiliating defeat cheered up Lincoln, his constituents, and the army. Butler, smarting from the fiasco at Big Bethel in June, rushed to the White House with the good news. (His haste to brag about his accomplishment made him appear childish to some.) When the general arrived late at night to submit his report, Gustavus Fox, who had helped plan the operation, suggested that Butler immediately tell the president what had happened.

"We ought not to do that," said Butler, "and get him up at this time of night. Let him sleep."

"He will sleep enough better for it," replied Fox.

At the White House, Lincoln was so exhilarated at the glad tidings that he hugged the diminutive Fox, and together they danced around the room. Butler was much amused at the president's night shirt, which was "considerably agitated."[158]

The navy, in cooperation with the army, achieved a far more important victory in November, when seventy vessels and 12,000 troops captured Port Royal, South Carolina. That port then became a vital link in the chain enforcing the blockade. While helping to plan that operation, carried out jointly by Flag Officer Samuel Francis Du Pont and General Thomas W. Sherman, Lincoln grew frustrated by delays. Time and again the launch date was postponed until finally, on September 18, Lincoln told Welles that the "joint expedition of the Army and Navy, agreed upon some time since, . . . must be ready to move by the 1st of, or very early in October. Let all preparations go forward accordingly."[159] Du Pont feared that such a deadline would not allow time for adequate preparation. On October 1, the expedition was still not ready to depart. That day the president got "his dander up a little" when, during a council of war, mention was made of a scheme that General Ambrose E. Burnside was concocting for a campaign to secure the Chesapeake Bay and the Potomac River. Lincoln heatedly denied knowing anything about it and asked that the matter be investigated. An official from the War Department soon arrived with a paper from McClellan's headquarters describing an "expedition of 8,000 men, General McClellan to name the Commanding General and names General Burnside." No one in the war council had seen this paper, including Lincoln, who said he had never been asked "or told a word on the subject" and talked "of going back to Illinois if his memory has become as treacherous as that."[160]

Around that time, Lincoln remarked ironically to Ohio Governor William Dennison, who thought that the various government departments were "little islands unto themselves," that if Jefferson Davis "was to get me and I told him all I know, I couldn't give him much information that would be useful to him."[161]

In mid-October, when Thomas Sherman asked for a regiment from McClellan's army, the president became irritated, as did the Young Napoleon, who objected to any diminution of his force. On October 17, Lincoln told Seward: "I think I will telegraph to Sherman that I will not break up McClellan[']s command and that I haven[']t much hope of his expedition anyway." The secretary of state replied, "No you won[']t say discouraging things to a man going off with his life in his hand. Send him some hopeful and cheering dispatch." Lincoln took only part of this advice, telling Sherman: "I will not break up McC's army without his consent. I do not think I will come to Annapolis." John Hay thought Lincoln's "petulance very unaccountable."[162] A telegraph operator who often saw the president testified that he "was sometimes critical and even sarcastic when [military] events moved slowly."[163]

The Port Royal armada, whose mission had been planned by Gustavus Fox, finally sailed on October 29, complete with the extra regiment that Sherman had requested. The country anxiously awaited word of this fleet, whose destination was a closely guarded secret. When a White House caller implored him to reveal it, Lincoln teasingly asked if he could keep a confidence.

"Oh, yes, upon my honor," came the answer.

"Well," said Lincoln, "I will tell you." Pulling his curious visitor near him, the president whispered loudly enough to be heard by everyone in the room, "Well, the expedition has gone to . . . SEA!"[164]

Nine days after departing, the combined army and navy forces scored a brilliant success. Northerners rejoiced at what they called a "glorious achievement" and "our first great victory."[165] Acting on Lincoln's suggestion, Congress expressed its thanks to Du Pont "for the decisive and splendid victory achieved at Port Royal."[166]

At the same time, Lincoln derived satisfaction from the victory of the Republican mayoral candidate in New York, George Opdyke, who defeated the incumbent, Fernando Wood, a bitter critic of the administration. William Cullen Bryant reported that this good news "fills Washington with rejoicing."[167]

McClellan and the Administration under Attack

At the time of Frémont's removal, he was belatedly pursuing the enemy; meanwhile in the East, the conservative Democrat McClellan presided over the disaster at Ball's Bluff and then refused to undertake even a modest offensive. When Congress reassembled in early December, the Radicals demanded an investigation of the army and established a body to carry it out, the Joint Committee on the Conduct of the War, which was authorized to examine all aspects of the conflict. It vindicated Frémont, whom the Radicals regarded as a martyr to emancipation. The naiveté of the committee members, mostly Radical Republicans, led them to support men (like the Pathfinder) whose antislavery ardor was matched only by their military incompetence. The committee was critical of the president, but Lincoln found it useful, for such criticism provided him with spurs to help goad his generals into fighting. Lincoln was just as eager as the Radicals to conduct the war vigorously; he, too, wanted aggressive, effective commanders.

McClellan did not fit that description. The Radicals, along with the rest of the North, grew increasingly impatient with the Young Napoleon as winter approached. Ideal fighting weather persisted into December, but the Army of the Potomac failed to take advantage of it. Instead, it concentrated on ringing Washington with dozens of forts, mounting hundreds of guns. (After inspecting those works and hearing the general-in-chief explain that every contingency should be planned for, the president remarked: "The precaution is doubtless a wise one, and I'm glad to get so clear an explanation, for it reminds me of an interesting question once discussed for several weeks in our lyceum or moot court in Springfield, Illinois, soon after I began reading law. The question was, 'Why does man have breasts?' After many evenings' debate, the question was submitted to the presiding judge, who wisely decided 'that if under any circumstances, however fortuitous, or by any chance or freak, no matter of what nature or by what cause, a man should have a baby, there would be the breasts to nurse it.'")[168]

"There is a growing dissatisfaction with McClellan's inaction here which finds universal utterance," Congressman Henry L. Dawes reported from Washington.[169] Adam Gurowski spoke for many when he expressed the hope that the joint committee "will quickly find out what a terrible mistake this McClellan is, and warn the nation of him."[170] In fact, the committee chairman, Ohio Senator Benjamin F. Wade, deplored McClellan's timidity. Soon after being named general-in-chief, Little Mac promised to launch an offensive within weeks, but he did not. In early December, Lincoln formally asked him about the feasibility of attacking the Confederate supply lines to Manassas. If the Union army managed to cut the enemy's rail link, Johnston would be forced out of his entrenched position. It was a wise suggestion, but predictably Little Mac asserted that since the Rebel forces were nearly as large as his own, no such advance should be risked. Yet, he said, he had a plan "that I do not think at all anticipated by the enemy nor by many of our own people." He did not deign, however, to reveal its details.[171] On December 20, McClellan came down with typhoid fever and was indisposed for three weeks.

Despair overspread the North as the army entered winter quarters; some feared that its inaction would lead European nations to recognize the Confederacy. Bankers told Chase that unless either the army advanced or there was a cabinet shake-up, they would not lend the government more money, for the administration had nothing to show for the funds already lent. They were especially upset with Seward for issuing an alarmist appeal to state governors urging them to improve their shore defenses. That document, which halted popular subscriptions to the Treasury Department loan, seemed to many proof positive that Seward was unfit for his post.

Criticism of the administration grew ever more strident. Most congressional Republicans disagreed with Ohio Representative John A. Bingham's contention that "Congress ought to act & not find fault with the President."[172] Michigan Senator Zachariah Chandler groused that Lincoln was "*timid* vacillating & inefficient."[173] In early January, Congressman Henry L. Dawes told his wife that the "times are exceedingly dark and gloomy—I have never seen a time when they were so much so. Confidence in everybody is shaken to the very foundation—The credit of the Country is ruined—its arms impotent, its Cabinet incompetent, its servants rotten, its ruin inevitable. . . . The Govt. can't survive sixty days of such a life as it is now living. Oh that such a Cause should be crucified to an unholy alliance between trifling indifference, utter incompetence and reeking corruption."[174] Ben Wade denounced the "blundering, cowardly, and inefficient" administration and sneered that one "could not inspire Old Abe, Seward, Chase, or Bates, with courage, decision and enterprise, with a galvanic battery."[175] Kansas Congressman Martin F. Conway called Lincoln and Seward "undoubtedly pro-slavery." The president, in Conway's view, was "a poor affair," just "an old Kentucky Whig" who "knows no country as his own but Kentucky, and yet he would sell this for a small price."[176]

A Republican from the Bluegrass State acknowledged that Lincoln was "worthy & eminently honest" but feared that those qualities were not enough: "We need a man with an iron will & inflexible purpose." After spending several weeks in New York and Washington, this Kentuckian reported that there "is a painful state of feeling pervading all classes." The administration's delay in attacking the Confederates "has become intolerable. Something must be done or every thing will be lost & that speedily. If the Govt is not in earnest let us know it & quit. If it is then let it go to work. . . . If there is a single person that has not lost all confidence in the powers that be I have yet to find him."[177] Lincoln's former ally in the antislavery Whig ranks, Truman Smith, admired his "unspotted rectitude & great goodness of heart" but insisted that "in such a crisis rectitude & goodness are poor substitutes for that spirit & determination which Genl. Jackson was accustomed to manifest."[178] People in Wisconsin, according to a Republican editor there, believed "that the President and Cabinet,—*as a whole,—are not equal to the occasion.*"[179]

A Massachusetts woman, who was strongly opposed to slavery, thought Lincoln "was *honest,* no doubt, but no more fit for his station than I should be. Mrs Lincoln has the stronger will of the two."[180] Less charitable was a constituent of George W. Julian, who complained that Lincoln "has no *positive qualities,* however trivial. He is the mere puppet in the hands of others," most notably Seward. David Hunter would have taken Memphis long since, but "General McClellan and Col. Seward and Capt. Lincoln did not want it so."[181] Henry Winter Davis hyperbolically declared that "*no* administration has been so incompetent and so corrupt—not even Buchanan[']s."[182] Charles Eliot Norton condemned the "incapacity," "cowardice," "wretched feebleness & inefficiency," and "mean personal ambitions of the men who are in power," while George Gibbs deplored "the utter incapacity of Lincoln."[183]

Illinoisans were especially critical of the administration. "The people are heartily sick of reviews at an expense of one and a quarter millions a day," noted Lincoln's friend Pascal P. Enos of Springfield. The public felt that if the North could whip the Confederates, "let it be done at once," but, said Enos, "if we cannot we want to know it now and save ourselves from bankruptcy."[184] Gustave Koerner reported from Belleville that "our people, and our army out West are getting very much demoralised by this inaction." The rate of desertion from the army was soaring, and the "enthusiasm of the People is pretty nearly all gone. Recruiting at the West has come to a dead standstill."[185] "Public sentiment here is becoming sadly debauched," a resident of Freeport informed Congressman Elihu B. Washburne. "You at Washington must make a stand somewhere, and soon—else all—all is lost. . . . O! for an hour of an Executive of Jackson nerve and ability to stand forth and save this nation!!"[186] Another Freeporter warned Washburne that "unless the War Policy at Washington is soon changed the People will break down every man that endorses it. The rumbling thunder is beginning to be heard and the People are getting aroused and I say to you the watchword must be forward at Every Point."[187] Other Suckers observed that "nearly a Majority of the Men who voted for Uncle Abe are beginning to come out against him. . . . They curse Lincoln & call him a *Damned old traitor.*" Thousands "among his most devoted friends, who have persistently stood by him through evil as well as good report," were now "denouncing him most bitterly. They declare that he has done for the Republican Party what John Tyler did for the Whig Party."[188] Wait Talcott feared "that Kentucky had conquered the Administration, & that the President had forgotten that there was a North pouring out its best blood & treasure free as water to sustain the government."[189]

Discontent also reigned in Ohio. A Cincinnati physician asked: "How is it with our President? Our *Republican* President! Is he not given over, sold out, or pledged, bound hand and foot, soul and body, to the 'Conservative,' 'Union men' of the 'Border States.'—to *Kentucky* 'Union men?' I fear so!"[190] A former congressman from the Queen City complained that the "inaction of the army is bad enough, but when it seems that the cause is to prolong the robbery of the public funds, the people feel indignant."[191]

The president would have appreciated the understanding expressed by a Chicagoan: "I have no doubt, the Prest. would gladly exchange his tribulations for those of St. Paul, and be comparatively happy," said E. B. Talcott. "It is no holiday Sport to run the Govt Machine at this time."[192]

Lincoln grew as frustrated and discouraged as the Congressional Committee on the Conduct of the War. On January 2, he spoke to John A. Dahlgren "of the bare possibility of our being two nations." (This was the first time the commander of the navy yard could recall the president suggesting such an outcome of the war.)[193] When Ben Wade's committee visited him at the White House on December 31, the senator said bluntly: "Mr. President, you are murdering your country by inches in consequence of the inactivity of the military and the want of a distinct policy in regard to slavery."[194] Lincoln offered no reply, but he did write McClellan about it the next day: "I hear that the doings of an Investigating Committee, give you some uneasiness. You may be entirely relieved on this point. The gentlemen of the Committee were with me an hour and a half last night; and I found them in a perfectly good mood. As their investigation brings them acquainted with facts, they are rapidly coming to think of the whole case as all sensible men would."[195]

Thus, Lincoln hinted that the Army of the Potomac must attack. He also tried to convey that message through a friend of the general, to whom he said: "McClellan's tardiness reminds me of a man in Illinois, whose attorney was not sufficiently aggressive. The client knew a few law phrases, and finally, after waiting until his patience was exhausted by the non-action of his counsel, he sprang to his feet and exclaimed: 'Why don't you go at him with a Fi Fa demurrer, a *capias*, a *surrebutter*, or a *ne exeat*, or something; and not stand there like a *nudum pactum*, or a *non est?*'"[196]

On January 6, Wade's committee met with Lincoln and the cabinet to recommend that McDowell be given command of the Army of the Potomac and to insist that the war be prosecuted vigorously. The members were surprised that both the president and the secretaries knew little about McClellan's plans or his reasons for delay. Even more surprising was Lincoln's assumption that he had no right to know about them because his lack of a military background led him to defer to Little Mac. It seemed outrageous to the committee that the administration let McClellan sit idle without explanation. Wade attacked the Young Napoleon and bluntly demanded that changes be made. Lincoln and the cabinet did not agree with that assessment, and so the meeting ended inconclusively. On another occasion, Lincoln told a delegation protesting against McClellan's inertness: "Well, gentlemen, for the organization of an army—to prepare it for the field—and for some other things, I will back General McClellan against any general of modern times—I don't know but of ancient times either—but I begin to believe that he will never get ready to fight."[197]

Other congressional leaders were growing impatient with the administration. "We are in a world of trouble here," Senator William Pitt Fessenden of Maine told his family. "Everybody is grumbling because nothing is done, and there are no symptoms that anything will be done. The truth is that no man can be found who is equal to this crisis in any branch of the government."[198] A Democratic congressman from Indiana called the president "a feeble & vascillating man" who "lacks the energy, earnestness, comprehensive views & experience necessary for the crisis."[199]

In February, Thurlow Weed growled that "most of the men trusted with the great responsibilities of the Government, either lack ability or fail to comprehend the magnitude of their trust. I am *sure* that this war wisely entered upon and energetically carried on, would have been virtually concluded now."[200] A Cincinnatian reported that Lincoln "is universally an admitted failure, has no will, no courage, no executive capacity . . . and his spirit necessarily infuses itself downwards through all departments."[201]

All Quiet in the West

Union commanders in the West seemed as inert and querulous as McClellan. One exception was Ulysses S. Grant, who commanded a district with headquarters at Cairo. From there on November 7 he moved 9 miles south to attack Confederate forces at Belmont, Missouri, where he demolished a camp, captured half a dozen guns, and inflicted 642 casualties while sustaining comparable losses before being repulsed. John A. McClernand, a brigade commander under Grant (and Lincoln's former political opponent and congressman) complained that the administration had inadequately supported the Illinois units he headed. The president thanked and congratulated him and his men for all "you have done honor to yourselves and the flag and service to the country." As for the shortages and other problems the Illinoisans faced, Lincoln explained that in "my present position, I must care for the whole nation; but I hope it will be no injustice to any other state, for me to indulge a little home pride, that Illinois does not disappoint us. . . . Be assured, we do not forget or neglect you. Much, very much, goes undone: but it is because we have not the power to do it faster than we do. Some of your forces are without arms, but the same is true here, and at every other place where we have considerable bodies of troops. The plain matter-of-fact is, our good people have rushed to the rescue of the Government, faster than the government can find arms to put into their hands. It would be agreeable to each division of the army to know its own precise destination: but the Government cannot immediately, nor inflexibly at any time, determine as to all; nor if determined, can it tell its *friends* without at the same time telling its *enemies*. We know you do all as wisely and well as you can; and you will not be deceived if you conclude the same is true of us."[202]

On another occasion, when officers complained about lack of equipment, Lincoln urged them to make do with what they had. To drive home the point, he told an anecdote from his days on the circuit in Illinois. Late one night a thirsty traveler banged on the door of a tavern in Postville and demanded whisky. When the host and guests explained that they had none, the desperate fellow exclaimed, "Great heavens, give me an ear of corn and a nutmeg grater and I'll make some!"[203]

On November 9, Lincoln broke up the gigantic Western Department, placing Henry W. Halleck, a pedantic, goggle-eyed, indecisive West Point graduate in command of the new Department of Missouri (which also encompassed Arkansas and western Kentucky). Halleck had earned the sobriquet "Old Brains" for writing several books, most notably *Elements of Military Art and Science,* which made him the premier military theorist in the country. Hunter was assigned to the Department of Kansas, and Don Carlos Buell was appointed head of the Department of the Ohio, with responsibility for eastern Kentucky. Buell and Halleck were supposed to coordinate their efforts; the latter was to move south along the Mississippi toward Memphis, while the former was to slice the critically important rail line connecting Virginia with the Confederate West and to liberate eastern Tennessee, where Unionists were suffering persecution. In the West, Lincoln emphasized seizing territory, and in the East, destruction of the enemy's army.

A stern martinet who suffered from indecisiveness, Buell understandably thought Lincoln's plan infeasible, for his army faced daunting logistical problems in marching across four mountain chains in winter, then occupying eastern Tennessee, with no rail line to supply it. McClellan, however, counted on Buell to cut the railroad from Virginia to Chattanooga, isolating the Confederate forces he planned to attack in the Old Dominion; Little Mac said he would be unable to advance until Buell accomplished his mission. Buell, however, favored moving against Nashville in central

Tennessee, following the line of the Cumberland River, as a more practicable alternative to Lincoln's strategy. Impertinently, he told the president that he moved to carry out his plan with reluctance: "I have been bound to it more by, say sympathy for the people of Eastern Tennessee, and the anxiety with which yourself and the General in Chief have desired it, than by my opinion of its wisdom."[204]

Meanwhile in Missouri, Halleck reported that "everything here is in complete chaos. The most astonishing orders and contracts for supplies of all kinds have been made and large amounts purport to have been received, but there is nothing to show that they have ever been properly issued, and they cannot now be found."[205] He swiftly canceled fraudulent contracts, suppressed guerrillas, brought order out of the administrative rat's-nest left behind by Frémont, fired do-nothing staffers, suspended the construction of needless fortifications around St. Louis, and restored order to the state, all the while complaining about a shortage of troops and weapons.

From Kansas, Hunter protested bitterly that his new command was too small for a man of his rank. Lincoln gently chided him and offered sound paternal advice: "I am constrained to say it is difficult to answer so ugly a letter in good temper. I am, as you intimate, losing much of the great confidence I placed in you, not from any act or omission of yours touching the public service, up to the time you were sent to Leavenworth, but from the flood of grumbling despatches and letters I have seen from you since. I knew you were being ordered to Leavenworth at the time it was done; and I aver that with as tender a regard for your honor and your sensibilities as I had for my own, it never occurred to me that you were being 'humiliated, insulted and disgraced'; nor have I, up to this day, heard an intimation that you have been wronged, coming from any one but yourself. No one has blamed you for the retrograde movement from Springfield, nor for the information you gave Gen. Cameron; and this you could readily understand, if it were not for your unwarranted assumption that the ordering you to Leavenworth must necessarily have been done as a *punishment* for some *fault*. I thought then, and think yet, the position assigned to you is as respo[n]sible, and as honorable, as that assigned to Buell. . . . You constantly speak of being placed in command of only 3000. Now tell me, is not this mere impatience? Have you not known all the while that you are to command four or five times that many? I have been, and am sincerely your friend; and if, as such, I dare to make a suggestion, I would say you are adopting the best possible way to ruin yourself." Quoting one of his favorite poets, Alexander Pope, Lincoln counseled: "'Act well your part, there all the honor lies.' He who does *something* at the head of one Regiment, will eclipse him who does *nothing* at the head of a hundred."[206]

Halleck and Buell each offered abundant excuses for delay. When Buell opposed forwarding arms to East Tennessee, the president wrote on January 6: "Your despatch of yesterday has been received, and it disappoints and distresses me. . . . I am not competent to criticise your views; and therefore what I offer is merely in justification of myself." Rather than attack Nashville, which Buell preferred to do, Lincoln repeated his earlier advice to move on East Tennessee, where persecuted Unionists were begging for assistance. He told Buell that "my distress is that our friends in East Tennessee are being hanged and driven to despair, and even now I fear, are thinking of taking rebel arms for the sake of personal protection. In this we lose the most valuable stake we have in the South. My despatch, to which yours is an answer, was sent with the knowledge of Senator [Andrew] Johnson and Representative [Horace] Maynard of East Tennessee, and they will be upon me to know the answer, which I cannot safely show them. They would despair—possibly resign to go and save their families somehow, or die with them. I do not intend this to be an order in any sense, but merely, as intimated before, to show you the grounds of my anxiety."[207] He urged Buell to name a date when he could begin an offensive: "Delay is ruining us; and it is indispensable for me to have something definite."[208] The president sent a similar request to Halleck, who was unwilling to commit troops to Kentucky while he was preparing for an advance in southwest Missouri.

Despair

For Lincoln, January 10, 1862, was one of the worst days in the war. He dejectedly wrote to Cameron apropos of the negative responses from Halleck and Buell: "It is exceedingly discouraging. As everywhere else, nothing can be done."[209] On January 1, Lincoln said "with much feeling" to John A. Dahlgren, commander of the Washington Navy Yard: "No one seemed ready."[210] In despair, he turned to Montgomery Meigs, whose counsel he valued. (The president said Meigs "never comes [to the White House] without he has something to say worth hearing.")[211] "General," Lincoln asked, "what shall I do? The people are impatient; Chase has no money and he tells me he can raise no more; the General of the Army has typhoid fever. The bottom is out of the tub. What shall I do?"[212]

When Meigs suggested a consultation with Little Mac's division commanders, Lincoln called a meeting for January 10 with Generals Irvin McDowell and William B. Franklin, along with Seward and Assistant Secretary of War Thomas A. Scott. Cameron was conspicuously absent. According to McDowell, the president told them that he "was in great distress, and, as he had been to General McClellan's house, and the General did not ask to see him, and as he must talk to somebody, he had sent for General Franklin and myself, to obtain our opinion as to the possibility of soon commencing active operations with the Army of the Potomac." He added that "if something was not done soon, the bottom would be out of the whole affair; and if General McClellan did not want to use the army, he would like to '*borrow it*.'"[213] When Lincoln asked for recommendations, McDowell suggested an attack on the Confederates' supply line to Manassas, a sensible plan that the president had been urging on McClellan. Franklin proposed a campaign against Richmond via the York River. Lincoln asked that they reflect on the matter and convene again the next day, which they did.

Word that two of his division commanders had met with the president acted as a tonic restoring McClellan's health. On Sunday morning, January 12, he unexpectedly called at the White House and outlined a plan to attack Richmond by sailing his army down Chesapeake Bay to Urbanna on the Rappahannock River, 40 miles east of the Confederate capital. Early that afternoon the president met with Chase, Seward, Montgomery Blair, McDowell, Franklin, and Meigs. After Meigs endorsed

McDowell's proposal to attack the Confederate supply lines to Manassas, Lincoln suggested that since McClellan had recovered his health, they meet with him the next day.

On January 13 at 3 P.M., they did so. After explaining why he had convened this council of war, Lincoln asked McDowell and Franklin to go over their proposals for an advance. When McDowell restated his plan to attack enemy supply lines, the sullen general-in-chief "coldly, if not curtly" exclaimed: "You are entitled to have any opinion you please!" As the discussion continued, McClellan ominously said nothing further. Meigs whispered into Little Mac's ear that Lincoln expected him to participate in the deliberations. The general-in-chief replied that the Confederates had at least 175,000 men at Manassas (a gross exaggeration), too many for the Army of the Potomac to confront. Moreover, he sneered: "If I tell him my plans they will be in the New York Herald tomorrow morning. He can't keep a secret, he will tell them to Tadd." Meigs responded: "That is a pity, but he is the President,—the Commander-in-Chief; he has a right to know; it is not respectful to sit mute when he so clearly requires you to speak." (Meigs thought McClellan's conduct a "spectacle to make gods and men ashamed!")[214] Chase told Franklin: "Well, if that is Mac's decision, he is a ruined man."[215]

Responding to pressure from the treasury secretary, McClellan deigned to say that he would prod Buell to launch an offensive in Kentucky but that he was reluctant to discuss his plans further. Lincoln asked the commanding general "if he had counted upon any particular time" for that movement to begin, without specifying it. When Little Mac replied affirmatively, Lincoln said: "Well, on this assurance of the General that he will press the advance in Kentucky, I will be satisfied, and will adjourn this Council."[216]

Incredibly, the next day McClellan spelled out to a New York *Herald* reporter the plan he had refused to describe to Lincoln because he feared the president would reveal it to that very newspaper! Little Mac began a three-hour conversation with correspondent Malcolm Ives by saying, "What I declined communicating to them [Lincoln and the others] I am now going to convey through you to Mr. [James Gordon] Bennett . . . *all* the knowledge I possess myself, with no reserve."[217] Also incredible was McClellan's decision to reveal his plan to Chase and to N. P. Banks (but not Lincoln) well before January 13.

McClellan's stubborn unwillingness to confide in Lincoln would prove a grave mistake and lead to his undoing. The president's tendency to defer to Little Mac was also mistaken; if he had been more assertive, the general may have been more compliant. Bates realized this. At a cabinet meeting on January 10, he emphatically urged the president to "take and act out the powers of his place, to command the commanders," and if they balked, to fire them.[218]

The Trent Affair

Frustrating as McClellan's conduct was, Lincoln found it even more frustrating to cope with a diplomatic crisis that threatened to lead to war with Great Britain. That autumn, the Confederate government decided to replace its three roving commissioners to

Europe with two ministers plenipotentiary—former senators James M. Mason of Virginia (to England) and John Slidell of Louisiana (to France). In mid-October those two boarded a blockade runner that whisked them to Havana, where they transferred to the British mail packet *Trent,* bound for St. Thomas in the Danish Virgin Islands. There they intended to book passage for Europe. On November 8, Union Captain Charles Wilkes, commanding the *San Jacinto,* rashly stopped the *Trent* in the Bahama Channel, boarded her, and seized Mason and Slidell as contraband, maintaining that they were in effect animate dispatches. He allowed the *Trent* to proceed on its way while he shipped the two would-be diplomats off to confinement at Fort Warren in Boston harbor.

The North rejoiced, for Mason and Slidell were particularly loathed as extreme fire-eaters. Mason was the principal author of the widely execrated Fugitive Slave Act of 1850, and Slidell had been a leading spokesman for slavery and disunion. Here was good news for a change. Temporarily, the defeats at Bull Run, Wilson's Creek, Lexington, and Ball's Bluff were forgotten. "We do not believe the American heart ever thrilled with more genuine delight," declared the New York *Times.*[219] Congress voted a resolution of thanks to Wilkes "for his brave, adroit, and patriotic conduct," Secretary of the Navy Welles congratulated him officially, the city fathers of Boston gave him a banquet, and editorial writers showered him with praise. Leading jurists like Edward Everett, Edwin M. Stanton, and Reverdy Johnson declared Wilkes's action legal. Many other prominent observers, however, like Charles Sumner, chairman of the Senate Foreign Relations Committee, did not celebrate; they thought Wilkes had violated international law by seizing men from a neutral ship in transit from one neutral port to another. They were right; the envoys should have been released as soon as the administration ascertained the facts.

Lincoln may have briefly shared his constituents' glee, but within hours of receiving the news, he realized that Mason and Slidell had to be surrendered. On November 16, the president told Benson J. Lossing: "I fear the traitors will prove to be white elephants."[220] Three days thereafter, D. W. Bartlett wrote that the president was "somewhat fearful of the result" because "some men in whom he has confidence" informed him "that England will try to get up a war with the United States over the affair."[221] To Gideon Welles, Lincoln expressed "anxiety . . . as to the disposition of the prisoners." The public's "indignation was so overwhelming against the chief conspirators, that he feared it would be difficult to prevent severe and exemplary punishment, which he always deprecated."[222] The president told Edward Bates, "I am not getting much sleep out of that exploit of Wilkes', and I suppose we must look up the law of the case. I am not much of a prize lawyer, but it seems to me pretty clear that if Wilkes saw fit to make that capture on the high seas he had no right to turn his quarter-deck into a prize court."[223]

Initially, the cabinet did not share Lincoln's view. Edouard de Stoeckl, Russian *chargé d'affaires* in Washington, informed his government that upon hearing of Wilkes's actions, "the President was disposed to disavow Captain Wilkes's act, restore the prisoners, and apologize to England. But he ran into strong opposition from his Cabinet and from the demagogues among his advisors who believed . . .

they [Union forces] were stronger than ever and could defy England."[224] At a cabinet meeting early in the crisis, Lincoln, according to a press account, "expressed himself in favor of restoring them [Mason and Slidell] to the protection of the British flag, if it should be demanded. He said it was doubtful if the course of Captain Wilkes could be justified by international law, and that, at all events, he could not afford to have two wars upon his hands at the same time." (More succinctly, he cautioned: "one war at a time.") Only Montgomery Blair agreed. Chase forcefully maintained that the president's approach would dishonor the nation. Bates argued that Wilkes had acted lawfully. At first, Seward was, as Gideon Welles recalled, "jubilant" and "elated" and "for a time made no attempt to conceal his gratification and approval of the act of Wilkes." He "discredited every suggestion that Great Britain would avail herself of any technical error of the officer [Wilkes], and take serious exception to the proceeding. It was, he claimed, in conformity with British ruling and British practice; and if the commander of the San Jacinto has erred in permitting the *Trent* to proceed, it was not for that government to take advantage of his mistaken generosity by which they had been benefited." But at the cabinet meeting Seward did not commit himself.[225]

When the British first learned of Wilkes's act more than two weeks afterward, their indignation knew no bounds. The Union Jack had been insulted! The outraged prime minister, Lord Palmerston, allegedly exclaimed to his cabinet: "I don't know whether you are going to stand for this, but I'll be damned if I do!" Lord Lyons regarded Wilkes's act as a grave affront to his country. Her Majesty's government was predisposed to react angrily in part because of Seward's well-known Anglophobia. Weed reported from London that a "spirit, almost infernal, has been roused here against Gov. Seward, who is regarded as the incarnation of hostility to England."[226] Such a view was not unjustified. While visiting England in 1859, Seward had offended Britons with tactless remarks about the high cost of English books and the gullibility of nobles who paid too much for paintings. In July, the impulsive secretary of state had told William Howard Russell of the London *Times* that a "contest between Great Britain and the United States would wrap the world in fire, and at the end it would not be the United States which would have to lament the results of the conflict."[227] According to the duke of Newcastle, the previous year Seward had said to him that "he was likely to occupy a high office; that when he did so it would become his duty to insult England, and he should insult her accordingly."[228]

Palmerston instructed his foreign minister, Lord John Russell, to compose a belligerent, curt message, which Queen Victoria and her mortally-ill husband, Prince Albert, toned down. The revised document stated that British authorities would accept an American explanation that Wilkes had acted without instructions; but the United States must agree within seven days to offer an apology, pay indemnities, and forthwith release Mason and Slidell. If the Lincoln administration balked, Lord Lyons must pack his bags and return home. Lyons was to give Seward informal notice of this message in order to allow the administration sufficient time to consider its response. Ominously, 11,000 British troops set sail for Canada; Great Britain refused to sell the United States any more saltpeter (then the principal ingredient of gunpowder, imported from India); and several warships were ordered to the North American Station. As hostilities between America and Britain loomed, Wall Street panicked. "It looks like war," observed Foreign Minister Russell.[229] One of the most dangerous moments of Lincoln's presidency had arrived.

Russell's dispatch did not reach Washington until December 19. Meanwhile, Lincoln took comfort from (mistaken) reports that British legal authorities had declared Wilkes's action justified. On December 10, the president told his old friend Orville H. Browning "that there would probably be no trouble about it."[230] Three days later he was jolted out of his complacency when English newspapers arrived describing British indignation. Two days thereafter, informal word came that Her Majesty's government would demand the release of the Confederate emissaries and an apology. The news astounded Lincoln. Browning, who was at the White House when this intelligence arrived, told him that he did not "believe England has done so foolish a thing," but "if she is determined to force a war upon us why so be it. We will fight her to the death."[231] Among the many Americans who agreed with Browning was Anson S. Miller of Illinois. The "National Govt and Washington must not be bullied by England," wrote Miller. "Even war with England . . . is far preferable to humiliation."[232] A Cincinnati attorney howled that England "has humbled us," "emasculated our pride, and thus invited any other insolent nation to spit upon us."[233]

On December 16, Seward exclaimed to a British journalist and some diplomats: "We will wrap the whole world in flames! No power so remote that she will not feel the fire of our battle and be burned by our conflagration."[234] That day he and his fellow cabinet members decided to keep Mason and Slidell because it was believed that Her Majesty's government would not go to war over their capture; instead, it would probably demand their release, and a prolonged diplomatic correspondence would solve the issue.

But a lengthy negotiation no longer seemed possible after December 19, when Lord Lyons informally showed Seward the dispatch from Russell insisting on the release of Mason and Slidell and demanding a response within one week. Four days later, the British envoy officially submitted Russell's document, giving the administration until December 30 to reply. On December 18, Seward and Lincoln visited the navy yard to see Commander John A. Dahlgren, whom the president regarded highly and in whom he confided. (Lincoln told a friend, "I like to see Dahlgren. The drive to the Navy Yard is one of my greatest pleasures. When I am depressed, I like to talk with Dahlgren. I learn something of the preparations for defence, and I get from him consolation and courage.")[235] Dahlgren noted in his diary that "I never saw the President or Mr. Seward more quiet or grave. The British affair seems to weigh on them."[236]

That same day, at Lincoln's urging, John W. Forney, editor of the Philadelphia *Press,* published an article maintaining that war with the British would be catastrophic and that therefore "the Administration may be compelled to concede the demands of England, *and, perhaps, release Messrs. Mason and Slidell.* God forbid!—but in a crisis like this we must adapt ourselves to stern circumstances, and yield every feeling of pride to maintain our existence."[237] The president had told Forney: "I want you to sit down and write one of your most careful articles, preparing the American people for the release of Mason and Slidell. I know this is much to ask of you, but it shows my confidence in you, my friend, when I tell you that this course is forced upon us by our peculiar position; and that the good Queen of England is moderating her own angry people, who are as bitter against us as our people are against them. I need say no more."[238]

Two days later, the president and Seward met to discuss the crisis. No record of their meeting remains, though it seems likely that Seward explained the British position. The following day, Lincoln confessed that he "feared trouble."[239] He now confronted a dilemma: if the Confederate envoys were released, it would outrage public opinion in the North; if they were not, Britain might declare war and break the blockade.

Arbitration seemed a possible middle way. A champion of that solution, Charles Sumner, called at the White House regularly during the critical week of December 19–25 to share correspondence from his well-placed English friends warning of the dangers of war and urging the surrender of Mason and Slidell. One such letter from John Bright recommended mediation. Sumner suggested that Prussia "or better still, three learned publicists of the Continent" could serve that function.[240] Thurlow Weed, who had been sent abroad as a propagandist for the Union cause, offered similar counsel from London. France was rumored to be willing to act as an umpire, and American diplomats like Norman B. Judd, Henry S. Sanford, and George G. Fogg were suggesting that Louis Napoleon's government should play that role. James R. Doolittle, Sumner's colleague on the Senate Foreign Relations Committee, urged Lincoln to "refer the matter to the Emperors of France, & Russia to determine the question whether upon the law of nations we were not as belligerents justified in making that arrest."[241]

On December 20 and 21, Lincoln acted on such advice, drafting a dispatch for Seward's signature. He tactfully wrote: "this government has intended no affront to the British flag, or to the British nation; nor has it intended to force into discussion, an embarrassing question, all which is evident by the fact, hereby asserted, that the act complained of was done by the officer, without orders from, or expectation of, the government. But being done, it was no longer left to us to consider whether we might not, to avoid a controversy, waive an unimportant, though a strict right; because we too, as well as Great Brittain, have a people justly jealous of their rights, and in whose presence our government could undo the act complained of, only upon a fair showing that it was wrong, or, at least, very questionable. The United States government and people, are still willing to make reparation upon such showing."[242] On December 21, he read this document to Browning, who agreed that "the question was easily susceptible of a peaceful solution if England was at all disposed to act justly."[243] Similarly, the president informed Sumner that there "will be no war unless England is *bent* upon having one." To help defuse tension, Lincoln proposed circumventing normal diplomatic channels in order to deal directly with the British minister to the United States. "If I could see Lord Lyons, I could show him in five minutes that I am heartily for peace," he said to Sumner. When the senator counseled against such an irregular procedure, Lincoln abandoned that idea.[244]

Meanwhile, Seward drafted his own response to the British government, which Lincoln promised to examine carefully in order to make sure that it contained no offensive language like that in the secretary's May dispatch to Charles Francis Adams. Seward endorsed the release of Mason and Slidell, even though he maintained that those men were in fact contraband of war. Wilkes had acted without instructions, Seward explained, and though justified in seizing the Confederate emissaries, the captain should have taken the *Trent* to a prize court for adjudication. Such a step would have been in keeping with the traditional American view of neutral rights, a view that the British had earlier rejected, leading to the War of 1812. But because he voluntarily let the *Trent* sail away, Wilkes vitiated America's case for holding Mason and Slidell. Seward gratuitously added that if the survival of the Union had hung in the balance, the prisoners would not have been yielded, and that he was glad the British were finally agreeing with the American position on impressment.

On December 25 and 26, the cabinet discussed at length Seward's draft, though not Lincoln's. Edward Bates recorded that everyone understood "the magnitude of the subject, and believed that upon our decision depended the dearest interest, probably the existance, of the nation." The attorney general, waiving the question of legal right, "urged the necessity of the case; that to go to war with England now, is to abandon all hope of suppressing the rebellion, as we have not the possession of the land nor any support of the people of the South. The maratime superiority of Britain would sweep us from all the Southern waters! our trade would be utterly ruined and our treasury bankrupt." There was, Bates noted in his diary, "great reluctance on the part of some of the members of the cabinet—and even the President himself—to acknowledge these obvious truths." Evidently, Cameron, Welles, and Smith balked. Opponents of surrendering the prisoners feared "the displeasure of our own people—lest they should accuse us of timidly truckling to the power of England."[245] Chase said, "It is gall and wormwood to me. Rather than consent to the liberation of these men, I would sacrifice everything I possess." But even the treasury secretary agreed to their release, explaining that as long as "the matter hangs in uncertainty, the public mind will remain disquieted, our commerce will suffer serious harm, our action against the rebels must be greatly hindered, and the restoration of our prosperity . . . must be delayed."[246]

Charles Sumner attended the Christmas meeting and read aloud letters from John Bright and Richard Cobden, eminent members of Parliament and fast friends of the Union. They both urged conciliation. (Lincoln so admired Bright that he hung a photograph of the Liberal leader in his office.) Most importantly, a freshly arrived dispatch from the French foreign minister, Edouard Thouvenel, was read; in moderate tones, it denied the legitimacy of Wilkes's action and supported the British position. Along with it came a message from William Dayton, U.S. minister to France, reporting that no European power accepted America's argument. Thus arbitration did not seem feasible. These documents persuaded hawkish opponents of Seward's proposal that European opinion would favor Britain; thus, they helped produce a unanimous cabinet vote to surrender Mason and Slidell.

After the session adjourned, Lincoln said: "Governor Seward, you will go on, of course, preparing your answer, which, as I understand, will state the reasons why they ought to be given up. Now I have a mind to try my hand at stating the reasons why they ought not to be given up. We will compare the points on each side." The next day, after making several changes, the cabinet endorsed Seward's dispatch, though some members expressed regret at the release of Mason and Slidell. The document was submitted to Lord Lyons on December 27. It was a clever, face-saving argument, designed to mollify the British government without offending the American public. Seward read it to several members of Congress, who agreed that Mason and Slidell must be released.

When the secretary of state asked Lincoln why he had not submitted a paper justifying retention of the Confederate diplomats, he replied: "I found I could not make an argument that would satisfy my own mind, and that proved to me your ground was the right one."[247] (In fact, Seward's dispatch contained serious logical and legal weaknesses.) Lincoln may have also feared both a gunpowder shortage, if Britain maintained its embargo of saltpeter, and a bombardment of American ports by ironclads invulnerable to America's antiquated shore batteries.

The Palmerston government waived the demand for reparations and an apology, viewing the release of Mason and Slidell as a gesture sufficiently conciliatory to end the crisis. Lincoln called that surrender "a pretty bitter pill to swallow" but told an army officer that "I contented myself with believing that England's triumph in the matter would be short-lived, and that after ending our war successfully we would be so powerful that we could call her to account for all the embarrassments she had inflicted upon us." The surrender made Lincoln feel "a good deal like the sick man in Illinois who was told he probably hadn't many days longer to live, and he ought to make his peace with any enemies he might have. He said the man he hated worst of all was a fellow named Brown, in the next village, and he guessed he had better begin on him. So Brown was sent for, and when he came the sick man began to say, in a voice as meek as Moses's, that he wanted to die at peace with all his fellow-creatures, and he hoped he and Brown could now shake hands and bury all their enmity. The scene was becoming altogether too pathetic for Brown, who had to get out his handkerchief and wipe the gathering tears from his eyes. It wasn't long before he melted, and gave his hand to his neighbor, and they had a regular love-feast of forgiveness. After a parting that would have softened the heart of a grindstone, Brown had about reached the room door, when the sick man rose up on his elbow and called out to him: 'But, see here, Brown; if I should happen to get well, mind that old grudge stands.'"[248]

(Similarly, when Anglo-American relations once again grew tense in the spring of 1863, Lincoln remarked to hotheads who wanted to confront the British: "we must have no war with England now; we can't afford it. We'll have to bear and bear and bear; she may even kick us, if she wants to, and we won't resent it, till we get rid of the job we already have on hand. *Then* it will be *our* turn to see about the kicking!")[249]

At a dinner party shortly after the crisis ended, Lincoln indicated that (in Sumner's paraphrase) he "covets kindly relations with all the world, especially with England."[250] Early in the crisis, he had assured a member of Canada's cabinet, Alexander

T. Galt, that the United States would not attack her. On December 5, the president told Galt that he "had implicit faith in the steady conduct of the American people even under the trying circumstances of the war, and though the existence of large armies had in other countries placed successful generals in positions of arbitrary power, he did not fear this result, but believed the people would quietly resume their peaceful avocations and submit to the rule of the government." Lincoln went on to pledge "himself as a man of honor, that neither he nor his cabinet entertained the slightest aggressive designs upon Canada, nor had any desire to disturb the rights of Great Britain on this continent."[251]

Most Americans and Britons felt relief that war had been averted, at least for the time being. To Bostonians, the surrender of Mason and Slidell "was taken a good deal as a man swallows an emetic—not because he loves it, but because it is the best way of ridding himself of an unpleasant matter."[252] Not everyone was so stoic. Like Lincoln, many of his constituents harbored a grudge and looked forward to an opportunity for revenge. His good friend, Joseph Gillespie, took it badly; writing from Illinois, he noted that the "[p]eople are almost frantic with rage[.] We feel disgraced dishonored & outraged. . . . This blunder as I regard it of succumbing to England has ruined the Administration beyond redemption and if the war is not pushed on with becoming energy the cause of the Country and the Union is likewise gone."[253] "We have eaten our peck of dirt—and all at once!" exclaimed Henry Winter Davis in disgust.[254] In a similar vein, *Frank Leslie's Illustrated Newspaper* remarked: "If we are compelled to eat dirt, let us improve the disgusting process to our profit."[255] An Illinois congressman reported from Washington that things "look very blue here. The humiliation of this country by the conduct of the Cabinet in giving up Slidell & Mason is almost too much to bear."[256]

But Lincoln was not blue. On New Year's Day, as he presided over a White House reception, he was reportedly "in his happiest mood."[257] As he shook innumerable hands, he showed no signs of weariness and seemed to be having a good time. Some observers, however, thought "the weight of the nation's cares makes him a sadder, silenter looking man" than he was back in Illinois, and that that he looked "perceptibly older than he did less than a year ago."[258]

The outcome of the *Trent* affair bitterly disappointed the Confederates. The French consul in Richmond reported that the "release of Messrs. Slidell and Mason has greatly upset the South. The government of the Confederate States was hoping for a war between England and the United States, and, as a consequence, the raising of the blockade."[259] Slidell later told Louis Napoleon he regretted his release "because if we had not been given up, it would have caused a war with England, which would have been of short duration, and whatever might have happened to myself, the result must have been advantageous to our cause."[260] There is reason to think that the seizure of Mason and Slidell was a setup by the Confederates, designed to precipitate hostilities between the North and Great Britain.

Many months later, Lincoln told a visitor "how he had pushed the prompt surrender of Mason and Slidell as an act of justice toward England, realizing that in the light of international law the Trent affair might justly have given ground for reprisal.

Seward would have temporized, and so risked a most unwelcome complication with England."[261] As he had done in the spring, Lincoln cooled off the fiery Seward and helped keep relations with Great Britain relatively cordial. Sumner, who told Gideon Welles "that Seward was ignorant of international law and lacked common sense," also helped counteract the secretary of state's impulsiveness and contributed significantly to defusing the crisis.[262]

Tentatively Addressing Slavery

At the conclusion of the *Trent* affair, Sumner twitted Lincoln about his reluctance to liberate the slaves. If he had publicly announced an emancipation plan, the United States would have enjoyed far more support in Europe, the senator claimed, and the *Trent* crisis "would have come and gone and would have given you no anxiety."[263] In fact, the president had been working on a scheme to free slaves in Delaware, which would, he hoped, serve as a model for other Border States. In December, Lincoln indicated to George Bancroft that he thought "slavery has received a mortal wound, that the harpoon has struck the whale to the heart."[264] With a mere 1,798 bondsmen (8% of the total 1860 population), Delaware would undergo less economic and social upheaval than any other Slave State if it adopted emancipation. (In 1847, the Whig-dominated legislature had come within a single vote of abolishing slavery gradually.)

On November 4, Lincoln consulted with Delaware Congressman George P. Fisher, a member of the so-called People's Party, the main opposition to the Democrats in the First State. Fisher agreed to draft an emancipation bill that would be submitted after Lincoln had revised it. When the president suggested that for each slave, owners would receive $300, Fisher held out for $500; Lincoln agreed. The president also met with Fisher's party colleague, Benjamin Burton, the largest slaveholder in Delaware. Lincoln asked Burton if the legislature, then in session, could be induced to free the slaves in case Congress provided compensation to be determined by local appraisers. "I am satisfied that this is the cheapest and most humane way of ending the war," the president said. "Delaware is the smallest and has the fewest slaves of any State in the Union. If I can get this plan started in Delaware I have no fear but that all the other border states will accept it."[265]

Burton thought his fellow slaveowners would go along with such a scheme. Working with Fisher and a Delaware state legislator, the president drafted two bills, each providing for total abolition in the First State by 1893. Slave children born following the passage of one of the proposed laws, along with all slaves more than 35 years of age, would be immediately emancipated. Others would gain their freedom upon their thirty-fifth birthday. To compensate slaveholders, the federal government would provide the state with $719,200 in bonds, which could be paid out in small increments until 1893 or in larger sums until 1872.

As Lincoln explained to Orville H. Browning, "it would require only about one third of what was necessary to support the war for one year." The president was, Browning noted, "very hopeful of ultimate success," and predicted to David Davis "that if Congress will pass a law authorizing the issue of bonds for the payment of the emancipated Negroes in the border states, Delaware, Maryland, Kentucky, and Missouri will all accept the terms."[266] In order to carry out the scheme, Congress had to appropriate the necessary funds and the Delaware Legislature had to accept the offer.

On December 3, Lincoln submitted to the newly reconvened Congress his annual message which did not mention the Delaware plan directly, but it did address the matter of compensated emancipation in a roundabout way. Noting that under the provisions of the recent Confiscation Act, some slaves had become semi-free, he said they must now be cared for. (Less than a month earlier, many slaves had been liberated when the Union joint army–navy expedition captured Port Royal, South Carolina, and a number of nearby coastal islands. When the local whites fled, 10,000 bondsmen suddenly found themselves without masters.) Conceivably, other slaves might also be freed by state legislatures. Such states, he recommended, should be compensated with tax breaks or some other means. (Here was a veiled hint at the Delaware plan, but so heavily veiled that some criticized its obscurity. Others understood its true intent, which was to encourage the legislatures of Maryland, Kentucky, Missouri, and Delaware to adopt emancipation.) As it was, slaves who had been taken from their Confederate owners by virtue of the Confiscation Act existed in a legal limbo as virtual wards of the government; Lincoln recommended that such people "be at once deemed free." Then they, and any bondsmen who might in the future be liberated by state action, should be voluntarily colonized "at some place, or places, in a climate congenial to them." Free blacks would be encouraged to follow suit. Implementing that plan might require the purchase of territory "and also the appropriation of money beyond that to be expended in the territorial acquisition." In a nod toward the prevalent white racial prejudice, he argued that if "it be said that the only legitimate object of acquiring territory is to furnish homes for white men, this measure effects that object; for the emigration of colored men leaves additional room for white men remaining or coming here." (This sentence created a sensation among the congressmen when it was read to them.) He asked rhetorically if some kind of emancipation was not "an absolute necessity . . . without which the government itself cannot be perpetuated?"

Lest his modest remarks be construed as rank abolitionism, Lincoln emphasized that he would treat the slavery issue cautiously: "In considering the policy to be adopted for suppressing the insurrection, I have been anxious and careful that the inevitable conflict for this purpose shall not degenerate into a violent and remorseless revolutionary struggle." This was probably an allusion to slave insurrections, which some Northerners thought should be encouraged. (In December, Lincoln told George Bancroft that he was "turning in his thoughts the question of his duty in the event of a slave insurrection."[267] In 1863, when a few Union commanders expressed a willingness to aid slave uprisings, Lincoln reportedly "refused on the ground that a servile insurrection would give a pretext for foreign intervention.")[268] "I have, therefore, in every case, thought it proper to keep the integrity of the Union prominent as the primary object of the contest on our part, leaving all questions which are not of vital military importance to the more deliberate action of the legislature." But, he hinted, emancipation might become necessary in time, for the "Union must be preserved, and hence, all indispensable means must be employed." To soften that sentence of iron, he immediately added: "We should not be in haste to determine that radical and extreme measures, which may reach the loyal as well as the disloyal, are indispensable."[269]

Lincoln may also have been alluding to proposals recommending what later generations would call "ethnic cleansing." In late June, he told Worthington G. Snethen, a Baltimore abolitionist who urged him to emancipate the slaves: "I should like to put down the rebellion, without disturbing any of the institutions, laws or customs of the States." Snethen maintained that Southern resistance would never cease as long as slavery existed: "You must drive slavery and slaveholders into the Gulf, and people the waste with a new people."[270] In January 1862, a Democratic congressman who spoke with the president at length reported that "he will stand up and not succumb to the abolitionists in their mad causes—he says he will stand firm."[271]

The Delaware plan fizzled when the legislature, which was evenly divided between Democrats and representatives of the People's Party, refused by a one-vote margin to endorse it. In addition, the lawmakers passed a resolution asserting that when "the people of Delaware desire to abolish slavery within her borders, they will do so in their own way, having due regard to strict equity," and "that any interference from without, and all suggestions of saving expense to the people, or others of like character, are improper to be made to an honorable people such as we represent, and are hereby repelled."[272]

Behind the state's action lay what its Democratic Senator James A. Bayard called "the antagonism of race." It was, said Bayard, "the principle of equality which the white man rejects where the negro exists in large numbers."[273] The state's other senator, Willard Saulsbury, a bad-tempered sympathizer with secession, echoed that sentiment, arguing that the country "shall be the white man's home; and not only the white man's home, but the white man shall govern, and the nigger never shall be his equal."[274] Other opponents of emancipation warned that Lincoln's plan was but "the first step; if it shall succeed, others will follow tending to elevate the negro to an equality with the white man or rather to degrade the white man by obliterating the distinction between races." If the remaining slaves of Delaware were to join the large ranks of free blacks in the state, soon the blacks "might equal the white population and cause a massacre."[275] (In 1860, there were 21,627 blacks and 90,589 whites in the state.) Even Republican Congressman Fisher appealed to racial prejudice while championing Lincoln's plan: "the Almighty intended this Union as the home of the white race, created for them, not for the negro." All patriots should consider "how the separation of the two distinct races, which can never, and ought never, to dwell together upon terms of political and social equality, can be effected with the least jarring to the harmony and happiness of our country."[276]

Lincoln's annual message dealt with a series of other problems in a rather perfunctory fashion, making it one of his less memorable state papers. Before its publication, a justice of the New York State Supreme Court, fearing that it would be undignified and marred by "low commonplaces," suggested that Seward should help write it.[277] In fact, a portion of the message was evidently composed by Seward and inserted at the last moment. Its most noteworthy rhetoric appeared in a disquisition on free labor, a seeming *non sequitur*, resembling the speech he had given at the 1859 Wisconsin agricultural fair. In closing, Lincoln stressed the larger significance of the war, giving a foretaste of the address he would deliver at Gettysburg in 1863: "The struggle of today, is not altogether for today—it is for a vast future also. With a reliance on Providence, all the more firm and earnest, let us proceed in the great task which events have devolved upon us."[278]

While moderate Republicans hailed the message's substance as "wise, patriotic, and conservative," and its style as "plain, concise and straightforward," others deplored its brevity and its failure to mention the *Trent* crisis or to deal more fully with the slavery issue, both of which loomed large in the public mind.[279] Kansas Congressman Martin F. Conway noted with disappointment that the president "in his recent message to Congress, refers only incidentally to the subject [of slavery]; and indicates no policy whatever for dealing with the momentous question."[280] A Democratic journalist noted that the "whole country awaited his message with breathless suspense. But the whole country turns away from it, sick with disappointment. It is silent on the very topic of all others that the nation is most anxious to have settled."[281] The Cincinnati *Commercial* also regretted that the president "evaded the rugged issue, and leaves the everlasting slavery question still adrift."[282] The New York *Evening Post* remarked that the message contained nothing which "speaks to the popular heart; nothing in it seems up to the spirit of the times; no sententious utterances of great truths are there to stir the public mind in the midst of trial and calamities."[283] The *Post*'s editor, William Cullen Bryant, wrote that Lincoln's "evident eagerness to dispose of the slavery question without provoking any violent conclusion is honorable to his feelings of humanity," but "it will be felt universally that he does not meet either the necessities or the difficulties of the case with sufficient determination."[284] Charles Eliot Norton, a Massachusetts litterateur, complained that the message was "very poor in style, manner and thought,—very wanting in pith, and exhibiting a mournful deficiency of strong feeling and of wise forecast in the President. This 'no policy' system in regard to the conduct of the war and the treatment of the slavery question is extremely dangerous."[285]

Just before submitting the message to Congress, Lincoln told his cabinet why he soft-pedaled the slavery issue: "Gentlemen, you are not a unit on this question, and as it is a very important one, in fact the most important which has come before us since the war commenced, I will float on with the tide till you are more nearly united than at present. Perhaps we shall yet *drift* into the right position."[286] Just after Frémont's dismissal, when a Western congressman asked if the administration would not be forced to issue an emancipation proclamation, Lincoln replied: "We are *drifting* in that direction."[287] According to an abolitionist, Lincoln admitted that he had "no policy" but rather "allowed matters to drift along pretty much as they pleased."[288] To a query about his overall policy, he said: "I have none. I pass my life in preventing the storm from blowing down the tent, and I drive in the pegs as fast as they are pulled up."[289] In January 1862, Democratic editor James Brooks of New York said the president "seems right, all right, and acts right, but he is not now a *positive* man. He drifts, and loves to drift."[290]

Lincoln evidently believed that the best way to boil a frog was to place it in a pot of water on a stove and then gradually heat it up. If the water temperature rose precipitously, the frog would leap out, but if it increased little by little, the frog would not notice the difference and would eventually be cooked. Abolitionist Francis G. Shaw shrewdly observed that "Lincoln is *Providential*; for if we had a more energetic man at the helm he would rouse all the pro-slavery forces in the country to violent activity, whereas now they are lulled by his slow and timid course, and will not fairly wake up till the current of events has carried them too far out to sea to steer for the port they *intended* to make, and supposed they *were* making."[291] Varying the image, Owen Lovejoy sensibly observed in November that "President Lincoln is advancing step by step just as the cautious swimmer wades into the stream before making a dive. President Lincoln will make a dive before long."[292]

Lincoln had been urged to ignore the vexed question of slavery by the venerable John J. Crittenden, author of the congressional resolution stating that the war was being fought solely to preserve the Union. When the president received contrary advice from George Bancroft, he told the prominent historian that emancipation was a subject "which does not escape my attention, and with which I must deal in all due caution, and with the best judgment I can bring to it."[293]

Such caution did not suit most Radicals. According to a Washington correspondent, the message "falls like a wet blanket upon the hopes of the ardent anti-slavery party, and is all but denounced by many Republicans as utterly below the occasion."[294] The "utterances of the White House are not statesmanlike in tone any more than elegant in expression," sneered the *National Anti-Slavery Standard*. It dismissed the annual message as "the development of a hand-to-mouth policy" by a president who "drifts about with every day's breeze, but ever with the traditionary instinct of all politicians, that slavery is still the guiding star of the ship of state."[295] Lucretia Mott called the message "*rather tame*" and denounced Lincoln's "proslavery conservatism."[296] "I really blushed for my country when I read that message," Elizabeth Cady Stanton remarked. She added that "all his messages have been of the most mamdy-pamby order."[297] Lydia Maria Child contemptuously asked, "What else could we expect from King *Log*?" She deplored the president's "stagnant soul" and "wooden skull."[298]

Some Republican members of Congress were so angry that they were prepared to censure the administration. Senator William P. Fessenden noted that the message was "considered here a dry and tame affair" and contained "several ridiculous things," but he condescendingly remarked, "we must make the best of our bargain."[299] He added that the well-meaning Lincoln was "sadly deficient in some qualities essential for a ruler in times like these" and had "lost all hold upon Congress, though no one doubts his personal integrity."[300] Henry L. Dawes of Massachusetts found the document "very weak and in some parts . . . exceedingly flat." He wished "that some Webster could put on record for immortality a true statement of the real character of this infamous rebellion, of the events transpiring here beneath the gaze of the world." (Dawes discovered much to admire in the president even if his rhetoric might be deficient. After visiting the White House on December 4, he wrote his spouse: "Everybody

likes Lincoln when they call on him. There is the simplicity of a child, the earnestness and sincerity which command the love of all who get near him.")[301]

The message disheartened many Midwesterners. A prominent attorney in Milwaukee declared that "people, in this section, have scarcely a remaining hope, that
this Administration will ever awake [from] its deep lethargy to a vigorous prosecution
of the war. The demon slavery, seems to have struck it with blindness."[302] In Illinois,
Lincoln's good friend James C. Conkling wrote that "I was highly disappointed and
so was the country generally upon the complete non-committal policy of the President as indicated in his Message," which lacked "that high toned sentiment which
ought to have pervaded a Message at such a critical period as this. Instead of ignoring
the subject [of slavery] and falling far below public opinion and expectation, it should
have recommended a bold and decisive policy and should have elevated public sentiment and aroused the national enthusiasm."[303] A resident of eastern Illinois complained that he and his neighbors "were all on tiptoe in expectation of the President's
Message, but imagine our disappointment and mortification when it came. Such a
Message! Not *one single manly, bold, dignified* position taken in it from beginning to
end. No response to the popular feeling. No battle cry to the 500,000 gallant soldiers
now in the field, but a tame, timid, time-serving, commonplace sort of an abortion of
a Message, cold enough with one breath to *freeze* h-ll over."[304] On December 10, a
physician who identified himself as "no Abolitionist" reported that many voters in
Aurora, Illinois, were "surprised and disappointed at the President's course," for "the
meekness of his Message disgusts the whole of us. The first man I met after leaving
my house this morning, in a rage declared that if a speedy change in views and acts
did not soon occur, he hoped some Brutus would arise and love his country more than
he did the President."[305] If Lincoln persisted for three more months with his moderate policy regarding slavery, predicted a resident of Greene County, he would "become the most unpopular man in the nation." No Illinois Republican, said he, "doubts
the honesty and patriotism of Abe Lincoln, yet his persevering opposition to striking
rebellion where a blow is most effectual, has utterly destroyed all confidence in his
statesmanship."[306]

The proposal to colonize freedmen outraged many opponents of slavery, who
protested that the message "is thoroughly tinged with that colorphobia which has so
long prevailed in Illinois," and condemned Lincoln for "so laboring under colorphobia,
as to make emancipation dependent on colonization."[307] The country's leading opponent of colonization, William Lloyd Garrison, called the president "a man of very
small caliber" who would do better "at his old business of splitting rails than at the
head of a government like ours, especially in such a crisis." He characterized the message as "wishy-washy," "very feeble and rambling, and ridiculous as a State paper,"
"weak and commonplace to a pitiable degree," and scorned Lincoln's "stupidity" and
"imbecility." The colonization proposal, he said, was "absurd and preposterous" and
suggested that "Lincoln may colonize himself if he choose, but it is an impertinent
act, on his part, to propose the getting rid of those who are as good as himself."[308]

In New York, the *Tribune* spoke dismissively of the president's "crazy scheme."[309]
Even the conservative *Herald* declared that there "is no necessity for it." The editor of

that paper voiced a widely shared practical objection: "the labor of the negroes is needed in the cotton and sugar States. The labor of the white man cannot supply it; and it would be extreme folly to deprive the country of such an immense laboring population."[310]

Many blacks indignantly protested against colonization. The editor of the New York *Anglo-African* remarked that Lincoln's message "does not contain one word of generous trust, generous cheer or cordially sympathy with the 'great uprising' of the nation," and recommended ironically that "any surplus change Congress may have can be appropriated 'with our consent' to expatriate and settle elsewhere the surviving slaveholders."[311] In Boston, prominent blacks insisted that "when we wish to leave the United States we can find and pay for that territory which shall suit us best," that "when we are ready to leave, we shall be able to pay our own expenses of travel," that "we don't want to go now," and that "if anybody else wants us to go, they must compel us."[312] Frederick Douglass, who was "bewildered by the spectacle of moral blindness, infatuation and helpless imbecility which the Government of Lincoln presents," denounced colonization and bitterly remarked that the president "shows himself to be about as destitute of any anti-slavery principle or feeling as did James Buchanan."[313]

(Yet a few months earlier Douglass had urged his fellow blacks to emigrate to Haiti, "this modern land of Canaan" where "our oppressors do not want us to go, and where our influence and example can still be of service to those whose tears will find their way to us by the waters of the Gulf washing all our shores. Let us be there to help beat back the filibustering invaders from the cotton States, who only await an opportunity to extinguish that island asylum of the deeply-wronged colored race." In an 1853 speech, Douglass had spoken favorably of Caribbean islands and British Guiana as suitable locations for American blacks to resettle.)[314]

Some other blacks supported colonization, including a group of newly freed slaves in Washington who memorialized Congress to provide for their settlement in Central America. Earlier, they had resisted colonization because it was privately managed, but they trusted the government to administer the program in their best interest.

Dissenting more temperately than some of his fellow abolitionists, Gerrit Smith acknowledged that Lincoln "is more intellectual than nine-tenths of the politicians, and more honest than ninety-nine hundreds of them. I admit too, that he would have made a good President had he not been trained to worship the Constitution," a "comparatively petty thing." Still, Smith deemed the message "twattle and trash," and urged that there be no more talk "of expelling our friends from the country."[315]

The Radical editors of the Chicago *Tribune*, however, came to the president's defense, remarking that the "cautious language which Mr. Lincoln employs, does not hide from us, who know the deep moral convictions of the man, the purpose that he has in view."[316] A Radical senator emphatically defended the message, arguing that "nothing should be attempted that could not be maintained."[317] Both the New York *Times* and *Tribune* detected in the message full acceptance of the Confiscation Act, which the president had so reluctantly signed a few months earlier.

In fact, Lincoln's long-standing support of colonization was not rooted in "colorphobia" but in hard political realities. Southern states simply would not voluntarily emancipate slaves unless the freedmen left the country. A case in point was Kentucky. Senator Garrett Davis of that state assured the president that loyal men there "would not resist his gradual emancipation scheme if he would only conjoin with it his colonization plan." (Lincoln cited this statement when explaining his support for colonization.)[318] Wisconsin Senator James R. Doolittle similarly remarked that "every man, woman, and child who comes from these [Slave] States, tells me that it is utterly impossible for them to talk of emancipation within any slave State without connecting it with the idea of colonization."[319] Democratic Congressman Charles John Biddle of Pennsylvania told his colleagues that alarm about emancipation "would spread to every one of my constituents who loves his country and his race if the public mind was not lulled and put to sleep with the word 'colonization.' I say the word, not the thing; for no practicable and adequate scheme for it has ever been presented or devised. The word is sung to us as a sort of 'lullaby.'"[320]

Lincoln was singing that necessary tune. Another Representative from the Keystone State received a similar message from a Democratic constituent: "If you can only send the whole race out of the country, I think all loyal democrats would be willing to see slavery abolished at once, regardless of any other consideration. . . . If the black race is once removed, we will have repose—not sooner."[321] In New York, Democrats at a Tammany meeting declared that they were "opposed to emancipating negro slaves, unless on some plan of colonization."[322] A former resident of the South assured Senator John Sherman that it was essential "that colonization should be held out in order to win the nonslaveholding and especially the poor whites of the South, and these are the men who must uphold the United States rule in the slave states." Ninety percent of them "when they once understand it will hail manumission and colonization as a God's blessing. The slaveholders rule them by creating a horror of what the Negroes would do if freed among them, but with all this there is a strong though secret hatred of slavery."[323] Appalled by the discrimination that blacks faced in the Free States, a treasury official in St. Louis exclaimed that if emancipation were not accompanied by colonization, "God pity the poor Negro!" for many Northern states would follow the lead of Illinois and Indiana by forbidding blacks to settle within their borders.

Thousands of slaves in Virginia, South Carolina, and elsewhere were in the custody of the Union army, which did not wish to continue feeding and housing them. (Ben Butler, who ingeniously declared them "contraband of war," called the flood of blacks streaming into Fort Monroe a "Disaster.")[324] Neither the North nor the Border States wanted them, and the public disapproved of allowing them to serve in the army; colonization therefore seemed the only viable option, especially since practical steps had already been taken to find sites abroad where freedmen might migrate.

Before 1861, colonization had been supported by many Radicals, among them Salmon P. Chase. During the war, other Radicals promoted it, including James Redpath, whom Frederick Douglass described as "a sincere friend of the colored race."[325] The ultra-Radical Moncure D. Conway, who became a bitter critic of Lincoln, published an influential book in 1862, *The Rejected Stone,* which contained a letter to the president urging him to colonize Haiti as part of a general plan of emancipation.

It is not entirely clear whether Lincoln really thought colonization feasible or desirable. Harriet Martineau speculated that he was insincere. His "absurd" and "impracticable" plan, she wrote, "is so wrong and foolish that we might safely assume that Mr. Lincoln proposed something that would not do, in order to throw upon others the responsibility of whatever will have to be done."[326] Indeed, he was covering his flank against attacks which would inevitably attend emancipation, and also trying to sugarcoat it to make it a less bitter pill for Conservatives to swallow. But he may also have harbored an unrealistic belief that colonization just might work. At least he wanted to be able to say that he had tried to implement it.

Radicals were upset not only at Lincoln's message but also at the conduct of Halleck, McClellan, and Ward Hill Lamon, all of whom appeared soft on slavery. On November 20, Halleck, a conservative Democrat, had issued a general order forbidding runaway slaves to enter Union lines in the Department of the West. Months earlier, McClellan had announced to white Virginians: "Notwithstanding all that has been said by the traitors to induce you to believe that our advent among you will be signalized by interference with your slaves, understand one thing clearly—not only will we abstain from all such interference but we will on the contrary with an iron hand, crush any attempt at insurrection on their part."[327] Other army officers, including Charles P. Stone, were returning fugitive slaves to their owners, and Ward Hill Lamon was holding some runaways in the District jail.

Infuriated Radicals in Congress denounced these actions and began formulating new confiscation measures. A Republican caucus endorsed the unconditional emancipation of slaves held by disloyal masters. On December 7, Lincoln reportedly took umbrage, predicting that "such suicidal legislation" would drive the Border States to secede.[328] Congress backed down for the time being, refusing to pass that bill or a resolution urging the president to countermand Halleck's order.

Cabinet Shake-up

Lincoln also angered Radicals by insisting that Cameron revise a paragraph in his annual report calling for the emancipation and arming of slaves. Under Chase's influence, Cameron had been growing more radical as time passed. In May, when slaves ran to Union army lines and General Benjamin F. Butler declined to return them to their owners but instead kept them as "contraband of war," Cameron approved his action. Three months later, Cameron impulsively congratulated Frémont on his emancipation proclamation. In October, he wrote orders for General Thomas W. Sherman, who was to lead the expedition against Port Royal, South Carolina, authorizing him to liberate and arm slaves who came under his control. When he read those orders to Lincoln, the president struck out the clause emancipating slaves. Soon thereafter, the war secretary said that he would send extra arms on any future expedition to the South "to enable those who desired to fight to take the field in aid of the Union cause."[329] On November 13, after Colonel John Cochrane told his regiment that he endorsed the emancipation and arming of slaves as a military measure, Cameron said to those troops: "I heartily approve every sentiment uttered by your commander. The doctrines which he has laid down I approve as if they were my own words."[330] Soon thereafter, Cameron made the same points at a cabinet meeting.

Days later, at a dinner party given by John W. Forney, the war secretary embarrassed his host by reiterating "his opinion that, as a last resort, we ought to arm every man who desires to strike for human liberty." Caleb B. Smith demurred, protesting heatedly that "the Administration contemplated no such policy. Slaves escaping from rebels might be received as they had been hitherto—within the lines of the army; but it was not intended to arm them. If twenty million of freemen could not, single handed, subdue this rebellion, it would be a disgrace to them, and they ought to give up the contest."[331] The controversy grew so heated that the music stopped and the guests became alarmed.

This intra-cabinet public contretemps delighted Democratic leaders like New York lawyer S. L. M. Barlow, who urged Edwin M. Stanton to foment even greater dissension within the Republican ranks: "Such quarrels should be fostered in every proper way."[332] Stanton was in a good position to do so, for he had become close to Cameron. Acting on Barlow's advice, Stanton recommended that the war secretary incorporate into his annual report a paragraph on the emancipation and arming of slaves. Stanton perused the draft report closely and suggested the following addition: "Those who make war against the Government justly forfeit all rights of property, privilege, and security derived from the Constitution and laws against which they are in armed rebellion; and as the labor and service of their slaves constitute the chief property of the rebels, such property should share the common fate of war. . . . It is as clearly the right of the Government to arm slaves, when it may become necessary, as it is to use gunpowder taken from the enemy."[333]

Without bothering to consult Lincoln, Cameron took Stanton's suggestion and included this language in his report. Stanton's motive is not clear. He may have been trying to carry out Barlow's scheme to exacerbate tension within the cabinet, or he may have been paving the way for Cameron's dismissal and thus creating an opportunity for himself to become secretary of war, or he may have sincerely favored those measures. (In fact, the policy Cameron recommended was logical and would eventually be adopted by the administration.)

Although newspapers had accurately predicted what Cameron would write, Lincoln felt blindsided by the report, copies of which had been mailed to the press. On December 1, immediately after reading it, the president exclaimed: "This will never do! Gen. Cameron must take no such responsibility. This is a question which belongs exclusively to me!"[334] He told a supporter of the secretary's policy: "Arm the slaves, and we shall have more of them than white men in our army."[335] Indeed, a Kentucky Unionist said the effect of Cameron's proposal "is worse than pouring fifty thousand more Secession voters in among us. . . . Proclaim the general emancipation of all slaves of rebels, and as sure as there is a heaven, you annihilate the Union sentiment in every Southern state, destroy every hope of a Union party anywhere with which to begin a reconstruction, and unite the whole South as one man in a struggle of desperation."[336]

Lincoln demanded that Cameron delete the controversial language, whose true authorship was unknown to him. The president was working on a proposal dealing with slavery in Delaware and did not want his war secretary to rile up the public on that sensitive subject. The impertinent Cameron refused. At a cabinet meeting the next day, Welles and Chase backed the war secretary, but Bates, Blair, Seward, and Smith did not. The secretary of state was especially alarmed. According to the Philadelphia *Inquirer,* Lincoln "finally settled it by going to General Cameron and insisting upon his confining his report to a statement of the past, and not dictate to Congress what they should do! Cameron insisted that his policy was correct, and must be carried out at once. The President assured him that it did not follow, if he changed his report or left out any of it, that he must necessarily change his policy, but that he could carry it out; only let Congress take hold of the matter first." The secretary then reluctantly complied with the presidential directive.[337]

The offending paragraph was replaced with a less controversial statement, which Lincoln may have written: "It is already a grave question what shall be done with those slaves who were abandoned by their owners on the advance of our troops into southern territory, as at the Beaufort district, in South Carolina. The number left within our control at that point is very considerable, and similar cases will probably occur. What shall be done with them? Can we afford to send them forward to their masters, to be by them armed against us, or used in producing supplies to sustain the rebellion? Their labor may be useful to us; withheld from the enemy it lessens his military resources, and withholding them has no tendency to induce the horrors of insurrection, even in the rebel communities. They constitute a military resource, and, being such, that they should not be turned over to the enemy is too plain to discuss. Why deprive him of supplies by a blockade, and voluntarily give him men to produce them? The disposition to be made of the slaves of rebels, after the close of the war, can be safely left to the wisdom and patriotism of Congress. The Representatives of the people will unquestionably secure to the loyal slaveholders every right to which they are entitled under the Constitution of the country."[338]

The original version of Cameron's report had been sent to some newspapers. Angrily, Lincoln ordered Montgomery Blair to telegraph postmasters instructing them to stop delivery of the report until the revised version arrived. A few papers ran both versions of the document, causing Radical Republicans to cheer Cameron and denounce the president. "What a *fiasco!*" exclaimed Charles Henry Ray of the Chicago *Tribune.* "Old Abe is now unmasked, and we are sold out. We want to keep the peace as long as there is hope of unity, but . . . we are ready to quarrel with Lincoln, the Cabinet, McClellan, and anybody else." Ray urged that Congress force Lincoln "to accede to the popular demand to make this a war in earnest."[339] An Illinois abolitionist lamented that "the modification of Cameron's report has absolutely broken down all enthusiasm in his [Lincoln's] favor among the people. No man . . . ever threw away so completely, an opportunity, such as occurs to no individual, more than once in an age, to make himself revered, and loved by millions, and secure to himself a place and a name in history, more enviable than often falls to the lot of man. The modification reveals to the eyes of the people the real position and sentiments of the president, in a way that destroys in a great measure all confidence in his ability to bring the war to a successful issue."[340] Wendell Phillips sneered, "If we had a man for President, or an American instead of a Kentuckian, we should have had the satisfaction of attempting to save the Union instead of Kentucky."[341] He conceded that Lincoln was honest, but added: "as a pint pot may be full, and yet not be so full as a quart, so there is a vast difference between the honesty of a small man and the honesty of a statesman."[342]

Tension had been building between the president and Cameron for some time. In May, a friend of Lincoln reported that there was "evidently much feeling between Lincoln & Cameron—judging from the conversation of each of them." The president said he had received complaints "about some Pennsylvania contracts" and "that he hoped the contracts were fair, but that he intended to have the matter examined."[343] Five months later, Lincoln complained that the secretary of war was "utterly ignorant and regardless of the course of things, and the probable result," "[s]elfish and openly discourteous," "[o]bnoxious to the Country," and "[i]ncapable of organizing details or conceiving and advising general plans."[344] An example of Cameron's rudeness occurred in the late fall when a young man presented him a letter of recommendation from McClellan with a strong endorsement from Lincoln. The general wanted the bearer to have an important position in the commissary department. The war secretary read the document impassively, tossed it aside, and said Lincoln's "recommendation has not the slightest weight with me."[345] A similar episode had occurred months earlier, when a sharpshooter presented Cameron a letter from Lincoln endorsing his plan to raise a regiment in Wisconsin. The secretary of war treated him gruffly, saying the government wanted no more troops. When the rejected would-be soldier reported this conversation to the president, Lincoln appointed him to a highly desirable civilian post.

Chase and others shared the president's concern about the administration of the War Department. The treasury secretary chastised Cameron for tardiness and sloppiness in submitting budget estimates. In May, an up-and-coming political leader from Maine, James G. Blaine, reported from Washington that he was having trouble getting the War Department to accept troops from the Pine Tree state because "Cameron is too busy awarding contracts to Pennsylvanians and in giving the new lieutenancies in such a manner that S. Cameron shall not lose the convention in 1864. Besides it is said that his capacity is for intrigue and not for business."[346] Iowa Senator James W. Grimes, alluding to Napoleon's fabled war minister, fumed that "[i]nstead of having a man in these times at the head of the War Dept. who Carnot like, can sit down and organize victory for us we have a man there whose highest capabilities would be reached as payment broker of third class notes in Wall Street or as the speculator of corner lots in some of our western paper towns."[347] Similarly, Henry Winter Davis asked: "Why will not the President find a Carnot to end the rebellion with?"[348]

In June, Lincoln seemed "agitated" and "in a temper" when asking T. J. Barnett, a lawyer-journalist and Republican activist, about War Department contracts.[349] Soon thereafter, when Ebenezer Peck urged him to replace Cameron, the president was impressed with his arguments about the Chief's incompetence but feared that his hostility would have a deleterious effect on Pennsylvania. In August, influential New Yorkers called at the White House to express their lack of confidence in Cameron's probity and efficiency and to recommend that he be supplanted by Joseph Holt. Even though the public was rapidly losing confidence in the war secretary that summer, Lincoln hesitated to replace him, saying: "It is no time to swap horses when we are crossing a torrent" and "I know everything that Mr. Cameron has done since he came into office, and I tell you that he is *as honest as I am.*"[350]

But shortly thereafter, Lincoln changed his tune. In early September 1861, he told Hiram Barney that he wished to remove Cameron because the war secretary "was unequal to the duties of the place" and "his public affiliation with army contractors was a scandal." Moreover, when away from Washington, Cameron often gave "telegraphic orders for the removal of troops and munitions, of which no record was made in the Department," thus causing "serious disorder and difficulty." The president, according to Barney, also "named other instances to the same end."[351] The New York *Times* complained about Cameron's refusal to accept regiments or to encourage the enlistment of cavalry, his reluctance to enroll a regiment of marksmen until Lincoln practically forced him to do so, his awarding of contracts for cannon to one Pennsylvania manufacturer instead of several different firms who collectively could have filled the order more quickly, and to his wasting time by "quarrelling over the appointment of sutlers and messengers, and arranging minor matters of the least possible consequence to the public."[352] The Boston *Transcript* denounced Cameron's favoritism in making army appointments and his "sheer want of executive capacity."[353]

Cameron blocked the appointment of capable men, like Ethan Allen Hitchcock and Montgomery C. Meigs. Lincoln did manage to get Meigs named quartermaster general but had less luck with Hitchcock's case. Once the war broke out, General Scott asked Cameron's permission to have Hitchcock, who had retired from the army in 1855 after thirty-eight years of service, recalled to duty and assigned to Washington. The secretary of war, whose corruption in dealing with the Winnebago Indians in 1838 had been denounced at the time by Hitchcock, refused. When Scott appealed to Lincoln, the president replied "that he must let the Head of the War Dept. have his voice."[354] (Eventually, Hitchcock was made supervisor of prisoner exchanges.)

In December, Montgomery Blair told Lincoln that "he ought to get rid of C[ameron] at once, that he was not fit to remain in the Cabinet, and was incompetent to manage the War Department."[355] For some time the president had been planning to do so. In September, he hinted to Edwin M. Stanton that soon he would probably be named to an important position. (Stanton, who had been contemplating a move from Washington to New York, postponed those plans. After months of waiting, however, he grew impatient and harshly criticized Lincoln.) In October, the president informed Cameron that he would be dismissed sooner or later. But what to do with him? Because he remained a powerful force in Pennsylvania, the Chief had to be given a consolation prize, like a diplomatic post. As it developed, Cassius M. Clay wished to return home from Russia, where he had been serving as U.S. minister, and take an army command. From Thurlow Weed, the president learned that Cameron would be willing to take Clay's place. (When informed of this move, Thaddeus Stevens quipped: "Send word to the Czar to bring in his things of nights.")[356]

So on January 11, Lincoln sent Cameron an uncharacteristically curt note: "As you have, more than once, expressed a desire for a change of position, I can now gratify you, consistently with my view of the public interest. I therefore propose nominating you to the Senate, next monday, as minister to Russia."[357] According to Henry Winter Davis, Cameron's "removal was after the fashion of the deposition of an eastern Vizier. No consultation of the Cabinet—not one of them knew it was contemplated except Mr. Seward."[358]

Because Lincoln's note contained no expression of regret or gratitude, Cameron felt deeply wounded and complained that Lincoln was "discourteous."[359] To Alexander K. McClure and Thomas A. Scott, the Chief predicted tearfully that it "meant personal as well as political destruction." Those three men agreed to ask Lincoln to replace that note with a more generous and complimentary one. The president obliged, sending Cameron another missive, backdated to January 11, paying tribute to his services.

Cameron later maintained that he was fired because of his antislavery principles, but that seems unlikely, though many at the time believed it was so. William P. Fessenden accurately observed that "Cameron did not leave the department on account of his Slavery views," which "were the same as those of Mr Chase and others, who remain." (A case in point was Welles, whose annual report describing his policy of sheltering fugitive slaves and hiring them for the navy was more radical than Cameron's, yet the navy secretary was not reprimanded; he stayed in the cabinet throughout Lincoln's administration.) As Fessenden put it, Cameron simply "*could not* manage so large a concern," for he "had neither the capacity nor strength of will." As a result, "there was great mismanagement. He did his best, but his best was not enough."[360] Welles concurred, noting that Cameron lacked "the grasp, power, energy, comprehension, and important qualities essential to the administration of the War Department."[361] Among Cameron's most widely criticized shortcomings were his "worse than equivocal antecedents; his swarms of corrupt hangers-on and contract-hunting friends; his repeated and persistent attempts to enrich his Pennsylvania favorites at the expense of the people," and his lack of "a single military instinct" or a "comprehensive and organizing executive faculty."[362]

Cameron's dismissal electrified both the public and Congress. "Washington has not been in such a ferment since the day after Bull Run," reported one journalist. "The crowds who are here for good or evil still stand agape at the great change which has darted across the political firmament like a meteor."[363] The president's bold act prompted calls for a further shakeup in the cabinet. A Maine resident insisted that there "should be more changes immediately," for "[w]e have so signally failed in our Cabinet."[364] Criticism of the navy and interior secretaries was especially harsh. "Everybody knows that the heads of those Departments are not the men for these times," remarked a Washingtonian.[365] Welles was denounced for lacking "energy, decisiveness, system, organization, [and] prescience."[366] But when urged to dump the navy secretary, Lincoln replied that "when I was a young man I used to know very well one Joe Wilson, who built himself a log-cabin not far from where I lived. Joe was very fond of eggs and chickens, and he took a great deal of pains in fitting up a poultry shed." Late one night, hearing loud squawks and the fluttering of wings, Wilson arose to see what caused the fuss. He observed half a dozen skunks circling the shed. Angrily he reached for his musket and banged away at the pests, managing to kill only one. When he told this story to his neighbors, Wilson held his nose at this point. They asked why he didn't shoot the other skunks. "Blast it," he rejoined, "why it was eleven weeks before I got over killin' *one*. If you want any more skirmishing in that line you can just do it yourselves!"[367]

In the spring of 1862, when the House of Representatives censured Cameron, Lincoln defended him, much to the Congress's surprise. With his customary magnanimity, the president assumed much of the blame for mistakes made at the beginning of the war, when contracts were let without the usual precautions. Lincoln's defense of Cameron antagonized many Republicans, including several senators who manifested their dissatisfaction by voting not to confirm the Chief as minister to Russia. Samuel Galloway of Ohio "was shocked at the assumption of the responsibility of Cameron's odious acts by Lincoln." Incredulously, Galloway asked: "Does he suppose that any sane man is so stupid as to suppose that the President anticipated that any government officer would employ *scoundrels* to execute its wishes and orders." The president "must have been persuaded by Chase to throw his mantle over Simon's 'multitude of sins.'"[368] Some wondered why Lincoln waited till Cameron had left for Europe to defend him. Others praised his forbearance and pointed out that the president assumed responsibility only for the emergency expenditure of $2 million by Cummings et al., and not for Cameron's other peccadilloes. The president's gesture won him Cameron's unflagging gratitude, which would prove significant in later elections.

To replace the Chief, Lincoln wanted to name Joseph Holt, who had served with distinction as war secretary in the latter days of the Buchanan administration. Lincoln so trusted Holt that he told a Kentucky Republican seeking a favor that he should call on Holt. "If *he* says you ought to be attended to I will do it."[369] But Holt was too conservative for the Radicals, whose support Lincoln regarded as vital. When the president asked Cameron about possible successors, the Chief mentioned Edwin M. Stanton, a celebrated lawyer who as attorney general had, like Holt, helped stiffen Buchanan's backbone during the final stages of the secession crisis.

Chase, who regarded himself as the ablest man in the cabinet, took a hand in the selection of a new war secretary, maneuvering to have Stanton named. The two men had known each other as young attorneys and political activists; Chase may have thought the gruff, irascible Pennsylvanian would be an ideological ally, for Stanton had opposed slavery and his father had been an abolitionist. Evidently, Chase was unaware that in 1860 Stanton supported John C. Breckinridge for president. Calling on Seward, the treasury secretary speculated that Holt or Stanton would be chosen. Holt, he feared, could embarrass the administration on the slavery issue "and might not prove quite equal to the emergency." He praised Stanton as "a good lawyer and full of energy." Seward also regarded Stanton highly, calling him a man "of great force—full of expedients, and thoroughly loyal."[370] The secretary of state may have believed that as a War Democrat, Stanton might well side with him and the other Moderates in the cabinet. Seward lobbied actively on behalf of Stanton, with whom he had worked in secret during the winter of 1860–1861. At that time, Stanton had leaked inside information to the New York senator. Thus, Chase and Seward, who opposed each other on virtually every question, helped engineer Stanton's appointment. Lincoln probably rejoiced to observe these antagonists cooperate for a change.

Stanton was politically attractive, for, like Cameron, he lived in Pennsylvania and had been a Democrat. In addition, his service in Buchanan's cabinet had made him famous as a staunch Unionist. Lincoln decided to pass over other candidates for the War Department portfolio, including Holt, Montgomery Blair, John A. Dix, and Benjamin F. Wade, and name the lawyer who had humiliated him during the McCormick reaper trial in 1855. Lincoln consulted with George Harding, a Philadelphia patent attorney whom he had gotten to know during that trial. When asked his opinion about a successor to Cameron, Harding replied: "I have in mind only one man, but I know you could not and would not appoint him after the outrageous way he has insulted you and behaved towards you in the Reaper case."

"Oh," replied Lincoln, "you mean Stanton. Now, Mr. Harding, this is not a personal matter. I simply desire to do what will be the best thing for the country."[371]

Stanton's appointment was one of the most magnanimous acts of a remarkably magnanimous president.

When informed that he would be offered the War Department portfolio, Stanton said: "Tell the President I will accept, if no other pledge than to throttle treason shall be exacted."[372]

At Lincoln's invitation, Stanton visited the White House with Harding, who recalled that the president and his secretary-of-war-designate greeted each other with little embarrassment: "The meeting was brief but friendly and Lincoln and Stanton shook hands cordially at parting, both thanking him [Harding] for the trouble he had taken in bringing them together."[373]

Before announcing Stanton's appointment, Lincoln asked Congressman Henry L. Dawes, who served on a committee looking into government transactions during the secession crisis, "whether any thing appeared in that investigation reflecting on the integrity" of Stanton. The president explained that he did not doubt Stanton's probity, but "it is necessary that the public as well as I should have confidence in the man I appoint to office, whatever may be my own opinion." Later, when Dawes congratulated Lincoln on his choice, he replied "that it was an experiment which he had made up his mind to try, and that whenever a Union man was willing to break away from party affiliations, and stand by the government in this great struggle, he was resolved to give him an opportunity and welcome him to the service." Lincoln added "that he had been warned against this appointment, and had been told that it never would do; that 'Stanton would run away with the whole concern, and that he would find he could do nothing with such a man unless he let him have his own way.'" Lincoln "then told a story of a minister out in Illinois who was in the habit of going off on such high flights at camp meetings that they had to put bricks in his pockets to keep him down. 'I may have to do that with Stanton; but if I do, bricks in his pocket will be better than bricks in his hat. I guess I'll let him jump a while.'"[374] Dawes reported that Stanton's appointment "makes everybody breathe easier," for the new war secretary "is an earnest man and believes that this is a war to be fought like any other war with all our might."[375]

Although he consulted with many men before selecting Stanton, Lincoln had not spoken with McClellan. On the day after the appointment, he told the general-in-chief that he knew Stanton was a friend of McClellan whom he would probably be happy to have in the War Department, and that he was afraid if he had informed the general ahead of time, Radical Republicans would allege that McClellan had inveigled him into making that choice. In early January, Stanton said "he regarded McClellan as the greatest military genius upon the continent."[376] That opinion would soon change.

News of Stanton's appointment exploded like an artillery round among the Republicans, including Senator William P. Fessenden, who reported that it "astounded every body."[377] When some protested against the selection of a prominent Democrat as secretary of war, Lincoln replied: "If I could find four more democrats just like Stanton, I would appoint them."[378] He said "he knew him to be a true and loyal man, and that he possessed the greatest energy of character and systematic method in the discharge of public business."[379]

Democrats like New York editor James Brooks were gratified. In choosing Stanton, Lincoln "shows that he means to administer the Government, not alone upon a narrow Chicago Platform, but upon the Constitutional National Platform," Brooks declared.[380] August Belmont, chairman of the Democratic National Committee, thought Stanton's appointment indicated that Lincoln understood the necessity of adding conservative Democrats to his administration. The Democratic former mayor of New York, Fernando Wood, praised Lincoln extravagantly: "Your highly patriotic, and conservative course meets with the hearty concurrence of the Democratic masses in this state—We will sustain you fully, and you may rely upon my best exertions in behalf of the administration of which you are the noble head—The late change in the cabinet was opportune—It has given the best proof of your own ability to govern, and also of your executive power and will."[381]

Westerners were also pleased. "The West will look to Mr. Stanton . . . as her guardian and representative in the voyage of the Cabinet in these perilous times," the Cincinnati *Enquirer* predicted. "He is identified with us by birth, feelings and interests, and by all his aspirations."[382]

Physically, the new secretary cut an unimpressive figure. General John Pope thought Stanton "was in no sense an imposing person, either in looks or manner." Relatively short, "stout and clumsy," with "a broad, rather red face, well covered with a heavy black beard, which descended on his breast and was scarcely sprinkled with gray," he "had a mass of long hair, pushed off toward the back of his head from a broad, massive brow and large, dark eyes, which looked even larger behind a pair of gold-rimmed spectacles, seemingly of unusual size." With a "rather squat figure, surmounted by the leonine bust and head above it," he seemed "shaggy" and "belligerent."[383]

Former California Senator William M. Gwin, who had known Stanton years before, predicted that the new war secretary "will tomahawk them all."[384] But most observers approved of the choice, among them George Templeton Strong of the U.S.

Sanitary Commission, who said Stanton was worth "a wagon load of Camerons." Although Strong did not admire Stanton's "rather pigfaced," "Luther-oid" appearance, the new war secretary was, in his view, "[i]ntelligent, prompt, clear-headed, fluent without wordiness, and above all, earnest, warm-hearted, and large-hearted," and thus represented "the reverse in all things of his cunning, cold-blooded, selfish old predecessor."[385] Journalist D. W. Bartlett called Stanton "a very able man, a pushing, all-alive man."[386] The conservative New York *Herald* predicted that "what Carnot was to the first French republic, as Minister of War, Stanton will be to 'Honest Abe Lincoln'" and "that he will be the man to bring order out of confusion, efficiency out of inaction, and an invincible army out of raw recruits, dispirited by frequent disasters, delays and disappointments."[387] Senator Fessenden hoped that Stanton would "be of great benefit in *stiffening* the Cabinet—a thing which it much needs."[388] Some senators, however, were reluctant to confirm Stanton unless the president assured them that the war would be prosecuted vigorously.

Lincoln's preferred candidate for the war portfolio, Joseph Holt, thanked the president for choosing Stanton: "In him you will find a friend true as steel, & a support, which no pressure from within or from without, will ever shake. It was my fortune to know him during the darkest days of the late administration & I think I know him well. With his great talents, he is the soul of honor, of courage, & of loyalty. In the progress of the terrible events inseperable from the struggle for the life of our country, in which you are heroically engaged, you can assign to Edwin M. Stanton no duty however stern, or solemn or self-sacrificing, which he will not nobly & efficiently perform."[389] New York attorney Edwards Pierrepont described to Lincoln "the reviving confidence which your appointment of Mr Stanton had given us. The whole nation thanks God, that you had the wisdom and the courage to make the change."[390]

In the New York *Tribune,* managing editor Charles A. Dana lauded his good friend Stanton as a man who cared deeply about the preservation of the Union: "If slavery or anti-slavery shall at any time be found obstructing or impeding the nation in its efforts to crush out this monstrous rebellion, he will walk straight on the path of duty, though that path should lead him over or through the impediment, and insure its annihilation." The energetic Stanton would infuse energy into the War Department, Dana predicted, and would be a "zealous cooperator" rather than "a lordly superior" in dealing with McClellan.[391]

In thanking Dana, Stanton expressed the hope that all Unionists would support him. "Bad passions, and little passions, and mean passions gather around and hem in the great movements that should deliver this nation," he said. But he sensed a new determination in his department. "We have no jokes or trivialities," he assured Dana, "but all with whom I act show that they are now in dead earnest. . . . As soon as I can get the machinery of the office working, the rats cleaned out, & the ratholes stopped, we shall *move.*"[392]

Joseph Medill of the Chicago *Tribune* spoke for many Northerners when he told Stanton that the "country looks to you to infuse vigor, system, honesty, and *fight* into the services. The army has lost more men in the past four months from inaction and ennui than it would have done from ten bloody pitched battles."[393] John Hay described Stanton as "an energetic and efficient worker, a man of initiative and decision, an organizer, a man of administrative scope and executive tact" who "is personally friendly" with all the members of the cabinet.[394]

Hay reckoned without Montgomery Blair, who expressed doubt about Stanton's integrity and opposed his appointment. Attorney General Bates also distrusted Stanton, and Gideon Welles complained that Stanton's "remarks on the personal appearance of the President were coarse, and his freely expressed judgment on public measures unjust." The navy secretary believed Stanton "was engaged with discontented and mischievous persons in petty intrigues to impair confidence in the Administration."[395] (Indeed, Stanton had criticized Lincoln severely in private, and the Washington rumor mill spread his caustic comments far and wide. McClellan recalled the "extreme virulence" with which Stanton "abused the President, the administration, and the Republican party. He carried this to such an extent that I was often shocked by it. He never spoke of the President in any other way than as the 'original gorilla.'")[396] Welles also objected to the way Stanton curried McClellan's favor. Later, the navy secretary wrote that Stanton "took pleasure in being ungracious and rough towards those who were under his control, and when he thought his bearish manner would terrify or humiliate those who were subject to him. To his superiors or those who were his equals in position, and who neither heeded nor cared for his violence, he was complacent, sometimes obsequious."[397]

Despite those unfortunate qualities, Stanton proved to be a remarkably capable war secretary who worked well with the president. Whereas the selection of his first secretary of war was one of Lincoln's greatest mistakes, the choice of a successor turned out to be one of his most inspired appointments. Shortly after Stanton assumed control of the War Department, Joshua Speed praised the way he transformed it: "Instead of that loose shackeling way of doing business in the war office, with which I have been so much disgusted & which I have had so good an opportunity of seeing—there is now order regularity and precision. . . . I shall be much mistaken if he does not infuse into the whole army an energy & activity which we have not seen heretofore."[398]

Unlike the president, Stanton had little trouble saying "no." Early in his tenure at the War Department, the new secretary was approached by a man who wanted an army appointment and said he had received Lincoln's endorsement. "The President, sir, is a very excellent man and would be glad if he had an appointment for every man who applied, which, unfortunately for his good nature, is not the case," Stanton explained.[399] Later, when Judge Joseph G. Baldwin of California requested a pass to visit his brother in Virginia, Lincoln suggested he see Stanton. The judge replied that he had done so and was refused. With a smile Lincoln observed, "I can do nothing; for you must know that I have very little influence with this administration."[400] By assuming the unpleasant but necessary duty of denying requests, Stanton thus helped the president seem accommodating. His gruffness was useful, for, as General Pope observed, no one "can compute what was the value to the government, of this terse, not to say abrupt treatment of men and business by the Secretary of War in the times when Mr. Stanton held that office. No politician nor suave man of any description could have disposed of such a mass of business and such a crowd of people as pressed on the Secretary of War from morning until night and until far into the early hours of the next day, for months together."[401]

With Stanton's assistance, Lincoln now began to assert himself more forcefully in dealing with his generals and to take charge of the war effort more decisively. The new war secretary's first directive to McClellan was signed by order of "the President, Commander-in-Chief of the Army and Navy," a not-so-subtle message to the Young Napoleon. Lincoln had been studying strategy and tactics whenever he could find the time. Among the books he read was Henry W. Halleck's *Elements of Military Art and Science*. William Howard Russell of the London *Times* observed him scuttling from the White House to the War Department and to the homes of his generals. "This poor President!" Russell exclaimed. "He is to be pitied; . . . trying with all his might to understand strategy, naval warfare, big guns, the movements of troops, military maps, reconaissances, occupations, interior and exterior lines, and all the technical details of the art of slaying. He runs from one house to another, armed with plans, papers, reports, recommendations, sometimes good humored, never angry, occasionally dejected, and always a little fussy."[402]

In time, Lincoln acquired a better understanding of strategy than most of his generals, as is made clear in a letter he wrote to Buell on that memorable January 13: "I state my general idea of this war to be that we have the greater numbers, and the enemy has the *greater* facility of concentrating forces upon points of collision; that we must fail, unless we can find some way of making *our* advantage an over-match for *his*; and that this can only be done by menacing him with superior forces at *different* points, at the *same* time; so that we can safely attack, one, or both, if he makes no change; and if he weakens one to *strengthen* the other, forbear to attack the strengthened one, but seize, and hold the weakened one."[403]

Lincoln was right: the North's advantages in manpower and economic strength would secure victory only if the military applied pressure on all fronts simultaneously. Buell, Halleck, McClellan, and many other generals failed to grasp this elementary point.

"This Damned Old House"
The Lincoln Family in the Executive Mansion

During the Civil War, the atmosphere in the White House was usually sober, for as John Hay recalled, it "was an epoch, if not of gloom, at least of a seriousness too intense to leave room for much mirth."[1] The death of Lincoln's favorite son and the misbehavior of the First Lady significantly intensified that mood.

The White House

The White House failed to impress Lincoln's secretaries, who disparaged its "threadbare appearance" and referred to it as "a dirty rickety concern."[2] A British journalist considered it beautiful in the moonlight, "when its snowy walls stand out in contrast to the deep blue sky, but not otherwise."[3] The Rev. Dr. Theodore L. Cuyler thought that the "shockingly careless appearance of the White House proved that whatever may have been Mrs. Lincoln's other good qualities, she hadn't earned the compliment which the Yankee farmer paid to his wife when he said: 'Ef my wife haint got an ear fer music, she's got an eye fer dirt.'"[4] The north side of the Executive Mansion, facing Pennsylvania Avenue, was marred by an immense portico that seemed to dwarf the building, and the statue of Thomas Jefferson on the lawn before the front entrance was a green, moldy eyesore.

Passing beneath the outsized portico, visitors entered a small lobby, then emerged into a large vestibule, where coat racks were set up for large public receptions. Those events were held in the enormous East Room, which William O. Stoddard said had "a faded, worn, untidy look" and needed fresh paint and new furniture.[5] It featured a conventionally frescoed ceiling, satin drapes, a plush carpet, and three huge chandeliers.

Three other state parlors, designated by their colors, were smaller. Mary Lincoln's favorite, the red one, served as her sitting room where she received guests. The president also entertained friends there after dinner. Its furniture was upholstered in red satin and gold damask, its windows had gilded cornices, and throughout were scattered many vases and much ormolu work. Few paintings other than a full-length portrait of George Washington adorned the walls. Stoddard believed that the plainness of the White House could have been softened with more art-work.[6] The oval Blue Room, which had a fine view across the spacious grounds to the Potomac River, was known as "Charles Ogle's Elliptical Saloon," a reference to the demagogic Pennsylvania congressman who had attacked Martin Van Buren for redecorating the White House. The Green Room was a small parlor where guests were received informally. (After Willie Lincoln died in 1862, his body was em-balmed in the Green Room. His mother refused to enter it thereafter. His death is discussed in chapter 26.)

Beyond these three parlors was the modestly appointed state dining room, which could accommodate up to thirty-five guests. A smaller family dining room adjoined it on the north side. On the far end of the west wing was a spacious conservatory, a great favorite of Mary Lincoln, who used its flowers to adorn the house profusely. She also sent them to hospitals and hospital fund-raising events called sanitary fairs. Visitors picked the flowers so often that eventually the conservatory was declared off-limits to the public. (Flowers were not the only souvenirs taken. In the public rooms visitors shamelessly cut swatches from draperies and carpets, and stole tassels, ornaments, and fringes.)

Also at the end of the west wing was a massive staircase leading to the second floor, which housed offices as well as the family quarters. (There were two smaller stairways, one of which led to the offices; another was a service staircase, which Lincoln used most often, for it allowed him to pass from the second story to the basement hallway and exit unobserved.) The upstairs was dark, with its heavy ma-hogany doors and wainscoting. On the east side was the president's sparsely fur-nished office, which Stoddard described as "a wonderful historic cavern" with "less space for the transaction of the business of his office than a well-to-do New York lawyer."[7] In the middle of the room stood a long table around which the cabinet sat. By the center window overlooking the Potomac was Lincoln's upright desk, resem-bling something from a used furniture auction. Maps were displayed on racks in the northwest corner of the room, a portrait of Andrew Jackson hung above the fire-place, and a large photograph of the English reformer John Bright adorned one wall.

Adjoining this office-cum-cabinet-meeting-chamber was a large waiting room, through which Lincoln had to pass in order to reach the living area. (The only modi-fication to the house made during his presidency was a partition installed toward the rear of the waiting room, creating a private passageway from the office to the family quarters.) Nearby were Nicolay's small office and reception room, another office—used by Stoddard and Hay—and a bedroom occupied by Nicolay and Hay. Adjacent to Lincoln's bedroom was a small dressing room.

The family quarters on the west side of the second floor included an oval library-cum-family-room which was, as Stoddard put it, "really a delightful retreat." In addition to bedrooms for the president and First Lady there were four others, one of which was for Willie and Tad. Running water for washing was available in all the family rooms save the library.

The rat-infested basement, where the kitchen and the servants' quarters were located, had "the air of an old and unsuccessful hotel," according to Stoddard.[8] In 1864, Commissioner of Public Buildings Benjamin Brown French reported that during the previous summer "the effluvia from dead rats was offensive in all the passages and many of the occupied rooms to both the occupants of, and visitors to, the Presidential mansion."[9] A British caller noted that the house "is rendered very unhealthy by the accumulation of refuse and garbage, which the tide washes to and fro between the piles of the long chain-bridge."[10] Commissioner French recommended that the president should have a new residence in a less unhealthy location, like the heights of Georgetown.

The lack of screens on windows and doors made summers in the White House disagreeable. One night in July 1862, Nicolay amusingly reported that the "gas lights over my desk are burning brightly and the windows of the room are open, and all bugdom outside seems to have organized a storming party to take the gas light, in numbers which seem to exceed the contending hosts at Richmond. The air is swarming with them, they are on the ceiling, the walls and the furniture in countless numbers, they are buzzing about the room, and butting their heads against the window panes, they are on my clothes, in my hair, and on the sheet I am writing on. They are all here, the plebeian masses, as well as the great and distinguished members of the oldest and largest patrician families—the Millers, the Roaches, the Whites, the Blacks, yea even the wary and diplomatic foreigners from the Musquito Kingdom. They hold a high carnival, or rather a perfect Saturnalia. Intoxicated and maddened and blinded by the bright gaslight, they dance, and rush and fly about in wild gyrations, until they are drawn into the dazzling but fatal heat of the gas-flame when they fall to the floor, burned and maimed and mangled to the death, to be swept out into the dust and rubbish by the servant in the morning."[11]

To escape the rat effluvia and the bugs, Lincoln and his family spent the warmer months of 1862, 1863, and 1864 at the Soldiers' Home, a complex of five buildings on 300 acres, located 3 miles north of the White House on the Seventh Street Road. Established in the early 1850s to house indigent, disabled veterans, it was officially known as the Military Asylum. On the grounds, a wealthy banker, George W. Riggs, built a comfortable house in the Rural Gothic style, which in time became known as the Anderson cottage. This dwelling was in all likelihood the one where the Lincolns stayed. "We are truly delighted, with this retreat, the drives & walks around here are truly delightful," Mary Lincoln wrote.[12] The Home occupied high ground, catching whatever breezes might be blowing in the area, and offering a splendid view of Washington. Lincoln commuted every day to the Executive Mansion, usually departing no later than 8 A.M.

The staff at the White House included doorkeepers, a coachman, messengers, a gardener, groundskeepers, a steward, cooks, waiters, a housekeeper, and guards. There was an unusually rapid turnover of staff during the Lincoln administration, just as there had been in the Lincoln household in Springfield. It was hard to please the mercurial Mary Lincoln. Among others, the English steward, Richard Goodchild, was fired to make way for Jane Watt, wife of the corrupt gardener, John Watt.

The butler Peter Vermeren was let go early on, after he dared to report corruption in the White House. The head doorkeeper, Thomas Burns, was also dismissed soon after the Lincolns moved in.

A few members of the White House staff were black, including the messenger-valet-steward William Slade, known as an excellent storyteller; the cook Cornelia Mitchell; and the butler Peter Brown. William Johnson, a valet-cum-barber who came from Springfield with the First Family in 1861, initially worked in the White House stoking the furnace. But the other black employees, all light-skinned, objected to his dark complexion so vehemently that Lincoln had to find him another post. To Navy Secretary Welles Lincoln wrote in mid-March 1861: "The bearer (William) is a servant who has been with me for some time & in whom I have confidence as to his integrity and faithfulness. He wishes to enter your service. The difference of color between him & the other servants is the cause of our seperation. If you can give him employment you will confer a favour on Yours truly."[13] After several months, Johnson eventually landed a job at the Treasury Department, which he held till his death in 1864. To help him earn more money, Lincoln also facilitated his efforts to moonlight for others.

Security was provided by uniformed soldiers at the exterior doors and gates. Indoors, plainclothes guards acted as doormen and other servants.

Stoddard recalled that in dealing with the staff, Lincoln "took their presence and the performance of their duties so utterly for granted" that none of them "was ever made to feel, unpleasantly, the fact of his inferior position by reason of any look or word of the President. All were well assured that they could not get a word from him unless the business which brought them to his elbow justified them in coming. The number of times that Mrs. Lincoln herself entered his business-room at the White House could probably be counted on the fingers of one hand."[14] Though kindly and considerate, Lincoln could take umbrage at insubordination. One day when the president asked his Irish coachman to buy a morning paper, that gentleman said that he would but then did not do so, for he considered it beneath his dignity to run errands. Lincoln himself went out on the street, hailed a newsboy, and purchased a copy of the Washington *Chronicle*. To convey a message to the haughty coachman, Lincoln ordered the coach up at 6 A.M. to take another staffer out to buy a paper. The driver was humiliated.

Daily Routine

Lincoln usually rose early, for he slept lightly and fitfully. Before consuming his spare breakfast of an egg, toast, and coffee, he spent a couple of hours glancing at newspapers, writing letters, signing documents, or studying the subjects most pressing at the moment. After eating, he would read telegrams at the dingy War Department building next door to the Executive Mansion. Upon his return, he would go through the mail with a secretary. Around ten o'clock visitors would be admitted. Cabinet members had precedence, then senators, followed by congressmen, and finally the general public. One morning, Lincoln was showing his good friend Anson G. Henry some maps when the clock stuck ten, indicating that office hours were to begin. "Citizens can get in," Henry reported, "but nine times out of ten not half the Senators get in unless several go in together, & this is very often done, and they can take in with them as many of their friends or constituents as they please. It is no uncommon thing for Senators to try for ten days before they get a *private* interview."[15] On Tuesdays and Fridays, when cabinet meetings were usually held, visiting hours ended at noon.

When the public's turn to enter came, Lincoln had the doors opened and in surged a crowd, filling up his small office. Those who simply wanted to shake his hand or to wish him well were quickly accommodated. Others seeking mercy or assistance told their tales of woe, unconcerned about who might hear them. Many who hoped for a more private consultation held back and would be brought up short when the president loudly called them forward: "Well, friend, what can I do for you?" This forced them either to speak up or withdraw.[16] All kinds of people sought presidential assistance: army officers longing for promotion, foreign diplomats concerned about their country's interests, autograph seekers, inventors touting their creations, cabinet members soliciting favors for friends, women appealing on behalf of their sons or husbands or fathers, and businessmen in quest of contracts, among others.

A satirist poked fun at the swarming hordes who desired to see the president: "They cannot be driven off; they cannot be bluffed. Bars and bolts will not shut them out. The frowns of janitors have no terrors for them. They are proof against the snubbings of secretaries. It is in vain the President sends word that he 'cannot be seen.' He must be seen; he shall be seen. Has not the Honorable Jonathan Swellhead come all the way from Wisconsin to consult him about the [draft] quota of his town? Has not the Reverend Dr. Blowhard travelled a thousand miles to impress upon him the necessity of increasing the number of fast days? Has not Christopher Carbuncle, Esq., traveled two days and nights in order to arrange with him the vexed question of the post office in Grabtown? Has not Mr. Samuel Shoddy come expressly from Boston to get him to endorse an application for a blanket contract? Has not a committee from the synod of the See-No-Further church come to implore him to open cabinet meetings with prayer and inaugurate his Wednesday levees with the singing of a psalm? Nor can these clamorous patriots be dismissed with a brief audience. They belong to the class of bores who make long speeches. Having once got the ear of the President, they resolve to keep it. They hang on like a dog to a root. There is no shaking them off until they have had their say; and so hour after hour of the precious time of the head of the nation is thus frittered away."[17]

Seated at his table, Lincoln greeted visitors kindly, saying to those he was not acquainted with: "Well?" and those he did know: "And how are you today, Mr. _____?'" He usually called old friends by their first names. Seward he addressed as "Governor," Blair and Bates as "Judge," Stanton as "Mars," Welles as "Neptune," and the other cabinet secretaries as "Mister." Patiently he listened to requests, asked questions, and then informed callers what he would do for them. If, for example, his petitioner was an impoverished widow seeking a clerkship, he would peruse her letters of recommendation, ask some probing questions, then write out a note to the relevant official instructing him to honor her request. This procedure was so time-consuming that he was able to deal with only a small fraction of the crowd in the anteroom.

To Lincoln's annoyance, many callers insisted that he solve minor disputes and deal with other petty matters. According to Hay, Lincoln "pretended to begin business at ten o[']clock in the morning, but in reality the anterooms and halls were full before that hour—people anxious to get the first axe ground. He was extremely unmethodical: it was a four-years struggle on Nicolay's part and mine to get him to adopt some systematic rules. He would break through every regulation as fast as it was made. Anything that kept the people themselves away from him he disapproved—although they nearly annoyed the life out of him by unreasonable complaints & requests."[18] In 1863, Stoddard reported from the White House that the president was besieged by the "same unceasing throng in the ante-rooms . . . bent on dragging him 'for only a few minutes only,' away from his labors of state to attend to private requests, often selfish, often frivolous, sometimes corrupt or improper, and *not* so often worthy of the precious time and strength thus wasted."[19] Private grievances, misfortunes, and wishes were so numerous that Lincoln once remarked "that it seemed as if he was regarded as a police justice, before whom all the petty troubles of men were brought for adjustment."[20]

A typical case involved an enlisted man who pestered Lincoln with a matter that the president thought should be handled by the soldier's superior officer. When his advice was ignored, Lincoln peremptorily barked, "Now, my man, go away! I cannot attend to all these details. I could as easily bail out the Potomac with a spoon."[21] Similarly, when a sutler asked Lincoln to grant him permission to peddle ale to the troops, he said sharply: "Look here! What do you take me for, anyhow? Do you think I keep a beer shop?"[22] A woman who aspired to be a physician called repeatedly, asking Lincoln to approve her application for a license to practice medicine. Because the medical faculty of the District of Columbia would not give her one, she demanded that the president do so.

Sometimes Lincoln resorted to gentle sarcasm when confronted by importunate visitors. A delegation once appealed to him to help the Washington fire department obtain new equipment. He interrupted their presentation, gravely remarking: "Ah! Yes, gentlemen, but it is a mistake to suppose that I am at the head of the fire department of Washington. I am simply the President of the United States."[23] When a landlord complained that he could not collect his rents, Lincoln expressed sympathy but asked, "what would you have me do for you? I have much to do, and the courts have been opened to relieve me in this regard." Sheepishly his caller said, "I am not in the habit of appearing before big men." With customary modesty, the president replied: "And for that matter, you have no need to change your habit, for you are not before very big men now." Lincoln patiently concluded the interview by observing that he could not "go into the collection business."[24] Lincoln had to make the same point to another creditor: "I am really very sorry, madam, very sorry. But your own good sense must tell you that I am not here to collect small debts. You must appeal to the courts in regular order." To an army officer, he exclaimed: "What odd kinds of people come in to see me, and what odd ideas they must have about my office! Would you believe, Major, that the old lady who has just left, came in here to get from me an order for stopping the pay of a treasury clerk, who owes her a board bill of about seventy dollars. . . . She may have come in here a loyal woman, but I'll be bound she has gone away believing that the worst pictures of me in the Richmond press only lack truth in not being half black and bad enough."[25]

An allegedly loyal Southerner asked Lincoln to sign papers permitting him to recover substantial sums for property damaged in the war. The president heatedly observed that the claimant's documents did not prove that he deserved the money. "I know what you want," Lincoln snapped, "you are turning, or trying to turn me into a justice of the peace, to put your claims through. There are a hundred thousand men in the country, every one of them as good as you are, who have just such bills as you present; and you care nothing of what becomes of them, so you get your money."[26] When a poor woman from Michigan came begging for help to meet her mortgage, Lincoln listened patiently, scanned her letters "with a half humorous, half vexed expression," and pledged a modest sum.[27]

To a farmer seeking presidential aid in pressing a claim for damages, Lincoln exclaimed: "Why, my good sir. If I should attempt to consider every such individual case I should find work enough for twenty Presidents!" When his interlocutor failed to take the hint, Lincoln said he was reminded of an expert pilot back in Illinois who was deftly guiding a steamboat through some rapids. As the craft pitched and rolled in the turbulent water, a young boy accosted him with a plea: "Say, Mister Captain! I wish you would just stop your boat a minute—I've lost my apple overboard!"[28] Visiting clergy often annoyed the president. One day when a minister called at the White House, Lincoln invited him to sit, then took his own chair and announced: "I am now ready to hear what you have to say."

"Oh, bless you sir, I have nothing to say. I merely called to pay my respects."

With relief written all over his face, Lincoln rose, took the clerical visitor's hand in both of his, and exclaimed: "My dear sir, I am very glad to see you. I am very glad to see you indeed. I thought you came to preach to me!"[29]

Lincoln put in long hours attending to public business. When the First Lady was away (which was often), he would eat breakfast, lunch, and even dinner alone in his office while working away steadily. Theodore Cuyler once asked him: "Mr. President, I am here at almost every hour of the day or night, and I never saw you at the table; do you ever eat?" Lincoln replied: "I try to. I manage to browse about pretty much as I can get it."[30] Receiving callers from early morning till late afternoon, he seemed to Stoddard like "a man who carried a load too great for human strength; and, as the years went on and the load grew heavier, it bowed him into premature old age. He was the American Atlas."[31]

At lunchtime, Lincoln ran a gauntlet formed by would-be callers lining the hallway between his office and the family quarters. Afternoons were spent much like mornings. Late in the day he would usually take a carriage ride, often with the First Lady. Dinner was served at 6 P.M. According to John Hay, Lincoln "was one of the most abstemious of men; the pleasures of the table had few attractions for him." His lunch consisted of little more than a biscuit and some fruit, washed down with a glass of milk, and for supper he "ate sparingly of one or two courses."[32] He liked simple food, especially cornpone, cabbage, and chicken fricassee. After the evening meal, he would usually return to his office and continue working. Sometimes at dinner he enjoyed the company of friends, who joined him for coffee and a postprandial chat in the red drawing room. During sessions of Congress, its members took up many of his evening hours. He went to bed between 10 and 11 P.M., but if he was expecting important news, he would stay up as late as 1 or 2 A.M., closeted with the telegraph operators at the War Department. After the death of Willie in February 1862, Tad usually slept with his father.

On Sundays, Lincoln attended services at the nearby New York Avenue Presbyterian Church, where the Rev. Dr. Phineas Gurley presided. Upon arriving in Washington, he asked friends and allies to recommend "a church whose clergyman holds himself aloof from politics."[33] At first, Willie and Tad went to Sunday school there, but later the headstrong Tad revolted, preferring to go to the livelier Fourth Presbyterian Church where his friends Holly and Bud Taft and their family worshipped.

Receptions

Like their predecessors, the Lincolns hosted receptions, levees, open houses, state dinners, and concerts. On March 7, 1861, the president held a reception for foreign representatives. One of them, the Russian minister Edouard de Stoeckl, reported that "the diplomatic corps has only praise" for the event. (A sarcastic, witty put-down artist, Stoeckl thought the president's "manners are those of a man who has spent all his life in a small Western town.")[34]

Lincoln was formally presented to those diplomats in special audiences, one of which the English journalist William Howard Russell described vividly. On March 27, 1861, the Chevalier Bertinatti of Sardinia (Italy), splendidly decked out with a sword, sash, cocked hat, white gloves, suit of blue with silver lace, and ribbon of the cross of Savoy, made his appearance at the White House. Lincoln presented a striking contrast, entering "with a shambling, loose, irregular, almost unsteady gait" and wearing a wrinkled black suit which caused him to resemble an undertaker. He made an unprepossessing appearance with his "sinewy muscular yellow neck," "flapping and wide projecting ears," "thatch of wild republican hair" that looked like "a ruff of mourning pins," "stooping shoulders," and "long pendulous arms, terminating in hands of extraordinary dimensions, which, however, were far exceeded in proportion by his feet." His "strange, quaint face" featured an "absolutely prodigious" mouth with lips "straggling and extending almost from one line of black beard to the other." The equally huge nose stood out "with an inquiring, anxious air, as though it were sniffing for some good thing in the wind." The "dark, full, and deeply set, penetrating" eyes were "full of an expression which almost amounts to tenderness." Above them loomed a "shaggy brow" and a forehead with "irregular flocks of thick hair carelessly brushed across it." He would not be mistaken for what Europeans considered a gentleman. Russell reported that since coming to the United States, he had "heard more disparaging allusions made by Americans to him on that account than I could have expected among simple republicans, where all should be equals."[35]

(One such critic was a New York clergyman who wished Lincoln "were more of a gentleman," for he was "decidedly shabby in his dress & manner."[36] Frederick Law Olmsted, a member of the U.S. Sanitary Commission as well as a noted landscape architect and journalist, was dismayed to see the president "dressed in a cheap & nasty French black cloth suit just out of a tight carpet bag" looking like "an applicant for a Broadway squad policemanship."[37] Echoing Olmsted was another member of the Sanitary Commission, George Templeton Strong, a sophisticated Wall Street lawyer who found the president "lank and hard-featured, among the ugliest white men I have seen," and emphatically "plebeian." He had "the laugh of a yahoo, with a wrinkling of the nose that suggests affinity with the tapir and other pachyderms; and his grammar is weak." In sum, he was "a barbarian, Scythian, yahoo, or gorilla, in respect of outside polish."[38] Prince Napoleon, cousin of Napoleon III, thought Lincoln had "the appearance of a bootmaker" and found him "badly put together, in a black suit." In his diary, the prince exclaimed: "What a difference between this sad representative of the great republic and her founding fathers!" Withal Lincoln impressed the prince as "a good man, but one without greatness nor very much knowledge."[39] The unrefined, "painfully homely & awkward" president, Richard Henry Dana thought, resembled "a man who has brought in something to sell" with a face radiating no "power or firmness.")[40]

Despite Lincoln's unprepossessing appearance, journalist Russell acknowledged that "it would not be possible for the most indifferent observer to pass him in the street without notice." As Lincoln proceeded through the East Room to greet the Italian diplomat, "he evidently controlled a desire to shake hands all round with everybody, and smiled good-humoredly till he was suddenly brought up by the staid deportment of Mr. Seward, and by the profound diplomatic bows of the Chevalier Bertinatti." Abruptly the president "jerked himself back, and stood in front of the two ministers, with his body slightly drooped forward, and his hands behind his back, his knees touching, and his feet apart." After Seward formally presented Bertinatti, Lincoln "made a prodigiously violent demonstration of his body in a bow which had almost the effect of a smack in its rapidity and abruptness, and, recovering himself, proceeded to give his utmost attention, whilst the Chevalier, with another bow, read from a paper a long address." Lincoln in turn delivered a brief reply, shook the minister's hand, and was introduced by Seward to Russell. The president "put out his hand in a very friendly manner, and said, 'Mr. Russell, I am very glad to make your acquaintance, and to see you in this country. The London 'Times' is one of the greatest powers in the world,—in fact, I don't know anything which has much more power—except perhaps the Mississippi. I am glad to know you as its minister.' Conversation ensued for some minutes, which the President enlivened by two or three peculiar little sallies." Russell was impressed by Lincoln's "shrewdness, humour, and natural sagacity."[41]

On March 8, 1861, Lincoln hosted his first public reception, which Attorney General Bates described laconically: "motley crowd and terrible squeeze."[42] The president, according to one report, "with his towering figure and commanding presence, stood like a hero, putting the foot down firmly, and breasting the stream of humanity as it swept by." By one estimate, he shook 3,000 hands, including that of a man who said, "Mr. President, you must diminish the number of your friends, or Congress must enlarge the edifice." Lincoln, referring tongue-in-cheek to his reputation as a rail-splitter, replied: "I've no idea of diminishing the number of my friends, but the only question with me now is whether it would be best to have the building stretched or split."[43] To Charles Francis Adams, the president looked "entirely worn out," and his facial expression seemed "formal and embarrassed."[44] A journalist remarked that Mary Lincoln "made a pleasant impression upon every one who came near her. Had she been born and lived her life in the court of the Tuleries, she could not have shown more fitness for the position which she so admirably adorns."[45] (Adams disagreed, recording in his diary that neither she nor her husband "is at home in this sphere of civilization." That crusty New Englander, according to one of his assistants in the American legation in London, "always spoke disrespectfully of Mrs. Lincoln.")[46] The levee was "voted by all the 'oldest inhabitants' to have been the most successful one ever known here," John G. Nicolay told his fiancée.[47]

William O. Stoddard recalled that Lincoln's "manner at receptions, and other occasions of ceremony or of social or official formality, was that of a man who performs an irksome but unavoidable duty, though he was never lacking in cordial hospitality." According to Stoddard, some people attended receptions "with the dim idea that they were about to make the acquaintance of the President and his wife, and prepared themselves for a quiet little chat, with stores of questions about this and advice about that for Father Abraham. Others, not expecting much time to themselves, would prepare patriotic little speeches, which they would launch with sudden fervor and wonderfully rapid utterance at the head of the President."[48] In July, the Baltimore *Patriot* reported that people "who have grasped the dexter of successive Presidents from John Quincy Adams, with his pump-handle shake, down to the present time, say that Mr. Lincoln goes through the necessary work of a reception with less fatigue than any of them did. Besides, he has kind looks for everybody, and pleasant words for all who accompany the pressure of his hand with a passing remark." Lincoln "sends all his fellow citizens of every class and condition away with the impression that they have been respectfully and kindly treated at the White House."[49] Journalist Mary Clemmer Ames wrote that "Lincoln looks very awkward in white kid gloves, and feels very uncomfortable in new boots; so much so, that at the very first one [reception] he slipped into his easy slippers, then back to the martyrdom, where his honest hand was squeezed in the vise of the 'sovereign people' for five weary hours."[50]

On March 9, Lincoln received the officers of the navy, including Charles Henry Davis, who described the president as "awkward in his figure and manners, but his awkwardness is not *gaucherie*. It is by no means vulgar."[51] David D. Porter concurred, deeming the president "a plain politician, with very little polish of manner," who "was much confused at meeting such an imposing looking set of men. Such was his embarrassment that he could not answer the little speech made to him by Commodore [Joseph] Smith." When the officers asked to meet his wife, Lincoln went off to fetch her and "returned half dragging in the apparently confused lady." After "a few commonplace remarks," the visitors left. "The interview," said Porter, "was not at all calculated to impress us favorably, and there were many remarks made about the President's gaucherie."[52]

On March 22, Herman Melville attended the second public reception at the White House. The president, he said, "shook hands like a good fellow—working hard at it like a man sawing wood at so much per cord." Melville thought Mary Lincoln "rather good-looking."[53] John W. Forney concurred, reporting that she was "arrayed in greater taste than on the occasion of the first reception" and "is, as all exclaim, an affable, good-looking little lady."[54] Gustavus Fox told his wife that Mrs. Lincoln was "Lady Like, converses easily, dresses well and has the Kentucky pronunciation."[55] Agreeing that the First Lady was "really well dressed," historian George Bancroft also found her "pleasant," "affable," "friendly & not in the least arrogant."[56] John Lothrop Motley told his wife that Mrs. Lincoln "is rather nice-looking, youngish, with very round white arms, well dressed, chatty enough, and if she would not, like all the South and West, say 'Sir' to you every instant, as if you were a royal personage, she would be quite agreeable."[57]

Others were less favorably impressed. After attending White House receptions, attorney Richard Henry Dana of Massachusetts described Mary Lincoln as a "short, fat," "cross, suspicious, under-bred" woman who "looks like the housekeeper of the establishment, & a notable, prying, & not good tempered housekeeper," with "a *snubby* face & mealy complexion" and a "not good-tempered look."[58] A New York lawyer, Charles E. Strong, thought Mrs. Lincoln "a very vulgar old woman." His cousin and partner, George Templeton Strong, shared that view, calling her "[u]nder-bred, weak, and vain."[59] John Bigelow confided to his diary that Mary Lincoln did not converse easily in French. When asked if she spoke that language, she replied "tres poo" and later pronounced "J'entend" to rhyme with "pond."[60]

John Hay reported that Lincoln "rather enjoyed" the large public receptions and "seemed surprised when people commiserated him upon them." At those events he shook thousands of hands, "seemingly unconscious of what he was doing, murmuring some monotonous salutation as they went by, his eye dim, his thoughts far withdrawn; then suddenly he would see some familiar face,—his memory for faces was very good,—and his eye would brighten and his whole form grow attentive; he would greet the visitor with a hearty grasp and a ringing word and dismiss him with a cheery laugh that filled the Red Room with infectious good nature." Many callers armed themselves with an appropriate speech to be delivered on these occasions, but unless it was compressed into the smallest possible space, it never got utterance; the crowd would jostle the peroration out of shape. If it were brief enough and hit the President's fancy, it generally received a swift answer. One night an elderly gentleman from Buffalo said 'Up our way, we believe in God and Abraham Lincoln,' to which the President replied, shoving him along the line, 'My friend, you are more than half right.'"[61]

At a typical reception, as fancifully described by the journalist Noah Brooks, Ward Hill Lamon, marshal of the District of Columbia, would announce the names of callers: "Mr. Snifkins of California." Lincoln would greet him: "I am glad to see you, Mr. Snifkins—you come from a noble State—God bless her." Snifkins "murmurs his thanks, is as warmly pressed by the hand as though the President had just begun his day's work on the pump handle, and he is replaced by Mr. Biffkins, of New York, who is reminded by the Father of the Faithful that the Empire State has some noble men in the Army of the Union."[62] When asked if he did not find shaking so many hands tiresome, he replied: "Oh—it's hard work, but it is a relief, every way; *for here nobody asks me for what I cannot give*."[63] When Benjamin Brown French, who referred to Mrs. Lincoln as "The Queen," introduced callers to her, she curtseyed and asked, "How do you do?" She addressed friends with a cordial, "I am glad to see you" and presented her gloved fingertips to indicate her pleasure. French noted that at one reception she "greeted every guest with such cheerful good will and kindness as to do infinite credit to her position and her heart."[64]

After Willie died, his mother lost interest in entertaining. (Francis B. Carpenter, who spent several months at the White House in 1864, said "she was less hospitable" than any previous First Lady.)[65] For months thereafter she forbade the Marine Band to hold its traditional and very popular weekly concerts on the south lawn of the White House. When this ban persisted, the public grew restive. Gideon Welles suggested that the concerts be given in Lafayette Park across the street, but she also refused permission in her imperious manner, employing the royal we: "It is our especial desire that the Band, does not play in these grounds, this summer. We expect our wishes to be complied with."[66]

The Lincolns' Children

During Lincoln's first year in office, the solemn atmosphere in the White House was somewhat relieved by his two sons, the studious and lovable Willie (born in 1850) and the irrepressible and equally lovable Tad (born in 1853). Their older brother Robert was attending Harvard and spent little time in Washington. The young boys, Hay recorded, "kept the house in an uproar. They drove their tutor wild with their good natured disobedience; . . . they made acquaintance with the office seekers and became the hot champions of the distressed." Willie, "with all his boyish frolic," was nonetheless "a child of great promise, capable of close application and study. He had a fancy for drawing up railway time tables, and would conduct an imaginary train from Chicago to New York with perfect precision. He wrote childish verses, which sometimes attained the unmerited honors of print."

Tad, on the other hand, "was a merry, warm-blooded, kindly little boy, perfectly lawless, and full of odd fancies and inventions, the 'chartered libertine' of the Executive Mansion. He ran continually in and out of his father's cabinet, interrupting his gravest labors and conversations with his bright, rapid and very imperfect speech—for he had an impediment which made his articulation almost unintelligible, until he was nearly grown. He would perch upon his father's knee and sometimes even on his shoulder while the most weighty conferences were going on. Sometimes, escaping from the domestic authorities, he would take refuge in that sanctuary for the whole evening, dropping to sleep at last on the floor, when the President would pick him up and carry him tenderly to bed."[67] Tad's appearance as well as his speech was unusual; a journalist deemed him a "rather a grotesque looking little fellow."[68] He suffered from learning disabilities and took an inordinately long time to master the art of read-ing. Lincoln did not mind, for as John Hay noted, he "took infinite comfort in the child's rude health, fresh fun, and uncontrollable boisterousness. He was pleased to see him growing up in ignorance of books, but with singularly accurate ideas of prac-tical matters. . . . 'Let him run,' the easy-going President would say; 'he has time enough left to learn his letters and get pokey. Bob was just such a little rascal, and now he is a very decent boy.'"[69] The Lincolns hired a tutor for the boys, one Alexan-der Williamson. The children had ponies, which they loved to ride. In February, 1864, a fire burned down the stables, killing all the steeds. Upon observing the flames, Lincoln ran toward the building, vaulted over a hedge, and asked the guards if the horses had been removed. When told they had not, he asked impatiently why and threw open the doors. Then he realized that none of the animals within could sur-vive. Concerned for his safety, the guards hustled him back into the White House, where he wept, for Willie's pony was among the animals killed.

Among the White House menagerie on the south lawn were donkeys, horses, and a pair of goats, Nanny and Nanko. Tad would hitch the goats to a chair, which he used as a cart, and would drive pell-mell through the White House during a recep-tion, to the consternation of many guests. One day the pun-loving president observed a goat gamboling on the lawn and remarked: "He feeds on my bounty, and jumps with joy. Do you think we could call him a bounty-jumper?"[70] In the spring of 1864, when Tad and the First Lady were away on one of their many trips, Lincoln sent her a telegram: "Tell Tad the goats and father are very well especially the goats."[71]

Lincoln was fond of the cats that Seward gave to the boys. In April 1862, a dinner guest observed one of the felines perched on a chair next to the president. As he fed it with Executive Mansion cutlery, the First Lady asked: "Don't you think it is shameful for Mr. Lincoln to feed tabby with a gold fork?" Her husband replied: "If the gold fork was good enough for Buchanan I think it is good enough for Tabby" and continued feeding the cat.[72]

Willie and Tad were prankish. One day they commandeered the spring-bell sys-tem used to summon servants. Discovering in the attic the node where the cords to the various bells were gathered, they pulled all of them, sending servants scurrying madly from room to room. On another occasion Tad, dressed in a lieutenant's uni-form (Stanton had appointed him to that rank), dismissed the regular guards and as-signed the White House staff to protect the house. When his stuffy brother Robert observed what Tad had done, he indignantly protested to Lincoln, who laughed it off and refused to take any disciplinary action. Late one night, when the servants com-plained that they could not get Tad into bed, Lincoln excused himself, saying to his guests: "I must go and suppress Tad." Upon his return, he remarked: "I don't know but I may succeed in governing the nation, but I do believe I shall fail in ruling my own household."[73] The public delighted in reading of the boys' antics, for they were only the second youngsters in the nation's history to inhabit the White House (the first youth being John Tyler's 10-year-old son).

The Lincoln boys had two playmates, the young sons of a Patent Office exam-iner, Horatio Nelson Taft: 8-year-old "Holly" (Halsey Cook) and 11-year-old "Bud"

(Horatio Nelson, Jr.). The Taft boys frequently visited the White House, escorted by their 16-year-old sister Julia, and the First Sons often played at the nearby Taft home. The White House roof became the lads' favorite playground. On it they erected a fort bristling with a log cannon and some condemned muskets, and on occasion they pretended that the roof was the deck of a man-o'-war. The attic became a playhouse for the youngsters, who put on a minstrel show there with Tad in blackface and Willie in drag, much to the amusement of a small crowd of sentinels and White House staff who gladly paid the admission charge of 5 cents. The attic was also the scene of "blizzards" that Tad created with hundreds of calling cards that had been left by White House visitors. One day Tad took his toy cannon and pretended to fire at the room where the cabinet was in session. During the bombardment, Holly Taft pinched his finger and cried out, prompting Lincoln to interrupt the meeting to see what was wrong. The president and his wife indulgently smiled on such shenanigans. Lincoln told stories to the four boys, who especially relished tales of bloody conflict between Indians and frontiersmen. He also played on the floor with them. One day Julie Taft found Lincoln pinned down by the youngsters; when she entered the room, Tad instructed her to sit on the presidential stomach.

Tad once enraged John Watt, the White House gardener, by eating all the strawberries he was growing for a formal dinner party. Watt called the boy a "wildcat." Watt also disapproved of Tad's goat Nannie, who ate flowers promiscuously. One day the animal escaped from the White House grounds—probably with the assistance of Watt. The gardener was doubtless perturbed when Tad dug up the rose bushes to make a grave for a Zouave doll named Jack who had fallen asleep on sentry duty (or deserted, or had acted as an enemy spy) and was executed by a firing squad armed with the lad's toy cannon. They performed this funeral several times until Watt hinted that the president might pardon Jack. Inspired by that suggestion, Tad appealed to his father for mercy. After a formal hearing, Lincoln granted the request. One day Tad accidentally broke a large mirror while playing with a ball indoors. Warned that it meant seven years of bad luck unless he threw salt over his left shoulder, he promptly dashed to the kitchen and returned with some sodium chloride, which he tossed onto the carpet in accordance with the prescribed ritual. The boys formed a military company dubbed "Mrs. Lincoln's Zouaves," with Willie as the colonel, Bud the major, Holly the captain, and Tad the "drum major" (at his insistence). Lincoln reviewed the unit ceremoniously. Tad wanted a pistol and finally got one after nagging his parents repeatedly. When the First Lady and the boys were away in June 1863, Lincoln wired her: "Think you better put 'Tad's' pistol away. I had an ugly dream about him."[74]

The boys' fun came to an end with Willie's death in February 1862. Thereafter, Mary Lincoln forbade the Tafts' sons to enter the White House, for their presence conjured up memories too painful for her to bear.

The First Lady

In 1864, after calling at the White House, a Quaker wrote Mary Lincoln explaining how she could help the president: "Thou hast it in thy power to strengthen his hands in the great work in which he is engaged, to encourage him in seasons of deep discouragement; to soothe & cheer him in times of depression; to divert his attention in seasons of relaxation, from the heavy pressure of care & the weight of Government; to train his sons to honor their father & their father's God, to shield him from all little cares & annoyances in his home."[75] Instead of performing those functions, Mrs. Lincoln was a constant source of anxiety and embarrassment to her husband, who often talked to Orville H. Browning "about his domestic troubles." As Browning reported, the president "several times told me there [in the White House] that he was constantly under great apprehension lest his wife should do something which would bring him into disgrace." David Davis also worried that Mary Lincoln "will disgrace her husband."[76] They had good reason to be apprehensive. As if Lincoln did not have enough trouble dealing with recalcitrant generals, editors, senators, governors, congressmen, office seekers, and cabinet members—not to mention Confederates— the First Lady added immeasurably to his woes.

Among other things, she meddled in patronage matters, forcing her husband "to do things which he knew were out of place in order to keep his wife's fingers out of his hair," as Herndon put it.[77] In June 1861, the journalist Murat Halstead wrote that some of Lincoln's "most unfortunate appointments have been made to please his wife who is anxious to be thought the power behind the throne and who is vulgar and pestiferous beyond description." He added that Mary Lincoln was "a fool—the laughing stock of the town, her vulgarity only the more conspicuous in consequence of her fine carriage and horses and servants in livery and fine dresses, and her damnable airs."[78] She herself told James Gordon Bennett in 1862 that although she had "a great terror of *strong* minded Ladies," she nonetheless believed that "a word fitly spoken and in due season" might induce her husband to make some changes in his cabinet.[79]

Mary Lincoln thought of herself as a kind of assistant president and as such had tried to influence the initial cabinet selections. From New York, where she went to shop in January 1861, she predicted that Norman B. Judd "would cause trouble & dissatisfaction," and noted that Wall Streeters testified that "his business transactions, have not always borne inspection." People in New York, she reported, "were laughing at the idea of *Judd*, being any way, connected with the Cabinet in *these times,* when honesty in high places is so important." She asked David Davis to use his influence to block Judd, who complained that his opponents were using every possible tactic to defeat him, "including female influence."[80] (Nine years later, Mary Lincoln obsequiously and fawningly appealed to Judd to help her win a pension from Congress.) Some believed Mrs. Lincoln deserved credit for blocking Judd, but that seems unlikely. Upon hearing complaints that his wife was meddling in the selection of cabinet members, Lincoln replied: "Tell the gentlemen not to be alarmed, for I myself manage all important matters."[81]

In Washington, Mary Lincoln's shopping trip to New York was judged to be wildly inappropriate. Her buying sprees involved extravagant purchases, including shawls costing $650 and $1,000 as well as expensive china and silver plate. Also criticized were her indiscreet public remarks. "The idea of the President[']s wife kiting about the country and holding levees at which she indulges in a multitude of silly speeches is looked upon as very shocking," wrote Herman Kreismann from the capital in January 1861. "Among other interesting speeches of Mrs L. reported here is that she says her husband had to give Mr Seward a place. The pressure was so great; but he did it very reluctantly."[82] Mary Lincoln did not like Seward and let her feelings be known to visitors. When her spouse indicated to a caller that he would appoint the New Yorker secretary of state, she interrupted: "Never! Never! Seward in the Cabinet! Never. If all things should go on all right—the credit would go to Seward—if they went wrong—the blame would fall upon my husband. Seward in the Cabinet! *Never!*"[83] Two weeks after the election, she told guests at her home, "The country will find how we regard that Abolition sneak Seward."[84] Later, when Mrs. Lincoln told the president that Seward lacked principles and was "worse than Chase," he replied: "Mother, you are mistaken; your prejudices are so violent that you do not stop to reason. Seward is an able man, and the country as well as myself can trust him."

She retorted: "Father, you are too honest for this world! You should have been born a saint. You will generally find it a safe rule to distrust a disappointed, ambitious politician. It makes me mad to see you sit still and let that hypocrite, Seward, twine you around his finger as if you were a skein of thread."[85]

In 1863, Mary Lincoln told Francis P. Blair, Sr., "that there was not a member of the Cabinet who did not stab her husband & the Country daily" except his son Montgomery. The First Lady qualified her observation by admitting that "she did not know anything about Politics—but her instincts told her that much."[86] She also believed that Seward spread unflattering tales about her.

In October 1861, the journalist D. W. Bartlett alleged that Mary Lincoln had "made and unmade the political fortunes of men. She is said to be much in conversation with cabinet members, and has . . . held correspondence with them on political topics. Some go so far as to suggest that the president is indebted to her for some of his ideas and projects." Her "friends compare Mrs Lincoln to Queen Elizabeth in her statesmanlike tastes and capabilities."[87] In Massachusetts, Mrs. Lincoln's political influence was the topic of conversation among those who had visited Washington. A former congressman from Indiana thought the First Lady "a corrupt woman who controles her husband."[88] Her influence reportedly led to "some very curious appointments, more curious than suitable."[89]

A dramatic case in point was Mary Lincoln's effective campaign to have Isaac Henderson, publisher of the New York *Evening Post,* named to a lucrative post in the New York customhouse. On February 11, as Lincoln was about to board the train for Washington, she threw a tantrum that may have led to the decision to leave her behind that day. Henry Villard recalled that Lincoln at that time appeared "so careworn as to excite one's compassion" in part because of "the inordinate greed, coupled with an utter lack of sense of propriety, on the part of Mrs. Lincoln," who "allowed herself to be persuaded, at an early date, to accept presents for the use of her influence with her husband in support of the aspirations of office seekers."[90] (Others at that time reported that Lincoln's expression was as "care worn, or rather *thought* worn as the face of old Dante," and that he looked "thinner than usual.")[91] One such bribe was extended by Isaac Henderson, an unsavory self-made man who had sent Mary Lincoln diamond jewelry to enlist her aid in his quest for office. When Lincoln balked, she carried on in hysterics at the hotel suite where they were staying during their final days in Springfield. Her antics caused Lincoln to miss an appointment with Norman B. Judd and Herman Kreismann, a Republican operative. Curious about the president-elect's tardiness, Kreismann called at the hotel and was shocked to find Mrs. Lincoln in the throes of a fit. Lincoln told him: "she will not let me go until I promise her an office for one of her friends." The president-elect eventually acceded to her demand, nominating Henderson to the post he wanted.[92] (Three years later, Henderson was dismissed after being indicted for corruption. He allegedly demanded kickbacks from contractors doing business with the Brooklyn Navy Yard; by one estimate, he extorted $70,000. Although eventually acquitted by a court in 1865, Henderson was believed guilty by Parke Godwin and other knowledgeable observers.)

The son of Gideon Welles recalled a similar episode. As a young boy, on one occasion he was standing outside a shop on Pennsylvania Avenue and overheard Mrs. Lincoln tell her husband that if he did not appoint a man of her choice to an office, she would descend from their carriage and roll about on the sidewalk. Lincoln, according to Welles, gave in.[93]

Bribes given to Mary Lincoln also helped pave the way for the strange appointment of George Denison as naval agent in the New York customhouse. Denison was a partner of William Henry Marston, son-in-law of Lincoln's friend and banker, Robert Irwin, who urged the appointment. (Irwin's daughter Eliza married Marston in 1859. She was a friend of Mary Lincoln, accompanying her on a tour of New York harbor in July 1861.)[94] The president hesitated to comply because, as he told Irwin: "I am scared about your friend Dennison. The place is so fiercely sought by, and for, others, while . . . his name is not mentioned at all, that I fear appointing him will appear too arbitrary on my part."[95] In May 1861, Secretary of the Treasury Salmon P. Chase strongly objected to Denison: "A friend sometimes best proves his friendship by speaking when selfishness counsels silence. Agreeably to your direction I send a Commission for Mr. Dennison; but I shall not fulfill my duty to you if I do not say that I fear, if you make this appointment, you will regret it. When it was first proposed I had heard so little expression either way that I did not feel myself called upon,—though I felt that setting aside so many prominent men for a gentleman so little known in political or financial circles was of questionable expediency,—to say anything against it. But during the time which has since elapsed many of the most eminent and influential gentlemen of New York have expressed to me such unfavorable opinions of Mr. D—and such strong convictions that his appointment to so high an office will affect the Administration injuriously in quarters whose good opinion is most valuable that I feel myself constrained to say that were the responsibility of decision mine, I should not put my name to the commission."

In reply, Lincoln explained that "the urgent solicitation of an old friend who has served me all my life, and who has never before received or asked anything in return," led to the appointment. "His (Mr. Dennison's) good character was vouched for from the start by many at New York, including Mr. Opdyke."[96] But, as Chase had warned, some prominent New York reformers questioned Denison's integrity. James A. Briggs said Denison "only cares to make money. He knows nobody, & nobody knows him.

His appointment was a party outrage."[97] Denison helped his cause by giving Mrs. Lincoln a handsome carriage and establishing a $5,000 line of credit for her in New York, leading Briggs to state: "this office was sold."[98] Irwin was acting on behalf of Marston, a Wall Street broker with whom Denison formally agreed to split evenly the profits of his lucrative government position.[99] (Denison abused his power as naval officer, engaging in extortion, seizing ships promiscuously, and pocketing cash from out-of-court settlements that should have gone into the government's coffers.)[100] Senator Preston King complained to Lincoln about the gift Denison gave to Mrs. Lincoln. A New York merchant called Denison an unqualified "good looking boy about 25 years of age, whose only naval experience was obtained as a runner, or collecting clerk" for the New York *Evening Post*, which allegedly received $80,000 "worth of pecuniary aid" from Denison. The appointment was made "in order to please the sinister desire of the editors" of that paper.[101] Sam Ward, a Washington insider known as "King of the Lobby," suggested that there was something unsavory about the relationship between Denison and Mrs. Lincoln.

In Washington, Mary Lincoln would continue to accept bribes and engage in other unethical conduct.[102]

On March 10, Charles Sumner of Massachusetts, chairman of the Senate Foreign Relations Committee, regaled a friend with stories about how "Mrs. Lincoln appointed a collector [of the Port] for Boston on ac[count] of [her son] 'Bobby,' and *had* made a naval officer" and how she "was meddling with every office in the gift of the Executive."[103] For the Boston collectorship, she favored Amos Tuck of New Hampshire, who had befriended young Robert Lincoln during his year at Phillips Exeter Academy (1859–1860). Robert had lived with the Tuck family for a time. The wealthy Republican national leader and lieutenant governor of Massachusetts, John Z. Goodrich, was named collector; Tuck became naval officer in the Boston customhouse, which was considered a "good place—fat salary and no work!" Mary Lincoln wrote friendly letters to the Tucks. In January 1861, Amos Tuck visited Springfield, stayed overnight at the Lincoln home, and accompanied Mrs. Lincoln part-way on her trip east to shop.[104] She also pestered Seward to give a friend the consulship at Honolulu.[105]

Mary Lincoln championed William S. Wood, impresario of the train journey from Springfield, for the post of commissioner of public buildings. She told a senator that he "would always find a very true friend in her" if he would support the pending nomination of Wood, who, she alleged, "was very popular and very worthy[.]"[106] In March, Wood presented the First Lady with a gift of fine horses.[107] She also urged Ward Hill Lamon to use his influence with the president to have Wood, whom she called "a clever man," well qualified to "make an efficient Commissioner," appointed despite Lincoln's misgivings.[108] David Davis, who found the appointment of Wood "incomprehensible," was told by the president that "it would be ruinous to appoint him—*ruinous to him.*"[109]

It is hard to know what to make of Lincoln's statement; perhaps it had something to do with rumors that his wife was committing adultery with Wood. In June 1861, the president received a pseudonymous letter about a "scandal" involving Mary

Lincoln and Wood, who went on shopping trips together to New York. The writer warned that if the rumors about that scandal were published, it would "stab you in the most vital part."[110]

The president spoke sharply to his wife about this matter; Schuyler Colfax later recalled "the war she had with Mr. Lincoln" about her relations with Wood. According to Colfax, the First Couple "scarcely spoke together for several days."[111] An Iowan, referring to Wood, claimed that Mary Lincoln "used to often go from the White House to the Astor House in New York to pass the night with a man who held a high government office in Washington, given to him by her husband."[112] Benjamin Brown French, who replaced Wood as commissioner of public buildings, called Wood a "libertine" and "a disgrace to the Nation, to Lincoln & to the office." A friend of French's, "whose wife he [Wood] undertook to seduce," termed Wood a "damned infernal villain."[113] Others deemed Wood "a great scamp."[114]

Mary Lincoln may have been unfaithful with men other than Wood. John Watt, the White House gardener, told a journalist in 1867 that "Mrs. Lincoln's relations with certain men were indecently improper" and claimed to be well informed about "the secrets of Mrs. Lincoln's domestic affairs."[115] Rumors circulated that Watt himself had "too great an intimacy" with her.[116] Oswald Garrison Villard, son of the noted journalist Henry Villard, asserted that Robert Todd Lincoln "systematically bought up any books that reflected [poorly] on Mrs. Lincoln," including one by "the Hungarian adventurer who very nearly succeeded in eloping with Mrs. Lincoln from the White House."[117] She purportedly wrote to her confidant Abram Wakeman, postmaster of New York, saying "I have taken your excellent advice and decided not to leave my husband while he is in the White House."[118] In 1870, Senator Richard Yates of Illinois hinted broadly that Mary Lincoln had been unfaithful, telling his colleagues that "there are recollections and memories, sad and silent and deep, that I will not recall publicly. . . . Amid all the perils of life, and its devastation, amid good and evil report, a woman should be true to her husband. . . . I shall not . . . go into details."[119] Edward McManus, a White House doorkeeper, evidently made a similar allegation to Thurlow Weed.[120]

Lincoln finally agreed to appoint Wood only after the First Lady shut herself in her room.[121] She used the same tactic to win an army officer's commission for John Watt, who colluded with her in padding bills.[122] Maine Senator William P. Fessenden and the historian George Bancroft both heard that she "wished a rogue [Watt] who had cheated the government made a lieutenant: the cabinet thrice put the subject aside. One morning in came Lincoln sad and sorrowful: [']Ah,['] said he, [']to-day we must settle the case of Lieutenant [Watt]. Mrs. Lincoln has for three nights slept in a separate apartment.'"[123]

Wood did not last long as commissioner. After learning from a congressional delegation that Wood was corrupt, Lincoln obtained his resignation. While serving as commissioner-of-public-buildings-designate (the senate had not yet acted on his nomination), Wood told one Samuel A. Hopkins: "I understand that you are here . . . trying to get work from the government in the way of engraving. I want to tell you, as a friend, that there is no use at all of trying; that the work will be given to the

American Bank Note Company and the National Bank Note Company." When Hopkins protested that his firm could do the work better and cheaper than those competitors, Wood explained the contract would not go to him because Wood himself had an interest in the American Bank Note Company and that George Denison and William H. Marston had an interest in the National Bank Note Company. Hopkins then said he was trying to sell the government some cannons for $500 apiece. Wood replied, "Well, I can help you in that matter. Say nothing about the price; we can make something out of that. If the government wants them, they can as well afford to pay more as less. I will take you down and introduce you to Mr. Leslie, the chief clerk of the War Department." After Hopkins told this story on August 30, 1861, to a congressional committee investigating government contracts, members of that body promptly informed Lincoln, and Wood was replaced on September 6.[124]

A week later, Mary Todd Lincoln denounced Wood "as a very bad man" who "does not know, what truth means." Everyone, she claimed, understood that he was "a most unprincipled man." Her wrath had been occasioned in part by Wood's charge that her friend John Watt was disloyal.[125] In addition, he allegedly refused to falsify bills at her behest.[126]

Mrs. Lincoln also lobbied on behalf of a pompous former New York congressman, Caleb Lyon, who had written some adulatory puff pieces about her for newspapers.[127] (Horace Greeley noted that Mary Lincoln "enjoys flattery—I mean deference."[128] She reportedly took offense at "the want of attention" from Jessie Benton Frémont when she called at the White House.)[129] Lyon was named governor of the Idaho Territory, where he proved woefully inadequate, spending less than half his time in the territory and embezzling money designated for Indian tribes.[130]

When the New York *World* reported that in "the scramble for jobs presidential relatives did well," it was doubtless referring to Lincoln's in-laws, including two of his wife's brothers-in-law, William S. Wallace (paymaster of volunteers) and Ninian Edwards (commissary of subsistence). Mary Lincoln boasted that she had fought a "hard battle" to get Wallace appointed.[131] Lincoln explained that Wallace "is needy, and looks to me; and I personally owe him much."[132] According to Herndon, Lincoln said Wallace was "appointed to a bureau simply to 'keep hell' out his own family!"[133] Wallace's brother Edward became naval officer at Philadelphia. Charles S. Todd, a distant relative, was named a tax assessor in Kentucky. Mary Lincoln's cousins also fared well in the patronage lottery. Lyman Beecher Todd was appointed postmaster of Lexington, Kentucky. Thomas M. Campbell held the same post at Boonville, Missouri. Lincoln nominated John Blair Smith Todd as a brigadier general, but the senate rejected him. Lockwood Todd was appointed U.S. drayman for the San Francisco customhouse, a highly remunerative post. That selection touched off a furor.

The appointment of Ninian Edwards, husband of Mary Lincoln's eldest sister Elizabeth, caused much aggravation to the president, who had been warned that Edwards associated with corruptionists. Along with another quartermaster, William H. Bailhache, Edwards used his post to enrich himself, triggering protests from several of Lincoln's Springfield friends. In 1862, when Edward L. Baker defended the two, Lincoln replied: "The appeal to me in behalf of Mr. Edwards and Mr. Bailhasche, for a hearing, does not meet the case. No formal charges are preferred against them, so far as I know; nor do I expect any will be made; or, if made, will be substantiated. I certainly do not suppose Mr. Edwards has, at this time of his life, given up his old habits, and turned dishonest; and while I have not known Mr. Bailhasche so long, I have no more affirmative reason to suspect him. The trouble with me is of a different character. Springfield is my home, and there, more than elsewhere, are my life-long friends. These, for now nearly two years, have been harrassing me because of Mr. E. & Mr. B. I think Mr. E. & Mr. B. without dishonesty on the other hand, could have saved me from this, if they had cared to do so. They have seemed to think that if they could keep their official record dryly correct, to say the least, it was not any difference how much they might provoke my friends, and harrass me. If this is too strong a statement of the case, still the result has been the same to me; and, as a *misfortune* merely, I think I have already borne a fair share of it."[134]

Mary Lincoln also worked hard to get her cousin Lizzie Grimsley the postmastership in Springfield. Behind the scenes, Lincoln and Nicolay both urged Illinois friends to have her chosen by an election among the various candidates for that post. To Lincoln's appeal, John Todd Stuart replied: "I would not let the case of Cousin Lizzie trouble me if I were you[.] No one will complain of you if you do not give her the appointment while very many doubtless would complain of her appointment and would have much show of reason because the appointment of a lady would be unusual."[135] (It would have been unusual but hardly unique; 411 women served as postmasters during Lincoln's administration.) When Shelby Cullom, the speaker of the Illinois House, asked for control of both that office and the revenue collectorship in Springfield, the president replied: "Well, you may have the collectorship, but the Post Office I think I promised to old Mrs. [Seymour] Moody for her husband. I can not let you have the post office, Cullom; take the collectorship."

"Now, why can't you be liberal, and let me have both?" responded Cullom.

"Mrs. Moody would get down on me," said the beleaguered chief executive.[136]

Ultimately, Mrs. Grimsley and Mr. Moody both lost out to Lincoln's friend, John Armstrong. When Lincoln explained "that a Post-Mistress in a place the size of Springfield would produce dis-satisfaction," Lizzie Grimsley immediately abandoned her quest.[137] Moody, who was considered not a good enough party worker for the postmastership, was offered a job either as commissary of subsistence or as a quartermaster, but he turned both posts down because they would take him out of Springfield.

Mary Lincoln boasted that she significantly influenced the president's appointments. "My husband placed great Confidence in my Knowledge of human Nature," she said in 1866. He "had not much Knowledge of men."[138] Actually, her voice counted for little except in minor cases like Watt, Henderson, Lyon, and Wood. When she criticized officials, Lincoln chided her, saying "you are too suspicious" and "you are disposed to magnify trifles."[139] Some cabinet members resisted her meddling. When she lobbied to have a "half loafer, half gentleman" appointed to office, Edwin M. Stanton replied: "If I should make such appointments, I should strike at the very root of all confidence in the government, in your husband, you and me."[140]

Ben Hardin Helm, husband of Mary Lincoln's half-sister Emilie, sought a pay-master's job, which Lincoln obligingly offered him. Helm reluctantly turned it down in order to join the Confederate army.

The largesse enjoyed by Mary Lincoln's family created bad blood in Illinois. Ebenezer Peck bitterly remarked that the president "and his wife have some relatives not yet provided for" and that "until *all* these shall have been provided for, all *newer* friends I suppose must needs wait."[141] William Jayne thought it "very strange how as bitter a democrat as Capt [Lockwood] Todd can have so much influence over Mr Lincoln."[142]

Lincoln was clearly embarrassed by the extensive patronage given to the Todds. To one of his wife's importunate cousins, he asked: "Will it do for me to go on and justify the declaration that Trumbull and I have divided out all the offices among our relatives?"[143] (One relative Lincoln did not accommodate was his son Robert, who wrote on behalf of a friend seeking the postmastership of Cambridge, Massachusetts, where the lad was enrolled at Harvard. Upon reading that letter, the president replied sharply: "If you do not attend to your studies and let matters such as you write about alone, I will take you away from college.")[144]

While Lincoln gave offices to many of his wife's relatives, he did little for his mother's family. Dennis Hanks sought in vain to be named postmaster of Charleston. When John Hanks asked for an Indian agency, Lincoln was eager to oblige his old partner in rail-splitting. "He is thoroughly honest, and his son has a tolerable educa-tion and might be his clerk," the president told Henry C. Whitney. But Hanks's semiliteracy posed an insuperable barrier to his appointment. (In 1864, Hanks wrote to Lincoln complaining that "you hav given som of the best offices to men that I con-sider mi self so peair to them her under mi nose I dont think you hav treated me rite all though you hav don your duty as a president wich you ar not to blame I hav allways hav loved you from Child hood and Still think well ove you.")[145] Whitney remarked apropos of the president's failure to gratify his cousins, "Lincoln regarded his obliga-tion to duty as a stronger obligation than that to friendship."[146] Dennis Hanks's son-in-law, Augustus H. Chapman, sought unsuccessfully to become marshal for the southern district of Illinois, though Lincoln wanted to appoint him.

As well as Mary Lincoln's meddling in patronage matters, her rustic, penny-pinching ways also set tongues wagging. Mary Clemmer Ames noted that the First Lady "brought shame upon the President's House, by petty economies, which had never disgraced it before."[147] On March 11, 1861, Charles Francis Adams, Jr., attended a reception at which she was discussed: "All manner of stories about her were flying around; she wanted to do the right thing, but, not knowing how, was too weak and proud to ask; she was going to put the White House on an economical basis, and, to that end, was about to dismiss 'the help,' as she called the servants; some of whom, it was asserted, had already left because 'they must live with gentlefolks'; she had got hold of newspaper reporters and railroad conductors, as the best persons to go to for advice and direction."[148] Some believed Mary Lincoln was tightfisted because she wanted to preserve her husband's salary "as much as possible to build them a house after [his] term at Washington expires."[149] She allegedly told a White House staffer

The president-elect and outgoing chief executive James Buchanan pass the northwestern base of Capitol Hill en route to Lincoln's inauguration. *Harper's Weekly*, March 16, 1861. Library of Congress.

"Gulliver Abe, in the White House, Attacked by the Lilliputian Office-Seekers" appeared on the front page of *Frank Leslie's Budget of Fun*, March 15, 1861, over the legend, "Well, this is orful! Who'd a' ever believed such diminutivorous var-mints could have had such impudence! Why, they're creeping all over me! I feel a kinder goosefleshy. Scratch himself couldn't get rid of 'em!" Abraham Lincoln Presidential Library and Museum, Springfield, Illinois.

This photograph of Willie Lincoln was taken in 1861, when the lad was 10 years old. After his death the following year, his mother wrote to a friend: "You have doubtless heard, how very handsome a boy, he was considered—with a pure, gentle nature, always unearthly, & in intellect far, far beyond his years." John Hay noted that Willie was "a child of great promise, capable of close application and study. He had a fancy for drawing up railway time-tables, and would conduct an imaginary train from Chicago to New York with perfect precision. He wrote childish verses, which sometimes attained the unmerited honors of print." Abraham Lincoln Presidential Library and Museum, Springfield, Illinois.

Robert Todd Lincoln was 18 years old when an unknown photographer took this portrait on July 24, 1861. That year a reporter wrote of Robert's "comparative elegance," which stood in "striking contrast to the loose, careless, awkward rigging of his Presidential father." Abraham Lincoln Presidential Library and Museum, Springfield, Illinois.

This little-known vignette of Mary Todd Lincoln was evidently taken in 1861. Both William H. Mumler of Boston and the New York Photographic Company issued it as a *carte-de-visite*. Abraham Lincoln Presidential Library and Museum, Springfield, Illinois.

This photo of Mary Todd Lincoln was probably taken at the Mathew Brady Studio in January 1862. She loved flowers and often plastered down her hair in order to wear a floral arrangement on her head. She did not like to pose for photographs because, as she put it, "my hands are always *made* in *them*, very large, and I look too stern." Library of Congress.

"The First Reading of the Emancipation Proclamation before the Cabinet" (July 22, 1862), a steel engraving that Alexander Hay Ritchie made of Francis B. Carpenter's enormous painting, completed in 1864. It depicts (left to right, seated), Secretary of War Edwin M. Stanton, the president, Navy Secretary Gideon Welles, Secretary of State William H. Seward, and Attorney General Edward Bates as well as (standing, left to right) Treasury Secretary Salmon P. Chase, Interior Secretary Caleb B. Smith, and Postmaster General Montgomery Blair. The painting hangs in the U.S. Capitol. The engraving offers a better image of Lincoln, for Carpenter kept tinkering with his canvas even after Ritchie completed the engraving, and the more Carpenter revised, the weaker Lincoln's portrait became. Library of Congress.

Detail of a photo Alexander Gardner took of the president and General George B. McClellan and some members of his staff on October 3, 1862. Lincoln then visited the Army of the Potomac in Maryland, near the site of the recent battle of Antietam, in an effort to urge it into action. From left, Colonel Alexander S. Webb, chief of staff, 5th Corps; General McClellan; Scout Adams; Dr. Jonathan Letterman, army medical director; and an unidentified person. Behind the president stands General Henry J. Hunt, McClellan's chief of artillery. Library of Congress.

Alexander Gardner took this memorable photograph of Lincoln on November 8, 1863, eleven days before he delivered the Gettysburg Address. The sculptor Daniel Chester French used it to model the statue of the seated Great Emancipator in the Lincoln Memorial. Indiana Historical Society, Indianapolis, Indiana.

The two principal White House secretaries, John G. Nicolay (seated) and John Hay (standing), flank the president at Gardner's studio, November 8, 1863. Hay recorded in his diary that "Nico & I immortalized ourselves by having ourselves done in group with the Presdt." Abraham Lincoln Presidential Library and Museum, Springfield, Illinois.

This portrait of Lincoln, which Anthony Berger of the Mathew Brady Gallery took in Washington on February 9, 1864, became the image that later appeared on the five-dollar bill. Robert Todd Lincoln thought it the best representation of his father as he actually looked. Library of Congress.

that she and her husband "were poor and hoped to save twelve thousand dollars every year from their salary."[150] One Sunday in the New York Avenue Presbyterian church, she and her husband both placed money in the collection plate. As the collector moved on to the next pew, Lincoln drew him back and whispered: "I want to contribute more than that; come to the White House in the morning."[151] In 1861, William Howard Russell recorded that she "beat down a poor widow" by paying her fourteen cents instead of twenty for cloth "after immense chaffing."[152] She sought to sell the milk produced by the White House cows and haggled over the price unbecomingly. Alexander Williamson, the tutor for the Lincolns' sons, reported that the First Lady bargained like a fishwife over his compensation.

The First Lady's sartorial taste also scandalized polite society. Alexander K. McClure reported that she "was vain, passionately fond of dress and wore her dresses shorter at the top and longer at the train than even fashion demanded. She had great pride in her elegant neck and bust, and grieved the president greatly by her constant display of her person and her fine clothes."[153] Observing a particularly low-cut dress she wore, Lincoln told his wife one day: "Mother, it is my opinion, if some of that tail was nearer the head, it would be in better style."[154]

Mary Lincoln shocked many people at Edward D. Baker's funeral by appearing in a lilac dress, bonnet, and gloves. Some members of her circle, thinking she should be made aware of that breach of etiquette, dispatched one of her closest friends to convey the message. Upon arriving at the White House, the emissary was greeted by Mary Lincoln with an exclamation: "I am so glad you have come, I am just as mad as I can be. Mrs. Crittenden has just been here to remonstrate with me for wearing my lilac suit to Colonel Baker's funeral. I wonder if the women of Washington expect me to muffle myself up in mourning for every soldier killed in this great war?"

"But Mrs. Lincoln," came the reply, "do you not think black more suitable to wear at a funeral because there is a great war in the nation?"

"No, I don't. I want the women to mind their own business; I intend to wear what I please."[155]

In August, Prince Napoleon noted that at a White House dinner "Mrs. Lincoln was dressed in the French style without any taste; she has the manner of a petit bourgeois and wears tin jewelry."[156] Three months later, the prominent English journalist William Howard Russell recorded in his diary: "Poor Mrs. Lincoln [—] a more preposterous looking female I never saw."[157] In February 1862, he wrote that at a grand White House party she resembled "a damned old Irish or Scotch (or English) washerwoman dressed out for a Sunday at Highbury Barn."[158] Oregon Senator James Nesmith was equally appalled by the First Lady's appearance at that event: "The weak minded Mrs Lincoln had her bosom on exhibition and a flower pot on her head, while there was a train of silk or satin drag[g]ing on the floor behind her of several yards in length." Nesmith "could not help regretting that she had degenerated from the industrious and unpretending woman that she was in the days when she used to cook Old Abe[']s dinner, and milk the cows with her own hands." Now, he acidly observed, "[h]er only ambition seems to be to exhibit her own milking apparatus to the public eye."[159] A guest at a White House reception noted that the First Lady "wore a *very* low-necked dress, reminding me of the 'French fool' fashion."[160] A Democratic newspaper described her on one occasion as a "coarse, vain, unamiable . . . sallow, fleshy, uninteresting woman in white robes, and wearing a band of white flowers about her forehead, like some over-grown Ophelia. . . . She has less taste than any woman in the land of her half pretensions. She does not distinguish the *grande monde* from the *demi monde*."[161] At a later reception she struck a Massachusetts economist as "a dowdy little woman."[162] Mary Clemmer Ames told readers of the Springfield, Massachusetts, *Republican* that the "very dumpy" First Lady "stuns me with her low-necked dresses and the flower-beds which she carries on the top of her head."[163] Another female correspondent for that paper noted that Mrs. Lincoln had "a beautiful bust, which was largely shown to admiring gaze" at a White House reception.[164] A general's wife was scandalized by the "bad manners" of the First Lady, who was "preposterously attired" and said "'yes *ma'am*,' and 'no *ma'am*' like a servant-woman."[165]

Yet other women criticized the First Lady's appearance. Her friend Elizabeth Blair Lee said that Elizabeth Todd Edwards "is ten times better looking than [her sister] Mrs. Lincoln."[166] The abolitionist Lydia Maria Child remarked that Mary Lincoln "looks more like a dowdy washerwoman" than "the 'representative of fashion.'" To Child, the First Lady's face seemed "mean, and vulgar," and she pitied Lincoln for "having a fool for a wife." The only thing "she cares for is flattery, and dress, and parties. Willis's Home Journal abounds with fulsome compliments about her stylish dressing, her gayeties &c. This is not becoming, when the people are suffering and sacrificing so much."[167] When Child read about Mrs. Lincoln's shopping trips, she exclaimed: "So *this* is what the people are taxed for! to deck out this vulgar doll with foreign frippery. And oppressed millions must groan on, lest her 'noble native State' [Kentucky] should take offence, if Government made use of the beneficent power God has so miraculously placed in its hands."[168]

In August 1861, a New York politico echoed Mrs. Child, expressing disgust with Mary Lincoln because at a time when "the country was in the throes of revolutionary travail she was coolly buying china and dresses in New York: and now that wounded men pant for Florence Nightingales in Washington *she* is relaxing at Long Branch [on the New Jersey shore] from—the cares of state."[169] She "is as meddling & injuriously officious as she is conceited & ill-bred," according to a young Bostonian, Robert C. Winthrop, Jr.[170] An antislavery clergyman, Henry W. Bellows, called Mary Lincoln "ambitious" and "vulgar."[171]

Mrs. Lincoln was not wholly without supporters, though their number was very small. In 1864, a matron from Indiana wrote that Mrs. Lincoln "is not what can be called an intellectual woman, and in many things has no doubt acted injudiciously," nonetheless "her goodness of heart, and pleasant manner, must make her liked by all who real[l]y come in contact with her."[172] Julia Taft recalled that the First Lady was "pleasant and kind" to her, treating her like a surrogate daughter.[173] Though Julia liked Mrs. Lincoln, she was nonetheless shocked by her exaggerated sense of entitlement.

The First Lady could be indiscreet in conversation. After meeting her for the first time and spending an hour conversing, Pennsylvania Congressman James H.

Campbell described her as "an ordinary woman with strong likes, and dislikes, and with bitter prejudices. She prides herself on being a 'little Southern[,]' hates the angular Yankees, and detests the *Trumbulls* who are nowhere!"[174]

Mary Lincoln had never forgiven Lyman Trumbull for defeating her husband in the senatorial election of 1855, nor could she bring herself to renew her former friendship with Mrs. Trumbull, who had been one of her bridesmaids.

In September 1861, while on a boat trip Mrs. Lincoln very loudly disparaged Trumbull. Mrs. Trumbull reported to her husband that one Rev. Mr. Collins "travelled on the same boat with Mrs Lincoln between N. Y. & Washington. He says she talked so as to be heard above every one else & although he was in the Gents. Cabin he could not avoid hearing her; she discussed people freely, even those in private life[;] talked of you & I[;] referred to your first election when Mr Lincoln was defeated & then to the last fall when he was honorably elected, with an emphasis on the word which implied that yours was not honorable. He says she was surrounded by a set whose object seemed to be to draw her out."[175]

Mary Lincoln was also rude to the Seward family. When the Sewards called on her at the White House in September 1861, they were ushered into the Blue Room, where a servant had them take a seat while he announced their presence to the First Lady. He returned after a long interval, saying "Mrs. Lincoln begged to be excused—she was *very* much engaged." Young Fanny Seward, who believed that this was "the only time on record that she ever refused to see company in the evening," confided to her diary: "The truth of Mrs. L's engagement was probably that she did not want to see Mother—else why not give general directions to the door keeper to let no one in? It was certainly very rude to have us all seated first."[176]

Scandals

The New York *Herald's* premature publication of excerpts from Lincoln's 1861 annual message created a scandal. Mary Lincoln, who, according to rumor, "told state secrets" and was thus considered "*one* of the *leaky vessels*—from which contraband army news, gets afloat," embarrassed the president by allowing her close friend and influential "social adviser," Henry Wikoff, to see an advance copy of the document.[177] (One source even claimed that she received a substantial sum for this favor.)[178] Wikoff leaked it to the *Herald,* which employed him as a free-lancer.[179] When the House Judiciary Committee investigated the matter, Wikoff at first refused to answer its questions. He was promptly clapped into the Old Capitol Prison. When Illinois Congressman William Kellogg informed the president of these developments, he expressed great surprise, for he had been unaware of any premature publication of the message. The next day he visited Capitol Hill and "urged the Republicans on the Committee to spare him disgrace." He told the chairman, John Hickman of Pennsylvania, that "he never gave any portion of the Message to anybody except members of the Cabinet" before submitting it to Congress. The committee summoned General Daniel Sickles, who had been regularly visiting his friend Wikoff in jail. The general, initially defiant, backed down when threatened with a contempt-of-Congress citation. He admitted that he had been in contact with John Watt, the White House gardener. Wikoff alleged that he had telegraphed the president's message to the *Herald* after receiving it from Watt. Watt told the committee that he had indeed been Wikoff's source, implausibly claiming that he had seen a copy of the message lying about in the White House library, had memorized a portion of it, and repeated it verbatim to Wikoff.[180]

But as White House watchman Thomas Stackpole told Orville H. Browning, the First Lady was the true culprit. In March 1862, according to a long-suppressed passage in Browning's diary, Stackpole revealed that "the President's message [to Congress last December] had been furnished to [Henry] Wycoff by her, and not by Watt as is usually supposed—that she got it of [John D.] Defrees, Sup[erintendent] of government printing, and gave it to Wycoff in the Library, where he read it—[and] gave it back to her, and she gave it back to Defrees."[181]

Alexander K. McClure reported that Mary Lincoln "was the easy prey of adventurers, of which the war developed an unusual crop, and many times they gained such influence over her as to compromise her very seriously."[182] Her friendship with Wikoff was a case in point. Born to wealthy Philadelphia parents in 1813, he attended Yale, from which he was expelled, and ultimately graduated from Union College. He spent much time in Europe, where he pursued pleasure single-mindedly. Eventually, he became something of a journalist and an off-again, on-again friend of James Gordon Bennett, editor of the New York *Herald*. In 1851, he achieved notoriety by kidnapping a woman he loved. Convicted of abduction, Wikoff served fifteen months in jail; his account of this misadventure, *My Courtship and Its Consequences*, sold well. Later in the 1850s, he worked for Bennett in Washington, acting as a go-between for the publisher in his dealings with President James Buchanan.[183]

Wikoff had charm as well as notoriety. John W. Forney described him glowingly: "You might travel a long way before meeting a more pleasant companion than the cosmopolite Wikoff. He has seen more of the world than most men, has mingled with society of every shade and grade, has tasted of poverty and affluence, talks several languages fluently, is skilled in etiquette, art, and literature, and, without proclaimed convictions, is a shrewd politician, who understands the motives and opinions of others."[184]

Wikoff's relationship with Mary Lincoln appalled polite society. In October 1861, George Gibbs, bemoaning the "fatuity of Lincoln & Seward," told a friend that "Mrs L. seems now to be at the head of the State. As the Chevalier Wikoff is an habitué of the White House you need not be surprised at anything." The First Lady, Gibbs added, "is a byword among the officials here [in Washington] for ignorance, vulgarity and meanness."[185] Two months later, David Davis wrote home: "Rumors are plenty—that Mrs. Lincoln is acting badly." It was said "that she has installed as Master of Ceremonies at the White House, the Chevalier Wikoff," a "terrible libertine, & no woman ought to tolerate his presence." Washington matrons were "in distress" at this news.[186] In November 1861, a journalist reported that "Mrs. Lincoln is making herself both a fool and a nuisance. Chevalier Wikoff is her gallant, and I have within the week seen two notes signed by him in her name sending compliments and invitation. . . . He is a beautiful specimen to occupy such a position."[187] In disbelief, a leading Connecticut Republican, Joseph R. Hawley, asked: "What does Mrs. Lincoln mean by . . . having anything to do with that world-renowned whoremonger and swindler Chevalier Wikoff? Is [Mrs.] Lincoln an old saphead or is she a headstrong fool who thinks she can have a kitchen cabinet? It's a national disgrace."[188] Echoing this sentiment, John Hay deemed Wikoff an "unclean bird," a "vile creature," a "marked and branded social Pariah, a monstrosity abhorred by men and women," and declared it "an enduring disgrace to American society that it suffers such a thing to be at large."[189] Frederick Law Olmsted was scandalized when he observed the First Lady and Wikoff, whom he called an "insufferable beast," at a White House band concert.[190] General John E. Wool found it "certainly strange" that she would call on Wikoff at Willard's Hotel, wait for him in the lobby for a long time, help him don his gloves, and then ride off with him in her carriage. "Some very extraordinary storeys are told of this *Lady*," Wool wrote his wife.[191]

The public also looked askance at Mrs. Lincoln's friendship with Daniel Sickles, yet another acquaintance whose reputation was none too savory. When the president nominated him for a generalship, that gesture was thought to reflect Lincoln's "desire to confer on him respectability because his wife condescended to be attended by Sickles at a Review in public when no other women in the country of unsullied character would have done such a thing." A New Yorker reported that, because of her indiscretions, "Mrs. Lincoln is seen in society at the North to be the worst enemy" of her husband.[192] A matron in the Empire State, Maria Lydig Daly, thought the First Lady "behaves in the most undignified manner possible, associating with Wyckoff and Sickles, with whom no lady would deign to speak; but she seems to be easily flattered. She is not a young woman by any means, but dresses like one."[193] Senator William P. Fessenden told his cousin that the First Lady "by common consent, is making both herself & her husband very ridiculous."[194] Philo S. Shelton, a Boston merchant and speculator, indignantly remarked that Lincoln "is a *humbug* & his wife worse [—] only think of such men as Wikoff & Gordon Bennett & Mrs. B[ennett] being the special guests of Mrs. Lincoln & of men placed in office thro[ugh] such influences."[195]

The president intervened when warned of scandal by Matthew Hale Smith, New York correspondent for the Boston *Journal*. Shortly after the Civil War, Smith revealed the full story: Wikoff, "with whom no reputable woman would willingly be seen on Broadway," had been "very officious in his attention to . . . Mrs. Lincoln. . . . His frequent visits to Washington, and his receptions at the White House, were noticed by the friends of the President. At all of the receptions of Mrs. Lincoln he was an early and constant visitor. At the informal receptions he was found. No one went so early but this person could be seen cosily seated in a chair as if at home, talking to the ladies of the White House. None called so late but they found him still there." Wikoff was often "seen riding in the President's coach, with the ladies, through Pennsylvania Avenue. Frequently he was found lounging in the conservatory, or smoking in the grounds, very much at home, and not at all anxious to hide his presence." Wikoff's frequent visits embarrassed the White House staff, and the press began to comment unfavorably.

Friends of the president, suspicious of Wikoff, investigated his background and discovered that he had been hired "by some parties in New York, who were using him as their tool." These men had "furnished him with money and instructions. He was to go to Washington, make himself agreeable to the ladies, insinuate himself into the White House, attend levees, show that he had the power to come and go, and, if possible, open a correspondence with the ladies of the mansion." Once he became known as an insider, he would be able to wield influence that his backers might find useful in time. (According to Charles A. Dana, Wikoff "made about $20,000 by contracts" which Mary Lincoln "knew how to help him to.")

Wikoff carried out his assignment well. Lincoln's friends "considered that the President should be made acquainted with this plot against his honor" and dispatched Smith to do so. Accompanied by a U.S. senator, Smith visited the White House one evening. As the journalist later recalled, Lincoln "took me by the hand, led me into the office of his private secretary, whom he drove out, and locked the door." When Smith showed him documents revealing the purposes of Wikoff, who at that moment was downstairs in the White House, the president said, "Give me those papers and sit here till I return." Lincoln "started out of the room with strides that showed an energy of purpose." He soon came back, shook Smith's hand, and had Wikoff "driven from the mansion that night."[196] According to another source, Lincoln "became jealous" of Wikoff and "taxed" his wife. The Chevalier then "volunteered an explanation," telling "the wounded & incensed" president that "he was only teaching the madame a little European Court Etiquette."[197] Wikoff was thereafter forbidden to enter the Executive Mansion.[198]

John Watt, who was made to take the blame for Mrs. Lincoln's indiscretion in leaking her husband's annual message to Congress, was also denied access to the White House. A native of Scotland who had been residing in Washington for over a decade by 1861, Watt had served as the presidential gardener since the early 1850s. In January 1861, the 37-year-old Watt became a major in the Washington, D.C., militia. On September 9, he was appointed first lieutenant in the Sixteenth U.S. Infantry, but the senate revoked his commission on February 3, 1862. (His appointment, according to George Gibbs, was made "at Mrs Lincoln's demand.")[199] Watt later told authorities that he "was commissioned by President Lincoln and detailed for special duty at [the] White House and never served with his Regiment," and that he "also acted as recruiting officer at Washington D.C." A congressional report stated that he served as "one of the commanders of the bodyguard of President Lincoln" and "one of his personal aids and attendants." In March 1862, he was appointed to visit Europe on behalf of the Interior Department's Patent Division to inspect seeds. Returning the following year, on August 12 he enlisted in the Thirteenth New York Artillery as a private, rose to the rank of corporal, and in 1865 accepted a commission as a second lieutenant in the Thirty-eighth U.S. Colored Troops, serving until 1867.[200]

Before the Lincolns entered the White House, Watt had acquired an unenviable reputation. As Executive Mansion gardener during the Buchanan administration, he had been chastised by the commissioner of public buildings, John B. Blake, for submitting unreasonable bills. Blake, "astonished" at a seed bill, told Watt in 1859, "You must raise your own seed hereafter." Blake also protested against an "enormous" bill "for making and sharpening tools." The commissioner sternly warned Watt not to "incur the smallest debt without first consulting the public gardener or myself."[201]

Early in Lincoln's first term, Watt continued to attract unfavorable attention. John F. Potter, chairman of the House Select Committee investigating the loyalty of government employees, informed the president in September 1861 of damning testimony about Watt's pro-Confederate sympathies. Two independent witnesses confirmed that the gardener, shortly after the first battle of Bull Run, had proclaimed that the South could not be defeated and that the Union army consisted of human trash.[202] Mary Lincoln, who was "determined that he should be retained," vehemently denied those allegations, much to Potter's annoyance.[203] The congressman forwarded the documents about Watt to the president, who did not dismiss the gardener. Instead, according to Charles A. Dana, Mary Lincoln accosted Cameron and "after a good deal of bullying on her part & resistance on his, actually gets him appointed a lieutenant in the army with orders to report for duty not to the colonel of his regiment, but to the President."[204] When Potter's committee issued its report in January, it expressed "surprise that, in the face of such testimony, a man clearly disloyal, instead of being instantly removed, should have been elevated to a higher and more responsible position." Lincoln had committed a "blunder," said the *National Anti-Slavery Standard*, for during "such times as these, no man against whom a respectable suspicion can lie should be kept in place under the government."[205] The journalist D. W. Bartlett explained that Lincoln "clings to the men around him. Not even the menials about the White House, some of whom have been proven before Potter's investigation committee to be guilty of indulging secession sentiments, have been dismissed, because Mr. Lincoln good-naturedly says he can't believe them to be guilty."[206]

Watt was the gentleman who, according to the White House servant Thomas Stackpole, "had in the beginning of the Administration suggested to Mrs. Lincoln the making of false bills so as to get pay for private expenses out of the public treasury and had aided her in doing so."[207] It is not clear just when Watt and the First Lady began conspiring to defraud the government. John P. Usher, assistant secretary of the interior, informed Browning in late July 1861 of scandals involving Mrs. Lincoln. The first known example of her padding bills occurred the following month, when she tried to charge a state dinner for Prince Napoleon to the manure fund (paid by Congress), but Watt charged it to his account.[208] He billed the Interior Department $900, but the secretary of that department, Caleb B. Smith, rejected the claim. Finding the cost exorbitant, Smith consulted with Secretary of State Seward, who had also given a dinner for the prince, involving an equal number of guests, and providing the same meal that had been served at the White House. Both dinners had been catered by the same restaurant, which charged Seward $300. Mrs. Lincoln asked for a $900 reimbursement. Thwarted by Smith's refusal, the First Lady then instructed Watt to prepare a bill for plants, flowers, pots, and other gardening expenses totaling $900. She vouched for it herself and received the money. This legerdemain created a scandal.[209]

Use of the gardener's account to hide the cost overrun was described by a White House gatekeeper, James H. Upperman, who complained to Interior Secretary Smith in October 1861 about "sundry petit, but flagrant frauds on the public treasury," the products of "deliberate col[l]usion." According to Upperman, in mid-September Watt had authorized payments to Alexander McKerichar, a laborer on the White House grounds, for flowers ($700.75) and for 215 loads of manure ($107.50) as well as hire of a horse and cart for twenty-seven days in August to haul it to the Executive Mansion ($47.25). These bills were for goods and services apparently not provided. Another gentleman, Charles F. Cone, was paid $33.75 for working at the White House for twenty-seven days in August and $47.25 for the hire of horse cart and driver, even though, Upperman testified, "this individual is no labourer and has rendered no such service as charged for as can be proved by sundry persons, that he does not work at any kind of labour and was at the time refer[r]ed to, and can yet be found in a certain locality on P[ennsylvani]a Avenue anytime during working hours." As for Cone's de-livery charges, Upperman contended that "it can be proved that no such horse cart or driver rendered any such service in said grounds." Moreover, Upperman claimed, William Johnson was paid $155 for loads of manure that were never delivered. "I imagine his whereabouts to be doubtful as nobody knows him." Augustus Jullien, a French cook employed in the White House kitchen, received $67.50 for work done on the grounds in July and August, although he "has at no time rendered any such ser-vice." Similarly, Francis P. Burke, a presidential coachman, was paid $33.75 for labor on the grounds for August, as was White House butler Peter Vermeren.[210]

In late October 1861, Mary Lincoln, through Watt, begged Secretary Smith to see the president, evidently about these embarrassing revelations made by the White House gatekeeper. In response to a query from Commissioner of Public Buildings Benjamin Brown French, Lincoln on October 26 said he would "determine in a few days what he would do." Watt insisted that "the arrangement of the accounts was made by [William S.] Wood & that he assured Mrs L[incoln] that the transaction was right & legal and that she had no idea that anything was done which was not authorized by law." Secretary Smith told his cabinet colleague William Henry Seward that he "would be glad to have her relieved from the anxiety under which she is suf-fering."[211]

Smith provided such relief by covering the scandal up. After interviewing Watt, McKerichar, and Benjamin Brown French about the $700 flower bill, Smith con-cluded "that the voucher was correct, and that it had been rightfully paid by Mr. French," and therefore he "pursued the matter no further."[212] He did not consult Up-perman, Burke, Jullien, Johnson, Vermeren, Cone, or others knowledgeable about the affair. Gatekeeper Upperman then protested to Solomon Foot, chairman of the Sen-ate Committee on Public Buildings and Grounds, citing as his sources Burke, Jullien, and Vermeren, as well as the former public gardener, Thomas J. Sutter, and George W. Dant, a messenger and clerk to the commissioner of public buildings.[213] Nothing came of his complaint. According to Thurlow Weed, the Interior Department and Congress "measurably suppressed" this story out of "respect for Mr. Lincoln."[214] Con-gressman Benjamin M. Boyer confirmed this story, adding that the president paid the bill himself and withdrew the government check.[215] (In the fall of 1861, Lincoln gave Benjamin Brown French $270 out of his own pocket to reimburse the government for

"Accounts erroneously paid." They included $33.75 paid to Burke, Vermeren, and Jullien for work they allegedly performed in August 1861 as well as similar sums to those gentlemen for labor purportedly done on the President's Square in July and September 1861.)[216] A congressional committee was made aware of this scandal, but it was agreed to hush it up for fear of appearing unchivalrous.

On March 11, 1862, the president asked the "watchdog of the Treasury Department," First Comptroller Elisha Whittlesey, to help him stop the padding of bills: "Once or twice since I have been in this House, accounts have been presented at your Bureau, which were incorrect—I shall be personally and greatly obliged to you if you will carefully scan every account which comes from here; and if in any there shall appear the least semblance wrong, make it known to me directly."[217]

Later, Watt threatened to blackmail the First Lady. To keep him quiet, he was given a commission in the army, but when Henry Wilson, chairman of the Senate Military Affairs Committee, learned of it, he blocked the nomination. Watt then demanded to be taken care of or else he would reveal all he knew. Terrified, Mary Lincoln appealed to Isaac Newton, head of the agriculture division of the Interior Department, to give Watt a clerkship. Newton refused, for he dreaded the wrath of Senator Wilson.[218] According to Newton, the gardener "entered into a conspiracy to extort [$]20,000 from the President by using three letters of Mrs. Lincoln."[219] In those documents the First Lady apparently asked Watt to defraud the government through forgery and perjury.[220] In 1867, Watt offered to sell a journalist an account of his relations with Mary Lincoln; it contained "a note to Watt signed by Mrs. L. (which is genuine) proposing to cover up their schemes etc."[221] Simeon Draper, a New York politico who in 1864 paid Mary Lincoln $20,000 for her help in obtaining his position as agent for selling cotton seized in Savannah, called on Watt and, "with much bluster & great oaths," threatened to have him imprisoned. Watt then "fell on his literal marrow bones & begged, & gave up the letters & the conspiracy got demoralized & came down, down, to 1500 dollars which was paid, and the whole thing [was] settled."[222] The money came in the form of a sinecure; in March 1862, Watt was named special agent for Newton's agriculture division to purchase seeds in Europe, at an annual salary of $1,500, plus travel costs.[223] (Thomas Stackpole urged Browning "to get the President to give Watt the appointment of public gardener, or agent to buy seeds for [the] patent office.") After failing to be paid for his services in Europe, Watt in 1863 billed the president $736 to compensate him for Mary Lincoln's hotel bills, cash advances, and "Commissary stores." The vouchers for these payments and advances from Watt to the First Lady were held by Simeon Draper.[224] Watt told Simon Cameron: "You know very well what difficulties I had to contend with in regard to Mrs. Lincoln. . . . I paid about $700.00 for Mrs. Lincoln on one trip to Cambridge, Mass."[225]

The Watt affair became the talk of the capital. David Davis wrote his wife in February 1862 that "I got a letter from Washington & the gossip is still about Mrs. Lincoln and the gardener Watt." Such gossip was "horrid, about money speculation, etc. etc."[226] The press reported that Watt, at Mary Lincoln's instigation, bought two cows "and charged them to the manure fund—that is, a fund voted in one of the general appropriation bills to provide manure for the public lands." This bill was rejected, probably by Interior Secretary Smith. Watt facilitated the sale of a White House rug to a Washington photographer to pay an outstanding bill; the carpet was replaced at public expense.[227]

Mary Lincoln suggested to a New York merchant that he provide the White House with a $500 chandelier and charge $1,000 for it, thus allowing her to conceal $500 worth of jewelry purchases. The businessman refused to cooperate and apparently lost the sale of the chandelier.[228] Rumor had it that Mary Lincoln "appropriated the manure piles which had always been the perquisites of the gardener" and used the funds from the sale of that commodity for her own purposes.[229] Horace Greeley alleged that in September 1861, the First Lady purchased a $600 carriage and charged it to the contingency fund.[230]

The First Lady also exasperated her husband by overspending the $25,000 earmarked by Congress in 1861 for refurbishing the White House.[231] When she realized that a supplemental appropriation would be necessary to cover her redecorating expenses, she desperately appealed to Commissioner of Public Buildings Benjamin Brown French.

"I have sent for you to get me out of trouble," she pleaded on December 14; "if you will do it, I will never get into such a difficulty again." She confessed that the contractor's bill exceeded the original congressional authorization by $6,700. "Mr. Lincoln will not approve it," she lamented. "I want you to see him and tell him that it is common to overrun appropriations—tell him how *much* it costs to refurnish, he does not know much about it, he says he will pay it out of his own pocket." She wept as she begged French's help: "Major, he cannot afford that, he ought not to do it. Major you must get me out of this difficulty[;] it is the last, I will always be governed by you, henceforth, I will not spend a cent without consulting you, now do go to Mr. Lincoln and try to persuade him to approve the bill. Do Major for my sake, but do not let him know that you have seen me." She gave the commissioner the bill with her annotation, dated December 13: "This bill is correct. Mr Lincoln will please have it settled—this closes the house furnishing."[232]

When French, whose position made him a virtual member of the presidential household, complied with her request, he found the president "inexorable." The commissioner explained that "a Mr. Carryl has presented a bill of some $7000 over the appropriation, for furnishing this house, and, before I can ask for an appropriation to pay it, it must have your approval."

The president, "a little excited," exclaimed: "It never can have my approval—I'll pay for it out of my own pocket first—it would stink in the nostrils of the American people to have it said that the President of the United States had approved a bill overrunning an appropriation of $20,000 for *flub dubs* for this damned old house, when the poor freezing soldiers cannot have blankets! Who is that Carryl, and how came he to be employed[?]"

French replied: "I do not know, sir—the first I ever heard of him he brought me a large bill for room paper."

Lincoln was especially shocked by a "Rich, Elegant Carpet made to order" that his wife had purchased. "I would like to know where a carpet worth $2,000 can be put," he queried.

"In the East Room," French suggested.

The president called it "a monstrous extravagance," adding: "Well I suppose Mrs. Lincoln *must* bear the blame, let her bear it, I swear I won't! . . . It was all wrong to spend one cent at such a time, and I never ought to have had a cent expended, the house was furnished well enough, better than any one we ever lived in, and if I had not been overwhelmed with other business I would not have had any of the appropriation expended, but what could I do? I could not attend to everything." He concluded "by swearing that he *never* would approve that bill" and that rather than sign such legislation "he would pay it out of his own pocket!"[233]

Rumor had it that when Lincoln refused to authorize payment, his wife "was mad & stormed . . . *and would not sleep with him for three nights*."[234]

(In April 1862, French told his son that Mary Lincoln "is a little troublesome, & I can tell you some rather funny things relative to my experience with the worthy President and his Lady. Abraham is my *beau ideal* of an honest man, and Mrs. L. is—not my *beau ideal* pendant to that picture. You have heard the song I presume 'Oh Kitty Clover *she troubles me so,* Oh—oh—oh——oh—oh—oh.' Substitute Mrs. L- for Kitty & I can sing it from my heart!")[235]

In February 1862, Congress passed a supplemental appropriation of $14,000 for White House "extras," over the objections of some Republicans, including Senators Lyman Trumbull, Morton Wilkinson, and James Grimes.[236] Senator James R. Doolittle of Wisconsin explained that he and his colleagues "were placed in this fix[:] either the President must pay this money out of his own pocket or we must appropriate it to cover deficiencies." According to Doolittle, Senator James A. Pearce of Maryland "very delicately passed the matter on in the Senate and we voted it somewhat upon the principle that is it not gentlemanly to overhaul a lady's wardrobe." The legislators also thought "it would not be just to compel the President to pay" for the act of his "silly" and "vainglorious" wife. It was, Doolittle said, "exceedingly mortifying."[237]

Mary Lincoln "was surrounded by flatterers and intriguers, seeking for influence or such places as she can give," William H. Russell noted.[238] She had, said the editor of the Indianapolis *Journal,* "been spoiled by the gross flatteries of the fools about the White House, and thinks she must conduct herself like a European Queen." That Republican newspaper editorialized: "If the President hasn't sense enough, or control enough, over his foolish wife," then it was up to members of Congress "to exert that control themselves over him and his wife both."[239] Other newspapers referred to her as "our parvenue queen" who had "no conception of dignity" and "all the peevish assurance of a baseless parvenue." David Davis criticized the "*queenly*" way she traveled, and she reportedly sought to have the presidential yacht, the *Harriet Lane,* renamed the *Lady Lincoln.*[240] Her imperious manner led people to call the First Lady "her royal majesty."[241] Even her friend Mercy Levering Conkling referred to her as "Our Royal Highness."[242] A satirical newspaper piece criticized her for being "stuck up," for accepting inappropriate gifts, and for wasting taxpayer dollars on elaborate china.[243] A gentleman in Crawfordsville, Indiana, said that everybody there regarded her as "decidedly a snob" and made fun of her. He regretted that "we have a president with so little mind, and a presidentess with so little of the lady."[244]

Benjamin Brown French later wrote that in his dealings with Mary Lincoln, "I always felt as if the eyes of a hyena were upon me, & that the animal was ready, if I made a single mismove, to pounce upon me!" He called her a "bundle of vanity and folly" and wrote verses about her regal ways:

> [She] moved in all the insolence of pride
> as if the world beneath her feet she trod;
> Her vulgar bearing, jewels could not hide,
> And gold's base glitter was her only god![245]

In May 1865, French confided to his diary that Mrs. Lincoln "is a most singular woman, and it is well for the nation that she is no longer in the White House. It is not proper that I should write down, *even here*, all I know!"[246]

In February 1862, the First Lady scandalized the North by throwing an elaborate White House party, inaccurately called a ball (there was no dancing because Lincoln emphatically forbade it). Instead of the traditional open house, she decided to invite a select group, thereby antagonizing those who were excluded. It was widely viewed as a social blunder.[247] The exclusiveness of the event made it seem like a throwback to the aristocratic "drawing rooms" of Martha Washington and a repudiation of the egalitarian practice introduced by Thomas Jefferson.[248] The last exclusive White House fete, given by Mrs. John Tyler two decades earlier, had offended many.[249]

Some newspapers became indignant because reporters were not invited. When two New York congressmen, flatterers of Mrs. Lincoln, asked that an exception be made for the New York *Herald* and the *Spirit of the Times*, the White House staff feared that she would bend the rule and cause other journalists to protest against such favoritism. John G. Nicolay, in charge of White House social arrangements, appealed to his assistant, William O. Stoddard: "I can't do anything! It will make all sorts of trouble. 'She' is determined to have her own way. You will have to see to this. 'She' wouldn't listen to me." Stoddard artfully persuaded the First Lady to reject the appeal of the two courtiers, much to their dismay.[250]

On February 1, with the party less than a week off, Mary Lincoln asked Benjamin Brown French to take charge of the arrangements. "That good lady, who is not popular, but 'more sinned against than sinning,' is hand and glove with me, and seems to expect me to get her out of every difficulty," French told his son. "She implores me, & I try my best to respond to her implorations." A month later, French reported that "[w]e are all well, and looking on at the doings of our *great* & good President with admiration. We rather wish Mrs. President was—a more prudent lady."[251]

Mary Lincoln's motive in breaking with tradition was evidently to silence criticism that under her stewardship, White House entertainments had failed to match the splendor of parties given earlier by Southern leaders' wives.[252] She reportedly thought that it was "her duty to show those haughty secessionist dames [who once ruled society at the capital] that there is sufficient of fashion and respectability among the ladies of loyal families in and about Washington to constitute a court that will easily cast into the shade of that of their bogus President [i.e., Jefferson Davis.]"[253] In addition, she evidently sought to economize. A woman defender of Mary Lincoln argued that state dinners were customary at the White House, that the new administration had continued the tradition, and that the First Lady sensibly thought it more efficient and economical to have a few stand-up parties for hundreds of guests than to hold a long series of weekly dinner parties accommodating no more than forty people at a time. Moreover, it gave employment to caterers, dressmakers, and dry goods merchants.[254]

But, unlike her critics, Mary Lincoln's defenders were few in number. She was widely denounced for indulging in extravagance and frivolity while the soldiers were suffering and dying. On one single day she received eighteen hostile letters.[255] The *National Anti-Slavery Standard* bitterly remarked that she "has selected this darkest hour of the Republic for fiddling and dancing at the Presidential mansion. It is fit and proper that the most favored of her guests should be Mr. and Mrs. James Gordon Bennett. So we go. If we cannot fight, let us show the world that we can dance."[256] (That abolitionist paper noted that Bennett's New York *Herald* had previously run "fulsome panegyrics of Mrs. Lincoln, which disgust all people of taste.")[257] "Poor woman," Congressman Henry L. Dawes observed. "She seems to act if she expected to be the last President's wife and was disposed to make the most of it. Trifling at the White House in these times seems as inappropriate as jollity at a funeral."[258] Through an intermediary, Dawes told the president that nothing could "break down his administration so rapidly as this dancing-party given at the time when the nation is in the agonies of civil war. With equal propriety might a man make a ball with a corpse in his house!" In declining an invitation to the party, Senator Ben Wade asked: "Are the President and Mrs. Lincoln aware there is a civil war? If they are not, Mr. and Mrs. Wade are and for that reason decline to participate in feasting and dancing."[259] George H. Boker, a poet and ardent Republican, penned a scathing verse satire, "The Queen Must Dance."[260] The Cincinnati *Commercial* thought it "unfortunate that Mrs. Lincoln has so poor an understanding of the true dignity of her position, and the duties devolving upon her. It is not becoming her to be assuming the airs of a fine lady and attempting to shine as the bright star of 'the Republican court,' as shameless and designing flatterers call the White House circle." The editors disapproved of her "rich dresses and glittering equipage, her adornment of the President's House with costly upholstery," and her penchant for "crowding it with gay assemblages."[261] To the public, according to another Cincinnati paper, "the occasion seems too serious, the national peril too imminent, the distress of the country too great, and the condition of the nation too humiliating, to inaugurate a carnival at the Government mansion."[262] The journalist Mary Clemmer Ames concluded that Mrs. Lincoln, "unconsciously elated, carried away with the sudden honors of her new condition; unsuspectingly pleased with the delicate, dangerous flatteries of brilliant yet unprincipled intriguers, had little thought for anything but shopping and dressing."[263] The Indianapolis *Journal* protested: "With an empty treasury and a failing credit, a war raging all around us, and foreign nations threatening to interfere, such displays as that at the White House are a disgrace to the President."[264] Wendell Phillips exclaimed that "Mrs. Lincoln is vulgar, and wants to be fashionable!"[265]

In light of this evidence, it is no wonder that Alexander K. McClure concluded that the First Lady "was a consuming sorrow to Mr. Lincoln." Yet, McClure recalled, the president "bore it all with unflagging patience. She was sufficiently unbalanced to make any error possible and many probable, but not sufficiently so as to dethrone her as mistress of the White House."[266]

26

"I Expect to Maintain This Contest Until Successful, or Till I Die, or Am Conquered, or My Term Expires, or Congress or the Country Forsakes Me"

From the Slough of Despond to the Gates of Richmond
(January–July 1862)

Lincoln's decision to replace Cameron with Stanton was a key turning point in the war. As William O. Stoddard aptly noted, it ended "the first scene in the great tragedy," after which "changes were gradual, but the old order of things passed away."[1] In the winter of 1861–1862, the New York *World* predicted that Lincoln's assertiveness in dismissing Cameron "will confirm the opinion which has been for the last ten months slowly maturing in the public mind, that President Lincoln is the most self-poised and self-dependent statesman that could have been placed at the head of the government in this trying crisis. His whole course since his inauguration has exhibited moral robustness combined with masculine sense." The editors acknowledged that the president "is slow and deliberate, pondering long and turning over an important subject many times in his thoughts before reaching a decision," but once he "puts down his foot, he puts it down firmly" and "the Alps or the Andes are not more firmly planted on their bases than are his deliberate decisions." The country "had many presidents who could reach decisions more rapidly; but none, no not even Jackson, whose mind was more self-determined."[2]

Others saw a parallel between the Rail-splitter and Old Hickory. George Templeton Strong detected in the president "a most sensible, straightforward, honest old codger," both "clear-headed and sound-hearted," whose "evident integrity and simplicity of purpose would compensate for worse grammar than his, and for even more intense provincialism and rusticity." Withal, Strong judged that Lincoln was the "best President we have had since old Jackson's time."[3] John Pendleton Kennedy predicted that Lincoln would "set down that great, broad, flat, long and heavy-shod foot of his, in good earnest, and that it will squelch the whole dozen reptiles who are now crawling across his path into an indistinguishable mass of slime."[4]

In January 1862, Lincoln began to assert himself in dealing with generals, just as he had earlier done with the cabinet. He followed the sound advice of Edward Bates, who "insisted that, being 'Commander in chief' by law," Lincoln "*must* command—especially in such a war as this."[5] Lyman Trumbull informed Illinois Governor Richard

285

Yates that Lincoln "at last seems to be waking up to the fact . . . that the responsibility is upon *him,* & I think he has resolved hereafter not to content himself with throwing all army movements on the Generals commanding, on the ground that he is no military man. He seems inclined to take a personal supervision of matters to some extent, & see that Generals & subordinate officers do their duty."[6] Yates rejoiced to learn that the president "is taking firm hold of the helm."[7]

Lincoln also began standing up to domineering members of Congress, among them the outspoken, combative Senator Benjamin F. Wade of Ohio, known as Bluff Ben. A leader of the Radical Republicans, Wade resented Lincoln's story-telling. One day in early January 1862, the senator replied to a presidential tale stiffly: "Sir, you are not a mile from Tophet [i.e., hell] and you are riding a swift locomotive at that!" Lincoln rejoined: "well, there is one consolation—I shall not have to part long from my senatorial friends. You will be along by the next train!"[8] The journalist Benjamin Perley Poore thought that politicos "do not exactly fancy 'Old Abe,' for they cannot use him, nor will he be guided by them, for he prefers to decide for himself on all important topics."[9]

As Lincoln took charge of his administration more forcefully, he won increased respect from Congress. When that body met in December, according to Samuel Bowles, editor of the influential Springfield (Massachusetts) *Republican,* "many of his old political friends treated him with marked neglect and discourtesy." But in late March, Bowles reported from Washington that "all are hastening to do him reverence. His integrity, his wisdom, his caution, his strength as a man and a statesman are warmly admitted on all hands; and he has, more than any other man in the nation, the respect and confidence of Congress."[10]

By the spring, the public, too, had come to share that feeling. "The confidence felt by all loyal men in the integrity and wisdom of President Lincoln forms one of the most marked and hopeful features of the existing political condition of our country," observed the Philadelphia *Press.* "Even those who do not approve all his acts accord to him perfect rectitude of purpose and fervent patriotism."[11] The Providence *Journal* was pleased that Lincoln was "not merely the nominal executive of our government" but had become "really the President. He has the reins in his own hands."[12] Democratic Judge Edwards Pierrepont of New York remarked that Lincoln "is rising above all exterior influence and learning to depend upon himself and taking his own judgment" and "that Seward, even, has little influence with him now." Somewhat condescendingly, the fastidious Pierrepont added: "He is greater than he seems. His manners are so against him, but he is great from being so *good,* so conscientious."[13]

If Lincoln's manners offended Pierrepont, the voters found them to their liking. Poore noted that the president "will sometimes throw his legs upon the table, as if in his law office in Springfield, and illustrate his position by a good story, or by a colloquial expression, drawn from the mother wit and humor of the prairie people. But this pleasant manner endears him the more to the great mass of those who elected him."[14] Also endearing Lincoln to his constituents was his patience in dealing with advisors and critics. "Mr. Lincoln is a *good listener,*" reported the New York *Commercial Advertiser.* "He will patiently hear any man, (unless he is reminded of an anecdote, which he at once relates,) and he thus patiently gathers tribute from all, often submitting to severe criticisms from tried friends."[15] (One of those friends, his former colleague in Congress Truman Smith, grumbled that the "amiable President seems to be averse to *hurting* any body and I shall not be surprised if the traitors on submission secure to themselves the benefit of a general amnesty.")[16] In late January, a New Yorker declared that Lincoln, Stanton, and McClellan "are not only the popular favorites of the hour but the hope of all thoughtful and patriotic men."[17]

Lincoln's greater assertiveness was especially appreciated by leaders from his own region. When he asked a Western governor, "Will the people of the West sustain the government through the onerous taxation which must be imposed upon them?" he received an emphatic response: "They will endure *anything*, if they are convinced *that they have got a government*."[18] In February, Illinois Congressman William Kellogg approvingly reported that Lincoln "is determined to move on to the accomplishment of the great work before him firmly and surely."[19]

Lincoln did not burn with a desire to wield power, but his keen sense of responsibility led him to perform his duties conscientiously, onerous though he found them to be. He said of the presidency: "It is a big job; the country little knows how big," and told an Illinois friend: "This getting the nomination for President, and being elected, is all very pleasant to a man's ambition; but to be the President, and to meet the responsibilities and discharge the duties of the office in times like these is anything but pleasant. I would gladly if I could, take my neck from the yoke, and go home with you to Springfield, and live, as I used [to], in peace with my friends, [rather] than to endure this harassing kind of life."[20]

In exercising his new-found assertiveness, Lincoln continued to face a daunting challenge in McClellan. Getting him to move proved as difficult as ever. Among the general's chief defects were the ones that he mistakenly ascribed to Robert E. Lee, who, Little Mac alleged, "is *too* cautious & weak under grave responsibility" and "wanting in moral firmness when pressed by heavy responsibility & is likely to be timid & irresolute in action."[21] This assessment is a classic example of the psychological mechanism of projection—accusing others of having one's own flaws.

Presidential Reading

As Lincoln took greater control of his administration, he had little time to relax. In January, when chided for inaccessibility, he said that he simply could not accommodate everybody who wanted to see him and exclaimed: "I have not looked into a newspaper for a month!"[22] He told his Illinois friend George W. Rives "that he had no time to read many letters & none to read newspapers."[23] Some mistakenly interpreted these remarks as a scandalous admission that the president cared little for public opinion. As John Hay noted, Lincoln "read very little. Scarcely ever looked into a newspaper unless I called his attention to an article on some special subject. He frequently said 'I know more about that than any of them.'"[24] Hay's coadjutor, John G. Nicolay, reported that except for telegraphic dispatches in the Washington press, "the President rarely ever looks at any papers, simply for want of leisure to do so."[25] Nicolay and Hay's assistant, William O. Stoddard, recalled that Lincoln "cared little" for newspaper opinion. In 1861, the president instructed him to prepare a digest of the most significant editorials in prominent journals. Stoddard complied for a few weeks but eventually quit because Lincoln ignored his handiwork. The president "knew the people so much better than the editors did," Stoddard explained, "that he could not bring himself to listen with any patience to the tissue of insane contradictions which then made up the staple of the public press."[26]

When an army officer volunteered to write a defense of the administration, Lincoln told him: "Oh, no, at least, not now. If I were to try to read, much less answer, all the attacks made on me, this shop might as well be closed for any other business. I do the very best I know how—the very best I can; and I mean to keep doing so until the end. If the end brings me out all right, what is said against me won't amount to anything. If the end brings me out wrong, ten angels swearing I was right would make no difference."[27] In 1865, Lincoln said: "As a general rule, I abstain from reading the reports of attacks upon myself, wishing not to be provoked by that to which I can not properly offer an answer."[28]

Lincoln also avoided reading newspapers because he was, as he put it, too "thin-skinned." Mary Lincoln testified that press attacks caused her husband "great pain." When she tried to share with him hostile journalistic commentary, he would say: "*Don't do that*, for I have enough to bear."[29] One Sunday afternoon he spent an hour perusing some anti-administration editorials clipped from Henry Ward Beecher's New York *Independent*. The eminent preacher snobbishly dismissed Lincoln: "It would be difficult for a man to be born lower than he was. He is an unshapely man. He is a man that bears evidence of not having been educated in schools or in circles of refinement."[30] Upon finishing Beecher's salvos, Lincoln indignantly threw them down and quoted heatedly from the Second Book of Kings: "Is thy servant a *dog*, that he should do this thing?"[31] He sharply criticized an editor of that journal, Henry C. Bowen, who protested that he only controlled the commercial, not editorial, side of the paper and therefore could do nothing about Beecher's attacks.

(Beecher was pleased that Lincoln read his barbs and rejoiced "that the arrow is well directed," but his brother Thomas, a recruiting officer in upstate New York, criticized his naiveté about the degree of public support for emancipation: "I am satisfied that the day you succeed in writing your magnificent principles on our national banner, you will have only a flag and a sentiment; the army, the men with one voice will say, 'We ain[']t going to fight for the Niggers.' You remember [your earlier years in] Indiana. Do you soberly think that those fighting Hoosiers would hurry to enlist for the sake of freeing the slave? Will negro hating Illinois that now gives nigh half her men to the war, consent to fight for the slaves she despises? I can answer for rural New York. The more emancipation you talk, the less recruits you can enlist.")[32]

Ward Hill Lamon heard Lincoln cry out after learning of criticism like Beecher's: "I would rather be dead than, as President, thus abused in the house of my friends."[33] When Henry J. Raymond's New York *Times* was severely critical of Lincoln, he made it clear that Raymond would receive no government position. The president once protested to Sydney Howard Gay, managing editor of the New York *Tribune*, about an unfair article in that paper: "I want to straighten this thing out and then I don't care what they do with me. They may hang me."[34]

Instead of perusing newspapers to gauge the mood of the country, Lincoln relied on what he called "public-opinion baths"—that is, talking with innumerable callers. He acknowledged to journalist Charles G. Halpine that it was a "heavy tax" on his time to do so, but insisted that "no hours of my day are better employed than those which thus bring me again within the direct contact and atmosphere of the average of our whole people." Government officials moved in such limited circles that they could easily lose touch with the electorate. By regularly admitting all comers, even those with "utterly frivolous" concerns, he was able to obtain "a clearer and more vivid image of that great popular assemblage out of which I sprung, and to which at the end of two years I must return."[35]

Lincoln read only a tiny percentage of the letters that poured into the White House, for most business correspondence was routed to the appropriate departments. At his request, White House secretaries summarized the incoming mail for him. "Mr. Nicolay, please run over this & tell me what is in it," he endorsed a 15-page missive.[36] One of those secretaries, William O. Stoddard, recalled that "there never was on earth such another *omnium gatherum* as the President's mail." It consisted of "applications for office, for contracts, for pardons, for pecuniary aid, for advice, for information, for autographs, voluminous letters of advice, political disquisitions, religious exhortations, the rant and drivel of insanity, bitter abuse, foul obscenity, slanderous charges against public men, police and war information, military reports," and a "large number of threatening letters." Stoddard could not get the president to take seriously the threats, which averaged one a day. If Lincoln bothered to notice them at all, he responded with "contemptuous ridicule."[37]

The president had little time for voluminous documents. When he received a very detailed committee report on artillery, he threw it down, exclaiming: "I should want a new lease of life to read this through! Why can't a committee of this kind occasionally exhibit a grain of common sense? If I send a man to buy a horse for me, I expect him to tell me his '*points*'—not how many *hairs* there are in his tail."[38]

To a caller presenting a long petition, he stated bluntly: "I'm not going to read that."

"Why not?"

"Why, if all these thing were read it would take fifty Presidents to do the business."

"But this once, do just read mine."

Holding up the lengthy document, Lincoln exclaimed: "Read that! Why I don't expect to live long enough to read it through."[39]

In the winter of 1861–1862, Lincoln looked especially haggard and careworn. A guest at a mid-January dinner recalled that it "was evident that he was harassed by haunting cares; the obligation of politeness to his guests made him endeavor to be agreeable; he would tell a funny story to my mother who sat next to him, or make some amusing remark to his other neighbor, then when the attention of these ladies was called away, Mr. Lincoln's thoughts lapsed into their 'sea of trouble' and flew far away from the lights and the guests and the scene around him; the face a moment before twinkling with the merriment of a jest, became rigid in its intensity of thought."[40] The president, wrote D. W. Bartlett on New Years Day, "is not so cheerful as he used to be, is a little more grave in his demeanor, and is somewhat worn."[41] This news caused alarm, for it was widely believed that the president's face unerringly indicated the state of public affairs.

As his anxiety grew, Lincoln's temper shortened. When confronted by the increasingly vehement criticism of McClellan's tardiness in attacking the Confederates, he responded that "there was probably but one man in the country more anxious for a battle than himself, and that man was McClellan." He "repudiated in words of withering rebuke those who make the charge that he or Mr. Seward or General McClellan were temporizing or delaying out of any consideration for rebels or rebel institutions, or that they indulged any thought of ending the war by any means other than by conquest on the battlefield."[42] He insisted that "McClellan is not a traitor; his difficulty is that he always prefers to-morrow to to-day. He never is ready to move. I think the immense importance of the interests at stake affects him thus. In this he is very much like myself. When I was practicing law at Springfield, I sometimes had a case involving a man's life or death, and I never could feel that I was ready to go on with the trial; I always wished to postpone it; and when the next court came round I felt a similar impression that I was not ready, whatever preparations I had made."[43]

Cheering News from Kentucky and Tennessee

As time passed, Lincoln grew more optimistic. On January 19, Union troops under the exceptionally capable Virginian George H. Thomas won a battle at Mill Springs, Kentucky, killing 148 of the enemy, including General Felix K. Zollicoffer, while losing only 55 men. The president was in excellent spirits upon hearing of that victory, which he looked upon as the first in a series that would extend into the warmer months. Also cheering was word that General Ambrose E. Burnside and his men had safely reached North Carolina, where they quickly defeated the Confederates at Roanoke Island. On February 5, Lincoln said "that he felt more confidence now than ever in the power of the Government to suppress the rebellion."[44] When Joshua Speed protested against a rumored plan to award a general's stars to Cassius M. Clay—then serving as U.S. minister to Russia—the president said "that he was now in great hopes that the rebellion would pretty much [be] ended" before Clay could return from St. Petersburg.[45]

(Lincoln came to regret offering a commission to Clay. In December 1862, the "much annoyed" president refused to see that general, saying Clay had "a great deal of conceit and very little sense, and that he did not know what to do with him, for he could not give him a command—he was not fit for it."[46] But feeling sorry for the unpopular Clay, he nominated him to serve once again as minister to Russia despite the objections of Sumner and Seward. Seeing that the president was "vexed and grieved" at the prospect that the senate might well reject Clay, Seward magnanimously agreed to abandon his opposition and help secure the indiscreet Kentuckian's confirmation.)[47]

On February 6, U.S. Grant, with the help of gunboats under the command of Navy Captain Andrew Hull Foote, took Fort Henry on the Tennessee River, a victory that Lincoln considered extremely important. And on February 16, when Grant captured a Rebel army at Fort Donelson on the Cumberland, Washingtonians became wildly excited. The wife of a prominent government official told friends back in Iowa: "Our hearts are bursting with gratitude, our tears start, we grasp hands, we laugh, we say 'God be thanked;' our country's honor is vindicated, the stain of our Flag is forever blotted out!"[48] An army officer noted, "some think that the back bone of the rebellion, as it is called, is broken forever."[49]

At Donelson, Grant took several thousand Confederates prisoner. This successful joint operation represented the first major Northern victory in the war; it not only opened the South to invasion along two rivers but also forced the rebels to forsake their positions in Kentucky and much of Tennessee. Tired of hearing reports that all was quiet on the Potomac, many Northerners scoffed when McClellan's partisans claimed that their hero, as general-in-chief, should receive credit for those victories.

Lincoln rejoiced at the triumph of Grant and Foote. When the news arrived and someone jubilantly suggested "let's have a drink," the teetotaling president drolly responded: "All right bring in some water."[50] Informed that the victory had been achieved with the help of many Illinois troops, he remarked: "I cannot speak so confidently about the fighting qualities of the Eastern men, . . . but this I do know—if the Southerners think that man for man they are better than our Illinois men, or western men generally, they will discover themselves in a grievous mistake."[51]

For weeks Lincoln had been working behind the scenes to provide Grant and Foote with floating mortars, the brainchild of Gustavus Fox, who realized that the Mississippi, Cumberland, and Tennessee rivers would be convenient invasion routes and that to attack forts along their banks, mortars on boats would be essential. While still in charge of the Department of the West, Frémont to his credit approved the idea and ordered the construction of a mortar fleet at Cairo. It was to assist the army in a thrust led by Grant, who had obtained permission from Halleck to launch an offensive down the Tennessee. Special beds had to be manufactured to accommodate the gigantic 13-inch mortars. This was successfully accomplished for a flotilla being constructed in New Jersey at the behest of David Dixon Porter, who was planning to attack New Orleans, but Lincoln grew anxious as the work on a similar fleet in Cairo was seemingly abandoned. On January 10, the cabinet learned that nobody knew anything about those vessels. When he made inquiries, Lincoln was infuriated to discover that no mortars had been constructed for Foote's armada and only two mortar beds. He instructed Navy Lieutenant Henry A. Wise "to put it through." With fierce determination, he told Wise on January 23, "I am going to devote a part of every day to these mortars and I won[']t leave off until it fairly rains Bombs."[52] He wanted "to rain the Rebels out" and "treat them to a refreshing shower of sulphur and brimstone."[53] When word of the president's special interest in the flotilla reached Cairo, it galvanized the officers and men there.

Lieutenant Wise turned to the firm of Cooper and Hewitt, which speedily completed the beds by mid-February and sent them westward in boxcars plainly labeled

"U. S. GRANT, CAIRO. NOT TO BE SWITCHED UNDER PENALTY OF DEATH."[54] A similar feat was accomplished by a Cincinnati foundry. Lincoln supervised all these efforts closely. Despite his best endeavors, however, the mortar flotilla was not ready in time for Foote and Grant's campaign. Happy as he was with the news from Tennessee, Lincoln was "[m]ad about mortars." He remarked that "he must take these army matters into his own hands. The Navy have built their ships and mortars for N[ew] O[rleans] and are ready to go. Gen. McC[lellan] & [General James W.] Ripley & all are to blame."[55]

One-Man Research-and-Development Bureau
for New Weaponry

Lincoln's attempt to expedite the creation of a mortar fleet was emblematic of his desire to provide the military with the latest, most lethal weapons. In keeping with his long-standing interest in things mechanical, he studied weaponry as well as strategy, and during the first two years of his administration became in effect a one-man research-and-development branch of the War Department in addition to its main strategist. But the chief of army ordnance, General James W. Ripley (known as "Ripley Van Winkle"), proved obstinate and recalcitrant. Trying to get the unimaginative, cantankerous Ripley to adopt technological innovations was as difficult as it was to get McClellan or Buell to attack the enemy.

Lincoln concerned himself with a wide variety of weapons: small arms, artillery, flame throwers, rockets, submarines, mines, iron-clad ships, and explosives. Often he tested new-fangled rifles himself. An inventor with a patent of his own, he encouraged all sorts of innovations, most notably the breechloading rifle and the machine gun. His interest in the latter began in June 1861, when he observed tests of "the Union Repeating Gun," modestly described by its salesman as "an army in six feet square." Lincoln dubbed it the "coffee-mill gun" because its hopper, into which bullets were poured, resembled that culinary apparatus. Impressed by what he saw, Lincoln in October ordered all of the ten guns then available at $1,300 apiece. On October 26, the president called on McClellan and "began to talk about his wonderful new repeating battery of rifled gun, shooting 50 balls a minute." Lincoln was "delighted with it" and asked the general to "go down and see it, and if proper, detail a corps of men to work it."[56] Characteristically, Little Mac hesitated to act, asking Cameron if fifty could be purchased at the rather steep price. Lincoln then demanded that the general back his decision to buy them. Impatiently, the president told a salesman promoting the weapon that McClellan "knows whether the guns will be serviceable. I do not. It avails nothing for him that he has no *objection* to my purchasing them." McClellan ultimately agreed, and on December 19 Lincoln ordered the purchase of fifty coffee-mill guns.

More significantly, Lincoln championed the introduction of breechloading rifles, which allowed a soldier to avoid the cumbersome, time-consuming, and dangerous procedures necessary to reload single-shot muzzleloaders: while standing or kneeling he must take a from a pouch a paper cartridge containing powder and bullet, tear it open with his teeth, pour the powder into the barrel, stick the ball point-first into the muzzle, pull out a ramrod, jam the bullet home, replace the ramrod in its tube, raise the weapon, half-cock the hammer, remove the spent percussion cap, place a new one on the nipple, and cock the hammer once more. Had breechloaders been widely adopted by the North early in the war, the conflict might have been significantly shortened.

Lincoln did his best to persuade the War Department to equip the army with breechloaders, which he enjoyed testing himself. Inventors often submitted prototypes of their wares to him, and he inspected many of them carefully, especially rifles. Early one morning in 1861, he and William O. Stoddard took target practice on the grassy mall behind the White House, the president using a new Spencer single-shot breechloader and his assistant a converted Springfield rifle (known as a Marsh gun after its inventor) that also loaded at the breech. As they banged away at a large pile of scrap lumber, in violation of the standing order to fire no weapons in the District, the leader of a small army squad rushed toward them shouting "Stop that firing!" When the president stood up, the troopers, recognizing their commander-in-chief, abruptly wheeled about and scurried off. "Well, they might have stayed to see the shooting," Lincoln remarked. The two men frequently tested new rifles in this fashion. (Lincoln was, Stoddard recalled, "a very good shot." At a demonstration by a sharpshooter unit, the president surprised the spectators with his marksmanship.) Lincoln was convinced that the single-shot breechloader was "the army rifle of the future."[57] When others tested the Marsh gun, they became as enthusiastic as Lincoln and recommended its adoption. Ripley, however, rejected that advice. In mid-October 1861, the president overruled him, insisting that he order 25,000 of them. Two months later, Lincoln also demanded that 10,000 Spencer rifles be purchased, despite Ripley's objections. The Spencer rifle was superior to the Marsh, for it was a repeater, carrying a clip of seven rounds, and was capable of firing fourteen shots per minute without overheating. While trying one out, Lincoln whittled a piece of wood into a gun sight, which improved the weapon's accuracy. That innovation was not adopted, however.

Lincoln also favored breechloading artillery, which Ripley opposed. In the fall of 1861, the president ordered the purchase of a few so-called Ellsworth guns, designed by Eli Thayer for Elmer Ellsworth's zouaves. In addition, Lincoln prevailed on the War Department to buy thirty small muzzle-loading three-pounders, but Ripley managed to thwart the president's plan to order two other breechloading fieldpieces.

Pushing on a String: Goading McClellan into Action

Lincoln agreed with Stanton's insistence that "while men are striving nobly in the West, the champagne & oysters on the Potomac must be stopped."[58] The new secretary of war said that if Little Mac did not move soon, he (Stanton) "should move *him*."[59] The president had waited patiently—and in vain—for McClellan's plan of operations, and, like the electorate, he was growing restless. "It is wonderful how public opinion is changing against McClellan," an Ohioan reported in late February.[60] A periodical editor quipped that he had no time to peruse the many monthly magazines he had received and was tempted to send them to Little Mac, "whose forte seemed to be *reviewing*."[61]

To smoke the general out, Lincoln employed an unusual expedient: on January 27, he issued "President's General War Order No. 1," commanding all land and naval forces to begin moving against the enemy on February 22. (Privately, Stanton explained that "the Government was on the verge of bankruptcy, and at the rate of expenditure, the armies must move or the Government perish.")[62] As Hay observed, this order marked a turning point: Lincoln "wrote it without any consultation and read it to the Cabinet, not for their sanction but for their information. From that time he influenced actively the operations of the Campaign. He stopped going to McClellan's and sent for the general to come to him. Everything grew busy and animated after this order."[63] When the order was publicly released in March, the Cincinnati *Gazette* called it "the stroke that cut the cords which kept our great armies tied up in a state of inactivity."[64] On January 31, Lincoln followed up with "President's Special War Order No. 1," directing the Army of the Potomac to attack Confederate supply lines at Manassas, a strategy he had proposed to McClellan several weeks earlier. The New York *Tribune* optimistically predicted that Lincoln as de facto commander-in-chief of the army, along with the "prodigiously energetic" Stanton, "will now lift this war out of mud and delay, and carry it to victory."[65]

Goaded into action by these presidential war orders, McClellan hastened to the Executive Mansion to register objections and ask permission to submit an alternative plan. Lincoln may well have exclaimed to himself, "At last!" The general wrote a twenty-two-page document proposing an attack on Richmond from the lower Chesapeake. He would move the Army of the Potomac by water to the hamlet of Urbanna on the Rappahannock River, then drive toward the Confederate capital, 40 miles to the west, before Confederate General Joseph E. Johnston's force at Manassas could shift to protect it. McClellan argued that it was "by no means certain" that victory could be achieved following the Manassas plan, but that an attack via Urbanna would provide "the most brilliant results" (as "certain by all the chances of war"), partly because the roads in the lower Chesapeake region "are passable at all seasons of the year." (To his dismay, he was to find that such was not the case at all. How he reached such an erroneous conclusion is hard to understand.)[66]

The president offered to defer to the general if Little Mac could satisfactorily answer five questions: "1st. Does not your plan involve a greatly larger expenditure of *time,* and *money* than mine? 2nd. Wherein is a victory *more certain* by your plan than mine? 3rd. Wherein is a victory *more valuable* by your plan than mine? 4th. In fact, would it not be *less* valuable, in this, that it would break no great line of the enemie's communications, while mine would? 5th. In case of disaster, would not a safe retreat be more difficult by your plan than by mine?"[67] Inexplicably, McClellan did not deign to respond.

Now Lincoln faced a dilemma: he must order McClellan to carry out the Manassas plan, or find a new general to do so, or acquiesce in the Urbanna strategy. But who should take Little Mac's place? There was no obvious alternative, as Lincoln told an indignant Benjamin Wade when the Ohio senator urged him to substitute anybody for McClellan: "Wade, *'anybody'* will do for you, but not for me. I must have *somebody.*"[68] Wade's colleague Henry Wilson was so disgusted with McClellan that he would have preferred to see even the aged John E. Wool in command. In late February and early March, Lincoln repeatedly said "that if the army of the Potomac could not otherwise be made to move, he would take command of it in person."[69] If Lincoln retained McClellan in command, would he order him to attack the Manassas supply lines? The president confided to Charles Sumner that the general's scheme was "very much against his judg[men]t, but that he did not feel disposed to take the responsibility of overruling him."[70] Chase shared the view that an attack on Confederate supply lines was preferable to the Urbanna scheme. But on February 13, McClellan assured him that he would be in Richmond by the end of that month.

So the president reluctantly consented to the Young Napoleon's plan, but only with the understanding that enough troops would be left behind to defend Washington in case the Confederates attacked it while the Army of the Potomac was 80 miles away. If the city were captured, the blow to the North's prestige might prove fatal, possibly leading to European recognition of the Confederacy and defeat in the war. McClellan promised to leave a sufficient force to protect the capital. The number was to be determined by all twelve division commanders, who jointly recommended a force of 40,000 to 50,000. That seemed reasonable, since McClellan had assured them that the enemy at Manassas and Centreville numbered over 100,000. Unfortunately, Lincoln and McClellan did not agree on a specific number, nor did they identify which troops would have that assignment.

In mid-February, Lincoln prodded McClellan indirectly by having Stanton congratulate General Frederick W. Lander for showing "how much may be done in the worst weather and worst roads by a spirited officer at the head of a small force of brave men, unwilling to waste life in camp when the enemies of their country are within reach."[71] This was widely interpreted as a rebuke to Little Mac.

Meanwhile, pressure on McClellan to break the Confederate hold on the upper and lower Potomac grew ever stronger. The blockade of that river below Washington cut the capital off from all seafaring traffic save warships; Rebel control of the river above the city obstructed a main rail line between the Atlantic seaboard and the Ohio Valley (the Baltimore and Ohio). An exasperated Lincoln impatiently asked Welles if the enemy batteries along the river could not be destroyed. The navy secretary said it could be easily done by 10,000 troops, but McClellan would never agree to it. Little Mac wishfully assumed that the lower Potomac would be opened when his Urbanna offensive got underway.

As for the upper Potomac, McClellan took action to keep Confederates from disrupting the Baltimore and Ohio. In late February, he ordered troops under General Nathaniel P. Banks to move toward Winchester, Virginia. To facilitate that offensive, a light pontoon bridge was thrown across the Potomac at Harper's Ferry; it was to be supplemented by a permanent bridge of heavy timbers resting upon canal boats anchored in the river. On February 27, when those vessels tried to enter a lift lock in order to move from the Chesapeake and Ohio Canal to the river, they proved 6 inches too wide. The entire operation had to be called off, prompting the usually humorless Chase to quip that the Winchester expedition had died of lockjaw. Horace White of the Chicago *Tribune*, who aptly described the fiasco as "Ball's Bluff all over again, minus the slaughter," reported that Lincoln was in "a h[el]l of a rage" and "swore like a Phillistine" upon learning of it.[72] He banged his fist on a table and exclaimed: "Why in hell didn't he measure first!" This was the only time Nicolay heard his boss swear, and the secretary's assistant, William O. Stoddard, said he "never knew Mr. Lincoln so really angry, so out of all patience." The president, Stoddard recalled, "was alone in his room when an officer of General McClellan's staff was announced by the door-keeper and admitted." Lincoln "turned in his chair to hear, and was informed, in respectful set terms, that the advance movement could not be made.

"'Why?' he curtly demanded.

"'The pontoon trains are not ready—'

"'Why in hell and damnation *ain't* they ready?'

"The officer could think of no satisfactory reply, but turned very hastily and left the room. Mr. Lincoln also turned to the table and resumed the work before him, but wrote at about double his ordinary speed."[73]

When Stanton confirmed the bad news, the president asked: "What does this mean?"

"It means that it is a d[amne]d fizzle. It means that he [McClellan] doesn't intend to do anything," replied the secretary of war.

"Why could he not have known whether his arrangements were practicable?" Lincoln queried in exasperation.

The president then summoned McClellan's chief of staff (and father-in-law), Randolph B. Marcy, and spoke sharply to him: "'Why in the [damn]nation, Gen. Marcy,' said he excitedly, 'couldn't the Gen. have known whether a boat would go through that lock, before he spent a million of dollars getting them there? I am no engineer: but it seems to me that if I wished to know whether a boat would go through a hole, or a lock, common sense would teach me to go and measure it. I am almost despairing at these results. Everything seems to fail. The general impression is daily gaining ground that the Gen. does not intend to do anything. By a failure like this we lose all the prestige we gained by the capture of Ft. Donelson. I am grievously disappointed—grievously disappointed and almost in despair.'" When Marcy attempted to defend his son-in-law, Lincoln abruptly dismissed him.[74]

On March 1, Lincoln told Charles Sumner that he would speak plainly to the general. Six days later, while conversing with Mrs. Virginia Fox, he said apropos of a recent visit to McClellan: "There has been an immense quantity of money spent on our army here on the Potomac & there is nothing done—the country & the Congress & every one is anxious & excited about it." Mrs. Fox said she had read accounts of it in the papers and assumed that the administration and the generals knew more about what was needed than did the editors. Lincoln replied: "We won't mention names, & I'll tell you how things are. [Let me] state a proposition to you. Suppose a man whose profession it is to understand military matters is asked how long it will take him & what he requires to accomplish certain things, & when he has had all he asked & the time comes, he does *nothing*."[75]

The public was beginning to regard the Army of the Potomac, whose delays and blunders contrasted sharply with the success of Grant's army in the West, "as a gigantic joke."[76] When some credited McClellan with devising the grand strategy that led to Grant's victory at Fort Donelson, a skeptic mocked the Young Napoleon, sarcastically observing that the "high and dry" canal boats formed "a stupendous and sublime exhibition of his never-can-be-sufficiently-bragged-about strategy! Such is the splendid result of all this fanfaronade that stupid dunderheads have been attempting to cram into the ears of the people about a General who fights all his battles a thousand miles away from fire! Lord, Lord, how this world is given to folly! How old Jack [Falstaff] would laugh at that 'strategy,' which won Donelson by telegraph, when there wasn't a wire within a hundred miles of Donelson, and yet couldn't get a canal boat right under its own nose (old 'strategy's' nose I mean) into the river, after six months' preparation!"[77] Another wag quipped that "McClellan is waiting for the Chinese population of California to increase to such a vast number that they will be able to cross the Rocky Mountains and bring up his right wing, by which time the Russian Possessions and Greenland will have a redundant population, which can be drafted down to the support of the grand left wing of the Union army." Then and only then "the war will commence in earnest!"[78] Chase was warned that the army's delay caused such dissatisfaction that the government would soon find it impossible to borrow money at anything lower than extortionate interest rates.

Disenchantment with McClellan was affecting Lincoln's popularity. Democratic Congressman John Hickman of Pennsylvania told his colleagues that "the country has felt a great lack of confidence" in both the general, and the President.[79] Lincoln seemed ready to fire Little Mac. On March 3, when another Pennsylvania congressman complained that he and other Representatives felt "humiliated at the long siege of the Capital, and the blockade of the Potomac," Lincoln replied that "if Gen. Washington, or Napoleon, or Gen Jackson were in command on the Potomac they would be obliged to move or resign the position." Emphatically, he added that "the army will move, either under General McClellan or some other man and that very soon."[80] Just as a resolution calling on the president to remove McClellan was about to be introduced by Pennsylvania Representative John Covode, word arrived from North Carolina that Burnside had captured New Berne. Since McClellan received some credit for planning that operation, Covode held his fire.

Private Tragedy: The Death of Willie Lincoln

Lincoln's despair over the canal boat fiasco was doubtless intensified by the crushing blow he had sustained a week earlier when his beloved 11-year-old son Willie died. The president described him as "a very gentle & amiable boy."[81] A Springfield friend, the black barber William Florville, wrote Lincoln that he deemed Willie "a Smart boy for his age, So Considerate, So Manly: his Knowledge and good Sence, far exceeding most boys more advanced in years."[82] Others called him a lad "of unusual intelligence" and a "favorite with all who visited the White House." He was exceptionally self-possessed, frank, "studious and intellectual," as well as "sprightly, sweet tempered and mild mannered."[83] Horatio Nelson Taft, father of Willie's best friends in Washington, thought him "an amiable good hearted boy," a "ceaseless talker, ambitious to *know* everything, always asking questions, always busy," one who "had more judgment and foresight than any boy of his age that I have ever known."[84] Taft's daughter Julia praised Willie as "the most lovable boy" of her acquaintance, "bright, sensible, sweet-tempered and gentle mannered."[85] His manners were indeed gracious, as one eminent visitor to the White House discovered when he introduced some of his friends to the lad, who was playing in the driveway. In response, Willie said, pointing to the ground: "Gentlemen, I am very happy to see you. Pray be seated."[86] His tutor in Washington, Alexander Williamson, reported that the youngster "had only to con over once or twice a page of his speller and definer, and the impression became so fixed that he went through without hesitation or blundering, and his other studies in proportion."[87] Willie aspired to be a teacher or clergyman.

In early February, the boy contracted a fever which laid him low and caused his mind to wander so badly that he became delirious. It is not certain exactly what the illness was; it may have been typhoid, smallpox, or tuberculosis. Some suspected that the White House basement promoted disease. The cellar was, according to Stoddard, "perennially overrun with rats, mildew and foul smells" and probably caused "the well-known mortality in the upper part of the building."[88]

At the same time, Willie's younger brother Tad grew sick. For days the president was so attentive to the boys, spending night after night at their bedsides, that he hardly tended to business. On February 18, Edward Bates noted that Lincoln was "nearly worn out, with grief and watching."[89] White House receptions were canceled.

As time passed, Willie became so weak that he resembled a shadow, and on February 20 the disease finally killed him. When he died, his father chokingly announced to the principal White House secretary: "Well, Nicolay, my boy is gone—he is actually gone!" and burst into tears.[90] That day a journalist reported that "it would move the heart of his bitterest political enemy . . . to witness the marked change which grief has wrought upon him."[91] The next morning he appeared "completely prostrated with grief" when speaking with Elihu B. Washburne, who wrote his wife that Lincoln "is one of the most tender-hearted of men and devotedly attached to his children."[92] The president was so grief-stricken that close friends worried about the effect Willie's death would have on him. For the next two days he remained sunk in grief and took little interest in public affairs.

On February 23, Lincoln started to recover. The following day, the Rev. Dr. Phineas D. Gurley conducted a White House funeral that Lincoln had asked Orville H. Browning to arrange. There, as the president stood with his eyes full of tears and his lips aquiver, gazing at his boy's corpse, a look of the utmost grief came over his face, and he exclaimed that Willie "was too good for this earth . . . but then we loved him so. It is hard, hard to have him die!"[93] He said repeatedly, "This is the hardest trial of my life. Why is it? Oh, why is it?"[94] His body shook convulsively as he sobbed and buried his face in his hands. Elizabeth Keckly, Mrs. Lincoln's modiste and close friend, never observed a man so grief-stricken. A woman who attended the funeral complained that it "was in very bad taste, ostentatious & showy." She thought that "one needed only to look at the poor President, bowed over & sobbing audibly to see he had nothing to do with the pageant. The services by Dr Gurley were endlessly long and offensively fulsome. I felt glad that the poor Mother was ill in bed & so escaped the painful infliction."[95]

By the end of February, Lincoln had regained enough strength to resume his duties. D. W. Bartlett noted that he "is frequently called up three and four times in a night to receive important messages from the West. Since his late bereavement he looks sad and care-worn, but is in very good health again."[96] It took a long time for Lincoln to recover completely. On March 6, while attending the funeral of General Frederick W. Lander, he appeared so bereaved as to be scarcely recognizable. "I certainly never saw a more impressive picture of sorrow," an observer recalled. "There seemed to be none of the light of the recent victories in his pale, cadaverous face." As the president descended from his carriage, he hesitated "as if about to stagger back" into it, "and then seemed to collect himself for the duty at hand, with a fatigued air, which seemed to say, 'What will come next?'"[97] Willie died on a Thursday, and for several weeks afterward Lincoln would take time out from work on Thursdays to mourn.

Between the time of Willie's death and his funeral, an applicant for a postmastership barged into the White House clamoring to see the president. When Lincoln emerged from his office inquiring about the commotion, the importunate office seeker demanded an interview, which was granted. Upon learning what his caller wanted, he angrily asked: "When you came to the door here, didn't you see the crepe on it? Didn't you realize that meant somebody must be lying dead in this house?"

"Yes, Mr. Lincoln, I did. But what I wanted to see you about was important."

With some heat, the president exclaimed: "That crepe is hanging there for my son; his dead body at this moment is lying unburied in this house, and you come here, push yourself in with such a request! Couldn't you at least have the decency to wait until after we had buried him?"[98]

Willie's younger brother Tad had also contracted a fever and seemed near death. Dorothea Dix, who called at the White House to express her condolences, detailed a nurse, Rebecca Pomroy, to help tend the sick youngster and his distraught mother. Mrs. Pomroy, who had lost all her family except for one son then serving in the army, tried to console the president by assuring him that thousands of Northerners prayed for Tad every day. "I am glad of that," he replied, then hid his face in his hands and wept. On February 24, just before returning to his office, he looked at his youngest son and told Mrs. Pomroy: "I hope you will pray for him that he may be spared, if it is God's will; and also for me, for I need the prayers of many."[99] The pious nurse explained how faith in God had sustained her through the loss of her husband and two children. Lincoln, who called her "one of the best women I ever knew," arranged to have her surviving son promoted to lieutenant.[100] Her faith may well have strengthened Lincoln's own. Mary Lincoln said that her husband reflected more intently on the ways of God after Willie's death.

A month after the boy's funeral, William O. Stoddard reported that Lincoln had "recovered much of his old equanimity and cheerfulness; and certainly no one who saw his constant and eager application to his arduous duties, would imagine for a moment that the man carried so large a load of private grief, in addition to the cares of a nation."[101]

But some knew it, including LeGrande Cannon, who in May observed Lincoln weep convulsively after reciting the lament of Constance for her dead son from

Shakespeare's *King John*: "And, Father Cardinal, I have heard you say/ That we shall see and know our friends in heaven./ If that be true, I shall see my boy again." He had dreamed of Willie and wanted to believe that he had actually communed with him, though he understood that he did not in reality do so.[102] He once asked an army officer late in the war, "Do you ever find yourself talking with the dead? Since Willie's death I catch myself every day involuntarily talking with him, as if he were with me."[103] On the final day of his life, Lincoln told the First Lady: "We must *both* be more cheerful in the future—between the war & the loss of our darling Willie—we have both, been very miserable."[104]

Like her husband, Mary Lincoln was wracked with grief. To Elihu Washburne she lamented that the White House seemed "like a tomb and that she could not bear to be in it." Willie, she said, "was the favorite child, so good, so obedient, so promising."[105] It certainly made her feel guilty as well as sorrowful, for two weeks earlier she had thrown an elaborate party for hundreds of guests which was deemed "splendid and dazzling," "equally remarkable and brilliant," a "display of elegance and taste and loveliness" unmatched in the history of the White House. But for the Lincolns, their sons' illness cast a pall over the event. Several times that evening, the First Lady climbed the stairs to check on Willie and Tad. She came to regard Willie's death as punishment for her vanity and for her decision to give the party while two of her sons lay sick abed. Months later she described her "crushing bereavement" to a friend: "We have met with so overwhelming an affliction in the death of our beloved Willie a being too precious for earth, that I am so completely unnerved."[106] She wrapped herself so profoundly in mourning that Lincoln one day led her to a window, pointed to an insane asylum in the distance, and said: "Mother, do you see that large white building on the hill yonder? Try and control your grief, or it will drive you mad, and we may have to send you there."[107] Public resentment against her excessive grieving swelled when, for over a year, she forbade the traditional weekly White House Marine Band concerts; as noted earlier, she even refused permission to have them performed in Lafayette Park across the street. (Lincoln had enjoyed those concerts, sometimes requesting "Dixie" after the band had played "Yankee Doodle" and "Hail Columbia.") Mary Lincoln had lost her enthusiasm for entertaining.

The First Lady's eldest sister, Elizabeth Edwards, was summoned from Springfield to help calm her down. Lincoln urged Mrs. Edwards to stay at the White House as long as she possibly could: "you have Such a power & control Such an influence over Mary—Come do Stay and Console me," he implored her.[108] From Washington, she reported that "my presence here, has tended very much to soothe, the excessive grief" of her sister. In her agony, Mary Lincoln was unable to help care for her younger son, Tad, who also ran a dangerous fever. According to Elizabeth, Mary "has been but little with him, being utterly unable to control her feelings."[109]

When a woman friend visited the White House to offer condolences, the First Lady turned on her, asking accusingly: "Madam, why did you not call upon me before my ball? I sent you word I wished to know you."

"Because my country was in grief, as you now are, and I shunned all scenes of gayety."

"I thought so! Those who urged me to that heartless step (alluding to the ball) now ridicule me for it, and not one of them has . . . come, to share my sorrow. *I have had evil counselors!*"[110]

When her sister went back to Illinois, Mrs. Lincoln turned for comfort to her dressmaker, Elizabeth Keckly, a black woman whose only son had been killed in battle the previous year. Mrs. Keckly, who had accepted her own loss stoically, looked askance on the First Lady's manifest inability to control her grief. The seamstress, however, did what she could to console her friend. For additional solace, Mary Lincoln met with spiritualists who could allegedly enable her to communicate with her dead son. On several occasions she held séances at the White House, some of which Lincoln attended. David Davis suspected that the death of Willie would not "be a lesson" to the First Lady, though he hoped that it "may change her notions of life."[111]

With Willie, Lincoln had known the special pleasure that a parent derives from having a child who is a near-clone. The boy's tutor thought that the lad "was the exact counterpart of his father," and the poet and editor Nathaniel P. Willis, a fixture in Mrs. Lincoln's White House circle, agreed that Willie "faithfully resembled his father" in all important respects.[112] A neighbor in Springfield recollected that Willie "was the true picture of Mr. Lincoln, in every way, even to carrying his head slightly inclined toward his left shoulder."[113] So close were they that the president could read Willie's mind. One day at breakfast in the White House, Willie's emotional brother Tad broke out crying because soldiers to whom he had given religious tracts mocked him. When paternal hugs and kisses failed to comfort the boy, Willie set his mind to devise some way to ease Tad's hurt feelings. Willie silently thought for a long while, then suddenly looked up with a smile at his father, who exclaimed: "There! you have it now, my boy, have you not?" Turning to a guest, Lincoln remarked: "I know every step of the process by which that boy arrived at his satisfactory solution of the question before him, as it is by just such slow methods I attain results."[114]

The death of Willie deprived Lincoln of an important source of comfort and relief from his heavy official burdens. The boy was his favorite child. The two were quite close and were frequently observed holding hands. Springfield neighbors said Lincoln "was fonder of that boy than he was of anything else." Bob and Tad took after their mother, and did not resemble Lincoln physically or temperamentally.[115] The president's eldest son, with whom he shared little in common, was attending college in Massachusetts. His youngest son, the hyperactive, effervescent Tad, was not a clone like Willie but much more like his mother. Julia Taft recalled that he "had a quick, fiery temper," was "implacable in his dislikes," but could be "very affectionate when he chose."[116]

In the wake of Willie's death, the president's love for Tad grew stronger as he displaced onto him the powerful feeling he had harbored for the older boy. He explained to a friend that he wished to give Tad "everything he could no longer give Willie."[117] Lincoln derived great comfort from Tad's fun-loving, irrepressible nature and delighted in his common sense. Although Tad suffered from learning disabilities and a speech impediment that made it hard to understand him, his indulgent father was unconcerned, and often said: "Let him run; he has time enough left to learn his letters and get poky."[118] A White House guard thought that Tad was "the best companion Mr. Lincoln ever had—one who always understood him, and whom he always understood."[119] Tad became, to some degree, another Willie for his grief-stricken father. David Davis sympathized with Lincoln and feared that "if he should lose his other son, he would be overwhelmed with sorrow & grief."[120]

Taking Charge: More War Orders

On March 8, Lincoln called McClellan to the White House and evidently spoke plainly to him, as he had told Senator Sumner he would. According to Little Mac, the president said that "it had been represented to him . . . that my plan of campaign . . . was conceived with the traitorous intent of removing its defenders from Washington, and thus giving over to the enemy the capital and the government, thus left defenceless." The general said he leapt up and, "in a manner perhaps not altogether decorous towards the chief magistrate," insisted that Lincoln retract the charge and told him "that I would permit no doubt to be thrown upon my intentions." McClellan then declared he would submit his Chesapeake plan to a vote of his division commanders to demonstrate that he was no traitor.[121] (This account seems implausible, but Lincoln evidently did have sharp words for McClellan about the botched Winchester campaign.)

When the Army of the Potomac's twelve division commanders were polled, eight favored and four opposed McClellan's Urbanna strategy. Among the minority was John G. Barnard, who sensibly objected that the main Confederate army could easily move to the lower Chesapeake from Manassas and thwart the Union advance. Joining Barnard in dissent were Irvin McDowell, Samuel P. Heintzelman, and E. V. Sumner. By a seven-to-five margin, the generals also supported McClellan's intention to ignore the blockade of the lower Potomac. Only two favored an immediate attack on the enemy batteries commanding that river. Later, Stanton acidly remarked, "we saw ten Generals afraid to fight."[122] Lincoln was less critical, saying to them: "I don't care, gentlemen, what plan you have, all I ask is for you to just pitch in!"[123] "Napoleon himself," he added, "could not stand still any longer with such an army."[124]

On March 8, Lincoln issued "General War Order No. 2," stipulating that the Army of the Potomac's dozen divisions be organized into four army corps, to be commanded by three of the dissenting generals plus Erastus Keyes, who had supported the Urbanna plan only if the enemy were first cleared from the banks of the Potomac.[125] (For three months Lincoln had been urged to undertake this reorganization, because it was feared that the army's cumbersome structure made its defeat inevitable.) The next morning, the president reconvened the war council to announce his approval of the Urbanna scheme and urge all the generals "to go in heartily" for it.[126] To a resentful McClellan, Lincoln later explained his reasons for establishing the corps system. He had taken that step "not only on the unanimous opinion of the twelve Generals of Division, but also on the unanimous opinion of every military man I could get an opinion from, and every modern military book, yourself only excepted. Of course, I did not, on my own judgment pretend to understand the subject."[127]

Lincoln issued a third General War Order, stating that the move to the lower Chesapeake must begin by March 18, that sufficient troops must be left behind to protect Washington, and that the blockade of the lower Potomac must be lifted. Finally, plans for the long-delayed advance seemed in place. McClellan would sail his army down the Chesapeake, move swiftly overland to Richmond, and capture the city before Johnston could hasten to its rescue. The jumping-off point for the expedition to Urbanna had come under discussion at a war council two days earlier. Then Lincoln objected to the proposal to launch the armada from Annapolis, arguing that "taking the whole army first to Annapolis, to be embarked in transports, would appear to the extremely sensitive and impatient public opinion very much like a retreat from Washington. It would be impolitic to explain that it was merely a first step by way of the Chesapeake Bay and Fort Monroe towards Richmond." He asked if 50,000, or even 10,000, troops could not be sent directly down the Potomac. Eventually, it was decided to use Alexandria rather than Annapolis as the launch site.[128]

On March 11, Lincoln issued yet another War Order, this time removing McClellan from his position as general-in-chief of all Union armies. At a cabinet meeting that day, the general became the target of sharp criticism. Seward "spoke very bitterly of the imbecility which had characterized the general[']s operations on the upper Potomac."[129] Stanton condemned the army's "great ignorance, negligence and lack of order and subordination—and reckless extravagance." He noted that Little Mac "has caused all reports to be made *to him,* and he reports nothing—and if he have any plans, keeps them to himself." In his diary, Bates wrote that "I think Stanton believes, as I do, that McC. has no plans but is fumbling and plunging in confusion and darkness." The attorney general reiterated his earlier advice that Lincoln "take his constitutional position, and command the commanders—to have no 'General in Chief'—or if he wd. have one, not allow him to be also a genl. *in detail* i.e. not command any particular army."[130] The president said "that though the duty of relieving Gen McClellan was a most painful one, he yet thought he was doing Gen McC. a very great kindness in permitting him to retain command of the Army of the Potomac, and giving him an opportunity to retrieve his errors."[131] Just after McClellan had left for the Peninsula, Lincoln told Samuel Bowles "that though he had relieved him from the general command, in part because he was not satisfied with his course, he had confidence that now he had taken the field at the head of his especial division of the army, he would push forward the campaign as rapidly as possible, and prove worthy of the position."[132]

In that same War Order, Lincoln created a new military district in eastern Tennessee and western Virginia—the Mountain Department—and placed Frémont in charge. Before doing so, the president told a friend of the Pathfinder that the general "has not had fair play—will give it to him."[133] Lincoln had long been assuring Frémont's advocates that the Pathfinder would be given a command when one opened up. Not all Radicals were insisting that this be done. Josiah G. Holland asked George William Curtis: "are we not making more fuss over Gen Frémont than there is any call for? A curse on the politicians! I hate them. I believe in McClellan and Halleck and Burnside and Banks, and excepting the President and Chase I do not believe in anything else but the good God above us all."[134]

Lincoln did not consult with Montgomery Blair, Frémont's bitter enemy, because he knew that the postmaster general would balk, and the president wished to avoid a confrontation. In August 1861, Blair had written Frémont a letter criticizing the administration: "The main difficulty is . . . with Lincoln himself. He is of the whig school, and that brings him naturally not only to incline to the feeble policy of whigs, but to give his confidence to such advisers."[135] To embarrass Blair, the Pathfinder leaked this missive to the press. On March 6, when Blair asked Lincoln to look at it, the president refused, "saying he did not intend to read it as it was never written for that purpose." Blair admitted that it was foolish and apologized: "I regret it most sincerely—but it is due to you to make some amend by resigning my place & explain fully what I meant—& omitted in a hasty private letter—I leave the whole thing to you & will do exactly as you wish."

"Forget it, & never mention or think of it again," Lincoln replied. "I know what you meant for you [were] very frank about your feelings & views at the time[.] Genl Scott was the Old Whiggism you meant—[you] talked plainly enough—But the Old Hero has done his country noble service—& it was natural to trust him—but his vigor is past."[136] Lincoln magnanimously added "that he was too busy to quarrell with him." If Blair did not "show him the letter he would probably never see it."[137] Such forbearance was characteristic of Lincoln. If friends mentioned attacks on him, he would steer the conversation in a different direction or simply remark, "I guess we won't talk about that now."[138]

In 1864, Lincoln explained that "the pressure from the people at the North and Congress . . . forced him into issuing his series of 'Military orders.'"[139] In addition, Frémont and his allies urged the president to bolster the Pathfinder's forces in the Mountain Department. So in late March, over the emphatic objections of some advisors, Lincoln detached General Louis Blenker's division from McClellan and sent it to Frémont. The president told Little Mac "that he knew this thing to be wrong, and . . . that the pressure was only a political one to swell Fremont's command."[140]

Commenting on the president's war orders, the New York *Herald* said "Lincoln holds the reins, and is handling them, as he has handled them from the beginning, with the skill and discretion of an old campaigner."[141] McClellan, however, resented them, even though some accorded with his own views. He had, for instance, planned to organize the divisions into corps after a major battle had revealed his generals' strengths and weaknesses; he had agreed to leave sufficient troops behind to protect the capital; and the March 18 deadline fell within the time frame he had established in his own mind. He did not like the choice of corps commanders, but they were the most senior generals, and army tradition dictated that seniority must be taken seriously.

Suddenly, word arrived that the Confederates had abandoned their entrenchments at both Manassas and Centreville and were heading south toward the Rappahannock. (General Johnston feared an attack, like the one recommended by Lincoln, which his inferior numbers could not withstand.) The incredulous, stupefied McClellan, for unknown reasons, sent 112,000 troops arrayed for battle toward Centreville and Manassas, where he discovered that the artillery which had so intimidated him was the same sort he had earlier feared on Munson's Hill: Quaker cannon (logs painted black).

Once again the general stood embarrassed before the disgusted people of the North, who, according to John Hay, "said a great deal about it and thought a great deal more."[142] Scornfully the president remarked that the gun platforms at Centreville were too flimsy to support real artillery. Members of Congress were enraged. "We shall be the scorn of the world," William Pitt Fessenden fumed. "It is no longer doubtful that Genl. McLellan is utterly unfit for his position," the Maine senator told his cousin. "He has had more than 200,000 fine troops here for five months, supplied with every thing needful, and yet has been held in check, at an expense of three hundred millions by an army of not half his numbers, badly armed & supplied."[143] Treasurer of the U.S. Francis E. Spinner angrily concluded that "McClellan either knew that there were less than 50,000 men opposing his 247,000, and that they were moving three days before he started, or he didn't. If he did know, he must be a traitor, if he didn't he is an incompetent."[144] The Washington bureau chief of the New York *Tribune* asked rhetorically: "How long can the country afford to worship this do-nothing, this moral coward, if not, as some think, traitor?"[145] The spectacle of "an army of 200,000 allowing an enemy encamped within 27 miles, to go quietly away" struck Adam Gurowski as "something like treason."[146]

In executive session on March 14, the senate considered a resolution calling for McClellan's removal. Three days later a congressional delegation visited the White House to urge that a new commander be named for the Army of the Potomac. Senator Fessenden bemoaned Lincoln's failure to dismiss Little Mac: "Every movement has been a failure. And yet the President will keep him in command, and leave our destiny in his hands. I am, at times, almost in despair. Well, it cannot be helped. We went in for a rail-splitter, and we have got one."[147] The New York *Herald* denounced McClellan as a "Quaker general."[148] The Confederates' move, remarked D. W. Bartlett, "disarranges all McClellan's plans, and puts his reputation in a delicate and dangerous position. He can only sustain himself by immediate and decided victories." No one "with the brains of a woodchuck can take a good look at Manassas without feeling certain that McClellan has made a gigantic blunder in submitting all winter to the Potomac blockade."[149] Former Senator Thomas Ewing wrote Lincoln that in Ohio significant "doubts are entertained of McClelland[']s loyalty, and as I think with reason. He commenced his career with unbounded popularity. Our public here bore with his inaction long & patiently—one excuse after another was used and admitted, until at last the retreat of the rebel army from Manassas, with their mighty armaments and munitions of war, without an attempt at prevention have convinced his best friends that he is either false or strangely incompetent. I for myself cannot conceive it possible that that retreat could have been effected without his knowledge— the like was never heard of in the history of the world."[150]

The news saddened and angered Lincoln, who hoped that the Army of the Potomac would win a smashing victory at Manassas. It was not an unreasonable expectation, for if McClellan had moved against Johnston on February 22, as Lincoln had ordered him to, Little Mac might well have routed the enemy. The president interpreted the Confederate withdrawal as a portent that there would be "a hot summer campaign, with the deadly fevers of the south to aid the enemy and to harass and destroy the government forces."[151] Michigan Senator Zachariah Chandler told a fellow Radical that "Old Abe is mad, and the war will now go on."[152]

The president wanted to replace McClellan with a senior officer, Ethan Allen Hitchcock, whom Winfield Scott recommended highly. On March 15, Stanton amazed that 63-year-old general by offering him command of the Army of the Potomac. According to Hitchcock, the war secretary "spoke of the pressure on the President against McClellan, saying that the President and himself had had the greatest difficulty in standing against it." Hitchcock declined on the grounds of poor health.[153]

With Johnston heading toward the Rappahannock, McClellan had to alter his plans, for the Army of the Potomac could not safely land at Urbanna. His fallback location was Fort Monroe at the tip of the Virginia Peninsula, formed by the James and York rivers.

On March 8, the Confederate ironclad ram *Virginia*, better known as the *Merrimack*, further upset McClellan's plans by destroying two Union frigates in Hampton Roads and driving others aground. When word of this naval disaster reached Washington, panic quickly spread. Would that powerful warship sail up the Potomac and destroy the capital and sink McClellan's transports, thus wrecking the planned offensive? On the morning of March 9, Lincoln sent for Gideon Welles, who joined other alarmed cabinet members at the White House. Feeling in need of a professional opinion, Lincoln fetched John A. Dahlgren, commander at the Washington Navy Yard. As they rode back to the White House, the president indicated that he "did not know whether we might not have a visit [from the *Merrimack*] here." Dahlgren was able to provide scant comfort, saying only that "such a thing might be *prevented*, but not met. If the 'Merrimac' entered the river it must be blocked; that was about all which could be done at present." He explained that since the Confederate ironclad drew less than twenty-two feet of water, it could attack Washington or even sail as far as New York, anchor there, "and levy contributions at will." In his diary, Dahlgren noted that "the President was not at all stunned by the news, but was in his usual suggestive mood." The captain felt sorry for Lincoln: "Poor gentleman, how thin and wasted he is!"[154]

Back at the White House, Dahlgren's inability to recommend a way to stop the *Merrimack* intensified the cabinet's anxiety. Stanton was nearly frantic, predicting that the Confederates would destroy the fleet, capture Fort Monroe, and arrive in Washington by nightfall, demolish the Capitol and other public buildings, or perhaps it would steam further north and level New York and Boston or exact tribute from those cities. The panicky secretary of war scurried from room to room, sat down only to leap up after scribbling a bit, then swung his arms about while raving and scolding. He wired instructions to New York that a counterpart to the *Merrimack* be constructed immediately. Welles calmly informed him that the previous night a new Union ironclad, the *Monitor*, had already reached Hampton Roads and would challenge the Confederate behemoth that very day. When Stanton learned that the *Monitor* mounted only two guns, he expressed incredulity and contempt, which only made Lincoln and the others even more nervous. Again and again, the president and the secretary of war strode to the window to see if the *Merrimack* was heading their way. Lincoln was relieved when Welles, contradicting Dahlgren, assured him that the heavily armored Confederate ship drew so much water that she could be effective only in Hampton Roads and the Chesapeake.

Stanton, however, felt no relief. Deepening his gloom was the excitable Montgomery Meigs, who stampeded. "I do not see that any thing can be done," the quartermaster general gloomily announced, unless the *Monitor* were to disable the *Merrimack,* which otherwise might "come up to Washington or go to Annapolis & destroy our transports." The enemy ironclad could also possibly reach New York and "call for the specie for coal for any thing she wants & compel it to be given up by burning the city." Meigs made several suggestions: "Notify the steamers at Annapolis to be ready to run for it—send the transports back into the canal or into some shallow water out of her reach. Notify the authorities at N Y, & Balt[imore] & Boston & Portland to be on the lookout & prepare obstructions. . . . Get steamers ready to run into her[,] the only thing except the Monitor's eleven inch guns that can do her any harm."[155]

With Lincoln's authorization, Stanton, in cooperation with Dahlgren and Meigs, ordered several boats to be loaded with rocks and sunk at Kettle Bottom Shoals to keep the *Merrimack* from reaching Washington. When Welles and Fox protested against this "stone fleet," Lincoln suspended the war secretary's instructions, stipulating that the boats obstruct the channel only if the Confederate ironclad was approaching. The furious Stanton sniffed that Lincoln was under the impression that Fox possessed "the entire amount of knowledge in the naval world."[156] (Months later, when asked about the many idle canal boats lining the Potomac bank near the shoals, Lincoln explained: "Oh, that is Stanton's navy. That is the fleet concerning which he and Mr. Welles became so excited about in my room. Welles was incensed and opposed the scheme, and it seems Neptune [i.e., Welles] was right. Stanton's navy is as useless as the paps of a man to a sucking child. There may be some show to amuse the child, but they are good for nothing for service.")[157]

Lincoln had endorsed the construction of ironclad ships months earlier, when it seemed as if the Confederates would build one. (The French and British fleets already included a few such vessels.) When plans for the unusual craft were presented to him, he remarked: "All I have to say is what the girl said, when she put her foot into the stocking, 'It strikes me there's something in it.'"[158] Work on the *Monitor* had begun in October. Despite its small size, it fought the *Merrimack* to a draw and forced the Confederate behemoth to retreat to its base, where it remained bottled up until the Rebels scuttled it later in the spring, lest it fall into Union hands.

On March 10, Lieutenant Henry A. Wise, who had observed the historic battle at Hampton Roads, described it to the cabinet, emphasizing the bravery of the *Monitor*'s skipper, Lieutenant John L. Worden. When he concluded, Lincoln arose and said: "Well, gentlemen, I am going to shake hands with that man," and proceeded to Wise's house, where Worden lay abed, his scorched eyes covered with bandages.

As he shook Lincoln's hand, the lieutenant remarked: "You do me great honor, Mr. President, and I am only sorry that I can't see you."

Lincoln burst into tears and replied: "No, sir, you have done me and your country honor and I shall promote you. We owe to you, sir, the preservation of our navy. I can not thank you enough." He then "expressed the warmest sympathy with his suffering, and admiration of his bravery and skill."[159] A few days thereafter Welles, on behalf of the president, formally thanked the lieutenant and his crew in a gracious letter.

Two months later, the president—along with Chase, Stanton, General John E. Wool, and others—visited the *Monitor*. This ship's paymaster reported that "Mr. Lincoln had a sad, care worn & anxious look in strong contrast with the gay cortege by which he was surrounded. As the boat which brought the party came alongside every eye sought the *Monitor* but his own. He stood with his face averted as if to hide some disagreeable sight. When he turned to us, I could see his lip quiver & his frame tremble with strong emotion & imagined that the terrible drama in these waters of the ninth [eighth] & tenth [ninth] of March was passing in review before him." He shook hands with the officers, examined the ship closely, and asked to be presented to the crew. The captain objected that they were busy with their chores and not presentable. "That is just as I want to see them, sir," replied the president. Hat in hand, he bowed right and left as he slowly passed between two rows of enlisted sailors.[160]

The Peninsular Campaign Begins

With the *Merrimack* neutralized, the Army of the Potomac set sail for the Peninsula on March 17, one day before Lincoln's deadline. In a good mood, McClellan wrote that the president "*is all right*—he is my strongest friend."[161] But Lincoln harbored grave doubts about the general. On April 2, he told Orville Browning that General Scott "and all the leading military men around him, had always assured him" that McClellan "possessed a very high order of military talent, and that he did not think they could all be mistaken—yet he was not fully satisfied with his conduct of the war—that he was not sufficiently energetic and aggressive in his measures." Lincoln added that he had studied McClellan "and taken his measure as well as he could—that he thought he had the capacity to make arrangements properly for a great conflict, but as the hour for action approached he became nervous and oppressed with the responsibility and hesitated to meet the crisis, but that he had given him peremptory orders to move now, and he must do it."[162]

On April 4, after the first 58,000 Union troops had reached their destination (many more were on the way), McClellan began his march toward Richmond, 75 miles distant. He came to an abrupt halt upon encountering a weakly held Confederate line stretching across the Peninsula from Yorktown to the James River. The flamboyant Confederate commander John Magruder skillfully deployed his 17,000 troops, marching and countermarching them in a successful attempt to fool McClellan into thinking his force was much larger than it actually was. In fact, the Army of the Potomac could easily have swept it away. But the hypercautious Union commander decided to besiege Yorktown, wasting a month in preparation for a massive bombardment. During that interval, Joseph E. Johnston was able to reinforce Magruder; McClellan had squandered a glittering opportunity to advance swiftly to the gates of Richmond. Upon seeing the weakness of Magruder's forces, Johnston remarked:

"No one but McClellan could have hesitated to attack."[163] Lincoln said "there was no reason why he should have been detained a single day at Yorktown, but he waited, and gave the enemy time to gather his forces and strengthen his position."[164]

One excuse McClellan gave for his timidity was the president's decision to withhold Irvin McDowell's corps, which had originally been slated to sail to the Peninsula. Lincoln changed that plan at the last minute when he discovered that Little Mac, in violation of orders, had not left enough men behind to guarantee the safety of Washington. The president was indignant when informed that only 19,022 raw troops were in and around the capital instead of the 40,000 to 50,000 recommended by McClellan's division commanders. Such legerdemain would have justified Little Mac's removal, but Lincoln had no confidence in the other generals of the Army of the Potomac. When notified of the president's action, the Young Napoleon called it "the most infamous thing that history has recorded. . . . The idea of depriving a General of 35,000 troops when actually under fire!"[165] To Lincoln he telegraphed an urgent appeal: "In my deliberate judgement, the success of our cause will be imperilled when it is actually under the fire of the Enemy, and active operations have commenced. Two or three of my Divisions have been under fire of artillery most of the day. I am now of the opinion that I shall have to fight all of the available force of the Rebels, not far from here. Do not force me to do so with diminished numbers."[166] The Young Napoleon grumbled that enemies in Washington, among them Lincoln and Stanton, were conspiring to undermine his offensive and that they were "traitors . . . willing to sacrifice the country & its army for personal spite & personal aims."[167]

When the pro-McClellan press denounced Stanton for sabotaging the general's offensive, Lincoln assured a congressman that the charge was "wholly false, and that nothing had been done that he, the president, did not feel it to be his solemn duty to do, and that he assumed the entire responsibility of the military movements recently made."[168]

Lincoln's decision to withhold McDowell's corps did not in fact compel Little Mac to besiege Yorktown instead of racing up the Peninsula. Even before Lincoln's message arrived, McClellan had already decided not to turn the Confederate forces at Yorktown. To encourage the Young Napoleon to move, Lincoln ordered McDowell to advance overland toward Richmond. Perhaps the spur of competition could galvanize McClellan, who would not want McDowell to have the honor of taking the Confederate capital.

Perhaps, too, word of the battle of Shiloh in Tennessee would stir McClellan to action. On April 6 and 7, the combined forces of Grant and Buell fought an exceptionally bloody battle against Confederates under the gifted Albert Sidney Johnston, who was killed in the fighting. Johnston had at first seemed victorious, catching Grant off guard, but on the second day, Buell's reinforcements allowed the Federals to drive the enemy from the field. Their victory paved the way for the capture of Memphis in June.

In reply to McClellan's pleas, Lincoln wired on April 6: "You now have over one hundred thousand troops, with you. . . . I think you better break the enemies' line from York-town to Warwick River, at once. They will probably use *time*, as advanta-geously as you can."[169] Three days later, disturbed by McClellan's lack of self-confidence, and losing patience with the army's sluggish progress, Lincoln again bluntly implored him to move: "Your despatches complaining that you are not properly sustained, while they do not offend me, do pain me very much." After the Army of the Potomac sailed, "I ascertained that less than twenty thousand unorganized men, without a single field battery, were all you designed to be left for the defence of Washington, and Manassas Junction. . . . This presented, (or would present, when McDowell and Sumner should be gone) a great temptation to the enemy to turn back from the Rappahanock, and sack Washington. My explicit order that Washington should, by the judgment of *all* the commanders of Army corps, be left entirely secure, had been neglected. It was precisely this that drove me to detain McDowell. . . . And now al-low me to ask 'Do you really think I should permit the line from Richmond, *via* Mannassas Junction, to this city to be entirely open, except what resistance could be presented by less than twenty thousand unorganized troops?' This is a question which the country will not allow me to evade. There is a curious mystery about the *number* of the troops now with you. When I telegraphed you on the 6th. saying you had over a hundred thousand with you, I had just obtained from the Secretary of War, a state-ment, taken as he said, from your own returns, making 108,000 then with you, and *en route* to you. You now say you will have but 85,000, when all *en route* to you shall have reached you. How can the discrepancy of 23,000 be accounted for? As to Gen. Wool's command [at Fort Monroe], I understand it is doing for you precisely what a like number of your own would have to do, if that command was away. I suppose the whole force which has gone forward for you, is with you by this time; and if so, I think it is the precise time for you to strike a blow. By delay the enemy will relatively gain upon you—that is, he will gain faster, by *fortifications* and *re-inforcements*, than you can by re-inforcements alone. And, once more let me tell you, it is indispensable to *you* that you strike a blow. *I* am powerless to help this. You will do me the justice to remember I always insisted, that going down the Bay in search of a field, instead of fighting at or near Mannassas, was only shifting, and not surmounting, a difficulty—that we would find the same enemy, and the same, or equal, intrenchments, at either place. The coun-try will not fail to note—is now noting—that the present hesitation to move upon an intrenched enemy, is but the story of Manassas repeated. I beg to assure you that I have never written you, or spoken to you, in greater kindness of feeling than now, nor with a fuller purpose to sustain you, so far as in my most anxious judgment, I consistently can. *But you must act*."[170] On May 1, the president similarly responded to McClellan's request for more artillery: "Your call for Parrott guns from Washington alarms me—chiefly because it argues indefinite procrastination. Is anything to be done?"[171]

Lincoln was understandably puzzled by McClellan's audit of his troops. The general counted only the enlisted men present for duty, whereas the president counted all those being fed and equipped by the War Department, which, in addition to the ones on McClellan's list, included officers, men on sick call, prisoners in the guard-house, and noncombatants. Disingenuously, Little Mac used the latter method of calculation when estimating the size of the enemy forces. In exasperation, the commander-in-chief declared that getting troops to McClellan was like trying to gather fleas in a barn: "the more you shovel them up in the corner the more they get away from you."[172] But he wanted to give McClellan no cause for complaint, so over the objections of Stanton and Generals Ethan Allen Hitchcock, Montgomery C. Meigs, James W. Ripley, and Lorenzo Thomas, Lincoln shipped McClellan two brigades of engineers plus William B. Franklin's division from McDowell's corps, even though the president acknowledged "that the force was not needed by General McClellan."[173] (According to Henry Winter Davis, Stanton "refused to sign the order for Franklin's division to go to McClellan & talked about resigning," whereupon Lincoln "signed the order & told him he could resign or not as he saw fit.")[174] To help replace those units, Lincoln ordered N. P. Banks to send James Shields's division to McDowell. The reassignment of Shields proved to be a blunder, but Lincoln at the time believed that no enemy forces were nearby in the Shenandoah Valley; he also mistakenly thought that Banks had 35,000 troops (including Shields) and could spare a division. As the president explained to Judge Edwards Pierrepont, "McClellan worried me so for more troops that I sent McDowell to him and then weakened Banks to strengthen McDowell. McClellan is all the time writing for more troops."[175]

While Lincoln's confidence in McClellan was badly undermined, popular confidence in the president remained strong. According to Maine Governor Israel Washburn: "our people are faithful, confiding, patriotic—they *do* believe in the President—they trust, honor & love him."[176] After traveling through the Midwest, Hiram Barney reported that the "hearts of the people there are with the President—they speak of him as a gift of God for the times."[177] Henry W. Bellows wrote after visiting Washington that "Uncle Abe is very popular—a shrewd, firm, clear & strong man."[178] The president, Charles A. Dana declared, "is the most popular man & the most confided in, since Washington. Since the death of his boy led Mrs Abe into retirement, there has been nothing to diminish the public trust and attachment."[179] To some commentators, Lincoln's leadership appeared indispensable. William O. Stoddard asked readers of the New York *Examiner:* "Did you ever try to realize the idea of losing our good Chief Magistrate? Perhaps not, but suppose you try, and then look around you in imagination for the man whom you could trust, and whom the people would trust, to take the reins from *his* dead hand. The fact is, that at present the country has entire confidence in no one else."[180]

McClellan did not love, honor, and trust Lincoln; in fact, he deeply resented presidential prodding. After the war, Alexander K. McClure asserted that if the general had "understood and treated Lincoln as his friend, as I know Lincoln was, he could have mastered all his combined enemies."[181] Little Mac said he felt like telling his commander-in-chief that if he wished the Confederate line broken, "he had better come & do it himself."[182]

The Commander-in-Chief Takes Norfolk
and Tries to Bag Stonewall Jackson

Lincoln did indeed feel impelled to visit the army and actually helped direct the capture of Norfolk and the consequent destruction of the *Merrimack*. On May 3, just as

McClellan was finally ready to begin shelling Yorktown, the 56,000-man Confederate army there under Joseph E. Johnston pulled back toward Richmond. Little Mac, who was surprised by that retreat, had made no plans to pursue. On May 5, when some elements of the Army of the Potomac engaged Johnston's rear guard at Williamsburg, they took serious losses (2,230 killed, wounded, or missing); for most of the fight, McClellan was absent from the field.

That same day, eager to infuse some energy into McClellan, to persuade the army and navy to cooperate more effectively, and to launch an offensive against Norfolk, Lincoln sailed for the front, accompanied by Stanton, who had suggested the trip Chase, General Egbert Viele, and several others. McClellan said he was too busy to see the president, thus unwisely forgoing an opportunity to repair his frayed relations with Lincoln.

Upon arriving in Hampton Roads, Lincoln visited the *Vanderbilt*, a huge, powerful ship that Cornelius Vanderbilt had tried to donate to the government in 1861. His offer had been turned down, but after the *Merrimack* made her destructive debut, Lincoln personally reversed the earlier decision; since the vessel was equipped with a ram, he believed that it could single-handedly sink the *Merrimack*.

But in case the *Vanderbilt* could not destroy the Confederate ironclad, Lincoln thought of another way to do so. At Fort Monroe, he consulted with the general in charge of that facility, John E. Wool, and with the chief naval commander in the area, Flag Officer Louis M. Goldsborough. After a bit of sightseeing, he asked General Wool: "Why don't you take Norfolk?" and speculated that "it may be easier taken than the Merrimac; and, once [Norfolk is] in our possession, the Merrimac, too, is captured, not, perhaps, actually, but virtually she is ours."

"Pooh," replied the general, "you don't understand military necessity."[183]

Lincoln, who was convinced that General William B. Franklin could have seized Norfolk when the Army of the Potomac first reached the Peninsula if he had not stayed on shipboard, decided to take charge himself of an effort to capture the city. Upon learning that it was nearly deserted, he resolved to spur the military to take it. He ordered Goldsborough, who was known for "masterly inactivity," to attack Rebel forts commanding the James; they were promptly knocked out of commission.

With those threats removed, the next question was where to land Wool's troops. On May 9, Lincoln, along with Wool, Stanton, and Chase, scouted the south bank of the James. It was his idea, and he directed the reconnaissance. When their ship, the revenue cutter *Miami*, came under enemy fire, Lincoln was told that he should seek safety in another part of the vessel. He replied: "Although I have no feeling of danger myself, perhaps for the benefit of our country, it would be well to step aside."[184] At first, no place seemed ideally suited for a landing. Lincoln nonetheless thought of a plan: "Those old canal boats that I saw near the wharf at the fort do not draw more than a foot of water when they are entirely empty. These may easily be placed in such a position at high water that the ebb tide will leave them—or, rather, the one nearest the shore—entirely dry, while at the outer one, which may be securely anchored, there will be a depth of seven or eight feet—plenty for the numerous fleet of light draughts that we have at our disposal." Bearing this in mind, a spot was selected at Willoughby's

Point, about 8 miles from Norfolk. Union sailors dubbed it "Lincoln's Choice." The president was rowed to shore and inspected the terrain. Upon his return to Fort Monroe, the troops who were assigned to seize the town cheered him enthusiastically.[185] It was determined to launch an assault immediately.

During the night of May 9–10, four regiments were dispatched, but a squabble between two generals about rank hampered their progress. Meanwhile, Lincoln asked Joseph R. Carr why his troops were not participating in the advance. When the colonel explained that General Wool had ordered them to Camp Hamilton, Lincoln vehemently flung down his hat and gave vent to his keen disappointment and disapproval. "Send me some one who can write," he barked. To Wool's aide, he dictated an order that Carr's troops should be dispatched to Norfolk and that the Union forces already underway should press forward swiftly.[186] A Union captain observed the president "rushing about, hollering to someone on the wharf—dressed in a black suit with a very seedy crape on his hat, and hanging over the railing, he looked like some hoosier just starting for home from California, with store clothes and a biled shirt on."[187]

The order was carried out, and Norfolk soon surrendered, though the delays that precipitated Lincoln's hat-throwing allowed the Confederates to destroy shipping and burn the navy yard at Portsmouth. Late at night, Wool returned to announce the good news of the city's capture. Lincoln, sitting on his bed, was amused when the excitable Stanton, clad in a nightshirt, rushed into the stateroom and impulsively hugged Wool, lifting him up in delight. "Look out, Mars!" the president jocularly exclaimed. "If you don't, the General will throw you!" Tongue in cheek, the president suggested that the artist Emanuel Leutze, who was then painting large historical canvases for the Capitol, be commissioned to execute one depicting Stanton's embrace of Wool. Later, the general quipped that he had "not yet recovered from the hug which Stanton gave him, nor will he ever recover from the shock given him by seeing so great a man as Stanton, so exalted a man as the president, in his night-shirt."[188]

Fearing that the *Merrimack* might be captured, the Rebels set it afire and watched it explode spectacularly. On behalf of Lincoln, Stanton formally thanked and congratulated Wool, who was promoted to major general. The president, said the war secretary, ranked the destruction of the *Merrimack* and the occupation of Norfolk "among the most important successes of the present war."[189]

The James River was now accessible to the Union navy, which could theoretically sail up to the docks of Richmond. But when Stanton ordered Goldsborough to do so, that timid captain hesitated, unsuccessfully appealing to the president to rescind the order. Meanwhile, the *Merrimack*'s crew had reinforced Fort Darling on Drewry's Bluff, 90 feet above the river and 7 miles from the Confederate capital. On May 15, when the Union navy finally moved up the James, Rebel artillery on those imposing heights successfully drove it back. If Goldsborough had promptly executed the order that Lincoln seconded, he might not have been repulsed. The president was deeply disappointed. Another naval disappointment was the failure to capture the blockade-runner *Nashville*, which repeatedly eluded the Union fleet off Wilmington, North Carolina. It had recently delivered 60,000 arms to the Rebels. In May, upon learning that it had made its fourth successful run in two months, Lincoln indignantly threatened to call the naval officer in charge of the blockade to account.

Lincoln was also exasperated with McClellan, who had said he was not discouraged by the navy's failure to reach Richmond. Sarcastically, the president remarked to Fox: "I would not be discouraged if they [the Union flotillas] were *all* destroyed. No."[190] Yet Lincoln objected to indirect criticism of Little Mac during a dinner at Wool's headquarters. "I will not hear anything said against Genl McClellan," he insisted; "*it hurts my feelings.*"[191]

On May 11, as Lincoln and his entourage sailed back to Washington, he believed that the Union cause was making as much progress as could reasonably be expected. He took pride in his own handiwork, explaining: "I knew that Saturday night that the next morning the Merrimac would either be in the James river or at the bottom. Mr. Stanton, Commodore Goldsborough and myself had a long conversation on the subject. I knew that, Norfolk in our possession, the Merrimac would have no place to retire to, and therefore I took the step which resulted in the capture of that place. The result proved my figuring correct."[192]

Others shared Lincoln's estimate of his role. The New York *Herald* reported that it was "generally admitted that the President and Secretary Stanton have infused new vigor into both the naval and military operations here."[193] Among those voicing that opinion were an officer on the *Monitor* who remarked that it "is extremely fortunate that the President came down as he did—he seems to have infused new life into everything, even the superannuated old fogies," and Captain Wilson Barstow, who thought that the "attack on Norfolk is entirely due to Abe, who insisted upon its being done at once."[194] The sailors aboard the president's flagship, the *Baltimore,* ascribed the success of the Norfolk campaign to Lincoln's ability to energize it. They also declared that the president was "a trump," and they marveled at the way he seemed so comfortable aboard ship.[195] En route back to Washington, Chase wrote his daughter: "So has ended a brilliant week's campaign of the President; for I think it quite certain that, if he had not come down, Norfolk would still have been in possession of the enemy, and the 'Merrimac' as grim and defiant and as much a terror as ever."[196]

Lincoln's trip to the front revitalized him. He was encouraged not only by the success of the Norfolk campaign but also by several other recent Union triumphs, including the capture of New Orleans in late April. Word of that victory he received gleefully. The previous month, he humorously read a caller a telegram announcing the defeat of Confederate forces at Pea Ridge, Arkansas: "Here's the dispatch. Now, as the showman says, 'Ladies and Gentlemen, this remarkable specimen is the celebrated wild he-goat of the mountings, and he makes the following noise, to wit.'"[197] He also rejoiced at the surrender of Fort Pulaski outside Savannah, Georgia, and at John Pope's capture of both Island No. 10 in the Mississippi and the town of New Madrid, Missouri.

The good news improved Lincoln's appearance as well as his spirits. In late April, it was reported that he "is looking better than he did the day of his inauguration. He has gained steadily in health, strength, and even in weight."[198] Helping to improve his morale were laudatory press notices like an editorial in the *Iowa State Register* which said the recent victories in the field "are due in a great measure to the prescience and sagacity of President Lincoln."[199]

Lincoln's optimism about future prospects was widely shared. Lyman Trumbull predicted that "the rebels will abandon Richmond without any serious battle, when they discover that we are advancing on them with our whole Army of the Potomac." Similarly, the senator expected Confederates in the West would retreat before oncoming Union forces.[200] Sanguine though Lincoln was, he exclaimed to an optimist who predicted that the war would soon be over, "No; we have a big job yet on hand to finish the war!"[201]

While at Fort Monroe, Lincoln wrote McClellan about the reorganization of the army. The general had created two new corps for his favorites, Fitz John Porter and William B. Franklin, and had removed division commander Charles S. Hamilton. The dismissal of Hamilton seemed to the president most unjust, but he could not restore him without deposing McClellan. Ominously Lincoln advised Little Mac that by relieving Hamilton he had "lost the confidence of at least one of your best friends in the Senate." He told McClellan that in Washington, the reorganization "is looked upon as merely an effort to pamper one or two pets, and to persecute and degrade their supposed rivals. I have had no word from [Generals] Sumner, Heintzelman, or Keyes. The commanders of these Corps are of course the three highest officers with you, but I am constantly told that you . . . consult and communicate with nobody but General Fitz John Porter, and perhaps General Franklin. I do not say these complaints are true or just; but at all events it is proper you should know of their existence. Do the Commanders of Corps disobey your orders in any thing?" Lincoln asked rhetorically: "are you strong enough, even with my help—to set your foot upon the necks of Sumner, Heintzelman, and Keyes all at once? This is a practical and very serious question for you. The success of your army and the cause of the country are the same; and of course I only desire the good of the cause."[202]

Lincoln may have considered firing McClellan. According to Senator Henry Wilson, there was "evidence on file in the Department in the President's own hand-writing proving that his visit to Fort Monroe convinced him of the entire incapacity of Gen. McClelland, and that he had made up his mind to remove him, and would have done so in three days had not [Congressman Owen] Lovejoy's unfortunate resolution inspired by Forney, interposed." (Lovejoy's resolution, which passed the House on May 9, praised Little Mac's "high military qualities which secure important results with but little sacrifice of human life.") According to journalist Adams S. Hill, Lincoln stated "that had it not been for Lovejoy's resolution he would have removed McClellan."[203]

In mid-May, McClellan clamored once again for reinforcements, alleging that he had only 80,000 effective troops while the enemy had double that number (a characteristically gross overestimate of Confederate forces). Earlier, when Lincoln offered to send McDowell's corps to him from Fredericksburg with the understanding that McDowell would remain in charge of those troops, Little Mac refused to accept them on those terms. Now he backed down and expressed willingness to take reinforcements under any arrangement, though he wanted them shipped via water. Lincoln agreed to direct McDowell to McClellan, but overland in order to screen Washington.

On May 22–23, Lincoln again visited the troops, this time McDowell's corps at Fredericksburg. Stanton and Dahlgren accompanied him. Since it had been decided to forward those troops to McClellan, the president wanted to expedite that transfer, just as he had facilitated the capture of Norfolk a few days earlier. While proceeding from the landing at Aquia Creek to the general's headquarters, he admired the new railroad bridge across Potomac Creek, an immense structure 400 feet long and 100 feet high, which, he said wonderingly, contained nothing but "beanpoles and corn-stalks." He reviewed the troops and consulted their commander, who declared he could be ready to march south on Sunday the 25th. But Lincoln suggested that he "take a *good ready*" that Sabbath and start out on Monday.[204] While inspecting the troops, he was within view of Confederates across the river who could have shot him. Commented one journalist, "Mr. Lincoln is certainly devoid of personal timidity."[205]

When the president returned to Washington, he became quite agitated by news that on the previous day, May 23, Stonewall Jackson had captured Colonel John R. Kenly, cut his regiment at Front Royal to pieces, routed Nathaniel P. Banks's other forces, and had begun driving them down the Shenandoah Valley toward the Poto-mac. Deeply affected by Colonel Kenly's fate, Lincoln suffered intense anxiety at word of Banks's pell-mell retreat, which resembled the disgraceful flight from the Bull Run battlefield. To Charles Sumner he vividly described how "Banks' men were running & flinging away their arms, routed & demoralized."[206] The Confederates seized so much material that General J. E. B. Stuart deemed Banks the best supply officer in Jackson's corps. George William Curtis voiced the dismay of many North-erners when he exclaimed: "how we have been out Generaled!"[207]

Panic gripped the capital, which seemed in danger of being taken by the enemy. Some residents fled northward. "We have been 'stampeded' all day with news from Gen. Banks' army," Nicolay wrote from the White House. "Only a few minutes ago, a woman came up here from Willards to see me to ascertain if she had not better leave the city as soon as possible."[208]

Lincoln accepted responsibility for the debacle. By sending Shields's division to McDowell, he made Banks's diminished force of 4,000 a tempting target for Jack-son's corps, which was four times as strong. Whenever anyone tried to blame Stanton or others for that fateful decision, Lincoln quickly interjected: "*I* did it!"[209]

Word that Banks had escaped across the Potomac greatly relieved the president. "I then determined to capture his pursuers," to "entrap Jackson in the Valley," he re-called.[210] Boldly directing that effort, he spent long hours at the War Department firing off telegrams. One of them altered McDowell's orders: instead of marching south from the Rappahannock with all his men to join McClellan, he was to send 20,000 of them west to block Jackson's line of retreat. The president told McDowell: "Every thing now depends upon the celerity and vigor of your movement."[211] Mc-Dowell assigned James Shields's division to carry out Lincoln's order. (When told that Shields was crazy, the president said he was reminded "that George III had been told the same of one of his generals, namely, that he was mad. The King replied he wished he would bite his other generals.")[212] Lincoln directed Frémont's 17,000 men to move 30 miles east from Franklin to Harrisonburg on the Valley Turnpike, Jackson's escape route. "Do not lose a minute," Lincoln warned the Pathfinder.[213] He urged McClellan to support that portion of McDowell's corps which was to keep marching south. In addition, the battered remnants of Banks's army were ordered to regroup and pursue Jackson from the north, a directive that they were slow to obey. To prevent the Confederates from entering Maryland, the president sent a force from Baltimore to occupy Harper's Ferry.

With significant help from Stanton, Lincoln was now acting as general-in-chief as well as commander-in-chief. To assist those two civilians, 63-year-old Ethan Allen Hitchcock reluctantly agreed to come out of retirement. On March 15, Lincoln conferred with that general and asked him to serve as an advisor, for the president admitted frankly that he himself "had no military knowledge." (In February, Lincoln had told Governor Richard Yates of Illinois that "he knew but little of military matters" and therefore "he must trust to the Commander in Chief.")[214] The president read Hitchcock an anonymous letter severely condemning McClellan and calling for his removal. That missive, explained Lincoln, gave some indication of the pressure he faced.

Meanwhile in the West, Henry W. Halleck appealed for reinforcements. In response, Lincoln patiently explained his inability to comply. "I beg you," wrote the president on that busy May 24, "to be assured we do the best we can. I mean to cast no blame when I tell you each of our commanders along our line from Richmond to Corinth supposes himself to be confronted by numbers superior to his own. Under this pressure we thinned the line on the upper Potomac until yesterday it was broken, at heavy loss to us, and Gen. Banks put in great peril, out of which he is not yet extricated, and may be actually captured. We need men to repair this breach, and have them not at hand."[215] He advised Halleck to be cautious while approaching Corinth, Mississippi.

To cheer up the badly disappointed McDowell, who regarded the altered plans as a "crushing blow," Lincoln on May 24 told him: "The change was as painful to me as it can possibly be to you or to any one."[216] The next day he wired McDowell's patron, Treasury Secretary Chase, who was visiting the general at Fredericksburg: "I think it not improbable that [Confederate generals Richard] Ewell [Stonewall] Jackson and [Edward] Johnson, are pouring through the gap they made day-before yesterday at Front-Royal, making a dash Northward. It will be a very valuable, and very honorable service for Gen. McDowell to cut them off. I hope he will put all possible energy and speed into the effort."[217]

Between them, Banks, Frémont, and McDowell might be able to block Jackson's retreat. Lincoln knew that the Confederates intended "by constant alarms [to] keep three or four times as many of our troops away from Richmond as his own force amounts to."[218] Even so, he decided to take a gamble: if McDowell, Frémont, and Banks moved quickly and cooperated with each other, their 40,000 combined troops could bag Jackson's 17,000. There was a reasonable chance that the plan would work, if those troops moved quickly.

For the next month, the president continued to supervise Union forces in the Valley. On May 25, he concluded that Jackson's move was "a general and concentrated one," not a feint. Therefore he wired McClellan: "I think the time is near when you must either attack Richmond or give up the job and come to the defence of Washington." After explaining how Banks had been routed by Jackson and was fleeing toward Harper's Ferry, Lincoln assured Little Mac: "If McDowell's force was now beyond our reach, we should be utterly helpless. Apprehension of something like this, and no unwillingness to sustain you, has always been my reason for withholding McDowell's force from you. Please understand this, and do the best you can with the force you have."[219] This message has been misinterpreted as evidence that a panicky Lincoln was thinking defensively, concerned above all with saving Washington. But it was sent the day after he urged McDowell and Frémont to take the offensive and bag Jackson; he did not order them to fall back to defend the capital. Lincoln's telegram to McClellan was designed to prod him into attacking Richmond.

Angered by Frémont's decision to proceed to Banks's relief via Mooresfield, far north of his assigned spot (Harrisonburg), Lincoln caustically remarked that "there are three kinds of animals: there is a horse & a mule & a jackass. A horse when he is broken will obey the *reins* easily, a mule is hard to guide but still you can make him go rightly. But a *jackass* you can't guide *at all*!!"[220] The president complained bitterly about Frémont's failure to obey orders. When it was suggested that the president criticize the Pathfinder in the press, Lincoln replied that he was far too busy to write for newspapers. Impatiently, the president ordered Frémont to Strasburg, south of Harrisonburg on the Valley Turnpike. (In mid-June, Lincoln explained that when he ordered Frémont to Harrisonburg, he had been unaware that the Pathfinder's "supplies had not reached him & that he was not prepared to cross the mountains. If I had known that, if he had so informed me I would have ordered him to rest two days until his stores came & then cross the mountains." To one of Frémont's subordinates he said that the general "should have notified me that he could not go to Harrisonburg by the route I directed.")[221]

On May 28, Lincoln spurred McDowell on: "it is, for you a question of legs. Put in all the speed you can."[222] As McDowell and Frémont converged on Strasburg, it looked as if they might close the pincers on Jackson. But that wily Confederate, driving his men hard, slithered between them and escaped up the Valley, burning bridges behind him to slow down his pursuers. On June 8, he wheeled about and bloodied Frémont in a rear-guard action at Cross Keys. The following day he did the same thing to Shields at Port Republic. Soon thereafter he left the Valley and rejoined Lee unmolested, for Lincoln directed Frémont to stay at Harrisonburg, sent Banks to protect Front Royal, and had Shields return to Fredericksburg.

As the Confederates evaded the trap Lincoln had set, he lamented the failure to bag them. He reportedly "felt certain that Jackson should have been captured, and cannot comprehend the excuses made by the generals who should have taken him."[223] He was especially disappointed in Shields, explaining that if that general "had not drilled his men about so much [and] he had moved in strength to Port Republic & held or destroyed the Bridge Fremont would have destroyed Jackson[']s entire army. Shields drilled his forces along the mountain road South from Front Royal until his forces were 40 miles apart & fearing that the forces of Frémont were also scattered in the race I ordered him to stop at Harrisonburg."[224]

Critics chastised Lincoln for his decision to send part of McDowell's corps to the Valley rather than to McClellan, but his thinking was not unreasonable. Jackson might have been bagged if the amateur Union generals had been more capable and if they had not been plagued with torrential rain at crucial times. Moreover, it is unlikely that the congenitally timid McClellan would have taken Richmond even if he had had all of McDowell's men at his disposal.

Defeat: Lee Whips McClellan

Meanwhile, on May 31 and June 1, McClellan had fought Joseph E. Johnston in a bloody, indecisive battle at Fair Oaks (also known as Seven Pines), five miles from the Confederate capital. During the action, the Rebel commander was wounded and replaced by Robert E. Lee. McClellan, horrified by the severe losses his army sustained, grew increasingly reluctant to assault the enemy directly; now more than ever was he disposed to rely on maneuver and siege operations. Lincoln viewed the fighting "as the last desperate effort of the rebels in which they had thrown their whole strength. Their defeat he regarded as final." It was not.[225]

To help replace the Army of the Potomac's losses, the president gave McClellan control of the Fort Monroe garrison, from which the general promptly summoned nine regiments. In addition, reinforcements from Baltimore and Washington, as well as another division of McDowell's corps from Fredericksburg, were rushed to augment the army on the Peninsula. From North Carolina, 7,000 men of Burnside's division were assigned to McClellan's command. But two divisions of McDowell's corps were left in the Valley to deal with any potential threat from Jackson, whose whereabouts were unknown. Because those units did not join him, the Young Napoleon characteristically complained about lack of support: "Honest A has again fallen into the hands of my enemies," he exclaimed to his wife, "& is no longer a cordial friend of mine!"[226] To be sure, Lincoln had on June 15 told him that he could not forward Shields's division because it "has gotten so terribly out of shape, out at elbows, and out at toes, that it will require a long time to get it in again."[227] But McClellan was well furnished with troops. On April 1 he had 158,419 on his rolls (including McDowell's corps and Blenker's division), and on June 20 he had 156,838. The loss of Blenker and McDowell's 45,000 troops had been made up by the replacements.

As time passed, Lincoln grew impatient to know why the Army of the Potomac remained idle after Fair Oaks. On June 5, Nicolay reported from the White House that "McClellan's extreme caution, or tardiness, or something, is utterly exhaustive of all hope and patience, and leaves one in that feverish apprehension that as something *may* go wrong, something most likely *will* go wrong."[228] The president also objected to McClellan's excessive tenderness in dealing with enemy property, most notably a dwelling near Richmond belonging to Robert E. Lee known as the White House. Before the war, Little Mac had promised Lee that if hostilities broke out, that structure would be protected. On June 16, according to D. W. Bartlett, "Mr. Lincoln 'put his foot down' . . . , declaring that he would break the engagement between the two generals" for, he "said he wasn't bound by any such promise." He ordered that Lee's White House be used as a Union hospital.[229]

On June 18, Lincoln gently prodded McClellan: "I could better dispose of things if I could know about what day you can attack Richmond, and would be glad to be informed, if you think you can inform me with safety."[230] That day the president told Orville H. Browning that he had reluctantly gone along with McClellan's plan only after the division commanders so strongly endorsed it. Now, however, he was convinced that he had been right when he urged that the fight should have been made near Manassas.

Anxious about the fate of McClellan's army, fearful that McDowell might be attacked before he could link up with it, and eager for counsel, Lincoln on June 23 slipped out of Washington to meet with Winfield Scott at West Point. The president, who had recently remarked that Old Fuss and Feathers was "worth all the rest" of the generals, asked about "the present state of the campaign, and the best policy to bring the war to a speedy end." No formal record of their five-hour conversation survives except a memo by the general approving Lincoln's decision to send McDowell's corps to McClellan. According to press reports, Scott offered advice regarding the need to reorganize the army and assured Lincoln that Frémont and Banks's forces were properly deployed. Some speculated that the president was about to remove McClellan, but on his return trip to Washington, he scotched that rumor by telling a crowd at Jersey City that his visit to West Point "was not to make or unmake any generals now in the army."[231] In all likelihood, Lincoln and Scott discussed a plan to unite the corps of Frémont, Banks, and McDowell under one commander, as Chase had recommended.

That new commander of the combined force was to be John Pope, who had been summoned from the West. On June 26, Pope met with Lincoln, who persuaded him to take charge of the newly created Army of Virginia, containing the 45,000 troops in the Shenandoah Valley. Pope hesitated to assume that role, explaining that all three of the major generals in that army—Banks, Shields, and Frémont—outranked him; they and their troops might well be reluctant to follow his lead uncomplainingly. Pope argued that "I should be much in the situation of the strange dog, without even the right to run out of the village."[232]

Frémont resigned his commission in protest and was replaced by Franz Sigel, much to the consternation of abolitionists like Henry T. Cheever, who exclaimed: "How dreadful [are] the new blunders of the President. How shameful [is] the treatment of Fremont." Kentuckians, however, were delighted to see the Pathfinder go.[233] Pope's selection was dictated more by politics than by considerations of military merit. Chase and Stanton pressed Lincoln to name him, for they were tired of McClellan's everlasting delays and suspicious of his political conservatism. They wanted a fighting general to replace the Young Napoleon, and Pope had proved aggressive in the West. The general's outspoken hostility to slavery endeared him to the Radicals. In addition, Stanton wished to embarrass McClellan, whom he had come to despise. The war secretary had been trying to persuade Lincoln to replace Little Mac with Napoleon B. Buford.

Instead of Pope, Lincoln might have chosen Grant, but that general's record was tarnished by the close call he had experienced at the battle of Shiloh in early April.

There he had incautiously allowed his army to be surprised by the Confederates, who almost defeated him before reinforcements from Don Carlos Buell arrived to turn the tide. Lincoln nearly yielded to critics insisting on Grant's removal. "Mr. Washburne," he told the general's patron in Congress, Elihu B. Washburne, "Grant will have to go. I can't stand it any longer. I am annoyed to death by the demands for his removal." When Washburne insisted that such a step "would be an act of injustice to a deserving officer," the president relented, saying: "Well, Washburne, if you insist upon it, I will retain him, but it is particularly hard on me."[234] Gustave Koerner claimed that if it had "not been for the most strenuous efforts of Washburne, who stood very high at Washington, . . . there is no doubt but Grant would have been deprived of his command."[235] Two years later, Washburne told Grant that "when the torrent of obloquy and detraction was rolling over you, and your friends, after the battle of Shiloh, Mr. Lincoln stood like a wall of fire between you and it, uninfluenced by the threats of Congressmen and the demands of insolent cowardice."[236]

Warned that Pope bragged and lied, Lincoln remarked that "a liar might be brave and have skill as an officer." He thought that "Pope had great cunning."[237] Pope's tasks were to shield Washington, defend the Shenandoah Valley, move south up the Valley, and then turn to assault Richmond from the west as McClellan did so from the east. But Lee thwarted that strategy by attacking on the very day of Pope's appointment. The Confederate general had resolved to act boldly in the face of superior forces instead of waiting for McClellan to besiege Richmond. (Lee had managed to scrape together 92,000 troops. McClellan had 115,000 present for duty.) Attack, attack, attack was Lee's motto. In preparation for an offensive, he ordered his cavalry under J. E. B. Stuart to determine the enemy's position. In mid-June, with 1,200 horsemen, Stuart rode completely around the Army of the Potomac, in the process discovering that its right flank was unprotected. With this information, Lee took a gamble, concentrating most of his army north of the Chickahominy River. If McClellan had been at all aggressive, he could have easily brushed aside the remaining Confederate forces south of the river and taken Richmond. In the final week of June, Lee, counting on Little Mac's timidity, launched a series of battles that became known as the Seven Days.

On the eve of that bloody offensive, McClellan desperately appealed to Stanton in an extraordinary telegram: "I incline to think that Jackson will attack my right & rear. The rebel force is stated at 200,000 including Jackson & Beauregard. I shall have to contend against vastly superior odds if these reports be true. But this army will do all in the power of men to hold their position & repulse any attack. I regret my great inferiority in numbers but feel that I am in no way responsible for it as I have not failed to represent repeatedly the necessity of re-inforcements, that this was the decisive point, & that all the available means of the Gov[ernmen]t should be concentrated here. I will do all that a General can do with the splendid army I have the honor to command & if it is destroyed by overwhelming numbers [I] can at least die with it & share its fate. But if the result of the action which will probably occur tomorrow or within a short time is a disaster the responsibility cannot be thrown on my shoulders,—it must rest where it belongs."[238]

On June 26, Lincoln replied to this panicky message, saying it "pains me very much. I give you all I can, and act on the presumption that you will do the best you can with what you have, while you continue, ungenerously I think, to assume that I could give you more if I would. I have omitted and shall omit no opportunity to send you reenforcements whenever I possibly can."[239]

That day Lee began his offensive. McClellan retreated, but instead of returning to his base at White House Landing on the Pamunkey River, he moved south to Harrison's Landing on the James, 35 miles from Richmond, where Union gunboats could fend off pursuers. On June 30, as the fighting raged and news from the front was scarce, Lincoln called at the Patent Office, where D. W. Bartlett saw him with "a peculiar look of pain, anxiety and discouragement on his countenance."[240] In the final battle of the Seven Days, at Malvern Hill, Lee rashly hurled his men against an exceptionally strong Union position from which artillery cut the attackers down; their bodies covered the field like windrows. (The doomed assault grimly foreshadowed George Pickett's charge at Gettysburg one year and two days later.) Instead of following up with a counterattack that might well have allowed him to capture Richmond, McClellan retreated to Harrison's Landing, where he established a new base. In doing so, he abandoned 2,500 wounded men and destroyed tons of precious material. As the bad news poured into Washington, Lincoln summoned Gustavus Fox, an excellent raconteur, whose amusing anecdotes cheered him up.

On June 28, as he was sidling toward the James, McClellan telegraphed once again to Stanton complaining bitterly about the administration's failure to reinforce him: "If we have lost the day we have yet preserved our honor & no one need blush for the Army of the Potomac. I have lost this battle because my force was too small. I again repeat that I am not responsible for this & I say it with the earnestness of a General who feels in his heart the loss of every brave man who has been needlessly sacrificed today. I still hope to retrieve our fortunes, but to do this the Gov[ernmen]t must view the matter in the same earnest light that I do—you must send me very large reinforcements, & send them at once. I shall draw back to this side of Chickahominy & think I can withdraw all our material. Please understand that in this battle we have lost nothing but men & those the best we have. In addition to what I have already said, I only wish to say to the Presdt that I think he is wrong, in regarding me as ungenerous when I said that my force was too weak. I merely reiterated a truth which today has been too plainly proved. . . . If at this instant I could dispose of 10,000 fresh men I could gain the victory tomorrow. I know that a few thousand more men would have changed this battle from a defeat to a victory—as it is, the Gov[ernmen]t must not & cannot hold me responsible for the result. I feel too earnestly to-night—I have seen too many dead & wounded comrades to feel otherwise than that the Gov[ernmen]t has not sustained this Army. If you do not do so now the game is lost." McClellan closed with a remarkably insubordinate blast: "If I save this Army now I tell you plainly that I owe no thanks to you or any other persons in Washington—you have done your best to sacrifice this Army."[241]

Before passing this message on to his boss, the scandalized supervisor of telegraphs in the War Department, Edward S. Sanford, omitted the last two sentences.

Even in its bowdlerized version, that telegram angered Stanton, who took it to Lincoln and said "with much feeling 'You know—Mr President that all I have done was by your authority.'"[242]

Lincoln magnanimously overlooked McClellan's insolence and tried to calm him. "Save your Army at all events," he wired in response to Little Mac's frantic telegram. "Will send re-inforcements as fast as we can. Of course they can not reach you to-day, to-morrow, or next day. I have not said you were ungenerous for saying you needed re-inforcement. I thought you were ungenerous in assuming that I did not send them as fast as I could. I feel any misfortune to you and your Army quite as keenly as you feel it yourself. If you have had a drawn battle, or a repulse, it is the price we pay for the enemy not being in Washington. We protected Washington, and the enemy concentrated on you; had we stripped Washington, he would have been upon us before the troops sent could have got to you. Less than a week ago you notified us that re-inforcements were leaving Richmond to come in front of us. It is the nature of the case, and neither you or the government . . . is to blame."[243]

The president ordered Dix, Burnside, Halleck, Hunter, and Goldsborough to rush to McClellan's assistance. But, as he told the Young Napoleon on July 1, there was little hope that they could make a difference: "It is impossible to re-inforce you for your present emergency. If we had a million of men we could not get them to you in time. We have not the men to send. If you are not strong enough to face the enemy you must find a place of security, and wait, rest, and repair. Maintain your ground if you can; but save the Army at all events, even if you fall back to Fortress-Monroe. We still have strength enough in the country, and will bring it out."[244]

The following day, Lincoln continued to reason with his panicky general: "When you ask for fifty thousand men to be promptly sent you, you surely labor under some gross mistake of fact." He pointed out that all the Union troops east of the Alleghenies (around Washington, in the Shenandoah Valley, at Fort Monroe, and elsewhere) did not number more than 75,000. "Thus, the idea of sending you fifty thousand, or any other considerable force promptly, is simply absurd. If in your frequent mention of responsibility, you have the impression that I blame you for not doing more than you can, please be relieved of such impression. I only beg that in like manner, you will not ask impossibilities of me. If you think you are not strong enough to take Richmond just now, I do not ask you to try just now. Save the Army, material, and personal; and I will strengthen it for the offensive again, as fast as I can."[245]

Despite such sensible advice, McClellan continued to make wildly unrealistic demands: "To accomplish the great task of capturing Richmond & putting an end to this rebellion reinforcements should be sent to me rather much over than much less than 100,000 men. I beg that you will be fully impressed by the magnitude of the crisis in which we are placed."[246] The weary president replied on July 4: "Under these circumstances the defensive, for the present, must be your only care. Save the Army— first, where you *are,* if you can; and secondly, by removal, if you must."[247] The next day, he assured the general that "the heroism and skill of yourself, officers, and men, are, and forever will be appreciated. If you can hold your present position, we shall 'hive' the enemy yet."[248]

Though polite in his correspondence with McClellan, the president felt bitter about the general's demands. When asked the size of the Confederate army, he replied sarcastically: "*Twelve hundred thousand, according to best authority*. . . . no doubt of it. You see, all of our Generals, when they get whipped, say the enemy outnumbers them from three to five to one, and I must believe them. We have four hundred thousand men in the field, and three times four make twelve."[249]

On July 2, Lincoln was relieved to learn from Prince de Joinville of McClellan's staff that the troops had fought well, enjoyed good morale, and were in a strong position, with their flanks covered by gunboats. But as the severity of the defeat became apparent, Lincoln understandably despaired. On July 3, D. W. Bartlett noticed "profound sorrow" in his face.[250] In the wake of the defeat, Bartlett reported, Lincoln "for days and weeks" looked "as if he had no friend on earth."[251] The president told a congressman that "when the Peninsular Campaign terminated suddenly at Harrison's Landing, I was as nearly inconsolable as I could be and live."[252] A White House caller in mid-July said "Mr. Lincoln presented a careworn, anxious appearance."[253] He was especially downcast because he believed that McClellan might have ended the war by seizing Richmond after the fight at Malvern Hill. The president described himself to Bishop Charles Gordon Ames of Illinois as "the loneliest man in America."[254]

To help relieve his gloom, Lincoln resorted to humor. Shortly after the battle of Malvern Hill, when a senator called at the White House, the president said that his visitor's sad face reminded him of a story.

"Mr. President," came the stuffy reply, "this situation is too grave for the telling of anecdotes. I do not care to listen to one."

Riled by those words, Lincoln said: "Senator, do you think that this situation weighs more heavily upon you than it does upon me? If the cause goes against us, not only will the country be lost, but I shall be disgraced to all time. But what would happen if I appeared upon the streets of Washington to-day with such a countenance as yours? The news would spread throughout the country that the President's very demeanor is an admission that defeat is inevitable. And I say to you, sir, that it would be better for you to infuse some cheerfulness into that countenance of yours as you go about upon the streets of Washington."[255] To keep up morale, Lincoln somehow managed to retain his equanimity.

In those trying times, the president and First Lady unostentatiously and unceremoniously visited many Washington hospitals, filled with the wounded veterans of the futile campaign. A journalist, observing the Lincolns at a hospital on July 26, remarked that it "was a scene of sublime interest to witness the President of the Republic taking a few hours from the care and anxieties of official business, to mingle his sympathies with the wounded and brave of our armies, and his wife placing fragrant flowers in their hands."[256] Lincoln's solicitude for the sick and wounded of all ranks endeared him to the troops. One enlisted man told his father, a bitter critic of the administration, that the president had "a *heart* which does *honnor* to the ruler of a christian people." Many "maimed and invalid soldiers in the Hospitals at Washington will ever cherish his name for the words of sympathy & consolation received from him when they wer[e] suffering from their honnored wounds." Lincoln "has alway[s] the same warm hand and ready smile for a *private soldier* as he has for a Major General." Recently, "while he was walking in one of the parks of the city he was approached by a poor invalid soldier who had some petition or other." Instead of brushing him off "as many of our 2d Lieut[enants] and many of our city bugs would have done," Lincoln "sat down on the grass beside the suplient, spoke kindly to him, gave him words of cheer, with a pencil endorsed his petition, and sent him on his way rejoicing." While "that was a simple act," it nevertheless "speaks volumes."[257]

The Northern public despaired. Massachusetts Congressman Henry L. Dawes exclaimed: "Oh the bitterness of the cup we are compelled to drink. With a larger army than the world ever saw before, a more abundant treasury than was ever before poured into the awful maw of war, with a patriotism pervading every soul deep and abiding as his religion, buoyant and enthusiastic as hope, this nation has gone to war with the most infamous and causeless rebellion God ever permitted to exist among a set of men arrogant conceited empty-headed, leading a set of ragged sand-hillers, with no arms they did not steal, no means they did not plunder, no credit they did not have to create, and what has the nation achieved but discomfiture disgrace and ruin. . . . The Administration seems paralyzed."[258] Maine Senator William P. Fessenden fretted that "Seward's vanity & folly & Lincoln's weakness & obstinacy have not yet quite ruined us, but I fear they will."[259] One exasperated Ohioan asked: "Is there any hope that Mr. Lincoln will require that there shall be no more unnecessary delays?"[260] The New York *Evening Post* complained that the president had "trusted too much to his subordinates," with whom he had "not been sufficiently peremptory," and that "his whole administration has been marked by a certain tone of languor and want of earnestness which has not corresponded with the wishes of the people."[261] A consensus emerged that McClellan lacked the talent for his post and that he was a physical and moral coward.

Abolitionists were especially irate. On June 29, Wendell Phillips accused Lincoln of "doing twice as much today to break this Union as [Jefferson] Davis is. We are paying thousands of lives & millions of dollars as penalty for having a *timid & ignorant* President, all the more injurious because *honest*."[262] Samuel J. May, Jr., observed harshly that if the North lost the war, "Lincoln is the criminal" responsible for the failure.[263]

Replenishing the Army: "We Are Coming, Father Abraham, Three Hundred Thousand More"

As McClellan fell back, Lincoln responded to the defeat on the Peninsula by arranging to expand the army. When Seward offered to arouse Northern governors, who would be responsible for raising new legions, the president gave him a strongly worded letter to show them: "What should be done is to hold what we have in the West, open the Mississippi, and, take Chatanooga & East Tennessee, without more [troops]—a reasonable force should, in every event, be kept about Washington for it's protection. Then let the country give us a hundred thousand new troops in the shortest possible time, which added to McClellan, directly or indirectly, will take Richmond, without endangering any other place which we now hold—and will substantially end the war."

He closed with words of iron: "I expect to maintain this contest until successful, or till I die, or am conquered, or my term expires, or Congress or the country forsakes me."[264] This letter was designed to stiffen the resolve of the public. Lincoln also sought to bolster the morale of the army by squelching any signs of defeatism. Upon learning that McClellan's chief of staff, General Randolph B. Marcy, had predicted that the Army of the Potomac might be forced to capitulate, Lincoln became so excited that he summoned him to the White House, where he told the general sternly: "I understand you have used the word 'Capitulate'—that is a word not to be used in connection with our army." Marcy blurted out that he was only talking hypothetically, which relieved Lincoln.[265]

After conferring with Governors Morgan of New York and Curtin of Pennsylvania, Seward recommended that they and their counterparts band together and urge Lincoln to ask them for a fresh levy of 500,000 men. They did so, and in response the president decided to split the difference between that figure and the one he had originally floated. On July 11, he called on the governors for 300,000 new troops.

In Chicago, Joseph Medill accurately predicted that there would "be a feeble response to the late call for 300,000 volunteers to serve under proslavery generals to fight for 'Union and Slavery.'"[266] Plaintively Congressman Dawes asked: "How is the President going to get 300,000 more volunteers, and of what use [would they be] under such leaders if he did?"[267] A colleague of Dawes's from Ohio told Lincoln: "We find it very difficult to get men to enlist here," for "they say they will be put to guarding rebel property or digging ditches in some swamp instead of fighting the enemy."[268] The governor of New Hampshire reported that "our reading, thinking, intelligent, patriotic young men are inquiring with commendable solicitude into the propriety of wasting their strength and energy in daily and nightly watchings of rebel estates and other property, or in keeping accurate and detailed accounts of all such property as is of absolute necessity for their comfort and convenience while prosecuting the war, or in building corduroy roads and bridges in Chickahominy Swamps."[269]

The disappointing response to Lincoln's new appeal led Congress to institute a quasi-draft. On July 17, it passed a Militia Act authorizing the secretary of war to call on states for nine-month militiamen above and beyond the regular three-year recruits. If the quotas were not met, the administration could draft men. The necessity for a draft was obvious to men like George Templeton Strong, who in late July asked rhetorically: "Why in the name of anarchy and ruin doesn't the President order the draft of one million fighting men at once?"[270] The Cincinnati *Commercial* editorialized: "Let us have a draft and that instantly."[271]

To a sympathetic Frenchman, Lincoln explained that the draft was necessary because in America "every soldier is a man of character and must be treated with more consideration than is customary in Europe." Therefore, "our great army for slighter causes than could have prevailed there has dwindled rapidly, bringing the necessity for a new call, earlier than was anticipated." While predicting that the government "shall easily obtain the new levy," he warned that a draft might be resorted to. Strangely enough, he said, "the Government is now pressed to this course by a popular demand," for thousands of men "who wish not to personally enter the service are nevertheless anxious to pay and send substitutes, provided they can have assurance that unwilling persons similarly situated will be compelled to do like wise." Moreover, "volunteers mostly choose to enter newly forming regiments, while drafted men can be sent to fill up the old ones, wherein, man for man, they are quite doubly as valuable."[272] Lincoln hoped that the new men would be added to already existing regiments. He explained that "if he could get 50,000 troops to fill up decimated regiments they would be as effective as 150,000 in new regiments under inexperienced officers," but he added "that so many desired to be officers that it was difficult to get recruits for those regiments which had already their quota of officers."[273]

As Massachusetts prepared to send new regiments of both three-year recruits and nine-months militiamen, problems with a hidebound army paymaster and disbursing officer obstructed the process. When Governor John A. Andrew appealed for federal help in breaking the logjam, Lincoln impatiently replied on August 12 that the governor should tell the responsible officials "that if they do not work quickly I will make quick work with them. In the name of all that is reasonable, how long does it take to pay a couple of Regts? We were never more in need of the arrival of Regts than now—even to-day."[274]

In August, Stanton issued a call for 300,000 militia and warned that a draft would be used if necessary. Despite fierce opposition, particularly among Irish and German immigrants, the governors eventually raised more men than the administration had requested. Helping the recruitment effort was a new song written by a fighting Quaker abolitionist, James S. Gibbons: "We Are Coming, Father Abraham, Three Hundred Thousand More."

Shoveling Fleas Across a Barnyard: Visit to the Front

Now Lincoln had to decide what to do with the Army of the Potomac. Some advisors, including Stanton and Montgomery Meigs, feared that Lee would attack Washington while that army licked its wounds. The quartermaster general urged Lincoln "to withdraw the army from a dangerous & useless position, & use it to defend the free states & as a nucleus for new armies."[275] (Meigs had a tendency to panic. One night, while the army lay at Harrison's Landing, he awakened the president "to urge upon him the immediate flight of the Army from that point—the men to get away on transports & the *horses to be killed* as they c[oul]d not be saved." Lincoln calmed him down and later remarked: "Thus often I who am not a specially brave man have had to sustain the sinking courage of these professional fighters in critical times.")[276]

Fearing that McClellan might surrender the army, Lincoln hurried down to Harrison's Landing to confer with him. Stanton, Assistant Secretary of War Peter H. Watson, and Frank Blair accompanied the president, who wanted to learn whether the army could possibly be starved out while the enemy attacked Washington. Before departing the capital, Lincoln assured congressional supporters that "henceforth the war shall be conducted on war principles." They were persuaded that he had finally "convinced himself of the folly of rose-water warfare."[277]

Upon the president's arrival at Harrison's Landing, the nearby soldiers, quartermasters, and surgeons cheered him repeatedly. McClellan asserted that during a review, he "*had to order* the men to cheer & they did it very feebly," but numerous eyewitness accounts contradict his statement.[278] A New Yorker wrote that McClellan's popularity among the troops "will never measure 1/100th part of Honest Abe's. Such cheers as greeted him never tickled the ears of Napoleon in his palmiest days."[279] Another trooper from the Empire State recalled that "we cheered his presence to the echo."[280] Yet another soldier reported that as Lincoln "rode slowly along the lines, the cheering was most enthusiastic. It evidently gratified and cheered both officers and men to witness this evidence of a lively interest in their welfare and sympathy with them of the President. On his part, he seemed to be much pleased with his reception, and to be satisfied that the Army of the Potomac was yet a living institution."[281] A general remarked "that the visit was worth a reinforcement of ten thousand men."[282] In his diary, a lieutenant described the reaction: "Long and hearty was the applause and welcome which greeted him. His presence after the late disaster . . . seemed to infuse new ardor into the dispirited army."[283] A sailor aboard the *Monitor* thought that the president "seemed to be in better spirits than I supposed he would be. His visit here has been a good thing, serving to give more confidence to the army by his presence among them."[284] Doubtless that was one of Lincoln's aims in visiting the front.

To help achieve that goal, the president scaled the outer line of an artillery battery and made a brief, informal address to the troops: "Be of good cheer; all is well. The country owes you an inextinguishable debt for your services. I am under immeasurable obligations to you. You have, like heroes, endured, and fought, and conquered. Yes, I say conquered; for though apparently checked once you conquered afterwards and secured the position of your choice. You shall be strengthened and rewarded. God bless you all." These remarks were greeted with hearty cheers.[285]

A chaplain observing a review thought that Lincoln cut a ludicrous figure, for it seemed "as though every moment the Presidential limbs would become entangled with those of the horse he rode and both come down together, while his arms were apparently subject to similar mishaps. That arm with which he drew the rein, in its angles and position, resembled the hind leg of a grasshopper—the hand before—the elbow away back over the horse's tail. The removal of his hat before each regiment was also a source of laughter in the style of its execution—the quick trot of the horse making it a feat of some difficulty, while, from the same cause, his hold on it, while off, seemed very precarious." And yet "*the boys* liked him, in fact his popularity in the army is and has been universal. Many of our rulers and leaders fall into odium but all have faith in Lincoln. 'When *he* finds it out,' they say, 'it will be stopped.'"[286] Shortly after the review, a Massachusetts soldier wrote that "Abraham Lincoln has acted the part of a Wise Man. No *one* man in this Country has so many supporters as Old Abe. . . . Let Abraham Lincoln say the *Word*, then let *every man*, wither Abolishionists, Proslaverites, Fanatics, Radicals, Moderates or Conservatives of whatever Party or Distinction, hold up both hands and with one unanimous voice say *Amen*."[287] Lincoln's paternal streak led him to call the troops "my boys." They in turn regarded him as a benevolent father.

But while Lincoln's spirits were buoyed by the army's relatively good condition, they were depressed by a long letter that McClellan handed him upon his arrival. In that remarkable document, which became known as the Harrison's Landing letter, the general insolently and menacingly offered detailed advice about "civil and military policy, covering the whole ground of our national trouble." He acknowledged that the views he expressed "do not strictly relate to the situation of this army, or strictly come within the scope of my official duties."

McClellan presumptuously urged that the war be conducted "upon the highest principles known to Christian civilization," with all the property rights of the Confederates scrupulously protected, including the right to own slaves. "Neither confiscation of property, political executions of persons, territorial organization of States, or forcible abolition of slavery should be contemplated for a moment. . . . Military power should not be allowed to interfere with the relations of servitude, either by supporting or impairing the authority of the master, except for repressing disorder." Such a conservative policy, the general predicted, "would receive the support of almost all truly loyal men" and "would deeply impress the rebel masses and all foreign nations." Ominously, he warned that if his advice were not followed, "the effort to obtain requisite forces will be almost hopeless. A declaration of radical views, especially upon slavery, will rapidly disintegrate our present armies."[288] Here McClellan meddled with policy on slavery almost as blatantly as Frémont, Hunter, and Cameron had done.

It is hard to know how Lincoln felt about McClellan's brazen letter. After receiving it from the general's hand, he read it, thanked its author, and said nothing about it to him. He jestingly told Frank Blair that Little Mac's advice reminded him "of the man who got on a horse, and the horse stuck his hind foot into a stirrup. The man said, 'If you're going to get on I'll get off.'"[289]

Although he could joke about the document, it "struck the President painfully," according to Gideon Welles. Lincoln may have regarded it as a veiled threat to march on Washington and overthrow the government. The navy secretary wrote that within the Army of the Potomac "there was a belief, hardly a design perhaps, among a few of their indiscreet partisans, that these generals, better than the Administration, could prescribe the course of governmental action."[290] McClellan's letter convinced him that the general intended to run for president in 1864.

The Young Napoleon told his wife that Lincoln had probably not profited much from his visit to Harrison's Landing, "for he really seems quite incapable of rising to the height of the merits of the question & the magnitude of the crisis." The general added that "I did not like the Presdt's manner—it seemed that of a man about to do something of which he was much ashamed."[291] To his good friend S. L. M. Barlow, he complained that Lincoln "asked for no explanations, expressed no dissatisfaction—treated me with no confidence, & did not ask my opinion, except in *three* questions—

"1st. 'How many troops have you left?'

"2nd. 'How many did you lose in the late actions?'

"3rd. 'Can you move this Army still further in retreat?'"[292]

Upon returning to the White House, Lincoln seemed to Nicolay "in better spirits" for having "found the army in better condition and more of it than he expected."[293] Lincoln may have been cheered to discover more troops in the Army of the Potomac than he anticipated, but he nevertheless worried about the enormous number of absentees. On July 13, he asked McClellan what had happened to the more than 160,000 men who had been sent to the Peninsula: "When I was with you the other day we made out 86,500 remaining, leaving 73,500 to be accounted for. I believe 23,500, will cover all the killed, wounded and missing in all your battles and skirmishes, leaving 50,000 who have left otherwise. Not more than 5000 of these have died, leaving 45,000 of your Army still alive, and not with it. I believe half, or two thirds of them are fit for duty to-day. Have you any more perfect knowledge of this than I have? If I am right, and you had these men with you, you could go into Richmond in the next three days. How can they be got to you? and how can they be prevented from getting away in such numbers for the future?"[294]

Lincoln's suggestion that McClellan go on the offensive amused the general. "It is so easy," he wrote his wife, "for people to give advice—it costs nothing!" It would be impossible for him with only 75,000 combat-ready men to attack 150,000 to 170,000 entrenched Confederates.[295] When he told Lincoln that, the president gave up hope for a renewed assault on the enemy capital. He predicted to Orville H. Browning that if he could somehow "by magic" send McClellan 100,000 reinforcements, the general "would be in an ecstacy over it, thank him for it, and tell him that he would go to Richmond tomorrow, but that when tomorrow came he would telegraph that he had certain information that the enemy had 400,000 men, and that he could not advance without reinforcements."[296] Sarcastically Lincoln remarked that the general "had so skilfully handled his troops in not getting to Richmond as to retain their confidence."[297]

Lincoln voiced his astonishment and exasperation to others, including some callers who came to the White House on July 11: "I *can't* tell where the men have gone in that army. I have sent there, at one time and another, one hundred and [sixty] thousand men, and I can only find just half that many now. Where *can* they have gone? Burnside accounts to me for every man *he* has taken—so many killed in battle, so many wounded, so many sick in the hospitals, so many absent on furloughs. So does Mitchell. So does Buell, and so others; but I *can't* tell what has become of half the army I've sent down to the Peninsula." When he wondered aloud if many of the missing men would ever come back, he was told by Radical Congressmen John A. Gurley of Ohio and Isaac N. Arnold of Illinois, "You won't get many men in our section unless there be a change." Lincoln rejoined: "And some won't come if there be one." They replied, "We'll give ten for every one that doesn't."[298]

Mea Culpa: Magnanimously Accepting Blame for Defeat

In the wake of defeat, McClellan was roundly criticized. Michigan Senator Zachariah Chandler called the general "an imbecile" and "an *awfull* humbug" who "deserves to be shot."[299] In an attempt to shift blame away from the general, his allies launched a campaign to vilify Stanton. From Philadelphia came rumors of ugly statements justifying the assassination of the war secretary. Edward Everett Hale hoped Lincoln would wring Stanton's neck and throw "his 'impulsive' head out of the window."[300]

Insisting that he himself was responsible, Lincoln absolved Stanton of any blame. In August, he made his mea culpa at a huge war rally in Washington. The atmosphere was electric with anticipation, as artillery salvos and martial music stirred up excitement. Standing on the east side of the Capitol, where he had taken the oath of office seventeen months earlier, he addressed a wildly enthusiastic crowd of 10,000, which expected an inspirational pep talk. Amid all the waving banners and other patriotic hoopla, they greeted the president with several minutes of deafening cheers. Benjamin Brown French, who had helped organize the rally, said he had "never witnessed more enthusiasm than was manifested at his appearance. It shows how he is beloved. He is one of the best men God ever created."[301] Finally Lincoln's sad and solemn expression induced the crowd to quiet down.

The president had not anticipated that he would be asked to speak and did so only when the crowd insisted on it after the first scheduled orator had finished. Modestly, he began by stating that he had little of interest to say that the others on the platform could not better express than he might. "The only thing I think of just now not likely to be better said by some one else, is a matter in which we have heard some other persons blamed for what I did myself. [Voices—"What is it?"] There has been a very wide-spread attempt to have a quarrel between Gen. McClellan and the Secretary of War. Now, I occupy a position that enables me to observe, at least, these two gentlemen are not nearly so deep in the quarrel as some pretending to be their friends. [Cries of "Good."] Gen. McClellan's attitude is such that, in the very selfishness of his nature, he cannot but wish to be successful, and I hope he will—and the Secretary of War is in precisely the same situation. If the military commander in the field cannot be successful, not only the Secretary of War, but myself, for the time being the master of them both, cannot be but failures. [Laughter and applause.] I know Gen. McClellan wishes to be successful, and I know he does not wish it any more than the Secretary of War for him, and both of them together no more than I wish it. [Applause and cries of "Good.'"] Sometimes we have a dispute about how many men Gen. McClellan has had, and those who would disparage him say that he has had a very large number, and those who would disparage the Secretary of War insist that Gen. McClellan has had a very small number. The basis for this is, there is always a wide difference, and on this occasion, perhaps, a wider one, between the grand total on McClellan's rolls and the men actually fit for duty; and those who would disparage him talk of the grand total on paper, and those who would disparage the Secretary of War talk of those at present fit for duty. Gen. McClellan has sometimes asked for things that the Secretary of War did not give him. Gen. McClellan is not to blame for asking for what he wanted and needed, and the Secretary of War is not to blame for not giving when he had none to give. [Applause, laughter, and cries of "Good."] And I say here, as far as I know, the Secretary of War has withheld no one thing at any time in my power to give him. [Wild applause, and a voice, "Give him enough now!"] I have no accusation against him. I believe he is a brave and able man, [applause,] and I stand here, as justice requires me to do, to take upon myself what has been charged upon the Secretary of War, as withholding from him."[302]

Lincoln disappointed some by failing to offer confidence-inspiring rhetoric. The following day an Illinoisan told him: "you ought to take a stronger stand. The nation expects you to. You are looked up to with confidence. Rouse the soul of the people."[303] Others praised Lincoln's impromptu speech extravagantly. Whitelaw Reid called it "remarkable, alike for the courageous assumption of unpopular responsibility, and for the characteristic honesty with which he refrained from boastful promises and stirring declarations that the war should now soon be ended." Reid could think of "no more striking scene" in "all the history of the Republic." Rhetorically he asked: "Was ever the ruler of a great people, in a moment when his personal popularity was so flatteringly brought home to him by his people, known voluntarily to assume, without special necessity therefor, such popular odium as the President honestly sought to transfer from the Secretary [of War] to himself?"[304] Reporters noted that the crowd "was delighted with the manly manner in which the President assumed the whole responsibility in the Stanton-McClellan imbroglio."[305] The Providence *Journal* lauded the president's "straightforward manliness and homely common sense," and Erastus Brooks, a partisan Democratic journalist, wrote that by such "frank confessions, which are often more generous to others than just to himself, the President draws friends around him, and makes many friends of those, who have been warm opponents of his policy, principles and his election."[306] Lincoln's profound magnanimity would continue to win him respect and affection.

27

"The Hour Comes for Dealing with Slavery"
Playing the Last Trump Card
(January–July 1862)

The failure of the Peninsular campaign was a defining moment in the war, for if McClellan had won, his triumph—combined with the many other successes of Union arms that spring, including the capture of New Orleans, Memphis, and Nashville—might well have ended the war with slavery virtually untouched. But in the wake of the Army of the Potomac's significant defeat, Lincoln decided that the peculiar institution must no longer be treated gently. It was time, he thought, to deal with it head-on. As he told the artist Francis B. Carpenter in 1864, "It had got to be midsummer, 1862. Things had gone on from bad to worse, until I felt that we had reached the end of our rope on the plan of operations we had been pursuing; that we had about played our last card, and must change our tactics, or lose the game! I now determined upon the adoption of the emancipation policy."[1] To New York attorney Edwards Pierrepont, Lincoln similarly explained: "It is my last trump card, Judge. If that don't do, we must give up."[2] By playing it, he said he hoped to "win the trick."[3] To pave the way for an emancipation proclamation, Lincoln during the first half of 1862 carefully prepared the public mind with both words and deeds.

Two Steps Forward: Proposal to Abolish Slavery
in the Border States and in Washington

Ever since the fall of Sumter, opponents of slavery had been urging emancipation on the president. Some based their appeals on moral grounds, but many others emphasized practical considerations, like the need to prevent European powers from intervening on behalf of the South. From his diplomatic post in Madrid, Carl Schurz wrote that by emancipating the slaves, Lincoln could best reduce the chances of foreign intervention. When Schurz visited the White House in early 1862, Lincoln expressed agreement: "I cannot imagine that any European power would dare to recognize and aid the Southern Confederacy if it becomes clear that the Confederacy stands for slavery and the Union for freedom." But, the president added, he doubted that public opinion at home "was yet sufficiently prepared" for emancipation. He wanted "to unite, and keep united, all the forces of Northern society and of the Union element in the South, especially the Border States, in the war for the Union." With good reason he feared that "the cry of 'abolition war,'" which an open antislavery policy would elicit, would "tend to disunite those forces and thus weaken the Union cause."[4]

In January 1862, Lincoln voiced similar doubts to abolitionists Moncure Conway and William Henry Channing, who urged him to emancipate the slaves and compensate their masters. (Other abolitionists also supported compensating slaveholders.) "We grow in this direction daily," the president told them, "and I am not without hope that some great thing is to be accomplished. When the hour comes for dealing with slavery, I trust I shall be willing to act, though it costs my life; and, gentlemen, lives *will* be lost."[5] But that hour had not yet arrived. Offering a variation of Shakespeare's dictum that "ripeness is all," he told other militant opponents of slavery that a "man watches his pear-tree day after day, impatient for the ripening of the fruit. Let him attempt to *force* the process, and he may spoil both fruit and tree. But let him patiently *wait*, and the ripe pear at length falls into his lap!"[6]

Lincoln also fended off emancipationists by protesting that he did not cross rivers until reaching them. On January 28, 1862, the New York diarist George Templeton Strong recorded a presidential interview, leaving a valuable record of what Lincoln sounded like in conversation: "Wa-al, that reminds me of a party of Methodist parsons that was travelling in Illinois when I was a boy thar, and had a branch to cross that was pretty bad—ugly to cross, ye know, because the waters was up. And they got considerin' and discussin' how they should git across it, and they talked about it for two hours, and one on 'em thought they had ought to cross one way when they got there, and another [one of them suggested] another way, and they got quarrelin' about it, till at last an old brother put in, and he says, says he, 'Brethren, this here talk ain't no use. I never cross a river until I come to it.'" (In that same interview, Lincoln exclaimed: "me and the Attorney-General's very chicken-hearted!")[7]

On another occasion, Lincoln employed an equally homey story to make his point to an Ohioan who raised the topic of emancipation: "Well, you see, we've got to be mighty cautious how we manage the negro question. If we're not, we shall be like the barber out in Illinois, who was shaving a fellow with a hatchet face and lantern jaws like mine. The barber stuck his finger in his customer's mouth, to make his cheek stick out, but while shaving away he cut through the fellow's cheek and cut off his own finger!"[8]

Emancipationist pressure had grown intense after Lincoln overruled John C. Frémont's proclamation liberating the slaves of disloyal Missourians. In November 1861, the president had responded by trying to get Delaware to accept his plan of gradual, compensated emancipation. That failed. In his annual message the following month, he had suggested to Congress in a rather backhanded way that it endorse a similar plan, coupled with voluntary colonization of the freedmen. That too produced no results, though the lawmakers throughout the winter and spring debated several bills dealing with the confiscation of Confederate property, including slaves.

Some Radicals lost all patience. On March 6, 1862, the Rev. Dr. George B. Cheever exclaimed to a fellow abolitionist: "how black the prospect looks before us!" Cheever feared that "we are under a military pro-slavery despotism, and the President is at length taking the active command, in behalf of slavery and against freedom."[9] When Charles Sumner pressed Lincoln to endorse a gradual emancipation plan, the president replied that the Massachusetts senator was ahead of him "only a month or six weeks."[10] As it turned out, Sumner was three months in front of the president.

At a cabinet meeting in early March, Lincoln proposed to send Congress a plan of gradual emancipation with financial grants to participating states. All approved save Stanton, who objected that Slave States would ignore such a proposal and that the scheme "commits the administration to the theory that this is not a nation, the very theory for which the secessionists are contending with force and arms."[11] Lincoln also showed the message to Sumner, who approved in general but persuaded the president to delete one sentence ("Should the people of the insurgent districts now reject the councils of treason, revive loyal state governments, and again send Senators and Representatives to Congress, they would, at once find themselves at peace with no institution changed, and with their just influence in the councils of the nation fully re-established.")[12] In vain did Montgomery Blair urge Lincoln to include a colonization provision.

Lincoln also read the message to Samuel Gridley Howe of the U.S. Sanitary Commission. On March 5, after a White House interview, Howe expressed puzzlement about the president's hesitation to speak out boldly, for Lincoln obviously regarded slavery as "a great stumbling block in the way of human progress, and especially of this country. He feels that whoever has a hand in its removal will stand out before posterity as a benefactor of his race." Rhetorically Howe asked: "Why in the world, then, does he not 'speak out in meetin' and relieve his mind?" Answering his own question, Howe said: "Simply because of his habit of procrastinating: he puts off and puts off the evil day of effort, and stands shivering with his hand on the string of the shower-bath." But Howe was convinced that the president "has at last had a change of heart, and has set his face steadily Zionward." In fact, Howe predicted that the emancipation message "will prove to be a bomb-shell. If he is not further demoralized by victories, he will be brought up to the scratch."[13]

On March 6, Lincoln submitted the revised proposal in a special message to Congress suggesting that it resolve "that the United States ought to co-operate with any state which may adopt gradual abolishment of slavery, giving to such state pecuniary aid, to be used by such state in it's discretion, to compensate for the inconveniences, public and private, produced by such change of system." (*Abolishment* was a term less likely to raise conservative hackles than *abolition*.) Lincoln justified the recommendation not as an act of moral righteousness but "as one of the most efficient means of self-preservation." If Maryland, Delaware, Missouri, and Kentucky could be induced to abolish slavery on their own initiative, with federal help, then the Confederacy might well despair of winning the war: "The leaders of the existing insurrection entertain the hope that this government will ultimately be forced to acknowledge the independence of some part of the disaffected region, and that all the slave states

North of such part will then say 'the Union, for which we have struggled, being already gone, we now choose to go with the Southern section.' To deprive them of this hope, substantially ends the rebellion; and the initiation of emancipation completely deprives them of it, as to all the states initiating it. The point is not that *all* the states tolerating slavery would very soon, if at all, initiate emancipation; but that, while the offer is equally made to all, the more Northern shall, by such initiation, make it certain to the more Southern, that in no event, will the former ever join the latter, in their proposed confederacy."

Although the federal government would have to pay a large sum to the states, Lincoln argued that the cost would be more than offset by the early termination of the war: "In the mere financial, or pecuniary view, any member of Congress, with the census-tables and Treasury-reports before him, can readily see for himself how very soon the current expenditures of this war would purchase, at fair valuation, all the slaves in any named State." The plan, Lincoln argued, would be constitutional, for under its provisions the federal government "sets up no claim of a right, by federal authority, to interfere with slavery within state limits, referring, as it does, the absolute control of the subject, in each case, to the state and it's people, immediately interested. It is proposed as a matter of perfectly free choice with them." In conclusion, Lincoln hinted that if his plan were not adopted, the war might produce sudden rather than gradual emancipation. If Border State slaveowners wanted to avoid losing the money they had invested in slaves, they should support his plan: "In the annual message last December, I thought fit to say 'The Union must be preserved; and hence all indispensable means must be employed.' I said this, not hastily, but deliberately. War has been made, and continues to be, an indispensable means to this end. A practical re-acknowledgement of the national authority would render the war unnecessary, and it would at once cease. If, however, resistance continues, the war must also continue; and it is impossible to foresee all the incidents, which may attend and all the ruin which may follow it. Such [measures] as may seem indispensable, or may obviously promise great efficiency towards ending the struggle, must and will come."[14]

The idea was not new. In 1825, New York Senator Rufus King had proposed that funds generated by the sale of western lands be used to compensate states that abolished slavery, a suggestion which impressed Chief Justice John Marshall very favorably. Six years later, James Madison endorsed a plan to use public land funds to underwrite colonization.

As Samuel G. Howe had predicted, the message landed in the Capitol "like a bomb-shell," creating a sensation and taking both chambers by surprise. The text was passed from hand to hand by senators, on whom it had an electrifying impact. In the House, where it was read aloud, it generated profound interest and serious discussion.

Some abolitionists and Radicals lauded the message. To Owen Lovejoy it proved that the president was "an anti-slavery man" who "hates human bondage." The Illinois congressman supported the proposal even though it called for gradual rather than immediate emancipation. Lovejoy insisted that "slavery must perish," but he stressed that he did "not mean that it must perish at once necessarily." And though he believed "that the slaves can take care of themselves, and that they should be let alone," he did not "mean to preclude the idea of colonization that is not compulsory."[15] Lydia Maria Child told Horace Greeley that the Radical press missed the "*full* import" of Lincoln's message, which she thought "says plainly enough, [']If the rebels continue to resist, the U.S. govt. must and will resort to emancipation; and, gentlemen of the Border States, I ask you to reflect how much *your* slaves will be worth under those circumstances. Hadn't you better accept of compensation from the U.S. before their market value is gone?'"[16] Moncure D. Conway called Lincoln's message "the insertion of a wedge so neatly as to do credit to the President's knowledge of railsplitting."[17]

Wendell Phillips, who seldom praised Lincoln, also likened the message to "a wedge—a very small wedge, but it is a wedge for all that." Varying the image, he declared that Lincoln "had opened the door of emancipation a foot, and he (Mr. Phillips) with a coach and six, and Wm. Lloyd Garrison for a driver, would drive right through."[18] More emphatically, Phillips told Conway: "Thank God for Old Abe! He hasn't got to Caanan yet but he has set his face Zionward."[19] On March 18, at the president's request, Phillips visited the White House, where Lincoln said that for three months he had labored on his address to Congress "all by himself, [with] no conference with his cabinet." Though the abolitionist spellbinder praised that document, Lincoln evidently did not believe that his guest "valued the message quite enough" and told a story about an Irish toper in the legally-dry state of Maine. Thirsty for alcohol, this son of Erin requested a glass of soda, asking his host: "Couldn't ye put a drop of the crathur in it *unbeknown to meself*?" Just so, said Lincoln, "I've put a good deal of Anti Slavery in it unbeknown to themselves." This was evidently a reference to the Border State congressmen and senators, for he went on to inform Phillips that he had instructed them "not to talk to him about slavery. They loved it & meant it should last—he hated it & meant *it should die*." The president added that "if only men over 50 voted we could abolish slavery. When men are soon to face their God they are Antislavery—it is the *young* who support the system—unfortunately *they* rule too much." Although the Bostonian was frustrated because Lincoln talked "so fast & constantly" during their one-hour interview that "it was hard to get a word in edgewise," nevertheless Phillips "felt *rather encouraged*," and reported that the president "is better than his Congress fellows." Still, though Lincoln seemed a "perfectly honest" magistrate "trying to do what he thought his duty," Phillips condescendingly deemed him "a man of very *slow mind*."[20]

William Lloyd Garrison did not share Phillips's enthusiasm, fearing the message "will prove a 'decoy duck' or 'a red herring,' so as to postpone that decisive action by Congress which we are so desirous of seeing." Noting that thousands of petitions calling for immediate emancipation were flooding Congress, Garrison asked: "Are these to be satisfied by proposing such a will-of-the-wisp as a substitute?" Lincoln, he charged, "is at war with common sense, sound reason, the teachings of history, the instincts and aspirations of human nature, [and] the laws of political economy."[21] Wisconsin Congressman John F. Potter thought the message "does not amount to much," and remarked: "one swallow don't make a summer."[22] Maria Weston Chapman regretted the word "gradual" in Lincoln's message, but she charitably regarded it as "a make-weight, like the word compensation: a couple of sops thrown to the heads of slaveholders. Meanwhile, events are compelling immediatism."[23]

Most Radical Republicans, however, agreed with the New York *Tribune*, which praised "the message of freedom" as "the day-star of a new national dawn" and "one of those few great scriptures that live in history and mark an epoch in the lives of nations and of races." It was, said the editors, "the most important document ever issued from the White House." Enthusiastically, they predicted that March 6 "will yet be celebrated as a day which initiated the Nation's deliverance from the most stupendous wrong, curse and shame of the Nineteenth Century." The president's "admirable and comprehensive" suggestions would "conduce to National integrity and internal peace."[24] Similarly, Charles Sumner thought "it must take its place among the great events of history," and Ralph Waldo Emerson declared that it "marks the happiest day in the political year."[25] To a critic of Lincoln's plan, George William Curtis replied: "I have rather more faith in the President's common-sense and practical wisdom." Deeming Lincoln "*very* wise," Curtis said that his "policy has been to hold the border states. He has held them. Now he makes his next move, and invites emancipation. I think he has the instinct of a statesman: the knowledge of how much is practicable without recoil. From the first he has steadily advanced—and there has been no protest against anything he has said or done. It is easy to say he has done nothing,—until you compare March 6 '61 & '62."[26]

The president's message contained a stern ultimatum. As one journalist noted, "Mr. Lincoln has at last determined to tender peaceable and friendly emancipation to the slaveholders if they will have it, and forcible emancipation if they will not." This reporter thought that "Mr. Lincoln has determined to shake off the Kentucky nightmare and be himself again" now that the Border States seemed unlikely to secede. Many believed that the president "has been reserving this shot for the contingency which had now been brought about and that it was his intention from the beginning, after securing so much ground, to put his views of the incompatibility of slavery and freedom into practical operation."[27] The Chicago *Tribune*'s editors calculated that "the Free States are unanimous in adhering to the emancipation idea" and that "the President has struck the key-note with which full twenty millions of people will accord."[28] In Massachusetts, the Springfield *Republican* called the message "a *coup d'etat*, in fact, displaying much sagacity in its inception, significant in its aim and purpose, and likely to be most important in its effects."[29] An antislavery militant in Connecticut, Elihu Burritt, wrote Lincoln that the "whole civilized world is honoring you with its sincere homage, as the first of all the list of American Presidents that ever had the moral courage to propose a plan for the extinction of Slavery, so just, generous and noble as to be hailed with admiration in both hemispheres. No earthly potentate ought to aspire to a higher glory than that which this magnanimous overture will forever attach to your name."[30]

Moderates joined the chorus of praise. Joseph Holt of Kentucky regarded the proposal as "a means of soothing & reassuring the slave states. It is the first explicit declaration by a republican President that this question belongs wholly to *the people* of the *slave states.*"[31] It "completely squelches the accusation, trumped up for partisan purposes, that the Administration is in favor of emancipation by radical means, and regardless of Constitutional obligations," declared the Cincinnati *Commercial.*[32]

The New York *World* predicted that Lincoln's message "will attach to our cause in Europe an immense party, and help sustain the efforts of our friends in preventing an intervention in our affairs."[33] (In fact the message was believed "to be aimed at foreign opinion," according to Henry W. Bellows.)[34] The Providence *Journal* speculated that the document "will attract more attention in Europe and win for Mr. Lincoln's administration more commendation than any or all the deeds it has done before."[35] In applauding the message, an Ohioan argued that the "time has past for compromise, aggressive measures must be adopted, but mild in character, towards the sacred institution."[36]

As Owen Lovejoy observed, the message "presented ground where all might stand, the conservative and radical."[37] The conservative Boston *Courier,* which rarely spoke well of the administration, hailed the message's "practical benefit toward the great object of restoring the Union."[38] The New York *Herald* thought it "so simple, so just, so profound and comprehensive that we may pronounce it as reaching the final solution and settlement of the most perplexing difficulty in our political system." It was, said the editors, the "heaviest blow which the rebellion has as yet received."[39] Maryland ex-Governor Thomas H. Hicks, a slaveholder, thanked Lincoln for his proposal and lauded its moderation: "The option being left with the States, the offer to provide compensation, when we may be ready to act, is all that any can reasonably ask." Hicks looked on the message as a blow "aimed as much at the ultraists of the North as at the Southern fanatics," and predicted that the "patriotic and Union-loving citizens here and everywhere will stand by you as long as you continue to be conservative."[40] Similarly, the Baltimore *American* remarked that the message dealt "a shrewd blow" to both the abolitionists and "the Cotton Oligarchy."[41] Inside the White House, William O. Stoddard wrote that it "disabled the fanatics by one well directed blow."[42] An Ohioan describing himself as "no abolitionist" exclaimed to Senator John Sherman: "Hurrah for Old Abe! I hope you will pass his Resolution, with a will, and get rid of the nigger & save the Constitution."[43]

The message's style drew mixed reviews. In Cambridge, Charles Eliot Norton called it "an immense move forward in the right direction" but asked rhetorically: "could anything be more feebly put, or more inefficiently written? His style is worse than ever; and though a bad style is not always a mark of bad thought,—it is at least a proof that thought is not as clear as it ought to be."[44] The *National Anti-Slavery Standard* agreed that the message was "very obscurely written."[45] Less unfavorable was *Frank Leslie's Illustrated Newspaper,* which deemed it "sturdy, clumsy, inelegant and characteristic, having none of the sophomoric touches of Mr. Seward" and lacking "the lowest level of platitude by Edward Bates."[46]

Some critics raised practical economic questions. The Cincinnati *Commercial* asked: "Will the people consent to be taxed to the extent required to indemnify the owners of slaves? If they are willing, are they able? Shall the tax be general, or restricted to the free States?"[47] In southern Pennsylvania, where deep-seated Negrophobia prevailed, especially among working men, many Republicans balked at the prospect of higher taxes to free slaves. Indiana Republicans suffered reverses because voters objected to "taxing the people hundreds of millions to pay for negroes to be turned loose to work North at 10 cts a day."[48] An attorney in Peoria snorted: "If any states think they would be better off by setting their niggers free let them do it. . . . When our forefathers in the North saw fit to liberate their slaves, they did it without asking or dreaming of asking any compensation. Why should we now voluntarily offer them a reward for doing the same thing?"[49] Congressional opponents demagogically taunted the administration, saying in effect: "You are exceedingly anxious to take away the property of the Southern people and to tax us in order that emancipation may be effective, but we hear nothing from you about protecting the poor white men and women of the free states."[50]

When the New York *Times* called the plan too expensive, Lincoln asked editor Henry J. Raymond if he had considered "that less than one half-day's cost of this war would pay for all the slaves in Delaware, at four hundred dollars per head?—that eighty-seven days cost of this war would pay for all in Delaware, Maryland, District of Columbia, Kentucky, and Missouri at the same price? Were those states to take the step, do you doubt that it would shorten the war more than eighty-seven days, and thus be an actual saving of expense."[51] Raymond, who was serving in the state legislature at Albany and had not written the editorial mentioned by Lincoln, instructed his newspaper to change its stance. To Lincoln he praised the message as "a masterpiece of practical wisdom and sound policy. It is marked by that plain, self-vindicating common-sense which, with the people, overbears, as it ought, all the abstract speculations of mere theorists and confounds all the schemes of selfish intriguers,—and which, you will permit me to say, has preeminently characterized every act of your Administration. It furnishes a solid, practical, *constitutional* basis for the treatment of this great question, and suggests the only feasible mode I have yet seen of dealing with a problem infinitely more difficult than the suppression of the rebellion."[52]

Complying with Raymond's directive, the *Times* hailed Lincoln's message as one whose "words will echo round the globe. They will recover us the respect once felt for us in the Old World. In dealing with this vexed subject we think he has hit the happy mean upon which all parties in the North and all loyalists in the South can unite."[53] In England, the Liverpool *Post* similarly predicted that the message "will have an incalculable effect in Europe, and that effect will be most favorable to the Northern cause," while the London *Star and Dial* declared that it would secure for Lincoln "the warmest sympathy and admiration of the civilized world."[54]

Congress's response, however, disappointed Lincoln. The leading Radical in the House, Thaddeus Stevens, called the message "about the most diluted, milk-and-water gruel proposition that was ever given to the American nation."[55] (Though Lincoln's friend William M. Dickson also considered the message a "milk & water" document and "a very tame thing," he conceded that it was a "good beginning in the right direction," which might "be a warning and in this respect it may be significant.")[56] On March 9, the president complained to Missouri's Frank Blair that "[s]ince I sent in my message, about the usual amount of calling by the Border State congressmen has taken place; and although they have all been very friendly not one of them has yet said a word to me about it." Kentucky Senator Garrett Davis "has been here three times since; but although he has been very cordial he has never yet opened his mouth on the subject." When Lincoln requested that Blair invite his fellow Border State legislators to the White House for "a frank and direct talk," the congressman objected "that it might be well to wait until the army did something further."

Lincoln disagreed. "That is just the reason why I do not wish to wait," he rejoined. "If we should have successes, they may feel and say, the rebellion is crushed and it matters not whether we do anything about this matter. I want them to consider it and interest themselves in it as an auxiliary means for putting down the rebels. I want to tell them that if they will take hold and do this, the war will cease—there will be no further need of keeping standing armies among them, and that they will get rid of all the troubles incident thereto."[57]

Blair promptly urged Maryland Congressman John W. Crisfield to round up Border State lawmakers for a White House meeting. On March 10, Crisfield and a few members of Congress from Missouri and Kentucky gathered at the Executive Mansion, where Lincoln (according to Crisfield) "disclaimed any intent to injure the interests or wound the sensibilities of the slave States." On the contrary, the president said that "his purpose was to protect the one and respect the other, that we were engaged in a terrible, wasting and tedious war; immense armies were in the field, and must continue in the field as long as the war lasts; that these armies must, of necessity, be brought into contact with slaves in the States we represented, and in other States as they advanced; that slaves would come to the camps, and continual irritation was kept up; that he was constantly annoyed by conflicting and antagonistic complaints; on the one side a certain class complained if the slave was not protected by the army; persons were frequently found, who, participating in these views, acted in a way unfriendly to the slaveholder; on the other hand slaveholders complained that their rights were interfered with, their slaves induced to abscond and [were] protected within the [Union] lines. These complaints were numerous, loud and deep; were a serious annoyance to him and embarrassing to the progress of the war; that it kept alive a spirit hostile to the government in the States we represented; strengthened the hopes of the Confederates that at some day the border States would unite with them, and thus tend to prolong the war, and he was of the opinion, if this resolution should be adopted by Congress and accepted by our States, these causes of irritation and these hopes would be removed, and more would be accomplished towards shortening the war than could be hoped from the greatest victory achieved by Union armies; that he made this proposition in good faith, and desired it to be accepted, if at all, voluntarily and in the same patriotic spirit in which it was made; that emancipation was a subject exclusively under the control of the States, and must be adopted or rejected by each for itself, that he did not claim nor had this government any right to coerce them for that purpose; that such was no part of his purpose in making this proposition, and he wished it to be clearly understood that he did not expect us there to be prepared to give him answer, but he hoped we would take the subject into serious consideration, confer with one another, and then take such course as we felt our duty and the interest of our constituents required of us."

When a Missouri congressman complained that the New York *Tribune* had interpreted Lincoln's proposal "to mean that we must accept gradual emancipation according to the plan suggested, or get something worse," the president replied that "he must not be expected to quarrel with the New York *Tribune* before the right time; he hoped never to have to do it." To Crisfield, who asked what would happen if the Border States rejected the plan, Lincoln said "that he had no designs beyond the action of the States on this particular subject. He should lament their refusal to accept it, but he had no designs beyond their refusal of it." Crisfield added that his constituents felt the administration was coercing them indirectly. Lincoln replied that as long as he remained in office "Maryland had nothing to fear, either for her institutions or her interests, on the points referred to." The congressman asked permission to make this pledge public, but Lincoln demurred, saying "it would force me into a quarrel before the proper time."

To constitutional objections raised by Charles Wickliffe of Kentucky, whom Lincoln described as a "secessionist," he said: "I have considered that, and the proposition now submitted does not encounter any constitutional difficulty. It proposes simply to co-operate with any State, by giving such State pecuniary aid and he thought that the resolution, as proposed by him, would be considered rather as the expression of a sentiment than as involving any constitutional question."

Queried about his own attitude toward slavery, Lincoln "said he did not pretend to disguise his anti-slavery feeling; that he thought it was wrong, and should continue to think so; but that was not the question we had to deal with now. Slavery existed, and that, too, as well by the act of the North as of the South, and in any scheme to get rid of it the North as well as the South was morally bound to do its full and equal share. He thought the institution wrong, and ought never to have existed, but yet he recognized the rights of property which had grown out of it, and would respect those rights as fully as similar rights in any other property; that property can exist and does legally exist. He thought such a law wrong, but the rights of property resulting must be respected; he would get rid of the odious law, not by violating the right, but by encouraging the proposition [made on March 6] and offering inducements to give it up."[58]

Lincoln also appealed to other members of Congress, including California Senator James A. McDougall, who objected to the program's expense. The president replied with an argument like the one he had made to Henry J. Raymond. To illustrate the practicality of his plan, he suggested a possible example of how it might be financed: "Suppose, for instance, a State devises and adopts a system by which the institution absolutely ceases therein by a named day—say January 1st 1882. Then, let the sum to be paid to such State by the United States, be ascertained by taking from the Census of 1860 the number of slaves within the state, and multiplying that number by four hundred,—the United States to pay such sum to the state in twenty equal annual instalments, in six per cent: bonds of the United States. The sum thus given, as to *time* and *manner*, I think would not be half as onerous, as would be an equal sum raised *now*, for the indefinite prosecution of the war."[59]

Lincoln was somewhat pessimistic about his plan's chances for success. As he explained to Carl Schurz, he "was not altogether without hope" that it would be accepted by at least some of the Border States. If they all rejected it, then "theirs was the responsibility."[60]

As Lincoln feared, the Border State delegations found his arguments unpersuasive. They balked at the meager sum to be paid for slaves, raised constitutional objections, predicted that a race war would ensue, and warned that Lincoln's scheme would cause taxes to skyrocket. They also protested that their economies would be ruined and that, if adopted, the plan would make life harder for Unionists in Virginia and Tennessee. (A Missouri Unionist regretted that Lincoln, whom he regarded as "a good & honest man," had become "a monomaniac" on the slavery issue.)[61] On March 11, D. W. Bartlett, after observing the congressional debates in which these objections were made, remarked that it "is certainly astonishing with what tenacity the border state men cling" to slavery. Prophetically, he speculated that the "whole scheme will prove a failure, for no border state unless it be Delaware will accept the offer."[62] John W. Forney found their opposition "inexplicable," for they failed to "see that, while the ultra Republicans swallowed the President's theory with reluctance, the sentiment which actuated it was a sentiment of devoted attachment" to the Border State men.[63] The Louisville *Journal* warned that Border State intransigence would drive Lincoln into the arms of the Radicals.

On March 12, the Border State delegations held a caucus at which they angrily rejected emancipation, "whether coated with sugar or gunpowder."[64] The efforts of George Fisher of Delaware, Horace Maynard of Tennessee, Samuel L. Casey of Kentucky, and John W. Noell of Missouri proved unavailing. With evident disgust, Fisher reported that most of the caucus members opposed the liberation of any slaves whatsoever. The proslavery spokesmen were more deeply committed, more earnest, more energetic, and more determined than Fisher and his few allies. (Simultaneously, a Kentucky lawmaker moved to suspend the rules of the state legislature in order to propose that any advocate of emancipation in the commonwealth, or any sympathizer with abolition, be "disfranchised for life." The motion to suspend, supported by forty-eight legislators and opposed by twenty-nine, failed because it did not quite win the necessary two-thirds vote.)[65] Congress nevertheless passed Lincoln's resolution by wide margins: 88 to 31 in the House, 32 to 10 in the senate.

Lincoln thanked Horace Greeley for his paper's approval of the emancipation plan and suggested that "as the North are already for the measure, we should urge it *persuasively,* and not *menacingly,* upon the South." The place to start might well be Washington, D.C. There slavery could be abolished constitutionally, for the federal government controlled the District of Columbia. Lincoln, however, told Greeley: "I am a little uneasy about the abolishment of slavery in this District, not but I would be glad to see it abolished, but as to the time and manner of doing it. If some one or more of the border-states would move fast, I should greatly prefer it; but if this can not be in a reasonable time, I would like the bill [abolishing slavery in the District] to have the three main features—gradual—compensation—and vote of the people—I do not talk to members of congress on the subject, except when they ask me."[66] Greeley offered to endorse emancipation in the District with Lincoln's provisos.

Some congressmen and senators favored a more radical approach, for constituents were pressing them to rid the capital of slavery on both moral and pragmatic grounds. Former Representative Jacob Brinkerhoff of Ohio optimistically predicted that if the emancipation bill passed, "Washington will soon become a northern city, and a radiating center for the dissemination of northern ideas."[67] In December 1861, Massachusetts Senator Henry Wilson had introduced a bill abolishing slavery in the District immediately and providing compensation for slaveowners. Four months later, the lawmakers heatedly debated the measure, adding a provision for voluntary colonization to be funded by Congress.

Maryland Unionists denounced the statute as "an act of bad faith on the part of Congress toward our State."[68] The state's former governor and future senator Thomas H. Hicks opposed the bill. When Maryland Congressman John A. Crisfield called at the White House to protest against the legislation, Lincoln "said he greatly objected to the time, and terms of the bill, and saw the trouble it would cause, and would gladly have avoided any action upon it," but "he also saw the troubles to arise on its rejection." He "could not say it was unconstitutional, and he had come to the conclusion, after full consideration of all the pros & cons, that he would do less mischief by approving than by rejecting it; and he hoped that the people of Maryland, would see the difficulties of his position, and treat him with forbearance." Crisfield told his wife that he was "really sympathetic" with the president, who was "surrounded with immense difficulties."[69]

After the bill was adopted, Lincoln expressed to Orville H. Browning his regret that it "had been passed in its present form—that it should have been for gradual emancipation—that now families would at once be deprived of cooks, stable boys &c and they of their protectors without any provision for them." He delayed signing the bill in order to allow Kentucky Congressman Charles Wickliffe time to remove two sick slaves who, in the president's view, "would not be benefitted by freedom."[70]

Lincoln's March 6 message recommending compensated emancipation helped pave the way for the bill's passage. Four days after that bombshell exploded at the Capitol, the *National Anti-Slavery Standard* reported that "several members who before it was delivered were on the fence have since leaped headlong over on the emancipation side." The "hint at the close of his message, that a time *may* come when a decree of emancipation must be made, has worked wonders in Congress. Men who, a week ago, looked with horror upon any proposition to touch slavery in any manner, begin to shift position." Such men "are the suitors for Executive favor—men who must be with the Administration, and sleep under the wing of the Executive, or die."[71]

On April 16, Lincoln signed the legislation and explained his concerns to the lawmakers: "I have never doubted the constitutional authority of congress to abolish slavery in this District; and I have ever desired to see the national capital freed from the institution in some satisfactory way. Hence there has never been, in my mind, any question upon the subject, except the one of expediency, arising in view of all the circumstances. If there be matters within and about this act, which might have taken a course or shape, more satisfactory to my jud[g]ment, I do not attempt to specify them. I am gratified that the two principles of compensation, and colonization, are both recognized, and practically applied in the act."[72] Unlike the bill he had framed in 1849 abolishing slavery in the District, this statute did not allow the District's voters to express their views, nor did it make emancipation gradual. Referring to his earlier measure, he told a friend: "Little did I dream in 1849, when I proposed to abolish slavery at this capital, and could scarcely get a hearing for the proposition, that it would be so soon accomplished."[73] In his 1858 debates with Stephen A. Douglas, Lincoln had declared that he "would be exceedingly glad to see Congress abolish slavery in the District of Columbia, and, in the language of Henry Clay, 'sweep from our Capital that foul blot upon our nation.'"[74]

Washington blacks were jubilant, especially those who had been hiding out for days, fearing that their owners might remove them from the District in anticipation of Lincoln's action. At Cooper Union, the preacher-colonizationist Henry Highland Garnet proposed to a group of fellow blacks who were celebrating the statute that they give "three cheers for the Union, the President, and old John Brown."[75] Alluding to Proverbs 14:34, Frederick Douglass hailed the new law as "that first great step towards that righteousness which exalts a nation." The New York *Anglo-African* said: "Americans abroad can now hold up their heads when interrogated as to what the Federal Government is fighting for, and answer, 'There, look at our capital and see what we have fought for.'" The president's action "marks the grandest revolution of the ages, a revolution from barbarism to civilization" and among blacks won for him a "confidence and admiration . . . such as no man has enjoyed in the present era"[76]

White abolitionists loudly sang the law's praises. Henry Ward Beecher declared that it "is worth living for a lifetime to see the capital of our government redeemed from the stigma and shame of being a slave mart. . . . we have found by experience that though Abraham Lincoln is sure, he is slow; and that though he is slow, he is sure!"[77] Lydia Maria Child thought "it is *some* thing to get slavery abolished in ten miles square, after thirty years of arguing, remonstrating, and petitioning," although the amount of territory liberated was "not much." She predicted that the "*effect* it will produce is of more importance than the act itself." As for the president, she was "inclined to think that 'old Abe' *means* about right, only he has a hide-bound soul."[78] Even the *National Anti-Slavery Standard,* which freely admitted that it had "not been overswift" to "acknowledge the sagacity of the President," now said he "has shown himself a resolute and a wise man" with his "face set Zionward and a disposition to press forward in that direction."[79]

Most Radicals thought that Lincoln's approval of the bill represented "the turning-point in the policy of the Administration upon the slavery question."[80] Indiana Congressman George W. Julian rejoiced that the "current is setting in the right direction."[81] Passage of the bill, said Charles Eliot Norton, "has a significance far deeper than is contained in the mere fact of freeing a few thousand negroes. The first step toward general freedom has been taken, and certainly in this case it is le premier pas qui coute."[82]

Some Radicals were less enthusiastic, believing that "the butter is spread on rather thin."[83] The eccentric Parker Pillsbury, whose "fretful, narrow spirit" disturbed fellow abolitionists, "said he dreaded to give way to any rejoicing, for he had noticed that any *good* thing in the Government was quite sure to be followed by some extraordinary baseness!"[84] Illinois Congressman Owen Lovejoy, a self-described "old and ultra abolitionist," demurred. With an apt image, he defended Lincoln as an "Executive rail-splitter" who "understands his business." The president knew full well "that the thin end of the wedge must first enter the wood." By signing the emancipation bill, he had "taken the Abolition wedge, and struck it into the log of Slavery and now the heavy mall of Abolition must let the blows fall till it is driven to the head, and the log riven in twain." But, Lovejoy cautioned, "in very ugly and cross-grained, or frozen wood, the blows have to be a little easy at first, or the wedge flies out." Echoing Lincoln's belief, the congressman added that it was "not worthwhile to strike so hard as to have a rebound, for that would retard the work in the long run."[85]

Midwestern Republicans hailed the new law joyfully. "*The world does move!*" exclaimed a happy Ohioan. "Congress has begun in the right place."[86] People in western Illinois felt "like shouting glory" to celebrate the news "that we have at last got a clean nest for the American Eagle." One Sucker praised Lincoln for having "the discretion of Washington & the firmness of Andrew Jackson." Initially, "we thought the pro Slavery influence about him would kill him—now we perceive his wisdom in making *haste slowly*."[87]

Even the London *Times*, which generally took a dim view of the Lincoln administration, praised the law extravagantly. The "Thunderer" predicted that April 16, 1862, would "stand in American history as the greatest day since that of signing the Declaration of Independence—the day of this century which will be honored through all time."[88] With similar hyperbole, Wall Street lawyer George Templeton Strong asked rhetorically, "Has any President, since this country came into being, done so weighty an act?" Strong rejoiced that the "federal government is now clear of all connection with slaveholding."[89]

Conservatives in Congress, however, were gravely disappointed. Democrats sneered that the "inevitable consequence must be a very great influx of fugitive negroes, and drain on the pockets of the philanthropic, besides calling for government assistance."[90] The Chicago *Times* predicted that the bill, along with Lincoln's compensated emancipation scheme, "will prolong the rebellion" and "make eventual adjustment a thousand times more difficult."[91] That paper's Washington correspondent remarked: "Negrophobia has seized the entire party of the Administration; they have nigger on the brain, nigger in the bowels, nigger in the eyes, nigger, nigger, everywhere."[92]

When told that the Maryland congressional delegation would protest that their constituents' slaves might escape to Washington, Lincoln remarked: "Well, I shall say to them, 'I am engaged in putting down a great rebellion, in which I can only succeed by the help of the North, which will not tolerate my returning your slaves, and I cannot try experiments. You cannot have them.'"[93] In fact, slave masters did complain to Maryland Governor Augustus W. Bradford about bondsmen fleeing to the capital. In May, the governor called on Lincoln, who was busy, but from

Congressman Crisfield he learned that Marshal Lamon was helping to return fugitives to their owners.

Lincoln appointed Daniel R. Goodloe, Horatio King, and Samuel F. Vinton as commissioners to appraise the monetary value of each slave in the District. He explained to them "that he had chosen Mr Goodloe as representing the 'black Republican' party, Mr Vinton, *his* old Whig party, and Mr King the democratic party."[94] When some Republican senators objected to King, who had served in Buchanan's cabinet, the president met with them at the Capitol on April 26. King and the others were soon confirmed, and over the next few months authorized compensation for 2,989 slaves.

One Step Backward: Revoking Hunter's Abolition Decree

While Lincoln was willing to sign what he regarded as an imperfect emancipation measure for the District, he would not condone formal emancipation by military commanders in the field. Just as he had overruled Frémont's proclamation in September 1861, so, too, he struck down General David Hunter's similar decree in the spring of 1862. On May 9, Hunter, in charge of the Department of the South (consisting primarily of the Sea Islands off the coast of Georgia, Florida, and South Carolina), cited military necessity as a justification for liberating slaves there. Two days later, he pressed hundreds of them into military service and gave them weapons, prompting Border State delegations to demand that Lincoln repudiate Hunter's action. From the North, Lincoln received heated protests, including one from a New Yorker who warned that if "General Hunter's proclamation declairing the slaves of his department forever free, is not disowned by the administration and himself disgraced, I will place my whole property to the value of three millions, in the hands of the rebels for the use of the traitor Jeff Davis and his base ends[.] This act has done us more harm than a loss of two battles and has made Kentucky & Maryland almost against us, if not wholly."[95] Reverdy Johnson of Maryland pleaded with Lincoln to overrule Hunter and recall the general: "Unless promptly corrected, it will serve the rebels, more than a dozen victories." Though he insisted that he was devoted to the Union cause, Johnson said he regarded "the policy thus inaugurated, if to be followed, as fatal to all our hopes."[96] Another Marylander, the former congressman and future Radical *bête noire* of the Lincoln administration, Henry Winter Davis, called Hunter's proclamation "an outrage," "unmilitary, unrepublican & insubordinate & wholly incapable of giving liberty in fact to a single slave who could not himself take it. A proclamation of emancipation over three States by a commander who hangs on by his fingernails to the coast under cover of . . . gun boats is a little ludicrous!!"[97] A Philadelphian recommended that Lincoln should turn the tables on proclamation-prone generals by forbidding the issuance of any such documents contradicting administration policy. The president may well have been tempted to do so, for he exclaimed in frustration: "No matter what I do—I am troubled every day with the rash and unexpected acts of my officers!"[98]

Some Republicans maintained that Hunter had acted within the scope of his authority as a department commander; that the slaves freed by his order could not in good conscience be re-enslaved; and that the order would eliminate all possibility of European powers' intervention on behalf of the Confederacy. Chase urged Lincoln to support Hunter, alleging that it was "of the highest importance, whether our relations at home or abroad be considered, that this order be not revoked. . . . It will be cordially approved, I assume, by more than nine tenths of the people on whom you must rely for support of your Administration."[99] The president, who "expressed great indignation" at Hunter's action, curtly replied: "No commanding general shall do such a thing, upon *my* responsibility, without consulting me."[100] He explained that Hunter "was specially enjoined not to meddle with matters political" and had been forbidden to issue proclamations.[101] Though Stanton approved of Hunter's act, he deplored his lack of discretion: "Damn him, why didn't he do it and say nothing about it."[102] Similarly, Lincoln remarked that he wished the general "to *do* it, not say it."[103]

At first, Lincoln hesitated to overrule Hunter, lest European powers conclude that the North was simply waging a war of conquest which civilized nations might feel compelled to halt. But on May 19, he formally revoked Hunter's order, surprising many Republican allies. The president averred that "the government of the United States, had no knowledge, information, or belief, of an intention on the part of General Hunter to issue such a proclamation," adding that "neither General Hunter, nor any other commander, or person, has been authorized by the Government of the United States, to make proclamations declaring the slaves of any State free; and that the supposed proclamation, now in question, whether genuine or false, is altogether void, so far as respects such declaration."

Having taken away with one hand, Lincoln then gave with the other. Portentously, he hinted that soon he might issue a proclamation like Hunter's: "I further make known that whether it be competent for me, as Commander-in-Chief of the Army and Navy, to declare the Slaves of any state or states, free, and whether at any time, in any case, it shall have become a necessity indispensable to the maintainance of the government, to exercise such supposed power, are questions which, under my responsibility, I reserve to myself, and which I can not feel justified in leaving to the decision of commanders in the field. These are totally different questions from those of police regulations in armies and camps."

When a friend reminded the president that he had allowed Halleck's notorious order of the previous November forbidding slaves to enter Union lines to stand, Lincoln replied: "D—n General order No 3."[104]

Lincoln used the occasion to warn Border State senators and congressmen that they should approve his compensated emancipation plan. In his proclamation revoking Hunter's order, he issued an earnest appeal: "I do not argue. I beseech you to make the arguments for yourselves. You can not if you would, be blind to the signs of the times. I beg of you a calm and enlarged consideration of them, ranging, if it may be, far above personal and partizan politics. This proposal makes common cause for a common object, casting no reproaches upon any. It acts not the pharisee. The change it contemplates would come gently as the dews of heaven, not rending or wrecking anything. Will you not embrace it? So much good has not been done, by one effort, in all past time, as, in the providence of God, it is now your high previlege to do. May the vast future not have to lament that you have neglected it."[105] The appeal fell on deaf ears.

Lincoln's revocation of Hunter's proclamation pleased Moderates like Governor Israel Washburn of Maine, who maintained that the general's "act was in fact unauthorized" and therefore "the President could say no less." Washburn believed that "it is wise that the power should be exercised by him [Lincoln] alone."[106] To a general who congratulated him on his decision, the president remarked: "I am trying to do my duty, but no one can imagine what influences are brought to bear on me."[107]

An Ohioan accurately noted that the "people are not yet prepared for Hunter's conclusion." In time, public opinion would change, he predicted, for the "logic of the war is doing its work slowly but surely."[108] Henry Winter Davis considered Lincoln's action "the best disposition that could be made" and hoped that Hunter would be cashiered.[109] (Lincoln did not fire or censure Hunter, nor did he order him to dismiss his black soldiers.) The leading Republican paper in Rhode Island found Lincoln's proclamation revoking Hunter's order "admirable in letter and spirit," and *Frank Leslie's Illustrated Newspaper* lauded the document as characteristically Lincolnian, "rugged, direct, simple and earnest. . . . pervaded by a spirit sympathetic and paternal." Also paternal was the president's statement to the Border State delegation, which resembled an appeal "a father might make to his children." The editors were glad that Lincoln had apparently not allowed Seward "to make revisions, and bedizen honest, earnest thoughts with a tawdry rhetoric."[110] A prominent New York merchant, Alexander T. Stewart, urged Lincoln to continue "your policy of maintaining the Constitution. It is our only rock of safety. A grateful Country will in return give you its approval, and its encreased confidence and love."[111] The conservative New York *Herald* called Lincoln's proclamation "opportune and admirable," the "most important State paper issued since the outbreak of the rebellion." The editors thought that it "gives another example of the unflinching conservativeness of Mr. Lincoln, while it widens and deepens, if possible, the impassable gulf between him and the baffled revolutionary nigger-worshipping radicals."[112]

Those Radicals were intensely disgruntled. "A more injudicious and unjust edict has not been issued since the war began," Joseph Medill expostulated to Chase.[113] The treasury secretary was equally upset, telling Horace Greeley: "I have not been so sorely tried by any thing here."[114] Adam Gurowski thought Hunter's decree was "too noble, too great, for the tall Kentuckian. Henceforth every Northern man dying in the South is to be credited to Mr. Lincoln."[115] Lydia Maria Child warned that the nation "will have to pass through shameful stages of degenerance if we blindly and recklessly throw away the glorious opportunity for atonement which the Divine Ruler has placed within our reach."[116] Another Massachusetts abolitionist, William Lloyd Garrison, predicted that Lincoln's act "will serve to increase the disgust and uneasiness felt in Europe at our shilly-shallying course, to abate the enthusiasm of the army and friends of freedom universally, and to inspire the rebels with fresh courage and determination." To Garrison, the future seemed "pregnant with sorrow and disaster."[117] Radical clergy denounced the president's "short-sighted" and "unreasonable" act "of overweening caution & timidity" as "an insult to the country," a "disgrace to himself and to the government," as well as a "crime against humanity and God."[118] Moncure Conway hyperbolically declared that Lincoln "cannot annul the order of Gen. Hunter without being pilloried in history as the man who reenslaved nearly a million human beings."[119] In the House of Representatives, Thaddeus Stevens declared that Lincoln "is as honest a man as there is in the world, but I believe him too easy and amiable, and to be misled by the malign influence of Kentucky counselors."[120] Privately, he expressed himself more harshly, telling a friend: "As to future hopes, they are poor as Lincoln is nobody."[121] A disappointed black abolitionist, who had been heartened by the president's messages on confiscation and emancipation, denounced him for overruling Hunter with a "Pro-slavery Proclamation."[122]

Massachusetts Governor John A. Andrew hinted that if the administration failed to support Hunter, the Bay State would not gladly provide troops for the army. In response to an appeal for reinforcements, Andrew told Secretary of War Stanton that "if the President will sustain General Hunter, recognize *all* men, even black men, as legally capable of that loyalty the blacks are waiting to manifest, and let them fight, with God and human nature on their side, *the roads will swarm if need be with multitudes whom New England would pour out to obey your call.*"[123]

Not all Radicals condemned Lincoln's decision. From South Carolina, Edward Lillie Pierce reluctantly criticized Hunter, whose antislavery zeal he shared. "I think there may be some irregularity, almost aberration in his mind," Pierce told Chase. "This is not the first time since his arrival, where he has acted without premeditation or examination, and the next day recalled an order just issued. He has evidently brooded over the arming of negroes for some time, and seems to be carried away by it, and in his action, ignores all sources of information. . . . I confess to a want of confidence in his discretion and the regular action of his mind."[124] The New York *Tribune,* though disappointed, said: "Let no one be discouraged nor alienated because of this Presidential step."[125] *The Independent* pointed out that Lincoln was "very careful not to reject the principle" of emancipation as a military necessity.[126] Samuel J. May, Jr., acknowledged that Hunter's proclamation interfered with Lincoln's offer of compensated emancipation and "would even seem to cast a doubt on the sincerity & honesty of it."[127] While deploring Lincoln's action, the *National Anti-Slavery Standard* was "glad to observe that the language of the President encourages the hope that he will himself, ere long, exercise the power he denies to his subordinates, and proclaim liberty, not alone in South Carolina, Georgia and Florida, but 'throughout all the land, unto all the inhabitants thereof.'"[128] Many Republicans shared that optimism, though some thought Lincoln's warning a mere *"sugar-coated pill"* to placate Radicals.[129]

Carl Schurz, who regretted the timing of Hunter's proclamation, offered Lincoln solace: "I do not see how you could have acted otherwise, at least at the present moment; and I am especially glad that you have given no additional declaration of policy but reserved to yourself the use of your constitutional powers and prerogatives." Schurz was fully persuaded that the president would eventually eliminate slavery, but he urged him in the meantime to make some gestures to placate the more skeptical Radicals.[130]

The Sugar-Coated Pill: Placating Radicals

Lincoln took that advice, pleasing Radicals by signing legislation to extend diplomatic recognition to Haiti and Liberia, by approving a treaty with Great Britain strictly enforcing the ban on the African slave trade, and by forbidding the military to return slaves reaching Union lines. In addition, he sanctioned General Butler's stratagem of declaring slaves who entered his lines "contraband," a policy which Winfield Scott referred to as "Butler's fugitive slave law."

Repeatedly Lincoln insisted that bondsmen reaching Union lines would never be surrendered. In early March 1862, he assured New York Judge John W. Edmonds that "no slave freed by the advance of our army would be returned."[131] A few days later he approved an article of war prohibiting the military from returning runaways. In April, he declared to representatives of the Freedmen's Association: "I am entirely satisfied that no slave who becomes for the time free within the American lines will ever be re-enslaved. Rather than have it so, I would give up and abdicate."[132] That month, D. W. Bartlett reported that Lincoln "has said a hundred times that not with his consent, not if he can hinder it, shall any slave ever be remanded to chains and servitude by the restoration of peace."[133] On July 1, Lincoln showed Orville H. Browning a paper he had drafted stating that while no slaves "necessarily taken and escaping during the war are ever to be returned to slavery," on the other hand "[n]o inducements are to be held out to them to come into our lines for they come now faster than we can provide for them and are becoming an embarrassment to the government."[134] Two days later, Stanton informed General Butler that the president "is of the opinion that, under the law of Congress, they [runaway slaves] cannot be sent back to their masters; that, in common humanity, they must not be permitted to suffer for want of food, shelter or other necessaries of life; that, to this end, they should be provided for by the quartermaster and commissary departments, and that those who are capable of labor should be set to work and paid reasonable wages."[135] When a leading Kentucky Unionist protested that federal troops refused to turn over his runaway slave, Lincoln offered to pay $500 out of his own pocket to settle the matter.

Diplomatic recognition of Haiti and Liberia had long been resisted on the grounds that those nations might send blacks to represent them at Washington. Lincoln, however, did not object to that possibility. When James Redpath told him that President Fabre Nicolas Geffrard of Haiti was willing to appoint a white representative rather than a black one to Washington, Lincoln replied: "Well—you can tell Mr. Geffrard that I shan't tear my shirt if he does send a negro here!"[136] (The Haitian government appointed a black army colonel, Ernest Roumain, as its first minister to the United States.)

Especially pleasing to Radicals was Lincoln's decision in early 1862 to approve the execution of Nathaniel Gordon, the only American ever hanged for slave trading. When the prosecutor in the case, E. Delafield Smith, visited Washington to urge the president to uphold the death sentence, Lincoln said: "Mr. Smith, you do not know how hard it is to have a human being die when you know that a stroke of your pen may save him."[137] (Similarly, he told the governor of Missouri that he "could not bear to have the power to save a man[']s life and not do it.")[138] The president was torn, explaining to Dr. Robert K. Stone, his family physician, that he did not want to execute slave traders "but that he did not wish to be announced as having pardoned them, lest it might be thought at Richmond that he feared the consequences of such action and then he might be compelled to hang fifty such men."[139]

To his Illinois friend, Congressman Henry P. H. Bromwell, Lincoln said: "you don't know how they [Gordon's supporters] followed and pressed to get him pardoned, or his sentence commuted."[140] The pressure had been intense indeed; thousands of New Yorkers signed petitions appealing for commutation of the sentence. The New York *World* reported that every "possible social, professional and other interested influence has been brought to bear upon Mr. Lincoln, and it is stated that never before has a President been so thoroughly and persistently approached for official interference as in this case. Every possible argument which the ingenuity of counsel, the regard of relatives, or the fear of mercantile accomplices could suggest, has been used."[141] On behalf of Gordon, funds were poured out, a rally took place on Wall Street, and congressmen and senators lobbied the president.

Lincoln's resolve may have been stiffened by Charles Sumner, who told him that Gordon must be executed in order to "deter slave traders," to "give notice to the world of a change of policy," and to demonstrate "that the Govt. can hang a man."[142] The New York *World* agreed: "A more deliberate, cold-blooded, nefarious, accursed, infernal crime it is not possible for a human being to commit. If we are to cheat the gallows of such guilt, we may as well at once abolish the gallows altogether."[143] A Massachusetts antislavery militant, John Murray Forbes, asked: "Is he [Gordon], like the rattlesnake in camp . . . to be released? The great want of the hour is to see one spy . . . hanged. . . . But if this wish of the nation must not be gratified, can we not at least hang one of the pirates who have sacrificed such hecatombs of Africans?"[144]

Fearing that the president might commute the death sentence, U.S. Marshal Robert Murray hastened from New York to Washington, where he explained to the president "that mercy would be misapplied in this instance, and if extended, that it would only embolden the slave traders and give the government a character for timidity and incompetency." Lincoln assured him "that no change in the sentence would be extended by him." Gordon's beautiful young wife also traveled to the capital, where she won the sympathy of Mary Lincoln. But it did her no good, for Lincoln would not allow the First Lady to raise the subject.

Ultimately, the president refused to commute Gordon's sentence, telling the prisoner's intercessors that the "slave-trade will never be put down till our laws are executed, and the penalty of death has once been enforced upon the offenders." The statute had been thought unenforceable.[145]

When Gordon's lawyer sent Lincoln a last-minute appeal for mercy, the president forwarded it and accompanying documents to Attorney General Bates, who advised that the chief executive "has no right to stop the course of law, except on grounds of excuse or mitigation found in the case itself—and not to arrest the execution of the statute merely because he thinks the law wrong or too severe."[146] Lincoln did allow a brief postponement of Gordon's execution, but nothing more. He counseled the prisoner to relinquish "all expectation of pardon by Human Authority" and "refer himself alone to the mercy of the common God and Father of all men."[147]

In New York, George Templeton Strong applauded Gordon's execution. "Served him right," Strong wrote, "and our unprecedented execution of justice on a criminal of this particular class and at this particular time will do us good abroad, perhaps with the pharisaical shop-keepers and bagmen of England itself." He hoped that the courts, acting on this precedent, would "promptly exterminate every man who imports niggers into this continent." Strong admired the backbone Lincoln displayed in resisting appeals for clemency. "Immense efforts were made to get the man pardoned or his punishment commuted. Lincoln told me of them. . . . He deserves credit for his firmness. The Executive has no harder duty, ordinarily, than the denial of mercy and grace asked by wives and friends and philanthropes."[148] *Frank Leslie's Illustrated Newspaper* insisted that Gordon's execution was necessary "to show to the friends of Freedom throughout the world that we are really entitled to their sympathies and support."[149]

A Massachusetts citizen who applauded the execution of "the wretched pirate" viewed it as part of the administration's general campaign against slave trading. "Mr Lincoln, in selecting his district attorneys and marshals, had an eye to their capacities for arresting the foreign slave trade. Under the energetic and sagacious action of his officers, slave ships which, under former administrations, boldly entered our northern ports to fit out for their atrocious and inhuman voyages, are now suppressed. . . . He has made with England a most stringent treaty, to insure the suppression of the slave trade. . . . Without the professions of a philanthropist, Mr L. has evinced a noble and generous nature, and should rank with the honored names of Clarkson and Wilberforce."[150] A similar view was taken by the London *Daily News*, which speculated that "Gordon would have had a better chance had his life depended on the decision of some impulsive negro-phile, instead of being at the disposal of the severe, deliberative, but inflexible tenant of the White House, a man who, amidst the severest trials has never swerved a hair's breadth from the policy which he professed when he was a candidate for office. Those who knew President Lincoln well said that he would not lose the precious opportunity to strike a blow at a system which costs hundreds of lives yearly and dooms the brave men of the two African squadrons to ruin their health on a pestilential coast." The president's refusal to alter the death sentence "is an index of the quality of Mr. Lincoln's government, of its strength of principle, and the consistency of its policy, and *it marks the end of a system*."[151]

Many abolitionists applauded the president, though a protégé of Thaddeus Stevens wondered why Lincoln would hang Gordon and yet allow men like John C. Breckinridge and Beriah Magoffin to go unmolested. Similarly, the president's old friend Erastus Wright asked: "If Lincoln directed Gordon hung Why should he treat with complacency those who are in fellowship and complicity, who are equally guilty?"[152] In fact, Lincoln did pardon some slave traders. When, however, Massachusetts Congressman John B. Alley appealed to him on behalf of one who had served his prison sentence but had been unable to pay his fine, the president replied sternly: "I believe I am kindly enough in nature and can be moved to pity and to pardon the perpetrator of almost the worst crime that the mind of man can conceive or the arm of man can execute; but any man, who, for paltry gain and stimulated only by avarice, can rob Africa of her children to sell into interminable bondage, I never will pardon, and he may stay and rot in jail before he will ever get relief from me."[153]

Lincoln's contempt for slave traders applied to the domestic as well as foreign trade. In 1864, upon hearing that Confederate cavalry raider and slave dealer John Hunt Morgan had been killed, he told an army chaplain: "Well, I wouldn't crow over anybody's death, but I assure you that I take this as *resignedly* as I could take any dispensation of Providence. This Morgan was a nigger-driver. You Northern men don't know anything about such low, mean, cowardly creatures." He added that "Southern slaveholders despise them. But such a wretch has been used to carry on their rebellion."[154]

Those antislavery steps gratified some Radicals, including Charles Sumner, who was deeply impressed with Lincoln's sincere commitment to the cause of freedom. In June, the Massachusetts senator told an abolitionist friend: "Could you have seen the President—as it was my privilege often—while he was considering the great questions on which he has already acted—the invitation to Emancipation in the [Border] States, Emancipation in the District of Columbia, and the acknowledgment of the independence of Hayti and Liberia—even your zeal would have been satisfied, for you would have felt the sincerity of his purpose to do what he could to carry forward the principles of the Declaration of Independence. His whole soul was occupied, especially by the first proposition, which was peculiarly his own. In familiar intercourse with him, I remember nothing more touching than the earnestness and completeness with which he embraced this idea. To his mind, it was just and beneficent, while it promised the sure end of Slavery."[155] Months earlier, Lincoln confided to Sumner "that he was now convinced that this [war] was a great movement of God to end slavery & that the man wd. be a fool who shd. stand in the way."[156] Despite their political and temperamental differences, Lincoln and the Massachusetts senator managed to get along fairly well, in part because—as Lincoln put it—"Sumner thinks he runs me."[157]

Lydia Maria Child told Sumner that she agreed with his assessment of the president: "I believe he is, as you think, honest and right-minded." She did, however, "wish he were a man *strong* enough to *lead* popular opinion, instead of *following* it so conscientiously." Nevertheless, she rejoiced "that so much *has* been accomplished. Slavery has been abolished in the District, an event which I had long given up the expectation of living to see. Liberia and Hayti are recognized as States among the sisterhood of nations. Military officers are forbidden to return fugitive slaves." In addition, slavery had been abolished in the territories.[158] After visiting the White House in April, abolitionist William Goodell reported that Lincoln was open-minded and "sincerely desirous of doing what was best for the country."[159] A black writing from Brooklyn said "every colored man" should "uphold the present administration, because it is doing more for his race than has ever been done since the organization of the government. Never has a President, or cabinet officer stood forth to vindicate the rights of black men before." He was especially thankful for the attorney general's 1862 ruling that blacks were citizens and the secretary of state's decision to issue them passports. Beyond that, "the recognition of the republics of Liberia and Hayti, [and] the acceptance of ambassadors from these countries, all demonstrate that this administration is the friend of the black race, and desires its prosperity no less than the good will of all the races of men."[160]

Lincoln did not please all militant opponents of slavery; they wanted every slave of disloyal owners freed, even if those slaves were not being used directly to support the Confederate military. The abolitionist George Luther Stearns told Charles Sumner that he "could hope for nothing good from the imbecility in Washington."[161]

On July 12, Lincoln made his third and final appeal to Border State lawmakers, urging them to support his gradual emancipation plan and gently chiding them for their failure to do so: "I intend no reproach or complaint when I assure you that in my opinion, if you all had voted for the resolution in the gradual emancipation message of last March, the war would now be substantially ended. And the plan therein proposed is yet one of the most potent, and swift means of ending it. Let the states which are in rebellion see, definitely and certainly, that, in no event, will the states you represent ever join their proposed Confederacy, and they can not, much longer maintain the contest. But you can not divest them of their hope to ultimately have you with them so long as you show a determination to perpetuate the institution within your own states. Beat them at elections, as you have overwhelmingly done, and, nothing daunted, they still claim you as their own. You and I know what the lever of their power is. Break that lever before their faces, and they can shake you no more forever."

Lincoln implored them to think rationally about the future, to realize that slavery was doomed, and that they should accept gradual, compensated emancipation now rather than risk sudden, uncompensated emancipation later. "Most of you have treated me with kindness and consideration; and I trust you will not now think I improperly touch what is exclusively your own, when, for the sake of the whole country I ask 'Can you, for your states, do better than to take the course I urge?['] Discarding *punctillio* and maxims adapted to more manageable times, and looking only to the unprecedentedly stern facts of our case, can you do better in any possible event? You prefer that the constitutional relation of the states to the nation shall be practically restored, without disturbance of the institution; and if this were done, my whole duty, in this respect, under the constitution, and my oath of office, would be performed. But it is not done, and we are trying to accomplish it by war. The incidents of the war can not be avoided. If the war continue long, as it must, if the object be not sooner attained, the institution in your states will be extinguished by mere friction and abrasion—by the mere incidents of the war. It will be gone, and you will have nothing valuable in lieu of it. . . . I do not speak of emancipation *at once*, but of a *decision* at once to emancipate *gradually*. Room in South America for colonization, can be obtained cheaply, and in abundance; and when numbers shall be large enough to be company and encouragement for one another, the freed people will not be so reluctant to go."

The president begged the Border State delegations to view the situation from his perspective, to realize how much pressure he was under to abolish slavery by decree, especially after he had overruled General Hunter. "I am pressed with a difficulty not yet mentioned—one which threatens division among those who, united are none too strong. An instance of it is known to you. Gen. Hunter is an honest man. He was, and I hope, still is, my friend. I valued him none the less for his agreeing with me in the general wish that all men everywhere, could be free. He proclaimed all men free within certain states, and I repudiated the proclamation. He expected more good, and less harm from the measure, than I could believe would follow. Yet in repudiating it, I gave dissatisfaction, if not offence, to many whose support the country can not afford to lose. And this is not the end of it. The pressure, in this direction, is still upon me, and is increasing."

In closing, Lincoln appealed to their idealism. "As you would perpetuate popular government for the best people in the world, I beseech you that you do in no wise omit this. Our common country is in great peril, demanding the loftiest views, and boldest action to bring it speedy relief. Once relieved, it's form of government is saved to the world; it's beloved history, and cherished memories, are vindicated; and it's happy future fully assured, and rendered inconceivably grand. To you, more than to any others, the previlege is given, to assure that happiness, and swell that grandeur, and to link your own names therewith forever."[162]

A day later, the president submitted to Congress a bill compensating any state which would abolish slavery voluntarily. Some thought Lincoln's approach might eventually work. "It is not at all improbable that the Presdt's way of managing this matter may turn out the best," Maine Congressman Frederick Pike wrote on July 13. "Kentucky is getting accustomed to the policy. What would shock her six months ago she tolerates now very readily."[163] But most of Pike's colleagues agreed with Vermont Senator Jacob Collamer, who called the bill "ridiculous" and reported that it was received with "considerable disappointment." Free State members were, he said, "about sick of this dickering, bargaining business. The feeling is, that inasmuch as a fair offer had been made, and the border states show no signs of accepting it, that they had better be left alone until great events shall terrify them into compliance."[164] They were unterrified. On July 14, twenty of the twenty-eight members of the Border State delegations rejected Lincoln's appeal. This negative response depressed Lincoln badly. The following day, Orville H. Browning found him looking "weary, care-worn, and troubled." Alarmed by his appearance, Browning said: "your fortunes Mr President are bound up with those of the Country, and disaster to one would be disaster to the other, and I hope you will do all you can to preserve your health and life." Lincoln "looked very sad, and there was a cadence of deep sadness in his voice" as he replied that he felt "tolerably well" and added "in a very tender and touching tone, 'Browning I must die sometime.'" As Browning bade good-bye, both men had tears in their eyes.[165]

To Illinois Congressmen Owen Lovejoy and Isaac Arnold, Lincoln vented his disappointment: "Oh, how I wish the border states would accept my proposition. Then, you, Lovejoy, and you, Arnold, and all of us, would not have lived in vain! The labor of your life, Lovejoy, would be crowned with success."[166]

Congress Applies Heat: The Second Confiscation Act

Radicals also exasperated Lincoln. In December 1861, Senator Lyman Trumbull introduced legislation embodying their demands for stronger action to liberate slaves and punish rebels. Known as the Second Confiscation Act, it reflected the mood of the Northern public, which clamored for sterner measures against the Confederates. The publisher of the Lincoln–Douglas debates declared that "the people are anxious that Congress should really feel that we are at *War,* that *Rebels* are *Enemies* that *their* property and *their* negroes, is not half so precious as the lives of our brave and noble soldiers, and that the speedy enactment of a law confiscating the one, and liberating the other class of property, would be an evidence, that the peoples representatives are in Earnest, having the *bravery* to vote, while the *people fight*."[167] According to Henry Winter Davis, the people of the North "*feel* that there is not brains enough at Washington to put down the insurrection by skillfully used military power, which has been furnished ample, adequate & magnificent; & this bill is their mode of saying so. It is the transition from military suppression to *revolutionary* suppression."[168]

On July 12, after months of heated debate, Congress passed a watered-down version of Trumbull's bill (primarily reshaped by senate Moderates like Jacob Collamer and William Pitt Fessenden), providing that all slaves of disloyal masters—not just those directly employed in direct support of the Confederate military—were free and that the property of rebels could be confiscated. An additional provision authorized the enlistment of freedmen as soldiers. Trumbull believed that "[p]roclaiming freedom to any slave who shall escape to our lines is worth more than many victories."[169] Henry Winter Davis was skeptical, calling the statute "one of those shapeless agglomerations which com[mi]tte[e]s of conference after long labor bring forth—with the features of both parents & usually the worst of both."[170]

Moderate and conservative Republicans urged Lincoln to veto the Second Confiscation Act, which seemed to violate the Constitution's ban on bills of attainder and *ex post facto* legislation. Fearing that if the measure became law "there will be fifty thousand increased bayonets against us, in the Border States," Orville H. Browning told the president that "he had reached the culminating point in his administration, and his course upon this bill was to determine whether he was to control the abolitionists and radicals, or whether they were to control him;" that "the tide in his affairs had come and he ought to take it at its flood;" that "if he vetoed it he would raise a storm of enthusiasm in support of the Administration in the border states which would be worth to us 100,000 muskets, whereas if he approved it I feared our friends could no longer sustain themselves there;" that "we could not succeed without unity of sentiment and purpose which would be secured by a veto as that would at once bring to his support every loyal Democrat in the free states, and consolidate all truly loyal men into one party—whereas if approved it would form the basis upon which the democratic party would again rally, and reorganize an opposition to the administration." Lincoln promised to give this advice "his profound consideration."[171]

As he thought over Browning's advice, Lincoln asked Congress to delay its planned adjournment. When told that the members were exceedingly reluctant to do so unless there was a true emergency, he somewhat testily remarked: "I am sorry Senators could not so far trust me as to believe I had some real cause for wishing them to remain. I am considering a bill which came to me only late in the day yesterday, and the subject of which has perplexed Congress for more than half a year. I may return it with objections; and if I should, I wish Congress to have the oppertunity of obviating the objections, or of passing it into a law notwithstanding them."[172] Secluding himself, he hurriedly prepared a veto message focusing on the confiscation of Rebel property beyond the life of guilty parties. Such confiscation, he argued, violated the Constitution's ban on "corruption of blood." Moreover, slaveowners accused of treasonous acts committed before the passage of the bill would be victims of *ex post facto* legislation. As for a general policy in dealing with the Confederates, he counseled that the "severest justice may not always be the best policy." But the president was careful to acknowledge his agreement with many provisions of the bill and with its ultimate aim: "That those who make a causeless war should be compelled to pay the cost of it, is too obviously just, to be called in question. To give governmental protection to the property of persons who have abandoned it, and gone on a crusade to overthrow that same government, is absurd."[173]

Indignant Radicals stormed into the White House and told Nicolay that if the president vetoed the bill "he destroys the Republican party and ruins his Administration."[174] They insisted that they would not compromise and threatened to denounce the administration publicly. Senators Wade, Wilkinson, Trumbull and other Radicals predicted that "if the confiscation bill is not signed, & the policy of the government in prosecuting the war is not changed, the Union is gone."[175] William P. Fessenden thought that the president might "be mad enough to veto the Confiscation bill—Such an act will disappoint, & I fear will dishearten, the country." Lincoln, said the Maine senator, "seems to be very much in the hands of the Philistines. Well—we have what we bargained for—a Splitter of rails—and have no right to complain."[176] Republicans in caucus denounced Lincoln "as the deliberate betrayer of the freedmen and poor whites."[177]

Abolitionist Gerrit Smith concluded that Lincoln "is bound hand and foot by the Pro-Slavery regard for the Constitution in which he was educated." Further inhibiting him, Smith concluded, was public opinion, for "in every part of the North you meet with this insanity about our *Constitutional* obligations to the Rebels." During the present emergency, the Constitution was no more useful as a guide than an outdated almanac, Smith cavalierly asserted. The Framers' handiwork was to be preserved in peacetime, but "in time of war, save the Country with or without the Constitution."[178] William Dickson complained that the president shirked his duty as a leader and was acting merely as "a moderator between contending factions, helping the one today & the other tomorrow & holding for the present, each in fealty to himself by the hope that he holds out that he will finally be with one of them. Neither break[s] with him because each yet hopes him to be on its side."[179]

Dickson was correct. Lincoln considered it his imperative duty to hold the party—and the North—together. To avoid a confrontation with Congress, he met secretly with some members to hammer out a compromise. On July 15, Tennessee

Representative Horace Maynard, evidently at the president's suggestion, introduced a "joint resolution for the purpose of correcting the confiscation act" which refined the language so as to meet Lincoln's desire for a more "justly discriminating application" of the measure.[180] That night Senators Daniel Clark of New Hampshire and Fessenden met with Lincoln, who warned them that he would veto the bill unless it were modified to conform to the Constitution. The following day, Clark offered another amendment stating that no property would be confiscated beyond the lifetime of any convicted traitor. Despite the objections of Benjamin Wade and other Radical senators, who thought the president's tactics "monstrous" (as Preston King put it), these provisos passed, and on July 17 Lincoln signed the bill and the joint explanatory resolution. The ban on the forfeiture of property beyond the owners' lifetime severely weakened the government's ability to restructure the society and economy of the South. Many supporters of the original bill sought to make such a dramatic reform possible; Radical Congressman George W. Julian of Indiana said that the supplementary resolution was "inexpressibly provoking to a large majority of Congress."[181] Other Radicals were profoundly disgusted by what they considered Lincoln's deficient backbone. Adams S. Hill of the New York *Tribune* was surprised "that a President can live in such utter ignorance of popular feeling."[182] But Charles Sumner acknowledged that Lincoln and Congress agreed on two fundamental principles: "Blacks are to be employed, and slaves are to be freed. In this legislative proclamation the President and Congress will unite. Together they will deliver it to the country and to the world."[183]

Curiously, Lincoln sent the House and senate a copy of his veto message, even though he now agreed to sign the modified bill. This uncharacteristically tactless gesture annoyed many members of Congress. As it was being read aloud, some lawmakers uttered irreverent cracks. One of them asked incredulously, "Whoever heard of the reading of a veto that was not a veto, or the production of a document the necessity for which had passed away?"[184] According to Adams S. Hill, it was "entirely unexpected, and fell like a wet blanket upon his friends." Everyone "was disgusted, and particularly those who were most ready to get down on their knees to avoid a vetoe yesterday. They got more than they bargained for, soiled their trousers, and got the vetoe to boot. Such men as Washburne, Gurley, Arnold, Sumner, and Conway, were ineffably disgusted. Washburne said he went out in order that he might not hear it read, and Collamer privately expressed the hope that it would not be read at all in the Senate."[185] Congressman Julian later wrote that "[n]o one at a distance could have formed any adequate conception of the hostility of Republican members toward Mr. Lincoln . . . while it was the belief of many that our last session of Congress had been held in Washington. Mr. Wade said that the country was going to hell, and that the scenes witnessed in the French Revolution were nothing in comparison with what we should see here."[186] Republicans retaliated against Lincoln by filibustering a motion to print his veto message.

Lincoln's motive in communicating the draft veto was unclear. Perhaps he intended to show Congress that on matters of slavery and reconstruction, he was master. On other legislative matters—such as taxation, public lands, and internal improvements—he generally followed traditional Whig doctrine, which called for the executive branch to defer to the legislature.

On July 18, Congressman Isaac N. Arnold said that "within the last two or three days the President has been subjected to the greatest pressure in favor of vigorous war measures that was ever brought to bear upon him."[187] That day the main author and promoter of the Confiscation Acts, Lyman Trumbull, urged Lincoln to "use rebel property for the support of your armies, subsist off the enemy's country, use negroes as laborers, and put arms in their hands when necessary. Give the country proof that you are in earnest and you can raise one hundred thousand soldiers in Illinois alone; adhere to the present peace policy of conducting the war, and you get none at all."[188] It is not known what Lincoln said in reply, but on July 17 John W. Forney publicly announced that the president had recently told him "that henceforth his policy should be as stringent as the most enthusiastic could desire. That hereafter there will be no restriction in the employment of all men to put down this rebellion. No more doubting about the confiscation of rebel property. No longer need the northern people be frightened with the cry of negro equality and emancipation."[189]

On July 25, Lincoln issued a proclamation warning all Rebels that if they did not "cease participating in, aiding, countenancing, or abetting the existing rebellion," they would suffer "the forfeitures and seizures" spelled out in the Second Confiscation Act.[190] But because the statute provided no mechanisms for enforcement or for oversight of its implementation (thus giving Lincoln wide discretionary power to carry it out as he saw fit), he virtually ignored it. Though almost no Confederate property was seized under the provisions of the Second Confiscation Act, its passage was significant, for it helped pave the way for the Emancipation Proclamation. It showed Lincoln that issuing such a proclamation would not be as politically risky as it had earlier seemed, and the lengthy congressional debates helped undermine the notion that blacks were property. As Senator John Sherman noted, the statute "was more useful as a declaration of policy than as an act to be enforced."[191]

Bombshell Proposal to Issue an Emancipation Proclamation

On July 13, Lincoln took a fateful carriage ride with Welles and Seward. A day earlier he had unsuccessfully attempted to persuade the Border States to accept his gradual emancipation plan; that failure persuaded him it was time for more drastic steps. As he rode with his secretaries of state and the navy to attend the funeral of Stanton's infant son, Lincoln discussed issuing an emancipation proclamation. According to Welles, he "dwelt earnestly on the gravity, importance, and delicacy of the movement, said he had given it much thought and had about come to the conclusion that it was a military necessity absolutely essential for the salvation of the Union, that we must free the slaves or be ourselves subdued, etc., etc." This was "the first occasion when he had mentioned the subject to any one, and wished us to frankly state how the proposition struck us. Mr. Seward said the subject involved consequences so vast and momentous that he should wish to bestow on it mature reflection before giving a decisive answer, but his present opinion inclined to the measure as justifiable, and perhaps he might say expedient and necessary." Welles agreed. "Two or three times on that ride the subject, which was of course an absorbing one for each and all, was adverted to, and before separating[,] the President desired us to give the question special and deliberate attention, for he was earnest in the conviction that something must be done. It was a new departure for the President, for until this time, in all our previous interviews, whenever the question of emancipation or the mitigation of slavery had been in any way alluded to, he had been prompt and emphatic in denouncing any interference by the General Government with the subject. This was, I think, the sentiment of every member of the Cabinet, all of whom, including the President, considered it a local, domestic question appertaining to the States respectively, who had never parted with their authority over it. But the reverses before Richmond, and the formidable power and dimensions of the insurrection, which extended through all the Slave States, and had combined most of them in a confederacy to destroy the Union, impelled the Administration to adopt extraordinary measures to preserve the national existence. The slaves, if not armed and disciplined, were in the service of those who were, not only as field laborers and producers, but thousands of them were in attendance upon the armies in the field, employed as waiters and teamsters, and the fortifications and intrenchments were constructed by them."[192]

Though disappointed by the Border State lawmakers, Lincoln took heart from the positive response he received from Welles and Seward, the cabinet's leading Moderates. He assumed he could rely on the support of the more radical Chase and Stanton. Therefore he began drafting an emancipation proclamation that would be far more effective than the Confiscation Acts, which required a trial for disloyal slaveholders before their slaves would become legally free, and even then it was doubtful that the forfeiture of property could last beyond the lifetime of convicted traitors. To justify so momentous a step, Lincoln decided not to appeal to the idealism of the North by denouncing the immorality of slavery. He had already done that eloquently and repeatedly between 1854 and 1860. Instead, he chose to rely on practical and constitutional arguments that he assumed would be more palatable to Democrats and conservative Republicans, especially in the Border States. He knew full well that those elements would object to sudden, uncompensated emancipation, and that many men who were willing to fight for the Union would be reluctant to fight for the liberation of slaves. To minimize their discontent, he would argue that emancipation facilitated the war effort by depriving Confederates of valuable workers. Slaves might not be fighting in the Rebel army, but they grew the food and fiber that nourished and clothed it. If those slaves could be induced to abandon the plantations and head for Union lines, the Confederates' ability to wage war would be greatly undermined. Military necessity, therefore, required the president to liberate the slaves, but not all of them. Residents of Slave States still loyal to the Union would have to be exempted, as well as those in areas of the Confederacy that the Union army had already pacified. Such restrictions might disappoint Radicals, but Lincoln was less worried about them than he was about Moderates and Conservatives.

The reliance on pragmatism rather than idealism to justify emancipation was not unique to Lincoln. Since the defeat at Bull Run, even Radicals like Massachusetts

Senator Henry Wilson and abolitionists like Frederick Douglass had been urging that the slaves be freed in order to weaken the Confederacy militarily. Moderates and Conservatives echoed their appeals.

Lincoln also feared that Roger Taney's Supreme Court might object. The constitutional basis for such a bold decree would have to be the war powers of the president, a somewhat vague concept implied in the chief executive's status as "Commander-in-Chief of the Army and Navy of the United States" and in the presidential oath of office. In 1842, Congressman John Quincy Adams had emphatically insisted that in a civil or foreign war, "not only the President of the United States, but the commander of the army has power to order the universal emancipation of the slaves."[193] Charles Sumner, Henry Ward Beecher, and other antislavery militants had endorsed Adams's dictum and urged Lincoln to act on it. With these thoughts in mind, Lincoln drafted his momentous proclamation. He may have been influenced by *The War Powers of the President, and the Legislative Powers of Congress in Relation to Rebellion, Treason and Slavery*, a book which appeared that spring. Written by the Boston abolitionist William Whiting, it argued that "the laws of war give the President full belligerent rights" and that "personal property of every kind, ammunition, provisions, contraband, or slaves, may be lawfully seized, whether of loyal or disloyal citizens, and is by law presumed hostile, and liable to condemnation, if captured within the rebellious districts. This right of seizure and condemnation is harsh, as all the proceedings of war are harsh, in the extreme, but it is nevertheless lawful."[194] Lincoln befriended Whiting and appointed him solicitor of the War Department.

On July 20, John Hay wrote that the president "has been, out of pure devotion to what he considers the best interests of humanity, the bulwark of the institution he abhors, for a year. But he will not conserve slavery much longer. When next he speaks in relation to this defiant and ungrateful villainy it will be with no uncertain sound."[195] The following day, the president summoned his cabinet for an unusual Monday meeting. Chase recorded that Lincoln "had been profoundly concerned at the present aspect of affairs, and had determined to take some definitive steps in respect to military action and slavery." But instead of springing his proclamation on the cabinet, Lincoln merely announced that he had prepared orders allowing commanders in the field to have their troops subsist off the land in Confederate territory; authorizing the employment of blacks within Union lines as laborers; and providing for colonization of blacks overseas. These measures were discussed at length. When the use of blacks as troops came up, Lincoln expressed reservations and proposed to discuss that matter, along with the others, on the morrow.

That fateful day, July 22, the cabinet reconvened to continue discussion of the arming of blacks, which Chase heartily supported. The president demurred but added that he planned to issue a proclamation, based on the Second Confiscation Act, warning that all slaveholders who continued rebelling against the Union would have their property (including slaves) confiscated; declaring that he would once again urge Congress to renew its endorsement of his earlier offer of gradual, compensated emancipation; and reaffirming that the war was being fought to restore the Union. The final sentence of this brief document stated that "as a fit and necessary military measure for effecting this object [i.e., restoration of the Union] I, as Commander-in-Chief of the Army and Navy of the United States, do order and declare that on the first day of January in the year of Our Lord one thousand, eight hundred and sixty three, all persons held as slaves within any state or states, wherein the constitutional authority of the United States shall not then be practically recognized, submitted to, and maintained, shall then, thenceforward, and forever, be free."[196] Lincoln explained that he "had resolved upon this step, and had not called them together to ask their advice, but to lay the subject-matter of a proclamation before them" and solicit suggestions.[197]

Surprisingly, the conservative Edward Bates agreed heartily. But he wanted colonization linked with emancipation. Long opposed to slavery, he hoped that the bondsmen would be freed and then emigrate. He voiced the widely held belief that the two races could not coexist without intermarriage, which would degrade whites without improving blacks. At the opposite end of the cabinet's ideological spectrum, Chase approved Lincoln's proclamation in general but raised some objections. In his diary, the treasury secretary noted that "I said that I should give to such a measure my cordial support, but I should prefer that no new expression on the subject of compensation should be made, and I thought that the measure of Emancipation could be much better and more quietly accomplished by allowing Generals to organize and arm the slaves (thus avoiding depredation and massacre on the one hand, and support to the insurrection on the other) and by directing the Commanders of Departments to proclaim emancipation within their Districts as soon as practicable; but I regarded this as so much better than inaction on the subject, that I should give it my entire support."[198] Stanton recorded a different version of Chase's remarks. According to the war secretary, Chase "thinks [emancipation] a measure of great danger, and would lead to universal emancipation."[199] Astonished at the treasury secretary's reservations, Lincoln exclaimed: "What! You Chase, the father of abolitionism, object!"[200]

Stanton himself favored prompt issuance of Lincoln's decree. Blair, who arrived late at the White House, objected that such a move would cost the Republican Party the fall elections. The conservative Caleb B. Smith did not voice an opinion at the meeting, but immediately afterward he told the assistant secretary of the interior that if Lincoln did issue an emancipation proclamation, "I will resign and go home and attack the administration."[201] When no one else seemed willing to make suggestions, Seward delivered what Stanton called "a long speech against its immediate promulgation." According to the war secretary, Seward predicted that "foreign nations will intervene to prevent the abolition of slavery for [the] sake of cotton." A proclamation "would break up our relations with foreign nations and the production of cotton for sixty years."[202]

Lincoln recalled Seward's remarks differently. To the artist Francis B. Carpenter, the president summarized the secretary of state's argument: "I approve of the proclamation, but I question the expediency of its issue at this juncture. The depression of the public mind, consequent upon our repeated reverses, is so great that I fear the effect of so important a step. It may be viewed as the last measure of an exhausted government, a cry for help; the government stretching forth its hands to Ethiopia, instead of Ethiopia stretching forth her hands to the government." Lincoln recollected that

Seward's "idea was that it would be considered our last *shriek,* on the retreat." So, the Sage of Auburn argued, "while I approve the measure, I suggest, sir, that you postpone its issue, until you can give it to the country supported by military success, instead of issuing it, as would be the case now, upon the greatest disasters of the war!" (Seward boasted to a senator, "I have done the state service, for I have prevented Mr. Lincoln from issuing an emancipation proclamation in the face of our retreating army.")[203] Lincoln told Carpenter that Seward's analysis "struck me with very great force. It was an aspect of the case that, in all my thought upon the subject, I had entirely overlooked. The result was that I put the draft of the proclamation aside, as you do your sketch for a picture, waiting for a victory. From time to time I added or changed a line, touching it up here and there, anxiously watching the progress of events."[204] For the next two months, those events would be unpropitious.

As July drew to a close, Massachusetts litterateur Charles Eliot Norton voiced questions that were preying on the minds of many Northerners: "Will Lincoln be master of the opportunities, or will they escape him? Is he great enough for the time?"[205]

"Would You Prosecute the War with Elder-Stalk Squirts, Charged with Rose Water?"
The Soft War Turns Hard
(July–September 1862)

In the summer of 1862, public disenchantment with the Lincoln administration's "fatal milk and water policy" intensified.[1] "The stern sentiment of justice and of retribution which swells even to bursting in millions of American hearts today, must be vindicated," declared a Washington correspondent on Independence Day. "The outraged sense and patience of a long suffering nation must be trifled with no longer."[2] The people of the North "are fast getting into the belief, that as quiet & moderate war measures have accomplished no good, that severe measures are now necessary, & if the rebels will not lay down their arms—that it is the duty of the Gov^t to smite them hip & thigh," Lincoln's friend David Davis observed.[3]

Northerners were indeed growing bloodthirsty. "The public temper is becoming bitter & everybody cries out for extermination," noted a Maine congressman.[4] Referring to the Confederacy, a leading Unitarian divine reluctantly concluded that the nation "shall be compelled to *exterminate* her 300,000 slaveholders."[5] A former mayor of Chicago insisted that "extermination of the rebel whites" was necessary in addition to the emancipation and arming of slaves. "Shoot, & hang, & burn, & destroy all that we cannot use, leaving nought but desolation behind as our armies advance, is the *only* way to save the Union," he declared.[6] In New York, George Templeton Strong complained that "[w]ar on rebels as criminals has not begun. We have dealt with these traitors as a police officer deals with a little crowd that threatens a breach of the peace. He wheedles and persuades and administers his club-taps mildly and seldom."[7] Constituents told Ohio Senator John Sherman that the "people feel that the Government has been *too tender* of the supposed rights of the rebels under the Constitution," and that it would be better to "save the *National territory intact*—though all the Seceded States shall be reduced to *Territories*—nay *depopulated*—than that the 'Confederacy' *shall prove a success!*"[8] Illinois Governor Richard Yates warned Lincoln that the "crisis of the war and our national existence is upon us. The time has come for the adoption of more decisive measures. . . . Mild and conciliatory means have been tried in vain."[9] Abolitionists believed that the war must become one of "conquest & extermination, not the killing of every man woman & child, but the destruction & decimation of the ruling classes & an entire social reorganization."[10] Kansans reportedly thought that "Lincoln has pursued the policy of conciliation long enough. He has given it a fair trial."[11] Senator William P. Fessenden lamented that the "miserable policy of tenderness & conciliation, the maggot in Seward's brain, has been disastrous [in] every way."[12]

The president agreed. On July 21, he announced: "I have got done throwing grass." From now on, he "proposed trying stones."[13] Sarcastically he asked proponents of a conciliatory policy if they intended to prosecute the war "with elder-stalk squirts, charged with rose water?"[14] Solicitude for the rights of slaveholders and other Confederate noncombatants as well as for civil liberties in the North had to be modified. In August, he assured visitors that within his administration there "was no division of sentiment" regarding "the confiscation of rebel property, and the feeding the National troops upon the granaries of the enemy."[15]

Lincoln would show that his legendary tenderheartedness did not prevent him from employing stern measures to win the war. In September, a well-connected Interior Department employee reported that the administration intended to wage a war "of subjugation and extermination if the North can be coerced and coaxed into it." The social system of the South "is to be destroyed and replaced by new propositions and ideas."[16] Lincoln's principal secretary, John G. Nicolay, wrote an editorial stating that the "people are for the war; for earnest, unrelenting war; for war now and war to the bitter end, until our outraged and insulted flag shall have been everywhere triumphantly vindicated and restored."[17]

In carrying out this new strategy, Lincoln emancipated slaves, further suspended the writ of habeas corpus, drafted men into the army, confiscated Confederate civilian property, and appointed what he hoped were more aggressive, capable generals. On August 25, General Henry W. Halleck reported that the "Government seems determined to apply the guillotine to all unsuccessful generals. It seems rather hard to do this where the general is not in fault, but perhaps with us now, as in the French Revolution, some harsh measures are required." In keeping with the new approach, Halleck criticized General Horatio G. Wright for "pursuing 'too milk and water a policy toward the rebels in Kentucky.'" Sternly, he lectured Wright: "Domestic traitors, who seek the overthrow of our Government, are not entitled to its protection, and should be made to feel its power. . . . Make them suffer in their persons and property for their crimes and the sufferings they have caused to others. . . . Let the guilty feel that you have an iron hand; that you know how to apply it when necessary. Don't be influenced by those old political grannies."[18]

In August the administration's new toughness led a journalist to remark that recently "the Jacksonian qualities of Abraham Lincoln have been more than ever apparent."[19] This cheered the public, which, though discouraged by McClellan's failure, took heart from the president's leadership. Shortly after the Seven Days battles, Frederick Law Olmsted told Lincoln that in "the general gloom, there are two points of consolation and hope. . . . One, is the trustworthy, patriotic devotion of the solid, industrious, home-keeping people of the country; the other, the love and confidence constantly growing stronger between these people and their president."[20] Echoing Olmsted's analysis, a correspondent for the London *Times* informed his readers that "the President is the most popular man in the United States. Without education or marked ability, without the personal advantage of a fine presence or courteous manners, and placed unexpectedly in a position of unparalleled difficulty and danger, he has so conducted himself amid the storm of passion that rages around him as to have won the good opinion of everybody."[21] Also in London, Charles Francis Adams concluded that Lincoln's obvious integrity inspired the confidence so essential for victory.

That good opinion was held even by political opponents, including an influential Illinois Democrat who said: "it has been a hard struggle for me to come to the support of a Republican Administration. It has been a hard struggle for the Democratic party. We were afraid of Mr Lincoln, but his firm, honest, patriotic course has won our hearts, and now nine out of every ten of us, every where, would vote for him. He has resisted factions, and shown that he can be President himself, and the President of *all* the people. I have two sons in the war, and am now ready to go myself."[22] The New York *Commercial Advertiser* rejoiced that the president would ignore "the promptings of his kindly nature" and that "the sword of justice will be wielded with a vigor and earnestness that will convince the rebels and the world that he is terribly in earnest."[23]

But in some circles Lincoln's popularity slipped. A few New Yorkers were saying that although he was "honest and true" and "thoroughly sensible," nevertheless he lacked "the decision and the energy the country wants." The administration, they felt, "does not lead the people," but rather the people had "to keep up a toilsome *vis a tergo* [i.e., a force acting from behind], and shove the government forward to every vigorous step." Wall Street attorney George Templeton Strong came to share Wendell Phillips's judgment that "old great-uncle Abe" was "a first-rate second-rate man."[24] Another New Yorker reported that Lincoln's friends were concluding that he had only one desirable quality, "honesty of intention," which was more than offset by the lack of decisiveness and "firmness of character" that the times required: "He leans on his subordinates to such a degree that they control his actions."[25] Others condescendingly referred to the president as "a Man of only medium capacity" who was "too amiable to be firm, & too conscientious to be as *savage,* as the crisis requires."[26] A judge in Maine warned that the country would perish "unless the President can be made to feel that here is war—internecine war—& the only remedy is subjugation." Let Lincoln "be made to see that the Dantonian maxim—audacity, audacity, & yet more audacity—is all that can save us."[27] More bitterly, a Wisconsin Republican sneered: "A respectable mule could do better than Lincoln—the former could only bray, while the latter only 'blabs.'"[28]

The cabinet also drew intense criticism. "We must have a new, distinct, earnest policy, or the country is ruined, & I do not believe such a policy possible with the present Cabinet," insisted Maine Governor Israel Washburn. "A war cabinet united in policy & purpose, will give us the right Commanders."[29] Another resident of the Pine Tree State lamented that Lincoln and the nation "are on the road to destruction from a weak cabinet," whose members had "neither the ability nor the comprehensive will to grasp the troubles of the nation, and Congress has failed equally in the great emergencies."[30] William T. Coggeshall, secretary to Ohio Governor William Dennison, likened the cabinet to "a collection of powerful chemicals—each positive, sharp, individual—but thrown together, they neutralize each other and the result is an insipid mess."[31]

Overhaul: Restructuring and Relocating the Army

The failure to bag Stonewall Jackson, along with McClellan's inability to take Richmond, prompted Lincoln to restructure the military command. He asked Ambrose E. Burnside to replace Little Mac at the head of the Army of the Potomac, but that Rhode Island general "said the responsibility was too great—the consequences of defeat too momentous," and so he declined. He did, however, agree to take charge of a corps.[32]

The president was more successful in his quest to appoint a general-in-chief empowered both to issue commands and give advice (and who also might help insulate Lincoln from criticism.) The aged, infirm Ethan Allen Hitchcock had quit after a brief stint as military advisor to the president and secretary of war. John Pope, fearing with good reason that as commander of the Army of Virginia he could not succeed unless McClellan were forced to cooperate, told Lincoln that "he should assign an officer as General-in-Chief of the Armies, who should have the power to enforce his orders."[33]

Acting on the advice of Pope and Winfield Scott, Lincoln decided to feel out Henry W. Halleck, the brusque, rigid, testy commander of armies in the West. There U. S. Grant and Pope had won substantial victories for which Halleck unfairly received credit. (Old Brains, as Halleck was called, had demanded that he be put in charge of the entire Western Department "in return for Forts Donelson and Henry." On March 11, he received that post.)[34] The president was favorably disposed toward Halleck, for he admired the general's *Elements of Military Art and Science* and realized that he needed a West Pointer to fill that post. He also approved of Halleck's military leadership in St. Louis, and declared that he "has Websterian brains."[35] On July 2, Lincoln summoned the general to Washington for a consultation. That evening, Halleck coyly responded that although he was reluctant to leave his army in Mississippi, nevertheless "being somewhat broken in health and wearied out with long months of labor and care," he would find a trip to the capital "exceedingly desirable."[36] A week later, he stated that he "could advise but one thing—to place all the forces in North Carolina, Virginia, and Washington under one head and hold that head responsible for the result."[37] Such willingness to take responsibility pleased Lincoln, who was growing ever more exasperated by McClellan's reluctance to do so.

The president decided to appoint Halleck general-in-chief without a personal consultation. On July 11, the day after Lincoln returned from Harrison's Landing, he issued an order naming Old Brains to that post, explaining to Charles Sumner that during the visit to the Army of the Potomac his "mind became perfectly perplexed" and he "determined right then and there to appoint a Commander-in-Chief who should be responsible for our military operations" and "determined further that General Halleck should be the man."[38] Three days later Lincoln wired Old Brains: "I am very anxious—almost impatient—to have you here."[39] Leaving Grant in charge of the army around Corinth, a Mississippi city that Halleck had captured with little bloodshed, Old Brains repaired to Washington, arriving on July 23.

The general had grave reservations about his new position, whose duties and powers were ill-defined. Though pleased by the honor that his elevation represented, he wanted to avoid entanglement in the bitter dispute between Stanton and McClellan, nor did he relish dealing with political intrigue and civilians ignorant of logistics. He also regretted losing the autonomy he had enjoyed as a department commander. In late July, he confessed to McClellan, "I hold my present position contrary to my own wishes . . . I did everything in my power to avoid coming to Washington; but after declining several invitations from the President I received the order of the 11th instant, which left me no option. I have always had strong personal objections to mingling in the politico-military affairs of Washington. I never liked the place, and like it still less at the present time. . . . I greatly feared that whatever I might do I should receive more abuse than thanks."[40] McClellan, who had not been consulted in the matter, regarded the appointment of Halleck "as a slap in the face." Old Brains was a man "whom I know by experience to be my inferior," Little Mac told his wife.[41] "Of all the men whom I have encountered in high position Halleck was the most hopelessly stupid," McClellan later wrote. "It was more difficult to get an idea through his head than can be conceived by any one who never made the attempt. I do not think he ever had a correct military idea from beginning to end."[42]

Lincoln's choice of Halleck, though understandable, was a blunder. The president was evidently unaware that in the western theater Old Brains had demonstrated the selfishness, hypercaution, reluctance to assume responsibility, deceitfulness, incompetence, and pettiness that would render him an ineffective general-in-chief. The appointment of Halleck was viewed as Lincoln's admission of his own failure to perform the office of general-in-chief adequately. The journalist Whitelaw Reid remarked that "it became a more straightforward acceptance of the responsibility than was expected from Mr. Lincoln." Reid thought it a shrewd move, placating West Pointers who believed civilians should not try to run military affairs. It was also interpreted as a gentle way to replace McClellan without offending his many supporters, who would be pleased to see Stanton's influence reduced. Radical Republicans, however, were not pleased; they had denounced Halleck's 1861 order forbidding runaway slaves to enter his lines. Lyman Trumbull considered Halleck "a good organizer but a poor fighter, judging from his movements before Corinth."[43] (After maneuvering the Confederates out of that Mississippi city, Halleck divided up his army so badly that it was able to accomplish little.)

John Hay quoted "a Western friend"—probably Lincoln—who remarked that Halleck "is like a singed cat—better than he looks." (In recommending a candidate for admission to the bar, Lincoln once said: "He's a good deal smarter than he looks to be."[44] He made a similar observation while introducing a supplicant to Stanton: "This woman is a leetle smarter than she lets on to be.")[45] The short, stout, carelessly dressed Halleck was indeed unprepossessing. One observer was "greatly disappointed in his appearance. Small and farmer-like, he gives a rude shock to one's preconceived notions of a great soldier."[46] A journalist described him memorably as an "oleaginous Methodist parson dressed in regimentals."[47]

But John Hay admired Halleck's "great head," well stocked with "vast stores of learning, which have drifted in from the assiduous reading of a quarter of a century." The general, said Hay, "is a cool, mature man, who understands himself. Let us be glad we have got him."[48] Grant called Halleck "a man of gigantic intellect and well studied in the profession of arms," and Edward Bates told a friend: "We have great hopes of Halleck."[49] The Chicago *Tribune* described him as "a closet general who in his library will be able to give celerity and potency to military movements which in the field he would be powerless to direct."[50] Noah Brooks admired Halleck's "plodding, patient, impervious character."[51]

Others were less sanguine. According to Gideon Welles, Halleck was "a man of some scholastic attainments, but without soldierly capacity," a "dull, stolid, inefficient, and incompetent General-in-Chief" who "earnestly and constantly smoked cigars and rubbed his elbows."[52] Though Chase deplored Halleck's inaction after the victory at Corinth, he nonetheless hoped that the general would "come & act vigorously." But, he confided to his daughter, "my apprehensions . . . exceed my hopes."[53]

Halleck's first assignment in his new role was to help determine what ought to be done with the Army of the Potomac. Should it be left at Harrison's Landing or united with Pope's army on the Rappahannock? Should McClellan be retained in command? Lincoln instructed the new general-in-chief to visit the army and learn Little Mac's views and wishes. He was also to inform the Young Napoleon that only 20,000 reinforcements could be supplied and that he must either attack Richmond with those additional forces or withdraw and join Pope. In late July, Lincoln told Halleck "that he was satisfied McClellan would not fight" and authorized him to remove Little Mac if he saw fit.[54] Halleck confided to his wife that the president and the cabinet "have lost all confidence in him [McClellan] & urge me to remove him from command."[55]

Lincoln also wanted Halleck to formulate strategic plans and coordinate the movement of all Union armies. When asked what would be done with McClellan's army, Lincoln replied: "You forget we have a general who commands all the armies and makes all the plans to suit himself—ask him!"[56] With some justification, Halleck complained that because the president and the cabinet had approved everything he proposed, "it only increases my responsibility, for if any disaster happens they can say we did for you all you asked."[57] Lincoln probably counted on the general to take charge of the Army of the Potomac, unite it with Burnside's troops at Falmouth, and attack Lee while Pope covered Richmond. When Halleck delivered the presidential ultimatum to McClellan, Little Mac said he could possibly take Richmond with 30,000 more troops but not with only 20,000 more. He soon changed his mind, however, and reluctantly agreed to try with 20,000. A day after Halleck left, the Young Napoleon reversed course yet again: he would need 50,000 more men, not 20,000!

Upon Halleck's return to Washington, the administration debated whether to remove the Army of the Potomac from the Peninsula. Lincoln opposed doing so, while Chase emphatically urged that such a step was necessary to strengthen the nation's credit. General Winfield Scott, a Virginian, reportedly said "that no army can exist on the James River after August 15. It must advance, retreat, or perish, poisoned by malaria."[58] As Lincoln wrestled with this momentous question, his old friend Leonard Swett called on him and reported that the president "is in great trouble & care weighs heavily upon him."[59]

When McClellan claimed that he had only 80,000 troops as opposed to Lee's 200,000, it became obvious to Halleck that the Army of the Potomac could not safely remain on the Peninsula but must unite with Pope. (In fact, the Army of Northern Virginia numbered only 75,000.) Given the alleged disparity between Union and Confederate forces, it appeared necessary to withdraw the army from the Peninsula. And so on August 3, Old Brains ordered McClellan to transfer to Aquia Creek, where he would be near Pope. Little Mac objected heatedly but to no avail. Halleck was so worried about Pope's army that he could hardly sleep.

Lincoln may have erred in approving Halleck's recommendation, which was backed by Pope, Stanton, and Chase. During the president's visit to the army in early July, he had polled the corps commanders about withdrawing from the Peninsula. Edwin V. Sumner said it could be done, "but I think we give up the cause if we do it." Similarly, Samuel P. Heintzelman insisted it "would be ruinous to the country." Fitz John Porter concurred. William B. Franklin believed it advisable to fall back to the Rappahannock, while E. D. Keyes was noncommittal, saying only that a transfer could be accomplished quickly. McClellan opined that it "would be a delicate & very difficult matter."[60] Two years would pass before the Union army would draw so close to Richmond again. But if Lee really did have 200,000 men, he could overwhelm Pope, then turn and crush McClellan. Military doctrine stipulated that forces be concentrated lest they be conquered piecemeal.

Slowly the Army of the Potomac withdrew from Harrison's Landing, thus formally concluding the Peninsular Campaign, during which 25,000 Union soldiers and 30,000 Confederates were killed, wounded, or missing. At least 5,000 more succumbed to disease.

Knocked into Last Year: The Second Battle of Bull Run

When Lee realized that the Army of the Potomac was pulling back, he launched a new campaign, driving north toward Pope's 45,000-man Army of Virginia. If he could reach it before McClellan did, which seemed distinctly possible, the Confederates might achieve a smashing triumph. Lincoln wondered if Little Mac would move fast enough to prevent such a calamity. On August 19, the president told John A. Dahlgren: "Now I am to have a sweat of five or six days. The Confederates will strive to gather on Pope before McClellan can get around, and his first corps is not in the Potomac yet."[61] That same day Chase reported that Lincoln was "uneasy about Pope."[62] In fact, the first units of the Young Napoleon's army did not join Pope until August 23, twenty days after the order to do so was issued. During that time, Halleck complained to his wife, "I can[']t get Genl McClellan to do what I wish."[63]

In July, while lingering at the capital awaiting Halleck's arrival, Pope had committed some blunders. Shortly after the retreat of the Army of the Potomac from the gates of Richmond, he issued a boastful address to his men: "I have come to you from the West, where we have always seen the backs of our enemies; from an army whose business it has been to seek the adversary and to beat him when he was found; whose policy has been attack, and not defense. . . . I hear constantly of 'taking strong positions and holding them,' of 'lines of retreat,' and of 'bases of supplies.' Let us discard such ideas. . . . Let us study the probable lines of retreat of our opponents, and leave our own to take care of themselves."[64] This message was widely ridiculed by the public and resented by soldiers in the Army of the Potomac. Colonel Herman Haupt spoke for many when he said "Pope has made a fool of himself in his first paper," which "is all bombast, stuff and nonsense, and is a virtual declaration of war between him and McClellan, destroying all harmony of action." Prophetically, Haupt speculated: "I should not be surprised if both should be superseded and some one else put over the two."[65]

After thus alienating the Eastern troops, Pope made matters worse by issuing a series of orders (written by Stanton) dictating that civilians should be treated harshly: property would be seized, disloyal residents deported south, violators of loyalty oaths executed, and guerrilla attacks punished by reprisals. The hard hand of war, he intimated, would now fall on noncombatants. (This policy sharply clashed with that adopted by McClellan, who responded coldly to Pope's friendly overtures. For good reason, Pope feared that Little Mac would not readily cooperate with him.) An angry General Lee deemed Pope a "miscreant" to be "suppressed."[66]

As the Army of Northern Virginia closed in on Pope, he retreated from the Rapidan to the north bank of the Rappahannock, where for several days he parried the Confederates' attempts to cross. On August 9, at Cedar Mountain, Stonewall Jackson whipped a much smaller force under Nathaniel P. Banks, who managed to inflict severe casualties before withdrawing. Lincoln praised the Massachusetts politician-general: "I regard Gen. Banks as one of the best men in the army. He makes me no trouble; but, with a large force or a small force, he always knows his duty, and does it."[67] To Judge Hugh Lennox Bond of Maryland, Lincoln described Banks as "his ablest man."[68] Pope and Banks bought enough time for McClellan's forces to join them, but Little Mac as usual moved at a glacial pace. (A young woman observing a photograph of the general said "any artist could get a good one of him because he was always *setting still*.")[69] Lee boldly divided his 54,000-man force, sending half of it under Jackson on a wide flanking movement around the Union right. This dangerous maneuver indicated how little respect Lee had for McClellan. On August 27, Jackson's men astounded Pope by getting into his rear, sacking his supply depot at Manassas Junction, and severing his communications. When news of that calamity reached the capital, Lincoln felt mortified, depressed, angry, and alarmed. His reaction was understandable, for Jackson now stood between him and Pope.

Realizing that Lee had divided his forces, Pope sought to defeat Jackson before the rest of the Army of Northern Virginia could join him. But his failure to block Thoroughfare Gap in the Bull Run Mountains allowed James Longstreet's corps to stream to Jackson's rescue. On August 29 and 30, while the Second Battle of Bull Run raged, Lincoln anxiously followed events as described by telegrams from Herman Haupt, chief of the army's railroad construction and transportation. The president greatly admired Haupt, who he said "had enough brains for a corps commander, if he could be spared from his railroad work."[70] Lincoln was especially impressed by the colonel's succinct, informative dispatches, so different from the imprecise, fretful, and misleading ones sent by McClellan.

The president worried most about McClellan, who had established headquarters in Alexandria and was supposedly hastening to Pope's assistance. Of the Army of the Potomac's 90,000 men, amazingly only 20,000 managed to connect with the Army of Virginia. The 25,000 soldiers in the corps of Franklin and Sumner could easily have reached the battlefield in time to help Pope if McClellan had not delayed their advance. An officer complained that Little Mac was "too dull to ever accomplish anything in War when decisions & speed are the essentials."[71] When Halleck chided him, McClellan sniffed that the general-in-chief "is not a refined person at all." In fairness, it should be noted that Halleck's infrequent orders were vague.[72]

On August 29, Little Mac shocked the president with an extraordinary telegram. "I am clear that one of two courses should be adopted," the general counseled; "1st To concentrate all our available forces to open communication with Pope—2nd To leave Pope to get out of his scrape & at once use all our means to make the Capital perfectly safe."[73] McClellan wrote his wife that "I have a terrible task on my hands now—perfect imbecility to correct. No means to act with, no authority—yet determined if possible to save the country & the Capital. . . . I have just telegraphed very plainly to the Presdt & Halleck what I think ought to be done—I expect merely a contemptuous silence."[74] Contrary to McClellan's expectations, Lincoln did reply. Suppressing his anger at the transparent suggestion that Pope be abandoned to his fate without the hearty cooperation of the Army of the Potomac, the president told the general: "I think your first alternative . . . is the right one. But I wish not to control. That I now leave to Gen. Halleck, aided by your counsels."[75] When Lincoln showed Old Brains the telegram from McClellan, the general-in-chief maintained that the Young Napoleon had been repeatedly ordered to hurry Franklin's corps to Pope.

On August 30, in conversation with John Hay, Lincoln "was very outspoken in regard to McClellan's present conduct. He said it really seemed to him that McC wanted Pope defeated." As evidence supporting that conclusion, the president cited Little Mac's message about leaving Pope "to get out of his own scrape." He also deplored McClellan's "dreadful cowardice" in recommending that Chain Bridge be blown up. (An order to that effect was countermanded.) Lincoln was furious at the general's "incomprehensible interference with Franklin's corps which he recalled once, and then when they had been sent ahead by Halleck's order, begged permission to recall them again & only desisted after Halleck[']s sharp injunction to push them ahead till they whipped something or got whipped themselves. The President seemed to think him a little crazy." (Indeed, McClellan displayed unmistakable signs of deep-seated paranoia.) When Hay asked if the general-in-chief had "any prejudices," Lincoln exclaimed: "No! Halleck is wholly for the service. He does not care who succeeds or who fails so [long as] the service is benefited."[76] In fact, Halleck had misinformed Lincoln about the orders to McClellan. Contrary to what he told the president, Halleck was in fact too timid to confront McClellan. In the midst of the battle, Halleck reportedly "lost the serene, cheerful cordial manner which was his a week ago. He is very short even with men who bring letters from Lincoln."[77] On August 31, the general-in-chief, fatigued by the heavy responsibility resting on his shoulders, appealed pathetically to McClellan: "I beg of you to assist me in this crisis with your ability and experience. I am utterly tired out."[78] With uncharacteristic promptitude, Little Mac responded, criticizing Pope harshly: "to speak frankly,—& the occasion requires it, there appears to be a total absence of brains & I fear the total destruction of the Army."[79] He recommended that Pope immediately fall back to Washington, which was, he thought, in such grave danger that he told his wife he would try to slip into the city and rescue her silver.

On August 30, Hay and the president met with Stanton, who severely criticized McClellan. The war secretary "said that nothing but foul play could lose us the battle & that it rested with McC. and his friends," who deserved to be court-martialed. Stanton, wrote John Hay, "seemed to believe very strongly in Pope. So did the President." That night, according to Hay, "[e]very thing seemed to be going well . . . & we went to bed expecting glad tidings at sunrise." But the next morning, Lincoln told his young secretary: "Well John we are whipped again, I am afraid. The enemy reinforced on Pope and drove back his left wing and he has retired to Centerville where he says he will be able to hold his men. I don[']t like that expression, I don[']t like to hear him admit that his men need holding." Lincoln did not despair, however. Hay noted that he "was in a singularly defiant tone of mind. He often repeated, 'We must hurt this enemy before it gets away.'" The following day, when his assistant personal secretary remarked that things looked bad, Lincoln demurred: "No, Mr Hay, we must whip these people now. Pope must fight them, if they are too strong for him he can gradually retire to these fortifications." Hay thought that it was due largely to Lincoln's "indomitable will, that army movements have been characterized by such energy and celerity for the last few days."[80]

The president emphatically declared to Gideon Welles that "there has been a design, a purpose in breaking down Pope, without regard of consequences to the country. It is shocking to see and know this." On August 30, "[w]e had the enemy in the hollow of our hands" and would have destroyed him "if our generals, who are vexed with Pope, had done their duty; all of our present difficulties and reverses have been brought upon us by these quarrels of the generals."[81] Radical Republicans in Congress shared his view.

Lincoln was also angry at General Fitz John Porter, who was court-martialed and cashiered for failing to support Pope on August 29. Robert Todd Lincoln recalled seeing his father deeply distressed upon learning of Porter's behavior. To a friend the president remarked that "he knew no reason to suspect any one [involved in the Second

Bull Run campaign] of bad faith except Fitz John Porter," and that "he believed his disobedience of orders, and his failure to go to Pope[']s aid in the battle . . . had occasioned our defeat, and deprived us of a victory which would have terminated the war."[82] After signing an order dismissing that general from the service, Lincoln remarked that in "any other country but this, the man would have been shot."[83] With unwonted severity, he asserted that Porter *should* have been shot. (In early August, Porter had called Pope "a fool" who "deserves defeat" and accurately predicted that he "will be whipped."[84] McClellan had made a similar prediction: "Pope will be thrashed during the coming week—& very badly, whipped he will be & ought to be.")[85] Republicans applauded Lincoln's decision, which they regarded as a sign that he would crack down on other disloyal army officers and civilian bureaucrats. "It was a bold act, and he deserves credit for it," commented a Radical journalist.[86] Democrats had anticipated that they could convince him to go easy on Porter, but as D. W. Bartlett noted, when the president "is thoroughly convinced" he "is obstinately courageous. When he is not convinced he is sometimes vacillating."[87]

A sense of *déjà vu* came over Lincoln as he contemplated the military situation. Things looked as bleak after the second battle of Bull Run as they had after the first. "I have heard of people being knocked into the middle of next week, but this is the first time I ever knew of their being knocked into the middle of last year," he remarked on September 4.[88] Four days later, General James Wadsworth reported that the president was "very downcast" and "has given way to apprehension remarkably."[89]

McClellan's actions infuriated not only Lincoln and Stanton but other members of the cabinet as well. Seward expressed amazement "that any jealousy could prevent these generals from acting for their common fame and the welfare of the country."[90] Bates complained of "a criminal tardiness, a fatuous apathy, a captious, bickering rivalry, among our commanders who seem so taken up with their quick made dignity, that they overlook the lives of their people & the necessities of their country."[91]

On August 30, Stanton and Chase drew up a remonstrance calling for McClellan's dismissal. Bates suggested that they tone down this "round-robin," which was done. Smith, Stanton, Bates, and Chase signed the amended version, which declared that it was their "deliberate opinion that, at this time, it is not safe to entrust to Major General McClellan the command of any of the armies of the United States."[92] Welles was sympathetic but thought the document insufficiently courteous and respectful, while Blair refused to sign, though he agreed that McClellan was too untrustworthy for command. Seward was out of town, perhaps to avoid any confrontation over Little Mac.

On September 1, the angry McClellan had a frank talk with Halleck and Lincoln. The president and general-in-chief explained that they were alarmed by Pope's dispatch complaining of the "unsoldierly and dangerous conduct of many brigade and some division commanders of the forces sent here from the Peninsula." The demoralization of the army seemed "calculated to break down the spirits of the men and produce disaster." Little Mac reluctantly agreed to accept command of the defenses of Washington and to urge officers in the Army of the Potomac to cooperate with

Pope.[93] Halleck, unable or unwilling to lead, had failed in his assignment to produce victory. McClellan had outmaneuvered him as sure-footedly as he had outmaneuvered Scott.

Bitter Pill: Restoring McClellan to Command

Lincoln was understandably perplexed. His Illinois friend Mark Skinner reported that the president "wanders about wringing his hands and wondering whom he can trust and what he'd better do."[94] On September 2, at a heated cabinet meeting, he appeared to be in deep distress and suffering bitter anguish, saying "he felt almost ready to hang himself."[95] He astounded the department secretaries by announcing that he had put McClellan in charge of Washington's defenses. Chase vigorously protested "that giving the command to him was equivalent to giving Washington to the rebels" and predicted that "it would prove a national calamity."[96] When Stanton endorsed those views, Lincoln said that "it distressed him exceedingly to find himself differing on such a point from the Secretary of War and the Secretary of the Treasury; that he would gladly resign his place; but he could not see who could do the work wanted as well as McClellan." Halleck had proven incapable of command. The president would not budge, for he insisted that McClellan "knows this whole ground—his specialty is to defend—he is a good engineer, all admit—there is no better organizer—he can be trusted to act on the defensive, but having the 'slows' he is good for nothing for an onward movement." Halleck shared his view, Lincoln added. Blair agreed that McClellan "had beyond any officer the confidence of the army."[97]

The president said that he understood why the cabinet opposed McClellan and, according to Bates, that he "was far from doubting our sincerity, but that he was so distressed, precisely because he knew we were earnestly sincere. He was manifestly alarmed for the safety of the City. He had been talking with Gen Halleck . . . & had gotten the idea that Pope's army was utterly demoralized—saying that 'if Pope's army came within the lines (of the forts) as *a mob*, the City w[oul]d be overrun by the enemy in 48 hours!!'" Bates argued that "if Halleck doubted his ability to defend the City, he ought to be instantly broke. 50,000 men were enough to defend it against all the power of the enemy. If the City fell, it would be by treachery in our leaders, & not by lack of power to defend."[98] The meeting adjourned without a discussion of the anti-McClellan round-robin, which Lincoln never saw.

Lincoln told Hay that McClellan, for all his faults, was at that moment indispensable because of his popularity within the army. "Unquestionably he has acted badly toward Pope," the president acknowledged. "He wanted him to fail. That is unpardonable. But he is too useful just now to sacrifice." In the present emergency, "we must use what tools we have."[99]

Lincoln justifiably feared that the military might revolt if McClellan were not restored to command. On August 31, General Carl Schurz chatted with some brigadiers in the Army of the Potomac, who spoke contemptuously of the administration. McClellan boasted "that people had assured him that the army was so devoted to him that they would as one man enforce any decision he should make as to any part of the war policy."[100] A reporter who was initially indignant at the reappointment of

McClellan changed his mind when he learned that "ninety thousand of our best troops were almost in a mutinous condition ... because Gen. McClellan was not their commander." This journalist, who strongly opposed slavery, concluded that "Lincoln did the very best thing he could do. Admit that the necessity was a melancholy one, nevertheless it was a most imperative necessity."[101] Whitelaw Reid heard a prominent public man remark: "I have been spending the afternoon talking with one of our leading Generals on this very subject of a possible *coup d'etat*. He has given me an inside view of military machinations, and I tell you, we have more than one General who has been trying to shape events so as to make himself dictator." Reid found it significant "that the idea begins to be tolerated as a possibility" beyond the circle of proslavery officers.[102] A high-ranking general in the Army of the Potomac warned that if someone other than McClellan were put in charge, it would be hard to tell whether the Confederate army or the Union army would reach Washington first. Michigan Senator Zachariah Chandler speculated that "traitor Generals" would soon remove Lincoln and establish a military dictatorship.[103]

To help squelch mutinous stirrings, Lincoln sacked Major John J. Key, who had asserted that the Army of the Potomac had no intention of defeating Lee. When asked by a fellow officer why the army had not pursued the Confederates after Antietam, Key allegedly replied: "The object is that neither army shall get much advantage of the other; that both shall be kept in the field till they are exhausted, when we will make a compromise and save slavery."[104] When Chase heard about this conversation, he promptly informed the president, who "said he should have the matter examined and if any such language has been used, his [Key's] head should go off."[105] After Chase's informant met with Lincoln and repeated the story, Key was summoned to the White House and in response to questions "said he thought that slavery was a divine institution, and any issue in this conflict that did not save it would be disastrous." Lincoln interrupted: "You may think about that as you please, but no man shall bear a commission of mine, who is not in favor of gaining victories over the rebels, at any and all times." To show that he was serious, the president immediately cashiered Key "for his silly treasonable talk" and because he feared "it was staff talk" and he "wanted an example."[106] Lincoln felt humiliated by the necessity to restore the army to McClellan, but he insisted that considerations merely personal to himself "must be sacrificed for the public good."[107] He told Congressman William D. Kelley that "though he acted as Commander-in-Chief, he found himself in that season of insubordination, panic, and general demoralization consciously under military duress," for McClellan "had contrived to keep the troops with him, and by charging each new failure to some alleged dereliction of the Secretary of War and President, had created an impression among them that the administration was hostile to him." Reappointing Little Mac, the president added, "was a good deal like 'curing the bite with the hair of the dog'" and called the decision to do so "the greatest trial and most painful duty of his official life. Yet, situated as he was, it seemed to be his duty."[108] Lincoln did not worry that McClellan himself would mutiny. When John Hay suggested that Little Mac might harbor seditious thoughts, the president replied: "McC[lellan] was doing nothing to make himself either respected or feared."[109]

McClellan's reinstatement mortified and disappointed Chase and Stanton. The treasury secretary said Lincoln's relation with the general called to mind "the case of the woman who after yielding everything but the last favor could hardly help yielding that also."[110] Abolitionists objected vehemently. William Lloyd Garrison found himself "growing more and more skeptical as to the 'honesty' of Lincoln," who in the abolitionist's opinion was "nothing better than a wet rag." McClellan's return to command showed that the president "is as near lunacy as any one not a pronounced Bedlamite."[111] Ohio Congressman John A. Gurley said of Little Mac: "we have lost through him more than fifty thousand lives, [$]400,000,000, & a year[']s valuable time. God only knows why the President has retained him at the head of the army! I *guess* Providence designs to prolong this War till we agree to let the Negro go!"[112] Whitelaw Reid, who thought that Joseph Hooker, Heintzelman, or Sedgwick would have been a better choice than McClellan, lamented that the president's "superabundant kindness of heart so often overcomes his better judgment."[113]

That kindness of heart prompted Lincoln to comfort Pope, whom the cabinet viewed as a boastful liar unfit for high command. On September 3, Lincoln met with the general and "assured him of his entire satisfaction with his conduct; assured him that McClellan's command was only temporary; and gave him reason to expect that another army of active operations would be organized at once," which Pope would lead. Lincoln allowed him to see letters that Fitz John Porter had sent during the campaign sharply criticizing Pope. In response, Pope composed a screed excoriating Porter and McClellan. On September 4, Lincoln allowed him to read that document to him and the secretary of the navy, who described it as "not exactly a bulletin nor a report, but a manifesto, a narrative, tinged with wounded pride and a keen sense of injustice and wrong." The following day, the cabinet agreed that it should not be published. The president acted on the report, however, by having Generals Porter, Franklin, and Griffin relieved from duty and brought before courts of inquiry. When newspapers ran Pope's report, Lincoln deplored its publication but said that the leak could never be traced to the cunning general.

The president thought that Pope's services should be acknowledged, and he contemplated preparing a statement to that effect for Halleck's signature. In the statement, he described Pope "as brave, patriotic, and as having done his whole duty in every respect in Virginia, to the entire satisfaction of himself and Halleck." But he felt that Pope must be sacrificed because the army was prejudiced against him. When a Sioux Indian uprising erupted in Minnesota, Lincoln sent Pope to quell it. Thinking himself the "most talented general in the world and the one most wronged," Pope left for Minnesota on September 6, as Lincoln put it, "very angry, and not without cause, but circumstances controlled us."[114] The exiled general called the president's treatment of him "dastardly & atrocious."[115] (Pope continued grousing at length about Lincoln into 1863, deeming him "the worst enemy I ever had in my life.")[116]

Although Pope became the principal scapegoat for Second Bull Run, sharp criticism was also directed at Lincoln and Stanton. Senator Henry Wilson speculated that the president "couldn't get one vote in twenty in New England," and Zachariah Chandler said Lincoln was as "unstable as water."[117] Adams S. Hill, a leading Washington correspondent, reported in early September that *"Abraham Lincoln has killed himself this week. Such weakness."*[118] Hill thought that Lincoln "lost much ground in the estimation of the people," had "fallen from a h[e]ight which no President since Jackson ever occupied before," and had "dumped himself into the back yard of the American people." Hill added that "[i]nefficiency [and] indecision are weak words for the case," and speculated that if Hamlin were "more of a man there would be a strong movement for his substitution."[119] Henry W. Bellows wrote from Washington that the "feeling of indignation at the inefficiency or incompetence of the Government is intense." He believed that the nation's "political concerns are so loosely & ineptly managed that it sends contagious weakness & demoralization through the Army."[120] Henry Ward Beecher thundered: "It is a supreme and extraordinary want of executive administrative talent at the head of the Government that is bringing us to humiliation. Let it be known that the Nation [is] wasted away by an incurable consumption of Central Imbecility."[121] The New York *Evening Post* maintained that despite Lincoln's "personal popularity" and "the general confidence in his good intentions," the "effect of his management has been such that . . . a large part of the nation is utterly discouraged and despondent." It was widely believed, the editors said, "that treachery lurks in the highest quarters." Such suspicion and demoralization grew "out of the weakness and vacillation of the Administration, which itself has grown out of Mr. Lincoln's own want of decision and purpose."[122] A leading Indiana Republican lamented that the "President, in his anxiety to do right, has vacillated and is fast losing the confidence of his friends, and the respect of his enemies."[123]

Lincoln tried to deflect such criticism by stating "that he was 'under bonds' to let Halleck have his own way in everything in regard to the army: to make no appointments or removals even without his advice or consent."[124] At the close of the order restoring the army to McClellan, only Halleck's name appeared. To former governor William Dennison of Ohio, Lincoln explained: "I found I must select one man to command all the armies of the United States, and though it may be possible that Halleck is not a great General, I firmly believe he is the best I have got." Therefore "he left military matters *entirely* to General Halleck." He added that "Stanton had no more to do with military movements than a clerk. He is like a Secretary of War in time of peace—he attends to all the duties of his office, but does not plan a campaign anywhere."[125]

But after Second Bull Run, the opposite was actually the case; Halleck became, in effect, a clerk, while Stanton resumed his earlier status as a co-planner of the war effort. In 1864, Lincoln remarked that Old Brains at first had accepted the full power and responsibility of a true general-in-chief and persisted "till Pope's defeat: but ever since that event, he had shrunk from the responsibility whenever it was possible." After Second Bull Run, "he broke down—nerve and pluck all gone" and became "little more since that [time] than a first-rate clerk."[126] (Hooker contemptuously likened Halleck to a man who wed with the understanding that he would not have sex with his bride.) In early September, Halleck told his wife of the "terrible anxiety" he had suffered in the past month, and complained that he was "greatly dissatisfied with the way things go here. There are so many cooks, they destroy all the broth. I am tired and disgusted with the working of this great political machine."[127]

Especially exasperating to the president was Halleck's "habitual attitude of demur."[128] According to Assistant Secretary of War Charles A. Dana, the "first impulse of his mind toward a new plan was not enthusiasm; it was analysis, criticism."[129] Halleck had other flaws. Caleb B. Smith thought that he demoralized the army by treating volunteer officers contemptuously. In Smith's view, he was unqualified for his post by a lack of talent, genius, and success. After a conversation with the general, George Templeton Strong confided to his diary that Halleck was "weak, shallow, commonplace, vulgar," and that his "silly talk was conclusive as to his incapacity."[130]

But Lincoln kept Halleck on as a technical advisor, a translator of presidential wishes into military parlance, a shield against criticism, and an administrator. In these roles he proved useful. Halleck described his function as "simply a military adviser of the Secretary of War and the President" and said that he "must obey and carry out what they decide upon."[131] General Jacob D. Cox accurately deemed Halleck a mere "bureau officer in Washington."[132]

Key Turning Point: Quasi-Victory at Antietam

On September 3, instead of besieging Washington, Lee's Army of Northern Virginia began splashing across the upper Potomac and entered Maryland, spreading panic throughout that state and Pennsylvania. Lincoln was not alarmed, for when asked earlier about the possibility of a Confederate invasion of the Free State, he had said "that there was exactly where he would have them; & where the military men would have them."[133]

For Lincoln, the vexing question of command arose once again: who should lead the Union forces pursuing Lee? (McClellan had been given control only of the Washington forts.) Halleck declined the job when Lincoln indirectly offered it to him. Burnside also begged off, modestly insisting that he was not up to the job. Chase thought that Joseph Hooker or Edwin V. Sumner might do, but his opinion was not widely shared. By default, the choice settled on McClellan. (When the elderly John E. Wool learned that he had been passed over yet again, he bitterly complained that Lincoln was "a joker" lacking "the first qualification to govern a great people," a man who "delights in relating smutty stories" and whose pets, most notably McClellan, "have all failed.")[134]

On September 5, Halleck and the president asked Little Mac to take charge of the army in the field. The decision, which essentially restored the Army of the Potomac to McClellan (Pope's army had been given to him three days earlier), was doubtless Lincoln's, though for some unknown reason he ascribed it to Halleck. Nathaniel P. Banks replaced McClellan in charge of the capital's fortifications.

Morale soared when the army realized that McClellan had resumed command. "Our troops know of none other they can trust," explained Major Alexander Webb.[135] "It makes my heart bleed," Little Mac wrote his wife on September 5, "to see the poor shattered remnants of my noble Army of the Potomac, poor fellows! and to see how they love me even now. I hear them calling out to me as I ride among them—

'George—don't leave us again!!' 'They *shan't* take you away from us again' etc. etc."[136] That same day, Lincoln observed that "McClellan is working like a beaver. He seems to be aroused to doing something, by the sort of snubbing he got last week." Though "he can[']t fight himself," the president observed, "he excells in making others ready to fight."[137]

Restoring the troops' morale seemed vitally important to Lincoln, who told Welles that he "was shocked to find that of 140,000 whom we were paying for in Pope's army only 60,000 could be found. McClellan brought away 93,000 from the Peninsula, but could not to-day count on over 45,000." The president believed "that some of our men permitted themselves to be captured in order that they might leave on parole, get discharged, and go home." Plaintively, he asked: "Where there is such rottenness, is there not reason to fear for the country?"[138] Chase shared Lincoln's concern, reluctantly acknowledging that if McClellan were not restored to command, the Northern cause at that delicate moment might be placed in severe jeopardy.

As he led the army into Maryland, McClellan wrote his wife that the "feeling of the Govt towards me . . . is kind & trusting. I hope with God's blessing, to justify the great confidence they now repose in me, & will bury the past in oblivion."[139] Lincoln predicted, predicting that if the general did not win a victory, both of them "would be in a bad row of stumps."[140] But the president was not sanguine. In early August, he ruefully told a group who criticized Little Mac: "McClellan must be a good military man. Everybody says he is. These military men all say so themselves, and it isn't possible that they can all be so completely deceived as some of you insist. He is well versed in military matters, and has had opportunities of experience and observation. Still there must be something wrong somewhere, and I'll tell you what it is, *he never embraces his opportunities*—that's where the trouble is—he always puts off the hour for embracing his opportunities."[141] More succinctly, the president explained to Welles: "I can never feel confident that he will do anything effectual."[142] The navy secretary also feared that McClellan would "persist in delays and inaction" and "do nothing affirmative." To be successful, Welles thought, the general "must rid himself of what President Lincoln calls the 'slows.'"[143]

McClellan's leisurely progress in Maryland confirmed such suspicions. On September 12, Lincoln told his cabinet that the general "can't go ahead—he can't strike a blow. He got to Rockville, for instance, last Sunday night [September 8], and in four days he advanced to Middlebrook, ten miles in pursuit of an invading enemy. This was rapid movement for him."[144] Lincoln seriously considered meeting with McClellan, but both Banks and Halleck warned him it would be too risky to leave Washington while Lee's troops were nearby.

Characteristically overestimating the enemy numbers by a wide margin, McClellan appealed for reinforcements. (The Army of the Potomac contained 75,000 effective troops to Lee's 38,000.) Lincoln ordered Fitz John Porter's corps to join Little Mac and telegraphed him on September 11, "I am for sending you all that can be spared, & I hope others can follow Porter very soon."[145] When Lee seemed to be retreating, Lincoln urged McClellan: "Please do not let him get off without being hurt."[146]

Pennsylvanians grew extremely anxious as Lee headed their way. When Governor Andrew G. Curtin appealed for 80,000 troops, Lincoln patiently explained his inability to comply: "We have not to exceed eighty thousand disciplined troops, properly so called, this side of the mountains, and most of them, with many of the new regiments, are now close in the rear of the enemy supposed to be invading Pennsylvania. Start half of them to Harrisburg, and the enemy will turn upon and beat the remaining half, and then reach Harrisburg before the part going there, and beat it too when it comes. The best possible security for Pennsylvania is putting the strongest force possible into the enemies rear."[147] To another skittish resident of the Keystone State, fearful that the Confederates would seize Philadelphia, the president offered reassurances: "Philadelphia is more than a hundred and fifty miles from Hagerstown, and could not be reached by the rebel Army in ten days, if no hinderance was interposed."[148]

On September 15, Lincoln rejoiced to hear that the Army of the Potomac had the previous day beaten the enemy at South Mountain, though he could not know that McClellan's dispatch announcing the victory exaggerated its significance. The Rebels, Little Mac telegraphed Halleck, were retreating "in a perfect panic," and "Lee last night stated publicly that he must admit they had been shockingly whipped."[149] (How he knew about Lee's remarks was unexplained.) Lincoln sent congratulations: "God bless you, and all with you. Destroy the rebel army, if possible."[150] He told a friend, "I now consider it safe to say that Gen. McClellan has gained a great victory over the great rebel army in Maryland. . . . He is now pursuing the flying foe."[151]

In fact, however, the Confederates were not flying but were instead consolidating their scattered forces after capturing the 11,500-man Union garrison at Harper's Ferry on September 15. (Lincoln deplored this calamity, saying that McClellan "could and ought to have prevented the loss of Harper's Ferry, but was six days marching 40 miles, and it was surrendered.")[152] Little Mac, having fortuitously obtained a copy of Lee's orders two days earlier (this document became famous as the Lost Order), knew that the Confederate commander had divided his army. McClellan could have scored a smashing victory if he had acted swiftly to take advantage of that news, but his habitual slowness permitted the enemy to regroup. Having won what he assumed was a major victory at South Mountain, the general ignored the president's injunction to destroy the Army of Northern Virginia. Instead, he was content to let it recross the Potomac, which he mistakenly thought it was doing. He was startled to learn that the Rebels were in reality forming a line of battle near Antietam Creek. During the three-and-a-half days following the discovery of the Lost Order, Lee's army had been in grave danger; now its components were reunited and ready to fight the Army of the Potomac. McClellan had forfeited what he properly deemed the "opportunity of a lifetime."[153]

On September 17, the bloodiest single day's battle of the war was fought at Antietam Creek, where the Army of the Potomac suffered 12,000 casualties and the Army of Northern Virginia 14,000. The result was in effect a draw, with neither side clearly victorious, though Lee abandoned the field. Lincoln believed that the Confederate army could be annihilated before it crossed the Potomac if only McClellan would act promptly. At Antietam, Little Mac had committed only two-thirds of his men to battle; the remainder, reinforced by 12,000 freshly arrived troops, could have attacked effectively on September 18. But that day the passive Union commander allowed Lee to slip back into Virginia unharmed, much to the chagrin of the president, who moaned once again: "he never embraces his opportunities."[154] A week after the battle, Lincoln remarked "that nothing could have been better fought than the battle of Antietam; but that he did not know why McClellan did not follow up his advantage."[155]

Others were equally puzzled. In Missouri, a Union colonel lamented that the "Campaign on the Potomac is another failure on our part, and I can[']t understand the motive inducing Lincoln to hold onto McClellan. He don't move. If we had displayed half the Energy on the Potomac that the Rebels have we could now see the end of this war." Morale among western troops, he noted, was sinking because "so little good results from what has been done."[156] Gustavus Fox thought the loss of the Harper's Ferry garrison more than offset the advantage gained at Antietam, since Lee was allowed to escape with his army intact. Shortly after the battle, Fox told Lincoln that his anxious wife insisted that he write her daily assurances that Washington was safe. The president "said that put him in mind of the fellow in the Democratic convention in Illinois. The question was upon dispensing with the roll call as the convention was large and much time would be consumed. This fellow said he was not certain as he was present and he would like to have the roll called to make sure of it."[157]

Colonization Schemes

With Lee in retreat, Lincoln's mind turned to the Emancipation Proclamation, which had been in his desk drawer for weeks. Since announcing to the cabinet his intention to issue it, he had been preparing the public mind to accept so momentous a step. To that end, he once again raised the colonization proposal. In mid-August, he gave a hint of future developments when he urged a group of Washington blacks to emigrate to Panama. The president realized that colonization would be politically necessary if emancipation were in the offing, for only something acceptable to conservative whites could be effectively provided for the freedmen. He told Kansas Senator Samuel C. Pomeroy that "he would emancipate as soon as he was assured that his colonization project would succeed." To Pomeroy, Lincoln often quoted Kentucky Senator Garrett Davis's remark that Unionists in the Bluegrass State "would not resist his gradual emancipation scheme if he would only conjoin with it his colonization plan."[158] John Palmer Usher of Indiana (arguably the most Negrophobic state in the North) told Lincoln that a colonization plan "will, if adopted, relieve the free states of the apprehension now prevailing, and fostered by the disloyal, that they are to be overrun by negroes made free by the war, [and] it will alarm those in rebellion, for they will see that their cherished property is departing from them forever and incline them to peace."[159] Orestes Brownson, who favored colonization, estimated that 75 percent of Northern voters were antislavery and 90 percent antiblack.

A few colonizationists argued that blacks would never receive decent treatment from American whites and would fare better abroad. From St. Louis, the sometime poet and civil servant William Davis Gallagher wrote his close friend Salmon P. Chase about slaves who escaped from bondage in the interior of Missouri but could find no work at St. Louis, and were unable to obtain passes to visit Illinois. Discouraged, they decided to return to their masters. Gallagher indignantly exclaimed: "in this manner the *disability of color* in the Border States . . . is operating to strengthen the hands of the very rebels who have brought upon the country its grievous troubles! If these poor people were out of the State, employment could be found for most if not all of them in neighboring parts of Illinois," but the Black Laws of the Prairie State forbade them entrance. Gallagher scorned the hypocrisy of many Northerners: "The very people that at one moment denounce slave-holders as tyrants and sinners, the next moment turn their backs and shut their doors against the poor slaves whom accident or repentance has set free. Before we have Emancipation . . . I hope we shall have matured a system of *Colonization*: for if we have not, God pity the poor Negro!"[160]

The timing of the White House meeting, which represented the first occasion that blacks were invited there to consult on public policy, suggests that Lincoln was trotting out colonization to smooth the way for emancipation. If he had been truly enthusiastic about colonization, he might well have acted more swiftly on the appropriation that Congress had voted months earlier to fund the emigration of Washington's blacks. Evidently, Lincoln urged colonization not primarily because he still believed in it, but rather because he wished to make emancipation more palatable to the Border States, to Unionists in the Confederacy, and to Northern Conservatives. There is good reason to accept the analysis of one observer who regarded the meeting as an attempt "to throw dust into the eyes of the Kentucky slaveholders."[161]

James Mitchell, a Methodist minister and a former agent of the American Colonization Society, set up the meeting. Lincoln had worked with Mitchell in Illinois, and in 1862 appointed him commissioner of emigration in the Interior Department. In May, at the president's behest, Mitchell published an open letter endorsing gradual emancipation and colonization. Two months later, he urged Lincoln to persuade black Washingtonians to take the lead in colonization, noting that "the Colored people of this District . . . for the most part are less inclined to remove therefrom than the Contrabands." A "great emigration from the ranks of the Colored residents of the District" would not occur, for "they are to a great extent satisfied with their new liberties and franchises, with hopes of further enlargement." It "will require time to enable them to realize that they are near the summit now—education must refine their sensibility, and a purer morality than has yet obtained amongst the free people of Color, must actuate them, before they will feel that an escape from their present relation to the American people is a *duty and a privilege*."[162] Lincoln sought to instruct them about their duty.

Colonization had been debated in Congress that spring and summer, with Missouri Representative Frank Blair and Wisconsin Senator James R. Doolittle, along with some Border State colleagues, supporting it enthusiastically. Blair asserted that it "was the negro question, and not the *slavery question* which made the rebellion, questions entirely different and requiring different treatment. . . . If the rebellion was made by two hundred and fifty thousand slave-holders, for the sake of perpetuating slavery, then it might be a complete remedy to extirpate the institution; but if the rebellion has grown out of the abhorrence of the non-slaveholders for emancipation and amalgamation, and their dread of 'negro equality,' how will their discontent be cured by the very measure [emancipation] the mere apprehension of which has driven them into rebellion?" Colonization, therefore, must follow emancipation.[163] Doolittle cited familiar arguments in support of colonization, which he said was "in accordance with the natural laws of climate, in accordance with the difference of constitution existing between these two races; a solution to which nature itself is pointing; a solution by which the tropics are to be given to the man of the tropics, and the temperate zone to the man of the temperate zone. . . . it is God's solution; and it is easier to work with Him than to work against Him, and wiser, too."[164]

On July 16, a special congressional committee endorsed an emancipation scheme that included colonization, recommended an appropriation of $20 million to facilitate the voluntary emigration of American blacks, and noted that the most serious objections to emancipation arose "from the opposition of a large portion of our people to the intermixture of the races, and from the association of white and black labor. The committee would do nothing to favor such a policy; apart from the antipathy which nature has ordained, the presence of a race among us who cannot, and ought not to, be admitted to our social and political privileges, will be a perpetual source of injury and inquietude to both. This is a question of color, and is unaffected by the relation of master and slave." The "most formidable difficulty which lies in the way of emancipation," the committee argued, was "the belief, which obtains especially among those who own no slaves, that if the negroes shall become free, they must still continue in our midst, and, so remaining after their liberation, they may in some measure be made equal to the Anglo-Saxon race." The "Anglo-American will never give his consent that the negro, no matter how free, shall be elevated to such equality. It matters not how wealthy, how intelligent, or how morally meritorious the negro may become, so long as he remains among us, the recollection of the former relation of master and slave will be perpetuated by the changeless color of the Ethiop's skin, and that color will alike will be perpetuated by the degrading tradition of his former bondage." The "highest interests of the white race, whether Anglo-Saxon, Celt, or Scandinavian, require that the whole country should be held and occupied by those races alone." Therefore a home "must be sought for the African beyond our own limits and in those warmer regions to which his constitution is better adapted than to our own climate, and which doubtless the Almighty intended the colored races should inhabit and cultivate."[165] Congressional pressure to do something about colonization may well have prompted Lincoln to summon the black Washingtonians.

The president's widely reported remarks to those men indirectly signaled his intention to emancipate at least some slaves. On August 14, after cordially shaking hands with the five black leaders who gathered at the White House, Lincoln reviewed the recent legislative history of colonization measures. In April and July, Congress had appropriated a total of $600,000 for colonizing blacks abroad. The Second Confiscation Act of July 17 authorized Lincoln to "make provision for the transportation, colonization, and settlement in some tropical country beyond the limits of the United States, such persons of the African race, made free by the provisions of this act, as may be willing to emigrate, having first obtained the consent of the Government of said country to their protection and settlement within the same, with all the rights and privileges of freeman." Lincoln said that he wanted to consult with his guests about how that money should be spent. In justifying colonization, which he had supported for many years in Illinois, he remarked: "You and we are different races. We have between us a broader difference than exists between almost any other two races. Whether it is right or wrong I need not discuss, but this physical difference is a great disadvantage to us both, as I think your race suffer very greatly, many of them by living among us, while ours suffer from your presence. In a word we suffer on each side. If this is admitted, it affords a reason at least why we should be separated."

Lincoln acknowledged that American slaves were the victims of a uniquely cruel form of oppression: "Your race are suffering, in my judgment, the greatest wrong inflicted on any people." Free blacks as well as slaves experienced discrimination: "even when you cease to be slaves, you are yet far removed from being placed on an equality with the white race. You are cut off from many of the advantages which the other race enjoy. The aspiration of men is to enjoy equality with the best when free, but on this broad continent, not a single man of your race is made the equal of a single man of ours. Go where you are treated the best, and the ban is still upon you." Lincoln was careful not to say that blacks *were* unequal to whites; rather, he implied, blacks had been *placed* in an unequal position and were *made* unequal to whites. He did not specify how they had been so placed and so made, but a fair inference would be that whites had done so through discriminatory laws and institutions.

Lincoln asked his guests to consider how best to deal with the harsh reality of slavery and discrimination. "I do not propose to discuss this, but to present it as a fact with which we have to deal. I cannot alter it if I would. It is a fact, about which we all think and feel alike, I and you. We look to our condition, owing to the existence of the two races on this continent. I need not recount to you the effects upon white men, growing out of the institution of Slavery. I believe in its general evil effects on the white race. See our present condition—the country engaged in war!—our white men cutting one another's throats, none knowing how far it will extend; and then consider what we know to be the truth. But for your race among us there could not be war, although many men engaged on either side do not care for you one way or the other. Nevertheless, I repeat, without the institution of Slavery and the colored race as a basis, the war could not have an existence." Lincoln was acknowledging that the Civil War was caused by the South's desire to maintain white supremacy at all costs. If no blacks had been in the country, no war would have occurred. His logic was sound, but the black committeemen doubtless thought to themselves: "It's not our fault that we're here! Don't blame your troubles on us!"

From these hard realities Lincoln concluded that it "is better for us both, therefore, to be separated." Colonization as he envisioned it would be voluntary. But how to persuade free blacks to leave the country when they did not want to? To this problem Lincoln now turned. Slavery could only be abolished if blacks agreed to emigrate. Those already free owed it to their enslaved brothers and sisters to spearhead a colonization effort: "I know that there are free men among you, who even if they could better their condition are not as much inclined to go out of the country as those, who being slaves could obtain their freedom on this condition. I suppose one of the principal difficulties in the way of colonization is that the free colored man cannot see that his comfort would be advanced by it. You may believe you can live in Washington or elsewhere in the United States the remainder of your life [as easily], perhaps more so than you can in any foreign country, and hence you may come to the conclusion that you have nothing to do with the idea of going to a foreign country. This is (I speak in no unkind sense) an extremely selfish view of the case. But you ought to do something to help those who are not so fortunate as yourselves. There is an unwillingness on the part of our people, harsh as it may be, for you free colored people to remain with us."

Lincoln said that educated free blacks should take the lead by volunteering to be colonized, for they would serve as role models for slaves who might eventually be liberated. "If we deal with those who are not free at the beginning, and whose intellects are clouded by Slavery, we have very poor materials to start with. If intelligent colored men, such as are before me, would move in this matter, much might be accomplished. It is exceedingly important that we have men at the beginning capable of thinking as white men, and not those who have been systematically oppressed."

Lincoln appealed to his guests' altruism. "There is much to encourage you. For the sake of your race you should sacrifice something of your present comfort for the purpose of being as grand in that respect as the white people. It is a cheering thought throughout life that something can be done to ameliorate the condition of those who have been subject to the hard usage of the world. It is difficult to make a man miserable while he feels he is worthy of himself, and claims kindred to the great God who made him. In the American Revolutionary war sacrifices were made by men engaged in it; but they were cheered by the future. Gen. Washington himself endured greater physical hardships than if he had remained a British subject. Yet he was a happy man, because he was engaged in benefiting his race—something for the children of his neighbors, having none of his own."

To the practical question of just where American blacks might move, Lincoln at first pointed to Africa. "The colony of Liberia has been in existence a long time. In a certain sense it is a success. The old President of Liberia, [Joseph Jenkins] Roberts, has just been with me—the first time I ever saw him. He says they have within the bounds of that colony between 300,000 and 400,000 people. . . . The question is if the colored people are persuaded to go anywhere, why not there? One reason for an unwillingness to do so is that some of you would rather remain within reach of the country of your nativity. I do not know how much attachment you may have toward our race. It does not strike me that you have the greatest reason to love them. But still you are attached to them at all events."

Another possible relocation site was in the Chiriqui province of Panama, then part of Colombia (also known as New Grenada). Early proponents of colonization, including Thomas Jefferson, James Madison, and Benjamin Lundy, had preferred the Western Hemisphere to Africa. In more recent times, the Blair family (especially Frank) had championed colonization there. Other antislavery leaders, including Lyman

Trumbull and Richard Bissell of Illinois, James R. Doolittle, Gerrit Smith, and Theodore Parker, concurred. In 1861 and early 1862, Mexico and lightly populated Central American nations expressed interest in such schemes.

In urging his black callers to support colonization in Panama, Lincoln pointed out that that country "is nearer to us than Liberia—not much more than one-fourth as far as Liberia, and within seven days' run by steamers. Unlike Liberia it is on a great line of travel—it is a highway. The country is a very excellent one for any people, and with great natural resources and advantages, and especially because of the similarity of climate with your native land—thus being suited to your physical condition. The particular place I have in view is to be a great highway from the Atlantic or Caribbean Sea to the Pacific Ocean, and this particular place has all the advantages for a colony. On both sides there are harbors among the finest in the world. Again, there is evidence of very rich coal mines. A certain amount of coal is valuable in any country, and there may be more than enough for the wants of the country." Mining the coal "will afford an opportunity to the inhabitants for immediate employment till they get ready to settle permanently in their homes. If you take colonists where there is no good landing, there is a bad show; and so where there is nothing to cultivate, and of which to make a farm. But if something is started so that you can get your daily bread as soon as you reach there, it is a great advantage. Coal land is the best thing I know of with which to commence an enterprise."

Lincoln tried to convince the black leaders that the Chiriqui project was not a corrupt scheme designed to enrich a few greedy swindlers: "you have been talked to upon this subject, and told that a speculation is intended by gentlemen, who have an interest in the country, including the coal mines. We have been mistaken all our lives if we do not know whites as well as blacks look to their self-interest. Unless among those deficient of intellect everybody you trade with makes something. You meet with these things here as elsewhere. If such persons have what will be an advantage to them, the question is whether it cannot be made of advantage to you. You are intelligent, and know that success does not as much depend on external help as on self-reliance. Much, therefore, depends upon yourselves. As to the coal mines, I think I see the means available for your self-reliance. I shall, if I get a sufficient number of you engaged, have provisions made that you shall not be wronged. If you will engage in the enterprise I will spend some of the money intrusted to me."

Lincoln carefully warned his black guests that settlers had no guarantee that they would prosper in Chiriqui: "I am not sure you will succeed. The Government may lose the money, but we cannot succeed unless we try; but we think, with care, we can succeed. The political affairs in Central America are not in quite as satisfactory condition as I wish. There are contending factions in that quarter; but it is true all the factions are agreed alike on the subject of colonization, and want it, and are more generous than we are here. To your colored race they have no objection."

Lincoln expressed a keen desire to make sure that American blacks would not become second-class citizens in Panama. He pledged to the black delegation that he "would endeavor to have you made equals, and have the best assurance that you should be the equals of the best. The practical thing I want to ascertain is whether

I can get a number of able-bodied men, with their wives and children, who are willing to go, when I present evidence of encouragement and protection. Could I get a hundred tolerably intelligent men, with their wives and children, to 'cut their own fodder,' so to speak? Can I have fifty? If I could find twenty-five able-bodied men, with a mixture of women and children, good things in the family relation, I think I could make a successful commencement. I want you to let me know whether this can be done or not. This is the practical part of my wish to see you. These are subjects of very great importance, worthy of a month's study, [instead] of a speech delivered in an hour. I ask you then to consider seriously not pertaining to yourselves merely, nor for your race, and ours, for the present time, but as one of the things, if successfully managed, for the good of mankind—not confined to the present generation, but as

> From age to age descends the lay,
> To millions yet to be,
> Till far its echoes roll away,
> Into eternity.

(Earlier that day, Lincoln had told Liberian President Roberts and William McLain, a financial agent for the American Colonization Society, that he believed Liberia would be a suitable locale for free blacks to settle. Angry at Lincoln's inconsistency in praising Liberia as a venue for colonization and then criticizing it a short time later, McLain denounced the Chiriqui plan: "Out upon all such men and such schemes!")[166]

The black delegation promised to consider Lincoln's request carefully. Two days later its chairman, Edward M. Thomas, who headed the Anglo African Institute for the Encouragement of Industry and Art, told the president that he had originally opposed colonization but that he had changed his mind and would like authorization to proselytize in New York, Boston, and Philadelphia on behalf of that scheme.

Some of Thomas's fellow blacks supported emigration, including well-known men like Henry Highland Garnet, Lewis Woodson, and Martin R. Delany. (In 1865, Lincoln met with Delany and appointed him a major in the army, the first black to achieve so high a rank.) Support for colonization among blacks had grown during the 1850s. In 1854, a black emigration convention in Cleveland had discussed a large-scale exodus. Delany inspected sites in the Niger Valley for the relocation of his fellow blacks; James Whitefield did the same in Central America; and James Theodore Holly looked into the West Indies. In 1858, blacks in New York under the leadership of Henry Highland Garnet founded the African Civilization Society to encourage black emigration to Yoruba. In 1862, Congress received petitions from 242 blacks in California, expressing the desire to be colonized "in some country in which their color will not be a badge of degradation," and from blacks in the District of Columbia, asking to be sent to Central America.[167] A few years earlier, Owen Lovejoy had introduced into the Illinois Legislature "a remonstrance from the colored people of the State against their colonization in Africa, until they are all able to read and write, and unless separate colonies be assigned to those of different shades of color. The reason assigned for the latter objection is, that blacks and mulattoes cannot live in harmony together."[168]

A journalist characterized Lincoln's remarks as "very sympathetic and paternal," manifesting "his sincere and earnest desire to see them [black people] invested with the rights and privileges of real freemen." Remarkable was the president's willingness to make the "humiliating statement" that "the semi-civilized States of South America 'are more generous' than the great model Republic."[169] Henry Highland Garnet lauded the Chiriqui scheme as "the most humane, and merciful movement which this or any other administration has proposed for the benefit of the enslaved."[170]

Most black leaders, however, were less enthusiastic. Among them was Robert Purvis, a well-to-do Philadelphian, who wrote Lincoln a stinging public letter: "It is in vain you talk to me about 'two races' and their 'mutual antagonism.' In the matter of rights, there is but one race, and that is the *human* race. God has made of one blood all nations, to dwell on the face of the earth. . . . Sir, this is our country as much as it is yours, and we will not leave it."[171] Another black in the City of Brotherly Love predicted that Lincoln's colonization scheme would "arouse prejudice" and "increase enmity against us, without bringing with it the remedy proposed or designed."[172] Fellow townsmen published *An Appeal from the Colored Men of Philadelphia to the President of the United States* acknowledging that many blacks were "[b]enighted by the ignorance entailed upon us, oppressed by the iron-heel of the master who knows no law except that of worldly gain and self-aggrandizement" and asking "why should we not be poor and degraded? . . . We regret the ignorance and poverty of our race." But, they pointed out, "[m]any of us, in Pennsylvania, have our own houses and other property, amounting, in the aggregate, to millions of dollars. Shall we sacrifice this, leave our homes, forsake our birth-place, and flee to a strange land, to appease the anger and prejudice of the traitors now in arms against the Government, or their aiders and abettors in this or in foreign lands?"[173] The Rev. Mr. William T. Catto, speaking at a rally in Manhattan, declared that the president was "pandering to the mob spirit."[174]

Frederick Douglass excoriated the president for appearing "silly and ridiculous" by uttering remarks that revealed "his pride of race and blood, his contempt for negroes and his canting hypocrisy." Douglass scouted the administration's entire record on slavery: "Illogical and unfair as Mr. Lincoln's statements are, they are nevertheless quite in keeping with his whole course from the beginning of his administration to this day, and confirms the painful conviction that though elected as an anti-slavery man by Republican and Abolitionist voters, Mr. Lincoln is quite a genuine representative of American prejudice and negro hatred and far more concerned for the preservation of slavery, and the favor of the Border States, than for any sentiment of magnanimity or principle of justice and humanity." Lincoln, in Douglass's view, was saying to blacks: "I don't like you, you must clear out of the country." The polite tone of Lincoln's remarks "is too thin a mask not to be seen through," for they lacked the "genuine spark of humanity" and a "sincere wish to improve the condition of the oppressed."[175] Hyperbolically, Douglass declared that "the nation was never more completely in the hands of the Slave power."[176]

White Radicals were also disenchanted. Lamenting the president's remarks, Chase confided to his diary: "How much better would be a manly protest against prejudice against color!—and a wise effort to give freemen homes in America!"[177] William Lloyd Garrison, a long-time opponent of colonization, scornfully wrote that Lincoln's "education (!) with and among 'the white trash' of Kentucky was most unfortunate for his moral development." If the president understood that it "is not their color, but their being free, that makes their presence here intolerable," he "would sooner have the earth opened and swallow him up, than to have made the preposterous speech he did." Garrison further declared Lincoln's words to be "puerile, absurd, illogical, impertinent, untimely." As for the ability of blacks and whites to coexist, Garrison insisted that everyone "differs from everybody else in height, bulk, and looks. Is any one of these 'physical differences,' more than another, a justifiable ground for colonization? The whole thing is supremely ridiculous."[178] Fellow abolitionist Beriah Green could scarcely contain his indignation. "Such braying—babbling—chattering Lincoln indulged in in his interview with 'the Negro Delegation!'" he exclaimed. "Enough to turn the stomach of an ostrich! Such driveling folly! Such brazen impudence! Such glaring selfishness! Such a 'blind Leader of the Blind!'"[179]

The Chicago *Tribune* objected on practical grounds: "The blacks can neither be colonized across the Gulf, or sent through our lines to the North. Their numbers utterly forbid and render futile these measures save on the most limited scale."[180] The New York *Times* also demurred: "No, Mr. President. The enfranchised blacks must find homes, without circumnavigating the seas at the National expense."[181] Democrats scoffed at the proposal. The New York *Evening Express* protested that Lincoln's scheme would "entail upon the White Labor of the North, the doom and debt of the tax-groaning serfs and labor-slaves of Europe."[182]

Despite the support of chairman Edward M. Thomas for colonization, eventually the black delegation rejected Lincoln's advice, asserting that it was "inexpedient, inauspicious and impolitic to agitate the subject of emigration of the colored people of this country anywhere. . . . We judge it unauthorized and unjust for us to compromise the interests of over four and a half millions of our race by precipitate action on our part."[183]

As if that rejection were not enough to kill the Chiriqui scheme, an aroma of corruption further undermined support for it. There was good reason to suspect corruption. The plan to colonize blacks in the Chiriqui province was the brainchild of a wealthy Philadelphia businessman, Ambrose W. Thompson, who alleged that he owned large tracts of land there. In the 1850s, he formed the Chiriqui Improvement Company and unsuccessfully attempted to persuade the Navy Department to buy Panamanian coal. In August 1861, when Thompson offered to sell coal at half the market price if American blacks could be colonized there to work the mines, he attracted congressional support. To investigate the matter, Lincoln appointed a commission and enlisted the aid of his brother-in-law, Ninian Edwards, who reported favorably on the plan to purchase cheap coal from the Chiriqui Company. In November, Interior Secretary Smith echoed those sentiments. The following month, Francis P.

Blair, Sr., supplied the president with an elaborate brief endorsing Thompson's scheme, which he said might yield several desirable results, including *"the acquisition of safe and well fortified Harbors on each side of the Isthmus—a good and sufficient Railway transportation between them—a command of the Coal-fields to afford adequate supply for our Navy – A million of acres of land for the colonization of American Freeman in Homesteads and freeholds."*[184] Chase told the president that he was "much impressed by the prospects" that the contract offered.[185] On November 15, Thompson reported that "Lincoln is willing to make a contract for coal, at one dollar less per ton than Govt now pays."[186] Twelve days later the president urged Chase to endorse the contract if it could be done "consistently with the public interest."[187] The day after Christmas, Assistant Secretary of the Interior John P. Usher reported that Lincoln "is quite anxious to make the arrangement but is held back by the objection of Seward," who "thinks that the Government had better make the arrangements direct with the New Grenadian Government," and by the objection of Chase, "who complains on account of the money."[188]

A more telling objection was raised by Navy Secretary Welles, whom Lincoln had asked to review the contract. Welles concluded "that there was fraud and cheat in the affair," that it "appeared to be a swindling speculation," and that the entire project "was a rotten remnant of an intrigue of the last administration."[189] Congressman Thaddeus Stevens, chairman of the House Committee on Ways and Means, agreed. In investigating Thompson's claim to the land, Stevens and his colleagues "found that he had not a particle of title to an inch of it; and if he had the whole thing was not worth a dollar. . . . the whole country is so unhealthy as to be wholly uninhabitable."[190]

In the spring of 1862, when Congress appropriated money for colonizing the freedmen of Washington, Lincoln instructed Secretaries Chase and Smith to reexamine Thompson's proposal. The busy Chase delegated the task to Treasury Solicitor Edward Jordan, who joined Smith in endorsing a plan to have the Chiriqui Improvement Company provide coal for the navy and to colonize blacks on its land. The president received similar advice from Assistant Secretary Usher, as well as from James Mitchell. Joining in the lobbying effort on behalf of Thompson's company was Kansas Senator Samuel C. Pomeroy, who was authorized in late August to issue a public appeal, sanctioned by the president, urging blacks to volunteer for colonization. Though "not inclined to it himself originally," Pomeroy said he would "devote himself with his whole energies to put it through."[191] The senator was quickly swamped with applications from blacks eager to leave, including two sons of Frederick Douglass. Henry Highland Garnet also expressed a desire to join them.

Lincoln's choice of Pomeroy was curious. To be sure, the senator had helped organize the settlement of the Kansas Territory in the 1850s and might have seemed a likely candidate to assist with a similar enterprise in the tropics. But his integrity was suspect. The New York *Tribune* described him as a man who "weighed everything by a money standard. He has judged all public measures by the cash that was in them; and estimated all men by the amount it would take to buy them."[192] In 1873, a committee of the Kansas Legislature found Pomeroy "guilty of the crime of bribery, and attempting to corrupt by offers of money, members of the Legislature of the State of Kansas."[193] Pomeroy served as the model for corrupt Senator Dilworthy in *The Gilded Age* by Mark Twain and Charles Dudley Warner. Thaddeus Stevens implied that several members of Congress received bribes from the Chiriqui lobby.

Strangely, Pomeroy had ridiculed the idea of colonization earlier in 1862. How and why he became an enthusiast for it later in the year is unclear. He told Wisconsin Senator James R. Doolittle that his April 1862 speech on the subject helped change his mind and that he desired more for blacks than his Radical colleagues did: "They want the freedom of the Col'd man—and are satisfied with that. I want for him something more than *that*—To be a *free laborer*—and *only that*, is not his manhood. I want for him the rights & enjoyments—of a *free man*." Because blacks' "full rights & privileges cannot be secured" in the United States, Pomeroy was "for the Negro's securing his rights and his *nationality*—in the clime of his nativity—on the soil of the Tropics."[194] By appointing this shady character, Lincoln may have been trying to win support for colonization from Chase, a friend of Pomeroy's.

The lobbying pressure on Lincoln worked, even though the director of the Smithsonian Institution reported that Chiriqui coal was of such poor quality that it was unsuitable for naval vessels. On September 11, the president provisionally endorsed a contract with the Chiriqui Company to settle at least 50,000 blacks. Final authorization would be made if Pomeroy reported favorably after visiting Panama to verify the company's assertions. According to John Palmer Usher, "very many consequential *niggers* from the North are manifesting a desire to go."[195] In fact, by mid-September, 500 "good substantial colored men & women" had prepared to emigrate, and 4,000 more placed their names on a waiting list. Pomeroy would escort them to their new homeland and help them get established. The senator was prepared to leave in early October with those 500 emigrants, most of whom were given farm tools as well as "everything necessary to comfort and industry."[196]

The president's decision to endorse the Chiriqui scheme may have been influenced by an old friend from his days in Congress, Richard W. Thompson, who served as the company's attorney and lobbyist. On September 12, the former Indiana congressman and Whig leader received a contract from Ambrose Thompson awarding him 20 percent of whatever the company might receive for its land. But Thompson's involvement in the Chiriqiui proposal led to its ultimate abandonment. Calling it a "swindle," the Albany *Evening Journal* remarked that "Thompson's connection with the project is enough to stamp its character and purpose" and urged the president "to look well into this scheme before committing himself to it."[197] Lincoln did so. He told Ambrose W. Thompson that he had intended to back the program fully "but that representations had been made to him, that the whole matter was a speculation, a job, that the money required to be paid was not intended to be used in the developing of the property, but in the payment of old debts, judgments, mortgages &c." He explained that "it had been said his friend Dick Thompson was to get money" for services rendered earlier. Lincoln added that "he was willing to do anything personal to serve" his former colleague in the House of Representatives, "yet he could not go before the people admitting that he had so applied public money, on a contract that was to be appropriated to paying private debts." He insisted that "no public money should with his knowledge go to pay private debts."[198] Despite this refusal, Lincoln and Thompson remained on good terms.

Other problems arose. Ambrose Thompson's title to the land proved questionable; the cabinet and some newspapers raised serious doubts about the ethics of Pomeroy and Richard Thompson; and American blacks showed little inclination to emigrate. Most importantly, Nicaragua, Costa Rica, San Salvador, Guatemala, Brazil, and Honduras objected, fearful of becoming "Africanized." They also regarded the scheme as something akin to the filibustering expeditions of the 1850s. As the New York *Tribune* observed, no nation "would choose to be made the Botany Bay of other nations which should see fit to pick out a poor, ignorant, despised class of their people for exportation."[199] Seward, anticipating that the North might soon be dragged into a war with Europe, wished to maintain good relations with Central and South America. In early October, Lincoln accepted the secretary of state's advice and shelved the project. It was eventually scrapped.

The blacks of Washington who had signed up for Chiriqui protested against the suspension. Unable to see the president, they left a statement for him: "Many of us acting upon your promise to send us so soon as one hundred families were ready, have sold our furniture, have given up our little homes, to go in the first voyage; and *now*, when more than five times that number have made preparations to leave, we find that there is *uncertainty* and *delay*, which is greatly embarrassing to us, and reducing our scanty means until fears are being created that those means being exhausted, poverty in a still worse form than has yet met us, may be our winter prospect." When a delegation presented this document at the White House, a secretary assured them that Lincoln "was as anxious as he ever was for their departure; that he had placed everything in the hands of Senator Pomeroy of Kansas; and that he could not now see the deputation of colored men, but that he would do so in the course of a few days."[200] But the president did not meet with them later.

In late October, the New York *Journal of Commerce* recommended that, in light of the opposition of Latin American nations to serve as colonization sites, the black volunteers who had signed up for Chiriqui be sent to Liberia instead. When shown this editorial, Lincoln replied: "I am perfectly willing that these colored people should be sent to Liberia, *provided they are willing to go*: but there's the rub. I cannot coerce them, if they prefer some other locality. Central America was designated because they showed a willingness to go there. But I would just as soon, and a little rather, send them to Liberia. But where are the people who wish to go there?"[201] When Attorney General Bates recommended that the blacks be expelled, Lincoln "objected unequivocally to compulsion" insisting that their "emigration must be voluntary and without expense to themselves."[202]

Lincoln considered yet another colonization scheme, this one suggested by the eccentric former Congressman Eli Thayer of Massachusetts, a militant opponent of slavery who in the 1850s had played a vital role in the struggle to keep Kansas free. In the summer of 1862, Thayer proposed to lead 10,000 black short-term troops to Florida, defeat the enemy there, then have those soldiers discharged and take possession of property confiscated for nonpayment of taxes. Thayer pledged that if his plan were accepted, he could bring Florida back into the Union as a free state within a few months. In January 1863, Lincoln observed that the plan "had received the earnest and cordial attention of himself and cabinet, and that while recent military events had forced the postponement of this enterprise for the time by demanding the entire attention and power of the government elsewhere, yet he trusted the delay was but for a few days."[203] The New York *Tribune* endorsed colonization in either Florida or West Texas. But nothing came of this scheme.

Colonization in Haiti: Cow Island

Something did come of a plan to colonize freed slaves in Haiti, however. Haitian authorities encouraged immigration from the United States. To expedite matters, James Redpath, a radical abolitionist and devotee of John Brown, was appointed "general agent of emigration to Haiti from the state and province of North America." In 1861, he persuaded over a thousand American blacks to settle in that Caribbean nation. Frederick Douglass's newspaper praised Redpath's efforts. Helping Redpath were several black recruiting agents, including Douglass's assistant editor, William J. Watkins, the novelist William Wells Brown, Henry Highland Garnet, James Theodore Holly, Richard J. Hinton, and H. Ford Douglas. In October 1862, one Bernard Kock submitted to Lincoln a proposal to colonize a 25-square-mile island off the Haitian coast called Ile à Vache (Cow Island), which was virtually deserted. Although Attorney General Bates considered Kock "an arrant humbug" and a "Charleston adventurer," on New Year's Eve the president approved a contract offering him $250,000 to take 5,000 American blacks to the island, which he claimed he had leased from the Haitian government.

Preoccupied with other matters on that memorable day, Lincoln failed to note the contract's flaws. Kock offered no reliable security to guarantee that he would fulfill his end of the bargain, nor did he provide evidence that the Haitian government had approved his scheme. Moreover, no one in the administration knew much about the self-styled "governor of Cow Island." When Kock approached the secretary of state to affix the great seal of the United States to the contract, the skeptical Seward kept it in his possession, effectively scuttling the plan. In April 1863, the contract was canceled. The Cow Island project might have died aborning if Lincoln had not been so enthusiastic about it. The success of the Haitian Emigration Bureau in persuading American blacks to emigrate may have influenced his thinking, though by late 1862 Redpath's enterprise was foundering. The project was kept alive by New York capitalists, including Paul S. Forbes and Charles K. Tuckerman, who had advanced Kock money to prepare the expedition. At the president's request, Seward drafted a contract for Forbes and Tuckerman which allowed them to carry out the provisions of the original agreement with Kock, though it stipulated that the Haitian government must approve and support the plan.

Tuckerman received brusque treatment when he suggested to Lincoln "that all the preliminaries having been satisfactorily arranged, the easiest way to settle the matter would be for him to affix his signature to the document before him."

"O, I know that," the president responded, "and it would be 'very easy' for me to open that window and shout down Pennsylvania Avenue, only I don't mean to do it—just now."

Tuckerman recalled that Lincoln "was irritated, and justly irritated, by certain difficulties which had been thrown in his way . . . by opponents of the [colonization] scheme."

Tuckerman proposed that the president might want more time to consider the matter. "No," Lincoln replied, "you've had trouble enough about it, and so have I." After perusing the document attentively, he said: "I guess it's all right," and signed it.[204]

The contract called for Tuckerman and Forbes to convey 500 American blacks to Cow Island at $50 per person. There the freedmen were to be given houses, land, education, and medical care, all supervised by Kock. A ship took 453 volunteers to that desolate spot, where nothing had been provided for them and where disease and poisonous insects killed off many. The demoralized survivors, badly mistreated by Kock, longed to return to the United States. After an investigation revealed their plight, Kock was dismissed. In February 1864, Lincoln dispatched a transport to bring back the 368 remaining emigrants, who were in wretched condition. Months later, Congress repealed the laws appropriating money for colonization. When it was determined that Tuckerman and Forbes had failed to carry out the provisions of the contract, they received no money, despite urgent appeals.

Lincoln was partly to blame for this fiasco, for his administration had been careless in negotiating the contract, then remiss in providing supervision to assure that its terms were implemented properly. He certainly did not honor his pledge to the black delegation in August 1862: "I shall, if I get a sufficient number of you engaged, have provision made that you shall not be wronged." The president's failure to examine closely the Cow Island contract stands in sharp contrast to the scrutiny he gave the Chiriqui contract a few months earlier.

Complicating the president's life in the summer of 1862 was a new patronage scramble created by the internal revenue law, which was to go into operation on September 1. The statute established for the first time in American history an income tax, which necessitated the appointment of a tax assessor and a collector for each congressional district. Candidates for these posts helped swell the flood of visitors to the White House, and the presidential desk groaned under enormous batches of recommendations. In late July, after spending half an hour with one caller, Lincoln said to the others waiting in the anteroom: "I want to make a little speech. You all want to see me on business. It is a matter of no importance to me whether I spend my time with half a dozen or with the whole of you, but it is of importance to you. Therefore when you come in, please don't stay long." He recommended that each take no more than two minutes.[205] The new places were, Lincoln told Chase, "fiercely contested."[206]

The Greeley Letter: Responding to Emancipationist Pressure

For months prior to the battle of Antietam, pressure had been building for Lincoln to issue an emancipation edict. Abolitionists were growing ever more critical. "How terribly he will be pilloried in history like Pharaoh!" exclaimed Henry T. Cheever, while Elizur Wright asked impatiently: "Is our own *people's President*, after repressing the generals [like Frémont and Hunter], going to delay striking the vital blow himself?"[207] On Independence Day, Frederick Douglass thundered that an "administration without a policy is confessedly an administration without brains. . . . we have a right to hold Abraham Lincoln sternly responsible for any disaster or failure attending the suppression of this rebellion. . . . Lincoln and his cabinet . . . have fought the rebels with the Olive branch. The people must teach them to fight them with the sword."[208]

More vituperatively, Wendell Phillips charged that "Mr. Lincoln is conducting this war, at present, with the purpose of saving slavery." The president, "a first-rate *second rate* man," has "no mind whatever," the fiery Brahmin orator told an audience on August 1. He "may be honest,—nobody cares whether the tortoise is honest or not; he has neither insight, nor prevision, nor decision." As long as such a tortoise headed the government, it was "digging a pit with one hand and filling it with the other." Phillips sneered, "I never did believe in the capacity of Abraham Lincoln. . . . I asked the lawyers of Illinois, who had practiced law with Mr. Lincoln for twenty years, 'Is he a man of decision, is he a man who can say no?' They all said: 'If you had gone to the Illinois bar, and selected the man least capable of saying no, it would have been Abraham Lincoln. He has no stiffness in him.'" Phillips's speech implied a hope that Confederates would bombard Washington, kill Lincoln, and thus make Hamlin president.[209] From the White House, William O. Stoddard wrote that Phillips "is no longer the apostle of the great reform . . . but seems voluntarily to take his true place as a mere vulgar agitator and sensation spouter." Lincoln was probably referring to Phillips when he described a "well-known abolitionist and orator" as "a thistle" and exclaimed: "I don't see why God lets him live!"[210]

Adam Gurowski characterized Lincoln as a man with "a rather slow intellect, with slow powers of perception." The president, he said, "has no experience of men and events, and no knowledge of the past. . . . Slavery is his mammy, and he will not destroy her."[211] Henry Ward Beecher lamented that Northerners "have been made irresolute, indecisive and weak by the President's attempt to unite impossibilities; to make war and keep the peace; to strike hard and not hurt; to invade sovereign States and not meddle with their sovereignty; to put down rebellion without touching its cause."[212] The president had no "spark of genius," "element of leadership," or "particle of heroic enthusiasm," Beecher charged.[213] William Lloyd Garrison fumed that the "[s]tumbling, halting, prevaricating, irresolute, weak, besotted" president "is blind as a bat" to the administration's "true line of policy."[214] A disgusted New Yorker told Gerrit Smith that if "our revolutionary fathers were to look down on such a miserable, emasculated set of so-called leaders as we now have, and should fail to spit upon them, it w[oul]d only be from simple inability."[215] Beriah Green, known as "abolition's ax," called Lincoln "the presiding bloodhound of the nation."[216]

Congress was also growing restive. "Mr. Lincoln desires *God* to liberate them [the slaves], without compromising him in any way! and if *He* will do it Himself, Mr. Lincoln will cheerfully submit to it!" exclaimed Senator James Harlan of Iowa sarcastically.[217] Congressman Frederick Pike of Maine predicted in August that unless

Lincoln "follows along after public sentiment more rapidly than he seems disposed to do there will be howling before the snow flies. He exhibits immense deference to the opinions of Kentucky."[218] Summing up the mood of Radicals, Thaddeus Stevens disgustedly noted on August 10, "we are just as far from the true course as ever. Unless the people speak in their primary assemblies, no good will come, and there seems little chance of that. A change of Cabinet is our only hope; but I do not hope for that."[219]

Sydney Howard Gay, managing editor of Horace Greeley's *Tribune,* received a complaint from a fellow New Yorker, who said the "people are uneasy, anxious, and suspicious" and that "there is not & never has been any serious determination to put down the rebels."[220] When Gay forwarded this missive to the White House, Lincoln invited him to visit Washington. There Gay asked several questions that Lincoln refused to answer either officially or semiofficially but indirectly replied by saying to each one: "I shouldn't wonder." Gay recounted this interview to a friend, who reported that the editor "returned to New York feeling like a mariner who has made an observation in some sunny interval between long days of clouds and storms."[221] After their conversation, the president described Gay as "a truly good man, and a wise one"; in turn, Gay became "quite enamored of the President, & convinced that although slowish, he is perfectly sure."[222]

Other Radicals dogged Lincoln's heels. On July 4, when Charles Sumner urged that Independence Day be reconsecrated by issuing an emancipation decree, the president said it was "too big a lick," arguing that "half the army would lay down its arms, if emancipation were declared," and that "three more States would rise"—Kentucky, Missouri, and Maryland.[223] The following month, when Sumner once more lobbied him on behalf of emancipation, Lincoln counseled patience: "Wait; time is essential."[224]

Helping Sumner apply pressure were Thaddeus Stevens and Henry Wilson. Those three lawmakers, Lincoln complained to Missouri Senator John B. Henderson, "simply haunt me with their importunities for a Proclamation of Emancipation. Wherever I go and whatever way I turn, they are on my trail; and still in my heart, I have the deep conviction that the hour has not yet come." One day when he spied those three Radicals approaching the White House, he told Henderson that he was reminded of a schoolmate of his who had trouble reading aloud the Biblical description of Shadrach, Meshach and Abednego in the fiery furnace. For mispronouncing their names, the lad received a blow from his teacher. After his tears finally stopped, he was dismayed to be called upon again to read a passage where those men reappeared. When he wailed aloud, the instructor asked what was wrong. "Look there," he said pointing to the verses he was to read, "there come them same damned fellows again."[225]

When another importunate Radical senator demanded that the slaves be freed, Lincoln asked: "will Kentucky stand that?"

"Damn Kentucky!" came the reply.

"Then damn you!" exclaimed the president, who seldom resorted to profanity.[226]

The assertiveness of some Quakers also aroused Lincoln's ire. On June 20, he addressed a delegation of Progressive Friends who presented him a memorial calling for emancipation. He was relieved, he said, "to be assured that the deputation were not applicants for office, for his chief trouble was from that class of persons. The next most troublesome subject was Slavery." He concurred with them in thinking "that Slavery was wrong, but in regard to the ways and means of its removal, his views probably differed from theirs." Their memorial seemed to imply that if he did not promptly issue an emancipation proclamation, he would be violating the spirit of his 1858 "House Divided" speech. Lincoln resented the suggestion that he had betrayed his earlier stance. According to Pennsylvania Congressman William D. Kelley, who observed this exchange, the president "sought to repel this covert imputation upon his integrity and veracity" and "replied with an asperity of manner of which I had not deemed him capable." Lincoln said that the quotation they cited was taken out of context. ("A house divided against itself cannot stand. I believe this government cannot endure permanently half slave & half free. I do not expect the Union to be dissolved—I do not expect the house to fall—but I do expect it will cease to be divided. It will become all one thing, or all the other.") The delegation should have included "another sentence, in which he indicated his views as to the effect upon Slavery itself of the resistance to its extension. The sentiments contained in that passage were deliberately uttered, and he held them now. If a decree of emancipation could abolish Slavery, John Brown would have done the work effectually. Such a decree surely could not be more binding upon the South than the Constitution, and that cannot be enforced in that part of the country now. Would a proclamation of freedom be any more effective?" Lincoln added "that he felt the magnitude of the task before him, and hoped to be rightly directed in the very trying circumstances by which he was surrounded."

When a member of the delegation expressed "sympathy for him in all his embarrassments, and an earnest desire that he might, under divine guidance, be led to free the slaves and thus save the nation from destruction," Lincoln replied "that he was deeply sensible of his need of Divine assistance. He had sometime thought that perhaps he might be an instrument in God's hands of accomplishing a great work and he certainly was not unwilling to be. Perhaps, however, God's way of accomplishing the end which the memorialists have in view may be different from theirs. It would be his earnest endeavor, with a firm reliance upon the Divine arm, and seeking light from above, to do his duty in the place to which he had been called."[227]

Lincoln also lost patience with an antislavery delegation from Connecticut, headed by the state's governor, William A. Buckingham. The president "said abruptly and as if irritated by the subject: 'Governor, I suppose what your people want is more nigger.'" Buckingham was surprised both by Lincoln's unwonted impatience and by his language. Lincoln quickly changed his tone and earnestly remarked "that if anybody supposed he was not interested in this subject, deeply interested, intensely anxious about it, it was a great mistake."[228]

With gentle sarcasm Lincoln responded to a Chicago clergyman who claimed he was delivering the word of the Lord: "open the doors of bondage that the slave may go free!" "That may be, sir," said the president, "but if it is, as you say, a message from your Divine Master, is it not odd that the only channel he could send it by was that

roundabout route by that awfully wicked city of Chicago?"[229] To another presumptuous clergyman, Lincoln said: "Perhaps you had better try to run the machine a week."
(This was a tactic he used on laymen as well. He put down an impudent caller who
was excoriating a government official. "Now," said the president, "you are just the
man I have been looking for. I want you to give me your address, and tell me, if you
were in my place, and had heard all you've been telling, and didn't believe a word of it,
what would you do?")[230]

The most dramatic and widely circulated appeal for emancipation came from the
pen of Horace Greeley, who had been growing ever more impatient with Lincoln. On
August 7, that controversial editor asked Charles Sumner: "Do you remember that old
theological book containing this: 'Chapter One—Hell; Chapter Two—Hell Continued.'" Well, Greeley added, "that gives a hint of the way Old Abe *ought to be* talked to
in this crisis."[231] Understandably worried that Greeley might publish something rash,
journalist James R. Gilmore and former Secretary of the Treasury Robert J. Walker
attempted to soothe him. Walker and Gilmore had learned that Lincoln would soon
issue an emancipation decree and that he wished to inform the *Tribune* editor. (The
president had uncharacteristically revealed his intention to several other people,
among them Owen Lovejoy, Hannibal Hamlin, Orville H. Browning, James Speed,
Leonard Swett, and Hiram Barney.) Gilmore and Walker obtained Lincoln's permission to do so, with the understanding that the paper would not leak the news. But it
was too late. Gilmore informed Greeley on August 20, the very day that the *Tribune*
ran the editor's blast at the administration, titled "The Prayer of Twenty Millions."
The next day, in violation of the understanding that Gilmore and Walker had reached
with Lincoln, the paper ran a news item about the forthcoming Emancipation Proclamation.

"The Prayer of Twenty Millions" scolded the president, alleging that many of his
early supporters were now "sorely disappointed and deeply pained" by his foot-dragging
on emancipation. Greeley demanded that Lincoln enforce the Confiscation Acts, ignore the counsels of "fossil politicians hailing from the Border States," stop deferring
to slaveholders, adopt some consistent policy with regard to slavery, and employ runaway bondsmen as "scouts, guides, spies, cooks, teamsters, diggers and choppers."[232]
Wendell Phillips applauded Greeley's handiwork as "superb" and "terrific."[233] Moderates, however, condemned the editor's "impudence," his "insolence and dictatorial
tone," along with his "arrogant" and "acrimonious" spirit.[234] Greeley's letter, noted the
Philadelphia *Ledger*, constituted "a severe lecture" written "in the style of a pedagogue
dictating to a pupil."[235] An Indiana editor likened Greeley to "a shrewish housekeeper"
chastising "a careless servant."[236]

Lincoln responded swiftly with a letter that soon became famous. He had been
looking for an occasion to explain his approach to emancipation and thus pave the
way for the Proclamation. Tactfully, he assured Greeley that he took no offense at
what might be considered the editor's "impatient and dictatorial tone." Nor would he
controvert any seemingly erroneous "statements, or assumptions of fact" or false infer-
ences in the editorial. Rather he would ignore them in "deference to an old friend,
whose heart I have always supposed to be right."

In dealing with the charge that he only *seemed* to have a policy dealing with slavery, Lincoln tersely described the course he had been pursuing all along: "I would save the Union. I would save it the shortest way under the Constitution. The sooner the national authority can be restored; the nearer the Union will be 'the Union as it was.'" (At this point, Lincoln included a sentence that he later struck out at the urging of the editors of the Washington *National Intelligencer*, in which the document first appeared: "Broken eggs can never be mended, and the longer the breaking proceeds the more will be broken." By having his letter published in a Washington paper and by not forwarding it to Greeley, he let that truculent editor know that finger-wagging lectures were not appreciated.) "If there be those who would not save the Union, unless they could at the same time *save* slavery, I do not agree with them. If there be those who would not save the Union unless they could at the same time *destroy* slavery, I do not agree with them. My paramount object in this struggle *is* to save the Union, and is *not* either to save or to destroy slavery. If I could save the Union without freeing *any* slave I would do it, and if I could save it by freeing *all* the slaves I would do it; and if I could save it by freeing some and leaving others alone I would also do that. What I do about slavery, and the colored race, I do because I believe it helps to save the Union; and what I forbear, I forbear because I do *not* believe it would help to save the Union. I shall do *less* whenever I shall believe what I am doing hurts the cause, and I shall do *more* whenever I shall believe doing more will help the cause. I shall try to correct errors when shown to be errors; and I shall adopt new views so fast as they shall appear to be true views. I have here stated my purpose according to my view of *official* duty; and I intend no modification of my oft-expressed *personal* wish that all men every where could be free."[237] In this final sentence, he made clear what anyone familiar with his speeches and actions in the 1850s already knew: that he hated slavery. Still, he emphasized that as a president bound by an oath, he could not ignore constitutional and political constraints.

Lincoln's unprecedented public letter caused a sensation. "So novel a thing as a newspaper correspondence between the President and an editor excites great attention," noted a journalist; but "Mr. Lincoln does so many original things that everybody has ceased to be surprised at him, and hence the violation of precedent in this matter does not provoke so much comment as might be expected."[238] A Washington correspondent reported that people "who insist on precedent, and Presidential dignity, are horrified at this novel idea of Mr. Lincoln's, but there is unanimous admiration of the skill and force with which he has defined his policy."[239] George Ashmun told Lincoln that the "first feeling of all your friends was, that it would be, to some extent, lessening the grave importance of your office, & the dignity with which you had performed all its functions. But an enlarged consideration of the surrounding circumstances, & the triumphant manner in which you have so modestly & so clearly set forth the justification of your fixed purpose dispels all doubts of the expediency & wisdom of your course."[240] The letter struck other moderate Republicans, like ex-Governor William Dennison of Ohio and Supreme Court Justice Noah Swayne, "as an advance step in the right direction—as a stronger official declaration of his determination to tread out the 'institution' if the Union can be no[t] otherwise preserved, than the President has yet given to the public."[241] Missouri Senator John B. Henderson assured Lincoln that the position spelled out in the Greeley letter "is the only one through which we can win for the Union. Emancipation proclamations can only serve to make things worse in the border states, without reaching the rebellious district."[242] The New York *Times* observed that Lincoln's reply "exhibits the peculiarities of his mind and style; but the logical sequence and precision, and the grammatical accuracy of this, is greatly in advance of any previous effort."[243] Thurlow Weed, who had been badly discouraged about the military situation, took "heart and hope" from the letter, which he said "clears the atmosphere, and gives ground to stand on. The ultras were. . . . getting the Administration into [a] false position. But it is all right now."[244] Senator Timothy O. Howe of Wisconsin deemed the letter "the best enunciation of the best platform we have had since the Chicago convention."[245] Lincoln's reply, said the Indianapolis *Journal,* "is admirable in temper, and takes the only ground he can take in regard to the bearing of the war upon slavery."[246]

Greeley himself considered Lincoln's response "a sign of progress," as did Massachusetts Governor John A. Andrew, who said, "hope rises of a vigorous, large, bold and hopeful policy."[247] Sydney Howard Gay wrote Lincoln: "your letter to Mr. Greeley has infused new hope among us at the North who are anxiously awaiting that movement on your part which they beleive will end the rebellion by removing its cause. I think the general impression is that as you are determined to save the Union tho' Slavery perish, you mean presently to announce that the destruction of Slavery is the price of our salvation."[248] There was good reason for such optimism. Lincoln told his friend Congressman Isaac N. Arnold "that the meaning of his letter to Mr. Greeley was this: that he was ready to declare emancipation when he was convinced that it could be made effective, and that the people were with him."[249]

Democrats, too, were impressed. A correspondent of Francis P. Blair, Sr., told the venerable gentleman that Lincoln's letter "meets with universal approbation. I have heard scores of Douglas Democrats declare that they would now support Lincoln for Dictator."[250] In New York, former lieutenant-governor Sanford E. Church, a leading Democrat, thought "Mr Lincoln has 'hit the nail on the head' this time in his answer to Greeley. While it looks a little humiliating to answer it at all, the effect of the answer will be good."[251]

Some abolitionists, like Owen Lovejoy and Gerrit Smith, praised Lincoln's "excellent Letter."[252] Others, like Wendell Phillips, condemned it as "cold, low, brutal" and "the most disgraceful document that ever came from the head of a free people." Phillips contemptuously remarked that Lincoln "can only be frightened or bullied into the right policy. . . . If the proclamation of Emanc[ipation] is possible at any time from Lincoln (which I somewhat doubt) it will be wrung from him only by fear. He's a Spaniel by nature—nothing broad, generous, or highhearted about him."[253] Echoing Phillips, another abolitionist asked rhetorically: "Was ever a more heartless policy announced? . . . With the President public policy is *everything,* humanity and justice nothing."[254] Beriah Green indignantly denounced Lincoln's willingness to leave slavery intact if the Union could be preserved without touching it. "What sort of a Union is Mr. Lincoln & his supporters & admirers fighting for?" he asked. Answering his own question, Green called the Union "the very sty of pollution—the very den of the grimmest oppression—the vestibule of Hell!"[255] Equally contemptuous of Lincoln's letter to Greeley was a young conservative, Robert C. Winthrop, Jr., who found a "humiliating contrast between his state papers and those of [Jefferson] Davis, who can at least write good English & express himself with dignity & firmness." Winthrop admired the president's honest intentions but deemed him "cruelly unfit for his place."[256]

Less hostile abolitionists feared not that Lincoln would fail to "reach the right conclusion, but that he will reach it too late."[257] Frederick Douglass said that he would "prefer the Union even with Slavery than to allow the Slaveholders to go off and set up a Government."[258] The president's hint that he might save the Union by freeing all the slaves impressed the editors of the *National Anti-Slavery Standard,* who sensibly observed that he was constrained by the Constitution and therefore "is not to be expected to act upon motives of mere morality and humanity. In a certain political sense it may be said that he had no *right* to do so."[259]

Lincoln's letter has been misunderstood by those who view it as a definitive statement of his innermost feelings about the aims of the war. Some deplored its insensitivity to the moral significance of emancipation. In fact, the document was a political utterance designed to smooth the way for the proclamation which he intended to issue as soon as the Union army won a victory. He knew full well that millions of Northerners as well as Border State residents would object to transforming the war into an abolitionist crusade. They were willing to fight to preserve the Union but not to free the slaves. As president, Lincoln had to make the mighty act of emancipation palatable to them. By assuring Conservatives that emancipation was simply a means to preserve the Union, Lincoln hoped to minimize the white backlash that he knew was bound to come. As he explained to General Lovell Harrison Rousseau and Kentucky Congressman Samuel L. Casey when they pressed for emancipation: "you are my friends—I can say and do what I please with you. But this other man I am in doubt about, yet it is important that I retain him in adhesion to our cause, so I go out of my way to please him, while I almost abuse you, who will stick by me, or the cause, come what will!"[260]

Lincoln's letter puzzled Greeley. "It is no answer to my 'Prayer,'" the editor remarked. Indeed, the president had not addressed Greeley's main complaint, viz., his failure to enforce the Confiscation Acts. Lincoln had drafted the main body of the letter well before "The Prayer of Twenty Millions" appeared. According to Whitelaw Reid, "days before Greeley's letter was published the President read to a friend a rough draft of what now appears in the form of a reply to Greeley and asked his advice about publishing it."[261]

On August 23, in response to Orestes Brownson's argument that colonization would not work unless preceded by emancipation, Lincoln "said that he was not fully persuaded that it was yet time to proclaim Emancipation." When Brownson asked the president to specify just when he would emancipate the slaves, Lincoln referred him to the Greeley letter. Brownson prophetically surmised that "if the next battle in

Virginia results in a decided victory," Lincoln would then issue a proclamation freeing the slaves in all the Confederate states save Virginia and Tennessee.[262] (But Brownson had little faith in the president, for he thought that "nothing can be made of him, & no good can come of him.")[263] The letter to Greeley offered a preview of coming events. It announced that Lincoln might free some slaves and leave others in bondage, which is just what his Emancipation Proclamation would do.

In dealing with other emancipationists, Lincoln frequently played devil's advocate. As a New York *Tribune* correspondent observed, "it is one of the President's peculiarities—to some degree the result of his legal education—that he always looks at both sides of every question at once; and that, far from arguing with himself in favor of those views which are most in accordance with his desires, he rather runs into the opposite extreme of magnifying and attaching undue weight to the obstacles which appear in his course."[264] The best-publicized episode of this sort occurred on September 13, 1862, when a delegation of clergy from Chicago presented a memorial calling on him to liberate the slaves. He told his visitors that he had long given the subject much thought and had "no objections against it on legal or constitutional grounds; for, as commander-in-chief of the army and navy, in time of war, I suppose I have a right to take any measure which may best subdue the enemy. Nor do I urge objections of a moral nature, in view of possible consequences of insurrection and massacre at the South. I view the matter as a practical war measure, to be decided upon according to the advantages or disadvantages it may offer to the suppression of the rebellion." The president said he was curious to know "[w]hat *good* would a proclamation of emancipation from me do, especially as we are now situated? I do not want to issue a document that the whole world will see must necessarily be inoperative, like the Pope's bull against the comet!"

Lincoln insisted that he lacked the power to free slaves in territory controlled by the Confederacy. "Would *my word* free the slaves," asked he, "when I cannot even enforce the Constitution in the rebel States? Is there a single court, or magistrate, or individual that would be influenced by it there? And what reason is there to think it would have any greater effect upon the slaves than the late law of Congress, which I approved, and which offers protection and freedom to the slaves of rebel masters who come within our lines? Yet I cannot learn that that law has caused a single slave to come over to us."

Even if slaves could be induced to flee to Union lines, Lincoln was perplexed to know "*what should we do with them*? How can we feed and care for such a multitude?" The blacks might, at least in theory, be accepted into the Union army, but Lincoln worried that they would be captured and re-enslaved. "I am told that whenever the rebels take any black prisoners, free or slave, they immediately auction them off! They did so with those they took from a boat that was aground in the Tennessee river a few days ago. And then *I am very ungenerously attacked for it*! For instance, when, after the late battles at and near Bull Run, an expedition went out from Washington under a flag of truce to bury the dead and bring in the wounded, and the rebels seized the blacks who went along to help and sent them into slavery, Horace Greeley said in his paper that the Government would probably do nothing about it. What *could* I do?"

Moreover, the president said he was "not so sure we could do much with the blacks. If we were to arm them, I fear that in a few weeks the arms would be in the hands of the rebels; and indeed thus far we have not had arms enough to equip our white troops."

Lincoln agreed with his callers that "slavery is the root of the rebellion, or at least its *sine qua non*." Secession may have been the work of ambitious politicians, "but they would have been impotent without slavery as their instrument." He acknowledged "that emancipation would help us in Europe, and convince them that we are incited by something more than ambition." As for domestic opinion, emancipation "would help *somewhat* at the North, though not so much, I fear, as you and those you represent imagine. Still, some additional strength would be added in that way to the war."

The greatest practical advantage to be gained by freeing the slaves was that it would undermine the Confederate war effort, for "unquestionably it would weaken the rebels by drawing off their laborers, which is of great importance." But that was offset by a grave disadvantage: "There are fifty thousand bayonets in the Union armies from the Border Slave States. It would be a serious matter if, in consequence of a proclamation such as you desire, they should go over to the rebels."

Even without emancipation as a war aim, Lincoln emphasized, the conflict still had a great moral foundation around which the people easily rallied "in the fact that constitutional government is at stake. This is a fundamental idea, going down about as deep as any thing." Lest his callers draw a false inference from his remarks, Lincoln assured them that his questions merely "indicate the difficulties that have thus far prevented my action in some such way as you desire. I have not decided against a proclamation of liberty to the slaves, but hold the matter under advisement. And I can assure you that the subject is on my mind, by day and night, more than any other. Whatever shall appear to be God's will I will do."[265] At the close of the interview, he added that "there is a question of expediency as to time, should such a proclamation be issued. Matters look dark just now. I fear that a proclamation on the heels of defeat would be interpreted as a cry of despair. It would come better, if at all, immediately after a victory. I wish I could say something to you more entirely satisfactory."[266]

Similarly, Lincoln told Leonard Swett that if he issued an emancipation proclamation, "50,000 troops, armed with our weapons, and in our service, in Kentucky and Tenn[essee], would in a body go over to the enemy."[267] He acknowledged to Swett that Robert Dale Owen had given him excellent arguments in favor of immediate emancipation, but the president added that while "all his sympathies were that way," there were "a few things to be considered before venturing into the unknown result. Such negroes as had come through the lines were very poor and helpless, and at one place in the neighborhood of the capital he had two regiments exclusively employed in feeding them. If emancipated, would the negro come? If he came, would he fight?"[268]

Lincoln sought advice from some emancipation advocates. On September 11, he asked James A. Hamilton to draft a proclamation that he thought should be issued. Hamilton may have been flattered, but most abolitionists despaired. "I am growing more and more skeptical as to the 'honesty' of Lincoln," William Lloyd Garrison snorted. "He is nothing better than a wet rag."[269] Frederick Douglass felt "ineffable disgust" as he contemplated the president's course.[270] The irascible Thaddeus Stevens wrote that it "is plain that nothing approaching the present policy will subdue the rebels. Whether we shall find *any body* with a sufficient grasp of mind, and sufficient moral courage, to treat this as a radical revolution, and remodel our institutions, I doubt. It would involve the desolation of the South as well as emancipation; and a re-peopling of half the Continent."[271] A Massachusetts editor sarcastically remarked, "Mr. Lincoln must worship a strange God indeed, if he imagines He is not in favor of universal freedom. The Bible Society, or some other benevolent institution ought at once to present him with a copy of the New Testament, with directions to peruse several chapters daily. Unless he indulged his usual hair-splitting propensity, he might derive great benefit."[272]

Conservative Counterpressure

Counterpressure came from the Border States and areas of the Confederacy controlled by the Union. Henry Winter Davis of Maryland argued that the "President can issue *no* decree of emancipation; if he could he would be my master & could take my home & imprison me at pleasure."[273] Most vocal in their opposition were Louisiana Unionists, including a prominent New Orleans attorney who told Lincoln: "we are in imminent danger of another revolution a thousand times more bloody than the present. If the agitation about slavery is not silenced, every man woman and child capable of using the knife or pistol will rush into the fight regardless of life or property, [and the] result will be that the stars and stripes will not wave over this city ninety days longer."[274]

A similar complaint came from another New Orleans Conservative, Thomas J. Durant (who, like Henry Winter Davis, would eventually become a Radical and effectively sabotage the president's Reconstruction efforts). Lincoln replied heatedly to Cuthbert Bullitt, who had forwarded Durant's letter, calling Durant "an able, a dispassionate, and an entirely sincere man." Lincoln nonetheless criticized him and his allies for their passivity: "The paralysis—the dead palsy—of the government in this whole struggle is, that this class of men will do nothing for the government, nothing for themselves, except demanding that the government shall not strike its open enemies, lest they be struck by accident!" The president insisted that "what is done, and omitted, about slaves, is done and omitted on . . . military necessity. It is a military necessity to have men and money; and we can get neither, in sufficient numbers, or amounts, if we keep from, or drive from, our lines, slaves coming to them." Durant must be aware "of the pressure in this direction" and "of my efforts to hold it within bounds till he, and such as he shall have time to help themselves."

Durant and his ilk might have no unpatriotic motives, Lincoln argued, but even so, "if there were a class of men who, having no choice of sides in the contest, were anxious only to have quiet and comfort for themselves while it rages, and to fall in with the victorious side at the end of it, without loss to themselves, their advice as to the mode of conducting the contest would be precisely such as his is." Durant "speaks of no duty—apparently thinks of none—resting upon Union men. He even thinks it injurious to the Union cause that they should be restrained in trade and passage without taking sides. They are to touch neither a sail nor a pump, but to be merely passengers,—dead-heads at that—to be carried snug and dry, throughout the storm, and safely landed right side up. Nay, more; even a mutineer is to go untouched lest these sacred passengers receive an accidental wound."

Lincoln refused to smooth "the rough angles of the war." The fighting would end only when the Rebels surrendered, and to achieve that end, stern measures must be taken. With some sarcasm, he asked Bullitt: "What would you do in my position? Would you drop the war where it is? . . . Would you deal lighter blows rather than heavier ones? Would you give up the contest, leaving any available means unapplied?" He closed this remarkable private letter with an eloquent disclaimer: "I am in no boastful mood. I shall not do *more* than I can, and I shall do *all* I can to save the government, which is my sworn duty as well as my personal inclination. I shall do nothing in malice. What I deal with is too vast for malicious dealing."[275] (Two years later, the recipient of this missive justifiably called it one of Lincoln's best.)

Bombshell: Public Announcement of Emancipation Plans

The despair of many abolitionists turned to joy in September when Lincoln seized upon the result of Antietam and announced his intention to issue the Emancipation Proclamation. The battle took place on Wednesday, September 17, but three days passed before he felt sure that it could be considered a Union victory. That weekend he tinkered with the Proclamation, which he presented to his cabinet on Monday, September 22. He began that memorable session by reading a humorous piece by Artemas Ward entitled "High-handed Outrage at Utica." Everyone enjoyed the tale but Stanton, who thought it inappropriately frivolous for such a solemn occasion.

Lincoln then turned serious. According to Welles, he said that "he had made a vow, a covenant, that if God gave us the victory in the approaching battle, he would consider it an indication of Divine will, and that it was his duty to move forward in the cause of emancipation. It might be thought strange, he said, that he had in this way submitted the disposal of the matter when the way was not clear to his mind what he should do. God had decided this question in favor of the slaves. He was satisfied it was right, was confirmed and strengthened in his action by the vow and the results."[276] (Lincoln offered a similar explanation to a Massachusetts congressman: "When Lee came over the river, I made a resolution that if McClellan drove him back I would send the Proclamation after him.")[277]

Chase recorded a somewhat different version of the president's words that fateful twenty-second day of September: "I have, as you are aware, thought a great deal about the relation of this war to Slavery; and you all remember that, several weeks ago, I read to you an Order I had prepared on this subject, which, on account of objections made by some of you, was not issued. Ever since then, my mind has been much occupied with this subject, and I have thought all along that the time for acting on it might very probably come. I think the time has come now. I wish it was a better time. I wish that we were in a better condition. The action of the army against the rebels has not been quite what I should have best liked. But they have been driven out of Maryland, and Pennsylvania is no longer in danger of invasion. When the rebel army was at Frederick, I determined, as soon as it should be driven out of Maryland, to issue a Proclamation of Emancipation such as I thought most likely to be useful. I said nothing to any one; but I made the promise to myself, and (hesitating a little)—to my Maker. The Rebel army is now driven out, and I am going to fulfill that promise. I have got you together to hear what I have written down. I do not wish your advice about the main matter—for that I have determined for myself. This I say without intending any thing but respect for any one of you. But I already know the views of each on this question. They have been heretofore expressed, and I have considered them as thoroughly and as carefully as I can. What I have written is that which my reflections have determined me to say." He asked for suggestions about the form but not the content of the proclamation, a four-page document much longer than the brief one he had read to them two months earlier. Modestly Lincoln acknowledged to the cabinet that "many others might, in this matter, as in others, do better than I can; and if I were satisfied that the public confidence was more fully possessed by any one of them than by me, and knew of any Constitutional way in which he could be put in my place, he should have it. I would gladly yield it to him. But though I believe that I have not so much of the confidence of the people as I had some time since, I do not know that, all things considered, any other person has more; and, however this may be, there is no way in which I can have any other man put where I am. I am here. I must do the best I can, and bear the responsibility of taking the course which I feel I ought to take."[278] (Two years later, Lincoln would remark that "it is very strange that I, a boy brought up in the woods, and seeing, as it were, but little of the world, should be drifted into the very apex of this great event.")[279]

Lincoln then read aloud his Proclamation, which was preliminary, for it would not go into effect until January 1. Like the Proclamation he had submitted to the cabinet in July, it called for voluntary colonization of the freedmen, endorsed his earlier gradual emancipation plan, and exempted both the Border States and some (but not all) areas occupied by the Union army. As Montgomery Blair remembered, the president stated that "he had power to issue the proclamation only in virtue of his power to strike at the rebellion, and he could not include places within our own lines, because the reason upon which the power depended did not apply to them, and he could not included such places" merely because he opposed slavery.[280] Confederate slaveholders would have one hundred days in which to cease rebelling; if they would lay down their arms, they could keep their chattels. If they did not, then as of New Year's Day, their slaves "shall be then, thenceforward, and forever free." Wherever the Union army penetrated, it would rigorously enforce the Proclamation. The attorney general, not commanders in the field, was to determine which slaveowners were loyal.

A striking new feature of the Proclamation was its seeming hint that the administration would aid slave insurrections: "The executive government of the United States, including the military and naval authority thereof, will recognize the freedom of such persons [freed slaves], and will do no act or acts to repress such persons, or any of them, in any efforts they may make for their actual freedom." Lincoln doubtless meant that the Union army would not return runaways to bondage, though many would interpret his words to mean that the North would incite slave uprisings. Also noteworthy was the Proclamation's pledge that "all citizens of the United States who shall have remained loyal thereto throughout the rebellion, shall . . . be compensated for all losses by acts of the United States, including the loss of slaves." He was promising to compensate loyal slaveholders without congressional authorization!

After Lincoln finished reading the text, Seward suggested that it would be better to promise to "recognize and maintain the freedom" of the slaves rather than merely to "recognize" it. The secretary of state also objected that the document as written implied that emancipation would only be valid as long as Lincoln remained president ("the executive government of the United States will, during the continuance in office of the present incumbent, recognize such persons, as being free.") Lincoln took Seward's advice, adding "and maintain" and deleting the reference to "continuance in office of the present incumbent." Chase expressed some reservations about the Proclamation, which "was going a step further than he had ever proposed," but he nevertheless pledged to "take it just as it is written, and to stand by it with all my heart." Stanton and Welles voiced strong approval, but Bates and Blair objected to the document's timing. The postmaster general, a strong emancipationist, feared that the Border States might be driven to secede. Lincoln acknowledged the validity of such criticism but replied that "the difficulty was as great not to act as to act. There were two sides to that question. For months he had labored to get those [Border] States to move in this matter, convinced in his own mind that it was their true interest to do so, but his labors were vain. . . . They would acquiesce, if not immediately, soon; for they must be satisfied that slavery had received its death-blow from slave-owners—it could not survive the rebellion." Blair also protested that the proclamation put into the hands of Northern Democrats "a club to be used against us." Lincoln said that argument "had not much weight with him" for "their clubs would be used against us, take what course we might."[281]

The next day Blair elaborated on his argument, maintaining that there was "no public sentiment at the North, even among extreme men which now demands the proposed measure." The Proclamation would "endanger our power in Congress, and put the power in the next House of Representatives in the hands of those opposed to the war, or to our mode of carrying it on."[282] When the Proclamation was released to the press on September 23, a Republican leader in Ohio echoed Blair, expressing fear that it "will defeat me and every other Union candidate for Congress along the border."[283]

The "rheumatic and stiff-jointed" language of the Proclamation disappointed some Radicals.[284] "How cold the President's Proclamation is," the abolitionist lecturer Sallie Holley remarked; it was "graceless coming from a sinner at the head of a nation of sinners."[285] Adam Gurowski called it an "illogical, pusillanimous, confused half-measure," written "in the meanest and the most dry routine style."[286] Frederick Douglass lamented that the words of the Proclamation "touched neither justice nor mercy. Had there been one expression of sound moral feeling against Slavery, one word of regret and shame that this accursed system had remained so long the disgrace and scandal of the Republic, one word of satisfaction in the hope of burying slavery and the rebellion in one common grave, a thrill of joy would have run round the world."[287] Beriah Green indignantly asked: "How in his Proclamation . . . does Mr. L. regard the horribly outraged—the damnably oppressed men & women & children, who in this country are blasphemously called slaves? Other at all than as a fulcrum, by wh. he tries to pry the Confederate States into his Union?"[288] The fiery Parker Pillsbury thought "God has no better opinion of our President than he had of Pharaoh." Pillsbury longed for the day when "somebody calls for *justice*," talks "of something besides 'Compensation & Colonisation,'" and acts "from higher consider-ations than 'Military Necessity.'"[289] Although Lydia Maria Child was grateful for the Proclamation, nonetheless she told a friend: "The ugly fact cannot be concealed that it was done reluctantly and stintedly, and that even the degree that *was* accomplished was done selfishly; was merely a war-measure, to which we were forced by our own perils and necessities; and that no recognition of principles of justice or humanity sur-rounded the politic act with a halo of moral glory."[290]

Lincoln carefully omitted any moral appeal in order to avoid antagonizing con-servative opinion, especially in the Lower North and the Border States. He also wished to make sure that slaves liberated under the proclamation had a sound legal basis to protect their freedom in court, if necessary. Months later, when the Final Emancipation Proclamation was about to be issued, Lincoln told a journalist that he was "strongly pressed" to justify it "upon high moral grounds, and to introduce into the instrument unequivocal language testifying to the negroes' right to freedom upon the precise principles expounded by the Emancipationists of both Old and New-England." The president resisted this advice, for "policy requires that the Proclama-tion be issued as a war measure, and not a measure of morality; and that Law and Justice require that the slaves should be enabled to plead the Proclamation hereafter if necessary to establish judicially their title to freedom. They can do this, the President says, on a proclamation proceeding as a war measure from the Commander-in-Chief of the Army, but not on one issuing from the bosom of philanthropy."[291]

John Murray Forbes, an influential Massachusetts industrialist and philanthro-pist, defended Lincoln's emphasis on military necessity. As Forbes told Charles Sum-ner, "our strongest Republicans some even of Mr Lincoln['s] Electors have constitutional scruples in regard to emancipation upon any other ground—& with these must be joined a large class of Democrats & self styled 'Conservatives' whose support is highly desireable—and ought to be secured where it can be done without any sacrifice of principle." Forbes realized that Sumner and his allies "would like to have it done upon higher ground but the main thing is to have it *done strongly* & *to have it so backed* up by public opinion that it will strike *the* telling blow at the Rebel-lion and at slavery together." Resorting to a nutritional metaphor to make his case, Forbes added: "I buy and eat my bread made from the flour raised by the hard work-ing Farmer—it is certainly satisfactory that in so doing I am helping the Farmer clothe his children but my *motive* is self preservation—not philanthropy nor justice. Let the President free the slaves upon the same principle & so state it that the masses of our people can easily understand it. He will thus remove constitutional scruples from some and will draw to himself the support of a very large class—who do not want to expend their Brothers & Sons and money for the benefit of the Negro, but who will be very glad to see Northern life and treasure saved by any practical measure—*even if it does incidentally* an act of justice and benevolence." Forbes did not wish to "disclaim the higher motives but where so much predjudice exists—*I would eat my* bread to sustain my life—I would take *the one short sure* method of preserving the national life—& say little about any other motive."[292]

Radicals objected to the Preliminary Emancipation Proclamation on more than stylistic grounds. Although William Lloyd Garrison publicly declared its issuance was a "matter for great rejoicing," an "important step in the right direction," and "an act of immense historic consequence," he objected to its limited scope, its contradictory "jumble of words," and "its mean, absurd and proscriptive devices to expatriate the colored population."[293] Privately, he remarked that Lincoln "can do nothing for *freedom* in a direct manner, but only by circumlocution and delay."[294] The Rev. Dr. George B. Cheever of New York detected in the Proclamation no "justice, nobleness, or humanity," but rather "the most unreserved national selfishness."[295] To him it seemed "a measure of mere political expediency" and little more than "a bribe to win back the slaveholding States to loyalty by giving and confirming to them the privilege of tyrannizing over millions of their fellow creatures in perpetual slavery. . . . So stupendous a bribe, so truly hellish in its nature, never before was imagined." Lincoln was, Cheever scornfully remarked, "nothing but a nose of wax," and abolitionists "had as good a right to pull that nose as Kentucky."[296] In scolding Lincoln, he urged that the Proclamation be made to apply to all slaves unconditionally.

But many other Radicals agreed with Massachusetts Governor John A. Andrew's conclusion that it was "a mighty *act*" though a "poor *document*," "slow, somewhat halting, wrong in its delay till January, but grand and sublime after all."[297] The firebrand Samuel J. May, Jr., wished that the emancipation had been immediate and had come much earlier, but he confessed that "I cannot stop to dwell on these. Joy, gratitude, thanksgiving, renewed hope and courage fill my soul."[298] The *National Anti-Slavery Standard* greeted the Proclamation "with an unspeakable joy."[299] Theodore Tilton laughed and cried "in a bewilderment of joy" and was "half crazy with enthusiasm!"[300] "We shout for joy that we live to record this righteous decree," wrote Frederick Douglass. The president might be slow, but Douglass was sure that he was "not the man to reconsider, retract and contradict words and purposes solemnly proclaimed over his official signature."[301] Other blacks were equally enthusiastic. The editor of the New York *Anglo-African* said: "joy sits enthroned upon our heart," for Lincoln's proclamation was "a bridge of gold" and "a glorious harbinger of the future."[302] The abolitionist Boston *Commonwealth* relished the way that Lincoln turned the tables on critics who insisted that the war be fought solely to preserve the Union. The editor remarked to such carpers: "We complained bitterly that the President was slow; but now we see that his slowness has been the means of committing the whole flock of you to a rule of loyalty, which you cannot abandon without making it appear that in all your previous course you were liars and hypocrites. . . . Those who do not stand by the Proclamation will be branded as those who would rather see the United States Government overthrown than the end of Human Bondage on this continent."[303]

To Charles Sumner the "skies are brighter and the air is purer now that Slavery is handed over to judgment."[304] Hannibal Hamlin told the president that the Proclamation would "stand as the great act of the age," would "prove to be [as] wise in Statesmanship, as it is Patriotic," and would "be enthusiastically approved and sustained." Future generations, he predicted, "will, as I do, say God bless you for the great and noble act."[305] Horace Greeley called the issuance of the Proclamation the "beginning of the end of the rebellion," the "beginning of a new life for the nation," and "one of those stupendous facts in human history which marks not only an era in the progress of the nation, but an epoch in the history of the world." That cantankerous editor, who had scolded the president a month earlier in "The Prayer of Twenty Millions," now said: "God bless Abraham Lincoln." Extravagantly Greeley's paper announced: "Let the President know that everywhere throughout all the land he is hailed as Wisest and Best, and that by this great deed of enfranchisement of an oppressed people—a deed, the doing of whereof was never before vouchsafed to any mortal ruler—he re-creates a nation."[306]

Others heaped similar praise on the document. John W. Forney called it a "second Declaration of Independence."[307] The Pittsburgh *Gazette* editorialized that the Proclamation was "the most important document in the world's history. Magna Charta is as nothing to it. It is, in fact, a new Magna Charta, before the light of which the other must pale."[308] The New York *Evening Post* deemed it "the most solemn and momentous declaration the world ever witnessed," which "puts us right before Europe," "brings us back to our traditions," and "animates our soldiers with the same spirit which led our forefathers to victory under Washington."[309] The New York *Times* more moderately acclaimed it as "one of the great events of the century."[310] Lincoln's hometown paper, the *Illinois State Journal,* grandly asserted that "no event in the history of this country since the Declaration of Independence itself has excited so profound attention either at home or abroad."[311] The Springfield, Massachusetts, *Republican* sensibly commented that Lincoln's "action is timely—neither too soon nor too late. . . . it will be sustained by the great mass of the loyal people, North and South, and thus by the courage and prudence of the president the greatest social and political revolution of the age will be triumphantly carried through in the midst of a civil war."[312]

The proclamation warmed the hearts of New England intellectuals. A former critic of the administration, Ralph Waldo Emerson, changed his tune after the announcement of the Proclamation. In the *Atlantic Monthly* he ranked it with such milestones in the history of liberty as "the Confession of Augsburg, the plantation of America, the English Commonwealth of 1648, the Declaration of American Independence in 1776, the British emancipation of slaves in the West Indies, the passage of the Reform Bill, the repeal of the Corn-Laws, the Magnetic Ocean-Telegraph," and the enactment of the homestead bill by Congress earlier in 1862. Lincoln, said the Sage of Concord, "has been permitted to do more for America than any other American man." The nation was redeemed, he declared: "With this blot removed from our national honor, this heavy load lifted off the national heart, we shall not fear henceforward to show our faces among mankind. We shall cease to be hypocrites and

pretenders, but what we have styled our free institutions will be such."[313] The abolitionist and transcendentalist William Henry Furness expected that the Proclamation
would open a "new world," which was "coming into existence arrayed in millennial
splendor, wherein the distinctions of race, which have always been such active causes
of contempt and hatred and war shall be obliterated, and men shall live together in
the relations of a Christian brotherhood."[314] "God be praised!" exclaimed Charles
Eliot Norton to George William Curtis. "I can hardly see to write,—for when I think
of this great act of Freedom, and all it implies, my heart and my eyes overflow with
the deepest, most serious gladness."[315] Curtis declared that there "was a time, not very
long since, when a large majority of the Northern people would have opposed it
strenuously—not so much from any admiration for slavery, as from the belief that,
under the Constitution, we had no right to meddle with it, and that its abolition involved dangers and inconveniences perhaps as formidable as those which were created
by its existence." But educated people had been radicalized and the working class was
sure to follow.[316]

More than a dozen Northern governors who had gathered in Altoona, Pennsylvania, also congratulated the president. Their original purpose in coming together
had been to discuss the parlous military situation as Lee invaded the North, and to
urge a more vigorous prosecution of the war. On September 6, Andrew G. Curtin of
Pennsylvania had asked some of his counterparts if it would not "be well that the loyal
governors should meet at some point in the Border States to take measures for the
more active support of the Government?"[317] Especially enthusiastic in promoting the
conclave was Massachusetts Governor John A. Andrew, who argued that something
must be done "to save the Presdt. from the infamy of ruining his country."[318] Andrew
favored replacing McClellan with Frémont. Other Radical governors, notably Richard Yates of Illinois, insisted that Lincoln must be goaded to take vigorous action
against slavery. But on September 14, Moderates (Curtin, David Tod of Ohio, and
Francis H. Pierpont of Virginia) rather than Radicals issued the call inviting fellow
governors to join them at Altoona ten days later.

After receiving a letter from Senator Zachariah Chandler of Michigan stating
that "nothing will save us but a demand of the loyal governors, *backed by a threat*—that
a change of policy and men shall instantly be made," Lyman Trumbull warned Yates
and his colleagues against dictating policy to the president. Such a step would violate
the spirit of the Constitution, he argued. Moreover, Trumbull said with uncharacteristic charity for Lincoln, none of the governors, though "men of great ability and
far-seeing comprehension," was as capable as the president. "I know of no governor in
any state who I believe equal in ability to Mr. Lincoln, and in high moral
integrity—besides he has in his councils as great men as the Republic can produce.
With this combination of talent and experience, I feel that our cause is doing the best
it can under the circumstances."[319]

Before the Altoona meeting, Curtin, Andrew, and David Tod called on the
president, who advised them to expect a new pronouncement on slavery. The president said that he approved of the conclave, and the governors gave him assurances
that they would support the forthcoming change in policy. The mood at the Altoona

meeting was soothed by the quasi-victory at Antietam a week earlier. Despite the outcome of that battle, some of the thirteen governors criticized McClellan, most notably Samuel J. Kirkwood of Iowa, who said the general "had done wrong in allowing bad men and bad newspapers who were doing all in their power to help the rebellion to success, to be his peculiar champions, although he knew that ten words from his lips would send them to hell, where they belonged."[320] Ohio's Governor Tod defended McClellan, as did Curtin and Maryland Governor Augustus Bradford. Half a dozen governors expressed indignation that Frémont had been offered no command since his petulant resignation that summer. All save Bradford approved of the Emancipation Proclamation. Curtin and Andrew drew up an address expressing "heartfelt gratitude" to Lincoln for that momentous document, which they predicted would inspire "new vigor" as well as "new life and hope" among their constituents. They also urged that 100,000 reserve troops be organized to respond to future emergencies like the recent Confederate incursion across the Potomac.

In reply, the president invited them to the White House, where he gratefully declared that "no fact had assured him so thoroughly of the justice of the conclusion at which he had arrived as that the Executives of loyal States gave it their hearty approbation."[321] The friendly tone of the meeting was disturbed briefly by Kirkwood's interjection that the people of Iowa thought that McClellan "was unfit to command his army that his army was well clothed, well armed, well disciplined," that his troops "were fighting in a cause as good as men ever fought for, and fought as bravely as men ever fought, yet were continually whipped." Then Kirkwood brashly added: "There is an impression out west, Mr. President, that you do not dare to remove McClellan." Stung by this remark, Lincoln replied: "if I believed our cause would be benefited by removing Gen. McClellan to-morrow, I would remove him to-morrow. I do not so believe to-day, but if the time shall come when I shall so believe I will remove him promptly, and not till then."[322] Several governors at Altoona had criticized cabinet members, but it was decided not to raise that delicate subject with Lincoln at their White House meeting. Instead, Andrew, Tod, and Pierpont would speak to him individually.

Democrats called the Altoona Conference a "second Hartford Convention" and claimed that the governors' pressure had forced Lincoln to preempt them by issuing the Emancipation Proclamation. Lincoln denied their assertion, insisting to George Boutwell that he "never thought of the meeting of the governors" when deciding to issue the Proclamation.[323]

Lincoln gracefully expressed gratitude to a group of serenaders who called at the Executive Mansion on September 24. Whitelaw Reid reported that the crowd, which was "honoring the great act that shall make Abraham Lincoln immortal among men," cheered repeatedly, surged back and forth, and looked on the man whom "the people trust" with "a thousand expressions—delight, gratification, curiosity, rage." When the cheering subsided, the president explained in a tone that was neither triumphant nor even confident that "[w]hat I did, I did after very full deliberation, and under a very heavy and solemn sense of responsibility. [Cries of "Good," "Good," "Bless you," and applause.]" He added "reverently and humbly" that "I can only trust in God I have made no mistake. [Cries "No mistake—all right; you've made no mistakes yet. Go ahead, you're right."] I shall make no attempt on this occasion to sustain what I have done or said by any comment. [Voices—"That's unnecessary; we understand it."] It is now for the country and the world to pass judgment on it, and, maybe, take action upon it." Reid thought the scene "well worth remembering—one that History will treasure up forever: the President of a great Republic . . . standing at his window, amid the clouds and gloom with which his decree of Universal Emancipation is ushered in, receiving the congratulations of his People for his bold word for Freedom and the Right, . . . hesitating as he thanks them, doubting even amid the ringing cheers of the populace, trusting in God he has made no mistake, tremulously (so tremulously that his utterance seems choked by his agitation) awaiting the judgment of the Country and the World."[324]

Some sneered at the Proclamation as an "inopportune paper weapon."[325] Even a sympathetic observer like George Templeton Strong predicted that it "will do us good abroad, but will have no other effect."[326] The Washington *National Intelligencer* spoke for many when it scornfully referred to "the inutility of such proclamations" and speculated that Lincoln's might do more harm than good.[327] The New York *Herald* argued that Lincoln thought the war would be over by year's end and that the document was therefore a mere sop "to silence the clamors of our shrieking and howling abolition faction." It could not "in any just sense be regarded as an emancipation or abolition measure. It is wholly conditional, and may never emancipate a single slave."[328]

Fear of slave revolts and the possible destruction of the cotton crop alarmed some European governments. England's foreign secretary, Lord John Russell, viewed the Emancipation Proclamation as an attempt to arouse "the passions of the slave to aid the destructive progress of armies." Even staunch English friends of the North like Richard Cobden feared that the Proclamation would transform the war into "one of the most bloody & horrible episodes in history." In October, French foreign minister Edouard Drouyn de Lhuys issued a circular to the British and Russian governments alluding to the "irreparable misfortunes" of "a servile war" and calling for joint mediation of the American conflict. Based on a six-month armistice and suspension of the blockade, this proposal was tantamount to diplomatic recognition of the Confederacy. When it was rejected in London and St. Petersburg, France shelved it. Still, Queen Victoria's government had misgivings about the Emancipation Proclamation and was predisposed to intervene somehow to end the war and obviate the threat of slave uprisings. Ominously, the influential chancellor of the exchequer, William Gladstone, told an enthusiastic English audience in October: "We may have our own opinions about slavery, we may be for or against the South; but there is no doubt that Jefferson Davis and other leaders of the South have made an army; they are making, it appears, a navy; and they have made what is more than either—they have made a nation."[329]

Democratic papers called the Emancipation Proclamation "a nullity," a "monstrous usurpation," a "criminal wrong," and an "act of national suicide" that would "excite the ridicule that follows impotency."[330] The New York *Express* protested that the human mind "*never conceived a policy so well fitted, utterly to degrade and destroy while labor, and to reduce the white man to the level of the negro.*"[331] Reaction in the Border States was predictably negative. The "mischievous, pestilent proclamation" reportedly "produced great despondency" in Kentucky.[332] The Louisville *Democrat* objected that "the President has as much right to abolish the institution of marriage, or the laws of a State regulating the relation of parent and child, as to nullify the right of a State to regulate the relations of the white and black races."[333] The Louisville *Journal* decried the proclamation as "wholly unauthorized and wholly pernicious" and predicted that "Kentucky cannot and will not acquiesce in this measure. Never!"[334] A Kentuckian warned Lincoln that if "Negroes be freed in any of the Southern States, which are in rebellion, they will at once, make their way to the loyal or 'border States,' and there become a pest to Society, an expense upon the public or be driven beyond the bounds by the bayonet, or exterminated in like manner as *we* Christians have 'done unto' the Indians."[335] In Missouri, the news was "received with serious head shakings by many."[336] A St. Louis admirer of the president appealed to Joseph Holt: "Stop him! Hold him!" Could Holt "not prevail on him to be entirely silent on 'negro-ology'?" Lincoln's "proclamations have paralized our armies; and given nerve & vigor to the rebels."[337] In western Virginia, the Wheeling *Press* engaged in hyperbole, arguing that the Proclamation was "more like the knell of freedom and the wail of the departing angel of peace" than any document since the revocation of the edict of Nantes in 1685, which led to the persecution of French Protestants.[338]

Midwestern Democrats howled in protest. "This is another step in the nigger business, and another advance in the Robespierrian highway of tyranny and anarchy," declared an Ohio editor.[339] Some Wisconsin newspapers called for Lincoln's impeachment. Others urged sterner measures. A leading Iowa Democrat confided to his diary that Lincoln was a tyrant whose power could be checked only "by revolution or private assassination."[340] Another Iowan, Dennis A. Mahoney, editor of the Dubuque *Herald,* wrote: "The people who submit to the insolent fanaticism which dictated this last act, *are and deserve to be enslaved* to the class which Abraham Lincoln self-sufficiently declares free. If they possessed a tithe of the spirit which animated Rome when Cataline was expelled from its walls . . . they would hurl him into the Potomac."[341] Murat Halstead reported that "there are persons who would feel that it was doing God's service to kill him [Lincoln], if it were not feared that Hamlin is a bigger fool than he is."[342]

When John Hay tried to speak to the president about such hostile commentators, Lincoln cut him off, saying that "he had studied that matter so long that he knew more about it than they did."[343] Some critics, like George Francis Train, irritated Lincoln. As that eccentric millionaire went about the country denouncing abolitionists and calling the Proclamation "the cleverest trick of the season," Lincoln remarked that Train "reminded him of the Irishman's description of Soda water. 'It was a tumbler of piss with a fart in it.'"[344]

The passage in the Proclamation that seemed to encourage slave revolts led the New York *Express* to ask: "Can it be that President Lincoln calculates such a contingency as a servile insurrection consequent upon his emancipation proclamation?"[345]

The Louisville *Democrat* termed Lincoln "an imbecile" and an "encourager of insurrection, lust, arson, and murder."[346] Jefferson Davis indignantly declared to the Confederate Congress: "We may well leave it to the instincts of common humanity to pass judgment on a measure by which millions of human beings of an inferior race, peaceful and contented laborers in their sphere . . . are encouraged to a general assassination of their masters."[347] A member of that Congress introduced a resolution condemning the Proclamation as "a gross violation of the usages of civilized warfare, an outrage on the rights of private property, and an invitation to an atrocious servile war." He recommended "that it should be held up to the execration of mankind and counteracted by severe retaliatory measures." Other Confederate legislators urged that the war be conducted under the black flag, with no prisoners taken. Many Confederate soldiers shared that view. In Kentucky, the president's words were reportedly "translated as designing a *rising of the slaves in order to destroy their masters*."[348] The Richmond *Enquirer* condemned "Lincoln's proclamation ordaining servile insurrection in the Confederate States," called its author a "fiend," and exclaimed: "let the civilized world fling its scorpion lash upon him!"[349] In North Carolina, the Raleigh *Standard* termed the Proclamation "one of the most monstrously wicked documents that ever emanated from human authority."[350]

English papers echoed their Southern counterparts, deriding the Proclamation as a call for servile war leading to "horrible massacres of white women and children, to be followed by the extermination of the black race in the South." The London *Times* asked if Lincoln would not "be classed among that catalogue of monsters, the wholesale assassins and butchers of their kind?" The president resembled "a Chinaman beating his two swords together to frighten his enemies." The "Thunderer" sneeringly remarked: "Where he has no power Mr. Lincoln will set the negroes free; where he retains power he will consider them as slaves."[351] The organ of Prime Minister Palmerston rejoiced that the "*disgraceful*" Proclamation "is *deservedly reprobated*" in England "as one of the *bloodiest manifestoes* that ever issued from a civilized government."[352] Even liberal papers, which might be expected to sympathize with the Proclamation, denounced it as harshly as moderate and conservative journals did.

Some administration supporters also objected to that section of the Proclamation. Charles A. Dana confided to Seward that it "*jars on me like a wrong tone in music*. . . . This is the only 'bad egg' I see in 'that pudding'—& I fear may go far to make it less palatable than it deserves to be."[353] Thaddeus Stevens, however, rejoiced to think that slaves might be "incited to insurrection and give the rebels a taste of real civil war."[354]

The army had a mixed reaction to the Proclamation. Some officers and men disapproved emphatically. General Fitz John Porter called the document "absurd" and, alluding to Lincoln's remarks to Chicago clergymen on September 13, ridiculed him as "a political coward, who has not the manliness to sustain opinions expressed but a few days before—and can unblushingly see published side by side, his proclamation and his reasons for not issuing it. What a ruler for us to admire!"[355] McClellan had intended to submit a letter to the president protesting against the Emancipation Proclamation "and saying that the Army would never sustain" it but decided not to do so when General William F. Smith warned that McClellan "would neither sustain him-self with the army nor the country and that it would only array him in opposition" to the government "and result in disaster to him."[356] Smith's advice was seconded by Generals John Cochrane, Jacob D. Cox, and Ambrose E. Burnside. So instead of carrying out his original intention, McClellan belatedly issued a general order coolly hinting that the administration should be voted out of office. It counseled against criticism of the Proclamation and stated that the "remedy for political errors, if any are committed, is to be found only in the action of the people at the polls."[357] But most of the army supported the Proclamation. A partisan Democrat, who as a medi-cal commissioner visited the Peninsula, reported that "with very few exceptions the *whole army* is in favor of the most stringent prosecution of the war, using every means in our power to stifle the rebellion, and it regards emancipation as one of our most potent weapons."[358]

Conservative Republicans like Richard W. Thompson thought the Proclamation unfair to loyal slaveholders in the Confederacy. In response to this objection, Lincoln told Thompson bluntly that "there were no loyal slave owners in the South" and "avowed his resolution to follow the course dictated by his own conscience." Thomp-son recalled that the president assured him with "the utmost composure" that "I would be wiser after awhile."[359]

Public response to emancipation did not encourage Lincoln. On September 28, he told his vice-president that "while I hope something from the proclamation, my expectations are not as sanguine as are those of some friends. The time for its effect southward has not come; but northward the effect should be instantaneous. It is six days old, and while commendation in newspapers and by distinguished individuals is all that a vain man could wish, the stocks have declined, and troops come forward more slowly than ever. This, looked soberly in the face, is not very satisfactory. We have fewer troops in the field at the end of six days than we had at the beginning—the attrition among the old outnumbering the addition by the new. The North responds to the proclamation sufficiently in breath; but breath alone kills no rebels."[360] Many more Rebels would have to be killed before emancipation could become a reality.

"I Am Not a Bold Man, But I Have the Knack of Sticking to My Promises!"
The Emancipation Proclamation
(September–December 1862)

Although Lincoln's announcement that he would issue an Emancipation Proclamation seemed to do more harm than good in the short run, he refused to back down. His deep commitment to black freedom led him to stand by his decision despite intense pressure.

Backlash: Electoral Reverses

The Proclamation, which some commentators dismissed as a ploy to strengthen the Republicans politically, instead contributed to the party's severe losses in the fall of 1862. As Montgomery Blair had warned, the document became a club that the Democrats wielded effectively in the election campaigns that October. In Ohio, they captured fourteen House seats to the Republicans' five, and in Indiana, they won seven of the eleven House seats and gained a majority of the state legislature. The parties divided the Pennsylvania House seats evenly. David Davis called the results "disastrous in the extreme" and remarked that the Emancipation Proclamation "has not worked the wonder that was anticipated."[1] Another of Lincoln's Illinois friends, W. W. Orme, bemoaned the "terrible reverses," which were, he thought, "as bad, indeed and worse, than a battle lost."[2] Maine Senator William P. Fessenden ascribed the setbacks to the "folly of the President" and called the result "disgraceful [in] every way."[3] Another Pine State lawmaker, Congressman Frederick Pike, believed that if Lincoln "would leave off story telling long enough to look after the war & drive the drunken generals out of the army & cashier those who wish for the success of the rebels . . . we might hope for a successful prosecution of the campaign."[4] In Minnesota, the ill-humored General John Pope also blamed the setback on Lincoln, who "seems striving to conciliate the enemies by driving off & discouraging the friends of the Administration."[5]

During the fall electoral contests, Democrats relentlessly employed their customary appeal to what the New York *Tribune* aptly called "that cruel and ungenerous prejudice against color which still remains to disgrace our civilization and to impeach our Christianity."[6] Their race-baiting was especially virulent in Ohio and Indiana. The Cincinnati *Commercial* justly complained that "the prejudice of race has been inflamed, and used by the Democratic party with an energy and ingenuity perfectly infernal."[7] Democratic editors warned Ohio workingmen that they would "have to leave Ohio and labor where niggers could not come" and urged them to vote Democratic if they did "not desire their place occupied by negroes."[8] Playing on voters' dread that freed slaves would swarm across the Ohio River, Democrats adopted as their slogan: "The Constitution as it is, the Union as it was, and the negroes where they are." Former Ohio Governor William Allen told his neighbors in Chillicothe that "[e]very white laboring man in the North who does not want to be swapped off for a free nigger should vote the Democratic ticket." If the slaves were freed, he predicted, hundreds of thousands of them, "with their hands reeking in the blood of murdered women and children," would "cross over into our state" looking for work.[9] Another Buckeye Democrat, Congressman Samuel S. "Sunset" Cox, advised opponents to heed an Eleventh Commandment: "Thou shalt not degrade the white race by such intermixtures as emancipation will bring."[10] An unsuccessful Republican congressional candidate in Ohio explained his defeat to Chase: "I had thought until this year the cry of 'nigger' & 'abolitionism' were played out, but they never had as much power & effect in this part of the State as at the recent election. Many who had heretofore acted with us voted the straight democratic ticket."[11] Samuel Medary, editor of *The Crisis* in Columbus, spoke for many Ohio Democrats when he rejoiced that a "[f]ree press and a white man's government is fully established by this vote."[12]

On October 16, Nicolay reported from the White House that "[w]e are all blue here today on account of the election news."[13] The results astounded Lincoln, who had not anticipated such a severe drubbing. But his spirits quickly recovered, and a few days later he told a caller who asked why he seemed so upbeat: "there is no use in being blue. The elections have not gone to suit me, but I have felt a good deal better since I saw a regiment polled to ascertain the sentiments of the soldiers. Eight hundred out of a thousand voted to sustain my policy. And so it is with most of the troops. . . . Then too about the military situation. Things *drag* too much to suit me. I have tried my best to crowd matters. But we shall hear of something good ere long. Things look very well in comparison with the aspect two months ago, and this fall and winter I believe will make them look a great deal better than they do now."[14] On October 27, Lincoln met with John A. Jones, who reported that he "looks well & cheerful."[15]

But the November results plunged Lincoln back into despair. The Democrats won the governorships of New York and New Jersey and captured a majority of legislative seats in both the latter state and Illinois. The most significant result was the triumph of New York gubernatorial candidate Horatio Seymour by 11,000 votes. It was widely regarded as a repudiation of "Old Lincompoop."[16] The race issue also loomed large in that contest. A leading Democratic newspaper in the Empire State declared that a vote for Seymour "is a vote to protect our white laborers against the association and competition of Southern negroes."[17] More important still in causing Republican losses was the lack of military success. George Templeton Strong estimated that two-thirds of Seymour's supporters "meant to say by their votes, 'Messrs. Lincoln, Seward, Stanton & Co., you have done your work badly, so far. You are humbugs. My business is stopped, I have got taxes to pay, my wife's third cousin was killed on the Chickahominy, and the war is no nearer an end than it was a year ago. I am disgusted with you and your party and shall vote for the governor or the congressman you disapprove, just to spite you.'"[18] When asked how he felt after the Democrats' victory in New York, Lincoln replied: "Somewhat like that boy in Kentucky, who stubbed his toe while running to see his sweetheart. The boy said he was too big to cry, and far too badly hurt to laugh."[19] He told Massachusetts Senator Henry Wilson: "I confess that I am grieved at the results of these elections. This intelligence will go to Europe; it will be construed there as a condemnation of the war; it will go into the land of the rebellion, and will encourage the leading rebels and nerve the arms of the rebel soldiers fighting our men in the field. It is true, many of those men elected profess to be war Democrats; but the resolutions of their conventions, the tone of their leading presses, and their general action will be construed everywhere against the cause of our country."[20]

Lincoln had good reason to lament the disastrous result in Illinois. Democrats elected their state ticket by 14,000 votes; their congressional candidates won nine of the fourteen seats; and they secured control of the legislature with a margin of 13 to 12 in the senate and 54 to 32 in the House, thus ensuring that Orville H. Browning would be ousted from the U.S. senate. (Some thought it would make little difference politically, for Lincoln's longtime friend allegedly planned to establish a conservative third party in opposition to the administration.) Most painful for Lincoln was the defeat of his dear friend Leonard Swett in a congressional race against John Todd Stuart. Swett's law partner feared that the Democratic victory in the Eighth Congressional District "will palsy the arm of the President."[21] A War Department order issued in September, resettling newly liberated slaves in Illinois, proved to be a blunder which became the most significant campaign issue and helped swell the Democrats' vote. In a terse postmortem, Swett told a friend that the "Proclamation hurt rather than helped us. Negroes from the south were taken into our state. Fifty or more went to Livingston. This did great harm."[22] Lyman Trumbull reported that many Illinois Republicans "believed that their sons & relations were being sacrificed to the incompetency, indisposition or treason of a great many Democratic generals" and therefore "were unwilling to sustain an administration which allowed this."[23]

In June, Lincoln had derived some solace from the defeat of a proposed new Illinois constitution that would have severely crippled the war effort. He also rejoiced at the November results in Missouri, where emancipationists gained a majority of the state's congressional seats. He was particularly glad that General Frank Blair was reelected, saying on November 5 "that it was the *only good* news he had heard for many days." The gains in Missouri, he added, "consoled him for the loss of his own [state]" and "more than compensated him for all defeats elsewhere."[24] Providing further comfort was news that Republicans had kept control of the U.S. House (101–77), even though Democrats gained a net of thirty-four seats, mostly from the Lower North. With some justice, Democrats howled that the administration had packed Congress by having military forces interfere in elections in Kentucky and other Border States.

Lincoln had been warned that backlash against the Emancipation Proclamation would hurt the Republicans at the polls, but that did not deter him from announcing it a scant three weeks before the crucial elections in Ohio, Indiana, and Pennsylvania. Later he told a Radical delegation that "many good men, some earnest Republicans and some from very far North, were opposed to the issuing of that proclamation, holding it unwise and of doubtful legality."[25] Looking back on that risk in 1864, he said: "I hoped for greater gain than loss; but of this, I was not entirely confident."[26] To the Rev. Dr. John McClintock, an ultra-Radical, he recalled his anxiety about the timing of the announcement: "When I issued that Proclamation, I was in great doubt about it myself. I did not think that the people had been quite educated up to it, and I feared its effects upon the Border States, yet I think it was right; I knew it would help our cause in Europe, and I trusted in God and did it." He added that "Providence is stronger than either you or I."[27]

Lincoln's fear was justified. In late October, a Kentucky Unionist reported that the "proclamation damaged us very much."[28] The president told Congressman George W. Julian that the "proclamation was to stir the country; but it has done about as much harm as good."[29] On November 6, Theodore Tilton reported that the president "has spoken to at least six persons, lamenting the issue of his Proclamation, and calling it the great mistake of his life."[30] One of those persons was Wendell Phillips. When asked about this alleged remark to Phillips, Lincoln did not deny that he had made it and implied that "he had put himself into a minority with the people, and he well knew that it was impossible for him to carry on a great war against the feelings of the majority of the people."[31]

In light of the Republicans' dismal showing at the polls, it was widely speculated that Lincoln might renege on his commitment to issue the Proclamation, but he insisted that he would not. On November 20, he unqualifiedly assured intimate friends that "his views on this important question had in no wise been modified by the result of the recent elections; that he had issued the Proclamation of September after long and thoughtful deliberation, and that he should stand by it up to and on the 1st of January."[32] That same day, he dashed off a heated letter to Kentucky Unionists who complained about Union troops infringing on the rights of slaveholders: "I believe you are acquainted with the American Classics, (if there be such) and probably remember a speech of Patrick Henry, in which he represented a certain character in the revolutionary times, as totally disregarding all questions of country, and 'hoarsely bawling, beef! Beef!! Beef!!!' Do you not know that I may as well surrender this contest, directly, as to make any order, the obvious purpose of which would be to return fugitive slaves?" After cooling off, Lincoln decided not to send this missive.[33]

The next day Lincoln told other Kentucky Unionists "that he would rather die than take back a word of the Proclamation of Freedom."[34] Similarly, he explained why a would-be caller who wished the Proclamation to be withheld could not obtain a White House interview: "I shall not do anything of the kind, and why should he or I waste time or words over the subject?"[35] Alluding to the slaves, he said: "My word is out to these people, and I can't take it back."[36] In mid-December, he informed Border State congressmen and senators lobbying against the Proclamation "that he was an Anti-Slavery man, and considered Slavery to be the right arm of the rebellion, and that it must be lopped off."[37] He feared that "if he should refuse to issue his proclamation there would be a rebellion in the north, and that a dictator would be placed over his head within the week."[38] On Christmas Eve, he "said he would not if he could, and could not if he would, withhold his decree of emancipation."[39] Six days later, he exclaimed to a pair of western politicians: "Gentlemen, I am not a bold man, but I have the knack of sticking to my promises!"[40] In late November, he informed T. J. Barnett of the Interior Department "that he should *abate no jot* of his emancipation policy" and that "the foundations of slavery have been cracked by the war, by the Rebels." He derided "the notion that servile insurrection is stimulated by his proclamation."[41]

Dismissing Dull Augers: Buell and McClellan

In addition to backlash against the Emancipation Proclamation, the lack of military success hurt the Republicans at the polls. Writing from Illinois in October, Horace White told Lincoln: "*If* we are beaten in this State . . . , it will be because McClellan & Buell *won't fight*."[42] White's colleague on the Chicago *Tribune*, Joseph Medill, was especially indignant at McClellan. The Democrats, he said, were "taking advantage of the treachery that keeps the army motionless," "fomenting public discontent," and "promising a peace, if brought into power. The future is dark and dismal. Lincoln issued his proclamation and then set down on his d[errier]e contented. But proclamations like faith without works are dead."[43] In Ohio, William M. Dickson warned that "the want of all firmness in dismissing incompetency and punishing criminality," along with "a facile disposition to reward importunity," was threatening "to destroy all respect for the President" and placing an "overwhelming weight upon us in the approaching elections."[44] An Iowan bemoaned "the lamentable want of vigor and energy in the conduct of the war" and reported that the "people out here in the North West on whom the burdens of this war have fallen more heavily than on the people of any other section of the loyal portion of the country, are heart-sick at the manner in which the war has been conducted. They are fast losing all heart, and all hope. Within the last year the loyal states have lost hundreds of thousands of their sons and hundreds of millions of their means."[45] A prominent Westerner noted that "many persons are getting tired of a war which seems to them to drag heavily. . . . they have no confidence in the generals, especially Halleck, McClellan and Buell. So many things look as if . . . the plan of these men is not to subdue the South, but to wear out the patience of the North."[46] William Cullen Bryant, whose New York *Evening Post* had been belaboring the administration for its timidity and tardiness, advised Lincoln that the Democrats might well carry the Empire State because of "the inactivity of our armies in putting down the rebellion. I have been pained to hear lately from persons zealously loyal, the expression of a doubt as to whether the administration sincerely desires the speedy annihilation of the rebel forces."[47] Lincoln's friend Noah Brooks reported "that the slow conduct of the war had more to do with the result of the elections than anything else. This is the view which the President took of it, and it must be admitted that by adopting, as he did, that hypothesis, he was more deeply chagrined than if he had supposed that his emancipation policy had received a signal rebuke."[48]

Some Radicals consoled themselves with the belief that the administration would now be forced to abandon its temporizing policy. "I can scarcely mourn over the elections in the West, and in New York," said Lydia Maria Child, "for they have driven 'old Abe' to the wall. *Now,* the Republican party must '*do or die.*'" She thanked God "for putting them in that fix! At last, I really believe 'old Abe' has got his back up. . . . I think we shall now go ahead in earnest; and, having tried everything else without success, we shall at last rely upon principle."[49]

After Antietam, McClellan, fearing that the Confederates would attack and that the Union army was too disorganized to move, dawdled in his usual fashion, allowing the enemy to escape across the Potomac. When he boasted that he had achieved a great victory by driving Lee from Union soil, the "hearts of 10 million people sank within them," according to Lincoln.[50] Bitterly, Interior Secretary Caleb B. Smith remarked that "darkness and doubts rest upon the future while the best blood of the country has been poured out like water and sorrow and mourning has been brought to almost every hearthstone, and we are left to enjoy the consolation afforded by Gen McClellan in his pompous announcement that 'Pa. and Md. are safe.' I wonder that he did not add and so is New England."[51]

No one's heart sank deeper than Lincoln's. In early October, over the objections of the cabinet, he visited the Army of the Potomac hoping to goad it into action. He told Ozias Hatch that in addition he wanted "to satisfy himself personally without the intervention of anybody, of the purposes intentions and fidelity of McClellan, his officers, and the army."[52]

The administration reportedly had "a dread of the army" and feared "revolution in the North."[53] This anxiety was not irrational. Lincoln's Cincinnati friend, William M. Dickson, concluded in late September that "[i]f McClellan had been defeated in Md. there would have been a revolution. . . . wise and good men are & have been considering the propriety of revolution, of a provisional government. The atmosphere was murky with treason after Pope's defeats, a vain, weak man, put in power by a weak President."[54] Pope reported that officers in the Army of the Potomac "talk openly of Lincoln's weakness and the necessity of replacing him by some stronger man."[55] The adjutant general of the Army of the Potomac, Thomas M. Key, recalled that "the 'traitor' element near McClellan had constantly grown bolder" and that "they daily talked of overthrowing the Government and making McClellan dictator." After the Preliminary Emancipation Proclamation was announced, "this element felt that McClellan would not long remain in command: that then was the time to move or never—that an appeal could be made to the army setting forth that this proclamation was a usurpation, the conversion of the war for the Union into a John Brown Abolition raid and thus was a subversion of the Constitution absolving the army from its allegiance: that a movement should be made upon Washington to restore the Constitution."[56]

During his three days with the army in Maryland, Lincoln visited hospitals, including one that housed some Confederates. To them he remarked "that if they had no objection he would be pleased to take them by the hand" and that "the solemn obligations which we owe to our country and posterity compel the prosecution of this war, and it followed that many were our enemies through uncontrollable circumstances, and he bore them no malice, and could take them by the hand with sympathy and good feeling." The Confederates, after a brief silence, stepped up and wordlessly, warmly shook his hand. He then approached those too seriously wounded to stand, bade them to be cheerful, and pledged that everything that could be done to help them would be done. There was not a dry eye in that hospital.[57]

Astride the horse of General E. V. Sumner's son, Lincoln inspected the troops, reviewing twelve divisions and riding 40 miles. When warned that the steed was rather frisky, the president laughingly replied: "That makes it the more interesting. I'll try him." Skillfully he mounted and took the reins so that the horse realized immediately who was in charge.[58] As he passed the crimson-clad Fifth New York Zouaves, which had suffered heavy losses, he stopped and remarked to General George Sykes: "And these are the red legged devils. I know from the reports that there has been no such thing as beating them, even round a stump." Turning to the troops, he said: "Boys, your thinned ranks and shattered flags tell the story of your bravery. The people thank you and so do I." At General Brooks Morell's division he paused again. "Those flags are more tattered now than when I saw them at Harrison's Landing," he told the general; "the regiments have reason to be proud of such flags, and you of such men."[59] He was dismayed to see how small some regiments had become since he last visited the army. "I thought they were merely a corporal's guard," he remarked in astonishment.[60]

The soldiers were pleased to have Lincoln in their midst. One observed that as he reviewed the ranks on October 3, the president's "kindly smile . . . touched the hearts of the bronzed, rough-looking men more than one can express. It was like an electric shock. It flew from elbow to elbow; and, with one loud cheer which made the air ring, the suppressed feeling gave vent, conveying to the good President that his smile had gone home, and found a ready response."[61] A sergeant from Massachusetts reported that he "could easily perceive why and how he was called 'Honest Abe.' . . . I think his coming down, or up, to see us done us all good." Another soldier wrote: "We marched proudly away, for we all felt proud to know that we had been permitted to see and salute him."[62]

The army's conservative Democrats were less enthusiastic. One of them, Colonel Charles S. Wainwright, described Lincoln unflatteringly: "Republican simplicity is well enough, but I should have preferred to see the President of the United States travelling with a little more regard to appearances than can be afforded by a common ambulance, with his long legs doubled up so that his knees almost struck his chin, and grinning out of the windows like a baboon." The chief executive, Wainwright recorded in his journal, "not only is the ugliest man I ever saw, but the most uncouth and gawky in his manners and appearance."[63] A Hoosier told his parents that "Old Abe looked *decidedly hard*."[64] Several troops noted that he also appeared "careworn and sorrowful."[65] One thought the president was "much more careworn" than his pictures, so much so that it seemed as if "one of his feet is in the grave."[66]

One evening Lincoln visited the battlefield strewn with hundreds of dead horses and the clothing of slain and wounded troops. He also noticed innumerable graves, among them one with a grim inscription: "Here lies the bodies of sixty rebels. The wages of sin is death!" Over another mass grave a sign read: "Here lies the body of General Anderson and eighty other rebels."[67]

During his stay at Sharpsburg, Lincoln spoke often with McClellan, who reported that the president "was very kind personally—told me he was convinced I was the best general in the country etc etc. He was very affable & I really think he does feel very kindly towards me personally."[68] Though pleasant in manner, Lincoln was stern in substance, asking tough questions and offering blunt criticism. He was puzzled to see most of the new recruits in Frederick, 20 miles from the veteran army units. "Why was this? Why were not green troops and veterans mixed together?" he asked McClellan.

"We have not tent equipage and cannot well move up the new levies!" came the reply.

"Why are the troops any worse off at Sharpsburg without tents than at Frederick without tents?" the president asked. No satisfactory answer was offered.[69]

Lincoln frankly told the general "that he w[oul]d be a ruined man if he did not move forward, move rapidly & effectively."[70] According to the New York journalist George Wilkes, Lincoln also said to McClellan: "I wish to call your attention to a fault in your character—a fault which is the sum of my observations of you, in connection with this war. You merely get yourself ready to do a good thing—no man can do that better—you make all the necessary sacrifices of blood and time, and treasure, to secure a victory, *but whether from timidity, self-distrust, or some other motive inexplicable to me, you always stop short just on this side of results.*"[71] He instructed McClellan to advance within two weeks. Unmoved by Lincoln's criticism, the general scornfully wrote his wife about the presidential entourage: "These people don't know what an army requires & therefore act stupidly."[72]

If McClellan was disgusted with Lincoln, the feeling was mutual. One evening, the president asked his friend Ozias M. Hatch, as they stood on a hill and surveyed the vast encampment: "Hatch, what do you suppose all these people are?"

"Why, I suppose it to be a part of the grand army."

Lincoln sarcastically corrected him: "No, you are mistaken."

"What are they then?"

"That is General McClellan's body guard."[73]

Although Lincoln "expressed himself eminently satisfied with the discipline and appearance of the troops," he was dismayed to learn that they numbered only 93,000, though 180,000 were on the muster rolls.[74] He cited similar figures to Samuel F. Du Pont as he bemoaned the "melting away" of the army. "These are the facts," he told the admiral; "how they are to be cured *I don't know.*" In part, Lincoln seemed to blame the U.S. Sanitary Commission, which he called "the sentimental department of the army." He evidently shared Halleck's view that commission members encouraged the discharge of many soldiers who were not seriously sick or wounded.[75] (In August, Lincoln had lamented to Benjamin Brown French that "although the army consisted nominally of 600,000 men, from the best information that he could get there were not, at that moment, over 362,000 available fighting men in our army.")[76] Some of the officers who should have been in the field were availing themselves of Washington's brothels and saloons. "These fellows *and the Congressmen* do vex me sorely!" Lincoln exclaimed.[77]

One solution to the absentee problem was to crack down on deserters and bounty jumpers. In late November, when asked to offer encouragement to the ladies of the Sanitary Commission, he balked, explaining that the army had far fewer men reporting for duty than were officially enrolled. "Order the army to march any place! Why it's jes' like *shovellin'* fleas." To the suggestion that he shoot stragglers, he replied: "Oh, I ca-an't do *that*, you know."[78] After Halleck and Stanton showed the president long lists of absentees, however, he reportedly pledged "to pursue the most rigorous policy with these offenders, and that by executions, dismissals, ball-and-chain labor for the whole term of their enlistment, and other of the severest penalties, he is resolved to deprive the rebels of the great advantage they have heretofore enjoyed over us in the means necessary to preserve discipline, and prevent the crimes of straggling, absenteeism and desertion."[79] In November, 1,000 officers absent without leave were dismissed. But the total number of soldiers executed for desertion was, according to surviving records, only 147.

Shortly after his return to Washington on October 4, Lincoln had Halleck order McClellan to "cross the Potomac and give battle to the enemy or drive him south. Your army must move now while the roads are good."[80] But to no avail. Three days later, the general-in-chief lamented that "I cannot persuade him to advance an inch."[81] For the next month, McClellan deluged Washington with justifications for staying put. Among other things, he complained that his men lacked shoes, clothing, and horses. In response to McClellan's explanation that his horses were exhausted, Lincoln sent a tart reply through Halleck: "The President has read your telegram, and directs me to suggest that, if the enemy had more occupation south of the river, his cavalry would not be so likely to make raids north of it."[82] Shortly thereafter, Lincoln wired McClellan more pointedly: "I have just read your despatch about sore tongued and fatigued horses. Will you pardon me for asking what the horses of your army have done since the battle of Antietam that fatigue anything?"[83] Indignant at this message, which he considered a "dirty little fling," McClellan sent a lengthy report on his cavalry but failed to deal with Lincoln's larger point—that the army's inactivity threatened the war effort.[84] The president tried to soothe the general's hurt feelings: "Most certainly I intend no injustice to any; and if I have done any, I deeply regret it. To be told after more than five weeks total inaction of the Army, and during which period we had sent to that Army every fresh horse we possibly could, amounting in the whole to 7918 that the cavalry horses were too much fatigued to move, presented a very cheerless, almost hopeless, prospect for the future; and it may have forced something of impatience into my despatches. If not recruited, and rested then, when could they ever be?"[85]

While McClellan dithered, 1,800 Confederate cavalry under Jeb Stuart once again rode a circle around the Army of the Potomac. Nicolay observed that Stuart's joyride was "a little thing, accomplishing not much actual harm, and yet infinitely vexatious and mischievous. The President has well-nigh lost his temper over it."[86] With some asperity, Lincoln remarked to McClellan that "Stuart's cavalry outmarched ours, having certainly done more marked service on the Peninsula, and everywhere since."[87]

The Congress and cabinet shared Lincoln's impatience with McClellan. "His slow trench digging defensive tactics will not do," Caleb B. Smith wrote in late September. "He has already done more to give strength & vigor to the rebellion than Jeff Davis." The quasi-victory at Antietam "is fruitless except of slaughter to our troops." Little Mac's failure to capture even one gun or one wagon from the retreating Lee was, Smith believed, "proof of either treachery or imbecility."[88] Michigan Senator Zachariah Chandler confided that he was "becoming discouraged and disheartened" by the "unaccountable delay in the movement of the Army." He told his wife that "[s]omething *must* be done or we are lost."[89] The public, too, was growing disenchanted. "We hate & abhor this milk & water course at Washington," groused a constituent of Chandler. "It invites attack & sustains our domestic enemies."[90]

On October 13, the president bluntly criticized McClellan for his timidity. "You remember my speaking to you of what I called your over-cautiousness. Are you not over-cautious when you assume that you can not do what the enemy is constantly doing? Should you not claim to be at least his equal in prowess, and act upon the claim?" To McClellan's insistence that he needed to repair the rail line from Harper's Ferry before he could move against Lee's army at Winchester, Lincoln replied: "I certainly should be pleased for you to have the advantage of the Railroad from Harper's Ferry to Winchester, but it wastes all the remainder of autumn to give it to you; and, in fact ignores the question of *time,* which can not, and must not be ignored."

McClellan feared that while his army moved toward Winchester, the Confederates might attack Pennsylvania. To alleviate this anxiety, Lincoln pointed out that if Lee "does so in full force, he gives up his communications to you absolutely, and you have nothing to do but to follow, and ruin him; if he does so with less than full force, fall upon, and beat what is left behind all the easier." The Army of the Potomac, Lincoln noted, was closer to Richmond than was the Army of Northern Virginia. "Why can you not reach there before him, unless you admit that he is more than your equal on a march. His route is the arc of a circle, while yours is the chord. The roads are as good on yours as on his." If Lee moved toward the Confederate capital, Lincoln suggested that McClellan "press closely to him, fight him if a favorable opportunity should present, and, at least, try to beat him to Richmond on the inside track. I say 'try'; if we never try, we shall never succeed."

If Lee stayed put at Winchester, Lincoln recommended, the Army of the Potomac should "fight him there, on the idea that if we can not beat him when he bears the wastage of coming to us, we never can when we bear the wastage of going to him. This proposition is a simple truth, and is too important to be lost sight of for a moment. In coming to us, he tenders us an advantage which we should not waive. We should not so operate as to merely drive him away. As we must beat him somewhere, or fail finally, we can do it, if at all, easier near to us, than far away. If we can not beat the enemy where he now is, we never can, he again being within the entrenchments of Richmond." After describing how the Union army could be easily supplied as it moved toward the Confederate capital, the president assured McClellan that his long letter was "in no sense an order."[91]

Lincoln feared that this admonition would have little effect, even though it implicitly gave McClellan only one last chance to redeem himself. In private, the president expressed doubt that Little Mac "would move after all" and added that "he'd got tired of his excuses" and "*he'd remove him at once but for the election*."[92] The general reluctantly abandoned his own intention to postpone serious action till the spring. Still he dawdled. On October 21, Halleck told him that the president "does not expect impossibilities, but he is very anxious that all this good weather should not be wasted in inactivity."[93] To a congressman who asked when the Army of the Potomac would advance, Lincoln replied: "Gen. McClellan knows I wish him to move on at the first practicable moment. *When* he will do so *you know as well as I!*"[94]

Treasury Secretary Chase was also anxious, for McClellan's inactivity made it difficult to raise money. Exasperated, Chase urged Jay Cooke, his chief bond salesman, to inform Lincoln that the Young Napoleon must be replaced if government loans were to be taken. In late October, Cooke visited the president at the Soldiers' Home. "I told him of my struggles to maintain the credit of the Nation and to provide, from popular sales, for the enormous daily demands for cash," Cooke recalled. He explained "that in spite of every effort, the gloom was increasing and the sales declining, and that the people and myself felt that unless McClellan was sent away very soon, no one could foretell the future." Lincoln's response indicated, as Cooke remembered, "that my request was appreciated."[95]

As Lincoln struggled to decide whether to fire McClellan, a sympathetic observer thought that the president "might be likened to a boy carrying a basket of eggs. Couldn't let go his basket to unbutton his breeches—was in great distress from a necessity to urinate—and stood crying 'What shall I do?'"[96]

On October 26, Nicolay wrote that Lincoln "keeps poking sharp sticks under little Mac's ribs, and has screwed up his courage to the point of beginning to cross the river today."[97] McClellan took more than a week to get his army over the Potomac. Intemperately he complained to his wife: "If you could know the mean & dirty character of the dispatches I receive you would boil over with anger—when it is possible to misunderstand, & when it is not possible, whenever there is a chance of a wretched innuendo—there it comes. But the good of the country requires me to submit to all this from men whom I know to be greatly my inferiors socially, intellectually & morally! There never was a truer epithet applied to a certain individual than that of the 'Gorilla.'"[98]

As McClellan moved south at a leisurely pace, Lee swiftly retreated toward Richmond. On November 4, the Confederates were positioned athwart the Union army's line of advance. Finally, out of all patience with the Young Napoleon, Lincoln fired him. He had been tempted to do so earlier, but told a friend that "there was a question about the effect of [McClellan's] removal *before* the election."[99] He said he wished not "to estrange the affections of the Democratic party," nor did he want to make the general a martyr.[100] By early November, Nicolay reported, Lincoln's "patience is at last completely exhausted with McClellan's inaction and never-ending excuses." The president "has been exceedingly reluctant" to dismiss the general, for in many ways he thought Little Mac "a very superior and efficient officer. This with the high personal regard for him, has led him to indulge him in his whims and complaints and short-comings as a mother would indulge her baby. He is constitutionally *too slow*, and has fitly been dubbed the great American tortoise."[101] (McClellan was also known as the "Great Do-nothing," the "peatland turtle," and "Fabius McClellan Cunctator.")[102]

To Francis P. Blair, Lincoln explained that he "had tried long enough to bore with an auger too dull to take hold." He added: "I said I would remove him if he let Lee's army get away from him, and I must do so. He has got the 'slows,' Mr. Blair." Moreover, McClellan's subordinate generals had lost confidence in him.[103] Similarly, Lincoln told Orville H. Browning that he had "coaxed, urged, & ordered" McClellan to move aggressively, "but all would not do. At the expiration of two weeks after a peremptory order to that effect, he had only 3/4 of his army across the River, and was six days doing that, whereas the rebel army had effected a crossing in one day."[104] The president offered another account to John Hay: "After the battle of Antietam, I went up to the field to try to get him to move & came back thinking he would move at once. But when I got home he began to argue why he ought not to move. I peremptorily ordered him to advance. It was 19 days before he put a man over the river. It was 9 days longer before he got his army across and then he stopped again, delaying on little pretexts of wanting this and that. I began to fear he was playing false—that he did not want to hurt the enemy. I saw how he could intercept the enemy on the way to Richmond. I determined to make that the test. If he let them get away I would remove him. He did so & I relieved him."[105] Lincoln's suspicion that McClellan "did not want to hurt the enemy" is easy to understand, given the general's timidity, but it was unjustified; McClellan desired military success but lacked the boldness to achieve it. Lincoln's good friend Anson G. Henry astutely judged that if McClellan had carried out the plan contained in the president's long October 13 letter, the general could have won a significant victory and "would have been a great Hero, for Mr Lincoln would have never claimed the Glory."[106]

Lincoln's futile efforts to spur McClellan into action reminded him of a story: "I was not more successful than the blacksmith in our town, in my boyhood days, when he tried to put to a useful purpose a big piece of wrought-iron that was in the shop. He heated it, put it on the anvil, and said: 'I'm going to make a sledge-hammer out of you.' After a while he stopped hammering it, looked at it, and remarked: 'Guess I've drawed you out a little too fine for a sledge-hammer; reckon I'd better make a clevis of you.' He stuck it in the fire, blew the bellows, got up a good heat, then began shaping the iron again on the anvil. Pretty soon he stopped, sized it up with his eye, and said: 'Guess I've drawed you out too thin for a clevis; suppose I better make a clevis-bolt of you.' He put it in the fire, bore down still harder on the bellows, drew out the iron, and went to work at it once more on the anvil. In a few minutes he stopped, took a look, and exclaimed: 'Well, now I've got you down a leetle too thin even to make a clevis-bolt out of you.' Then he rammed it in the fire again, threw his whole weight on the bellows, got up a white heat on the iron, jerked it out, carried it in the tongs to the water-barrel, held it over the barrel, and cried: 'I've tried to make a sledge-hammer of you, and failed; I've tried to make a clevis of you, and failed; I've tried to make a clevis-bolt of you, and failed; now, darn you, I'm going to make a fizzle of you'; and with that he soused it in the water and let it fizz."[107]

McClellan's chief engineer, John G. Barnard, agreed with Lincoln about the general. "If you were to 'count noses' among the officers of the A[rmy of the] P[otomac] whose opinions are worth any thing," Barnard told a senator in January 1863, "I believe you would find that most think and express the opinion that he made the most stupendous failure. He showed himself incapable in the outset of appreciating & grasping his position by utterly failing to do anything—permitting the Potomac to be blockaded in face of his 25000 men—Norfolk to be kept—until he lost the essential requisite to success—*the confidence of the Administration and of the Country.*" Barnard judged that "[h]istory records few such opportunities of *greatness offered*—and so *stupendously . . . lost.*"[108] Halleck insisted that by November the removal of McClellan had become "a matter of absolute necessity. In a few weeks more, he would have broken down the government."[109] A judicious biographer of McClellan deemed him "inarguably the worst" of the many generals who headed the Army of the Potomac.[110]

Lincoln's dismissal of the general came as a pleasant surprise to some. A Washington correspondent astutely remarked that "it required immense courage on his part to do it. It may not seem so to a quiet, stay-at-home body, far from the centre of political and military movements, but *here* no intelligent man could fail to perceive that it required great moral courage in the President," for McClellan had many powerful friends and admirers.[111]

McClellan's dismissal was in part a response to the elections. Lincoln sensibly interpreted the negative results as the voters' demand for a more aggressive pursuit of victory. On November 13, he told Zachariah Chandler that the "war shall henceforth be prosecuted with tremendous energy. The country could afford to wait no longer. The government must and shall prosecute the war to a conclusion."[112] Twelve days later, however, Chandler's colleague Lyman Trumbull spoke with Lincoln for an hour and came away skeptical. "Mr. Lincoln's intentions as you and I both know," Trumbull told William Butler, "have always been right, but he has lacked the *will* to carry them out. I think he means to act, with more vigor hereafter, but whether he will be able to do so as at present surrounded is perhaps doubtful." When the Illinois senator speculated that Grant would "clean out the South West if let alone from Washington," the president "replied that he would be let alone except to be urged forward." The same policy would apply to William S. Rosecrans.[113]

(By the fall of 1862, Lincoln had concluded that Trumbull was not his friend. In 1861, the senator had criticized him for not having "confidence in himself and the *will* necessary in this great emergency."[114] Many years later Trumbull rendered a similar judgment: "as President during a great civil war he lacked executive ability, and that resolution and prompt action essential to bring it to a speedy and successful close."[115]

Trumbull, who evidently was jealous of Lincoln's success, fought against the assertion that the president, rather than Congress, had the power to suspend the writ of habeas corpus. In debates over the Second Confiscation Act, Trumbull had virtually accused Lincoln of acting tyrannically. In reply, Senator James Dixon of Connecticut declared: "The Senator from Illinois has, at last, unmasked himself as an opponent of this Administration. . . . I have thought for some time that he was an opponent of the Administration.")[116]

Abolitionists and Radicals cheered the president for dismissing McClellan. Elizur Wright found it hard to express "the sense of relief, not to say joy, it gives me to see the government at last beginning to displace commanders that have used, and nearly *used up,* our armies *helping the rebels,*" and Indiana Governor Oliver P. Morton thought that McClellan's removal "has taken a load off the heart of the nation, and the pulse once again beats high."[117] Reflecting on Republican losses at the polls, Horace White said that since "the effect of the election has been to rid the country of that moral & military incubus Geo[rge] B. McClellan I will not regret it."[118]

McClellan was not the only important general lacking boldness; Don Carlos Buell, like the Young Napoleon, had a case of the "slows" and favored a "soft war" policy. He thought like a hidebound adjutant general rather than an aggressive field commander. When Confederates under Braxton Bragg invaded Kentucky in the summer of 1862, Buell forsook his Chattanooga campaign in order to defend Louisville and Cincinnati. Panicky Ohio Republicans implored Lincoln to send reinforcements to protect the Queen City. "I have no regiments to put there. The fact is *I do not carry any regiments in my trouser pocket,*" he impatiently snapped.[119]

Much to the dismay of the North, Bragg captured 8,000 Union troops at two garrisons. Moreover, Buell had come within 10 miles of Bragg's army at Munfordsville, Kentucky, but failed to attack. Disenchanted with Buell, Lincoln on September 24 decided to replace him with George H. Thomas, who had won the battle of Mill Springs, Kentucky, in January. Kentucky Congressmen John J. Crittenden and Charles A. Wickliffe, who were grateful to Buell for saving Louisville, protested. Thomas, however, refused the offer, maintaining that Buell was closing in on the enemy and should not be removed. An embarrassed Lincoln suspended the order while intimating that Buell "must win his spurs if he would continue to wear them."[120]

Goaded by the president, Buell stepped up his pursuit of Bragg and fought him at Perryville, Kentucky, on October 8. When the Rebels withdrew into Tennessee, Buell failed to chase them vigorously and instead returned to Nashville. He could not follow the Confederates, he said, because they had entered an area where it would difficult to supply his army. Remarking on Buell's inertia, Nicolay sarcastically observed that it "is rather a good thing to be a Major General and in command of a Department. One can take things so leisurely!"[121] In the same vein, Chase remarked that the planet earth was "a body of considerable magnitude—but moves faster than Gen. Buell."[122]

The exasperated president, always eager to aid the Unionists of East Tennessee, had Halleck order Buell to move against Chattanooga once again: "You say it is the heart of the enemy's resources; make it the heart of yours. . . . [Y]our army must enter

East Tennessee this fall, and . . . it ought to move there while the roads are passable. Once between the enemy and Nashville there will be no serious difficulty in reopening your communications with that place. He [the president] does not understand why we cannot march as the enemy marches, live as he lives, and fight as he fights, unless we admit the inferiority of our troops and of our generals."[123] Lincoln, mystified by the general's failure to move, "was down on Buell as worse than a slow man."[124]

When Buell contended that his troops were not as highly motivated as the enemy's, the president on October 24 replaced him with hard-drinking, hot-tempered, excitable William S. ("Old Rosy") Rosecrans of Ohio, much to the delight of the Western governors who had been clamoring for Buell's dismissal. Though the industrious Rosecrans had recently shown vigor in battles at Iuka and Corinth, Mississippi, it is hard to understand why Lincoln did not try once again to appoint George H. Thomas to replace Buell. Thomas outranked Rosecrans and was a far more gifted general, and Stanton recommended him. The war secretary's advice was outweighed by that of Halleck and Chase, a fellow Ohioan.

Reflecting Lincoln's view, the general-in-chief told Rosecrans that the "time has now come when we must apply the sterner rules of war, whenever such application becomes necessary, to enable us to support our armies and to move them rapidly upon the enemy. You will not hesitate to do this in all cases where the exigencies of the war require it. . . . Neither the country nor the Government will much longer put up with the inactivity of some of our armies and generals."[125]

The appointment of Rosecrans came too late to affect the October elections. After the November votes were in, the president expressed regret that he had not replaced Buell earlier. Meanwhile, Old Rosy dithered in Nashville, and by late November the president had lost patience with him. Halleck informed the general that Lincoln was "greatly dissatisfied" and "has repeated to me time and again that there were imperative reasons why the enemy should be driven across the Tennessee River at the earliest possible moment."[126] The general-in-chief warned Rosecrans that twice already he had "been asked to designate some one else to command your army. If you remain one more week at Nashville, I cannot prevent your removal. . . . [T]he Government demands action."[127] But the headstrong, argumentative Rosecrans stayed put until December 26, when he finally moved to expel Braxton Bragg's army from central Tennessee.

Controlling the Mississippi River

Lincoln also appointed another general to an important command in the West—John A. McClernand, his old political opponent from Illinois. In September, McClernand had proposed recruiting an army with which he would capture Vicksburg and seize control of the Mississippi River. Eager to have prominent Democrats support the war and raise troops, especially in his own state, Lincoln gave the scheme his blessing, for he believed that the Mississippi was "the backbone of the Rebellion" and "the key to the whole situation." The war, he said, "can never be brought to a close until that key is in our pocket."[128] Since the campaign against the Confederate citadel would involve both the army and the navy, Lincoln summoned Admiral David Dixon Porter and asked his advice about naming a general to command it. When Porter suggested Grant or Sherman, Lincoln replied that McClernand would be "the very person for the business." After calling on McClernand at the president's suggestion, Porter concluded that he was foolish and promptly departed for Illinois without reporting back to the White House. In a memoir, Porter declared: "I do not suppose that so great a piece of folly was ever before committed" as the appointment of McClernand.[129] He was right. Halleck and Stanton shared Porter's view.

In fact, Lincoln had some reservations about McClernand; he told Chase that the general was "brave and capable, but too desirous to be independent of every body else."[130] That drawback would later cause serious complications. Yet in December 1862, Lincoln declared that he wanted the general to command the expedition and pledged to sustain, strengthen, and stand by him. That month the president alluded to the McClernand plan, saying "that the whole energies of the Government were now devoted to opening the Mississippi river."[131] To facilitate that campaign, Lincoln decided to replace Benjamin F. Butler, who had been in charge at New Orleans since David Farragut had captured the city in April. Butler caused problems for Union diplomacy by antagonizing foreign consuls in the Crescent City. In addition, his heavy-handed tactics in dealing with the local population, as well as his rumored corruption, had discouraged the growth of Unionist sentiment. Earlier, Butler had exasperated Lincoln by quarreling with Massachusetts Governor John A. Andrew about recruiting in the Bay State. (Apropos of this controversy, the president remarked that "Butler was cross eyed and he supposed he didn't see things as other people did.")[132] When the president met the governor's wife in January 1862, he asked: "Well, how does your Husband & Butler get on—has the Governor commissioned those men yet?"

When Mrs. Andrew hesitated, her escort replied: "We are informed Sir that you have commissioned them."

"No," said Lincoln, "but I am getting mad with the Governor & Butler both."

When Mrs. Andrew remarked that the president did not appear especially angry, he replied: "No, I don't ever get fighting mad, no how."[133]

The president explained to a young lieutenant why he had long hesitated to move against Butler: "I don't know what to do with General Butler. He gives me more trouble than any general in the army; and yet should I deprive him of command, I should have the State of Massachusetts and the whole of New England down upon me."[134] Lincoln also had to worry about Radical Republicans elsewhere who admired the Massachusetts general's "contraband" policy and his recruitment of black troops in Louisiana. When Illinois Congressman Isaac N. Arnold protested against the removal of Butler from command, Lincoln gently but firmly urged his old friend to be more understanding: "I am compelled to take a more impartial and unprejudiced view of things. Without claiming to be your superior, which I do not, my position enables me to understand my duty in all these matters better than you possibly can, and I hope you do not yet doubt my integrity."[135]

In response to popular pressure, Lincoln offered to restore Butler to command in New Orleans, but the general balked because the department had too few troops.

When Butler asked why more could not be provided, Lincoln reportedly answered: "We haven't them to give."

"Then why don't you raise more—put the draft in New York!—raise that forty thousand who should have been raised in that state last fall!"

"Mr. Seymour says it will not do to draft in New York."

"*Then I would draft Seymour*!" Butler exclaimed.[136]

As the president and his advisors took their time considering alternative assignments for him, Butler grew impatient and finally "told them all to go to h[el]l" and returned to Massachusetts.[137]

To take Butler's place, Lincoln chose another Massachusetts politico, Nathaniel P. Banks, who was informed by Halleck that the president "regards the opening of the Mississippi river as the first and most important of all our military & naval operations, and it is hoped that you will not lose a moment in accomplishing it."[138] Controlling the Father of Waters, said the general-in-chief, "is worth to us forty Richmonds."[139] The administration decided to focus on the river partly in response to the electoral setbacks of the fall. Indiana Governor Oliver P. Morton warned Lincoln that the "fate of the North-West is trembling in the balance. The result of the late elections admonishes all who understand its import that not an hour is to be lost." The region, so dependent on the commercial artery of the Mississippi, might decide to cast its lot with the South.[140]

Confederate fortresses at Vicksburg, Mississippi, and Port Hudson, Louisiana, posed the main obstacles to securing the Mississippi. Lincoln envisioned a three-pronged campaign: from New Orleans, Banks would move north toward Port Hudson; McClernand would move south toward Vicksburg; and a fleet of gunboats under Admiral David Dixon Porter would attack Confederate strongholds along the river. Where Grant would fit in was unclear. Lincoln and Stanton's failure to consult with Halleck and Grant about this campaign laid the groundwork for later confusion, for it was unclear just who would be in overall charge. Grant should have been given command of this campaign, for he was a professional soldier who had achieved significant victories. Halleck objected to political generals like Banks and McClernand, complaining that "political power over-rules all military considerations." The general-in-chief lamented: "How long the president will submit to this dictation is uncertain. He must either put it down, or it will sink him so low that the last trump of Gabriel will never reach his ears!"[141]

Defending Himself: Analyzing Political Reverses

Other factors aside from military stalemate contributed to the Republican reverses that fall, most notably the president's September 24 proclamation suspending the writ of habeas corpus nationwide, thus empowering the military to arrest civilians who discouraged enlistments, resisted the militia draft, or were "guilty of any disloyal practice." Along with the Emancipation Proclamation, the suspension of habeas corpus provided the Democrats with their most effective ammunition during the election campaign. John W. Forney had warned that "altho' the President's two last proclamations have aroused the wildest feelings of enthusiasm among our true friends, yet at the same time they increase the responsibilities and dangers of the administration. The Federal power must be felt at once in every Congressional district in the loyal states or we may lose the next House of Representatives."[142] Even some Republicans objected to the suspension. Maryland's Henry Winter Davis said it instituted "court martial despotism."[143] Many Midwestern party leaders, however, thought it just as important and effective a war measure as the Emancipation Proclamation.

Lincoln was widely blamed for the party's dismal showing. "It is hard to say a hard word of your friends, but it is the simple truth that the President is responsible for the political disasters in the West," remarked the *National Anti-Slavery Standard*.[144] In an editorial titled "The Vote of Want of Confidence," the New York *Times* declared that the "very qualities which have made Abraham Lincoln so well liked in private life—his trustful disposition, his kindheartedness, his concern for fair play, his placidity of temper—in a manner unfit him for the stern requirements of deadly war. Quick, sharp, summary dealings don't suit him at all. He is all the while haunted with the fear of doing some injustice, and is ever easy to accept explanations." He lacked "the old Jacksonian passion" and "the high sacred vehemence, inspired by the consciousness of infinite interests at stake, and infinite responsibilities." The people demand that he end the "indecision and procrastination and general feebleness which, from the beginning thus far, have marked military operations, for which he is ultimately responsible."[145] George Bancroft denounced Lincoln as "ignorant, self-willed" and "surrounded by men, some of whom are as ignorant as himself."[146] Among those close to Lincoln who came in for the most vigorous censure were the heads of both military and civilian departments. "As a whole, the Cabinet has been a sad failure, and so has been our generalship," remarked *Frank Leslie's Illustrated Newspaper*. "And when the people voted, or declined to vote, they did so as much in opposition to the one as the other."[147]

General Carl Schurz scolded the president, alleging that the "defeat of the Administration is the Administration's own fault" because it "placed the Army, now a great power in this Republic, into the hands of its enemy's." Democratic generals, unenthusiastic about the war's aims, had failed to deliver victories. "Let us be commanded by Generals whose heart is in the war, and only by such," Schurz urged. "Let every General who does not show himself strong enough to command success, be deposed *at once*. Let every trust of power be accompanied by a corresponding responsibility, and all may be well yet."[148] (In fact, McClellan and Buell both opposed emancipation. Buell thought liberated slaves would prove a military nuisance.)

After numerous critics made points like Schurz's, Lincoln took that general's letter as the occasion to reply to them all. He argued that three factors caused the Republican setback: "1. The democrats were left in a majority by our friends going to the war. 2. The democrats observed this & determined to re-instate themselves in power, and 3. Our newspaper's, by vilifying and disparaging the administration, furnished them all the weapons to do it with. Certainly, the ill-success of the war had much to do with this."

The president explained to Schurz that he had distributed military patronage to Democrats because "very few of our friends had a military education or were of the

profession of arms. It would have been a question whether the war should be conducted on military knowledge, or on political affinity, only that our own friends (I
think Mr. Schurz included) seemed to think that such a question was inadmissable.
Accordingly I have scarcely appointed a democrat to a command, who was not urged
by many republicans and opposed by none. It was so as to McClellan. He was first
brought forward by the Republican Governor of Ohio, & claimed, and contended for
at the same time by the Republican Governor of Pennsylvania. I received recommendations from the republican delegations in congress, and I believe every one of them
recommended a majority of democrats. But, after all many Republicans were appointed; and I mean no disparagement to them when I say I do not see that their
superiority of success has been so marked as to throw great suspicion on the good
faith of those who are not Republicans."[149]

The egotistical Schurz replied impertinently: "I fear you entertain too favorable a
view of the causes of our defeat in the elections." He denied Lincoln's major points
and insisted that unsuccessful generals were retained in command too long. "Was I
really wrong in saying that the principal management of the war had been in the
hands of your opponents?" Schurz asked. "Or will perhaps anybody assert, that such
men as McClellan and Buell and Halleck have the least sympathy with you or your
views and principles?" Republican generals were never given a fair chance to prove
themselves, he charged. Like a schoolmaster chastising a recreant pupil, Schurz lectured the president: "let us indulge in no delusions as to the true causes of our defeat
in the elections. The people, so enthusiastic at the beginning of the war, had made
enormous sacrifices. Hundreds of millions were spent, thousands of lives were lost
apparently for nothing. The people had sown confidence and reaped disaster and disappointment. They wanted a change, and as an unfortunate situation like ours is apt
to confuse the minds of men, they sought it in the wrong direction. I entreat you, do
not attribute to small incidents, as the enlisting of Republican voters in the army and
the attack of the press, what is a great historical event. It is best that you, and you
more than anybody else in this Republic, should see the fact in its true light and appreciate its significance: *the result of the elections was a most serious and severe reproof
administered to the Administration.* Do not refuse to listen to the voice of the people.
Let it not become too true what I have heard said; that of all places in this country it
is Washington where public opinion is least heard, and of all places in Washington
the White House."

Schurz self-righteously claimed that he, as a general, had special moral authority
to criticize the president: "the spectacle of war is apt to awaken solemn and serious
feelings in the heart of one who has some sympathy with his fellow beings. I command a few thousands of brave and good fellows, entitled to life and happiness just as
well as the rest of us; and when I see their familiar faces around the campfires and
think of it, that to-morrow they may be called upon to die,—to die for a cause which
for this or that reason is perhaps doomed to fail, and thus to die in vain;—and when
I hear the wailings of so many widows and orphans, and remember the scenes of
heart-rending misery and desolation I have already witnessed—and then think of a
possibility, that all this may be for nothing,—then, I must confess, my heart begins

sometimes to sink within me and to quail under what little responsibility I have in this business. I do not know, whether you have ever seen a battlefield. I assure you, Mr. President, it is a terrible sight."[150]

Taking understandable umbrage at Schurz's lecture, the president sent a crushing rebuke: "I certainly know that if the war fails, the administration fails, and that I *will* be blamed for it, whether I deserve it or not. And I ought to be blamed, if I could do better. You think I could do better; therefore you blame me already. I think I could not do better; therefore I blame you for blaming me. I understand you *now* to be willing to accept the help of men, who are not republicans, provided they have 'heart in it.' Agreed. I want no others. But who is to be the judge of hearts, or of 'heart in it'? If I must discard my own judgment, and take yours, I must also take that of others; and by the time I should reject all I should be advised to reject, I should have none left, republicans, or others—not even yourself. For, be assured, my dear sir, there are men who have 'heart in it' that think you are performing your part as poorly as you think I am performing mine. I certainly have been dissatisfied with the slowness of Buell and McClellan; but before I relieved them I had great fears I should not find successors to them, who would do better; and I am sorry to add, that I have seen little since to relieve those fears. I do not clearly see the prospect of any more rapid movements. I fear we shall at last find out that the difficulty is in our case, rather than in particular generals. I wish to disparage no one—certainly not those who sympathize with me; but I must say I need success more than I need sympathy, and that I have not seen the so much greater evidence of getting success from my sympathizers, than from those who are denounced as the contrary. It does seem to me that in the field the two classes have been very much alike, in what they have done, and what they have failed to do. In sealing their faith with their blood, [Edward D.] Baker, an[d] [Nathaniel] Lyon, and [Henry] Bohlen, and [Israel B.] Richardson, republicans, did all that men could do; but did they any more than [Philip] Kearney, and [Isaac I.] Stevens, and [Jesse L.] Reno, and [Joseph K. F.] Mansfield, none of whom were republicans, and some, at least of whom, have been bitterly, and repeatedly, denounced to me as secession sympathizers? I will not perform the ungrateful task of comparing cases of failure."[151]

Lincoln had chosen many Democrats as generals in order to win the support of their party, without which the war effort was doomed. Though several of them proved inept in the field (e.g., Benjamin F. Butler), they served a useful political function. Lincoln regarded their appointment as an indispensable investment in national unity. Naturally, Democrats were more likely to support the administration if their leaders became high-ranking military officers. In the spring of 1861, Democrats in one Illinois town threw rocks at army recruits marching off to war and said they hoped all the "dam[ned] black Republicans would be killed." But when Democratic Congressman William R. Morrison received a colonel's commission and undertook to raise a regiment, Democrats stopped complaining about a "horrible, unjust war."[152] Some Democratic generals, like John A. Logan, proved to be highly capable military leaders.

At the president's invitation, Schurz called at the White House to discuss matters further. "Now tell me, young man, whether you really think that I am as poor a fellow as you have made me out in your letter!" Lincoln exclaimed. After a friendly explanation of his policies, the president slapped Schurz's knee, laughed, and asked: "Didn't I give it to you hard in my letter? Didn't I? But it didn't hurt, did it? I did not mean to, and therefore I wanted you to come so quickly." He suggested that the general, whom Lincoln regarded as a kind of surrogate son, continue writing him. The brash Teuton often did so.[153]

But Lincoln's explanation to Schurz was inadequate. In truth, the voters, as the Cincinnati *Gazette* put it, "are depressed by the interminable nature of this war, as so far conducted, and by the rapid exhaustion of the national resources without progress."[154] Yet the president was clearly right in stating that the absence of many supporters serving in the military hurt the Republicans. A defeated Ohio state legislator told Lincoln that in his district 80 percent "of the forces Sent into the field are from the Union [i.e., Republican] ranks. . . . We could not induce the opposition to enlist, except an occasional one to keep up an appearance of Loyalty."[155] Ohio and other states which did not allow troops to vote in the field went Democratic; states like Iowa, which did, went Republican. If all soldiers had voted, and they had cast their ballots in the same fashion that eligible soldiers did, Republicans would have won majorities in every Northern state save New Jersey.

In response to the defeat, Nicolay wrote an editorial for the Washington *Daily Morning Chronicle*, probably at Lincoln's behest. It argued that because the Democrats had for the most part insisted during the campaign that they favored a vigorous prosecution of the war, their representatives in Congress therefore "must sustain the President in his war measures and war policy," including emancipation. "Either they must do this or be false to their pledges to the people."[156] (The *Chronicle*, edited by John W. Forney, began publication in November 1862 and was widely regarded as an administration organ. John Hay as well as Nicolay wrote for it.)

Soaring Rhetoric: The Second Annual Message to Congress

When the Thirty-seventh Congress reconvened for its brief lame-duck session, the mood was sour. "It seems to me that this is the darkest day yet, and no ray of light as yet penetrates the thick clouds which hang over us," Congressman Henry L. Dawes of Massachusetts wrote from Washington on December 10. "There is no change for the better here. We have reached this state of things for want of capacity and that can't be supplied."[157]

In his annual message, Lincoln once again urged Congress to adopt gradual, compensated emancipation, and the members paid unusually close attention as that document was read to them. "Without slavery the rebellion could never have existed," he asserted; "without slavery it could not continue." Instead of passing statutes like the Confiscation Acts, which courts could overrule, he suggested that constitutional amendments be enacted providing federal aid to states which abolished slavery by 1900; guaranteeing freedom to slaves already liberated by the war, with compensation to be paid to loyal slaveowners; and funding colonization efforts. In justifying compensation, he remarked that Northerners as well as Southerners were responsible for the introduction and continuance of slavery. In something of a non sequitur, he rebutted the Democratic contention that freed slaves would take the jobs of whites. "If there ever could be a proper time for mere catch arguments, that time surely is not now. In times like the present, men should utter nothing for which they would not willingly be responsible through time and in eternity." Liberated slaves would not move to the North, he predicted; even if they did, whites would outnumber them seven-to-one.

Rhetorically Lincoln asked: "Is it doubted, then, that the plan I propose, if adopted, would shorten the war, and thus lessen its expenditure of money and of blood? Is it doubted that it would restore the national authority and national prosperity? Is it doubted that we here—Congress and the Executive—can secure its adoption, and perpetuate both indefinitely? . . . Will not the good people respond to a united, and earnest appeal from us? Can we, can they, by any other means, so certainly, or so speedily assure these vital objects? We can succeed only by concert. It is not 'can *any* of us *imagine* better?' but 'can we *all* do better?'"

In an inspired conclusion, Lincoln supplied the soaring rhetoric so conspicuously absent from the legalistic Emancipation Proclamation: "The dogmas of the quiet past, are inadequate to the stormy present. The occasion is piled high with difficulty, and we must rise with the occasion. As our case is new, so we must think anew, and act anew. We must disenthrall our selves, and then we shall save our country. Fellow-citizens, *we* cannot escape history. We of this Congress and this administration, will be remembered in spite of ourselves. No personal significance, or insignificance, can spare one or another of us. The fiery trial through which we pass, will light us down, in honor or dishonor, to the latest generation. We *say* we are for the Union. The world will not forget that we say this. We know how to save the Union. The world knows we do know how to save it. We—even *we here*—hold the power, and bear the responsibility. In *giving* freedom to the slave, we *assure* freedom to the *free*— honorable alike in what we give, and what we preserve. We shall nobly save, or meanly lose, the last best, hope of earth."[158]

Few of his state papers are more eloquent. The New York *Tribune* lauded its final passage extravagantly: "Sentiments so noble, so forcible, so profoundly true, have very rarely found their way into the manifestoes of rulers and Governments. . . . Their appearance in a President's Message is an immense fact, significant, fruitful, enduring. The howls and jeers of a million 'lewd fellows of the baser sort' are soon stilled and forgotten; while the reverberations of one such voice are prolonged and diffused through centuries." The editors also praised the compensated emancipation plan as "eminently a measure of conciliation and peace."[159] Lincoln's "homely terseness and honest frankness of expression" pleased the Providence *Journal*.[160] The moderate New York *Times* called the message "concise, clear and perspicuous" but expressed doubt that Congress would enact the emancipation plan.[161]

Most observers shared the *Times's* pessimism. Upon hearing the message, Orville H. Browning was surprised "by the hallucination the President seems to be laboring under that Congress can suppress the rebellion by adopting his plan of compensated emancipation, when if there was no opposition to it, it would require at least four years to have it adopted."[162] An Ohio congressman called the compensation proposal "a most impracticable scheme" that "nobody likes. Nobody will give it a cordial support & yet he has loaded his friends down with its odium while probably nothing will be done with it."[163] His colleague Henry L. Dawes was equally dismissive: "How it makes one's heart bleed for his country to have its chief magistrate proposing measures to be accomplished in 1900 as a remedy for evils and perils which have thrust us . . . into the very jaws of death. Whether the Republic shall live six months or not is the question thundering in our ears and the chief magistrate answers I've got a plan which is going to work well in the next century."[164] James A. Garfield, who was present when the message was read aloud, found Lincoln's scheme "most weak and absurd." Garfield could scarcely believe his ears when he "heard no word or sentence that indicated that the administration intended to push the war to a triumphant conclusion. Indeed, it hardly contained a sentence which implied that we are in the midst of war at all."[165] A Boston abolitionist concluded that Lincoln "seems to be a man of inadequate calibre; he does not comprehend his position."[166] Henry Ward Beecher patronizingly remarked that although it was "pleasing to know the opinions of any intelligent man on public topics," Lincoln "was not placed in the Presidential chair to read lectures to Congress on political economy, nor to manage a war with reference to New York politics, nor to undertake to draw out on paper how anyone may settle the questions of the next century. . . . There is the enemy. Defeat him."[167] Similar criticism appeared in many newspapers.

Most Radicals found the message unsatisfactory. The New York *Evening Post* asserted that "to free men gradually, or by installments, is like cutting off a dog's tail by inches, to get him used to the pain."[168] The message "greatly disappointed" Congressman James Ashley, but after speaking with the president, the Ohioan said he "felt confident that *in heart* he was *far in advance of the message*."[169] Henry Winter Davis called Lincoln's proposed constitutional amendments "*impossible* in his way of viewing them, illusory to the loyal states & ridiculous in relation to the disloyal states." The message in general seemed to Davis "wise, liberal, eloquent & impressive— everything but practical & practicable," with "every quality but the highest & the rarest—a knowledge that temporizing is fatal in great emergencies."[170] An exception was Charles Sumner, who approved of the message: "Massachusetts was satisfied—& all reasonable men ought to be so if we could get rid of slavery at the end of this century & that without any more fighting." Sumner doubted that Lincoln's "olive branch would be accepted." But if it were, he asked "who would be fool enough to refuse it on our side [–] no *real* abolitionist certainly."[171]

Some wondered why Lincoln revived his compensated emancipation proposal one month before the Emancipation Proclamation was due to take effect. Abolitionist Moncure Conway asked: "if the President means to carry out his Edict of Freedom on the New Year, what is all this stuff about gradual emancipation?"[172] Conway and others feared that the compensated emancipation plan would replace the Emancipation Proclamation. William Lloyd Garrison said: "we shall not be surprised if he substituted some other project for it. A man so manifestly without moral vision . . . cannot be safely relied upon in any emergency."[173] Conservative papers like the New York *Herald* and *World* speculated that the president would not issue the proclamation.

Lincoln reportedly told a Border State delegation "that, as to his Emancipation proclamation, he had acted from the belief that it would effect good results; but, if he could be convinced to the contrary, he would modify his position on that subject."[174] But he immediately amended his statement, telling a Kentucky member: "You know me, and when I tell you that I have made up my mind that slavery is the right arm of the rebellion, you will be convinced that it is my purpose *to lop it off*!"[175] And Lincoln assured Congress that his plan was "recommended as a means, not in exclusion of, but additional to, all others." Moreover, one of the proposed amendments stipulated that every slave "who shall have enjoyed actual freedom by the chances of war, at any time before the end of the rebellion, shall be forever free."[176] On December 22, Lincoln assured Ashley that he would issue the Proclamation.

Democrats dismissed the message because it rested on the assumption that "*this Federal Government was created to do about every thing, instead of little or nothing, and that the chiefest object of its creation was to free negroes.*"[177] The Cincinnati *Enquirer* called it "[p]oor in manner, poorer still in argument, avoiding the topics for the discussion of which the people looked with the utmost anxiety, and giving prominence to ideas of which they are tired and disgusted."[178] The Border State delegations, to Lincoln's chagrin (if not surprise), were unenthusiastic.

It is not entirely clear why Lincoln once again trotted out his compensated emancipation scheme. David Davis observed that the president's "whole soul is absorbed in his plan of remunerative emancipation. . . . He believes that if Congress will pass a Law authorizing the issuance of bonds for the payment of the emancipated negroes in the border states that Delaware, Maryland Kentucky & Mo. will accept the terms. He takes great encouragement from the vote in Mo."[179] The electoral triumph by Missouri Republicans who supported gradual, compensated emancipation led the president to hope that his scheme might be practicable there. Reports from Missouri indicated that his hopes were not unreasonable. The St. Louis *Missouri Democrat* appealed to Congress and the Northern people to fund Lincoln's program. The president was also heartened by a group of Kentuckians, led by Congressman Samuel L. Casey, who met with him repeatedly in November and offered assurances that they could effectively promote gradual emancipation by establishing two newspapers and dispatching speakers throughout the state. Joseph Holt believed that if new leadership emerged in the Bluegrass State, it would accept the presidential plan. In Maryland, several knowledgeable leaders maintained that if Congress appropriated funds for compensating slaveholders, state legislators would abolish the peculiar institution; but in the absence of such federal help, they would not.

If Missouri, Maryland, and Kentucky did free their slaves with financial help from Congress, backlash against emancipation would be minimized. If they did not, Lincoln at least wanted to appear magnanimous by demonstrating his willingness to go to great lengths in helping them avoid the shock of sudden, uncompensated emancipation. He had adopted a similar strategy during the secession crisis, and he would do so later in dealing with Confederate peace feelers. Lincoln's decision to stick with the compensation plan also resembles his willingness to retain McClellan for such a long time. He knew that Little Mac enjoyed the support of the army, and therefore he wished to give the general every chance to prove himself. So, too, he wished to give slaveholders every chance to have emancipation implemented gradually and with compensation. Probably he shared Chase's doubt that two-thirds of Congress would pass such amendments. Still more improbable was the likelihood that three-quarters of the states would ratify them.

It was, however, possible that Congress might appropriate money to implement Lincoln's plan. On December 10, 1862, Missouri Senator John B. Henderson introduced a bill (which Lincoln may have drafted) earmarking funds to compensate Missouri slaveholders. In the House, Congressman John W. Noell of Missouri offered a slightly different proposal. Lincoln, who said "that if no appropriation was made, then the bottom would be out of the tub," took a keen interest in Congress's action on these measures. On January 9, 1863, he told Senators Orville H. Browning and John P. Hale that in the past week blacks "were stampeding in Missouri, which was producing great dissatisfaction among our friends there, and that the democratic legislatures of Illinois & Indiana seemed bent upon mischief, and the party in those states was talking of a union with the lower Mississippi states." He added that "we could at once stop that trouble by passing a law immediately appropriating $25,000,000 to pay for the slaves in Missouri—that Missouri being a free state the others would give up their scheme—that Missouri was an empire of herself—could sustain a population equal to half the population of the United States, and pay the interest on all of our debt, and we ought to drive a stake there immediately." Fervently he appealed to those senators: "you and I must die but it will be enough for us to have done in our lives if we make Missouri free."[180]

The following day Lincoln wrote General Samuel R. Curtis in St. Louis: "I understand there is considerable trouble with the slaves in Missouri. Please do your best to keep peace on the question for two or three weeks, by which time we hope to do something here towards settling the question, in Missouri." Each house of Congress passed a bill, but fierce resistance by Border State delegations blocked reconciliation of the two statutes, and the plan died with the expiration of the Thirty-seventh Congress in March. "If the Missouri bill had gone through," Senator Henderson thought, "the others would have followed undoubtedly and the loyal slaveholders in all of the border States would have received pay for their slaves."[181]

Lincoln was bitterly disappointed. In exasperation he declared that the "dissensions between Union men in Missouri are due solely to a factious spirit which is exceedingly reprehensible. The two parties ought to have their heads knocked together. Either would rather see the defeat of their adversary than that of Jefferson Davis. To this spirit of faction is to be ascribed . . . the defeat of the Missouri Aid bill in Congress, the passage of which [I] strongly desired."[182]

Calamity: Replacing McClellan with Burnside

Finding a replacement for McClellan proved difficult. Lincoln did not consider appointing Halleck, for, as he told the cabinet, he thought Old Brains "would be an indifferent general in the field; that he shrank from responsibility in his present position; that he is a moral coward, worth but little except as a critic, though intelligent and educated."[183] So he turned once again to Ambrose E. Burnside, who had twice declined the job. This time the president insisted, and the personable, modest, 38-year-old corps commander from Rhode Island accepted after protesting that he "was not competent to command such a large army."[184] He rightly feared that if he turned it down yet again, Joseph Hooker, whom he despised, would be given the job. Burnside was chosen because he was next in rank behind McClellan and because none of the other corps commanders (with the possible exception of Hooker) seemed more capable than the man who had won battles at Roanoke Island, Fort Macon, and New Bern, North Carolina. Old Burn had acquired the reputation of a fighter and had invented a breechloading carbine used by cavalry. Moreover, he was a friend of McClellan and thus acceptable to that general's many army admirers.

Some in Congress would have preferred the appointment of Hooker. William P. Fessenden said Fighting Joe "has shown more brains than any of them, and it is in his favor that he despises McLellan, and does not hesitate to say so, openly."[185] When Congressman William D. Kelley recommended that Hooker be given command, Lincoln replied that "Burnside would be better, for he is the better housekeeper."

"You are not in search of a housekeeper or a hospital steward, but of a soldier who will fight, and fight to win," Kelley protested.

"I am not so sure," the president said softly, "that we are not in search of a housekeeper. I tell you, Kelley, the successful management of an army requires a good deal of faithful housekeeping. More fight will be got out of well-fed and well-cared-for soldiers and animals than can be got out of those that are required to make long marches with empty stomachs, and whose strength and cheerfulness are impaired by the failure to distribute proper rations at proper seasons."[186]

The president wanted to place Hooker in command of the Army of the Potomac, for, as he told a friend, "Fremont, and some others . . . are uneasy and impatient, and make me trouble, but I like Joe, for when he has *nothing to do, he does nothing!*" Halleck and others, however, dissuaded Lincoln.[187] The main obstacle to Hooker's appointment was his reputation as a toper.

Instead of having the army go into winter quarters, Lincoln hoped it would fight once again before cold weather made an offensive impossible. He shared the opinion of George William Curtis, who predicted that if "we only strike earnestly, we shall destroy the enemy." Curtis thought the "time has come to say, 'Up Abe, and at 'em.'"[188]

Burnside promptly submitted a plan calling for an assault on Richmond via Fredericksburg. He would march the army southeast to Falmouth, opposite Fredericksburg, and cross the Rappahannock River over pontoon bridges which were to be in place before the Confederates realized that the army had left Warrenton. On November 14, the president approved this scheme, though he wanted Burnside to attack Richmond along the route he had ordered McClellan to follow, directly toward the city via the line of the Orange and Alexandria railroad.

Burnside moved quickly, but when his army began arriving at Falmouth on November 17, it found no pontoons. Halleck and his subordinates had fumbled the assignment to deliver those essential items; during the fateful week that passed before they arrived, Lee occupied Fredericksburg.

Alarmed by the delay, Lincoln sailed to Falmouth and on November 26–27 conferred at length with Burnside, who said that "he could take into battle now any day, about one hundred and ten thousand men, that his army is in good spirit[s], good condition, good moral[e], and that in all respects he is satisfied with officers and men; that he does not want more men with him, because he could not handle them to advantage; that he thinks he can cross the river in face of the enemy and drive him away, but that, to use his own expression, it is somewhat risky." The president, who desired the army's "crossing of the river to be nearly free from risk," assured Burnside that the nation would patiently bear with him and that he should not feel pressured to attack before he felt ready. Lincoln also suggested that instead of a frontal assault against Fredericksburg, the army wait till a 25,000-man column could be assembled on the south bank of the Rappahannock, far downstream from Fredericksburg; at the same time, a force of similar size would gather on the Pamunkey. When those columns were in place, they could launch a simultaneous assault in coordination with Burnside and thus drive Lee from Fredericksburg and prevent him from falling back to the Richmond entrenchments. "I think the plan promises the best results, with the least hazzard, of any now conceiveable," Lincoln told Halleck.[189] Burnside argued that Lincoln's plan, though sound in principle, would unreasonably postpone the operation. When Halleck concurred, the president shelved his scheme. Upon returning to Washington, he was profoundly depressed and discouraged.

Meanwhile, the Confederates dug into exceptionally strong positions behind Fredericksburg. Burnside therefore considered crossing the Rappahannock at a location several miles below the town, but Lee moved quickly to defend that site. Foul weather hindered Burnside's preparations for assault, but finally, on December 11, some of his men managed to lay down pontoons, cross the river, and drive the enemy from the town. Upon learning of this accomplishment, Lincoln rejoiced. "The rebellion is now virtually at an end," he exulted, predicting that Richmond would fall by New Year's.[190]

Two days later, the president's elation turned to despair as the army stormed the heights above the town and sustained a crushing defeat, taking over 12,000 casualties, while the Confederates lost less than half that number.

While the battle raged, Lincoln visited the War Department and anxiously conned telegrams from the front, but they were quite vague. When Herman Haupt arrived from Falmouth, Lincoln eagerly quizzed him about the progress of the fighting. Once he understood the peril confronting Burnside, the president went to Halleck's residence and instructed him to command the general to withdraw across the Rappahannock. "I will do no such thing," the general-in-chief replied. "If such orders are issued you must take the responsibility of issuing them yourself. I hold that an officer in command of an army in the field ought to be more familiar with the details of the situation than parties at a distance and should be allowed to exercise his own discretion." When Haupt predicted that Burnside would soon be able to retreat unmolested, the president sighed deeply and told him: "What you tell me gives me a great many grains of comfort."[191] Turning to Halleck, Lincoln "remarked that as far as his observation extended, our friend Haupt had always come up to time in his department better than almost any one else." The general-in-chief agreed. After this interview, Haupt wrote his wife: "I pity the President very much. He is an honest and good man but never was poor mortal more harassed."[192]

Upon his return to the White House, Lincoln received another eyewitness account of the slaughter from journalist Henry Villard, who described the grim battlefield and suggested that Burnside retreat. "I hope it is not so bad as all that," Lincoln remarked.[193]

But it was, and so the president despaired. "I wonder if the damned in hell suffer less than I do," he mused plaintively.[194] Similarly, he declared that "[i]f there is a worse place than hell I am in it."[195] When Pennsylvania Governor Andrew G. Curtin depicted the carnage at Fredericksburg, Lincoln, his face "darkened with pain," "moaned and groaned in anguish," "showed great agony of spirit," and "walked the floor, wringing his hands and uttering exclamations of grief," repeatedly asking: "What has God put me in this place for?"[196] Curtin led a delegation of Pennsylvanians who warned Lincoln that unless there was a shakeup in the cabinet, "the people in forty days would *have his head*."[197]

Lincoln told a congressman that he would rather be a solider in the ranks than president: "There is not a man in the army with whom I would not willingly change places."[198] The president interrupted another congressman, freshly returned from Fredericksburg, who was recounting the battle: "I beg you not to tell me anything more of that kind. I have as much on me now as I can bear."[199] A War Department telegrapher reported that when news arrived that so many men had been killed, "the calamity seemed to crush Lincoln. He did not get over it for a long time and, all that winter of 1863, he was downcast and depressed. He felt that the loss was his fault."[200]

Lincoln's despair was so palpable that Noah Brooks expressed shock at his appearance. Comparing him with the vigorous campaigner he had known back in Illinois, Brooks wrote that the president's "hair is grizzled, his gait more stooping, his countenance sallow, and there is a sunken, deathly look about the large cavernous eyes." Philosophically Brooks remarked that it "is a lesson for human ambition to look upon that anxious and careworn face, prematurely aged by public labors and private griefs, and to remember that with the fleeting glory of his term of office have come responsibilities which make his life one long series of harassing cares."[201] Murat Halstead told readers of the Cincinnati *Commercial* that no one could observe the president's face "and believe that he is insensible to the responsibilities pressing upon him. I know he always had a doleful sort of physiognomy, but his features had not, two years ago, the pale and pinched appearance that they now wear."[202] To Joshua Speed, Lincoln seemed "haggard and care-worn beyond what he expected to see in him."[203]

David Davis, who also reported that Lincoln "looks weary & care worn" and that the "cares of this Government are very heavy on him," thought it was "a good thing that he is fond of anecdotes & telling them, for it relieves his spirits very much."[204] The day after Fredericksburg, Davis and two other Illinoisans called at the White House, where Lincoln voiced his determination to press ahead no matter what reverses the Union suffered. He compared himself to a character made famous by the Rev. Mr. Sydney Smith in an 1831 speech: "I am sometimes reminded of old Mother Partington. You know the old lady lived on the sea beach, and one time a big storm came up and the waves began to rise till the water began to come in under her cabin door. She got a broom and went to sweeping it out. But the water rose higher and higher; to her knees; to her waist; at last to her chin. But she kept on sweeping and exclaiming, 'I'll keep on sweeping as long as the broom lasts and we will see whether the storm or the broom will last the longest!' And that is the way with me."[205]

Not everyone shared Davis's positive view of the president's humor. A soldier complained that "while Old Abe tells outsiders that something reminds him of an anecdote . . . thousands of lives are sacrificed & our beloved country [is] still sinking to disgrace & ruin."[206] Others contemptuously deemed Lincoln "the Border State Joking Machine" and called his administration "a huge untimely joke."[207] To such criticism, Lincoln replied: "if I could not get momentary respite from the crushing burden I am constantly carrying I should die."[208]

Lincoln's humor inspired good-natured jests in others. A Southern clergyman reportedly speculated that God would favor the Confederacy because Jefferson Davis prayed so fervently for His blessing. When it was pointed out that Lincoln was a religious man and had probably prayed for the same thing, the minister replied: "If he has, *the Lord undoubtedly thought he was joking!*"[209]

Downcast as he was by the Fredericksburg debacle, Lincoln extended the nation's gratitude to the army: "Although you were not successful, the attempt was not an error, nor the failure other than an accident." (The "accident" was the tardy arrival of the pontoons.) "The courage with which you, in an open field, maintained the contest against an entrenched foe, and the consummate skill and success with which you crossed and re-crossed the river, in face of the enemy, show that you possess all the qualities of a great army, which will yet give victory to the cause of the country and of popular government. Condoling with the mourners for the dead, and sympathizing with the severely wounded, I congratulate you that the number of both is comparatively so small."[210] These words struck some as ironic. Colonel Charles S. Wainwright of the Army of the Potomac remarked: "Mr. Lincoln is more flattering to this army when defeated than when victorious. He had not a word to say to it after South Mountain and Antietam." Puzzled by the president's reference to "comparatively small" casualties, Wainwright asked: "Compared with what, I wonder; with the loss of the enemy? Or with the advantages gained? Or with our losses in previous battles?"[211]

The president was doubtless referring to the Confederate losses, which though much smaller than the Union's, could not be replaced so easily. White House secretary William O. Stoddard recalled that soon after the battle, Lincoln analyzed the North's comparative advantage: "if the same battle were to be fought over again, every day, through a week of days, with the same relative results, the army under Lee would be wiped out to its last man, the Army of the Potomac would still be a mighty host, the war would be over, the Confederacy gone, and peace would be won at a smaller cost of life than it will be if the week of lost battles must be dragged out through yet another year of camps and marches, and of deaths in hospitals rather than upon the field. No general yet found can face the arithmetic, but the end of the war will be at hand when he shall be discovered."[212] On December 21, the president told General William K. Strong that the army was "not as bad off as he apprehended," that it "is not demoralized, but no onward movement can take place very soon where they are."[213]

Lincoln did not blame Burnside for the defeat. "In my opinion Mr. Lee caused this trouble," he said.[214] He also compared Burnside favorably to his predecessor: "Had Burnside had the same chances of success that McClellan wantonly cast away, to-day he would have been hailed as the saviour of his country. A golden opportunity was lost by the latter General at Antietam."[215] Returning the favor, Burnside promised Lincoln that he would publish a letter accepting sole responsibility for the reverse. The grateful president told him that he "was the first man he had found who was willing to relieve him of a particle of responsibility."[216] True to his word, Burnside wrote Halleck on December 17: "For the failure in the attack I am responsible. . . . The fact that I decided to move from Warrenton onto this line rather against the opinion of the President, Secretary, and yourself, and that you have left the whole management in my hands, without giving me orders, makes me the more responsible."[217] Burnside submitted this document to the newspapers, which circulated it widely.

Not everyone was willing to exonerate the president. Ohio journalist Whitelaw Reid said that either Halleck or Burnside might be blamed, "but ABRAHAM LINCOLN was Commander-in-Chief of the Army and Navy! From that sad fact, and from its logical sequences, there was no escape!"[218] Moncure Conway declared that the "disasters have root in the White House."[219] After speaking with numerous members of Congress, military men, Radicals, and Conservatives, William M. Dickson reported that "all united in ascribing to the President the honor of being the author of all our calamities. His imbecility, vacillation, meddling interference with everything, his frivolity and total incapacity of receiving or appreciating [advice] make him the most incorrigible stumbling block that God ever afflicted any nation with."[220] The people of the North "have borne, silently and grimly, imbecility, treachery, failure, privation, loss of friends and means, almost every suffering which can afflict a brave people," observed *Harper's Weekly*. "But they cannot be expected to suffer that such massacres as this at Fredericksburg shall be repeated."[221] Benjamin Brown French gave voice to the widespread pessimism: "Unless something occurs very soon to brighten up affairs, I shall begin to look upon our whole Nation as on its way to destruction."[222]

As if the Fredericksburg disaster had not generated enough criticism, Lincoln's decision to send Nathaniel P. Banks to Louisiana rather than to Burnside's army was widely condemned. "The Banks diversion south has disappointed the whole country," the president observed.[223]

Senatorial Putsch Attempt: The Cabinet Crisis of December

In the wake of the Fredericksburg defeat, Lincoln's popularity reached a low ebb. "A year ago we laughed at the Honest Old Abe's grotesque genial Western jocosities, but they nauseate us now," remarked George Templeton Strong. He predicted that if things continued to go as they had been going, pressure would mount to have the president "resign and make way for Hamlin, as for one about whom nobody knows anything and who may therefore be a change for the better, none for the worse being conceivable."[224] Charles Eliot Norton lamented that while the nation required the leadership of "a Bengal tiger," it had only a "domestic cat" in the White House.[225] Constituents told Pennsylvania Representative Edward McPherson that "almost everybody is dissatisfied with the administration. President Lincoln is denounced by many of his most devoted friends in former times." The public was "utterly disgusted," believing "that the present administration is utterly incompetent." Ominously McPherson was warned that "if things are not more successfully managed the President will be generally deserted."[226] Orestes A. Brownson lost all patience with Lincoln, whom he derided as a "petty politician," "thick-headed," "ignorant," "tricky," "astute in a small way," "obstinate as a mule," "wrong-headed," and "ill-deserving the *sobriquet* of Honest."[227] Lincoln was "not equal to his position," Brownson argued; "he is not the right man in the right place. . . . It had been better for the nation if a better man had been elected President."[228] William Cullen Bryant indignantly asked: "How long is such intolerable and wicked blundering to continue?"[229] A correspondent for an abolitionist journal complained that Lincoln was not moved "by the yawning, bleeding wounds of the devoted, noble people—unmoved by the prayers and supplications of patriots of his once friends," and instead resists with "all his might . . . any change of the mephistic influences surrounding him."[230]

Lincoln might be honest and patriotic, an Indiana Republican conceded, "*but I fear he is not courageous.*" The administration's "policy of 'no policy' . . . emboldens our southern as well as our domestic foes." Not long ago, he said, "men would not venture to suggest openly a possible alliance with the south on the part of the northwest," but nowadays "the advantages of such an alliance are unblushingly discussed." Secret groups plotted to overthrow the government. "Denunciation of New England is indulged in, and an open avowal that a union leaving her out, would be preferable to the 'old union.'" It was "unaccountable that a government possessed of the resources that ours is, with loyal and patriotic local governments in the union states, should have made so little progress in putting down this rebellion."[231]

A Bostonian predicted that Lincoln's resignation "would be received with *great satisfaction*" and might "avert what . . . will otherwise come, viz, a *violent and bloody revolution at the North.*"[232] The president was aware of such threats. When told that a Pennsylvanian expressed the hope that he would be hanged from a lamppost outside the White House, Lincoln remarked to Congressman William D. Kelley: "You need not be surprised to find that that suggestion has been executed any morning; the violent preliminaries to such an event would not surprise me. I have done things lately that must be incomprehensible to the people, and which cannot now be explained."[233]

Congress, too, was growing disenchanted with the president. Zachariah Chandler, who regarded Lincoln as "a weak man, too weak for the occasion," told his wife that "the country is gone unless something is done at once. Folly, folly, folly reigns supreme."[234] Another Republican senator said that his colleagues would ask Lincoln "to resign if they supposed he would take the advice." Yet another declared that the president "has fewer positive vices than most men but is strikingly without a high positive good quality."[235] In January, William P. Fessenden jeered that he had recently perused a letter by the King of Siam to Admiral Foote "which had more good sense in it, & a better comprehension of our troubles, . . . than *Abe* has had from the beginning." In Washington, "every thing wears a most gloomy aspect," the Maine senator reported. "Our financial troubles are thickening every day." The Army of the Potomac "is almost ruined, & melting away rapidly." He condemned the administration roundly: "there never was such a shambling, half & half, set of incapables collected in one government before, since the world began."[236]

Rather than attack Lincoln directly, congressmen and senators, upset by defeat at both Fredericksburg and the polls, made the cabinet, especially Seward, their scapegoat. Abolitionist John Jay foresaw a "storm rising that presently will not be stilled by any thing less than an entire reconstruction of the Cabinet." At the very least, either Stanton or Halleck had to go, Jay insisted.[237] A Republican leader in Indiana argued that if Lincoln "had a strong, united, and fearless cabinet," the "country could yet be saved." Therefore Seward and Blair must be dismissed.[238] Zachariah Chandler called the secretary of state "the evil genius of this Nation" and "the bane of Mr Lincolns administration."[239] Lydia Maria Child and Joseph Medill concurred: "Seward is *really* President; Lincoln only *nominally* so," said Child, and Medill deemed the secretary of state Lincoln's "evil genius" who "has been President *de facto*, and has kept a sponge saturated with chloroform to Uncle Abe's nose all the while, except one or two brief spells."[240] When Seward's alter ego, Thurlow Weed, was thought to be "advising and guiding the stolid Executive," the "rage of the best Republicans & even of Mrs. Lincoln" was reportedly "unrestrained."[241]

Anger at the secretary of state had been building for a long time. In September 1861, some New York Republicans complained to Lincoln about Seward's excessive drinking and smoking. Lincoln acknowledged the truth of their charge, but added: "I have been at work with him during a whole day & evening and never knew a man more ready to take up different subjects and to master them."[242] A year later, when another delegation from New York called at the White House to urge a change of policy, a sharp exchange took place between Lincoln and John E. Williams, President of New York's Metropolitan Bank. Then James A. Hamilton criticized Seward's April 10, 1861, dispatch to Charles Francis Adams. The president excitedly interjected: "Sir! You are subjecting some letter of Mr. Seward's to an undue criticism in and undue manner." Pointing to Williams and Hamilton, he added: "You, gentlemen, to hang Mr. Seward, would destroy this Government." Hamilton replied: "Sir, that is a very harsh remark."[243] Two months later, Thaddeus Stevens wrote that it would be "a great blessing if Seward could be removed."[244]

With the news of the Fredericksburg debacle fresh in their minds, thirty-two Republican senators caucused secretly on December 16 and 17 "to ascertain whether any steps could be taken to quiet the public mind, and to produce a better condition of affairs." They denounced Seward bitterly "and charged him with all the disasters which had come upon our arms alleging that he was opposed to a vigorous prosecution of the war—controlled the President and thwarted the other members of the Cabinet." Lincoln, too, was criticized for failing "to consult his Cabinet councilors, as a body, upon important matters" and for appointing generals "who did not believe in the policy of the government and had no sympathy with its purposes." John Sherman of Ohio asserted that the problem was not the cabinet but Lincoln, who "had neither dignity order nor firmness." Sherman proposed that they "go directly to the President, and tell him his defects."[245]

The senators' chief informant was Chase, leader of the Radical faction in the cabinet. Seward, representing the opposite end of the ideological spectrum, had triumphed over the treasury secretary in the competition to win Lincoln's favor. As Welles put it, "Seward's more pleasant nature and consummate skill have enabled him to get windward of Chase." The president, Welles confided to his diary, "is fond of Seward, who is affable. He respects Chase, who is clumsy. Seward comforts him. Chase he deems a necessity."[246]

The haughty Chase regarded his cabinet colleagues and the president with lordly contempt and schemed to win the 1864 Republican presidential nomination. He called the secretary of state "a back-stairs influence which often controlled the apparent conclusions of the cabinet itself" and told senators that there was "no cabinet except in name. The Heads of Departments come together now and then—nominally twice a week—; but no reports are made; no regular discussions held; no ascertained conclusions reached. Sometimes weeks pass by and no full meeting is held."[247]

Fully aware of these comments and criticisms, Lincoln said "he had no doubt Chase was at the bottom of all the mischief, and was setting the radicals on to assail Seward."[248] He told Frank Blair that the treasury secretary "runs the machine against me."[249] The president believed that the attempted putsch was rooted in personal hostility rather than a genuine concern for the country's welfare. Moreover, he disliked the senators' resort to a secret caucus rather than an open debate and vote of no confidence.

After twenty-eight senators agreed on a resolution stating that "the public confidence in the present administration would be increased by a change in and partial reconstruction of the Cabinet," they resolved to send a nine-man delegation to Lincoln.[250] They had toned down their criticism of Seward lest they make a martyr of him. Upon learning the results of the caucus, Seward said: "They may do as they please about me, but they shall not put the President in a false position on my account." He promptly wrote a letter of resignation. Upon reading it, Lincoln appeared shaken, pained, and surprised. He urged Seward to reconsider, but the New Yorker blandly remarked that "he must be excused from holding any conversation with him upon the subject of his resignation:—that it was based on what seemed to be a unanimous expression of the opinion on the part of the Republican Senators that he ought no longer to hold the place:—that the President knew better than any other man how far the assumptions on which their actions rested were true:—that he had no explanation to offer and certainly none to ask:—that so far as his personal feelings were concerned, the happiest day of his life would be that which should release him honorably, and without any unmanly shrinking from labor or responsibility, from public office."

Lincoln replied: "Ah, yes, Governor, that will do very well for you, but I am like the starling in [Laurence] Sterne's story [in *Sentimental Journey*] 'I can't get out.'"[251]

For Lincoln, this was one of the darkest days of the war. He told Browning: "Since I heard last night of the proceedings of the caucus I have been more distressed than by any event of my life." The Radical senators, he said, "wish to get rid of me, and I am sometimes half disposed to gratify them." In despair, he added: "We are now on the brink of destruction. It appears to me the Almighty is against us, and I can hardly see a ray of hope." Dismayed at the allegations against Seward, the president wondered: "Why will men believe a lie, an absurd lie, that could not impose upon a child, and cling to it and repeat it in defiance of all evidence to the contrary?" But Lincoln would not be bullied, insisting emphatically that "he was master."[252]

On December 18, Lincoln met from 7 P.M. to 10 P.M. with the senatorial delegation, which consisted of Jacob Collamer of Vermont, spokesman for the group; Charles Sumner, chairman of the Foreign Relations Committee; Benjamin Wade, chairman of the Committee on the Conduct of the War; William P. Fessenden of Maine, chairman of the Finance Committee; Ira Harris of New York; Lyman Trumbull; Samuel C. Pomeroy of Kansas; James M. Howard of Michigan; and James W. Grimes of Iowa. Collamer, the Nestor of the senate, read a paper summarizing their grievances and suggestions. Among other things, it contained the startling assertion that "all important public measures and appointments" should be made by presidents only after obtaining the consent of a cabinet majority.[253] The senators then had a wide-ranging, frank conversation with the president, who listened respectfully and calmly to their complaints about the lack of unity in the cabinet, Lincoln's failure to consult its members, and the need for a vigorous prosecution of the war by generals sympathetic to the administration. They charged Seward with "indifference, with want of earnestness in the War, with want of sympathy with the country in this great struggle, and with many things objectionable, and especially with a too great ascendancy and control of the President and measures of administration."

In reply, the president "stated how this movement had shocked and grieved him; that the Cabinet he had selected in view of impending difficulties and of all the responsibilities upon himself; that he and the members had got on harmoniously, whatever had been their previous party feelings and associations; that there had never been serious disagreements, though there had been differences; that in the overwhelming troubles of the country, which had borne heavily upon him, he had been sustained and consoled by the good feeling and the mutual and unselfish confidence and zeal that pervaded the Cabinet."[254]

"What the country wanted," Lincoln said, "was military success. Without that nothing could go right:—with that nothing could go wrong. He did not yet see how the measure proposed by the Committee would furnish the remedy required: if he had a Cabinet of angels they could not give the country military successes, and that was what was wanted and what must be had."[255]

When the dyspeptic Fessenden raised McClellan's complaint about the administration's failure to support the Army of the Potomac properly, Lincoln read several of his letters to Little Mac showing how well that general had been sustained. Sumner laced into Seward, denouncing his official correspondence, "averring that he had subjected himself to ridicule in diplomatic circles, at home and abroad—that he had uttered sentiments offensive to Congress, and spoke of it repeatedly with disrespect, in the presence of foreign ministers—that he had written offensive despatches which the President could not have seen, or assented to." The Massachusetts senator cited as an example a dispatch which the indiscreet secretary of state had allowed to be published a few days earlier, stating that "the extreme advocates of African slavery and its most vehement opponents were acting in concert together to precipitate a servile war—the former by making the most desperate attempt to overthrow the federal Union, the latter by demanding an edict of universal emancipation." Lincoln replied that "it was Mr. Seward's habit to read his despatches to him before they were sent," that "they were not usually submitted to a Cabinet Council," and that he "did not recollect that [one] to which Mr Sumner alluded." In conclusion he "said he would carefully examine and consider the paper submitted" and "expressed his satisfaction with the tone & temper of the Committee." As he ushered them out, he seemed cheerful and invited them to return on the morrow.[256]

Rumors swirled through the capital, creating widespread fear that a *coup d'etat* was underway. When Nicolay set foot in the House of Representatives, he answered dozens of questions, hardly pretending to disguise the fact that the administration was in the throes of a grave crisis. The chief justice of the Massachusetts Supreme Court viewed the senators' action "as Revolutionary in its tendencies and so far second only to the Southern Rebellion." A Boston merchant regarded the loss at Fredericksburg "as a *trifle* in comparison of this truly unfortunate & *disgraceful* proceeding."[257] One Republican journalist reported that the "cooler and wiser of our people dread the probable consequence of an assault upon the Administration—the driving of the President into the arms of Vallandigham & Co."[258]

The next morning, Lincoln summoned the cabinet, minus Seward, and told them that the senatorial delegation had been "earnest and sad—not malicious nor passionate—not denouncing any one, but all of them attributing to Mr. S[eward] a lukewarmness in the conduct of the war, and seeming to consider him the real cause of our failures." Though "they believed in the Pres[iden]t's honesty, they seemed to think that when he had in him any good purposes, Mr. S[eward] contrived *to suck them out of him unperceived*." Lincoln, in obvious distress, urged the cabinet not to quit and, according to Bates, "said that he could not afford to lose us," for he "did not see how he could get along with any new cabinet, made of new materials."[259] The president asked them to reconvene that evening, when the senators would again call. Chase, who realized that he would be put in a delicate position, tried to excuse himself from attending, but because all his colleagues agreed to be there, he felt compelled to join them. His inclusion proved to be a brilliant tactical stroke on Lincoln's part.

On the fateful night of December 19, the senators returned to the White House, where Lincoln opened the four-hour conference by stating "that he had invited the Cabinet, with the exception of Mr Seward, to meet the Committee for a free and friendly conversation, in which all, including the President, should be on equal terms—and he desired to know if the Committee had any objection to talk over matters with the Cabinet." Taken by surprise, the senators did not object, though it would be awkward for them to make their case in the presence of Chase, their main informant.[260] With some severity (and rather inaccurately), Lincoln spoke at length "of the unity of his Cabinet, and how, though they could not be expected to think and speak alike on all subjects, all had acquiesced in measures when once decided. The necessities of the times, he said, had prevented frequent and long sessions of the Cabinet, and the submission of every question at the meetings."[261] He asserted "that most questions of importance had received a reasonable consideration," though he cited "several instances in which most important action was had not only without consultation with his Cabinet, but without the knowledge of several [of its members]—such as the appointment of Generals McClellan & Halleck—the sending for Genl. Halleck to act as Commander in Chief—placing the army under McLellan's command after his return from the Peninsula—and the Banks expedition." Yet, he said, he "was not aware of any divisions or want of unity. Decisions had, so far as he knew, received general support after they were made. He thought Mr Seward had been earnest in the prosecution of the war, and had not improperly interfered—had generally read him his official correspondence, and had sometimes consulted with Mr Chase." When Lincoln asked the cabinet "to say whether there had been any want of unity, or of sufficient consultation," Chase found himself on the spot.[262]

All eyes focused on the treasury secretary, who seemed to take offense and looked quite angry. He stated "that he should not have come here had he known that he was to be arraigned before a committee of the Senate." Reluctantly acknowledging that "there had been no want of unity in the Cabinet, but a general *acquiescence* on public measures," he endorsed the president's statement "fully and entirely." Yet rather equivocally he said that he "regretted that there was not a more full and thorough consideration and canvass of every important measure in open Cabinet."[263] The senators, having often heard Chase bemoan the lack of unanimity and consultation, were understandably astounded. The treasury secretary felt humiliated. Replying to the charge that the committee was "arraigning" Chase, Fessenden "with much warmth" remarked: "It was no movement of ours, nor did we suspect that we came here for that purpose." Welles thought that the Maine senator "was skillful, but a little tart," and that he was feeling "more than he cared to say."[264]

When Lincoln asked if he should accept Seward's resignation, the senators were divided. Chase's backpedaling led Collamer and Howard to abstain and Harris to abandon his opposition to the secretary of state. Sumner, Pomeroy, Grimes, Fessenden, and Trumbull persisted in their anti-Seward stance. (Wade was at the front with the Committee on the Conduct of the War.) Lincoln remarked "that he had reason to fear 'a general smash-up' if Mr Seward was removed, and he did not see how he could get along with an entire change in his Cabinet." He "thought Mr. Chase would seize the occasion to withdraw, and it had been intimated that Mr Stanton would do the same—and he could not dispense with Mr Chase's services in the Treasury just at this time." At 1 A.M., the meeting broke up inconclusively.[265]

The next day, Welles, who thought "Seward's foibles are not serious failings," urged the president to reject the senatorial advice about the secretary of state and about compromising the independence of the executive branch. Lincoln, quite satisfied, responded that if the delegation's scheme were adopted, "the whole Government must cave in. It could not stand, could not hold water; the bottom would be out." The navy secretary, with Lincoln's blessing, hastened to Seward and urged him to withdraw his resignation. Meanwhile, Chase decided to quit, explaining to Fessenden that "Seward and he came into the Cabinet as representing two wings of the Republican party, and if he remained he might be accused of maneuvering to get Mr Seward out—and he thought he ought to relieve the President of any embarrassment, if he desired to reconstruct the Cabinet." He added that "Mr Seward's withdrawal would embarrass him so much that he could not get along with the Treasury. He found that very difficult as it was—and if he had to contend with the disaffection of Mr Seward's friends the load would be more than he could carry."[266] With his resignation letter in hand, Chase met with Lincoln, Stanton, and Welles. The treasury secretary "said he had been painfully affected by the meeting last evening, which was a total surprise to him, and, after some not very explicit remarks as to how he was affected, informed the President he had prepared his resignation."

Lincoln's eyes lit up and he asked: "Where is it?"

"I brought it with me," said Chase. "I wrote it this morning."

"Let me have it," said the president as he reached for the document, which its author hesitated to surrender.

Eagerly, Lincoln ripped open the envelope. "This cuts the Gordian knot," he said, laughing triumphantly. "I can dispose of this subject now without difficulty. I see my way clear."

Stanton then offered to submit his resignation. "You may go to your Department," replied the president. "I don't want yours." Holding up Chase's letter, he said: "This is all I want; this relieves me; my way is clear; the trouble is ended."[267] Soon thereafter Lincoln told a member of the senatorial delegation: "Now I can ride: I have a pumpkin in each end of my bag."[268]

When word of Chase's action leaked out, a senator exclaimed to Lincoln, "What is this? I hear that Chase has resigned too. That will never do; we can't spare him from the Treasury. Seward's the man we want out." Lincoln replied: "Sir, I have made up my mind that one shall not go out without both, and you gentlemen may as well understand that at once!"[269] Similarly, when the editor of the Washington *Chronicle*, John W. Forney, said "that he hoped the President would not let Mr. Chase resign, nor Mr. Seward," Lincoln turned red and abruptly remarked: "If one goes, the other must; they must hunt in couples."[270] (Months later, in response to yet another assault on Seward, the president remarked "that it would not do to dismiss him without dismissing Chase also, because, whether rightfully or wrongly, the people regarded them as representatives of the two wings of the party, the Radicals and the Conservatives, and 'we can't afford to ignore either wing, for that would sort the party down to altogether too small a heap.'")[271]

The president did not intend that either man should resign. He let it be known "that he could not permit the idea to go out to the country now that the Cabinet was divided."[272] On December 20, Lincoln wrote to both Seward and Chase asking them to withdraw their resignations and "resume the duties of your Departments respectively."[273] Seward agreed promptly, but Chase repeated the temporizing act he had engaged in two years earlier when he was offered the treasury portfolio.

As Lincoln awaited Chase's response, the capital buzzed with rumors. "To-day has been the gloomiest of all the days in the history of the nation in Washington," wrote a journalist on Sunday, December 21. "The most prominent men here assert that the disease of the nation is at its crisis, and the events to be determined to-night will fix the destinies of the country."[274] Fessenden lamented that "such a curious compound is our good Abraham that no one knows how it will eventuate. His attachment to individuals, and his tenderness of heart are fatal to his efficiency in times like these." Moreover, the senator added, Lincoln lacked "dignity, order, and vigor—three terrible defects."[275] Opponents of the administration rejoiced at the prospect of its impending breakup; friends of McClellan expressed confidence that their hero would be reinstated as commander of the Army of the Potomac and, as the price of his acceptance, would insist on controlling all the armies.

Conservative hopes were dashed on December 22 when Chase grudgingly consented to remain at his post, even though his credibility and prestige were badly damaged. Later, Orville Browning asked Senator Collamer how Chase "could venture to make such a statement in the presence of Senators to whom he had said that Seward exercised a back stair and malign influence upon the President, and thwarted all the measures of the Cabinet." Collamer responded bluntly: "He lied."[276] Disgusted with Chase, Stanton on December 20 told Fessenden that "what the Senators had said about the manner of doing business in the Cabinet was true, and *he* did not mean to lie about it." The war secretary added "that he was ashamed of Chase, for he knew better." Caleb B. Smith later told Fessenden much the same thing.[277]

As Stanton and Smith acknowledged, the senators were right in thinking that the cabinet lacked harmony and was often ignored when important decisions were made. Personal antagonisms were strong. Blair called Seward an "unprincipled liar," and Bates and Welles held similarly dim views of the secretary of state.[278] Chase regarded him as an archenemy. They all resented Seward's toplofty condescension, his meddling in their affairs, and his intimacy with the president.

But the senators' belief, nurtured by Chase, that the secretary of state dominated Lincoln was inaccurate. "Seward knows that I am his master!" the president exclaimed to an army chaplain.[279] Indeed, he was master of the cabinet in general. John Hay marveled at the "tyrannous authority" with which Lincoln "rules the Cabinet," for he decided the "most important things" and "there is no cavil." Hay wrote a friend that the "trash you read every day about wrangles in the Cabinet about measures of state policy looks very silly from an inside view, where Abraham Rex is the central figure continually. I wish you could see as I do, that he is devilish near an autocrat in this Administration."[280]

Lincoln's adroit handling of the senatorial putsch greatly strengthened his control over the administration. With an ingenious tactical stroke, he had successfully weathered one of the gravest political crises of the war. Months later, reviewing these dramatic events, he told John Hay: "I do not now see how it could have been done better. I am sure it was right. If I had yielded to that storm & dismissed Seward the thing would all have slumped over one way & we should have been left with a scanty handful of supporters. When Chase sent in his resignation I saw that the game was in my own hands & I put it through."[281] Seward detected a positive aspect to the cabinet crisis. "Perhaps it is not unfortunate that it occurred," he wrote a friend on December 22. "Like the Trent affair it ought to be regarded as a proof of the stability of the country."[282]

That day Lincoln was not so philosophical, telling John A. Dahlgren: "It was very well to talk of remodelling the Cabinet, but the caucus had thought more of *their* plans than of *his* benefit, and he told them so."[283] In general, the president tried to be fair to critics and wanted them to be fair in return. He explained that whenever he confronted a difficult case, "I always try to understand both sides, and begin by putting myself into the shoes of the party against whom I feel a prejudice; but then I expect that party to get into mine, so that he may also feel my responsibility."[284]

The outcome of the cabinet crisis disgusted the Radicals, who seemed crestfallen. One of them complained bitterly that the "chief fault of all our public men it that they are cowards. Lincoln is the chiefest among them—the cowards—but Seward is after all not much more cowardly than Chase and the senators. Mr. Lincoln is *afraid* to make over his cabinet—afraid to lose Seward and Chase. But he is no worse than the senators, for they no sooner made mischief than they were frightened at their own work."[285] Hannibal Hamlin expressed disappointment in the result of the senatorial effort but predicted that at least "there will be more of energy in *all* the departments," which Lincoln himself needed. Hamlin said he "deeply lamented" that "the President has not more of energy in his character—a little of Henry Clay or Andrew Jackson. But so it is. He is as God made him."[286] Fessenden remarked that if "all men upon whom we have a right to rely [had] proved brave & true and forgotten themselves in their love of country, I think it [the putsch attempt] would have been productive of great good." He was especially disappointed at "the weak squeamishness of our friend Chase," who, he said, lacked "nerve and force." Fessenden predicted that the treasury secretary "will never be forgiven by many for deliberately sacrificing his friends to the fear of offending his & their enemies. To him it is owing that the Cabinet remains as it is—admitted by him to be weak, divided, vacillating and powerless." But, the Maine senator acknowledged, Lincoln "thinks he cannot get along without Seward, and, really, it would be very difficult to supply his place at this juncture. For, though I have little confidence in him, still he represents a great and powerful army of friends." Moreover, the country's "foreign affairs are too complicated" to entrust to a new man.[287]

Some Radicals were not through attacking Seward. On December 22, Michigan's Senator Chandler told the governor of his state that "Old Abe promises to stand firm & I think he will. We shall get rid of his evil genius Gov S. ere long, if not now. He can[']t withstand the pressure long & without him Old Abe is naturally right."[288] Six weeks later, he was less complimentary of the president. "The Cabinet is weak & Lincoln weaker," he complained to his wife.[289] At that same time, Henry Wilson of Massachusetts predicted "that unless things are amended *instantly* the Senate will in open session denounce the traitorous Secretary—and after[ward] denounce and part from the President unless he removes him."[290] The New York *Tribune* moaned that the inadequate cabinet "is not what our bleeding, almost dying, country calls for."[291]

Egging the Radicals on, Mary Lincoln remarked "that unless Seward was dismissed, the country would be ruined within three months."[292] In January 1863, she loudly announced that "she regretted the making up of the family quarrel," and that except for Montgomery Blair "there was not a member of the Cabinet who did not stab her husband & the Country daily."[293] Two months later, she invited Chandler and Wade to confer with her about Seward. (In 1865, Chandler spoke at length to the First Lady and reported that she "hates him [Seward] worse than ever & says the feeling is mutual.")[294]

A colonel accurately observed in March: "Abe holds on with the pertinacity of a Bull dog" in the face of demands for cabinet changes.[295] When two New York Radical leaders, David Dudley Field and George Opdyke, called at the White House to demand the secretary of state's resignation, Lincoln rebuked them. "For once in my life," he confessed, "I rather gave my temper the rein and I talked to those men pretty Damned plainly."[296] He told them that "the Government was better informed as to the necessities of the country than outsiders could be, no matter how able or intelligent."[297] Noah Brooks reported that the president "is exceeding lo[a]th to give up his [Seward's] wise and conservative counsels, and retains him against the wishes of a respectably large fraction of his own party friends, merely because he believes that to his far-seeing and astute judgment the Administration has owed more than one deliverance from a very tight place." In addition, the policy of the secretary of state has "always been of a character to avoid all things which might result in a divided North, and though it may have been too emollient at times, it has resulted in retaining to the Administration its cohesive strength, when it would have driven off its friends by following the more arbitrary and rash measures of Stanton."[298]

Amid the December cabinet imbroglio, one change was made, though not in deference to congressional pressure. Secretary of the Interior Caleb B. Smith, in poor health and out of sympathy with the administration's emancipation policy, accepted a federal judgeship. In September, he had complained that "the President does not consult his Cabinet about the conduct of the war" and bitterly observed that "he might as well have no Cabinet." For many months Lincoln ignored the cabinet majority calling for the dismissal of Buell. "I am desponding and almost despairing," Smith confided to Thurlow Weed.[299] David Davis, who had lobbied hard to have Smith named to the cabinet, wrote that the interior secretary "repels me very much. There can be neither heart nor sincerity about him & he cannot be a man of any convictions." Ruefully he confessed to Leonard Swett: "We made a great mistake in urging [him] . . . for a cabinet appointment."[300]

To fill Smith's place Lincoln chose another Hoosier, Assistant Secretary of the Interior John Palmer Usher, who had vigorously supported colonization. (The president reportedly wanted to name Kentuckian Joseph Holt, but Radicals objected strongly.) Usher was a longtime friend of Lincoln from his days on the Eighth Judicial Circuit and handled much of the president's legal business once he left Illinois for Washington. His appointment may have been designed to alleviate anxiety about the results of the impending Emancipation Proclamation. In his annual message, the president had stated, "I cannot make it better known than it already is, that I strongly favor colonization," and in the Preliminary Emancipation Proclamation he pledged that the "effort to colonize persons of African descent, with their consent, upon this continent, or elsewhere, with the previously obtained consent of the Governments existing there, will be continued." Naming Usher might reassure skeptics that plans to colonize the freedmen would be pursued. Usher had helped plot strategy to win approval for the Chiriqui project, emphasizing that colonization plans would "show that there will be no danger of an influx" of blacks northward.[301] The appointment also pleased Indiana Moderates like Senator Henry S. Lane, but did not sit well with his Radical colleagues, who fought the nomination. The New York *Tribune* protested that Usher was too little known for such an important post. More famous was Congressman Schuyler Colfax, but it was reasonably anticipated that if he gave up his seat in Congress, a Democrat would replace him. Despite strong opposition, Usher was confirmed with the help of Northwestern senators who feared that otherwise Joseph Holt might be named.

Stretching the Constitution: The Admission of West Virginia

In late 1862, Lincoln worried about the constitutionality not only of the Emancipation Proclamation but also of a bill authorizing the creation of West Virginia. The northwesternmost counties of the Old Dominion had long been estranged from the eastern part of the state. Beyond the Allegheny Mountains, Virginians owned few slaves and chafed at their high taxes and their underrepresentation in the state legislature. They felt greater kinship with their neighbors in Ohio and Pennsylvania than with the residents of the tidewater region of their own state. In November 1861, delegates from thirty-four counties banded together at Wheeling and voted to secede from Confederate Virginia and establish a new state, to be called Kanawha. Six months later a Unionist legislature, in which only the northwestern portion of the state was represented, approved the creation of Kanawha and applied for admission to the Union.

The legality of this procedure was questionable. According to Article IV of the U.S. Constitution, new states can be carved from existing ones only with "the consent of the Legislatures of the States concerned, as well as of the Congress." The legislature of "the restored state of Virginia," which had representatives from counties containing roughly one-third of the state's population, did not appear sufficiently legitimate to authorize the division of the Old Dominion. Nevertheless, Congress voted on December 10 to admit West Virginia (i.e., Kanawha).

Two days later, Lincoln, who felt some distress about the law, told the cabinet that he thought "the creation of this new State at this time of doubtful expediency."[302] In mid-December, proponents of West Virginia statehood greatly feared that Lincoln would veto the bill. He let it be known, however, "that he was not so much opposed to it as [were] some members of his Cabinet."[303] Lincoln was probably referring to Attorney General Bates, who insisted that the department secretaries be asked to submit written opinions on the wisdom and the constitutionality of the bill. The president complied. On December 27, the leading champions of statehood from Virginia reported that the "president has strongly assured us of his desire to sign the bill if he can[;] we are hopeful but not sanguine."[304] Two days later they said they had "additional reason to believe that the president will sign our bill."[305] Meanwhile, six cabinet members wrote out their opinions. Seward, Chase, and Stanton favored the measure, while Bates, Blair, and Welles were opposed. (Caleb B. Smith had resigned in order to accept a federal judgeship and did not participate in this decision; his successor, John Palmer Usher, assumed office later.) Friends of the statehood bill argued that Lincoln would be inconsistent if he vetoed it, for he had recognized the Wheeling government as the true government of Virginia and treated Francis H. Pierpont as its legitimate governor.

Lincoln's written opinion did not reflect his earlier reservations about the expediency of admitting West Virginia. He was moved by the plight of the Unionists, whose leader, Pierpont, pleaded earnestly for statehood. "A thick gloom hangs over my mind about the new State," Pierpont wrote in a letter which Lincoln saw. "I don[']t know how the Union sentiment of W. Va can be satisfied. *Butternutism* will sweep W. Va. In fact I fear the soldiers in the field will throw down their arms [–] it will be *tereble—Tereble indeed*."[306] Pierpont telegraphed the president directly, saying: "I am in great hope that you will sign the bill to make West Virginia a new State. The loyal troops from Virginia have their hearts set on it; the loyal people in the bounds of the new State have their hearts set on it; and if the bill fails, God only knows the result. I fear general demoralization and I must be held responsible."[307]

"We can scarcely dispense with the aid of West-Virginia in this struggle," Lincoln asserted in his own written opinion; "much less can we afford to have her against us, in congress and in the field." The "brave and good men" of West Virginia, who "have been true to the union under very severe trials," consider "her admission into the Union as a matter of life and death." It would be shameful to turn them down, for "[w]e have so acted as to justify their hopes; and we can not fully retain their confidence, and co-operation, if we seem to break faith with them." Admitting West Virginia would advance the antislavery cause, because Congress insisted that the new state's constitution provide for gradual emancipation. Therefore, the bill "turns that much slave soil to free; and thus, is a certain, and irrevocable encroachment upon the cause of the rebellion."

The division of Virginia should not be "dreaded as a precedent," Lincoln argued, for "a measure made expedient by a war, is no precedent for times of peace. It is said that the admission of West-Virginia, is secession, and tolerated only because it is our secession. Well, if we call it by that name, there is still difference enough between secession against the constitution, and secession in favor of the constitution." Though he freely acknowledged that a majority of the state's voters had not participated in the election of the legislature, he pointed out that "it is a universal practice in the popular elections in all these states, to give no legal consideration whatever to those who do not choose to vote, as against the effect of the votes of those, who do choose to vote." Therefore, he argued, "it is not the qualified voters, but the qualified voters, *who choose to vote*, that constitute the political power of the state." Moreover, it should be borne in mind that many non-voters "were not merely neglectful of their rights under, and duty to, this government, but were also engaged in open rebellion against it." To be sure, among the nonvoters there may have been some pro-Union men whose voices were smothered by their Confederate neighbors, "but we know too little of their number to assign them any appreciable value." Common sense dictated that the disloyal should not enjoy the same status as the loyal: "Can this government stand, if it indulges constitutional constructions by which men in open rebellion against it, are to be accounted, man for man, the equals of those who maintain their loyalty to it?" Should the Rebels "be accounted even better citizens, and more worthy of consideration, than those who merely neglect to vote? If so, their treason against the constitution, enhances their constitutional value! Without braving these absurd conclusions, we can not deny that the body which consents to the admission of West-Virginia, is the Legislature of Virginia." Citing the aphorism that "the devil takes care of his own," Lincoln asserted that "much more should a good spirit—the spirit of the Constitution and the Union—take care of it's own—I think it can not do less, and live."[308]

On New Year's Eve, leading champions of statehood from western Virginia (including Senator Waitman T. Willey and Congressmen Jacob B. Blair and William G. Brown) called on Lincoln by invitation. At his request, they presented the various arguments in favor of statehood. He then read aloud the opinions of the cabinet and part of his own. They liked what he had written, which seemed to favor statehood. But he stopped before reaching the conclusion. Using imagery from card playing, he teased them about their evident optimism. "I suppose you think this is the odd trick," meaning that his positive opinion would result in a cabinet vote of four to three in favor of statehood. But they were disappointed that he would not definitely assure them he would sign the bill. He urged them to come the next morning to learn his decision. Jacob Blair recalled that on New Year's Day, before 10 A.M., "I presented myself at the White House, but found the doors locked. I raised the sash of one of the large windows, gained an entrance, and went directly to the President's room. When I was ushered in I found Secretaries Seward and Stanton with him, but the President went directly to his desk and, taking out the West Virginia bill, held it up so that I read the signature, Approved: Abraham Lincoln." The president manifested "the simplicity and joyousness of a child, when it feels it has done its duty, and gratified a friend." The bill admitted West Virginia, with the stipulation that the voters of the new state would have to approve a clause in its constitution providing for compensated emancipation. They did so promptly, and the state was officially admitted to the Union in June 1863.[309]

Later, the president told Pierpont that the governor's telegram "was the turning point in my mind in signing the bill. I said to myself, [']here, this is not a constitutional question, it is a political question. The government has been fighting nearly two years for its existence. The friends of the bill say it will strengthen the Union cause and will weaken the cause of the Rebels. It is a step and is political. I will not trouble myself further about the constitutional point,['] so I determined to sign the bill."[310]

Condoler-in-Chief: Comforting Fanny McCullough

In the midst of the turmoil created by the cabinet crisis, the defeat at Fredericksburg, the impending issuance of the Emancipation Proclamation, and the debate over statehood for West Virginia, Lincoln took time to pen a letter of condolence to Fanny McCullough, the grief-stricken daughter of his friend, Lieutenant Colonel William McCullough. The colonel, who had served as sheriff and clerk of the courts in Bloomington, Illinois, was killed in action on December 5. His 21-year-old daughter, "a guileless, truthful, warm hearted, noble girl" who suffered from a nervous condition, was shattered by the bad news, and spent her days either pacing back and forth violently or lethargically sitting without uttering a word.[311]

When the president, who felt the loss of his good friend McCullough keenly, learned of her condition, he offered her moving and revealing advice and comfort: "It is with deep grief that I learn of the death of your kind and brave Father; and, especially, that it is affecting your young heart beyond what is common in such cases. In this sad world of ours, sorrow comes to all; and, to the young, it comes with bitterest agony, because it takes them unawares. The older have learned to ever expect it. I am anxious to afford some alleviation of your present distress. Perfect relief is not possible, except with time. You can not now realize that you will ever feel better. Is not this so? And yet it is a mistake. You are sure to be happy again. To know this, which is certainly true, will make you some less miserable now. I have had experience enough to know what I say; and you need only to believe it, to feel better at once. The memory of your dear Father, instead of an agony, will yet be a sad sweet feeling in your heart, of a purer, and holier sort than you have known before."[312] A friend of Fanny reported that the "beautifully written" letter "had a very good effect in soothing her troubled mind."[313]

Modifying the Emancipation Proclamation

Lincoln had many things on his mind that busy New Year's Eve, most notably the Emancipation Proclamation, due to be issued the following day. On December 29 and 31, the cabinet discussed a draft of the final version of the momentous document. The president had modified the preliminary version somewhat, toning down its pledge that the government "will recognize and maintain the freedom of such persons [freed slaves], and will do no act or acts to repress such persons, or any of them, in any efforts they may make for their actual freedom." Lincoln inserted the word *suitable* before *any efforts they may make for their actual freedom.* He had doubts about the word *maintain.* As he later remarked: "It was Seward's persistence which resulted in the insertion of the word 'maintain,' which I feared under the circumstances was promising more than it was quite probable we could carry out."[314]

Chase argued that no areas in the Confederacy should be exempted, save West Virginia. The president understandably rejected this suggestion, fearing that slaveholders in areas under Union control might successfully argue in court that the government had no right to seize their slaves. Lincoln also hoped to placate Northern Conservatives, Border State residents, and Southern Unionists. The treasury secretary proposed a closing sentence that echoed the Declaration of Independence: "And upon this act, sincerely believed to be an act of justice warranted by the Constitution, and of duty demanded by the circumstances of the country, I invoke the considerate judgement of Mankind and the gracious favor of Almighty God." Lincoln adopted the sentence, substituting *upon military necessity* for *of duty demanded by the circumstances of the country.*

Montgomery Blair thought the freedmen should be enjoined "to show themselves worthy of freedom by fidelity & diligence in the employments which may be given to them by the observance of order & by abstaining from all violence not required by duty or for self-defence. And whilst I appeal & & it is due to them to say that the conduct of large numbers of these people since the war began justifies confidence in their fidelity & humanity generally."[315] In keeping with this advice, Lincoln altered his version to read: "I hereby enjoin upon the people so declared to be free to abstain from all violence, unless in necessary self-defence; and I recommend to them that, in all cases when allowed, they labor faithfully for reasonable wages."

Curiously, Lincoln dropped the word *forever* from his earlier drafts, which stated that the slaves of disloyal masters "shall be then, thenceforward, and forever free." The final draft merely read that those slaves "are, and henceforward shall be free." He may have feared that the courts would take a dim view of such an extravagant claim. Unlike the preliminary version announced in September, the final Emancipation Proclamation said nothing about colonization.

That change pleased Radicals, but the Proclamation's legalistic language did not. "It must have required considerable ingenuity to give two and a half millions of human beings the priceless boon of Liberty in such a cold ungraceful way," remarked the Boston *Commonwealth*. "The heart of the Country was anticipating something warm and earnest. One could scarcely imagine that the herald of so blessed a dawn should have caught none of its glow. Was it not a time when some word of welcome, of sympathy, of hospitality for these long-enslaved men and women, might have been naturally uttered?"[316] James Freeman Clarke, an ultra-Radical Unitarian minister, told his parishioners that the document should have been "put on principles of justice and right, not on mere war necessity."[317]

Sable Warriors: Enlisting Black Troops

A striking feature of the revised document was a provision that blacks might serve in the military: "And I further declare and make known, that such persons of suitable condition, will be received into the armed service of the United States to garrison forts, positions, stations, and other places, and to man vessels of all sorts in said service."

This represented a reversal of Lincoln's earlier stand on the enlistment of blacks. On July 1, he told Orville H. Browning that no blacks "are to be armed. It would produce [a] dangerous & fatal dissatisfaction in our army, and do more injury than good."[318] Later that month, during a cabinet meeting, he "expressed himself as averse to arming negroes" and said nothing about that subject in the Preliminary Emancipation Proclamation. Halleck, too, was unenthusiastic about the use of black troops. "I do not think much of the negro," he told the cabinet.[319] Many others shared General Samuel R. Curtis's belief that if blacks were enrolled in the service, "some of them might adopt *Savage* cruelty, repugnant to honorable modern warfare. It might also reduce the *esprit du Corps* of free man."[320]

Politically, Lincoln had to contend with fierce popular resistance to recruiting blacks, especially in the Midwest and Border States. His Illinois friend, Colonel W. W. Orme, confided that "I don't want to mingle in an army of Negroes. And if it has come at last to the point that the white race of the North cannot successfully contend in arms with the white race of the South, then let us quit the contest and stop the war."[321] Presciently one Democratic congressman from Ohio warned colleagues that the "question is one of political and social equality with the negro everywhere. If you make him the instrument by which your battles are fought, the means by which your victories are won, you must treat him as a victor is entitled to be treated, with all decent and becoming respect."[322] In 1862, the Republican governor of the Buckeye State rhetorically asked John Mercer Langston, a black man who wished to raise a regiment: "Do you not know, Mr. Langston, that this is a *white man's* government; that white men are able to defend and protect it, and that to enlist a negro solider would be to drive every white man out of the service? When we want you colored men we will notify you."[323]

In July, Congress had paved the way for the administration's new departure by approving Senator Henry Wilson's amendment to the Militia Act which authorized the president "to receive into the service of the United States, for the purpose of constructing intrenchments, or performing camp service, or any other labor, or any military or naval service for which they may be found competent, persons of African descent, and such persons shall be enrolled and organized under such regulations, not inconsistent with the Constitution and laws, as the President may prescribe."[324] The Second Confiscation Act contained a similar provision.

The changing mood of the voters had affected the thinking of Congress and the president about enlisting blacks. Many Northerners shared the view of an Ohioan who maintained that "we have the same right to employ Black men on our side as they [the Confederates] have to use them against us."[325] In May, another Buckeye informed Chase that the "very timid course of the President as to slavery, and the strange conduct of certain generals, are fast bringing public opinion to the fearful alternative of an armed intervention of the slaves themselves. Those of you who have been in Washington for the last year can have no idea of the rapid change which is taking place in public opinion. I have heard the most ultra democrats of former times advocate the confiscation of all rebel property and the arming of the slaves."[326]

Though authorized to enlist blacks as combat troops, Lincoln decided to employ them only in support roles. He feared alienating the Border States and was aware of opposition in the army to the use of blacks as fighters. An Iowa colonel spoke for many officers when he wrote: "I have now *sixty men on extra duty* as teamsters &c. whose places could just as well be filled with *niggers*. We do not need a single negro in the army to fight but we could use to good advantage about one hundred & fifty with a regiment as teamsters & for making roads, chopping wood, policing camp &c."[327]

On August 4, Lincoln refused the offer of two black regiments recruited in the West, explaining to Senators James Harlan and Samuel C. Pomeroy that "he had made up his mind not to accept at present the service of armed negroes. He would use them as teamsters, cooks, laborers on entrenchments and in every capacity save fighting. He declared that to accept regiments of armed negroes would be to lose forty thousand white soldiers now in the army, and would drive some of the border States out of the Union." The employment of black troops in combat was premature; he decided that "he should wait till such a course seemed to be a direct command of Providence before adopting it."[328] He concluded by saying, "Gentlemen, you have my decision. I have made my mind up deliberately and mean to adhere to it. It embodies my best judgment, and if the people are dissatisfied, I will resign and let Mr. Hamlin try it." Pomeroy, laboring under the impression that the president was backing away from his earlier support of enlisting blacks, snapped: "I hope in God's name, Mr. President, you will."[329]

In early August, the president told a close friend that he had "no confidence" in blacks as fighters and predicted "that as much harm would come to us from the fact that we were arming negroes, as from a general proclamation of freedom."[330] On another occasion, Lincoln asked a congressman who was lobbying to have blacks enrolled in the military: "if I lose as many white men from the army of Virginia as I can enlist black men, will it pay?"[331] (There was good reason to believe that white Kentuckians would quit the army if blacks were admitted to its ranks.) In mid-August, Orville H. Browning told him that many Illinoisans were speculating that if the president "will accept one black Regiment he will lose twenty white Regiments by it." Browning declared that the "time *may* come for arming the negroes. It is not yet."[332]

Lincoln thought that time was late August. An informal effort by General David Hunter to raise black troops in the Sea Islands of South Carolina foundered because of that general's ineptitude. On August 10, Hunter reported that he was disbanding his black regiment. Surprisingly, two weeks later the War Department authorized the enrollment of 5,000 blacks in the Sea Islands under Hunter's replacement, General Rufus Saxton. Without official sanction, a modest number of black troops in Louisiana and Kansas were also mustered in. Some blacks had begun serving aboard Union warships as early as the fall of 1861. It was not clear that slaves thus employed would become free. Lincoln deliberately avoided an explicit policy statement for fear of antagonizing Border State sentiment. A journalist remarked apropos of the president's calculated ambiguity, "[n]ever was a man more cat-like in stealthily feeling his way before him."[333]

The president evidently encouraged Kansas Senator James H. Lane to enlist blacks in his state and thereby induce slaves from neighboring Missouri to desert their plantations and farms, slip across the border, and join up. Missouri slaveowners might then see merit in Lincoln's compensated emancipation scheme and press their legislators to adopt it.[334] In July, when Lane told the president and Stanton that he intended to raise two black regiments in Kansas, he was not forbidden to do so. Six months earlier, Lane had planned to lead a column against Texas. According to one report, his instructions were, in effect, to "let slavery be disposed of by military necessities and the course of events. If slaves come within our lines from the plantations beyond the federal lines, use them. If they can work on fortifications use their services, clothe, feed and pay them. If absolutely necessary, arm them. If [they are] slaves of rebels, free them." Lane's "Southern Expedition" was eventually scrubbed after he and David Hunter quarreled about who should command it.[335] When word of Lane's instructions leaked out, an incredulous Democrat asked: "Can it be possible that a chief magistrate of a great nation has no settled policy? Can it be possible that he lets out his administration by contract to politicians who are to take turns in the management of it?"[336]

After the Fredericksburg debacle, Maine Governor Israel Washburn recommended that the president "now quietly commence organizing colored regiments—they will fight & will save him if he will let them." Why, Washburn asked, "are our leaders unwilling that Sambo should save white boys?"[337] Another governor, Samuel J. Kirkwood of Iowa, told Halleck: "When this war is over & we have summed up the entire loss of life it has imposed on the country I shall not have any regrets if it is found that a part of the dead are *niggers* and that *all* are not white men."[338] Kirkwood could not "understand or appreciate the policy that insists that all the lives lost . . . shall be those of white men when black men are found willing to do the work and take the risks."[339]

In fact, Lincoln was no longer unwilling to enroll blacks, as the Emancipation Proclamation made clear. At first, he wanted them in jobs and areas where they were unlikely to be captured. In July 1862, while discussing the Mississippi River and the many blacks living along it, Lincoln had told Orville H. Browning: "I am determined to open it, and, if necessary will take all these negroes to open it, and keep it open."[340] Shortly after issuing the Proclamation, he suggested to General John A. Dix that Fort Monroe be manned by blacks: "The proclamation has been issued. We were not succeeding—at best, were progressing too slowly—without it. Now, that we have it, and bear all the disadvantage of it, (as we do bear some in certain quarters) we must also take some benefit from it, if practicable. I therefore will thank you for your well considered opinion whether Fortress-Monroe, and York-Town, one or both, could not, in whole or in part, be garrisoned by colored troops, leaving the white forces now necessary at those places, to be employed elsewhere."[341] Two months later, Lincoln encouraged Andrew Johnson, then serving as military governor of Tennessee, to recruit blacks into the army. "The colored population is the great *available* and yet *unavailed* of, force for restoring the Union. The bare sight of fifty thousand armed, and drilled black soldiers on the banks of the Mississippi, would end the rebellion at once.

And who doubts that we can present that sight, if we but take hold in earnest?"[342] He prodded General N. P. Banks to expedite the recruitment of Louisiana blacks: "To now avail ourselves of this element of force, is very important, if not indispensable. . . . I shall be very glad if you will take hold of the matter in earnest."[343] In the summer of 1863, Lincoln told U.S. Grant that black troops constituted "a resource which, if vigorously applied now, will soon close the contest. It works doubly, weakening the enemy and strengthening us."[344]

The recruiting of blacks was proceeding too slowly for Lincoln's taste. In May 1863, he complained to a delegation urging the appointment of Frémont to command an army of 10,000 black men that "the policy of the government, so far as he controlled it, was fixed, it was that [the] government should avail itself of any means to obtain the aid of emancipated slaves," but acknowledged that he "was only under embarrassment how to carry the policy out." He "confessed to a partial failure in the endeavors which had been made to recruit colored soldiers both North and South," and inquired of the delegation how he should proceed: "You ask a suitable command for General Fremont. Now he is the second [ranking] officer of the army. . . . He would expect a department. I cannot dismiss him from that position to offer him an inferior position. You place me in the position of the English Lord who, when told by his paternal relative to take a wife, replied, 'whose wife shall I take, father?'" He wanted black troops to occupy the region around Vicksburg and said he "had explained the matter to various officers of high rank, but have always found on these occasions I ran afoul of somebody's dignity. I would like anybody who can to undertake the matter. I believe Gen. Fremont peculiarly adapted to this special work. I would like to have him do it." He pledged that if the committee could raise 10,000 troops (they had claimed they could recruit 60,000 within two months), he would put Frémont in charge of them.[345] The journalist D. W. Bartlett paraphrased what Lincoln had been saying to various men throughout the spring: "I have made up my mind to give the black man every possible encouragement to fight for us. I will do him justice, and I will dismiss any officer who will not carry out my policy. If the people dislike this policy they will say so at the next presidential election—but so long as I am president the government shall deal fairly with this unfortunate race."[346]

Eventually, Johnson, Banks, Grant, Massachusetts Governor John A. Andrew, and Adjutant General Lorenzo Thomas did "take hold in earnest," and by war's end over 180,000 black soldiers and approximately 20,000 black sailors served in the war, constituting about 9 percent of the total Union armed forces.

Lincoln endorsed the use of black troops partly because public resistance was waning rapidly after McClellan's defeat on the Peninsula. In addition, the president may have been moved by the history of black soldiers in the War of 1812 and the American Revolutionary War. In the former, 500 of them played a key role in Andrew Jackson's victory at the battle of New Orleans; in the latter, approximately 5,000 took up arms to help the colonists gain independence. In February, Frederick Douglass asked an audience at Cooper Institute: "The negro fought the British under Jackson. Why not fight the rebels under Hooker?"[347] Lincoln agreed that they should.

Free at Last: Emancipation Officially Declared

As New Year's Day 1863 approached, supporters and opponents of emancipation lobbied the president. Among them was the Rev. Dr. Byron Sunderland, who told him: "We are full of faith and prayer that you will make a clean sweep for the Right." With an expression half-sad and half-shrewd, Lincoln replied: "Doctor, it's very hard sometimes to know what is right! You pray often and honestly, but so do those people across the lines. They pray and all their preachers pray devoutly. You and I do not think them justified in praying for their objects, but they pray earnestly, no doubt! If you and I had our own way, doctor, we would settle this war without bloodshed, but Providence permits blood to be shed. It's hard to tell what Providence wants of us. Sometimes we, ourselves, are more humane than the Divine Mercy seems to us to be."[348] The previous year, Lincoln had impressed Orville H. Browning with a similar observation. One Sunday afternoon in the White House library, as Lincoln was reading the Bible and Browning was perusing some other volume, the Illinois senator predicted that the North would not win unless it attacked slavery: "This is the great curse of our land, and we must make an effort to remove it before we can hope to receive the help of the Almighty." "Browning," the president replied, "suppose God is against us in our view on the subject of slavery in this country, and our method of dealing with it?"

Browning was "very much struck by this answer," which seemed to indicate that Lincoln "was thinking deeply of what a higher power than man sought to bring about by the great events then transpiring." Browning recalled that this answer "caused me to reflect that perhaps he had thought more deeply upon this subject than I had."[349] (In 1865, Lincoln would return to this theme in his second inaugural address.)

On New Year's Eve, 1862, Lincoln made a similar point to a trio of abolitionist clergy who had called at the White House to present a memorial urging him to carry out God's will by extending the Proclamation to apply to the whole country. He replied that while he opposed slavery wholeheartedly, he admitted that he had doubts about the Almighty's stance: "I am not so certain that God's views and feelings in respect to it are the same as mine. If his feelings were like mine, how could he have permitted it to remain so long? I am obliged to believe that God may not, after all, look upon it in the same light as I do." Lincoln added that just because a proclamation declared slaves free did not in fact make them free. "In one of our western courts," he remarked, "there had been an attempt made to show that a calf had five legs—the way the point was to be established was by calling the tail a leg, but the decision of the judge was that calling the tail a leg, did not make it a leg, and the calf had but four legs after all."[350] As he ushered the ministers out, he good-naturedly teased them, saying "this is the first time I ever had the honor of receiving a delegation from the Almighty." One of the visitors, William Goodell, expressed admiration for the president's "frankness and earnestness" and his willingness "to allow and to appreciate frankness and earnestness in others."[351]

On January 1, 1863, after Lincoln spent a sleepless night, his wife, who (according to her eldest son) "was very much opposed to the signing of the Emancipation Proclamation," inquired "in her sharp way, 'Well, what do you intend doing?'" He replied: "I am a man under orders, I cannot do otherwise."[352]

When Lincoln viewed the engrossed copy of the Proclamation that the State Department had prepared, he noticed a technical error in the wording of the closing subscription and ordered that it be corrected. While that task was being carried out, he presided over the traditional New Year's reception at the White House. According to Noah Brooks, the "press was tremendous, and the jam most excessive; all persons, high or low, civil, uncivil, or otherwise, were obliged to fall into an immense line of surging, crowding sovereigns [i.e., citizens], who were all forcing their way along the stately portico of the White House to the main entrance."[353]

After three hours, Lincoln returned to his office, exhausted from shaking hundreds of hands. When he began to sign the corrected copy of the Proclamation, his hand trembled. "I could not for a moment, control my arm," he later recalled. "I paused, and a superstitious feeling came over me which made me hesitate." Had he made a mistake? he wondered.[354] But swiftly regaining his composure, he told Seward and his son Frederick: "I never, in my life, felt more certain that I was doing right, than I do in signing this paper." He added that "I have been receiving calls, and shaking hands since nine o'clock this morning, till my arm is stiff and numb." He feared that if his signature appeared shaky, some people would think he had reservations. So, with renewed firmness, he said: "any way, it is going to be done!" Slowly and carefully he wrote out his full name in a bold, clear hand. Smiling, he looked up and observed softly: "That will do."[355]

Lincoln gave the pen he used to sign the document to Massachusetts Senator Charles Sumner, a longtime champion of freedom, who passed it along to George R. Livermore, author of *An Historical Research Respecting the Opinions of the Founders of the Republic on Negroes as Slaves, as Citizens and as Soldiers.* In early November 1862, Sumner had forwarded a copy of that recently published work to the White House. It "much interested President Lincoln," Sumner recalled. The "President expressed a desire to consult it while he was preparing the final Proclamation of emancipation; and as his own copy was mislaid, he requested me to lend him mine."[356] On Christmas, the senator complied.

The president had been nettled by Sumner's brusque manner and impatient rhetoric, but, as Carl Schurz observed, though "it required all his fortitude to bear Sumner's intractable insistence, Lincoln did not at all deprecate Sumner's public agitation for an immediate emancipation policy, even though it did reflect upon the course of the administration." To the contrary, "he rather welcomed everything that would prepare the public mind for the approaching development."[357] Sumner's counterpart in the House, Thaddeus Stevens of Pennsylvania, often denounced the president, but in effect, the two men worked in tandem. As Alexander K. McClure put it, "Stevens was ever clearing the underbrush and preparing the soil, while Lincoln followed to sow the seeds that were to ripen in a regenerated Union."[358]

Often portrayed as antagonists, Lincoln and the Radicals were actually united in their desire for emancipation and for a vigorous prosecution of the war. They differed only in temperament and in tactics. Lincoln was no reluctant emancipator; he welcomed the liberation of slaves as enthusiastically as any abolitionist. In discussing the Emancipation Proclamation with Joshua Speed, he said: "I believe that in this measure my fondest hopes will be realized."[359] Constitutional and political constraints had forced him to delay issuing the document; if he had acted solely on his own convictions and inclinations, emancipation would have come about much sooner. Lincoln was not forced by political considerations to issue the Proclamation; on the contrary, such considerations (along with his respect for the Constitution) compelled him to postpone doing what he had long wanted to see done.

Radicals rejoiced. "Now, hurrah for Old Abe and the *proclamation*," exulted Ben Wade.[360] Thaddeus Stevens told his constituents that the Proclamation "contained precisely the principles which I had advocated."[361] William Lloyd Garrison saluted the promulgation of the document as "a great historic event, sublime in its magnitude, momentous and beneficent in its far-reaching consequences."[362] Similarly, the budding intellectual historian Moses Coit Tyler thought the date of January 1, 1863 "the *greatest* one for America and perhaps for the human family since July 4, 1776."[363] The Chicago *Tribune*, which regarded the war as God's way of punishing a slaveholding country, praised Lincoln for sparing the people nine of the ten plagues visited upon the Egyptians for keeping the Jews in bondage. (The one plague that had already been visited upon Americans was the slaying of many first-born.) The abolitionist Samuel May, Jr., gave Lincoln credit for raising the moral sensibility of the North "up to the level of his Proclamation," although "a large minority are still below it." He "declared that Lincoln, not the abolitionists, had brought about whatever antislavery sentiment existed in the North."[364] Exclaimed Maria Weston Chapman: "Hurrah! Hosanna! Hallelujah! Laudamus! Nunc dimittis! Jubilate! Amen!"[365] Theodore Tilton proposed "Three cheers for God!" The Proclamation, though "not all one could wish," was still "too much not to be thankful for. It makes the remainder of slavery too valueless and precarious to be worth keeping." Optimistically, Tilton predicted that the "millennium is on the way" and declared that Lincoln's action, "faulty as it is, & long delayed, redeems the failing fortunes of his Administration." Disappointed that not all Slave States were covered by the Proclamation, Tilton anticipated that "Providence means to supplement it *de facto*, by adding the omitted states in due time."[366]

Blacks were especially jubilant. At mass rallies in New York, Philadelphia, Boston, and elsewhere in the North, speakers as well as cannon salvos hailed the Proclamation. Henry Highland Garnet told a vast crowd of blacks that Lincoln was "the man of our choice and hope" and that the Proclamation was "one of the greatest acts in all of history," an act that should be celebrated annually like the Fourth of July.[367] When the news reached the capital of Massachusetts, thousands of blacks exulted passionately. "I never saw enthusiasm before," Frederick Douglass reported. "I never saw joy before. Men, women, young and old, were up; hats and bonnets were in the air, and we gave three cheers for Abraham Lincoln." Shouts of "Glory, Hallelujah!" "Old John Brown," "Marching On," and "Blow Ye the Trumpet, Blow" filled the air. Douglass deemed the issuance of the Proclamation "a mighty event for the bondman" and "a still mightier event for the nation at large, and mighty as it is for both, the slave and the nation, it is still mightier when viewed in its relation to the cause of truth and justice throughout the world."[368] It was, Douglass told an audience at Cooper Union in March 1863, "the greatest event in our nation's history."[369] Another black abolitionist, H. Ford Douglas, wrote that "Abraham Lincoln has crossed the Rubicon and by one simple act of Justice to the slave links his memory with immortality."[370] In Philadelphia, a white abolitionist reported to Lincoln that the "Black people all trust *you*. They *beleive* that you desire to do them Justice."[371] When Sojourner Truth, the black woman renowned for helping many slaves escape from bondage, expressed her gratitude to Lincoln for being the only president who ever did anything for her people, he modestly replied: "And the only one who ever had such opportunity. Had our friends in the South behaved themselves, I could have done nothing whatever."[372]

Some Radicals regretted that Lincoln exempted all of Tennessee as well as parts of Louisiana and Virginia. "He might have stricken the shackles at once from the limbs of several hundreds of thousands of slaves, and thereby given to those left in bondage to Rebels an earnest that our failure to reach and liberate them resulted from want of power rather than will," observed the New York *Tribune*.[373] The president had received strong protests from the Volunteer State, whose people (so it was alleged) were loyal but had been prevented from holding elections by the warfare raging in their midst.

A few abolitionists who had been disappointed by the Preliminary Proclamation underwent a change of heart as Emancipation Day drew near. Lydia Maria Child said apropos of Lincoln's delay: "it would not be fair to blame the President for moving so slowly. The *people* were not prepared to sustain him in any such measure; they had become too generally demoralized by long subservience to the Slave Power."[374] (Similarly, Theodore Parker in 1856 had acknowledged that officeholders must be more circumspect than reformers: "I think that the anti-slavery party has not always quite done justice to the political men. See why. It is easy for Mr. Garrison and Mr. Phillips or me to say all of our thought. I am responsible to nobody, and nobody to me. But it is not easy for Mr. Sumner, Mr. Seward, and Mr. Chase to say all of their thought; because they have a position to maintain, and they must keep that position.")[375]

Opinion in the Border States was, as Lincoln predicted, hostile. The Catholic archbishop of Baltimore indignantly exclaimed: "While our brethren are slaughtered in hecatombs, Abraham Lincoln coolly issues his Emancipation Proclamation, letting loose from three to four millions of half civilized Africans to murder their Masters and Mistresses! And all that under the pretense of philanthropy!! Puritan hypocrisy never exhibited itself in a more horrible and detestable attitude."[376]

Many Democrats in the Free States also objected strenuously. The issuance of the Proclamation, said the Cincinnati *Enquirer*, was "as much a usurpation and revolution in the Government" as would be Lincoln's assumption of "the Imperial crown" and his declaration that he was "Dictator of America." It was "a complete overthrow of the Constitution he swore to protect and defend."[377] Other Democratic papers in the Midwest deemed it "a wicked, atrocious and revolting deed," as "impudent and insulting to God as to man, for it declares those 'equal' whom God created unequal."[378] In New York, a leading Catholic journal protested that the Proclamation would transform the conflict: "It is no longer to be a war between white men; it is the St. Domingo massacres inaugurated on our soil, under the sanction, approval and encouragement of the Government."[379] The *Journal of Commerce* noted that by freeing the slaves of loyal masters without compensation in Union-occupied Florida, Lincoln "has done a great injustice, for which there is no excuse."[380]

Florida was not the only state where slaves would become free on January 1, whether or not their masters were loyal. The exemption of areas under federal control (where 800,000 slaves lived) caused some to scoff that the "Proclamation is a dead letter upon the face of it. It don't free a negro where a negro is to be freed, but enslaves, or re-enslaves all, where the negro could be freed."[381] But in fact the Proclamation freed tens of thousands of slaves in Union-occupied Florida, Arkansas, Alabama, North Carolina, South Carolina, and Georgia on New Year's Day. And hundreds of thousands more would be freed as federal armies penetrated ever deeper into the Confederacy.

On January 12, Jefferson Davis expressed his outrage in a message to the Confederate Congress in which he called the Emancipation Proclamation "a measure by which several millions of human beings of an inferior race, peaceful and contented laborers in their sphere, are doomed to extermination, while at the same time they are encouraged to a general assassination of their masters by the insidious recommendation 'to abstain from violence unless in necessary self-defense.' Our own detestation of those who have attempted the most execrable measure recorded in the history of guilty man is tempered by profound contempt for the impotent rage which it discloses." Davis warned that white officers commanding black units would be turned over to Confederate state governments for punishment as instigators of slave uprisings and that black troops would be restored to their masters.[382] The Richmond *Enquirer* deemed the Emancipation Proclamation "little more than the indecent expression of Lincoln's rage and fiendishments" and predicted that it would "tell the world how bad he is."[383] Caleb Cushing, former U.S. attorney general and chairman of the 1860 Democratic conventions in Baltimore and Charleston, bemoaned "the unspeakable calamities which the Republicans and their President have brought upon us." Among those calamities Cushing listed "possible servile war, probable foreign war, the attempted total prostration of all constitutional rights and liberty throughout the Northern States, and the proposed massacre of eight millions of white men women and children in the Southern States in order to turn four millions of black men into vagabonds [and] robbers."[384]

The most telling criticism of the Proclamation came from eminent lawyers who questioned its constitutionality. In an influential pamphlet, Benjamin R. Curtis, a former associate justice of the U.S. Supreme Court, denied that military necessity justified emancipation and argued that since the seceded states were still technically in the Union, the president could not abrogate their laws. Moreover, Congress had provided for emancipation in the Second Confiscation Act. Curtis did not "see that it depends upon his [Lincoln's] executive decree, whether a servile war shall be invoked to help twenty millions of the white race to assert the rightful authority of the Constitution and the laws of their country, over those who refuse to obey them."[385]

Several prominent attorneys, including Charles P. Kirkland, Charles Mayo Ellis, and Grosvenor P. Lowrey, issued pamphlets challenging Curtis's arguments. Lincoln read Kirkland's work, *A Letter to the Hon. Benjamin R. Curtis,* which he called a "paper of great ability."[386] Kirkland chastised Curtis for ignoring the reality of wartime conditions: "It is difficult to imagine under what hallucination you were laboring when you gave utterance to those sentiments," he wrote.[387]

Lincoln appreciated the constitutional argument and would eventually find a way to make emancipation unambiguously legal through an amendment to the Constitution. But for the moment, the implied war powers of the president were cited to justify the mighty act. Professor Theophilus Parsons of the Harvard Law School, temperamentally a conservative, insisted that while the president had no power *in peacetime* to liberate slaves, "there can be no doubt that he has a constitutional power to do this as a military act, grounded on a military necessity; that the Commander-in-chief of our army must have the right to judge of the existence and the force of this necessity."[388]

When warned that the Proclamation would "would rouse the South as one man and send a force into the field twice as great as then existed," Lincoln replied: "we'll double ours then."[389] According to one resident of Richmond, the "actual effect of the President's proclamation has been to make the people more determined. They claim that they will now be able to raise ten men voluntarily where they could not raise three before."[390]

In the evening of New Year's Day, Lincoln confided to Indiana Congressman Schuyler Colfax that the "South had fair warning, that if they did not return to their duty, I should strike at this pillar of their strength. The promise must now be kept, and I shall never recall one word."[391] And he did not.

Lincoln said the issuance of the Emancipation Proclamation was "the central act of my administration" as well as "the great event of the nineteenth century," and speculated to Charles Sumner "that the name which is connected with this matter will never be forgotten."[392] And it has not been.

A few weeks after issuing the Proclamation, Lincoln told a group of abolitionists that it had "knocked the bottom out of slavery" but he did not expect "any sudden results from it."[393] Though not sudden, the results would be profound.

"Go Forward, and Give Us Victories"
From the Mud March to Gettysburg
(January–July 1863)

The winter and early spring of 1863 found Lincoln and his constituents once again mired in the Slough of Despond. In February, when Benjamin Brown French suggested to the president that doubtless "he would feel glad when he could get some rest," he "replied that it was a pretty hard life for him." French confided to his diary that Lincoln was "growing feeble. He wrote a note while I was present, and his hand trembled as I never saw it before, and he looked worn & haggard."[1] As 1862 drew to a close, George William Curtis remarked that everything "is very black," and journalist Benjamin Perley Poore noted that the year was ending "somewhat gloomily, and no one appears hopeful enough to discern dry land upon which our storm-tossed ark of State may rest, while many think that we are drifting—drifting—drifting—toward a cataract which may engulf our national existence."[2] "Exhaustion steals over the country," Montgomery Meigs observed. "Confidence and hope are dying."[3] Representative Frederick Pike of Maine reported that in January, "nine tenths of the men in Washington, in Congress & out, said it was no use to try any further."[4] That same month Henry B. Stanton confessed that he "was more gloomy than ever," for it seemed clear to him that the nation was "rapidly going to destruction" and was "never so badly off as at this moment." He told Susan B. Anthony that Radicals like Owen Lovejoy and John P. Hale "have pretty much given up the struggle in despair. You have no idea how dark the cloud is which hangs over us."[5] In February, William O. Stoddard wrote from the White House that "the growth of a discontented spirit in portions of the North" was more "ominous than anything else."[6]

That discontent led to sharp criticism of Edwin M. Stanton, whom Lincoln defended repeatedly. To those who suggested that Nathaniel P. Banks be made secretary of war, Lincoln tactfully replied: "General Banks is doubtless a very able man, and a very good man for the place, perhaps; but how do I know that he will do any better than Stanton? You see, I know what Stanton has done, and think he has done pretty well, all things considered. There are not many men who are fit for Stanton's place. I guess we may as well not trade until we know we are making a good bargain."[7] To other critics of the war secretary Lincoln pointed to the Democratic newspapers, which had been denouncing Stanton: "See how these anti-war journals hound him on—they are my bitter enemies also, and shall I take advice of them about the reconstruction of my cabinet?"[8]

Discontent: Presidential Popularity Ebbs

Lincoln's own popularity sagged badly. David Davis thought that if it were peacetime, the administration "would be the most completely broken down one, that was ever known."[9] In Washington, Richard Henry Dana observed that the "lack of respect for the Pres[iden]t, in all parties, is unconcealed."[10] From Baltimore, John Pendleton Kennedy asked: "Is there any thing in history to parallel the extraordinary dilemma we are in? The finest army of brave men almost ever collected in one body: the most willing and noble people that ever sustained a good cause—a propitious season for operations—for we never had had so beautiful a winter as this—abundance of all kinds of munitions; every thing necessary for success—and all this mighty equipment brought to a still-stand, checkmated, not by the superior vigor or skill of the enemy, but by the ineptitude of the cabinet! What a contemptible exhibition of jealous factions in the Senate, what incapacity in the General in Chief, what trifling with this tremendous emergency in the President!"[11] Lincoln's friend Hawkins Taylor of Iowa found a "general feeling [of] *contempt* entertained by the people of the West towards the administration for its want of vigor" as well as "a widespread feeling of despair for the success of our Army and a strong disposition for the North West to unite and take care of herself."[12]

Constituents mused to Ohio Senator John Sherman that while Lincoln probably meant well, it was not clear that he "has ability sufficient for this crisis," and noted that the "people are beginning to denounce our President as an imbecile—made on too small a scale for his position."[13] One Buckeye expressed the fervent wish that "Lincoln had the military genius, the firmness and decision of Napoleon the first."[14] A former Whig congressman from Ohio despairingly warned that "unless something is soon done to change the current of events our national destruction is inevitable. The multiplicity of Executive blunders coupled with the failures of our armies are producing the effect upon our people which is fast driving them to a sort of hopeless indifference."[15] Murat Halstead of the Cincinnati *Commercial* charged that "the foolish, drunken, stupid Grant" could not "organize or control or fight an army." Even worse, in Halstead's view, was Lincoln's "weak, puling, piddling humanitarianism" that kept him from shooting deserters.[16] The president, he declared, was little more than "an awful, woeful ass" and a "damned fool."[17] A treasury official in New Orleans, fearing that Lincoln was "too good," wished to see him replaced with a "strong war man" like Benjamin F. Butler.[18] Also expressing the wish that Butler were president instead of Lincoln was Thurlow Weed, who told John Bigelow: "*We are in a bad way.*"[19] In February, the abolitionist Jane Grey Swisshelm complained that "when committees wait upon the President to urge strong measures, he tells them a story. A delegation waited on him some time ago, on important business, and he told them four anecdotes! A Western Senator visited him on official business and reciprocated by telling an anecdote the President had not before heard. After he rose to leave Mr. Lincoln remarked: 'Wait a moment; I want you to give me the notes of that story!' The notes were given, carefully taken down and filed away on his desk."[20]

Even allies in Illinois were growing critical. Joseph Medill of the Chicago *Tribune* wrote dismissively that "Lincoln is only half awake, and never will do much better than he has done. He will do the right thing always too late and just when it does no good."[21] In Quincy, Jackson Grimshaw growled that the administration "is kind to all but its *friends*. It has dug up snakes and it can[']t kill them, it has fostered d[amne]d rascals & crushed honest men. If it were not that our country, our homes, our all is at stake . . . Lincoln, Baker, Bailhache Edwards etc. might go to —."[22]

Republican congressmen also disdained Lincoln. In late January, William P. Cutler of Ohio confided to his diary that "all is dark, and it would almost seem that God works for the rebels and keeps alive their cause. . . . [H]ow striking is the want of a leader. The nation is without a head."[23] Henry L. Dawes concurred, telling his wife that "[n]othing lifts as yet the dark cloud which rests on our cause. The Army is palsied, the government imbecile, and the nation distracted." Lincoln, Dawes sneered, "is an imbecile and should be sent to the school for feeble minded youth."[24] In January, congressmen laughed out loud at the reading of a presidential message and declined to refer it to a select committee. Little wonder then that Noah Brooks thought Lincoln "does not have the cordial and uniform support of his political friends." Though they might agree with him on issues involving emancipation, confiscation, and the suspension of habeas corpus, nonetheless there ran beneath this superficial harmony "an undercurrent of dissatisfaction and an open manifestation of the spirit of captious criticism." Brooks frequently heard Republicans "abuse the President and the Cabinet, as they would not allow a political opponent to do." Brooks was dismayed "to see Republicans, who would vote for sustaining the President in any of his more important acts, deliberately squelch out a message from the White House, or treat it with undisguised contempt."[25] A Missourian wrote from Washington that leading men "are beginning to speak of the President in tones of mingled pity, contempt and scorn. Few if any look to him for relief in this 'winter of our discontent.' He is regarded as a debauched man politically."[26]

A case in point was Conservative Unionist Congressman John W. Crisfield of Maryland, who told his wife in late January that the "conviction of the President[']s incapacity is every day becoming more universal." In Crisfield's view, the "election of Lincoln, the blundering ignorance of his administration, and the want of statesmanship, in the management of this civil war . . . have done more [to] discredit the capacity of man for self-government" than "all the emperors, kings, and despots" in history.[27] Crisfield's Radical colleague, Martin F. Conway of Kansas, publicly denounced Lincoln as "a politician of a past age" who was "anti-slavery, but of a genial Southern type" and "has not made war upon the South in any proper sense." Nor could he be considered "a Northern man in any sense; neither by birth, education, political or personal sympathies, or by any belief in the superiority of Northern civilization, or its right to rule this continent. The idea of Northern nationality and domination is hateful to him."[28] Conway was partially right; much as he hated slavery, Lincoln was a nationalist who did not view the South as a moral pariah.

Senators as well as congressmen were growing disenchanted. In January, William Pitt Fessenden of Maine denounced Lincoln's "entire want of executive ability" and scornfully remarked that "there never was such a shambling, half and half set of incapables collected in one government before since the world began."[29] He predicted that "unless we speedily achieve some decided military successes, the President will find himself compelled by public opinion to reorganize his Cabinet," for, Fessenden believed, confidence in the administration "is rapidly wasting away, and the people will not much longer sustain a war so unfortunately conducted."[30] With more venom, Ohio Senator John Sherman told his brother: "How fervently I wish Lincoln was out of the way. Any body would do better. I was among the first of his political friends to acknowledge how fearfully we were mistaken in him. He has not a single quality befitting his place. . . . He is unstable as water—afraid as a child & yet sometimes stubborn as a mule. I never shall cease to regret the part I took in his election and am willing to pay a heavy penance for this sin. This error I fear will be a fatal one as he is unfit to control events and it is fearful to think what may come during his time."[31]

Yet Senator Sherman publicly defended Lincoln: "We do no good to our cause by a constant crimination of the President, by arraigning him . . . as a tyrant and imbecile. Sir, he is the instrument in the hands of Almighty God, holding the executive power of this Government for four years." Somewhat patronizingly, he added: "If he is a weak man, we must support him; if we allow his authority to be subdued and overrun, we destroy the authority of the Government."[32] The new secretary of the interior, John Palmer Usher, concurred, assuring an Indiana banker that there was "not on earth a more guileless man [than Lincoln], and but few of more wisdom. It is by and through him that the nation is to be saved at all. Abraham Lincoln with all his energies is seeking to maintain the life of the nation. Whoever attacks and paralyzes him in that effort is the foe of his country."[33]

Pelion Heaped on Ossa: Presidential Woes Mount

On January 25, when a group of abolitionists called at the White House, Lincoln analyzed the sources of Northern discontent. To Wendell Phillips, who insisted that the public was not satisfied with the way the Emancipation Proclamation was being implemented, the president replied that "the masses of the country generally are only dissatisfied at our lack of military successes. Defeat and failure in the field make everything seem wrong." Bitterly, he added: "Most of us here present have been long working in minorities, and may have got into a habit of being dissatisfied." When some of his guests objected, Lincoln said: "At any rate, it has been very rare that an opportunity of 'running' this administration has been lost."[34] When the delegation chided him for not issuing the Emancipation Proclamation earlier, he said the public had not been ready to support it. If that were so, objected Moncure Conway, then why had conservative papers like the Chicago *Times*, Boston *Post*, and New York *Herald* supported Frémont's emancipation order? The president replied that he had been unaware of that fact. According to Conway's journal, "there was a burst of surprise around the room at this ignorance which was *brutal*. When assured that it was so—and that we could bring (if necessary) the files of those papers to prove it, he was staggered completely & sank back in his chair in silence." Conway speculated that the president "was surrounded a mile thick with Kentuckians who would not let him know the truth." He also expressed doubts about the honesty of Nicolay, "who super-intends his reading."[35] Soon afterward, in a lecture titled "The Vacant Throne of Washington," Conway told a Boston audience that "we find *no man,* in the station of power and influence, adequate to the work."[36]

Other participants in that meeting found Lincoln more impressive than Conway did. George Luther Stearns said: "It is of no use to disparage his ability. There we were, with some able talkers among us, and we had the best position too; but the President held his ground against us." Frank Bird acknowledged that Lincoln "is the shrewdest man I ever met; but not at all a Kentuckian. He is an old-fashioned Yankee in a Western dress."[37]

At the same time, Conservatives and Moderates pressed Lincoln to rescind the Emancipation Proclamation. They were convinced, as Senator Sherman put it, that Negrophobia was generating significant backlash against emancipation. Democrats would "fight for the flag & the country," Sherman told his brother, "but they hate niggers," were "easily influenced by a party cry," and "stick to their party while its or-ganization is controlled by the [worst] set of traitors in this country North or South."[38] Sherman received a warning from Murat Halstead of the Cincinnati *Commercial* that there was "a change in the current of public sentiment out west." If the president "were not a damned fool, we could get along yet. . . . But what we want is not any more nigger."[39] On January 12, Sherman's colleagues Orville H. Browning and James R. Doolittle, as well as Thomas Ewing, agreed that Republicans "were upon the brink of ruin, and could see no hope of an amendment in affairs unless the President would change his policy, and withdraw or greatly modify his proclamation."[40] Even Radical Senator John P. Hale of New Hampshire acknowledged that the Republicans "had made a great mistake upon the slavery question, and that it would have been better both for the cause of the Country, and of emancipation if nothing had been said in regard to the negro since the war commenced."[41] Seward doubted the efficacy of the Proclamation, regarding it "as useful abroad" but ineffective at home. Indeed, he thought "it was rather in spite of it that the actual emancipation had taken place."[42]

Lincoln rejected advice to withdraw the Proclamation, insisting that it was "a fixed thing" and "that he intended to adhere to it."[43] To a Pennsylvania congressman he remarked: "Suppose I had given a deed of my place in Springfield, having received equivalent therefor, could I recall that deed and retake it into my own possession? Just as impossible would it be for me to revoke this deed of emancipation."[44] In the sum-mer of 1863, when urged to accept the return of North Carolina to the Union with slavery, Lincoln replied laconically: "My proclamation setting free the slaves of the rebel states was issued nearly a year ago."[45]

Adding to Lincoln's dismay, in February the French government, eager to placate manufacturers and laborers suffering from a cotton shortage, formally offered to help mediate the American conflict. Upon receiving this news, the president appeared worn out and downcast. Angrily, he declared that he "would be d[amne]d if he wouldn't get 1,000,000 men if France dares to interfere."[46] Less vehemently, Seward declined the French offer.

Most distressing to Lincoln was the Peace Democrats' increasingly harsh criticism of the war effort. According to Charles Sumner, the president feared "the 'fire in the rear'—meaning the Democracy, especially at the Northwest—more than our military chances."[47] When told that his situation resembled that of the French statesman, Cardinal Richelieu, Lincoln (who had seen Edward Bulwer-Lytton's play *Richelieu*) replied: "Far from it, Richelieu never had a fire in his front and rear at the same time, as I have. Besides, he had a united constituency; I never have had. If ambition in Congress and jealousy in the army could be allayed, and all united in one common purpose, this infernal rebellion would soon be terminated."[48]

Lincoln found army jealousy particularly vexing. On January 23, David Davis, who was badgering him to give their mutual friend W. W. Orme a general's stars, wrote that the "pressure upon Lincoln for officers & promotions is as great as ever. He sometimes gets very impatient. If ever a man sh[oul]d be sympathized with it is Lincoln."[49] The president complained "that the changes and promotions in the Army of the Potomac cost him more anxiety than the campaigns."[50]

Such problems also plagued the western theater, where German-born General Franz Sigel huffily resigned in December 1861 when Samuel R. Curtis superseded him in Missouri. Determined to placate Sigel and his many vociferous backers who held mass protest meetings and deluged the White House with petitions, Lincoln sent Gustave Koerner to St. Louis to straighten things out. "The Germans are true and patriotic," the president wrote Halleck, "and so far as they have got cross in Missouri it is upon mistake and misunderstanding."[51] In March, though both Halleck and General John M. Schofield took a dim view of Sigel's competence (his mistakes had contributed to the Union defeat at Wilson's Creek in August 1861), Lincoln promoted the German brigadier to major general. He did so at the urging of many congressmen and senators. Earlier that month, Sigel had helped Curtis win the battle of Pea Ridge, Arkansas, which ended the formal military threat to Missouri. (Despite this achievement, Curtis entertained no high opinion of Sigel. "I cannot understand him and do not wish to have the honor of commanding him," he told Halleck.)[52] In September 1862, the hypersensitive German protested that a junior officer had been promoted over him. Lincoln directed the complaint to Halleck, whom Sigel accused of lying.

A month later Sigel dispatched an aide to the White House to denounce once more the administration's mistreatment of him and his men. Lincoln urged that Sigel "do the best he could with the command he had" and "not to keep up this constant complaining," which made it appear that the general was "only anxious about himself." The president emphasized that he "was tired of this constant hacking," which "gave him more trouble than anything else." He added that "he had given equal or greater cause of complaint to other officers," but "they had not complained."[53] Soon thereafter, when yet another caller tried to plead Sigel's case, Lincoln exclaimed: "Don't talk to me any longer about *that man!*"[54] In January 1863, the president rebuked Sigel but soon apologized, saying: "If I do get up a little temper I have no sufficient time to keep it up."[55] Lincoln feared "that Sigel would never forget that he and his Germans are step-sons."[56] The president tolerated Sigel's behavior because the general was popular with his countrymen, who formed an important voting bloc.

For the same reason, Lincoln decided to promote another German, Alexander Schimmelfennig. When Stanton objected that more worthy Germans should be advanced before Schimmelfennig, Lincoln replied: "Never mind about that, his name will make up for any difference there may be, and I'll take the risk of his coming out all right." Laughingly, he repeated the general's unmistakably Teutonic surname, emphasizing each syllable, especially the final one: "Schem-mel-fin-*nig* must be appointed."[57]

Other squabbles among generals exasperated Lincoln. David Hunter and John G. Foster quarreled about which of them would control a part of Foster's corps that happened to be situated in Hunter's department. John M. Schofield threatened to resign his command in Missouri because Samuel R. Curtis would not authorize him to undertake offensive action. Curtis, in turn, objected to orders transferring some of his troops to the Vicksburg front. To Lincoln's relief, Grant conducted the Vicksburg campaign without grumbling. The president said he liked Grant (whom he described as "a copious worker, and fighter, but a very meagre writer, or telegrapher") because he "doesn't worry and bother me. He isn't shrieking for reinforcements all the time. He takes what troops we can safely give him . . . and does the best he can with what he has got."[58] Grant's best turned out to be quite good indeed.

Amidst his many troubles, Lincoln managed to retain a sense of humor. At a reception in January, an army paymaster said to him: "Being here, Mr. Lincoln, I thought I'd call and pay my respects." In reply, the president quipped: "From the complaints of the soldiers, I guess that's about all any of you do pay."[59]

Magnanimity: Dealing with the Minnesota Sioux Uprising

Discontent was especially strong in the West, where Lincoln's handling of an uprising by Minnesota Sioux in the summer and fall of 1862 enraged the citizenry. The Indians, angry at white encroachment on their territory, at the failure of the government to deliver promised supplies and money, and at the notorious corruption of Indian agents and traders, launched savage attacks on white men, women, and children along the frontier. They killed hundreds and drove over 30,000 from their homes. It was the bloodiest massacre of American civilians on U.S. soil prior to September 11, 2001. Settlers demanded protection, and Governor Alexander Ramsey appealed to Lincoln for troops.

General John Pope, who was dispatched to restore order, issued a stern declaration: "It is my purpose utterly to exterminate the Sioux if I have the power to do so. . . . They are to be treated as maniacs or wild beasts, and by no means as people with whom treaties or compromises can be made."[60] When the administration warned him to make no unreasonable demands for troops and supplies, Pope responded: "You have no idea of the wide, universal, and uncontrollable panic everywhere in this country. Over 500 people have been murdered in Minnesota alone and 300 women and children are now in captivity. The most horrible massacres have been committed;

children nailed alive to trees and houses, women violated and then disemboweled—everything that horrible ingenuity could devise."[61]

Lincoln ordered thousands of paroled prisoners of war to the scene. "Arm them and send them away just as fast as the Railroads will carry them," he instructed Stanton.[62] When the Confederates refused to continue paroling POWs unless the Union agreed not to deploy them as Indian fighters, Lincoln threatened to "send the prisoners back with a distinct notice that we will recognize no paroles given our prisoners by the rebels, as extending beyond a prohibition against fighting them."[63] But eventually the administration decided that assigning parolees to combat Indians violated the prisoner exchange cartel, and so the plan was scrapped.

Under the leadership of Minnesota Congressman Henry H. Sibley, militiamen and regular troops put down the Sioux rebellion by early October. As he conducted war crimes trials that led to a death sentence for 303 Sioux men, Sibley was urged by Pope not to "allow any false sympathy for the Indians to prevent you from acting with the utmost rigor." Sibley told his wife that "the press is very much concerned, lest I should prove too tender-hearted."[64]

Lincoln was under intense pressure to expel all Indians from Minnesota. Governor Alexander Ramsey told him that his constituents had come "to regard this perfidious and cruel race with a degree of distrust and apprehension which will not tolerate their presence of their neighborhood in any number or in any condition."[65]

Faced with a potential mass execution of over three hundred prisoners, Lincoln hesitated. A pro-administration Washington paper announced that he had "resolved that such an outrage, as the indiscriminate hanging of these Indians most certainly would be, shall not take place."[66] On November 10, he instructed Pope to "forward, as soon as possible, the full and complete record of these convictions" and to prepare "a careful statement."[67] In response, the general warned that white Minnesotans "are exasperated to the last degree & if the guilty are not all executed I think it nearly impossible to prevent the indiscriminate massacre of all the Indians [—] old men, women, & children." The soldiers, too, would be likely to resort to vigilante justice if the executions were not carried out, Pope added.[68] Governor Ramsey joined the chorus demanding that the convicted Indians be hanged. "I hope," he wrote the president, "the execution of every Sioux Indian condemned by the military court will at once be ordered. It would be wrong upon principle and policy to refuse this. Private revenge would on all this border take the place of official judgment on these Indians."[69] Fiercely the Minnesota abolitionist-feminist Jane Grey Swisshelm condemned the Indians as "crocodiles," asserted that they had "just as much right to life as a hyena," and urged the government to "[e]xterminate the wild beasts and make peace with the devil and all his host sooner than with these red-jawed tigers whose fangs are dripping with the blood of innocents."[70] On December 4, the Minnesota congressional delegation vigorously protested to Lincoln against clemency for the condemned prisoners. Especially emphatic was Senator Morton Wilkinson, who introduced a resolution demanding that the president inform the senate about the Indian war and the proposed execution of condemned prisoners. In a gruesome speech, Wilkinson recounted stories of atrocities perpetrated by the Sioux. The senate passed his resolution. Like Pope, Minnesota Congressman Cyrus Aldrich counseled Lincoln that if all the Indians found guilty were not executed, his constituents would "dispose of them in their own way."[71]

Newspapers also predicted that lynching would result if the convicted murderers were not executed. One Minnesota journal warned against any leniency in dealing with the Sioux: "If the Government wants wholesale hanging by the acre; if it wants the Western plains turned into a wide Golgotha of dead Indians; if it wants them hunted down like wild beasts from the face of the continent, it had better refuse to perform the act of justice which the people of this State demand."[72] Civic and religious leaders joined the outcry. One missionary to the Sioux urged Lincoln "to execute the *great majority* of those who have been condemned" lest "the innocent as well as the guilty" be killed by vengeful settlers.[73]

While considering what to do, Lincoln received letters from Minnesotans insisting that no mercy be shown to the "lurking savages." A physician in St. Paul painted him a lurid picture: "Mr. President, if a being in the shape of a human, but with that shape horribly disfigured with paint & feathers [in order] to make its presence more terrible, should enter your home in the dead hours of night, & approach your pillow with a glittering tomahawk in one hand, & a scalping knife in the other, his eyes gleaming with a thirst for blood, you would spring from your bed in terror, and flee for your life; . . . there you would see the torch applied to the house your hands had built; . . . your wife, or your daughter, though she might not yet have seen twelve sweet summers . . . ravished before your eyes; & carried into a captivity worse than death." If he had seen such horrors, would the president not demand revenge?[74]

The New York *Tribune* reported that the threat made by Aldrich and his exasperated Minnesota colleagues "is not received with favor, and will not influence the Executive action."[75] The situation resembled the one Lincoln had faced thirty years earlier during the Black Hawk War, when fellow militiamen wished to kill an Indian bearing a safe-conduct pass; then he had courageously stopped them. As the president and two Interior Department lawyers, Francis Ruggles and George Whiting, scrutinized the record of the trials, they discovered that some had lasted only fifteen minutes, that hearsay evidence had been admitted, that due process had been ignored, and that counsel had not been provided the defendants. Ruggles and Whiting recommended that many of the condemned men be pardoned.

Persuaded by their arguments, Lincoln authorized the execution of only 37 of the 303 condemned men (35 were found guilty of murder and 2 were convicted of rape). In response to Senator Wilkinson's resolution, Lincoln explained his reasoning: "Anxious to not act with so much clemency as to encourage another outbreak on one hand, nor with so much severity as to be real cruelty on the other, I caused a careful examination of the records of the trials to be made, in view of first ordering the execution of such as had been proved guilty of violating females." He further sought to discriminate between those involved in massacres and those involved only in battles.[76]

As execution day for those Indians drew near, Lincoln instructed Nicolay, who had been in Minnesota on a troubleshooting mission during the uprising, to warn Sibley not to hang Chas-kay-don, whose name was similar to one of the condemned men. At the last minute, the president pardoned Round Wind, who had helped some whites to escape. On December 26, the convicted rapists and killers died on the gallows while a peaceful crowd of more than 5,000 looked on. In 1864, Alexander Ramsey told Lincoln that if he had executed all 303 Indians, he would have won more backing for his reelection bid. "I could not afford to hang men for votes," came the reply.[77]

Minnesotans denounced the president's decision. In February, the abolitionist-feminist Jane Grey Swisshelm told a Washington audience that if "justice is not done," whites in Minnesota "will go to shooting Indians whenever these government pets get out from under Uncle Sam's wing. Our people will hunt them, shoot them, set traps for them, put out poisoned bait for them—kill them by every means we would use to exterminate panthers."[78] When she urged Secretary of the Interior John Palmer Usher to recommend to the president that Indian prisoners be executed in retaliation for Sioux depredations in 1863, Usher replied: "Why it is impossible to get him to arrest and imprison one of the secesh women who are here—the wives of officers in the rebel army, and hold them as hostages for the Union women imprisoned in the South. We have tried again, and again, and cannot get him to do it.—The President will hang nobody!"[79]

To placate Minnesota voters, Lincoln declared that the government would help compensate victims of depredations and would support the removal of Indians from their state. Eventually, Congress appropriated money for compensation and provided that the Sioux and the Winnebagos be sent elsewhere.

In sparing the lives of 264 Sioux, Lincoln had been influenced by Episcopal Bishop Henry B. Whipple and a religious delegation from Pennsylvania, which recommended clemency. Whipple wrote that although the leaders of the uprising had to be punished, nevertheless "we cannot afford by an act of wanton cruelty to purchase a long Indian war—nor by injustice on other matters purchase the anger of God."[80] Endorsing Whipple's unpopular view was Commissioner of Indian Affairs William P. Dole, who insisted that executing all the condemned men would "be contrary to the spirit of the age, and our character as a great magnanimous and Christian people."[81]

Whipple also lobbied the president to reform the corrupt Indian agency system. In the spring of 1862, the bishop had recommended more humane treatment of the Minnesota Sioux. Lincoln promptly asked the secretary of the interior to investigate, which he did and suggested numerous reforms. The president told a friend that Whipple "came here the other day and talked with me about the rascality of this Indian business until I felt it down to my boots." In reply to Whipple's appeal, Lincoln characteristically recounted a story: "Bishop, a man thought that monkeys could pick cotton better than negroes could because they were quicker and their fingers smaller. He turned a lot of them into his cotton field, but he found that it took two overseers to watch one monkey. It needs more than one honest man to watch one Indian agent." He pledged that "[i]f we get through this war, and if I live, *this Indian system shall be reformed*."[82] Similarly, in the winter of 1863–1864, he told Joseph La Barge, a steamboat captain who protested against corrupt government Indian agents, "wait until

I get this Rebellion off my hands, and I will take up this question and see that justice is done the Indian."[83] To Father John Beason, a noted Indian clergyman, he said "that as soon as the war was settled his attention should be given to the Indians and it should *not cease until justice* to their and my satisfaction was secured."[84] In his 1862 annual message to Congress, Lincoln urged that it change the system. "With all my heart I thank you for your reccommendation to have our whole Indian system reformed," Whipple wrote the president. "It is a stupendous piece of wickedness and as we fear God ought to be changed." Though Lincoln did not live to see his recommendation implemented, he gave a significant boost to the movement that eventually overthrew the corrupt system.[85]

In 1864, Lincoln pardoned two dozen of the 264 Sioux who, after being spared the death penalty, had been incarcerated. That same year he intervened to spare the life of Pocatello, chief of a Shoshoni band in Utah.

Fighting Joe: Replacing Burnside with Hooker

On the momentous first day of 1863, Lincoln had more on his mind than the Emancipation Proclamation: he must decide what to do about the demoralized Army of the Potomac. Exacerbating his anxiety for that army was fear that Union forces in the West might also suffer defeat. He had good reason to be apprehensive, for on December 29, General William T. Sherman led a disastrous assault at Chickasaw Bluffs, a few miles north of the Confederate bastion of Vicksburg on the Mississippi River, and two days later, Confederates recaptured the port of Galveston, Texas, which they held for the rest of the war.

News of those two setbacks arrived on January 12, which D. W. Bartlett called "the bluest day I have ever seen in Washington." He explained that it was not merely the defeats in Mississippi and Texas that caused "the almost universal feeling of discouragement." Intensifying the gloom was "the fact that we have had such a series of reverses, that the northern democracy everywhere seems to be rising against the government, certainly against the administration." Moreover, "the impression is now rapidly gaining ground that the leaders of the democracy and of the rebellion have some kind of an understanding with each other."[86]

The one bright spot in the West occurred at Stone's River, Tennessee, where on December 31, Confederates under Braxton Bragg attacked the Army of the Cumberland, led by General William S. ("Old Rosy") Rosecrans. The battle raged for three days, during which the White House was, as Nicolay put it, "in a state of feverish anxiety."[87] If Rosecrans had been defeated, the effect on Northern morale would have been catastrophic. But at Stone's River, the Union was not defeated. Although the outcome was hardly a resounding victory, by January 2 Bragg had at least been driven from the field. (Later, when the president referred to the battle as a triumph, Grant said that Stone's River was not exactly a victory. "A few such fights would have ruined us," he remarked.)[88] Nonetheless, it was with vast relief that Lincoln congratulated Old Rosy: "God bless you, and all with you!" Months later he wrote Rosecrans: "you gave us a hard earned victory which, had there been a defeat instead, the nation could scarcely have lived over." Rosecrans's success had checked "a dangerous sentiment which was spreading in the North."[89] A year after the battle, the president, still cognizant of the importance of that battle, told James A. Garfield that the nation was "deeply indebted" to Rosecrans "for its salvation from almost fatal disaster," for if "that battle had been lost it is difficult to see where our fortunes would have landed." It was "*one* of the most if not the *most* important props of support the country" had in the war so far.[90]

In the East, Burnside, prodded by Halleck, intended to move against the enemy on December 31. Two days earlier, however, a pair of his subordinate generals, John Newton and John Cochrane, hastened to the White House to protest against that plan. In response, Lincoln wired Burnside: "I have good reason for saying you must not make a general movement of the army without letting me know."[91] When Burnside demanded an explanation, Lincoln told him of Newton and Cochrane's visit, without mentioning their names. In addition to those generals, Joseph Hooker and William B. Franklin opposed Burnside's plans. When Old Burn spelled out those plans to him, Lincoln remained noncommittal, merely saying he would discuss the matter with Stanton and Halleck.

The frustrated president took time from his busy schedule on New Year's Day to pen a blunt letter to the general-in-chief: "Gen. Burnside wishes to cross the Rappahannock with his army, but his Grand Division commanders all oppose the movement. If in such a difficulty as this you do not help, you fail me precisely in the point for which I sought your assistance. You know what Gen. Burnside's plan is; and it is my wish that you go with him to the ground, examine it as far as practicable, confer with the officers, getting their judgment, and ascertaining their temper, in a word, gather all the elements for forming a judgment of your own; and then tell Gen. Burnside that you *do* approve, or that you do *not* approve his plan. Your military skill is useless to me, if you will not do this." At long last the president was chastising Old Brains for refusing to do his job. Taking understandable umbrage, the general promptly submitted his resignation, which was rejected. To salve Halleck's hurt feelings, Lincoln retracted the letter, endorsing it: "Withdrawn, because considered harsh by Gen. Halleck."[92] It was indeed harsh, but it was fully justified. Halleck did finally urge Burnside to cross the Rappahannock and engage the enemy, emphasizing that "our first object was, not 'Richmond,' but the defeat or scattering of his army."[93]

Like Halleck, Burnside felt slighted and offered to resign because his division commanders had lost confidence in him. After reading the general's letter of resignation, Lincoln handed it back to him without comment. Burnside decided to launch yet another campaign and notified the administration; he also sent an undated letter of resignation to be used by the president whenever he saw fit. Lincoln urged him to be "cautious, and do not understand that the government, or country, is driving you. I do not yet see how I could profit by changing the command of the A[rmy of the] P[otomac] & if I did, I should not wish to do it by accepting the resignation of your commission."[94]

As discontent welled up within the ranks, Burnside prepared to send them across the Rappahannock once again. When he ordered them to do so on January 20, they promptly bogged down in a fierce rainstorm that persisted for three days. As the mud grew deeper, the advance—known as the "Mud March"—halted, and the army fell back to its camps. Hooker, ever the malcontent, openly criticized his commander. Burnside, fed up with such insubordination, lashed out, dismissing four generals (including Hooker, Newton, and Cochrane) and relieving five others.

Many thought it was Burnside who should be relieved. "I have no doubt that the President is as well convinced as I am that this Army will do nothing as it is," William P. Fessenden told his son, "but he has not force of character requisite for its improvement."[95] But in fact, Lincoln did have "the requisite force of character" to make the necessary change. On January 24, Burnside demanded that the president support his astounding order, though Lincoln had not been consulted about the dismissal of the four generals. When Old Burn and the president met again the next day, Lincoln announced that Hooker was to be the new commander of the Army of the Potomac. Burnside offered to resign his commission, but the president refused; instead he granted the general a one-month furlough and transferred him to the Department of the Ohio, where presumably he could do little harm.

Hooker had treated Burnside shabbily and was known as a hard drinker, chronic intriguer, indiscreet talker, compulsive womanizer, and reckless gambler. One officer described Hooker's headquarters as "a combination of barroom and brothel."[96] Nevertheless, Fighting Joe was an obvious choice to take charge of the Army of the Potomac. When the editor of the New York *Times* complained about his attempts to undermine Burnside, Lincoln replied: "That is all true. Hooker does talk badly, but the trouble is, he is stronger with the country today than any other man."[97] The other grand division commanders were unsuitable: William B. Franklin had been disgraced by his lackluster conduct at Fredericksburg, and the 66-year-old Edwin V. Sumner was too infirm. (Because the president knew that both of those generals resented Hooker and would probably not cooperate fully with him, he relieved them of their commands.) Moreover, Lincoln informed a friend of Franklin that the general's "loyalty is suspected."[98] Chase liked Hooker for his willingness to condemn McClellan and his purported sympathy with the Radicals. Lincoln made his decision without consulting Halleck or Stanton, both of whom favored George Gordon Meade, even though Hooker outranked him. While in California before the war, Halleck and Hooker had clashed, leading to strained relations. To accommodate Hooker, Lincoln accepted his request that he be allowed to report directly to the president without going through the general-in-chief.

Hooker had earned a reputation for "dash courage & skill."[99] He was, as Noah Brooks portrayed him, exceptionally handsome, "tall, shapely, well dressed, though not natty in appearance; his fair red and white complexion glowing with health, his bright blue eyes sparkling with intelligence and animation, and his auburn hair tossed back upon his well shaped head. His nose was aquiline, and the expression of his somewhat small mouth was one of much sweetness, though rather irresolute." Hooker, in Brooks's view, was "a gay cavalier, alert and confident, overflowing with animal spirits, and cheery as a boy."[100] A division commander thought that anyone "would feel like cheering when he rode by at the head of his staff."[101]

In naming Hooker, Lincoln read aloud to that general one of his most eloquent letters, a document illustrative of his deep paternal streak. Like a wise, benevolent father, he praised Hooker while gently chastising him for insubordination toward superior officers: "I have placed you at the head of the Army of the Potomac. Of course I have done this upon what appear to me to be sufficient reasons. And yet I think it best for you to know that there are some things in regard to which, I am not quite satisfied with you. I believe you to be a brave and a skilful soldier, which, of course, I like. I also believe you do not mix politics with your profession, in which you are right. You have confidence in yourself, which is a valuable, if not an indispensable quality. You are ambitious, which, within reasonable bounds, does good rather than harm. But I think that during Gen. Burnside's command of the Army, you have taken counsel of your ambition, and thwarted him as much as you could, in which you did a great wrong to the country, and to a most meritorious and honorable brother officer. I have heard, in such way as to believe it, of your recently saying that both the Army and the Government needed a Dictator. Of course it was not *for* this, but in spite of it, that I have given you the command. Only those generals who gain successes, can set up dictators. What I now ask of you is military success, and I will risk the dictatorship. The government will support you to the utmost of it's ability, which is neither more nor less than it has done and will do for all commanders. I much fear that the spirit which you have aided to infuse into the Army, of criticising their Commander, and withholding confidence from him, will now turn upon you. I shall assist you as far as I can, to put it down. Neither you, nor Napoleon, if he were alive again, could get any good out of an army, while such a spirit prevails in it." In closing, Lincoln urged Hooker to "beware of rashness. Beware of rashness, but with energy, and sleepless vigilance, go forward, and give us victories."[102]

Hooker thought it was "just such a letter as a father might write to a son. It is a beautiful letter, and, although I think he was harder on me than I deserved, I will say that I love the man who wrote it."[103] (As Nicolay remarked, "it would be difficult to find a severer piece of friendly criticism.")[104] Boastfully Hooker told some fellow officers: "After I have been to Richmond I shall have the letter published in the newspapers. It will be amusing."[105] Anson G. Henry, to whom Hooker showed the missive, thought it "ought to be printed in letters of gold," for it "breathes a spirit of Patriotic devotion to the Country and a spirit of frankness & candor worthy of Mr Lincoln's character, and is peculiarly his own."[106]

Navy Failure: The Repulse at Charleston

The appointment of Hooker boded well, but as he prepared for a spring offensive, the lack of military success discouraged Congress, the public, and the administration. In February, Nicolay complained to his fiancée that the Army of the Potomac "is for the present stuck in the mud, as it has been during nearly its whole existence. We hope however that it may yet do something, by accident at least, if not by design. I think we all doubt its ability to help in the great struggle more because the sort of fatality which has hitherto attended it, than by any just estimate of its strength and discipline."[107] A month later he told her apropos of the capture of one of General William

S. Rosecrans's brigades: "Of course carelessness or inefficiency must have been the cause. It is very hard not entirely to lose one's patience at this succession of adverse accidents which seems to have no end."[108] Along the Mississippi River, Union forces appeared stymied. "Grant's attempt to take Vicksburg looks to me very much like a total failure," Nicolay lamented in April. "At Port Hudson we are held at bay."[109]

Partially offsetting the dearth of success on the battlefield, New Hampshire and Connecticut voters provided political victories in March and April, respectively. To help raise funds for those campaigns, Lincoln summoned Thurlow Weed, who persuaded several New York merchants to contribute generously. The Connecticut election was especially noteworthy, for the Democrats had nominated a virulent Peace Democrat, Thomas H. Seymour, who lost to the incumbent William A. Buckingham by 2,000 votes.

Despite that encouraging development, the bleak military situation continued to torment Lincoln. At a Union mass meeting on March 31, he appeared pallid and emaciated. After receiving bad news from the front one night, he could not sleep. The next morning, Schuyler Colfax "found him looking more than usually pale and careworn." In reply to the congressman's query about his spirits, he exclaimed: "How willingly would I exchange places to-day, with the soldier who sleeps on the ground in the Army of the Potomac!"[110] One March day, Lincoln gave vent to his frustration with underperforming commanders. When told that Confederate guerrillas had captured General Edward H. Stoughton, he sarcastically remarked: "Oh, *that* doesn't trouble me. I can make a better Brigadier, any time, in five minutes; but it *did* worry me to have all those horses taken. *Why, sir, those horses cost us a hundred and twenty-five dollars a head!*"[111]

Lincoln was particularly exasperated by Admiral Samuel F. Du Pont's campaign against Charleston, which was the brainchild of Assistant Secretary of the Navy Gustavus V. Fox. Convinced that the ironclad monitors were invulnerable, Fox argued that a few of them could run past the forts guarding the entrance to Charleston harbor and compel the city to surrender. Ever since the failure of his plan to relieve Fort Sumter, Fox longed to redeem himself. He also wanted to erase memories of the navy's poor showing at Galveston in January. When he proposed to send an ironclad fleet against the storm center of secessionism, Lincoln responded enthusiastically. He was eager to have a success to offset the disaster at Fredericksburg and the failures at Vicksburg and Galveston; he did not want to wait until the May offensive in Virginia for something to bolster Northern morale. In September, Fox told Du Pont: "We must have Charleston. . . . The Pres't is most anxious and you know the people are," and five months later, he explained that "[f]inances, politics, foreign relations, all seem to ask for Charleston before Congress adjourns [on March 4], so as to shape legislation."[112] Du Pont raised legitimate objections, which Fox blithely ignored.

Lincoln was led to believe that the Charleston assault would take place that winter. At a meeting in mid-February, he was astounded to learn from General John G. Foster that the Charleston campaign would be a joint army–navy effort. The president had assumed it would be an all-navy affair. He was also dismayed by a request for further plating of the ironclads. Suspecting that the admiral had lost faith in his chances of success, Lincoln insisted that Fox visit South Carolina to confer with Du Pont. Fox begged off, arguing that he did not wish to injure the admiral's hypersensitive pride, but he did implore Du Pont not to let the army's plans disrupt the navy's. (The admiral had recommended that the army and navy carry out the assignment jointly; troops could capture some of the forts, reducing the gauntlet that the ships must run. When Fox and Welles vetoed that idea, Du Pont understandably wanted additional monitors.) Fox also informed the admiral that Lincoln and Welles *are very much struck with this programme*" and that the joint army–navy plan, involving a siege, "meets with disfavor."[113] A siege! Shades of Yorktown and McClellan's dithering on the Peninsula! Lincoln would not stand for it, nor would the public. On March 20, the president instructed Du Pont's aide to inform the admiral: "I fear neither you nor your officers appreciate the supreme importance to us of *Time*; the more you prepare, the more the enemy will be prepared."[114] A week later, he complained that "Du Pont was asking for one ironclad after another, as fast as they were built."[115]

Du Pont rightly thought that monitors were ill-suited for attacking forts, no matter how effective they proved in naval battles. The admiral regarded the administration with contempt: "our rulers . . . only think of a blow being struck to help them politically," he told his wife on the eve of battle. "They know no more what the bravest hearts here think and feel about the matter than, when alongside a comfortable fire, they remember a man outside in a snowdrift. The ignorance about Charleston is appalling on their part, for it is the only way to account for the impatience which seems to manifest itself."[116] Lincoln, he wrote, "is evidently a most *mediocre* man and unfortunately interferes a great deal with matters he should leave to his subordinates and agents."[117]

Fox's wildly optimistic prognostications helped overcome presidential doubts. More than once Lincoln told the assistant secretary of the navy: "I should be very anxious about this job if you did not feel so sure of your people being successful."[118] If Du Pont had more candidly shared his misgivings about the assault with the administration, the president may have reconsidered its viability. As it was, Lincoln feared that Du Pont lacked the aggressive spirit of an old salt like David Farragut, whose fleet had captured New Orleans a year earlier. To Welles, Lincoln pessimistically observed that Du Pont "is everlastingly asking for more . . . ironclads. He will do nothing with any. He has intelligence and system, and will maintain a good blockade" but "he will never take Sumter or get to Charleston."[119] Welles agreed, judging that the admiral "shrinks from responsibility, dreads the conflict he has sought, yet is unwilling that any other should undertake it, is afraid the reputation of Du Pont will suffer. This jeopardizes the whole—makes a botched thing of it."[120]

Lincoln instructed Du Pont to attack Charleston or, if he doubted his ability to succeed there, send his ironclads to assist in the Vicksburg campaign. Before the telegram reached Du Pont, however, he had assaulted Charleston on April 7 with eight monitors and a huge armored frigate, the *New Ironsides*. After a furious encounter of little more than half an hour, they withdrew. One monitor, the *Keokuk*, was sunk. As Lincoln awaited news of the assault, he was skeptical. "What will you wager that half our iron-clads are at the bottom of Charleston Harbor?" he asked Noah Brooks. "The people will expect big things when they hear of this; but it is too late—*too late*!" he exclaimed.[121]

On April 12, when he learned of the Union repulse, Lincoln told journalists at the Navy Department that the news displeased him, then left the building looking demoralized and unstrung. He had not supposed that the ironclads would quit "after a fight of forty minutes," but assumed they would continue the campaign for days or weeks.[122] Summing up his disappointment, Lincoln observed that "the six months' preparation for Charleston was a very long grace for the thin plate of soup served in the two hours of fighting."[123] He said "his only consolation was extracted from the thought that it proved that the Northern harbors were capable of being more quickly made defensible against foreign attack than had been supposed."[124] On April 16, Nicolay expressed what his boss was probably thinking: the young secretary was puzzled by Du Pont's decision to withdraw so abruptly, "for after all the damage done us was very slight (the Keokuk being a comparatively weak vessel, not built on the Monitor plan.) To counterbalance the sinking of our ship and the trifling derangement of some of the Monitors, we had tested their comparative invulnerability and had found and secured possession of a safe and important anchorage inside Charleston Bar, from which we could greatly lessen the line of blockade, and more important than all it substantially commanded a part at least of Morris Island enabling us to gain a lodgment there by landing troops, and beginning a series of siege operations that might of themselves render Fort Sumpter untenable. This advantage was partially thrown away by the subsequent withdrawal of the whole iron-clad fleet, leaving the enemy undisturbed in the work of erecting new batteries, which they began, even before we left, to protect that only weak point in their defences."[125]

Lincoln conferred with Halleck about continuing the Charleston campaign, asking "why it was not possible to land a strong infantry force upon Morris Island, under cover of the gunboats, to co-operate with the navy in the attack upon the works at Cummings Point." Then "Sumter could be reduced, and, by gradual approaches, we could get within range of the city." The general-in-chief pooh-poohed the idea, insisting that troops "could do nothing after they got there." Even though Fox seconded Lincoln's proposal, Halleck continued to demur. According to Noah Brooks, "though he treated the suggestions of Lincoln with respect," Halleck "evidently entertained a profound contempt for his generalship."[126] (On another occasion, when "absolutely insulted" by Halleck, Lincoln allegedly "resolved to [re]move" him for such an "act of personal indignity." But he curbed his temper and retained the general's services, for he saw no suitable replacement.)[127]

Lincoln ordered Du Pont to hold his position inside the Charleston bar and prevent the erection of more Confederate batteries at the harbor's entrance; both the admiral and General Hunter were to renew the attack, which, in the president's words, should "be a real one, (though not a desperate one)."[128] By the time Lincoln's telegram reached Du Pont, the ironclads had already withdrawn.

The thin-skinned admiral, unwilling to renew the assault, took offense at what he considered the president's implied censure and asked to be relieved. As Lincoln considered this request, he received a stout defense of Du Pont from John Hay, who was on a visit to South Carolina. In early May, Congressman Henry Winter Davis met with the president, who had kind words for Du Pont. As Davis reported to the admiral, Lincoln said that "that no one stood higher than you with him and the department; that you were the idol of the navy and the favorite of Mr. Welles and enjoyed their full confidence; neither had ever felt the slightest abatement of it; they knew you had done all that in your opinion was possible, and they had never dropped a word of censure or discontent respecting you."[129]

Lincoln's attempt to placate the touchy admiral failed; Du Pont would not be consoled. Eager to salvage his reputation, Du Pont recklessly lashed out at critics, thus helping to scuttle his career. A letter he wrote to the Navy Department on April 16 seemed to Lincoln to disparage his administration. In June, Welles accepted the admiral's request to be relieved. Months later, when Du Pont denounced the navy secretary, Welles in reply enumerated the admiral's many offenses. Privately he called Du Pont "an intriguer, selfish[,] aspiring and disappointed."[130]

Relief: Visiting Hooker's Army

While the drama at Charleston was playing itself out, Hooker planned a spring offensive for the Army of the Potomac. "There is a good deal expected of him [Hooker] & hoped from him," David Davis observed. "He is the last chance."[131] In early April, Lincoln accompanied his wife and several others, including Noah Brooks, on a visit to the general to learn more about his plans. Seward had intended to join them, but Mrs. Lincoln objected, and so he remained in Washington.

As was his wont on such excursions, Lincoln inspected the troops. While at a grand infantry review near Falmouth, he returned the salute of officers by merely touching his hat but removed that item as he passed by enlisted men. A soldier observed that the president "looked care-worn and anxious, and we thought there must be a '*heap of trouble on the old man's mind.*'"[132] To others he seemed "very thin and pale, so much so that many people remarked that there was a fair chance of Hamlin being our President soon."[133] One soldier who was especially moved by Lincoln's appearance wrote that he "looks poorly . . . thin and in bad health . . . he is to all outward appearances much careworn, and anxiety is fast wearing him out, poor man; I could but pity as I looked at him, and remembered the weight of responsibility resting upon his burdened mind; *what* an ordeal he has passed through, and *what is yet before him*! All I can say is, *Poor Abe!*"[134] Lincoln cut a comical figure as he inspected the Fifth Corps, sitting astride a pony so small that his toes almost scraped the ground. Because he did not strap down his pantlegs, they rode up exposing long underwear. His black suit was entirely mud-spattered. But, as a trooper from Indiana remarked, the "fact that Mr. Lincoln is a very awkward horseman did not lessen the Soldiers admiration for him as a man and as president."[135]

Lincoln asked a corps commander as they watched a grand review, "what do you suppose will become of all these men when the war is over?" The general was heartened that a leader spoke about the end of the war.[136] As he rode in an army ambulance to another review, Lincoln asked the driver, who was profanely urging on the mules: "Excuse me, my friend, are you an Episcopalian?" The startled teamster replied that he was a Methodist. "Well, I thought you must be an Episcopalian, because you swear just like Governor Seward, who is a churchwarden," the president drolly remarked. The driver used no more profanity for the rest of the way.[137]

At hospitals Lincoln shook hands with the wounded men. Noah Brooks reported that as he "moved softly from between the beds, his face shining with sympathy and his voice often low with emotion," many patients "shed a tear of sad pleasure as they returned the kind salutation of the President and gazed after him with a new glow upon their faces." To Brooks it was no wonder that "a thundering cheer burst from the long lines of men" as Lincoln rode past them on his way back to headquarters.[138]

Pardoner-in-Chief: Dealing with Condemned Soldiers

Lincoln's merciful treatment of troops condemned to death by courts-martial increased his popularity with the army. On September 4, 1861, Private William Scott, an unsophisticated Vermont country boy who had fallen asleep on sentry duty, was sentenced to die before a firing squad in five days. When Lincoln received appeals for clemency from the officers of Scott's regiment as well as from leading Washington clergymen, he assured them that he would consider the matter carefully. The death sentence was widely criticized in the city. According to a journalist, "the general expression was that to shoot the soldier would be a terrible mistake. Mutineers have been let off with a term at Tortugas as laborers. Rebels captured, fighting against the Government, are released on parole, but a zealous soldier, for sleeping at his post, must receive the extreme penalty. It was felt that to carry it into execution would at once stop all recruiting."[139] The day before the scheduled execution, McClellan, who had approved the sentence, issued an order announcing that "the President of the United States has expressed a wish that as this is the first condemnation to death in this army for this crime, mercy may be extended to the criminal. This fact, viewed in connection with the inexperience of the condemned as a soldier, his previous good conduct and general good character, and the urgent entreaties made in his behalf, have determined the Major General commanding to grant the pardon so earnestly prayed for."[140] The press lauded this decision as "a high tribute to the great goodness of our excellent President."[141]

Seven months later Scott was killed in action. In his last moments, the lad enjoined a comrade to tell Lincoln "that I thank him for his generous regard for me, when a poor soldier under the sentence of death. Tell him that I died for my country with six bullets shot into me, by my enemies and his enemies and my country's enemies. And oh, tell him, that I hope that God will guide and direct him and take care of him in all the scenes through which he may be called to pass. Yes, God bless President Lincoln for he will one day give him victory over all our enemies."[142]

Lincoln's willingness to reprieve death sentences for sleeping sentinels, deserters, and others became legendary, and for good reason. When Massachusetts Congressman Henry L. Dawes urged him to spare the life of a 19-year-old constituent guilty of desertion, the president replied "that the War Department insisted that the severest punishment for desertion was absolutely necessary to save the army from demoralization." He added: "But when I think of these mere lads, who had never before left their homes, enlisting in the enthusiasm of the moment for a war of which they had no conception and then in the camp or on the battle field a thousand miles from home, longing for its rest and safety, I have so much sympathy for him that I cannot condemn him to die for forgetting the obligations of the soldier in the longing for home life. There is death and woe enough in this war without such a sacrifice."[143]

One day in 1863, after spending six hours with Lincoln reviewing court-martial proceedings, John Hay confided to his diary: "I was amused at the eagerness with which the President caught at any fact which would justify him in saving the life of a condemned soldier. . . . Cases of cowardice he was specially averse to punishing with death. He said it would frighten the poor devils too terribly, to shoot them. On the case of a soldier who had once deserted & reenlisted he endorsed, 'Let him fight instead of shooting him.' One fellow who had deserted & escaped after conviction into Mexico, he sentenced, saying 'We will condemn him as they used to sell hogs in Indiana, as they run.'"[144] Lincoln called such sessions "butcher days."[145] Late one day at the military telegraph office, he said: "To-morrow night I shall have a terrible headache." When asked why, he sadly replied: "To-morrow is hangman's day and I shall have to act upon death sentences."[146] Joseph Holt, judge advocate general of the army, recalled that when considering courts-martial cases, Lincoln "shrank with evident pain from even the idea of shedding human blood. . . . In every case he always leaned to the side of mercy. His constant desire was to save life."[147]

Lincoln also extended clemency to over 300 prisoners convicted by civil courts. He especially favored those who had served in the military, who had spouses or sons in the service, or who indicated a desire to join the army. Among the most common beneficiaries of presidential mercy were the young, those who had women as intercessors pleading their cases, those who appeared penitent, and those who displayed "good conduct."[148]

Army officers often complained that presidential pardons and reprieves undermined discipline. When chided for lacking the sternness of an Andrew Jackson, Lincoln replied: "I am just as God made me, and cannot change."[149] A political ally observed him one day grant a pardon in response to a mother's plea on behalf of her son. After she left, the president remarked: "Perhaps I have done wrong, but at all events I have made that poor woman happy."[150] Lincoln's mercy also paid political dividends, for members of Congress felt grateful to the president whenever he reprieved a constituent, an act that predisposed the beneficiary, his family, and his friends to vote Republican.

Though Lincoln's mercy was legendary, it had limits. Joseph Holt reported that there "was only one class of crimes I always found him prompt to punish—a crime which occurs more or less frequently about all armies—namely, outrages upon women. He never hesitated to approve the sentence in these cases."[151] The president also showed little compassion for thieves, murderers, and Confederate recruiters plying their trade in the North. Hay noted that the president "was only merciless in cases where meanness or cruelty were shown."[152] Over the course of the war, he approved 267 death sentences.

In rejecting pleas for mercy, Lincoln sometimes displayed anger. When a man and a woman came seeking a pardon for a convicted spy, he listened to their story with ever-dwindling patience. He finally interrupted, exclaiming sternly: "There is not a word of this true! and you know it as well as I do. He *was* a spy, he has been a spy, he ought to have been hanged as a spy. From the fuss you folks are making about him, who are none too loyal, I am convinced he was more valuable to the cause of the enemy than we have yet suspected. You are the third set of persons that has been to me to get him pardoned. Now I'll tell you what—if any of you come bothering me any more about his being set at liberty, that will decide his fate. I will have him hanged, as he deserves to be. You ought to bless your stars that he got off with a whole neck; and if you don't want so see him hanged as high as Haman, don't you come to me again about him."[153] When asked by a Presbyterian minister to pardon a deserter, Lincoln snapped: "Not a word more. . . . I can do nothing in the matter. I will not interfere. You should not come here trying to undermine the morale of my armies. Those increasing desertions must be stopped. If you had stopped to think, you would not have come on this foolish errand. So go back to Pittsburgh and try to be a more loyal citizen." Eventually, however, he relented and pardoned the soldier.[154]

Lincoln's willingness to issue pardons sometimes led to clashes with Stanton. A notable example of such friction occurred when Henry L. Dawes appealed on behalf of a jailed quartermaster who was dying of consumption, according to a statement signed by two physicians.

"Do you believe that statement?" Lincoln asked.

"Certainly," replied the Massachusetts congressman.

"Then say so here," the president instructed, pointing to the back of the document alleging that the prisoner was terminally ill. Lincoln then endorsed it: "Let this man be discharged."

"Neither you nor I can afford to let that man die in prison," said the president, who agreed to deliver the document to Stanton.

The next day, however, Lincoln rebuffed a similar plea by a Representative from Michigan, explaining that he had issued a pardon at Dawes's request and just taken it to Stanton. The gruff war secretary refused to comply, arguing that the prisoner was "the biggest rascal in the army" and that his appeal was obviously bogus. "I begin to think I haven't much influence with this Administration," the president quipped.

When informed of this exchange, Dawes hastened to the White House and urged that a messenger be sent to the prison to investigate Stanton's charge. Lincoln agreed, saying that if Dawes was willing to take the risk, so would he, for "he had rather two well men should escape through deception, than to live in doubt whether he had not let one man die of consumption in a cell, rather than believe his story." The prisoner was released and lived many years thereafter, confirming Stanton's suspicion.[155]

First Lady: Visiting the Front and Hospitals

At Falmouth, Mrs. Lincoln visited hospitals and unostentatiously distributed small gifts. In Washington, too, she often made "Good Samaritan" calls on the wounded.

On one occasion, Lincoln gave her $1,000 out of his own pocket to buy Christmas turkeys for the hospitalized troops and helped her distribute them. She won praise for "the generous devotion with which she has tenderly cared for the sick and wounded soldiers." Pro-Confederate elements in the capital might sneer at her as the "hospital matron," but Unionists applauded "her errands of mercy to those brave men who are cheered by her visits and benefited by her liberal donations."[156]

During this visit to the front, Mrs. Lincoln became enraged when she heard that at a post-review collation which she had not attended, several generals' wives, among them the beautiful spouse of General Felix Salm-Salm, had kissed her husband after obtaining permission to do so from General Daniel Sickles. The notoriously jealous First Lady blamed Sickles for that indiscretion, and for a quarter of an hour she berated the president, who replied: "But, mother, hear me."

"Don't mother me, and as for General Sickles, he will hear what I think of him and his lady guests," came the indignant reply. "It was well for him that I was not there at the time."

As the First Couple returned to Washington, escorted by Sickles, the president sought to reduce tension in the social atmosphere. "I never knew until last night that you were a very pious man," Lincoln remarked to the general, who protested that he merited no such description. "Not at all," quipped the president. "Mother says you are the greatest Psalmist in the army. She says you are more than a Psalmist, you are a Salm-Salmist." The pun had the desired effect.[157]

The Spring Offensive

Although Lincoln had originally planned to stay at Falmouth for only one day, he enjoyed himself so much that he remained nearly a week in order to inspect each corps. He was relieved to escape from the capital and its clamorous politicians. Yet no matter what he did, he told Noah Brooks, "nothing could touch the tired spot within, which was all tired."[158] He expressed a wish to General Egbert Viele that "George Washington or some of those old patriots were here in my place so that I could have a little rest."[159]

But Lincoln did not visit Falmouth merely in quest of relaxation. He also went over plans for the upcoming campaign with Hooker and his corps commanders, and was disturbed by a discussion about whether to get to Richmond by going around Lee's right flank or his left. So he penned a memorandum noting that the presence of Lee's army on the opposite bank of the Rappahannock meant that there was "*no* eligible route for us into Richmond." Therefore Hooker should consider that "our prime object is the enemies' army in front of us, and not with, or about, Richmond—at all, unless it be incidental to the main object." Since the Army of the Potomac had shorter supply lines than the enemy, "we can . . . fret him more than he can us." So it was decided that Hooker should not attack Lee frontally but rather "continually harrass and menace him, so that he shall have no leisure, no safety in sending away detachments. If he weakens himself, then pitch into him."[160] This advice was in keeping with Lincoln's approach to the war in the eastern theater: the goal should be the destruction of the enemy's army, not the conquest of territory.

Anson G. Henry, who accompanied his old friend Lincoln to Falmouth, observed the generals and the president conferring, and was struck by Hooker's "most exalted opinion of Mr Lincoln's sound judgment & practical sense." He predicted that Fighting Joe would "act in accordance with his suggestions in good faith for the reason that they meet his own views in the main."[161] The general, however, thought Lincoln was "not much of a soldier" and, referring to him, Halleck, and Stanton, said that it was "a preposterous irregularity" to have "three heads of military affairs at the Capital." When that trio arrived at Falmouth, Hooker feared that they would make some last-minute suggestions just as he was completing his arrangements.[162] The general told Lincoln that "he would not submit to being interfered with."[163]

Disturbed by Hooker's statements which were prefaced by such remarks as "When I get to Richmond" and "After we have taken Richmond," Lincoln said that the general's overconfidence depressed him.[164] When he learned of Hooker's boast that after he had captured the Confederate capital he would publish Lincoln's letter advising him to beware of rashness, the president exclaimed: "Poor Hooker! I am afraid he is incorrigible."[165]

Lincoln had observed evidence of this cockiness earlier. In the summer of 1861, Generals Scott and McClellan had thwarted his intention to give Hooker a regimental command. But shortly after First Bull Run, the president overruled them, for he admired a veteran like Hooker who had won three brevets in the Mexican War and who traveled all the way from California to offer his services. "I thought I'd take the responsibility, and try the fellow," he said. He gave him a chance after Hooker, then a lieutenant colonel, called at the White House and tearfully declared: "I was at Bull Run the other day, Mr. President, and it is no vanity or boasting in me to say that I am a — sight better General than you, Sir, had on that field!" Lincoln recalled that Hooker's "eye was steady and clear, his manner not half so confident as his words, and altogether he had the air of a man of sense and intelligence who thoroughly believed in himself, and who would at least try to make his words good. I was impressed with him, and rising out of my chair, walked up to him and putting my hand on his shoulder, said: 'Colonel, not Lieut. Col. Hooker, stay! I have use for you, and a regiment for you to command!'" Hooker's subsequent record won the president's respect. "In every position in which he had been put," Lincoln declared, "Gen. Hooker has equaled the expectations which his self-confidence excited."[166] Just before he launched his offensive in late April, that cocksure quality led Hooker to state, "My plans are perfect, and when I start to carry them out, may God have mercy on General Lee, for I will have none."[167]

On April 10, Lincoln's last day at Falmouth, he spoke with Hooker and his senior corps commander, Darius N. Couch. Evidently fearing that they might repeat McClellan's blunder at Antietam, Lincoln said: "I want to impress upon you two gentlemen, in your next fight, put in all of your men."[168] If the president feared that Hooker might be too timid, he also feared his recklessness. "They told me in Washington to hurry up General Hooker," he remarked during this visit, "but when he once gets started there will be more necessity for treading on the tail of his coat to keep him from moving too rashly."[169]

Back at the White House, Lincoln was in high spirits, but he worried about the slow progress of George Stoneman's cavalry, which had been ordered to cut Lee's supply lines. On April 15, the president expressed "considerable uneasiness" to Hooker, who notified him that heavy rains had delayed Stoneman. "The rain and mud, of course, were to be calculated upon," Lincoln sternly observed. "Gen. S. is not moving rapidly enough to make the expedition come to any thing. He has now been out three days, two of which were unusually fine weather, and all three without hindrance from the enemy, and yet he is not twentyfive miles from where he started. To reach his point, he still has sixty to go; another river, the Rapidan, to cross, and will be hindered by the enemy. By arithmetic, how many days will it take him to do it? I do not know that any better can be done, but I greatly fear it is another failure already. Write me often. I am very anxious."[170] When Hooker replied that the weather could not be controlled and that Stoneman had done nothing worthy of censure, Lincoln hastened to Falmouth with Halleck and conferred with the commander on April 19. (No record of their conference survives.)

The rains continued, upsetting Hooker's plans. At just that time, one Francis L. Capen called at the White House offering his services as a "Certified Meteorologist & Expert in Computing the Changes of the Weather." On April 28, Lincoln scornfully endorsed Capen's letter, in which the weatherman claimed to be able to save thousands of lives and millions of dollars: "It seems to me Mr. Capen knows nothing about the weather, in advance. He told me three days ago that it would not rain again till the 30th. of April or 1st. of May. It is raining now & has been for ten hours. I can not spare any more time to Mr. Capen."[171] (Crackpot inventors annoyed Lincoln regularly. One sought his assistance in persuading the War Department to use his "universal solvent," which could dissolve anything. After patiently listening to this gentleman extol the virtues of his product, Lincoln deflated him with a simple question: "What do you propose to keep it in?")[172]

Another unwelcome caller in late April asked Lincoln for a pass to Richmond. "My dear sir," replied the president, "I would be most happy to oblige you if my passes were respected; but the fact is I have within the last two years given passes to more than two hundred and fifty thousand men to go to Richmond, and not one of them has got there yet in any legitimate way."[173]

Hooker revised his plans ingeniously, proposing to send some troops against Fredericksburg as a feint, throw most of his forces across the river well above the town, and menace Lee's communications. That would force the Confederates to abandon their strongly entrenched position and either retreat or fight in the open, where superior Union numbers and artillery could prevail. Upon receiving Hooker's dispatch about this new strategy, Lincoln replied with characteristic modesty: "While I am anxious, please do not suppose I am impatient, or waste a moment's thought on me, to your own hindrance, or discomfort."[174]

As Hooker poised to strike, Lincoln appeared optimistic and of good cheer. He told Robert C. Winthrop that "he had lost no flesh, notwithstanding all his cares, & that he weighed about 180 pounds still."[175] D. W. Bartlett reported that the president had "seen his hours of despondency" but now was "hopeful and courageous. This is worth half an army to the country and the cause. A bold courageous president at this crisis of our affairs is everything to us."[176]

Lincoln's hopes were soon dashed, for Lee did not cooperate with Hooker's plans. Instead of waiting on the defensive, he boldly attacked, dividing his numerically inferior force and smashed the Army of the Potomac between May 2 and 6 at Chancellorsville. As the fighting raged, Lincoln told Welles that "he had a feverish anxiety to get the facts" and "was constantly up and down, for nothing reliable came from the front."[177] On May 3, Hooker received a concussion when a shell struck a column of the Chancellor House as he leaned against it. When informed of this injury, the anxious president wired Hooker's chief of staff, Daniel Butterfield, asking: "Where is Gen. Hooker? Where is Sedgwick? where is Stoneman?" Butterfield replied vaguely that Lee was between Hooker and Sedgwick and that Stoneman had not been heard from.[178] Impatiently, the president asked about the generals: "Was Sickles in it? Was Couch in it? Was Reynolds in it? Where is Reynolds? Is Sedgwick fighting Lee's rear? or fighting in the entrenchments around Fredericksburg?"[179] Butterfield could not say. "We know very little as yet as to what was attempted, or what has been accomplished," Nicolay reported that day. "For the present we are obliged to content ourselves in patience, with a silent prayer for the success of our arms."[180]

Nicolay's prayer went unanswered. As the fighting continued, Lincoln had to rely on newspapers for information. After his concussion, Hooker halted and allowed Lee to seize the initiative. On May 6, the Union army retreated back across the Rappahannock, having taken 17,000 casualties to Lee's 13,000. The only consolation to Union forces was the death of Stonewall Jackson, who was accidentally shot by his own men. (When John W. Forney published kind remarks about the fallen Confederate chieftain, Lincoln wrote the journalist: "I honor you for your generosity to one who, though contending against us in a guilty cause, was, nevertheless, a gallant man. Let us forget his sins over his fresh made grave.")[181]

When Lincoln finally received a dispatch reporting the defeat, he was stunned and turned pale as a corpse. "Had a thunderbolt fallen upon the President he could not have been more overwhelmed," Noah Brooks told the readers of the Sacramento *Union*. "One newly risen from the dead could not have looked more ghostlike." At the president's request, Brooks read the fateful document aloud. With tears streaming down his ashen face, Lincoln paced the room exclaiming: "My God! my God! What will the country say! What will the country say!" To Brooks, Lincoln never seemed "so broken, so dispirited." He was inconsolable.[182] On May 7, John Sherman reported that Lincoln "is subject to the deepest depression of spirits amounting to Monomania. He looked upon Hooker as his 'last card.'"[183] To Bishop Charles Gordon Ames, Lincoln sadly confessed: "I am the loneliest man in America."[184]

As Lincoln anticipated, the country had a lot to say about the defeat. Along with Hooker, Stanton, and Halleck, the president received harsh criticism. Wendell Phillips told a New York audience: "Lincoln and Halleck,—they sit in Washington, commanders-in-chief, exercising that disastrous influence which even a Bonaparte would exercise on a battle, if he tried to fight it by telegraph a hundred miles distant."[185] Phillips's contempt for Lincoln shone through his assertion that a "man for

President would have put down the rebellion in six months!"[186] (After reading that speech, Henry W. Bellows asked a friend: "Don[']t such loose talk, however eloquent & true on general principles, do a great deal of harm, by preventing people from seeing that it is government of law & usage, not an ideal kingdom, we live in?")[187] Joseph Medill called Halleck "the most detested and odious man in the Administration," an "inveterate, proslavery, westpoint fogy—universally hated in and out of the army." According to Medill, it was "the daily wonder of the whole country" that Lincoln "clings to that odious old Blunderhead."[188] When told that Halleck "is universally execrated by the lay people," Lincoln replied: "Well, I guess that's about so. I don't know that he has any friends, and so I think that a man who has no friends needs to be taken care of."[189]

Lincoln was particularly upset because Hooker had not committed all his men to the fight. The president believed that if Fighting Joe had reinforced General John Sedgwick when Lee dangerously split his army, he might have won a great victory and ended the war. Lincoln also opined that if Hooker "had been killed by the shot which knocked over the pillar that stunned him, we should have been successful."[190]

Immediately on hearing the bad news, Lincoln hurried to visit the Army of the Potomac. There he was charitable to Hooker, remarking "that the result was in his judgment most unfortunate" but "that he did not blame anyone," for he "believed everyone had done all in his power" and "that the disaster was one that could not be helped." Yet he "thought its effect, both at home and abroad, would be more serious and injurious than any previous act of the war."[191] Upon arriving at Hooker's head-quarters on May 7, Lincoln handed the general a letter asking: "What next? If possible I would be very glad of another movement early enough to give us some benefit from the fact of the enemies communications being broken, but neither for this reason or any other, do I wish anything done in desperation or rashness. An early movement would also help to supersede the bad moral effect of the recent one, which is sure to be considerably injurious. Have you already in your mind a plan wholly, or partially formed? If you have, prossecute it without interference from me. If you have not, please inform me, so that I, incompetent as I may be, can try [to] assist in the formation of some plan for the Army."[192] Fighting Joe promptly replied that he wanted to stay on the Rappahannock and renew the campaign once his army was again prepared to advance. Lincoln returned to Washington, satisfied that the troops had "suffered no defeat or loss of *esprit du corps*, but have made a change in the programme (a forced one, to be sure) which promises just as well as did the opening of the campaign."[193]

On May 13, Hooker wrote the president that even though the enemy now outnumbered him, he would attack the next day. Lincoln, doubtless reminded of McClellan's overestimate of Confederate troop strength, summoned the general to Washington where he handed him yet another letter, this time pointing out that the Confederates were no longer as vulnerable as they had been a week earlier and that therefore it "does not now appear probable to me that you can gain any thing by an early renewal of the attempt to cross the Rappahannock. I therefore shall not complain, if you do no more, for a time, than to keep the enemy at bay, and out of other mischief, by menaces and occasional cavalry raids, if practicable; and to put your own army in good condition again. Still, if in your own clear judgment, you can renew the attack successfully, I do not mean to restrain you. Bearing upon this last point, I must tell you I have some painful intimations that some of your corps and Division Commanders are not giving you their entire confidence. This would be ruinous, if true; and you should therefore, first of all, ascertain the real facts beyond all possibility of doubt."[194]

Hooker's immediate subordinates were indeed complaining about him just as he had complained about Burnside. Lincoln's prediction that "the spirit which you have aided to infuse into the Army, of criticising their Commander, and withholding confidence from him, will now turn upon you" was proving accurate. The commander of the Twelfth Corps, Henry W. Slocum, and Darius N. Couch of the Second Corps (who thought Hooker lacked the "weight of character" necessary in an army commander) organized a revolt against Fighting Joe which failed when Meade of the Fifth Corps, their choice to head the army, refused to cooperate. Daniel Sickles, an old friend of Hooker's, was the only corps commander still loyal to him.

Despite these complaints, Lincoln hesitated to replace Hooker, for he liked him personally and thought it only fair to give him another chance. When General John Reynolds denounced Fighting Joe, Lincoln replied "that he was not disposed to throw away a gun because it missed fire once" and that "he would pick the lock and try it again."[195] Hooker begged the president not to shelve him as he had McClellan. "I am satisfied with your conduct," Lincoln assured him. "I tried McClellan twenty times; I see no reason why I can't try you at least twice."[196] In fairness to Hooker, it must be said that the corps commanders of the Army of the Potomac were as responsible as their commander for the defeat at Chancellorsville.

Nevertheless, Lincoln made a mistake in not replacing Hooker immediately after Chancellorsville. Evidence suggests that the president may have decided to choose a new commander, in consultation with Halleck and Stanton, but for some reason hesitated. Perhaps he feared that public confidence would be shaken if he seemed inordinately hasty in selecting the fifth man within a year to head the Army of the Potomac. That rapid turnover disturbed some Republicans, including an official in the Pacific Northwest who reported that many of the "truest and staunchest Union-men hereabouts, begin to doubt Mr Lincolns capacity. . . . How can he suffer himself to be made a perfect weather cock, in the hands of others, is more than I can account for, but certain it is, he makes too many changes in our commanding Generals. . . . The Union cause receives a *stub* every time Mr Lincoln shows his vacillating disposition, by the removal of a Commanding General."[197] A Pennsylvanian also found that "this frequent changing of commanders has destroyed confidence."[198]

Further undermining confidence in the administration was the victory of conservative forces in Washington municipal elections on June 1. "Nothing could better illustrate the shambling management of the President and his incongruous Cabinet," observed a correspondent of the Boston *Commonwealth*. Lincoln "said he wouldn't lift a hand on either side" and thus helped ensure that candidates hostile to emancipation would triumph.[199]

Invasion: Lee Strikes Northward Again

On June 2, when asked if a Confederate raid was imminent, Lincoln replied "that all indications were that there would be nothing of the sort, and that an advance by the rebels could not possibly take place so as to put them on this side of the Rappahannock, *unless Hooker was very much mistaken, and was to be again out-generaled.*"[200] But in fact, shortly thereafter, Lee began his second invasion of the North, again using the Shenandoah Valley as a corridor into Maryland as he had done nine months earlier. On June 5, when Hooker asked permission to attack the Confederate rear at Fredericksburg, Lincoln urged him instead to concentrate on the main body of the Army of Northern Virginia, not its tail: "in case you find Lee coming to the North of the Rappahannock, I would by no means cross to the South of it. If he should leave a rear force at Fredericksburg, tempting you to fall upon it, it would fight in intrenchments, and have you at disadvantage, and so, man for man, worst you at that point, while his main force would in some way be getting an advantage of you Northward." Using vivid rustic imagery, he warned against "any risk of being entangled upon the river, like an ox jumped half over a fence, and liable to be torn by dogs, front and rear, without a fair chance to gore one way or kick the other." If the Confederates crossed the river, Hooker should "keep on the same side & fight him, or act on the defence, according as might be my estimate of his strength relatively to my own." Modestly, the president closed, saying: "these are mere suggestions which I desire to be controlled by the judgment of yourself and Gen. Halleck."[201]

Ignoring this advice, Hooker on June 10 proposed to forget about Lee and march on Richmond. Lincoln, who thought "it would be a very poor exchange to give Washington for Richmond," immediately vetoed that suggestion.[202] "If left to me, I would not go South of the Rappahannock, upon Lee's moving North of it," the president wrote, repeating his earlier counsel: "If you had Richmond invested to-day, you would not be able to take it in twenty days; meanwhile, your communications, and with them, your army would be ruined. I think *Lee's* Army, and not *Richmond*, is your true objective point. If he comes towards the Upper Potomac, follow on his flank, and on the inside track, shortening your lines, whilst he lengthens his. Fight him when oppertunity offers. If he stays where he is, fret him, and fret him."[203]

Alarmed by Hooker's evident unwillingness to confront Lee's army, Lincoln planned to consult with him. But he aborted that trip when Stanton and Halleck warned that it was too perilous to visit the general's ever-shifting headquarters when that region could become the scene of battle.

Hooker eventually decided to take Lincoln's advice and shadow Lee as he moved north down the Valley. Lincoln worried that General Robert H. Milroy at Winchester would be seized, just as the Harper's Ferry garrison had been captured during Lee's earlier thrust into the North. On June 14, the president quietly told Welles that "he was feeling very bad; that he feared Milroy and his command were captured, or would be." When Welles asked why Milroy did not fall back, Lincoln explained "that our folks appeared to know but little how things are, and showed no evidence that they ever availed themselves of any advantage." Sadly, Welles reflected that Lincoln "is kept in ignorance and defers to the General-in-Chief, though not pleased that he is not fully advised of events as they occur. There is a modest distrust of himself, of which advantage is taken."[204] (In September 1862, James A. Garfield had similarly observed that Lincoln "is almost a child in the hand[s] of his generals. Indeed he recently told a delegation from Chicago that he could not grant a certain request of theirs, which [he] regarded perfectly proper to be granted, unless General Halleck concurred. But he would give them a letter to the General introducing them and their business. What shameful humiliation when the President becomes a petitioner before one of his subordinates.")[205]

Lincoln telegraphed Milroy's superior, Robert C. Schenck, on June 14: "Get Milroy from Winchester to Harper's Ferry if possible. He will be gobbled up, if he remains, if he is not already past salvation."[206] Simultaneously, he wired Hooker: "So far as we can make out here, the enemy have Milroy surrounded at Winchester, and [Erastus B.] Tyler at Martinsburg. If they could hold out a few days, could you help them? If the head of Lee's army is at Martinsburg and the tail of it on the Plank road between Fredericksburg and Chancellorsville, the animal must be very slim somewhere. Could you not break him?"[207] But it was too late; the following day Confederates routed Milroy, killing and capturing over half of his 8,000-man force.

As the Confederates tramped northward, Lincoln thought Hooker began to resemble McClellan more and more, complaining that he was outnumbered (he was not) and that the administration did not support him wholeheartedly (it did). The president said that "he got rid of McC[lellan] because he let Lee get the better of him in the race to Richmond" and hinted "that if Hooker got beat in the present race—he would make short work of him."[208] On June 16, Hooker fired off a bitter telegram: "You have long been aware Mr. President that I have not enjoyed the confidence of the Major-General Commanding the Army & I can assure you so long as this continues we may look in vain for success."[209]

Lincoln replied bluntly: "To remove all misunderstanding, I now place you in the strict military relation to Gen. Halleck, of a commander of one of the armies, to the General-in-Chief of all the armies. I have not intended differently; but as it seems to be differently understood, I shall direct him to give you orders, and you to obey them."[210] To soften the blow, he sent a more conciliatory letter: "When you say I have long been aware that you do not enjoy the confidence of the major-general commanding, you state the case much too strongly. You do not lack his confidence in any degree to do you any harm. On seeing him, after telegraphing you this morning, I found him more nearly agreeing with you than I was myself. Surely you do not mean to understand that I am withholding my confidence from you when I happen to express an opinion (certainly never discourteously) differing from one of your own. I believe Halleck is dissatisfied with you to this extent only, that he knows that you write and telegraph ('report,' as he calls it) to me. I think he is wrong to find fault with this; but I do not think he withholds any support from you on account of it. If you and he would use the same frankness to one another, and to me, that I use to both of you, there would be no difficulty. I need and must have the professional skill of both, and yet these suspicions tend to deprive me of both. I believe you are aware that since you took command of the army I have not believed you had any chance to effect anything till now. As it looks to me, Lee's now returning toward Harper's Ferry gives you back the chance that I thought McClellan lost last fall. Quite possibly I was wrong both then and now; but, in the great responsibility resting upon me, I cannot be entirely silent. Now, all I ask is that you will be in such mood that we can get into our action the best cordial judgment of yourself and General Halleck, with my poor mite added, if indeed he and you shall think it entitled to any consideration at all."[211]

A week later, Hooker visited Washington to confer with Lincoln and doubtless to ask for reinforcements. At a cabinet meeting later that day, the president appeared so "sad and careworn" that Welles was "painfully impressed."[212] Lincoln tried to remain optimistic. On June 26, he said: "We cannot help beating them, if we have the man. How much depends in military matters on one master mind! Hooker may commit the same fault as McClellan and lose his chance. We shall soon see, but it appears to me he can't help but win."[213]

Soon Lincoln thought differently. When Hooker insisted that the 10,000 troops guarding Harper's Ferry be sent to join his army, Halleck vetoed the idea, prompting Hooker to quit in protest on June 27. Stanton later told a military historian that the Maryland Heights had been fortified at great cost and that Hooker had been instructed on June 24 to hold that position. Shortly thereafter, Fighting Joe directed the commander of that garrison to abandon it. When Stanton and Halleck learned of this, they countermanded the order, thinking that there had been some misunderstanding. Stanton said that if Hooker had asked them first, they would have approved his request to evacuate the Heights.

Upon reading Hooker's dispatch resigning his command, Lincoln turned pale. To Stanton's query, "What shall be done?" he replied: "Accept his resignation."[214] When Chase, who had strongly supported Hooker, protested, Lincoln cut him off abruptly: "The acceptance of an army resignation is not a matter for your department."[215]

Lincoln told Noah Brooks "that he regarded Hooker very much as a father might regard a son who was lame, or who had some other incurable physical infirmity. His love for his son would be even intensified by the reflection that the lad could never be a strong and successful man." When Brooks shared this conversation with Hooker, the tearful general replied: "Well, the President may regard me as a cripple; but if he will give me a chance, I will yet show him that I know how to fight."[216] Lincoln wanted Hooker to command a corps in the Army of the Potomac, but nothing came of it for months. To General Meade, the president wrote in late July: "I have not thrown Gen. Hooker away."[217] In the autumn, as a corps commander in the western theater, Hooker would partially redeem himself.

Burnside Blunders Again

While the Army of the Potomac was busy shadowing Lee, Burnside in his new position as head of the Department of the Ohio created yet another headache for Lincoln by arresting ex-Congressman Clement L. Vallandigham, a prominent Peace Democrat from Dayton, Ohio. Dubbed by their opponents "Copperheads," after the poisonous snake that strikes without warning, Peace Democrats were concentrated in the lower Midwest and in large cities. They generally backed compromises that would bring about a negotiated restoration of the Union with slavery intact. War Democrats, in contrast, tended to support the administration's military policies. Each faction deplored arbitrary arrests and emancipation. During the winter of Northern discontent, the Emancipation Proclamation, the draft, and the suspension of the writ of habeas corpus greatly strengthened their appeal.

As a leader of the antiwar forces, the 42-year-old Vallandigham had notable strengths. According to Noah Brooks, he was "well built," with a "fresh and fair" complexion, a "small head, regular and somewhat delicate features, and dark hair slightly sprinkled with gray." Though deploring his ideology, Brooks found the Ohioan "a personable man," a "most agreeable and delightful talker," a "genial and pleasant companion, a steadfast friend, and a man well versed in literature, history, and politics." As a speaker, Valandigham was "smooth, plausible, and polished," though when delivering a formal speech, "he often became greatly excited, his face wore an expression at times almost repulsive, and his voice rose with a wild shriek; his hands fluttered convulsively in the air, and the manner of the man underwent a physical transformation." Peace Democrats in the House of Representatives paid him great deference. "At a word from him, or a wave of his hand," they "would incontinently scud into the lobbies or cloakrooms; or his signal would bring them all back when they were needed in their seats."[218] Not every journalist was so complimentary; Horace White called Vallandigham a man who was as "cold as ice and hard as iron" and whose character exhibited "neither humor nor persuasion nor conciliation."[219]

Even before the bombardment of Fort Sumter, Vallandigham had made his mark as a Peace Democrat. On November 2, 1860, he told a crowd in New York that "if any one or more of the States of this Union should, at any time, secede—for reasons of the sufficiency and justice of which . . . they alone may judge—much as I should deplore it, *I never would as a Representative in the Congress of the United States vote one dollar of money whereby one drop of American blood should be shed in a civil war.*" In Congress, Vallandigham declined to vote for resolutions commending Major Robert Anderson, refused to offer thanks to the men who fought at First Bull Run, and supported the Fugitive Slave Act and slavery.[220]

In 1862, Lincoln helped defeat Vallandigham's reelection bid by recruiting a strong opponent to run against him, Robert C. Schenck, a general who had been wounded at Second Bull Run. Lincoln had known Schenck when they both served in the U.S. House. As he was recovering in Washington, Schenck was approached by Stanton, Chase, and the president, all of whom urged him to enter the lists against Vallandigham. To increase Schenck's prestige, Lincoln promoted him to major general. Schenck won with the help of the Ohio Legislature, which redrew the boundaries of the Dayton congressional district, lopping off a heavily Democratic county and adding one with a Republican majority. This gerrymandering may have sealed Vallandigham's doom, for he had carried the district two years earlier by only a slim majority.

Vallandigham could be exceptionally vituperative. On January 14, 1863, seeking to become the main leader of the Peace Democrats, he told the House that he saw "nothing before us but universal political and social revolution, anarchy and blood-shed, compared with which the Reign of Terror in France was a merciful visitation." He declared that "the South could never be conquered—never," and argued that "the secret but real purpose of the war was to abolish slavery in the States" and to turn "our present democratical form of government into an imperial despotism." Proudly he announced that from the day that Fort Sumter was bombarded, "I did not support the war; and to-day I bless God that not the smell of so much as one drop of its blood is upon my garments." He grandiloquently condemned the administration for trying to whip the Confederates "back into love and fellowship at the point of the bayonet." He maintained that "history will record that, after nearly six thousand years of folly and wickedness in every form and administration of government, theocratic, democratic, monarchic, oligarchic, despotic, and mixed, it was reserved to American statesman-ship, in the nineteenth century of the Christian era, to try the grand experiment, on a scale the most costly and gigantic in its proportions, of creating love by force and developing fraternal affection by war; and history will record, too, on the same page, the utter, disastrous, and most bloody failure of the experiment."[221] While running for the Democratic gubernatorial nomination in Ohio that spring, Vallandigham continued to assail the administration in such terms.

In April, Burnside issued General Order Number 38, stating that "the habit of declaring sympathy for the enemy will not be allowed in this department. Persons committing such offenses will be at once arrested," tried by military courts "as spies or traitors, and, if convicted, will suffer death" or will be "sent beyond our lines into the lines of their friends." No "treason, expressed or implied," would be tolerated.[222]

Even before Vallandigham was apprehended, Order 38 had aroused strong protests from Burnside's staff. Captain James Madison Cutts told Lincoln that it "has kindled the fires of hatred and contention, and Burnside is foolishly and unwisely excited, and if continued in command will disgrace himself, you, and the Country, as he did at Fredericksburg." The arrest of Vallandigham, said the captain, "has inflicted a lasting injury upon *your administration*."[223] It was one thing for Burnside to resort to such draconian measures in North Carolina, which he had done earlier, but quite another in Ohio. Several embarrassing arrests of innocent people discredited both the order and its author. After Lincoln intervened to postpone the death sentence of one alleged traitor, Burnside stayed the execution of many men convicted under Order 38.

But the impulsive general showed no such reserve in dealing with Vallandigham, who made a particularly inflammatory speech on May 1, denouncing the administration of "King Lincoln" and Order 38. In his closing remarks, Vallandigham warned his audience "that an attempt would shortly be made to enforce the conscription act; that 'they should remember that this war was not a war for the preservation of the Union;' that 'it was a wicked abolition war! and that if those in authority were allowed to accomplish their purposes the people would be deprived of their liberties and a monarchy established; but that as for him he was resolved that he would never be a priest to minister upon the altar upon which his country was being sacrificed."[224] Four days later, soldiers apprehended the Democratic firebrand; soon thereafter a military commission found him guilty of violating Order 38 and sentenced him to confinement for the rest of the war.

Thus the obstreperous orator became a martyr whose treatment many Democrats deplored. Burnside's action, New York Governor Horatio Seymour wrote, "has brought dishonor upon our country; it is full of danger to our persons and to our homes; it bears upon its front a conscious violation of law and justice." It "is not merely a step toward revolution, it is revolution; it will not only lead to military despotism, it establishes military despotism. . . . If it is upheld, our liberties are overthrown."[225] On May 16, Seymour's message was read at a giant Albany rally where resolutions were adopted denouncing "the recent assumption of a military commander to seize and try a citizen of Ohio . . . for no other reason than words addressed to a public meeting, in criticism of the course of the Administration, and in condemnation of the military orders of that general." The New Yorkers urged Lincoln to "be true to the Constitution" and to "recognize and maintain the rights of the States and the liberties of the citizen."[226] An unusually choleric Democrat, paraphrasing Patrick Henry's "treason speech," told a crowd at Indianapolis that the president deserved assassination: "Let us remind Lincoln that Caesar had his Brutus and Charles the First his Cromwell. Let us also remind the George the Third of the present day that he, too, may have his Cromwell or his Brutus."[227]

Even some Republicans condemned what they called Burnside's "blunder" and "great mistake."[228] A strong supporter of the Lincoln administration, former Wisconsin Governor Nathaniel P. Tallmadge, warned of "civil war in the loyal states" if Vallandigham were not released.[229] *Harper's Weekly* observed correctly that Vallandigham had been "fast talking himself into the deepest political grave ever dug when Burnside resurrected him."[230]

Upon Vallandigham's arrival in Cincinnati, where he was incarcerated, he issued an address to his fellow Buckeyes: "I am here in a military bastille for no other offence than my political opinions, and the defence of them, and of the rights of the people, and of your constitutional liberties."[231] The Democrats of Ohio responded by unanimously nominating him for governor. In federal court, when Vallandigham's attorney asked for a writ of habeas corpus, Burnside emphatically defended his action, arguing that it was his duty "to stop license and intemperate discussion which tend to weaken the authority of the Government and army."[232] Upholding the power of the president and his subordinates to arrest Vallandigham, the court refused to issue the desired writ.

Surprised and dismayed by Burnside's action, Lincoln sought to undo the damage it caused. Rightly fearing that he could not overrule the general without embarrassing him and simultaneously encouraging bitter dissenters, the president at first had Stanton send him a positive telegram: "In your determination to support the authority of the Government and to suppress treason in your Department, you may count on the firm support of the President."[233] The cabinet, however, demurred; upon learning of their dissatisfaction, Burnside offered once again to resign. Lincoln replied that all cabinet members "regretted the necessity of arresting . . . Vallandigham, some, perhaps, doubting, that there was a real necessity for it—but, being done, all were for seeing you through with it."[234] On May 19, Lincoln shrewdly undercut Vallandigham's martyr status by commuting his sentence and, in keeping with a provision of Order 38, directed that the prisoner "be put . . . beyond our military lines," and warned that if he returned he would be "kept in close custody for the term specified in his sentence."[235] (Others had been similarly banished, including the notorious spy, Rose O'Neal Greenhow, and Missouri newspaper editor Edmund J. Ellis.) Accordingly, Vallandigham was turned over to puzzled Confederates in Tennessee. After conferring with Jefferson Davis and other Southern leaders, he made his way to Canada where he issued stirring if bootless addresses.

Lincoln's modification of Vallandigham's sentence represented one step in defusing the crisis caused by Burnside. Another was his prompt decision to revoke the general's June 1 order shutting down the vitriolic Chicago *Times*. That journal had fiercely denounced the administration, especially since the issuance of the Emancipation Proclamation. In February 1863, it declared that the "only way to compel the administration to withdraw its emancipation proclamation and kindred policies is for the democracy of the country to absolutely and unqualifiedly refuse to support the war for the enforcement of these policies."[236] When some of U.S. Grant's subordinates expressed a desire to silence the *Times,* the general agreed that it "should have been suppressed long since by authority from Washington," but in the absence of such authority, it was wise to forbear. Suppression was only "calculated to give the paper a notoriety evidently sought, and which probably would increase the sale of it."[237]

Upon learning of Burnside's high-handed act, Lincoln immediately had Stanton suggest to the general that he might want to rescind the order. The secretary of war explained that the president thought the "irritation produced by such acts is . . . likely to do more harm than the publication would do." Though he "approves of your motives and desires to give you cordial and efficient support," and "while military movements are left to your judgment," nevertheless "upon administration questions such as the arrest of civilians and the suppression of newspapers not requiring immediate action the President desires to be previously consulted."[238] On June 3, several prominent Chicagoans, including the mayor, urged Lincoln to overrule Burnside, and Senator Lyman Trumbull and Republican Congressman Isaac N. Arnold implored him to give the appeal "serious & prompt consideration."[239] In Springfield, the General Assembly condemned Burnside's act as a "direct violation of the constitution of the United States and of this State."[240] The president's decision to honor these requests made him appear sensitive to First Amendment rights. Because Lincoln acted so quickly, the *Times* was able to resume publication after an interruption of only one day.

Yet another step minimizing the effect of Burnside's blunders was Lincoln's public letter to the organizers of the May 16 protest meeting at Albany, chaired by the industrialist Erastus Corning. In that important document, he defended the arrest of Vallandigham and the suspension of habeas corpus. Asserting that the government must execute deserters to maintain its armies intact, he argued that it was equally necessary to punish those who encouraged desertion. "Must I shoot a simple-minded soldier boy who deserts, while I must not touch a hair of a wily agitator who induces him to desert?" he asked rhetorically. Whoever "dissuades one man from volunteering, or induces one soldier to desert, weakens the Union cause as much as he who kills a union soldier in battle." To be sure, in peacetime, the suspension of habeas corpus would be unconstitutional. But the Constitution provides that "[t]he previlege of the writ of Habeas Corpus shall not be suspended, unless when in cases of Rebellion or Invasion, the public Safety may require it."

The secessionists, Lincoln argued, cynically expected constitutional scruples to hamper the government's attempt to preserve the Union. They planned to cry "Liberty of speech," "Liberty of the press," and "*Habeas corpus*" in order "to keep on foot amongst us a most efficient corps of spies, informers, supplyers, and aiders and abettors of their cause in a thousand ways." While those charges were being debated, the Rebel "spies and others might remain at large to help on their cause." Alternatively, if the president "should suspend the writ, without ruinous waste of time, instances of arresting innocent persons might occur, as are always likely to occur in such cases; and then a clamor could be raised." Fully aware that the Rebels would avail themselves of such cynical tactics, Lincoln insisted that he nevertheless "was slow to adopt the strong measures," for he was "thoroughly imbued with a reverence for the guarranteed rights of individuals." As the war progressed, however, he was forced to take steps "indispensable to the public Safety," steps that he believed were "within the exceptions of the constitution." Civilian courts were "utterly incompetent" to handle the vast number of cases that such a "clear, flagrant, and gigantic case of Rebellion" generated, and juries "too frequently have at least one member, more ready to hang the panel than to hang the traitor." Moreover, men enticing soldiers to desert might behave in such a way as to commit no crime that civil courts would recognize. The power to suspend "is allowed by the constitution on purpose that, men may be arrested and held, who can not be proved to be guilty of defined crime, 'when, in cases of Rebellion or Invasion the public Safety may require it.'" During a rebellion, "arrests are made, not so much for what has been done, as for what probably would be done." And who should be arrested? Lincoln dubiously asserted that the "man who stands by and says nothing, when the peril of his government is discussed, can not be misunderstood. If not hindered, he is sure to help the enemy." Worse still, "if he talks ambiguously—talks for his country with 'buts' and 'ifs' and 'ands.'"

It would have been advisable, Lincoln argued, if at the outbreak of hostilities the government had arrested men like John C. Breckinridge, Robert E. Lee, Joseph E. Johnston, John B. Magruder, William B. Preston, Simon B. Buckner, and Franklin Buchanan, all high-ranking military leaders in the Confederacy. "Every one of them if arrested would have been discharged on Habeas Corpus, were the writ allowed to operate. In view of these and similar cases, I think the time not unlikely to come when I shall be blamed for having made too few arrests rather than too many."

Lincoln denied the Albany protestors' argument that military arrests could not be made "outside of the lines of necessary military occupation, and the scenes of insurrection." The Constitution, he pointed out, "makes no such distinction." Such arrests were justified wherever "in cases of Rebellion or Invasion, the public Safety may require them." Far from the front lines, "mischievous interference with the raising and supplying of armies" and "the enticing [of] men out of the army" presented a grave military danger. Vallandigham clearly belonged in that category of eligible detainees, Lincoln maintained. "Mr. Vallandigham avows his hostility to the war on the part of the Union; and his arrest was made because he was laboring, with some effect, to prevent the raising of troops, to encourage desertions from the army, and to leave the rebellion without an adequate military force to suppress it. He was not arrested because he was damaging the political prospects of the administration, or the personal interests of the commanding general; but because he was damaging the army, upon the existence, and vigor of which, the life of the nation depends. He was warring upon the military; and this gave the military constitutional jurisdiction to lay hands upon him." Orators can indirectly encourage soldier boys to desert "by getting a father, or brother, or friend, into a public meeting, and there working upon his feelings, till he is persuaded to write the soldier boy, that he is fighting in a bad cause, for a wicked administration of a contemptable government, too weak to arrest and punish him if he shall desert. I think that in such a case, to silence the agitator, and save the boy, is not only constitutional, but, withal, a great mercy."

To support his argument that the extraordinary measures taken during war would set no dangerous precedents for peacetime, Lincoln graphically insisted that he could "no more be persuaded that the government can constitutionally take no strong measure in time of rebellion, because it can be shown that the same could not be lawfully taken in time of peace, than I can be persuaded that a particular drug is not good medicine for a sick man, because it can be shown to not be good food for a well one." During the War of 1812, Andrew Jackson had suspended the writ of habeas corpus and arrested a judge as well as critics of his action. When after the war that same judge fined him $1,000, he paid it; years later Democrats, led by Stephen A. Douglas, persuaded Congress to rescind the fine. Jackson's precedent did not undermine the Bill of Rights and pave the way to postwar despotism.

Lincoln denied that any partisan motive underlay Vallandigham's arrest. After all, he pointed out, Burnside was a Democrat, the judge who refused to issue a writ of habeas corpus was a Democrat, and "of all those democrats who are nobly exposing their lives and shedding their blood on the battle-field, I have learned that many approve the course taken with Mr. V[allandigham] while I have not heard of a single one condemning it." Lincoln suggested that if he had been in Burnside's position, he might not have arrested Vallandigham, but while he would not shirk ultimate responsibility for the arrest, he believed that "as a general rule, the commander in the field is the better judge of the necessity in any particular case." He would gladly release Vallandigham as soon as he believed "the public safety will not suffer by it." In conclusion, Lincoln expressed the belief that as the war continued, the necessity for such strong measures would diminish. But, he insisted, "I must continue to do so much as may seem to be required by the public safety."[241]

Some of Lincoln's case was logically and constitutionally weak, especially his contention that anyone "who stands by and says nothing, when the peril of his government is discussed . . . is sure to help the enemy." The New York *World* with some justice asked: "Was anything so extraordinary ever before uttered by the chief magistrate of a free country? Men are torn from their home and immured in bastilles for the shocking crime of *silence!*"[242] Still, the Corning letter's homey rhetoric succeeded in allaying many public doubts. George William Curtis called it "altogether excellent" and said the president's timing was "another instance of his remarkable sagacity."[243] Nicolay and Hay noted that few of Lincoln's state papers "produced a stronger impression upon the public mind."[244] A visit to several Midwestern cities convinced Hiram Barney that although opposition leaders there were vocal, "the great majority are with the Administration and disposed to support the President in a vigorous enforcement of the laws against Copperheads."[245]

On June 30, Erastus Corning and the rest of the Albany committee issued a reply scorning Lincoln's "pretensions to more than regal authority" and the "misty and cloudy forms of expression in which those pretensions are set forth." They vehemently deplored the "gigantic and monstrous heresy" that the Constitution contained "a principle or germ of arbitrary power, which in time of war expands at once into an absolute sovereignty, wielded by one man; so that liberty perishes, or is dependent on his will, his discretion, or his caprice."[246]

Lincoln did not offer a rejoinder to Corning, but when the Ohio Democratic State Convention made similar arguments, he denied ever saying that "the constitution is different in time of insurrection or invasion from what it is in time of peace & public security." Rather, he had "expressed the opinion that the constitution is different, *in its application* in cases of Rebellion or Invasion, involving the Public Safety, from what it is in times of profound peace and public security; and this opinion I adhere to, simply because, by the constitution itself, things may be done in the one case which may not be done in the other."[247] Lincoln failed to answer the telling objection raised by the Ohioans that Vallandigham was entitled to a civil trial under the provisions of the Second Confiscation Act and the March 3, 1863, law authorizing the president to suspend habeas corpus.

The Southern Tide Crests: Gettysburg

As Lincoln and Stanton discussed a replacement for Hooker, they rejected advice to choose McClellan. Lee's invasion of Pennsylvania so panicked residents of that state and neighboring New Jersey that they urged the reinstatement of Little Mac. A. K. McClure telegraphed the White House: "Our people are paralyzed for want of confidence & leadership & unless they can be inspired with hope we shall fail to do anything worthy of our State or Govt. I am fully persuaded that to call McClellan to a command here would be the best thing that could be done."[248] Tersely Lincoln asked: "Do we gain anything by opening one leak to stop another? Do we gain any thing by quieting one clamor, merely to open another, and probably a larger one?"[249]

If not McClellan, then who? An obvious choice would be one of the corps commanders in the Army of the Potomac. The president had already asked Darius Couch, who declined because of poor health. John F. Reynolds had complained bitterly about Hooker but refused to take his place. Winfield Scott Hancock and John Sedgwick had expressed no interest in assuming command of the army. By process of elimination, the choice settled on George Gordon Meade, who had distinguished himself in earlier campaigns. When Stanton mentioned that the general was a Pennsylvanian,

Lincoln predicted that, like a rooster, he would "fight well on his own dunghill."[250] One soldier likened the choleric general to "a damned old goggle-eyed snapping turtle."[251] Another regarded him as "conservative and cautious to the last degree, good qualities in a defensive battle, but liable to degenerate into timidity when an aggressive or bold offensive becomes imperative."[252] Though industrious and personally fearless, the reserved Meade lacked charisma. The other corps commanders, however, thought highly of him.

Meade accurately anticipated that Lee, who had divided his forces as he entered Pennsylvania unopposed, would have to concentrate them as the Army of the Potomac drew nearer. From different directions the Confederates began streaming toward the small town of Gettysburg. There, during the first three days of July, the bloodiest battle of the war was fought. Lee lost fully a third of his men (28,000) while Meade lost a fifth of his (23,000). The Army of the Potomac, occupying high ground, fended off repeated attacks, including the fabled charge of George Pickett's division on July 3. The following day, Lee's shattered army began retreating toward the Potomac.

While awaiting news from the battlefield as the armies clashed, Lincoln spent many anxious hours in the telegraph office. One evening he rode out to review troops commanded by General T. R. Tannatt. There he asked the regimental band to play the familiar hymn, "Lead Kindly Light." As he listened, his face grew sad and tears came to his eyes, perhaps prompted by the text: "Lead thou me on/Keep thou my feet; I do not ask to see/ The distant scene,—one step enough for me."[253]

Word of the decisive victory filled Lincoln's heart with joy, though Meade's order congratulating his troops did not. The general said their job was now to "drive from our soil every vestige of the presence of the invader." When Lincoln read this proclamation, his heart sank. In anguish he exclaimed: *"Drive the invaders from our soil! My God! Is that all?"*[254] Lincoln called it "a dreadful reminiscence of McClellan. The same spirit that moved McC. to claim a great victory because P[ennsylvani]a & M[arylan]d were safe." Exasperated, he asked: "Will our Generals never get that idea out of their heads? The whole country is *our* soil."[255]

On July 6, the president wrote to Halleck: "I left the telegraph office a good deal dissatisfied. You know I did not like the phrase, in Orders, No. 68, I believe, 'Drive the invaders from our soil.' Since that, I see a dispatch from General [William H.] French, saying the enemy is crossing his wounded over the river in flats, without saying why he does not stop it, or even intimating a thought that it ought to be stopped. Still later, another dispatch from General [Alfred] Pleasonton, by direction of General Meade, to General French, stating that the main army is halted because it is believed the rebels are concentrating 'on the road toward Hagerstown, beyond Fairfield,' and is not to move until it is ascertained that the rebels intend to evacuate Cumberland Valley. These things all appear to me to be connected with a purpose to cover Baltimore and Washington, and to get the enemy across the river again without a further collision, and they do not appear connected with a purpose to prevent his crossing and to destroy him. I do fear the former purpose is acted upon and the latter is rejected. If you are satisfied the latter purpose is entertained and is judiciously pursued, I am content. If you are not so satisfied, please look to it."[256] Later the president asked Meade, "Do you know, General, what your attitude towards Lee after the battle of Gettysburg reminded me of?" "No, Mr. President—what is it?" "I'll be hanged if I could think of anything else but an old woman trying to shoo her geese across a creek."[257]

Halleck promptly notified Meade that if the Confederates were in fact crossing the Potomac, he should engage the portion still on the north bank: "the importance of attacking the part on this side is incalculable. Such an opportunity may not occur again." Even if Lee's troops had not begun passing over the river, Meade should gather his forces and attack. After describing the units that were rushing to join the Army of the Potomac, Halleck told Meade: "You will have forces sufficient to render your victory certain. My only fear now is that the enemy may escape by crossing the river."[258] But with characteristic unwillingness to give a direct command, a failing that exasperated Lincoln, Halleck added: "Do not be influenced by any dispatch from here against your own judgment. Regard them as suggestions only."[259]

Meade replied that he would press on as soon as he could concentrate and supply his forces. But, he warned, "I expect to find the enemy in a strong position, well covered with artillery, and I do not desire to imitate his example at Gettysburg, and assault a position where the chances were so greatly against success. I wish in advance to moderate the expectations of those who, in ignorance of the difficulties to be encountered, may expect too much. All that I can do under the circumstances I pledge this army to do."[260]

Lincoln believed that Meade could deliver the *coup de grâce* to the Army of Northern Virginia before it escaped to Virginia. Thus, he thought, Meade would end the war, in conjunction with Grant's capture of Vicksburg on July 4. At a White House fireworks display on Independence Day, Lincoln exclaimed to Elizabeth Blair Lee: "Meade would pursue Lee instantly but he has to stop to get food for his men!!"[261] Heavy rains delayed Lee's retreat to the Potomac.

With mounting impatience, Lincoln followed the army's slow progress, hoping Meade would attack but fearing he would not. He spent much time at the War Department, where telegrapher Albert B. Chandler observed him closely. Lincoln's "anxiety seemed as great as it had been during the battle itself," Chandler recalled; he "walked up and down the floor, his face grave and anxious, wringing his hands and showing every sign of deep solicitude. As the telegrams came in, he traced the positions of the two armies on the map, and several times called me up to point out their location, seeming to feel the need of talking to some one. Finally, a telegram came from Meade saying that under such and such circumstances he would engage the enemy at such and such a time. 'Yes,' said the president bitterly, 'he will be ready to fight a magnificent battle when there is no enemy there to fight!'"[262]

On July 7, the deeply discouraged president, wearing a sad, almost despondent look, told his cabinet "that Meade still lingered at Gettysburg, when he should have been at Hagerstown or near the Potomac, to cut off the retreating army of Lee. While unwilling to complain and willing and anxious to give all praise to the general for the great battle and victory, he feared the old idea of driving the Rebels out of Pennsylvania and Maryland, instead of capturing them, was still prevalent among the officers.

He hoped this was not so" and "said he had spoken to Halleck and urged that the right tone and spirit should be infused into officers and men," and that Meade "especially should be reminded of his . . . wishes." When Halleck demurred curtly, Lincoln said: "I drop the subject." He still felt that he must yield to Old Brains: "It being strictly a military question, it is proper I should defer to Halleck, whom I have called here to counsel, advise, and direct in these matters, where he is an expert."[263]

Frustrated, Lincoln issued a desperate order. His son Robert recollected that he "summoned Gen. [Herman] Haupt, in whom he had great confidence as a bridge builder, and asked him how long in view of the materials which might be . . . available under Lee, would it take him to devise the means and get his army across the river." Haupt estimated that it would require no more than twenty-four hours. The president "at once sent an order to Gen. Meade," a document probably carried north by Vice-President Hannibal Hamlin, "directing him to attack Lee's army with all his force immediately, and that if he was successful in the attack he might destroy the order, but if he was unsuccessful he might preserve it for his vindication."[264]

On July 12, Meade caught up with Lee at Williamsport, where he could have attacked that day or the next. When he said he would convene a council of war, Halleck telegraphed: "Call no council of war. It is proverbial that councils of war never fight."[265] Meade ignored that sage advice, and, as the general-in-chief had predicted, a majority of the corps commanders opposed an assault. On the night of July 13, the Confederates began crossing the river, and finished doing so the next day.

On July 14, John Hay recorded in his diary: "This morning the Presdt. seemed depressed by Meade's despatches of last night. They were so cautiously & almost timidly worded—talking about reconnoitering to find the enemy's weak place and other such." Lincoln "said he feared that he would do nothing." Around midday, when Lee's escape was confirmed, Lincoln was overcome with grief and anger. Profoundly dismayed, he said: "We only had to stretch forth our hands & they were ours. And nothing I could say or do could make the Army move." His son Robert reported that Lincoln "grieved silently but deeply about the escape of Lee. He said, 'If I had gone up there I could have whipped them myself.'" (In fact, some newspapers had been urging the president to take command of the army and lead it in the field.) For the only time in his life, Robert saw tears in his father's eyes. Lincoln had justifiably feared that it would be a repeat of Antietam, with the Army of the Potomac failing to cut off the Confederates as they retreated.[266]

Halleck sent Meade a stern telegram conveying Lincoln's displeasure: "I need hardly say to you that the escape of Lee's army without another battle has created great dissatisfaction in the mind of the President, and it will require an active and energetic pursuit on your part to remove the impression that it has not been sufficiently active heretofore."[267] Understandably stung by this rebuke, Meade offered to resign: "Having performed my duty conscientiously and to the best of my ability, the censure of the President conveyed in your dispatch of 1 P.M. this day, is, in my judgment, so undeserved that I feel compelled most respectfully to ask to be immediately relieved from the command of this army." To soften the blow, Halleck replied: "My telegram, stating the disappointment of the President at the escape of Lee's army, was not intended as a censure, but as a stimulus to an active pursuit. It is not deemed a sufficient cause for your application to be relieved."[268]

Lincoln himself tried to soften the blow further in an extraordinary letter to the aggrieved general. He began with an expression of sincere gratitude: "I am very— *very*–grateful to you for the magnificent success you gave the cause of the country at Gettysburg; and I am sorry now to be the author of the slightest pain to you." After this conciliatory opening, Lincoln became stern: "I was in such deep distress myself that I could not restrain some expression of it. I had been oppressed nearly ever since the battles at Gettysburg, by what appeared to be evidences that yourself, and Gen. Couch, and Gen. Smith, were not seeking a collision with the enemy, but were trying to get him across the river without another battle. What these evidences were, if you please, I hope to tell you at some time, when we shall both feel better. The case, summarily stated is this. You fought and beat the enemy at Gettysburg; and, of course, to say the least, his loss was as great as yours. He retreated; and you did not, as it seemed to me, pressingly pursue him; but a flood in the river detained him, till, by slow degrees, you were again upon him. You had at least twenty thousand veteran troops directly with you, and as many more raw ones within supporting distance, all in addition to those who fought with you at Gettysburg; while it was not possible that he had received a single recruit; and yet you stood and let the flood run down, bridges be built, and the enemy move away at his leisure, without attacking him."

In one of the harshest passages Lincoln ever penned, he told Meade how much his failure to attack Lee would hurt the Union cause: "I do not believe you appreciate the magnitude of the misfortune involved in Lee's escape. He was within your easy grasp, and to have closed upon him would, in connection with our other late successes, have ended the war. As it is, the war will be prolonged indefinitely. If you could not safely attack Lee last monday, how can you possibly do so South of the river, when you can take with you very few more than two thirds of the force you then had in hand? It would be unreasonable to expect, and I do not expect you can now effect much. Your golden opportunity is gone, and I am distressed immeasureably because of it." Lincoln filed away this stinging letter with the endorsement: "To Gen. Meade, never sent, or signed."[269] But he did tell the general, "The fruit seemed so ripe, so ready for plucking, that it was very hard to lose it."[270]

A week later, Lincoln was in a better mood. "I was deeply mortified by the escape of Lee," he told one of Meade's corps commanders. "A few days having passed," he added, "I am now profoundly grateful for what was done, without criticism for what was not done."[271] As time went by, however, Lincoln continued to be exasperated by Meade's habitual caution. On July 18, he moaned to Hay: "Our Army had the war in the hollow of their hand & they would not close it. . . . We had gone through all the labor of tilling & planting an enormous crop & when it was ripe we did not harvest it."[272] There was "bad faith somewhere," he darkly speculated to Gideon Welles. "Meade has been pressed and urged, but only one of his generals was for an immediate attack. . . . What does it mean, Mr. Welles? Great God! what does it mean."[273] On July 26, he told the navy secretary: "I have no faith that Meade will attack Lee; nothing looks like it to me. I believe he can never have another as good opportunity as that which he trifled away. Everything since has dragged with him."[274] In September, when Welles asked what that general was doing, Lincoln replied: "It is the same old story of this Army of the Potomac. Imbecility, inefficiency—don't want to *do*—is defending the Capital." He then groaned, "Oh, it is terrible, terrible this weakness, this indifference of our Potomac generals, with such armies of good and brave men."[275]

Lincoln was not alone in his view that Meade could have ended the war with a vigorous pursuit. "Had Meade finished Lee before he had crossed the Potomac, as he might have done & he should have done, . . . we should now be at the end of the war," wrote Charles A. Dana on July 29.[276] Whitelaw Reid called Lee's escape "the greatest blunder of the war," and David Davis deemed it "one of the great disasters & humiliations of the war."[277] In fact, if Meade had begun pursuing the Army of Northern Virginia by July 8, Lee may well have been forced to surrender. (In fairness, it should be noted that Meade had been in charge of the army for only three days when the battle began and hardly knew the capabilities of any corps other than his own. His best corps commanders had been killed, along with over 3,000 other Union soldiers, among them many brigade colonels. Moreover, Lee's position at Williamsport was strong, and it was easier for a defeated army to retreat than it was for a victorious army to pursue, especially after such an epic battle as Gettysburg. Still, if an aggressive commander like Grant or Philip Sheridan had been in charge, the Army of the Potomac would probably have hurt Lee badly before he managed to cross the Potomac.)

For all his keen disappointment, Lincoln on July 19 felt cheerful enough to pen a bit of doggerel titled "Gen. Lee[']s invasion of the North written by himself":

> In eighteen sixty three, with pomp, and mighty swell,
> Me and Jeff's Confederacy, went forth to sack Phil-del,
> The Yankees they got arter us, and giv us particular hell,
> And we skedaddled back again, and didn't sack Phil-del.[278]

In assessing credit for the victory at Gettysburg, Lincoln expressed reluctance to single out anyone in particular. "There was glory enough at Gettysburg to go all round, from Meade to the humblest enlisted man in the ranks," he told Daniel Sickles.[279]

Ironically, on that fateful July 4, Confederate Vice-President Alexander H. Stephens arrived at Fort Monroe with a letter from Jefferson Davis regarding prisoner exchanges. When Stephens asked permission to proceed to Washington, Lincoln flatly refused. Davis then issued a proclamation designed to bolster Confederate morale; it alleged that the Lincoln administration's "malignant rage aims at nothing less than the extermination of yourselves, your wives, and children. They seek to destroy what they cannot plunder. They propose as the spoils of victory that your homes shall be partitioned among the wretches whose atrocious cruelties have stamped infamy on their Government. They design to incite servile insurrection and light the fires of incendiarism wherever they can reach your homes, and they debauch the inferior race, hitherto docile and contented, by promising indulgence of the vilest passions as the price of treachery. Conscious of their inability to prevail by legitimate warfare, not daring to make peace lest they should be hurled from their seats of power, the men who now rule in Washington refuse even to confer on the subject of putting an end to outrages which disgrace our age, or to listen to a suggestion for conducting the war according to the usages of civilization."[280]

Opening the Mississippi

While generals in the Army of the Potomac disappointed Lincoln badly, their counterparts in the western theater, especially Ulysses S. Grant, gladdened his heart. Lincoln had not always been sanguine about Grant's campaign against Vicksburg, which had received a severe check in December 1862. In March 1863, the president complained that Union forces "were doing nothing at Vicksburg," even though Grant promised that "I will have Vicksburg this month, or fail in the attempt."[281] The general had made several unsuccessful bayou expeditions against the Confederate citadel. The first was an effort to dig a canal across the peninsula fronting the city, an enterprise which Lincoln thought "of no account." He expressed wonder "that a sensible man would do it" and thought "that all these *side* expeditions thro[ugh] the country [were] dangerous" because "if the Rebels can blockade us on the Mississippi, which is a mile wide, they can certainly stop us on the little streams not much wider than our gunboats; & shut us up so we can't get back again." He added that his "only hope about the matter is that the Military commanders on the ground know prospects and possibilities better than he can."[282] He predicted the failure of the canal scheme and said that the expedition up the Yazoo "would do no good" and might even prove harmful, for "we run a great risk of losing all our transports & steamers."[283] Gustavus Fox reported that Lincoln "is rather disgusted with the flanking expeditions and predicted their failure from the first."[284] The president told Lorenzo Thomas, adjutant general of the army, that he feared Grant was not taking the proper steps to capture Vicksburg and that he lacked the necessary energy. In April, his Illinois friends Jesse K. Dubois, Ozias M. Hatch, and David L. Phillips visited the Vicksburg front and reported that Grant was not fit for his position, for he seemed to be drifting without any plan.

To learn more about Grant, Lincoln sent General Thomas to investigate conditions in the Army of the Tennessee. For the same purpose, he also dispatched Assistant Secretary of War Charles A. Dana, former managing editor of the New York *Tribune*. Officially, Dana went merely as a "special commissioner of the War Department to investigate and report upon the condition of the pay service in the Western Armies." In April, he began regularly sending favorable dispatches from Grant's headquarters describing the general's plans and the state of the army. "I never knew such transparent sincerity combined with such mental resources," Dana wrote of Grant.[285]

In the autumn of 1862, Lincoln had created a problem for Grant by authorizing John A. McClernand, a prominent Illinois Democrat, to recruit an army and march down the Mississippi toward Vicksburg. The vague orders made it unclear whether he or Grant would be in control. In addition, General N. P. Banks, in charge of the Department of the Gulf and headquartered in New Orleans, was ordered to move up the Mississippi toward Vicksburg. Lines of authority and jurisdiction were indistinct.

When the president finally put Grant in charge, the hyperambitious and arrogant McClernand protested bitterly and urged that Halleck be fired. Lincoln pleaded with him to stop complaining: "I have too many *family* controversies, (so to speak) already on my hands, to voluntarily, or so long as I can avoid it, take up another. You are now doing well—well for the country, and well for yourself—much better than you could possibly be, if engaged in open war with Gen. Halleck. Allow me to beg, that for your sake, for my sake, & for the country's sake, you give your whole attention to the better work."[286] Demoted to a corps command, McClernand remained so querulous and insubordinate that eventually Grant dismissed him.

In late April, when Grant stopped making "side expeditions" and boldly threw his army across the Mississippi, he began a brilliant campaign leading to the capture of Vicksburg on Independence Day. Upon learning that the general had moved south of that citadel and that David D. Porter had successfully run his fleet of gunboats past the Vicksburg batteries, Lincoln exclaimed: "This is more important than anything which is occurring in Virginia!"[287]

When Grant reached the east bank of the river, below Vicksburg, he could have moved toward that city or headed south to link up with Banks, whose goal was to take Port Hudson. Lincoln hoped he would choose the latter course, but he did not, despite Halleck's urging. In May, as Grant daringly marched from triumph to triumph in Mississippi, Lincoln said: "I have had stronger influence brought against Grant, praying for his removal, since the battle of Pittsburg Landing, than for any other object, coming too from good men." (A year earlier, when Grant was caught unprepared for the Confederate onslaught at Shiloh—also known as Pittsburg Landing—he was roundly criticized, even though the Rebels were eventually driven from the field.) But, Lincoln added, "now look at his campaign since May 1. Where is anything in the Old World that equals it? It stamps him as the greatest general of the age, if not of the world."[288]

According to popular rumor, Lincoln asked critics of Grant's alleged drunkenness what brand of whiskey the general used, so he could send some to his other generals. The president denied that he had made that witty riposte, saying that it was probably ascribed to him "to give it currency." Actually, he pointed out, it was based on King George III's purported response to those who charged that General Wolfe was insane: "I wish he would bite some of my other generals then."[289] (This anecdote appears in *Joe Miller's Complete Jest Book,* a favorite of Lincoln's.) The president disclaimed credit for many other stories attributed to him, calling himself "only a retail dealer." He said "that as near as he could reckon, about one-sixth of those [stories] which were credited to him were old acquaintances; all of the rest of them were the productions of other and better story-tellers than himself."[290]

On July 7, Gideon Welles rushed into the White House with a dispatch announcing the surrender of Vicksburg and in his great enthusiasm almost knocked Lincoln over. Hugging Welles tightly, the president exclaimed: "what can we do for the Secretary of the Navy for this glorious intelligence? He is always giving us good news. I cannot, in words, tell you my joy over this result. It is great, Mr. Welles, it is great!"[291]

That evening Lincoln addressed serenaders at the White House: "I am very glad indeed to see you to-night, and yet I will not say I thank you for this call, but I do most sincerely thank Almighty God for the occasion on which you have called. [Cheers.] How long ago is it?—eighty odd years—since on the Fourth of July for the first time in the history of the world a nation by its representatives, assembled and declared as a self-evident truth that 'all men are created equal.' [Cheers.] That was the birthday of the United States of America. Since then the Fourth of July has had several peculiar recognitions. The two most distinguished men in the framing and support of the Declaration were Thomas Jefferson and John Adams—the one having penned it and the other sustained it the most forcibly in debate—the only two of the fifty-five who sustained [signed?] it being elected President of the United States. Precisely fifty years after they put their hands to the paper it pleased Almighty God to take both from the stage of action. This was indeed an extraordinary and remarkable event in our history. Another President, five years after, was called from this stage of existence on the same day and month of the year; and now, on this last Fourth of July just passed, when we have a gigantic Rebellion, at the bottom of which is an effort to overthrow the principle that all men were created equal, we have the surrender of a most powerful position and army on that very day, [cheers] and not only so, but in a succession of battles in Pennsylvania, near to us, through three days, so rapidly fought that they might be called one great battle on the 1st, 2d and 3d of the month of July; and on the 4th the cohorts of those who opposed the declaration that all men are created equal, 'turned tail' and run. [Long and continued cheers.]"[292]

Democrats sneeringly called Lincoln's remarks "miserable and puerile trash" which "humiliated and disgraced" the people, and asserted that the president "never opens his mouth without committing a blunder, and never seizes a pen that he does not write something that causes his friends to blush for his incapacity."[293] They were particularly incensed at Lincoln's colloquialism. One called it "a burning disgrace to the Nation. The Pres. of this Republic—talking about 'turning tail'—*shame, shame, shame*!!!"[294] When Lincoln learned that the Boston *Evening Journal,* a Republican paper, had criticized his use of the expression "turned tail and run," he said: "Some very nice Boston folks, I am grieved to hear, were very much outraged by that phrase, which they thought improper. So I resolved to make no more impromptu speeches if I could help it."[295] This, in fact, was the longest set of off-the-cuff remarks he made during the war, and it foreshadowed the address he would deliver in November at Gettysburg.

Modestly, Lincoln congratulated Grant. "I do not remember that you and I ever met personally. I write this now as a grateful acknowledgment for the almost inestimable service you have done the country. I wish to say a word further. When you first reached the vicinity of Vicksburg, I thought you should do, what you finally did—march the troops across the neck, run the batteries with the transports, and thus go below; and I never had any faith, except a general hope that you knew better than I, that the Yazoo Pass expedition, and the like, could succeed. When you got below, and took Port-Gibson, Grand Gulf, and vicinity, I thought you should go down the river and join Gen. Banks; and when you turned Northward East of the Big

Black, I feared it was a mistake. I now wish to make the personal acknowledgment that you were right, and I was wrong."[296] When Jesse K. Dubois told Lincoln that Grant should not have paroled the Confederate army which surrendered at Vicksburg, he replied: "Dubois, General Grant has done so well, and we are all so pleased at the taking of Vicksburg, let us not quarrel with him about that matter."[297]

The Vicksburg campaign had not entirely opened the Mississippi, for 200 miles to the south Confederates at Port Hudson still threatened river traffic. The movement against that stronghold was undertaken by General N. P. Banks, who in November 1862 had been appointed to command the Department of the Gulf, headquartered in New Orleans. Banks got off to a bad start in his new assignment. After receiving secret orders in late October to raise a force for an expedition to New Orleans, he went about organizing it poorly. When he requisitioned 600 wagons and 300 ambulances (and 4,350 horses and mules to pull them), the quartermaster-general protested that to meet such demands would delay the mission for months and would "require such a fleet of transports as has never sailed at one time from a port."[298] Lincoln, who was anxious that the expedition get underway promptly, scolded Banks: "this expanding, and piling up of *impedimenta*, has been, so far, almost our ruin, and will be our final ruin if it is not abandoned." It would take many weeks to gather and ship all the material requested, which was not even needed in Louisiana. If Banks did not scale back his plan to something like the modest one he had originally proposed, the "expedition is a failure before you start." Eager to have Banks underway before Congress reconvened in early December, Lincoln sensibly pointed out to the general that he "would be better off any where, and especially where you are going, for not having a thousand wagons, doing nothing but hauling forage to feed the animals that draw them, and taking at least two thousand men to care for the wagons and animals, who otherwise might be two thousand good soldiers." Tactfully, the president urged Banks not to regard his letter as "ill-natured," for "it is the very reverse. The simple publication of this requisition would ruin you."[299]

Banks explained that he had no intention of waiting until the requisition was filled and that he had asked for so much equipment for the long run and could sail well before everything he had requested could be provided. He finally got underway on December 4. When a Pennsylvania congressman denounced Banks as a failure, Lincoln demurred: "Well, that is harsh," he said, but acknowledged that the general "*hasn't* come up to my expectations."

"Then, sir, why don't you remove him?"

"Well, sir, one principal reason for not doing so is that *it would hurt Gen. Banks' feelings very much!*"[300]

(Asked by Moncure Conway if Ben Butler would be restored to command in Louisiana, Lincoln said that "he meant to return Butler to N. Orleans as soon as it could be done without hurting Gen. Banks' feelings!" Conway sarcastically exclaimed: "What a fine watchword would be 'Liberty, Union and Banks' feelings!'")[301]

When Banks finally reached Louisiana, he failed to understand that the administration wanted above all to secure the Mississippi. Throughout the spring, Halleck urged Banks to cooperate with Grant's Vicksburg campaign. The "Government is exceedingly disappointed that you and General Grant are not acting in conjunction," Old Brains told the general.[302] Finally, in May, Banks's Army of the Gulf began a siege of Port Hudson, which dragged on into July. Five days after the surrender of Vicksburg, the Port Hudson garrison finally capitulated. Once again, as Lincoln would later put it, the "Father of Waters" could flow "unvexed to the sea."[303] The president gratefully told Banks that the "final stroke in opening the Mississippi never should, and I think never will, be forgotten."[304]

The North reveled in the victories at Port Hudson, Vicksburg, and Gettysburg. "How marvelously the clouds seem to part!" exclaimed George William Curtis. "Three armies under three true and skillful leaders and upon three points successful! I think that for the first time we have a *real* confidence in our Generals."[305]

Vindication: The Successful Performance of Black Troops

A notable feature of Banks's campaign was the part played by his black combat troops. They represented a departure from Lincoln's original plan to use black soldiers only in supporting roles. To Charles Sumner he earnestly explained his intention "to employ African troops to hold the Mississippi River, and also other posts in the warm climates, so that our white soldiers may be employed elsewhere."[306] Lincoln believed that the "immense black population resident on the great river will, when freed and armed, be amply sufficient to protect peaceful commerce from molestation." Blacks could also "garrison the forts below New-Orleans and on the coast which are exposed to the diseases of a Southern climate."[307]

On May 27, 1863, the First and Third Infantry of the Corps d'Afrique, which had been recruited by Butler, along with Banks's own First Engineers, distinguished themselves in a gallant, if unsuccessful, assault on the Confederate works at Port Hudson. In his official report, Banks said: "Whatever doubt may have existed heretofore as to the efficiency of organizations of this character, the history of this day proves conclusively to those who were in condition to observe the conduct of these regiments that the Government will find in this class of troops effective supporters and defenders. The severe test to which they were subjected, and the determined manner in which they encountered the enemy, leaves upon my mind no doubt of their ultimate success. They require only good officers, commands of limited numbers, and careful discipline, to make them excellent soldiers."[308] Commenting on this report, the New York *Times* observed: "this official testimony settles the question that the negro race can fight with great prowess. Those black soldiers had never before been in any severe engagement. They were comparatively raw troops, and were yet subjected to the most awful ordeal that ever veterans have to experience—the charging upon fortifications through the crash of belching batteries. . . . It is no longer possible to doubt the bravery and steadiness of the colored race, when rightly led."[309]

Eleven days later at Milliken's Bend, Louisiana, black troops heroically fended off Confederate attacks. Charles A. Dana, who visited the site shortly afterward, recalled that "the bravery of the blacks in the battle at Milliken's Bend completely revolutionized the sentiment of the army with regard to the employment of negro troops. I heard prominent officers who formerly in private had sneered at the idea of the negroes fighting express themselves after that as heartily in favor of it."[310] The colonel of the Ninth Louisiana regiment thought it "impossible for men to show greater bravery than the Negro troops in that fight."[311]

A week after the fall of Port Hudson, a black regiment in South Carolina covered itself with glory at the battle of Fort Wagner, part of the ongoing campaign against Charleston. The Fifty-Fourth Massachusetts bravely charged the Confederate batteries, crossing a narrow sandy strip raked by artillery and small arms fire. Despite taking heavy casualties, the unit pressed on, reaching the parapet before being driven back because support units failed to appear. Northern newspapers heralded the accomplishment of the black soldiers. Later, the New York *Tribune* noted that it was "not too much to say that if this Massachusetts Fifty-fourth had faltered when its trial came, two hundred thousand colored troops for whom it was a pioneer would never have been put into the field, or would not have been put in for another year, which could have been equivalent to protracting the war into 1866. But it did not falter. It made Fort Wagner such a name to the colored race as Bunker Hill has been for ninety years to the white Yankees."[312]

The conduct of these black soldiers earned the respect of military leaders, including Grant, who in August told Lincoln: "I have given the subject of arming the negro my hearty support. This, with the emancipation of the negro, is the heavyest blow yet given the Confederacy." By "arming the negro we have added a powerful ally. They will make good soldiers and taking them from the enemy weakens him in the same proportion they strengthen us. I am therefore most decidedly in favor of pushing this policy to the enlistment of a force sufficient to hold all the South falling into our hands and to aid in capturing more."[313]

Lincoln, too, paid high tribute to black troops. Three days after Grant penned his missive, the president composed one of his most eloquent public letters, in which he defended the emancipation of slaves and the enlistment of blacks into military service. Referring to Grant's message, he wrote: "some of the commanders of our armies in the field who have given us our most important successes, believe the emancipation policy, and the use of colored troops, constitute the heaviest blow yet dealt to the rebellion; and that, at least one of those important successes, could not have been achieved when it was, but for the aid of black soldiers. Among the commanders holding these views are some who have never had any affinity with what is called abolitionism, or with republican party politics; but who hold them purely as military opinions." Rhetorically, he asked opponents of black enlistment: "You say you will not fight to free negroes. Some of them seem willing to fight for you. . . . I thought that whatever negroes can be got to do as soldiers, leaves just so much less for white soldiers to do, in saving the Union. Does it appear otherwise to you? But negroes, like other people, act upon motives. Why should they do any thing for us, if we will do nothing for them? If they stake their lives for us, they must be prompted by the strongest motive—even the promise of freedom. And the promise being made, must be kept." When at last the North wins the war, "then, there will be some black men who can remember that, with silent tongue, and clenched teeth, and steady eye, and well-poised bayonet, they have helped mankind on to this great consummation;

while, I fear, there will be some white ones, unable to forget that, with malignant heart, and deceitful speech, they have strove to hinder it."[314]

When Confederates threatened to execute or enslave captured black soldiers, the New York *Tribune* complained that Lincoln did nothing to stop them. One abolitionist officer, angry that "the President was very weak on the subject of protecting black troops and their officers," expressed the wish that Lincoln "had said a rebel solider shall die for every negro soldier sold into slavery."[315] Lincoln called the subject of retaliation "one of the most vexing which has arisen during the war."[316] In response to such criticism, on July 30, 1863, he wrote to Stanton: "It is the duty of every government to give protection to its citizens, of whatever class, color, or condition, and especially to those who are duly organized as soldiers in the public service. The law of nations and the usages and customs of war as carried on by civilized powers, permit no distinction as to color in the treatment of prisoners of war as public enemies. To sell or enslave any captured person, on account of his color, and for no offence against the laws of war, is a relapse into barbarism and a crime against the civilization of the age. The government of the United States will give the same protection to all its soldiers, and if the enemy shall sell or enslave anyone because of his color, the offense shall be punished by retaliation upon the enemy's prisoners in our possession. It is therefore ordered that for every soldier of the United States killed in violation of the laws of war, a rebel soldier shall be executed; and for every one enslaved by the enemy or sold into slavery, a rebel soldier shall be placed at hard labor on the public works and continued at such labor until the other shall be released and receive the treatment due to a prisoner of war."[317]

Democrats protested that slaves who joined the Union army were different from free blacks who had done so. If General Burnside was justified in hanging two Confederate officers for recruiting in Kentucky, then the Confederates were justified in executing Union officers recruiting slaves, argued the New York *World*.

Despite the prospect of being murdered in cold blood or enslaved if captured, blacks joined the army in large numbers. Many, however, were angry because they were paid less than white troops and because they could serve only as enlisted men, not officers. "We have an imbecile administration, and the most imbecile management that is possible to conceive of," wrote the black novelist William Wells Brown.[318] A prominent recruiter, Massachusetts businessman and abolitionist George Luther Stearns, suggested to Frederick Douglass that he lobby the administration to do more to protect black prisoners of war. Taking that advice, on August 10, 1863, the black orator called on Stanton and then, accompanied by Kansas Senator Samuel C. Pomeroy, visited the White House. Douglass reported that he was "received cordially" by Lincoln, who rose and extended his hand. "I have never seen a more transparent countenance," Douglass wrote two days later. "There was not the slightest shadow of embarrassment." When he began to explain who he was, Lincoln put him at ease, saying: "I know you; I have read about you, and Mr. Seward has told me about you." Douglass said that he felt "quite at home in his presence."

Hoping to get the president to talk in general terms about his policies regarding blacks, including the pay differential and the refusal to allow blacks to become officers, Douglass thanked Lincoln for the order of retaliation. This tactic worked. As Douglass reported, Lincoln "instantly . . . proceeded with . . . an earnestness and fluency of which I had not suspected him, to vindicate his policy respecting the whole slavery question and especially that in reference to employing colored troops." Responding to criticism of his administration, the president said: "I have been charged with vacillation even by so good a man as Jno. Sherman of Ohio, but I think the charge cannot be sustained. No man can say that having once taken the position I have contradicted it or retreated from it." Douglass interpreted this comment as "an assurance that whoever else might abandon his antislavery policy President Lincoln would stand firm." In justifying his hesitancy to endorse the recruitment of black troops and to issue the order of retaliation, Lincoln (according to Douglass) "said that the country needed talking up to that point. He hesitated in regard to it when he felt that the country was not ready for it. He knew that the colored man throughout this country was a despised man, a hated man, and he knew that if he at first came out with such a proclamation, all the hatred which is poured on the head of the negro race would be visited on his Administration. He said that there was preparatory work needed, and that that preparatory work had been done." He described that "preparatory work" accomplished by black troops: "Remember this, Mr. Douglass; remember that Milliken's Bend, Port Hudson, and Fort Wagner are recent events; and that these were necessary to prepare the way for this very proclamation of mine." If he had issued it earlier, he said, "such was the state of public popular prejudice that an outcry would have been raised against the measure. It would be said 'Ah! We thought it would come to this. White men are to be killed for negroes.'" Douglass found this argument "reasonable." In a letter describing this conversation, he wrote: "My whole interview with the President was gratifying and did much to assure me that slavery would not survive the War and that the country would survive both slavery and the War."[319] In December, Douglass told a Philadelphia audience that while in the White House, "I felt big."[320]

Lincoln's order of retaliation was never implemented, even though Confederates did kill some black prisoners in cold blood, most notoriously at Fort Pillow, Tennessee, in April 1864. After accounts of that massacre inspired public outrage, Lincoln told an audience in Baltimore that no retaliation would be made while the matter was being investigated, but that if the reports turned out to be true, "the retribution shall . . . surely come. It will be [a] matter of grave consideration in what exact course to apply the retribution; but . . . it must come." But it did not come. After the Congressional Committee on the Conduct of the War reported that the allegations were true, the cabinet discussed possible responses. Opinion was divided, with Seward, Chase, Stanton, and Usher supporting an eye-for-an-eye policy and Blair, Bates, and Welles opposed. As Lincoln put it, the "difficulty is not in stating the principle, but in practically applying it." Blood, he said, "can not restore blood, and government should not act for revenge."[321] When Frederick Douglass called for the execution of Confederate prisoners, Lincoln replied that retaliation "was a terrible remedy, and one which it was very difficult to apply; one which, if once begun, there was no telling where it would end; that if he could get hold of the Confederate soldiers who had been guilty of treating colored soldiers as felons he could easily retaliate, but the thought of hanging men for a crime perpetrated by others was revolting to his feelings. He thought that the rebels themselves would stop such barbarous warfare, and less evil would be done if retaliation were not resorted to; that he had already received information that colored soldiers were being treated as prisoners of war."[322]

After mulling over the matter, Lincoln on May 17, 1864, ordered Stanton to notify Confederate authorities that if they did not abandon their policy, the Union would set aside a number of Rebel prisoners and "take such action as may then appear expedient and just."[323] That threat proved idle, however, for Grant's spring offensive distracted attention from the subject of retaliation.

In 1863, Lincoln approved the execution of a Virginia physician, David M. Wright, who had shot a Union army officer commanding black troops. Incensed by the very idea of former slaves in uniform marching down the sidewalks of Norfolk, the doctor whipped out a pistol and murdered Lieutenant Anson L. Sanborn. When a military commission condemned Wright to death, Lincoln carefully reviewed the trial record, spoke with the defendant's attorney, read the numerous petitions testifying to the doctor's respectability, ordered a special examination to be made of the condemned man's mental condition (he had pleaded temporary insanity), and then, after satisfying himself that the accused had received a fair trial and that he was never insane, approved the death sentence. Despite intense pressure to pardon Wright, Lincoln stood by his decision, and the doctor was hanged.

When news reached Washington that the Confederates were using thousands of captured black troops to help fortify Mobile instead of exchanging them, it enraged and disgusted Lincoln. In return, the Union army employed Rebel prisoners for similar purposes.

Meanwhile, black soldiers protested against the lack of equal pay. In 1863, Lincoln told Frederick Douglass that, given the strong Negrophobia prevailing in the earlier stages of the war, "the fact that they [black troops] were not to receive the same pay as white soldiers seemed a necessary concession to smooth the way to their employment at all as soldiers." But, the president added hopefully, "ultimately they would receive the same."[324] His prediction was more or less accurate. In late 1863, a bill equalizing the pay of white and black troops was introduced into Congress, where it encountered stiff opposition. A leading Democratic newspaper protested that to "claim that the indolent, servile negro is the equal in courage, enterprise and fire to the foremost race in all the world, is a libel upon the name of an American citizen. . . . It is unjust in every way to the white soldier to put him on a level with the black."[325] Finally, in June 1864, Congress mandated equal pay but made it retroactive only to the first of that year for those blacks who had been freed during the war; for those who had been free as of April 19, 1861, no such limit was applied.

The victories at Gettysburg, Vicksburg, and Port Hudson represented a major turning point in the war. Edward Bates called the successful campaign in Mississippi "the crowning act of the war," and predicted that it "will go farther towards the suppression of the rebellion than twenty victories in the open field. It breaks the heart of the rebellion."[326] He accurately observed that "the rebellion *west* of the great river, will hardly need to be conquered in the field—it must die out, of mere inanition."[327] Indeed, three of the eleven Confederate states—Arkansas, Texas, and Louisiana—were cut off. In addition, one of the most gaping holes in the blockade was plugged. (Goods imported into Mexico often crossed into Texas and then on to Confederate armies further east.)

No longer could the Confederacy aspire to win independence on the battlefield. Its principal hope was that the North would grow so weary of the war that it would insist on a compromise peace.

"The Signs Look Better"
Victory at the Polls and in the Field
(July–November 1863)

Lincoln's popularity soared after the victories at Gettysburg, Vicksburg, and Port Hudson. His old friend from Illinois, Jesse W. Fell, reflected the changed public mood when he told Lyman Trumbull that during the early stages of the war, "I did not like *some* things that were done, and many things that *were not done*, by the present Administration." Along with most "earnest, loyal men, I too was a grumbler, because, as we thought, the Gov't. moved *too slow*." But looking back, Fell acknowledged that "we are not *now* disposed to be sensorious to the 'powers that be,' even among *ourselves*." To the contrary, "it is now pretty generally conceded, that, all things considered, Mr. Lincoln's Administration has done well." The president had been tried, and it was clear "that he is both honest and patriotic; that if he don't go forward as *fast* as some of us like, *he never goes backwards*."[1] To a friend in Europe, George D. Morgan, brother of New York Senator Edwin D. Morgan, explained that the president "is very popular and good men of all sides seem to regard him as the man for the place, for they see what one cannot see abroad, how difficult the position he has to fill, to keep the border States quiet, to keep peace with the different generals, and give any satisfaction to the radicals."[2] One of those Radicals, Franklin B. Sanborn (who had helped fund John Brown), declared that Lincoln "is really all that we desire."[3]

Despite the Union's July victories, the Confederacy was not on the verge of collapse. White House secretary William O. Stoddard accurately predicted that "[t]his tiger is wounded undo death, but it will die hard, and fight to the last." If "we slacken our efforts because of our successes, there is great danger that the hard-won fruit of them will be torn from us."[4] Lincoln fully realized the truth of this prophecy and worked hard to keep his generals from slackening their efforts. Simultaneously, he girded for the looming political struggle in the fall, when crucial elections in Pennsylvania and Ohio would measure the public mood.

As the president did so, another White House secretary, John Hay, analyzed Lincoln's leadership qualities. In the summer of 1863, Hay told his coadjutor, John G. Nicolay, that their boss "is in fine whack. I have rarely seen him more serene & busy.

He is managing this war, the draft, foreign relations, and planning a reconstruction of the Union, all at once. . . . I am growing more and more firmly convinced that the good of the country absolutely demands that he should be kept where he is till this thing is over. There is no man in the country, so wise, so gentle and so firm. I believe the hand of God placed him where he is." Hay scoffed at rumors that Radicals dominated administration policy: "You may talk as you please of the Abolition Cabal directing affairs from Washington: some well meaning newspapers advise the President to keep his fingers out of the military pie: and all that sort of thing. The truth is, if he did, the pie would be a sorry mess. The old man sits here and wields like a backwoods Jupiter the bolts of war and the machinery of government with a hand equally steady & equally firm."[5]

Others also detected the hand of God at work. In 1864 Joseph T. Mills, a Wisconsin judge who had expected to find the president a mere joker, reached a conclusion like Hay's. After a White House interview, Mills recorded in his diary that Lincoln appeared to be "a man of deep convictions," the "great guiding intellect of the age," whose "Atlantian shoulders were fit to bear the weight of [the] mightiest monarchies." This visitor was so impressed by Lincoln's "transparent honesty, his republican simplicity, his gushing sympathy for those who offered their lives for their country, his utter forgetfulness of self in his concern for his country," that he concluded Lincoln "was Heaven[']s instrument to conduct his people thro[ugh] this red sea of blood to a Canaan of peace & freedom."[6] Amos Tuck of New Hampshire also believed Lincoln "was sent from God to lead this nation out of Egypt, figuratively speaking."[7] In 1864, a Philadelphia abolitionist predicted that Lincoln's "historic heights will dwarf all others in our annals."[8] During Lincoln's lifetime, many others joined Hay, Tuck, and Mills in recognizing the president's greatness.

Fire in the Rear: Resistance to the Draft

In addition to blacks' complaints about their unequal treatment in the military, Lincoln had to deal with whites' protests against the administration of the draft. In March 1863, Congress passed an Enrolling Act, which made most of the 3,115,000 Northern men between the ages of 20 and 45 eligible for conscription. The provisions for commutation (allowing a man to buy his way out for $300, roughly an average worker's annual income) and substitution (allowing a man to hire a substitute to serve in his stead) aroused special ire, provoking widespread protests about "a rich man's war and a poor man's fight." Resistance to the draft became violent. By war's end, thirty-eight enrolling officers were killed, sixty wounded, and a dozen suffered damage to their property. In addition, antidraft riots broke out in several cities, including New York. There, between July 13 and 15, 1863, while most local militiamen were busy in Pennsylvania assisting the Army of the Potomac, a mob ran amok, venting its wrath primarily on blacks. With shouts of "kill the naygers," the rioters, mostly Irish, lynched people and burned the Colored Orphan Asylum. Francis Lieber reported that "negro children were killed in the street, like rats with clubs."[9] Other targets included the draft office, the New York *Tribune* building, police headquarters, homes of government officials and wealthy residents, tenements and boarding houses occupied by blacks, upscale stores like Brooks Brothers, and hotels denying liquor to the rioters. Observing the anarchy from a rooftop, Herman Melville wrote that "the town is taken by its rats."[10] Order was finally restored when some of General Meade's troops helped New York militia and police suppress the roving hordes. Over 100 people were killed and 300 wounded. Lincoln reportedly said "that sooner than abandon the draft at the dictation of the mob, he will transfer Meade's entire army to the city of New York."[11]

During this bloody rampage, the worst riot in American history, Horatio Seymour, the newly elected governor of New York, hastened to the city and seemed to egg the rioters on by addressing them as "my friends" and saying "I assure you I am your friend. You have been my friends." He announced that he had come "to show you a test of my friendship."[12] Seymour did not order them to disperse but gently suggested that they cease and desist. His speech seemed to please the mob. The indiscreet allusion to "friends" was widely criticized and would dog the governor for the rest of his life.

In the preceding months, Seymour, a narrowly partisan Democrat, had done his best to obstruct the enrollment process by delay, neglect, and denunciation. He told an ally that the Lincoln administration "is governed by a spirit of malice in all things small and great" and was acting "in a spirit of hostility" to New York.[13] That charge was patently untrue; the president, along with the head of the draft bureau, Provost Marshal James B. Fry, and the military commander in New York, General John A. Dix, consistently showed restraint, tact, and patience in dealing with the recalcitrant governor.

Shortly after Seymour took office on New Year's Day 1863, Lincoln tried to reach out to him, believing that "as the Governor of the Empire State, and the Representative Man of the Democratic Party," he "had the power to render great public service, and that if he exerted that power against the Rebellion and for his Country, he would be our next President."[14] In early January, Seymour's brother called at the White House to assure Lincoln of the governor's support. The president replied that if he could visit Albany, he would tell Seymour that "his desire was to maintain this Government;" that "he had the same stake in the country" as Seymour did; that he had two children and assumed Seymour had at least as many; that "there could be no next Presidency if the country was broken up;" and that "he was a party man and did not believe in any man who was not;" that "a party man was generally selfish, yet he had appointed most of the officers of the army from among Democrats because most of the West Point men were Democrats, and he believed a man educated in military affairs was better fitted for military office than an uneducated man, and because anti-slavery men, being generally much akin to peace, had never interested themselves in military matters and in getting up companies, as Democrats had;" and that "when the army was unsuccessful, everyone was dissatisfied and criticised the administration." "If a cartman's horse ran away," the president continued, "all the men and women in the streets thought they could do better than the driver, and so it was with the management of the army." "The complaints of his own party gave the Democrats the weapons of their success." "In this contest," Lincoln said, "he saw but three courses to take: one was to fight until the leaders were overthrown; one was to give up the contest altogether; and the other was to negotiate and compromise with the leaders of the rebellion," which "he thought impossible so long as [Jefferson] Davis had the power." The Confederate leaders' "lives were in the rebellion; they, therefore, would never consent to anything but separation and acknowledgment." If Seymour disagreed with this analysis, Lincoln "would be very glad to know of any fact . . . to the contrary."[15]

When nothing came of this overture by March, Lincoln wrote Seymour a friendly letter inviting cooperation. Weeks later the governor responded coolly that he was too busy to answer at length but would do so when time allowed. But he did not. Meanwhile, Seymour repeatedly denounced the draft as unconstitutional, arguing that no man could legally be forced "to take part in the ungodly conflict which is distracting the land." On Independence Day, he delivered an address in Brooklyn proclaiming that Democrats "look upon this Administration as hostile to their rights and liberties; they look upon their opponents as men who would do them wrong in regard to their most sacred franchises."[16] He maintained that the "bloody," "treasonable," and "revolutionary" argument of "public necessity" which the Lincoln administration cited could as well be employed "by a mob as well as by a government."[17] In July, two days before drafting was to begin at New York, Seymour dispatched an aide to Washington with a request that the process be suspended, but the message did not get through. On July 16, Lincoln rejected appeals to declare martial law and to place Ben Butler in charge of New York, remarking "that for the present the authorities of New-York seemed competent to the work of suppressing the riot, and that until it got the better of them, the General Government would not deem it necessary to interfere."[18]

After the riots, the governor bombarded Lincoln with acrimonious letters, arguing that the Empire State's draft quotas were disproportionate compared to its population. Seymour also urged that no further conscription be undertaken until courts had ruled on the constitutionality of the Enrollment Act, and ominously hinted that violent resistance might otherwise be renewed.

Ignoring the tone of menace in Seymour's appeal, Lincoln on August 7 tactfully refused to honor his request. The president, who told John Hay that he was "willing and anxious to have the matter before the Courts," explained to Seymour that he did "not object to abide a decision of the United States Supreme Court, or of the judges thereof, on the constitutionality of the draft law," and would "be willing to facilitate the obtaining of it." But he insisted that he could "not consent to lose the *time* while it is being obtained." (He could have pointed out that under the Constitution, laws were to be enforced until the courts ruled against them in response to complaints by persons affected by those laws.) The Confederate leader who had instituted a draft in 1862, "drives every able bodied man he can reach, into his ranks, very much as a butcher drives bullocks into a slaughter-pen. No time is wasted, no argument is used." Thus the enemy "produces an army which will soon turn upon our now victorious soldiers already in the field, if they shall not be sustained by recruits." To placate Seymour, Lincoln agreed to reduce the quotas in some New York districts.[19]

The governor, however, was not satisfied; he angrily insisted that the draft in his state was being conducted unfairly. In response, Lincoln again reduced some quotas in New York districts. When Seymour continued to behave uncooperatively, the president dispatched 10,000 troops to New York to maintain order while the draft was renewed there on August 19. To repeated protests that the administration failed to credit volunteers against the draft quotas properly, Lincoln patiently explained to Seymour that "[w]hen, for any cause, a fair credit is not given at one time, it should be given as soon thereafter as practicable. My purpose is to be just and fair; and yet to not lose time."[20] In fact, draft quotas in Democratic districts tended to be relatively high because earlier they had not furnished as many volunteers as Republican districts.

When the chairman of the Democratic National Committee, August Belmont, criticized Seymour's letters to Lincoln, the governor intemperately replied: "In dealing with the Republican leaders it is necessary to bear in mind that they are coarse, cowardly, and brutal. They cannot understand generous purposes. They represent the worst phases of the Puritan character."[21] Seymour's nerves were evidently frayed. Halleck, who thought Seymour acted like "a man stark mad," wondered if the governor had not "inherited his father's insanity."[22] John Hay called the governor "half lunatic half demagogue," a "delicate soul without courage or honesty fallen on evil times" and whose "reason, never the most robust is giving way under its overwork."[23] According to a fellow New York Democrat, Seymour was "in a terrible state of nervous excitement" and in "danger of the loss of his wits." He was "tormented both by the terrible reminiscence of the riots & by the constant assertions of the Press that he is concerned in a conspiracy of which the outbreak was a mismanaged portion."[24]

When it was suggested that Lincoln name a special commission to investigate those conspiracy charges, he declined for fear of touching "a match to a barrel of gunpowder." The administration was already sitting on two volcanos, he said, one of which was "blazing away already, and the other will blaze away the moment we scrape a little loose dirt from the top of the crater. Better let the dirt alone,—at least for the present. One rebellion at a time is about as much as we can conveniently handle."[25]

Seward remarked that the governor "is silly and short sighted. One fundamental principle of politics is to be always on the side of your country in a war." The president was reminded of the Illinois politico Justin Butterfield, who "was asked at the beginning of the Mexican War if he were not opposed to it; he said, 'no, I opposed one War [the War of 1812]. That was enough for me. I am now perpetually in favor of war, pestilence and famine.'"[26]

Seymour had acted badly, delivering speeches that helped create the atmosphere in which the draft riot occurred. His motive seemed political, for he did not object to the constitutionality of the draft until *after* the riots. He told Samuel J. Tilden that he wrote to Lincoln in August as part of an attempt at "making up a record." The governor looked "for nothing but hostility" but said he should do his duty, demand his rights, "and let consequences take care of themselves."[27]

The intemperate attacks of Seymour and other leading Democrats on Lincoln angered T. J. Barnett, a Washington insider, who told S. L. M. Barlow, a New York attorney and Democratic kingmaker, that "Lincoln is not a madman wholly. You are mistaken if you suppose that he is blind to the mischiefs of the Radicals. Does the appointment of Meade look that way? The business of the hour is to whip the

Rebels or to give up our nationality, and . . . to settle with our incendiaries afterwards. . . . I am no parasite, . . . but I do have a high respect for Mr. Lincoln's character and motives, as an honest man with sufficient discernment to read the plain ABC of the hornbook before him. He sees and knows that the North cannot afford peace and dismemberment. . . . The struggle within and without, with us, is for national existence—and this the President sees; and more and more; every day, he discerns the waning power of the Radicals; so much so, that if the opposition to his Administration had not been so precipitate and so organized as to render him, at one time, afraid to trust them with the conduct of the war, he would long ago have made a sensational demonstration in their jaws." Barnett deplored Democrats who were "carping and yelling about dead issues, or the secondary one of constitutional law, which will keep well enough till we have the power to settle it. And this makes Mr. Lincoln timid of the very men with whom, on the absorbing question of the instant, his predispositions are. Why do not the respectable leaders of the Conservative Party present themselves here with half the energy which brings the Radicals to Washington? The answer is [that they are] selfish and unworthy. It only amounts to this, that they have failed . . . to drive him from the Chicago platform." If Democrats would stop their reckless criticism of the administration, Lincoln would not be forced into the arms of the Radicals. Sensibly Barnett said "I want the conservatives, on the simple issue of the conduct of the war, of the probable terms of peace, and all such questions, to offer the President a fair chance to stand on a platform more moderate than [the one] that he occupies."[28] His sound advice fell on deaf ears.

As Barnett warned, Lincoln was moving ever closer to the Radicals. In August, one of their leaders, Michigan Senator Zachariah Chandler, expressed "little fear that the President will recede" on emancipation. Admiringly, he told Lyman Trumbull that Lincoln "is as stubborn as a mule when he gets his back up *& it is up now* on the Proclamation." Seward and Weed might be "shaky," but not Lincoln: "this peculiar trait of stubbornness (which annoyed us so much 18 months ago), is *now* our Salvation."[29]

Seymour was not the only Northern leader protesting alleged unfairness in the administration of the draft. When a delegation from Chicago, led by Joseph Medill of the *Tribune,* called to file such a complaint, Lincoln patiently listened, then angrily turned on them with a scowling face. Bitterly he snapped: "Gentlemen, after Boston, Chicago has been the chief instrument in bringing this war on the country. The Northwest has opposed the South as New England has opposed the South. It is you who are largely responsible for making blood flow as it has. You called for war until we had it. You called for Emancipation, and I have given it to you. Whatever you have asked you have had. Now you come here begging to be let off from the call for men which I have made to carry out the war you have demanded. You ought to be ashamed of yourselves. I have a right to expect better things of you. Go home, and raise your 6,000 extra men. And you, Medill, you are acting like a coward. You and your 'Tribune' have had more influence than any paper in the Northwest in making this war. You can influence great masses, and yet you cry to be spared at a moment when your cause is suffering. Go home and send us those men." As Medill recalled, "I couldn't say anything. It was the first time I ever was whipped, and I didn't have an answer. We all got up and went out, and when the door closed one of my colleagues said: 'Well, gentlemen, the old man is right. We ought to be ashamed of ourselves. Let us never say anything about this, but go home and raise the men.' And we did—6,000 men—making 28,000 in the war from a city of 156,000."[30]

Lincoln did not always react harshly to such complaints. When Indiana Governor Oliver P. Morton dispatched his assistant adjutant general, Austin Brown, to Washington to protest that his state had filled its aggregate quota, even though each district had not done so, the president received him cordially. After listening to Brown, he said: "As this case appears to me, Mr. Stanton has acted unjustly and inconsistently. The government cannot be partial in such grave matters to any one State more than another, and I will not permit it." As instructed by Lincoln, Brown left his papers and returned to the White House later that day to discuss the matter in Stanton's presence. When the war secretary adamantly refused to budge, Lincoln grew impatient and finally said: "it seems to me that Stanton will not authorize these credits as claimed by Indiana. I now say to you that I am thoroughly convinced that justice to Indiana demands that the fact that she has filled her quota must be put upon the record. Mr. Brown, if you will wait I will have an order prepared for my signature addressed to the Adjutant General of the Army, and when I sign it you will please deliver it." Stanton abruptly said: "Good day, Mr. President," and left with no further display of temper.[31]

Lincoln sometimes used humor to deflect protests about the draft. When a delegation from an Illinois village complained, he described to them a Maryland hamlet whose quota was one man. At a farmhouse there the enrolling officer solemnly asked an old woman to name every male creature on the premises. She provided several names, including one Billy Bray, who had the ill fortune to be selected for army service. When the provost marshal came to call for Mr. Bray, he was surprised to learn that Bray was a donkey. "So," said Lincoln, "gentlemen, you may be the donkey of your town, and so escape. Therefore don't distress yourselves by meeting trouble half way."[32]

Lincoln was less jovial in dealing with state courts which seriously hindered the enforcement of the draft through habeas corpus proceedings. The problem became acute in Pennsylvania, where resistance to conscription was widespread, especially in the mining regions. By a 3–2 margin, that state's Supreme Court ruled the Enrollment Act unconstitutional. At a cabinet meeting on September 14, 1863, the president, according to Attorney General Bates, "was greatly moved—more angry than I ever saw him" by the action of judges who had been releasing civilians arrested for obstructing conscription. He "declared that it was a formed plan of the democratic copperheads, deliberately acted out to defeat the Govt., and aid the enemy" and that "no honest man did or could believe that the State Judges have any such power."[33] He was, he added, "determined to put a stop to these factious and mischievous proceedings." He even threatened to banish such jurists to Confederate lines, just as he had exiled Clement L. Vallandigham.[34] Pounding the table, he emphatically declared: "I'll not permit my officers to be arrested while in the discharge of their public duties."[35]

Chase demurred, arguing that the writ of habeas corpus was "a most important safeguard of personal liberty" and that traditionally state courts were authorized to issue such writs "for persons detained as enlisted soldiers" and to discharge them. (Chase ignored the 1859 Supreme Court decision in *Ableman v. Booth*, which held that state courts could not prevent federal officers from carrying out their constitutional duties.) He counseled that any change in policy should be adopted only if "a clear case" could be made that the writ was being "abused with a criminal purpose of breaking up the Army." Otherwise, he feared, "a civil war in the Free States would be inevitable." Montgomery Blair concurred, as did John Palmer Usher. The president, however, "thought there was no doubt of the bad faith in which the Writ was now being used."[36]

The next day, Lincoln read to the cabinet a proposed order authorizing provost marshals to ignore habeas corpus injunctions in draft-related cases. If necessary, force could be used to resist state court edicts. Chase agreed that the president had the power to suspend the writ under the 1863 Habeas Corpus Act; but, he argued, Lincoln's order was too vague and might be challenged successfully. Better, he said, to issue a proclamation explicitly suspending the writ. Lincoln concurred, as did the rest of the cabinet. Seward then composed a document which, with slight modifications, was promulgated that day covering all cases involving the military arrest of deserters, draft resisters, spies, aiders and abettors of the Confederacy, prisoners of war, "or any other offense against the military or naval service." It was officially announced on September 17, in the midst of the hotly contested Pennsylvania gubernatorial race. "The proclamation suspending the writ of *Habeas corpus* is a heavy blow but as it is right we can stand it," Governor Curtin told the president.[37]

Around the same time, Lincoln wrote an angry message to draft protestors in which he explained the necessity for conscription and defended its constitutionality on the obvious grounds that Congress had the power to raise and support armies. (The U.S. Supreme Court did not rule on this question until 1918, when it upheld the Selective Service Act of 1917.) After pointing out that some men had been drafted in the Revolutionary War and the War of 1812, Lincoln asked rhetorically: "Wherein is the peculiar hardship now? Shall we shrink from the necessary means to maintain our free government, which our grand-fathers employed to establish it, and our own fathers have already employed once to maintain it? Are we degenerate? Has the manhood of our race run out?"[38] Turning to the commutation and substitution provisions, he pointed out that the latter was a traditional feature of drafting armies and that the former, which was unprecedented, made it easier for poor men to avoid becoming conscripts: "The substitution of men is the provision if any, which favors the rich to the exclusion of the poor. But this being a provision in accordance with an old and well known practice, in the raising of armies, is not objected to. There would have been great objection if that provision had been omitted. And yet being in, the money provision really modifies the inequality which the other introduces. It allows men to escape the service, who are too poor to escape but for it. Without the money provision, competition among the more wealthy might, and probably would, raise the price of substitutes above three hundred dollars, thus leaving the man who could raise only three hundred dollars, no escape from personal service. True, by the law as it is, the man who can not raise so much as three hundred dollars, nor obtain a personal substitute for less, can not escape; but he can come quite as near escaping as he could if the money provision were not in the law. To put it another way, is an unobjectionable law which allows only the man to escape who can pay a thousand dollars, made objectionable by adding a provision that any one may escape who can pay the smaller sum of three hundred dollars? This is the exact difference at this point between the present law and all former draft laws. It is true that by this law a some what larger number will escape than could under a law allowing personal substitutes only; but each additional man thus escaping will be [a] poorer man than could have escaped by the law in the other form. The money provision enlarges the class of exempts from actual service simply by admitting poorer men into it. How, then can this money provision be a wrong to the poor man? The inequality complained of pertains in greater degree to the substitution of men, and is really modified and lessened by the money provision. The inequality could only be perfectly cured by sweeping both provisions away."[39]

Lincoln did not publish this cogent analysis. He was right in pointing out that substitution was a traditional feature of drafting in both the United States and Europe. Congress was merely following precedent by incorporating it into the Enrollment Act. The commutation provision had been added to keep the price of substitutes from soaring, and to raise money for bounties. In practice, the draft did not discriminate significantly against the poor. Nationwide, only 46,000 men were actually drafted, a tiny percentage of the total Union army. Many men took advantage of the commutation provision. In 1863, 59 percent of those called up (and not exempt) paid the $300 fee, while only 9 percent hired substitutes. The following year Congress, persuaded that the army needed the men who had been buying their way out, and reacting to protests against a "concession to the man of means," rescinded the commutation clause for all save conscientious objectors but retained substitution. As Lincoln predicted, the price of substitutes increased rapidly, making it more difficult for poorer men to escape service. Thus the repeal of commutation, not its enactment, represented class legislation favoring the well-to-do.

Though notoriously soft-hearted in issuing pardons, Lincoln had little sympathy for draft resistance. When the wives of two poor Irishmen who had been jailed for that crime asked the president to pardon them, he replied in the accent they had used: "If yers hushbands had not been resisting the draft, they would not now be in prison; so they can stay in prison."[40]

Claybanks vs. Charcoals: Imbroglio in Missouri

Exasperating as problems associated with the draft might be, Lincoln found it even more vexatious to deal with political and military turmoil in the bitterly divided state of Missouri, where his generals clashed repeatedly with local authorities. In the autumn of 1861, he met with the provisional governor, Hamilton R. Gamble, who requested funding for the state militia. The president, eager to free up federal troops in Missouri for service elsewhere, readily agreed, with the understanding that the general in charge of the Department of the West would *ex officio* become the major general commanding the new Missouri State Militia. Implemented in November, the Gamble plan seemed like a sensible arrangement, for many Missourians were unwilling to join the Union army but would happily serve in the state militia in order to suppress local rebels and repel both invading Confederates and marauding Kansas irregulars, called Jayhawkers. Halleck, burdened with administrative responsibilities for a vast department, assigned his assistant, John M. Schofield, to command the militia.

A West Pointer who had taught physics at Washington University in St. Louis, the gentlemanly, sociable, 30-year-old Schofield would prove a controversial figure in Missouri. He had won respect for recruiting troops after the outbreak of hostilities, for assisting Nathaniel Lyon's ill-fated campaign, and for helping to mobilize the old militia. Under Schofield's able direction, the new Missouri State Militia was quickly organized and performed valuable service. But his lack of enthusiasm for emancipation made him suspect in the eyes of Radicals, as did his reputation for indolence. Others found him too willing to employ extreme measures against guerrillas. To combat the bushwhackers and guerrillas terrorizing the state, he authorized provost marshals to punish them severely.

In April 1862, when Halleck left St. Louis to take command in the field, he put Schofield in charge of most of Missouri. Schofield sent many U.S. volunteers to augment the armies of Halleck and Samuel R. Curtis, leaving militiamen to control Missouri, where guerrilla bands spread havoc. To combat them, Schofield assessed damages against Rebel sympathizers for killing or wounding Union soldiers or civilians and for damaging property. To supplement the 10,000-man Missouri State Militia, he drafted men into a new outfit, the Enrolled Missouri Militia, which soon had 40,000 members, mostly from the interior. They were to be supplied and transported by the federal government but paid by the state. Strapped for funds, the Provisional Government levied assessments on disloyal citizens. Careless recruiters allowed some disloyalists to join the Enrolled Missouri Militia, which soon led irate St. Louis Unionists to demand the ouster of Schofield and Gamble.

In September 1862, the ambitious Schofield was not removed but in effect demoted when, to his dismay, General Samuel R. Curtis took charge of the newly created Department of the Missouri, incorporating Kansas, Arkansas, Missouri, and the Indian Territory (the future Oklahoma). A West Point graduate and former congressman from Iowa, Curtis had won a major general's stars as a reward for his victory at Pea Ridge, Arkansas, six months earlier. The serious, deliberate, 56-year-old Curtis demonstrated little emotion, seldom laughed, and was known among the troops as "Old Grannie."

Lincoln was soon embroiled in a controversy between Curtis and Governor Gamble over control of the militia. In late November 1862, the president asked Attorney General Bates (Gamble's brother-in-law) to help settle the dispute: "Few things perplex me more than this question between Gov. Gamble, and the War Department, as to whether the peculiar force organized by the former in Missouri are 'State troops,' or 'United States troops.'" To Lincoln it seemed obvious that it was "either an immaterial, or a mischievous question." Who cared what title the soldiers were given? If more substantive issues were involved, it would be ruinous for the administration to intervene: "Instead of settling one dispute by deciding the question, I should merely furnish a nest full of eggs for hatching new disputes." It should be understood, he argued, that the militia was neither entirely a federal nor a state force, but was "of mixed character." It was safer to ignore the abstract question and deal with practical problems as they arose. The issue now before them was whether the governor had the power to create vacancies, either by removing officers or accepting resignations. Why should there be such bitter contention over such a minor problem, the president wondered. Let Gamble create vacancies and have the War Department ratify them.

A month later, after consulting with Halleck and Stanton, the president transformed that suggestion into an official ruling, in effect designating Missouri militiamen as federal troops. When the governor protested, Stanton agreed that Gamble's earlier decisions regarding removals and resignations would stand, but that in the future the War Department would control such matters. To Lincoln's annoyance, Gamble appealed to him to overrule the war secretary.

Further irritating Gamble was the Second Confiscation Act, which Curtis enforced vigorously. In effect, the general instituted martial law, jailing or exiling suspected disloyalists without due process. In mid-December 1862, attempting to placate Gamble, Lincoln asked Curtis: "Could the civil authority be introduced into Missouri in lieu of the military to any extent, with advantage and safety?" The general promptly replied: "The peace of this State rests on military power. To relinquish this power would be dangerous."[41]

Later that month, the president intervened when Curtis approved an order banishing the Reverend Dr. Samuel B. McPheeters, minister of the Pine Street Presbyterian Church in St. Louis. Although the pastor had taken a loyalty oath, his devotion to the Union appeared to some parishioners insufficiently fervent. He had offended many by baptizing an infant named after Confederate General Sterling Price. McPheeters's case quickly became a *cause célèbre*. He hastened to Washington and appealed to Lincoln, who, on December 27, suspended the banishment decree. When Curtis protested, Lincoln explained that he saw no hard evidence of McPheeters's disloyalty but would rescind his order if the general insisted. He added, however, that the federal government "must not, as by this order, undertake to run the churches. When an individual, in a church or out of it, becomes dangerous to the public interest, he must be checked; but let the churches, as such take care of themselves."[42] Curtis failed to carry out this order, and the president once again had to intervene. As Lincoln explained to the mayor of St. Louis: "I have never interfered, nor thought of interfering as to who shall or shall not preach in any church; nor have I knowingly, or believingly, tolerated any one else to so interfere by my authority. If any one is so interfering, by color of my authority, I would like to have it specifically made known to me. If, after all, what is now sought, is to have me put Dr. M[cPheeters] back, over the heads of a majority of his own congregation, that too, will be declined. I will not have control of any church on any side."[43]

The assessment system of taxing disloyalists, designed to fund the Enrolled Missouri Militia, exacerbated tensions between Curtis and Gamble. Understandably, the governor thought the implementation of the policy was arbitrary, that loyalty could not be easily measured, nor could a sum for assessment be reasonably determined. Gamble asked Lincoln to halt the entire process. On December 10, the president complied, ordering Curtis to suspend assessments in St. Louis. Three weeks later, Gamble urged that a similar order be issued covering the entire state.

Irked by these incessant appeals, Lincoln on January 5, 1863, asked Curtis to cooperate with Governor Gamble and thus to spare him the necessity of intervening in Missouri's endless disputes. "I am having a good deal of trouble with Missouri matters," the exasperated president said. In response to the hard-liners' charges that Gamble's Unionism was suspect, Lincoln assured Curtis that "Gov. Gamble is an honest and true man, not less so than yourself." The president also thought that the general and the governor "could confer together on this, and other Missouri questions with great advantage to the public; that each knows something which the other does not, and that, acting together, you could about double your stock of pertinent information. May I not hope that you and he will attempt this? I could at once safely do, (or you could safely do without me) whatever you and he agree upon. There is absolutely no reason why you should not agree."[44]

By this time, however, Curtis and Gamble had become so estranged that cooperation was impossible. Throughout the winter of 1863, relations between the two men worsened as Curtis seemed to cast his lot with the antislavery Radicals (known as Charcoals), who denounced the Provisional Government as hopelessly in the control of Conservatives (known as Claybanks). Their rivalry grew increasingly bitter after the issuance of the Emancipation Proclamation, which exempted Missouri. Both factions wanted the state government to abolish slavery, but the Claybanks, led by the conservative, Virginia-born Gamble, supported a gradual approach, while the Charcoals, with the bitter, opportunistic firebrand Charles D. Drake at their head, favored immediate emancipation.

Each faction sought to drag Lincoln into the quarrel. In January 1863, as the newly elected Missouri Legislature was choosing a senator, the Radical candidate, B. Gratz Brown, a hot-tempered former editor of the St. Louis *Missouri Democrat*, asked the president: "Does the Administration desire my defeat[?] if not why are its appointees here working for that end?"[45] Lincoln patiently explained that his administration "takes no part between it's friends in Mo, of whom, I at least, consider you one; and I have never before had an intimation that appointees there, were interfering, or were inclined to interfere."[46] The legislature deadlocked, leaving in office the incumbent senators, who had been appointed months earlier to replace their pro-Confederate predecessors.

During the 1862 campaign, Brown, known as "the Prince of the Radicals," had accused Lincoln of acting dictatorially. When St. Louis Germans denounced the president in similar terms, Lincoln told their emissary that "it may be a misfortune for the nation that he was elected president. But, having been elected by the people, he meant to be president, and to perform his duty according to his best understanding, if he had to die for it. No general will be removed, nor will any change in the cabinet be made, to suit the views or wishes of any particular party, faction, or set of men." Responding to the Germans' sharp criticism of Halleck, Lincoln denied that the general was guilty of the charges against him, based as they were on the "misapprehension or ignorance of those who prefer them."[47]

Opponents of Curtis, among them Attorney General Bates and influential members of the Missouri congressional delegation, beseeched Lincoln to remove the general. Bates thought such a move "was the only course that could save Mo. from Social war and utter anarchy."[48] In deciding to replace Curtis, the president rejected charges that he had behaved unethically but explained that the "system of provost marshals established by him throughout the state gave rise to violent complaint."[49] In addition, Lincoln wanted to provide U. S. Grant as many troops as possible for his Vicksburg campaign. When the president asked Curtis to release some of his regiments for service under Grant, the reply came back that no troops could be spared from Missouri. Although there were enough Missouri militiamen to deal with local challenges, Governor Gamble would not cooperate with Curtis. The president considered appointing Frémont or McDowell to take Curtis's place, but rather than either of those discredited men, he selected Edwin V. Sumner. That appointment, made in early March, apparently solved the problem, but en route to St. Louis, Sumner died.

Weeks later Lincoln chose Schofield in Sumner's stead, explaining to that general that he made the change not because Curtis had done anything wrong, but "because of a conviction in my mind that the Union men of Missouri, constituting, when united, a vast majority of the whole people, have entered into a pestilent factional quarrel among themselves, Gen. Curtis, perhaps not of choice, being the head of one faction, and Gov. Gamble that of the other." After laboring in vain for months to settle the quarrel, Lincoln felt obliged "to break it up some how." Since he could not fire Gamble, he removed Curtis, over the objections of a Missouri congressman who protested with some justice that "Gov. Gamble is noted for his unrelenting spirit towards every one who disagrees with or opposes him."[50] The president warned Schofield to avoid siding with either the Claybanks or the Charcoals: "Let your military measures be strong enough to repel the invader and keep the peace, and not so strong as to unnecessarily harrass and persecute the people. It is a difficult *role*, and so much greater will be the honor if you perform it well. If both factions, or neither, shall abuse you, you will probably be about right. Beware of being assailed by one, and praised by the other."[51] That was easier said than done, for the factions had become bitterly estranged amid the bloody guerrilla warfare that ravaged the state.

When Lincoln's private letter to Schofield appeared in the St. Louis *Missouri Democrat,* that general asked the editor how it had been obtained. Receiving no answer, Schofield jailed him, much to Lincoln's dismay. "I regret to learn of the arrest of the Democrat editor," he wrote Schofield in mid-July. "I fear this loses you the middle position I desired you to occupy. . . . I care very little for the publication of any letter I have written. Please spare me the trouble this is likely to bring."[52] To Missouri Congressman Henry T. Blow, who denounced Schofield's action, Lincoln suggested that the significance of that episode had been exaggerated: "The publication of a letter without the leave of the writer or the receiver I think cannot be justified, but in this case I do not think it of sufficient consequence to justify an arrest; and again, the arrest being, through a parole, merely nominal, does not deserve the importance sought to be attached to it. Cannot this small matter be dropped on both sides without further difficulty?"[53]

When the hypersensitive Gamble read the president's letter to Schofield in the *Democrat,* the governor waxed wroth and sent Lincoln a heated protest in which, as John Hay put it, he "alternately whined and growled through many pages."[54] Gamble called the suggestion that he led a faction "grossly offensive" and a "most wanton and unmerited insult." It was, he scolded the president, "unbecoming your position," for it would be as "improper for the President of the United States to assail officially the Governor of a State, as it would be for a Governor of a State to assail officially the President of the United States." Indignantly and self-righteously, he defended his record, adding: "I have not approved the administration of affairs in Missouri under the rule of General Curtis. I have not approved of the system of robbery and arson and murder that has extensively prevailed. While you were treating with humanity and exchanging as prisoners of war those who were elsewhere taken actually fighting against the government, I have not approved of the cold blooded murder of persons in this State at their own homes and in their own fields upon mere suspicion of sympathy with the rebellion. I have not approved of covering the State with Provost Marshals to plunder the people, and keep up a constant irritation and prevent the restoration of peace."[55]

Lincoln replied to the governor's gross overreaction to his letter with characteristic tact: "My Private Secretary has just brought me a letter saying it is a very '*cross*' one from you, about mine to Gen. Schofield, recently published in the Democrat. As I am trying to preserve my own temper, by avoiding irritants, so far as practicable, I have declined to read the cross letter. I think fit to say, however, that when I wrote the letter to Gen. Schofield, I was totally unconscious of any malice, or disrespect towards you, or of using any expression which should offend you, if seen by you.")[56]

(This reaction typified the mature Lincoln's patient way of dealing with hostile invective. When Illinois Congressman William Kellogg protested that he was being unfairly treated, Lincoln endorsed one of his missives: "I understand my friend Kellogg is ill-natured—therefore I do not read his letters."[57] To friends who tried to inform him of personal attacks, he merely said: "I guess we won't talk about that now.")[58]

Humiliated by his removal, Curtis wrote that the president's friends in the West "consider the change one of the worst acts of his administration."[59] To mollify the general, Lincoln sent him a conciliatory letter: "I have scarcely supposed it possible that you would entirely understand my feelings and motives in making the late change of commander for the Department of the Missouri. I inclose you a copy of a letter which I recently addressed to Gen. Schofield, & which will explain the matter in part. It became almost a matter of personal self-defence to somehow break up the state of things in Missouri. I did not mean to cast any censure upon you, nor to indorse any of the charges made against you by others. With me the presumption is still in your favor that you are honest, capable, faithful, and patriotic."[60] When this letter also found its way into print, Gamble was further infuriated. The following month, Lincoln invited the governor to Washington. There the president offended his guest by allowing Ohio Governor William Dennison to join their meeting, which went so poorly that Gamble expressed to Edward Bates his "profound conviction" that the president was "a mere intriguing, pettifogging, piddling politician."[61]

Schofield's appointment dismayed Radicals not only in Missouri but throughout the North. In August, Joseph Medill complained that of "all the acts of omission and commission charged against the President during the last six months none has given the loyal masses of the Northwest more pain than the appointment of Gen Schofield over the great and important Department of the West. No Republican, no antislavery man, no friend of the President approves the appointment."[62] Medill urged Lincoln to name Ben Butler to replace Schofield.

The Missouri Radicals' simmering discontent with Lincoln came to a boil in the summer of 1863, when atrocities along the border with Kansas grew exceptionally lethal. Though conflict had begun there in 1854, when Missouri Border Ruffians and Kansas Jayhawkers first clashed, the level of violence soared with the outbreak of war. Bushwhackers on both sides pillaged, looted, and committed arson as well as cold-blooded murder. On August 21, the notoriously brutal Confederate officer, Captain William Clarke Quantrill, led a raid against Lawrence, Kansas, where his guerrilla band, acting upon orders to "[k]ill every man big enough to carry a gun" and to "[b]urn every house," slaughtered 182 men and boys and torched a like number of buildings. This act of wanton terrorism, the greatest single atrocity against civilians in the war, shocked the North.

Shortly thereafter, General Thomas Ewing, Jr., Union commander of the District of the Border, issued his notorious Order No. 11, banishing approximately 20,000 residents of four Missouri counties bordering Kansas. Except for the internment of Japanese-Americans in World War II, this constituted the most repressive action ever undertaken by the government against American citizens on the grounds of military necessity. It caused immense hardship for the families of loyal Unionists as well as guerrilla supporters. From the vicinity of Kansas City, a Unionist reported observing many "poor people, widows and children, who, with little bundles of clothing, are crossing the river to be subsisted by the charities of the People amongst whom they might find shelter." A federal colonel told his wife that it was "heartsickening to see what I have seen. . . . A desolated country and men & women and children, some of them all most naked. Some on foot and some in old wagons."[63]

Lincoln tacitly authorized this stern measure. On August 3, Ewing had asked Schofield for permission to deport the civilians and to free their slaves. Schofield, in turn, requested Frank Blair to consult with Lincoln about the matter. On August 12, Blair called at the White House and reported back to Schofield: "I had a conversation with the President on the topic suggested by you. He said in regard to the Guerrillas in Lafayette and Jackson counties of whom you propose to dispose & at the same time remove the causes of their organization, that his position could be very well illustrated by an anecdote. An Irishman once asked for a glass of soda water and remarked at the same time that he would be glad if the Doctor could put a little brandy in it *'unbeknownst to him.'* The inference is that old Abe would be glad if you would dispose of the Guerrillas and would not be sorry to see the negroes set free, if it can done without his being known in the affair as having instigated it. He will be certain to recognize it afterward as a military necessity."[64] On August 14, Schofield approved of Ewing's plan, which was implemented four days after Quantrill's raid. Union troops under the notorious Charles "Doc" Jennison carried out this assignment so brutally—pillaging and torching homes of the dispossessed residents—that the affected counties became known as the Burnt District.

On October 1, Lincoln informed Schofield that he would not interfere with the deportations. "With the matters of removing the inhabitants of certain counties *en masse;* and of removing certain individuals from time to time, who are supposed to be mischievous, I am not now interfering, but am leaving to your own discretion." Although the general was enjoined to "expel guerrillas, marauders, and murderers, and all who are known to harbor, aid, or abet them," he was also to "repress assumptions of unauthorized individuals to perform the same service; because under pretence of doing this, they become marauders and murderers themselves. To now restore peace, let the military obey orders; and those not of the military, leave each other alone; thus not breaking the peace themselves."[65]

Lincoln's willingness to approve such a draconian measure reflected his awareness that dealing with guerrillas required unorthodox tactics, and that hard-and-fast rules like those laid out in General Order No. 100 (Instructions for the Government of the Armies of the United States in the Field, written by Francis Lieber at the behest of General Halleck) had to be applied flexibly. He probably understood the situation in much the same way as Schofield, who explained the necessity of deportations: "The evil which exists upon the border of Kansas and Missouri is somewhat different in kind and far greater in degree than in other parts of Missouri. It is the old border hatred intensified by the rebellion and by the murders, robberies, and arson which have characterized the irregular warfare carried on during the early period of the rebellion, not only by the rebels, but by our own troops and people. The effect of this has been to render it impossible for any man who openly avowed and maintained his loyalty to the Government to live in the border counties of Missouri outside of military posts. A large majority of the people remaining were open rebels, while the remainder were compelled to abstain from any word or acts in opposition to the rebellion at the peril of their lives. All were practically enemies of the Government and friends of the rebel guerrillas. The latter found no difficulty in supplying their commissariat wherever they went, and . . . they obtained prompt and accurate information of every movement of our troops, while no citizen was so bold as to give us information in regard to the guerrillas. In a country remarkably well adapted by nature for guerrilla warfare, with all the inhabitants practically the friends of guerillas, it has been found impossible to rid the country of such enemies. At no time during the war have these counties been free of them. No remedy short of destroying the source of their great advantage over our troops could cure the evil."[66]

The deportation order was, in fact, necessitated by the circumstances Schofield enumerated. Confederate General Joseph O. Shelby acknowledged that if Order No. 11 had not been issued, Rebel forces "would shortly have found their way through the district into Kansas" and would have "not only cut off a large amount of supplies, but . . . removed a large number of our friends and sympathizers. . . . The order was fully justified and Ewing did a wise thing when he issued it."[67] The following year, Grant approved similar measures to deal with Virginia guerrillas.

Order Number 11 aroused such vehement protests that it was suspended in November. Two months thereafter, deported loyalists were permitted to return to what was left of their homes, much to the dismay of Ewing, who complained that "the President has treated me rather unkindly in practically removing me."[68] The policy failed to reduce guerrilla violence in Missouri, though no more Quantrill-style raids were made into Kansas. Over a year later, Lincoln gave Missouri Governor Thomas C. Fletcher the same sort of advice he had dispensed to his predecessor (Gamble died in January 1864) and to the military authorities in Missouri: "It seems that there is now no organized military force of the enemy in Missouri and yet that destruction of property and life is rampant every where. Is not the cure for.this within easy reach of the people themselves? It cannot but be that every man, not naturally a robber or cut-throat would gladly put an end to this state of things. A large majority in every locality must feel alike upon this subject; and if so they only need to reach an understanding one with another. Each leaving all others alone solves the problem. And surely each would do this but for his apprehension that others will not leave him alone. Can not this mischievous distrust be removed? Let neighborhood meetings be every where called and held, of all entertaining a sincere purpose for mutual security in the future, whatever they may heretofore have thought, said or done about the war or about anything else. Let all such meet and waiving all else pledge each to cease harassing others and to make common cause against whomever persists in making, aiding or encouraging further disturbance. The practical means they will best know how to adopt and apply. At such meetings old friendships will cross the memory; and honor and Christian Charity will come in to help. Please consider whether it may not be well to suggest this to the now afflicted people of Missouri."[69]

But in Missouri the depth of hatred and the intensity of vengeful feelings were too great for such a solution. Even after the war, guerrillas like Jesse James and Bloody Bill Anderson continued their lawless ways.

Missouri and Kansas Radicals, angry at Schofield's failure to protect them from outrages like Quantrill's raid and the general's refusal to allow Kansans to retaliate, decided to appeal directly to Lincoln. In August, Kansas Senator Jim Lane and Congressman A. C. Wilder urged Schofield's ouster. The following month at the Radical Union Emancipation Convention in Jefferson City, a delegation of seventy members (one from each county represented at that conclave) was chosen to go to Washington. They were to demand that Schofield be replaced by Benjamin F. Butler, a darling of antislavery militants. They also wanted the Enrolled Missouri Militia demobilized and its function assumed by federal troops. Furthermore, they insisted that only loyal men be allowed to vote in state elections.

Radicals objected to the way Schofield had acted that summer during a fateful session of the Missouri state convention, which had originally been elected to consider secession and had been acting more or less as a legislature for over two years. There the Claybanks defeated the Charcoals and adopted a measure abolishing slavery in 1870, much to the chagrin of immediate emancipationists. Radicals denounced Schofield for supporting a Lincoln-like scheme involving compensation and gradualism. During the debates, Schofield had asked Lincoln if loyal slaveholders could count on the administration to protect their rights for the short time that slavery would continue in Missouri. On June 22, Lincoln replied positively: "Desirous as I am, that emancipation shall be adopted by Missouri, and believing as I do, that *gradual* can be made better than *immediate* for both black and white, except when military necessity changes the case, my impulse is to say that such protection would be given. I can not know exactly what shape an act of emancipation may take. If the period from the initiation to the final end, should be comparatively short, and the act should prevent persons being sold, during that period, into more lasting slavery, the whole would be easier. I do not wish to pledge the general government to the affirmative support of even temporary slavery, beyond what can be fairly claimed under the constitution. I suppose, however, this is not desired; but that it is desired for the Military force of the United States, while in Missouri, to not be used in subverting the temporarily reserved legal rights in slaves during the progress of emancipation. This I would desire also. I have very earnestly urged the slave-states to adopt emancipation; and it ought to be, and is an object with me not to overthrow, or thwart what any of them may in good faith do, to that end."[70]

Shortly before the seventy Missourians arrived at Washington, along with a smaller delegation of Kansans, Lincoln said that "if they can show that Schofield has done anything wrong & has interfered to their disadvantage with State politics—or has so acted as to damage the cause of the Union and good order their case is made." But he suspected that "it will be found that Schofield is a firm competent energetic & eminently fair man, and that he has incurred their ill will by refusing to take sides with them in their local politics." Moreover, Lincoln did "not think it in the province of a military commander to interfere with the local politics or to influence elections actively in one way or another."[71]

The eyes of the North focused on the White House meeting, with Radicals everywhere regarding the Missourians as their surrogates. Not since the cabinet imbroglio of the previous December had factionalism so seriously threatened to tear the Republican coalition apart. The utmost tact and diplomacy were required to damp down Radical discontent without alienating Moderates and Conservatives. More specifically, the Missouri, Kansas, Iowa, and Illinois delegations to the next Republican national convention would be profoundly affected by Lincoln's treatment of the aggrieved parties.

While willing to hear them out, the president was determined not to appease them. He told John Hay, "I think I understand this matter perfectly and I cannot do anything contrary to my convictions to please these men, earnest and powerful as they may be."[72] He was particularly disturbed by one of Charles D. Drake's speeches accusing him of tyrannical behavior. Lincoln reasonably concluded that the visitors were not friendly to the administration, their protestations to the contrary notwithstanding. Horace White reported that "[n]othing will convince him that there is anything serious in the Missouri question until civil war actually begins."

Moreover, Lincoln suspected that the committee had an ulterior motive: to replace him with Benjamin Butler in 1864.[73] Reinforcing his negative view were letters from Missouri Conservatives and Edward Bates's opinion that the Committee of Seventy was a "Jacobin Delegation."[74] Lincoln complained to Bates that he "had no *friends in Missouri*."[75]

An ally who urged Lincoln to deal with the delegation in a cordial manner gloomily left the White House on September 27 thinking there was no hope for an amicable meeting of the minds. In fact, the bitterness of the Charcoals and Claybanks was so great that no compromise was possible. Reflecting Lincoln's views, Halleck told Schofield in late September that "[n]either faction in Missouri is really friendly to the President and administration, but each one is striving to destroy the other, regardless of all other considerations. In their mutual hatred they seem to have lost all sense of the perils of the country and all sentiment of national patriotism."[76]

The Committee of Seventy approached the interview with an unbending attitude. As one of them stated: "It is for the President to decide whether he will ride in their wagon or not."[77] As they proceeded toward Washington, they received a warm welcome from antislavery elements in several cities. Upon arrival at the nation's capital, they drew up a nineteen-page formal address praising the Emancipation Proclamation, endorsing immediate abolition in their state, and condemning Governor Gamble's course as proslavery. "From the antagonisms of the radicals to such a policy," the address stated, "have arisen the conflicts which you, Mr. President, have been pleased heretofore to term a 'factional quarrel.'" Like Gamble, they took vigorous exception to the notion that they constituted a faction. "With all respect we deny that the radicals of Missouri have been or are, in any sense, a party to any such quarrel. We are no factionists; but men earnestly intent upon doing our part toward rescuing this great nation from the assaults which slavery is aiming at its life." Schofield, the delegates complained, "has disappointed our just expectations by identifying himself with our state administration, and his policy as department commander has been, as we believe, shaped to conform to Gov. Gamble's proslavery and conservative views. . . . [F]rom the day of Gen. Schofield's accession to the command of that department, matters have grown worse and worse in Missouri, till now they are in a more terrible condition than they have been at any time since the outbreak of the rebellion. This could not be if Gen. Schofield had administered the affairs of that department with proper vigor and a resolute purpose to sustain loyalty and suppress disloyalty. We, therefore, respectfully pray you to send another general to command that department; and, if we do not overstep the bounds of propriety, we ask that the commander sent there be Maj. Gen. Benjamin F. Butler. We believe that his presence here would restore order and peace to Missouri in less than sixty days." In closing, their appeal grew melodramatic: "Whether the loyal hearts of Missouri shall be crushed is for you to say. If you refuse our requests, we return to our homes only to witness, in consequence of that refusal, a more active and relentless persecution of Union men, and to feel that while Maryland can rejoice in the protection of the government of the Union, Missouri is still to be the victim of a proslavery conservatism, which blasts wherever it reigns."[78]

Before meeting with the Committee of Seventy, Lincoln spoke with its secretary, Emil Preetorius, a refugee from the German Revolution of 1848 and editor of the St. Louis *Westliche Post*. By exempting Missouri from the Emancipation Proclamation, said Preetorius, Lincoln had punished the Radicals, who felt that they must combat three administrations: Jefferson Davis's, Hamilton Gamble's, and Abraham Lincoln's. The president replied: "We need the border states. Public opinion in them has not matured. We must patiently educate them up to the right opinion."[79]

On September 30, the president spent over two hours with seventy angry Missourians and eighteen unhappy Kansans, led by Charles D. Drake and Senator James Lane. Lincoln seemed anxious and depressed. He had good reason, for the public mood was growing sour. Ten days earlier the Union army had suffered its first major defeat in the western theater when Confederates under Braxton Bragg badly whipped William S. Rosecrans's Army of the Tennessee at Chickamauga, Georgia. The bad news caused gloom and anxiety to envelop the White House.

Entering the spacious East Room at 10:30 A.M., Lincoln beheld a rather scruffy group, which John Hay described as an "ill combed, black broadcloth, dusty, long-haired and generally vulgar assemblage of earnest men."[80] Some of them were battle-scarred from guerrilla warfare; one had his arm in a sling fashioned from a red handkerchief. The president offered no special greeting and shook no hands.

The committee had disposed itself around three sides of the East Room. Lincoln ambled to the open end of the room, impressing one delegate as "a great, ungainly, almost uncouth man." There he stood, a little more erect than usual, and bowed to his callers. Stiffly and respectfully, they returned the bow. A few applauded, but when their colleagues failed to join in, they stopped.

Pompously and slowly, Drake delivered the committee's formal address, which had been hammered out over the preceding three days. When the deep-voiced Missourian finished reading, Lincoln said he would consider the document "without prejudice, without pique, without resentment," and provide a written response soon.

There followed a long, desultory conversation. One member of the delegation, St. Louis attorney Enos Clarke, recalled that Lincoln "began to discuss the address in a manner that was very disappointing to us. He took up one phase after another and talked about them without showing much interest. In fact, he seemed inclined to treat many of the matters contained in the paper as of little importance. The things which we had felt to be so serious Mr. Lincoln treated as really unworthy of much consideration." The president "was almost impatient, as if he wished to get through with something disagreeable. When he had expressed the opinion that things were not so serious as we thought he began to ask questions, many of them. He elicited answers from different members of the delegation. He started argument, parrying some of the opinions expressed by us and advancing opinions contrary to the conclusions of the Committee of Seventy. This treatment of our grievances was carried so far that most of us felt a sense of deep chagrin."[81]

Lincoln insisted that Governor Gamble enjoyed no special treatment at the hands of the administration. After coming to Washington in 1861 and negotiating an arrangement whereby militia would be organized in Missouri and supported by federal funds, Gamble had repeatedly tried to assert complete control over those troops, and Lincoln had consistently refused. The governor had taken even more offense than the seventy delegates did at the suggestion that Missouri Republicans engaged in a "pestilent factional quarrel."

Lincoln also insisted that he had shown no favoritism toward Schofield. He told his visitors that they had presented only nebulous charges against that general, whom he had never met and with whom he had no personal relationship. "I cannot act on vague impressions," he insisted. "Show me that he had disobeyed orders; show me that he has done something wrong & I will take your request for his removal into serious consideration." He praised the general for doing his duty without complaint and for providing Grant with valuable reinforcements during the Vicksburg campaign. Schofield, Lincoln argued, could not fairly be held responsible for the Lawrence massacre; Quantrill's raid was the sort of act that "could no more be guarded against than assassination." Ominously foreshadowing his own fate, he said to Senator Lane: "If I make up my mind to kill you for instance, I can do it and these hundred gentlemen could not prevent it. They could avenge but could not save you."

To the complaint that Schofield had carried out Lincoln's order suspending the writ of habeas corpus, the president expressed understandable puzzlement. Why should he cashier an officer for implementing his orders? As for the crackdown on the Missouri press, Lincoln defended Schofield, saying that "when an officer in any department finds that a newspaper is pursuing a course calculated to embarrass his operations and stir up sedition and tumult, he has the right to lay hands upon it and suppress it, but in no other case." He noted that he had approved Schofield's order regarding the press only after the leading Radical newspaper in St. Louis, the *Missouri Democrat*, had endorsed it.

"We thought it was then to be used against the other side," interrupted a member of the delegation.

"Certainly you did," replied Lincoln caustically. "Your ideas of justice seem to depend on the application of it. You have spoken of the consideration which you think I should pay to my friends as contradistinguished from my enemies. . . . I recognize no such thing as a political friendship personal to myself," he remarked. "You insist upon adherence to the policy of the proclamation of Emancipation as a test of such political friendship." The committeemen, he said, "seem to be determined to have it executed" in Missouri, which was specifically exempted from its operation.

"No sir, but we think it a national test question."

Of course, Lincoln rejoined, he thought the Proclamation was "right and expedient." He had issued it "after more thought on the subject than probably any one of you have been able to give it." He was better satisfied with people who agreed with him on that subject than those who did not. But, he pointed out, "some earnest Republicans, and some from very far North, were opposed to the issuing of that Proclamation holding it unwise and of doubtful legality." Were these critics to be dismissed as enemies of the Union cause? "Now when you see a man loyally in favor of the Union—willing to vote men and money—spending his time and money and throwing his influence into the recruitment of our armies, I think it ungenerous unjust and impolitic to make his views on abstract political questions a test of his loyalty." Bluntly, Lincoln suggested that his visitors, in demanding that the Conservatives of Missouri be proscribed, were latter-day Torquemadas: "I will not be a party to this application of a pocket Inquisition."

In defending Missouri's Conservatives, Lincoln insisted that they did not resemble the Copperheads, who were deliberately undermining the war effort. One bold visitor contradicted him. In reply, Lincoln delivered a little sermon: "In a civil war one of the saddest evils is suspicion. It poisons the springs of social life. It is the fruitful parent of injustice and strife. Were I to make a rule that in Missouri disloyal men were outlawed and the rightful prey of good citizens as soon as the rule should begin to be carried into effect I would be overwhelmed with affidavits to prove that the first man killed under it was more loyal then the one who killed him. It is impossible to determine the question of the motives that govern men, or to gain absolute knowledge of their sympathies."

When a delegate interjected, "Let the loyal people judge," Lincoln asked sharply: "And who shall say who the loyal people are? You ask the disfranchisement of all disloyal people: but difficulties will environ you at every step in determining the questions which will arise in that matter." They should rely on their long-established test oath for voters to keep secessionists from casting ballots.

"Are we to be protected at the polls in carrying out these laws?" asked a delegate.

"I will order Gen. Schofield to protect you at the polls and save them from illegal interference. He will do it you may be assured. If he does not I will relieve him."

Senator Jim Lane interrupted: "Do you think it sufficient cause for the removal of a General, that he has lost the entire confidence of the people."

Pointedly Lincoln shot back: "I think I should not consider it a sufficient cause if he had lost the confidence unjustly, it would [not] be a very strong reason for his removal."

When Lane asserted, "General Schofield has lost that confidence," Lincoln exclaimed: "You being judge!" (Lane alleged that Lincoln told him "that whoever made war on General Schofield, under the present state of affairs, made war on him—the President.")[82]

The meeting grew ever more tense as the delegates murmured their agreement with Lane.

Lincoln swiftly added that he had evidence that Schofield "has not lost the confidence of the entire people of Missouri."

"All loyal people," they objected.

"You being the standard of loyalty."

A delegate from a rural district, bellowing like an enraged bull, complained about "the sufferings me and the rest of the board suffers, with the guerillas achasing of us, and we a writing to Mr. Scovil for help & he not giving it to us, so we couldn't collect the broken bonds."

"Who's *us?*" asked the president.

"The *Board.*"

"What board?"

"The Board for collecting the broken bonds," came the somewhat nervous reply.

Sternly Lincoln queried: "Who appointed you & by what law, & how were you acting & by what right did you ask a military force from Gen. Schofield?"

The answer to these questions revealed the gentleman to be, in the words of John Hay, a cattle thief and "a sportive and happy free plunderer on the estates of misguided traitors."

Similar exchanges followed, which Hay described: "a question or two from the President pricked the balloon of loud talk and collapsed it around the ears of the delegate to his no small disgust and surprise. The baffled patriot would retreat to a sofa & think the matter over again or would stand in his place and quietly listen in a bewildered manner to the talk and discomfiture of another."

Without naming Drake, Lincoln addressed charges made by him: "I am well aware that by many, by some even among this delegation,—I shall not name them,—I have been in public speeches and in printed documents charged with 'tyranny' and willfulness, with a disposition to make my own personal will supreme. I do not intend to be a tyrant. At all events I shall take care that in my own eyes I do not become one. I shall always try and preserve one friend within me, whoever else fails me, to tell me that I have not been a tyrant, and that I have acted right. I have no right to act the tyrant to mere political opponents. If a man votes for supplies of men and money; encourages enlistments; discourages desertions; does all in his power to carry the war on to a successful issue,—I have no right to question him for his abstract political opinions. I must make a dividing line, some where, between those who are the opponents of the Government and those who only oppose peculiar features of my administration while they sustain the Government."

As the contentious meeting drew to a close, Lincoln reiterated his support for gradual emancipation and chided the Radicals for letting him down. "My friends in Missouri last winter did me a great unkindness. I had relied upon my Radical friends as my mainstay in the management of affairs in that state and they disappointed me. I had recommended Gradual Emancipation, and Congress had endorsed that course. The Radicals in Congress voted for it. The Missouri delegation in Congress went for it,—went, as I thought, right. I had the highest hope that at last Missouri was on the right track. But I was disappointed by the immediate emancipation movement. It endangers the success of the whole advance towards freedom. But you say that the gradual emancipation men were insincere;—that they intended soon to repeal their action; that their course and their professions are purely fraudulent. Now I do not think that a majority of the gradual Emancipationists are insincere. Large bodies of men cannot play the hypocrite.

"I announced my own opinion freely at the time. I was in favor of gradual emancipation. I still am so. You must not call yourselves my friends, if you are only so while I agree with you. According to that, if you differ with me you are not my friends.

"But the mode of emancipation in Missouri is not my business. That is a matter which belongs exclusively to the citizens of that state: I do not wish to interfere. I desire, if it pleases the people of Missouri, that they should adopt gradual emancipation. . . . I think that a union of all anti-slavery men upon this point would have made emancipation a final fact forever. Still, I do not assume any control. I am sorry to see anti-slavery men opposing such a movement."

(According to one delegate, Lincoln "spoke kindly, yet now and then there was a little rasping tone in his voice that seemed to say: 'You men ought to fix this thing up without tormenting me.'")[83]

Lincoln recollected that as he listened to the delegates, he "saw that their attack on Gamble was malicious. They moved against him by flank attacks from different sides of the same question. They accused him of enlisting rebel soldiers among the enrolled militia: and of exempting all the rebels and forcing Union men to do the duty: all this in the blindness of passion." Lincoln scolded them for jeopardizing the chances of Unionist candidates for the U.S. senate (the Radical B. Gratz Brown and the Conservative John B. Henderson) at the upcoming session of the Missouri Legislature. Sternly he told them that "their duty was to elect Henderson and Gratz Brown." (In November, when the legislature chose those two men, Lincoln said "nothing in our politics . . . has pleased me more.")[84]

After the delegation left, Lincoln in a good humor told Edward Bates that some of its members "were not as bad as he supposed" and that he "really thought some of them were pretty good men."[85] John Hay was not so positive. He concluded that the delegation's "incoherent, vague, abusive, prejudiced" case "did no good." They had "claimed to advocate no man—but asked for Butler—to speak without prejudice—yet abused Schofield like drabs; to ask for ascertained rights and they rambled through a maze of ridiculous grievances and absurd suggestions. In the main ignorant and well-meaning, they chose for their spokesman Drake, who is neither ignorant nor well-meaning, who covered the marrow of what they wanted to say in a purposeless mass of unprofitable verbiage which they accepted because it sounded well, and the President will reject because it is nothing but sound. He is a man whom only facts of the toughest kind can move and Drake attacked him with tropes & periods which might have had weight in a Sophomore Debating Club. And so the great Western Delegation from which good people hoped so much for freedom, discharged their little rocket, and went home with no good thing to show for coming—a little angry and a good deal bewildered—not clearly seeing why they have failed—as the President seemed so fair and their cause so good."[86] Hay thought that Lincoln "never appeared to better advantage in the world. Though he knows how immense is the danger to himself from the unreasoning anger of that committee, he never cringed to them for an instant. He stood where he thought he was right and crushed them with his candid logic."[87]

Three days later, Drake delivered supplementary statements to the White House. When he called there yet again on October 5, a servant informed him that the president "is sorry, but he really can't see you. He has a hundred pages of the manuscript you left him to read yet!" Washingtonians chuckled when they learned of that rebuff.[88]

Reflecting on the upcoming elections in Missouri, Lincoln told Hay: "I believe, after all, those Radicals will carry the state & I do not object to it." (In fact, at the hotly contested statewide judicial elections in November, the three Radical candidates for the Supreme Court narrowly outpolled their conservative opponents.) The Radicals,

Lincoln added, "are nearer to me than the other side, in thought and sentiment, though bitterly hostile personally. They are utterly lawless—the unhandiest devils in the world to deal with—but after all their faces are set Zionwards."[89] He believed that the Radicals "have in them the stuff which must save the state and on which we must mainly rely. They are absolutely uncorrosive by the virus of secession. It cannot touch or taint them." The Conservatives, on the other hand, "in casting about for votes to carry through their plans, are tempted to affiliate with those whose record is not clear. If one side *must* be crushed out & the other cherished there could be no doubt which side we would choose as fuller of hope for the future. We would have to side with the Radicals." (Lincoln was indeed ideologically closer to the Radicals than to Governor Gamble, whose conservatism led him in early 1861 to declare that Southern secessionists had legitimate complaints; to protest against troops who permitted slaves to escape to Union lines; to issue an order forbidding Home Guard soldiers to harbor runaway bondsmen; and to discriminate against Radicals when appointing officers.)

But the Radicals' intolerance offended Lincoln. "They insist that I shall hold and treat Governor Gamble and his supporters—men appointed by loyal people of Mo. as reps. of Mo. loyalty—and who have done their whole duty in the war faithfully & promptly—who when they have disagreed with me have been silent and kept about the good work—that I shall treat these men as copperheads and enemies to the Govt. This is simply monstrous." Lincoln found it noteworthy that some fierce Radicals, notably their leader Charles D. Drake, had once been bitter opponents of abolition. Others had been Confederates. He did not object "to penitent rebels being radical: he was glad of it." But he thought it only fair for them to be more forbearing in dealing with Gamble. In matters political, Lincoln "was in favor of short statutes of limitations."[90] His problems with Radicals had more to do with their style than with their ideology. While he shared much in common with them, he did object to what he deemed the "self-righteousness of the Abolitionists."[91]

In his written response to the Committee of Seventy, Lincoln reiterated some of the arguments he had made verbally to those "unhandy devils" a week earlier, but now he wished to defend his Missouri policies to the larger public. He rejected the delegation's contention that Schofield and the Enrolled Missouri Militia caused the Unionists' woes. "The whole can be explained on a more charitable, and, as I think, a more rational hypothesis," he assured them. "We are in civil war. In such cases there always is a main question; but in this case that question is a perplexing compound— Union and Slavery." Thus several political combinations emerged, causing severe strains within the pro-Union coalition: gradual versus immediate emancipationists; proslavery Unionists versus antislavery Unionists; Unionists who cared little about slavery, but were inclined to favor it versus those who cared little about slavery, but were inclined to oppose it. All the permutations of Unionism "may be sincerely entertained by honest and truthful men." Yet "sincerity is questioned, and motives are assailed." Once war breaks out, "blood grows hot, and blood is spilled. Thought is forced from old channels into confusion. Deception breeds and thrives. Confidence dies, and universal suspicion reigns. Each man feels an impulse to kill his neighbor, lest he be first killed by him. Revenge and retaliation follow. . . . Every foul bird comes abroad, and every dirty reptile rises up. These add crime to confusion. Strong measures, deemed indispensable but harsh at best, such men make worse by mal-administration. Murders for old grudges, and murders for pelf, proceed under any cloak that will best cover for the oc[c]asion. These causes amply account for what has occurred in Missouri, without ascribing it to the weakness, or wickedness of any general." Schofield was no more to blame for this chaos than were Frémont, Hunter, Halleck, and Curtis, under whom such anarchy was just as bad.

Lincoln acknowledged that the assessment regime and the provost marshal network were flawed. "To restrain contraband intelligence and trade, a system of searches, seizures, permits, and passes, had been introduced. . . . That there was a necessity for something of the sort was clear; but that it could only be justified by stern necessity, and that it was liable to great abuse in administration, was equally clear. Agents to execute it, contrary to the great Prayer, were led into temptation. Some might, while others would not resist that temptation. It was not possible to hold any to a very strict accountability; and those yielding to the temptation, would sell permits and passes to those who would pay most, and most readily for them; and would seize property, and collect levies in the aptest way to fill their own pockets. Money being the object, the man having money, whether loyal or disloyal, would be a victim. This practice doubt-less existed to some extent, and it was a real additional evil, that it could be and was, plausably charged to exist in greater extent than it did." Critics of assessments and provost marshals had a valid point but ignored the necessity for them, while defenders made valid points about the necessity for them and ignored the mistakes, and each side "bitterly assailed the motives of the other. I could not fail to see that the controversy enlarged in the same proportion as the professed Union-men there distinctly took sides in two opposing political parties. I exhausted my wits, and very nearly my patience also, in efforts to convince both that the evils they charged on each other, were inher-ent in the case, and could not be cured by giving either party a victory over the other."

To modify the "irritating system," Lincoln had replaced General Curtis with General Schofield. "I gave the new commander no instructions as to the administra-tion of the system mentioned, beyond what is contained in the private letter, after-wards surreptitiously published, in which I directed him to act solely for the public good, and independently of both parties. Neither anything you have presented me, nor anything I have otherwise learned, has convinced me that he has been unfaithful to this charge." Moreover, Lincoln could not believe "charges that Gen. Schofield has purposely withheld protection from loyal people, and purposely facilitated the objects of the disloyal." Therefore Schofield would retain command in Missouri.

The Enrolled Militia could not safely be scrapped and replaced by U.S. troops. "Whence shall they come?" asked Lincoln rhetorically. "Shall they be withdrawn from Banks, or Grant, or Steele, or Rosecrans? Few things have been so grateful to my anxious feeling as when, in June last, the local force in Missouri aided Gen. Scho-field to so promptly send a large general force to the relief of Gen. Grant, then invest-ing Vicksburg, and menaced from without by Gen. Johnston."

Lincoln agreed with the Radicals that disloyal elements should not be allowed to vote, and he instructed Schofield accordingly. The president masterfully explained why he could not side with either faction in Missouri: "I do not feel justified to enter upon the broad field you present in regard to the political differences between radicals and conservatives. From time to time I have done and said what appeared to me proper to do and say. The public knows it all. It obliges nobody to follow me, and I trust it obliges me to follow nobody. The radicals and conservatives, each agree with me in some things, and disagree in others. I could wish both to agree with me in all things; for then they would agree with each other, and would be too strong for any foe from any quarter. They, however, choose to do otherwise, and I do not question their right. I too shall do what seems to be my duty. I hold whoever commands in Missouri, or elsewhere, responsible to me, and not to either radicals or conservatives. It is my duty to hear all; but at last, I must, within my sphere, judge what to do, and what to forbear."[92]

Hay justly called this document "a superb affair" in which the president showed himself to be "courteous but immoveable. He will not be bullied even by his friends. He tries to reason with those infuriated people. The world will hear him if they do not."[93] Indeed, the world did hear, for the letter appeared in the press to general acclaim. Even Kansas Senator Samuel C. Pomeroy, despite his Radicalism, approved of Schofield's conduct in Missouri.

Other Radicals were less enthusiastic. Treasury agent Ralph S. Hart reported from St. Louis that it was "just like the President—a dodge. It has disaffected his friends in Mo to an awful extent."[94] Theodore Tilton, editor of the New York *Independent,* agreed, observing that Lincoln "swings his scythe among some men of straw" and has thus "grieved to the heart his best friends and supporters, by closing his ears against the one single and groaning burden their [the Missourians'] grievances," namely, "that he permits Slavery to override Freedom in that state, and appoints his enemies to govern his friends."[95] After Wendell Phillips alleged that Seward had written the letter to Drake and his colleagues, Lincoln explained privately that when "the Missouri delegation was appointed and it was known they were coming to see me, Seward asked that until I should hear and decide their case in my own mind, I would not say a word to him on the subject, or in any way ask his opinion concerning the controversy, so that hereafter we might both say that he had taken no part whatever in the matter; to which I agreed."[96]

En route back to Missouri, members of the Committee of Seventy damaged their cause with inflammatory speeches and resolutions at Manhattan's Cooper Institute. As the New York *Commercial Advertiser* observed, "Mr. Drake and his political friends have the sympathies of the unconditional Unionists in all loyal states, but the intemperate language used by the Missouri delegates at their public meetings in this city tended to shake confidence in their judgment."[97] Noting that the Radicals denounced Lincoln even before they received his written response to their demands, Henry J. Raymond's New York *Times* remarked that if the tone of the speeches was "the measure of their loyalty and respect for the established authorities of the nation, the President will be excused from paying any further attention to their demands."[98] The editors of the Washington *Chronicle* said that they had "too much respect for the cause of radical emancipation in Missouri to say an unkind word in reference to its friends. We would much rather rescue it from the hands of such men as Mr. Drake. . . . Until the Republic is safe Drake and his friends must not be surprised if the country does not hearken to their appeals."[99] The resolutions adopted at the Cooper Institute meeting "do injustice to Mr. Lincoln," noted the New York *Evening Post*.[100] Lincoln reportedly was "a little sore" at what he considered the Missourians' attempt to browbeat him.[101]

Four days before replying to the Missouri Radicals, Lincoln instructed Schofield to have his troops "compel the excited people" in Missouri "to leave one another alone," insofar as that was possible. The general was cautioned to use restraint: "only arrest individuals, and suppress assemblies, or newspapers, when they may be working *palpable* injury to the Military in your charge; and, in no other case will you interfere with the expression of opinion in any form, or allow it to be interfered with violently by others. In this, you have a discretion to exercise with great caution, calmness, and forbearance." His troops were neither to return fugitive slaves nor to encourage slaves to become fugitives. Honoring a request of the Radicals, Lincoln stipulated that at elections, only those taking the test oath be permitted to vote. He also agreed to make Kansas a separate military department and to place a Radical general in charge of it. A Radical judge was also appointed in that state.

Gamble was not pleased. The governor's character, as even his friends acknowledged, had a harsh, stern quality. His integrity and strength of will inspired respect but no fondness. On September 30, he drafted an imperious, slightly hysterical letter to the president insisting that the administration protect Missouri's Provisional Government from the imminent danger posed by violent Radicals who wished to overthrow it. "My patience is exhausted by accusations of disloyalty," he told the president. "I am tired with the repeated imputations of sympathy with bushwhackers and guerillas, against whom I have employed all the power of the State. Without attempting to dictate to you, who shall be commanding General in this Department, I do demand, as I have a right to demand, that you *will* frankly and boldly discountenance the revolutionists [i.e., the Radicals] who are about to involve the State in anarchy."[102] The following day he toned down this missive, but he was still adamant: "I . . . demand of you Mr President that you shall order the General commanding this department to maintain by all the force under his control the integrity of the State Government, and to suppress in its incipiency every combination designed to subvert its authority and to take such measures as may be necessary to this end."[103] When Edward Bates insisted that Gamble stood on firm constitutional ground, Lincoln replied that he would of course protect the Missouri government just as vigorously as he would protect the government of Pennsylvania, "neither more nor less."[104] He offered Gamble similar assurances while expressing serious doubts about the reasonableness of the governor's alarmism.

Gamble's faction rejoiced when Attorney General Bates sacked the Radical William W. Edwards the district attorney for the eastern district of Missouri. Though Chase partisans claimed that it meant "war from the White House upon the friends of Mr. Chase," Lincoln disavowed any knowledge of the case beyond what Bates told him, namely, "that Edwards was inefficient and must be removed for that reason."[105]

(The attorney general explained to Edwards that he was fired for "active participation in political enterprises hostile to the known views and wishes of the Executive Government of both the nation and the state.")[106] When Radicals demanded the dismissal of Bates, Lincoln refused.

The election of the Conservative John B. Henderson and the Radical B. Gratz Brown to the senate did not end bitter factionalism in Missouri. Brown, understandably resenting Schofield's opposition to his senatorial bid, sought to have the general removed. In the senate, Brown blocked Schofield's promotion and urged that he be fired. On December 11, 1863, Brown reported to a friend: "Have just returned from a long and satisfactory interview with the President, and if he will adhere to the purpose expressed all will be well in Mo. very briefly. He . . . expressed an inclination to order Schofield elsewhere and substitute in his place Rozencrans [William S. Rosecrans]."[107] The next day, Representatives John Covode, George S. Boutwell, and James M. Ashley called at the White House to demand that Schofield be replaced as head of the Department of Missouri. The president may not have been entirely chagrined, for Congressman Elihu Washburne had reported to him that Schofield tried to thwart Brown's senatorial aspirations. In addition, the general had subsequently rejected Brown's offer to forgo his opposition to Schofield's promotion if the general would abandon his attempts to prevent Missourians from holding a constitutional convention dealing with emancipation. Lincoln said that Schofield's actions were "obviously transcendent of his instructions and must not be permitted"; he thereupon summoned the general to Washington for an explanation.[108]

At the White House, Schofield was insufficiently persuasive to save his job. He told Lincoln that he "did not believe any general in the army could, as department commander, satisfy the Union people of both Kansas and Missouri; neither the man nor the policy that would suit the one would be at all satisfactory to the other." He also denied intervening in the Missouri senatorial election, despite what Washburne and others reported.[109] Unwilling to discredit Washburne, the president wrote Stanton on December 18: "I believe Gen. Schofield must be relieved from command in the Department of Missouri, otherwise a question of veracity, in relation to his declaration as to his interfering, or not, with the Missouri Legislature, will be made."[110] Schofield had proved effective as a leader of troops in the field but not as an administrator of civilian affairs. But before removing Schofield, Lincoln wanted him promoted to major general. He lobbied Senator Brown repeatedly, asking him to allow Schofield's promotion to go forward. The president believed that the "Prince of Radicals" had agreed, but that gentleman inveigled Senator Charles Sumner to protest against Schofield. According to John Hay, Lincoln was "very much disappointed at Brown. After three interviews with him he understood that Brown would not oppose the confirmation. It is rather a mean dodge to get Sumner to do it in his stead."[111]

When Radical Senators Morton Wilkinson and Zachariah Chandler called on Lincoln to protest against Schofield's promotion, Lincoln told them that General William T. Sherman "says that Schofield will fight, and that he is a good soldier. Sherman says he would like to have him, and that he will give him a corps and put him at active duty in the field. Now if you will confirm Schofield I will send him down there to Sherman and I will send Rosecrans up to take his place in Missouri. And I think that this will so harmonize matters that the whole thing will hang together."[112] The senators reported this conversation to their colleagues, prompting Gratz Brown to ask: "what in the hell is up now?" The Missouri congressional delegation argued that Schofield's promotion would "be an imputation upon the radical men of their State, and a declaration of the Administration against them."[113] In May 1864, the senate finally confirmed Schofield as a major general. Lincoln gave him command of the Army of the Ohio, and off he went to join Sherman, with whom he performed ably.

Defeat in the West: Rosecrans at Chickamauga

General William S. Rosecrans, who weeks earlier had been dismissed from his post as commander of the Army of the Cumberland, now went to St. Louis. After his crucial victory at the battle of Stone's River in January 1863, he had done little with his troops for many months. In the summer, however, he maneuvered Braxton Bragg's army out of Shelbyville, then Tullahoma, and finally Chattanooga. But he incautiously pursued the Confederates into Georgia, where his army was routed on September 19 and 20 at the battle of Chickamauga and driven back into Chattanooga, which Bragg besieged.

Upon learning of the defeat at Chickamauga, Lincoln told John Hay: "Well, Rosecrans has been whipped, as I feared. I have feared it for several days. I believe I feel trouble in the air before it comes. Rosecrans says we have met with a serious disaster—extent not ascertained."[114] When the extent was finally ascertained, Lincoln reportedly was "sober and anxious over it, but not in the least despondent."[115] He did severely criticize two of Rosecrans's corps commanders, Thomas L. Crittenden and Alexander McCook, who, with their commander, had skedaddled back to Chattanooga during the battle, leaving George H. Thomas to fend off the enemy. Thomas did so effectively, earning the sobriquet, "The Rock of Chickamauga." When General James A. Garfield called at the White House and vividly described the battle, Lincoln "listened with the eagerness of a child over a fairy tale," according to Hay.[116]

Other distressing news arrived from the Georgia battlefield: Mary Lincoln's brother-in-law, Confederate General Benjamin Hardin Helm, had been killed. Lincoln had befriended Helm and his wife before the war, and word of his death profoundly saddened the president. "I never saw Mr. Lincoln more moved," recollected David Davis, "than when he heard of the death of his young brother-in-law Ben Hardin Helm, only thirty-two years old, at Chickamauga. I called to see him about 3 o'clock on the 22d of September. I found him in the greatest grief. 'Davis,' said he, 'I feel as David of old did when he was told of the death of Absalom.' "Would to God I had died for thee, oh Absalom, my son, my son!"' I saw how grief stricken he was so I closed the door and left him alone."[117] In the 1850s Lincoln had gotten to know Helm, whom he regarded with fraternal affection. At the outbreak of the war, he tried to appoint the Kentuckian a paymaster with the rank of major. Helm had originally sought that position, but he rejected the generous offer and joined the Confederate army; he said he regarded the day he did so as the "most painful moment of my life."[118]

To Helm's widow Emilie (Mary Todd's favorite half-sister) Lincoln said, "You know, Little Sister, I tried to have Ben come with me. I hope you do not feel any bitterness or that I am in any way to blame for all this sorrow."[119] He had passes issued allowing Emilie to return to her Kentucky home. He also invited her to visit Washington. She accepted the offer and stayed at the White House for two weeks, much to the indignation of some patriots. When Daniel Sickles chided him for hosting the widow of a Rebel general, Lincoln replied with quiet dignity: "Excuse me, General Sickles, my wife and I are in the habit of choosing our own guests. We do not need from our friends either advice or assistance in the matter."[120] The following year, when Mrs. Helm sought another pass in order to retrieve cotton from Atlanta, Lincoln refused because she would not take a loyalty oath. She chided him for his unwillingness to provide help in her hour of need: "I have been a quiet citizen and request only *the right* which humanity and Justice always gives to Widows and Orphans." Bitterly, she added: "your *Minnie bullets* have made us what we are."[121]

(Lincoln had trouble with another of his wife's half-sisters who wanted a cotton trading permit. In the spring of 1864, Martha Todd White of Alabama, who was estranged from Mrs. Lincoln, called at the White House, where the First Couple refused to see her. The president did, however, grant her a pass to return to the South. When she asked for special permission to have her baggage exempt from inspection, Lincoln balked. She then sent emissaries to plead her case. The president sternly remarked to one of them that "if Mrs. W[hite] did not leave forthwith she might expect to find herself within twenty-four hours in the Old Capitol Prison." Despite this refusal, newspapers asserted that she had, while passing through General Butler's lines, refused to allow soldiers to inspect her bags, insisting that she had a special presidential pass. Lincoln had Nicolay write a denial, which ran in the New York *Tribune*, the source of the original false story.)[122]

While grief-stricken over Helm's death, Lincoln was dismayed at the conduct of General Burnside. "Burnside instead of obeying the orders which were given him on the 14th & going to Rosecrans has gone up on a foolish affair to Jonesboro to capture a party of guerrillas," he complained.[123] When word arrived that Burnside was moving away from Chattanooga and towards Jonesboro, Lincoln angrily exclaimed: "Jonesboro? Jonesboro? D— Jonesboro!" and hastily penned a stern rebuke to the general: "Yours of the 23rd is just received, and it makes me doubt whether I am awake or dreaming. I have been struggling for ten days, first through Gen. Halleck, and then directly, to get you to go to assist Gen. Rosecrans in an extremity, and you have repeatedly declared you would do it, and yet you steadily move the contrary way."[124] Deciding this was too harsh, he simply urged Burnside to move quickly toward Chattanooga. To Rosecrans, Lincoln sent words of encouragement: "Be of good cheer, we have unabated confidence in you. . . . We shall do our utmost to assist you."[125]

On the night of September 23, the excitable Stanton asked John Hay to summon the president from the Soldiers' Home to attend a council of war. The young secretary wakened his boss, who expressed concern, for this was the first time that Stanton had sent for him. At the War Department, Lincoln joined Halleck, Stanton, Seward,

Chase, Peter H. Watson, Daniel C. McCallum, and James A. Hardie; together they considered ways to reinforce Rosecrans. When Stanton estimated that 30,000 troops could be moved in five days from the Army of the Potomac to Chattanooga, Lincoln skeptically remarked: "I will bet that if the order is given tonight, the troops could not be got to Washington in five days."[126] Despite his reservations, which were shared by Halleck, it was agreed that the Eleventh and Twelfth Corps should be detached from the Army of the Potomac and rushed to Rosecrans posthaste, with Hooker in charge. Though Fighting Joe would have a much smaller command than usual, and despite his reservations about the proposed strategy, he agreed to take on the new assignment. The grateful president remarked: "Whenever trouble arises I can always rely upon Hooker's magnanimity."[127] Stanton thereupon organized the most successful and dramatic use of railroads in the war, dispatching 23,000 men southwestward. They completed the 1,192-mile journey in record time.

Those reinforcements kept the Confederates from crushing Rosecrans's army, but Bragg might be able to starve it out. Could Rosecrans deal with that threat? The tone of his dispatches convinced the president that he no longer had confidence in his ability to hold the city. Those telegrams made the general seem (in Lincoln's colorful image) "confused and stunned like a duck hit on the head."[128] Further shaking Lincoln's faith in Rosecrans were dispatches from Assistant Secretary of War Charles A. Dana, who was traveling with the Army of the Cumberland. Dana thought the "dazed and mazy" general "was greatly lacking in firmness and steadiness of will" and should be replaced.[129]

In mid-October, Lincoln said: "Rosecrans has seemed to lose spirit and nerve since the battle of Chickamauga." So the president put all three western armies under the command of Grant, who was told he could retain Rosecrans in charge of the Army of the Cumberland or remove him as he saw fit. Stating that Old Rosy "never would obey orders," Grant replaced him with George H. Thomas, who had heroically kept the defeat at Chickamauga from becoming a total rout. Lincoln had praised Thomas lavishly: "It is doubtful whether his heroism and skill . . . has ever been surpassed in the world."[130]

Months later, the president explained to journalist James R. Gilmore why he had authorized Rosecrans's removal: "The army had lost confidence in him. We could not have held Chattanooga three days longer if he had not been removed. His own dispatches after the battle confirmed that. I think Stanton had got a pique against him, but Chickamauga showed that Rosecrans was not equal to the occasion. I think Rosecrans a true man, and a very able man, and when the War Department merged the departments, I fully expected Rosecrans would remain in command. But you wouldn't have me put him in active service against Grant's express request, while Grant is commander-in-chief? I try to do my best. I have tried to do justice by Rosecrans. I did the most I could."[131] Similarly, Lincoln told James A. Garfield in December that he had "never lost confidence" in Rosecrans's patriotism or courage and wanted it understood that he was still a friend of the general.[132] Taking charge of the beefed-up Army of the Cumberland, Grant swiftly opened a supply line to Chattanooga, then methodically planned a counteroffensive against Bragg.

While Grant prepared to reverse the tide in Tennessee, N. P. Banks bungled an attempt to secure a beachhead in Texas. After the surrender of Port Hudson, that general wanted to move against Mobile, an important railroad center and one of the few deep-water ports still in Confederate hands. But Lincoln wished to establish a Union presence in the Lone Star State in order to send a message to Louis Napoleon, whose troops in June 1863 occupied Mexico City. Soon thereafter, the French emperor installed the Archduke Ferdinand Maximilian of Austria to head a puppet government in Mexico. The Union fear was that the French might try to restore Texas to Mexico. In September, responding to Halleck's orders, Banks dispatched troops to Sabine Pass, where they were routed by a small contingent of Rebels. Weeks later, at the battle of Bayou Bourbeau Confederates thwarted another Union advance toward Texas through western Louisiana. In November, Banks did manage to capture Brownsville, but that minor accomplishment hardly offset his earlier failures.

Ohio Saves the Union: Success at the Fall Elections

During the summer and fall of 1863, Lincoln worried about political as well as military developments. Eight gubernatorial elections were to be held that would prove a crucial turning point in the war, especially those in Ohio and Pennsylvania. Would the electorate repudiate the administration as it had done the previous year? Would Clement L. Vallandigham be elected governor of Ohio? Would Democrat George W. Woodward oust Pennsylvania's Governor Andrew G. Curtin? The New York *Tribune* noted that people in both the North and South as well as in England "feel that the fate of the Union rests upon the results of the election in Ohio."[133] The *Tribune*'s editor feared that Democrats would triumph by claiming that their victory would produce "instant Peace and Reunion," while a Republican triumph would mean "interminable War."[134] In September, T. J. Barnett predicted that all "the instant questions will be settled by the coming elections. If they go for the Democracy, then Mr Lincoln will not wind up the war—a new feeling & spirit will inspire the South, to try the Fabian policy, until they can have a chance at the new order of things."

In June 1863, after Vallandigham had been exiled, Lincoln told Barnett that the administration had nothing to fear from the Peace Party, which had just held a massive rally at Manhattan's Cooper Union. Barnett reported that the president "looks upon it as an amalgam of the elements of discontent in New York, & of folks apprehensive of the personal effect of the Conscription act." Opposition to the draft, Lincoln speculated, "will give the Democrats far more trouble than it will anybody else." Grant's splendid campaign in Mississippi would dampen antiwar sentiment. The president was "in great spirits about Vicksburg, & looks to that as the beginning of the end of organized Opposition to the war." Lincoln pooh-poohed criticism of his supposedly dictatorial ways, calling himself "more of a 'Chief Clerk' than a 'Despot.'" In sum, said Barnett, "he smokes the pipe of Peace with his Conscience & will keep on 'pegging away at the Rebels,' wholly satisfied that . . . his head will not be brought to the block." Opponents of the war might fuss and fume, but they were unlikely to commit political suicide. With frontier earthiness, Lincoln told Barnett that

Lincoln and his youngest son, Tad, examine a photograph album (not a bible, as is sometimes alleged). This image, taken by Anthony Berger on February 9, 1864, was reproduced by the thousands and became a great popular favorite. Library of Congress.

"Long Abraham Lincoln a Little Longer" appeared in *Harper's Weekly*, November 26, 1864, on the heels of Lincoln's landslide reelection victory. Cartoonists, both favorable and hostile, typically emphasized Lincoln's great height (6 feet, 4 inches). Abraham Lincoln Presidential Library and Museum, Springfield, Illinois.

In this photo, taken by Alexander Gardner on February 5, 1865, Lincoln seems to radiate an inner peace, for he knew that the war would soon end. Library of Congress.

Lincoln delivering his second inaugural address, March 4, 1865. Some close students of this image assert, a bit dubiously, that they can detect John Wilkes Booth and his co-conspirators in the crowd. Booth did attend the event and, according to Commissioner of Public Buildings Benjamin Brown French, was rebuffed when he attempted to get at the president. Alexander Gardner photograph, Library of Congress.

"If people see the Capitol going on, it is a sign we intend the Union shall go on," Lincoln said when someone suggested suspending construction of the dome during the war. These photographs depict the building at the time of Lincoln's first inauguration (left, taken by Montgomery Meigs) and second inauguration (right, taken by Alexander Gardner). Abraham Lincoln Presidential Library and Museum, Springfield, Illinois.

Enₜ accᵈ ta Act of Cong. A.D. 1863 by Th. Nast in the Clerks Off. of the Dist. Court of the South Dist. of N.Y.

Thomas Nast, the eminent artist and political cartoonist, drew this image of Lincoln entering Richmond, April 5, 1865, based on an eyewitness account provided to him by the journalist Charles Carlton Coffin. A reversed image appeared in *Harper's Weekly*. In 1868, Nast painted a large version of this scene, which hangs in the Union League Club in New York. Lincoln supposedly referred to Nast as "our best recruiting sergeant. His emblematic cartoons have never failed to arouse enthusiasm and patriotism." John Hay Library, Brown University, Providence, Rhode Island.

Often misidentified as the final picture of Lincoln before his death, this Alexander Gardner portrait dates from February 5, 1865, a month before the last photograph of the president. In the developing process, the negative broke. Gardner simply placed the two pieces back together, made one print, and disposed of the negative. Abraham Lincoln Presidential Library and Museum, Springfield, Illinois.

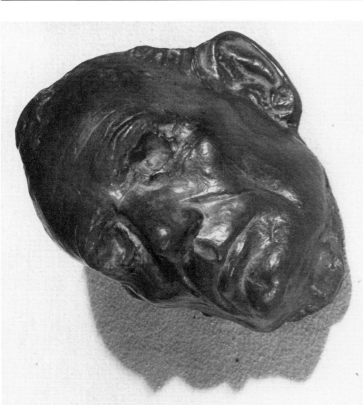

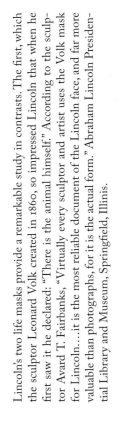

Lincoln's two life masks provide a remarkable study in contrasts. The first, which the sculptor Leonard Volk created in 1860, so impressed Lincoln that when he first saw it he declared: "There is the animal himself." According to the sculptor Avard T. Fairbanks, "Virtually every sculptor and artist uses the Volk mask for Lincoln....it is the most reliable document of the Lincoln face, and far more valuable than photographs, for it is the actual form." Abraham Lincoln Presidential Library and Museum, Springfield, Illinis.

Clark Mills made this life mask in January 1865. Commenting on the difference between this one and Volk's five years earlier, Lincoln's secretary John Hay wrote: "Under this frightful ordeal his demeanor and disposition changed, so gradually that it would be impossible to say when the change began; but he was in mind, body, and nerves a very different man at the second inauguration from the one who had taken the oath in 1861. He continued always the same kindly, genial, and cordial spirit he had been at first; but the boisterous laughter became less frequent year by year; the eye grew veiled by constant meditation on momentous subjects; the air of reserve and detachment from his surroundings increased. He aged with great rapidity." Library of Congress.

FROM OUR SPECIAL WAR CORRESPONDENT.

"CITY POINT, VA., *April* —, 8.30 A.M.
"All seems well with us."—A. LINCOLN.

On the day Lincoln died, this touching cartoon appeared, quoting the president's April 2 telegram from the front to Secretary of War Stanton. Grant had just broken through the Confederate lines at Petersburg and forced Lee to evacuate Richmond. *Harper's Weekly*, April 15, 1865. Abraham Lincoln Presidential Library and Museum, Springfield, Illinois.

Memorabilia celebrating the martyred president and the victorious side in the Civil War included this hand-colored lithograph that Anton Hoenstein produced and John Smith of Philadelphia published in 1865. Entitled "Abraham Lincoln's Last Reception," it fancifully brought together the president and Mrs. Lincoln, Vice President and Mrs. Andrew Johnson, cabinet members, and various high-ranking military officers—all gathered in timeless triumph. Library of Congress.

"'Mrs Grundy [i.e., excessively conventional people] will talk'—but that, after all, she has more sense than to scald her own a[s]s in her *own* pot."[135]

Lincoln's optimism was partly rooted in Republican successes that spring, when the party swept to victory in gubernatorial elections in New England and in municipal contests throughout the Midwest. As the summer progressed, military triumphs at Vicksburg, Gettysburg, and Port Hudson cheered the public. Even Rosecrans's defeat at Chickamauga did not persuade many voters that the war was a failure. Nor could the daring raid of Confederate partisan John Hunt Morgan, who in July led 2,500 men across the Ohio River and rampaged through Indiana and Ohio, stealing horses and spreading panic, before being driven off with huge losses. The raid backfired politically. "If there was before any doubt about the Ohio election," wrote Lyman Trumbull in early August, "Morgan's raid has settled it. No campaign before ever damaged a political friend so much as Morgan's has damaged Vallandigham's."[136] Lee's unsuccessful invasion of Pennsylvania had a similar effect.

Helping improve Republican prospects were newly formed Union Leagues and Union Clubs dedicated to promoting loyalty irrespective of party. In Eastern cities, socially prestigious Union League Clubs emerged to complement the more down-to-earth branches in the Midwest. Members wrote and distributed patriotic literature; encouraged men to enlist; bolstered Union morale; and intimidated blatant Copperheads. Though not officially connected with the Republican Party, the League did yeoman service in building support for the administration. Lincoln's secretary, William O. Stoddard, an active member of the League, called it "the most perfect party skeleton ever put together for utter efficiency of political machine work."[137]

In part, the Union Leagues were intended to combat the activities of organizations like the Knights of the Golden Circle, a secret society formed in the 1850s to help spread slavery into the Caribbean basin. During the war, chapters were formed in the lower Midwest to promote the "Northwest Confederacy" project, an attempt to merge the South and West into a new nation and exclude New England. "The Northwest must be prepared to take her destiny in her own hands," the Chicago *Times* declared a day before the Emancipation Proclamation was formally promulgated. Confederate secret service agents encouraged the Knights and other elements trying to undermine the war effort.[138]

Some Republicans exaggerated the threat posed by the Knights in order to discredit all Democrats, many of whom were loyal to the Union while opposed to the Republican economic program. During the war, Congress established a national banking system, granted public land to railroads, enacted an income tax, passed homestead legislation, jacked up tariff rates, and took other Hamiltonian steps, the likes of which Democrats had been denouncing since Thomas Jefferson's day. Lincoln deferred to the legislature, spending little time or political capital on such economic legislation. (A conspicuous exception was the National Banking Act, which he championed vigorously.) But the activities of many Knights and their ilk were far more sinister than simple Jeffersonian dissent against modernization.

Further enhancing the Republicans' chances for victory in 1863 was the blundering leadership of the Democratic Party. As T. J. Barnett told a prominent New York

Democrat, "the partizans are carping & yelling about dead issues, or the secondary one of Constitutional law." In Washington, leading opponents of the administration were, in Barnett's opinion, "selfish & unworthy!" They should stop criticizing Lincoln personally, stop harping on the race issue, and stop acting in such a partisan manner. "The hatchet must be buried with Mr Lincoln, on the War question," Barnett counseled. The "Democracy must stand like Ate with her hound-furies, under the flag and by the side of its constituted authorities." As it was, the Democrats did not seem like "a grand loyal Union party." Barnett was right. The Democrats sorely missed the leadership of Stephen A. Douglas, whose unalloyed Unionism contrasted sharply with the negativism of so many other party spokesmen. Plaintively, Barnett expressed the hope that the Democrats would "discard such oracles as Fernando Wood, James Brooks, & [Charles] Ingersoll, and [James W.] Wall, and Vallandigham, and [Daniel] Voorhees."[139]

Even more embarrassing were Democratic legislatures in Indiana and Illinois, which brazenly refused to appropriate money or men for the war effort. The Republican governors (Oliver P. Morton and Richard Yates, respectively) used extraconstitutional means to thwart the obstructionists: Yates prorogued the Prairie State's General Assembly, while Morton raised money from the federal government and private citizens.

Some Democrats hated Lincoln and his fellow leaders passionately. Shortly after Gettysburg, the celebrated inventor of the telegraph, Samuel F. B. Morse, called the president a man "without brains, so illiterate as not to be able to see the absurdities of his own logic, so weak and vacillating as to be swayed this way and that by the vulgar cant and fanaticism of such mad zealots as Wilson, Wade, Sumner, Chandler, [and] Wendell Phillips."[140]

In August, a Kentucky Unionist won election as governor with the help of substantial military intervention. Lincoln rejoiced that "the election in Kentucky has gone very strongly right. Old Mr. Wickliffe got ugly, and is terribly beaten." (Representative Charles A. Wickliffe received only 17,344 votes to his opponent's 67,586.) The president also rejoiced at the victory of other Unionist candidates for Congress, especially Green Clay Smith, who defeated incumbent John Menzies. Lincoln noted that Menzies "behaved very badly in the last session of Congress."[141]

To bolster Republican prospects in other states, the administration furloughed thousands of soldiers and granted leave to government employees from Pennsylvania and Ohio, allowing them to return home to vote. While that policy significantly helped Republican chances, Lincoln's most important contribution to the campaign was a letter he wrote in response to an invitation to visit Springfield, where Democrats had held a huge rally in June. To trump that event, Republicans organized an even bigger rally in August and wanted Lincoln to address it. He was tempted to go but felt he could not leave Washington when military events in Tennessee were unfolding. So he wrote a public letter, one of his very best, to be read at the Springfield conclave.

The invitation had come from his old friend, James C. Conkling, who, like many Illinoisans, worried about the strength of antiwar Democrats capitalizing on opposition to emancipation and the use of black soldiers. Even some Republicans were growing disenchanted with the administration. Jackson Grimshaw complained that "it looks blue. . . . Cotton & family speculations, concessions to army rascals—arrests one day & releases the next—Kentucky policy and all that have shit us to hell."[142]

Lincoln's letter, which he asked Conkling to read slowly to the crowd at the Illinois capital, masterfully defended the Emancipation Proclamation and the decision to enroll black troops, but avoided discussing the unpopular Conscription Act. With iron logic, Lincoln bluntly challenged Peace Democrats to answer some tough questions: "You desire peace; and you blame me that we do not have it. But how can we attain it? There are but three conceivable ways. First, to suppress the rebellion by force of arms. This, I am trying to do. Are you for it? If you are, so far we are agreed. If you are not for it, a second way is, to give up the Union. I am against this. Are you for it? If you are, you should say so plainly. If you are not for *force,* nor yet for *dissolution,* there only remains some imaginable *compromise.*" But, Lincoln averred, no compromise that restored the Union was possible. Neither the Confederacy's army nor its civilian leadership had shown interest in such a compromise. "In an effort at such compromise we should waste time, which the enemy would improve to our disadvantage; and that would be all."

Lincoln boldly addressed the race issue, challenging his critics: "you are dissatisfied with me about the negro. Quite likely there is a difference of opinion between you and myself upon that subject. I certainly wish that all men could be free, while I suppose you do not." As he had done a year earlier in his public letter to Horace Greeley, Lincoln emphasized that he issued the Emancipation Proclamation and approved the recruitment of black troops as practical, Union-saving measures. He chided critics for their reluctance to avail themselves of his generous offer to pay for slaves: "I suggested compensated emancipation; to which you replied you wished not to be taxed to buy negroes. But I had not asked you to be taxed to buy negroes, except in such way, as to save you from greater taxation to save the Union exclusively by other means." To those who objected that the Emancipation Proclamation violated the Constitution, Lincoln insisted that "the constitution invests its commander-in-chief, with the law of war, in time of war," which permitted the seizure of property. Was there any doubt, he asked rhetorically, "that by the law of war, property, both of enemies and friends, may be taken when needed? And is it not needed whenever taking it, helps us, or hurts the enemy? Armies, the world over, destroy enemies' property when they can not use it; and even destroy their own to keep it from the enemy."

Military leaders, Lincoln assured his critics, had praised the Emancipation Proclamation and the enlistment of black troops as essential weapons in prosecuting the war. "Among the commanders holding these views," he pointed out, "are some who have never had any affinity with what is called abolitionism, or with republican party politics; but who hold them purely as military opinions. I submit these opinions as being entitled to some weight against the objections, often urged, that emancipation, and arming the blacks, are unwise as military measures, and were not adopted, as such, in good faith."

Lincoln offered a brief, somewhat whimsical progress report on the war, paying tribute to all who made that progress possible: "The signs look better. The Father of Waters again goes unvexed to the sea. Thanks to the great North-West for it. Nor yet wholly to them. Three hundred miles up, they met New-England, Empire, Key-Stone, and Jersey, hewing their way right and left. The Sunny South too, in more colors than one, also lent a hand. On the spot, their part of the history was jotted down in black and white. The job was a great national one; and let none be banned who bore an honorable part in it. And while those who have cleared the great river may well be proud, even that is not all. It is hard to say that anything has been more bravely, and well done, than at Antietam, Murfreesboro, Gettysburg, and on many fields of lesser note. Nor must Uncle Sam's Web-feet be forgotten. At all the watery margins they have been present. Not only on the deep sea, the broad bay, and the rapid river, but also up the narrow muddy bayou, and wherever the ground was a little damp, they have been, and made their tracks. Thanks to all. For the great republic—for the principle it lives by, and keeps alive—for man's vast future,—thanks to all."

In an eloquent conclusion, Lincoln meditated on the larger significance of the war: "Peace does not appear so distant as it did. I hope it will come soon, and come to stay; and so come as to be worth the keeping in all future time. It will then have been proved that, among free men, there can be no successful appeal from the ballot to the bullet; and that they who take such appeal are sure to lose their case, and pay the cost."[143]

With this powerful letter, Lincoln helped scotch the Copperhead snake. It was read at the huge Springfield rally, which, Conkling told the president, "was a magnificent success," drawing between 50,000 and 75,000 people. "The most unbounded enthusiasm prevailed. The speeches were of the most earnest, radical and progressive character and the people applauded most vociferously every sentiment in favor of the vigorous prosecution of the war until the rebellion was subdued—the Proclamation of Emancipation and the arming of negro soldiers and every allusion to yourself and your policy."[144] A mass meeting of young men in New York greeted the Conkling letter "with shouts, cheers, thanksgiving, & tears."[145] Lincoln's insistence that emancipation would not be reversed pleased many Radicals, who called the document "a blow at the copperheads which they will find it hard to parry" and "one of the heaviest blows they have ever received—unless we except Gov. Seymour's mob."[146] Charles Sumner told Lincoln that his "true & noble letter" was a "historic document" in which the "case is admirably stated, so that all but the wicked must confess its force. It cannot be answered."[147] Sumner's venerable constituent, the abolitionist Josiah Quincy, praised Lincoln's "happy, timely, conclusive & effective" letter.[148] Said the Chicago *Tribune*: "It has been feared that even he looked upon his Proclamation as a temporary expedient, born of the necessities of the situation, to be adhered to or retracted as a short-sighted or time-serving policy dictated; and that when the moment for attempting compromise might come, he would put it aside. The Springfield letter dispels all doubts and silences all croakers. In a few plain sentences, than which none more important were ever uttered in this country, Mr. Lincoln exonerates himself from the charge urged against him, shows the untenableness of the position that his enemies occupy, and gives the world assurance that that great measure of policy and justice, which . . . guarantees freedom to three millions of slaves, is to remain the law of the republic."

Democrats protested that if "the proclamation cannot be retracted, then every provision in the constitution pertaining to slavery is abrogated. . . . The Constitution has been murdered—assassinated—by him who solemnly swore to 'preserve, protect and defend it.'" The Louisville *Daily Democrat* inferred that "at the end, if there ever be an end, we shall have, not a restoration of the Union, but something else, which may be desirable or not, no one can foresee." The New York *Old Guard* declared: "If it has any meaning at all it means that the object of this struggle is to free negroes. And to do this he is willing to shed the blood of a quarter of a million of white men."[149]

Although some Republicans who had anticipated that Lincoln would discuss Reconstruction issues were disappointed, most cheered the Conkling letter. The New York *Times* rejoiced "that it is plain that the President has no power to make a man once legally free again legally a slave. The President's argument for the employment of colored troops is unanswerable."[150] The New York *Evening Post* lauded the "singularly clear and ingenuous letter," which radiated "manly honesty, a sincere desire to do right, a conscientious intention to observe faithfully his oaths of office, and to do his duty as an American citizen, and a lover of democratic institutions and of that liberty upon which our government is founded."[151] The *North American Review* thought that Lincoln has "been reproached with Americanisms by some not unfriendly British critics," but the editor agreed with George Templeton Strong, who judged that some sentences "a critic would like to eliminate, but they are delightfully characteristic of the man." The letter, Strong accurately predicted, was "likely to be a conspicuous document in the history of our times."[152] (The Democratic *Illinois State Register* was less tolerant of presidential colloquialisms: "Mr. Lincoln speaks of 'Uncle Sam's webbed feet' as if the government were a goose," and "in the radical view of who constitutes 'the government,' perhaps he is right.")[153] A Radical admirer of the letter acknowledged that it "is a queer mingling of sense and humor."[154]

Charles Eliot Norton, who had been a harsh critic of Lincoln's rhetoric, praised "the extraordinary excellence of the President's letter." In Norton's opinion, the president rose "with each new effort, and his letters are successive victories." Those public letters since the one to the Albany Democrats "are, as he says to General Grant of Vicksburg, 'of almost inestimable value to the country,'—for they are of the rarest class of political documents, arguments seriously addressed by one in power to the conscience and reason of the citizens of the commonwealth." Such public letters, Norton boldly asserted, were "of the more value to us as permanent precedents—examples of the possibility of the coexistence of a strong government with entire and immediate dependence upon and direct appeal to the people. There is in them the clearest tone of uprightness of character, purity of intention, and goodness of heart."[155] John Hay deemed the Conkling letter "a great thing" despite some "hideously bad rhetoric" and "some indecorums that are infamous." It "takes its solid place in history, as a great utterance of a great man. The whole Cabinet could not have tinkered up a letter which could have been compared with it. He can snake a sophism out of its hole, better than all the trained logicians of all schools."[156]

English reaction was generally positive. The London *Star* echoed Hay, calling the letter a "manifesto of a truly great man in the exigency of almost unequaled moment" and "a masterpiece of cogent argument." As "an appeal to the spirit of the nation it is sublime in the dignified simplicity of its eloquence," which was "worthy of a Cromwell or a Washington."[157] The eminent British analyst of slavery, John Elliot Cairnes, was especially impressed by the Conkling letter, which he thought "an immense advance" over the Greeley letter; it proved that Lincoln was "a man of truly statesmanlike caliber of mind. To my taste there has been none like him since Washington. The metal indeed received the temper slowly, but now that it has got it, 'it can stand the strain of being in deadly earnest.'"[158]

The Democrats' most egregious blunder in the 1863 electoral campaigns was nominating Clement L. Vallandigham for governor of Ohio instead of a more moderate candidate. The Ohio contest became a referendum on the war rather than alleged government violations of civil liberties. From exile in Canada, where Vallandigham had settled weeks after Lincoln banished him to the South, the former congressman was unable to mount a serious campaign against his opponent, John Brough, a rotund, witty, persuasive orator and former Democrat who had served as Ohio's state auditor as well as president of a railroad. Unlike the incumbent governor, David Tod, Brough warmly supported emancipation. Republicans denounced Vallandigham as a traitor for opposing the war effort. Noting that he had been a brigadier in the Ohio militia in antebellum days, they ridiculed him as a general who was "invincible in peace, invisible in war."[159] Republicans soft-pedaled the slavery issue, for as Murat Halstead warned, "if the vote were taken in Ohio between Vallandigham and the 'radical policy' of the President, the foolish and hopelessly impracticable proclamation &c, the election of Vallandigham would be the result. The essential thing in this canvass is to keep the Administration out of sight as much as possible, and talk of the *cause of nationality* and nothing else." Halstead grew optimistic when General Burnside left Ohio for Tennessee: "now we will beat Vallandigham without the soldiers vote, if there can be a few moments quiet on the nigger question."[160]

But the Democrats would not keep quiet on that issue. Appealing to race prejudice, they called Brough a "nigger-lover," a "fat Knight of the corps d'Afrique," and a candidate of the "nigger-worshipping Republican party." Their rallies featured young women standing beneath banners imploring: "Father, save us from Negro Equality." Announced a Democratic paper in Iowa: "We had rather sleep with Democrats than Niggers." One Democrat warned that the "'irrepressible conflict' between white and black laborers will be realized in all its vigor upon Ohio soil if the policy of Lincoln and Brough is carried." Another urged fellow Buckeyes to let "every vote count in favor of the *white* man, and against the Abolition hordes, who would place negro children in your schools, negro jurors in your jury boxes, and negro votes in your ballot boxes!" Democrats portrayed their candidate as a "Martyr to Freedom of Speech."[161]

As the campaign heated up, Republicans in mid-September rejoiced at the news from Maine, where they won the gubernatorial election by a landslide and captured an overwhelming majority of the legislature. On October 13, as Ohio voters flocked to the polls, Lincoln said he felt nervous. Thomas F. Meagher, a War Democrat and founder of the Irish Brigade, explained why the stakes were unusually high: "The importance of the coming contest in Ohio . . . cannot be exaggerated. The triumph of the National Government in this contest . . . will be of no less (possibly of greater) consequence, than the repulse of the armed enemy at Gettysburg and the capitulation of Vicksburg have been. Defeated in Ohio, the malcontents and conspirators of the North are beaten everywhere. Their backbone is broken; and the surest way to kill a copperhead or any other reptile . . . is to break his back."[162]

When Brough triumphed over Vallandigham by a margin of slightly less than 100,000, capturing 95 percent of the soldier vote, Lincoln was vastly relieved and immensely delighted, regarding the outcome as a popular verdict on his presidency. The following day he told Gideon Welles that he "had more anxiety in regard to the election results of yesterday [in Ohio] than he had in 1860 when he was chosen. He could not have believed four years ago that one genuine American would or could be induced to vote for such a man as Vallandigham; yet he has been made the candidate of a large party, their representative man, and has received a vote that has discredited the country."[163]

When Brough called at the White House and lamented that he had not prevailed by 100,000 votes, Lincoln said he was reminded of a "man who had been greatly annoyed by an ugly dog" and "took a club and knocked the dog on the head and killed him; but he still continued to whack the animal, when a passer-by cried out to him, 'Why, what are you about, man? Don't you see the dog is dead? Where is the use of beating him now?' 'Yes,' replied the man, whacking away at the dog, 'I know he is dead, but I wanted to teach the mean dog that there is *punishment after death*.' Poor Val was dead before the election, but Brough wanted to keep on whacking him, as the man did the dog, after death."[164]

Lincoln was also gratified by the outcome in Pennsylvania, where Governor Andrew G. Curtin stood for reelection despite suffering from such poor health that he could not campaign extensively. The Democrats had nominated George W. Woodward, the cold, calculating chief justice of the state supreme court who maintained that both the Enrollment and the Legal Tender Acts were unconstitutional. He had done his best to impede the draft. During the secession crisis, he called slavery an "incalculable blessing" and expressed the hope that if the country were to be split, the dividing line would run north of the Keystone State. On September 4, Secretary Chase, who actively campaigned for Brough in Ohio, informed a friend that "Gov. Curtin's reelection or defeat is now the success or defeat of the administration of President Lincoln."[165] That same day, Curtin warned Lincoln that if "the election were to occur now, the result would be extremely doubtful."[166] As October began, Curtin reported that he was "having a hotly-contested canvass."[167]

On election day, a letter by General McClellan, who was angling for the 1864 Democratic presidential nomination, appeared in Democratic newspapers stating that "I would, were it in my power, give to Judge Woodward my voice and vote."[168] Little Mac's intervention proved futile, for Curtin, known as the "Soldiers' Friend," bested Woodward by over 15,000 votes, winning 51.5 percent of the ballots cast. But McClellan did improve his chances to win his party's nod for the presidency a few months later. According to Alexander K. McClure, Lincoln took "unusual interest" in the Pennsylvania campaign "and his congratulations to Curtin upon his re-election were repeated for several days, and were often as quaint as they were sincere."[169] George William Curtis urged friends to "rejoice over Penn. & Ohio. It is the great vindication of the President, and the popular verdict upon the policy of the war." He asked rhetorically, "Is it not the sign of the final disintegration of that rotten mass known technically as the Democratic party?"[170]

Republicans also won gubernatorial races in Iowa, Minnesota, Wisconsin, and Massachusetts, as well as carrying numerous local elections. Lincoln's spirits soared, especially at the landslide in the Bay State.

Transforming the Free State into a Free State: Elections in Maryland

The November elections in Maryland (for congressmen, state comptroller, and local offices) caused Lincoln some anxiety, for he was especially eager to promote emancipation there. But the public was led to believe otherwise when on October 3, Montgomery Blair delivered an intemperate speech at Rockville attacking the "ultra-abolitionists" and sharply criticizing Charles Sumner's "state suicide" theory, which he compared unfavorably to Lincoln's Reconstruction policy. At times Blair sounded like a Democrat as he championed states rights and denounced Radicals for supporting measures that "would make the manumission of the slaves the means of infusing their blood into our whole system by blending with it 'amalgamation, equality, and fraternity.'"[171]

Embarrassed by Blair's indiscretion, Lincoln claimed not to have read the Rockville speech. To John Hay, he explained that he saw little difference between Sumner's approach to Reconstruction and Blair's. He deemed the controversy "one of mere form and little else. I do not think Mr Blair would agree that the states in rebellion are to be permitted to come at once into the political family & renew the very performances which have already so bedeviled us. I do not think Mr. Sumner would insist that when the loyal people of a state obtain the supremacy in their councils & are ready to assume the direction of their own affairs, that they should be excluded. I do not understand Mr. Blair to admit that Jefferson Davis may take his seat in Congress again as a Representative of his people; I do not understand Mr Sumner to assert that John Minor Botts may not. So far as I understand Mr Sumner he seems in favor of Congress taking from the Executive the power it at present exercises over insurrectionary districts, and assuming it to itself. But when the vital question arises as to the right and privilege of the people of these states to govern themselves, I apprehend there will be little difference among loyal men. The question at once is presented in whom this power is vested. And the practical matter for decision is how to keep the rebellious populations from overwhelming and outvoting the loyal minority."[172]

Unlike Lincoln, many Radicals viewed the issues raised by Blair's speech as matters of substance rather than form. Senators Wade and Chandler predicted that if Blair made another such speech "it would kill Lincoln."[173] Thaddeus Stevens complained that Blair's "vile" remarks were "much more infamous than any speech yet made by a Copperhead orator. I know of no rebel sympathizer who has charged such disgusting principles and designs on the republican party as this apostate. It has and will do us more harm at the election than all the efforts of the Opposition. If these are the principles of the Administration no earnest anti-slavery man will wish it to be sustained. If such men are to be retained in Mr. Lincoln's cabinet, it is time, we were consulting about his successor."[174] Stevens also denounced Seward, telling Lincoln: "I and ever so many *Penn[sylvanian]s* went to Chicago to get rid of Seward & after all that trouble & taking you to get rid of him, here we are saddled with both of you."

"Well," replied Lincoln, "I suppose you would be willing to get rid of me to get rid of him."

"I don[']t know, Mr. Pres[iden]t what the people might think if they had the opportunity to speak!!"[175]

Another Pennsylvanian, John W. Forney, told Blair in Lincoln's presence: "if you had made that speech thirty days earlier, *you would have lost us the election in Pennsylvania!*"

"Well," the postmaster general replied, "they were my honest convictions, and I couldn't express anything else."

"What business have you remaining in the Cabinet, then, and loading us down with the weight of your convictions against the policy of the Administration you belong to?" asked Forney.[176]

Lincoln observed this sharp exchange in silence.

Radicals also objected to the postmaster general's efforts to defeat the candidacy of former Congressman Henry Winter Davis. To them, Lincoln's reluctance to disavow Blair made it seem as if he were "on the fence, apparently caring little which party wins—the anti-slavery or the pro-slavery."[177] To help defuse such criticism, Lincoln injected himself into the campaign publicly by having Samuel Galloway of Ohio convey a message to a huge Union Party rally at Baltimore in late October: "I am with them in heart, sympathy, in the great cause of Unconditional Union and Emancipation."[178]

Lincoln also tried to promote harmony between Unconditional and Conservative Unionists in Maryland. The army's practice of recruiting slaves rather arbitrarily, making little distinction between loyal and disloyal owners, had strained relations between the Republican factions. When irate Unionist slaveholders protested, the president told them "that if the recruiting squads did not conduct themselves properly, their places should be supplied by others, but that the orders under which the enlistments were being made could not be revoked, since the country needed able-bodied soldiers, and was not squeamish as to their complexion."[179] He emphasized, however, that he wished to offend no Marylanders. In October, he issued a general order providing that loyal slaveholders would be paid up to $300 for any slave who enlisted, with the understanding that all such recruits would "forever thereafter be free."[180] Any loyal slaveowners unwilling to let their slaves join the army must themselves enter the ranks.

Earlier, Lincoln had instructed General Robert C. Schenck to rein in aggressive army recruiters in Maryland, for he feared that discontent among the loyal slaveholders might jeopardize the Union Party's chances. Learning that his instructions were not being conscientiously obeyed, Lincoln became angry at Schenck, whom he described as "wider across the head in the region of the ears, & loves fight for its own sake, better than I do."[181] Summoning the general and his chief of staff, Donn Piatt, to the White House, he dressed them down. "I do not care to recall the words of Mr. Lincoln," Piatt later wrote. "They were exceedingly severe, for the President was in a rage."[182]

Lincoln also sought to curb Schenck's high-handed interference in the electoral process. The general prescribed a stringent loyalty oath for voters and dispatched troops around the state to intimidate Democrats and Conservative Unionists. Although Lincoln upheld Schenck's test oath, he modified the general's order to arrest anyone near the polls who seemed disloyal. In an unapologetic letter to Governor Augustus W. Bradford, who protested against Schenck's procedures, the president insisted that loyal voters would be protected against violent attempts to intimidate them: "General Schenck is fully determined, and has my strict orders besides, that all loyal men may vote, and vote for whom they please."[183]

Abolitionists applauded Lincoln's "manly letter to Gov. Bradford," which allegedly "gave solid encouragement to the Emancipationists of Maryland, and enabled them to elect their candidates."[184] They also cheered his decision to remove some federal officeholders in Maryland who opposed emancipation. The president's action gave the lie to Conservatives' claims that he was on their side. In late October, when Maryland Senator Reverdy Johnson informed the president of his constituents' apprehension about potential military interference, Lincoln "hooted the idea, said that no such purpose was entertained, nor had he received any intimation of any desire to that effect."[185]

On election day, however, Schenck's forces actively intervened at the polls and helped depress the turnout. At the White House, the returns from Maryland were anxiously awaited. There was great relief when news arrived that Unconditional Unionists won four congressional races, while Representative John W. Crisfield, a Conservative Unionist, lost his reelection bid. Emancipationists also gained control of the legislature. The antislavery forces' triumph, which paved the way for emancipation the following year, would probably not have occurred without federal interference. With some justification, critics like Reverdy Johnson condemned the behavior of the military in Maryland. Lincoln pledged "to hold to account" any officer who violated his order.[186] Congress outlawed the use of troops at election time except "to repel the armed enemies of the United States or to keep peace at the polls."

Lincoln's public letters, most notably the one to James C. Conkling, helped make the crucial electoral victories possible. That document, along with the two letters about Vallandigham and the correspondence with Seymour, was published in pamphlet form and widely distributed. Maine Governor Israel Washburn told the president that the Conkling letter "aided not a little in swelling our wonderful majority" in the September election.[187] Lincoln modestly disclaimed credit for the electoral victories, saying he was "very glad" that he had "not, by native depravity, or under evil influences, done anything bad enough to prevent the good result."[188] When congratulated on the outcome, he remarked: "The people are for this war. They want the rebellion crushed, and as quick as may be, too."[189]

Widely Noted and Long Remembered:
Address at Gettysburg

Shortly after the elections, Lincoln prepared a brief public utterance that would clinch his reputation as a supremely gifted writer: the Gettysburg Address. In the summer of

1863, David Wills, an aggressive and successful young attorney in Gettysburg, organized an effort to create a national cemetery for the Union soldiers killed there. He and his fellow planners decided to consecrate the site with a solemn ceremony. They agreed that the principal speaker should be Edward Everett, the most celebrated orator of the day, and that Lincoln should also be invited to speak briefly. Everett's invitation went out on September 23. In accepting, the former Massachusetts senator asked that the scheduled date for the ceremony (October 23) be postponed till November 19 to give him sufficient preparation time. Wills honored this request and waited till November 2 to write an invitation to the president asking him to "formally set apart these grounds to their Sacred use by a few appropriate remarks." Lincoln had probably been approached earlier, perhaps by Pennsylvania Governor Andrew G. Curtin in late August.

Lincoln was predisposed to accept the invitation, for he had told White House serenaders on July 7 that the defeat of Lee's army on the anniversary of the Declaration of Independence was "a glorious theme, and the occasion for a speech." But, he added, he was not at that moment "prepared to make one worthy of the occasion."[190] His inclination to make such a speech was probably enhanced by suggestions he received from correspondents, among them John Murray Forbes. The Massachusetts railroad magnate and philanthropist told Lincoln that since the Conkling letter had "exhausted (so far as you are concerned) the question of the Negro," it was now time to direct the public's attention to "the *true issue of the existing struggle*," namely, the worldwide fight for democracy. Forbes suggested that Lincoln "seize an early oppertunity and every subsequent chance to reach your great audience of *plain poeple* that the war is not North against South but *the Poeple against the Aristocrats*[.] If you can place this in the same strong light that you have the Negro question you will settle it in men[']s minds as you have *that*."[191]

From the outset of the war, Lincoln had regarded the conflict as one to vindicate democracy, not simply to preserve the Union for its own sake or to liberate slaves. As he told John Hay in May 1861, "the central idea" of the war was to prove "that popular government is not an absurdity."[192] In writing his address, Lincoln did not take Forbes's suggestion to emphasize class consciousness and antagonism, but he did make it clear that the stakes of the war involved more than slavery and the nation's territorial integrity. Union soldiers died in the effort to prove that self-government was viable for all nations, not just the United States. "Man's vast future" would be determined by the outcome of the war.

The president evidently did not share Forbes's view that the Conkling letter had disposed of the slavery issue. In his speech he would emphasize that the war would midwife "a new birth of freedom" by liberating slaves and thus moving the country closer to realizing the Founders' vision of equality. Since his Peoria speech of 1854, Lincoln had been stressing the need to live up to the ideals expressed in the Declaration of Independence.

It is not clear when and how Lincoln composed his Gettysburg address. He told close friends like James Speed and Noah Brooks that he began composing it in Washington and finished it in Pennsylvania. John G. Nicolay, who accompanied the president to Gettysburg, testified that he saw him revise the address on the morning of its delivery. Nicolay emphatically denied that Lincoln composed or revised it on the train ride from Washington. That seems entirely plausible, for the train jerked and bumped along so vigorously that writing was virtually impossible.

When drafting his speech, Lincoln doubtless recalled the language of Daniel Webster and Theodore Parker. In Webster's celebrated 1830 reply to Robert Hayne, the Massachusetts senator referred to the "people's government, made for the people, made by the people, and answerable to the people." Parker, whom the president admired and who frequently corresponded with his law partner, William H. Herndon, used a similar definition of democracy. Lincoln was familiar with at least two of Parker's formulations. In his "Sermon on the Dangers which Threaten the Rights of Man in America," delivered on July 2, 1854, the Unitarian divine twice referred to "government of all, by all, and for all." In another sermon delivered four years later, "The Effect of Slavery on the American People," Parker said "Democracy is Direct Self-government, over all the people, for all the people, by all the people." Lincoln, who owned copies of these works, told his good friend Jesse W. Fell that he thought highly of Parker. Fell believed that Lincoln's religious views more closely resembled Parker's than those of any other theologian. Lincoln may also have recalled the words that Pennsylvanian Galusha Grow, speaker of the U.S. House, uttered on the memorable 4th of July 1861, as Congress met for the first time during the war: "Fourscore years ago fifty-six bold merchants, farmers, lawyers, and mechanics, the representatives of a few feeble colonists, scattered along the Atlantic seaboard, met in convention to found a new empire, based on the inalienable rights of man."[193] Many newspapers published Grow's speech.

Lincoln told James Speed that "he was anxious to go" to Gettysburg, but as the ceremony date drew near, he worried that he might not be able to do so, for he was reluctant to leave the bedside of his son Tad, ill with scarletina.[194] In addition, Benjamin Perley Poore of the Boston *Journal* reported on November 14 that even though "it has been announced that the President will positively attend the inauguration of the Gettysburg soldiers' cemetery, it can hardly be possible for him to leave at this time, when his public duties are so pressing."[195] (Among other things, Lincoln was paying close attention to military developments at Chattanooga and was busily composing his annual message to Congress, due to be delivered in early December. To carve out time to do so, he restricted his office hours and admitted callers in groups rather than individually.) But four days later, Poore wrote that "[s]uch had been the pressure exerted on the President that he will probably go to Gettysburg tomorrow."[196] The president did in fact depart for Pennsylvania on November 18, even though Tad's health remained questionable.

Accompanying Lincoln to Gettysburg were cabinet members (Seward, Usher, and Blair), personal secretaries (Nicolay and Hay), a body servant (William Johnson), diplomatic representatives, Edward Everett's daughter and son-in-law, and Pennsylvania politician Wayne McVeagh. Also aboard the four-coach train were bodyguards, journalists, and musicians. Stanton had originally arranged for the president to leave on the morning of November 19, but Lincoln, fearing that was cutting it too close, insisted on departing the day before.

Arriving in Gettysburg in the late afternoon of November 18, Lincoln, flanked by a cheering crowd, proceeded to the home of David Wills, where he was to spend the night. Everett observed that at supper, the president was as gentlemanly in appearance, manners, and conversation as any of the diplomats, governors, and other *eminenti* at the table. Thus did Lincoln belie his reputation for backwoods social awkwardness. After the meal, when serenaders regaled him at the Wills house, he asked to be excused from addressing them: "I appear before you, fellow-citizens, merely to thank you for this compliment. The inference is a very fair one that you would [like] to hear me for a little while at least, were I to commence make a speech. I do not appear before you for the purpose of doing so, and for several substantial reasons. The most substantial of these is that I have no speech to make. [Laughter.] In my position it is somewhat important that I should not say any foolish things." An irreverent voice rang out: "If you can help it." Lincoln replied good-naturedly: "It very often happens that the only way to help it is to say nothing at all. [Laughter.] Believing that is my present condition this evening, I must beg of you to excuse me from addressing you further."[197] The crowd cheered enthusiastically and then moved next door to the home of Robert G. Harper, where Seward was staying. The secretary of state obliged them with more extensive remarks, strongly endorsing the Emancipation Proclamation and emphasizing that the war was fought to vindicate the principle of majority rule. This probably represented the formal speech that Seward would have delivered at the ceremony in case Lincoln had remained in Washington. (A journalist objected to Seward's egotism, pointing out that he used the first-person singular pronoun ten times.)

Later that evening, Lincoln greeted guests at a reception for an hour, after which he retired to work on his speech. Around 11 o'clock he stepped next door to confer with Seward and returned after less than half an hour. It is not known what, if any, suggestions the secretary of state may have made. Lifting the president's spirits was a telegram from the First Lady announcing that their son might be "slightly better."[198]

The next morning, well before dawn, all roads to Gettysburg became clogged with wagons, buggies, horseback riders, and pedestrians eager to attend the well-publicized ceremony. Others came pouring out of the uncomfortable trains that chugged into the local station. Quickly, visitors overflowed the town's streets. According to one reporter, most "were fathers, mothers, brothers, and sisters, who had come from distant parts to look at and weep over the remains of their fallen kindred, or to gather up the honored relics and bear them back to the burial grounds of their native homes—in relating what they had suffered and endured, and what part their loved ones had borne in the memorable days of July." An elderly Massachusetts gentleman remarked, "I have a son who fell in the first day's fight, and I have come to take back his body, for his mother's heart is breaking, and she will not be satisfied till it is brought home to her." A Pennsylvanian explained, "[m]y brother was killed in the charge of the Pennsylvania Reserves on the enemy when they were driven from Little Round-top, but we don't know where his remains are."[199]

The sky, at first overcast, cleared during the ceremony. John Hay called it "one of the most beautiful Indian Summer days ever enjoyed."[200] As people swarmed into

town, Lincoln rose early, toured the battlefield with Seward, and polished his address. To a reporter who had managed to gain access to the Wills' house, the president
said: "The best course for the journals of the country to pursue, if they wished to sustain the Government, was to stand by the officers of the army." Rather than harping
on military failures, newspapers should urge people to render "all the aid in their
power" to the war effort.[201] At 10 o'clock, Lincoln joined the procession to the cemetery, led by Ward Hill Lamon, the marshal in charge of arrangements. Upon emerging from the Wills house, wearing a black suit and white gauntlets, Lincoln encountered
a huge crowd whose deafening cheers made him blush. A journalist noted that his
"awkwardness which is so often remarked does not extend to his horsemanship."[202]
Another reporter wrote that once in the saddle, Lincoln "sat up the tallest and grandest rider in the procession, bowing and nearly laughing his acknowledgments to the
oft-repeated cheers—'Hurrah for Old Abe;' and 'We're coming, Father Abraham,'
and one solitary greeting of its kind, 'God save Abraham Lincoln.'"[203] His admirers
insisted on shaking hands until marshals finally intervened to protect his arm from
more wrenching.

Benjamin Brown French, acting as one of Lamon's assistants, was struck by the
way people lionized the president. "Abraham Lincoln is the idol of the American
people at this moment," French confided to his journal. "Anyone who saw & heard as
I did, the hurricane of applause that met his every movement at Gettysburg would
know that he lived in every heart. It was no cold, faint, shadow of a kind reception—it
was a tumultuous outpouring of exultation, from true and loving hearts, at the sight
of a man whom everyone knew to be honest and true and sincere in every act of his
life, and every pulsation of his heart. It was the spontaneous outburst of heartfelt
confidence in *their own* President."[204] A Virginia woman visiting Gettysburg recorded
in her diary that "[s]uch homage I never saw or imagined could be shown to any one
person as the people bestow on Lincoln. The very mention of his name brings forth
shouts of applause."[205]

Amid the firing of minute guns and the huzzahing of the crowd, the procession,
as John Hay put it, "formed itself in an orphanly sort of way & moved out with very
little help from anybody."[206] Led by the Marine Band, the long line of marchers and
riders advanced slowly, reaching the cemetery in about twenty minutes. Thanks to
recent rains, the immense cavalcade stirred up little dust. A Gettysburg resident described the procession as "a grand and impressive sight. I have no language to depict
it and though the mighty mass rolled on as the waves of the ocean, everything was in
perfect order."[207]

At the cemetery, Lincoln and three dozen other honored guests—including governors, congressmen, senators, cabinet members, and generals—took their places on
the 12' × 20' platform. As the president slowly approached that stage, the 15,000 spectators maintained a respectful silence. In keeping with the solemnity of the occasion,
men removed their hats. While waiting for the ceremony to begin, Martin D. Potter
of the Cincinnati *Commercial* sketched a pen portrait of Lincoln: "A Scotch type of
countenance, you say, with the disadvantage of emaciation by a siege of Western ague.
It is a thoughtful, kindly, care-worn face, impassive in repose, the eyes cast down, the

lids thin and firmly set, the cheeks sunken, and the whole indicating weariness, and anything but good health."[208]

(Around that time, a White House caller thought Lincoln was so weary that he resembled "a New York omnibus beast at night who had been driven all day" during an August heat spell. Journalists reported that he was "not looking well," that he was "careworn," that he appeared "thin and feeble," and that "his eyes have lost their humorous expression." Lincoln refused to heed the advice of friends who urged him to leave the capital to recruit his health.)[209]

Once the other dignitaries were seated, a dirge opened the proceedings, followed by the Rev. Dr. Thomas H. Stockton's long prayer, which, Hay quipped, "thought it was an oration."[210] Stockton may have bored Hay, but he brought tears to many eyes, including those of the president. For the next two hours, Everett delivered his polished, carefully researched and memorized speech describing the battle, analyzing the causes and nature of the war, rebutting secessionist arguments, predicting a quick postwar sectional reconciliation, citing ancient Greek funeral rites, and denouncing the enemy. Now and then Lincoln smiled at especially apt passages. At one point, he whispered his approval in Seward's ear. When Everett alluded to the suffering of the dying troops, tears came to Lincoln's eyes, as they did to the eyes of most auditors.

Everett's speech as a whole did not move everyone. The crowd gave it only tepid applause, and the Philadelphia *Daily Age* remarked dismissively: "Seldom has a man talked so long and said so little. He told us nothing about the dead heroes, nothing of their former deeds, nothing of their glories before they fell like conquerors before their greater conqueror, Death. He gave us plenty of words, but no heart." The editors objected to the "frigid sentences" and "classical conceits."[211] George William Curtis found the oration "smooth and cold," lacking "one stirring thought, one vivid picture, one thrilling appeal."[212] Another observer likened Everett to a "hired mourner—the laureate chanting a funeral dirge to order, with no touch of 'in memoriam' about it. His monument was an iron statue with no glow or pulse or passion in it."[213] The Milwaukee *Sentinel* complained that the speech lacked "the fire and spirit of true eloquence" and failed "to stir the blood and absorb the feelings, as one had reason to expect on such an occasion, and from so famous an orator."[214]

The New York press also found little to admire. The *Herald* called it "milk and water; utterly inadequate, although his sentences were as smooth as satin and his metaphors as chaste as snow."[215] The *World* opined that Mr. Everett "has fallen below his own reputation in the greatest opportunity ever presented to him, for rearing a monument more enduring than brass. . . . Every figure is culled in advance; every sentence composed in the closet; every gesture practiced before a mirror. . . . But where nature requires a voice, Mr. Everett's tears lie too near his eyes; they never gush up from the depths of a swelling heart."[216]

After a musical interlude, Lincoln slowly rose to speak, causing a stir of expectation. His "reception was quite cordial," noted Benjamin Perley Poore.[217] The Washington *Chronicle* reported that when Lamon introduced Lincoln, the president was "vociferously cheered by the vast audience."[218] As spectators on the outer fringes of the crowd pressed forward, those closer to the platform pushed back, causing a brief disturbance. A nurse in the audience recalled that she and the others "seemed packed like fishes in a barrel," so tightly jammed together that they nearly suffocated.[219] When calm was restored, the president put on his glasses, drew a paper from his pocket, and read his brief remarks "in a very deliberate manner, with strong emphasis, and with a most business-like air." His voice was so clear and loud that it carried to the outer extremities of the crowd.[220] John Hay recorded in his diary that Lincoln spoke "in a firm free way, with more grace than is his wont."[221]

Lincoln's words were taken down by reporters whose accounts differ slightly. The Associated Press correspondent, Joseph L. Gilbert, claimed that after delivering the speech, Lincoln allowed him to copy the text from his manuscript. Charles Hale of the Boston *Daily Advertiser* recorded Lincoln's words in shorthand. Conflating these two versions, we can obtain a good idea of what Lincoln actually said. It differs from the revised versions he made later when donating copies to charitable causes. The following text is what he probably said, with bracketed italics representing revisions he made for the final version (the so-called "Bliss copy" of the speech, the one that is best known):

> Four score and seven years ago our fathers brought forth upon [*on*] this continent a new nation, conceived in liberty, and dedicated to the proposition that all men are created equal. [Applause.] Now we are engaged in a great civil war, testing whether that nation or any nation so conceived and so dedicated, can long endure. We are met on a great battle-field of that war. We are met [*have come*] to dedicate a portion of it [*that field*] as the [*a*] final resting place of [*for*] those who here gave their lives that that nation might live. It is altogether fitting and proper that we should do this. But, in a larger sense, we cannot dedicate, we cannot consecrate, we cannot hallow this ground. The brave men, living and dead, who struggled here have consecrated it far above our poor power to add or detract. [Applause.] The world will little note nor long remember what we say here, but it can never forget what they did here. [Applause.] It is for us, the living, rather to be dedicated here to the unfinished work that [*which*] they [*who fought here*] have thus far so nobly carried on [*advanced*]. [Applause.] It is rather for us to be here dedicated to the great task remaining before us, that from these honored dead we take increased devotion to that cause for which they here gave [*they gave*] the last full measure of devotion; that we here highly resolve that these dead shall not have died in vain [applause]; that the nation shall, under God, [*nation, under God, shall*] have a new birth of freedom; and that Government of the people, by the people, [*for the people*] and for the people, shall not perish from the earth. [Long-continued applause.][222]

The audience was profoundly moved. Isaac Jackson Allen of the Columbus *Ohio State Journal* reported that Lincoln's "calm but earnest utterance of this deep and beautiful address stirred the deepest fountains of feeling and emotion in the hearts of the vast throngs before him; and when he had concluded, scarcely could an untearful eye be seen, while sobs of smothered emotion were heard on every hand." When the president said that the "world will little note nor long remember what we say here, but it can never forget what they did here," a captain who had lost an arm "burst all restraint; and burying his face in his handkerchief, he sobbed aloud while his manly frame shook with no unmanly emotion. In a few moments, with a stern struggle to master his emotions, he lifted his still streaming eyes to heaven and in a low and solemn tone exclaimed, 'God Almighty bless Abraham Lincoln!'"[223]

As Everett noted, the president's handiwork was "greatly admired."[224] The Cincinnati *Gazette* reported that "the universal encomium" bestowed on it was that it "was the right thing, in the right place, and a perfect thing in every respect."[225] Isaac Jackson Allen termed it "the best word of his administration," accurately predicting that it "will live long after many more elaborate and pretentious utterances shall have been forgotten."[226] The Philadelphia *Press* correspondent called it a "brief, but immortal speech," and the paper ran an editorial stating that "the occasion was sublime; certainly the ruler of the nation never stood higher, and grander, and more prophetic."[227] The Chicago *Tribune* reporter declared that the "dedicatory remarks of President Lincoln will live among the annals of man."[228] Other papers shared this high opinion. The Washington *Chronicle* said that the speech "glittered with gems, evincing the gentleness and goodness of heart peculiar to him."[229] The Philadelphia *Evening Bulletin* remarked that the "President's brief speech is most happily expressed. It is warm, earnest, unaffected and touching."[230]

Men of letters were equally enthusiastic. Josiah G. Holland of the Springfield, Massachusetts, *Republican* wrote that "the rhetorical honors of the occasion were won by President Lincoln. His little speech is a perfect gem; deep in feeling, compact in thought and expression, and tasteful and elegant in every word and comma. Then it has the merit of unexpectedness in its verbal perfection and beauty. We had grown so accustomed to homely and imperfect phrases in his productions that we had come to think it was the law of his utterance. But this shows he can talk handsomely as well as act sensibly. Turn back and read it over, it will repay study as a model speech. Strong feelings and a large brain were its parents."[231] James Burrill Angell, president of Brown University, confessed that he did not know "where to look for a more admirable speech than the brief one which the President made at the close of Mr. Everett's oration. It is often said that the hardest thing in the world is to make a five minute speech. But could the most elaborate and splendid oration be more beautiful, more touching, more inspiring than those few words of the President? They had in my humble judgement the charm and power of the very highest eloquence."[232] George William Curtis thought that the "few words of the President went from the heart to the heart. They cannot be read, even, without kindling emotion. . . . It was as simple and felicitous and earnest a word as was ever spoken." More extravagantly, he called the Gettysburg address the "most perfect piece of American eloquence, and as noble and pathetic and appropriate as the oration of Pericles over the Peloponnesian dead."[233] The speech won over some who had been critical of Lincoln's rhetoric. In August, Charles King Newcomb, a Rhode Island Emersonian, bemoaned the president's "want of eloquence," but on November 23, after reading the Gettysburg Address, he concluded that "Lincoln is, doubtless, the greatest orator of the age: a point not now seen generally."[234] Charles Francis Adams, Jr., thought the speech showed that Lincoln had "a capacity for rising to the demands of the hour which we should not expect from orators or men of the schools."[235]

Edward Everett added his voice to the chorus of praise, writing with customary graciousness to Lincoln the day after the ceremony: "Permit me . . . to express my great admiration of the thoughts expressed by you, with such eloquent simplicity & appropriateness, at the consecration of the Cemetery. I should be glad, if I could flatter myself that I came as near to the central idea of the occasion, in two hours, as you did in two minutes."[236] Lincoln told a friend that "he had never received a compliment he prized more highly."[237] Equally gracious, the president replied to Everett: "In our respective parts yesterday, you could not have been excused to make a short address, nor I a long one. I am pleased to know that, in your judgment, the little I did say was not entirely a failure. Of course I knew Mr. Everett would not fail; and yet, while the whole discourse was eminently satisfactory, and will be of great value, there were passages in it which trancended my expectation. The point made against the theory of the general government being only an agency, whose principals are the States, was new to me, and, as I think, is one of the best arguments for the national supremacy. The tribute to our noble women for their angel-ministering to the suffering soldiers, surpasses, in its way, as do the subjects of it, whatever has gone before."[238]

(Privately, Lincoln expressed a less favorable view of Everett. Shortly after the orator's death, he remarked: "I think Edward Everett was very much overrated. He hasn't left any enduring monument."[239] To a foreign visitor, Lincoln described his standard of judgment in oratory: "It is very common in this country to find great facility of expression, and common, though not so common, to find great lucidity of thought. The combination of the two faculties in one person is uncommon indeed; but whenever you do find it, you have a great man.")[240]

Some Democrats criticized the Gettysburg Address for injecting politics into a solemn, nonpartisan occasion. Samuel Medary of the Columbus, Ohio, *Crisis* sneered that "the President read a mawkish harrangue about this 'war for freedom' of the negro by the destruction of the liberties of American citizens."[241] The leading Democratic journal of the Midwest, the Chicago *Times,* called it "an offensive exhibition of boorishness and vulgarity" and added that the "cheek of every American must tingle with shame as he reads the silly flat and dishwattery remarks of the man who has to be pointed out as the President of the United States."[242] The Gettysburg *Weekly Patriot and Union* expressed similar contempt: "We pass over the silly remarks of the President. For the credit of the nation we are willing that the veil of oblivion shall be dropped over them, and they shall be no more repeated or thought of."[243]

Democrats criticized most vehemently the implication that the war was being fought, at least in part, to free the slaves. (Although Lincoln did not say so explicitly, that was the evident meaning of his references to equality and a "new birth of freedom.") "We submit that Lincoln did most foully traduce the motives of the men who were slain at Gettysburg," protested the Chicago *Times.* "They gave their lives to maintain the old government, and the old constitution and Union."[244] After citing passages in the Constitution alluding to slavery, the editor argued that "Mr. Lincoln occupies his present position by virtue of this constitution, and is sworn to the maintenance and enforcement of these provisions. It was to uphold this constitution, and the Union created by it, that our officers and soldiers gave their lives at

Gettysburg. How dare he, then, standing on their graves, misstate the cause for which they died, and libel the statesmen who founded the government? They were men possessing too much self-respect to declare negroes were their equals, or were entitled to equal privileges."[245] The New York *World* maintained that "the Constitution not merely does not say one word about equal rights, but expressly admits the idea of inequality of human rights."[246] The Keene, New Hampshire, *Cheshire Republican* indignantly declared: "If it was to establish negro equality that our soldiers lost their lives, Mr. Lincoln should have said so before. These soldiers won the day at Gettysburg under the noble impulse that they were contending for the Constitution and the Union."[247]

Democrats also objected to what they considered poor taste in Lincoln's opening sentence. It was "questionable," said the New York *World,* to represent "the 'fathers' in the stages of conception and parturition."[248] Similarly, the Boston *Daily Courier* protested against the "obstetric allusion."[249] The London *Times* correspondent said "[a]nything more dull and commonplace it wouldn't be easy to produce."[250]

Though posterity has come to regard Lincoln's remarks as a succinct, sublime masterpiece and Everett's oration as a florid, diffuse history lecture, the contemporary press devoted more coverage to the latter than to the former. Several myths grew up around the Gettysburg Address, among them that the president composed it on the train, that he regarded it as a failure, that the crowd and other contemporaries failed to appreciate it, and that it surreptitiously bootlegged the concept of equality into the Constitution.

Following the ceremony, Lincoln returned to David Wills's home, where he ate dinner and shook visitors' hands for an hour. Afterward, he walked to the Presbyterian church to hear an oration by the lieutenant governor of Ohio. En route he was accompanied by John Burns, an elderly cobbler who had won acclaim for fighting alongside the Union troops in July. Lincoln had heard of his exploits and asked to be introduced to him. Around 6 P.M., the president and his suite boarded a train for Washington.

Lincoln honored at least three requests for autograph copies of the Gettysburg Address. The version known as the "Bliss copy," composed for sale at the 1864 Baltimore Sanitary Fair, became the most famous; it is carved into a wall of the Lincoln Memorial. Since it was the final copy made, it represents, as Robert Todd Lincoln observed, his father's "last and best thought as to the address."[251]

The speech was, in effect, another of Lincoln's highly successful public letters. He realized, as some commentators prophesied, that people "who would not read the long elaborate oration of Mr. Everett will read the President's few words," which would "receive the attention and command the admiration of all the tens of thousands who will read it."[252] His audience was the Northern public at large, not merely the crowd at Gettysburg. He aimed to lift the morale of his constituents with a terse, eloquent exposition of the war's significance. His words admirably served that function in his own day and inspired the respect and admiration of subsequent generations. In 1865, Ralph Waldo Emerson accurately predicted that Lincoln's "brief speech at Gettysburg will not easily be surpassed by words on any recorded occasion."[253]

Something to Give to Everyone: Presidential Smallpox

Back in Washington, Lincoln came down with a mild version of smallpox, known as varioloid. It persisted for several days, and part of that time he was quarantined. When told that his illness was contagious, he quipped "that since he has been President he had always had a crowd of people asking him to give them something, but that *now he has something he can give them all*."[254] Alluding both to the scars that smallpox often caused and to his appearance, he told a physician: "There is one consolation about the matter, doctor. It cannot in the least disfigure me!"[255] In fact, he was not disfigured. A visitor on December 6 wrote that although he "looks feeble," yet "not a mark can be seen." Earlier, "he only had half a dozen."[256]

The varioloid did more than disfigure one of the members of the presidential party at Gettysburg, William H. Johnson. That young black man had accompanied Lincoln from Illinois and served in the White House until his fellow black staffers there objected to his presence because his skin was too dark. Lincoln then obtained a job for him in the Treasury Department. Johnson contracted smallpox, perhaps from Lincoln, which killed him in January 1864. One day that month, as the unfortunate fellow lay in the hospital, a journalist discovered the president counting out some greenbacks. Lincoln explained that such activity "is something out of my usual line; but a President of the United States has a multiplicity of duties not specified in the Constitution or acts of Congress. This is one of them. This money belongs to a poor negro [Johnson] who is a porter in one of the departments (the Treasury) and who is at present very bad with the smallpox. He did not catch it from me, however; at least I think not. He is now in hospital, and could not draw his pay because he could not sign his name. I have been at considerable trouble to overcome the difficulty and get it for him, and have at length succeeded in cutting red tape . . . . I am now dividing the money and putting by a portion labeled, in an envelope, with my own hands, according to his wish."[257]

Johnson had borrowed $150 from the First National Bank of Washington, using Lincoln as an endorser. After Johnson died, the bank's cashier, William J. Huntington, happened to mention the outstanding notes to Lincoln: "the barber who used to shave you, I hear, is dead."

"'Oh, yes,' interrupted the President, with feeling; 'William is gone. I bought a coffin for the poor fellow, and have had to help his family.'"

When Huntington said the bank would forgive the loan, Lincoln replied emphatically: "No you don't. I endorsed the notes, and am bound to pay them; and it is your duty to make me pay them."

"Yes," said the banker, "but it has long been our custom to devote a portion of our profits to charitable objects; and this seems to be a most deserving one."

When the president rejected that argument, Huntington said: "Well, Mr. Lincoln, I will tell you how we can arrange this. The loan to William was a joint one between you and the bank. You stand half of the loss, and I will cancel the other."

After thinking it over, Lincoln said: "Mr. Huntington, that sounds fair, but it is insidious; you are going to get ahead of me; you are going to give me the smallest note to pay. There must be a fair divide over poor William. Reckon up the interest on both notes, and chop the whole right straight through the middle, so that my half shall be as big as yours. That's the way we will fix it."

Huntington agreed, saying: "After this, Mr. President, you can never deny that you *indorse* the negro."

"That's a fact!" Lincoln exclaimed with a laugh; "but I don't intend to deny it."[258]

Victory in Tennessee

On November 21, Lincoln predicted that "the next two weeks would be the most momentous period of the rebellion."[259] Indeed, the war in the West was approaching a climax as Grant prepared to dislodge Bragg's forces from the heights above Chattanooga. Two days later, encouraging word arrived from there, but Lincoln warned friends against overconfidence, and would not rejoice until receiving conclusive news of Grant's victory. On November 24 and 25, Union troops captured strong Confederate positions on Missionary Ridge and Lookout Mountain, forcing Bragg to retreat into Georgia.

Lincoln could not participate in celebrations of this victory because he lay sick abed. Meanwhile, he grew quite anxious about Burnside's fate. That hapless general, ensconced in Knoxville, was being menaced by James Longstreet's corps of the Army of Northern Virginia, which Lee had sent to Tennessee weeks earlier. On November 24, the president expressed great relief to learn that firing had recently been heard in the vicinity of Knoxville. When asked why he reacted so positively to news indicating that Union forces might be in serious danger, he replied: "I had a neighbor out West, a Sally Taggart, who had a great many unruly children whom she did not take very good care of. Whenever she heard one squall in some out-of-the-way place, she would say, 'Well, thank Goodness, there's one of my young ones not dead yet!' As long as we hear guns, Burnside is not captured."[260]

On November 29, Burnside repulsed Longstreet's attack. Soon thereafter, General Sherman linked up with Old Burn, forcing the Confederates to pull back toward Virginia. When the president learned of that junction, he joyfully declared that it "is one of the most important gains of the war—the difference between Burnside saved and Burnside lost is one of the greatest advantages of the war—it secures us East Tennessee." At the same time, he expressed dismay over inactivity in the East, predicting that Meade would probably not intercept Longstreet: "if this Army of the Potomac was good for anything—if the officers had anything in them—if the army had any legs, they could move thirty thousand men down to Lynchburg and catch Longstreet. Can anybody doubt, if Grant were here in command that he would catch him? There is not a man in the whole Union who would for a moment doubt it."

The Union triumphs in Tennessee, combined with those at Gettysburg, Vicksburg, and Port Hudson in July, sealed the fate of the Confederacy. Military victory for Jefferson Davis's government was no longer possible. Fighting would continue for another year and a half, but the outcome no longer seemed doubtful. Grant had secured his reputation as the leading Union general. Though it seemed logical to replace Meade with Grant, Lincoln said on December 7, "I do not think it would do to bring Grant away from the West. I talked with Gen. Halleck this morning about the matter, and his opinion was the same."

"But you know Mr President," remarked Old Brains, "how hard we have tried to get this army to move towards the enemy and we cannot succeed."[261]

Indeed, it had proved almost impossible to budge Meade. In September, when the general argued that it would be quite difficult to attack Richmond, the exasperated Lincoln told Halleck: "to attempt to fight the enemy slowly back into his intrenchments at Richmond, and there to capture him, is an idea I have been trying to repudiate for quite a year. My judgment is so clear against it, that I would scarcely allow the attempt to be made, if the general in command should desire to make it. My last attempt upon Richmond was to get McClellan, when he was nearer there than the enemy was, to run in ahead of him. Since then I have constantly desired the Army of the Potomac, to make Lee's army, and not Richmond, it's objective point. If our army can not fall upon the enemy and hurt him where he is, it is plain to me it can gain nothing by attempting to follow him over a succession of intrenched lines into a fortified city."[262]

A month later Lincoln tried to goad Meade into taking the offensive against Lee. "If Gen. Meade can now attack him on a field no worse than equal for us," he instructed the general through Halleck, "and will do so with all the skill and courage, which he, his officers and men possess, the honor will be his if he succeeds, and the blame may be mine if he fails."[263] Meade replied with a typical excuse for inaction.

Months later, Grant would be placed in charge of all Union forces, and the Army of the Potomac would move decisively against the enemy without such presidential inducements.

32

"I Hope to Stand Firm Enough to Not Go Backward, and Yet Not Go Forward Fast Enough to Wreck the Country's Cause"
Reconstruction and Renomination
(November 1863–June 1864)

In the 1840s and 1850s, Lincoln's love for mathematics had led him not only to master the first six books of Euclid's geometry but also to try solving the ancient riddle of squaring the circle. In late 1863, as prospects for victory improved, he wrestled with the political equivalent of that puzzle: devising a Reconstruction policy that would protect the rights of the newly-freed slaves while simultaneously restoring sectional harmony. To make emancipation more than a paper promise without alienating white Southerners was a daunting challenge, for every measure designed to guarantee the rights of blacks was regarded as an insult by the region's whites.

Lincoln faced several questions. Should the rebellious states be regarded as conquered provinces, to be molded to the whim of the victor? Should Rebels stand trial for treason? Should amnesty be extended? To whom? What should be done to protect the freedmen? Should Confederate states be required to accept emancipation before they were restored? Should they be required to enfranchise blacks? Should Reconstruction be postponed till the war was over, or begun while the fighting still raged? Could the Confederates be induced to surrender by offering generous peace terms? Should Congress or the president determine how these questions would be answered?

In dealing with these issues, Lincoln was hard-pressed to keep the Republican coalition intact. Some Radicals, led by Charles Sumner, argued that each rebellious state had committed suicide, reverting to territorial status, and therefore could be regulated by Congress. They also wished to emancipate all slaves, confiscate Rebel property, and deny political rights to most Confederates. Understandably fearing that such measures might alienate Unionists in the Border States and the Confederacy as well as Northern Democrats and conservative Republicans, Lincoln took charge of wartime Reconstruction as federal forces occupied more and more Southern territory.

Lincoln's initial ad hoc response was to appoint military governors and rely on Southern Unionists to rehabilitate their states, with some general guidance from the administration. In March 1862, shortly after the capture of Nashville, he made

Tennessee Senator Andrew Johnson a brigadier general and named him governor of the Volunteer State. Later that year he selected governors for North Carolina, Louisiana, Arkansas, and Texas. Congress acquiesced at first, but eventually balked. Lincoln and the Radicals were to clash sharply over Reconstruction policy.

Early Experiments with Military Governors

Andrew Johnson, a fierce opponent of secession and the only U.S. senator to remain loyal to the Union when his state seceded, was given a free hand to restore civilian government to Tennessee as soon as practicable. Lincoln may have made a mistake in appointing the truculent, embittered Johnson for such a delicate task. A wiser choice may have been William B. Campbell, a Mexican War hero and Conservative from Middle Tennessee. Johnson undertook harsh measures, including the arrest of several clergymen, and used inflammatory rhetoric, telling a mass meeting: "Treason must be crushed out and traitors must be punished."[1]

In July 1862, Lincoln urged Johnson to call an election. "If we could, somehow, get a vote of the people of Tennessee and have it result properly it would be worth more to us than a battle gained," he wrote.[2] The president hoped that a civilian government might be persuaded to abolish slavery and accord freed blacks some basic rights. If that could be done, the inevitable white backlash might be minimized, for the momentous changes would be the work of native whites, not Yankees. Johnson disappointed the president by warning that it would be impossible to hold elections before East Tennessee was pacified.

Conflict between Johnson and military commanders Buell, Halleck, and Rosecrans also chagrined Lincoln, who tactfully tried to reconcile their differences. When Johnson sought to transfer soldiers to Kentucky in order to protect a rail line, the president gently reproved him: "Do you not, my good friend, perceive that what you ask is simply to put you in command in the West. I do not suppose you desire this. You only wish to control in your own localities; but this, you must know, may derange all other parts. *Can* you, not, and *will* you not, have a full conference with Gen. Halleck?"[3] Simultaneously, he wired the general: "The Gov. is a true, and a valuable man—indispensable to us in Tennessee. Will you please get in communication with him, and have a full conference with him?"[4]

To placate Tennessee Unionists who were outraged by the Emancipation Proclamation, Lincoln agreed to exempt their state, even though much of it remained under Confederate control. That drastic step illustrated the lengths to which the president was willing to go to accommodate beleaguered loyalists in East Tennessee. To a pair of them he wrote in August 1863: "I do as much for East Tennessee as I would, or could, if my own home, and family were in Knoxville." After pointing out the practical difficulties of inserting and maintaining troops in their region, he added: "I know you are too much distressed to be argued with; and therefore I do not attempt it at length. You know I am not indifferent to your troubles; else I should not, more than a year and a half ago, have made the effort I did to have a Railroad built on purpose to relieve you. The Secretary of War, Gen. Halleck, Gen. Burnside, and Gen. Rosecrans are all engaged now in an effort to relieve your section."[5]

The following month, with Burnside occupying Knoxville and Rosecrans in Chattanooga, the president grew more optimistic. He told Governor Johnson that "it is the nick of time for re-inaugerating a loyal State government. Not a moment should be lost. You, and the co-operating friends there, can better judge of the ways and means, than can be judged by any here." Lincoln warned that opponents of emancipation and the Union war effort should not be allowed to triumph: "The re-inauguration must not be such as to give control of the State, and it's representation in Congress, to the enemies of the Union, driving it's friends there into political exile. The whole struggle for Tennessee will have been profitless to both State and Nation, if it so ends that Gov. Johnson is put down, and Gov. [Isham] Harris is put up." The president emphasized that action had to be taken soon, for there was no telling what his successor might do. "Get emancipation into your new State government—Constitution—and there will be no such word as fail for your case."[6]

Rosecrans's defeat at Chickamauga delayed implementation of the president's plan. In early October, Lincoln told the general: "If we can hold Chattanooga, and East Tennessee, I think the rebellion must dwindle and die. I think you and Burnside can do this."[7] He also summoned Johnson to Washington for consultations. Unwisely, the governor declined, pleading preoccupation with business. Lincoln's hopes to have Tennessee become the first Confederate state to reestablish loyal civilian government thus came to nothing.

A similar attempt in North Carolina also fizzled. In early 1862, Union troops under Burnside had occupied coastal areas of the Tarheel State. To serve as military governor, Lincoln in May appointed an able, temperamental, and combative North Carolina native, Edward Stanly, then residing in California. A faithful Unionist and a longtime friend of Seward's, Stanly knew the occupied area well, for he had once represented it as a Whig in Congress. There John Quincy Adams called him "a lofty spirit, with a quick perception, an irritable temper, and a sarcastic turn of mind, sparing neither friend nor foe."[8] In North Carolina he enjoyed the reputation of "a man of tact, address and resources" who "knows how to manage men, and possesses the energy and courage requisite to the execution of his designs."[9] Like Johnson, he received carte blanche from the administration, and when he pleaded for more explicit instructions, he was simply told to act as a dictator.

Lincoln did, however, urge Stanly to call for congressional elections, but before that step could be undertaken, the governor committed blunders which outraged many Radicals. At New Bern, an idealistic New Yorker named Vincent Colyer, whom Burnside had appointed as superintendent of the poor, founded two schools for blacks and one for whites. When Stanly advised him that state law forbade the education of blacks, Colyer shut the schools down, prompting Radicals to howl indignantly. Why should Northerners be "compelled to perpetuate & sustain the barbarism of North Carolina?" they asked.[10] When Colyer protested to Charles Sumner, the senator escorted him to the White House on June 5, 1862 to explain the situation. As Colyer was relating his tale of woe, the president interrupted with unwonted severity and irritation: "Do you take me for a School-Committee-man?" After this outburst, he quickly shifted gears and kindly listened to the rest of Colyer's recital.

Lincoln replied that he was "as much astonished by the acts of Mr. Stanly as any other man in the country," that he "most heartily disapproved of them," and that he regretted not only the governor's decisions but also the way they were implemented. Among Stanly's other acts that Lincoln deplored were his return of a fugitive slave, his order mandating inspection of ships headed north to see if bondsmen had stowed away, and his decision to banish Hinton Rowan Helper's brother for daring to give Stanly advice on how to govern the state. When Colyer said that Stanly claimed he had been instructed to enforce local laws in North Carolina, the president "remarked that that was a misapprehension on the part of the Governor" and "that the idea of closing the schools and sending back fugitive slaves and searching vessels going North, never had emanated from his administration. Such an order never had been given by him, nor would it be tolerated by him or his administration." Lincoln insisted that "no slave who once comes within our lines a fugitive from a rebel, shall ever be returned to his master. For my part I have hated slavery from my childhood." At the president's behest, Stanton, who threatened to quit his post if Lincoln allowed such an outrage to stand, commanded the governor to reopen the black schools. Sumner was pleased that the president "has no sympathy with Stanly in his absurd wickedness, closing the schools, nor again in his other act of turning our camp into a hunting ground for Slaves. He repudiates both—positively."[11]

But Lincoln would not fire Stanly. When a delegation of abolitionists urged him to do so, he asked them to suggest a replacement. One of them asserted that it would be better to have nobody serving as military governor rather than a man out of sympathy with the president's policy. When another proposed Frémont, Lincoln replied that he had "great respect" for the Pathfinder, "but the fact is that the pioneer in any movement is not generally the best man to carry that movement to a successful issue." The delegation left convinced that Lincoln, for "all his forensic ability and his personal virtues, was not competent to grapple with the tremendous combination of issues before him."[12] Antislavery militants lamented that "the President is cautious & a little vacillating about suppressing *Stanly*."[13] Indignantly the abolitionist minister George B. Cheever called Lincoln's unwillingness to remove Stanly "the worst outrage yet committed, the most impious and heaven defying."[14]

The demand for Stanly's ouster was rooted in a fundamental policy disagreement between Lincoln and the Radicals. The president believed that Southern Unionism could be mobilized to restore Confederate states and help speed the end of the war. With good reason Radicals thought Lincoln overestimated the depth of Southern Unionism and misguidedly tailored his policies to accommodate it.

In the Stanly–Colyer dispute, Burnside recommended that Lincoln back the governor, whose views, said the general, had been misrepresented. Though not endorsing Stanly's school policy, Lincoln publicly expressed general support for him. The president apparently agreed with a journalist who reported from North Carolina that the governor was damned if he did and damned if he didn't: "If Mr. Stanly returns slaves he is denounced by the north and its army; if he fails to enforce the . . . law, he is hated by the very people he is sent to conciliate. He may try to trim his sails to either breeze, but in vain."[15] Lincoln himself faced a similar dilemma on the national level.

The governor threatened to resign when the Preliminary Emancipation Proclamation was announced in September 1862. Lincoln dissuaded him by explaining that intense Radical pressure had forced him to issue that document. Immediately after their conversation, Stanly summarized it for the editor of the Washington *National Intelligencer*, who in turn recorded in his diary that "Mr. Stanly said that the President had stated to him that the proclamation had become a civil necessity to prevent the Radicals from openly embarrassing the government in the conduct of the war. The President expressed the belief that, without the proclamation for which they had been clamoring, the Radicals would take the extreme step in Congress of withholding supplies for carrying on the war—leaving the whole land in anarchy. Mr. Lincoln said that he had prayed to the Almighty to save him from this necessity, adopting the very language of our Saviour, 'If it be possible, let this cup pass from me,' but the prayer had not been answered."[16] This disingenuous statement was an example of Lincoln's tendency to dissemble in order to win support for emancipation.

Two days after this conversation took place, the president further mollified Stanly by generously praising him: "Your conduct as Military Governor of that State . . . has my entire approbation; and it is with great satisfaction that I learn you are now to return in the same capacity, with the approbation of the War Department." The president reminded Stanly that the Emancipation Proclamation exempted all areas where elections for Congress had been held: "I shall be much gratified if you can find it practicable to have congressional elections held in that State before January. It is my sincere wish that North Carolina may again govern herself conformably to the constitution of the United States." As he had done with the Border States, Lincoln used the looming prospect of emancipation as an inducement to encourage occupied Confederate regions to return to the Union. But the offer would expire on January 1. Fearing that unsuitable candidates might be elected and that very few voters would turn out, Stanly delayed calling an election; eventually he ordered one for New Year's Day, too late to qualify for the exemption. In the event, a small voter turnout made the election of congressmen seem illegitimate, and nothing came of it except Stanly's resignation on January 15, 1863. The governor told Lincoln that the Emancipation Proclamation "crushes all hope of making peace by any conciliatory measures. It will fill the hearts of Union men with despair, and strengthen the hands of the detestable traitors whose mad ambition has spread desolation and sorrow over our country. To the negroes themselves it will bring the most direful calamities."[17] Further disenchanting Stanly was the administration's willingness to employ blacks as troops.

Stanly's tenure proved a failure, though the fault was not so much his as it was the Union army's inability to pacify the Tarheel State or to whip the Army of Northern Virginia. Lincoln appointed no successor to Stanly, evidently because he realized that there were too few Unionists in North Carolina to make the restoration of the state's civil government possible until more territory was occupied.

Lincoln enjoyed greater success in reconstructing Louisiana, where he appointed Colonel George S. Shepley military governor in June 1862 to preside over New Orleans and nearby parishes. Shepley, a native of Maine, had already served as military mayor of the Crescent City, a post to which General Benjamin F. Butler had named him. Like Stanly and Johnson, he received minimal instructions from the administration. The timid Shepley proved a disappointment, for he regarded himself as Butler's agent rather than a policymaker in his own right.

Louisiana represented a model for neighboring states to emulate, as George Boutwell, who was to play a key role in the Reconstruction drama, pointed out in 1863: "If one State even would frame a constitution and ask for admission a precedent would be established for all the others. Louisiana is so situated, geographically and commercially, that her lead would compel Texas, Arkansas, and Mississippi to follow."[18]

A massive influx of blacks into New Orleans seriously challenged the new government. Shepley and Butler tried to staunch the flow, but General John S. Phelps, the Vermont abolitionist whose proclamation had so incensed Lincoln a few months earlier, welcomed freed slaves into his camp. In July 1862, when informed that Phelps's policy was crushing Union sentiment in Louisiana, the president tartly dismissed the complaint as "a false pretense." Residents of Louisiana and "all intelligent people every where," he wrote, "know full well, that I never had a wish to touch the foundations of their society, or any right of theirs. With perfect knowledge of this, they forced a necessity upon me to send armies among them, and it is their own fault, not mine, that they are annoyed by the presence of General Phelps. They also know the remedy—know how to be cured of General Phelps. Remove the necessity of his presence. And might it not be well for them to consider whether they have not already had *time* enough to do this? If they can conceive of anything worse than General Phelps, within my power, would they not better be looking out for it? They very well know the way to avert all this is simply to take their place in the Union upon the old terms. If they will not do this, should they not receive harder blows rather than lighter ones?" Hinting that he might issue an emancipation order, he said portentously: "I am a patient man—always willing to forgive on the Christian terms of repentance; and also to give ample *time* for repentance. Still I must save this government if possible. What I *cannot* do, of course I *will* not do; but it may as well be understood, once for all, that I shall not surrender this game leaving any available card unplayed."[19]

By late July 1862, Lincoln had grown exasperated with the slow pace of Reconstruction efforts in Louisiana. He reproved New Orleans Unionists Cuthbert Bullitt and Thomas J. Durant for dragging their feet and for whining about the trials and tribulations of loyal slaveowners: "Of course the rebellion will never be suppressed in Louisiana, if the professed Union men there will neither help to do it, nor permit the government to do it without their help." Those "people of Louisiana who wish protection to person and property, have but to reach forth their hands and take it. Let them, in good faith, reinaugurate the national authority, and set up a State Government conforming thereto under the constitution. They know how to do it, and can have the protection of the Army while doing it. The Army will be withdrawn so soon as such State government can dispense with its presence; and the people of the State can then upon the old Constitutional terms, govern themselves to their own liking. This is very simple and easy."[20]

In July 1862, when told that another Louisiana Unionist had complained about the vagueness of the administration's policies, Lincoln asked heatedly: "Why will he not read and understand what I have said? The substance of the very declaration he desires is in the inaugural, in each of the two regular messages to Congress, and in many, if not all, the minor documents issued by the Executive since the inauguration. Broken eggs cannot be mended; but Louisiana has nothing to do now but to take her place in the Union as it was. . . . This government cannot much longer play a game in which it stakes all, and its enemies stake nothing. Those enemies must understand that they cannot experiment for ten years trying to destroy the government, and if they fail still come back into the Union unhurt. If they expect in any contingency to ever have the Union as it was, I join with the writer in saying, 'Now is the time.'"[21]

Impatient with Governor Shepley's failure to organize an election, Lincoln tried to galvanize him as well as General Butler and their associates. In October 1862, he sent them a message via Louisiana Congressman John E. Bouligny, who sought to promote elections for the U.S. House in the two congressional districts under Union control. All men there, Lincoln wrote, who "desire to avoid the unsatisfactory prospect [of emancipation] before them, and to have peace again upon the old terms under the constitution of the United States" were invited to participate. Union authorities were to "give the people a chance to express their wishes at these elections. Follow forms of law as far as convenient, but at all events get the expression of the largest number of the people possible. All see how such action will connect with, and affect the proclamation of September 22nd. Of course the men elected should be gentlemen of character, willing to swear support to the constitution, as of old, and known to be above reasonable suspicion of duplicity."[22]

When this ploy failed to goad Shepley into action, Lincoln wrote him directly on November 21 expressing annoyance. "I wish elections for Congressmen to take place in Louisiana," he reiterated, but added significantly that "I wish it to be a movement of the people of the Districts, and not a movement of our military and quasi-military, authorities there. I merely wish our authorities to give the people a chance—to protect them against secession interference. Of course the election can not be according to strict law—by state law, there is, I suppose, no election day, before January; and the regular election officers will not act, in many cases, if in any. These knots must be cut, the main object being to get an expression of the people. If they would fix a day and a way, for themselves, all the better; but if they stand idle not seeming to know what to do, do you fix these things for them by proclamation. And do not waste a day about it; but, fix the election day early enough that we can hear the result here by the first of January. Fix a day for an election in all the Districts, and have it held in as many places as you can."[23]

Unknown to Lincoln, Shepley had arranged to hold congressional elections on December 3. That day, over 7,700 voters turned out and chose the moderate Michael Hahn and the more radical Benjamin F. Flanders as U.S. Representatives. In December, when those gentlemen arrived in Washington to take their seats, their appearance touched off a fierce debate. Radicals had come to regret giving Lincoln a free hand in the Reconstruction process, especially their earlier decision to admit congressmen elected under his auspices in Virginia and Tennessee. As a result, those areas of the occupied South would be exempt from the impending Emancipation

Proclamation. Some Democrats joined the Radicals in objecting to presidential Reconstruction. Lincoln was furious when told that Congress might refuse to seat Flanders and Hahn. "Then I am to be bullied by Congress, am I?" he exploded. "I'll be d—d if I will."[24] Eventually, the House accepted their credentials. Lincoln confided to Flanders that "there was a strong effort to break down" his administration, and he urged the congressman to support him.[25] He regarded the seating of Flanders and Hahn as a major victory for his Reconstruction policy, but it was a false dawn. Congress rejected the credentials of all other Representatives elected from Confederate states, and little progress was made in 1863 toward restoring civil government in Louisiana, even though the politically experienced General Nathaniel P. Banks became military commander there in December 1862.

Squabbles between the Radicals, who dominated Louisiana's Free State Committee, and the Conservatives, represented by the Executive Central Committee, frustrated Lincoln. In June 1863, when a spokesman for the latter group, Thomas Cottman, asked him to restore Louisiana under the antebellum constitution (which sanctioned slavery) and hold elections in November, the president demurred, insisting that "a respectable portion of the Louisiana people desire to amend their State constitution, and contemplate holding a convention for that object." By itself, that "is a sufficient reason why the general government should not give the committal you seek, to the existing State constitution." While the president could not "perceive how such committal could facilitate our military operations in Louisiana," he said he did "really apprehend it might be so used as to embarrass them." As for elections in November, he assured Cottman that "there is abundant time, without any order, or proclamation from me just now. The people of Louisiana shall not lack an oppertunity of a fair election for both Federal and State officers, by want of anything within my power to give them." This rebuff to Cottman indicated that Lincoln was throwing his weight behind the Free State Committee, but doing so discreetly, for he wished to preserve harmony among the badly outnumbered Unionists. As he told Cottman, he strongly wished that "in Louisiana and elsewhere, all sincere Union men would stoutly eschew cliqueism, and, each yielding something in minor concerns, all work together. Nothing is likely to be so baleful in the great work before us, as stepping aside of the main object to consider who will get the offices if a small matter shall go thus, and who else will get them, if it shall go otherwise. It is a time now for real patriots to rise above all this."[26]

In early August 1863, Lincoln virtually ordered the implementation of the radical Free State Committee's program. When word reached Washington that an effort was underway to hold a constitutional convention, he spelled out to Banks his hopes for Reconstruction in Louisiana. He would be glad if the state would "make a new Constitution recognizing the emancipation proclamation, and adopting emancipation in those parts of the state to which the proclamation does not apply." He also desired to see Louisianans "adopt some practical system by which the two races could gradually live themselves out of their old relation to each other, and both come out better prepared for the new. Education for young blacks should be included in the plan." A contract system appeared to him best suited for that purpose. Lincoln strongly suggested that Louisiana form a new constitution and hold elections before Congress met in early December. Even if the voters did not provide for the abolition of slavery, the president said he would "not, in any event, retract the emancipation proclamation; nor, as executive, ever return to slavery any person who is free by the terms of that proclamation, or by any of the acts of Congress." Though he did not want his letter made public, he authorized Banks to show it to people who should know the administration's wishes—presumably the convention delegates. He told the general that he was offering advice not orders, but when he sent copies of the letter to the Free State Committee leaders—Flanders, Hahn, and Durant—he added the endorsement: "Please observe my directions to him." Significantly, he did not say *suggestions* but rather *directions*. Banks replied that he would execute Lincoln's *orders*, not *suggestions*.

The emphasis on *directions* appeared in orders that Stanton, speaking for the president, sent to Governor Shepley, instructing him clearly to arrange for a constitutional convention. Loyal citizens (presumably including free blacks) were to be registered and an election held within the month following the completion of that process. Apportionment of the delegates would favor New Orleans, where the radical Free State General Committee was stronger than the conservative Executive Central Committee. Lincoln had long been trying to strike a balance between those two organizations, but now he decided to support the former. Discussing Louisiana Reconstruction with George Boutwell, the president said "that he desired the return of the states upon the old basis, substantially, making provision of emancipation of the slaves, and, if possible, securing them homes."[27]

With Banks distracted by military concerns, Shepley was left to carry out these presidential directives. Upon learning that the governor had not done so, Lincoln scolded Banks. The failure to register voters "disappoints me bitterly," he told the general, adding that he did not blame Banks or the Free State leaders. But he urged them to "lose no more time." Bluntly, he stated his wish that they should, "without waiting for more territory" to be occupied, promptly "go to work and give me a tangible nucleus which the remainder of the State may rally around as fast as it can, and which I can at once recognize and sustain as the true State government. And in that work I wish you, and all under your command, to give them a hearty sympathy and support. The instruction to Gov. Shepley bases the movement (and rightfully too) upon the loyal element. Time is important. There is danger, even now, that the adverse element seeks insidiously to pre-occupy the ground. If a few professedly loyal men shall draw the disloyal about them, and colorably set up a State government, repudiating the emancipation proclamation, and re-establishing slavery, I can not recognize or sustain their work. I should fall powerless in the attempt. This government, in such an attitude, would be a house divided against itself." Here Lincoln seemed to renege on his pledge to exempt part of Louisiana from the Emancipation Proclamation; the entire state, including the occupied areas, must abolish slavery if it wished to be restored.[28]

From New Orleans, Congressman Flanders reported to Chase: "The letter from the President to General Banks urging him and all under his authority to aid us to establish a State government has had the desired effect. All Departments of the Government now appear on the same side."[29] Chase rejoiced that the president was shifting toward the Radical position. Lincoln "advances slowly but yet advances," the treasury secretary told Horace Greeley. "On the whole, when we think of the short time, and immense distance in the matter of personal Freedom, between the 1st of March 1861 & the 1st of October 1863 the progressives cannot be dissatisfied with results."[30]

The president grudgingly supported Banks's controversial system of halfway freedom, which provided that slaves in areas of Louisiana not exempted from the Emancipation Proclamation would contract with planters and farmers of their choice for wages, clothing, and housing in return for their labor but would not be allowed to leave the farm or plantation without the army's permission. Their children were authorized to attend schools that the army would establish. Physical punishment was forbidden, and employers were to set aside one acre for each black family to grow its own produce. Contracts were to last one year. "I have said, and say again," Lincoln wrote, "that if a new State government, acting in harmony with this [federal] government, and consistently with general freedom, shall think best to adopt a reasonable temporary arrangement, in relation to the landless and homeless freed people, I do not object; but my word is out to be *for* and not *against* them on the question of their permanent freedom. I do not insist upon such temporary arrangement, but only say such would not be objectionable to me."[31]

Months earlier, Lincoln had told General McClernand that he would accept the implementation of "systems of apprenticeship for the colored people, conforming substantially to the most approved plans of gradual emancipation."[32] Similarly, he had written Stephen A. Hurlbut, commanding general at Memphis, that the employment of freed slaves was "a difficult subject—the most difficult with which we have to deal. The able bodied male contrabands are already employed by the Army. But the rest are in confusion and destitution. They better be set to digging their subsistence out of the ground. If there are plantations near you, on either side of the river, which are abandoned by their owners, first put as many contrabands on such, as they will hold—that is, as can draw subsistence from them. If some still remain, get loyal men, of character in the vicinity, to take them temporarily on wages, to be paid to the contrabands themselves—such men obliging themselves to not let the contrabands be kidnapped, or forcibly carried away. Of course, if any voluntarily make arrangements to work for their living, you will not hinder them. It is thought best to leave details to your discretion subject to the provisions of the acts of Congress & the orders of the War Department."[33]

Horace Greeley spoke for many Radicals when he denounced Banks's "free labor" scheme: "Gen. Banks appears to have yielded without hesitation or reluctance to every demand which the grasping avarice, the hostility to freedom, the hatred to the policy of the Government, the cunning selfishness and the inhumanity of the Louisiana slavemasters can have induced them to make."[34] Such criticism was unfair, for Banks was helping pave the way to freedom and economic independence for slaves in areas exempt from the Emancipation Proclamation. He anticipated that the plantations would soon be broken up and that blacks would eventually possess their own farms.

Before Congress met in December 1863, Lincoln made yet another attempt to restart the sputtering Reconstruction process in Louisiana. Ben Butler had suggested that as a preliminary measure, a referendum be conducted to determine whether voters would like to call a constitutional convention and repeal the ordinance of secession. On November 9, the president commended this proposal to Congressman Flanders, even though it meant tacitly acknowledging the legitimacy of secession. Nothing came of it. By December, hopes for the speedy restoration of Louisiana were fading fast.

In nearby Arkansas, Lincoln's attempt to promote elections also foundered. The military governor, Missouri Congressman John S. Phelps, was frustrated by the failure of the Union army to occupy much territory. In 1863, the president tried to enlist the aid of William K. Sebastian, who had resigned his U.S. senate seat when the state seceded. Learning that Sebastian planned to ask for reinstatement, Lincoln told General Stephen Hurlbut that Sebastian's application "may be so presented as to be one of the very greatest national importance." If Sebastian could persuade Arkansans to form a government and adopt gradual emancipation, Lincoln wrote, "I at least should take great interest in his case; and I believe a single individual will have scarcely done the world so great a service." He added that of course the "emancipation proclamation applies to Arkansas. I think it is valid in law, and will be so held by the courts. I think I shall not retract or repudiate it. Those who shall have tasted actual freedom I believe can never be slaves, or quasi slaves again. For the rest, I believe some plan, substantially being gradual emancipation, would be better for both white and black. . . . It should begin at once, giving at least the new-born, a vested interest in freedom, which could not be taken away."[35] This initiative led nowhere, for Sebastian rejected the presidential overture.

Attempts at self-reconstruction in Texas suffered a like fate. The failure of N. P. Banks's assault at Sabine Pass in September 1863, followed by that general's more disastrous Red River campaign in the spring of 1864, left Military Governor Andrew Jackson Hamilton little to preside over beyond a small costal enclave around Brownsville.

Foiling a Coup: The Etheridge Plot

By December 1863, Lincoln realized that his ad hoc arrangement of military governors promoting Reconstruction in cooperation with Southern Unionists needed an overhaul. "However it may have been in the past, I think the country now is ready for radical measures," he told a caller.[36] To replace the failed approach, he devised a more systematic one, which he spelled out in his annual message to Congress and in an accompanying Proclamation of Amnesty and Reconstruction.

But before he issued those momentous documents, Lincoln was forced to help squelch a parliamentary coup by the clerk of the House of Representatives, former Congressman Emerson Etheridge of Tennessee. A strong Unionist but bitter opponent of abolition, Etheridge had supported the administration's policies until emancipation became a war aim. Liberating the slaves he regarded as "treachery to the Union men of the South."[37] During the organization of the new Thirty-eighth Congress, Etheridge, a crafty schemer, planned to exclude Republican Representatives on a technicality while admitting Conservatives from Louisiana, thus giving Democrats control of the House. The possibility of such a coup alarmed many, including Congressman Henry L. Dawes of Massachusetts, who remarked: "I can think of nothing but a Bull run so disastrous to our cause as that they might hear in Richmond and abroad that our own House of Representatives was in a state of Revolution."[38]

Sharing Dawes's concern, Lincoln mobilized Republicans to thwart Etheridge. He received word of the plot from the postmaster at Chattanooga, who suggested a way to head it off. Etheridge planned to deny Republicans their seats because their certificates of election were not precisely worded in accordance with the requirements of the Constitution and the laws of their states. These cases would be referred to the House committee on elections. To checkmate Etheridge, the president was advised to make sure that all Republican congressmen obtained correct certificates from their governors. Lincoln immediately conferred with the assistant clerk of the House, who offered practical advice on amended certificates. An act of Congress passed earlier that year authorized the clerk of the House to "make a roll of the representatives elect, and place thereon the names of all persons, and of such persons only, whose credentials show that they were regularly elected in accordance with the laws of their States respectively, or the laws of the United States." Citing this statute, Lincoln wrote to several Republican leaders suggesting that loyal state governors make out certificates conforming exactly to the letter of the law. He included printed copies of such a certificate.

Lincoln even contemplated using force against Etheridge. The night before the new House convened, he told Congressman Schuyler Colfax of Indiana to make "sure to have all our men there. Then if Mr. Etheridge undertakes revolutionary proceedings, let him be carried out on a chip, and let our men organize the House. If the worst comes to the worst a file of 'Invalids' [soldiers in the Invalid Brigade] may be held convenient to take care of him."[39] Congressman Owen Lovejoy, a clergyman who also thought force might be needed, said that if it came "to a question of muscle," he could "whip Etheridge."[40] The next day, Etheridge's attempt to exclude sixteen Republican congressmen was defeated by a 94–74 vote, obviating the need for Lovejoy's muscle or Invalid Brigade troops. Significantly influencing the result was the willingness of several Border State congressmen to side with the Republicans. A journalist scornfully observed that the "impotent exhibition of petty spite and malice, exhibited by Clerk Etheridge, resulted only in his disgraceful failure."[41] The following year, when the secretary of the interior suggested that Whitelaw Reid publish information embarrassing to Etheridge, Lincoln vetoed the idea, saying: "No, Reid, I would not do it. Emerson ain't worth more that a squirrel load of powder anyway."[42]

Before Congress assembled, Lincoln worried about the choice of a new speaker of the House to replace Galusha Grow, who had lost his reelection bid. The most likely candidate, Schuyler Colfax of Indiana, he considered "a little intriguer,—plausible, aspiring beyond his capacity, and not trustworthy."[43] Colfax was aligning himself with the pro-Chase Radicals. To challenge the Indiana congressman, Lincoln suggested to Frank Blair, then serving as a corps commander in Grant's army, that he take the seat in Congress to which he had been elected by the voters of Missouri and help organize the House. Through his brother Montgomery, General Blair asked if Lincoln would prefer him to remain in the army or serve in Congress. On November 2, the president replied that he wanted Frank to come to Washington, resign his army commission, "take his seat, go into caucus with our friends, abide the nominations, help elect the nominees, and thus aid to organize a House of Representatives which will really support the government in the war. If the result shall be the election of himself as Speaker, let him serve in that position; if not, let him re-take his commission, and return to the Army. For the country this will heal a dangerous schism; for him, it will relieve from a dangerous position. By a misunderstanding, as I think, he is in danger of being permanently separated from those with whom only he can ever have a real sympathy—the sincere opponents of slavery." (In September, Blair had infuriated Radicals by publicly attacking Chase.) "It will be a mistake if he shall allow the provocations offered him by insincere time-servers, to drive him out of the house of his own building. He is young yet. He has abundant talent—quite enough to occupy all his time, without devoting any to temper. He is rising in military skill and usefulness. His recent appointment to the command of a corps, by one so competent to judge as Gen. Sherman, proves this. In that line he can serve both the country and himself more profitably than he could as a member of congress on the floor."[44] After sending this letter, Lincoln said: "I don't know whether Frank will do this or not, but it will show durned quick whether he's honest or not."[45] Blair took the president's advice, though army commitments delayed his arrival in Washington until January, by which time Colfax had become speaker. Edward McPherson, a Pennsylvania congressman defeated for reelection in 1862, replaced Etheridge as clerk. Blair's inability to reach the capital in time to help organize the House should have led him to resign his seat, but he relished the opportunity to thwart his Radical opponents.

Restructuring Reconstruction: The Ten Percent Plan

As the president was composing his annual message, Michigan Senator Zachariah Chandler urged him to ignore Conservatives' advice: "You are today master of the Situation *if You stand firm*. The people have endorsed You gloriously."[46] Lincoln assured Chandler that he hoped "to 'stand firm' enough to not go backward, and yet not go forward fast enough to wreck the country's cause."[47] At the same time, the president agreed with Seward that it was important to woo War Democrats.

And so Lincoln offered a plan that he hoped would appeal to Radical and Moderate Republicans, to War Democrats, and to Southern Unionists. Like his earlier effort, it was rooted in his sensible belief that Southern white backlash against emancipation would be diluted if voters in the Confederate states themselves organized loyal governments, applied for restoration, and abolished slavery. Some reports from the South indicated that if Confederate leaders were held strictly accountable for the war and other Confederates granted amnesty, such a step would be hailed in the South as "magnanimous, noble, and great." It might well induce wavering Confederates to surrender, confident that they would receive lenient treatment.[48] Recent military developments predisposed many non-slaveholders to accept a generous amnesty. In October, when General Rosecrans proposed extending amnesty to most Rebels, Lincoln replied that "I intend doing something like what you suggest, whenever the case shall appear ripe enough to have it accepted in the true understanding, rather than as a confession of weakness and fear."[49]

The president's long-standing faith in Southern Unionism was strengthened during the fall of 1863. In late October, some Arkansas Unionists, heartened by General Frederick Steele's capture of Little Rock, proposed a constitutional convention to meet in January. Elections for delegates were underway as Lincoln penned his message. Meanwhile, in North Carolina, a strong peace movement emerged, led by William Woods Holden of Raleigh. Lincoln heartily endorsed an appeal to North Carolina Governor Zebulon Vance urging him to accept a peace based on reunion, emancipation, and full citizenship rights for Confederates.

The president optimistically told John Hay that the rebellion was on the verge of collapse. Jefferson Davis's government depended completely on the army, he said, "not only against us but against his own people. If that were crushed the people would be ready to swing back to their old bearings."[50] This was wishful thinking, for Southern disaffection with the Richmond government was not an expression of Unionism but rather of anger at the failure of Confederate arms, at the Davis administration's inability to guarantee social order, and at its encroachment upon individual and states rights. Peace supporters in the South desired a negotiated end to hostilities only if it guaranteed independence. Just as he had done in the secession crisis, Lincoln overestimated the strength of white Southerners' devotion to the Union.

Laboring under that misapprehension, the president devised a scheme known as the Ten Percent plan. It allowed for the restoration of rebellious states after a number of voters equal to one-tenth of those casting ballots in 1860 took an oath of future loyalty to the Union and of willingness to accept emancipation. (Some Confederates would be ineligible for this amnesty, including military and civilian leaders, those who resigned commissions in the U.S. military or federal legislative and judicial posts to join the rebellion, or those who mistreated captured black troops or their white officers.) Once that threshold was reached, the state could hold elections and rejoin the Union, with all the rights and privileges it had enjoyed before the war. The oath-takers would also have all their former rights restored, except the right to own slaves.

Lincoln appended this Proclamation of Amnesty and Reconstruction to his annual message to Congress, which explained why the loyalty oath required acceptance of emancipation. Characteristically, he stressed its practical benefits. The wartime laws and proclamations regarding slavery and emancipation, he said, "were enacted and put forth for the purpose of aiding in the suppression of the rebellion. To give them their fullest effect, there had to be a pledge for their maintenance. In my judgment they have aided, and will further aid, the cause for which they were intended." To abandon them now would be "to relinquish a lever of power." But in addition to such pragmatic concerns, Lincoln forcefully stated moral objections to any backsliding on emancipation. Such reneging "would also be a cruel and an astounding breach of faith." As long as he remained president, Lincoln promised, "I shall not attempt to retract or modify the emancipation proclamation; nor shall I return to slavery any person who is free by the terms of that proclamation, or by any of the acts of Congress." But, he added, Congress or the Supreme Court could modify the oath.

While Lincoln's proclamation did not allow ex-Confederate states to retain slavery, they could keep their antebellum political framework. The administration would not object if a restored state government were to provide a system of apprenticeship for freed slaves, as long as that government "shall recognize and declare their permanent freedom, provide for their education, and which may yet be consistent, as a temporary arrangement, with their present condition as a laboring, landless, and homeless class." Lincoln justified this concession as a necessary expedient to reduce "the confusion and destitution which must, at best, attend all classes by a total revolution of labor throughout whole States." In addition, more Confederates might be inclined to surrender if "this vital matter be left to themselves." But ex-Confederates would not be allowed to mistreat the freed people: "no power of the national Executive to prevent an abuse is abridged by the proposition."

To counter objections that his proposal was premature, Lincoln stressed that Rebels might be more likely to surrender if they knew they would be treated generously. He noted that in some occupied Confederate states "the elements for resumption seem ready for action, but remain inactive, apparently for want of a rallying point—a plan of action." The proclamation provided such a plan. But he assured Congress that he was flexible: "Saying that, on certain terms, certain classes will be pardoned, with rights restored, it is not said that other classes, or other terms, will never be included. Saying that reconstruction will be accepted if presented in a specified way, it is not said it will never be accepted in any other way." This concession, leaving the plan open to change, indicated Lincoln's willingness to have at least some blacks vote, even though his proposal enfranchised only whites. As he told Banks, the statement that other modes of Reconstruction were acceptable was added "on purpose that some conformity to circumstances should be admissible."[51] Lincoln was cautiously laying the foundation for black voting rights.

The president acknowledged an obvious truth—that defeating the Confederacy still required military force. Rebels who wished to surrender would be more likely to step forward if they were secure from insurgent attacks. "Until that confidence shall be established, little can be done anywhere for what is called reconstruction." In closing, he paid a handsome tribute to Union soldiers and sailors: "our chiefest care must still be directed to the army and navy, who have thus far borne their harder part so nobly and well. And it may be esteemed fortunate that in giving the greatest efficiency to these indispensable arms, we do also honorably recognize the gallant men, from commander to sentinel, who compose them, and to whom, more than to others, the world must stand indebted for the home of freedom disenthralled, regenerated, enlarged, and perpetuated."

To justify his plan, Lincoln cited the provision of the Constitution authorizing the chief executive "to grant reprieves and pardons for offences against the United States" as well as the Second Confiscation Act, which stipulated that the president could "extend to persons who may have participated in the existing rebellion, in any State of party thereof, pardon and amnesty." Lincoln's citation of the pardoning power was strained, for the framers of the Constitution clearly meant it to apply to individual cases, not whole classes of people.[52]

In tightening his grip on the reins of Reconstruction, Lincoln felt strengthened by military victories in the summer and fall as well as by the Supreme Court decision in the Prize Cases, handed down in March 1863, upholding the legality of his action during the opening weeks of the war. But he did not ignore Congress. Repeatedly he acknowledged that only the House and senate could determine whether to seat members from the Confederate states.

Congress was at first enthusiastic about Lincoln's plan. Members of both houses as well as other politicians considered his message "the best document yet produced by him."[53] Noah Brooks reported that it was "received with a general expression of satisfaction and relief, as indicating the most feasible method of settling reconstruction." The message, according to Brooks, "gives, probably, more general satisfaction than any Message since the days of Washington."[54] William Dennison, former governor of Ohio and future postmaster general in Lincoln's cabinet, lauded "the excellence and timeliness" of both the message and the proclamation.[55]

For the time being, Lincoln had managed to accommodate all factions. Brooks noted that the president had "pleased the radicals and satisfied the conservatives by plainly projecting a plan of reconstruction, which is just alike to popular rights, to the cause of liberty and to the loyal people of all sections of the Union."[56] The leading senate Radical, Charles Sumner, told a reporter that the proclamation and the message "fully and perfectly satisfied" him and noted with satisfaction that the "language of the proclamation and of the accompanying message plainly assumes that the rebel States have lost their original character as States of the Union."[57] The Massachusetts senator cited Lincoln's use of the term "reestablish" to prove his point: "We do not *reestablish* a government which continues to exist."[58] The conservative New York *Herald* shrewdly remarked that the "art of riding two horses is not confined to the circus." The president "has for some time been riding two political horses, and with the skill of an old campaigner, he whips them—the radical horse 'a leetle ahead'—through his message." Throughout his administration so far, "he has given us some marvelous surprises in bringing forward the radical horse in front when it was supposed he had been hopelessly dropped behind."[59] Another conservative journal, the Washington *National Intelligencer*, was unusually generous in its praise.

After observing the reaction on Capitol Hill, John Hay wrote in his diary: "I never have seen such an effect produced by a public document. Men acted as if the Millennium had come." Senate Radicals were quite "delighted" and "beaming." Henry Wilson told Hay: "The President has struck another great blow. Tell him from me God Bless him." Senate Conservatives like Reverdy Johnson and James Dixon, too, "said it was highly satisfactory." In the lower chamber the response was similar. George Boutwell called it "a very able and shrewd paper. It has great points of popularity: & it is right." Owen Lovejoy "said it was glorious" and declared: "I shall live to see slavery ended in America." James A. Garfield quietly remarked that the president "has struck a great blow for the country and himself." Michigan Congressman Francis W. Kellogg gushed: "The President is the only man. He is the great man of the century. There is none like him in the world," for "he sees more widely and more clearly than anybody." Representative Henry T. Blow of Missouri declared: "God Bless Old Abe. I am one of the Radicals who have always believed in the President."[60]

Iowa Senator James Grimes objected only to the implication that the Supreme Court might overrule the Emancipation Proclamation.

The public, happy with the recent victories at Chattanooga and Knoxville as well as the triumphs of July, was also enthusiastic. "It only needed this message to clinch and rivet the wide-spread and daily growing popularity of Mr. Lincoln," observed John W. Forney. "That he has a hold on the popular heart stronger than that of any living American, has been made clear by a thousand evidences."[61] Samuel Galloway reported to Lincoln that his message and proclamation "have strengthened public confidence in you in Ohio—and have rendered any competition for the next Presidential term utterly hopeless and forlorn—It is the best document you have written, always excepting your letter on military arrests to the Albany Committee."[62] George Templeton Strong, who recorded that the message "finds very general favor," thought that "Uncle Abe is the most popular man in America today. The firmness, honesty, and sagacity of the 'gorilla despot' may be recognized by the rebels themselves sooner than we expect, and the weight of his personal character may do a great deal toward restoration of our national unity."[63] Charles Eliot Norton was also struck by the importance of Lincoln's character: "Once more we may rejoice that Abraham Lincoln is President. How wise and how admirably timed is his Proclamation. As a state paper its naiveté is wonderful. Lincoln will introduce a new style into state papers; he will make them sincere, and his honesty will compel even politicians to like virtue. I conceive his character to be on the whole the great net gain from the war."[64] Harriet Beecher Stowe thought that Lincoln's messages "more resembled a father's talks to his children than a state-paper. And they have had that relish and smack of the soil, that appeal to the simple human heart and head, which is a greater power in writing than the most artful devices of rhetoric."[65] A master of such rhetorical devices, Edward Everett, called Lincoln's message a "very remarkable document; better written than usual & calculated to produce a great effect abroad."[66]

Not everyone shared Everett's positive view of the message's style. A journalist deemed it "short, sharp, and decisive as a State paper, crude and angular as a literary effort."[67] Some thought the stiff opening section, dealing with foreign relations, had been penned by Seward, whose assistance had in fact been necessitated by Lincoln's illness.

Radicals in general were pleased because Lincoln agreed with their fundamental demand: the Union must be restored without slavery. They might differ with the president—and among themselves—about other matters, but not that one. "Stock in Father Abraham has evidently improved greatly since his message & proclamation of amnesty," observed Republican Congressman Charles Upson of Michigan, who said he was "satisfied with any plan of Reconstruction which essentially destroys slavery. We want the snake killed this time, not 'scotched' merely." Upson remarked that "'Old Abe' never goes back and though sometimes he has been thought slow in his movements he carries the country along with him on the whole pretty successfully."[68] *"Let slavery be destroyed* and other things will give but transitory difficulty," proclaimed the Chicago *Tribune*.[69] The Radical Boston *Commonwealth* rejoiced that "the

President's plan ignores completely the present political existence of the rebel States, and subverts all their constitutions and their regulations as to suffrage, boundaries." The *Commonwealth* applauded what it called Lincoln's "conversion to the radical programme," pointing out that he had rejected the central tenet of the Conservatives' argument by insisting on emancipation as a prerequisite for restoration: "the President has fully made up his mind that as far as he is concerned, during his occupancy of the Presidential chair, be the term longer or shorter, no rebel State shall be again received into the Union as a slave State, or with slavery existing as a political and social element."[70] In praising Lincoln's two "great state papers," the New York *Independent* echoed those sentiments: "We are all stronger to-day, and happier, because the President has again solemnly said that the Nation's Word must be kept, and that those set free shall not be abandoned again to bondage."[71] Months later, Radicals would change their tune. The leader of the disenchanted would be Henry Winter Davis, who feared that the popularity of Lincoln's message guaranteed his reelection. If that proved true, he told a friend, "I certainly shall leave the country."[72]

To avoid irritating the Radicals, Lincoln omitted from his final draft a discussion of the abstract question of whether a Confederate state was in or out of the Union, a matter they considered vital. In his original draft, Lincoln said that the question "seems to me, in every present aspect, to be of no practical importance. They all have been States in the Union; and all are to be hereafter, as we all propose; and a controversy whether they have ever been out of it, might divide and weaken, but could not enhance our strength, in restoring the proper national and State relations." The president struck out this passage in part because, as Hay noted, he believed that the clause of the Constitution guaranteeing each state a republican form of government authorized him "to grant protection to states *in* the Union and it will not do ever to admit that these states have at any time be[en] out."[73]

The issue of black suffrage, which eventually would prove so contentious, barely arose in 1863. Chase suggested to Lincoln that in the Reconstruction proclamation the word "voters" be changed to "citizens," thus enfranchising blacks in the reconstructed states. (Attorney General Bates had recently ruled that some blacks were citizens, the Dred Scott decision to the contrary notwithstanding.) When Secretary of the Interior Usher remarked that "Chase was very pertinacious about the word citizen instead of voters," Lincoln heatedly replied: "Yes, Chase thinks the negroes, as citizens, will vote to make him President." Usher cited this as an example of Lincoln's temper.[74] Chase's was a lonely voice, for other Radical spokesmen and journals were avoiding the question of black voting rights. Since no other cabinet member supported the treasury secretary's position, he did not press it, saying "that he was in the main so well satisfied with it [the proclamation] that he would take no exception to it."[75] Another source of future conflict between the president and Congress, the Ten Percent provision, received little criticism at first. Lincoln chose that modest figure evidently based on the earlier response of voters in Tennessee, Arkansas, and Louisiana.

While Radicals seemed satisfied, conservative Republicans like Montgomery Blair, Gideon Welles, and Orville H. Browning objected to making emancipation a requirement for Reconstruction. Most of them, however, appreciated the conciliatory spirit of Lincoln's message as well as his willingness to leave the states and their governments intact (except for slavery) and to let Southern whites determine how the blacks were to be treated. They also liked his acknowledgment that Congress and the Supreme Court might alter the plan. To avoid an unfavorable court ruling, Lincoln could have taken the advice of Isaac N. Arnold and Leonard Swett to recommend a constitutional amendment abolishing slavery, but he feared that doing so would be moving too fast. Nonetheless, in October 1863 he told Swett that he knew the time for such an amendment was fast approaching: "I can see emancipation coming; whoever can wait for it will also see it; whoever gets in the way of it will be run over by it."[76] In addition, he doubtless assumed that some Radical would introduce such a measure into Congress sooner or later. To a Louisiana Conservative, Lincoln explained that he did not regard his plan "as a Procrustean bed, to which exact conformity is to be indispensable; and in Louisiana particularly, I wish that labor already done, which varies from that plan in no important particular, may not be thrown away."[77]

Moderates shared the view of the New York *Times* that the president's plan was "simple and yet perfectly effective" as well as "inevitable."[78] They found especially noteworthy its rejection of Sumner's state suicide doctrine, while insisting that slavery be abolished.

Some ultra-Radicals denounced the amnesty plan as "all wrong," and a "great error" rooted in "dangerous conservatism."[79] But the New York *Evening Post* spoke for most vigorous opponents of slavery when it praised Lincoln's generosity: "Nothing, it must be admitted, could be more magnanimous or lenient towards the rebels; they have put themselves beyond the pale of the law by their insanity; their properties are already declared confiscate and their lives are in jeopardy; and if they continue contumacious, the whole of the beautiful region they inhabit will be inevitably overrun by our armies, their fields laid waste, their cities and towns desolated, and their homes pillaged. But in this dire strait the President offers them not only a peace which shall save them from the miseries of war, but an honorable pardon which shall endue them with all the attributes of the citizen. The very condition, moreover, on which they are asked to accept these boons, is a beneficent one—the renunciation of that monstrous idol of slavery, which has been the source of all their sacrifices and sufferings and woes." The editors noted with approval that Lincoln was emulating George Washington's magnanimity in dealing with the leaders of the 1794 Whiskey Rebellion.[80] Some Southerners agreed. The Nashville *Daily Press*, a conservative paper, predicted that Lincoln's plan would appeal to a large majority of Tennessee voters, for it would relieve them of military government.

Democrats were less supportive, arguing that the "simply absurd" Ten Percent plan amounted to minority rule.[81] "When this proposition is accepted," said the Cincinnati *Enquirer*, "we had better burn up all the copies of the Declaration of Independence, for they will remind us of our apostasy and shame, and openly admit that our political system is a Despotism pure and simple—as much so as Russia or Austria." The *Enquirer* fumed that Lincoln's plan was "as crude and unconstitutional as it is impolitic," for it was essentially an attempt to impose "upon the Union men of the South the Emancipation Proclamation as a test."[82] In Iowa, a Democratic journal derided the "absurd" amnesty offer and sniffed that "no people alive to self-respect" could accept it. If they did so, they would deserve "not only to lose the slaves they have but to become bound to them in the bonds of the most galling servitude."[83] Democrats also alleged that Lincoln's Ten Percent plan cynically aimed to restore Southern states in such a way that they would vote Republican in 1864.

Congress's legislative response to Lincoln's plan was at first positive. Among the many bills introduced during the early weeks of session, the most important was offered by Representative James M. Ashley, a Radical from Ohio. It contained most of the president's suggestions—including the loyalty oath, the Ten Percent formula, the requirement that state constitutions abolish slavery, and the use of military governors—but stipulated that suffrage would be granted to loyal males (which would include blacks) but denied to Rebel officials and soldiers. Abandoning his earlier championship of the state suicide theory, Ashley grounded his proposal on the Constitution's guarantee that all states would have a republican form of government. In most regards (except for the suffrage qualifications), his bill appeared to be a detailed implementation of the framework Lincoln suggested. So it seemed to many at the time, including the editors of the New York *Evening Post* and New York *Times.* Ashley's bill was referred to a special committee on Reconstruction, which had been established in response to the president's message. In moving the creation of such a committee, Thaddeus Stevens was not declaring war on Lincoln's plan but merely carrying out a routine procedure followed by the House for decades. The committee would eventually become an enemy of the administration, but it was not so conceived.

The executive-legislative honeymoon was short-lived, for Radicals quickly grew disenchanted with Lincoln's approach to Reconstruction. Even on December 9, the Chicago *Tribune* reported that "as they began to scan it more closely," Radicals "became more cautious in their praise." The "intense radicals" argued "that it owes its apparent popularity to its avoidance of points on which he knew that anything he would say would arouse differences among his supporters."[84] Maine Senator William Pitt Fessenden called the amnesty proclamation "silly" because it told "the rebels they may fight as long as they can, and take a pardon when they have had enough of it."[85] Henry Winter Davis agreed, but he and Fessenden were in a distinct minority, at least in December 1863.

Maintaining that the "Administration has put the negro, his liberty, his future, into the hands of the Supreme Court," Benjamin Butler exclaimed to Wendell Phillips: "God help him if he have no other refuge!" and lamented that "no one seems to see the point."[86] Phillips, however, did. He replied to Butler that the president's scheme "leaves the large landed proprietors of the South still to domineer over its politics, and make the negro's freedom a mere sham. Until a large share of those estates are divided, the aristocracy is not destroyed, neither is any *fair* chance given for the development of a system of free labor."[87] To an audience at New York's Cooper Union, Phillips denounced Lincoln's proposal as "neither wise, safe, nor feasible." The country "owes to the negro, not merely freedom; it owes him land, and it owes him education also." Passionately he urged the president to ask Congress for a constitutional amendment abolishing slavery everywhere.[88]

Frederick Douglass was equally impatient with Lincoln, who he said "has virtually laid down this as the rule of his statesmen: *Do evil by choice, right from necessity.*" The Ten Percent plan, Douglass protested, was "an entire contradiction of the constitutional idea of the Republican government." By failing to support black suffrage, Lincoln betrayed black soldiers. "Our Government asks the Negro to espouse its cause; it asks him to turn against his master, and thus fires his master's hate against him. Well, when it has attained peace, what does it propose? Why this, to hand the Negro back to the political power of his master, without a single element of strength to shield himself from the vindictive spirit sure to be roused against the whole colored race."[89]

Implementing the Ten Percent Plan: Florida and Louisiana

The implementation of Lincoln's plan got off to a rocky start. In January 1864, to bring Florida back into the Union, the president dispatched John Hay with instructions to enroll enough voters to meet the Ten Percent threshold established in the Reconstruction Proclamation. Some Republicans thought the assistant private secretary lacked sufficient gravitas. A Philadelphia editor remarked that Hay's "young, almost beardless, and almost boyish countenance" suggested that he was too young for the "official responsibilities and the tumult of action in time of pressure."[90] An Ohio journalist described him as "that fellow five feet tall, that walks like lightning down the street" wearing "a turtle-backed hat, just the shape of his cranium, with well oiled locks, and handsome kid gloves." A "stranger might mistake him for a stray Englishman," and a "close observer will notice at once the air of weighty secrets by which he is surrounded." Hay spoke "in the choice and expressive language which prevails at the 'Chebang,' as he pleasantly terms the White House. Inquire affectionately after the health of the President of the mightiest nation on the earth, and John will inform you that the 'old Tycoon is in high feather.'"[91]

Union military authorities in Florida had been planning a campaign in the northeast portion of the state, designed to cut off the peninsula from the rest of the Confederacy. In January 1864, after authorizing General Quincy A. Gillmore to launch that offensive, Lincoln had Hay commissioned as a major and sent him to join it. At first, Hay expressed optimism about his mission. "I think we will soon have the state back in the Union," he wrote on February 8. "If we get the 'President's Tithe' it will be fully half the voters in the state, as the poor old carcass of a neighborhood has been plucked to the bone, by North & South."[92] To Lincoln he described Floridians as "ignorant and apathetic," seeming "to know nothing and care nothing about the matter." They vaguely objected "to being shot and having their houses burned," but they did not understand "why it is done" and "will be very glad to see a government strong enough to protect them against these everyday incidents of the last two years." Hay received "the best assurances that we will get the tenth required: although so large a portion of the rebel population is in the army & so many of the loyal people, refugees in the North, that the state is well-nigh depopulated. We will have almost a clean slate to begin with."[93]

A week later, however, Hay predicted that he would fail. On February 20, Gillmore's offensive was repulsed at the battle of Olustee, making that prediction a certainty.

A Union officer, Joseph R. Hawley of Connecticut, called the attempt to restore Florida "a gigantic humbug. Besides the Floridians who were already with the Union forces at St. Augustine, Fernandina, Key West, etc., we have scarcely met a man who would be allowed to vote in Connecticut,—that is with sufficient intelligence and education. Not enough white men have we picked up to make one good country school district at the north. We have some prisoners, a good many deserters and a lot of stragglers, poor white-livered, fever-stricken, scrawny, ignorant creatures, with hardly intelligence enough to be made even the tool of a political intriguer."[94]

Hay acknowledged the truth of Hawley's observation, explaining that "we must wait for further developments in military operations before we can hope for a reorganization of the state under a loyal government. I find nearly everybody willing to take the oath of allegiance prescribed by the President, but I find scarcely anyone left in the country. Whole counties seem almost thoroughly depopulated. The few that remain seem heartily tired of the war, and willing to swear allegiance in any terms to the power that will protect them, but there are really not enough, as it seems to me, to justify a movement just at present, for rehabilitation."[95]

The New York *Herald* also regarded Hay's mission as a humbug. That paper, which was championing Grant for president, reported rumors "that the expedition was intended simply for the occupation of Florida for the purpose of securing the election of three Lincoln delegates to the National Nominating Convention, and that of John Hay to Congress. The cost of the operation to the government is estimated at about one million of dollars."[96] Greatly disturbed by that charge, Hay penned a response for the *Washington National Republican* asserting that the military offensive was planned and approved before he was given his assignment, which he had applied for because he desired "a more active life."[97]

Criticism of the administration's plan grew more intense after Lincoln altered his policy in Louisiana. Frustrated by the endless delays in setting up a new government there, caused in part by the legalistic approach of Thomas J. Durant, he decided to stop relying on the Free State Committee and to count instead on Nathaniel P. Banks to get things moving. Thus he abandoned his earlier insistence that the formation of new state governments should "be a movement of the people of the Districts, and not a movement of our military and quasi-military, authorities there."

Banks had a plan that strongly appealed to Lincoln. The *"only speedy and certain* method of accomplishing your object," Banks told the president, would be to order the election "of a State Government, under the Constitution [of 1852] and Laws of Louisiana, except so much thereof as recognizes and relates to slavery, which should be declared by the authority calling the election, and in the order authorizing it, *inoperative and void.*" Within two months, voters could be registered in the manner that Lincoln had spelled out in his proclamation and an election could be held. Soon thereafter a convention to revise the 1852 constitution could be summoned. "The People of Louisiana will accept such a proposition with favor," Banks predicted, for they "will prefer it to any arrangement which leaves the subject to them for an affirmative or negative vote. . . . Of course a government organized upon the basis of immediate and universal freedom, with the general consent of the people, followed by the adaptation of commercial and industrial interests to this order of things, & supported by the Army and Navy, the influence of the civil officers of the Government, and the Administration at Washington, could not fail by any possible chance, to obtain an absolute and permanent recognition of the principle of freedom upon which it would be based." Such a strategy, Banks assured the president, "will be far more acceptable to the Citizens of Louisiana, than the submission of the question of slavery to the chances of an election. Their self-respect, their *Amour propre* will be appeased if they are not required to vote for or against it. Offer them a Government without slavery, and they will gladly accept it as a necessity resulting from the war." Banks explained that he was "opposed to any settlement, and have been from the beginning, except upon the basis of immediate emancipation, but it is better to secure it by consent, than by force, better still by consent *and* force. It carries moral, as well as physical power with it." Consideration of black suffrage could be postponed a year or more: "Other questions relating to the condition of the negro, may safely be deferred until this one is secured. If he gains freedom, education, the right to bear arms, the highest privileges accorded to any race and which none has yet proved itself worthy unless it be our own, his best friend may rest content for another year at least."[98]

It is not entirely clear if Lincoln knew the details of this plan before putting Banks in charge of Louisiana Reconstruction. The general had evidently written a letter, no longer extant, outlining his plans to George Boutwell, who read it to the president on December 21. Boutwell reported to Banks that the letter "made a deep impression upon the President and in no manner unfriendly to you. After some further consideration he said he should write to you saying that he understood and expected you to exercise supreme and undivided authority and to take the matter of State organization into your own hands." Lincoln, wrote Boutwell, "is still anxious to have La. organized as a free State, and I believe he fully agreed with my suggestion that it could be well and speedily accomplished only by putting the power into your hands."[99]

Delighted at the prospect of swift action, Lincoln wrote Banks on Christmas Eve 1863 endorsing his plan and authorizing him to carry it out. The president apologized for his sharp letter of December 6: "I have all the while intended you to be *master,* as well in regard to re-organizing a State government for Louisiana, as in regard to the military matters of the Department; and hence my letters on reconstruction have nearly if not quite all been addressed to you. My error has been that it did not occur to me that Gov. Shepley or any one else would set up a claim to act independently of you; and hence I said nothing expressly upon the point. Language has not been guarded at a point where no danger was thought of. I now tell you that in every dispute, with whomsoever, you are master. Gov. Shepley was appointed to *assist* the Commander of the Department, and not to thwart him, or act independently of him. Instructions have been given directly to him, merely to spare you detail labor, and not to supersede your authority. This, in it's liability to be misconstrued, it now seems was an error in us. But it is past. I now distinctly tell you that you are master of all, and that I wish you to take the case as you find it, and give us a free-state re-organization of Louisiana, in the shortest possible time. What I say here is to have a reasonable construction.

I do not mean that you are to withdraw from Texas, or abandon any other military measure which you may deem important. Nor do I mean that you are to throw away available work already done for re-construction; or that war is to be made upon Gov. Shepley, or upon any one else, unless it be found that they will not co-operate with you, in which case, and in all cases, you are master while you remain in command of the Department."[100]

Banks's "confidence in the practicability of constructing a free state-government, speedily, for Louisiana," and his "zeal to accomplish it" gratified Lincoln, who urged the general to "proceed with all possible dispatch." To assist Banks, the president let it be known that all federal appointees in Louisiana should give him "full, and zealous co-operation."[101] The decision to place Banks in charge would profoundly affect the course of Reconstruction not only in Louisiana but throughout the South.

True to his word, Banks delivered a free-state government in less than two months. Emboldened by his new authority, he scrapped the Free State Committee's plan to hold a constitutional convention, and mandated that on February 22 elections be held for governor and other state officials based on the 1852 state constitution. To nullify provisions of that document sanctioning slavery, the general promulgated special orders. Michael Hahn, a Moderate, won the governorship, defeating the Radical Benjamin Flanders and the Conservative J. Q. A. Fellows. The turnout of more than 11,000 voters far exceeded the Ten Percent requirement. Lincoln congratulated Hahn for "having fixed your name in history as the first-free-state Governor of Louisiana."[102] Five weeks later, 6,000 voters participated in the election of delegates to a constitutional convention, which met from April through July. In September, the resulting document won ratification by a handsome majority (6,836 to 1,566). Lincoln and Banks had transformed the sputtering Reconstruction efforts of the Free State Committee and General Shepley into a successful movement restoring the Bayou State on the basis of liberty. By all rights, Radicals should have been pleased, but they were not.

As 1864 began, a journalist rashly predicted that since "the republican party is a unit," therefore "no quarrels between radicals and conservatives will be in order."[103] In fact, a quarrel quickly broke out over Louisiana Reconstruction. The man most responsible for creating this major rupture in the Republican coalition was 46-year-old Thomas J. Durant, the tall, emaciated, dyspeptic head of Louisiana's Free State Committee. A follower of the French utopian socialist philosopher Francois Marie Charles Fourier, and an admirer of Thomas Jefferson, after whom he was named, Durant had campaigned for Stephen A. Douglas in 1860 and served briefly in the Confederate militia. Though he owned a few slaves and early in the war defended planters complaining about the Union troops' practice of harboring runaway bondsmen, by 1863 he had become an ardent leader of the antislavery forces in New Orleans. In 1862, Durant, who eventually was to pick a fight with Lincoln and Banks over black suffrage, had formulated a Reconstruction plan based on white voters alone. As state attorney general and commissioner of voter registration, he had refused to enroll free blacks.

Lincoln, on the other hand, had twice approved the enfranchisement of free blacks by February 1864, when Durant began his revolt against the president's Reconstruction policy. In August 1863, Stanton had directed Governor Shepley to register for voting "all the loyal citizens of the United States." The word *white*, which Durant had used in defining eligible voters, was conspicuously absent. In early December, Durant abruptly changed course and recommended that some black males—those born free—be enfranchised.

Chase told Durant that the administration meant to allow, but not insist upon, the enfranchisement of free-born blacks. "I am particularly gratified," wrote the treasury secretary, "by your wise & courageous advocacy of the right of native free born colored citizens to participate in the reorganization of the State Governments. I informed the President of your views in this respect, and he said he could see no objection to the registering of such citizens [or to] their exercise of the right of suffrage. You will have observed doubtless that in his message & proclamation he does not limit reorganization to the precise forms or modes proposed by him, but is willing to accept any form or mode whereby the great ends of restoration to the Union with permanent free state institutions can be best secured."[104] To Lyman D. Stickney, a friend acting as tax commissioner in Florida, Chase praised Durant's action regarding free-born blacks and added: "I told the President of it, and he said he could see no objection to their enrollment and voting." Chase urged Stickney and others working to restore the government of Florida to "go further, and let all of full age vote who have borne arms for the country, or who can read and write, without any other distinctions at present."[105] When Lincoln received an appeal from a white Louisiana Unionist urging him to deny blacks the right to vote for constitutional convention delegates, he endorsed it as follows: "On very full consideration I do not wish to say more than I have publicly said."[106] Just as he would not openly support black voting yet, neither would he oppose it.

If Lincoln meant to suggest subtly to Banks that he would be willing to have some blacks vote in Louisiana, the general failed to take the hint. He allowed only whites to cast ballots in the February 1864 election. Revealingly, Durant raised no objection, though he was enraged by Lincoln's decision to name Banks "master of all." In an access of injured self-esteem, Durant became an implacable and highly effective foe of Lincoln's plan. If Banks had handled Durant with more tact, Lincoln's Reconstruction policy might have worked. As it was, the general hurt Durant's feelings by reading him Lincoln's letter making him "master of all." The "word *master* . . . grated harshly upon my ears," Durant told Chase. "I was deeply mortified."[107] Further antagonizing the Free State Committeemen, Banks scuttled their effort to hold a constitutional convention before the general election. Durant said that he would not oppose the general's policy but would do nothing to further it either. When Banks issued a call for elections to be held on February 22, Durant quit his posts as attorney general and commissioner of registration.

Equally alienated was Benjamin F. Flanders, who wrote Chase from New Orleans that "Mr Lincoln has lost by his letter to Gen Banks much of the friendship which he previously enjoyed of loyal men here. He will find . . . that he has another Missouri case on his hands."[108] The general further angered the free-state faction by reneging on his agreement to hold elections for delegates to the constitutional convention simultaneously with the general election (February 22). At the free-state nominating convention, the Durant–Flanders faction lost to more conservative Unionists, who nominated Michael Hahn for governor. Though he emphatically endorsed immediate emancipation, Hahn was suspect in the eyes of the Radicals, who regarded him as "a trickster and a trimming politician." To challenge him, they put Flanders forward.[109] (Conservatives had decided not to contest the election.)

During the brief campaign, Hahn's supporters engaged in race-baiting, which Banks failed to stop. Such tactics lent credence to the Radicals' claim that they were the only true-blue antislavery faction. Durant openly charged that Banks had scrapped the original plan to hold a constitutional convention before the general election at the insistence of the Lincoln administration, which he said greatly dreaded the prospect of black suffrage. This charge was unfounded, as Durant knew from Chase's letters. In fact, Flanders denied that black suffrage was an issue in the contest, though when challenged to state his position on the subject, he refused to oppose it. Privately, he acknowledged that blacks eventually should be enfranchised, but not in 1864. Hahn won, to the intense disgust of the Durant faction, which then refused to have anything to do with the subsequent election for delegates to the constitutional convention. They believed that Banks had rigged the election. Their boycott drastically reduced the chances that the constitutional convention would enfranchise blacks.

To counter that development, Lincoln on March 13 injected himself into the contest on the side of black voting rights. Congratulating Hahn on his election, the president significantly alluded to the upcoming convention: "Now you are about to have a Convention which, among other things, will probably define the elective franchise. I barely suggest for your private consideration, whether some of the colored people may not be let in—as, for instance, the very intelligent, and especially those who have fought gallantly in our ranks. They would probably help, in some trying time to come, to keep the jewel of liberty within the family of freedom. But this is only a suggestion, not to the public, but to you alone."[110] Though phrased tentatively, the president's letter was really an order, similar to the August missive regarding emancipation that he had sent to Banks, with copies to Free State Committee leaders.

Lincoln's letter to Hahn may have been prompted by a delegation of New Orleans free blacks who had recently handed the president a petition, ignored by Shepley and Banks, bearing the signatures of a thousand blacks. Their leaders, Jean Baptiste Roudeanez and Arnold Bertonneau, asserted that of the 30,000 free blacks in Louisiana, all but 1,000 were literate; that they paid taxes on property worth over $15 million; that many were descended from French and Spanish settlers and from men who had fought with Andrew Jackson in the epic battle against the British on January 8, 1815; that many had lighter complexions than some whites; and that they had rallied to protect the city from a feared attack by Confederates while Banks's men were besieging Port Hudson. "We are men; treat us as such," they argued in their appeal for the right to vote.[111]

Lincoln's respectful treatment of his black visitors shocked the sensibilities of some Southern whites who observed the interview. After reading their petition, he remarked: "I regret, gentlemen, that you are not able to secure all your rights, and that circumstances will not permit the government to confer them upon you. I wish you would amend your petition so as to include several suggestions, which I think will give more effect to your prayer, and after having done so please hand it to me." When a leader of the delegation volunteered to rewrite the document on the spot, Lincoln asked: "Are you, then, the author of this eloquent production?"

"Whether eloquent or not, it is my own work," he replied, and thereupon swiftly incorporated the president's suggestions into the petition.[112]

Although Lincoln was courteous and respectful to his black guests, and although they agreed to his suggested changes in their petition, he denied their request, explaining "that the restoration of the Union in all its parts being his primary aim, all other questions, in his mind, were subordinate to this. Hence, whatever he did to attain this end arose from his estimate of the political necessity demanding the action, and not from any moral aspects of the case. Inasmuch as the reasons given for admitting the free people of color to the voting privilege in Louisiana were purely of a moral nature, in no wise affecting the relation of that State to the Union, he would not depart from his established views, and would decline to take any steps in the matter until a political urgency rendered such a course proper."[113] This statement strikingly resembled Lincoln's famous 1862 letter to Horace Greeley responding to "The Prayer of Twenty Millions." (According to another account of this interview, Lincoln said that he "saw no reason why intelligent black men should not vote; but this was not a military question, and he would refer it to the Constitutional Convention in Louisiana.")[114]

Lincoln's support of black suffrage was more comprehensive than that of Radicals like Durant, who endorsed voting rights only for *free-born* blacks. The president's recommendation that some former slaves be allowed to vote if they had served in the army or were "very intelligent" closely resembled Chase's stand on that issue. On December 28, the treasury secretary wrote Durant: "I hope your Convention will be wise enough to adopt the principle of universal suffrage of all men, unconvicted of crime, who can read & write and have a fair knowledge of the Constitution of the State & of the United States. What a glory for Louisiana to be the first state to adopt a constitution basing the right to suffrage on virtue & intelligence alone. The object might be easily attained by establishing Commissions to make examinations & give certificates for which a small fee, fifty cents or a dollar, might be required. These certificates would naturalize the recipients into the great electoral community."[115] (In later decades, white Southerners would use the requirement that blacks interpret the state and national constitutions and pay a poll tax as a means to strip blacks of voting rights granted them after the war.)

Thus in later 1863 and early 1864, Chase and Lincoln saw virtually eye to eye on black suffrage. The treasury secretary had not objected to the voting provision in Lincoln's Amnesty and Reconstruction Proclamation. The president hesitated to endorse black suffrage as long as Louisiana officially remained a Slave State, but he made it clear that he would not object if white Louisianans enfranchised their black neighbors.

Acting on Lincoln's gently phrased letter, Governor Hahn threw his weight behind efforts to incorporate voting rights for at least some blacks into the new state constitution. Banks, evidently at Lincoln's behest, worked behind the scenes to obtain the same result. When delegates met in April to draft a new constitution, the general maneuvered to prevent a Conservative from becoming chairman of the convention. Instead he helped get Edward H. Durrell, a New Orleans attorney, named to that post. Banks urged Durrell to have a provision adopted enfranchising blacks who were intelligent or who owned property. He gave similar advice to another delegate, Thomas B. Thorpe. The majority of delegates, however, were unreceptive and went so far as to prohibit the legislature from ever granting blacks the right to vote. Banks and Hahn worked hard to reverse that decision. The final version of the document authorized the legislature to allow blacks to vote based on service in the army, intellectual merit, or payment of taxes. This did not satisfy Lincoln's desire for limited black suffrage, but it did pave the way for its eventual adoption. The constitution also provided for the education of all children without distinction of race, allowed blacks to serve in the militia, and guaranteed equal rights in court.

This was as much as white public opinion in Louisiana would abide. Chase's main informant about Louisiana affairs, George S. Denison (collector of the port of New Orleans), told him that "constitutions & laws are without good effect, unless sustained by an enlightened public opinion—and any law giving suffrage to negroes, could not be so sustained at present, in any State county or town throughout the whole South. I do not think you appreciate or understand the intense antipathy with which Southerners regard negroes. It is the natural antipathy of races, developed & intensified by the servile, brutal condition of one—the insolent, despotic position of the other." Given those conditions, Denison judged that the constitution's provision allowing the legislature to enfranchise blacks was "a great step in the right direction."[116]

Lincoln's March 13, 1864, letter to Hahn had smoothed the way for the adoption of that clause in the new constitution. The following year, Hahn said that the missive, "though marked 'private,' was no doubt intended to be seen by other Union men in Louisiana beside myself, and was consequently shown to many members of our Constitutional Convention and leading free-State men." He added that the "letter, written in the mild and graceful tone which imparted so much weight to Mr. Lincoln's simple suggestions, no doubt had great effect on the action of the Louisiana Convention in all matters appertaining to the colored man."[117]

Having helped to get the constitution written with some, if not all, of the desired protections for blacks, Lincoln injected himself into the ratification contest. On August 9, he wrote to Banks that he had just seen a copy of the constitution and was "anxious that it shall be ratified by the people." To achieve that end, he was willing to employ the patronage power, as he told the general: "I will thank you to let the civil officers in Louisiana, holding under me, know that this, is my wish, and to let me know at once who of them openly declare for the constitution, and who of them, if any, decline to so declare."[118] Banks used this authorization effectively to enlist support for ratification and took other steps to support the pro-constitution campaign, which was successful. The new state legislature chose two U.S. senators and held elections for five Representatives. But, Lincoln wondered, would Congress recognize them?

Chase Lays Pipe: The Attempt to Supplant Lincoln

To attain congressional approval of the Louisiana experiment, Lincoln could have used the assistance of Chase, who had great influence with the Radical wing of the party both in Louisiana and Washington. The treasury secretary, however, was scheming to win the Republican presidential nomination, "at work night and day, laying pipe," as a Pennsylvania politician noted.[119] In October 1863, Edward Bates confided to his diary that "Chase's head is turned by his eagerness in pursuit of the presidency. For a long time he has been filling all the offices in his own vast patronage, with extreme partizans, and contrives also to fill many vacancies, properly belonging to other departments."[120] The patronage at his disposal included 15,000 jobs. As a rival for the nomination, Chase had little incentive to help Lincoln achieve a legislative victory, even though they shared similar views about Reconstruction policy in the Bayou State.

Chase's prospects appeared good in Washington, where Lincoln enjoyed far less popularity than he did in the country at large. Henry Winter Davis did not "know a public man who is not disgusted with the lack of Presidential qualities in the Prest."[121] In February, Lyman Trumbull reported that "the surface current is running in favor of Mr. Lincoln's renomination, but I find with many that the feeling for Lincoln is only apparent. It is by no means certain that he will be the candidate."[122] Few public men in the capital, the senator said, favored Lincoln's reelection, for there was "a distrust & fear that he is too undecided & inefficient ever to put down the rebellion." Trumbull would not be surprised "if a re-action sets in before the nomination in favor of some man supposed to possess more energy, & less inclination to trust our brave boys in the hands, & under the leadership of Generals who have no heart in the war."[123] One of Trumbull's constituents asserted that "a majority of Republican members of Congress are opposed to Lincoln's renomination."[124] During a visit to Washington in early 1864, William M. Dickson found "a strong feeling" against Lincoln's reelection. The Republican Party's "best men" insisted that the president "has been in the way, that our success has been [achieved] not by him but in spite of him & that he is so inefficient that he must not be permitted to remain in power another four years. But the thing most unfavorable to him, was the fact that the Blairs have assumed with or without his consent the care of his political fortunes."[125] Lincoln's support of the Blair family alienated many Ohioans, including Republican state legislators. One of them who had voted in February to endorse the president's renomination declared in May that Lincoln "must cut loose from the Blairs or sink with them."[126]

Radicals condemned Lincoln's purported conservatism, inconsistency, administrative incapacity, and reluctance to make difficult decisions. Henry Ward Beecher lamented that the president's mind "seldom works clearly & cleanly," and George Luther Stearns dismissed Lincoln as "unfit by nature and education to carry on the government for the next four years."[127] The state treasurer of Minnesota hoped that Lincoln would be denied renomination, for though the president was "honest and upright no doubt," nevertheless "we need a great leader in these hard times & not one who must be pushed by the people."[128] A Kansas abolitionist deplored Lincoln's "everlasting playing Hawk and Buzzard. You never know what to depend on. Sometimes he is just and sometimes he is unjust. Sometimes he is wise and sometimes he is foolish. Sometimes he is earnest and sometimes he is joking. Sometimes he is clear and sometimes he is muddy."[129] In Massachusetts, Richard Henry Dana sneered that Lincoln was "a shapeless mass of writhing ugliness" who "lacks administrative power" and "is not up to the office."[130] Lydia Maria Child complained that though God "is doing a great work," nevertheless "the agents by which He is accomplishing it are so narrow, so cold! The ruling motive of this administration, from the beginning to the present time, seems to have been how to conciliate the Democratic party."[131]

Radical senators were especially critical of the president. According to Charles Sumner, "there is a strong feeling among those who have seen Mr. Lincoln, in the way of business, that he lacks practical talent for his important place. It is thought that there should be more readiness, and also more capacity, for government." Sumner likened the president to Louis XVI and opposed his renomination, arguing that any member of the Massachusetts congressional delegation was better qualified for chief executive than the incumbent.[132] Sumner's colleague from Massachusetts, Henry Wilson, harshly criticized Lincoln behind his back. When asked why he did not voice his disapproval publicly, he replied that the president clearly was so popular with the people that he would be renominated, and that "bad as that would be, the best must be made of it."[133] William P. Fessenden scornfully remarked that the people of the North were "woefully humbugged in their notions" of the president, who was "weak as water." Yet, he acknowledged resignedly, "it will not do to tell the truth, and I see no way but to take another four years of selfish stupidity," for "Lincoln is, after all, about as good a candidate as we shall be likely to get." Despite the president's failings, "the people have a strong faith in his honesty of purpose, and at a time when their endurance is so largely drawn upon, that is a great point."[134] James W. Grimes of Iowa told Fessenden that the president could win reelection only if he dramatically reorganized his cabinet: "The truth is the people have not the slightest confidence in either Stanton Usher Blair Welles or Bates. There is no administrative ability possessed by either one of them, and some of them are generally supposed to be and I know them to be positively dishonest."[135] Timothy O. Howe of Wisconsin grumbled, "I am tired of this administration which I do not really know whether to characterize as many-headed or no-headed."[136]

Like Senators Fessenden and Wilson, Massachusetts Judge Ebenezer Rockwood Hoar had "come at last, though slowly and reluctantly, to the decided conviction, not only that Mr. Lincoln will be certain to be nominated in June, but that he would be equally certain to be nominated in September." There was no better alternative, Hoar told businessman John Murray Forbes: "I am afraid . . . that he represents about the average (and perhaps even a little better than that) of all that we have to trust for suppressing the rebellion."[137] Forbes, who deplored Lincoln's "system of floating along by the impulse of the people," was of like mind.[138]

Defenders of the administration pointed out that Lincoln's congressional critics who thought that "he has been right, but slow" ought to remember that "within three years they themselves solemnly resolved [in the Johnson–Crittenden resolutions] that the war should not touch slavery, and even went so far as to adopt an amendment to the constitution to preclude any further amendment that should abolish slavery." Thus "reproach comes from them with an ill grace."[139]

Some die-hards would not support Lincoln for reelection under any circumstances. Alfred B. Mullet, an architect working for the Treasury Department in Washington, considered the president "entirely unfitted by nature, education, and domestic relations for the Chief Magistracy of the American Nation." Therefore, Mullett "resolved in common with a large number of Republicans, to vote for his re-election under no circumstances. Should any loyal man be a Candidate in opposition to Mr Lincoln (should he unfortunately receive the endorsement of the Baltimore Convention) I shall feel it my duty to support him to the extent of my very humble ability. And should there be no choice between Mr Lincoln and a Copperhead, I shall not trouble myself about the matter, believing the difference between the results to be obtained from the cowardice and temporizing of one, will be very nearly the same as the treachery of the other." Mullet assured Chase that "the Germans the Old Liberty Guard and the War Democracy of the West, despise Mr Lincoln most heartily."[140] The abolitionist Bradford Wood longed to quit his post as U.S. minister to Denmark, return home, and help nominate as Lincoln's replacement someone "who adds capacity, energy and courage to honesty," who "knows men," and "for whose election an honorable man can work . . . without any misgivings."[141]

A lack of unity weakened the opposition to Lincoln's renomination. As New York Senator Edwin D. Morgan observed, the president's critics did not know "in what manner to organize their party. They are not by any means unanimous for Mr Chase, but would take Grant Fremont Banks or Butler more readily than Mr Lincoln."[142] Similarly, George Bancroft expressed disappointment "at finding everybody in Wash[ington] opposed to Lincoln & yet no concert of purpose." There was "a very general disgust among thinking men," according to that historian.[143]

Lincoln knew all about discontent among congressional Radicals. In mid-February, he indicated to Edward Bates that he was "fully apprehensive of the schemes of the Radical leaders." He understood "that they would strike at him at once, if they durst; but they fear that the blow would be ineffectual, and so, they would fall under his power as *beaten enemies*; and, for that only reason the hypocrit[e]s try to occupy equivocal ground—so that, when they fail, as *enemies,* they may still pretend to be *friends*."[144] When Shelby Cullom warned him that everybody in Washington seemed to oppose his renomination, Lincoln replied: "Well, it is not quite so bad as that," and showed him a congressional directory in which he had marked the inclinations of all members.[145]

In letters and conversations throughout the fall and winter of 1863–1864, Chase criticized the president repeatedly and expressed a willingness to replace him. On November 26, he told his son-in-law, "If I were myself controlled by merely personal sentiments I should prefer the reelection of Mr. Lincoln to that of any other man. But I doubt the expediency of reelecting any body, and I think that a man of different qualities from those the President has will be needed for the next four years."[146] That same day he spoke more bluntly to William T. Coggeshall, who summarized the treasury secretary's remarks in his diary: "Chase despondent. Says it is no use for him to struggle with present administration. Mr. Lincoln purposeless. Firm only from his inertia. Generous, kind, in some regards, wise, but as a precocious child. Has no practical power. No cabinet meetings for two years for counsel. Meetings for jokes. Unless people recover from infatuation of confidence in Lincoln, bankruptcy inevitable. Perhaps that to come because we deserve to suffer for participation in slavery. Must be a change at the White House."[147]

To the Congregationalist minister Joshua Leavitt, who opposed Lincoln's renomination, Chase recycled some of the arguments he had made in 1862: "Had there been here an administration in the true sense of the word—a President conferring with his cabinet and taking their united judgments & with their aid enforcing activity, economy, & energy in all Departments of Public Service—we could have spoken boldly & defied the world. But our condition here has always been very different. I preside over the funnel—everybody else & especially the Secretaries of War & the Navy, over the spigots—and keep them well opened, too—Mr. Seward conducts the foreign relations with very little let or help from any body. There is no unity & no system except so far as it is departmental. There is progress—but it is slow and involuntary."[148] Coyly Chase hinted that he would not object if friends championed his candidacy. In December, he wrote: "I have not the slightest wish to press any claims upon the consideration of friends, or the public. There is certainly, however, a purpose to use my name, and I do not feel at all bound to object to it."[149]

Although Lincoln said he knew that Chase's head was "full of *Presidential maggots*," and while the president was "trying to keep that maggot out of his head," he was "much amused" at the secretary's "mad hunt after the Presidency."[150] When told about Chase's frequent criticism of him, he replied that he did not care, for the secretary was "on the whole, a pretty good fellow and a very able man" whose "only trouble is that he has 'the White House fever.'"[151] To be sure, Lincoln thought Chase's maneuvering to win the nomination was in "very bad taste," but he said in October 1863 that he "shut his eyes to all these performances." Because Chase did good work at the Treasury Department, he would be kept in the cabinet. If he were to become president, Lincoln thought it would be "all right. I hope we may never have a worse man." For months he had observed Chase currying favor with malcontents. The secretary resembled, Lincoln said, "a bluebottle fly" who lays "his eggs in every rotten spot he can find." Whenever Chase saw "that an important matter is troubling me, if I am compelled to decide it in a way to give offense to a man of some influence he always ranges himself in opposition to me and persuades the victim that he has been hardly dealt by and that he (C[hase]) would have arranged it very differently. It was so with Gen. Fremont—with Genl. Hunter when I annulled his hasty proclamation—with Gen. Butler when he was recalled from New Orleans—with these Missouri people when they called the other day. I am entirely indifferent as to his success or failure in these schemes, so long as he does his duty as the head of the Treasury Department." Lincoln even saw an advantage in Chase's ambition, which he likened to "a horsefly on the neck of a ploughhorse—which kept him lively about his work."[152] Months later, when Shelby Cullom urged that Chase be fired, Lincoln replied: "Let him alone; he can do no more harm in here than he can outside."[153]

But Lincoln was not always so indulgent of Chase and his backers. In January 1864, he apparently sent the secretary a sharp note, no longer extant, about a fulsome puff piece touting the treasury secretary that appeared in an obscure journal. Chase denied that he had done anything to encourage its publication. The following month, Lincoln discussed with Edward Bates the Radical attempts to supplant him. Those men, the president said, "were almost *fiendish*" hypocrites, but he optimistically believed that his allies could defeat Radical schemes.[154]

Much to the dismay of his supporters, Lincoln seemed passive in the face of the Chase challenge. Joseph Medill urged him to act: "Without your own assistance the efforts of your friends won't avail much. You have it in your power by a few simple moves on the chess board to defeat the game of your rivals, and finally check mate them."[155] Mark Delahay observed that Lincoln's "only fault is he *will not* help himself."[156] David Davis groused, "Mr. Lincoln annoys me more than I can express, by his persistence in letting things take their course,—without effort or organization when a combined organization in the Treasury Dept. is in antagonism." The president, Davis reported, "seems disposed to let the thing run itself & if the people elect him, he will be thankful, but won[']t use means to secure the thing."[157] But when Davis described how Treasury Department employees were being forced to contribute to Chase's campaign fund, and how those who resisted were threatened with dismissal, Lincoln said with a grin that if such threats were carried out, "the head I guess would have to go with the tail."[158]

Chase's candidacy was no secret to political observers, though he did not openly announce it until mid-January 1864, when he wrote an Ohio state senator that he approved of efforts being made on his behalf. He insisted that he was motivated only by a desire to promote the public good and not by personal ambition: "If I know my own heart, I desire nothing so much as the suppression of this rebellion and the establishment of union, order, and prosperity on sure and safe foundations; and I should despise myself if I felt capable of allowing any personal objects to influence me to any action which would affect, by one jot or tittle, injuriously, the accomplishment of those objects."[159] Few men have been as capable of self-deception as Chase.

A Chase-for-president committee was organized in Washington under the leadership of Senator Samuel C. Pomeroy of Kansas. Among Chase's other backers in the capital were members of the Ohio congressional delegation (Representatives Robert C. Schenck, Rufus P. Spalding, James M. Ashley, James A. Garfield, and Senator John Sherman), the journalists Whitelaw Reid and James M. Winchell, and Senators B. Gratz Brown of Missouri and Henry Wilson of Massachusetts. Chase's wealthy son-in-law William Sprague and financier Jay Cooke helped raise funds. The poet and stockbroker Edmund C. Stedman persuaded Chase to release $640,000 to a client, the Kansas-Pacific Railroad, for work it had not completed. The corporation was entitled to the money under the Railroad Act of 1862 only after the roadbed had been laid, which was patently not the case of the Kansas-Pacific. In turn, Stedman became a leading force in the Chase organization, raising money from railroad men and operating a New York office.

(Lincoln's campaign also raised funds in questionable ways. According to Charles G. Halpine, a knowledgeable New York Democrat and good friend of John Hay, in early 1864 Congress had passed a "Whiskey Bill" allowing certain Republican operatives to corner the local liquor market. In return for this favor, the beneficiaries were expected to contribute half their profits to the "Lincoln Movement." Halpine cited as an example the fifth ward of New York, where soon after passage of the whiskey legislation the "Weed wire-pullers" who had gained advantages from it paid $600 to establish a "Lincoln Head Quarters." They printed posters and handbills, hired bands, sponsored ward meetings, and did whatever they could to promote a "Lincoln Endorsement.")[160]

In February, Chase's supporters issued two documents that embarrassed him mightily. The first, a pamphlet titled "The Next Presidential Election," denounced the Lincoln administration. Without mentioning Chase, it called for the nomination of "a statesman profoundly versed in political and economic science, one who fully comprehends the spirit of the age in which we live," and criticized the president as inept.[161] The second document, known as the "Pomeroy Circular," was not so coy. It asserted that Chase deserved the nomination because he had "more of the qualities needed in a President during the next four years than are combined in any other available candidate; his record is clear and unimpeachable, showing him to be a statesman of rare ability, and an administrator of the very highest order, while his private character furnishes the surest obtainable guaranty of economy and purity in the management of public affairs." Lincoln could not be reelected, the circular argued, and even if he were able to win a second term, the "cause of humanity liberty and the dignity and honor of the nation" would suffer, for he would then temporize even more than he had during his first term.[162] The document's author, James M. Winchell, said "the arraignment of the Administration made in the circular was one which he [Chase] thoroughly indorsed, and would sustain."[163]

An ally had advised Chase that Lincoln's "integrity & apparent unselfishness entitle him to every courtesy," but these two documents were highly discourteous, to say the least.[164] John Sherman mailed out copies of the pamphlet under his senatorial frank and received numerous complaints from offended constituents, who denounced it as "a violent, bitter attack on President Lincoln."[165] It "might do for Vallandigham to send such documents with his endorsement," wrote one. "But for a Senator elected by the loyal people of Ohio to be guilty of such an act is truly mortifying. There is no use however for a few politicians at Washington to think they can influence the people against 'Old Honest Abe.' You can't do it and, Mr. Sherman, you need not try it. If you were to resign tomorrow, you could not get ten votes in the Legislature provided it could be shown that you have been circulating such stuff as this."[166]

(The previous year, while campaigning in Ohio, Sherman had praised Lincoln as "one of the kindest and honestest men that the world affords" and scoffed at charges that the president was trying to establish a despotism. On the contrary, Sherman "had often thought that Mr. Lincoln was altogether too kind for the emergency. He hoped his democratic friends would live to be ashamed of all this violent criticism and gross personal abuse as unjust and unpatriotic.")[167]

The two documents, however, did win Chase the endorsement of some New York newspapers, including the *Tribune,* the *Independent,* and George Wilkes's *Spirit of the Times.* But in general the circular and the pamphlet backfired, alienating many who might have sympathized with Chase. As Samuel Galloway told the president, Pomeroy's action "has utterly annihilated the pretensions and prospects of Mr Chase—and has rallied, with a new and more efficient zeal your friends to the support of the Administration. 'The gun has recoiled and kicked the owner over.'"[168]

When friends attempted to call the Pomeroy circular to Lincoln's attention, he refused. Earlier he had protested impatiently: "I wish they would stop thrusting that subject of the Presidency into my face. I don[']t want to hear anything about it."[169] On February 20, newspapers published the circular, impelling Chase to offer his resignation. Secretary of the Interior Usher, who regarded the Pomeroy circular as "a most indecent thing" that was "badly conceived" and "badly worded," predicted that it would "cause a rupture in the cabinet."[170] But Lincoln told Chase that he had not read the document and did not intend to. Moreover, he wished the treasury secretary to remain at his post. To Usher, the president explained that he believed Chase's denial that he had authorized the circular, "for he thought it impossible for him (Mr. Chase) to have done such a thing."[171]

"I do not meddle in these matters," Lincoln informed a caller. "If any man thinks my present position desirable to occupy, he is welcome to try it, as far as I am concerned."[172] Struck by Lincoln's preternatural forbearance, David Davis observed that he "is a wise man, & he won[']t quarrel with Chase. I w[oul]d dismiss him [from] the cabinet, if it killed me. He pursues the wiser course."[173] According to Usher, "Lincoln says but little[,] finds fault with none & judging from his deportment, you would suppose he was as little concerned as any one about the result."[174] It was widely recognized that, as Supreme Court Justice Noah H. Swayne put it, if Lincoln "were not the self denigrating & most magnanimous man that he is there would be an explosion."[175]

The Chase boomlet, which never stood much chance of success, ended with a whimper. Even among Radicals, its support was weak. Joseph Medill observed in December 1863 that "Chase's friends are working for his nomination. But it is all lost labor[;] Old Abe has the inside track so completely that he will be nominated by aclamation when the convention meets." He predicted that the electorate will say to Chase: "you stick to finances and be content until after 1868," and to Grant, "give the rebels no rest, put them through. Your reward will come in due time, but Uncle Abe must be allowed to boss the reconstruction of the Union."[176] Similarly, David Davis noted that Chase "is doomed to disappointment," even though politicians would "put Mr. Lincoln aside, if they dared. They know their constituents don[']t back them, & hence they grumble, rather than make open war."[177]

Republicans throughout the North shared this view of Lincoln's popularity. Elihu B. Washburne concluded that "Lincoln is ahead of all competitors for President. He is very popular and very justly so."[178] Horace Greeley believed that the people thought of the president "by night & by day & *pray* for him & *their hearts* are where they have made so heavy investments."[179] The New York *Times* regarded the "universality of popular sentiment, in favor of Mr. Lincoln's reelection" as "one of the most remarkable developments of the time," while the Springfield, Massachusetts, *Republican* noted that the "people hold him to be honest in intention and in act, sound and reliable, and as fast as it is safe to be."[180] The *Republican*'s Washington correspondent explained that Lincoln's "immense hold . . . upon the affections of the people to-day arises principally from the fact that they believe that he is one of them, that he loves them, and that he never attempted to flatter or tickle them for the sake of office."[181] Republican Senator Lafayette Foster of Connecticut found it anomalous that the president "has a wonderful popularity in the country—nothing seems to shake it. His policy and measures are severely criticised and censured," and paradoxically the critics "lose all popularity, and indeed become quite obnoxious to the people, while the Presdt. himself escapes unscathed. This is a strange world."[182]

John W. Forney's Washington *Chronicle* declared that Republicans believed in Lincoln, "for he was their party choice. The loyal Democrats believe in him, for he has been kind and considerate to them, and has always, in the most magnificent manner, recognized their devotion to the country. His action in Missouri, where he refused to become a partizan of extreme radicals, and his action in Maryland, where he refused to become a partizan of the slave aristocracy, have united around him men of extreme differences of opinion—and they will support him as the leader of the Union party in the Presidential campaign. He, above all men, can unite the friends of the cause."[183] David Davis concurred: "I conscientiously believe that no man could have kept the incongruous elements of which the Republican party consists, better than he has. I know of none that could have done it so well."[184] The New York *Times* also paid tribute to Lincoln's remarkable ability to unify the North. The editors speculated that perhaps "his peculiar transparency of character, his remarkable faculty—never equaled in any other President since the first—of inspiring every one with a sense that he is a thoroughly honest and trustworthy man, has been the only thing that prevented faction from obtaining a fatal ascendancy at the crisis of the war. The people were willing to trust Abraham Lincoln with an amount of power they would have hardly confided to any other man."[185] Chase supporters acknowledged grudgingly that the president "is daily becoming more popular with the *unthinking* masses."[186]

A member of the thinking elite, Charles Eliot Norton, reported that "Mr. Lincoln seems to be the popular choice, & I shall be glad if he be the Union Candidate. Indeed it seems to me of great importance that he should remain in office." When George Perkins Marsh, U.S. minister to Italy, criticized the president for having "the ideas of a poor white, who has been brought up to look to Heaven for a fine plantation well stocked with negroes, as an expression of the highest bliss," Norton replied with one of the more thoughtful analyses of Lincoln's statesmanship: "You & I would have had the President long ago secure the abolition of Slavery; he might no doubt have done it; he would have been supported by the better men of all the parties;—but I do not feel sure that he could have done so without awaking such opposition as would have succeeded in making it impossible to carry on the war to a successful termination. By degrees the men who would have most bitterly opposed him have been won over to the support of the policy of freedom. A moral revolution such as is going on with us cannot be hurried without disaster. There is continual danger of reaction; of Charles II; of the Bourbons. Suppose Mr. Lincoln to have taken high anti-slavery ground two years ago,—and we should have been likely to have the old union between the corrupt & ignorant Democratic party & the Slave holders cemented with a cement that no future efforts could break till we were turned into a Slave-dependency. Mr. Lincoln is no doubt very slow in arriving at conclusions. He has no rapid intuitions of truth; but his convictions are the more firm from being attained only with difficulty. Experience has already taught him so much that we may hope it will teach him still more."[187]

Even in Ohio, where Chase assumed that he had widespread support, party leaders rallied behind Lincoln, who was popular with their constituents. Buckeye Congressman James A. Garfield, no fan of the president, observed that people in the West "are Lincoln-crazy."[188] By late March, John Sherman conceded that "public opinion has definitely settled the nomination of Mr. Lincoln" and that it was therefore "useless to contend against it."[189] A Dayton newspaper editor who wished to see Chase in the White House reported that "five out of six people of the West—in Ohio and Indiana especially—where I have been most observant are enthusiastically in favor of the renomination of Mr Lincoln. The movement is not managed; it is spontaneous beyond the possibility of a doubt; it is a great ground swell which will assuredly overwhelm everything in its path."[190]

Other admirers of Chase warned him that he stood no chance of wresting the nomination from Lincoln. James A. Briggs, his main operative in New York, told the treasury secretary that Empire State Republicans would support the incumbent for renomination "in spite of all that might, could, or should be done. He seems to be a Man of Destiny." (Briggs himself thought Lincoln better qualified for rail-splitter than for president and bemoaned his lack of gentlemanly sensibilities.)[191] In February, the Unitarian minister and abolitionist James Freeman Clarke, who professed to admire Chase far more than Lincoln, wrote the treasury secretary that "in common times I should be your ardent supporter, but if I were to vote tomorrow, I should vote for Lincoln" because "we cannot afford to try any experiments." The president was a known quantity and you are not, Clarke bluntly informed Chase. "This is the feeling which will actuate seven tenths of the people. They believe Lincoln, on the whole, a safe man—they believe him a man of sense & conscience, & one who is consistent with himself."[192] In fact, many Northerners had come to regard Lincoln as "the instrument with which our God intends to destroy Slavery," as Schuyler Colfax put it.[193] The chairman of the American Baptist Home Mission Society told delegates to its annual convention in 1864 that he "believed fully that God had raised up His Excellency for such a time as this."[194]

Meanwhile, Lincoln supporters were girding for the campaign. Francis P. Blair, Sr., and his sons, along with Cameron, schemed to have state legislatures and party conventions preempt Chase and other rivals by endorsing the president for reelection. In the fall of 1863, Cameron called on Lincoln, who said: "I don't like the idea of having Chase and Wade against me. I'm afraid I can't be nominated if they continue to oppose me." The Chief explained that Andrew Jackson wanted to be renominated but had pledged to serve only one term. To get around that problem, Democrats in the Pennsylvania legislature wrote him a letter asserting that as long as the Bank War continued, it would be best for him to remain in the White House to press the fight to victory. Taking the hint, Lincoln asked: "Cameron, could you get me a letter like that?" After assuring the president that he could do so, the Chief rushed to Harrisburg and arranged for the Republican legislators to send Lincoln a letter similar to the one Jackson had received; it went out on January 5.[195] "I have kept my promise," Cameron informed Lincoln.[196]

A day later, William E. Chandler, believing that "a corrupt moneyed ring" sought to defeat Lincoln and nominate Chase, persuaded the New Hampshire Republican state convention to follow suit.[197] It was the first such convention to be held, and the treasury secretary's operatives tried to keep it from either endorsing anyone for president or congratulating the administration. When the 29-year-old Chandler, then speaker of the state House of Representatives, heard of this scheme, he introduced a pro-Lincoln resolution and lined up support for it. Amos Tuck was opposed, arguing that it was "better not to grieve another aspirant to the Presidency by having N. Hamp. propose Mr. Lincoln . . . . Mr Chase thinks a great deal of the support of his native state."[198] (Tuck claimed that he favored Lincoln's reelection but admired Chase, whom he hoped to see occupy the White House some day.) On January 6, the convention enthusiastically adopted Chandler's resolution. Later that year, when Chandler described these events to Lincoln, the president said: "if Chase or any of his friends makes a raid upon you for what you have done, call upon me."[199] (In fact, disgruntled Radicals tried to block Chandler's election as chairman of the New Hampshire Republican State Committee, but they failed badly.)

Party conventions in Connecticut, Maryland, Indiana, Minnesota, and Iowa quickly followed New Hampshire's lead, and legislators in New Jersey, California, Maryland, Michigan, Wisconsin, Kansas, Maine, and Rhode Island emulated their counterparts in Pennsylvania. Some found this tactic unseemly. Senator Fessenden expressed "disgust" with the attempts of administration operatives "to control and direct public opinion."[200] He condemned Chase as well as Lincoln for paying too much attention to the presidential race while neglecting the public's business. "The fact that men in their condition, who ought to be thinking only of their country, can be indulging their personal ambition, excites my bitter contempt for both of them," he told his cousin.[201] Chase's supporters deplored what they considered the premature launching of the presidential campaign and unsuccessfully called for the postponement of the Republican convention from June to August. Others thought Lincoln "is trotted out too soon. All other aspirants will combine against him."[202]

But the principal aspirant, Chase, ignoring the advice of some key advisors, withdrew soon after Republicans in the Ohio Legislature on February 26 overwhelmingly resolved that "the *People* of Ohio and her *Soldiers* in the field demand the renomination of Abraham Lincoln to the Presidency of the United States."[203] According to David Davis, the Pomeroy circular made the legislators "so indignant at Columbus that they determined to express their preference for Lincoln at once." Davis rightly predicted that "Ohio speaking must . . . put a quietus upon Mr. Chase."[204] The treasury secretary, who had repeated his 1860 mistake of failing to secure his home state, hoped that his letter declining to run would intensify public pressure on him to run, but it did not. Ironically, he had told John Hay in January that it "is singularly instructive to meet so often as we do in life and in history, instances of vaulting ambition, meanness and treachery failing after enormous exertions and integrity and honesty march straight in triumph to its purpose."[205] Thus he succinctly described his own unsuccessful effort to supplant Lincoln.

Some thought Chase's withdrawal insincere. Attorney General Bates scoffed that the "forced declention of Mr. Chase is really, not worth much. It only proves that the *present* prospects of Mr. Lincoln are too good to be openly resisted." Bates speculated that Chase partisans would act behind the scenes to encourage several men to challenge Lincoln, then offer their champion as a compromise candidate.[206] David Davis also called Chase's withdrawal "a mere sham, & very *ungracefully* done. The plan is to get up a great opposition to Lincoln through Fremont & others & represent when the convention meets, the necessity of united effort, & that any body can unite &c, except Lincoln, & then present Chase again. . . . Look at the meanness in not saying one word about Mr. Lincoln."[207] (In fact, as one Radical admitted, his confreres did plan "to make use of the many candidates—Chase, Fremont, Butler, Andrew &c, to weaken the Lincoln forces. At the convention it is thought that these different men can unite their friends on one man against Lincoln, and so defeat his nomination.")[208] Davis marveled both at Chase's effrontery and the president's magnanimity: "How Chase can reconcile it with propriety to sustain the attitude to Lincoln that he does, I don[']t know. And it must be grievous for Lincoln to bear, but he is 'obstinately pacific.' My nature would not tolerate the thing for a moment."[209]

A Big Fish: Chase's Resignation

Relations between Lincoln and Chase rapidly deteriorated over the following weeks. Throughout the winter and early spring, Frank Blair in several congressional speeches denounced the treasury secretary and other Radicals. The two most blistering philippics, delivered on February 27 and April 23, charged with some justification that Chase was improperly using patronage and trade regulations to help him win the Republican presidential nomination. Furiously Blair assailed corruption in the cotton dealings of Chase's son-in-law, William Sprague, and the treasury secretary's questionable financial relationship with Jay Cooke. "[A] more profligate administration of the Treasury Department never existed under any Government," he declared, adding that "the whole Mississippi valley is rank and fetid with the fraud and corruptions practiced there" by Chase's agents, who accepted bribes for trading permits. Such permits to sell cotton "are brought to St. Louis and other western cities by politicians and favorites from distant parts of the country, and sold on 'change to the highest bidder, whether he be a secessionist or not, and that too, at a time when the best Union men in these cities are refused permits." Similarly corrupt, Blair thundered, were monopolies of trading privileges awarded to Chase's friends and partisans. "It is the most corrupting and demoralizing system that ever was invented, and has become a public scandal."[210]

Chase and the Radicals, livid with anger, believed that the president had encouraged Blair to launch these attacks. Lincoln, irritated and embarrassed by the April 23 barnburner, summoned Blair to the White House. When the congressman volunteered to resign from the army, Lincoln said "we must not back down" and handed him his commission. That reappointment, without congressional approval, rankled many lawmakers.

The president recalled that within hours of Blair's April speech, he had learned of it and "knew that *another beehive was kicked over.*" His initial impulse was to withdraw the order restoring Blair to the army, but he thought better of it. When Blair had informed him that he wished to give a speech on the trade regulations in the Mississippi Valley, Lincoln replied: "If you will do the subject justice, showing fairly the workings of the regulations, and will collect and present all the information on the subject, you will doubtless render a service to the country and do yourself much credit; but if you intend to make it the occasion of pursuing a personal warfare, you had better remain silent."[211]

Convinced that Lincoln had set Blair on him, Chase angrily threatened to resign. Ohio Republican Congressmen Rufus P. Spalding and Albert G. Riddle managed to calm him down; they then called at the White House to solicit the president's denial that he had instigated the attack. Lincoln received them civilly but coolly. After they stated that Chase's resignation would be politically disastrous to the party and expressed an earnest wish for the president's reelection, he warmed up, saying: "God knows I desire union and harmony as much as any man can." To underscore the point, he read them his February 29 letter to Chase regarding the Pomeroy circular. As for the Blairs, he pointed out that they were "strong, tenacious men, having some peculiarities, among them the energy with which their feuds are carried on." He added that they "labored for ten years to build up an anti-slavery party in Missouri, and in an action of ejectment to recover that party in the State, they could prove title in any common law court. Frank has in some way permitted himself to be put in a false position. He is in danger of being kicked out of the house built by himself and by a set of men rather new to it." He had summoned Blair to Washington because "he was most anxious that the country should have the benefit of every Union man elected to the House," including generals like Schenck and Garfield. He explained that "the arrangement had been made without much reference to its legal consequences." En route to the capital, Blair in St. Louis had delivered an anti-Chase speech which Lincoln deplored. At the close of this hour-long interview, the president insisted that he could not see "how the public service could be advanced by his [Chase's] retirement."[212] Riddle and Spalding reported this conversation to Chase, who agreed not to resign. But the episode further intensified his alienation from Lincoln. To other friends of Chase, the president insisted that he meant nothing by reappointing Blair and that he disapproved of his speech.

Radicals were furious at both Blair and the president. When Charles Sumner called at the White House to complain about the Blair family, Lincoln defended Frank, saying that Sumner's faction had begun warring on Blair in 1861 during his quarrel with Frémont. The Radicals, Lincoln added, kept up their attacks on Blair long after investigations revealed Frémont to be in the wrong. "Now, Mr. S[umner]," the president concluded, "the B[lairs] are brave people & never whine—but are ready always to fight their enemies and very generally whip them."[213] Radicals denounced the president for allowing Blair to serve both in the army and the Congress. Blair's commission as a major general had been due to expire on New Year's Day, but Lincoln did not accept it. The president faced a dilemma, for the Constitution forbade anyone to hold two positions in the government (like general and congressman) simultaneously. After Blair's vitriolic April speech, Radicals insisted that the president submit all relevant documents about Blair's special appointment. When the material provided by the White House showed that Lincoln pledged to restore Blair to the army after the organization of Congress, Radicals demanded that the president be impeached. Though that drastic step was not taken, the senate did adopt a resolution condemning Lincoln for violating the Constitution.

The steadily mounting tension between the president and his treasury secretary reached a crescendo in June when Chase, to protest a patronage decision, submitted his resignation for the fourth time. The secretary had demanded exclusive control over the distribution of offices within his department, arguing that fitness alone, not political influence, should be the determining criterion. He failed to acknowledge that in order to placate Congress, the wishes of senators and Representatives regarding government appointments had to be respected.

In March 1863, Chase had arbitrarily replaced the chief federal officeholders in San Francisco without consulting either the California delegation or Lincoln. Upon hearing a rumor about that decision, the president summoned Noah Brooks and testily asked if it were true. When Brooks confirmed the story, Lincoln angrily demanded to know why he had not told him earlier and voiced astonishment at the failure of anyone to inform him about such an important step. He was indignant at Chase for treating the California congressmen so cavalierly. Those Representatives shared Lincoln's view and, after failing to change Chase's mind, left Washington for New York upon the adjournment of Congress. The president instructed Brooks to wire them asking their return for a consultation. Brooks complied, and the two congressmen who could be reached met with Lincoln. He "expressed his regret at the hasty and somewhat arbitrary action" of the treasury secretary and asked them to submit a slate of candidates for the posts in question. Chase, Lincoln said later, was "exceedingly hurt" by this interference with what he considered his prerogatives.[214]

Chase was further hurt when Lincoln directed the removal of one of the secretary's champions, Victor Smith, collector of customs at Port Angelos in the Washington Territory. Smith was a visionary whom the journalist Murat Halstead called "a queer man," as "cranky as possible, imprudently partisan and zealous, always ready for a controversy," and "one of the fiercest of the devoted admirers of Chase."[215] The White House received complaints of Smith's corruption and ineptitude, most notably from Lincoln's old friend, Anson G. Henry. It was alleged that Smith had transferred the customhouse to Angelos in order to enhance the value of his property there, had used public funds to secure a personal loan, had cooked his books, and had generally run his office inefficiently. Relying on his long-standing friendship with Chase, Smith boasted that he was "so linked into the fibers of the National Government that he could not be removed." Once a special treasury agent confirmed the truth of the charges, Lincoln resolved to fire Smith, even though he was a favorite of Chase.[216]

When Chase was told to replace Smith, he angrily submitted his resignation. The president refused to accept it and, as a peace offering, agreed to appoint Chase's selection for the Port Angelos collectorship. The secretary had been miffed by other presidential meddling in Treasury Department patronage, including the removal of Chase's corrupt ally George S. Denison from the collectorship at New Orleans; the refusal to back Mark Howard for the collectorship at Hartford after a Connecticut senator raised objections; and the appointment in New York of Abram Hyatt, despite Chase's accurate warning that it would cause trouble.

The most lucrative patronage job in the Treasury Department, collector of New York, also became a source of friction between Chase and the president. Hiram Barney had been appointed to that post in 1861 at Chase's behest and over the vehement objections of Seward and Weed. But by early 1864, Lincoln decided that Barney must go. He was, as James A. Briggs put it, "estimable as a man" but had "no ability, or tact, or talent as a politician."[217] In early January, the collector's principal assistant, Albert N. Palmer, was arrested for expediting the issuance of bonds for goods illegally shipped to the South through Nassau. Palmer, an ally of Weed, had exercised significant control over patronage in the customhouse. Two months earlier, Deputy Collector Henry B. Stanton, husband of the feminist leader Elizabeth Cady Stanton, was dismissed after being charged with various ethical lapses. When the president suggested that Preston King, a shrewd conservative Republican and former Jacksonian Democrat, be appointed to replace Barney, Chase lamely objected that King knew nothing about the collector's duties and threatened to resign if Barney were sacked. Thurlow Weed warned the president that Barney's assistants were "constantly intriguing" against him, and insisted that a "change in the Custom House was imperatively needed."[218] Other influential Republicans echoed those charges. Lincoln told Weed that he would replace the incumbent. The New York boss favored Abram Wakeman, postmaster of New York, but counseled that gentleman not to press his case because Lincoln was probably going to submit a different name and Wakeman "would only embarrass the question" if he agitated for the post.[219] Wakeman's friends, however, deluged the White House with recommendations for their man. Others championed Judge James W. White, who was especially popular among the Irish.

The previous year, Barney had offered to resign because of failing health, but felt that he must stay on to defend his honor now that he was under attack. (In January the House Committee on Public Expenditures had launched an investigation into the New York customhouse.) Lincoln liked Barney, whose integrity he did not doubt, but concluded that "he has ceased to be master of his position" and that Joshua F. Bailey, a special treasury agent in New York, had become "Collector *de facto*, while Mr. Barney remains nominally so."[220] But to Weed's intense disappointment, Lincoln postponed action on the collectorship because Chase threatened to resign. The president also feared that he would be merely getting "out of one muss into another," since both Simeon Draper, who had been actively promoting Lincoln's renomination, and Wakeman were angling for Barney's job.[221]

Tension between Chase and Lincoln continued to mount until June 1864, when it burst like an overheated boiler on a Mississippi River steamboat. The occasion for that explosion came when John J. Cisco, assistant treasurer in the New York customhouse and a key pro-Chase operative, quit because of failing health. To replace him,

Chase proposed Maunsell B. Field, a sycophantic socialite with neither business experience nor political standing. He had served as a clerk in the New York customhouse and had been promoted to third assistant secretary by Lincoln as a good-will gesture to Chase. New York Senator Edwin D. Morgan adamantly objected to Field, who often failed to show up for work. In March, Morgan complained that "Chase will do *nothing* but what suits his purposes, and the President is *slow* to take any step in opposition to his wishes." Frustrated, Morgan was "not disposed to let the matter drop."[222] He had also protested against the appointment of Democrats to customhouse positions.

Lincoln regarded Field as morally objectionable, telling the Senate Finance Committee that "I could not appoint him. He had only recently at a social gathering, in [the] presence of ladies and gentlemen, while intoxicated, kicked his hat up against the ceiling, bringing discredit upon us all, and proving his unfitness."[223] (On a later occasion, Lincoln similarly explained why he opposed the appointment of a man highly recommended by influential supporters: "He is a drunkard. I hear bad stories of his moral character, yet his backers are among the best Republicans in the State. I like the fellow's friends, but it goes against my conscience to give the place to a man who gambles and drinks.")[224] When Chase insisted on Field, Lincoln patiently explained that he could not "without much embarrassment" accommodate him, "principally because of Senator Morgan's very firm opposition to it." Lincoln offered to let Chase select among three candidates acceptable to Morgan. When the secretary asked for a White House meeting, the exasperated president replied bluntly that "the difficulty does not, in the main part, lie within the range of a conversation between you and me." He explained that it had been "a great burden" to retain Barney in the face of intense criticism of the collector by many influential New Yorkers, and that the appointment as appraiser in the customhouse of the Radical Judge John T. Hogeboom, at Chase's request, had brought Empire State Republicans to "the verge of open revolt." Field's selection against the wishes of Morgan would, on top of those other problems, strain party unity to the breaking point.[225]

On June 29, Chase huffily offered his resignation yet again, doubtless assuming that the president would back down as he had done before. But Lincoln shocked him by accepting it, for as the president saw it, Chase in effect was saying: "You have been acting very badly. Unless you say you are sorry, & ask me to stay & agree that I shall be absolute and that you shall have nothing, no matter how you beg for it, I will go."[226] The president was in no mood to trifle, contending that Chase "is either determined to annoy me, or that I shall pat him on the shoulder and coax him to stay. I don't think I ought to do it. I will not do it. I will take him at his word."[227] When Ohio Governor John Brough offered to effect a reconciliation, Lincoln replied: "This is the third [fourth] time he has thrown this [resignation] at me, and I do not think I am called to continue to beg him to take it back, especially when the country would not go to destruction in consequence." When the governor persisted, Lincoln cut him off: "I know you doctored the matter up once, Brough, but I reckon you had better let it alone this time."[228]

Increasing the friction between Lincoln and Chase was the secretary's voracious appetite for deference, which the president gave in insufficient quantity. John Hay claimed that it was Lincoln's "intellectual arrogance and unconscious assumption of superiority" that Chase "never could forgive."[229] Hay clearly exaggerated, for Lincoln was hardly "intellectually arrogant." But despite his courteous, self-abnegating manner and self-deprecating humor, Lincoln had a deep-rooted sense of self that lent him dignity, strength, and confidence. These qualities were perhaps interpreted as arrogance by Hay, who may have projected onto Lincoln some of his own extreme self-regard. At all events, when Lincoln accepted Chase's resignation, he was not acting merely out of pique; Chase wanted to dominate the administration, and the president would not let him. To be sure, Lincoln did not like Chase personally, much as he admired his ability and his commitment to freedom. Certainly, he disliked other Radicals, more because of their style than their ideology. While he shared with them a strong desire to end slavery and to prosecute the war vigorously, he was exasperated by what he called "the self-righteousness of the Abolitionists" and "the petulant and vicious fretfulness of many radicals."[230]

Chase was especially objectionable because, as General Rutherford B. Hayes of Ohio observed, he was "cold, selfish, and unscrupulous." Hayes thought "[p]olitical intrigue, love of power, and a selfish and boundless ambition were the striking features of his life and character."[231] A former Whig congressman from Ohio who knew Chase well called him "*ambitious, cold-hearted* and *utterly selfish*," one who "always disparages and never speaks well of any man who is likely to be in the way of his vaulting ambition. He is cunning and industrious in laying plans for the accomplishment of his ends, and always sees that the *friends he can use* are put in positions where they can have power to help him."[232] A Philadelphia abolitionist concurred, deeming Chase "[b]ig-brained, cold-hearted, selfish, suspicious and parsimonious."[233]

Having made up his mind to let Chase go, Lincoln summoned John Hay to take a message to Capitol Hill. "When does the Senate meet today?" the president asked.

"Eleven o'clock," replied the youthful secretary.

"I wish you to be there when they meet. It is a big fish. Mr. Chase has resigned & I have accepted his resignation. I thought I could not stand it any longer."

To succeed Chase, Lincoln picked another former governor of Ohio, David Tod, a Douglas-Democrat-turned-Republican whom he described as a friend "with a big head full of brains." Tod was also a successful businessman and a gifted raconteur whom Lincoln praised for "telling the best story of any man in Ohio." But the Senate Finance Committee thought he lacked the necessary stature and experience for the job. When members of that body called at the White House, some were mad and others frightened. Lincoln explained "that he had not much personal acquaintance with Tod," that he "had nominated him on account of the high opinion he had formed of him while Governor of Ohio," that "the Senate had the duty & responsibility of considering & passing upon the question of fitness, in which they must be entirely untrammeled." But he "could not in justice to himself or Tod withdraw the nomination." When the incumbent governor of Ohio, John Brough, urged him to do so, Lincoln said "emphatically that he would not." Brough accurately predicted that Tod would decline because of poor health and because the nomination itself gave him prestige without requiring him to work hard. Moreover, Brough noted, Tod was a sensible, realistic fellow who would not deliberately take on a job he knew was too much for him.

Men in and out of Congress felt depressed and gloomy, regarding the abrupt change as a worrisome sign that the administration was breaking up. A panicky Elihu Washburne told Lincoln that it was "a great disaster: At this time, ruinous; this time of military unsuccess, financial weakness, Congressional hesitation on [the] question of conscription & imminent famine in the West." Another congressman, the influential Samuel Hooper of Boston, said that he felt "very nervous & cut up," and a colleague declared that June 30 was "the gloomiest day seen in Washington since the first Bull Run." The solicitor of the treasury informed Lincoln about a threatened mass resignation in the department. On July 3, a New York judge expressed fear that "there cannot fail to be an explosion if a more sane course is not pursued than that upon which the President seems now bent." Hay concluded that "the President has made a mistake," while financiers and merchants worried that Lincoln's willingness to appoint so little-known a man as Tod showed that he failed to appreciate how serious a financial crisis loomed.[234]

Indeed, Lincoln had blundered. Although his frustration with Chase was entirely understandable, his decision to let the treasury secretary go at such a time showed poor judgment. As D. W. Bartlett remarked, the president "seems to have been deserted of his usual good sense" when he submitted Tod's name, for the "feeling was unanimous in Congress that for such a man to succeed Mr. Chase would be ruinous to the finances."[235] The blow-up did not surprise Interior Secretary Usher, who remarked that there had "been a bad state of feeling for a long time, and since the Pomeroy circular no attempt at concealment." Chase "has rarely attended Cabinet meetings and has been apparently greatly disgusted at every body."[236]

That night, as Governor Brough had predicted, Tod wired his declination to the president. Immediately Lincoln, whose spirits had sunk quite low, authorized Hay to inform the senate. There Tod received a backhanded compliment from one member: "Not such a fool as I thought he was."

On July 1, upon waking, Lincoln decided to nominate William Pitt Fessenden, chairman of the Senate Finance Committee, in his stead. As that senator sat in the White House reception room (unaware of Lincoln's decision) awaiting an interview, the president dispatched Hay with the nomination to the Senate, where it was instantly ratified. When Lincoln told him of this move, the amazed senator, pleading poor health, said: "But it hasn't reached there—you must withdraw it—I can[']t accept." Lincoln protested: "If you decline, you must do it in open day: for I shall not recall the nomination."[237] The senator turned down the offer in a letter to Lincoln, who refused to receive it, "saying that Providence had pointed out the man for the crisis," that "none other could be found," and that he "had no right to decline." When Fessenden insisted that the job would kill him, Lincoln replied: "Very well, you cannot die better than in trying to save your country." At the president's urging, several leading Republicans lobbied Fessenden, insisting that he must rescue the nation. From chambers of commerce and individuals, telegrams and letters poured into his office warning that if he refused, the public credit would be ruined. In response to this overwhelming pressure, he reluctantly acquiesced with what he called "all the feeling of a man being led to execution."[238]

Lincoln, whose spirits had revived, exclaimed to Seward: "The Lord has never yet deserted me, and I did not believe he would this time!" To Hay, he recounted his thought process while mulling over Chase's replacement: "It is very singular, considering that this appointment of F[essenden]'s is so popular when made, that no one ever mentioned his name to me for that place. Thinking over the matter two or three points occurred to me. *First* he knows the ropes thoroughly: as Chairman of the Senate Committee on Finance he knows as much of this special subject as Mr. Chase. *2nd* he is a man possessing a national reputation and the confidence of the country. *3d* He is a radical." But there were some potential drawbacks, he told Hay: "the Vice President [Hamlin] & Sec Treasury coming from the same small state—though I thought little of that: then that Fessenden from the state of his health is of rather a quick & irritable temper: but in this respect he should be pleased with this incident; for, while for some time he has been running in rather a pocket of bad luck—such as [the] failure to renominate Mr. Hamlin [for vice-president] makes possible a contest between him & the V. P. the most popular man in Maine for the election [to the Senate] which is now imminent—& the fact of his recent spat in the Senate where Trumbull told him his ill-temper had left him no friends—this thing has developed a sudden & very gratifying manifestation of good feeling in his appointment, his instant confirmation, the earnest entreaties of every body that he may accept & all that. It cannot but be very grateful to his feelings."[239]

The appointment of Fessenden undid much of the damage caused by Chase's resignation. Republican newspapers lauded the new secretary as a "Senator who never left his post, never made a speech without a purpose, and always sharp, clear, brief in debate . . . a positive, daring statesman." Even the Democratic New York *World* called Fessenden "[u]nquesionably the fittest man in his party for that high trust."[240] Another Democratic newspaper, the New York *Daily News,* expressed doubt that Fessenden could repair all the damage that "Mr. Chase and his nigger ideas" had done.[241]

After a few weeks on the job, Fessenden praised Lincoln as "a man of decided intellect, and a good fellow—able to do well any one thing, if he was able, or content, to confine his attention to that thing until it was done." Unfortunately, however, "[i]n attempting to do too many [things]," the president "botches them all."[242]

Renomination

With Chase out of the presidential race, Lincoln's chances for renomination, which he keenly desired, seemed excellent. A Republican leader in Pennsylvania thought that "anxiety for a renomination was the one thing ever uppermost in his mind during the third year of his administration."[243] The provost marshal general noted that although Lincoln "had no bad habits," he did have "one craving that he could not overcome: that was for a second term."[244] Lincoln, whose sense of duty was strong, would not have regarded his ambition as a "bad habit," although he once referred to ambition as an "infirmity," and on another occasion told William Herndon: "If ever American society and the United States government are demoralized and overthrown it will come from the voracious desire of office—this struggle to live without toil—work and labor—from which I am not free myself."[245] Yet, as he told Joseph Hooker, he considered that ambition "within reasonable bounds, does good rather than harm."[246] Seldom in history has anyone's ambition produced as much good as Lincoln's.

Lincoln frankly acknowledged his desire for a second term. "If the people think that I have managed their case for them well enough to trust me to carry up to the next term, I am sure that I shall be glad to take it," he remarked in 1863.[247] "A second term would be a great honor and a great labor, which together, perhaps I would not decline, if tendered," he wrote to E. B. Washburne in October of that year.[248] Two months later he made a similar statement to Leonard Swett and Thurlow Weed: "Until very recently I expected to see the Union safe and the authority of the Government restored before my term of office expired. But as the war has been prolonged, I confess that I should like to see it out, in this chair. I suppose that everybody in my position finds *some* reason, good or bad, to gratify or excuse their ambition."[249] (Swett thought Lincoln "was much more eager" for a second term than he had been for his first.)[250] To a congressman, Lincoln explained that the only reason he wished for renomination was "that such action on the part of the Republican party would be the most emphatic indorsement which could be given to the policy of my Administration."[251] When Thaddeus Stevens spoke to him of his electoral chances, the president remarked: "I confess that I desire to be re-elected. God knows I do not want the labor and responsibility of the office for another four years. But I have the common pride of humanity to wish my past four years Administration endorsed."[252]

To others, Lincoln expressed a stoic willingness to be passed over. On the eve of the party's national convention, he said "that he was not at all anxious about the result; that he wanted the people to be satisfied, but as he now has his hand in, he should like to keep his place and finish up the war; and yet, if the people wished a change in the presidency, he had no complaint to make."[253] To a friend, he called himself "only the people's attorney in this great affair." He was trying to do his best for them, but if they "desire to change their attorney, it is not for me to resist or complain. Nevertheless, between you and me, I think the change would be impolitic, whoever might be substituted for the present counsel."[254]

After Chase's withdrawal from the race, the most serious potential threat to Lincoln's renomination was posed by General Grant, whose popularity after the victories at Vicksburg and Chattanooga was a source of concern. In the fall of 1863, the New York *Herald* began championing the general for president, and the chairman of the Ohio Democratic Central Committee told Grant that the party wanted him for their standard-bearer. In Pennsylvania, Alexander K. McClure, fearing that Lincoln might be unelectable, hinted that the Republicans would be wise to nominate Grant lest the Democrats did so. Elihu B. Washburne, the general's chief sponsor in Congress, warned Grant that some of his most vociferous promoters had earlier been his most caustic detractors. The Illinois congressman urged him not to challenge Lincoln, who, he said, had been exceptionally supportive of the general: "No man can feel more kindly and more grateful to you than the President. I have never asked anything in regard to you, but what he has most promptly and cheerfully granted." Recalling

Lincoln's support of the general after the battle of Shiloh, Washburne said Lincoln would "have my ever lasting gratitude."[255] (Lincoln told Jesse K. Dubois, "do you know that at one time I stood solitary and alone here in favor of General Grant.")[256]

In December 1863, Washburne introduced a bill reestablishing the rank of lieutenant general, which only George Washington and Winfield Scott had previously held. Grant's close friend and investment counselor, J. Russell Jones, told the Illinois congressman that Lincoln would promote Grant to that exalted rank if the general would back the president for reelection. Washburne replied, "that is the programme I desire. Lincoln will then go in easy, and Grant must be made Lieut Genl."[257] Jones assured Grant that he could gain the Democratic presidential nomination but that he could not defeat Lincoln.

Grant discouraged talk of his candidacy, declaring that the only office he wanted was the mayoralty of his hometown so that he could have a sidewalk laid from his house to the train station. Lincoln allegedly shrugged off the possibility of a Grant challenge, saying that if he "could be more useful than I in putting down the rebellion, I would be quite content. He is fully committed to the policy of emancipation and employing negro soldiers; and with this policy faithfully carried out, it will not make much difference who is President."[258] In fact, however, Lincoln was anxious about the general's intentions. Desiring reassurance from him, Lincoln, at the suggestion of Washburne asked Jones about his friend's views on the presidency. When Jones, showed him a letter from Grant denying any political aspirations and voicing strong support for Lincoln, the president replied: "you will never know how gratifying that is to me. No man knows, when that presidential grub gets to gnawing at him, just how deep it will get until he has tried it; and I didn't know but what there was one gnawing at Grant."[259] Lincoln also asked Frank Blair to sound out Grant. The congressman obliged by writing to the general, who replied that he had "no political aspirations either now or for the future" and enjoined Blair to share his letter with nobody except the president.[260]

Grant did not publicly announce his unwillingness to run because, as his chief aide, John Rawlins, explained in March, if the general published a statement forswearing presidential ambition, it "would place him much in the position of the old maid who had never had an offer declaring she 'would never marry;' besides it would be by many construed into a modest way of getting his name before the country in connection with the office."[261] Grant did, however, write a private letter to the Ohio Democrats emphatically rejecting their appeal for him to act as their standard-bearer.

Convinced that he would not have Grant as a rival, Lincoln threw his support behind the bill reviving the lieutenant-general post, which passed Congress in late February. Soon after signing the legislation, he nominated Grant for that honor. In July 1863, he had told General Sickles that he appreciated Grant's uncomplaining nature: "He doesn't worry and bother me. He isn't shrieking for reinforcements all the time. He takes what troops we can safely give him . . . and does the best he can with what he has got, and doesn't grumble and scold all the while."[262]

Although he admired Grant, Lincoln did find it necessary to overrule an infamous order the general had issued as commander of the Department of the Tennessee. Like many of his countrymen, Grant was a mild nativist, feeling antipathy for Catholics, Mexicans, Jews, and immigrants. The most blatant manifestation of his anti-Semitism was his December 1862 order stipulating that the "Jews, as a class violating every regulation of trade established by the Treasury Department and also department orders, are hereby expelled from the department." The "Jews seem to be a privileged class," he told the War Department.[263] He hoped to discourage cotton traders, some of them Jewish, who frequently violated the complicated rules promulgated in Washington. Over two dozen Jews were abruptly expelled from Paducah, Kentucky.

Democrats condemned the "detestable" order. "A whole class of people are brought to mortification by a military decree, which, if it had any justification at all, should have been made to apply to individuals alone," declared the Cincinnati *Enquirer*.[264] On January 3, when a Jewish delegation from the Queen City called at the White House to protest, Lincoln averred that neither he nor Halleck could believe that Grant had issued such a document. When he was shown a copy of the general's order, he asked rhetorically: "And so the children of Israel were driven from the happy land of Canaan?"

"Yes, and that is why we have come unto Father Abraham's bosom, asking protection," replied the group's leader.

"And this protection they shall have at once," said the president, who promptly instructed Halleck to countermand Grant's order.[265]

On January 7, Lincoln had an amicable interview with another Jewish delegation, led by Rabbi Isaac M. Wise of Cincinnati, who called to thank him for revoking Grant's order. Addressing them like an ordinary, candid fellow citizen, the president voiced "surprise that Gen. Grant should have issued so ridiculous an order." He remarked that "to condemn a class is, to say the least, to wrong the good with the bad. I do not like to hear a class or nationality condemned on account of a few sinners." The rabbi reported that Lincoln "fully illustrated to us and convinced us that he knows of no distinction between Jew and Gentile, that he feels no prejudice against any nationality, and that he by no means will allow that a citizen in any wise be wronged on account of his place of birth or religious confession." Wise added that the president "manifested a peculiar attachment" to Jews and "tried in various forms to convince us of the sincerity of his words in this matter."[266]

Later, Halleck told Grant that Lincoln "has no objection to your expelling traitors and Jew peddlers, which, I suppose, was the object of your order; but, as it in terms proscribed an entire religious class, some of whom are fighting in our ranks, the President deemed it necessary to revoke it."[267]

Grant's blunder did not significantly affect Lincoln's opinion of the general, whom he summoned to Washington to receive his promotion and to consult about military strategy. On March 8, Grant arrived and called that evening at the White House, where a public reception was being held. Noah Brooks described him on that occasion as "rather slightly built," with "stooping shoulders, mild blue eyes and light brown hair and whiskers, with a foxy tinge to his mustache. He has a frank, manly bearing, wears an ordinary-looking military suit, and doesn't put on any airs whatever." When Lincoln heard the crowd buzz, he knew Grant was on the premises and hurried to welcome him, warmly shaking his hand.

The two men, who had not met before, greeted each other cordially, but, as Nicolay recorded, "with that modest deference—felt rather than expressed by word or action—so appropriate to both." Lincoln dispatched Nicolay to notify Stanton, and asked Seward to introduce the honored guest to Mrs. Lincoln.[268] In the East Room, the general was cheered lustily. "There has never been such a coat-tearing, button-bursting jam in the White House," one journalist reported, while another wrote that the "crowd at the levee was immense, and for once the interest was temporarily transferred from the President to the newcomer. The mass of people thronged about him wherever he moved, everybody being anxious to get at least a glimpse of his face. The women were caught up and whirled into the torrent which swept through the great East room; laces were torn, crinoline mashed, and things were generally much mixed. People mounted sofas and table to get out of harm's way or to take observations, and for a time the commotion was almost like a Parisian *emeute* [riot]."[269] Blushing, Grant stood on a couch so that all could see him. But the crowd was not content with a mere glimpse of the general; they had to shake his hand, which they did for the remaining hour of the reception.

Grant, sweating from such an unaccustomed ordeal, afterward returned to the Blue Room, where Lincoln discussed with him the ceremony to be held next day. "Tomorrow at such time as you may arrange with the Sec[retary] of War, I desire to make to you a formal presentation of your commission as Lieut. Genl." With characteristic consideration, the president tried to make the occasion as easy as possible for the rather shy Grant: "I shall then make a very short speech to you, to which I desire you to reply, for an object; and that you may be properly prepared to do so I have written what I shall say—only four sentences in all—which I will read from my MSS. as an example which you may follow and also read your reply, as you are perhaps not as much accustomed to speaking as I myself—and I therefore give you what I shall say that you may consider it and form your reply." In that reply, Lincoln asked the general to incorporate two points: "1st To say something which shall prevent or obviate any jealousy of you from any of the other generals in the service, and secondly, something which shall put you on as good terms as possible with this Army of the Potomac. Now consider whether this may not be said to make it of some advantage; and if you see any objection whatever to doing it be under no restraint whatever in expressing that objection to the Secretary of War who will talk further with you about it."[270] Upon leaving, the general told Lincoln: "This is a warmer campaign than I have witnessed during the war."[271]

At the ceremony the following day, Lincoln addressed the general formally: "The nation's appreciation of what you have done, and it's reliance upon you for what remains to do, in the existing great struggle, are now presented with this commission, constituting you Lieutenant General in the Army of the United States. With this high honor devolves upon you also, a corresponding responsibility. As the country herein trusts you, so, under God, it will sustain you. I scarcely need to add that with what I here speak for the nation goes my own hearty personal concurrence."[272]

Grant replied: "Mr. President, I accept this commission with gratitude for the high honor conferred. With the aid of the noble armies that have fought on so many fields for our common country, it will be my earnest endeavor not to disappoint your expectations. I feel the full weight of the responsibilities now devolving on me, and I know that if they be met, it will be due to those armies, and, above all, to the favor of that Providence which leads both nations and men."[273] Grant had so hastily scribbled down his remarks that he could barely read them. Manifestly embarrassed, he stumbled his way through his delivery. Despite that problem, William O. Stoddard reported that the event "was simple, manly, dignified," worthy of the general and the president. There was no "pomp, no show, no vulgar ostentation."[274]

After a quick visit to the Army of the Potomac, Grant returned to Washington briefly. When the president invited him to dinner, he declined, saying "a dinner to me means a million dollars a day lost to the country."[275] He added: "I have become very tired of this show business." This response pleased Lincoln, who had encountered few officers willing to pass up such "show business" or who appreciated that the financial cost of the war must be taken into consideration. He told the general that "he did not pretend to know anything about the art of war, and it was with the greatest reluctance that he ever interfered with the movements of army commanders, but he did know that celerity was absolutely necessary, that while armies were sitting down, waiting for opportunities which might perhaps be more favorable from a military point of view, the government was spending millions of dollars every day, that there was a limit to the sinews of war, and there would come a time when the spirits and the resources of the people would become exhausted."[276]

With Chase and Grant both out of the presidential race, Lincoln still faced potential challenges from Benjamin Butler and John C. Frémont, both darlings of the German Radicals. When Missouri Germans attacked Lincoln publicly in May 1863, he said "there was evidently a serious misunderstanding springing up between him and the Germans of St. Louis, which he would like to see removed." In responding to charges that they made in formal resolutions, he told their emissary, James Taussig, that the shelved generals whom they so much admired—Frémont, Butler, and Sigel—were not "systematically kept out of command." Those men "by their own action" had "placed themselves in the positions which they occupied," and "he was not only willing but anxious to place them again in command as soon as he could find spheres of action for them, without doing injustice to others," but at that time "he had more pegs than holes to put them in."[277]

Both Butler and Frémont were angling for the presidential nomination. The publicity-savvy Butler had managed to endear himself to Radicals despite his lack of military talent. His policy of dealing with refugee slaves as "contrabands" in 1861 won Radical approval, as did his no-nonsense treatment of defiant New Orleans residents the following year.

(When women in the Crescent City insulted Union soldiers, he famously ordered that any such female "shall be regarded and held liable to be treated as a woman of the town plying her profession." Confederates and Europeans misinterpreted this as a license for occupation troops to treat refined ladies as prostitutes, but many Northerners understood that Butler was merely trying to shame the contemptuous natives into behaving civilly. He also won plaudits for summarily executing a man who hauled down the American flag, tore it, and trampled on it.)

When Lincoln recalled Butler from Louisiana in December 1862, the general was lionized throughout the North and spent eleven months at his Massachusetts home before receiving a new command (at Fort Monroe).

One of Butler's champions, the abolitionist Charles Grandison Finney of Oberlin College, told Gerrit Smith in January 1864: "We need a more radical man [than Lincoln] to finish up this war. I hope the radicals, in and out of Congress, will make their influence so felt in respect to the coming nomination that Mr. L. will see that there is no hope of his nomination and election unless he takes and keeps more radical ground. The people are prepared to elect the most radical abolitionist there is if he can get a nomination." Finney feared "that the radicals will so easily acquiesce in the nomination of Mr. Lincoln that he will get the impression that we are satisfied with his views and action."[278] Two months later, William P. Fessenden expressed a preference for Butler because "he seems to have exhibited from the start more proper sense of the crisis, more genius, more energetic ability, and more determination than any one."[279]

Lincoln worried about Butler's potential candidacy. In November 1863, Horace White observed that the president "has got his head full of the idea that the recent 'Missouri delegation' was a corrupt caucus to make Gen Butler the next President—a point on which he is very sensitive."[280] In the spring of 1864, Lincoln asked Thomas H. Ford, former lieutenant governor of Ohio, to sound out Butler. After making inquiries, Ford reported that a delegation from Senator Pomeroy's Republican National Executive Committee, headed by the Rev. Mr. Robert McMurdy, had called on the general at Fort Monroe. To Lincoln's relief, Butler "declined to enter into a combination with other candidates against the President," though he would not "decline the use of his name for the office."[281] Soon afterward, Lincoln expressed interest in accepting Butler's invitation to visit Fort Monroe, but nothing came of it. In May, when John Hay opined that "Butler was the only man in the army in whom power would be dangerous," the president replied: "Yes, he is like Jim Jett's brother[.] Jim used to say that his brother was the dam[n]dest scoundrel that ever lived but in the infinite mercy of Providence he was also the dam[n]dest fool."[282] (Many years later, Butler claimed that Lincoln offered to make him his running mate, but his account is highly suspect.)

With Butler's declination, Radicals turned to Frémont, who deeply resented the treatment he had received at the hands of the administration. In 1862, the abolitionist Moncure Conway proposed that Frémont replace Lincoln on the 1864 Republican ticket. In the spring of the following year, the general let it be known that he was interested in the presidential nomination. He also purchased a summer home in Massachusetts, where he and his extremely ambitious wife cultivated Radicals. One of them, Karl Heinzen, seconded Conway's proposal in the columns of his newspaper, *Der Pionier*. Frémont had "saved the honor of the Republic" with his emancipation order, Heinzen declared. Lincoln, on the other hand, was merely a "weak person, of average ability" who was "controlled by events which he did not foresee."[283] Another Frémont enthusiast expressed reluctance "to trust the issues of the next four years to the namby-pamby weakness and negative conservatism of Mr Lincoln and his present advisers. I want to see a *positive* man in the White House, a Radical."[284] That fall, a convention of anti-administration, pro-Frémont Germans met in Cleveland and adopted a platform endorsing the complete abolition of slavery, unconditional surrender of the Confederacy, treatment of the South as conquered territories, redistribution of slaveowners' property to the slaves, support for European revolutionaries, and strict adherence to the Monroe Doctrine. In February 1864, ex-Congressman George Ashmun of Massachusetts noted that the "friends of Fremont seem determined to run him at all events."[285]

Although some Republicans pooh-poohed the movement in favor of Frémont as "principally confined to the craziest portion of the infidel Dutch," others joined it, including a band of New York Radicals who launched the Frémont Campaign Club on March 18 at Cooper Union.[286] Among the attendees were such abolitionist luminaries as Parker Pillsbury and George B. Cheever. After adopting a platform condemning the "irresolute and feeble" policy of the administration and calling for a "vigorous, consistent, concentrated prosecution of the war," they were startled by the sudden entrance of Horace Greeley. The *Tribune* editor announced his support for a one-term limit on the presidency, recommended postponing the Republican national convention until it was clear what Grant's summer campaign might yield, and declared that "the people of New York were in favor of putting down the rebellion and its cause, and sustaining Freedom," and that Frémont "would carry out such views."[287] In the *Tribune*, Greeley conceded that Lincoln had merits but insisted "that they are not such as to eclipse and obscure those of all the statesmen and soldiers who have aided in the great work of saving the country from disruption and overthrow."[288]

Most Republicans resisted the appeal of Frémont, who "would rather split the party as he does his hair in the middle than see Lincoln elected," David Davis quipped.[289]

By the late spring, Lincoln believed that he had sewn up the nomination. When David Davis and Leonard Swett expressed anxiety about the convention, he assured them that there was no need to worry. But, he added, supposedly loyal delegates might not prove reliable. The situation reminded him of a story "about a man and a woman in the old days traveling up and down the country with a fiddle and a banjo making music for their living. And the man was proud of his wife's virtue and was always saying that no man could get to her, and he would trust her with any man who wanted to try it on a bet. And he made a bet with a stranger one day and the stranger took the wife into a room while the husband stood outside the door and played his fiddle. For quite a while he stood there playing his fiddle, and at last sang a song to her asking her how she was coming along with the stranger." She replied with a song of her own:

> He's got me down,
> He's clasped me round the middle;
> Kiss my ass and go to hell;
> Be off with your damned old fiddle.

An angry Davis scolded Lincoln: "if the country knew you were telling those stories, you could never be elected and you know it." In reply, the president just laughed.[290]

Lincoln's opponents might not be able to stop his renomination, but they could launch a third party and run Frémont as their standard-bearer. Even if the general was unable to win outright, some Radicals hoped his candidacy would throw the election into the House of Representatives and thus deny Lincoln a second term. The feminist leader Elizabeth Cady Stanton favored dumping Lincoln because he "has proved his incapacity for the great responsibilities of his position." Dismissively, she declared, "I say Butler or Fremont or some man on their platform for the next President & let Abe finish up his jokes in Springfield. We have had enough of 'Nero fiddling in Rome' in times like these, when the nation groans in sorrow, & mothers mourn for their first born."[291] She objected to Lincoln's appearance as well as his sense of humor.

Other feminist-abolitionists agreed. One of them, the young Quaker orator Anna E. Dickinson, had publicly called for the president's reelection during a speech that he attended in January 1864, but she later denounced Lincoln for being "not so far from . . . a slave-catcher after all," and privately called him "an Ass . . . for the Slave Power to ride" as well as "the wisest scoundrel in the country." She announced that "I would rather lose all the reputation I possess & sell apples & peanuts on the street than say aught—that would gain a vote for him."[292] In the early spring of that year, she visited the White House to urge a more vigorous enforcement of the Emancipation Proclamation. She later told an audience in Boston that Lincoln tried to divert her with a story, which she saucily interrupted, saying: "I didn't come to hear stories. I can read better ones in the papers any day than you can tell me." The president then showed her some letters about events in Louisiana. When asked her opinion of the administration's Reconstruction policy, she declared it "all wrong; as radically bad as can be." She alleged that Lincoln replied to this criticism with some compliments for his attractive young caller and closed with a piece of advice: "If the radicals want me to lead, let them get out of the way and let me lead." Indignantly she told a friend, "I have spoken my last word to President Lincoln." As she related this tale in Boston, she belittled Lincoln's appearance, particularly "his old coat, out at the elbows[,] which look[ed] as if he had worn it three years and used it as a pen wiper." She also had unkind words for his "stocking limp and soiled."[293] At least one member of the audience thought her comments about the president were "in the worst possible taste."[294]

The abolitionist J. Miller McKim, who had been a mentor to Dickinson and who thought her "desire to do what is right is strong, but her desire for distinction is enormous," heard a different version of this interview from Congressman William D. Kelley. According to Kelley, who was present during the conversation, she said very little, being "more a witness" than a participant. "What she did say was 'fool'ish according to her own acknowledgment at the time. She burst into tears—struck an attitude and begged Mr. L. to excuse her for coming there to make a fool of herself." Lincoln "was paternally kind and considerate in what he said to her." In discussing affairs in Louisiana, Kelley objected to General Banks's decision to hold a constitutional convention after rather than before the election of state officers. That approach, Kelley thought, was less likely to promote the cause of black citizenship rights. Lincoln acknowledged that others agreed with the congressman's views and "that a powerful argument could be made in favor" of them. But as things stood, he thought Banks's plan preferable. As for black citizenship rights, Lincoln predicted: "That must come soon. It must come pretty soon, and will." Kelley told McKim: "It pleased me to know that the President had firmly stipulated for a free state and that he saw the coming of Negro suffrage in Louisiana."[295]

In April, Dickinson's friend, journalist Whitelaw Reid, urged her to temper her criticism of the president: "It can do no good now for *you* to get tangled in the strifes of personal politics, & it may do much harm. Mr. Lincoln's popularity with the masses is established,—by what means it no longer does good to inquire,—& attacks on him only serve to inflame the ardor of his friends." Radical denunciation of the president, Reid warned, might backfire "by driving him to the Democratic & Blair parties for support."[296]

Some Radicals objected to Frémont. Summarizing their case, Wendell Phillips's son-in-law, George W. Smalley, argued that while the general might be "able & personally as honest as most public men," yet he was also "vain & selfish," the "worst judge of men in America," "surrounded by swindlers," a "*weak* man, sure to be a tool in others' hands," and "habitually a libertine" who had "seduced a governess in his own family."[297]

On May 4, a self-styled "people's provisional committee" issued a call for a national convention to meet in Cleveland at the end of the month, one week before the Republicans gathered at Baltimore. Endorsing the movement were several abolitionists, including Elizabeth Cady Stanton, William Goodell, Susan B. Anthony, George and Henry Cheever, and Wendell Phillips. Phillips complained that "Old Abe is more cunning & slow than ever" and "evidently wishes to save slaveholders as much loss & trouble as he can." The celebrated orator thought that most voters "would take Lincoln if he'd announce a policy, still more if he'd change his cabinet," for such moves "would indicate a *man*. But he is I think no believer in the *negro* as a citizen—is indeed a colonizationist yet—use the negro & be rid of him." The president "wishes to benefit the negro as much as he can & yet let the white race down *gently*—do them as little harm or change as possible. This is his first care—the negro his second."[298] (When Phillips charged that the truth of Chase's "Anti-Slavery life was tested and proved base metal," the treasury secretary's defenders aptly called him "the Boston Thersites" and a "common scold" with whom "the world has been all wrong from the beginning" and who "aspires to the unenviable distinction of scolding it into good behavior.")[299] Signatories for the Cleveland meeting also included Missouri Senator B. Gratz Brown and some German Radicals, among them Caspar Butz, who deemed Lincoln "the weakest and worst man that ever filled the Presidential chair."[300] Privately, influential Republicans like David Dudley Field, Andrew G. Curtin, and John A. Andrew supported Frémont. Governor Andrew maintained that "the administration lacks coherence, method, purpose, and consistency."[301]

In signing the Cleveland call, Frederick Douglass explained that he supported "the complete abolition of every vestige, form and modification of Slavery in every part of the United States, perfect equality for the black man in every State before the law, in the jury box, at the ballot-box and on the battle-field: ample and salutary retaliation for every instance of enslavement or slaughter of prisoners of color." He also insisted "that in the distribution of offices and honors under this Government no discrimination shall be made in favor or against any class of citizens, whether black or white, of native or foreign birth."[302] Not all black abolitionists agreed with Douglass. Just before the Cleveland Convention, John Mercer Langston of Oberlin, Ohio, said Lincoln was "cautious and for that reason he was the man of the hour. His head and his heart were right." Langston thanked God for the president's leadership.[303]

Few attended the Cleveland Convention to launch the new "Radical Democratic Party." When informed that the total number of delegates was no more than 400, Lincoln was reminded of an Old Testament passage describing the supporters of David at the cave of Adullam: "And every one that was in distress, and every one that was in debt, and every one that was discontented, gathered themselves unto him, and he became a captain over them, and there were with him about four hundred men."[304]

Wendell Phillips was not among the 400, but he wrote a letter that was read to the wildly approving assemblage. In it he excoriated the Lincoln administration, calling it "a civil and military failure" and predicting that if the incumbent were reelected, "I do not expect to see the Union reconstructed in my day, unless on terms more disastrous to liberty than even disunion would be." The president's approach to Reconstruction, Phillips charged, "puts all power into the hands of the unchanged white race, soured by defeat, hating the laboring classes, plotting constantly for aristocratic institutions." Lincoln's scheme "makes the freedom of the negro a sham, and perpetuates slavery under a softer name." The convention should "demand a reconstruction of States as speedily as possible on the basis of every loyal man, white or black, sharing the land and the ballot." In stark contrast to Lincoln, Phillips asserted, stood Frémont, "whose first act was to use the freedom of the negro as his weapon . . . whose thorough loyalty to democratic institutions, without regard to race, whose earnest and decisive character, whose clear-sighted statesmanship and rare military ability justify my confidence that in his hands all will be done to save the State that foresight, skill, decision, and statesmanship can do."[305]

The delegates shared Phillips's enthusiasm for Frémont, who won the nomination handily, but they ignored his advice regarding the platform; they glossed over both black suffrage and land redistribution to freedmen, using nebulous language about "equality before the law." The convention did, however, endorse a proposal to amend the Constitution to abolish slavery nationwide. That measure had been vigorously debated in Congress over the preceding months, easily passing the senate in April but failing to gain the necessary two-thirds vote in the House.

Some Radicals found the convention's proceedings unsatisfactory. The Detroit abolitionist Giles B. Stebbins reported that "the resolve of the Cleveland Convention for 'equal rights for *all*' is looked upon as vague, and of no meaning. *That Convention has no moral power*."[306] The nomination of John Cochrane as Frémont's running mate was especially disturbing, for Cochrane had regularly voted for Democratic presidential candidates and was, according to the *National Anti-Slavery Standard,* a man "without a drop of anti-slavery blood in his veins" and "whose life has been one long chapter of intrigue."[307] (Commenting on the many officeholders attending the Cleveland Convention, Lincoln said of Cochrane that he had been awarded his general's stars "not for his merits but his brass.")[308] Also disturbing was a platform plank condemning the suspension of the writ of habeas corpus, for that smacked too much of Copperheadism. The editor of the *National Anti-Slavery Standard,* Oliver Johnson, denounced the Cleveland movement as "an ally of Jeff. Davis" and called Fremont "a scoundrel, in alliance with the corrupt leaders of the Copperhead Democracy to divide the loyal voters of the country in the Presidential election." Johnson added that the feeble antislavery plank of the Cleveland platform was "Homeopathic," while its "Copperheadism" was "conspicuous and emphatic." He wondered what "delusion" had overcome such radical abolitionists as William Goodell, George B. Cheever, and Cheever's brother Henry.[309] William Lloyd Garrison's close ally, Henry C. Wright, deplored "the spirit of bitterness" that was "entering into & controlling the whole being of some of our old Abolitionists."[310]

Lydia Maria Child regarded Frémont as "a selfish unprincipled adventurer."[311] His acceptance letter seemed like a bid for the Democratic nomination, for it emphasized standard Copperhead charges about "the abuses of a military dictation," rejected the platform's call for confiscation of Rebel property, and said nothing about citizenship rights for blacks.[312] That document "killed him dead," according to a Chase partisan, and it angered George William Curtis, who exclaimed: "Poor Frémont! What a shadow and a sham he is!"[313] Franklin B. Sanborn thought the candidate's letter "has taken ground much worse than Lincoln's." In Sanborn's view, the general had "committed *fello de se*."[314] When Samuel May learned that Stephen Foster praised the letter as "just what we want," he exclaimed in disgust: "Well, it is certainly instructive, to find out at last, after the throes and travails of so many years on the part of our friend Stephen & his special associates, 'just what he wants.' What a dizzy height of moral grandeur!"[315]

Some Democrats did hope to ally with the Radical Republicans. Such disparate elements could, according to a party leader in New York, unite both in "opposition to the enormous frauds" tolerated by the Lincoln administration "and to the gross infringements upon the constitutional rights of Citizens & of the press at the North."[316]

William Lloyd Garrison, who had repeatedly denounced Lincoln throughout the war, now disagreed with the president's critics and opposed the Frémont movement. While Phillips scorned the incumbent as "a half-converted, honest Western Whig, trying to be an abolitionist," Garrison insisted that Lincoln must be judged on the basis "of his possibilities, rather than by our wishes, or by the highest abstract moral standard."[317] Phillips retorted that "the Administration has never yet acknowledged the manhood of the negro."[318] At a meeting of the Massachusetts Anti-Slavery Society in January, Phillips succeeded in having a bitter anti-Lincoln resolution adopted over Garrison's protest: "the Government, in its haste, is ready to sacrifice the interest and honor of the North to secure a sham peace . . . leaving the freedmen and the Southern States under the control of the late slaveholders." In support of this claim, Phillips acknowledged that Lincoln deserved credit for issuing the Emancipation Proclamation but insisted that blacks needed more than the administration was willing to give. "There stands the black man, naked, homeless; he does not own a handful of dust; he has no education; he has no roof to shelter him." The president, Phillips charged, has "no desire, no purpose, no thought, to lift the freed negro to a higher status, social or political, than that of a mere labourer, superintended by others." The present administration "was knowingly preparing for a peace in disregard of the negro." Its unwillingness to treat black troops as the equal of whites proved "that the Government is *ready* for terms which ignore the rights of the negro." The Emancipation Proclamation merely provided "technical liberty," which was "no better than apprenticeship. Equality is our claim, but it is not within the intention of the Government to grant it to the freedmen." Therefore, Phillips concluded, "I cannot trust the Government."[319] Abolitionists, he complained, got nothing from Lincoln "except by pressure. We have constantly to be pushing him from behind."[320]

Two months later, in a widely reprinted editorial, Garrison called Lincoln's re-election essential for "the suppression of the rebellion, and the abolition of slavery." The editor acknowledged that the president was "open to criticism and censure" but added that there "is also much to rejoice over and to be thankful for; and a thousand incidental errors and blunders are easily to be borne with on the part of one who, at one blow, severed the chains of three millions three hundred thousand slaves,—thus virtually abolishing the whole slave system . . . as an act dictated alike by patriotism, justice and humanity."[321] Garrison counseled abolitionists to understand the political and constitutional constraints which Lincoln had to deal with: "His freedom to follow his convictions of duty as an individual is one thing—as the President of the United States, it is limited by the functions of his office; for the people do not elect a President to play the part of reformer or philanthropist, nor to enforce upon the nation his own peculiar ethical or humanitarian ideas, without regard to his oath or their will. His primary and all-comprehensive duty is to maintain the Union and execute the Constitution, in good faith, according to the best of his ability, without reference to the views of any clique or party in the land." Emphatically Garrison expressed his "firm conviction" that "no man has occupied the chair of the Chief Magistracy in America, who has more assiduously or more honestly endeavored to discharge all its duties with a single eye to the welfare of the country, than Mr. Lincoln."[322] In September, Garrison told a guest: "I have every confidence in Mr. Lincoln's honesty; his honor is involved in his fidelity to the Emancipation Proclamation."[323] He voiced the same sentiments to the president: "God save you, and bless you abundantly! As an instrument in his hands, you have done a mighty work for the freedom of the millions who have so long pined in bondage in our land—nay, for the freedom of all mankind. I have the utmost faith in the benevolence of your heart, the purity of your motives, and the integrity of your spirit. This I do not hesitate to avow at all times."[324]

When a longtime reader of *The Liberator* angrily canceled his subscription and denounced the editor for abandoning the abolitionist cause, Garrison replied that if supporting the candidacy of Lincoln "makes us recreant to anti-slavery principles," then Owen Lovejoy, Joshua Giddings, Gerrit Smith "and a host of others long conspicuous for their consecration to the abolitionist cause are recreant." If the president had also been recreant, Garrison asked, "how does it happen that not a rebel in all the

South, nor a Copperhead in all the North, is aware of the fact?—that their malignant hatred of him, avowedly for no other reason than that he is determined upon the extermination of slavery, and is 'a black-hearted abolitionist'?—that the one great issue to be met at the ballot-box in November is, whether the President's emancipation policy shall stand or be repudiated?"[325]

To an English critic who denounced Lincoln as a hopeless bigot laboring under the delusion "that he has sworn to support slavery for the rebels," Garrison conceded that the president "might have done more and gone further, if he had had greater resolution and larger foresight; that is an open question, and opinions are not facts. Possibly he could not have gone one hair's breadth beyond the point he has reached by a slow and painful process, without inciting civil war at the North, and overturning the government." Such speculation, Garrison rightly noted, was "idle." Instead he listed what could be known, not guessed: "that his Emancipation proclamation of January 1, 1863, liberated more than three-fourths of the entire slave population; that since that period, emancipation has followed in Maryland, Western Virginia, Missouri, and the District of Columbia, and is being rapidly consummated in Kentucky and Tennessee, thus terminating the holding of property in man everywhere under the American flag; that all the vast Territories have been consecrated to freedom and free labor; that all Fugitive Slave laws have been repealed, so that slave-hunting is at an end in all the free States; that no rebel State can be admitted to the Union, except on the basis of complete emancipation; that national justice (refused under every other Administration) has been done to the republics of Hayti and Liberia, by the full recognition of their independence; that an equitable treaty has been made with Great Britain for the effectual suppression of the foreign slave trade, through right of search; that a large portion of the army is made up of those who, until now, have been prohibited bearing arms, and refused enrolment in the militia of every State in the Union [i.e., blacks]; . . . that free negro schools are following wherever the army penetrates, and multitudes of young and old, who, under the old slave system, were prohibited learning the alphabet, are now rapidly acquiring that knowledge which is power, and which makes slavery and serfdom alike impracticable; and that on numerous plantations free labor is 'in the full tide of successful experiment.'"[326] Garrison's endorsement, as the Philadelphia *Press* remarked, proved conclusively "that the President is not the candidate of the weak, semi-pro-slavery conservative faction."[327]

Seconding Garrison, Owen Lovejoy wrote to him that Lincoln, if not "the best conceivable President," was nonetheless "the best possible. I have known something of the facts inside during his administration, and I know that he has been just as radical as any of his Cabinet. And although he does not do everything that you or I would like, the question recurs, whether it is likely we can elect a man who would."[328] Lovejoy thought it "impolitic, not to say cruel, to sharply criticize even the mistakes of an executive weighed down and surrounded with cares and perplexities, such as have fallen to but few of those upon whom have been laid the affairs of Government."[329] Publicly he pleaded with his fellow Radicals: "Do not let any power from earth or from beneath the earth alienate your attachment or weaken your confidence in the President. He has given us the Proclamation of Freedom. He has solemnly

declared he will not revoke it. And although he may seem to lead the Isaac of freedom
bound to the altar, you may rest assured that it is done from a conviction of duty, and
that the sacrificial knife will never fall on the lad."[330] In February 1864, Lovejoy
warned that attempts to divide the Republican Party were "criminal in the last degree." Radical critics of Lincoln should realize that he "is at heart as strong an
anti-slavery man as any of them," but he "has a responsibility in this matter which
many men do not seem to be able to comprehend." Lovejoy conceded that the president's "mind acts slowly," but added that "when he moves, it is *forward.*" The congressman indignantly told a friend, "I have no sympathy or patience with those who
are trying to manufacture issues against him; but they will not succeed; he is too
strong with the masses. For my part, I am not only willing to take Mr. Lincoln for
another term, but the same cabinet, right straight through."[331] The Washington correspondent of the *National Anti-Slavery Standard* judged that Lincoln's antislavery
policy "has been a wise one, for he has drawn many conservatives after him who
would have been shocked by any sudden radical action upon his part."[332] Lydia Maria
Child acknowledged that Lincoln was "a man of slow mind, apparently incapable of
large, comprehensive views," and that he was inclined "to potter about details" and
thus waste "valuable time and golden opportunities." Still, the president "is an honest
man, and conscientiously hates Slavery." Besides, she asked rhetorically: "Who is
there that would be better except Charles Sumner and he would not be available as a
candidate?"[333]

Other female abolitionists agreed with Child. Lucy Stone had "expected the
largest antislavery utterance" from Frémont but was disappointed to get only a simple
"announcement that slavery is dead." She objected strenuously to the Cleveland Convention's selection of Cochrane for vice-president, wondering how a man who voted
for Franklin Pierce, James Buchanan, and John C. Breckinridge could possibly be
considered a true abolitionist. She told Susan B. Anthony, "bad as Mr. Lincoln is, a
union with him and his supporters, seems to me *less bad* than a union with peace
Democrats."[334] (Stone failed to convince Anthony, who enthusiastically backed Frémont.) Elizabeth Buffum Chace confessed that "impatient as I have been with Lincoln for his slowness of perception as to the needs of the hour; yet, since the best
sentiment of the people is carrying him with it toward freedom and justice and peace,
I had certainly as lief trust him as another man who has not been tried."[335] Lucretia
Mott observed that "we must admit that Lincoln has done well, *for him,*" and doubted
"if one *could* have been elected, who wd. have done more."[336] Abby Hopper Gibbons
called the president "a just and cautious man" who was "slow to move, but when ready,
[was] sure to take the right direction."[337] Maria Weston Chapman preferred Lincoln
to any other likely candidate "because, to a progressive domestic policy, he adds a
friendly foreign one."[338]

In response to his numerous critics, Wendell Phillips maintained that the Cleveland Convention's platform, with its demand for black citizenship rights including
suffrage, was infinitely preferable to what the Republicans offered. Acknowledging
that Lincoln would be renominated, he argued that Radicals should press him to
change his policies. Though reluctant to criticize Phillips, Theodore Tilton called

such arguments naïve: "Now, we would be glad if a great political party could go before the country on the high issue of giving every black man a vote. But the country is not ready for such an issue."[339] Agreeing was a Chase enthusiast in Ohio, who warned that "[h]atred to rebels has made thousands eager to abolish slavery, but no one is the less prejudiced against negro social equality. On any such issue, the party advocating it would be crushed out for years." The "love and zeal for the nigger may be carried too far."[340] Oliver Johnson was "deeply pained" that Phillips had "become the partizan of Fremont in his efforts to win support from the Copperhead Democracy." He predicted that the "consequences to himself will be fearful."[341] Lydia Maria Child was also "exceedingly sorry" that Phillips supported the general. "Since Fremont has written a letter, so obviously courting the Copperheads, I don't see how he *can* stand by him," she remarked.[342] Maria Weston Chapman predicted that "Wendell's labor against Lincoln will procure more votes for him than it will deprive him of."[343]

The Baltimore Convention (June 7–8)

To undercut Frémont's appeal, Lincoln bolstered the Republican Party's antislavery bona fides by endorsing a constitutional amendment outlawing slavery throughout the nation. He told Noah Brooks that he hoped the delegates to the Republican national convention would support such an amendment "as one of the articles of the party faith."[344] A few days before the convention met, party chairman Edwin D. Morgan called at the White House, where the president urged him to make an antislavery amendment the keynote of his opening speech at the convention.

Morgan took the president's advice, admonishing delegates that the party would "fall far short of accomplishing its great mission, unless among its other resolves it shall declare for such an amendment of the Constitution as will positively prohibit African slavery in the United States."[345] In response, the platform committee wrote a plank declaring that "as slavery was the cause and now constitutes the strength of the rebellion, and as it must be, always and everywhere, hostile to the principles of republican government, justice and the national safety demand its utter and complete extirpation from the soil of the Republic; and that, while we uphold and maintain the acts and proclamations by which the Government, in its own defence, has aimed a death-blow at this gigantic evil, we are in favor, furthermore, of such an amendment to the Constitution, to be made by the people in conformity with its provisions, as shall terminate and forever prohibit the existence of slavery within the limits or the jurisdiction of the United States." When introduced, this plank inspired wild enthusiasm.[346] Delegates leapt from their seats, waved their hats, applauded tumultuously, and adopted the resolution without dissent. This move stole some thunder from the Radical Democracy, but Lincoln did not suggest that his party support the Cleveland Convention's demand that blacks be accorded equal rights, nor did the Republicans adopt such a plank. Indeed, the platform did not directly address the contentious issues of Reconstruction, though by admitting delegates from some Southern states, the party in effect endorsed Lincoln's approach rather than that of the Radicals, who maintained that the rebellious states were out of the Union.

At the behest of the Missouri delegation, a plank was adopted indirectly calling for the resignation of conservative cabinet members: "we deem it essential to the general welfare that harmony shall prevail in the national councils, and we regard as worthy of public confidence and official trust those only who cordially endorse the principles proclaimed in these resolutions, and which should characterize the administration of the Government."[347] This was widely viewed as a demand for Montgomery Blair's dismissal.

Though willing to intervene to shape the party platform, Lincoln expressed no preference for a running mate. Shortly before Nicolay left to act as the president's eyes and ears at the convention, Lincoln told him "that all the various candidates and their several supporters being his friends, he deemed it unbecoming in him to advocate the nomination of any one of them; but that privately and personally he would be best pleased if the convention would renominate the old ticket that had been so triumphantly elected in 1860, and which would show an unbroken faith . . . in the Republican party, and an unbroken and undivided support of that party to the administration and in [the] prosecution of the war."[348] The delegates chose former Democrat Andrew Johnson of Tennessee to enhance the Republicans' new identity as the "National Union" Party. Nicolay reported the day before the convention opened that the "disposition of all the delegates was to take any war Democrat, *provided he would add strength to the ticket*."[349] Among those fitting that description were Johnson, John A. Dix, Daniel S. Dickinson, and Joseph Holt, but not the incumbent, Hannibal Hamlin. When Leonard Swett championed Holt for vice-president, the head of the Illinois delegation, Burton C. Cook, asked if the president preferred that Kentuckian. Lincoln wrote in reply that "Mr. Holt is a good man, but I had not heard or thought of him for V.P. Wish not to interfere about V.P. . . . Convention must judge for itself."[350] Nicolay told Cook that "Lincoln would not wish even to indicate a preference for V. P. as the rival candidates were all friendly to him."[351] Johnson eventually turned out to be a disastrous choice, but Lincoln had nothing to do with his selection.

Some Radicals expressed pleasure at Johnson's nomination. George Luther Stearns, who had recruited black troops in Tennessee, congratulated the governor: "If anything can reconcile me to the renomination of Abraham Lincoln, it is the association of your name on the same ticket. Indeed I should have been much better pleased if your name had been placed by the Convention before our people, for the Presidency."[352] Lincoln, however, had reservations. When told of the convention's choice for his running mate, he said: "So they have chosen him—I thought perhaps he would be the man. He is a strong man. I hope he may be the best man. But—." He did not finish that sentence.[353] According to Noah Brooks, Lincoln at first "made an exclamation that emphatically indicated his disappointment," but shortly thereafter remarked: "Andy Johnson, I think, is a good man."[354]

The Baltimore Convention, which resembled a ratification meeting, was, as Nicolay remarked, "almost too passive to be interesting."[355] It resembled the Connecticut Legislature, which reelected a man to office so regularly that the clerk of the House called for the vote by saying: "Gentlemen will please step up to the desk and deposit their votes for Samuel Wyllis for Secretary of State."[356] Credentials fights did provide some excitement. Of the six Southern delegations, only South Carolina's was barred. When its members called at the White House en route to Baltimore, Hay told the president: "They are a swindle." Lincoln replied: "They won[']t swindle me."[357] The most contentious case was Missouri, which sent two delegations, one Conservative and the other Radical. The credentials committee, acting on Lincoln's suggestion (which Nicolay conveyed to the Illinois delegation), endorsed the "Radical Unionists," who supported Grant for president. After the roll call showed Lincoln with 484 votes and Grant with 22, the Missourians moved to make the nomination unanimous. The decision to seat the Missouri Radicals pleased Lincoln's critics and helped undermine support for Frémont.

On their way home, some delegates stopped at the White House to pay their respects. To Ohioans who serenaded him on June 9, he said: "the hardest of all speeches I have to answer is a serenade. I never know what to say on these occasions. I suppose that you have done me this kindness in connection with the action of the Baltimore convention, which has recently taken place, and with which, of course, I am very well satisfied. [Laughter and applause.] What we want, still more than Baltimore conventions or presidential elections, is success under Gen. Grant. [Cries of "Good,'" and applause.] I propose that you constantly bear in mind that the support you owe to the brave officers and soldiers in the field is of the very first importance, and we should therefore bend all our energies to that point."[358]

One delegate, William Lloyd Garrison, had his faith in Lincoln strengthened by two White House interviews. "There is no mistake about it in regard to Mr. Lincoln's desire to do all that he can see it right and possible for him to do to uproot slavery, and give fair play to the emancipated," he reported to his wife. "I was much pleased with his spirit, and the familiar and candid way in which he unbosomed himself."[359] (According to Garrison's son William, the abolitionist editor frankly criticized Lincoln's "shortcomings,—his mistakes in not making the Proclamation universal, the wicked treatment of the colored troops. . . . Not one word of congratulation did he give the President regarding his renomination.")[360]

Other abolitionists cheered Lincoln's nomination. J. W. C. Pennington, a black Presbyterian minister, wrote that the prospect of having the incumbent reelected "should awaken in the inmost soul of every American of African descent emotions of the most profound and patriotic enthusiasm." Lincoln could be considered the black man's president, Pennington argued, "because he is the only American President who has ever given any attention to colored men as citizens." To reelect him "will be the best security that the present well-begun work of negro freedom and African redemption will be fully completed." Pennington, who believed that he voiced "the sentiments of nine-tenths of my colored fellow-citizens," prayed that God might "grant us four long years more of the judicious administration of that excellent man."[361] Massachusetts Radicals Franklin B. Sanborn and Frank W. Bird, who had opposed Lincoln earlier in the year, now believed that "the contest will be fought on the old issue, with Lincoln representing really the best of the Antislavery men." They supported his reelection, though deploring "the baseness of the Administration." Lincoln might be bad, but he was "better than [Fernando] Wood and Vallandigham." No evil was worse than "throwing power into the hands of the Peace Democrats."[362] Similarly, the New York *Evening Post* grudgingly acknowledged that the people overlooked Lincoln's defects, pardoned his mistakes, and were "prone to forgive even his occasional lapses into serious and dangerous abuses of power." All this they managed to do even though there was "nothing high, generous, [or] heroic in the tone of his administration," and though he "suffers the best opportunities to pass," lacks "knowledge of men," surrounds himself with "unworthy persons like Cameron," stands by "useless instruments like McClellan, long after their uselessness has been shown," has no "profound political convictions or a thoroughly digested system of policy," pays heed "too patiently to mere schemers," and "either drifts into the right course or assumes it with an embarrassed air, as if he took shelter in it as a final expedient."[363] That paper had earlier chastised the administration for "its arbitrary arrests, its suppression of journals, its surrender of fugitives without judicial warrant, and its practical abandonment of the Monroe Doctrine."[364] (Understandably, Lincoln resented such "newspaper assaults" and gently chided the editor for making them.)[365]

The New York *Round Table,* while conceding that Lincoln was not "a great man" and that he lacked "the sagacity of a statesman," said he was nevertheless "so steadfast, so honest" that "the people feel somehow that he is an eminently safe man to be charged with the conduct of affairs, at a time when perhaps a really more brilliant and wiser statesman would be thrown off his balance." The editors believed that "few Presidents have had more earnest friends than Mr. Lincoln has had and will have in time to come."[366]

Lincoln was profoundly moved when responding to the convention committee's formal notification of his candidacy. In his remarks, he laid special emphasis on the constitutional amendment abolishing slavery: "I approve the declaration in favor of so amending the Constitution as to prohibit slavery throughout the nation. When the people in revolt, with a hundred days of explicit notice, that they could, within those days, resume their allegiance, without the overthrow of their institution, and that they could not so resume it afterwards, elected to stand out, such [an] amendment of the Constitution as [is] now proposed, became a fitting, and necessary conclusion to the final success of the Union cause. Such alone can meet and cover all cavils. Now, the unconditional Union men, North and South, perceive its importance, and embrace it. In the joint names of Liberty and Union, let us labor to give it legal form, and practical effect."[367]

When informed of the Radical-dominated National Union League's endorsement, Lincoln told a deputation from that body: "I am very grateful for the renewed confidence which has been accorded to me, both by the convention and by the National League. I am not insensible at all to the personal compliment there is in this; yet I do not allow myself to believe that any but a small portion of it is to be appropriated as a personal compliment. The convention and the nation, I am assured, are alike animated by a higher view of the interests of the country for the present and the great future, and that part I am entitled to appropriate as a compliment is only that part which I may lay hold of as being the opinion of the convention and of the League, that I am not entirely unworthy to be intrusted with the place I have occupied for the last three years. I have not permitted myself, gentlemen, to conclude that I am the best man in the country; but I am reminded, in this connection, of a story of an old Dutch farmer, who remarked to a companion once that 'it was not best to swap horses when crossing streams.'"[368]

The following month, Lincoln received a formal notification of his nomination, which contained a passage written by George William Curtis, designed so as to offer the president a chance to address the Democrats' complaint about arbitrary arrests: "No right . . . is so precious and sacred to the American heart as that of personal liberty. Its violation is regarded with just, instant & universal jealousy. Yet in this hour of peril every faithful citizen concedes that, for the sake of national existence and the common welfare, individual liberty may, as the Constitution provides in case of rebellion, be sometimes summarily constrained."[369] But Lincoln did not avail himself of the opportunity.

The president was delighted by his renomination, for he had predicted to A. K. McClure that "his name would go into history darkly shadowed by a fraternal war that he would be held responsible for inaugurating if he were unable to continue in office to conquer the Rebellion and restore the Union."[370]

Democrats sneered at the Republican nominees as "two ignorant, boorish, third-rate, backwoods lawyers." The New York *World* exclaimed: "God save the Republic!"[371] Former Democrat Ben Butler was equally contemptuous, exclaiming to his wife sarcastically: "Hurrah for Lincoln and Johnson! That's the ticket! This country has more vitality than any other on earth if it can stand this sort of administration for another four years."[372]

It was not clear that the country would in fact have the same administration for another quadrennium, since enthusiasm for Lincoln might prove ephemeral. In late May, Theodore Tilton noted that there "is an insane popular sympathy for him [Lincoln] everywhere—very shallow, it is true—but salty & flavorsome, even though shallow, like Dr. Livingston's lake."[373] The shallow lake of the president's popularity might evaporate in the fierce heat of summer if Grant did not promptly defeat Lee.

"Hold On with a Bulldog Grip and Chew and Choke as Much as Possible"
The Grand Offensive
(May–August 1864)

That Americans would hold a presidential election during a titanic civil war amazed German-born Francis Lieber, professor of history and political science at Columbia University. "If we come triumphantly out of this war, with a presidential election in the midst of it," he wrote in August 1864, "I shall call it the greatest miracle in all the historic course of events. It is a war for nationality at a period when the people were not yet fully nationalized."[1] Democrats predicted that the administration would cancel the election in a brazen attempt to retain power, but Lincoln would not hear of it. "We can not have free government without elections," he believed; "and if the rebellion could force us to forego, or postpone a national election, it might fairly claim to have already conquered and ruined us."[2]

As dismayed Confederates saw their chances of winning on the battlefield fade, they pinned their hopes on Northern war weariness; if Lincoln could be defeated at the polls, they believed their bid for independence just might succeed. Union military triumphs alone could prevent that, Lincoln realized, and so in the winter and spring of 1864, he and Grant devised a grand strategy to achieve final victory before the fall elections. The fate of the nation, and the cause of democracy in the world, hung in the balance.

Planning and Launching the Spring Offensive

After the war, Grant wrote that Lincoln had given him carte blanche, but in fact the president rejected parts of the general's initial proposal, including a suggestion to attack Richmond's supply lines with an army landed in North Carolina. But both men agreed on the central principle that Union forces should attack on all fronts simultaneously. Meade would strike southward against Lee's army, Franz Sigel would drive up the Shenandoah Valley and then swing eastward toward Richmond, Butler would approach the Confederate capital from the opposite direction by moving up the Peninsula, Sherman would capture Atlanta, and Banks would push toward Mobile after taking Shreveport. Grant was in overall charge of operations, but instead of remaining in Washington, he accompanied the Army of the Potomac, whose tactical moves Meade controlled while he dictated its strategy.

It was the sort of coordinated plan that Lincoln had been urging on his generals since early 1862. On the eve of the spring offensive, Lincoln told John Hay that Grant's proposal "powerfully reminded" him of his "old suggestion so constantly made and as constantly neglected, to Buell & Halleck et al to move at once upon the enemy's whole line so as to bring into action to our advantage our great superiority in numbers. Otherwise by interior lines & control of the interior railroad system the enemy can shift their men rapidly from one point to another as they may be required. In the concerted movement[,] however, great superiority of numbers must tell: As the enemy however successful where he concentrates must necessarily weaken other portions of his line and lose important position. This idea of his own, the Prest. recognized with especial pleasure when Grant said it was his intention to make all the line useful—those not fighting could help the fighting."

"Those not skinning can hold a leg," Lincoln remarked.[3]

In addition to approving most of Grant's plan, Lincoln helped him reform the administration of the army. Congress had provided that staff departments like commissary, ordnance, quartermaster, and the adjutant general would report directly to the secretary of war, not the general-in-chief. When Grant asked that these departments be placed under him in the chain of command, the president explained that while he could not unilaterally alter the law, "there is no one but myself that can interfere with your orders, and you can rest assured that I will not."[4] The president did intervene when Grant clashed with Stanton over force reductions in the Washington area. The general wanted to transfer as many support troops as possible to the front lines, but the war secretary overruled his order to send artillerymen from the defenses of the capital to the Virginia front.

"I think I rank you in this matter, Mr. Secretary," Grant said.

"We shall have to see Mr. Lincoln about that," came the reply.

At the White House, the president ruled in favor of Grant: "You and I, Mr. Stanton, have been trying to boss this job, and we have not succeeded very well with it. We have sent across the mountains for *Mr.* Grant, as Mrs. Grant calls him, to relieve us, and I think we had better leave him alone to do as he pleases."[5]

Lincoln did not, however, accede to Grant's request to merge some of the twenty independent military departments, to eliminate extraneous commands, and to retire scores of generals. In an election year, such steps might have been politically ruinous. But he did agree to remove Nathaniel P. Banks from command of the Department of the Gulf and replace him with E. R. S. Canby. The failure of Banks's Red River campaign in April sorely disappointed the president, who, upon receiving word of that debacle, "said he had rather cousined up to Banks, but for some time past had begun to think" he was mistaken in doing so. To express his disappointment, he quoted verses from "The Fire-Worshippers" by Thomas Moore:

> Oh, ever thus, from childhood's hour,
> I've seen my fondest hopes decay;

I never loved a tree or flower
But 't was the first to fade away.
I never nurs'd a dear gazelle,
To glad me with its soft black eye,
But when it came to know me well
And love me, it was sure to die.[6]

Political considerations also affected the choice of Grant's principal subordinates in the East. While Meade, a professional soldier, would remain in command of the Army of the Potomac, the two men most responsible for aiding him against Lee were political generals with limited military talent, Butler and Sigel. The former had been a prominent Democrat, and Lincoln considered it essential to retain the support of War Democrats; the latter was exceptionally popular with the Germans, an important voting bloc that had shown signs of grave disaffection.

On April 30, as Grant was about to launch his offensive, Lincoln wrote him: "Not expecting to see you again before the Spring campaign opens, I wish to express, in this way, my entire satisfaction with what you have done up to this time, so far as I understand it. The particulars of your plans I neither know, or seek to know. You are vigilant and self-reliant; and, pleased with this, I wish not to obtrude any constraints or restraints upon you. While I am very anxious that any great disaster, or the capture of our men in great numbers, shall be avoided, I know these points are less likely to escape your attention than they would be mine. If there is anything wanting which is within my power to give, do not fail to let me know it. And now with a brave Army, and a just cause, may God sustain you."[7]

Graciously the general replied: "The confidence you express for the future, and satisfaction with the past, in my Military administration is acknowledged with pride. It will be my earnest endeavor that you, and the country, shall not be disappointed. From my first entrance into the volunteer service of the country, to the present day, I have never had cause of complaint, have never expressed or implied a complaint, against the Administration, or the Sec. of War, for throwing any embarassment in the way of my vigorously prossecuting what appeared to me my duty. Indeed since the promotion which placed me in command of all the Armies, and in view of the great responsibility, and importance of success, I have been astonished at the readiness with which every thin[g] asked for has been yielded without even an explaination being asked. Should my success be less than I desire, and expect, the least I can say is, the fault is not with you."[8]

Among Grant's legions was Burnside's corps, which contained some black regiments. While marching past the White House, those black soldiers waved their caps and heartily cheered "Hurrah for Massa Linkum!" and "Three cheers for the President!" He bowed to them from the balcony with tears in his eyes and exclaimed in a low voice: "It'll do! it'll do!"[9]

Awaiting news of the offensive, Lincoln seemed to former Congressman Albert G. Riddle of Ohio "like a man worn and harassed with petty faultfinding and criticism, until he had turned at bay, like an old stag pursued and hunted by a cowardly rabble of men and dogs."[10] He did turn on one critic, William Cullen Bryant, whose New York *Evening Post* had sharply criticized the administration for several things, including its coddling of officials guilty of unethical conduct. When Isaac Henderson, co-owner of the *Post* with Bryant, was dismissed from his lucrative post at the New York customhouse for taking bribes, Bryant begged the president to restore him. In reply, Lincoln expressed his irritation with the *Post*: "may I ask whether the Evening Post has not assailed me for supposed too lenient dealing with persons charged of fraud & crime? and that in cases of which the Post could know but little of the facts? I shall certainly deal as leniently with Mr. Henderson as I have felt it my duty to deal with others, notwithstanding any newspaper assaults."[11]

On May 5, the North held its collective breath as Grant attacked Lee near Chancellorsville. The armies slugged it out in the dense, tangled wilderness, inflicting heavy casualties on each other. "These are fearfully critical, anxious days," George Templeton Strong remarked, speaking for millions of his fellow citizens. "The destinies of the continent for centuries depend in great measure on what is now being done."[12] The first to bring Lincoln word of the bloody doings was a young New York *Tribune* reporter, Henry Wing, who briefed the president and cabinet on the morning of May 7. After he had finished describing the various movements, and the cabinet was leaving, Wing repeated to the president a message Grant had asked him to convey: "whatever happens, there is to be no turning back." Overjoyed at this declaration of steely resolve, the president kissed the youthful reporter on the forehead.[13]

On May 9, when Lincoln received a telegram from Grant saying "I intend to fight it out on this line if it takes all summer," he told John Hay: "How near we have been to this thing before and failed. I believe if any other General had been at the Head of that army it would have now been on this side of the Rapidan. It is the dogged pertinacity of Grant that wins."[14] That evening he addressed serenaders at the White House: "I am very much obliged to you for the compliment of this call, though I apprehend it is owing more to the good news received to-day from the army than to a desire to see me. I am, indeed, very grateful to the brave men who have been struggling with the enemy in the field, to their noble commanders who have directed them, and especially to our Maker. Our commanders are following up their victories resolutely and successfully. I think, without knowing the particulars of the plans of Gen. Grant, that what has been accomplished is of more importance than at first appears. I believe I know, (and am especially grateful to know) that Gen. Grant has not been jostled in his purposes; that he has made all his points, and to-day he is on his line as he purposed before he moved his armies. I will volunteer to say that I am very glad at what has happened; but there is a great deal still to be done."[15]

But Grant did not win a victory at the battle of the Wilderness, which was in effect a standoff, though the Army of Northern Virginia withdrew from the field. Unlike previous Union commanders, who retreated toward Washington after being bloodied by Lee, Grant swung around the Confederate right flank and drove toward Richmond.

When it became clear that the Army of the Potomac had taken immense losses, the anguished president exclaimed to Schuyler Colfax: "Why do we suffer reverses after reverses! Could we have avoided this terrible, bloody war! Was it not forced upon us! Is it ever to end!"[16] As he observed wounded soldiers in a long procession of ambulances, he pointed to them saying sadly: "Look yonder at those poor fellows. I cannot bear it. This suffering, this loss of life is dreadful." When a friend tried to console him with the assurance that the North would eventually triumph, he replied: "Yes, victory will come, but it comes slowly."[17]

Among the Union dead was General James S. Wadsworth, a wealthy New Yorker who had run unsuccessfully for governor in 1862. His death shook Lincoln badly. Hay noted in his diary: "I have not known the President so affected by a personal loss since the death of [Edward D.] Baker." Lincoln praised the general highly: "no man has given himself up to the war with such self sacrificing patriotism as Genl. Wadsworth. He went into the service not wishing or expecting great success or distinction in his military career & profoundly indifferent to popular applause, actuated only by a sense of duty which he neither evaded nor sought to evade."[18]

Dismayed by the losses, Lincoln looked as solemn and anxious as if a beloved family member had died. He nonetheless took heart from the fact that Grant was in charge and predicted that the general "will not fail us now; he says he will fight it out on that line, and this is now the hope of our country."[19] On May 15, Nicolay reported that the "President is cheerful and hopeful—not unduly elated, but seeming confident; and now as ever watching every report and indication, with quiet, unwavering interest."[20]

Lincoln also derived some consolation from his conviction "that every great battle, even if it is a drawn one, is a defeat to the rebels in its necessary consequences. A battle in which thirty thousand men a side were put *hors du combat,* killed, wounded and missing, but in which neither party could claim a victory, would, nevertheless, drive Lee back to the Lynchburg line, and place Richmond almost at our mercy."[21]

The Bogus Proclamation

On May 18, Lincoln was startled to read in the New York *World* and the *Journal of Commerce* a bogus presidential proclamation calling for 400,000 more volunteers and designating May 26 as a day of fasting, humiliation, and prayer occasioned by "the situation in Virginia, the disaster at Red River, the delay at Charleston, and the general state of the country."[22] Such language profoundly disheartened a public anxiously awaiting word of Grant's progress. Panic spread throughout the North as the story radiated nationwide via wire services. That day Lincoln told a journalist that the announcement "was a fabrication" and "that he had decided to call for 300,000 in July, not before."[23] He may have suspected that the document he had drafted the previous night to that effect had been leaked. An eyewitness recalled that the publication of the fake proclamation "angered Lincoln more than almost any other occurrence of the war period."[24] Not only did it threaten to depress Northern spirits, but it also indicated that the administration might be harboring a disloyal mole. That the two newspapers running the forgery were bitter critics of the administration may have predisposed Lincoln to think treason had been committed. Because the editors of those journals had plenty of reason to doubt the genuineness of the bulletin, or at least to make inquiries before publishing it, Lincoln's anger was understandable.

To combat the dire effects of the bogus proclamation, Lincoln had Seward draft a clarification announcing that the "paper is an absolute forgery. No proclamation of that kind or any other has been made or proposed to be made by the President, or issued or proposed to be issued by the State Department or any Department of the Government." When Seward recommended that the two newspapers be suppressed, Lincoln agreed and through Stanton ordered General John A. Dix to suspend the papers' publication and arrest their editors. It was the first and only time that Lincoln initiated such action. Over his signature a harshly worded telegram was sent to Dix, instructing him "to arrest and imprison in any fort or military prison in your command, the editors, proprietors and publishers of the aforesaid newspapers. . . . You will also take possession by military force, of the printing establishments of the 'New York World,' and 'Journal of Commerce,' and hold the same until further order, and prevent any further publication therefrom."[25]

Those remarkable orders were carried out promptly but rescinded two days later when it became clear that the newspapers had been duped by a forger, Joseph Howard, Jr., city editor of the Brooklyn *Daily Eagle*, who hoped to reap profits in the highly speculative gold market. (Howard was the journalist who in February 1861 had falsely reported that Lincoln slunk into Washington wearing a scotch cap.) Stanton wired Dix that while the president thought "the editors, proprietors, and publishers of The World and Journal of Commerce are responsible for what appears in their papers injurious to the public service, and have no right to shield themselves behind a plea of ignorance or want of criminal intent," he nevertheless "is not disposed to visit them with vindictive punishment; and hoping that they will exercise more caution and regard for the public welfare in [the] future, he authorizes you to restore them to their respective establishments."[26] Meanwhile, Stanton had ordered the apprehension of other journalists as well as some telegraphers, who were also released when the full story became known. Howard was jailed for three months, winning a reprieve only after his former employer, Henry Ward Beecher, appealed in person to Lincoln. The president later remarked "that no other man but Henry Ward Beecher could have induced him to be guilty of pardoning Joe Howard" and that "he had done nothing during the war which had pained him so much."[27]

Democrats pointed to these arrests as proof positive that Lincoln behaved tyrannically. Manton Marble, editor of the *World*, scolded the president: "For the purpose of gratifying an ignoble partisan resentment, you have struck down the rights of the press, you have violated personal liberty, subjected property to unjust seizure, ostentatiously placed force above law . . . and thus, and by attempting to crush the organs of free discussion, have striven to make free elections impossible, and break down all the safeguards of representative government."[28] Compounding the impression of the administration's arbitrariness was the arrest of Samuel Medary, editor of the ferociously anti-administration Columbus, Ohio, *Crisis*. Provost marshals, acting on a grand jury indictment for the crime of "conspiracy against the Union," apprehended him two days after the New York papers were shut down. The charges were eventually dropped, but meanwhile Democrats had more evidence of an assault on freedom of the press. The *Iowa Courier* protested that it "has always been a mania with Lincoln to arrest American citizens without warrant and to suppress American papers without authority."[29]

Some Republicans thought the administration had overreacted to Howard's hoax. Gideon Welles, who believed that the "hasty, rash, inconsiderate, and wrong" steps "cannot be defended," blamed Seward and to a lesser extent Stanton.[30] The action does indeed bear the hallmarks of Stanton's impetuous, punitive nature.

Frustration: The Offensive Stalls

As promised, Grant did fight it out all summer, constantly driving southward and battling Lee almost nonstop for six weeks. After the battle of the Wilderness, the next collision took place at Spotsylvania Courthouse between May 8 and 20. On May 18, when it seemed as if Grant had the upper hand, Lincoln told a caller that at the time "my wife had her first baby, the doctor from time to time, reported to me that everything was going on as well as could be expected under the circumstances. That satisfied me *he* was doing his best, but still I felt anxious to hear the first squall. It came at last, and I felt mightily relieved. I feel very much so about our army operations at this moment."[31] But again the news turned bad, for Lee inflicted severe losses before falling back to Hanover Junction, where fighting raged from May 23 to 27, and then to Cold Harbor for more bloody work yet (June 1–12). The Army of the Potomac finally came to a halt after a pitched battle at Petersburg (June 15–18), 20 miles south of Richmond. Lee's skillful maneuvering had kept Grant at bay, saving the Confederate capital and inflicting 65,000 casualties. That total represented 60 percent of the Army of the Potomac's entire losses over the three previous years.

Grant had little to show for the immense sacrifice of blood and treasure. He was bogged down at Petersburg, which he besieged with no imminent prospect of victory. Meanwhile, Sigel had been repulsed in the Shenandoah Valley, Butler was helplessly bottled up on the Peninsula, and Sherman was making disappointingly slow progress in his campaign against Atlanta. In June, Sherman unsuccessfully assaulted Confederates at Kennesaw Mountain and sustained heavy losses. The grand strategy that had seemed so promising in the spring had stalled.

As these developments unfolded, Lincoln occasionally found respite by attending the theater. "People may think strange of it," he remarked to Schuyler Colfax, "but I *must* have some relief from this terrible anxiety, or it will kill me."[32]

On July 18, to help fill the army's depleted ranks, Lincoln called for 500,000 men. When Ohio Republicans urged him to rescind the call lest it defeat the party in the autumn, he asked: "What is the Presidency worth to me if I have no country?"[33] Logically he argued that "[w]e must either have men, or the war must stop; I shall issue the call, and if the old ship goes down, it will be with the colors flying. So whether they come by draft, or volunteering, the nation needs soldiers. These she must have, or else she dies, and then comes anarchy, and the frightful ruin of a dismembered country, or its final surrender to the slave power, against which it now struggles, and calls every freeman to the rescue. Peace! In this struggle that which comes by the sword will be the more lasting, and worthy as a legacy to posterity."[34] On another occasion, he said: "We must lose nothing even if I am defeated." He wanted the people to realize that if they reelected him, it "will mean that the rebellion is to be crushed by force of arms."[35] In response, Democrats howled that "[t]ens of thousands of white men must bite the dust to allay the Negro mania of the president."[36]

The administration began implementing the draft in mid-September. The new call implied that the war might end within a year, for it stipulated that draftees would serve for only twelve months, whereas volunteers would serve for three years. Democrats' attempts to make conscription a significant issue in the campaign fizzled.

Lincoln had been encouraged when Grant crossed the James River in mid-June. "I begin to see it," he wired the general. "You will succeed. God bless you all."[37] The following day, taking his cue from Grant, Lincoln with iron determination told a Philadelphia audience that the North "accepted this war for an object, a worthy object, and the war will end when that object is attained. Under God, I hope it never will until that time. [Great cheering.] Speaking of the present campaign, General Grant is reported to have said, I am going through on this line if it takes all summer. [Cheers.] This war has taken three years; it was begun or accepted upon the line of restoring the national authority over the whole national domain, and for the American people, as far as my knowledge enables me to speak, I say we are going through on this line if it takes three years more. [Cheers.]"[38]

To help drive home the point that the war might not end quickly, Lincoln solicited the aid of the press. He solemnly told Noah Brooks, "I wish, when you write or speak to people, you would do all you can to correct the impression that the war in Virginia will end right off and victoriously. To me the most trying thing of all this war is that the people are too sanguine; they expect too much at once. I declare to you, sir, that we are to-day farther ahead than I thought, one year and a half ago, that we should be; and yet there are plenty of people who believe that the war is about to be substantially closed. As God is my judge, I shall be satisfied if we are over with the fight in Virginia within a year. I hope we shall be 'happily disappointed,' as the saying is; but I am afraid not—I am afraid not."[39]

When Lee fended off a nearly successful assault on Petersburg, the president became alarmed, and on June 21 made a two-day visit to the Army of the Potomac. "I just thought I would jump aboard a boat and come down and see you," he told Grant, modestly adding: "I don't expect I can do any good, and in fact I'm afraid I may do harm, but I'd put myself under your orders and if you find me doing anything wrong just send me right away."[40] When Grant asked after his health, the president observed that he was suffering from the aftereffects of seasickness. To a staff member who offered some champagne as a cure, Lincoln replied: "No, my friend; I have seen too many fellows seasick ashore from drinking that very stuff." One of the general's aides, Colonel Horace Porter, thought the president resembled a "boss undertaker" in his black suit.

After inspecting some units, Lincoln took Grant's suggestion that he "ride on and see the colored troops, who behaved so handsomely in [William F.] Smith's attack on the works in front of Petersburg last week." The president expressed keen interest in doing so, for he had not formally reviewed any United States Colored Troops. He was delighted by reports of their gallantry, which vindicated his controversial policy of enlisting blacks. "I think, general," he told Grant, "we can say of the black boys what a country fellow who was an old-time abolitionist in Illinois said when he went to a theater in Chicago and saw Forrest playing *Othello*. He was not very well up in Shakespere, and didn't know that the tragedian was a white man who had blacked up for the purpose. After the play was over the folks who had invited him to go to the show wanted to know what he thought of the actors, and he said: 'Waal, layin' aside all sectional prejudices and any partiality I may have for the race, darned ef I don't think the nigger held his own with any on 'em.'" Reflecting on the decision to allow blacks to serve in the army, Lincoln added: "I was opposed on nearly every side when I first favored the raising of colored regiments; but they have proved their efficiency, and I am glad they have kept pace with the white troops in the recent assaults."[41]

When Lincoln reached the camp of the Eighteenth Corps, hundreds of excited black troops delightedly rushed to see him, hurrahing and cheering. A journalist reported that it "was a genuine spontaneous outburst of love and affection for the man they looked upon as their deliverer from bondage."[42] They "received him most enthusiastically, grinning from ear to ear, and displaying an amount of ivory terrible to behold," Colonel Porter wrote his wife. Fervently they shouted: "God bress Massa Linkum!" "De Lord save Fader Abraham!" "De day ob jubilee am come, shuah" as they swarmed about the president, kissing his hands and reverently touching his dust-covered suit. As he rode bare-headed with tears in his eyes, he bowed left and right. When he tried to acknowledge their plaudits, his voice was, according to Porter, "so broken by emotion that he could scarcely articulate the words of thanks and congratulation which he tried to speak to the humble and devoted men through whose ranks he rode. The scene was affecting in the extreme, and no one could have witnessed it unmoved."[43]

The next day, Lincoln visited Butler's command and, upon observing a particularly strong set of works, remarked: "When Grant once gets possession of a place, he holds on to it as if he had inherited it."[44] As the party sailed up the James River, every vessel they passed cheered Lincoln. A nervous Gustavus Fox, recognizing that the presidential boat had come within range of Confederate guns, wondered why the enemy did not fire on such an important target. Upon returning to City Point, Lincoln had an hour's conversation with Grant, during which the general confidently assured the president he would eventually gain possession of the Confederate capital: "You will never hear of me farther from Richmond than now, till I have taken it. I am just as sure of going into Richmond as I am of any future event. It may take a long summer day, but I will go in."[45] Lincoln replied: "I cannot pretend to advise, but I do sincerely hope that all may be accomplished with as little bloodshed as possible."[46]

Throughout his stay at Petersburg, Lincoln appeared anxious, laboring as he was under such a heavy burden of responsibility. On the way back to Washington, however, the president seemed cheerful and told Fox that he was delighted with what he had seen and heard. Gideon Welles thought his brief visit to the front had done "him good, physically, and strengthened him mentally."[47] Edward Bates believed that Lincoln was "encouraged by Grant's persistent confidence," but nonetheless was "perceptably, disappointed at the small measure of our success."[48]

Many others shared his disappointment, including the troops. Lincoln was blamed by some of them, including an Ohio colonel who expressed "great confidence in the integrity and unselfishness of the President" but regretted that he lacked "force" and "prompt efficient will" and was "controlled by circumstances instead of taking them by the forelocks and giving direction to them." If the North were to prevail, its leader must have "power" and "will," but Lincoln was "too kind-hearted to offend anybody" and "too unselfish and unambitious to want to magnify himself or exalt his power." Commendable though such modesty was in theory, it was "terribly disastrous to our operations in the field."[49]

The friendship between Grant and Lincoln was growing stronger as each came to admire the strengths of the other. During the Wilderness battle, Lincoln praised Grant's "perfect coolness and persistency of purpose." The general, he said, "is not easily excited,—which is a great element in an officer,—and he has the *grit* of a bulldog! Once let him get his 'teeth' *in*, and nothing can shake him off."[50] Murat Halstead reported Lincoln saying: "Grant is the first General I have had. You know how it has been with all the rest. As soon as I put a man in command of the Army, he'd come to me with a plan of campaign and about as much as to say, 'Now, I don't believe I can do it, but if you say so, I'll try it on,' and so put the responsibility of success or failure on me. They all wanted me to be the General. Now, it isn't so with Grant. . . . I am glad to find a man that can go ahead without me. . . . He doesn't ask impossibilities of me."[51] By this time, Lincoln had come to insist on having a voice in the formulation of strategy but not tactics. At one point he said "[w]hatever objection may be urged as to the talents, or culture, or sobriety and military skill of Grant, or his evident stubborn[n]ess of purpose, or his alleged recklessness of means, it must be confessed that after repeated trials and failures with other Generals, he alone had the faith, the confidence and the persistence to compel success."[52]

President under Fire: Confederate Raid on Washington

Two weeks later, Lincoln's anxiety increased when Jubal Early's 15,000 Confederate troops swept down the Shenandoah Valley and seriously menaced Washington. On July 6, Early crossed the Potomac, brushed aside a Union detachment along the Monocacy River, and within days was a scant 4 miles from the Soldiers' Home, where the Lincolns were then staying. The capital was so panicky that U.S. Treasurer Francis E. Spinner bagged up all the money in the Treasury Department vaults and arranged to have it transferred to a tugboat. The incursion threatened not only Washington but Lincoln's political standing. Franklin B. Sanborn, a Radical journalist, thought "it shows that Grant's campaign has had no substantial results. If this is made to appear clearly, it will be fatal to Lincoln's reelection." Sanborn feared that "we are to suffer the penalty of Lincoln's misgovernment for years and years."[53]

On July 10, Stanton became alarmed for the president's safety and dispatched a carriage to bring the First Family back to the White House. The secretary of war himself arrived around 11 P.M. to demand that Lincoln return. The president with some irritation "said he didn't think there was any danger," but he complied.[54] He was also annoyed upon learning that Assistant Secretary of the Navy Gustavus Fox had stationed a small boat in the Potomac to whisk him to safety in case Early's men penetrated the city's defensive cordon.

When Grant offered to direct the defense of Washington, Lincoln replied that "we have absolutely no force here fit to go to the field. . . . Now what I think is that you should provide to retain your hold where you are certainly, and bring the rest with you personally, and make a vigorous effort to destroy the enemie's force in this vicinity. I think there is really a fair chance to do this if the movement is prompt. This is what I think, upon your suggestion, and is not an order."[55] Grant thought better of it and instead sent his finest unit, Horatio Wright's Sixth Corps, scurrying northward to confront Early. While it was en route, an improvised force of 8,000 militiamen, dismounted cavalry, invalids, government clerks, convalescents, and regular troops assembled to man the city's fortifications, including Fort Stevens on the Seventh Street road, down which Early was marching. By July 11, the Confederates came within a few hundred feet of that bastion, but the arrival of the Sixth Corps gave Early pause.

That day, eager to observe the action first-hand, Lincoln hastened to Fort Stevens, where he became the first and only sitting American president to come under serious enemy fire. (He had been exposed less dangerously during the Norfolk Campaign in the spring of 1862.) As he gazed at the skirmishing from the parapet, a soldier rudely instructed him to get down lest he be shot. He did so. Excited, Lincoln returned to the War Department and vividly described the action. That evening he was in an exceptionally good mood. Hay recorded that he was "not in the least concerned about the safety of Washington. With him the only concern seems to be whether we can bag or destroy this force in our front."[56] The next day, he revisited Fort Stevens, accompanied this time by his wife. As he once again watched the action from the parapet, an army surgeon standing nearby—Dr. C. C. V. Crawford of the 102nd Pennsylvania Volunteers—was shot in the thigh. At the urging of General Horatio Wright, Lincoln descended from his exposed perch.

As Early withdrew on July 12, Lincoln wanted Union troops to "push our whole column right up the river road & cut off as many as possible of the retreating raiders." Though he pressed Halleck, who had become chief of staff of the Union armies when Grant was named general-in-chief, to see that it was done, the Confederates managed to slip across the Potomac unmolested, to the president's visible disgust. Sarcastically, he remarked that General Wright had halted his pursuit and "sent out an infantry reconnaissance, for fear he might come across the rebels & catch some of them."[57] Shades of McClellan after Antietam and Meade after Gettysburg! He was also mad at Halleck, remarking that Old Brains' "manifest desire to avoid taking any responsibility without the immediate sanction of General Grant was the main reason why the rebels, having threatened Washington and sacked the peaceful farms and villages of Maryland, got off scatheless." Lincoln often cited Early's escape as one of the most exasperating developments of the war.[58] He had predicted a day before Early entered

Maryland that "with decent management" Union forces could "destroy any enemy who crosses the Potomac."[59]

Lincoln once confessed to Noah Brooks "that he lacked physical courage," but added that "he had a fair share of the moral quality of that virtue." Brooks considered the president's action at Fort Stevens "ample proof that he would not have dropped his musket and run, as he believed he certainly would, at the first sign of physical danger."[60]

Early's men had burned Montgomery Blair's elegant home in Maryland, causing the postmaster general to declare that "the officers in command about Washington are poltroons," that "there were not more than five hundred rebels on the Silver Spring road and we had a million of men in arms," and that "it was a disgrace." Taking understandable offense, Halleck wrote a heated letter demanding Blair's dismissal. When Stanton handed that document to Lincoln, the president replied firmly: "I do not consider what may have been hastily said in a moment of vexation at so severe a loss, is sufficient ground for so grave a step. Besides this, *truth* is generally the best vindication against slander. I propose continuing to be myself the judge as to when a member of the Cabinet shall be dismissed."[61] He penned a similarly stern memo for the cabinet as a whole: "I must myself be the judge, how long to retain in, and when to remove any of you from his position. It would greatly pain me to discover any of you endeavoring to procure another[']s removal, or, in any way to prejudice him before the public. Such endeavor would be a wrong to me; and much worse, a wrong to the country. My wish is that on this subject, no remark be made, nor question asked, by any of you, here or elsewhere, now or hereafter."[62]

Mary Lincoln shared her husband's irritation at Early's escape. When Stanton told her that he intended to commission a painting of the president on the ramparts of Fort Stevens, she snapped: "That is very well, and I can assure you of one thing, Mr. Secretary, if I had had a few *ladies* with me the Rebels would not have been permitted to get away as they did!"[63]

Like the Lincolns, the country was disgusted by Early's escape and by the lack of military success elsewhere. In Washington, a Treasury Department clerk lamented that "we are humbled in the eyes of the world. Everybody here feels it," and an attorney declared that "[w]e have now to be laughed at, as there never was a greater scare."[64] If Lincoln did not do something "to retrieve this blunder of omission," Benjamin Brown French predicted, "he will find 'a hard road to trabbel I believe,' to get, again, into the Presidential chair. The curses all around are long and deep as to the inefficiency *somewhere*, and I have had quite a talk with the President since the invaders left, which was anything but satisfactory to me. I do not think the President regards the whole affair with sufficient seriousness. He talks and laughs, and tells stories just as if nothing of moment had happened. I am warmly, most warmly, his friend, but would, were it proper, pray him to weigh this matter with all the seriousness that so grave an affair deserves."[65] From New York, George William Curtis reported that as a result of the Confederate incursion, "the sense of absurdity and humiliation is very universal. These things weaken the hold of the administration upon the people and the only serious peril that I foresee is the setting in of a reaction which may culminate in November and defeat Lincoln as it did [James S.] Wadsworth in this state [in 1862]."[66]

In late July, Early's forces inflicted additional humiliation by burning the town of Chambersburg, Pennsylvania, after its residents failed to meet a demand for $50,000. This further eroded support for Lincoln. A lawyer visiting the capital observed of the president: "These raids hurt him badly, and his star is declining."[67]

Voter Disenchantment

On July 30, Northern spirits were further depressed by the battle of the Crater at Petersburg. There troops from the coal mining regions of Pennsylvania had dug a tunnel, placed kegs of gunpowder directly beneath enemy lines, and detonated a huge explosion, whereupon 15,000 Union troops blundered by poring *into* the resulting crater rather than around it. The Rebels easily slaughtered them and stymied the attack. Like the country, Lincoln was deeply disturbed. The following day, he met with Grant at Fort Monroe for five hours. They evidently discussed the need to find a new commander to deal with Early in the Shenandoah Valley, where Franz Sigel and David Hunter had conspicuously failed. Among the possibilities considered were Meade, McClellan, and William B. Franklin. Despite great pressure to restore McClellan, Lincoln passed over him and those other senior generals in favor of the very junior Philip Sheridan, only 33 years old. (On July 21, Francis P. Blair, Sr., had urged McClellan to announce that he would not run for president; in return, Blair would recommend that Lincoln give Little Mac a command in the field. Blair insisted that he acted without the president's knowledge or authorization. When informed by Blair of this action, Lincoln responded courteously but indicated neither approval nor disapproval.) From his conference with Grant, the president emerged optimistic, for the general had confidently predicted "that he should meet with several rebuffs but that he would finally get the place [Richmond]."[68] After the meeting, Grant assigned Sheridan to pursue Early "to the death. Wherever the enemy goes let our troops go also."[69]

Lincoln was delighted with those instructions, but he feared that the War Department, which looked askance at the appointment of so young a general, might not be fully cooperative. So he wrote Grant on August 3: "I have seen your despatch . . . . This, I think, is exactly right, as to how our forces should move. But please look over the despatches you may have rece[i]ved from here, ever since you made that order, and discover, if you can, that there is any idea in the head of any one here, of 'putting our army *South* of the enemy' or of 'following him to the *death*' in any direction. I repeat to you it will neither be done nor attempted unless you watch it every day, and hour, and force it."[70] A few days later, Grant told Lincoln that he was reluctant to break his hold on the Confederate army at Petersburg. The president replied in a way that spoke volumes about his indomitable resolve: "Hold on with a bull-dog gripe, and chew & choke, as much as possible."[71]

Lincoln may have felt better after his July 31 visit to Grant, but the voters did not. As public morale sank, the president began to worry about his reelection chances. Gloomily, he predicted to General Andrew J. Hamilton, provisional governor of Texas, that "unless some great change takes place," he would be "*badly beaten*." The people of the North, he told Hamilton, "promised themselves when Gen. Grant started out that he would take Richmond in June—he didn't take it, and they blame me, but I promised them no such thing, & yet they hold me responsible."[72]

Radical Challenge: The Wade–Davis Bill and Manifesto

Among those most disenchanted with Lincoln were congressional Radicals, who passed a bill written by Senator Benjamin F. Wade and Maryland Congressman Henry Winter Davis laying out a Reconstruction program different in some ways from the president's. Both plans shared in common the requirement that the Confederate states must emancipate their slaves, and both stipulated that the federal government would appoint governors to preside over the Reconstruction process. Neither plan allowed blacks to vote. Unlike Lincoln's scheme, which called for military governors to be appointed by the president, the Wade–Davis bill authorized the appointment of civilian provisional governors. Passed on July 2, the bill mandated that when armed resistance ended within a state, the provisional governor (named by the president) was to enroll adult white males and permit them to take an oath of allegiance to the Constitution. Once a majority of those registered (not 10%, as Lincoln's plan called for) had taken the oath, the governor would facilitate the election of a state constitutional convention. Only those taking an "iron-clad" oath that they had never fought against the Union could vote in the referendum on the constitutions or serve as delegates to the constitutional conventions. (This was much more stringent than Lincoln's plan, which called for an oath of prospective, not retrospective, loyalty.) The new constitutions must repudiate all debt incurred in support of the war, disqualify from voting and officeholding all high-ranking members of the Confederate military or civilian governments, and abolish slavery. (The Wade–Davis bill also denied all citizenship rights to prominent Confederates who continued supporting the war after the bill's adoption.) Once these requirements were met, the state could be readmitted to the Union, vote in presidential elections, and choose members of Congress. Under Lincoln's plan, blacks were to be educated and their rights protected, but the states were to determine how these goals were to be met. Congress demanded that blacks and whites be treated equally before the law, that blacks enjoy the privilege of the writ of habeas corpus, and that white kidnappers of blacks be harshly punished.

The requirement that a *majority* had to take the oath effectively meant that Reconstruction would be strictly a postwar enterprise; Lincoln wanted it implemented while the fighting still raged in order to help shorten the war. The retrospective oath dismayed Lincoln, who objected in principle to "an oath which requires a man to swear he *has* not done wrong" because it "rejects the Christian principle of forgiveness on terms of repentance. I think it is enough if the man does no wrong *hereafter*."[73]

The Wade–Davis statute did not satisfy many abolitionists, who objected to its failure to enfranchise blacks. Wade explained that while he supported black suffrage in principle, he opposed an amendment providing for it because he feared that "it will sacrifice the bill."[74] Senator John P. Hale voiced the sentiments of many fellow Radicals when he expressed disagreement "with those who hold that the right of voting is a right which belongs to the catalogue of a man's natural rights & that it is quite as wrong to withhold that from him [the black man] as it is to keep him in a state of bondage. That is not so, it is not a natural right but a political one bestowed by those who frame the political institutions of a Country. If it were a natural right it would belong to women as well as to man, & society in forming its institutions and organizations has a right to with-hold it from any person or class of persons who it believes cannot exercise it understandingly & in a manner that will subserve and promote the best interests of society."[75] (As already noted, Lincoln at this time was, behind the scenes, pressing the Louisiana government to grant at least some blacks the vote.)

When rumors circulated that Lincoln might veto the Wade–Davis bill, congressmen and senators, among them Sumner, Davis, Thaddeus Stevens, and Zachariah Chandler, expressed their dismay to the president. On July 4, as Lincoln sat in the Capitol affixing his signature to various bills, Chandler accosted him, saying a veto "would make a terrible record for us to fight."

"Mr. Chandler, this bill was placed before me a few minutes before Congress adjourns," Lincoln replied. "It is a matter of too much importance to be swallowed in that way."

"If it is vetoed it will damage us fearfully in the North West. It may not in Illinois, but it will in Michigan and Ohio. The important point is that one prohibiting slavery in the reconstructed states."

"That is the point on which I doubt the authority of Congress to act."

"It is no more than you have done yourself."

"I conceive that I may in an emergency do things on military grounds which cannot be done constitutionally by Congress."

(Lincoln was not being entirely candid. The bill had been passed two days earlier and had been under discussion for months.)

When Chandler left, Lincoln told three of his cabinet members, "This bill and this position of these gentlemen seems to me to make the fatal admission (in asserting that the insurrectionary states are no longer states in the Union) that states whenever they please may of their own motion dissolve their connection with the Union. Now we cannot survive that admission I am convinced. If that be true I am not President, these gentlemen are not Congress. I have laboriously endeavored to avoid that question ever since it first began to be mooted & thus to avoid confusion and disturbance in our own counsels. It was to obviate this question that I earnestly favored the movement for an amendment to the Constitution abolishing slavery . . . . I thought it much better, if it were possible, to restore the Union without the necessity of a violent quarrel among its friends, as to whether certain states have been in or out of the Union during the war: a merely metaphysical question and one unnecessary to be forced into discussion." When John Hay opined that the Radicals had lost touch with public opinion, Lincoln said: "If they choose to make a point upon this I do not doubt that they can do harm. They have never been friendly to me & I don[']t know that this will make any special difference as to that. At all events, I must keep some consciousness of being somewhere near right: I must keep some standard of principle fixed within myself."[76]

When they realized that the president was not going to sign the bill (thus killing it with a pocket veto), the Radicals erupted in indignation. On the House floor, a wrathful Henry Winter Davis excoriated Lincoln. To one journalist, Davis seemed "to be ever wandering about dragging an imaginary coat upon the floor of the House and daring any one to tread upon it," and a fellow Maryland Radical exclaimed that the congressman "lives on wormwood & gall and aloes!"[77] The self-righteous, vain, and impulsive Davis regarded those who disagreed with him as "fools," "chattering, whining, and timorous merchants," "mutton heads," and "rattlesnakes."[78] In November 1864, Lincoln remarked that Davis "has been very malicious against me but has only injured himself by it. His conduct has been very strange to me. I came here, his friend, wishing to continue so. I had heard nothing but good of him; he was the cousin of my intimate friend Judge Davis. But he had scarcely been elected when I began to learn of his attacking me on all possible occasions."[79] The president, with characteristic magnanimity, said of Davis's assault against him, "it appears to do him good, and as it does me no injury, (that is I don't feel that it does) what's the harm in letting him have his fling? If he did not pitch into me he would into some poor fellow whom he might hurt."[80]

Davis's anger resulted in part from Lincoln's unwillingness to help him wrest control of the Maryland Republican Party from the Blairs. In late January 1864, the congressman asked that Donn Piatt or John S. Berry be appointed as military commander of the Middle Department. The president bluntly declined, saying he viewed the Maryland contretemps as "a personal quarrel & would do nothing to aid one set to vent their spite on another." Davis immediately left in a huff, thinking no response was called for. When Lincoln had a friend tell Davis that he wished to be on good terms with him, the congressman called the president "thoroughly Blairized" and insisted that Lincoln had insulted him.[81] Recounting this sad tale, Lincoln recalled that during the 1862 election campaign in Maryland, he had helped Davis win by persuading a Republican opponent not to run as an independent. A Buffalo newspaper speculated that "if Mr. Lincoln had granted Winter Davis what he modestly asked a year ago—the control of all the military and civil appointments for Maryland," the congressman would not have opposed the administration.[82]

But more than personal pique fueled the clash between the president and Congress. The central difference was rooted in conflicting interpretations of the Constitution's "guarantee clause," which stated that "the United States shall guarantee to every State in this Union a Republican Form of Government" but did not specify which branch of the government was empowered to enforce the guarantee. Along with his allies, Davis, an old Whig who strove to limit the power of the executive branch, argued that sixteen years earlier the Supreme Court in *Luther vs. Borden* had determined that Congress had the authority to do so; the Taney court ruled that "it rests with Congress to decide what government is the established one in a State. For as the United States guarantee to each State a republican government, Congress must necessarily decide what government is established in a State before it can determine whether it is republican or not."

Davis had not always championed black freedom. He opposed the Emancipation Proclamation because only "ignorant fanatics prate about decrees of emancipation" and because it set a dangerous precedent whereby "Lincoln would be my master &

could take my home & imprison me at pleasure."[83] He thought "loyal states were obligated to observe the slavery clauses of the Constitution" and feared "extreme people who run ahead of events into dream land or utopia." He hoped "people would remember other interests besides the Negro."[84] A former Know-Nothing, Davis hated Democrats more than he hated slavery.

The more extreme Radicals wanted to reconstruct the South on the basis of Charles Sumner's "state suicide" theory, which would allow Congress to treat the Rebel states as though they had reverted to the status of territories. But most Republicans rejected that approach in favor of relying on the Constitution's guarantee clause.

On July 8, Lincoln released his veto message, which was superfluous, since the Constitution does not require the president to justify a pocket veto. Lincoln explained that he was "unprepared, by a formal approval of this Bill, to be inflexibly committed to any single plan of restoration." Nor was he ready "to declare, that the free-state constitutions and governments, already adopted and installed in Arkansas and Louisiana, shall be set aside and held for nought, thereby repelling and discouraging the loyal citizens who have set up the same, as to further effort." Though he doubted that there was "constitutional competency in Congress to abolish slavery in States," he was "at the same time sincerely hoping and expecting that a constitutional amendment, abolishing slavery throughout the nation, may be adopted." Notwithstanding these objections, Lincoln in a conciliatory vein added that he was "fully satisfied with the system for restoration contained in the Bill, as one very proper plan for the loyal people of any State choosing to adopt it" and was "prepared to give the Executive aid and assistance to any such people, so soon as the military resistance to the United States shall have been suppressed in any such State, and the people thereof shall have sufficiently returned to their obedience to the Constitution and the laws of the United States,—in which cases, military Governors will be appointed, with directions to proceed according to the Bill."[85]

The veto ignited an epic struggle between Congress and the president. Thaddeus Stevens cynically scoffed: "What an infamous proclamation! The Pres[iden]t is determined to have the electoral votes of the seceded states—at least of Tenn[essee] Ark[ansas]—Lou[isiana] & Flor[ida]—Perhaps also of S. Car[olina]—The idea of pocketing a bill and then issuing a proclamation as to how far he will conform to it, is matched only by signing a bill and then sending in a veto—How little of the rights of war and the law of nations our Prest. knows! But what are we to do? Condemn privately and applaud publicly!"[86]

Davis chose to condemn publicly, calling Lincoln's message "a gross usurpation of legislative power" that "must be rebuked by supporters of the administration." On August 5 he, along with the co-author of his defunct bill, Senator Wade, issued a scathing manifesto denouncing the president. Echoing Stevens, they ascribed Lincoln's opposition to political expediency: he wanted to win reelection with the help of electoral votes from Southern states like Arkansas and Louisiana, whose representatives Congress refused to seat. "That judgment of Congress which the President defies was the exercise of an authority exclusively vested in Congress by the constitution to determine what is the established government in a State, and in its own nature and by the highest judicial authority binding on all other departments of the Government." Heatedly Wade and Davis declared that a "more studied outrage on the legislative authority of the people has never been perpetrated. Congress passed a bill; the President refused to approve it, and then by proclamation puts as much of it in force as he sees fit, and proposes to execute those parts by officers unknown to the laws of the United States, and not subject to the confirmation of the Senate." Lincoln "has greatly presumed on the forbearance which the supporters of his Administration have so long practiced, in view of the arduous conflict in which we are engaged, and the reckless ferocity of our political opponents. But he must understand that our support is of a cause and not of a man; that the authority of Congress is paramount and must be respected; that the whole body of the Union men of Congress will not submit to be impeached by him of rash and unconstitutional legislation; and if he wishes our support, he must confine himself to his Executive duties—to obey and execute, not make the laws—to suppress by arms armed rebellion, and leave political reorganization to Congress. If the supporters of the Government fail to insist on this, they become responsible for the usurpations which they fail to rebuke, and are justly liable to the indignation of the people whose rights and security, committed to their keeping, they sacrifice." Darkly, they hinted at impeachment: "Let them consider the remedy for these usurpations, and, having found it, fearlessly execute it."[87] The New York *World* thought the charge "amounts to an impeachment, and may be followed by one."[88] The New York *Herald* did not go that far, but it did predict that Lincoln would not win reelection.

The president said that from what he had heard about the manifesto, "he had no desire" to read it and "could himself take no part in such a controversy as they seemed to wish to provoke."[89] It was "not worth fretting about," he believed. He was reminded "of an old acquaintance, who, having a son of a scientific turn, bought him a microscope. The boy went around, experimenting with his glass upon everything that came in his way. One day, at the dinner-table, his father took up a piece of cheese. 'Don't eat that, father,' said the boy; 'it is full of *wrigglers*.' 'My son,' replied the old gentleman, taking, at the same time, a huge bite, 'let 'em *wriggle*; I can stand it if they can.'"[90] (Mary Lincoln testified that whenever her husband was told what critics said of him, he said: "Do good to those who hate you and turn their ill will to friendship.")[91]

But Lincoln did allow Seward to read him the manifesto. After hearing it through, he wondered aloud "whether these men intend openly to oppose my election,—the document looks that way."[92] After a White House interview, the Quaker abolitionist B. Rush Plumly reported that Lincoln's "blood is up on the Wade & Winter Davis protest."[93] Hurt as well as angry, the president told Noah Brooks: "To be wounded in the house of one's friends is perhaps the most grievous affliction that can befall a man. I have tried my best to meet the wishes of this man [Davis], and to do my whole duty by the country." When Brooks speculated that Davis might be crazy, Lincoln observed: "I have heard that there was insanity in his family; perhaps we might allow the plea in this case."[94]

The Radical manifesto backfired, in part because Congress was out of session. Maine Representative James G. Blaine said it "was so powerful an arraignment of the

President that of necessity it rallied his friends to his support with that intense form of energy which springs from the instinct of self-preservation."[95] After the New York *World* lauded the manifesto, the New York *Times* denounced it as "by far the most effective Copperhead campaign document thus far issued."[96] In Senator Wade's home district, Republicans railed against the "improper, ill-timed, ill-tempered, and ill-advised" screed.[97] Noah Brooks called it "a matter of regret that a man of so much oratorical ability and legal sharpness as Henry Winter Davis should be so much of a political charlatan as he is; but he is, like the Blairs, insatiate in his hates, mischievous in his schemes and hollow hearted and cold blooded. It is not supposed he honestly differs in opinion with any member of the present Cabinet, except Blair, but he has seized upon every occasion to quarrel with nearly every one of them, and he stands to-day in an attitude of such intense hostility to Lincoln that he is ready to jeopardize the success of the Union party in the campaign about opening, simply that he may gratify his personal malice toward the President. Revengeful, sore-headed and proud, Davis, like others of his sort here [in Washington], appears to forget that the defeat of Lincoln . . . would necessarily be the triumph of a Copperhead minority."[98]

Secretary of the Interior Usher thought Wade, Davis, and other Radicals were most ungrateful. "Lincoln has," he noted, "to the neglect of his true friends tried to propitiate and oblige this class of men and they never will be satisfied. Of all the acts of his administration they had the least cause & reason to assail him."[99] Another Hoosier, John D. Defrees, gently chided Wade, pointing out that Conservatives accepted the Emancipation Proclamation reluctantly while Radicals applauded it. "Is it not a little strange," Defrees asked the Ohio senator, "that most of the opposition to Mr. Lincoln, among Union men, is to be found among the very men who were loudest in their commendations of the proclamation of freedom, as they called it?"[100]

Conservatives applauded Lincoln's veto. "No doubt the President was right in the controversy with Wade & Davis," fumed Orville H. Browning. "The bill was an outrage, and its approval would have disgraced him."[101] Some Conservatives urged that all office holders appointed at Wade's request be fired, but Lincoln ignored their counsel.

Not all Radicals disparaged Lincoln. Minnesota Congressman Ignatius Donnelly praised him, though he did not share his views on Reconstruction. The president, Donnelly told his House colleagues, "is a great man. Great not after the old models of the world, but with a homely and original greatness. He will stand out to future ages in the history of these crowded and confused times with wonderful distinctness. He has carried a vast and discordant population safely and peacefully through the greatest of political revolutions with such consummate sagacity and skill that while he led he appeared to follow; while he innovated beyond all precedent he has been denounced as tardy; while he struck the shackles from the limbs of three million slaves has been hailed as a conservative! If to adapt, persistently and continuously, just and righteous principles to all the perplexed windings and changes of human events, and to secure in the end the complete triumph of those principles, be statesmanship, then Abraham Lincoln is the first of statesmen."[102] Gerrit Smith protested against the Wade–Davis manifesto, arguing that "the country cannot now afford to have the hold of Mr. Lincoln on the popular confidence weakened."[103] E. A.

Stansbury maintained that "nobody has done such an infamous thing since the war began" and predicted that the manifesto would help "bring in the virtual supremacy of the very traitors we are fighting at such cost."[104] He urged Lincoln to respond, for the "incessant attacks of traitors, aided by such infamous assaults as this, are having an effect which it is of the first importance to counteract."[105]

Disappointed by the response to the manifesto, Davis complained two weeks after it appeared: *"Wilkes' Spirit of the Times* is the only decided paper now! All the rest are trimming—none heartily for Lincoln—all afraid to speak—all tied by *local* elections which complicate the Presidential elections. None *attack* our protest but the [New York] Times—none venture to controvert or approve it."[106]

Attempts to Dump Lincoln

The manifesto was designed in part to trigger a dump-Lincoln movement before the Democratic convention met in late August. In July, Davis proposed that abolitionists press both Frémont and Lincoln to withdraw: "If the people shall en masse desert Lincoln & demand a new candidate & Fremont be induced to stand aside, then I see some hope for the country & the cause. Fremont has no more capacity or character than Lincoln. He may defeat Lincoln, but he cannot be himself elected; & the difference between the two is not worth the struggle."[107]

Other Radicals favored that course. Chase said that his fears about Lincoln "arise from the manifestations I see of a purpose to compromise, if possible, by sacrificing all that has been done for freedom in the rebel states—to purchase peace for themselves— the whites—by the reenslavement of the blacks."[108] Charles Sumner thought the president should step down to make way for "any one of 100 names," among them "half the Senate."[109] On August 6, disenchanted Republicans in Hamilton, Ohio, criticized Lincoln's "indecision of character," "disposition to temporize," and "the large preponderance of that peculiar element known as the milk of human kindness, in his disposition." The Buckeyes debated a call for a new nominating convention to meet at Buffalo on September 22 and a recommendation that both Frémont and Lincoln withdraw.[110] The New York *Evening Post* endorsed the proposal but added that a new convention might prove unnecessary if the Democrats nominated a pro-war candidate on a platform demanding only the restoration of the Union.

On September 2, Greeley, Parke Godwin, and Theodore Tilton wrote jointly to several governors asking if Lincoln should be replaced. Richard Yates of Illinois replied emphatically: "The substitution of another man at this late day would be disastrous in the highest degree. It is too late to change now." The governors of Ohio, Vermont, Maine, Rhode Island, West Virginia, Minnesota, Michigan, Wisconsin and Delaware shared Yates's view, as did Senator Jacob Collamer of Vermont and Joseph Medill of the Chicago *Tribune*.[111] Other governors concurred, but with great reluctance. John A. Andrew of Massachusetts hoped Lincoln would lead but thought that he could not do so because "he is essentially lacking in the quality of leadership, which is a gift of God and not a device of man." The country, Andrew argued, would be better off "under the more magnetic influence of a positive man, of clear purpose and more prophetic nature." Still, he assured Greeley and his colleagues that the Bay

State "will vote for the Union cause at all events and will support Mr Lincoln so long as he remains its candidate." In neighboring New Hampshire, the governor predicted that even though the president "has disappointed the expectations of the people and has no hold on their affections," he would carry the state in November. Lincoln, he added, "has not run the machine according to God's time-table as I try to run my rail-roads." William Buckingham of Connecticut said he could "name a score of gentlemen whose qualifications and personal fitness for the Presidency would be more in accordance with my judgment than Mr Lincoln[']s," but none of them could win half the votes that the president would receive. Thomas Carney of Kansas reported that "the shock to Mr Lincoln[']s popularity, even in Kansas, within the last six months, has been severe." In the trans-Mississippi West, "every thing has been sadly and most corruptly managed." Carney said he would be happy to see another candidate fielded in place of Lincoln if there were a chance the newcomer would win, but that seemed unlikely. In Iowa, William M. Stone doubted that Lincoln, "running solely on his own merits or personal popularity," could triumph, but since the people appreciated "the mighty issues at stake and the disastrous consequences which would inevitably result from his defeat," he would prevail. Only Andrew G. Curtin of Pennsylvania thought that Lincoln would lose. He speculated that if "an unobjectionable candidate divested of the antagonisms which surround President Lincoln was present the State would be entirely safe."[112]

"Lincoln's *best friends*," Henry Winter Davis predicted optimistically, "are impressed with his loss of strength and will be induced easily to urge him to get out of the way."[113] One of those was Richard Smith, editor of the Cincinnati *Gazette*, who on August 27 wrote that the "people regard Mr. Lincoln's candidacy as a misfortune. His apparent strength when nominated was fictitious, and now the fiction has disappeared, and instead of confidence there is distrust."[114] That same day, former Congressman Lewis D. Campbell of Ohio urged the governor of Massachusetts to lead a dump-Lincoln movement: "Our Union people are against Mr. Lincoln and cannot unite on Fremont. If we must be driven to the vote, . . . the Copperheads will carry the State. We do not believe that if Mr Lincoln could be elected the country could survive four years more of his stupid and imbecile management." To Campbell, it appeared that the administration was dominated by pressure from "*fanatical* men such as Beecher, Sumner *et al.*"[115] A Republican paper in Albany warned that the only way for the party to win in November was "to have President Lincoln decline the nomination, his successor to be either Generals Hancock, Grant, Sherman, or Butler."[116]

Lincoln dejectedly remarked that the only Republican congressman "in whose personal and political friendship he could be absolutely confide" was Isaac N. Arnold.[117] (In March, Arnold had praised Lincoln extravagantly in a House speech that was widely distributed in pamphlet form.) Wendell Phillips alleged that only five senators and proportionally even fewer congressmen supported Lincoln for reelection. One of the discontented congressmen, James Ashley of Ohio, tried to enlist War Democrats and skittish Republicans in an attempt to nominate Butler and force Lincoln to step aside. After consulting with Thurlow Weed, Thomas Corwin, Pennsylvania Congressman John Hickman, and others, Ashley assured Butler that there was strong support for his candidacy, and issued a call for a meeting at Cooper Union on August 17. But that document was so radical that it attracted few adherents. Still, Ashley plugged away, making common cause with New Yorkers like George Opdyke, Horace Greeley, George Wilkes, David Dudley Field, George B. Cheever, and Butler's principal aide, John W. Shaffer. Meanwhile, John A. Andrew, Henry Winter Davis and others banded together for the same end. At a meeting on August 19 at the New York home of Opdyke, it was decided to issue a call for a new Republican convention to meet at Cincinnati on September 28. Boston Radicals, led by George Luther Stearns, wrote Frémont a public letter endorsing the idea and urged both him and the president to withdraw. On August 25, the Pathfinder replied that he would quit if Lincoln did also. (His equivocal letter did not please Stearns: "What an abortion Fremont[']s letter is, cold as winter," he told Wendell Phillips. "I wonder the thermometer has not fall[en] to 40°. Well, we have done all we could for the *good honest* man, but he is constitutionally unable to do his part.")[118]

But Lincoln would not cooperate. As he told Carl Schurz: "They urge me with almost violent language to withdraw from the contest, although I have been unanimously nominated, in order to make room for a better man. I wish I could. Perhaps some other man might do this business better than I. That is possible. I do not deny it. But I am here, and that better man is not here. And if I should step aside to make room for him, it is not at all sure—perhaps not even probable—that he would get here. It is much more likely that the factions opposed to me would fall to fighting among themselves, and that those who want me to make room for a better man would get a man whom most of them would not want in at all. My withdrawal, therefore, might, and probably would, bring on a confusion worse confounded. God knows, I have at least tried very hard to do my duty—to do right to everybody and wrong to nobody. And now to have it said by men who have been my friends and who ought to know me better, that I have been seduced by what they call the lust of power, and that I have been doing this and that unscrupulous thing hurtful to the common cause, only to keep myself in office! Have they thought of that common cause when trying to break me down? I hope they have."[119]

In July, while discussing the clamor for peace, Lincoln told a visitor: "I have faith in the people. They will not consent to disunion. The danger is, they are misled. Let them know the truth, and the country is safe." Looking exhausted, he was asked if he worked too hard. "I can't work less, but it isn't that—work never troubled me. Things look badly, and I can't avoid anxiety. Personally I care nothing about a re-election; but if our divisions defeat us, I fear for the country."[120]

The lowest point in Lincoln's presidency arrived in August, when he and many party leaders became convinced that he would lose. His 1860 campaign manager, David Davis, noted that the public was "getting tired of the war." If the North did "not have military successes soon, & the democrats at Chicago act with wisdom, we are in danger of losing the Presidential election," he warned.[121] "Lincoln has done every thing that a man could do to deserve to be beaten," growled a pessimistic New York attorney.[122] On Long Island, a Republican paper praised Lincoln's honesty but concluded that "he is not a man for the times—too easy, forbearing, and shortsighted.

We need a man of sterner stuff, and possessed of deeper penetration."[123] The people were "coming to think that something more than good intentions are demanded of a national leader in such a crisis," observed the Concord, New Hampshire, *Monitor.*[124] Thurlow Weed told Lincoln that his reelection "was an impossibility."[125] In early August, the New York boss reportedly said that "Lincoln can be prevailed upon to draw off," and told a friend that he would support a Democratic nominee for president if that party would declare that it was for reunion and against emancipation and subjugation of the South.[126] At that same time, several Republican leaders met in Boston and concluded that something must be done to appease those demanding peace. Treasury Secretary Fessenden feared that otherwise he would be unable to carry out his duties and would have to resign. Senator Henry Wilson conveyed their message to Lincoln.

Leonard Swett, who shared Weed's view of Lincoln's reelection prospects, wrote home to Illinois saying: "Unless material changes can be wrought, Lincoln's election is beyond any possible hope. It is probably clean gone now." Swett was alarmed to find New Yorkers inert and demoralized, especially Republican national chairman Henry J. Raymond. The New York *Times* editor, whom Lincoln called "my lieutenant general in politics," had just published a long campaign biography of the president. Goaded by Swett, Raymond decided to call a meeting of the party's national committee in Washington with the understanding that Swett would prepare the way by visiting the president to see if he "understood his danger and would help to set things in motion."[127]

When Swett asked Lincoln if he expected to win reelection, the president responded gloomily: "Well, I don[']t think I ever heard of any man being elected to an office unless some one was for him."[128] To his old friend William Bross, lieutenant governor of Illinois, Lincoln sadly remarked that he understood why Westerners were anxious: "Well, they want success and they haven't got it; but we are all doing the best we can. For my part I shall stay right here and do my duty. Traitors will find me at my table." Pointing to a tall maple on the White House grounds, he added: "They can come and hang me to that tree if they like."[129] When the private secretary of a cabinet member told him of the widespread pessimism in New York, Lincoln paced the floor and "with grim earnestness of tone and manner" said: "Well, I cannot run the political machine; I have enough on my hands without *that*. It is the *people's* business,—the election is in their hands. If they turn their backs to the fire, and get *scorched* in the rear, they'll find they have got to '*sit*' on the 'blister'!"[130] In mid-August, when Governor Francis Pierpont of loyal Virginia told Lincoln that the Copperheads were waging "a very unfair campaign and it needed attention," he replied: "Yes, but we need military success more—and without it I doubt the result. If the election had come off two weeks after I was nominated at Baltimore, I think I should have carried every state that will vote this fall, but if it should come off tomorrow I hardly feel certain of what state I should carry. The people seem despondent, and our opponents are pressing the howl that the war is a failure and it has had its effect in the army and among the people. We must have military success."[131] Some faint-hearted Republicans argued that it might be wise to abandon the war effort on the assumption that it would better to have two countries, one of which was free, than one country with slavery.

Intensifying Lincoln's gloom was an August 22 letter from Henry J. Raymond offering a dismal forecast: "I am in active correspondence with your staunchest friends in every State and from them all I hear but one report. The tide is setting strongly against us. Hon. E. B. Washburne writes that 'were an election to be held now in Illinois we should be beaten'. Mr. Cameron writes that Pennsylvania is against us. Gov. Morton writes that nothing but the most strenuous efforts can carry Indiana." New York "would go 50.000 against us to-morrow. And so of the rest. Nothing but the most resolute and decided action, on the part of the Government and its friends, can save the country from falling into hostile hands. Two special causes are assigned for this great reaction in public sentiment,—the want of military successes, and the impression in some minds, the fear and suspicion in others, that we are not to have peace *in any event* under this Administration until Slavery is abandoned. In some way or other the suspicion is widely diffused that we *can* have peace with Union if we would. It is idle to reason with this belief—still more idle to denounce it. It can only be expelled by some authoritative act, at once bold enough to fix attention and distinct enough to defy incredulity & challenge respect."[132] Even such a stout supporter of the administration as John W. Forney's Washington *Chronicle* declared that it "would be glad to see Mr. Lincoln out of the canvass, with all our attachment to his person and his sense of his prescience, if by such a surrender we could save the country from the election of a dishonorable peace on the basis of separation."[133]

The Niagara Manifesto

"The people [of the North]" Thurlow Weed warned, "are wild for Peace. They are told that the President will only listen to terms of Peace on condition Slavery be 'abandoned.'"[134] The despairing public had good reason to believe that Lincoln would not end the war before slavery was extirpated. In the summer of 1864, Confederate leaders, aiming to capitalize on Northern war weariness and to fuel the growing demand for a negotiated peace, floated bogus peace overtures that the gullible Horace Greeley took seriously. The *Tribune* editor alerted Lincoln that he had received word from one William C. "Colorado" Jewett that two emissaries from Jefferson Davis were in Canada, fully authorized to negotiate for peace. (Jewett, described by Edward Bates as "a crack-brained simpleton" and reportedly a notorious Lothario known for stiffing creditors and committing fraud, had sent abusive letters to Lincoln, prompting John Hay to write a crushing response: "In the exercise of my duties [as] secretary in charge of the President's correspondence, it is necessary for me to use a certain discretion in the choice of letters to be submitted to the personal inspection of the President. In order to avoid a further waste of time on your part, I have to inform you that your letters are never so submitted. My proceeding in this matter has the sanction of the President.")[135]

In forwarding this information, Greeley patronizingly told Lincoln: "I venture to remind you that our bleeding, bankrupt, almost dying country also longs for peace—shudders at the prospect of fresh conscriptions, of further wholesale devastations, and of new rivers of human blood. And a wide-spread conviction that the Government and its prominent supporters are not anxious for Peace, and do not improve proffered opportunities to achieve it, is doing great harm now, and is morally certain, unless removed, to do far greater in the approaching Elections. It is not enough that we anxiously *desire* a true and lasting peace; we ought to demonstrate and establish the truth beyond cavil."[136] The rivers of blood ran especially deep that spring. Four days prior to the Republican convention, Grant lost 7,000 men in a frontal attack against entrenched Confederates at Cold Harbor. "I regret this assault more than any one I have ever ordered," the general said that evening.[137]

Though Lincoln rightly assumed that Jefferson Davis had given no authority to the emissaries in Canada, he knew that Greeley was accurate in stating that the administration could not afford to seem indifferent to peace feelers, even if made by agents whose goal, he correctly noted, "was to inflame the peace sentiment of the North, to embarrass the administration, and to demoralize the army."[138] Because he personally was unwilling to treat the peace negotiators as representatives of a legitimate government, Lincoln shrewdly asked Greeley to act as an unofficial mediator to deal with them. On July 9, he authorized the *Tribune* editor to bring to Washington for consultation "any person anywhere professing to have any proposition of Jefferson Davis in writing, for peace, embracing the restoration of the Union and abandonment of slavery." Six days later the president told Greeley, who had written that the Confederate agents seemed serious: "I not only intend a sincere effort for peace, but I intend that you shall be a personal witness that it is made."[139] When James Ashley protested Greeley's mission, Lincoln said: "Don't worry; nothing will come of it."[140] The *Tribune* editor, said Lincoln, "means right" but "makes me almost as much trouble as the whole Southern Confederacy."[141]

When John Hay presented Lincoln's letter to Greeley, the editor protested that he was "the worst man that could be taken for the purpose" and predicted that "as soon as he arrived there, the newspapers would be full of it" and that "he would be abused & blackguarded."[142] Nonetheless, he accepted the mission and at Niagara Falls met with the Confederate spokesmen James P. Holcombe, George N. Sanders, Clement C. Clay, and Jacob Thompson. He grievously misled them by failing to make clear that Lincoln insisted on "the restoration of the Union and abandonment of slavery," for he thought the president should not propose terms but instead let Jefferson Davis do so. When the Confederates told Greeley that they were not in fact officially accredited to negotiate, the editor requested further instructions from Washington. In reply, the president sent John Hay with a document that was to shock Northern peace advocates: "To whom it may concern: Any proposition which embraces the restoration of peace, the integrity of the whole Union, and the abandonment of slavery, and which comes by and with an authority that can control the armies now at war against the United States, will be received and considered by the Executive Government of the United States, and will be met by liberal terms on other substantial and collateral points; and the bearer or bearers thereof shall have safe conduct both ways."[143] Democrats called this "the Niagara Manifesto."

Because Greeley had not informed them initially of the president's conditions for negotiations, the Confederate agents were surprised by this document. Erroneously concluding that Lincoln had shifted his stance, they accused him of acting in bad faith. The New York *Daily News* declared that the Manifesto "is in such marked contrast with the previous spirit of the correspondence that it resembles the caprice of a foolish girl trifling with her submissive lover."[144]

Resenting the false position in which Greeley had put him, Lincoln asked the editor to publish their correspondence, with minor omissions. Greeley refused to run anything but the entire text, with its melodramatic analysis of the state of the country. Lincoln decided to drop the matter rather than have the demoralizing parts of Greeley's letters appear in print and thus dampen Northern spirits any further. Vexed by the editor's intransigence, Lincoln compared him to an old shoe. "In early life," he told the cabinet, "and with few mechanics and but little means in the West, we used to make our shoes last a great while with much mending, and sometimes, when far gone, we found the leather so rotten the stitches would not hold. Greeley is so rotten that nothing can be done with him. He is not truthful—the stitches all tear out."[145] Several months later, speaking of Greeley's unwillingness to allow the publication of a lightly redacted version of their correspondence, Lincoln offered a less harsh judgment: "In some respects Mr. Greeley is a great man, but in many others he is wanting in common sense."[146]

When some of the correspondence nonetheless appeared in newspapers, Greeley was made to look foolish as he deceitfully tried to blame Lincoln for the misunderstanding. Radicals praised the Niagara Manifesto as "one of the most dignified and appropriate acts in the records of the war."[147] A Congregational minister told his Boston flock that the president "exactly struck the pulse-beat of the nation in his note 'to whom it may concern' which so effectually demolished some would-be negotiators."[148] The Philadelphia *Bulletin* praised Lincoln for showing "wisdom, humanity, and genuine patriotism."[149] From Kansas, Mark W. Delahay reported to Lincoln that the document "was a fortunate thing; it has disarmed a class of Democrats of one important weapin, all who preached up, that you would not be for, or yield your assent to an honorable peace."[150]

Conservatives renewed their charge that Lincoln was transforming what was originally a war to preserve the Union into an abolitionist crusade. The Democratic Cincinnati *Enquirer* called the Niagara Manifesto "a *finality*, which . . . will preclude any conference for a settlement. Every soldier . . . that is killed, will lose his life not for the Union, the Stars and Stripes, but for the negro."[151] To the Detroit *Free Press*, it was proof positive that Lincoln was "bound hand and foot to the dogmas of the extreme abolitionists."[152] George Templeton Strong deemed it a "blunder" that "may cost him his election. By declaring that abandonment of slavery is a fundamental article in any negotiation for peace and settlement, he has given the disaffected and discontented a weapon that doubles their power of mischief."[153] One of the discontented, Maryland Senator Reverdy Johnson, asked rhetorically of the Niagara Manifesto: "could there be a refusal so insane, so reckless, so inhuman, so barbarous?"[154] In Pennsylvania, Democratic newspapers jeered that "our flippant, cunning undignified despot" was prosecuting the war to "liberate the negro and rivet their chains upon white freemen."[155] Some conservative Republican papers were also critical. In Illinois, Democrats predicted that the Manifesto would add 50,000 votes to their total in the fall.

Despite the criticism, Lincoln thought that his involvement in the bungled affair was worthwhile. At least, he said, it "will shut up Greeley, and satisfy the people who are clamoring for peace."[156] When some of those clamorers objected to making abolition a precondition for peace, he said: "there has never been a time since the war began when I was not willing to stop it if I could do so and preserve the Union, and earlier in the war I would have omitted some of the conditions of my note to the rebel Commissioners, but I had become satisfied that no lasting peace could be built up between the States in some of which there were free and in others slave institutions, and, therefore, I made the recognition of the abolition of slavery a *sine qua non*."[157]

In early August, Lincoln solemnly assured George M. Gill, a member of the Baltimore City Council who had four sons in the army, "that he would never consent to an armistice, or to peace, on any other terms but the explicit abolition of slavery in all the Southern States; that he was satisfied that if any other candidate except himself should be elected, that the result of such an election would be an immediate armistice, which would be followed by peace; that he considered peace, without the abolition of slavery, to be a great deal worse calamity than a separation of the South from the North would be; that, in plain terms, he preferred such a separation to a peace which would leave the South in the enjoyment of that institution, and that therefore he felt it to be his duty to oppose, by all means in his power, the election of any other candidate, and that he intended to do so." He added "that he was determined to prosecute the war with all the means at his command till the rebels were conquered or exterminated, even if it took four years more."[158]

Lincoln's moral sense dictated this bold insistence on emancipation as a basis for peace. If he had been motivated by political expediency alone, he could simply have avoided mentioning the slavery issue; he knew that the Confederates would reject any peace terms denying them independence.

While Greeley went about his abortive mission to Canada, another peace effort was being undertaken in Richmond. It was the brainchild of Colonel James F. Jacquess, a Methodist minister commanding the 73rd Illinois regiment. In 1863, he had obtained from General Rosecrans a furlough, which Lincoln approved, in order to consult with Jefferson Davis. When the Confederate president learned that Jacquess had no authority to speak for the administration, he refused to see him. (Lincoln approved a similar mission in the fall of 1863, undertaken by his chiropodist and troubleshooter, Issacher Zacharie, who did meet with Confederate cabinet members. The details of this venture are murky, and nothing came of it.)

Though Jacquess's sojourn in the Confederacy proved futile, the colonel managed to win the sympathy of a journalist, James R. Gilmore, who wrote under the pen name Edmund Kirke. A year later, when those two men requested official permission to repeat the experiment, Lincoln granted them a pass but no official sanction to negotiate on his behalf. They met with Davis, who insisted that the only terms acceptable must include complete independence for the Confederacy. (Here Davis blundered, for if he had hinted that a negotiated settlement might be possible, he could have jeopardized Lincoln's reelection chances.) When Gilmore reported this conversation to Lincoln, the president saw at once that it would help nullify criticism of his handling of the Greeley mission. He told Gilmore that "it is important that Davis's position should be known at once. It will show the country that I didn't fight shy of Greeley's Niagara business without a reason . . . . This may be worth as much to us as half a dozen battles." Charles Sumner, who was present at the interview, suggested that Gilmore write a brief account of his mission for a Boston paper and a fuller account for the *Atlantic Monthly*. Lincoln concurred, and on July 22 the Boston *Transcript* carried Gilmore's report, which closely resembled the one prepared by Judah P. Benjamin, the Confederate secretary of state. The *Atlantic Monthly* ran a longer version in September. Both items were widely copied in the Northern press. "We can negotiate only with the bayonet," Gilmore assured his readers. "We can have peace only by putting forth all our strength, crushing the Southern armies, and overthrowing the Southern Government."[159]

On July 25, Lincoln wrote a letter to Abram Wakeman intended for the eyes of James Gordon Bennett, whose New York *Herald* proclaimed that the Niagara Manifesto doomed the president's reelection chances. Though Lincoln believed that it was "important to humor the Herald," he would not have the editor as a guest at the White House, evidently sharing John Hay's view that Bennett was "too pitchy to touch."[160] (When it was suggested that Bennett be invited to the Executive Mansion, the president hesitated, saying: "I understand Mr. Bennett has made a great deal of money, some say not very properly; now he wants me to make him respectable." Since Lincoln had never invited William Cullen Bryant or Horace Greeley, he refused to extend Bennett a special invitation. If, however, the editor wished to call at the White House, the president let it be known that he would be received.)[161] But as the political skies darkened that summer, Lincoln grew more willing to accommodate Bennett. In his letter to Wakeman, the president contended that Jefferson Davis had made no bona fide peace feelers: "The men of the South, recently (and perhaps still) at Niagara Falls, tell us distinctly that they *are* in the confidential employment of the rebellion; and they tell us as distinctly that they are *not* empowered to offer terms of peace. Does any one doubt that what they *are* empowered to do, is to assist in selecting and arranging a candidate and a platform for the Chicago convention [of the national Democratic Party]? Who could have given them this confidential employment but he who only a week since declared to Jaquess and Gilmore that he had no terms of peace but the independence of the South—the dissolution of the Union? Thus the present presidential contest will almost certainly be no other than a contest between a Union and a Disunion candidate, disunion certainly following the success of the latter." In closing, Lincoln hinted that Bennett might be rewarded if he supported the Republican ticket: "The issue is a mighty one for all people and all time; and whoever aids the right, will be appreciated and remembered."[162] Wakeman read this letter to Bennett, who said after a few moments' reflection, "it did not amount to much." The editor clearly wanted a more specific pledge of a quid pro quo. To help close a deal between the president and the *Herald*, Wakeman suggested as intermediary William O. Bartlett, a well-known New York lawyer and journalist whom he called "a curious genius."[163]

Lincoln was eager to enlist the support of the cynical, egocentric Bennett, who had been trumpeting Grant while sneering at the president as an "imbecile joker," the "head ghoul," a "Political abolitionist failure," and condemning his "nigger-worshipping policy."[164] Iowa Senator James Harlan believed "that Bennett's support is so important especially considered as to its bearing on the soldier vote that it would pay to offer him a foreign mission for it."[165] Horace Greeley concurred, telling Bartlett that "if the President should see the way clear to tend to the Editor of the Herald some important diplomatic post in recognition of his services to the country in sustaining the Union at all hazards, but especially in upholding the Draft, I think a very good and extensive influence would thereby be exerted."[166] Also working behind the scenes was Mrs. Lincoln, who in August paid a call on Bennett's wife in New York. The two women had been friendly, and this meeting helped facilitate the *Herald*'s change of editorial course.

Bartlett shuttled back and forth between Bennett and Lincoln. On November 1, he told the president: "There are but few days now before the election. If Mr. Bennett is not *certainly* to have the offer of the French Mission, I want to know it *now*. It is important to me." According to Bartlett's report to the editor, Lincoln "concluded with the remarks that in regard to the understanding between him and me, about Mr. Bennett, he had been a 'shut pan, to everybody'; and that he *expected to do that thing (appoint you to France) as much as he expected to live*. He repeated: *'I expect to do it as certainly as I do to be reelected myself.*'"[167] This offer was somewhat curious, for the incumbent minister to France, William L. Dayton, had no intention of resigning. (Lincoln may have been planning to replace him after the election.)

During the final week of the campaign, Bennett toned down his criticism of Lincoln but did not endorse him, merely telling readers of the *Herald* that it made little difference how they voted. The editor believed that he could best help the president by simply not mentioning him in the *Herald*. In February 1865, Bennett was tendered the French post made vacant by the death of William Dayton two months earlier. Bennett turned it down, for he craved recognition and deference more than a diplomatic assignment. (When sounded out in the fall about his willingness to back the Republican ticket, the self-styled "Napoleon of the American Press" had asked: "Will I be a welcome visitor at the White House if I support Mr. Lincoln?")[168] Bennett was doubtless gratified that he had been offered a more prestigious post than any of his rivals like Horace Greeley, Henry J. Raymond, James Watson Webb, and William Cullen Bryant. When news of the bargain leaked out, Gideon Welles was disgusted at Lincoln's willingness to give the French mission to "an editor without character for such an appointment, whose whims are often wickedly and atrociously leveled against the best men and the best causes, regardless of honor or right."[169]

Reaching the Nadir: The Blind Memorandum

On August 23, the despairing Lincoln wrote one of his most curious documents, a memorandum revealing his belief that a Democratic victory was likely: "This morning, as for some days past, it seems exceedingly probable that this Administration will not be re-elected. Then it will be my duty to so co-operate with the President elect, as to save the Union between the election and the inauguration; as he will have secured his election on such ground that he can not possibly save it afterwards."[170] He folded and sealed this document and then, inexplicably, asked his cabinet to sign it without knowing its contents. It became known as the "blind memorandum." Lincoln may have feared that its contents would be leaked to the press if the cabinet had been allowed to read it.

Four days earlier, Lincoln had explained his pessimism to Commissioner of Indian Affairs William P. Dole and a pair of Wisconsin Republican leaders, Judge Joseph T. Mills and Alexander W. Randall. The president assured them that "there is no program intended by the democratic party but that will result in the dismemberment of the Union." When they objected that George McClellan would probably be the Democratic nominee and that he was "in favor of crushing out the rebellion," Lincoln replied that the "slightest acquaintance with arithmetic will prove to any man that the rebel armies cannot be destroyed with democratic strategy. It would sacrifice all the white men of the north to do it. There are now between 1 & 200 thousand black men now in the service of the Union. These men will be disbanded, returned to slavery & we will have to fight two nations instead of one. I have tried it. You cannot concilliate the South, when the mastery & control of millions of blacks makes them sure of ultimate success. You cannot concilliate the South, when you place yourself in such a position, that they see they can achieve their independence. The war democrat depends upon conciliation. He must confine himself to that policy entirely. If he fights at all in such a war as this he must economise life & use all the means which God & nature puts in his power. Abandon all the posts now possessed by black men surrender all these advantages to the enemy, & we would be compelled to abandon the war in 3 weeks. We have to hold territory. Where are the war democrats to do it. The field was open to them to have enlisted & put down this rebellion by force of arms, by concilliation, long before the present policy was inaugurated. There have been men who have proposed to me to return to slavery the black warriors of Port Hudson & Olustee to their masters to conciliate the South. I should be damned in time & in eternity for so doing. The world shall know that I will keep my faith to friends & enemies, come what will. My enemies say I am now carrying on this war for the sole purpose of abolition. It is & will be carried on so long as I am President for the sole purpose of restoring the Union. But no human power can subdue this rebellion without using the Emancipation lever as I have done. Freedom has given us the control of 200,000 able bodied men, born & raised on southern soil. It will give us more yet. Just so much it has sub[t]racted from the strength of our enemies, & instead of alienating the south from us, there are evidences of a fraternal feeling growing up between our own & rebel soldiers. My enemies condemn my emancipation policy. Let them prove by the history of this war, that we can restore the Union without it."[171]

Several weeks later, Lincoln read the "blind memorandum" to the cabinet and explained its genesis. "[Y]ou will remember that this was written at a time (6 days before the Chicago nominating convention) when as yet we had no adversary, and seemed to have no friends," he said. "I then solemnly resolved on the course of action indicated above. I resolved, in case of the election of General McClellan[,] being certain that he would be the Candidate, that I would see him and talk matters over with him. I would say, 'General, the election has demonstrated that you are stronger, have more influence with the American people than I. Now let us together, you with your influence and I with all the executive power of the Government, try to save the country. You raise as many troops as you possibly can for this final trial, and I will devote all my energies to assisting and finishing the war."

Seward remarked, "And the General would answer you '*Yes, Yes*'; and the next day when you saw him again & pressed these views upon him he would say, 'Yes—yes' & so on forever and would have done nothing at all."

"At least," Lincoln replied, "I should have done my duty and have stood clear before my own conscience."[172]

John Brown's Raid Redivivus: Lincoln Recruits Frederick Douglass

Because Lincoln quite rightly feared that a Democratic victory would end the emancipation process, he wanted to gather as many slaves as possible beneath the tent of freedom. All who were within Union lines by March 4, 1865, would be liberated by the Emancipation Proclamation. In August, he told Colonel John Eaton, superintendent of freedmen in the Department of the Tennessee and the state of Arkansas, "that he wished the 'grapevine telegraph'" which informed slaves about the progress of the war "could be utilized to call upon the Negroes of the interior peacefully to leave the plantations and seek the protection of our armies." When Eaton mentioned Frederick Douglass's recent criticism of administration policy, the president asked if Douglass might be persuaded to come to the White House for a discussion. Eaton, who knew Douglass well, facilitated the meeting.

On August 19, Lincoln and Douglass met for the second time. Among other things, they discussed a recent letter the president had drafted but not sent to a War Democrat, Charles D. Robinson, who had written to Lincoln criticizing the Niagara Manifesto. In defending that document to Robinson, the president appeared to renege on its insistence that abolition was a prerequisite for peace. In a lawyerly quibble, he maintained that "it seems plain that saying re-union and abandonment of slavery would be considered, if offered, is not saying that nothing *else* or *less* would be considered, if offered." He reminded Robinson that "no one, having control of the rebel armies, or, in fact, having any influence whatever in the rebellion, has offered, or intimated a willingness to, a restoration of the Union, in any event, or on any condition whatever. . . . If Jefferson Davis wishes, for himself, or for the benefit of his friends at the North, to know what I would do if he were to offer peace and re-union, saying nothing about slavery, let him try me."

In this draft of the letter to Robinson, Lincoln repeated the arguments he had made to his Wisconsin visitors that same day: "I am sure you would not desire me to say, or to leave an inference, that I am ready, whenever convenient, to join in re-enslaving those who shall have served us in consideration of our promise. As matter of morals, could such treachery by any possibility, escape the curses of Heaven, or of any good man? As matter of policy, to *announce* such a purpose, would ruin the Union cause itself. All recruiting of colored men would instantly cease, and all colored men now in our service, would instantly desert us. And rightfully too. Why should they give their lives for us, with full notice of our purpose to betray them?" The employment of black troops "is not a question of sentiment or taste, but one of physical force, which may be measured, and estimated as horsepower, and steam power, are measured and estimated. And by measurement, it is more than we can lose, and live. Nor can we, by discarding it, get a white force in place of it. There is a witness in every white man[']s bosom that he would rather go to the war having the negro to help him, than to help the enemy against him."[173]

While Douglass heartily agreed with Lincoln's arguments regarding the importance of black soldiers, he emphatically objected to the implicit backsliding on emancipation. He urged the president not to send the letter to Robinson, for it "would be given a broader meaning than you intend to convey; it would be taken as a complete surrender of your anti-slavery policy, and do you serious damage. In answer to your Copperhead accusers, your friends can make the argument of your want of power, but you cannot wisely say a word on that point."[174] Taking that advice, Lincoln decided to leave the missive in his desk, unsigned and unsent. He may also have been influenced by Dole and Randall, who had criticized the letter.

(Yet the gist of the Robinson letter leaked out when Henry J. Raymond, after conferring with Lincoln, wrote in the New York *Times* that the president "did say that he *would* receive and consider propositions for peace coming with proper authority, *if* they embraced the integrity of the Union *and* abandonment of slavery. But he did *not* say that he would *not* receive them unless they embraced both these conditions." The editor of the Albany *Evening Journal* ran a similar report of a conversation with Lincoln. Democrats denounced the president's evident waffling as "the dodge of a political trickster.")[175]

Turning to the danger presented by a Democratic victory, Lincoln told Douglass that the "slaves are not coming so rapidly and so numerously to us as I had hoped." (The situation had changed since 1862, when he had informed Orville Browning that the flood of escaped slaves posed a significant problem.)

Douglass "replied that the slaveholders knew how to keep such things from their slaves, and probably very few knew of his Proclamation."

Earnestly the president suggested "that something should be speedily done to inform the slaves in the Rebel states of the true state of affairs in relation to them" and "to warn them as to what will be their probable condition should peace be concluded while they remain within the Rebel lines: and more especially to urge upon them the necessity of making their escape." Months later, Douglass recalled that Lincoln's words that day "showed a deeper moral conviction against slavery than I had even seen before in anything spoken or written by him." The president said: "Douglass, I hate slavery as much as you do, and I want to see it abolished altogether."[176] The black orator agreed to recruit a band of black scouts "whose business should be somewhat after the original plan of John Brown, to go into the rebel States, beyond the lines of our armies, and carry the news of emancipation, and urge the slaves to come within our boundaries."[177]

Douglass also asked Lincoln to discharge his ailing son Charles from the army. Lincoln granted the request for Charles's discharge, but thanks to the military developments soon afterward, nothing came of the plan to create a sort of underground railroad encouraging slaves to flee to Union lines.

Douglass excitedly told General John Eaton that the president "treated me as a man; he did not let me feel for a moment that there was any difference in the color of our skins! The President is a most remarkable man. I am satisfied now that he is doing all that circumstances will permit him to do." The admiration was mutual, for Lincoln said "that considering the conditions from which Douglass rose, and the position to which he had attained, he was, in his judgment, one of the most meritorious men in America."[178]

No Backsliding: Commitment to Emancipation Reaffirmed

Douglass was not the only one fearful that Lincoln might backslide on his commitment to abolition. In Henry J. Raymond's letter of August 22, he had urged the president "to appoint a Commission, in due form, *to make distinct proffers of peace to Davis, as the head of the rebel armies, on the sole condition of acknowledging the* supremacy of the Constitution,—all other questions to be settled in convention of the people of all the States." To make such "an offer would require no armistice, no suspension of active war, no abandonment of positions, no sacrifice of consistency." Raymond predicted that if "the proffer were *accepted* (which I presume it would not be,) the country would never consent to place the practical execution of its details in any but loyal hands, and in those we should be safe." If "it should be *rejected,* (as it would be,) it would plant seeds of disaffection in the South, dispel all the delusions about peace that prevail in the North, silence the clamorous & damaging falsehoods of the opposition, take the wind completely out of the sails of the Chicago craft, reconcile public sentiment to the War, the draft, & the tax as inevitable *necessities,* and unite the North as nothing since firing on Fort Sumter has hitherto done."[179]

When word of this advice leaked out, Charles Eliot Norton asked incredulously: "What does Raymond mean . . . ? Is he hedging for a reconstruction with slavery? If so, he is more shortsighted and more unprincipled than I believed."[180] Defending the president's insistence on the "abandonment of slavery" in the Niagara Manifesto, Charles A. Dana told Raymond that if Lincoln "had left slavery out of his letter, he would have done himself and his party a great injury, hopelessly alienating the great part of the Radicals. As you are very well aware, he is more or less under suspicion of a want of earnestness upon this supreme question and if in such a communication he had omitted all reference to it, people would have taken for granted that he was willing to sacrifice his emancipation proclamation, and let the Southern States come back with their old power."[181]

Along with the rest of the Republican National Executive Committee, Raymond called at the White House on August 25. Nicolay reported that "Hell is to pay. The N. Y. politicians have got a stampede on that is about to swamp everything. . . . Everything is darkness and doubt and discouragement. Our men see giants in the airy and unsubstantial shadows of the opposition, and are about to surrender without a fight. I think that today and here is the turning-point in our crisis. If the President can infect R[aymond] and his committee with some his own patience and pluck, we are saved."

Three days later, Nicolay rejoiced that Lincoln and the cabinet had managed to convince Raymond "that they already thoroughly considered and discussed his proposition; and upon showing him their reasons, he very readily concurred with them in the opinion that to follow his plan of sending Commissioners to Richmond, would be worse than losing the Presidential contest—it would be ignominiously surrendering it in advance." (Lincoln said Raymond's plan to send a commission to Richmond "would be utter ruination" and that "our military prospects and situation would not allow it [an armistice] at present.") According to Nicolay, Raymond and his colleagues "found the President and Cabinet wide awake to all the necessities of the situation, and went home much encouraged and cheered up."[182]

Lincoln did not show his visitors a letter that he had drafted to Raymond on August 24, instructing the editor to "proceed forthwith and obtain, if possible, a conference for peace with Hon. Jefferson Davis, or any person by him authorized for that purpose," to "address him in entirely respectful terms, at all events, and in any that may be indispensable to secure the conference," to "propose, on behalf of this government, that upon the restoration of the Union and the national authority, the war shall cease at once, all remaining questions to be left for adjustment by peaceful modes." If Davis were to reject this offer, then Raymond was to "request to be informed what terms, if any embracing the restoration of the Union, would be accepted" and report back to Washington. These instructions remained in the president's desk.[183] Lincoln doubtless hoped to make Davis state unequivocally what he had already told Colonel Jacquess, namely, that he would accept no peace terms denying independence to the Confederacy.

Many Republicans shared Lincoln's view that any attempt to hold peace talks would be ruinous. Rumors that the administration might be willing to accept a compromise settlement were "paralyzing the Republican and the Union party," John Murray Forbes noted. He feared that if "the milk and water policy of trying to negotiate with the rebels while their armies exist is attempted, earnest men will feel that it is a mere contest for party power, and that perhaps the war Democrats may react upon the peace party, and make McClellan just as likely to save the Union as we should be." The Confederates would take advantage of a truce to "arm and make treaties with foreign nations, and negotiate with our border and Copperhead States for free trade seduction."[184] Negotiating with the Confederates "means defeat."[185] Forbes believed that if Lincoln had sent commissioners to Richmond, the party would have been forced to name a new ticket.

It is not clear if Lincoln seriously toyed with the idea of backsliding on emancipation. He probably had not meant to suggest that he would rescind the Emancipation Proclamation; his "try me" dare was in all likelihood merely a ploy to smoke out Jefferson Davis and thus undo the harm done by the Niagara Manifesto, which the Democrats repeatedly attacked, calling it "The Republican Platform."[186] While a retraction of his antislavery pledge might gain him some support from Conservatives, he said it would "lose ten times as much on the other side."[187]

But if Lincoln did really consider abandoning emancipation as a prerequisite for peace, it is not to be wondered at, for he may well have believed that insisting on it as a war aim guaranteed that the Democrats would win the election. To him it may have seemed preferable to save the Union by abandoning emancipation rather than losing both reunion and abolition by insisting on the latter. If such thoughts did occur to him, his keen moral sense trumped them. He hated slavery just as he hated to renege on promises. Even if it meant his defeat, he would not abandon emancipation. Lincoln may not have been thinking along these lines, but if he was, it is noteworthy that he made his decision *before* the tide turned in favor of the Republicans.

Gustavus Fox thought Lincoln's "playing with 'peace negotiations' in 1864 was a repetition of that profound and secretive policy which marked his course with regard to Fort Sumter in 1861. Many of the leaders, even those close to him, thought him to be a 'simple-minded man.'" Fox knew better. To him, Lincoln seemed "the deepest, the closest, the cutest, the most ambitious man American politics has produced."[188]

In late August, John Murray Forbes, who had earlier favored postponing the Republican convention, warned that it was too late to field another standard-bearer. "We cannot change our Candidate," even though the Democrats might win, he told Charles Eliot Norton. If the Peace Democrats "keep in the background & let the opposition put up some one at Chicago who can catch the votes of the war & peace opposition men we shall have a hard time in electing Lincoln. Were we free today we could nominate Dix or Butler and elect him by a strong vote." But the time for such a change had past.[189] As August drew to a close, the future looked bleak indeed.

34

"The Wisest Radical of All"
Reelection
(September–November 1864)

The political tide began turning on August 29, when the Democratic national convention met in Chicago. Lincoln accurately predicted that the delegates "must nominate a Peace Democrat on a war platform, or a War Democrat on a peace platform; and I personally can't say that I care much which they do."[1] The convention took the latter course, choosing George McClellan for president and adopting a platform which declared the war "four years of failure" and demanded that "immediate efforts be made for a cessation of hostilities, with a view to an ultimate convention of the states, or other peaceable means, to the end that, at the earliest practicable moment, peace may be restored on the basis of the Federal Union of the States." This "peace plank," the handiwork of Clement L. Vallandigam, implicitly rejected Lincoln's Niagara Manifesto; the Democrats would require as a prerequisite for peace only union, whereas the Republicans demanded union *and* emancipation. The platform also called for the restoration of "the rights of the States unimpaired," which suggested that slavery would be preserved under a Democratic administration. As McClellan's running mate, the delegates chose Ohio Congressman George Pendleton, a thoroughgoing opponent of the war who had voted against supplies for the army.

As the nation waited day after day to see how McClellan would react to this platform, Lincoln wittily opined that the general "must be *intrenching*." More seriously, he added that Little Mac "doesn't know yet whether he will accept or decline. And he never will know. Somebody must do it for him. For of all the men I have had to do with in my life, *indecision* is most strongly marked in General McClellan;—*if that can be said to be strong which is the essence of weakness*."[2]

A week and a half after the Chicago Convention, McClellan finally issued a temporizing acceptance letter which seemed to disavow the "peace plank." Yet he did indicate that he had no objection to a compromise settlement, leaving slavery intact within a restored Union. It is highly unlikely that if he had won the election, McClellan could have brought the war to a successful close with the nation reunited and slavery abolished.

Throughout the campaign he never indicated that he approved of the Emancipation Proclamation or that he would make abolition a precondition for peace.

Rallying around the Flag

Although some observers agreed with Fighting Joe Hooker's prediction that McClellan would "have an easy and a successful run" because "the people seem to desire to have a President *who has some influence with the Administration*," the news from Chicago restored Lincoln's flagging spirits.[3] Along with Vallandigham's "peace plank," the defiant nomination of Pendleton, Vallandigham's alter ego, estranged War Democrats and Conservative Unionists (supporters of John Bell in 1860). A New York critic of Lincoln spoke for many when he said: "I admire McClellan & should vote for him but I cannot swallow Pendleton & that Chicago platform. I never could digest them. The dyspepsia that would follow such a banquet would torment me all my days."[4]

Emphatically and confidently, Lincoln told a Pennsylvania Republican leader that "the danger was past" because "after the expenditure of blood and treasure that has been poured out for the maintenance of the government and the preservation of the Union, the American people were not prepared to vote the war a failure." Shortly before the Chicago Convention, he had speculated that if the Democrats were to put McClellan "on a platform pledging the party to a vigorous prosecution of the war, . . . the result in November would not only be doubtful, but the chances were in favor of the Democracy."[5] He was doubtless right. Others guessed that if McClellan had more definitively repudiated the peace plank, Peace Democrats would have fielded a candidate of their own, and the general might have won the ensuing three-way race.

Among the Conservatives repelled by the doings at Chicago was Edward Everett, who had felt tempted to join a third-party movement but instead threw his support to the Republican ticket. The "golden opportunity which had been given to the Democrats by the folly of the Republicans was miserably thrown away," said former Massachusetts Governor John H. Clifford, who reluctantly decided to vote for Lincoln. He explained that if he had acted on his political principles and his personal inclinations, he would have backed McClellan, but Lincoln's reelection seemed to him essential because the general's letter of acceptance and his public support of the Democratic candidate in the 1863 Pennsylvania gubernatorial election created "a painful distrust of his moral strength." Moreover, his administration would be dominated by the "peace-at-any-price" faction that had controlled the Chicago Convention.[6] Though disenchanted with Lincoln, John Pendleton Kennedy of Baltimore could not bring himself to vote for McClellan and thereby elevate the Peace Democrats to power. (Kennedy thought the president had not prosecuted the war vigorously enough. In addition, he confided to a friend, "I especially dislike Abraham's bosom friends, or those, who have got into his bosom after the manner of the black snakes which are said to establish themselves as boarders with the prairie dogs.")[7]

Northern morale soared. As George Templeton Strong observed, the "general howl against the base policy offered for our endorsement at Chicago is refreshing. Bitter opponents of Lincoln join in it heartily."[8] One of those bitter opponents, abolitionist editor Theodore Tilton, confided to Anna E. Dickinson: "I was opposed to

Mr. Lincoln's nomination: but now it becomes the duty of all Unionists to present a united front." The Republican platform "is the best in American history—we can pardon something to a second-rate candidate." While Lincoln might not be the best possible nominee, it would be "criminal" to desert the Republican Party, which was "the only one that can save the country." To divide it would be "to give over the country to the Copperheads" and "bring everlasting shame upon us all."[9] Tilton campaigned so hard for the president that shortly before election day he fainted from exhaustion while addressing a crowd. Dickinson herself announced that she would stump for the Republican ticket. To a fellow Quaker who expressed surprise at her support of Lincoln, she explained that "this is no personal contest. I shall not work for Abraham Lincoln; I shall work for the salvation of my country's life, that stands at stake—for the defeat of this disloyal peace party, that will bring ruin and death if it come[s] into power."[10] Greeley's New York *Tribune* followed suit, declaring on September 6 that from then on, "we fly the banner of ABRAHAM LINCOLN for the next Presidency, choosing that far rather than Disunion and a quarter of century of wars . . . which our opponents would give us." The editorial gave credit to the president for doing "seven-eighths of the work in his fashion; there must be vigor and virtue enough left in him to do the other fraction. . . . We MUST re-elect him, and, God helping us, we WILL."[11] Greeley told Lincoln's chief personal secretary, "I shall fight like a savage in this campaign. I hate McClellan."[12]

Radical Republican leaders added their voices to the swelling pro-Lincoln chorus. Although in mid-September Charles Sumner said that "Lincoln's election would be disaster, but McClellan's damnation," and that he had "not quite given up the hope that even now someone might be substituted for Lincoln," the senator insisted that if the president would not withdraw, duty demanded that Republicans unite behind him. Sumner was as good as his word, delivering pro-Lincoln speeches in New York and Connecticut as well as the Bay State.[13] He argued that it was necessary to support the Republican ticket: "I do not see how anything can be done except through Mr. Lincoln and with his good-will." Republican unity "must be had at all hazards and at every sacrifice."[14] To a Boston audience he declared that "if Lincoln is slow, McClellan is slower," and rhetorically asked: "why consider these petty personalities? They divert attention from the single question, 'Are you for your country, or are you for the rebellion?'"[15] Ben Butler publicly asserted that "the plain duty of every loyal man" was "to support the election of Lincoln and Johnson," and Thaddeus Stevens told voters that if they reelected "the calm statesman who now presides over the nation," he "will lead you to an honorable peace and to permanent liberty."[16]

Frederick Douglass, who had signed the call for the Radical Democracy convention, publicly endorsed Lincoln in September. "When there was any shadow of a hope that a man of a more decided anti-slavery conviction and policy could be elected, I was not for Mr. Lincoln," he told a fellow abolitionist. "But as soon as the Chicago convention [adjourned], my mind was made up." In a letter which ran in the *Liberator*, Douglass acknowledged that "all hesitation ought to cease, and every man who wishes well to the slave and to the country should at once rally with all the warmth and earnestness of his nature to the support of Abraham Lincoln and Andrew Johnson."

Douglass did not actively campaign for the ticket because, as he explained, "Republican committees do not wish to expose themselves to the charge of being the 'N[igge]r party. The Negro is the deformed child, which is put out of the room when company comes."[17]

Other blacks followed Douglass's lead. On September 24, the publisher of the *Anglo-African* told his readers that "we may have thought that Mr. Lincoln has not done what *we think* he could have done for the overthrow of oppression in our land; *but that is not the question now.* The great and overshadowing inquiry is, *do you want to see the many noble acts which have been passed during Mr. Lincoln's administration repealed, and slavery fastened again upon Maryland, Louisiana, Tennessee, Virginia, and portions of States now free?* This is the only question now, and if you are a friend of liberty you will give your influence and cast your vote for Abraham Lincoln, who, under God, is the only hope of the oppressed."[18] John Rock, who would soon become the first black attorney to argue a case before the U.S. Supreme Court, told a convention of the National Association of Colored Citizens and Their Friends that there were only two parties: the "one headed by Lincoln is for Freedom and the Republic; and the other, by McClellan, is for Despotism and Slavery." The delegates applauded this statement loud and long.[19]

Even before the party nominating conventions, some blacks had called for Lincoln's reelection. On January 1, 1864, at a mass meeting of San Francisco blacks, a resolution was adopted endorsing the president for a second term. Commenting on that document, a black newspaper praised Lincoln as the only president who "has stood up in defiance of the slave-power, and dared officially to maintain the doctrine, by his official actions, that we are citizens, though of African descent—that the army and navy shall protect and defend such citizens in common with all others—that provision ought to be made for the education of freedmen."[20] A black resident of Brooklyn declared that Lincoln's actions had to be understood politically, for he had a racist constituency: "I feel that much of the failure of Mr. Lincoln to do [his] duty is owing to the failure of the people of the land whose agent he is. Do we complain that Mr. Lincoln and the government do not recognize the manhood of the negro? Let us find the cause of that in the people at home. Just so long as citizens of New York exclude respectable colored persons from railway cars on the streets; just so long as the people of the city exclude the colored children from the ward schools, and force the colored children from several wards together, on the ground of color merely; just so long as even in some of the churches of the city there are negro pews—just so long as there is evidence that the people themselves do not recognize the manhood of the black man of this country."[21] "As a negro, I am for the man whose party and policy have given us a free capital, a confiscation law, and a proclamation of freedom, as against the man who, with honest enough intentions, expects to drive out the devils by Beelzebub," said the Rev. Mr. J. Sella Martin of Boston.[22]

In Baltimore, a number of free blacks raised money for an expensive Bible that they presented to Lincoln on September 7. It was, they explained, "a testimonial of their appreciation of your humane conduct towards the people of our race. . . . Towards you, sir, our hearts will ever be warm with gratitude. . . . The loyal colored

people of this country everywhere will remember you at the Throne of Divine Grace."
Lincoln replied that "it has always been a sentiment with me that all mankind should
be free. So far as able, within my sphere, I have always acted as I believed to be right
and just; and I have done all I could for the good of mankind generally. In letters and
documents sent from this office I have expressed myself better than I now can. In
regard to this Great Book, I have but to say, it is the best gift God has given to man.
All the good the Saviour gave to the world was communicated through this book. But
for it we could not know right from wrong. All things most desirable for man's welfare, here and hereafter, are to be found portrayed in it."[23]

The following month Lincoln showed this volume to Sojourner Truth, the abolitionist preacher and famous rescuer of many of her fellow blacks from slavery. When
she complimented him as "the best President" ever, he replied: "I expect you have
reference to my having emancipated the slaves in my proclamation." He modestly
cited several predecessors, including Washington, who he said "were all just as good,
and would have done just as he had done if the time had come. If the people over the
river [pointing across the Potomac] had behaved themselves, I could not have done
what I have; but they did not, and I was compelled to do these things." She later said:
"I never was treated by any one with more kindness and cordiality than was shown me
by that great and good man."[24]

Most, but not all, Radicals and abolitionists fell into line. With his "well-known
extravagance," Parker Pillsbury, who felt a call to expose Lincoln's "hypocrisy and
cruelty," insisted that "I do not believe the slaves, or free colored people, have a worse
enemy on earth, than Lincoln." Even more hyperbolically, he declared that "Egypt
had its *ten* Plagues. For us, God seems to have massed them in one—a ten Pharaoh-
power Plague in Lincoln." Pillsbury scolded Theodore Tilton for making "apologies
for this Administration!"[25] Elizabeth Cady Stanton called the president "Dishonest
Abe," deplored "the incapacity and rottenness" of his administration, and pledged
that if he "is reelected I shall immediately leave the country for the Fijee Islands."[26]
She disagreed with her cousin Gerrit Smith, who counseled fellow abolitionists to
support the president's reelection. In August, Smith wrote: "Though it may be at the
expense of passing by our favorite candidate, we should nevertheless all feel ourselves
urged by the strongest possible motives to cast our votes . . . to defeat the compromising or sham Peace Candidate."[27] Two months later, he urged Stanton to reconsider
and expressed regret that "neither you nor Wendell Phillips can favor Lincoln's
re-election. I am spending a great deal for the election of Lincoln. I see safety in *his*
election."[28] She rejected his advice: "We need leaders to galvanize the virtue and patriotism of the nation into life and concentrate thought and action in the right directions." Among her criticisms of the president, she cited his failure to liberate all the
slaves and to do anything about atrocities committed against black troops. Her husband, Henry B. Stanton, voted for Lincoln but did not campaign for him. (Years later,
she regretted having opposed Lincoln: "I see now the wisdom of his course, leading
public opinion slowly but surely up to the final blow for freedom. . . . My conscience
pricks me now when I recall how I worked and prayed in 1864 for the defeat of Lincoln's re-election, and now I perceive what a grave misfortune it was that he was not

left to reconstruct the South according to what would surely have been a better and wiser plan than that [which was] pushed through by the Radicals with whom I then stood.")[29]

Moncure Conway, residing in England, continued his attacks on Lincoln, arguing that the president should be denied reelection because a black sergeant, William Walker, had been executed for inciting mutiny. (In fact, Walker's death sentence had been carried out illegally, before his case was submitted to the president for review. If the army had followed proper procedures, it is unlikely that Walker would have been shot.) Conway termed the "imbecile President" a "murderer," an "irredeemable Kentuckian," and "an impossible American" who suffered from "an utter lack of culture" and was "brutally ignorant of history and of his own age."[30] William Lloyd Garrison, also a target of Conway's scathing invective, warned an English correspondent that Conway did not represent most American abolitionists: "Impulsive, eccentric, reckless, highly imaginative and ambitious at the same time for 'radical' distinction, his flaming zeal is not always according to knowledge; and his wisdom is too apt to 'magnify molehills into mountains' and 'to give an inch the importance of a mile.'"[31] British abolitionists could scarcely believe that their American counterparts would do anything that might help McClellan's chances.

Elizur Wright had little use for Lincoln, who was, he said, "fighting for the exclusive privilege of *white* men under a Constitution made for *all* men . . . . I cannot see the use of protracting this agony by reelecting Lincoln." The president, in Wright's view, was neither honest nor loyal.[32] Wendell Phillips, who supported Frémont for president, wrote privately: "I would cut off my right hand before doing any thing to aid A. L.'s election—I wholly distrust his fitness to settle this thing—indeed his purpose."[33] In October at Boston, he publicly denounced the president's "halting, half-way course, neither hot nor cold, wanting to save the North without hurting the South." It was dictated not "from want of brains, but want of purpose, of willingness to strike home. . . . [O]bserve how tender the President has been towards the South, how unduly and dangerously reluctant he has been to approach the negro or use his aid. Vigorous, despotic, decisive everywhere else, he halts, hesitates, delays to hurt the South or help the negro." Phillips defiantly proclaimed, "I mean to agitate till I bayonet him and his party into justice."[34] ("We must *bully* the Govt!" he exclaimed to Maria Weston Chapman.)[35] At New York's Cooper Institute, he thundered against the administration's lack of "vigor," "will," "purpose," and "loyalty in the highest sense of the word." Moreover, Phillips argued, Lincoln was a tyrant who trampled on the liberties of the people and was planning to steal the election: "if President Lincoln is inaugurated for the next time on the votes of Louisiana, Tennessee, or Arkansas, every citizen is bound to resist him."[36]

Incredibly, Phillips denounced Lincoln for extraditing Don Jose Augustin Arguelles, a Cuban official accused of illegally selling 141 Africans into slavery. With the profits from that crime, Arguelles moved to the United States, which had no extradition treaty with Spain. Nonetheless, when the Cuban authorities asked that he be turned over, the Lincoln administration complied, justifying its action by citing the Constitution, international comity, and an 1842 treaty with Great Britain regarding attempts to shut down the international slave trade. This action represented, in the view of Phillips (and, ironically, many defenders of slavery), a case of kidnapping and a gross miscarriage of justice. (Seward remarked: "So far as depends on me, . . . Spanish slave-dealers who have no immunity in Havana, will find none in New York.")[37]

Phillips's anti-Lincoln stance alienated many of his fellow antislavery militants. Garrison said of the Boston speech: "We cannot allow it to pass without expressing our regret to perceive what seems to us a set purpose—*prima facie*—to represent Mr. Lincoln in the worst possible light, to attribute to him the worst possible motives, to hold him up as an imbecile and a despot, and to damage his chance of re-election to the utmost extent."[38] Though Oliver Johnson acknowledged that Lincoln "is not the man I wish he were," he was "very bitter towards Phillips" and thought the Brahmin orator's "glasses get smoky sometimes." Johnson deplored the way abolitionists "have wasted their power in foolish, factious and abortive ways, so that they will not have their due influence over Lincoln during his last term."[39] J. Miller McKim bemoaned Phillips' "recklessness of assertion" and likened such "destructives" as Stephen S. Foster, James Redpath, and Parker Pillsbury to Jacobins.[40] Harriet Martineau thought Phillips a demagogue; Maria Weston Chapman disagreed, believing that Phillips was "merely weakly mistaken, & *used* by demagogues."[41] Samuel May, Jr., bluntly told Phillips that "no man is infallible" and that "*your turn* to be wrong has come now."[42] Lincoln, May believed, was "greatly to be preferred to John C. Fremont *on Anti-Slavery grounds.*" In some allies of Phillips, May detected an "uneasy spirit of jealousy."[43] Theodore Tilton insisted that he "could do nothing but denounce the whole Cleveland movement, even though in so doing, I had to pierce the bosom of my dear friend Wendell Phillips."[44] Commenting on a Frémont rally at Cooper Union in late June, Tilton called it a "complete and disastrous Copperhead display" and noted that "genuine anti-slavery men who have joined this company are in great sorrow & confusion."[45] Some Radicals could not believe that Phillips was making common cause with John Cochrane, Frémont's running mate. "If Phillips drank, I could account for it," said one, but since he did not, "the coalition surpasses my comprehension."[46]

In addition to Garrison, Johnson, May, and Tilton, Phillips's quondam allies who disagreed with his stand included Henry Ward Beecher, Lydia Maria Child, Thomas Wentworth Higginson, J. Miller McKim, Maria Weston Chapman, Josephine Griffing, Mary Grew, Sarah Pugh, Henry C. Wright, Giles Stebbins, Andrew T. Foss, Gerrit Smith, Marius R. Robinson, Calvin Fairbank, Sallie Holley, Caroline Weston, Anne Weston, and Elizabeth Buffum Chace. Congressman William D. Kelley of Pennsylvania spoke for many of them when he said "Abraham Lincoln is the wisest radical of us all."[47] A Connecticut legislator who shared Kelley's view of Lincoln confessed that he had at times thought the president "was too slow, too cautious: too lenient &c, but on reflection I am led to regard him rather [as] discreet and possessed of a full share of foresight."[48] Wendell Phillips's namesake, Wendell Garrison, son of William Lloyd Garrison, regretted that Pillsbury, Foster, and Phillips were inclined "to distrust everybody, to endeavor by every ingenious device to find evidence that the government is the enemy of the black man & every officer under it unworthy to be trusted." He disapproved of their "[c]austic criticism, snap judgments,

& wholesale asseveration," as well as their tendency to have "only eyes for the shadows of the night & do not see the flood of daylight which is driving the blackness away."[49]

It was thus no wonder that in late August, Parker Pillsbury lamented to Phillips: "I came up from Boston last night, sick at heart. Almost every abolitionist I see now, swears by Lincoln, & denounces your course."[50] A month later, Elizabeth Cady Stanton similarly bemoaned the loss of support for a radical alternative to Lincoln. "[O]ne by one our giants are being swept down with the current," she complained to Susan B. Anthony.[51]

Victory in the Field

The Democrats' nomination of McClellan and adoption of a peace plank were not the only developments reviving Lincoln's chances. Less than a week after the Chicago Convention, Sherman captured Atlanta. Lincoln was not entirely surprised, for a short while earlier he had "said the public did not properly estimate our military prospects, results of which would change the present current." He added that he "relied upon this confidently."[52] More specifically, he predicted that Sherman would take Atlanta and that Farragut would capture Mobile. George Templeton Strong reflected the public mood when he wrote in his diary on September 3: "Glorious news this morning—*Atlanta taken at last*!!!" It was, Strong said, "(coming at this political crisis) the greatest event of the war."[53] Nicolay predicted that the "Atlanta victory alone ought to win the Presidential contest for us."[54] To his fiancée he explained on September 11 that the "political situation has not been as hopeful for six months past as it is just now. There is a perfect revolution in feeling. Three weeks ago, our friends everywhere were despondent, almost to the point of giving up the contest in despair. Now they are hopeful, jubilant, hard at work and confident of success."[55]

Sherman's triumph gave the lie to Democratic allegations that the war was a failure. So, too, did Admiral Farragut's defeat of the Confederate ironclad *Tennessee* and his capture of Mobile Bay in August. (A year earlier Lincoln had told Welles that he "thought there had not been, take it all in all, so good an appointment in either branch of the service as Farragut." According to Welles, "no man surpasses Farragut" in Lincoln's estimation.)[56] From upstate New York, former Congressman Charles B. Sedgwick, who had earlier been "in a despairing mood about Lincoln," reported that the "old enthusiasm is reviving" because "Atlanta and Mobile have lifted us out of the slough of despond."[57] Later in September, General Philip Sheridan trounced Jubal Early in the Shenandoah Valley, further discrediting the Democrats' charge of failure. After Union forces crushed Early at the battles of Winchester and Fisher's Hill, George William Curtis remarked that "Sheridan has opened Lincoln's campaign with such enthusiasm among the people as I never saw."[58] On September 23, as word of the general's victories arrived, Lincoln was immensely cheered and told such funny stories that listeners laughed till they were sore. He complimented the general: "This Sheridan is a little Irishman, but he is a big fighter."[59] Musing on Sheridan's accomplishments, Lincoln told a reporter: "General Grant does seem to be able to pick out the right man for the right place and at the right time. He is like that trip-hammer I saw the other day . . . . always certain in his movements, and always the same."[60]

Grant further boosted Northern morale with a widely-published letter stating that "all we want now to insure an early restoration of the Union is a determined unity of sentiment [in the] North. The rebels have now in their ranks their last man. . . . A man lost by them can not be replaced. They have robbed the cradle and the grave equally to get their present force. Besides what they lose in frequent skirmishes and battles they are now loosing from desertions and other causes at least one regiment per day. With this drain upon them the end is visible if we will but be true to ourselves. Their only hope now is in a divided North." Confederates "are exceedingly anxious to hold out until after the Presidential election. They have many hopes from its effects. They hope [for] a counter revolution. They hope [for] the election of the peace candidate."[61]

Lincoln proclaimed Sunday, September 11, a day of thanksgiving for the good news from Atlanta and Mobile Bay. When the Rev. Dr. Joseph P. Thompson commended his action, he replied: "I would be glad to give you such a proclamation every Sunday for a few weeks to come." Thompson asked whether the capture of Atlanta or the Democrats' blunder at Chicago had most improved his prospects for reelection. "I guess it was the victory," he said, "at any rate I'd rather have that repeated."[62]

To defuse the effect of Lincoln's Niagara Manifesto, some Republican newspapers hinted that the administration would negotiate for peace without making abolition a prerequisite. In addition, both Seward and Interior Secretary John P. Usher gave speeches to the same effect. Those two cabinet members denied that they spoke for the president, but their prominence led some to believe that they were in fact doing so, their protestations to the contrary notwithstanding. George B. Cheever, who thought Lincoln "absolutely incapable of the work given him to do" and devoid of "moral dignity and honesty," inferred from Seward's speech that the administration was willing to accept restoration of the Union with slavery intact. "This is Lincoln's arrangement," Cheever confided to his wife, "and being such, I am still entirely doubtful whether God will allow him to be reelected."[63] On the other hand, a Wisconsin Republican assured Lincoln that Seward's speech "has done much good to the Union cause," for it "has tended to calm the excited minds" of voters who objected to the Niagara Manifesto.[64]

Placating Both Radicals and Conservatives

With the fall of Atlanta, the dump-Lincoln movement abruptly collapsed. Thurlow Weed had described that effort to Seward as "equally formidable and vicious, embracing a larger number of leading Men than I supposed possible."[65] On September 20, the New York *Evening Post*, which had been sharply critical of Lincoln, approvingly noted that he "has gained wisdom by experience. Every year has seen our cause more successful; every year has seen abler generals, more skillful leaders, called to the head; every year has seen fewer errors, greater ability, greater energy, in the administration of affairs. . . . While Mr. Lincoln stays in power, this healthy and beneficial state of things will continue."[66] John Sherman, who had denigrated Lincoln and supported Chase's candidacy, now confided to his famous brother that the president was "better than so timid & unworthy a man as McClellan will be in the hands of such traitors as

Vallandigham."[67] The senator told fellow Ohioans that Lincoln's "solicitude for the public welfare is never-ceasing. I differed from him at first myself, but at last felt and believed that he was right, and shall vote for this brave, true, patriotic, kind-hearted man. All his faults and mistakes you have seen. All his virtues you can never know. His patience in labor is wonderful. He works far harder than any man in Erie County." To exchange such a leader for the "idle, incompetent" McClellan would "be a devilish poor trade."[68]

Frémont withdrew from the race, largely thanks to the efforts of Michigan Senator Zachariah Chandler, a self-appointed peacemaker who worked behind the scenes to unite the party. In August, he began his extensive shuttle diplomacy with a visit to Ben Wade, who realized that he had made a blunder by signing Henry Winter Davis's manifesto denouncing Lincoln. The senator was in the mood to reconcile with the president despite his personal aversion to him. When his good friend and ally Chandler asked him to stump for Lincoln, Wade agreed on condition that the president would dismiss Montgomery Blair. David H. Jerome of Detroit, a future governor of Michigan, was present at this interview and described it as "rather titanic."[69] Chandler approached Lincoln with Wade's request. (Massachusetts Senator Henry Wilson advised the president that "every one hates" the postmaster general and predicted that "tens of thousands of men will be lost to you or will give a reluctant vote on account of the Blairs.")[70]

Earlier, the president had petulantly dismissed suggestions that he fire Blair, who had acquired a reputation as a "political Ishmaelite, whose hand seems to be against every man."[71] When Thaddeus Stevens warned that the Republicans of Pennsylvania would not "work with a good will" unless Lincoln pledged to dismiss Blair, the president bristled. Expressing regret that he could not make such a promise, the president said with some heat: "If I were even myself inclined to make it, I have no right to do so. What right have I to promise you to remove Mr. Blair, and not make a similar promise to any other gentleman of influence to remove any other member of my cabinet whom he does not happen to like? The Republican party, wisely or unwisely has made me their nominee for President, without asking any such pledge at my hands. Is it proper that you should demand it, representing only a portion of that great party? Has it come to this that the voters of this country are asked to elect a man to be President—to be the Executive—to administer the government, and yet that this man is to have no will or discretion of his own? Am I to be the mere puppet of power—to have my constitutional advisers selected for me beforehand, to be told I must do this or leave that undone? It would be degrading to my manhood to consent to any such bargain—I was about to say it is equally degrading to your manhood to ask it."[72] When the Republican National Executive Committee asked for Blair's resignation in compliance with the party's platform, Lincoln flatly denied their request.

In August, Francis P. Blair, Sr., recognizing that his controversial offspring might damage Lincoln's reelection chances, told the president "that he might rely on my sons to do all they could for him," and suggested that Frank Blair be recalled from the army "to heal party divisions in Missouri & Stump the States." He added that Montgomery "would go the rounds also—and would be very willing to be a martyr to the

Radical phrenzy or jealousy, that would feed on the Blairs, if that would help." Lincoln replied that "nobody but enemies wanted Montg[omer]y out of the Cabinet" and that "he did not think it good policy to sacrifice a true friend to a false one or an avowed enemy." Still, he did appreciate Montgomery's generous offer to "cheerfully resign to conciliate the class of men who had made their war on the Blairs because they were his friends—and sought to injure him among the ignorant partizans of those seeking to supplant him."[73]

Lincoln changed his position on September 3, when he met with Senator Chandler, Elihu Washburne, Iowa Senator James Harlan, and James M. Edmunds, head of the Union League. According to Henry Winter Davis, who heard the story from Chandler, the four men "intimated that the country thought well" of Lincoln but that it was upset by his acceptance of Chase's resignation. If "he would remove Blair all might still be well." After the president defended his postmaster general in a lengthy review of events in Missouri, his callers replied that even if a case could be made for Blair, "still *all* who will vote for you think Blair false and untrustworthy and you can't convince them; so you must remove him or be defeated."

"But I don't want to desert a friend!" Lincoln exclaimed.

"Very possibly, but you will go down with him. What you say about Blair may be true—but nobody thinks so and everybody wants to get rid of him. Won't you let him go?"

"Well I'll think of it."

Chandler then said: "I am going to New York to see Wade; and probably if I could say you will remove Blair I could secure *his* support and get Fremont out of the way."

Lincoln exclaimed, "Well I think it may be done!"

The next morning Chandler told Lincoln "if Fremont could be induced to withdraw by giving up Blair he would do [arrange] it." To his wife, the senator confided that Lincoln "was most reluctant to come to terms *but came*."[74]

Chandler proceeded to New York on his mission, which Senator Harlan told him was so important that if he succeeded he would do more for the campaign that any ten men could do on the stump. In New York, Chandler was chagrined to discover that Wade had not arrived. Undaunted, Chandler carried on negotiations with Frémont and his advisors, David Dudley Field and George Wilkes. Frankly, Chandler informed Frémont that Lincoln would not withdraw; Chandler also insisted that the Republicans would lose unless the general abandoned his campaign. Moreover, Blair would be dismissed if Frémont quit. The Pathfinder promised to think it over.

Frémont received conflicting advice from his friends. Some abolitionists, like Wendell Phillips, counseled him to remain in the race, while others, like John Greenleaf Whittier, favored the opposite course. Colonel Nathaniel P. Sawyer, a leading Republican in Pittsburgh, urged him to "withdraw as soon as practicable in favor of Lincoln and Johnson" if he had "assurance of Mr. Blair's immediate removal and also Mr. Stanton's and the assurance that Mr. Seward will not be reappointed." Although Sawyer held a rather low opinion of the president, he pledged that if Frémont withdrew, he and former Pennsylvania Governor William F. Johnston would support Lincoln.[75]

The persistent Chandler followed Frémont to Massachusetts and kept pressing him. After further reflection, the general said he would quit without conditioning his action on Blair's dismissal. He now recognized that his cause was hopeless after the Democratic convention had failed to endorse him, and he did not wish to see Mc-Clellan in the White House. According to Jessie Benton Frémont, Whittier's advice—"There is a time to *do,* and a time to *stand aside*"—was the "deciding word" that persuaded her husband to withdraw.[76] Chandler feared that if Frémont did not make his resignation contingent on Blair's removal, Lincoln might retain the post-master general in office. After remonstrating with the Pathfinder in vain, Chandler hastened to inform Lincoln of Frémont's decision and ask for the *quid pro quo* that he had specified before undertaking his mission: Blair's dismissal.

When the Michigan senator made that demand, Lincoln replied: "Well, but I must do it in my own way to soften it." It is not known whether Chandler informed Lincoln that Frémont would quit even if Blair remained in the cabinet. Perhaps the president realized that he could keep Blair on, but still he may have decided to sacrifice him in order to placate Wade, Davis, and their allies.

Frémont's grudging letter of withdrawal, written on September 17 and published five days later, understandably displeased Lincoln. In a most ungracious fashion, the Pathfinder offered to support the Republican ticket: "In respect to Mr. Lincoln, I consider that his Administration has been politically, militarily, and financially a failure, and that its necessary continuance is a cause of regret for the country."[77] Lincoln was so put off that when Chandler called at the White House on September 22, the president "showed symptoms of flying from the bargain." But Chandler insisted that "the form of the withdrawal was not a condition; and offensive as it was, still it was a substantial advice to support L[incoln]."[78]

The president agreed and the next day asked Blair to honor his pledge to step down: "You have generously said to me more than once, that whenever your resignation could be a relief to me, it was at my disposal. The time has come. You very well know that this proceeds from no dissatisfaction of mine with you personally or officially. Your uniform kindness has been unsurpassed by that of any friend; and, while it is true that the war does not so greatly add to the difficulties of your Department, as to those of some others, it is yet much to say, as I most truly can, that in the three years and a half during which you have administered the General Post-Office, I remember no single complaint against you in connection therewith."[79]

The request surprised Blair, for he believed that opposition to him was waning. On September 23, he startled Bates and Welles with the news: "I suppose you are both aware that my head is decapitated—that I am no longer a member of the Cabinet." When Welles asked what was behind the president's decision, he "said he had no doubt he was a peace-offering to Frémont and his friends. They wanted an offering, and he was the victim whose sacrifice would propitiate them." Welles opined that "the suggestion of pacifying the partisans of Frémont might have been brought into consideration, but it was not the moving cause." Lincoln, he said, "would never have yielded to that, except under the pressing advisement, or deceptive appeals and representations of some one to whom he had given his confidence." Blair replied that "there is no doubt Seward was accessory to this, instigated and stimulated by Weed." Welles believed that Chase was "more influential than Seward in this matter."[80] To his wife, Blair complained that Lincoln "has given himself and me too, an unnecessary mortification in this matter," but added that "I am sure he acts from the best motives."[81] His brother-in-law, Gustavus Fox, thought Blair's dismissal "rather a summary process and does not appear to me to be frank and true, but politics is not made up of the finest mettle."[82]

Bitter though he may have been about Seward and Weed's influence with the White House, Blair responded to the president's letter handsomely: "I can not take leave of you without renewing the expressions of my gratitude for the uniform kindness which has marked your course towards [me.]"[83] He was pleased that Lincoln followed his father's advice by appointing as his replacement William Dennison, former governor of Ohio and a friend of the family. David Davis congratulated Lincoln on the selection, calling Dennison "honorable, highminded pure, & dignified" and "a wise & safe counsellor."[84] Davis's cousin, Henry Winter Davis, however, disagreed, but rejoiced that the president, whom he called a "mean and selfish old dog," had dismissed his chief antagonist: "Blair is gone! Our necks are relieved from that galling humiliation."[85] Blair's dismissal indicated to the Maryland congressman that "bullying may do something" and that Lincoln "thinks more of himself than of his friends."[86]

Lincoln told Welles that he needed to placate Radicals upset by Chase's departure while Blair was allowed to remain in the cabinet. Chase and his numerous friends believed that the retention of the postmaster general was "invidious, and the public would consider it a condemnation of himself [Chase] and an approval of the Blairs." The president trusted that Blair's dismissal "would reconcile all parties, and rid the Administration of irritating bickerings." As Welles later recalled, Lincoln at that time "was greatly embarrassed by contentions among his friends, by nominal Republicans, by intense radicals, and the strong front of the Democrats."[87]

Blair's abrasiveness had in fact alienated most of the cabinet. Bates considered him a "tricky politician" who lacked "the first conception of statesmanship."[88] Chase deeply resented Blair's private letters that Frémont had released years earlier in which the postmaster general said the treasury secretary "has more horror of seeing treasury notes below par than of seeing soldiers killed."[89] Blair and Chase had quarreled over patronage matters. When Blair dismissed Chase's friend Lewis Clephane from his position as postmaster of Washington, the treasury secretary appealed to Lincoln. As they discussed the matter, Blair entered the room and insisted that each department head could fire employees in his domain without consulting other cabinet members. Chase snapped back, "Very well, then according to your own rule, I appoint Mr. Clephane collector in this district in the place of your friend Bowen, *who is removed*!" Lincoln admonished them: "Take your own course, gentlemen, and do not bother me with your changes."[90] In addition, Blair and Stanton were not on speaking terms; upon learning that Chandler celebrated the dismissal of the postmaster general by having "a good drunk," the secretary of war "said he would like to have known when & where, that he might have had a hand in it."[91] Chandler rejoiced, boasting that he had "been successful in *all* that I undertook to do."[92] Blair was so quick to impugn the motives of others that Lincoln chided him gently: "It is much better not to be led from the region of reason into that of hot blood, by imputing to public men motives which they do not avow."[93]

As he campaigned for Lincoln that fall, Blair disingenuously contradicted Democratic charges that he had been sacrificed to appease the Radicals: "I retired on the recommendation of my father," who "would not permit a son of his to stand in the way of the glorious and patriotic President who leads us on to success and to the final triumph that is in store for us."[94] Indeed, Francis P. Blair, Sr., told his son Frank that the sacrifice of Montgomery "tends to give a greater certainty of the defeat of McClellan, which I look upon as the salvation of the Republic."[95] Discontent among Conservatives threatened to break into the open, but when Frank Blair learned that some of his friends intended to attack the president for dismissing his brother, he squelched their plans.

Bates regretted Lincoln's decision to let Blair go, for the Radicals now seemed in the ascendant. "I think Mr. Lincoln could have been elected without them and in spite of them," he confided to his diary. "In that event, the Country might have been governed, free from their *malign influences*, and more nearly in conformity to the constitution."[96] In Lincoln's view, however, the Conservatives were not totally marginalized. He speculated that if Montgomery Blair "will devote himself to the success of the national cause without exhibiting bad temper towards his opponents, he can set the Blair family up again."[97]

Lincoln's willingness to let Blair go was rooted in his understandable fear that Frémont might siphon off essential votes. The general was especially popular among Missouri Germans, who scorned Lincoln as the "great violator of the Constitution," a "still greater butcher of men," and one who "remains unmoved in the face of the greatest misery, and who can crack jokes like a Nero while Rome is burning."[98] In late August, the president asked a Baltimore Republican about the progress of the Frémont movement, which allegedly troubled him far more than did the upcoming Democratic convention. The president told Gustav Koerner that "he would lose . . . the German element, which held the balance of power in Missouri, Wisconsin, and Illinois."[99] The president may well have been thinking of the 1844 election, for, as the postmaster of Brooklyn observed, the "Fremont movement is a weak concern," but so too was the Liberty Party candidacy of James G. Birney that doomed Henry Clay's bid for the presidency.[100]

Lincoln was also eager to have Wade, Davis, and other Radicals rejoin the fold. Some administration critics hoped that Chase would publicly denounce Lincoln as he had done in private, and the president expressed fear that Chase would come out against him. But Hugh McCulloch, comptroller of the currency, met with Lincoln in September to help reconcile Chase and the president. During their conversation, Lincoln "made a frank statement of his kind feelings for Mr. Chase," thus "removing all cause for estrangement between them." Shortly thereafter Chase, eager for the seat on the Supreme Court that seemed likely to open soon, returned to the Midwest to campaign for Lincoln and Johnson.[101]

Reluctantly, other Radicals followed suit, for no alternative candidate—not Ben Butler, or Henry Winter Davis, or Daniel S. Dickinson—seemed viable. "[W]ere it not for the country there would be a poetical justice in his [Lincoln's] being beaten by that stupid ass McClellan," Wade told Chandler. "I can but wish the d[evi]l had Old Abe," but "to save the nation I am doing all for him that I possibly could do for a better man."[102] As good as his word, Wade stumped extensively throughout the Midwest. Chandler shared his friend's dim view of the president; in the midst of his diplomatic offensive to unite the party, he told his wife: "If it was only Abe Lincoln I would say, [']go to _____ in your own way, I will not stop a second to save you[.']" But he believed that more was involved than Lincoln's personal fortunes. At stake was "this great nation with all its hopes for the present & future," and therefore he could not "abandon the effort now."[103] And so he campaigned throughout the East as well as the Midwest.

Henry Winter Davis said he felt "so disgusted that he cannot talk," but pledged that he would give a pro-Lincoln speech if he could "get his disgust off sufficiently."[104] When Chandler urged him to follow Wade's lead, the Maryland congressman "expressed willingness to accept Blair's displacement as an olive branch and give his earnest support to the Baltimore ticket."[105] His support, however, was far from warm. In late September, he told a Maryland audience "that neither McClellan nor Lincoln were leading men of vigor equal to the place & that the only difference was that each would be what his Congress made him in spite of himself—McClellan would be compelled to peace even if he wished war & Lincoln would be compelled to wage the war & to execute the emancipation policy & [would be] firmly restrained from any ignominious or weak compromises."[106] According to a Radical ally of Davis, "on all occasions he deplores the cruel necessity of voting for him [Lincoln]." His speeches contained a simple message: the president "is neither wise nor honest, good people, but if *I* can vote for him, it would be rediculous for *you* to be more squeamish."[107]

Frémont's withdrawal, accompanied by Blair's dismissal, did not satisfy all malcontents. On the eve of the election, the abolitionist George B. Cheever feared that Lincoln's victory would spark riots throughout the North: "Choosing a man whose latest act has been the deliberate refusal to set free three millions of slaves by law, when God commanded, and the Congress in obedience to God, and in answer to the people, ordered the measure—choosing that man, I fear we set ourselves anew against God, and God against us. I fear lest it be followed by a new rebellion, and consequent disintegration of the Northern government."[108]

In addition to cultivating Radicals, Lincoln attempted to placate some Conservatives, including the prominent Peace Democrat, James W. Singleton of Illinois. According to one source, "Lincoln's immediate friends were working to make the [Democratic] nominee and platform of the party as odious as possible." In that effort "they were largely assisted" by Singleton, "who was one of the leaders of the anti-McClellan faction in the democratic party and a strong supporter of Vallandigham."[109] On August 4, Singleton presided over a mass meeting in Peoria, where banners proclaimed "Ours is a White Man's Government, Defile it not with Miscegenation" and resolutions were adopted denouncing the war as unwinnable and unconstitutional.[110] Two weeks later, at a similar gathering in Springfield, Singleton threatened to abandon the Democratic Party unless the Peoria resolutions were approved. The meeting ended amid fist-fights and bitter recrimination between the Singleton faction and more moderate Democrats. In September, Lincoln showed Singleton an embarrassing letter written by McClellan. Soon thereafter, Singleton delivered a scathing anti-McClellan speech. Coming from a Peace Democrat, his words carried weight with members of that faction. On October 18, he met at Cincinnati with other Peace Democrats to nominate a new presidential candidate. There he presided over an informal convention and helped draft a platform that defended slavery as a positive good, described the people of the Confederacy as "brothers in blood," and recommended that "we should make all possible efforts to join them in a mutual policy of unconditional negotiation for the attainment of peace." When Alexander Long declined to serve as the rump party's candidate, the convention adjourned without fielding a ticket. Since they could not agree on a standard-bearer, Singleton told the delegates that he was unable to support McClellan and preferred Lincoln. Subsequently, the president told Singleton: "you have done more than any one else to insure my reelection."[111]

Democratic Attacks

As usual, Democrats appealed shamelessly to race prejudice. A leading party newspaper alleged that Lincoln was descended from blacks. His peculiar character, "which has led so many to the belief that Mr. Lincoln is insane, is, we suspect, more rationally accounted for by the idea that he is the outcrop of a remote African in his ancestry." This conclusion was supported by his "physical and physiognomical proportions: his face and hands, and especially his feet, which, like his manners, testify strongly of the plantation." Moreover, "his buffoonery, his superstition, and his conscientiousness—which takes no cognizance of consequences, except such as are personal, to himself—is of the purest Congo; and his negro logic and rhetoric—which we have heretofore been inclined to attribute to his negro politics—is better accounted for upon the presumption of an earlier origin."[112] Democrats summarized the Republican platform thus:

> Hurrah for the nigger
> The sweet-scented nigger,
> And the paradise for the undertaker!
> Hurrah for Old Abe[113]

The issue of interracial sex, long a staple of Democratic campaign rhetoric, was more prominent than usual in 1864. The party's traditional appeal to anti-black prejudice received a new twist in the campaign. David Goodman Croly and George Wakeman, both of the New York *World,* coined a neologism for their anonymous anti-Republican pamphlet, *Miscegenation: The Theory of the Blending of the Races, Applied to the American White Man and Negro,* which was sent to leading antislavery spokesmen. (The common term for miscegenation before Croly and Wakeman's handiwork was *amalgamation.*) A fraud designed to trap its recipients into endorsing interracial marriage, the tract was purportedly written by an unnamed abolitionist advocating that policy. It was filled with bogus "facts" that shamelessly played on the

North's deep-seated Negrophobia. The most blatant appeal targeted the Irish, whom the document crudely denigrated. It concluded on a rousing note: "Let the Republican party go into the next contest with a platform worthy of itself; worthy of the events which have occurred during the last three years; worthy of the great future. Let the motto then of the great progressive party of this country be Freedom, Political and Social Equality; Universal Brotherhood." The few gullible abolitionists who fell for the hoax became the butt of Democratic ridicule, but the attempt to inveigle a prominent Republican into supporting it failed, and no branch of the party adopted it as a platform plank.[114] (In fact, a handful of abolitionists had spoken out in favor of interracial marriage before 1864.) In some Democratic circles, Republicans were referred to as "nigger fuggers."[115] When asked if he supported miscegenation, Lincoln wryly answered: "That's a [D]emocratic mode of producing good Union men, & I don't propose to infringe on the patent."[116]

The Democratic appeal to race prejudice alarmed some Republicans, including an Ohio judge who warned John Sherman: "This love and zeal for the nigger may be carried too far; the prejudice against social equality is just as strong now as ever; the hatred of the rebellion is such that the people, as a war measure, are in favor of emancipation; but this is the extent of their change of opinion, and it arises not from any love of the nigger."[117]

Lincoln could be sarcastic when confronting racist arguments. In August, an ungrammatical Pennsylvanian wrote him saying: "Equal Rights & Justice to all white men in the United States forever. White men is in class number one & black men is in class number two & must be governed by white men forever." Lincoln wrote a biting reply over the signature of Nicolay: "The President has received yours of yesterday, and is kindly paying attention to it. As it is my business to assist him whenever I can, I will thank you to inform me, for his use, whether you are either a white man or black one, because in either case, you can not be regarded as an entirely impartial judge. It may be that you belong to a third or fourth class of *yellow* or *red* men, in which case the impartiality of your judgment would be more apparent."[118]

Democrats abused the president roundly, calling him "a miserable failure, a coarse, filthy joker, a disgusting politician, a mean, cunning and cruel tyrant and the shame and disgrace of the Nation."[119] Congressman S. S. Cox ridiculed Lincoln as an "executive trifler," a "retailer of smutty stories," and a "tyrant over men's thoughts, presses, letters, persons, and lives."[120] Samuel F. B. Morse called Lincoln an "illiterate," "inhuman," "wicked," "*irreligious*" president "without brains," and a "coarse, vulgar, uncultivated man, an inventor or re-teller of stories so low and obscene, that no decent man can listen to them without disgust."[121] A Democratic newspaper in Connecticut bestowed the sobriquet "Old Smutty" on Lincoln, while the Cincinnati *Enquirer* scornfully remarked that if "there ever was a man who has become an object of detestation, that man is Lincoln. Since the days of the French revolution no such monstrosity has been elevated to the head of affairs."[122] Hysterically, that paper bemoaned "the threatened extinguishment of the experiment of free government," predicted that the fall elections might well be the last "to receive the votes of freemen," and declared that under "Abraham the First," the United States had become "the Russia of the Western Hemisphere."[123] A former mayor of Cincinnati was sure that Lincoln and his party "will proclaim themselves in power during the war. . . . I believe that Lincoln will not give up the idea of accomplishing the great idea of the war, though he may be compelled to resort to the *levy en masse*."[124] In Ohio's capital, Samuel Medary asserted that "everybody not crazy with 'negro on the brain'" knew that "Lincoln is running our country to perdition—destroying 'life, liberty and the pursuit of happiness'" as he sought to make himself a king.[125]

A New York magazine literally demonized Lincoln while praising his opponent: "McClellan is for adhering scrupulously to the rules of civilized warfare. Lincoln is for practicing to the extremest limits the brutal customs of savage warfare. McClellan is a Christian and a gentleman. Lincoln is a barbarian and a buffoon. McClellan is humane and tolerant in all his instincts and rules of action. Lincoln is infernal and implacable in every feeling and purpose. The difference between them may defined to be precisely that between a human being and a fiend; for Lincoln is an *infernal*. His face is a faithful chart of his soul; and his face is that of a demon, cunning, obscene, treacherous, lying and devilish. Gen. McClellan is the reverse of all this."[126] The New York *Daily News* called Lincoln an "[i]nsenate destroyer," a "bloody minded fanatic," a "thrice accursed agent of the destruction that has swept over this land, more terrible than the plagues of Egypt," and a "miserable demagogue" who "sits amid the ruin he has provoked with the leer of a satyr chuckling over the gratification of unnatural passions." The editors declared that they "know not what most to loathe in him, whether his coarseness and obscenity, his ruthless fanaticism, or his unscrupulous ambition."[127]

Some newspapers suggested that Lincoln be killed. In late August, the La Crosse, Wisconsin, *Democrat* declared that if the president were reelected, it would be well if someone assassinated him: "The man who votes for Lincoln now is a traitor. Lincoln is a traitor and murderer. He who, pretending to war for, wars against the constitution of our country is a traitor, and Lincoln is one of those men. He who calls and allures men to certain butchery, is a murderer, and Lincoln has done all this. . . . And if he is elected to misgovern for another four years, we trust some bold hand will pierce his heart with dagger point for the public good."[128] Similarly ominous was an editorial in the Albany *Atlas and Argus* paraphrasing a sentence from Patrick Henry's 1765 "treason" speech: "Caesar had his Brutus, Charles I his Cromwell . . . and we the People recommend Abraham Lincoln to profit by their example."[129] The Chicago *Times* darkly proclaimed that it was necessary to "ourselves and to posterity to relieve the nation in some way of a most intolerable weight of tyranny." If Lincoln could not be voted out of office, "then the next step is plain and inevitable. We leave its character to the development of the future."[130] In Pennsylvania, the Greensburg *Argus* declared that Lincoln's "defeat or his death is an indispensable condition to an honorable peace." When the editor heard of petitions calling for the suspension of the draft, he said: "Go one step further, brethren, and suspend Old Abe—by the neck if necessary to stop the accursed slaughter of our citizens."[131] The New York *Daily News* wished that Heaven would "direct its vengeance openly against the man who has drenched this fair land of ours with blood."[132]

Less sanguinary Democrats called for Lincoln's impeachment rather than his assassination. Others deplored his alleged indifference to the troops' suffering. Ex-Governor William Allen of Ohio maintained that the people "don't want a cold blooded joker at Washington who, while the District of Columbia is infested with hospitals, and the atmosphere burdened by the groans and sighs of our mangled countrymen, when he can spare a minute from Joe Miller's Jest Book looks out upon the acres of hospitals and inquires 'What houses are those?'"[133] Such charges reached a peak when the New York *World* alleged that Lincoln had asked Ward Hill Lamon to sing a popular ditty while they were accompanying McClellan on a tour of the corpse-strewn Antietam battlefield. According to that flagship Democratic journal, the president said: "Come, Lamon, give us that song about Picayune Butler; McClellan has never heard it."

"Not now, if you please," McClellan purportedly remarked. "I would prefer to hear it some other place and time."[134]

This bogus story inspired some Democratic doggerel:

> Abe may crack his jolly jokes
> O'er bloody fields of stricken battle,
> While yet the ebbing life-tide smokes
> From men that die like butchered cattle;
> He, ere yet the guns grow cold,
> To pimps and pets may crack his stories.[135]

When Lamon wrote a blistering denial, Lincoln advised him not to release it: "I would not publish this; it is too belligerent in its tone. You are at times too fond of a fight. There is a heap of wickedness mixed up with your usual amiability. If I were you, I'd state the facts as they were. I would give the statement as you have it without the cussedness. Let me try my hand at it."[136] Taking pen in hand, Lincoln carefully and slowly composed a long letter for his friend's signature. After drafting it, Lincoln told Lamon: "You know, Hill, that this is the truth and the whole truth about that affair; but I dislike to appear as an apologist for an act of my own which I know was right. Keep this paper, and we will see about it."[137] The document was not released to the press.

When Democrats charged that Lincoln received his salary in gold while other government employees were paid in greenbacks, the treasurer of the United States, Francis E. Spinner, denied it, explaining that by law the president's salary was issued in monthly warrant drafts, minus income tax. Rather than drawing money on those drafts, Lincoln left them sitting in his drawer for long periods (in one case eleven months) without receiving any interest. Several times Spinner urged him to cash the warrants, pointing out that he was losing hundreds of dollars in interest. When Lincoln asked who gained thereby, Spinner said the U.S. Treasury. "I reckon the Treasury needs it more than I do," the president replied. By failing to cash his warrants, Lincoln had in effect contributed $4,000 to the treasury.[138]

More responsible criticism of the administration came from former Whigs like Robert C. Winthrop, whose oration at New London, Connecticut, was (in Lincoln's

view) the best pro-McClellan speech of the campaign. Winthrop deplored what he
considered violations of the Constitution and attempts to overthrow the social structure of the South. Senator Reverdy Johnson of Maryland, who had supported Lincoln
in 1860, four years later deplored his "utter unfitness for the presidency" and accused
him of employing the "most unscrupulous and unexampled abuse of patronage and
power."[139] Ex-Whig friends in Illinois like John Todd Stuart and Orville H. Browning had grown disenchanted with Lincoln. "I am personally attached to the President,
and have faithfully tried to uphold him, and make him respectable," Browning wrote
on September 6, "tho' I never have been able to persuade myself that he was big
enough for his position. Still, I thought he might get through, as many a boy has got
through College, without disgrace, and without knowledge, but I fear he is a failure."[140] Browning nonetheless told Lincoln he could campaign for him, and he did,
though lukewarmly.

The First Lady under Attack

Democrats also attacked Mary Lincoln. According to the New York *World*, when she
ordered $800 worth of china from E. V. Haughwout & Co., she tried to hide other
purchases, amounting to $1,500, by having the total bill ($2,300) applied to the china
alone; when Interior Secretary Smith raised questions, the merchant reportedly acknowledged that the overcharge was made to disguise the unspecified items. Haughwout & Co. denied the allegations in a letter to Manton Marble, editor of the *World*.
In turn, Marble defended the story, and rather than retracting it, threatened to "expose what I know about Mrs. Lincoln's practices in her New York purchases—her
silver service—the champagne[,] manure bills etc. etc. to say nothing of wallpaper,
seed commissions, shawls, contracts, etc. etc. etc."[141] Commenting on these scandals,
a New York Democratic matron remarked: "It is humiliating to all American women
who have to economize and struggle and part with their husbands, sons, and brothers
in these sad times, to see this creature sitting in the highest place as a specimen of
American womanhood."[142]

The *World*'s charges were credible. John Watt, the White House gardener who
colluded with Mrs. Lincoln in various schemes to defraud the government, claimed
that "a bill of $6,000 contracted with Haughwout & Co. for silverware was paid for
by a bill charged against gilding gas-fixtures."[143] According to a Maryland journalist,
Mrs. Lincoln "once bought a lot of China for $1,500 in New York & made the seller
give her $1,500 in cash & send in a bill for $3,000. When Lincoln refused to put his
signature to the Bill prior to sending it to the Department to be paid, on the ground
that it was exorbitant, [the merchant said,] 'You forget, sir, . . . that I gave Mrs Lincoln $1500.[']"[144]

The *World* also accused Mary Lincoln of appropriating $7,000 of public money
for her "personal adornment" and of sending used White House furniture to Springfield rather than putting it up for auction, as the law required.[145] Shortly before election day, Democratic papers ran a scathing account of the First Lady's imperious and
tightfisted ways. In 1862, they alleged, a dentist had been summoned to the White
House to remove an aching tooth from one of the residents. After performing the

emergency surgery, he was asked by Mary Lincoln what he charged. She balked when he said $2.50, insisting that she had never paid more than 50 cents for such services. Offended, he replied that did not make house calls for such a small amount and would charge nothing. As he prepared to leave, Lincoln paid him the requested fee. The First Lady was accused of treating hoteliers, theater proprietors, and merchants in the same fashion. At a Boston hotel she allegedly "had a most wordy discussion with the head bookkeeper, a scene appropriate rather to the Fulton [Fish] Market than to the best chambers of the best hostelry." In Washington she was reportedly "in the habit of ordering a row of the best seats at Grover's or Ford's [theaters] and sweeping out of them without any gratuity." When she sent word to one of those establishments to reserve two private boxes, the treasurer asked for money. When told that "Mrs. Lincoln never pays anything," he replied: "Then, d[am]n me, if she can have any box in this theater at all." In New York she offended dry goods dealers, who regarded her as "very mean." Allegedly, when she visited Alexander T. Stewart's fabled department store, she would "pull down all the goods in the place, bully the clerks, falsify or question their additions, and, in the end, leave without settling her bills." As a result, some upscale store owners vowed that they would have no further dealings with her.[146]

One such emporium was Genin's hat shop. While sitting in her carriage, Mrs. Lincoln imperiously summoned a clerk who was speaking with a friend at the front door. The clerk ignored her. When informed that the First Lady was beckoning, he "replied somewhat indifferently, that he did not care" and that he recognized no "difference between Mrs. Lincoln and the wife of a mechanic. If she will come into the store, I will attend to her, but I am not employed to wait on people in the street."[147] A Democratic paper in Ohio, astounded at reports that Mary Lincoln had spent $5,000 for a shawl and $3,000 for earrings and a pin, asked where "the money comes from that enables this very ordinary lawyer from Illinois . . . to live in this style, when the poor man can barely with the strictest economy after paying his taxes, get bread to eat?"[148]

The First Lady uneasily observed the campaign. In March, when a spiritualist told her that the president would be defeated, she returned to the White House inconsolably "crying *like a child*."[149] In response to such outbursts, Lincoln chided her gently: "Mary, I am afraid you will be punished for this overweening anxiety. If I am to be re-elected, it will be all right; if not, you must bear the disappointment." Her nervousness stemmed from fear that if Lincoln lost, her creditors would descend on her. She confessed to her close friend Elizabeth Keckly, "I have contracted large debts of which he [Lincoln] knows nothing, and which he will be unable to pay if he is defeated." She identified them as "store bills," principally from Alexander T. Stewart's emporium in New York. "You understand, Lizabeth, that Mr. Lincoln has but little idea of the expense of a woman's wardrobe. He glances at my rich dresses, and is happy in the belief that the few hundred dollars that I obtain from him supply all my wants. The people scrutinize every article that I wear with critical curiosity. The very fact of having grown up in the West, subjects me to more searching observation. To keep up appearances, I must have money—more than Mr. Lincoln can spare for me. He is too honest to make a penny outside of his salary; consequently I had, and still have, no alternative but to run in debt." She kept Lincoln in the dark about her spendthrift ways because, she explained, "If he knew that his wife was involved to the extent that she is, the knowledge would drive him mad. He is so sincere and straightforward himself, that he is shocked by the duplicity of others. He does not know a thing about any debts, and I value his happiness, not to speak of my own, too much to allow him to know anything. This is what troubles me so much. If he is re-elected, I can keep him in ignorance of my affairs."[150]

The First Lady owed the New York firm of Ball, Black & Company several thousand dollars for jewelry she had purchased without her husband's knowledge. From another jeweler she made purchases totaling $3,200 in a three-month span. Included among the items selected were four clocks as well as two diamond-and-pearl bracelets. In one month she bought eighty-four pairs of gloves. In March 1865, she spent $2,288 at the Galt & Bro. jewelry store in Washington. (It was not just as First Lady that she was given to extravagance; earlier in Springfield, Lincoln had to chide her for mismanaging the household funds.) At one point she tearfully begged Isaac Newton, head of the agriculture bureau in the Interior Department, to help her pay bills she had run up at a furrier. New York politico Simeon Draper agreed to do so, but after Lincoln's death he reneged.

Mary Lincoln's spending reflected her impulsive nature. Julia Taft Bayne, who as an adolescent visited the White House often, recalled that it "was an outstanding characteristic of Mary Todd Lincoln that she wanted what she wanted when she wanted it and no substitute!" Julia remembered how the First Lady coveted a special ribbon in her mother's bonnet and brazenly asked her to give it over. The astonished Mrs. Taft complied.[151]

To help her husband win reelection, Mary Lincoln tricked lobbyists into giving her money. She confided to Elizabeth Keckly: "I have an object in view, Lizabeth. In a political canvass it is policy to cultivate every element of strength. These men have influence, and we require influence to re-elect Mr. Lincoln. I will be clever to them until after the election, and then, if we remain at the White House, I will drop every one of them, and let them know very plainly that I only made tools of them. They are an unprincipled set, and I don't mind a little double-dealing with them." When asked if the president was aware of such schemes, she exclaimed: "God! no; he would never sanction such a proceeding, so I keep him in the dark, and will tell him of it when all is over. He is too honest to take proper care of his own interests, so I feel it to be my duty to electioneer for him."[152]

Mary Lincoln's spendthrift ways did not please Union soldiers. "I can hardly wish that Mrs. Lincoln should occupy the White House for four years longer," a supporter of Lincoln's reelection remarked. "Her want of sympathy with the loyal ladies of the North—our mothers and sisters, who to their arduous labors in behalf of our soldiers in the field and in the hospitals, have added dispensing with expensive luxuries that our National finances may be thereby improved, is not at all to her credit."[153]

The Prisoner of War Issue

The Democratic platform deplored the "shameful disregard of the Administration to its duty in respect to our fellow-citizens who now are and long have been prisoners of war and in a suffering condition."[154] In 1861, when urged by a member of the U.S. Sanitary Commission to exchange prisoners, Lincoln replied: "I feel just as you do about this matter. I don't like to think of our men suffering in the Southern prisons, neither do I like to think that the Southern men are suffering in our prisons; but you don't want me to recognize the Southern Confederacy, do you? I can't propose an exchange of prisoners without recognizing the existence of the Confederate Government."[155] Lincoln did, however, informally encourage a limited exchange of sick and wounded POWs. When asked in the fall of 1861 why he could not expand that to a general exchange, "he said that the main trouble grew out of the fact that he had not capital enough, in the shape of prisoners, to venture upon very liberal expenditures of this sort."[156]

The following year, both sides agreed to an exchange cartel that worked effectively for ten months, but once the Union began recruiting blacks, the agreement fell apart. The Confederates would not exchange ex-slaves they captured in uniform. In response, the Lincoln administration ended the cartel. Stanton said that to acquiesce in a discriminatory system of exchanges would constitute "a shameful dishonor . . . . When they [the Confederates] agree to exchange all alike there will be no difficulty."[157] The result was untold suffering by thousands of federal and Rebel troops in prison camps like Andersonville in Georgia and Johnson's Island in Lake Erie. Further stiffening Northern resistance to exchanges was the discovery that many of the 40,000 Rebel soldiers paroled at Vicksburg and Port Hudson were later found fighting once again in the Confederate ranks in violation of their word of honor. In late 1863, Lincoln complained that critics who had blamed him earlier for not completely suspending the exchange of prisoners were now demanding that he accept the terms of Jefferson Davis, who refused to exchange black POWs and their white officers.

In the summer of 1864, the North became outraged by the stories of Union POWs suffering badly at the grossly overcrowded Andersonville prison and elsewhere. As pressure mounted, Lincoln would not budge as long as the Confederates refused to exchange former slaves serving in the Union army. The Jefferson Davis government "excited the rage and disgust of Mr. Lincoln" by compelling black POWs to help fortify Mobile rather than exchanging them for captured Rebels.[158] The Confederates finally yielded in January 1865, when they were planning to recruit black troops. The POW issue played a relatively small role in the presidential campaign.

Counterattack: The Treason Issue

Republicans countered Democratic rhetoric by charging that secret societies like the Sons of Liberty and the Order of American Knights were committing treason. In October, Judge Advocate General Joseph Holt released a 14,000-word report accusing such organizations of treasonable conduct. Lincoln expressed skepticism about the Sons of Liberty, calling it "a mere political organization, with about as much of malice and as much of puerility as the Knights of the Golden Circle." In June, Clement L. Vallandigham had returned from exile to serve as "Supreme Grand Commander" of the Sons. Rather than re-arrest him, Lincoln thought it best to let him sow dissension in the Democratic ranks. In late 1863, Fernando Wood, a leading

Peace Democrat, urged the president "to publish some sort of amnesty for the northern sympathizers and abettors or rebellion, which would include Vallandigham, and permit him to return." Wood promised that if the president "would so do, they would have two Democratic candidates in the field at the next Presidential election."[159] Senator Edwin D. Morgan gave similar advice. To John Hay, Lincoln explained "that the question for the Government to decide is whether it can afford to disregard the contempt of authority & breach of discipline displayed in Vallandigham's unauthorized return: for the rest, it cannot but result in benefit to the Union cause to have so violent and indiscreet a man go to Chicago as a firebrand to his own party." According to Hay, Lincoln had long beforehand "seriously thought of annulling the sentence of exile but had been too much occupied to do it."[160] He may have hesitated because Ohio Senators John Sherman and Benjamin Wade warned him in 1863 "that if his order of banishment was revoked, it would result in riots and violence."[161]

In late June 1864, Lincoln drafted a letter instructing authorities in Ohio to watch Vallandigham closely, report his activities to Washington, and take him into custody only if he worked "any palpable injury" or presented an "iminent danger to the Military." But on second thought, he decided to withhold the order.[162] When Kentuckians protesting against the arrest of one of their own (Colonel Frank Walford of the First Kentucky Cavalry) asked Lincoln why he did not apprehend Vallandigham, he allegedly replied "that he had not been officially notified" of the Ohioan's return, "but whenever he learned certainly that he [Vallandigham] was making . . . speeches [discouraging enlistments] he would arrest him at once." Senator Lazarus Powell indignantly rejected that explanation: "No, sir, you won't; you are afraid to arrest him again, and you know full well if you undertake it 260,000 freemen of the state of Ohio will rush to his rescue. You dare not make the experiment."[163]

Lincoln's skepticism to the contrary notwithstanding, there was some truth in the Republican allegations about dangerous sedition. Confederate agents did in fact conspire with leading Northern Democrats to liberate prisoners of war, to seize high-ranking state officials, to stir uprisings on election day in Chicago and New York, and to induce Midwestern states to secede. The most conspicuous example was the attempt of pro-Confederate forces in southern Indiana to arm insurrectionaries. Four leaders of that scheme were tried and condemned to death. (In 1866, in a landmark decision, the Supreme Court threw out their conviction on procedural grounds, maintaining that military courts could not operate in areas where civil courts were open.)

Wooing New York and the Border States

Lincoln worried about his chances in New York, which he had won only narrowly in 1860. Republicans were not at all sure that they could again prevail. George William Curtis of Long Island told Charles Eliot Norton: "we have a very desperate political campaign before us, and we need all our friends. I wish with all my heart they were pluckier. The cause is so transcendent that even to fail in it is incomparably more glorious than to win with its opponents."[164] To the Republican gubernatorial candidate, Reuben Fenton, Lincoln expressed concern about Thurlow Weed's disaffection: "I am anxious for New York, and we must put our heads together and see if the matter can't be fixed."[165] Weed and his allies were, Lincoln noted in June, on "the verge of open revolt."[166] The New York boss objected not only to administration policies but also to the men who received lucrative government posts.

Trouble had been brewing for months as the Greeley wing of the Republican Party continued battling the Seward–Weed forces over New York patronage, especially in the customhouse. Such intraparty squabbles dismayed Lincoln, who naturally feared their impact on Republican electoral chances. Just as Missouri Republicans felt hurt when the president criticized their "pestilent factional quarrel," so too Weed was disgruntled when he heard that Lincoln regarded a controversy between him and Greeley as a personal quarrel. In October 1863, the hyper-defensive Weed complained to the president that his "'quarrells' are in no sense *personal*. I am without personal objects or interests. I have done something in my day towards Electing Presidents and Governors, none of whom have found me an expensive Partizan."[167] Lincoln tactfully apologized to the thin-skinned Weed for hurting his feelings: "I have been brought to fear recently that somehow, by commission or omission, I have caused you some degree of pain. I have never entertained an unkind feeling or a disparaging thought towards you; and if I have said or done anything which has been construed into such unkindness or disparagement, it has been misconstrued. I am sure if we could meet we would not part with any unpleasant impression on either side."[168]

The following year, speaking of the New York customhouse, Weed insisted "that the infamies of the Appraisers Office required the Removal of [John T.] Hogeboom and [Isaac O.] Hunt. . . . It is not alone that these men are against Mr Lincoln, but they disgrace the office—a Department everywhere spoken of as a 'Den of Thieves.'"[169] Hogeboom allegedly wrote articles for the New York *Standard & Statesman* criticizing Lincoln. In March 1864, Weed exploded in wrath when the president, to humor Chase, appointed Hogeboom general appraiser. "Mr. Lincoln not only spurns his friends . . . but *Promotes* an enemy who ought to be Removed!" Weed exclaimed. "After *this* outrage and insult," he added, "I will cease to annoy him [Lincoln] . . . . I feel this keenly because it subjects me to the mortification of learning that the President has no respect for my opinions."

Weed complained to Lincoln's intimate friend, David Davis, that almost "all the Office-holders appointed through our enemies, are now Mr. Lincoln's Enemies. My Friends, though 'out in the cold,' are the Friends of the President."[170] In despair, he confessed to Davis that he was "greatly discouraged," for he feared that "ultra Abolitionists will destroy our Government and Union. The war cannot go on, at the rate of blood and treasure it has cost . . . without Revolution or Anarchy." Weed's feelings were hurt because Lincoln and Stanton approved his plan to win the war but then failed to implement it.[171] He begged Davis to inform the president "distinctly and emphatically, that if this Custom House is left in custody of those who have for two years sent 'aid and comfort' to the enemy, *his* fitness for President will be questioned."[172]

After consulting with Lincoln, Justice Davis reported back to Weed that it "pains him very evidently when you are not satisfied with what he does. He stated to me that he had the highest esteem for you, knew that you was patriotic & that it hurt him when he could not do what you thought advisable. He feels the necessity for a change [in the New York customhouse], but it seems to me that he fears that he w[oul]d at the present get from one muss to another. I think he ought to act & act promptly. But his mind is constituted differently from yours and mine. We will have to await the slowness of his movements about this important matter." Lincoln protested that he was Weed's friend and wanted Lord Thurlow to be his.[173]

In an attempt to pacify Weed, the president sent Nicolay to New York with a note stating that he had been "pained and surprised" to learn that Lord Thurlow felt "wounded." Lincoln said he was "pained, because I very much wish you to have no unpleasant feeling proceeding from me, and surprised, because my impression is that I have seen you, since the last Message issued, apparently feeling very cheerful and happy. How is this?"[174]

Through Nicolay, Weed expressed concern for Lincoln's political future. High-ranking officials in the New York customhouse, including the collector and his principal assistants, were working against his renomination, he warned. Moreover, the appraiser's bureau "had been engaged in treasonably aiding the rebellion." In January 1864, Lincoln had told Weed that he would look into the matter, but by late March he had done nothing about replacing the "incapable and unworthy" men who infested not only the customhouse but also the cabinet, which, in Weed's view, was "notoriously weak and inharmonious—no Cabinet at all—gives the President no support. Welles is a cypher, Bates a fogy, and Blair at best a dangerous friend." Moreover, even though "Chase was not formidable as a candidate in the field," still "by the shrewd dodge of a withdrawal" the treasury secretary was "likely to turn up again with more strength than ever." Weed protested to Nicolay that his highest ambition was "not to get office for himself, but to assist in putting good men in the right places. If he was good for anything, it was as an outsider to give valuable suggestions to an administration that would give him its confidence." He feared that he did not enjoy Lincoln's complete confidence and that the president "only regarded him with a certain degree of leniency" and as "not quite so great a rascal as his enemies charged him with being."[175]

In August 1864, Lincoln once again sent Nicolay to placate Weed. Lord Thurlow and Henry J. Raymond urged that immediate changes be made in the leadership of the customhouse. Nicolay found the assignment "very delicate, disagreeable and arduous" but derived satisfaction from his ability to help broker a deal. Hiram Barney, collector, and Rufus Andrews, surveyor, were replaced by Simeon Draper and Abram Wakeman, respectively. Those changes, along with others in several lesser customhouse posts, and the appointment of James Kelly as postmaster of New York, satisfied Weed. Nicolay asked Barney to resign "as a *personal* and *political* favor of great value & importance" to the president, for it would "relieve him from political embarrassments" and lay "him under great obligations." Nicolay assured him of Lincoln's "personal kind regard and continued friendship."[176] To demonstrate his goodwill, the president intended to offer Barney the post of minister to Portugal.

Draper's appointment displeased some Republicans. John Murray Forbes called him "a mere pipe layer & wire puller—windy, pompous, and with a very damaged mercantile reputation."[177] Gideon Welles termed the appointment of the "corrupt" Draper "abominable" and predicted that it "will beget distrust in the Administration."[178]

At the Brooklyn Navy Yard, similar problems emerged. The head of the New York Union State Committee reported to Henry J. Raymond that almost half of the employees at that huge facility "are hostile to the present Administration, and will oppose the reelection of Mr. Lincoln. Of this number there are Mechanics in the different departments who must be retained, but I have no doubt that of the 6,000 to 7,000 employed it will not be necessary for the efficient working of the departments to retain as many as 1,000 who are opposed to us."[179] Raymond wanted to fire workers there who did not support the administration, and to assess each employee 5 percent of his pay to line the party's coffers. Political assessments were common in other departments, but Gideon Welles forbade them at navy yards. Unable to make progress with the navy secretary, Weed and Raymond pestered Lincoln, who said he would defer to Welles. But the navy secretary doubted that the president would long resist the New Yorkers' pressure. Lincoln's "convictions and good sense will place him with me," Welles speculated, but Weed and Raymond "will alarm him with forebodings of disaster if he is not vindictive."[180] The secretary was right, for in October dozens of workmen in the Brooklyn Yard were dismissed on political grounds.

Lincoln did not, however, make all the changes desired by New York politicos. To one of them, who demanded the removal of an official who opposed the president's renomination, Lincoln impatiently snapped: "You cannot think _____ to be half as mean to me as I know him to be, but I can not run this thing upon the theory that every officeholder must think I am the greatest man in the nation, and I will not." The offending critic kept his job.[181] Similarly, Lincoln restored an officer to the army after Stanton had dismissed him for giving a pro-McClellan speech. "Supporting General McClellan for the Presidency is no violation of army regulations," said the president, adding puckishly that "as a question of taste of choosing between him and me, well, I'm the longest, but he's better looking."[182] When warned that he was about to appoint a bitter opponent of his renomination to an important post, Lincoln remarked: "I suppose that Judge —, having been disappointed before, did behave pretty ugly; but that wouldn't make him any less fit for this place, and I have a Scriptural authority for appointing him. You recollect that while the Lord on Mount Sinai was getting out a commission for Aaron, that same Aaron was at the foot of the mountain making a false god, a golden calf, for the people to worship; yet Aaron got his commission, you know." On another occasion, Lincoln appointed a former opponent over the objections of current friends. To them Lincoln observed that no one "will deny that he is a first-rate man for the place, and I am bound to see that his opposition to me personally shall not interfere with my giving the people a good officer."[183]

The changes in the New York customhouse did not please everyone. The Greeley faction of the party was especially upset. "I am so utterly disgusted with Lincoln's behavior that I cannot muster respectful terms in which to write him," grumbled William Cullen Bryant.[184] Rumor had it that Weed was still discontent and spoke disparagingly of Lincoln two days before the election in the hopes of defeating him in New York.

Another internecine battle in New York irritated Lincoln. A substantial number of Republican leaders in former Congressman Roscoe Conkling's upstate district

announced that they would not support his candidacy even though the party had officially nominated him. Lincoln wrote: "I am for the regular nominee in all cases; and
that no one could be more satisfactory to me as the nominee in that District, than Mr.
Conkling. I do not mean to say there [are] not others as good as he in the District; but
I think I know him to be at least good enough."[185]

Indiana Congressman George W. Julian confronted a similar problem when a
newspaper controlled by Commissioner of Patents David P. Holloway refused to support him for reelection, after the incumbent had won the party's primary. When Julian complained to Lincoln, the president assured him: "Your nomination is as binding
on Republicans as mine, and you can rest assured that Mr. Holloway shall support
you, openly and unconditionally, or lose his head." Upon learning that Holloway ignored his directive to do so, Lincoln called for his messenger and exclaimed: "Tell
Mr. Holloway to come to me!" Taken aback by the president's unwonted vehemence,
the messenger hesitated, prompting an even more emphatic order: "*Tell Mr. Holloway
to come to me!*"[186] The commissioner's newspaper soon endorsed Julian.

Lincoln also had to intervene when the postmaster of Philadelphia, Cornelius
Walborn, refused to back Congressman William D. Kelley for reelection. The president summoned Walborn and gently chided him: "Complaint is made to me that you
are using your official power to defeat Judge Kell[e]y's renomination to Congress. I
am well satisfied with Judge Kell[e]y as an M.C. and I do not know that the man who
might supplant him would be as satisfactory; but the correct principle, I think, is that
all our friends should have absolute freedom of choice among our friends. My wish
therefore is that you will do just as you think fit with your own suffrage in the case,
and not constrain any of your subordinates to do other than as he thinks fit with
his."[187] Walborn promised to do as told, but he did not; when informed that almost all
of the hundreds of postmasters under his jurisdiction were opposing Kelley, Lincoln
asked an influential Philadelphia Republican to instruct Walborn that "he must find
a way to relieve me from the suspicion that he is not keeping his promise to me in
good faith."[188] Kelley won reelection. When John Locke Scripps, postmaster at Chicago and an old friend of Lincoln, refused to support Congressman Isaac N. Arnold's
reelection bid, the president sent him a copy of the letter to Walborn.

Lincoln's remarkable ability to harmonize factions helped assure his reelection
and Northern victory in the war. To Leonard Swett, he remarked: "I may not have
made as great a President as some other men, but I believe I have kept these discordant elements together as well as anyone could."[189]

In addition to New York, Lincoln worried about the Border States, whose voters,
like many Conservatives throughout the North, disliked both the Emancipation
Proclamation and the enlistment of black troops. In Missouri, Charcoals and Claybanks continued to wrangle. To combat their chronic divisiveness, Lincoln dispatched
Nicolay to St. Louis, where he spent a week conferring with various Republican leaders. The young emissary managed to promote enough harmony so that Republicans
swept the state that fall. In the summer, when a leading Claybank, Charles Gibson,
publicly resigned his government post with a blast at the Baltimore platform, Lincoln
wrote a response that went out over the signature of Hay: the president "thanks

Mr. Gibson for his acknowledgment that he has been treated with personal kindness and consideration; and he says he knows of but two small draw-backs upon Mr. Gibson's right to still receive such treatment, one of which is that he never could learn of his giving much attention to the duties of his office, and the other is this studied attempt of Mr. Gibson's to stab him."[190]

Hostility to Lincoln had grown especially acute in Kentucky. "*The nigger is Kentucky politics*," reported an Ohioan serving as the collector of customs at Louisville. He caustically and accurately summarized the attitude of Unionists in the Blue Grass State: "Save the nigger: save the country if you can, but—save the nigger. Hold on to slavery: hold on to the Union if you can, but—hold on to Slavery. Take care of your great domestic institution: take care of your liberties if you can, but—take care of your great domestic institution. . . . Damn Abe Lincoln and his Cabinet: help fight the rebels if that will keep your State from being overrun by them and your homes from pillage and your wives and daughters from ravishment, but—damn Abe Lincoln and his Cabinet. Call them fools, knaves, imbeciles, abolitionists, despots, anything you please that's ugly: call upon them to protect you from invasion whenever invasion is threatened by the naked and hungry hordes under arms in Dixie who long for the flesh-pots on which you fatten, but—call them the hardest names your vocabulary can supply."[191]

In late March 1864, when a Kentucky delegation consisting of Governor Thomas E. Bramlette, former Senator Archibald Dixon, and newspaper editor Albert G. Hodges called at the White House, the president made a brief speech to them, which he subsequently wrote out at Hodges's request. It was one of his most masterful public letters, addressing head-on their complaints about his policies. In it he sought to convince them that circumstances had forced him to liberate the slaves and employ blacks in the army. He began by frankly acknowledging his hostility to slavery. "I am naturally anti-slavery. If slavery is not wrong, nothing is wrong. I can not remember when I did not so think, and feel." But he insisted that his hatred for slavery had not determined his policies because he felt duty-bound to honor his oath of office: "I have never understood that the Presidency conferred upon me an unrestricted right to act officially upon this judgment and feeling. It was in the oath I took that I would, to the best of my ability, preserve, protect, and defend the Constitution of the United States. I could not take the office without taking the oath. Nor was it my view that I might take an oath to get power, and break the oath in using the power. I understood, too, that in ordinary civil administration this oath even forbade me to practically indulge my primary abstract judgment on the moral question of slavery. I had publicly declared this many times, and in many ways. And I aver that, to this day, I have done no official act in mere deference to my abstract judgment and feeling on slavery. I did understand however, that my oath to preserve the constitution to the best of my ability, imposed upon me the duty of preserving, by every indispensable means, that government—that nation—of which that constitution was the organic law. Was it possible to lose the nation, and yet preserve the constitution? By general law life *and* limb must be protected; yet often a limb must be amputated to save a life; but a life is never wisely given to save a limb. I felt that measures, otherwise unconstitutional, might become lawful, by becoming indispensable to the preservation of the constitution, through the preservation of the nation. Right or wrong, I assumed this ground, and now avow it. I could not feel that, to the best of my ability, I had even tried to preserve the constitution, if, to save slavery, or any minor matter, I should permit the wreck of government, country, and Constitution all together."

Lincoln reminded his callers that he had overruled emancipation orders by John C. Frémont in 1861 and David Hunter in 1862 and had objected to Simon Cameron's call, in his 1861 annual report, for arming blacks. At the time, he thought there was no "indispensable necessity" for those measures. As a further indication of his essentially moderate approach to slavery, he cited his appeals in March, May, and July 1862 to the Border State delegations to accept compensated emancipation, for, he said, he "believed the indispensable necessity for military emancipation, and arming the blacks would come, unless averted by that measure." After they rejected his advice, he said he was "driven to the alternative of either surrendering the Union, and with it, the Constitution, or of laying strong hand upon the colored element. I chose the latter." That policy proved successful, for over a year after emancipation had been declared, the North had suffered "no loss by it in our foreign relations, none in our home popular sentiment, none in our white military force,—no loss by it any how or any where. On the contrary, it shows a gain of quite a hundred and thirty thousand soldiers, seamen, and laborers. These are palpable facts, about which, as facts, there can be no cavilling. We have the men; and we could not have had them without the measure."

Lincoln challenged any Unionist "who complains of the measure" to "test himself by writing down in one line that he is for subduing the rebellion by force of arms; and in the next, that he is for taking these hundred and thirty thousand men from the Union side, and placing them where they would be but for the measure he condemns. If he can not face his case so stated, it is only because he can not face the truth."

In the letter to Hodges, Lincoln supplemented his earlier verbal remarks, for he wished the public to understand that the steps he took were to some extent necessitated by the will of the Almighty: "In telling this tale I attempt no compliment to my own sagacity. I claim not to have controlled events, but confess plainly that events have controlled me. Now, at the end of three years struggle the nation's condition is not what either party, or any man devised, or expected. God alone can claim it. Whither it is tending seems plain. If God now wills the removal of a great wrong, and wills also that we of the North as well as you of the South, shall pay fairly for our complicity in that wrong, impartial history will find therein new cause to attest and revere the justice and goodness of God."[192]

Divining the Divine Will

Like his 1862 letter to Horace Greeley, this missive was a campaign document designed to reassure Moderates and Conservatives that the president was scrupulously obeying the Constitution and not willfully imposing his own ideological views on the public. Both letters have been misunderstood as profoundly revealing documents shedding light on Lincoln's innermost thoughts and feelings. To be sure, the frank acknowledgment of his long-standing hatred of slavery was candid. But the implication that he was essentially the plaything of forces beyond his control is misleading. Lincoln was a forceful leader who used the power of his office tactfully but assertively, recognizing with characteristic fatalism that while he could shape events up to a point, larger forces were at work than his own will. His attitude toward fate resembled what the twentieth-century theologian Reinhold Niebuhr expressed in his "serenity prayer": "God grant me the serenity to accept the things I cannot change; the courage to change the things I can; and the wisdom to know the difference."

In September 1864, Lincoln told Eliza Gurney, a Quaker leader, of his belief in the power of the Almighty to shape events. "The purposes of the Almighty are perfect, and must prevail, though we erring mortals may fail to accurately perceive them in advance. We hoped for a happy termination of this terrible war long before this; but God knows best, and has ruled otherwise. We shall yet acknowledge His wisdom and our own error therein. Meanwhile we must work earnestly in the best light He gives us, trusting that so working still conduces to the great ends He ordains. Surely He intends some great good to follow this mighty convulsion, which no mortal could make, and no mortal could stay."[193]

In a private memo, probably written in the summer of 1864, Lincoln ruminated on the Lord's intentions. Dismayed by the terrible bloodshed of the stalled campaigns, he asked why a benevolent deity would allow it. "The will of God prevails. In great contests each party claims to act in accordance with the will of God. Both *may* be, and one *must* be wrong. God can not be *for*, and *against* the same thing at the same time. In the present civil war it is quite possible that God's purpose is something different from the purpose of either party—and yet the human instrumentalities, working just as they do, are of the best adaptation to effect His purpose. I am almost ready to say this is probably true—that God wills this contest, and wills that it shall not end yet. By his mere quiet power, on the minds of the now contestants, He could have either *saved* or *destroyed* the Union without a human contest. Yet the contest began. And having begun He could give the final victory to either side any day. Yet the contest proceeds."[194]

By March 1865, Lincoln had reached a conclusion about the will of God that he was to share with the public in his second inaugural address. But before he could be inaugurated once more, he must win reelection.

Although Lincoln issued no public letters other than the one to Albert G. Hodges during the election campaign, he did draft one in response to an invitation to address a mass meeting in Buffalo. In that missive he defended his decision to go to war, blaming the Confederates for starting the conflict. "Much is being said about peace; and no man desires peace more ardently than I. Still I am yet unprepared to give up the Union for a peace which, so achieved, could not be of much duration. The preservation of our Union was *not* the sole avowed object for which the war was commenced. It was commenced for precisely the reverse object—*to destroy our Union*. The insurgents commenced it by firing upon the Star of the West, and on Fort Sumpter, and by other similar acts. It is true, however, that the administration accepted the war thus commenced, for the sole avowed object of preserving our Union; and it is not true that it has since been, or will be, prossecuted by this administration, for any other object.

In declaring this, I only declare what I can know, and do know to be true, and what no other man can know to be false."

Addressing emancipation and the employment of black troops, he reiterated arguments he had made to his Wisconsin visitors and in his open letter to Hodges: "my present position in reference to the rebellion is the result of my best judgment, and according to that best judgment, it is the only position upon which any Executive can or could save the Union. Any substantial departure from it insures the success of the rebellion. An armistice—a cessation of hostilities—is the end of the struggle, and the insurgents would be in peaceable possession of all that has been struggled for. Any different policy in regard to the colored man, deprives us of his help, and this is more than we can bear. We can not spare the hundred and forty or fifty thousand now serving us as soldiers, seamen, and laborers. This is not a question of sentiment or taste, but one of physical force which may be measured and estimated as horse-power and Steam-power are measured and estimated. Keep it and you can save the Union. Throw it away, and the Union goes with it. Nor is it possible for any Administration to retain the service of these people with the express or implied understanding that upon the first convenient occasion, they are to be re-inslaved. It *can* not be; and it *ought* not to be."

Lincoln decided not to release this document. As he explained to the chief organizer of the Buffalo event, "I believe it is not customary for one holding the office, and being a candidate for re-election, to do so." Moreover, "a public letter must be written with some care, and at some expense of time, so that having begun with your meeting, I could not well refuse others, and yet could not get through with all having equal claims."[195]

Defining the Significance of the War

During the campaign, the president did speak informally to regiments calling at the White House. In those brief speeches, he pithily and eloquently summarized the Union cause. "I wish it might be more generally and universally understood what the country is now engaged in," he told the 164th Ohio in mid-August. "We have, as all will agree, a free Government, where every man has a right to be equal with every other man. In this great struggle, this form of Government and every form of human right is endangered if our enemies succeed. There is more involved in this contest than is realized by every one. There is involved in this struggle the question whether your children and my children shall enjoy the privileges we have enjoyed." Do not let side issues distract your attention, he urged. "There may be mistakes made sometimes; things may be done wrong while the officers of the Government do all they can to prevent mistakes. But I beg of you, as citizens of this great Republic, not to let your minds be carried off from the great work we have before us. This struggle is too large for you to be diverted from it by any small matter. When you return to your homes rise up to the height of a generation of men worthy of a free Government, and we will carry out the great work we have commenced."[196]

A few days thereafter, Lincoln told another Ohio regiment that "I almost always feel inclined, when I happen to say anything to soldiers, to impress upon them in a few brief remarks the importance of success in this contest. It is not merely for to-day, but for all time to come that we should perpetuate for our children's children this great and free government, which we have enjoyed all our lives. I beg you to remember this, not merely for my sake, but for yours. I happen temporarily to occupy this big White House. I am a living witness that any one of your children may look to come here as my father's child has. It is in order that each of you may have through this free government which we have enjoyed, an open field and a fair chance for your industry, enterprise and intelligence; that you may all have equal privileges in the race of life, with all its desirable human aspirations. It is for this the struggle should be maintained, that we may not lose our birthright—not only for one, but for two or three years. The nation is worth fighting for, to secure such an inestimable jewel."[197]

These brief, informal addresses rank among the best of Lincoln's spontaneous utterances and demonstrate his exceptional ability to address the public without a prepared text.

Celebrating Emancipation in Maryland

In October, Lincoln responded to civilian serenaders congratulating him on the emancipationists' victory in Maryland. Behind the scenes he had helped promote their cause, for he believed that its success "would aid much to end the rebellion."[198] Six months earlier, as voters in the Free State prepared to decide whether to summon a new constitutional convention, he wrote the recently elected Congressman John A. J. Creswell that he was "very anxious for emancipation to be effected in Maryland in some substantial form." He feared that his "expressions of a preference for *gradual* over *immediate* emancipation, are misunderstood." He "had thought the *gradual* would produce less confusion, and destitution, and therefore would be more satisfactory; but if those who are better acquainted with the subject, and are more deeply interested in it, prefer the *immediate,* most certainly" he had "no objection to their judgment prevailing." He wished "that all who are for emancipation in *any form,* shall co-operate, all treating all respectfully, and all adopting and acting upon the major[ity] opinion, when fairly ascertained." He was afraid "that by jealousies, rivalries, and consequent ill-blood—driving one another out of meetings and conventions—perchance from the polls—the friends of emancipation themselves may divide, and lose the measure altogether." Lincoln instructed Creswell not to make his letter public, but the congressman was free to let people know that anyone agreeing with its sentiments would not "be in any danger of contradiction" from the White House.[199]

Lincoln also shared his concern with the newly appointed commander of the Middle Department, Lew Wallace. When that general called at the White House, the president said at the close of their conversation, "I came near forgetting that there is an election nearly due over in Maryland, but don't *you* forget it." He urged Wallace "to be fair, but to give the benefit of all doubts to the emancipationists." Stanton, who had opposed assigning Wallace to a command, gravely explained to the general that the "Maryland legislature passed an act for an election looking to the abolition of slavery in the state by constitutional amendment. The President has set his heart on the abolition in that way; and mark, he don't want it to be said by anybody that the bayonet had anything to do with the election. He is a candidate for a second nomination. You understand?"[200]

Perversely, Henry Winter Davis, who scorned compensation for slave owners, predicted that "in spite of the Pres[iden]t.'s ill will, we will carry the constitutional conv[ention] for emancipation."[201] But it was in part *because* of Lincoln's support, as well as Wallace's tactful adherence to his instructions, that the pro-convention forces triumphed handily in the spring.

Shortly after that emancipationist victory, Lincoln helped open the Baltimore Sanitary Fair with a speech congratulating the people of Maryland for promoting the cause of liberty: "The world has never had a good definition of the word liberty, and the American people, just now, are much in want of one. We all declare for liberty; but in using the same *word* we do not all mean the same *thing*. With some the word liberty may mean for each man to do as he pleases with himself, and the product of his labor; while with others the same word may mean for some men to do as they please with other men, and the product of other men's labor. Here are two, not only different, but incompatable things, called by the same name—liberty. And it follows that each of the things is, by the respective parties, called by two different and incompatable names—liberty and tyranny." With some sarcasm, he observed that the "shepherd drives the wolf from the sheep's throat, for which the sheep thanks the shepherd as a *liberator*, while the wolf denounces him for the same act as the destroyer of liberty, especially as the sheep was a black one. Plainly the sheep and the wolf are not agreed upon a definition of the word liberty; and precisely the same difference prevails to-day among us human creatures, even in the North, and all professing to love liberty. Hence we behold the processes by which thousands are daily passing from under the yoke of bondage, hailed by some as the advance of liberty, and bewailed by others as the destruction of all liberty. Recently, as it seems, the people of Maryland have been doing something to define liberty; and thanks to them that, in what they have done, the wolf's dictionary, has been repudiated."[202]

In early September, the Maryland constitutional convention voted to outlaw slavery. Late in the month, when William L. W. Seabrook, commissioner of the Maryland land office, expressed skepticism about the proposed constitution's chances for ratification, Lincoln exclaimed: "You alarm me sir! you alarm me! you alarm me! I did not dream there was the slightest danger of such a calamity as the defeat of this Constitution. I fear you and others of our friends in Maryland are not alive to the importance of this matter and its influence upon the conflict in which we are engaged. The adoption of your Constitution abolishing slavery will be equal to a victory by one of our armies in the field. It will be a notification to the South that, no matter what the result of the war shall be, Maryland is lost to that section forever. I implore you, sir, to go to work and endeavor to induce others to go to work for your Constitution, with all your energy. Try to impress other unionists with its importance as a war measure, and don't let it fail! Don't let it fail."[203] To help bolster the pro-ratification cause, Lincoln urged Henry W. Hoffman, collector of the port of Baltimore and chairman of the Maryland Unconditional Union Central Committee, to harmonize Maryland's Republican factions.

On the eve of the vote, Lincoln sent a letter to be read at a pro-constitution rally: "I presume the only feature of the instrument, about which there is serious controversy, is that which provides for the extinction of slavery. It needs not to be a secret, and I presume it is no secret, that I wish success to this provision. I desire it on every consideration. I wish all men to be free. I wish the material prosperity of the already free which I feel sure the extinction of slavery would bring. I wish to see, in process of disappearing, that only thing which ever could bring this nation to civil war. I attempt no argument. Argument upon the question is already exhausted by the abler, better informed, and more immediately interested sons of Maryland herself. I only add that I shall be gratified exceedingly if the good people of the State shall, by their votes, ratify the new constitution."[204] As the ratification vote approached, Lincoln was informed that Henry Winter Davis was still bad-mouthing him; in response, the president said that if the congressman "and the rest can succeed in carrying the state for emancipation, I shall be very willing to lose the electoral vote."[205]

On October 12, Maryland voters ratified the constitution by the narrow margin of 30,174 to 29,799 (50.3% to 49.7%). Only the soldier vote (2,633 to 263) enabled it to win. Abolitionists rejoiced. "Glory to God!" exclaimed Lydia Maria Child. "This is marvelous progress. Glory to God! Hallelujah!"[206]

Lincoln, too, was delighted. To Charles H. Philbrick, an Illinoisan who had recently joined the White House staff to assist his friends Nicolay and Hay, Lincoln remarked that the outcome of the Maryland vote "was a victory worth double the number of electoral votes of the state because of its moral influence."[207] Similarly, the president confided to Noah Brooks: "I had rather have Maryland upon that issue than have a State twice its size upon the Presidential issue; it cleans up a piece of ground." Brooks observed that anyone "who has ever had to do with 'cleaning up' a piece of ground, digging out vicious roots and demolishing old stumps, can appreciate the homely simile applied to Maryland."[208]

When several hundred black residents of Washington descended on the White House to celebrate the new Maryland constitution, he told them: "It is no secret that I have wished, and still do wish, mankind everywhere to be free. [Great cheering and cries of 'God bless Abraham Lincoln.'] And in the State of Maryland how great an advance has been made in this direction. It is difficult to realize that in that State, where human slavery has existed for ages, ever since a period long before any here were born—by the action of her own citizens—the soil is made forever free. [Loud and long cheering.] I have no feeling of triumph over those who were opposed to this measure and who voted against it, but I do believe that it will result in good in the white race as well as to those who have been made free by this action of emancipation, and I hope that the time will soon come when all will see that the perpetuation of freedom for all in Maryland is best for the interests of all, though some may thereby be made to suffer temporary pecuniary loss. And I hope that you, colored people, who have been emancipated, will use this great boon which had been given you to improve yourselves, both morally and intellectually."[209]

That night Lincoln addressed another issue when a group of Marylanders serenaded him. Democrats had been warning that the president would cling to power no matter how the election turned out. A former Ohio congressman speculated that even if the Democratic candidate won the presidency, the Republicans "will proclaim themselves in power during the war."[210] The *Illinois State Register* echoed the charge. Lending credence to this speculation was a widely read speech delivered by Seward in October, arguing that Lincoln had been chosen president of all the states but had not actually served in that capacity, since several states had seceded. The opposition press interpreted Seward's remarks as a sure sign that Lincoln would not relinquish the White House if defeated. To the Maryland serenaders, the president (who was reportedly unhappy about Seward's speech) insisted that it was not his intention "to ruin the government." To the contrary, said he, "I am struggling to maintain government, not to overthrow it. I am struggling especially to prevent others from overthrowing it. I therefore say, that if I shall live, I shall remain President until the fourth of next March; and that whoever shall be constitutionally elected therefor in November, shall be duly installed as President on the fourth of March; and that in the interval I shall do my utmost that whoever is to hold the helm for the next voyage, shall start with the best possible chance to save the ship. This is due to the people both on principle, and under the constitution. Their will, constitutionally expressed, is the ultimate law for all. If they should deliberately resolve to have immediate peace even at the loss of their country, and their liberty, I know not the power or the right to resist them. It is their own business, and they must do as they please with their own. I believe, however, they are still resolved to preserve their country and their liberty; and in this, in office or out of it, I am resolved to stand by them."[211]

Presidential Anger

Lincoln's anger burst forth toward the end of the presidential campaign when a delegation from Tennessee called to protest the strict loyalty oath that Governor Andrew Johnson had prescribed for would-be voters. (An applicant for the franchise had to swear that he was "an active friend of the Government of the United States, and the enemy of the so-called Confederate States," that he "ardently desire[d] the suppression of the present rebellion," that he "sincerely rejoice[d] in the triumph of the armies and navies of the United States," and "cordially oppose[d] all armistices or negotiations for peace with rebels in arms.")[212] The Tennesseeans submitted a petition implying that Lincoln was abusing his power.

In reply, the president impatiently asked: "May I inquire how long it took you and the New-York politicians to concoct that paper?" (In fact, New York Democratic leaders complained with some justice that the oath virtually "commands every loyal citizen of Tennessee to vote for the Republican candidate or to abstain from the polls.")[213] The delegation's spokesman, John Lellyett, insisted that it accurately represented the opinion of the people of Tennessee. Lincoln snorted: "I expect to let the friends of George B. McClellan manage their side of this contest in their own way; and I will manage my side of it in my way."[214] Democrats denounced this "undignified and rude" response from "our coarse despot" as "an exhibition of party spite and petulance."[215] (A week later the president sent the Tennesseeans a far more civil response in which he asserted somewhat disingenuously that he had no control over the governor, Andrew Johnson, whom he had appointed.)

William O. Stoddard ascribed such intemperate presidential outbursts to stress and overwork. "To such an extent was his absorbed devotion to business carried that the perpetual strain upon his nervous system, with the utter want of all exercise, began to tell seriously upon his health and spirits . . . . Even his temper suffered, and a petulance entirely foreign to his natural disposition was beginning to show itself as a symptom of an overtasked brain."[216] Noah Brooks also observed that as the war progressed, Lincoln's "hearty, blithesome, genial, and wiry" spirit changed: "The old, clear laugh never came back; the even temper was sometimes disturbed; and his natural charity for all was often turned into an unwonted suspicion of the motives of men." Mary Lincoln also acknowledged that when "worn down," her husband "spoke crabbedly to men, harshly so."[217]

During the Christmas season of 1864, Lincoln was beseeched to pardon a condemned soldier whose mother wanted to plead in her son's behalf. He exclaimed angrily: "There is no use of her coming here crying about me. I can't do anything for her." The chaplain escorting her then explained that he wished to represent the interests of the accused lad and some other young men. "Well," the president asked, "suppose they were old men, with families to support, would that make it any better?" Eventually he relented.[218]

Much as he enjoyed storytelling, Lincoln disliked being asked to tell stories as if he were a professional entertainer. On one occasion, a visitor to Washington accosted him just as he mounted a horse: "I thought I would call and see you before leaving the city and hear you tell a story." The president asked where he lived. "Western New York," came the answer. "Well, that's a good enough country without stories," replied Lincoln and rode off.[219]

Though Lincoln lost patience more frequently as time passed, it was remarkable that (as Stoddard put it) "he generally succeeds in keeping down the storm which is continually stirred up within him by the treacheries, cowardices, villainies and stupidities, which, almost daily and hourly, he is compelled to see and understand and wrestle with and overcome."[220]

The Soldier Vote

Lincoln had blamed the 1862 political reverses on the inability of many soldiers to vote. In order to prevent a recurrence of that electoral setback, nineteen states had passed laws allowing troops to cast ballots in the field or by proxy; Indiana, Illinois, Delaware, Oregon, Massachusetts, and New Jersey, however, had not done so. At Lincoln's suggestion, William E. Chandler of New Hampshire wrote a campaign pamphlet chronicling the Democrats' strong opposition to such legislation. Indiana Republican leaders warned that their state would go Democratic in the October gubernatorial election unless the draft were delayed and 15,000 soldiers were furloughed so that they could return home to vote. So in mid-September, Lincoln appealed to General Sherman: "The State election of Indiana occurs on the 11th. of October, and the loss of it to the friends of the Government would go far towards losing the whole Union cause. The bad effect upon the November election, and especially the giving the State Government to those who will oppose the war in every possible way, are too much to risk, if it can possibly be avoided. The draft proceeds, notwithstanding its strong tendency to lose us the State. Indiana is the only important State, voting in October, whose soldiers cannot vote in the field. Any thing you can safely do to let her soldiers, or any part of them, go home and vote at the State election, will be greatly in point. They need not remain for the Presidential election, but may return to you at once. This is, in no sense, an order, but is merely intended to impress you with the importance, to the army itself, of your doing all you safely can, yourself being the judge of what you can safely do."[221] Sherman, who did not much admire the president, furloughed only sick and wounded troops, numbering around 9,000. (The general complained that Lincoln allowed himself to be "pulled hither & thither by every shade of policy—trimming his sails to every puff of wind.")[222]

One soldier who obtained leave was especially important to the Republican campaign: General John A. Logan. A brave commander especially admired by Lincoln, Logan stumped throughout Illinois on behalf of the Republican ticket. A former Democratic congressman from southern Illinois, he had become a devoted Republican and highly capable general. When the president asked him to leave his command temporarily to take to the hustings, Logan complied and did yeoman service.

Another political general who was granted a leave, Carl Schurz, had significant influence among German voters. In early 1864, Schurz asked Lincoln for a furlough in order to take the stump. The president at first discouraged him: "Allow me to suggest that if you wish to remain in the military service, it is very dangerous for you to get temporarily out of it; because, with a Major General once out, it is next to impossible for even the President to get him in again. With my appreciation of your ability, and correct principle, of course I would be very glad to have your service for the country in the approaching political canvass; but I fear we can not properly have it, without separating you from the military."[223] But as political prospects became ever more bleak in August, Lincoln invited Schurz to Washington, where he approved the general's plan to give several campaign speeches.

Unlike many of his fellow Radicals, Schurz admired Lincoln extravagantly. In October, he penned a ringing defense of the president. "The main thing," Schurz told a European friend who had criticized Lincoln, "is that the policy of the government moves in the right direction—that is to say, the slaveholder will be overthrown and slavery abolished. Whether it moves in that direction prudently or imprudently, slowly or rapidly, is a matter of indifference as against the question of whether a policy should be adopted which would move in another, an opposite and destructive, direction." To be sure, he conceded, Lincoln "does not understand artifices of speech and attitude," nor was he highly educated. His manners "harmonize little with the European conception of the dignity of a ruler." For all that, he was "a man of profound feeling, just and firm principles, and incorruptible integrity." He possessed "sound common sense" to "a marvelous degree." Schurz confessed that he had "often criticized him severely," and later "found that he [Lincoln] was right." Such as they were, the president's weaknesses were those "of a good man." His personality had "a quite peculiar significance" in the Civil War, for he personified the people, and "that is the secret of his popularity." His administration "is the most representative that has ever existed in world history." Presciently, Schurz speculated that within fifty years or less, "Lincoln's name will stand written upon the honor roll of the American Republic next to that of Washington, and there it will remain for all time. The children of those who now disparage him will bless him."[224]

During their conversation, Lincoln primed Schurz for his campaign swing, emphasizing heavily that "the Executive could do many things by virtue of the war power, which Congress could not do in the way of ordinary legislation." As Schurz left, the president told him: "Well, things might look better, and they might look worse. Go in, and let us all do the best we can."[225] Schurz pitched in, repeating Lincoln's arguments before several audiences; his efforts helped keep the German vote in the Republican column.

Serving that same political end was Berlin-born Francis Lieber, the aggressive chief of the Loyal Publication Society in New York. He wrote ten of the society's ninety pamphlets, including the highly influential *Lincoln oder McClellan? Aufruf an die Deutschen in Amerika,* which was distributed extensively in both German and English. The 500,000 copies of the society's pamphlets circulated widely among the troops. Keenly aware of the importance of those voters, Lincoln told a crowd at a White House rally that "no classes of people seem so nearly unanamous as the soldiers in the field and the seamen afloat" in the war "to save the country and it's liberties." Let their devotion to the cause inspire others, he counseled. "Do they not have the hardest of it? Who should quail while they do not? God bless the soldiers and seamen, with all their brave commanders."[226] When California's Supreme Court struck down the state's law permitting soldiers to vote, Lincoln said "he was sorry to see the Courts there had thrown *out* the soldier's right to vote" and called that action "a bad augury for the success of the loyal cause on Nov. 8th."[227]

Victory at the Polls

The first electoral test took place in Kentucky, where a judicial race on August 1 was regarded as a portent of things to come. Four weeks earlier, Lincoln had somewhat redundantly issued an order suspending the writ of habeas corpus in the Bluegrass State. The document, written by Seward, stipulated that martial law "will not . . . interfere with the holding of lawful elections." Nonetheless, General Stephen G. Burbridge ordered the name of the incumbent stricken from the ballot three days before the election. To avoid arrest, the judge fled Kentucky. The Democrats hastily found a replacement, who won, foreshadowing McClellan's decisive victory there in November.

For Republicans in other states, the signs were more propitious. In September, they handily won gubernatorial contests in Maine and Vermont. Writing from Portland, former Governor Israel Washburn informed his brother that Lincoln "is wonderfully popular in the North, & is nowhere stronger than in Maine. Nothing but some great blunder can prevent his re-election."[228] Based on these New England results, Nicolay accurately predicted that "Lincoln will receive a very large majority of the Electoral votes."[229] Along with the fall of Atlanta and the Democrats' decision to adopt a peace platform, these elections helped persuade Radical malcontents to rally around Lincoln lest continued opposition discredit their cause.

Far more significant elections took place on October 11, when voters trooped to the polls in Ohio, Indiana, and Pennsylvania. Republicans swept to victory in the Buckeye State, claiming seventeen of the nineteen congressional seats and carrying the state ticket by over 50,000. Among the Democratic casualties was S. S. Cox, one of the most prominent Democrats in the House. Lincoln's refusal to postpone the draft made Republicans in Indiana fearful that they would lose the state. Yet Governor Oliver P. Morton received 20,000 more votes than his Democratic challenger, and the Republicans took eight of the eleven congressional seats while gaining control of the legislature. The contest in Pennsylvania was fierce and the outcome close. A month before the election, John W. Forney warned Lincoln that Republicans might lose the Keystone State, and Simon Cameron, who headed the Union Party there, predicted that the "campaign will be short and must be urged with vigor now, on our side, if we hope to succeed. The enemy are full of money—we have none—and they will act with all the zeal usual to the opposing party who have hopes of success."[230] In late September, Congressman William D. Kelley of Philadelphia cautioned Lincoln that "our state is not safe. It is very doubtful. The campaign is not being conducted by the state committee with reference to *your* election, but to so organising legislative and committee and other influence as to constrain you to accept Simon Cameron as Secty of War—or if that fail to restore him to the Senate." The committee ignored "every man, and every influence that is not devoted to Cameron." The Chief "is everywhere courting the impression that he alone of Pennsylvania[']s sons is potential with you, and that he is certain of going into the Cabinet. *This impression must be removed*, or you will in certain districts fail to win with the congressional ticket, and may lose the state."[231]

As it turned out, the Republican/Union candidates in Pennsylvania squeaked by with a 15,000-vote margin. Their majority in the home vote was an exiguous 391. "Is not the result of the 'home-vote' in this state sickening to a man who loves his country and desires to respect his countrymen?" asked the disgruntled head of the Pennsylvania Union League, who resolved to work night and day till the November election.[232] Opposition to the draft there hurt Republicans so badly that Secretary of War Stanton was considered "a heavy load for Mr Lincoln to carry."[233]

As Lincoln sat at the War Department with Stanton and Charles A. Dana awaiting the October election returns, he read aloud from one of his favorite humorists, David Ross Locke, creator of the comic character Petroleum V. Nasby. ("For the genius to write these things I would gladly give up my office," Lincoln said of Locke's humorous pieces.)[234] The secretary of war had little patience for such humor, but the president paid him no mind, continuing to read with an occasional pause to glance at telegrams. When the humorless Chase arrived, Lincoln stopped reading. The equally humorless Stanton pulled Dana into an adjoining room and exploded in indignation: "God damn it to hell. Was there ever such nonsense? Was there ever such inability to appreciate what is going on in an awful crisis? Here is the fate of this whole republic at stake, and here is the man around whom it all centers, on whom it all depends, turning aside from this monumental issue to read the God damned trash of a silly mountebank!"[235]

The soldier vote seemed to be going heavily Republican save for the patients at the Carver Hospital in Washington, which Lincoln and Stanton both rode by daily. (The president was still residing at the Soldiers' Home at the time.) "That[']s hard on us Stanton," said the president; "they know us better than the others." Lincoln's own bodyguard, the 150th Pennsylvania, voted 63–11 in favor of the Republican ticket. As the evening wore on, Lincoln grew concerned, saying "he was anxious about Pennsylvania because of her enormous weight and influence which, cast definitely into the scale, wd. have closed the campaign & left the people free to look again with their whole hearts to the cause of the country."[236]

On October 13, Lincoln appeared more tired and downcast than usual as he sat in the War Department telegraph office jotting down an estimate of the likely November results. He said he was not entirely sure that he would be reelected, for he anticipated losing New York, Pennsylvania, New Jersey, Delaware, Maryland, Kentucky, and Illinois, and thus managing to defeat McClellan in the electoral college by an extremely narrow margin (117–114). Nine days earlier Democratic candidates for assessors and judges in Delaware had won 1,300 more votes than their Union/Republican opponents.

Especially alarmed by the narrowness of the Republican victory in Pennsylvania, Lincoln asked Alexander K. McClure to help strengthen the state central committee. That was necessary, for McClure, who barely won his bid for a legislative seat in October, warned that the committee was "a miserable affair" and that McClellan might well carry his home state in November. At Washington, Pennsylvanians who in October had taken a furlough to vote at home accused Cameron of badly mismanaging the campaign. The Chief apparently worked to promote his own interests rather than those of the national party. When Lincoln asked Cameron to cooperate with McClure, with whom he had long been feuding, the Chief readily agreed, for he was mortified by the poor showing in his state, compared with Ohio and Indiana. Despite the resulting improvement in Republican operations, Lincoln continued to fear the result in Pennsylvania. According to McClure, he "knew that his election was in no sense doubtful, but he knew that if he lost New York and with it Pennsylvania on the home vote, the moral effect of his triumph would be broken and his power to prosecute the war and make peace would be greatly impaired." At McClure's suggestion, the president arranged to have 10,000 Keystone State troops furloughed in order to vote at home.[237]

Shortly after the October elections, James W. Singleton urged Lincoln to announce that Confederate states could be restored without abandoning slavery. The president replied through their mutual friend Ebenezer Peck that while he respected the integrity of Singleton's motives, he could not take his advice. According to Peck, the president said that the "favorable results of the recent elections, might subject him to the imputation of being willing now, to disregard the desires of the radical men, who have so reluctantly come in to his support, and thus subject him to the imputation of catering to new elements [i.e., Conservatives] in disregard of their opinion."[238]

The Republican victories in October foreshadowed the party's triumph the following month. On election day, November 8, Lincoln said of the vituperative campaign: "It is a little singular that I who am not a vindictive man, should always have been before the people for election in canvasses marked for their bitterness." When a positive report arrived from Maryland that morning, Lincoln expressed surprise. A month earlier, the Free State had gone Republican by a narrow margin. Now the higher turnout might indicate that Democrats were voting in larger numbers. "I shall be glad if that holds," the president remarked somewhat skeptically.[239]

That afternoon, Lincoln, looking demoralized, found it understandably difficult to concentrate on routine business. Tad relieved the tension somewhat when he raced into his father's room to announce that the soldiers guarding the White House were off to vote. Lincoln noticed that the boy's pet turkey, which he had rescued from the chopping block a year earlier, was accompanying the troops to the polls. (They had made a mascot of the bird.) When the president asked if the turkey was also going to vote, Tad shot back: "Oh, no; he isn't of age yet!" The proud father regarded that response as far superior to many of the humorous "Lincoln stories" in circulation.[240]

Noah Brooks, who spent the afternoon and evening with the president, reported that Lincoln "took no pains to conceal his anxious interest in the result of the election." The president confessed: "I am just enough of a politician to know that there was not much doubt about the result of the Baltimore Convention, but about this thing I am far from being certain; I wish I were certain." Around 6:30, word arrived from Indianapolis announcing a predictable Republican landslide.

After dinner, the president and John Hay splashed over to the War Department through the rainy, dark, gloomy night. Passing by a soaked sentry encased in his own vapor, they entered the building through a side door and climbed to the telegraph room, where the president was handed a dispatch from John W. Forney predicting a 10,000-vote majority in Philadelphia. Lincoln remarked laconically: "Forney is a little excitable." Around nine o'clock, a telegram from Baltimore announced a solid 10,000-vote Republican victory. Lincoln merely smiled and remarked "that was a fair beginning."[241] From Massachusetts came news that Congressman Alexander H. Rice was leading by 4,000 votes. Incredulous, Lincoln said: "Rice has one of the closest districts in the country, and those figures are more likely to be 40 or perhaps 400." When subsequent reports confirmed the original estimate, he took heart: "If the doubtful districts come in in this shape, what may we expect from the certain ones?" (A few days later, he told Rice: "Well, your district proved to be a good deal like a jug after all, with the handle all on one side.")[242] Assistant Secretary of the Navy Gustavus Fox took special pleasure in Rice's victory, for the congressman was a friend of the navy. When Fox expressed joy that two of his department's congressional enemies had been defeated, Lincoln told him: "You have more of that feeling of personal resentment than I. Perhaps I may have too little of it, but I never thought it paid. A man has not time to spend half his life in quarrels. If any man ceases to attack me, I never remember the past against him."[243]

When a dispatch announced that Pennsylvania was indeed going heavily Republican, Lincoln appeared unusually sober, as if contemplating the prospect of another four years of heavy responsibility. He observed: "As goes Pennsylvania, so goes the Union, they say."[244] He then ordered the news conveyed to his wife, explaining that she was "more anxious than I."

When Thomas T. Eckert of the telegraph office staff arrived, Lincoln asked why his pants were so mud-splattered. He had taken a tumble crossing the street, the major explained. That reminded Lincoln of something that happened to him six years earlier: "For such an awkward fellow, I am pretty sure-footed. It used to take a pretty dextrous man to throw me. I remember, the evening of the day in 1858, that decided the contest for the Senate between Mr Douglas and myself, was something like this, dark, rainy & gloomy. I had been reading the returns, and had ascertained that we had lost the Legislature and started to go home. The path had been worn hog-back was slippering. My foot slipped from under me, knocking the other one out of the way, but I recovered myself & lit square; and I said to myself, '*It's a slip and not a fall.*'"[245]

Returns from the doubtful state of New York were slow to come in. A dispatch indicating that McClellan had carried it by 40,000 was regarded skeptically, for the state had been carefully canvassed and a close result was expected. When another dispatch proclaimed that the Republicans had won the state by 10,000, Lincoln scoffed: "I don't believe that." More plausible to him was a midnight wire from Greeley predicting a 4,000-vote Republican victory which, added to Pennsylvania, Maryland, New England, Michigan, and Wisconsin, seemed to clinch the election. When congratulated on that likely result, Lincoln responded calmly, saying "that he was free to confess that he felt relieved of suspense, and was glad that the verdict of the people was so likely to be clear, full and unmistakable, for it then appeared that his majority in the electoral college would be immense."[246]

At that point, Eckert served supper with the help of Lincoln, who "went awkwardly and hospitably to work shovelling out the fried oysters." Hay recorded that the president "was most agreeable and genial all the evening."[247] Lincoln still felt anxious about Illinois, which did not report good news till 1 A.M. An hour later, when a group of Pennsylvanians serenaded him, Lincoln replied with what Noah Brooks called "one of the happiest and noblest little speeches of his life."[248] He emphasized to his well-wishers the significance of the election: "I earnestly believe that the consequences of this day's work . . . will be to the lasting advantage, if not to the very salvation, of the country." All those "who have labored to-day in behalf of the Union organization, have wrought for the best interests of their country and the world, not only for the present, but for all future ages. I am thankful to God for this approval of the people." Yet Lincoln would not gloat: though "deeply grateful for this mark of their confidence in me, if I know my heart, my gratitude is free from any taint of personal triumph. I do not impugn the motives of any one opposed to me. It is no pleasure to me to triumph over any one; but I give thanks to the Almighty for this evidence of the people's resolution to stand by free government and the rights of humanity."[249] Hay thought the president spoke "with rather unusual dignity and effect."[250]

Lincoln won 55.4 percent of the popular vote and carried all states save Kentucky, Delaware, and New Jersey. The lopsided electoral college vote was 212 to 21. This showing was slightly below the average that Republicans had received in 1863, when they won 56.6 percent of the vote in the sixteen Northern states where the two parties clashed. The recorded soldier vote (4 percent of the total) went 78 percent for the president as compared with 53 percent of the civilian vote. (This result was surprising, since over 40 percent of the troops had been Democrats or belonged to Democratic families in 1860.) As one Vermont trooper wrote: "Soldiers don't generally believe in fighting to put down treason, and voting to let it live."[251] Colonel Charles Russell Lowell, a Massachusetts abolitionist and Harvard valedictorian, feared that if McClellan won, the nation would become "either half a dozen little republics, or *one despotism*," leaving the United States "in the condition of the South American republics."[252] A less highly-educated private looked forward to giving "the rebel[l]ion another thump this fall by voting for old Abe. I cannot afford to give three years of my life to maintaining this nation and then giving them Rebles all they want."[253] A sergeant reported that "[in] this army (as it is with all others) 'Old Abe' has the preference, his majority will be large in the army. McClellan lost friends by accepting the nomination on such a platform as that Chicago convention got up."[254] On the eve of the election, an Illinois officer predicted that the army "will be overwhelmingly for 'Old Abe.' A large proportion feel that he can put down this rebellion much better than any other man, and none are for peace with armed rebels."[255]

Though gratified to receive the soldier vote, Lincoln did not need it; in most states that he carried, the civilian vote sufficed. In New York and Connecticut, where no separate records of the soldier and the home votes were kept, the soldier vote may have made the difference. It also allowed several Republican congressional candidates to prevail.

During the campaign Lincoln said, "I rely upon the religious sentiment of the country, which I am told is very largely for me."[256] Indeed, evangelical Protestant churches supported his candidacy enthusiastically.

On November 10, a huge crowd converged on the White House with banners, lanterns, transparencies, and bands blaring martial tunes. A booming cannon added to the din. Approximately one-third of the serenaders were black, prompting an aged citizen of the capital to observe: "The white men there would not have made up a very large assemblage." Such a turnout of blacks was unprecedented.[257] In addressing this crowd, Lincoln analyzed the importance of the election. He had written out his remarks, for, as Noah Brooks reported, "being well aware that the importance of the occasion would give it significance," Lincoln "was not willing to run the risk of being betrayed by the excitement of the occasion into saying anything which would make him sorry when he saw it in print." Upon appearing at the second story window, he was greeted with "a tremendous yell."[258] When the loud cheering finally died down, he began with a point he had made in his July 4, 1861, message to Congress: "It has long been a grave question whether any government, not *too* strong for the liberties of its people, can be strong *enough* to maintain its own existence, in great emergencies. On this point the present rebellion brought our republic to a severe test; and a presidential election occurring in regular course during the rebellion added not a little to the strain. If the loyal people, *united*, were put to the utmost of their strength by the rebellion, must they not fail when *divided*, and partially paralyzed, by a political war among themselves?"

Though the danger was great, it would not have justified suspending or canceling the election. In remarking on the bitter canvass, Lincoln added: "The strife of the election is but human-nature practically applied to the facts of the case. What has occurred in this case, must ever recur in similar cases. Human-nature will not change. In any future great national trial, compared with the men of this, we shall have as weak, and as strong; as silly and as wise; as bad and good. Let us, therefore, study the incidents of this, as philosophy to learn wisdom from, and none of them as wrongs to be revenged."

Deplorable though the bitter campaign may have been, Lincoln insisted that it "has done good too," for it "demonstrated that a people's government can sustain a national election, in the midst of a great civil war. Until now it has not been known to the world that this was a possibility. It shows also how *sound*, and how *strong* we still are. It shows that, even among candidates of the same party, he who is most devoted to the Union, and most opposed to treason, can receive most of the people's votes. It shows also, to the extent yet known, that we have more men now, than we had when the war began. Gold is good in its place; but living, brave, patriotic men, are better than gold."

In closing, Lincoln urged his supporters to show magnanimity toward their defeated opponents: "now that the election is over, may not all, having a common interest, re-unite in a common effort, to save our common country? For my own part I have striven, and shall strive to avoid placing any obstacle in the way. So long as I have been here I have not willingly planted a thorn in any man's bosom. While I am deeply sensible to the high compliment of a re-election; and duly grateful, as I trust, to Almighty God for having directed my countrymen to a right conclusion, as I think, for their own good, it adds nothing to my satisfaction that any other man may be disappointed or pained by the result. May I ask those who have not differed with me, to join with me, in this same spirit towards those who have?"[259]

After finishing, Lincoln stepped away from the window as the crowd gave him three enthusiastic cheers. He told John Hay: "Not very graceful, but I am growing old enough not to care much for the manner of doing things."[260] Hay thought more highly of the effort, calling it "one of the weightiest and wisest of all his discourses," an opinion shared by the Washington correspondent of the London *Times*, who deemed it "one of the best speeches he has ever made."[261] Lydia Maria Child told a friend that it "charmed me exceedingly. A most beautiful spirit pervaded it."[262]

Those remarks were hastily written, for Lincoln was then very busy. A week later he told a delegation of Marylanders that he had planned to prepare some remarks for them, but he had been unable to find the time and would therefore speak off the cuff. He said that he "thought the adoption of their free State constitution was a bigger thing than their part in the Presidential election. He could, any day, have stipulated to lose Maryland in the Presidential election to save its free constitution, because the Presidential election comes every four years and the adoption of the constitution, being a good thing, could not be undone. He therefore thought in that they had a victory for the right worth a great deal more than their part in the Presidential election, although he thought well of that."[263] Abolitionists rejoiced that his remarks were "thoroughly emancipation in tone" and that he had evidently abandoned any thought of gradual emancipation.[264]

Lincoln's annual message to Congress in December also pleased Radicals. It eloquently summarized the lesson taught by the election: "The most reliable indication of public purpose in this country is derived through our popular elections. Judging by the recent canvass and its result, the purpose of the people, within the loyal States, to maintain the integrity of the Union, was never more firm, nor more nearly unanimous, than now. The extraordinary calmness and good order with which the millions of voters met and mingled at the polls, give strong assurance of this. Not only all those who supported the Union ticket, so called, but a great majority of the opposing party also, may be fairly claimed to entertain, and to be actuated by, the same purpose. It is an unanswerable argument to this effect, that no candidate for any office whatever, high or low, has ventured to seek votes on the avowal that he was for giving up the Union. There have been much impugning of motives, and much heated controversy as to the proper means and best mode of advancing the Union cause; but on the distinct issue of Union or no Union, the politicians have shown their instinctive knowledge that there is no diversity among the people. In affording the people the fair opportunity of showing, one to another and to the world, this firmness and unanimity of purpose, the election has been of vast value to the national cause."[265]

Harper's Weekly agreed with the president's assessment, calling the election result "the proclamation of the American people that they are not conquered; that the rebellion is not successful; and that, deeply as they deplore war and its inevitable suffering and loss, yet they have no choice between war and national ruin, and must therefore fight on." Lincoln's reelection demonstrated "that the people are conscious of the power and force of their own Government" and vindicated "the American system of free popular government. No system in history was ever exposed to such a strain directly along the fibre as that which ours has endured in the war and the political campaign, and no other could possibly have endured it successfully. The result is due to the general intelligence of the people, and to the security of perfectly free discussion." The United States had showed itself to be "a nation which comprehends its priceless importance to human progress and civilization, and which recognizes that law is the indispensable condition of Liberty."[266]

More succinctly, General John W. Geary told his wife that it "is now certain that the United States must be all *free* or all *slave,* and the momentous question has been decided in favor of freedom by the edict of the people in November."[267] Charles Eliot Norton predicted that November 8, 1864, "will always be esteemed as one of our great historic days. Never before was a people called upon for a decision involving more vital interests not only to itself but to the progress of mankind, and never did any people show itself so worthy to be entrusted with freedom and power."[268]

Some Confederates recognized that Lincoln's victory spelled their doom. A Rebel prisoner told a Union soldier that if the president were reelected, "we are gone up but . . . if you elect McC[lellan]D we are all right yet and will whip you yet." Many of this fellow's comrades shared his view.[269] Colonel Robert G. H. Kean, chief of the Confederate bureau of war, recorded in his journal that the "Yankee election was evidently a damper on the spirits of many of our people, and is said to have depressed the army a good deal. Lincoln's triumph was more complete than most of us expected. Most judicious persons . . . hoped that it would be closely contested, possibly attended with violence."[270] Lee's chief of ordnance lamented that "our subjugation is popular at the north."[271] From Atlanta, a Union general reported that the "rebs here are much chapfallen at the disaster to their political friends in the north. They seem to consider it worse than a disaster in the field, and a death blow to their dearest hopes of success."[272] Jefferson Davis, however, did not take that view and determined to fight on to the bitter end, needlessly prolonging an unwinnable war.

Lincoln savored his victory, though the possibility of defeat held few terrors for him. As he told Noah Brooks the day after the election: "Being only mortal, after all, I should have been a little mortified if I had been beaten in this canvass before the people; but the sting would have been more than compensated by the thought that the people had notified me that my official responsibilities were soon to be lifted off my back."[273] To another journalist he said that the cares of his office were "so oppressive" that "he felt as though the moment when he could relinquish the burden and retire to private life would be the sweetest he could possibly experience."[274] Still, Lincoln acknowledged to a committee of Marylanders that he "would not attempt to conceal from them the fact that he was gratified at the results of the Presidential election, and he would assure them that he had kept as near as he could to the exercise of his best judgment, for the promotion of the interests of the whole country; and now, to have the seal of approbation marked on the course he had pursued was exceedingly gratifying to his feelings."[275]

To Noah Brooks, the president modestly confessed his need of divine assistance: "I should be the veriest shallow and self-conceited blockhead upon the footstool if, in my discharge of the duties which are put upon me in this place, I should hope to get along without the wisdom which comes from God, and not from men."[276] This modest sensibility led him to reject Brooks's suggestion that he share the good electoral news with his old friend Anson G. Henry in Oregon: "I don't think it would look well for a message from me to go travelling around the country blowing my own horn. You sign the message and I will send it."[277]

Democratic blunders and Union military success did not alone account for Lincoln's reelection, important though they were. It is hard to say precisely how significant a role his character and personality played, but it was a big one. The perceptive journalist E. L. Godkin informed readers of the London *Daily News* that men in rural America showed little concern about the president's sartorial taste or his manners. Instead "his logic and his English, his jokes, his plain common sense, his shrewdness, his unbounded reliance on their honesty and straightforwardness, go right to their hearts." They "are in earnest in a way the like of which the world never saw before, silently, calmly, but deliberately in earnest; and they will fight on, in my opinion, as long as they have men, muskets, powder, and corn and wool, and would fight on, though the grass were growing in Wall Street, and there was not a gold dollar on this

side of the Atlantic."[278] This strong resolve was partly inspired by Lincoln's own indomitable will.

Endearing Lincoln to the voters was his remarkable unselfishness. "[A]mong the
great civilians of the day," William O. Stoddard noted in 1863, "the greatest and
strongest, our good Chief Magistrate, is great and strong chiefly because the people
have perfect faith in him that he has no ambition, no selfish lust of power, nor any
hope for the future unconnected with the welfare of his country." In addition, people
identified with Lincoln. "He is the most perfect *representative* of the purely American
character now in public life," Stoddard maintained. "This is why the mutual understanding between him and the people is so perfect. This it is which enables him to
exercise powers which would never by any possibility be entrusted to another man,
though his equal in other respects. The people know that they can trust their great
chief, and so they bid him 'see to it that the Republic suffers no detriment.'"[279] In
early 1864, Harriet Beecher Stowe noted that of all "the many accusations which in
hours of ill-luck have been thrown out upon Lincoln, it is remarkable that he has
never been called self-seeking, or selfish. When we were troubled and sat in darkness,
and looked doubtfully towards the presidential chair, it was never that we doubted the
good-will of our pilot—only the clearness of his eyesight. But Almighty God has
granted to him that clearness of vision which he gives to the true-hearted, and enabled him to set his honest foot in that promised land of freedom which is to be the
patrimony of all men, black and white—and from henceforth nations shall rise up to
call him blessed."[280] A frustrated Wendell Phillips said that "Lincoln had won such
loving trust from the people that it was impossible to argue anything against him."[281]

With Lincoln's reelection, antislavery forces heaved a sigh of relief. Gerrit Smith
said he was "more thankful than joyful over the Election—too deeply thankful to be
joyful."[282] Lucy Stone was equally pleased: "how glad I am, that Mr. Lincoln [in] spite
of his short comings, is re-elected."[283] George William Curtis urged friends to "thank
God and the people for this crowning mercy."[284] Lydia Maria Child was delighted
that she could finally "breathe freely now that this great danger is passed. If McLellan had been elected, the slave holders would have had it all their own way." She rejoiced "to have a rail-splitter for President, and a tailor for Vice President." She
deemed Lincoln's victory "the triumph of free schools; for it was the intelligence and
reason of the people that reelected Abraham Lincoln." The voters, Child said, were
sophisticated and thoughtful enough to overlook the president's many shortcomings:
"There is no beauty in him, that men should desire him; there is no insinuating, polished manner, to beguile the senses of the people; there is no dazzling military renown; no silver flow of rhetoric; in fact, no glittering prestige of *any* kind surrounds
him; yet the people triumphantly elected him, in spite of all manner of machinations,
and notwithstanding the long, long drag upon their patience and their resources,
which this war has produced." For all his flaws and lack of polish, the president was
likable, Child acknowledged. "I have sometimes been out of patience with him; but I
will say of him that I have constantly gone on liking him better and better."[285]

Some Radicals were less enthusiastic. Bradford R. Wood rejoiced but "with fear
and trembling for the future," because Lincoln's honesty meant little "if he surrounds

himself with incompetent or second rate men, to be the tools of our State Banks or our plutocrats or our old political hacks."[286] Henry Winter Davis did not look forward to a second Lincoln administration: "We must for four years more rely on the forcing process of Congress to *wring* from that old fool what can be gotten for the nation."[287] Davis, however, would not be able to lead the forcers in Congress, for he lost his bid for renomination. (Baltimore Republicans wanted to be represented by someone who would cooperate with the administration instead of fighting it.) Moncure Conway told his English readers that "[n]ever before in America has a president been elected so detested by his own electors as Abraham Lincoln."[288] (Apropos of Conway's criticism, George S. Hillard of Boston remarked that if it were read by everyone in Massachusetts, "it would be of no effect," for the "faith of the most ignorant and bigoted Catholic in the pope does not equal the faith of the great majority of this community in Abraham Lincoln." Another Bostonian remarked that Conway had "made himself a national laughing stock.")[289]

"Congratulate the President for me for the double victory," Grant wired Stanton. "The election having passed off quietly, no bloodshed or riot throughout the land, is a victory worth more to the country than a battle won. Rebeldom and Europe will so construe it."[290]

In his formal reply to the congressional committee notifying him of his reelection, Lincoln was eloquent: "Having served four years in the depths of a great, and yet unended national peril, I can view this call to a second term, in nowise more flatteringly to myself, than as an expression of the public judgment, that I may better finish a difficult work, in which I have labored from the first, than could any one less severely schooled to the task. In this view, and with assured reliance on that Almighty Ruler who has so graceously sustained us thus far; and with increased gratitude to the generous people for their continued confidence, I accept the renewed trust, with it's yet onerous and perplexing duties and responsibilities."[291] Thurlow Weed told the president that this reply "is not only the *neatest* but the most pregnant and effective use to which the English Language was ever put."[292]

Lincoln's victory reminded him of an ominous vision that he had seen four years earlier. "It was just after my election in 1860," he told Noah Brooks, "when the news had been coming in thick and fast all day, and there had been a great 'Hurrah, boys!' so that I was well tired out, and went home to rest, throwing myself down on a lounge in my chamber. Opposite where I lay was a bureau, with a swinging-glass upon it, and looking in that glass, I saw myself reflected, nearly at full length; but my face, I noticed, had *two* separate and distinct images, the tip of the nose of one being about three inches from the tip of the other. I was a little bothered, perhaps startled, and got up and looked in the glass, but the illusion vanished. On lying down again I saw it a second time—plainer, if possible, than before; and then I noticed that one of the faces was a little paler, say five shades, than the other. I got up and the thing melted away, and I went off and, in the excitement of the hour, forgot all about it—nearly, but not quite, for the thing would once in a while come up, and give me a little pang, as though something uncomfortable had happened. When I went home I told my wife about it, and a few days after I tried the experiment again, when, sure enough, the thing came back again; but I never succeeded in bringing the ghost back after that, though I once tried very industriously to show it to my wife, who was worried about it somewhat. She thought it was 'a sign' that I was to be elected to a second term of office, and that the paleness of one of the faces was an omen that I should not see life through the last term."[293]

"Let the *Thing* Be Pressed"
Victory at Last
(November 1864–April 1865)

Republican unity, which had made Lincoln's reelection possible, would be essential if Reconstruction were to proceed smoothly, but that unity was gravely threatened by Radicals who had supported Lincoln during the presidential campaign but might not be accommodating afterward. To keep them cooperating with Moderates and Conservatives was the president's greatest challenge in the wake of his electoral triumph.

Chase as Chief Justice

On October 12, a special opportunity to conciliate Radicals presented itself with the death of octogenarian Supreme Court Chief Justice, Roger B. Taney. A year earlier, Senator Ben Wade had quipped: "I prayed with earnestness for the life of Taney to be prolonged through Buchanan's Administration, and by God I[']m a little afraid I have overdone the matter." Nathaniel P. Banks opined that the Republican electoral victories of the previous day had killed Taney. Upon hearing the news, Lincoln said he would not nominate a replacement for Taney right away but would remain "shut pan" for a while.[1] Preoccupied with the election and his annual message, he postponed consideration of the matter until Congress met in December. In the meantime, he said that "he was waiting to receive expressions of public opinion from the Country."[2]

The White House mailbag overflowed with such expressions. Among the names mentioned by correspondents were New York attorney William M. Evarts, Montgomery Blair, Associate Justice Noah H. Swayne, Edward Bates, and Edwin M. Stanton. When Methodist Bishop Matthew Simpson urged Lincoln to choose Stanton, the president asked: "where can I get a man to take Secretary Stanton's place? Tell me that and I will do it."[3] To a member of the Massachusetts Supreme Court, the president lauded his war secretary: "Mr. Stanton has excellent qualities; and he has his defects. Folks come up here and tell me that there are a great many men in the country who have all Stanton's excellent qualities, without his defects. All I have to say is, I haven't met 'em! I don't know 'em! I wish I did!"[4] Although Stanton hoped for the appointment, he gave no outward signs of doing so. When speculation about his potential candidacy appeared in the press, he said he favored his friend Chase.

Charles A. Dana thought that Lincoln preferred Montgomery Blair. Fellow Democrat Gideon Welles praised the former postmaster general as an ideal candidate for the chief justice's post, for in the navy secretary's view Blair was a politician and not a partisan, a man in sympathy with the Republican program, personally friendly and loyal to the president. When Welles commended Blair for "his ability, his truthfulness, honesty, and courage," Lincoln "expressed his concurrence" and "spoke kindly and complimentarily of Mr. Blair, but did not in any way commit himself."[5]

Francis P. Blair, Sr., pleaded his son's case at the White House. Old Man Blair had been approached by Mary Lincoln, who implored him to help thwart Chase's candidacy. The former treasury secretary and his allies, she told him, "are besieging my Husband for the Chief-Justiceship[.] I wish you could prevent them." So he called on Lincoln and said "that if he would make one of his Ex-Cabinet men a Judge, I thought Montgomery was his man, that he had been tried as a Judge and not found wanting, that his practice in the West had made him conversant with our land law, Spanish law, as well as the common and civil law in which his university studies had grounded him, that his practice in the Supreme Court brought him into the circle of commercial and constitutional questions. That, besides on political issues he sustained him in every thing." Lincoln replied that he could not make a choice before consulting others. He implied that while he might favor Blair, there was significant opposition to the former postmaster general: "Although I may be stronger as an authority yet if all the rest oppose, I must give way. Old Hickory who had as much iron in his neck as any body, did so some times. If the strongest horse in the team *would* go ahead, he *cannot*, if all *the rest hold back*." Blair inferred that the president "is well disposed to appoint Montgomery."[6]

Several leading Republicans supported the ex-postmaster-general, including Seward, William Cullen Bryant, John Murray Forbes, and Joseph Medill. Montgomery Blair tried to add Edwin D. Morgan to the list: "There is one consideration which I hope you will bring to the President's attention to prevent Chase's appointment," he wrote to the New York senator. "He is known to be so vindictive towards me for supporting the President, that no one would employ me as counsel to the Court if he were Chief Justice. Now the President cannot consent not only to turn me out of his Cabinet, but to drive me from the bar for life, because I supported him for the Presidency."

But Lincoln decided against nominating Blair because, according to Charles A. Dana, many senators "were resolved that no second-rate man should be appointed to that office." Dana added that "if Montgomery Blair had succeeded in presenting his programme to that body, I have no doubt it would have been smashed to pieces in a moment. Mr. Blair's idea was that one of the existing justices, as for instance Judge Swayne, should be appointed Chief Justice, and that he himself should be made an Associate justice."[7] In time, Blair thought he would move up.

David Davis, who disliked Chase intensely, persuaded his colleagues on the high court to back Swayne for chief justice. But two of them, Stephen J. Field and Samuel Miller, eventually withdrew their support and boarded the Chase bandwagon.

Edward Bates personally asked for the chief justiceship, which he thought would be a "crowning and retiring honor." Lincoln told Isaac Newton he would gladly name the attorney general to that post "if not overborne by others" like Chase, who "was turning every stone, to get it." In addition, "several others were urged, from different quarters." When Newton informed Bates of this conversation, the attorney general cheerfully confided to his diary: "I am happy in the feeling that the failure to get the place, will be no painful disappointment for my mind is made up to private life and a bare competency."[8]

(At the end of November, Bates stepped down as attorney general, to be replaced by Lincoln's Kentucky friend James Speed, brother of Joshua Speed. The president had wanted to name Joseph Holt, who declined and recommended Speed. In choosing Bates's successor, geographical considerations weighed on Lincoln's mind. "My Cabinet has *shrunk up* North, and I must find a Southern man," he told Assistant Attorney General Titian J. Coffey. "I suppose if the twelve Apostles were to be chosen nowadays the shrieks of locality would have to be heeded." In explaining his choice of Speed, Lincoln said he knew him well, but not as well as his brother Joshua: "That, however, is not strange, for I slept with Joshua for four years, and I suppose I ought to know him well. But James is an honest man and a gentleman, and if he comes here you will find he is one of those well-poised men, not too common here, who are not spoiled by a big office."[9] Republican senators expressed surprise that such an obscure lawyer would be chosen to replace Bates.)

Chase was indeed turning every stone, disingenuously assuring Lincoln that he would rather be chief justice than president. When a friendly letter from him arrived at the White House, the president laconically instructed that it be filed "with his other recommendations."[10] Those recommendations were especially numerous. Chase had strengthened his chances for the job by actively campaigning for Lincoln in the fall. Coyly remaining in Cincinnati while the decision about the chief justiceship was pending, Chase urged friends to lobby the president on his behalf. Among them was Charles Sumner, who pleaded with special urgency, telling Lincoln that the country needed "a Chief Justice whose position on this great question [of slavery], in all its bearings, is already fixed and who will not need arg[umen]ts of counsel to convert him."[11] Schuyler Colfax also championed the former treasury secretary's candidacy, praising his "fine judicial talents, robust health and promise of long life (not an unimportant condition), and soundness on many questions, financial, political and military, which the events of the War may bring before that tribunal."[12] Another Hoosier, Senator Henry Lane, assured Lincoln that "[e]very Union man in Indiana *desires* Gov. Chase's appt. and every Democrat expects it."[13]

Numerous critics denounced Chase as a treacherous schemer who was "never distinguished at the bar or on the Bench for his judicial attainments."[14] Gideon Welles called him "selfishly stubborn," lacking "moral courage and frankness," "fond of adulation, and with official superiors . . . a sycophant."[15] Thomas Ewing told the president that the former treasury secretary "has no considerable reputation as a lawyer. He is a politician rather than a lawyer and unless he change[s] his nature always will be even if made Chief Justice. I am unwilling to see a Chief Justice of the U S intriguing and trading for the Presidency."[16]

Lincoln, too, worried that Chase's insatiable desire for the presidency would undermine his ability to be a good chief justice. To Massachusetts Senator Henry Wilson, who urged Chase's appointment as a gesture to placate Radicals, Lincoln said: "He is a man of unbounded ambition, and has been working all his life to become President; that he can never be; and I fear that if I make him Chief Justice, he will simply become more restless and uneasy, and neglect the place in his strife and intrigue to make himself President. He has got the Presidential maggot in his head and it will wriggle there as long as it is warm. If I were sure that he would go upon the bench and give up his aspirations to do anything but make himself a great judge, I would send in his name at once."[17] To another Radical senator, Lafayette Foster of Connecticut, he predicted that if Chase "keeps on with the notion that he is destined to be President," he "will never acquire that fame and usefulness as a Chief Justice which he would otherwise certainly attain."[18] Should Chase continue his quest for the White House from the bench, he said, it would "be very bad for him and very bad for me."[19] Presciently, he speculated that if Chase attained "so high and honorable a place," it might well "heighten rather than banish political ambition."[20] Sumner and Schuyler Colfax assured the president that once Chase was chief justice, he would quit pursuing the presidency. A more accurate opinion came from Edwards Pierrepont, who noted that Chase was "ambitious as Satan" and "so soon as he is rested a little he will start again for the Presidency, and will tire of the Bench within a year."[21]

Chase's supporters may have cynically exploited Lincoln's desire to avoid appearing petty or vindictive. Colfax asked fellow Congressman James A. Garfield to suggest to Lincoln that if, in the face of the "overwhelming public sentiment" in favor of Chase, "he app[ointe]d some one else, History might . . . say that he did so" because Chase "had dared to be a candidate for the Presdt. nomination agst. him."[22]

Lincoln's desire to avoid giving such an impression was intense. He told a close friend: "Mr. Chase's enemies have been appealing to the lowest and meanest of my feelings. They report ill-natured remarks of his upon me and my Administration. If it were true that he made them, I could not be so base as to allow the fact to influence me in the selection of a man for the Chief-Justiceship."[23] To tale-bearers recounting the treasury secretary's severe attacks on him, he stoically remarked: "I do not mind that" and said those attacks "will make no difference whatever in my action."[24] When some Ohioans showed him Chase's letters sharply critical of the president, Lincoln good-naturedly replied "that if Mr. Chase had said harsh things about him, he, in his turn, had said harsh things about Mr. Chase, which squared the account."[25] To New York Congressman Augustus Frank, he explained that Chase had stood with him "in the time of trial, and I should despise myself if I allowed personal differences to affect my judgment of his fitness for the office of Chief Justice."[26] (Lincoln's reference to a time of trial probably referred to the 1858 Illinois senatorial contest, when Chase was one of the very few nationally prominent Republicans to stump the Prairie State.) In early December, Lincoln told Noah Brooks: "I have been all day, and yesterday and the day before, besieged by messages from my friends all over the country, as if there were a determination to put up the bars between Governor Chase and myself." Gesturing toward a pile of letters and telegrams, he said those correspondents had nothing new to impart, for "I know meaner things about Governor Chase than any of those men can tell me."[27] Lincoln resented their tactics, telling John D. Defrees that "he had often been mortified at some of our friends who urged him not to appoint Chase because he had abused him at a public table at Newport—and on other occasions." The president took offense at the implication that he was "capable of being influenced in making an appointment of such importance to the country by mere personal considerations." Those "appeals were made to the worst side of him and he did not like it."[28]

In late November, Lincoln informed the cabinet that there was "a tremendous pressure just now for Evarts of New York, who, I suppose, is a good lawyer."[29] Chase acknowledged that Evarts clearly outshone him as an attorney. When Richard Henry Dana and Judge Ebenezer Rockwood Hoar pressed Evarts's case and denigrated Chase, Lincoln replied: "Chase is a very able man" who happened to be "a little insane" on the presidency and who "has not always behaved very well lately." Still, when people recommended that "now is the time to *crush him out*," Lincoln replied: "Well I'm not in favor of crushing anybody out! If there is anything a man can do and do it well, I say let him do it. Give him a chance."[30] Hoar had hoped that Stanton and Chase would cancel each other out, leaving Evarts as the obvious compromise candidate.

Lincoln told Colfax that he wanted to name Evarts, but "in deference to what he supposed to be public sentiment" he instead appointed Chase, who, he said, "occupies the largest place in the public mind in connection with the office."[31] The nation, he explained, "needed assurances in regard to two great questions," emancipation and the legal tender act. Many eminent attorneys were sound on those issues, but Chase had been so identified with them that he would never overturn them.[32] Lincoln could not be certain of others. "We cannot ask a man what he will do," he explained to George Boutwell; "if we should, and he should answer us, we should despise him for it." But it was unnecessary to quiz Chase, for his views were well known.[33]

Lincoln had evidently decided to appoint Chase as early as the spring of 1864, when he told Charles Sumner that he intended to name the former treasury secretary to fill Taney's place. At the end of June, he repeated this intention to Samuel Hooper and William P. Fessenden. Upon accepting Chase's resignation, Lincoln had said that the Ohioan should "go home without making any fight and wait for a good thing hereafter, such as a vacancy on the Supreme Bench."[34] A week after Taney's death, the president informed Senator Fessenden that he planned to appoint Chase, "but as things were going on well, he thought it best not to make any appointment or say anything about it until the election was over."[35] He did not want to antagonize Conservatives during the campaign.

Radicals bemoaned the delay, calling Lincoln a "very Sphynx," but on December 6, when he finally submitted Chase's name to the senate, his belief that doing so would please the Radicals was confirmed.[36] "I will now excuse many foolish things in the President, for this one 'big' thing," said one.[37] "It is equal to a military victory" and shows "that Mr. Lincoln is in sympathy with the spirit of those who supported him at the last election," declared a colonel in the U.S. Colored Troops.[38] But the editor of the Cincinnati *Gazette* erred in maintaining that Chase's appointment "preserves the Administration party, and heals up any real or imaginary breach that may have existed in it."[39] While applauding Lincoln's Supreme Court selection, some Radicals continued their fierce opposition to his Reconstruction plans.

"Probably no other man than Lincoln," Nicolay wrote to his fiancée, "would have had, in this age of the world, the degree of magnanimity to thus forgive and exalt a rival who had so deeply and so unjustifiably intrigued against him. It is however only another most marked illustration of the greatness of the President, in this age of little men."[40] Lincoln was magnanimous indeed, for Chase had deeply angered him. The president said that personally he would rather "have swallowed his buckhorn chair" or "eat[en] flat irons" than appoint Chase.[41] Montgomery Blair speculated plausibly that Chase "was the only human being that I believe Lincoln actually hated," and Charles A. Dana thought the "appointment was not made by the President with entire willingness. He is a man who keeps a grudge as faithfully as any other living Christian, and consented to Mr. Chase's elevation, only when the pressure became very general and very urgent."[42] Although Dana overestimated Lincoln's capacity for nursing grudges and underestimated his political savvy and commitment to freedom, there is some truth in his analysis; appointing Chase taxed the president's legendary powers of forgiveness to the utmost.

Upon receiving word of his appointment, Chase promptly expressed his gratitude to Lincoln: "I cannot sleep before I thank you for this mark of your confidence, and especially for the manner in which the nomination was made. I shall never forget either and trust that you will never regret either. Be assured that I prize your confidence and good will more than nomination or office."[43] On the bench, Chase confirmed Lincoln's fears that he would continue scheming to win the presidency. Ironically, his appointment proved unnecessary either for protecting emancipation (the Thirteenth Amendment took care of that) or upholding the legal tender act (he voted with the majority to declare it unconstitutional).

The Bixby Letter

In the immediate aftermath of the election, Lincoln was unusually preoccupied. When Charles S. Spencer, head of the Lincoln and Johnson Campaign Club of New York City, asked the president to provide a banquet toast, Lincoln wished to compose the text himself rather than have John Hay do it. But, as Hay told Spencer on November 25, Lincoln "was literally crowded out of the opportunity to writing a note" because "the crush here just now is beyond endurance."[44]

Nor did Lincoln have time to write a suitable reply when Massachusetts Governor John A. Andrew requested a presidential acknowledgment of the heroic sacrifice made by one of his constituents, a widow named Lydia Bixby, who (falsely) claimed that she had lost five sons in the war. For the president's signature Hay wrote a letter of condolence: "Dear Madam,—I have been shown in the files of the War Department a statement of the Adjutant General of Massachusetts, that you are the mother of five sons who have died gloriously on the field of battle. I feel how weak and fruitless must be any words of mine which should attempt to beguile you from the grief of a loss so overwhelming. But I cannot refrain from tendering to you the consolation that may be found in the thanks of the Republic they died to save. I pray that our Heavenly Father may assuage the anguish of your bereavement, and leave you only the cherished memory of the loved and lost, and the solemn pride that must be yours, to have laid so costly a sacrifice upon the altar of Freedom."[45]

The Bixby letter, as Lincoln biographer James G. Randall noted, "has taken a pre-eminent place as a Lincoln gem and a classic in the language."[46] Carl Sandburg deemed it "a piece of the American Bible. 'The cherished memory of the loved and lost'—these were blood-color syllables of a sacred music." Comparing the Bixby letter to the Gettysburg Address, Sandburg added: "More darkly than the Gettysburg speech the letter wove its awful implication that human freedom so often was paid for with agony."[47] Another biographer asserted that "Lincoln's three greatest writings"—the Gettysburg address, the Bixby letter, and the second inaugural—are the compositions "upon which assessment of his literary reputation must ultimately be based."[48] Those documents, according to a pair of literary scholars, are "great prose-poems" that "were the direct outgrowth of his whole life, of all those mysterious qualities of heredity and environment that went into the making of his genius."[49] The author of a monograph on the development of Lincoln's prose style pictured him writing to Mrs. Bixby: "we can imagine how that great heart throbbed and that strong, beautiful right hand rapidly traversed the paper while he was bringing comfort to a bereaved patriot mother. There was as true lyrical inspiration at work in the plain office of the White House that twenty-first day of November, 1864 as that which impelled Wordsworth to compose the 'Ode on Intimations of Immortality.'"[50]

The Bixby letter is beautiful indeed, but it was written by John Hay, not Lincoln; nor was its recipient the mother of five sons killed in the war. She lost two of her boys and tried to cheat the government out of money by claiming the others had been killed. Of the three survivors, one had deserted to the enemy, another may have done so, and the third was honorably discharged. Mrs. Bixby was born in Virginia, sympathized with the Confederacy, and disliked Lincoln so much that she apparently destroyed the letter in anger. Evidence suggests that she ran a whorehouse in Boston and was "perfectly untrustworthy."[51] (Though he did not compose the famous communication to Mrs. Bixby, Lincoln on occasion wrote exceptionally moving letters of condolence, like those he sent to the parents of Elmer Ellsworth in 1861 and to Fanny McCullough the following year.)

The adjutant general of Massachusetts, after hand-delivering the letter to Mrs. Bixby, provided copies to newspapers, which gave it wide distribution. One partisan Democratic journal sneeringly asked why "Mr. Lincoln's sons should be kept from the dangers of the field, while the sons of the laboring men are to be hurried into the harvest of death at the front? Are the sons of the rail-splitter, porcelain, and these other common clay?"[52] Of course, Tad was far too young to serve, but not 21-year-old Robert. Actually, Robert was eager to drop out of Harvard and enlist, but his mother adamantly objected. "We have lost one son, and his loss is as much as I can bear, without being called upon to make another sacrifice," she insisted to the president.

Lincoln replied: "But many a poor mother has given up all her sons, and our son is not more dear to us than the sons of other people are to their mothers."

"That may be; but I cannot bear to have Robert exposed to danger. His services are not required in the field, and the sacrifice would be a needless one."

"The services of every man who loves his country are required in this war. You should take a liberal instead of a selfish view of the question, mother."[53]

"Don't I know that only too well?" she cried; "before this war is ended I may be like that poor mother, my poor mother in Kentucky, with not a prop left in her old age."

On another occasion, she remarked to her husband: "I know that Robert's plea to go into the Army is manly and noble and I want him to go, but oh! I am so frightened he may never come back to us!"

When New York Senator Ira Harris bluntly asked her why Robert was not in uniform, Mary Lincoln replied that her son was "making his preparations now to enter the Army," and was "not a shirker as you seem to imply for he has been anxious to go for a long time. If fault there be, it is mine. I have insisted that he should stay in college a little longer as I think an educated man can serve his country with more intelligent purpose than an ignoramus."[54]

In January 1865, when the First Lady finally yielded, Lincoln wrote Grant asking that Robert be placed on his staff: "Please read and answer this letter as though I was not President, but only a friend. My son, now in his twenty second year, having graduated at Harvard, wishes to see something of the war before it ends. I do not wish to put him in the ranks, nor yet to give him a commission, to which those who have already served long, are better entitled, and better qualified to hold. Could he, without embarrassment to you, or detriment to the service, go into your Military family with some nominal rank, I, and not the public, furnishing his necessary means? If no, say so without the least hesitation, because I am as anxious, and as deeply interested, that you shall not be encumbered as you can be yourself."[55]

Grant replied graciously: "I will be most happy to have him in my Military family in the manner you propose. The nominal rank given him is immaterial but I would suggest that of Capt. as I have three staff officers now, of conciderable service, in no higher grade. Indeed I have one officer with only the rank of Lieut. who has been in the service from the begining of the war. This however will make no difference and I would still say give the rank of Capt."[56] On February 11, Robert entered the army as a captain and served creditably on Grant's staff until he resigned five months later.

Last Annual Message to Congress

In late November, Lincoln was busy drafting his annual message. On November 14, he told Orville H. Browning that he "had not yet written a word of his message, and thought he would close [the] doors tomorrow and go to work at it."[57] As he did so, he jotted his thoughts on slips of paste board or box board, then revised them before having a printer set them up in widely spaced lines. On this document he made further changes before the final version was set in type.

The message dealt at length with foreign relations, especially developments in the country's immediate neighbors, Canada and Mexico. Confederates operating in

Ontario laid various schemes to undermine the Union war effort. Jacob Thompson, secretary of war in Buchanan's administration, helped to foment armed uprisings by the Sons of Liberty in the Northwest. One was scheduled to coincide with the Democratic convention at Chicago in late August. Among other things, the plan called for the liberation of Camp Douglas, a 60-acre prison facility near the city, housing thousands of Rebel POWs who were guarded by only 800 troops. The conspirators lost their nerve, but others quickly hatched another scheme targeting Camp Douglas for election day in November. It was squelched when detectives got wind of it and arrested the leaders, including John B. Castleman, a captain in John Hunt Morgan's guerrilla band. Lincoln mercifully ordered that he be banished rather than tried as a spy.

The president was not so merciful with John Yates Beall of the Confederate Navy, ringleader of the "Lake Erie Conspiracy" aimed at liberating Rebel prisoners held at Johnson's Island off Sandusky, Ohio. Beall and his co-conspirators operated out of Windsor, Canada. In September, their plan to commandeer a Union gunboat on Lake Erie fell through. Beall escaped but three months later was captured while plotting to derail trains in upstate New York. Tried as a spy and guerrilla, he was sentenced to death. Lincoln resisted numerous appeals for clemency from eminent sources, including Thaddeus Stevens and eighty-nine other members of the U.S. House. To an Illinois friend, the president said Beall's case, like that of the slave trader Nathaniel Gordon, was one "where there must be an example." The young man's supporters "tried me every way. They wouldn't give up; but I had to stand firm on that, and I even had to turn away his poor sister when she came and begged for his life, and let him be executed. I can't get the distress out of my mind."[58] Lincoln was evidently convinced by the argument of General John A. Dix, who presided at Beall's court martial. On February 14, 1865, Dix wrote him that the "testimony seemed to me very clear and conclusive; and, in view of the transactions, in which Beall bore so important a part, as well as in consideration of the intelligence daily reaching me that new outrages on our frontier are meditated by rebel emissaries in Canada, I deemed it my duty to order the sentence pronounced upon him to be promptly executed."[59] Joseph Holt sternly endorsed Dix's recommendation, and Beall was hanged on February 24.

Lincoln was equally stern with another terrorist, Captain Robert C. Kennedy, one of eight conspirators operating out of Canada who attempted to torch several buildings in New York City on election day. The fires were quickly extinguished and did little harm. Kennedy was apprehended shortly afterward and tried before another court-martial, which found the arsonist guilty and condemned him to death. No intercessors pleaded for mercy, and he went to the gallows on March 25.

American anger at the British for allowing Confederates to use Canada as a staging area for sabotage, terrorism, and sedition grew stronger when twenty Rebel raiders plundered St. Albans, Vermont. After robbing banks, killing one man, and unsuccessfully trying to burn the town, they retreated to Canada, where authorities released them rather than extradite them to the United States. The American public was understandably outraged and cried for revenge against Great Britain, whose policies throughout the war had seemed to favor the Confederacy. On December 16, the

New York *Times* talked darkly of war: "if it must come, let it come. Not ours the guilt; it will belong only to English malignity and lawlessness. We were never in better condition for a war with England."[60]

Ten days earlier, Lincoln in his annual message urged a less confrontational policy but one that would signal American displeasure with the "recent assaults and depredations committed by inimical and desperate persons, who are harbored there." He threatened that the United States might expand its navy on the Great Lakes, require Canadians to have passports to enter the United States, and abrogate the reciprocity treaty of 1854, thus hindering trade between the two countries. But he hoped that such steps would be unnecessary, for "there is every reason to expect that, with the approval of the imperial government," Canadian authorities "will take the necessary measures to prevent new incursions across the border."[61]

Earlier in 1864, Lincoln had expressed his irritation with the governor-general of a Canadian maritime province who winked at Confederate blockade runners using its ports. When that official sarcastically asked if he might vote in the impending presidential election, Lincoln, who was exasperated by the governor-general's lax enforcement of neutrality rules, said he was reminded of a story about an Irishman who arrived in America one election day and was "perhaps, as eager as Your Excellency, to vote, and to vote early and late and often. So, upon his landing at Castle Garden, he hastened to the nearest voting place, and, as he approached, the judge, who received the ballots, inquired: 'who do you want to vote for? on which side are you?' Poor Pat was embarrassed, he did not know who were the candidates. He stopped, scratched his head, then, with the readiness of his countrymen, he said: 'I am fornent the Government, anyhow. Tell me, if your Honor plases, which is the rebellion side, and I'll tell you how I want to vote. In Ould Ireland, I was always on the rebellion side, and, by Saint Patrick, I'll stick to that same in America.' Your Excellency would, I should think, not be at all at a loss on which side to vote?"[62]

Less conciliatory than Lincoln, General John A. Dix instructed his troops to pursue Confederate raiders into Canada. The president swiftly revoked the order but with the caveat that if Canadian authorities did not extradite miscreants like the St. Albans terrorists, he would authorize cross-border pursuit in the future. The Canadian prime minister took steps to appease outraged Americans: nine of the St. Albans raiders were arrested and tried in local courts; the government paid back $50 million of the $200 million stolen from Vermont banks; militia were instructed to patrol the border more conscientiously; and Confederate terrorist cells were uprooted. To show his appreciation, Lincoln rescinded the passport order. In England, government leaders spoke "in the highest terms of the manner in which Mr. Lincoln's Administration had conducted its relations to foreign Powers."[63]

Relations with France became strained in 1864 when Louis Napoleon's government installed the Austrian Archduke Ferdinand Maximilian as emperor of Mexico. Three years earlier, the French had joined the British and Spanish in sending a military expedition to Mexico to collect debts. Spain and England withdrew their forces after the mission was accomplished, but French troops stayed on and overthrew the republican government of Benito Juarez, in open violation of the Monroe Doctrine.

In the spring of 1864, in part to send a message to the French, Lincoln ordered Nathaniel Banks's army in New Orleans to move into Texas. That expedition up the Red River floundered, and the administration assured France that it had no desire to threaten Maximilian's regime. Led by the implacable Henry Winter Davis, chairman of the House Committee on Foreign Affairs, congressional Republicans denounced Lincoln's appeasement of the French. Davis persuaded the House to approve a resolution condemning France for establishing a puppet regime in Mexico. When Seward assured Louis Napoleon's government that the United States had no intention of picking a fight over Mexico, the infuriated Davis asked Charles Sumner to bring his resolution to the floor of the senate. Sharing Lincoln's "one war at a time" approach to foreign affairs, Sumner urged his fellow Radical to postpone the matter. "Our friends are very anxious to get into a war with France," Lincoln observed, "using this Mexican business for that purpose. They don[']t consider that England and France would surely be together in that event. France has the whip hand of England completely. England got out of the Mexican business into which she had been deceived by France, by virtue of our having nothing to do with it. They have since been kept apart by good management, and our people are laboring to unite them again by making war on France. Worse than that, instead of doing something effective, if we must fight, they are for making mouths and shaking fists at France warning & threatening and inducing her to prepare for our attack when it comes."[64]

In his 1864 annual message, Lincoln glossed over the Mexican problem, prompting Congressman Davis to introduce a resolution criticizing the administration for ignoring Congress's power to shape foreign policy. It was tabled because, as a Washington correspondent noted, Republicans "are all in too good a humor with Mr. Lincoln to criticise or complain." To be sure, they disliked Seward's apologies for congressional action regarding the Monroe Doctrine, but they believed that Davis "is a very dangerous lion any way, needing to be kept under the most watchful restraint, lest he fall upon the administration party and rend it."[65] Shortly thereafter, the House reversed itself when Davis offered assurances that his resolution implied no criticism of Lincoln. Despite his denial, the New York *Times* condemned the action of the House as "a splenetic ebullition against the President, on the part of those who failed to prevent his re-election."[66]

In his annual message, Lincoln explained how he hoped to end the Civil War swiftly. He told Congress that upon "careful consideration of all the evidence accessible it seems to me that no attempt at negotiation with the insurgent leader [Jefferson Davis] could result in any good. He would accept nothing short of severance of the Union—precisely what we will not and cannot give. . . . Between him and us the issue is distinct, simple, and inflexible. It is an issue which can only be tried by war, and decided by victory." While Davis could not bring about peace because of his mulish insistence on independence, the people of the Confederacy "can, at any moment, have peace simply by laying down their arms and submitting to the national authority under the Constitution. . . . If questions should remain, we would adjust them by the peaceful means of legislation, conference, courts, and votes, operating only in constitutional and lawful channels." Here Lincoln was drawing a distinction between the end of bloodshed, which the people could bring about on their own, and ultimate peace terms, which must include not only the restoration of the Union but also the abolition of slavery: "In presenting the abandonment of armed resistance to the national authority on the part of the insurgents, as the only indispensable condition to ending the war on the part of the government, I retract nothing heretofore said as to slavery." Emphatically he reiterated his commitment to emancipation: "I repeat the declaration made a year ago, that 'while I remain in my present position I shall not attempt to retract or modify the emancipation proclamation, nor shall I return to slavery any person who is free by the terms of that proclamation, or by any of the Acts of Congress.' If the people should, by whatever mode or means, make it an Executive duty to re-enslave such persons, another, and not I, must be their instrument to perform it."[67]

Congress applauded this last statement loud and long. Radicals hailed its "unblemished moral grandeur" and predicted that it would "have immortal life" and "go down as a heritage to future generations."[68] A colonel in the U.S. Colored Troops echoed that sentiment: "God bless you Abraham Lincoln for these noble words that bring joy to so many thousands of Colored Soldiers and so many hundreds of thousands of women and children; words that would of themselves had you no other claim endear you for all time to all who love Freedom and the Nation."[69] The editor of the *National Anti-Slavery Standard* thanked Lincoln "for the noble words in your Message to Congress, which give assurance that nothing shall be wanting on your part to extirminate slavery, root and branch, from the American soil. . . . You have justified the confidence which the great body of Abolitionists, led by Wm. Lloyd Garrison, have placed in you."[70]

Congressmen also applauded Lincoln's reference to the new Maryland constitution: "Maryland is secure to liberty and Union for all the future. The genius of rebellion will no more claim Maryland. Like another foul spirit, being driven out, it may seek to tear her, but it will woo her no more."

Lincoln's statement that the people of the Confederacy "can, at any moment, have peace simply by laying down their arms and submitting to the national authority under the Constitution" may have represented an attempt to make an end-run around Jefferson Davis. Perhaps he was aiming his message at Robert E. Lee, whose power in the Confederacy waxed as Davis's waned, or at other war-weary Confederate leaders like Assistant Secretary of War John A. Campbell, Governor Joseph E. Brown of Georgia, Representatives William W. Boyce of South Carolina and Jehu A. Orr of Mississippi, and Senators William C. Rives of Virginia and William A. Graham of North Carolina. The Tarheel State had long been a hotbed of a powerful, if ill-organized, peace movement that gained strength below the Mason-Dixon line as one Confederate defeat followed another throughout the late summer and autumn of 1864.

Lee did make overtures to Grant, suggesting that they meet to discuss peace terms. When Grant forwarded the proposal to Washington, he received a blunt response from Stanton: "The President directs me to say that he wishes you to have no conference with Gen Lee unless it be for the capitulation of Lee[']s army, or on solely minor and purely military matters. He instructs me to say that you are not to decide, discuss, or confer upon any political questions: such questions the President holds in his own hands; and will submit them to no military conferences or conventions—mean-time you are to press to the utmost, your military advantages."[71]

In his annual message, Lincoln tactfully acknowledged that Congress had a role to play in setting peace terms. Some "questions are, and would be, beyond the Executive power to adjust; as, for instance, the admission of members into Congress, and whatever might require the appropriation of money." Furthermore, he conceded that his power "would be greatly diminished by the cessation of actual war. Pardons and remission of forfeitures, however, would still be within Executive control." He warned Southerners that the amnesty policy he had announced a year earlier might not remain in effect much longer, for "the time may come—probably will come—when public duty shall demand that it be closed; and that, in lieu, more rigorous measures than heretofore shall be adopted."[72] This may well have been a signal to Radicals that the president would move in their direction.

As Elizabeth Cady Stanton noted, the message for the most part was a "dry, barren document," consisting largely of a routine summary of his cabinet secretaries' reports.[73] But some praised it. A Massachusetts judge and former member of the U.S. senate called it an "honor to the country" and thought it was so "remarkably well written" that it "would not suffer in comparison with any message of any President." Another judge, Samuel F. Miller of the U.S. Supreme Court, detected in Lincoln's message "a vigor not usual to him."[74] Thaddeus Stevens declared "that it is the best message which has been sent to Congress in the past sixty years." According to Noah Brooks, the "verdict of all men is that the message is immensely strengthening for the President, and that while it has all of the dignity and polish of a first-rate State paper, it has the strong common sense, the practical knowledge of details which will commend the document to the minds of 'the simple people.'" Brooks told a friend that it was "interesting and curious to observe how the President has grown morally and intellectually since he has been at the White House; take his messages and read them through *ad seriatim* and you will see his advancement in ability, logic and rhetoric. . . . The last message is a model of compact, strong sense, practical knowledge and argument." Brooks asserted that Lincoln "is *the man* for these times; I know him well—very well, and I do not hesitate to say that he is a far greater and better man than our own people think." Prophetically Brooks speculated that the "time will come when people generally will concede his true merit and worth."[75]

Renewed Patronage Headaches

As 1864 drew to a close, Lincoln was also busy dealing with importunate office seekers, for many would-be civil servants regarded the second term as a justification for "a new deal."[76] A congressman advised job applicants that the only way to get Lincoln to remove incumbent office holders was to harass him with delegation after delegation. In March 1865, the president told Colonel James Grant Wilson, who joined him at an opera performance, that he attended music dramas not so much for the singing but, as he explained, "for the rest. I am being hounded to death by office-seekers, who pursue me early and late, and it is simply to get two or three hours' relief that I am here."[77] On March 22, Noah Brooks reported that Lincoln's "health has been worn down by the constant pressure of office-seekers and legitimate business, so that for a few days he was obliged to deny himself to all comers." He refused to see visitors after 3 P.M.[78] He was so harried that he sometimes forgot promises he had made. To a senator who had extracted a patronage pledge, Lincoln said he would carry it out if he remembered to do so: "as a man said to his debtor, 'I will see you tomorrow if I do not forget it.'"[79]

Of all the clamorous horde, none dismayed Lincoln more than the eminent Shakespearean actor, James H. Hackett. After seeing Hackett play Falstaff, the president wrote him a fan letter, which the indiscreet actor released to the New York *Herald*. That paper ridiculed Lincoln's taste in soliloquies, for he had told Hackett that Hamlet's soliloquy "to be or not to be" was surpassed by Claudius's speech, "oh my offense is rank." Abashed, Hackett apologized to Lincoln, who replied: "Give yourself no uneasiness on the subject. . . . My note to you I certainly did not expect to see in print; yet I have not been much shocked by the newspaper comments upon it. Those comments constitute a fair specimen of what has occurred to me through life. I have endured a great deal of ridicule without much malice; and have received a great deal of kindness, not quite free from ridicule. I am used to it."[80] The friendly correspondence between them ended when Hackett asked to be named consul in London, a post that could not be given to him. John Hay recalled that a "hundred times this experience was repeated; a man would be introduced to the President whose disposition and talk were agreeable; he took pleasure in his conversation for two or three interviews and then this congenial person would ask some favor impossible to grant, and go away in bitterness of spirit."[81]

Another painful request came from Lincoln's old friend Anson G. Henry, who wished to replace William P. Dole as head of the Bureau of Indian Affairs. The president was sympathetic but hesitated, saying that the "thing that troubles me most is, that I dislike the idea of removing Mr. Dole who has been a faithful and devoted personal and political friend." Dr. Henry replied: "Well Mr. Lincoln, I will go home and remain where I am, not only, without a murmur, but entirely satisfied that you have done what you believe to be best calculated to promote the welfare and prosperity of the Government." With emphasis the president said: "Henry—you must not understand me as having decided the matter." He explained that there was fierce competition for Dole's job: "The Delegation from Minnesota are pressing very strongly for that place for Ex-Senator Wilkinson, and the Delegation from Illinois headed by Yates and Trumbull are pressing their man judge Kellogg." Henry replied: "our Pacific men are beginning to think that the old North West are getting the Lyons share of the offices." Lincoln laughingly responded, "It does look a little that way."[82]

When pressed to remove officeholders who had not committed treason but were insufficiently loyal to the administration, Lincoln balked: "I have made up my mind to make very few changes in the offices in my gift for my second term. I think now that I will not remove a single man, except for delinquency. To remove a man is very easy, but when I go to fill his place, there are *twenty* applicants, and of these I must make *nineteen* enemies."[83] Earlier in the war, businessman John Murray Forbes remarked that Lincoln "is notoriously tender hearted about removing anybody. It is his weak point."[84] Another Massachusetts Republican, Congressman Samuel Hooper, predicted that Lincoln "will go along without many changes because of his aversion to do anything that he thinks would be unpleasant to anyone."[85] Hay noted that Lincoln was not predisposed to cashier civil servants for political treachery: "It seems utterly impossible for the President to conceive of the possibility of any good resulting from a rigorous and exemplary course of punishing political dereliction. His favorite expression is, 'I am in favor of short statutes of limitations in politics.'"[86]

In March, Chase's successor as treasury secretary, William P. Fessenden, resigned in order to accept a seat in the U.S. senate. To replace him, Lincoln wanted Senator Edwin D. Morgan, who refused. So the president turned to Hugh McCulloch, an Indiana banker serving as comptroller of the currency. Suspecting that he might be offered the job, McCulloch told his wife that he would rather not have it, but if it were tendered to him, "I should be ambitious enough or rather foolish enough to accept it."[87] The president summoned McCulloch and said: "I have sent for you, Mr. McCulloch, to let you know that I want you to be Secretary of the Treasury, and if you do not object to it, I shall send your name to the Senate." McCulloch later wrote that he was "taken all aback by this sudden and unexpected announcement," for it "was an office that I had not aspired to, and did not desire." He "knew how arduous and difficult the duties of the head of that department were," and he had been offered a lucrative bank presidency in New York. He "hesitated for a moment, and then replied: 'I thank you, Mr. President, heartily for this mark of your confidence, and I should be glad to comply with your wishes if I did not distrust my ability to do what will be required of the Secretary of the Treasury in the existing financial condition of the Government.'" Lincoln said: "I will be responsible for that."[88]

Intervening to Win Passage of the Thirteenth Amendment

Lincoln's chief legislative goal in the aftermath of the election was to secure passage of the Thirteenth Amendment outlawing slavery throughout the country. In June it had failed to win the requisite two-thirds majority of the House and did not become a significant issue in the presidential campaign, for Republicans soft-pedaled it while Democrats focused on miscegenation, civil liberties, conscription, and Lincoln's Niagara Manifesto. Voters assumed that Congress would not address the amendment again until the members elected in 1864 took their seats in December 1865, and so they did not consider it a pressing matter. Thus the president's reelection could not legitimately be interpreted as a mandate for the amendment.

Yet in his annual message, Lincoln did just that, boldly claiming that the electorate had endorsed the amendment: "It is the voice of the people now, for the first time, heard upon the question." And so he urged its immediate passage. In justifying such a recommendation, Lincoln noted that the "next Congress will pass the measure if this does not. Hence there is only a question of *time* as to when the proposed amendment will go to the States for their action. And as it is to so go, at all events, may we not agree that the sooner the better?"

Lincoln's motives were partly political. He evidently calculated that the amendment might help heal the breach in the Republican ranks by rendering moot the thorny question of whether Congress had the power to abolish slavery by statute. Moreover, with the slavery issue solved, some Democrats might be more willing to join the Republicans, who had won in 1860 and 1864 only because of highly unusual circumstances.

The president also argued that rapid adoption of the amendment might shorten the war. In December he lobbied the slaveholding Missouri Congressman James S. Rollins, who had voted against the amendment in the spring. "I am very anxious that the war should be brought to a close," he told Rollins, "at the earliest possible date, and I don't believe this can be accomplished as long as those fellows down South can rely upon the Border States to help them; but if the members from the Border States would unite, at least enough of them to pass the 13th amendment to the Constitution, they would soon see they could not expect much help from that quarter, and be willing to give up their opposition, and quit their war upon the Government; this is my chief hope and main reliance, to bring the war to a speedy close, and I have sent for you, as an old Whig friend, to come and see me, that I might make an appeal to you to vote for this amendment. It is going to be very close; a few votes one way or the other will decide it." When Rollins agreed to support it, Lincoln offered profuse thanks and asked him to persuade Missouri colleagues to follow suit. He urged Rollins to tell "them of my anxiety to have the measure pass," for it "will clinch the whole subject." Rollins said he had "never seen any one evince deeper interest and anxiety upon any subject than did Mr. Lincoln upon the passage of this amendment." The congressman was as good as his word, lobbying his colleagues on behalf of the amendment.[89]

Patronage considerations may have helped induce Rollins and his fellow Missourian Austin A. King to change their votes. In September the death of a federal judge in Missouri had created a vacancy on the bench. On December 7, Lincoln consulted with Abel Rathbone Corbin, a wealthy financier and former resident of Missouri then living in New York. Corbin also called on Interior Secretary John P. Usher, with whom he schemed to gain the votes of Rollins and King. Usher thought he could persuade Rollins and that Corbin would be able to win over King "*by co-operation*" (i.e., favors). Corbin told the president he would guarantee nothing to either Representative, but would like "to have 'a serpent hanging' up 'on a pole' in the sight of all." Therefore he counseled Lincoln not to fill the judgeship until after the House had passed the amendment. Corbin promised the president that "if you will allow a vacancy to remain unfilled, and allow it to be known to Sec. Usher that it is unpromised, I will please you by the result. Your amendment *shall* pass. I can get you some New York votes." Even if he could not persuade Democrats to reverse their earlier vote, they might be convinced to absent themselves. (Corbin reminded Lincoln that the two-thirds vote requirement applied only to the members present, not the entire House.) Thus the amendment might pass and even gain ratification by the time of Lincoln's second inauguration.[90] Both Rollins and King made passionate speeches in favor of the amendment. It is not clear whether their enthusiasm had anything to do with the vacant judgeship, but it may well have. According to Elizabeth Blair Lee, writing two days after the amendment passed, Rollins "has the credit of carrying the constitutional amendment."[91]

Lincoln recruited another Democratic congressman, the lame-duck Samuel S. Cox of Ohio, to lobby his colleagues. Cox, who enjoyed great respect among his party confreres in the House, had voted against the amendment that spring but after the election changed his mind. In December, eager to eliminate the slavery question from politics, he met with New York Democratic leaders S. L. M. Barlow, Samuel J. Tilden, and Manton Marble to discuss the amendment. He argued that the party should cast off the "proslavery odium" and "get rid of the element [of slavery] which ever keeps us in a minority and on the defensive."[92] During the holiday recess, Cox called at the White House with John Todd Stuart, Lincoln's former law partner and, like Cox, a lame-duck Representative. They urged the president to make a good-faith effort to end the war through honorable negotiations.

Lincoln told Cox and Stuart that he wanted their assistance in winning Democratic support for the amendment. Cox "promised the President his help, provided a sincere effort was made for peace within the Union." If that effort failed, Cox added, he would still pitch in: "not only by his help would the amendment be adopted, but the war would be pursued with renewed vigor."[93]

(Lincoln had met earlier with Cox, who claimed that he was both "a good friend" to the administration and "a good Democrat at the same time." The congressman's statement reminded Lincoln of an old sow belonging to one Jacob Straus. When she could not be found for several days, Straus told his two sons that she "was down the creek somewhere, for he saw where she had been rooting among the ironweeds, and he was going to find her." He instructed his boys to help him: "Now you go over the creek and go down that side of it, and I'll go down this side and we'll find her, for I believe she is on both sides of the creek." Lincoln believed Cox was "trying to be on both sides of the creek.")[94]

In the end, Cox voted against the amendment, maintaining that it "would prove an insurmountable obstacle to peace and union."[95] He had intended to vote for it but was planning to move to New York and received hints from Democrats there that he had better not support the amendment. A colleague believed that he would have voted for the measure if his vote had been required to pass it. He evidently did appeal to some Democrats effectively, however, for Seward—who organized a high-pressure lobbying operation on behalf of the amendment—later declared that it was the Ohio congressman "to whom, personally, more than any other member, is due the passage of the constitutional amendment in Congress abolishing African slavery."[96] Perhaps to encourage Cox, Lincoln authorized James W. Singleton and Francis P. Blair, Sr., to undertake peace missions to Richmond. (Their exploits are discussed later in this chapter.)

In mid-January, when the amendment seemed doomed to fail yet again, Lincoln stepped up his efforts to win support for it. Congressman Ashley prodded him, saying: "*You* must help us *one* vote [.] Don[']t you know of a sinner in the opposition who is on praying ground?"[97] The president told a pair of House members that two more votes were needed and that they were to be obtained by hook or crook. He evidently implied that favors could be expected from the administration in return for those votes. As a Democratic opponent of the amendment remarked on the House floor, the "wish or order of the President is very potent. He can punish and reward."[98] Lincoln tried to woo a Representative who had lost a sibling in the war, saying: "your brother died to save the Republic from death by the slaveholders rebellion. I wish you could see it to be your duty to vote for the Constitutional amendment ending slavery."[99]

No evidence survives that Lincoln offered a specific quid pro quo for votes, but it seems that he authorized his lieutenants to do so (particularly Seward and Ashley, the floor manager of the amendment.) Ashley cut a deal with Democratic Representative Anson Herrick of New York, who was lobbied by New Yorkers Abram Wakeman and Charles A. Dana as well as Congressmen Ashley, Augustus Frank, and Homer A. Nelson. (Nelson, who spoke with Herrick several times, claimed he had Seward's authorization to offer a reward.) They assured Herrick that his brother would receive a federal job in return for the congressman's vote. After the amendment passed, Lincoln allegedly told Herrick "in person that whatever Ashley had promised should be performed, and he signified his good faith by sending the name [of Herrick's brother] to the Senate."[100] (In March, Lincoln did nominate Hugh Herrick as an assessor of internal revenue, but the senate did not confirm him.)

Ashley did not always receive Lincoln's support. The Ohioan had been approached by spokesmen for the Camden and Amboy Railroad of New Jersey, who wanted to stop Charles Sumner's bill ending their monopoly control of train service between New York and Philadelphia. If Ashley could have Sumner's measure postponed, the railroad would encourage a pair of New Jersey Democratic congressmen either to support the Thirteenth Amendment or to absent themselves when it came up for a vote. After Sumner rebuffed him, Ashley asked the president to lobby the senator, asserting that Sumner "thinks the defeat of the Camden & Amboy monopoly would establish a principle by legislative enactment, which would effectually crush out the last lingering relics of the States' Rights dogma."

"I can do nothing with Mr. Sumner in these matters," Lincoln explained, according to a memo by Nicolay. "While Mr. Sumner is very cordial with me, ... I think he would be all the more resolute in his persistence . . . if he supposed I were at all watching his course on this matter."[101]

When the Senate Commerce Committee refused to report Sumner's bill, and two New Jersey Democratic congressmen (George Middleton and Andrew J. Rogers) failed to show up for the vote on the Thirteenth Amendment, it was widely rumored that the president had struck a deal. In light of Nicolay's memo, that seems highly unlikely. Ashley may have misled the Camden and Amboy lobbyists into thinking that the president would cooperate. Possibly those lobbyists convinced the Commerce Committee that bottling up Sumner's bill would yield political gains. In any event, the railroad appears to have persuaded Congressman Rogers, who had strongly opposed the amendment and had ties to the Camden and Amboy, to remain absent when the vote was taken. In the House, Lincoln's operative James S. Rollins explained that Rogers was "confined to his room several days by indisposition."[102] Rollins's involvement suggests that some arrangement had been made with the White House. Middleton's absence is more easily explained, for he was an opponent of slavery who tended to skip tough votes.

A Pennsylvania Democratic congressman whose election was being contested, Alexander Coffroth, voted for the amendment apparently in return for Republican pledges that the party would support his claim to a legislative seat. Moses Odell, a Democrat representing Brooklyn, received the coveted post of naval agent in New York after supporting the amendment (in both 1864 and 1865). Lame-duck Congressman George Yeaman of Kentucky, who had voted against the amendment in 1864, supported it in 1865. In August of that year, he was named minister to Denmark. (In 1862, he had practically begged Lincoln for an office. "I would like *right well* to have a good office," he wrote. "I don[']t want any *office*, but I *do* want the comforts and salary of a good office, I need them, and I *deserve* them." Immodestly, he claimed that he was "qualified for *anything* from Brig Genl or District Judge *down* to anything except a Clerkship—I would not make a good clerk—it is so *mechanical*.")[103]

Seward's agents evidently offered cash for votes. In early January, one of the more prominent of them, Robert W. Latham, told the secretary of state that he had "no doubt about passing" the amendment, for "[m]oney will certainly do it, if patriotism fails."[104] Latham was a shady character who had worked closely with the notoriously corrupt John B. Floyd, Buchanan's secretary of war. Of the sixteen Democrats voting for the amendment, six represented New York districts. The Seward lobby evidently persuaded the Democrats' flagship newspaper, the New York *World*, to change its anti-amendment stance to quasi-neutrality. Other important papers were also cajoled into taking similar action.

Just how much corruption was involved in the passage of the amendment is hard to measure. According to Montgomery Blair, Seward "made Lincoln believe that he had carried that Amendment by Corruption." Blair denied Seward's contention, insisting that the only case resembling bribery was the post offered to Anson Herrick's brother. Blair gave most credit to Dean Richmond, leader of the upstate New York Democracy. The Democrats who voted for the amendment, Blair insisted, did so for "patriotic and party considerations."[105]

S. S. Cox told a different tale of corrupt New Yorkers. Many years after the event, he alleged that a Radical who was boarding at the same house with him acknowledged that men in the Empire State were offering substantial bribes to Democrats willing to vote for the amendment.

On January 31, as the hour for voting on the Thirteenth Amendment drew near, rumors swept through the House that Confederate peace commissioners were en route to the capital. Ashley panicked, fearing that the news might prompt some Democrats to backslide and defeat the measure. To prevent that, he appealed to Lincoln, who was busy writing instructions for Seward's use in negotiating with the Confederate emissaries. To calm the storm, he penned a disingenuous message: "So far as I know, there are no peace commissioners in the city, or likely to be in it." This was a clever lawyer's quibble, for Lincoln knew full well that commissioners were en route to Hampton Roads, Virginia, where they would meet with Seward to discuss peace terms.[106] This "little secret piece of history" amused Lincoln, who told a caller several days later, "I *eased* it [the amendment] along—and concluded to send Seward down" to Fort Monroe. Recalling Ashley's fear that his Democratic "converts" might "have gone off in a tangent at the last moment had they smelt Peace," Lincoln laughed and repeated that phrase "as far as I know."[107]

With peace rumors thus squelched, the amendment narrowly won House approval by a margin of 119 to 56, with all Republicans and sixteen Democrats voting for it and eight Democrats absent and not paired. (If four of those absentees had voted no, the amendment would have failed.) Six Representatives who had voted against it earlier were absent or not voting, and ten who had been absent for the June 1864 ballot now supported it. As the voting proceeded, one Republican congressman wrote to his wife: "I never felt so much excitement over any measure before."[108] The "scene that followed the announcement of the result of the vote was worthy of the great event," Carl Schurz reported. "All arose as at a word of command" and "embraced, they shook hands, and ten minutes passed before the hurrahing and the enthusiastic racket ceased."[109] Women spectators fluttered their white handkerchiefs, transforming the packed galleries into a blizzard scene, while men cheered thunderously, threw their hats in the air, and vigorously waved their canes. Blacks in the galleries, including Henry Highland Garnet, also cheered heartily. "Oh what a pepper and salt mixture it was," Garnet remembered.[110] Lincoln was equally delighted when Isaac N. Arnold and other congressmen friendly to the administration brought him the news. It "filled his heart with joy," Arnold recalled, for he "saw in it the complete consummation of his own great work, the emancipation proclamation."[111]

Lincoln's active lobbying of congressmen was highly unusual, for he generally obeyed the Whig dictum that the executive should defer to the legislature when statutes were being framed. He seldom initiated or vetoed legislation. His willingness to intervene so vigorously for the Thirteenth Amendment was yet another indication of his deep commitment to black freedom.

William Lloyd Garrison fully appreciated that commitment, writing to the president shortly after the amendment passed: "God save you, and bless you abundantly! As an instrument in his hands, you have done a mighty work for the freedom of the millions who have so long pined in bondage in our land—nay, for the freedom of all mankind. I have the utmost faith in the benevolence of your heart, the purity of your motives, and the integrity of your spirit."[112] On February 4, before an enthusiastic crowd in Boston's Music Hall, Garrison asked rhetorically: "And to whom is the country more immediately indebted for this vital and saving amendment of the Constitution than, perhaps, to any other man?" The reply was obvious: "I believe I may confidently answer—to the humble railsplitter of Illinois—to Presidential chain-breaker for millions of the oppressed—to Abraham Lincoln!" The president "will never consent under any circumstances to the re-enslavement of any one of the millions whose yokes he has broken."[113]

Lincoln modestly disclaimed credit while praising Garrison's role in the abolition of slavery. In April 1865, he told Lieutenant Daniel H. Chamberlain of the U.S. Colored Cavalry: "I have only been an instrument. The logic and moral power of Garrison, and the anti-slavery people of the country and the army have done all."[114] To John Murray Forbes, the president described Garrison "as one of '*the Powers[,]*' a Radical with a substratum of common sense and practical wisdom."[115]

The day after the House passed the amendment, Lincoln responded to White House serenaders that he "could not but congratulate all present, himself, the country and the whole world upon this great moral victory." He hailed it as "a very fitting if not an indispensable adjunct to the winding up of the great difficulty." It was essential "to remove all causes of disturbance in the future; and to attain this end it was necessary that the original disturbing cause should, if possible, be rooted out." The Emancipation Proclamation "falls far short of what the amendment will be when fully consummated." If the Proclamation were all that protected the freedom of the slaves, its legal validity might be questioned and it could also be argued "that it only aided those who came into our lines and that it was inoperative as to those who did not give themselves up, or that it would have no effect upon the children of the slaves born hereafter. In fact it would be urged that it did not meet the evil. But this amendment is a King's cure for all the evils. [Applause.] It winds the whole thing up." It "was the fitting if not indispensable adjunct to the consummation of the great game we are playing."[116]

Lincoln was proud that Illinois was the first state to ratify the amendment, and by mid-April, nineteen others had followed suit. By year's end, it won endorsement by three-quarters of the states and thus became part of the Constitution.

To commemorate the amendment's passage, Lincoln, with the approval of the cabinet and congressional chaplains, invited Henry Highland Garnet, a prominent black Presbyterian minister and emigration champion, to deliver a sermon in the House chamber. Garnet did so on Sunday, February 14, before an enthusiastic, racially mixed audience.

Prior to 1865, it was not clear that the amending process was designed to do more than permit minor adjustments to the Constitution. Now it became evident that major social changes could be accomplished through it. The passage of the Thirteenth Amendment set in motion a chain of events foreseen by the Democratic Cincinnati *Enquirer,* which predicted accurately that it would be followed by other amendments enfranchising blacks and women.

The Hampton Roads Conference

The peace initiative that nearly sidelined the Thirteenth Amendment had been undertaken by Francis P. Blair, Sr., who entertained the delusive idea that the North and South might compose their differences by joining together to expel the French from Mexico. (His scheme resembled the one that Seward had suggested in his April 1, 1861, memorandum to the president.) In early December, Horace Greeley had pleaded with Blair to lobby the president: "*You* have Mr. Lincoln's ear, as *I* have not, and can exert influence on every side where it is needed. Do urge and inspire him to make peace among our friends any how, and with our foes so soon as may be." Without explaining his plan, Blair asked Lincoln for permission to visit Richmond and confer with Jefferson Davis. The president replied: "Come to me after Savannah falls."

Sherman took that Georgia port on December 22, and Lincoln gave Blair the pass he had requested. In Richmond, Jefferson Davis indicated a willingness to participate in a joint invasion of Mexico. In mid-January, upon receiving a report of this conversation, Lincoln authorized Blair to tell Davis "that I have constantly been, am now, and shall continue, ready to receive any agent whom he, or any other influential person now resisting the national authority, may informally send to me, with the view of securing peace to the people of our one common country."[117]

Davis should have realized that his cause was hopeless, for the Union had recently captured Fort Fisher at Wilmington, North Carolina, thus plugging the last hole in the blockade and cutting one of Lee's most important supply lines. General Sherman had spent December marching unopposed across Georgia en route to Savannah, a city that he tendered to the president as a Christmas gift. That month General George H. Thomas had obliterated John Bell Hood's army at Nashville and Franklin. Sherman followed up his spectacular march by thrusting into the Carolinas as he headed toward a rendezvous with Grant.

When some White House callers expressed anxiety about the military situation, Lincoln went to a map, showed how Grant had Lee trapped at Petersburg and how Sherman was moving thither. Lincoln remarked that his own situation, after being elected twice to the presidency, called to mind "an old fellow in the early days of Indiana who had been a wicked and lascivious sinner, and had joined the church and was getting baptized. The preacher had dipped him in a river, and he had come up gasping and rubbing his face, and then calling on the preacher to dip him again and baptize him once more. The preacher said once was enough. But the old fellow insisted." So the preacher dunked him again. "As he came up and rubbed the water out of his eyes and mouth and got his breath, he blurted out, 'Now I've been baptized twice, and the Devil can kiss my ass.'" Lincoln pointed to a spot on the map "and said that when Sherman's army got to that place the war would be ended. 'And then,' said Lincoln, 'the Southern Confederacy can kiss my ass.'"[118]

Instead of taking Lincoln's offer seriously, Jefferson Davis defiantly sent a trio of peace commissioners with instructions to confer informally with Lincoln "for the purpose of securing peace to the two countries." (Davis ignored the recommendation of his exceptionally capable secretary of state, Judah P. Benjamin, to omit any reference to "two countries.") Many members of the Confederate Congress, persuaded that the war was lost, had urged the appointment of peace commissioners to effect a surrender. Much later, they were surprised to learn of Davis's unyielding instructions, which doomed the conference to failure before it began. One Confederate emissary, Vice-President Alexander H. Stephens, considered his mission a "humbug" from the outset.[119]

When word of Blair's mission leaked out, Radicals expressed alarm. "Blair is an old fool for going to Richmond upon a peace mission and the Administration is little better for permitting him to go upon any pretense whatever," Zachariah Chandler grumbled. "Nothing but evil *can* come of this nonsense."[120] The senator and his ideological compeers suspected that Lincoln might offer universal amnesty to the Confederates, restore their confiscated property, allow their army to join with Union forces to attack Mexico, and offer slaveholders enormous financial compensation for their escaped bondsmen, while leaving those still outside Union lines in slavery. Such skepticism prompted Lincoln to remark: "Some of my friends in Congress act as if they were afraid to trust me with a dinner, yet I shall never compromise the principles upon which I was elected."[121] Joseph Medill warned the president not to "be in too much hurry for Peace. Don't *coax* the rebel chiefs but pound them a little more. When they are sufficiently whipped they will gladly accept *your terms,* and the peace then made will be enduring."[122]

On February 1, when Henry Ward Beecher called at the White House to express alarm at Blair's peace overtures, Lincoln explained that "Blair thinks something can be done, but I don't, but I have no objection to have him try his hand. He has no authority whatever but to go and see what he can do." Beecher recalled that Lincoln's "hair was 'every way for Sunday.' It looked as though it was an abandoned stubble-field. He had on slippers, and his vest was what was called 'going free.' He looked wearied, and when he sat down in a chair, looked as though every limb wanted to drop off his body."[123] Beecher feared that the "*pride of the nation,* is liable to be hurt. Anything that looks like the humiliation of our Government, would be bitterly felt," he told the president.[124]

Moderates also had qualms. Gideon Welles confided to his diary that Lincoln "with much shrewdness and much good sense, has often strange and incomprehensible whims; takes sometimes singular and unaccountable freaks. It would hardly surprise me were he to undertake to arrange terms of peace without consulting any one."[125] When Blair returned, Lincoln said he believed that "peace was much nearer at hand than the most confident have at any time hoped for."[126]

On January 30, the Confederate commissioners (Alexander H. Stephens, Senator Robert M. T. Hunter, and Assistant Secretary of War John A. Campbell) arrived at Grant's lines and asked permission to proceed to Washington. Lincoln sent word that they would receive a safe conduct pass only if they agreed to negotiate "with a view of securing peace to the people of our one common country." When they seemed to accept that condition, the president on January 31 dispatched Seward to parlay with them informally at Hampton Roads. The secretary of state was to make clear "that three things are indispensable." First, "the national authority" must be restored "throughout all the States." Second, there was to be no "receding, by the Executive of the United States on the Slavery question." And finally, there was to be no "cessation of hostilities short of an end of the war, and the disbanding of all forces hostile to the government." Seward was told to "inform them that all propositions of theirs not inconsistent with the above, will be considered and passed upon in a spirit of sincere liberality. You will hear all they may choose to say, and report it to me. You will not assume to definitely consummate anything."[127] Lincoln also instructed Grant to let "nothing which is transpiring, change, hinder, or delay your Military movements, or plans."[128]

When the Confederates seemed to renege on their agreement to negotiate based on Lincoln's conditions, the talks nearly collapsed. The president was poised to recall Seward when he received a dispatch from Grant that changed his mind. On February 1, sensing that such a denouement would "have a bad influence," Grant urged Lincoln to meet with the commissioners.[129] (The general's wife had prodded him to do something to break the logjam.) In addition, that night Major Thomas T. Eckert reported that the commissioners were hinting that they would be willing to drop Davis's insistence on Confederate independence.

The day that Grant sent his crucial telegram, Lincoln met with an amateur peace negotiator, James W. Singleton of Illinois, just back from a sojourn in Richmond. On January 5, the president had issued him a pass enabling him to travel through Union lines to the Confederate capital. Lincoln had known Singleton in prewar years, when he was a prominent Whig-turned-Democrat at Quincy and a close friend of fellow-townsman Orville H. Browning. During the war, the Virginia-born Singleton, whose brother served in the Confederate Congress, became the leader of Illinois's radical Peace Democrats. In the fall of 1864, Browning had entered a business deal with Singleton, New York Senator Edwin D. Morgan, Robert E. Coxe, and Judge James Hughes of the federal court of claims; they planned to purchase cotton and tobacco in Virginia and sell it for a hefty profit to Northern merchants and manufacturers. Such commerce was legal under the 1863 Captured and Abandoned Property Act. Lincoln felt obligated to Singleton for helping to undermine McClellan's 1864 presidential campaign by refusing to support the general's candidacy.

Lincoln's relations with Singleton are somewhat murky and confusing. During the election campaign of 1864, the president evidently sent him on a mission to Confederate agents in Canada. In September of that year, Singleton informed one of those operatives that he had met twice with Lincoln, who "says he will go as far 'as any man in America to restore peace on the basis of Union[.]' He declares that he never has and never will present any other *ultimatum*—that he is misunderstood on the subject of slavery—that it shall not stand in the way of peace."[130] On Thanksgiving, Singleton told Orville H. Browning that before the election, Lincoln had informed him that his Niagara Manifesto had "put him in a false position—that he did not mean to make the abolition of slavery a condition, and that after the election he would be willing to grant peace with an amnesty, and restoration of the union, leaving slavery to abide the decisions of judicial tribunals." Two days later, Singleton added that Lincoln had sent him word "that slavery should not stand in the way of adjustment, and that he intended to say so in his message [to Congress]—that he would determine after the meeting of Congress whether he would send commissioners to Richmond, and if he concluded to do so he would send him, Singleton."[131] On Christmas Eve, Lincoln (according to Browning's diary) told Browning that he had not intended to make abolition a precondition for peace.

These reports clash with explicit evidence that Lincoln had decided *not* to retract his insistence on abolition as a precondition for peace. Perhaps the president was referring to the peculiar distinction that he made in his annual message between an end to fighting and peace. In any event, Singleton traveled to Canada where he talked with Confederates Clement Clay and Nathaniel Beverly Tucker. He told Browning that, according to those gentlemen, the South was ready to cease fighting if it could retain slavery and receive amnesty.

Singleton later claimed that he had made four or five trips to Richmond at Lincoln's behest. When the president asked him what could be done to expedite peace, he replied that the Confederate leadership entertained false hopes inspired by some Northern Democrats who claimed that the war-weary North was on the verge of revolt. Lincoln, who viewed Singleton as ideally qualified to disabuse them of such a notion, told him: "if there is anybody in the country who can have any influence on those people, and bring about any good, you are the man. They must have confidence in you; you have been as much their friend as it was possible for you to be and yet be loyal to the government under which you live." Singleton responded that he was honored and would do his best to enlighten the Davis administration. Lincoln insisted that he would never retract the Emancipation Proclamation but added that the courts might rule it invalid and he would have to enforce that judicial decision.[132] Singleton wrote to his wife on January 7: "I cannot . . . too highly appreciate the confidence Mr. Lincoln has reposed in me and the honor conferred by the bare privilege of making the effort in behalf of my country and suffering humanity."[133]

Two days later, Singleton left for Richmond on a mission that was supposed to be secret. Alexander Long, a leading Peace Democrat and former congressman from Ohio, expressed the hope that Singleton's effort "may result in good—God grant that some means may be used through whatever instrumentality to once more give peace to the country."[134] In Richmond, Singleton made purchases for his business partners, met with Jefferson Davis and other leaders to discuss peace terms, and evidently helped persuade the Confederate president to send peace commissioners to Hampton Roads.

Upon his return on January 31, Singleton told William Cornell Jewett that the people of the South "are all anxious for peace," that it was "in the power of the North to reconstruct by an offer of liberal terms—to be considered and acted upon during an armistice of sixty days," that the Confederates "will not consent to Reconstruction upon any other basis than the clearest recognition of the rights of States respectively to determine each for itself all questions of local and domestic government, Slavery included," and finally that they "will not permit Slavery to stand in the way of Independence—to that [i.e., independence] it would be promptly surrendered, but to nothing else—*unless it should be a fair compensation* coupled with other liberal terms of Reconstruction secured by Constitutional Amendments."[135] Although Lincoln was unenthusiastic about Singleton's proposals for restoring sectional harmony, he may well have been encouraged by the news that "fair compensation" and "other liberal terms" might persuade the Davis government to cease fighting.[136]

Upon reading Grant's dispatch, Lincoln hastened to join Seward at Fort Monroe. On February 3 they parlayed with the Confederate delegation aboard the steamer *River Queen*, anchored in Hampton Roads. He greeted the commissioners warmly, especially Alexander H. Stephens, with whom he had worked for the nomination of Zachary Taylor seventeen years earlier when they both were serving in Congress. As the diminutive Stephens began to remove his heavy overcoat and large scarf, the president poked gentle fun at him: "Now, gentleman, you see what a large amount of 'shuck' Mr. Stephens has—just wait a minute and you will be surprised to find what a small 'nubbin' he is."[137] The president laughed heartily when Stephens retaliated with a story from their congressional days: at the Capitol several Representatives were discussing the proper pronunciation of "Illinois." Some said it was "Illinoy," others "Illinoise." John Quincy Adams smilingly quipped: "If one were to judge from the character of the representatives in this congress from that state, I should decide that the proper way to pronounce the word would be 'All noise.'"[138] During the informal conversation that preceded the negotiations, Lincoln "was very talkative and pleasant with all of the commissioners," Stephens recalled. "He seemed to be in a splendid humor, and was in excellent spirits."[139]

After these preliminaries, the five men got down to business. According to Stephens, Lincoln was "perfectly frank," submitting "his views, almost in the form of an argument."[140] The only way to restore peace and harmony was "for those who were resisting the laws of the Union to cease that resistance." The president reiterated that the "restoration of the Union is a *sine qua non* with me, and hence my instructions that no conference was to be held except upon that basis." Ignoring this plain language, Stephens expatiated on a plan like the one suggested by Blair, involving an armistice and a joint expedition against the French in Mexico. Lincoln firmly rejected an armistice, which "would be a *quasi* recognition of the States then in arms against the National Government, as a separate power." That he "never could do."[141]

As for the projected invasion of Mexico, Lincoln said "that it could not be entertained. That there could be no war without the consent of Congress, and no treaty without the consent of the Senate of the United States. That he could make no treaty with the Confederate States because that would be a recognition of those States, and that this could not be done under any circumstances. That unless a settlement were made there would be danger that the quarrel would break out in the midst of the joint operations. That one party might unite with the common enemy to destroy the other. That he was determined to do nothing to suspend the operations for bringing the existing struggle to a close to attain any collateral end."[142]

As Stephens recalled, Hunter, speaking "at length, in rather congressional style," urged "that the recognition of Mr. Davis's power to make a treaty, was the first and indispensable step to peace, and referring to the correspondence of King Charles the First, and his Parliament, as a reliable precedent, of a constitutional ruler, treating with rebels." Lincoln's face "then wore that indescribable expression which generally preceded his hardest hits," and he remarked drolly: "Upon questions of history, I must refer you to Mr. Seward, for he is posted in such things, and I don't profess to be bright. My only distinct recollection of that matter is, *that Charles lost his head*." That observation "settled Mr. Hunter for a while."[143]

Turning to more realistic questions, Lincoln said the Confederate states could resume their place in the Union once they had laid down their arms and allowed the federal government to resume its traditional functions. Seward reminded the commissioners that the president in his annual message had announced, "In stating a single condition of peace, I mean simply to say that the war will cease on the part of the Government whenever it shall have ceased on the part of those who began it." Congress would determine who was legitimately elected to serve in it, Lincoln pointed out, but he believed "that when the resistance ceased and the National Authority was recognized, the States would be immediately restored to their practical relations to the Union."[144] He added that "individuals subject to pains and penalties under the laws of the United States might rely upon a very liberal use of the powers confided to him to remit those pains and penalties if peace be restored." Of course he could not infringe on the powers of Congress or repeal its laws or undo the findings of courts; but "he did offer all the power of mercy and pardon and influence, both as the Chief Magistrate, and as a popular party leader." When Hunter remarked that he had no fear of harsh treatment, "Lincoln retorted, that he, also, had felt easy as to the rebels, but not always so easy about the lamp posts around Washington city—a hint that he had already done more favors for the rebels, than was exactly popular with the radical men of his own party." (This was clearly an allusion to the fear he had expressed earlier to Congressman William D. Kelley that he might be hanged by disaffected Republicans.)

As for emancipation, Lincoln said that he "never would change or modify the terms of the proclamation in the slightest particular." But that document had freed only about 200,000 slaves thus far; the status of the remaining 3 million-plus would be settled by the courts. (Lincoln underestimated the number of slaves already liberated.) Seward interjected that if the Thirteenth Amendment, whose recent passage by Congress was unknown to the Confederates, were ratified by three-quarters of the states, all slaves throughout the country would be free.

Apropos of the Thirteenth Amendment, Lincoln "suggested that there was a question as to the right of the insurgent States to return at once, and claim a right to vote upon the amendment." Seward hinted that if the Confederates surrendered and quickly regained admission to the Union, they might defeat the amendment. Taking a different tack, Lincoln "intimated that the States [in rebellion] might do much better to return to the Union at once, than to stand the chances of continued war, and the increasing bitterness of feeling in Congress. And that the time might come" when Confederates "would cease to be [regarded as] an erring people, invited back to the Union as citizens."[145]

If slavery were abolished, Stephens asked: "what are we to do? I know that negroes will not work, unless forced to it, and I tell you that we shall all starve together." The question reminded Lincoln of an Illinois farmer who told his neighbor about an easy way to feed hogs: "plant plenty of potatoes, and when they are mature, without either digging or housing them, turn the hogs in the field and let them get their own food as they want it." When the neighbor asked, "how will they do when the winter comes and the ground is hard frozen?" the farmer replied, "let' em root." Southern whites, Lincoln said, "can go to work like honest people or starve."[146]

Lincoln renewed his proposal to compensate slaveholders, stating "that he would be willing to be taxed to remunerate the Southern people for their slaves. He believed the people of the North were as responsible for slavery as the people of the South, and if the war should then cease, with the voluntary abolition of slavery by the States, he should be in favor, individually, of the Government paying a fair indemnity for the loss to their owners. He said he believed this feeling had an extensive existence at the North. He knew some who were in favor of an appropriation as high as Four Hundred Millions of Dollars for this purpose. I could mention persons, said he, whose names would astonish you, who are willing to do this, if the war shall now cease without further expense, and with the abolition of slavery as stated. But on this subject he said he could give no assurance—enter into no stipulation." When Seward objected to compensating slaveholders, Lincoln replied: "if it was wrong in the South to hold slaves, it was wrong in the North to carry on the slave trade and sell them to the South."

In frustration, Hunter protested that the Confederacy was being asked to surrender unconditionally. Denying that assertion, Seward said he did not "think that in yielding to the execution of the laws under the Constitution of the United States, with all its guarantees and securities for personal and political rights, as they might be declared to be by the court, could be properly considered as unconditional submission to conquerors, or as having anything humiliating about it."[147] Seward was right. The terms offered the South by Lincoln—reunion and emancipation—were far more limited and generous than the demands that the United States would in 1945 impose on Germany and Japan, who surrendered unconditionally.

As the meeting closed, Hunter asked about the U.S. Capitol expansion. Seward described how the dome had been completed and was now crowned by a large statue of Armed Liberty. (A few months earlier Lincoln had said "that there were some people who thought the work on the Capitol ought to stop on account of the war, people who begrudged the expenditure, and the detention of the workmen from the army." But Lincoln believed that the completion of the Capitol would symbolize the preservation of the Union: "If people see the Capitol going on, it is a sign we intend the Union shall go on.")[148]

The only agreement to emerge from the conference dealt with prisoner exchanges. At Stephens's suggestion, Lincoln said he would recommend to Grant that a cartel for such exchanges be negotiated with the Confederates. The president also agreed to have Stephens's nephew released from a Northern prison camp in return for a Union soldier.

The disappointed Rebel commissioners relayed Lincoln's terms to Jefferson Davis and said that "the conference was but a confirmation of the desire for peace upon the part of the United States." The Confederate chief regarded the proposition as an insult and wanted to issue an announcement to that effect, but the commissioners refused. So a bland statement was released instead. In public speeches, the Confederate president breathed defiance. He would "teach the insolent enemy who has treated our proposition with contumely in that conference in which he had so plumed himself with arrogance, he was, indeed, talking to his masters." With a sneer he referred to Lincoln as "His Majesty Abraham the First,"[149] and declared that rather than rejoin the Union, "he would be willing to yield up everything he had on earth, and if it were possible would sacrifice a thousand lives before he would succumb."[150] As it turned out, far more than a thousand lives were sacrificed because of Davis's stubborn unwillingness to accept the reality of defeat. As the disappointed John A. Campbell put it a few months later, Davis "became in the closing part of the war an incubus and a mischief" because he was "[s]low, procrastinating, obstructive, filled with petty scruples and doubts," lacking "a clear, strong, intrepid judgment, a vigorous resolution, and a generous and self-sacrificing nature."[151]

Lincoln returned to Washington optimistic that the conference at Hampton Roads might lead to peace. He told James W. Singleton, "I have not brought back peace in a lump from the conference, but I am glad I went down, and hope for good results."[152] Radicals disparaged Lincoln's trip. "The peace fizzle has ended as I supposed it would in national disgrace," remarked Zachariah Chandler. He thought it was bad enough for Seward and Blair to undertake such a fool's errand, but it was "not only disgracefull but ridiculous" for "the President to go 200 miles to meet the representatives of these accursed Rebels and then to come back with a flea in his ear."[153]

On February 6, Lincoln introduced to the cabinet a resolution embodying the proposal he made at the conference—to offer $400 million as compensation to slaveholders if the Confederacy would surrender by April 1. Half would be paid upon that surrender and the other half if the Thirteenth Amendment were ratified by July 1. Should Congress pass this resolution, Lincoln pledged that he would fully exercise the power granted him and that the "war will cease, and armies be reduced to a basis of peace; that all political offences will be pardoned; that all property, except slaves, liable to confiscation or forfeiture, will be released therefrom, except in cases of intervening interests of third parties; and that liberality will be recommended to congress upon all points not lying within executive control."[154]

In justifying his proposal, Lincoln asked the cabinet, "how long has this war lasted, and how long do you suppose it will still last? We cannot hope that it will end in less than a hundred days. We are now spending three millions a day, and that will equal the full amount I propose to pay, to saying nothing of the lives lost and property destroyed. I look upon it as a measure of strict and simple economy." The cabinet unanimously rejected this pragmatic argument, which Lincoln had used to justify compensated emancipation back in 1862. Secretary of the Interior John P. Usher speculated that Lincoln's "heart was so fully enlisted in behalf of such a plan that he would have followed it if only a single member of his Cabinet had supported him in the project." Sadly, Lincoln commented, "You are all against me" and dropped the matter.[155]

Welles recorded in his diary that Lincoln's "earnest desire" to "conciliate and effect peace was manifest, but there may be such a thing as so overdoing as to cause a distrust or adverse feeling. In the present temper of Congress the proposed measure, if a wise one, could not be carried through successfully." Welles feared that the Confederates would misunderstand it, and that if it were openly submitted and rejected, it would be harmful.[156] Secretary Usher was equally anxious, believing that if Lincoln submitted the resolution to Congress, Radicals like Ohioan Robert C. Schenck "would make it the occasion of a violent assault on the President and perhaps thus weaken his influence to procure men and money to prosecute the war."[157] According to the man who was to procure the money, Treasury Secretary Fessenden, the cabinet thought that since the president's proposal could not be acted on by Congress before its adjournment on March 4, it should not be submitted to that body. In addition, "it was evidently the unanimous opinion of the cabinet that the only way effectively to end the war was by force of arms—and that until the war was thus ended no proposition to pay money should come from us."[158] Lincoln evidently intended the $400 million to help revive the blighted economy of the South. It was an enlightened proposal designed to help restore sectional harmony.

When the House asked Lincoln for a report on the Hampton Roads conference, he promptly submitted a document including most of the relevant correspondence. (He omitted the dispatch from Thomas T. Eckert indicating that the commissioners might drop their unconditional demand for independence.) It tersely concluded that on the part of Seward and himself, "the whole substance of the instructions to the Secretary of State . . . was stated and insisted upon, and nothing was said inconsistently therewith; while, by the other party it was not said that, in any event, or on any condition, they *ever* would consent to re-union, and yet they equally omitted to declare that they *never* would so consent. They seemed to desire a postponement of that question, and the adoption of some other course first, which, as some of them seemed to argue, might, or might not, lead to re-union, but which course, we thought, would amount to an indefinite postponement. The conference ended without result."[159]

As Lincoln's report was read to the House, members listened breathlessly. When they heard the reference in the president's letter to Blair about "one common country," they audibly expressed satisfaction. The three conditions for peace in Seward's instructions triggered spontaneous applause, and mirthful laughter greeted the injunction to the secretary of state not to "definitely consummate anything." A reporter present guessed "that some men were ashamed of themselves when they remembered that they had said that Lincoln had gone to Fortress Monroe for fear that Seward would not make his terms *liberal enough*."[160] At the close of the reading, both the floor and galleries erupted in applause.

Originally skeptical about Lincoln's decision to meet with Confederate emissaries, Radicals felt relief at the outcome. Thaddeus Stevens acknowledged that he and his allies had underestimated the president. The Pennsylvania congressman maintained that no Republicans "desired to sue for peace" with the Confederacy so near collapse. "But the President thought it was best to make the effort, and he has done it in such a masterly style, upon such a firm basis and principle, that I believe [all] who thought his mission there was unwise will accord to him sagacity and patriotism, and applaud his action."[161] Franklin B. Sanborn chided the bitter Radical, Moncure D. Conway, who had just published an especially vitriolic attack on the president. "It is not true that Mr Lincoln was *detested* by the men who elected him," Sanborn wrote in late February. Rather, the president "was *distrusted* and still is,—witness the alarm which attended his late visit to Fortress Monroe. But even in that affair he seems to have been true to the policy which he has announced, and he is heartily bent on the destruction of slavery. Of this there is now no reason to doubt."[162] George Luther Stearns also chastised Conway for his criticism of Lincoln. Like Sanborn, Stearns spoke with Wendell Phillips, and they decided that it was time to stop agitating about emancipation and instead to focus on advocating black suffrage "with as much zeal and confidence too that we shall obtain it as we did emancipation last year. These questions are carried forward by their own gravity[.] Mr Lincoln Mr Seward, Mr Garrison or Mr Phillips are only straws on the current which shows the set in their particular locality. We do not care therefore to hold up Mr Lincoln's deficiencies to the public gaze but rather by enlightening the people prepare the way for that perfect day of freedom for all, which we believe is the destiny of our country."[163] Such criticism of Conway, in the view of Samuel J. May, Jr., was too gentle. "His preposterous folly and self-conceit deserved a much more stinging rebuke than it ever got," May confided to a friend.[164]

The Washington *Chronicle* accurately predicted that the Hampton Roads conference would unify the North, which was made more aware than ever that the war persisted only because of Jefferson Davis's obstinacy. Flagging Confederate patriotism also received a boost, for many in the South regarded Lincoln's terms as unacceptable. "There are no peace men among us now!" exclaimed the Richmond *Sentinel*.[165]

Lincoln was willing to meet Confederate commissioners and offer generous peace terms because he wanted to end the war swiftly, restore goodwill between the sections, reduce the chances of guerrilla warfare breaking out after the war's end, and stave off impending anarchy and poverty in the South. Gideon Welles recalled that in early 1865, Lincoln "frequently expressed his opinion that the condition of affairs in the rebel States was deplorable, and did not conceal his apprehension that, unless immediately attended to, they would, in consequence of their disturbed civil, social, and industrial relations, be worse after the rebellion was suppressed."[166]

In late February, Lincoln met with Roger A. Pryor of Virginia, who appealed in vain on behalf of convicted saboteur John Y. Beall. After explaining that he could not pardon Beall, the president spoke of the Hampton Roads conference. According to Pryor's wife, Lincoln stated that Jefferson Davis, having turned down the generous peace terms offered, would "be responsible for every drop of blood that should be shed in the further prosecution of the war, a futile and wicked effusion of blood, since it was then obvious to every sane man that the Southern armies must be speedily crushed." He spoke so warmly and at such great length that Pryor "inferred that he still hoped the people of the South would reverse Mr. Davis's action, and would renew the negotiations for peace." He hinted that he wanted Pryor to feel out Southern leaders on the matter. Pryor did so but was informed that Davis was inflexible.[167]

Misguided Cotton-Trading Policies

James W. Singleton's mission to Canada involved more than peacemaking; he was a businessman eager to purchase cotton, tobacco, and other Southern products. Nathaniel Beverly Tucker, with whom he met in late 1864, hoped to obtain meat for the Confederate army by selling cotton to the North. At that time, Lincoln was hoping to shorten the war by encouraging cotton trading (but not in exchange for meat and other commodities that might help the Confederate military). Acting on authority granted by Congress, the president early in the war had forbidden commercial intercourse with the enemy but did allow the Treasury Department to issue cotton-trading permits to Southern merchants who took a loyalty oath. Those merchants could sell cotton to treasury agents, then buy goods for resale in areas under Union control.

Such commerce was designed to encourage Southern Unionists, supply Northern textile manufacturers with much-needed fiber, allow some cotton to reach Europe, thereby reducing the chance of British or French intervention, and fill the government's coffers.

In practice, the system worked poorly. Soldiers and treasury officials accepted bribes to allow war material through Union lines; merchants who took the oath with mental reservations provided war material to the Confederates; and some Northerners paid for cotton with gold, which Rebels used to buy weaponry in the Bahamas. Military commanders, including Grant and Sherman, tried to staunch the flow of illegal cotton, but were only moderately successful. During the war, approximately 600,000 bales of Southern cotton made their way overland into the North illicitly, twice the amount that was lawfully traded. (Only 500,000 bales were shipped to Europe.) The proceeds helped keep the Confederacy relatively well supplied, despite the ever-tightening blockade and the fall of Vicksburg and Port Hudson.

Over the objections of Welles and Stanton, who echoed the views of army and navy commanders, Lincoln moved to liberalize trade with the enemy. Earlier, he had generally sided with the military in disputes about such commerce. When attorney Lawrence Weldon asked him one day about a struggle between the army and the treasury over cotton trading, Lincoln replied with a story about a mutual friend of theirs back in Illinois, one Robert Lewis, clerk of the De Witt county court. Lewis had inherited some property in a remote part of Missouri and went out to inspect it, taking along warrants and patents establishing his title. Arriving at his destination, Lewis discovered a lanky, leathery frontiersman in a cabin where a rifle hung above the fireplace. He showed the documents to the gentleman and asked what he might have to prove that the land was his. Pointing to the rifle, Lewis's host said: "Well, that is my title, and if you don't get out of here pretty damned quick you will feel the force of it." Lewis promptly galloped off. "Now," said Lincoln, "the military authorities have the same title against the civil authorities that closed out Bob's . . . title in Missouri."[168]

But Lincoln changed his mind in July 1864, when Edward Atkinson, a textile manufacturer and philanthropist from Massachusetts, informed him "that although the Rebels sold less cotton they received about as much for it in consequence of high prices as when they had more of the article." The president told his cabinet that he "thought it might be well to take measures to secure the cotton, but was opposed to letting the Rebels have gold."[169]

Two months later, the administration revised its trade policy to expedite cotton sales, making it a government monopoly. Treasury agents, not private merchants or brokers, would buy cotton, sell it on the open market, and use the gold they received to redeem greenbacks. The new regulations backfired, for they unintentionally made it easier for speculators to sell contraband to the South. When General Edward R. S. Canby complained about the policy's effects, Lincoln explained the administration's thinking: "By the external blockade, the price is made certainly six times as great as it was. And yet the enemy gets through at least one sixth part as much in a given period, say a year, as if there were no blockade, and receives as much for it, as he would for a full crop in time of peace. The effect in substance is, that we give him six ordinary crops, without the trouble of producing any but the first; and at the same time leave his fields and his laborers free to produce provisions. You know how this keeps up his armies at home, and procures supplies from abroad. For other reasons we cannot give up the blockade, and hence it becomes immensely important to us to get the cotton away from him. Better give him *guns* for it, than let him, as now, get both guns and ammunition for it. But even this only presents part of the public interest to get out cotton. Our finances are greatly involved in the matter. The way cotton goes now carries so much gold out of the country as to leave us paper currency only, and that so far depreciated, as that for every hard dollar's worth of supplies we obtain, we contract to pay two and a half hard dollars hereafter. This is much to be regretted; and while I believe we can live through it at all events, it demands an earnest effort on the part of all to correct it. And if pecuniary greed can be made to aid us in such effort, let us be thankful that so much good can be got out of pecuniary greed."[170]

Despite Lincoln's contention, the blockade was no boon to the Confederates, for its grip drove desperate enemy agents to try obtaining supplies from the North in exchange for cotton. In March 1865, when Congress passed a bill to clamp down on illicit trading, Lincoln pocket-vetoed it. An indignant John Murray Forbes wrote to the bill's author, Edward Atkinson: "You can hardly imagine my disgust . . . at finding that old Abe had pocketed our Grand bill—I could have wrung his long neck! I suppose the cotton speculators around him were too many for him. It is sad to see the impression which this and other things give that whether *he* gets any thing out of it or *not* his course is influenced by those who do. The next best thing now is to try and get him to give an order that all cotton seized shall be certified to the owners leaving Congress to decide hereafter upon what should be done with the proceeds. As this course would help the cotton speculators and increase the quantity of cotton by encouraging holders to bring it in instead of burning it I should think he would do it if properly moved thereto."[171]

Lincoln's handling of the cotton trade was one of the least creditable chapters in the history of his administration. In the spring of 1864, New York Senator E. D. Morgan was understandably disgusted because "there has been fraud enough in sending supplies in and bringing cotton out of Rebel States to *destroy any* administration at any other time." (Morgan withheld public comment because there was so much congressional criticism of the administration that he did not wish to compound it.)[172] Lincoln issued valuable trading permits to intimates like Leonard Swett, to friends and associates of Ward Hill Lamon, and to political allies with tarnished ethical credentials like Thurlow Weed. As Charles A. Dana observed, "Mr. Lincoln had a vast number of friends who were bent upon making money in various ways, and he was much more willing that they should have favorable opportunities of this sort, than I could have wished."[173] The president's policy encouraged a spirit of get-rich-quick greed. More seriously, over the objections of Grant, Sherman, Canby, Welles, Bates, and others, he countenanced a system that prolonged the war needlessly. His reasons for doing so were partly political, rooted in a desire to placate Massachusetts cotton manufacturers as well as merchants and politicos in New York, a state he carried by a razor-thin margin in 1864.

Pecuniary greed certainly motivated Singleton and his fellow speculators, who anticipated making enormous profits on the $7 million worth of cotton and tobacco he had contracted to buy in Richmond. At the White House on February 5, when he asked help in getting these goods through Union lines, Lincoln, according to Browning's diary, "expressed himself pleased with what was done—said he wanted to get out all [cotton etc.] he could, and send in all the Green backs he could in exchange, and he would do for us [Singleton, Browning and their associates] all that he could."[174] Shortly thereafter, Lincoln wrote to Grant requesting that Singleton be permitted to bring "a large amount of Southern produce" through the lines. "For its bearing on our finances I would be glad for this to be done if it can be without injuriously disturbing your military operations, or supplying the enemy. I wish you to be judge and master on these points."[175] Grant balked, alleging that Singleton was carrying out "a deep laid plan for making millions" that might "sacrifice every interest of the country to succeed."[176] Lincoln promptly authorized the commanding general to cancel all trade permits within his department. When the Confederates set fire to Richmond as they abandoned it in early April, all of Singleton's purchases were destroyed.

As Forbes alleged, some cotton speculators did wield significant political influence with the administration. A conspicuous example was Simeon Draper, collector of customs in New York and a staunch ally of Weed and Seward. After playing a key role in carrying the Empire State for Lincoln in 1864, Draper wished to become the agent selling the huge supply of cotton that fell into Union hands when Sherman captured Savannah on December 22. Draper was given that lucrative commission after paying Mary Lincoln a $20,000 bribe, according to David Davis.[177]

(In February 1864, it was reported that Draper had already received $50,000 from the administration in auction fees. In September 1864, Draper pleaded with Secretary of the Treasury Fessenden to be allowed to continue as the officer in the New York customhouse auctioning consignments of property seized in the South. Mary Lincoln was in touch with Draper, urging him to reinstate a Mr. Martin to a clerkship in the customhouse. Draper traveled to Savannah to oversee the auction of cotton there.)[178]

Gideon Welles was "sickened" at "the idea of sending such a man [as Draper] on such a mission," which he predicted "will be a swindle." The navy secretary felt certain that a "ring will be formed for the purchase of the cotton, regardless of public or private rights."[179]

In addition to the money she received from Draper, Mrs. Lincoln also obtained funds from an influence-peddling scheme. In January 1865, she arranged to have the longtime doorkeeper of the White House, Edward McManus, replaced by one Cornelius O'Leary. Although McManus was regarded as "good and kind," and was well liked by the president and his friends, he had evidently angered the First Lady by telling Thurlow Weed that she was romantically linked with a man other than the president. When petitioners sought to have friends or relatives released from prisoner-of-war camps, O'Leary said he could expedite the pardons if they paid him $50; otherwise they might have to wait a long time before gaining admission to the president's office. O'Leary divided whatever he received with the First Lady. When a Democratic newspaper exposed this corrupt arrangement, Lincoln promptly fired O'Leary.[180]

A Sacred Effort: The Second Inaugural

On March 4, Lincoln's desire for true sectional reconciliation shone through his inaugural address, the greatest of his oratorical masterpieces. Although the morning was dark and rainy, well before ten o'clock huge crowds lined Pennsylvania Avenue, hoping to catch a glimpse of the president. They were doomed to disappointment, for quite early he had gone to the Capitol to sign bills passed in the final hours of the Thirty-eighth Congress. The presidential carriage, however, did roll down the avenue, conveying Mary and Robert Lincoln as well as Iowa Senator James Harlan, whose daughter would marry Robert in 1868. As the carriage prepared to join the procession, some confusion arose about just where it was to fit in. After waiting twenty minutes, Mrs. Lincoln grew impatient. Finally, she asked if something might be done to clear a passage for her. When she received a positive response, she ordered it done, and her carriage horses galloped forward, causing marshals and their assistants to protest loudly that she was ruining their arrangements.

Spectators filled the plaza in front of the Capitol's east facade. Nicolay estimated that the turnout was twice as large as the one four years earlier. When the doors to the senate gallery were finally opened, women rushed in, taking all the seats. One of them described the chaos below: "The whole thing was confusion itself," for no usher was there "to show the foreign ministers where to go," and the senate floor was "so filled by people who did not belong there that the members of the house could not get in."[181] Gideon Welles called the scene "a jumble."[182] Though the senate was still in session, women in the galleries made so much noise with their chatter that the presiding officer tried unsuccessfully to shush them. They finally quieted down when admirals, generals, cabinet members, Supreme Court justices, and the president filed in and took their seats.

At noon, the outgoing vice-president, Hannibal Hamlin, entered with his successor, Andrew Johnson. After the former delivered a brief valedictory, the latter embarrassed all present with a drunken harangue. The night before, Johnson and his friend John W. Forney had consumed several drinks, and the next morning, feeling unwell, the vice-president-elect took three glasses of whiskey straight. He had been recovering from a debilitating bout of typhoid; in his weakened state, the liquor was more than he could handle. Obviously intoxicated, he gave a twenty-minutes speech, taking far more than his allotted time. When Hamlin nudged him from behind and audibly reminded him that his time was up, Johnson paid no attention.

The new vice-president's words were difficult to hear over the chatter and giggling of women in the galleries. According to the journalists present, Johnson boasted "that he was a plebeian—he thanked God for it." He reminded the senators and Supreme Court justices that they owed their exalted positions to the people. Turning to the cabinet, he added: "And I will say to you, Mr. Secretary Seward, and to you, Mr. Secretary Stanton, and to you, Mr. Secretary—" He could not remember Gideon Welles's name and sotto voce asked a seatmate, "Who is Secretary of the Navy?" The whispered reply came, "Mr. Welles." Johnson continued: "and to you, Mr. Secretary Welles, I would say, you all derive your power from the people." Indirectly, he bragged about his accomplishments as military governor of Tennessee. Finally, he took the oath of office; then he grabbed the Bible he had been swearing on and melodramatically declared in a loud voice, "I kiss this Book in the face of my nation of the United States." He carried out that promise histrionically. In reciting the long oath of allegiance, he interpolated such phrases as "I can say that with perfect propriety" and gave a five-minute discourse on the oath.[183]

As he listened to Johnson's incoherent tirade, the embarrassed president closed his eyes, lowered his head in despair, and appeared to withdraw into himself. Others were equally dismayed. Attorney General Speed whispered to Welles, "all this is in wretched bad taste" and said Johnson "is certainly deranged." Welles in turn told Stanton, who seemed frozen in horror, that "Johnson is either drunk or crazy."[184] Postmaster General Dennison turned alternately red and white, and his secretary, who had received a cold chill as he listened to Johnson, called the speech "the most disgraceful exhibition I ever witnessed."[185] The face of Senator Henry Wilson was flushed, and his Massachusetts colleague Charles Sumner smiled sardonically. Senator Zachariah Chandler wrote his wife about Johnson's "drunken foolish speech," saying: "I was never so mortified in my life[;] had I been able to find a small hole I should have dropped through it out of sight."[186] Other agonized senators squirmed in their seats. The jaw of horrified Supreme Court Justice Samuel Nelson dropped until a disapproving glace from the chief justice induced him to close his mouth. The New York *World* deplored "the person who defiled our chief council-chamber . . . with the spewings of a drunken boor" and said that compared to Johnson, "even Caligula's horse was respectable."[187]

As the scandalized spectators exited to listen to the inaugural address, Lincoln instructed a marshal: "Do not permit Johnson to speak a word during the exercises that are now to follow."[188] Afterward he allegedly palliated the vice-president's behavior, saying that he "would not lose confidence in him for what he regarded [as] an unfortunate accident."[189]

(But while Lincoln was willing to make allowances for Johnson, he shunned him. At City Point a month later, when the vice-president and another politician came to visit him, Lincoln leaped up and frantically exclaimed: "Don't let those men come into my presence. I won't see either of them; send them away. . . . I won't see them now, and never want to lay eyes on them. I don't care what you do with them . . . but don't let them come near me!" The agitated chief executive then sat back down with a forbidding look on his face. During that sojourn at City Point, Mary Lincoln heard him say: "For God's sake don't let Johnson dine with us.")[190]

As the presidential party emerged from the rotunda onto the platform erected for the occasion, many spectators followed, swarming over the stairs, the column bases, and every other vantage point. As Lincoln gazed out over the vast, surging throng, cheering broke out, bands blared away, and flags fluttered everywhere. When he stood to read his remarks, a thunderous outburst of applause greeted him. Just before he began speaking, the sun emerged from behind the clouds which had obscured it all morning. (Later Lincoln said that "he was just superstitious enough to consider it a happy omen."[191] Many in the crowd interpreted it similarly.)

Lincoln's central aim was to prepare the public mind for a generous Reconstruction policy. Rather than introducing a series of policy recommendations, he sought to exorcise feelings of vindictiveness and self-righteousness. He also wished to share his understanding of the nature of the war and the reasons for its long duration.

His deep thinking on those questions led him to conclusions that he shared with the nation in his unusually brief address. He began by explaining why no lengthy account of recent events was necessary: "At this second appearing to take the oath of the presidential office, there is less occasion for an extended address than there was at the first. Then a statement, somewhat in detail, of a course to be pursued, seemed fitting and proper. Now, at the expiration of four years, during which public declarations have been constantly called forth on every point and phase of the great contest which still absorbs the attention, and engrosses the energies of the nation, little that is new could be presented. The progress of our arms, upon which all else chiefly depends, is as well known to the public as to myself; and it is, I trust, reasonably satisfactory and encouraging to all. With high hope for the future, no prediction in regard to it is ventured."

Tersely he summarized the events culminating in war: "On the occasion corresponding to this four years ago, all thoughts were anxiously directed to an impending civil-war. All dreaded it—all sought to avert it. While the inaugeral address was being delivered from this place, devoted altogether to *saving* the Union without war, insurgent agents were in the city seeking to *destroy* it without war—seeking to dissolve the Union, and divide effects, by negotiation. Both parties deprecated war; but one of them would *make* war rather than let the nation survive; and the other would *accept* war rather than let it perish. And the war came."

After this succinct description of *how* the war began, Lincoln explained *why* it occurred. Slavery caused the war, he maintained: "One eighth of the whole population were colored slaves, not distributed generally over the Union, but localized in the Southern part of it. These slaves constituted a peculiar and powerful interest. All knew that this interest was, somehow, the cause of the war. To strengthen, perpetuate, and extend this interest was the object for which the insurgents would rend the Union, even by war; while the government claimed no right to do more than to restrict the territorial enlargement of it. Neither party expected for the war, the magnitude, or the duration, which it has already attained. Neither anticipated that the *cause* of the conflict might cease with, or even before, the conflict itself should cease. Each looked for an easier triumph, and a result less fundamental and astounding. Both read the same Bible, and pray to the same God; and each invokes His aid against the other."

Stressing a theme which had long been at the core of his antislavery feeling, Lincoln said that it "may seem strange that any men should dare to ask a just God's assistance in wringing their bread from the sweat of other men's faces; but let us judge not that we be not judged."

(Lincoln had repeatedly denounced slavery as organized, systematized robbery which perverted the word of God, who had decreed that men should eat bread in the sweat of their own brows. A few weeks earlier he had made this point yet again when two women from Tennessee urged him to release their soldier-husbands from prison.

One petitioner emphasized that her spouse was religious. Upon granting their request, the president observed: "You say your husband is a religious man; tell him when you meet him, that I say I am not much of a judge of religion, but that, in my opinion, the religion that sets men to rebel and fight against their government, because, as they think, that government does not sufficiently help *some* men to eat their bread on the sweat of *other* men's faces, is not the sort of religion upon which people can get to heaven!" After the women left, Lincoln wrote out these remarks and asked Noah Brooks to have them published in the Washington *Chronicle* with a headline reading: "THE PRESIDENT'S LAST, SHORTEST, AND BEST SPEECH.")[192]

At this point the inaugural took an abrupt turn as Lincoln analyzed why the war dragged on and on and on: "The prayers of both could not be answered; that of neither has been answered fully. The Almighty has His own purposes." He then quoted Jesus' words as reported in the Gospel of Saint Matthew: "Woe unto the world because of offences! for it must needs be that offences come; but woe to that man by whom the offence cometh!" Lincoln somewhat inaccurately applied that scriptural passage to the war (subsequent scholarship has interpreted the word translated in the King James Bible as *offences* to mean *temptations* or *stumbling blocks,* which in context is a condemnation of those who tempt small children): "If we shall suppose that American Slavery is one of those offences which, in the providence of God, must needs come, but which, having continued through His appointed time, He now wills to remove, and that He gives to both North and South, this terrible war, as the woe due to those by whom the offence came, shall we discern therein any departure from those divine attributes which the believers in a Living God always ascribe to Him? Fondly do we hope—fervently do we pray—that this mighty scourge of war may speedily pass away. Yet, if God wills that it continue, until all the wealth piled by the bond-man's two hundred and fifty years of unrequited toil shall be sunk, and until every drop of blood drawn with the lash, shall be paid by another drawn with the sword, as was said three thousand years ago, so still it must be said 'the judgments of the Lord, are true and righteous altogether.'"

This pronouncement might not have sounded out of place in the mouth of a pious abolitionist or a Christian minister preaching a sermon, but for a president to utter it on such an important occasion was astonishing. It rested on a proposition that he had articulated before: that both North and South were complicit in the sin of slavery. But never had he suggested that whites of both sections must suffer death and destruction on a vast scale in order to atone for that sin, and that the war would not end until the scales were evenly balanced. Lincoln offered this as a hypothesis, not a firm conclusion, but if it were true, then the words of the 19th Psalm would have to be recalled: "the judgments of the Lord, are true and righteous altogether."

A curious feature of this extraordinary analysis, which resembled late-seventeenth-century Puritan election-day jeremiads, was the reference to "the believers in a Living God." It might be inferred that Lincoln did not count himself among those believers, for he did not say "*we* believers in a Living God." But the impersonal manner of presenting his argument recalls the impersonal way in which he wrote his autobiographical sketch in 1860, alluding to himself in the third person. He probably did mean to include himself among the believers, but his instinctive modesty and reserve led him to use such impersonal language. Lincoln blamed white Americans for the war, not God; the Almighty was merely enforcing the elementary rules of righteous justice. After this stunning revelation of his understanding of the war's cause and the reason for its bloody continuation, Lincoln closed by shifting the emphasis from justice to mercy. His final paragraph was not the most remarkable one, but it became the most revered and beloved. In it he honored the men who had served in the army and navy and expressed his hope for the future: "With malice toward none; with charity for all; with firmness in the right, as God gives us to see the right, let us strive on to finish the work we are in; to bind up the nation's wounds; to care for him who shall have borne the battle, and for his widow, and his orphan—to do all which may achieve and cherish a just, and a lasting peace, among ourselves, and with all nations."[193]

Once Chief Justice Chase had administered the oath of office, Lincoln kissed the Bible and bowed to the audience, whose many cheers were punctuated by thunderous artillery salvos. During the speech, the crowd had listened intently but had for the most part remained silent, save for the many blacks who murmured "bress de Lord" at the close of most sentences.[194] Applause interrupted Lincoln after he said: "Both parties deprecated war, but one of them would *make* war rather than let the nation survive, and the other would *accept* war rather than let it perish." A long cheer made Lincoln pause before saying, "and the war came."[195] The final paragraph brought tears to many eyes.

Frederick Douglass, who thought the address "sounded more like a sermon than like a state paper," admired above all its final two paragraphs. After hearing them, he applauded "in gladness and thanksgiving," for to him they seemed "to contain more vital substance than I have ever seen compressed into a space so narrow." Afterward Douglass joined the crowd moving toward the White House to attend the traditional post-inaugural reception. When two policemen rudely blocked his way at the door, he told them that he was sure the president had issued no order banning blacks. (In fact, four black men "of genteel exterior and with the manners of gentlemen" had attended the White House reception on New Year's Day 1864 and were presented to Lincoln. A Democratic newspaper asked: "Are not such scenes at the White House disgusting? When will the white people of this country awake to the sense of shame that the dominant party is bringing upon us by the practical establishment of the social equality of the negro?")[196] After his appeal failed to persuade the officers, Douglass asked a passerby whom he recognized: "Be so kind as to say to Mr. Lincoln that Frederick Douglass is detained by officers at the door." That message was swiftly conveyed, and in less than a minute Douglass was admitted. As he later recalled, "I could not have been more than ten feet from him when Mr. Lincoln saw me; his countenance lighted up, and he said in a voice which was heard all around: 'Here comes my friend Douglass.' As I approached him he reached out his hand, gave me a cordial shake, and said: 'Douglass, I saw you in the crowd to-day listening to my inaugural address. There is no man's opinion that I value more than yours: what do you think of it?' I said: 'Mr. Lincoln, I cannot stop here to talk with you, as there are thousands waiting to shake you by the hand;' but he said again: 'What did you think of it?' I said: 'Mr. Lincoln, it was a sacred effort,' and then I walked off. 'I am glad you liked it,' he said."[197] According to Elizabeth Keckly, Douglass "was very proud of the manner in which Mr. Lincoln received him. On leaving the White House he came to a friend's house where a reception was being held, and he related the incident with great pleasure to myself and others."[198]

James Shepherd Pike, U.S. minister to the Netherlands, also thought the inaugural resembled "the tail of an old sermon." It seemed to him "a most curious production," written as if Lincoln "did not exactly know what to say and so he abandoned himself to musing and took down what first came uppermost and printed it." But there was no harm done, because "even his imperfections do not weaken him in the public estimation. His nature is so good and his heart is so sound, that no exhibition he can make of himself discovers any flaw in his moral composition, and none in his tenacity of purpose."[199]

The inauguration had "passed off well," as General Halleck put it. "Thanks to abundant preventions we had no disturbances, no fires, no raids, or robberies," he noted. "I was on the *qui vive* all day and night and consequently did not join in the proceedings. There were a large number of rebel deserters here who excited some suspicion of wrong intentions, but they were closely watched. New York and Philadelphia also sent their quotas of roughs and rowdies, but they were completely overawed."[200] One of the more sinister onlookers was a rising young actor, John Wilkes Booth, seething with hatred for blacks and for the man they called the Great Emancipator.

Lincoln was pleased with his inaugural address. A week before delivering it, he said there was "[l]ots of wisdom in that document, I suspect."[201] A woman who admired the religious tone of the speech asked a friend in Congress to obtain for her a presidential autograph written with the pen used to compose it. With emotion he replied to the request: "She shall have my signature, and with it she shall have that paragraph. It comforts me to know that my sentiments are supported by the Christian ladies of our country."[202] When Thurlow Weed praised the inaugural, Lincoln replied: "Every one likes a compliment. Thank you for yours on my little notification speech, and on the recent Inaugeral Address. I expect the latter to wear as well as—perhaps better than—any thing I have produced; but I believe it is not immediately popular. Men are not flattered by being shown that there has been a difference of purpose between the Almighty and them. To deny it, however, in this case, is to deny that there is a God governing the world. It is a truth which I thought needed to be told; and as whatever of humiliation there is in it, falls most directly on myself, I thought others might afford for me to tell it."[203]

Among those with whom the address was not popular was a Pennsylvanian who complained that "while the sentiments are noble," it was "one of the most awkwardly expressed documents I ever read—if it be correctly printed. When he knew it would be read by millions all over the world, why under the heavens did he not make it a little more creditable to American *scholarship*? . . . Jackson was not too proud to get Van Buren to slick up his state papers. Why could not Mr Seward have prepared the Inaugural so as to save it from the ridicule of a Sophomore in a British University? However, Lincoln[']s prototype was *Oliver Cromwell* who was just as *able*, as *true*, and as awkward in his scholarship as he."[204] A Connecticut Democrat sneered: "The inaugural is a mixture of Bible quotations made blasphemous in a degree by his use of them and bloody anathemas well suited to the times of corruption and lunacy in which we live."[205]

Some Northern newspapers were also critical. The New York *Herald* complained that Lincoln did not mention the Hampton Roads conference, Mexico, or the Baltimore platform. It dismissed the address as "a little speech of 'glittering generalities' used only to fill in the program" and "an effort to avoid any commitment regarding our domestic or foreign affairs."[206] The Chicago *Times* contemptuously observed: "We did not conceive it possible that even Mr. Lincoln could produce a paper so slip-shod, so loose-jointed, so puerile, not alone in literary construction, but in its ideas, its sentiments, its grasp."[207] A leading Democratic paper in the East, the New York *World,* compared Lincoln to the pope: "The President's theology smacks as strong of the dark ages as does Pope Pius IX's politics." Its editors expressed regret "that a divided nation should neither be sustained in this crisis of agony by words of wisdom nor cheered with words of hope" and criticized the president for "abandoning all pretense of statesmanship . . . in this strange inaugural" by taking "refuge in piety."[208] The address, said the *World,* was little more than a "prose parody of John Brown's Hymn."[209]

Republican papers found more to admire. Henry J. Raymond's New York *Times* was impressed by the simplicity of the inaugural and its notable lack of platitudes: "He makes no boasts of what he has done, or promises of what he will do. He does not reexpound the principles of the war; does not redeclare the worth of the Union; does not reproclaim that absolute submission to the Constitution is the only peace." Instead all "that he does is simply to advert to the cause of the war; and its amazing development; to recognize in the solemn language the righteous judgment of Heaven; and to drop an earnest exhortation that all will now stand by the right and strive for a peace that shall be just and lasting."[210] The Boston *Evening Transcript* called the inaugural "a singular State Paper—made so by the times. No similar document has ever been published to the world. . . . The President was lifted above the level upon which political rulers usually stand, and felt himself 'in the very presence of the very mystery of Providence.'" Other New Englanders shared this view, including Ralph Waldo Emerson, who allegedly "said he thought it was likely to outlive anything now in print in the English language."[211] Charles Francis Adams, Jr., told his father: "That rail-splitting lawyer is one of the wonders of the day. . . . This inaugural strikes me in its grand simplicity and directness as being for all time the historical keynote of this war; in it a people seemed to speak in the sublimely simple utterance of ruder times. . . . Not a prince or minister in all Europe could have risen to such an equality with the occasion."[212] Another son bearing the name of his politically prominent father, James R. Doolittle, told his brother that Lincoln "rivals the greatest statesmen of our country; he is surpassed by none, not even by Washington." The president "is possessed of great dignity," but not the "selfish, conceited, proud, imperial dignity which Mr. Chase assumes, but is kind, approachable and winning." Moreover, "he is great mentally, and no less morally."[213]

Readers in Old as well as New England were appreciative. The Duke of Argyll told Charles Sumner: "It was a noble speech, just, and true, and solemn. I think it has produced a great effect in England."[214] English newspapers offered some of the most thoughtful commentary. A conspicuous example was London's *Saturday Review*: "If it had been composed by any other prominent American politician, it would have been boastful, confident, and menacing." Indeed, one of the striking features of the address was the absence of self-congratulation and braggadocio. "His unshaken purpose of continuing the war until it ends in victory assumes the form of resigned submission to the inscrutable decrees of a superior Power."[215] The London *Spectator* was equally generous in its praise: "No statesman ever uttered words stamped at once with the seal of so deep a wisdom and so true a simplicity." The editors also analyzed the president's growth over the past four years: "Mr. Lincoln has persevered through all, without ever giving way to anger, or despondency, or exultation, or popular arrogance, or sectarian fanaticism, or caste prejudice, visibly growing in force of character, in self-possession, and in magnanimity." Though he was scorned in 1861 as a rustic attorney, "we can detect no longer the rude and illiterate mould of a village lawyer's thought, but find it replaced by a grasp of principle, a dignity of manner, and a solemnity of purpose which would have been unworthy neither of Hampden nor of Cromwell, while his gentleness and generosity of feeling towards his foes are almost greater than we should expect from either of them."[216] The English statesman William E. Gladstone reportedly said: "I am taken captive by so striking an utterance as this. I see in it the effect of sharp trial when rightly borne to raise men to a higher level of thought and feeling. It is by cruel suffering that nations are sometimes born to a better life; so it is with individual men. Mr. Lincoln's words show that upon him anxiety and sorrow had wrought their true effect. The address gives evidence of a moral elevation most rare in a statesman, or indeed in any man."[217]

Sumner as Nemesis: Presidential Reconstruction Blocked

When Congress reconvened in December, Lincoln was predisposed to meet it halfway on the contentious subject of Reconstruction. In his annual message, he acknowledged that his power in that area would decline sharply with the end of the war; that his generous amnesty offer might soon end; and that the legislators, not he, had the power to determine who would be seated in Congress. He also appointed two commissioners to investigate conditions in Louisiana and Arkansas, thus signaling his willingness to rethink the Reconstruction policy that had been followed in those states.

Congress was also predisposed to compromise with Lincoln. The two branches worked together to pass the Thirteenth Amendment, and a conciliatory House referred measures relating to Reconstruction to the Judiciary Committee rather than to Henry Winter Davis's Select Committee on the Rebellious States. A Massachusetts Representative who had voted for the Wade–Davis bill now urged recognition of the new Louisiana government as the legitimate authority in that state, which should be readmitted without further delay. In mid-December, James Ashley introduced a bill stipulating that such recognition would be granted if Lincoln would agree that only "loyal male citizens" (presumably including blacks) could vote and serve on juries.

(Ashley reportedly accepted recognition of Louisiana only after Lincoln threatened to veto the bill.)

On December 18, the president told Nathaniel P. Banks, who since September had been in Washington lobbying Congress on behalf of the Louisiana government, that he had been reading Ashley's bill with care and "liked it with the exception of one or two things which he thought rather calculated to conceal a feature which might be objectionable to some." The first feature "was that under the provisions of that bill negroes would be made jurors & voters under the temporary governments." Banks, who had evidently discussed the bill with congressmen, said: "Yes, that is to be stricken out and the qualification white male citizens of the U.S. is to be restored. [The Wade–Davis bill had extended suffrage to whites only.] What you refer to would be a fatal objection to the Bill. It would simply throw the Government into the hands of the blacks, as the white people under that arrangement would refuse to vote." The president was not voicing his own opposition to black voting but expressing fear that it might be so "objectionable to some" that the bill would be defeated.

(Just as he had done with emancipation, Lincoln did not wish to get very far ahead of public opinion on the issue of black voting. And, as William Lloyd Garrison noted in January, "the primary difficulty lies in the state of public sentiment towards the negro."[218] Responding to their constituents, members of Congress shied away from black suffrage; they had overwhelmingly rejected it for the Montana Territory and had refused to enfranchise the blacks of Washington. In July 1864, Garrison himself had defended Lincoln against Radical criticism of his failure to endorse black suffrage, arguing that the "elective franchise is a conventional, not a natural right." He explained to an English abolitionist that in America, states rather than the central government determined who could vote. Garrison asked, "when was it ever known that liberation from bondage was accompanied by a recognition of political equality? Chattels personal may be instantly translated from the auction block into freemen; but when were they ever taken at the same time to the ballot-box, and invested with all political rights and immunities?" Premature granting of the suffrage to blacks might provoke a ruinous white backlash, Garrison warned presciently: "Submitted to as a necessity at the outset, as soon as the [reconstructed] State was organized and left to manage its own affairs, the white population, with their superior intelligence, wealth and power, would unquestionably alter the franchise in accordance with their prejudices." Black voting rights, he accurately predicted, could be won over time only "by a struggle on the part of the disfranchised, and a growing conviction of its justice.")[219]

Lincoln's second objection to Ashley's bill was "the declaration that all persons heretofore held in slavery are declared free." That did not seem critical, for he said it was evidently "not a prohibition of slavery by Congress but a mere assurance of freedom to persons then [free] in accordance with the proclamation of Emancipation. In that point of view it is not objectionable though I think it would have been preferable to so express it."

Lincoln and Banks "spoke very favorably, with these qualifications[,] of Ashley's bill." John Hay, who was present at this conversation, recorded that the general "is especially anxious that the Bill may pass and receive the approval of the President. He regards it as merely concurring in the President[']s own action in the one important case of Louisiana and recommending an observance of the same policy in other cases." Neither Banks nor Lincoln thought of it "as laying down any cast iron policy in the matter. Louisiana being admitted & this bill passed, the President is not estopped by it from recognizing and urging Congress to recognize another state of the South coming in with constitution & conditions entirely dissimilar." Banks thought Congress wanted the bill passed in order to assert its prerogative in shaping Reconstruction. It was best, he thought, to accept the legislation, even if it was unnecessary, in order to win the readmission of Louisiana.[220]

Two days later Ashley accepted amendments designed to meet the president's objections: slaves would be freed only in the areas already covered by the Emancipation Proclamation, and voting rights would be extended only to blacks serving in the military and to white males. In addition, Louisiana would be readmitted, but Congress would have the power to set terms for the admission of the other Confederate States. Action on this compromise measure was postponed until after Christmas.

During the holiday recess, Wendell Phillips visited Washington and reported that "the radical men feel that they are powerless and checkmated." Henry Winter Davis "told him the game was up—'Lincoln with his immense patronage can do what he pleases; the only hope is an appeal to the people.'"[221] In January, Phillips made such an appeal at a meeting of the Massachusetts Anti-Slavery Society. He warned that to admit Louisiana under the Banks–Hahn government would set a dangerous precedent. The "principle underlying Louisiana" was, he charged, "a brutal, domineering, infamous overseer spirit."[222] In response to Radical pressure, Ashley significantly modified the compromise bill, virtually eliminating the possibility of admitting Louisiana, Arkansas, and Tennessee in accordance with the Ten Percent plan. In effect, the oft-modified measure was the Wade–Davis bill with black suffrage added. Moderate Republicans rebelled and the bill was tabled. Partly in response to Lincoln's reelection, most Republican lawmakers were backing away from their earlier endorsement of the Wade–Davis approach to Reconstruction and moving toward the president's plan. Noah Brooks reported that members who had voted in July for the Radical bill "are now willing to admit that the President's sagacity was greater than theirs."[223] Moderates agreed with Lincoln that no rigid formula should be applied to all eleven Confederate States. As Massachusetts Representative Thomas D. Eliot put it, Congress should lay down the fundamental principles and then let the people of each state "establish their constitution; let it prohibit slavery; let them grant freedom and equality of rights, and we need nothing else." It mattered not "how a State shall have brought itself before us, so only that it comes with a constitution that we can recognize."[224]

Although the Thirty-eighth Congress would pass no Reconstruction bill, few regarded a postponement of the issue as a misfortune. Noah Brooks predicted that the Confederate States "will come back in different ways, each State acting for itself in some sovereign capacity, and as the people of the States reorganize themselves, they will revive the paralyzed powers of the State, and before the present Summer closes there will be some order brought out of the chaotic mass."[225]

But in the meantime, would Congress admit Louisiana and Arkansas? Smarting from their setback on the Reconstruction bill, Radicals sought revenge. "We hope now to defeat the proposed admission of Louisiana and Arkansas, and if so the whole question will go over to the next Congress," said Ashley. "In the meantime I hope the nation may be educated up to our demand for universal suffrage."[226] Most moderate and conservative Republicans, however, disagreed. They wanted Louisiana admitted in part because they thought the state would vote to ratify the Thirteenth Amendment.

The question arose when senators and congressmen from Louisiana asked to be seated. As the senate addressed their request in January, Lincoln tried to frame the debate by suggesting to the chairman of the Judiciary Committee, Lyman Trumbull, that the most important question before that body was: "Can Louisiana be brought into proper practical relations with the Union sooner by *admitting* or by *rejecting* the proposed Senators?"[227] The committee, which had rejected Arkansas's senators a few months earlier, now recommended that Louisiana's be accepted. That necessarily entailed recognizing the Hahn government, which the committee said "fairly represented a majority of the loyal voters of the State."[228]

Although over half of the senate favored acceptance of the committee's recommendation, a few Radicals, led by Charles Sumner, demurred. They objected to the Louisiana constitution's failure to enfranchise blacks and to the Lincoln administration's alleged usurpation of congressional prerogatives. Sumner vowed to employ "all the instruments . . . in the arsenal of parliamentary warfare" to block the will of the majority. The Hahn government, he charged, was "a mere seven-months' abortion, begotten by the bayonet in criminal conjunction with the spirit of caste, and born before its time, rickety, unformed, unfinished—whose continued existence will be a burden, a reproach, and a wrong."[229] Conservative Democrats like Kentuckians Garrett Davis and Lazarus Powell, fearing that Louisiana would ratify the Thirteenth Amendment, teamed up with Sumner and a few other Radicals to conduct a successful filibuster, thus preventing recognition of the Bayou State.

Thomas J. Durant of New Orleans significantly influenced Radical opponents of the Hahn government, which he denounced as illegitimate because it had been elected under the aegis of the military. Some abolitionists regarded Durant's argument skeptically.

Moderate Republicans indignantly denounced Sumner's obstructionism. Richard Henry Dana thought the senator had behaved "like a madman, in the Louisiana question." Dana did not object to the delaying tactics or Sumner's votes, but rather to "the positions he took, the arguments he advanced, and the language he used to the 20 out of 25 Republican Senators who differed from him." Even such haughty slaveowning senators as James M. Mason, John Slidell, and Jefferson Davis "were never so insolent and overbearing as he was, and his arguments, his answers to questions, were boyish or crazy." Dana said he would be relieved to learn that Sumner "was out of his head from opium or even N[ew] E[ngland] rum."[230] The Springfield, Massachusetts, *Republican* editorialized that Sumner had forfeited any claim "to the character of an honorable statesman" by resorting "to the trickery of a pot-house politician."[231] The editor thought the senator's behavior "perfectly unjustifiable," "undignified," and "disgraceful."[232]

Lincoln, too, was furious. He told James Ashley that Sumner "hopes to succeed in beating the President so as to change this government from its original form, and making it a strong centralized power."[233] William Henry Crook, who joined the White House staff in January 1865, recalled that one day the president's "intense antipathy" for Sumner led him to forbid the senator admission to the Executive Mansion. Crook believed Sumner was "the only man, so far as my knowledge goes, to obtain the president's bitter dislike."[234] It is not hard to understand Lincoln's aversion to the vain, haughty, pedantic senator, who was thwarting the will of the overwhelming majority of his colleagues and frustrating the president's laboriously achieved attempt to rehabilitate Louisiana. When the press began to speak of a personal rupture between Sumner and himself, however, Lincoln quickly moved to squelch the rumor by magnanimously inviting the senator to join him at the inaugural ball on March 6. Sumner complied and escorted the First Lady into the festivities at the mammoth Patent Office building, following closely behind the president. The New York *Herald* inferred that Lincoln now endorsed Sumner's approach to Reconstruction. But Lincoln had not done so. He would postpone for six weeks his formal response to the senate's action.

Lincoln was angry at the military in Louisiana as well as at Congress for failing to support the Hahn government. In September he had summoned Banks to Washington and set him to lobbying Congress on behalf of that government. Taking over Banks's role in New Orleans were Generals E. R. S. Canby and Stephen Hurlbut, a friend of Lincoln's from Illinois.

To Hurlbut, the president wrote a blistering letter in November: "Few things, since I have been here, have impressed me more painfully than what, for four or five months past, has appeared as bitter military opposition to the new State Government of Louisiana." He praised the "excellent new constitution" as one that was "better for the poor black man than [the constitution] we have in Illinois." He also commended the Hahn government, which he said had won the support of all true unionists and the enmity of all disunionists. There was no sound reason, Lincoln insisted, for the military government to show "gratuitous hostility" to that government. The president reassured Hurlbut that he would continue to regard the commanding general as the ultimate "judge and master" in Louisiana, but he sternly warned that he would not tolerate "a purpose, obvious, and scarcely unavowed, to transcend all military necessity, in order to crush out the civil government."[235]

On November 29, Hurlbut replied: "I recognize as thoroughly as any man the advance toward the right made by the adoption of the Free Constitution of Louisiana, and have done and shall do all in my power to vindicate its declaration of freedom, and to protect and prepare the emancipated Bondsmen for their new status and condition. The fact has been withheld from you, Mr President, but it still exists that nothing has been done for this purpose since the adoption of the Constitution—*except by military authority.*"[236] Dissatisfied with this response, Lincoln ordered Banks to return to Louisiana. He did not write out instructions to the general, but his intentions can be inferred from Banks's remarks made in New Orleans in April 1865. There he addressed a mass meeting of blacks: "To the colored people of this State, I will say that the work is still going on; and by being patient, they will see that the day is not far distant when they will be in the enjoyment of all rights. . . . Abraham Lincoln gave his word that you will be free, and enjoy all the rights invested to citizens."[237] Presumably among those rights was the suffrage.

While lobbying Congress on behalf of the Hahn government, "Lincoln had been earnestly anxious to permit the extension of the right of suffrage to American citizens of African descent in Louisiana," according to Pennsylvania Representative William D. Kelley. That Radical congressman recalled that it "was not a mere sentiment with Mr. Lincoln. He regarded it as an act of justice to the citizens, and a measure of sound policy for the States, and doubtless believed that those whom he invested with power were using their influence to promote so desirable an object. Of this he assured me more than once, and in the presence of others to whose memories I may safely appeal."[238] To demonstrate his sincerity, Lincoln showed congressmen and senators the March 1864 letter he had written to Hahn, gently urging him to support black suffrage. Among them was Missouri Senator B. Gratz Brown, a leading supporter of black suffrage. In a letter to his constituents, Brown quoted the president's missive to Hahn and said that the provision of the Louisiana constitution authorizing the legislature to enfranchise blacks "was prompted by the executive head of our nation himself."[239] Congressman Thomas D. Eliot of Massachusetts was also assured by "the highest sources" (presumably Lincoln) that the Hahn government would soon enfranchise blacks.[240] While the president and Banks lobbied Congress, their allies and agents on the ground in Louisiana—including Governor Hahn, B. Rush Plumy, Thomas W. Conway, A. P. Dostie, as well as the editors of the *Daily True Delta* and the *Black Republican*—were championing the cause of black suffrage.

By April, Lincoln doubtless sensed that Northern support for black suffrage was growing. That month, Frank Sanborn wrote that "the question of Reconstruction on the basis of negro suffrage is coming up for discussion everywhere, and the converts to Phillips' view are increasing fast." In February, Charles Slack told Sumner that among Boston businessmen "the idea of negro suffrage in the disloyal states grows daily in favor and advocacy."[241] As Lydia Maria Child pointed out, the military service of blacks was largely responsible for the change in public opinion. To keep his party together, Lincoln understood that the time was growing ripe to support black voting rights publicly. He had already done so privately to many men. But when should he announce his decision to the nation?

Visit to the Front

As he mulled over that question, Lincoln was becoming weary of the White House grind. So on March 20, when Grant invited him to visit the front for a day or two, he gladly accepted. The general had acted at the prompting of his wife, who was disturbed by press reports indicating that the president was unusually haggard. One such report appeared in the Chicago *Tribune,* which noted that at the inauguration, many observers "were painfully impressed with his gaunt, skeleton-like appearance."[242] The crushing burden of responsibility had taken a fierce toll on Lincoln, changing his appearance dramatically between the time he took office and his second inauguration.

A life mask made in 1860 showed him to be youthful, vigorous, and healthy; a similar mask executed in 1865 showed him to be such a hollow-cheeked, worn-out old man that one artist assumed it was a death mask. Photographs corroborated the impression.

Gideon Welles noted that Lincoln was "much worn down" primarily because he took "upon himself questions that properly belong to the Departments, often causing derangement and irregularity" and thus made "his office much more laborious than he should." In deciding to leave Washington for the army headquarters at City Point (where the James and Appomattox rivers met), he sought to escape the clamorous office seekers and their patrons. Disapprovingly, the navy secretary noted that the more often Lincoln yielded to the crowd's importunities, "the greater the pressure upon him" grew. "It has now become such that he is compelled to flee."[243] (Democrats also criticized Lincoln's administrative style, charging that he delegated too little authority while trying to serve as "Secretary, Clerk, Scrivener, Joker, Story-teller, Clown, Doctor, Chaplain, the whole in one." The New York *Evening Express* sarcastically noted that "[n]o man, it is said, works harder than does this *universal* genius, Mr. Lincoln. He rises with the sun, and don't go down with the sun!")[244]

At first Grant hesitated to take his wife's advice, assuming that if Lincoln wished to visit, he would do so without being invited, but the general relented when Robert Todd Lincoln, then serving on his staff, opined that the president would come if his presence would not be intrusive. After deciding to take a brief vacation at the front, Lincoln requested Assistant Secretary of the Navy Gustavus Fox to make travel arrangements. Fox asked Captain John S. Barnes, commander of the U.S.S. *Bat*, a swift, armed blockade enforcer, if his vessel might be made suitable for the president. Barnes said he thought it could, and Fox took him to the White House for instructions. "I'm only a fresh-water sailor and I guess I have to trust you salt-water folks when afloat," Lincoln said, adding that he "wanted no luxuries but only plain, simple food and ordinary comfort." Whatever was good enough for Barnes, he stressed, was sufficient for him.[245]

The following day, however, the president told Barnes that more luxurious accommodations would be necessary, for Mrs. Lincoln had decided to join him and would be attended by her maidservant. The captain recalled that in modifying his request, Lincoln had "a certain kind of embarrassment and a look of sadness which struck me forcibly and rather embarrassed me. He appeared tired and worried." Taken aback, Barnes replied that the *Bat* was not appropriate for female passengers. So he and Fox arranged to charter the *River Queen*, the side-wheeled passenger ship on which the Hampton Roads conference had taken place a few weeks earlier, even though Barnes feared that Lincoln was running an unnecessary risk by traveling on such a vulnerable craft. Her sister ship had recently been sunk by a bomb made to resemble a lump of coal. Fox warned Barnes to be cautious in protecting Lincoln and said he regretted "that the determination of Mrs. Lincoln to accompany the President had made the *Bat* an impossible home for him and his family party."

Lincoln, however, felt no concern for his own safety. As for bombs disguised as coal lumps, he "expressed great contempt for cowardly assaults of such nature." At

1 P.M. on March 23, the president along with his wife and son Tad boarded the *River Queen* and sailed for City Point, escorted by the *Bat*. Accompanying them were Mrs. Lincoln's maidservant and army Captain Charles B. Penrose, whom Stanton assigned to act as a presidential bodyguard.[246] En route, Lincoln felt unwell, evidently because the water aboard the ship was bad. At 9 P.M. on March 24, the *River Queen* arrived at City Point, an immense base of supplies for the army that swarmed with soldiers, teamsters, sentries, wagons, ambulances, and other conveyances. When Grant and his wife called to pay their respects, he and the president retired to discuss military affairs. Coolly and somewhat condescendingly, the First Lady received Mrs. Grant, who committed an act of *lese majesty* by sitting down next to her hostess. Mrs. Lincoln imperiously exclaimed: "How dare you be seated until I invite you!"[247] The First Lady would make other such scenes in the coming days. (Apparently, she had treated Stanton's wife with the same hauteur, for the war secretary's wife told one of Grant's aides: "I do not go to the White House; I do not visit Mrs. Lincoln.")[248] Mary Lincoln's sense of entitlement led her to insist that the *River Queen* be berthed next to the dock, though Grant's headquarters boat, the *Mary Martin*, had been assigned that spot. The two vessels were placed side by side, but the First Lady refused to cross what became known as "Mrs. Grant's boat" in order to reach the gangplank. So, despite Lincoln's protests, the *Martin* was regularly forced to move out in order to make way for the *Queen*, necessitating extra work for the crews and causing some confusion.

The journalist Sylvanus Cadwallader, whose wife was friendly with Mrs. Grant, reported that the First Lady "seemed insanely jealous of every person, and everything, which drew him [Lincoln] away from her and monopolized his attention for an hour." She regularly dispatched Tad to summon his father back to the *River Queen*. On one occasion the boy, after having made a vain attempt to deliver such instructions, interrupted the president in the midst of an animated conversation: "Come, come, come now, mama says you must come instantly." Lincoln's face fell, he hesitated for a moment, then rose to leave, asking: "My God, will that woman never understand me?" Submissively he returned to the *River Queen*.[249]

Soon after landing at City Point, Lincoln was asked how long he intended to stay. "Well, I am like the western pioneer who built a log cabin," he laughingly replied. "When he commenced he didn't know how much timber he would need, and when he had finished, he didn't care how much he had used up. So you see I came down among you without any definite plans, and when I go home I shan't regret a moment I have spent with you."[250] Grant urged him to remain at least until the fall of Richmond, which seemed imminent.

On the morning March 25, a desperate Confederate attempt to break through the noose around Petersburg disrupted Lincoln's plans to review the troops. In a pre-dawn assault, Lee's forces punched a hole in the Union line, capturing Fort Stedman and two nearby batteries, but were soon driven back. Although Lincoln described it as "a little rumpus," in fact the losses were significant; the Federals suffered 2,080 casualties and the Rebels 4,800 (10% of the Army of Northern Virginia). Lincoln had wanted to observe the action, but Grant thought it too dangerous. When the firing stopped, however, the general suggested that they inspect the battle site. Around noon Grant, his staff, Lincoln, Barnes, and others boarded a train that took them 7 miles to the front. There they mounted horses and rode across terrain where the fighting had raged most fiercely, witnessing burial squads digging graves for the many corpses scattered about as doctors tended wounded Rebels. Lincoln showed great interest in the 1,600 ragged, dirty Confederates who had been taken prisoner earlier in the day. Though for the most part he remained silent, he did remark on their forlorn condition, showing compassion for the suffering he observed all around him. While frequently consulting a map, he indicated an awareness of the position of various units. When Lincoln returned to the train, he noticed cars full of wounded men. Looking fatigued, he said "that he had seen enough of the horrors of war, that he hoped this was the beginning of the end, and that there would be no more bloodshed or ruin of homes." During his visit, he repeated this hope earnestly and often. He also sought to comfort the wounded. He was told that a young boy in a Confederate uniform was moaning "Mother! Mother!" and when asked where he was hurt, the lad turned his head, revealing a ghastly wound, and died. Hearing this sad tale, Lincoln wept and with an emotion-choked voice he "repeated the well-known expression about 'robbing the cradle and the grave.'"[251]

Upon returning to City Point, Lincoln was rather solemn as he sat by the smoky campfire with Grant and his staff. At first his demeanor was unusually somber as he "spoke of the appalling difficulties encountered by the administration, the losses in the field, the perplexing financial problems, and the foreign complications; but said they had all been overcome by the unswerving patriotism of the people, the devotion of the loyal North, and the superb fighting qualities of the troops." In time, he unwound and entertained his companions with amusing anecdotes about public men and measures. When Grant asked, "Mr. President, did you at any time doubt the final success of the cause?" he replied swiftly and emphatically: "Never for a moment."

Worn out by the day's excitement, Lincoln declined the general's dinner invitation and returned to the *River Queen*, where he went to bed earlier than usual. After a good night's sleep, he arose to encouraging bulletins from the front, which led him to predict optimistically that the war would soon end. He was especially pleased to learn that General Philip Sheridan, having repeatedly whipped Jubal Early's army in the Shenandoah Valley, had reached the James River. At Grant's headquarters he found that diminutive cavalryman along with Admiral David Dixon Porter and Generals E. O. C. Ord and George G. Meade. It was suggested that since the president had been unable to review troops yesterday, he might like to watch Sheridan's army cross the river and then review both the naval flotilla and Ord's corps.

Lincoln accepted the invitation, but before departing, he took time to play with three recently orphaned kittens. He put them in his lap and said consolingly: "Poor little creatures, don't cry; you'll be taken good care of." He asked Colonel Theodore Bowers to make sure they were given food and kind treatment. Often during his visit at City Point, the president gently played with these kittens, wiping their eyes, stroking their fur, and listening to them purr their appreciation. Colonel Horace Porter thought it "a curious sight at an army headquarters, upon the eve of a great military crisis in the nation's history, to see the hand which had affixed the signature to the

Emancipation Proclamation, and had signed the commissions of all the heroic men who served the cause of the Union, from the general-in-chief to the lowest lieutenant, tenderly caressing three stray kittens."[252]

Looking worn out, the president then sailed downriver to the spot where Sheridan's men were to cross. En route, he seemed gloomy and spoke earnestly about the possibility that the Confederates might strike City Point. Uncharacteristically, he told no anecdotes. But upon observing Sheridan's soldiers traverse the bridge, he perked up, showing great interest and asking several questions of the young general. He thoroughly enjoyed the bustling scene. Some cavalry on the banks cheered loudly on catching sight of him. He met the same reception when his ship passed Porter's flotilla, which he happily saluted by waving his tall hat. After lunch aboard Porter's flagship, the *Malvern*, Lincoln proceeded to Aiken's Landing, where Ord's officers were waiting to escort the presidential party to the review. Lincoln rode with Grant and Ord, while the First Lady and Julia Grant, along with Grant's aide Adam Badeau, followed in an ambulance. The president cheerfully laughed and chatted with the generals. When they arrived at Ord's campsite, Lincoln was dismayed to learn that the troops had been awaiting their arrival for hours and had missed lunch. He therefore urged that the review begin without further delay while the women caught up.

Meantime, Major Badeau tried to make polite conversation with the First Lady and Mrs. Grant. He predicted that a battle would soon take place, for Grant had ordered to the rear the wives of officers in the Army of the Potomac. Mrs. Charles Griffin, who had received special permission from the president, was an exception. This news rasped Mary Lincoln. "What do you mean by that, sir?" she asked indignantly. "Do you mean to say that she saw the President alone? Do you know that I never allow the President to see any woman alone?" Julia Grant tried to rescue poor Badeau, who balked when Mary Lincoln instructed him to order the vehicle to halt so that she could leave it. The First Lady then took matters into her own hands by seizing the driver, but Mrs. Grant persuaded her to remain inside until they had reached the reviewing ground. There General Meade, unaware of the delicacy of the situation, replaced Badeau as the ladies' escort. When they returned to the carriage, the First Lady glared at Badeau and remarked, "General Meade is a gentleman, sir. He says it was not the President who gave Mrs. Griffin the permit, but the Secretary of War."

Later that day a more embarrassing scene occurred when the same party visited the command of General Ord's Army of the James. His beautiful, vivacious wife, like Mrs. Griffin, had been allowed to remain at the front. On a highly spirited horse she rode alongside the president while Mary Lincoln's carriage was making its way to the site. According to Badeau, as "soon as Mrs. Lincoln discovered this her rage was beyond all bounds. 'What does the woman mean,' she exclaimed, 'by riding by the side of the President? and ahead of me? Does she suppose that *he* wants *her* by the side of *him*?' She was in a frenzy of excitement, and language and action both became more extravagant every moment."

Mary Lincoln grew angrier still when Julia Grant once again attempted to calm her down. Haughtily, the First Lady asked: "I suppose you think you'll get to the

White House yourself, don't you?" Mrs. Grant explained that she was quite content with her current situation, provoking a sharp retort: "Oh! you had better take it if you can get it. 'Tis very nice."

At this awkward moment an officer approached and innocently remarked, "The President's horse is very gallant, Mrs. Lincoln; he insists on riding by the side of Mrs. Ord."

"What do you mean by that, sir?" she asked heatedly.

The astounded officer slunk away. When the carriage finally reached Ord's headquarters, that general's wife rode up. As Badeau remembered it, Mary Lincoln "positively insulted her, called her vile names in the presence of a crowd of officers, and asked what she meant by following up the President. The poor woman burst into tears and inquired what she had done, but Mrs. Lincoln refused to be appeased, and stormed till she was tired. Mrs. Grant still tried to stand by her friend, and everybody was shocked and horrified."

At dinner that evening, the First Lady vehemently condemned General Ord and urged her husband to remove him, for in her opinion he was unfit for his command. After the meal, at about eleven o'clock, she had Lincoln summon John S. Barnes, who had observed the embarrassing events of the afternoon. Already asleep when the message arrived, the captain arose, dressed quickly, and went to the president, who, he recalled, "seemed weary and greatly distressed, with an expression of sadness that seemed the accentuation of the shadow of melancholy which at times so marked his features." Mary Lincoln did most of the talking. According to Barnes, she "objected very strenuously to the presence of other ladies at the review that day, and had thought that Mrs. Ord had been too prominent in it, that the troops were led to think that she was the wife of the President, who had distinguished her with too much attention." Lincoln, Barnes recalled, "very gently suggested that he had hardly remarked the presence of the lady, but Mrs. Lincoln was hardly to be pacified and appealed to me to support her views." The mortified Barnes could not mediate this disagreement and strove to remain neutral, simply recounting what he had seen.

Badeau reported that Mary Lincoln over the next few days "repeatedly attacked her husband in the presence of officers because of Mrs. Griffin and Mrs. Ord." The spectacle dismayed Badeau, who later wrote: "I never suffered greater humiliation and pain . . . than when I saw the Head of State, the man who carried all the cares of the nation at such a crisis—subjected to this inexpressible public mortification." Lincoln "bore it as Christ might have done; with an expression of pain and sadness that cut one to the heart, but with supreme calmness and dignity." With "old-time plainness" he called his wife "mother." He also "pleaded with eyes and tones, and endeavored to explain or palliate the offenses of others, till she turned on him like a tigress; and then he walked away, hiding that noble, ugly face that we might not catch the full expression of its misery."[253]

Mary Lincoln returned to Washington on April 1, accompanied by Carl Schurz. In the manuscript version of his autobiography, that general explained that he had "misgivings" about accepting the invitation to join her. "I had not come into contact with Mrs. Lincoln frequently, but whenever I did, she had treated me with friendly politeness. She had even on some occasions spoken to me about others with a sort of confidential and not at all conventional freedom of tongue, which had embarrassed me not a little. But now, when I was substantially her sole social companion on that steamboat, with no means of escape, she overwhelmed me with a flood of gossip about the various members of the cabinet and leading men in Congress who in some way had incurred her displeasure—gossip so reckless, that I was not only embarrassed as to what to say in reply, but actually began to fear for the soundness of her mind. . . . While this giddy talk was rattling on almost without interruption from City Point to Washington, save sleeping time, I had the pathetic figure of tender-hearted Abraham Lincoln constantly before my eyes as he was sorely harassed not only by public care but also secretly by domestic torment."[254] In a suppressed chapter of his autobiography, Schurz allegedly "set down verbatim a conversation on her part so vulgar and so venomous that it can be fairly described as outrageous."[255] (As noted above, Schurz believed that "the greatest tragedy of Mr. Lincoln's existence" was his marriage.)[256]

Jealous behavior by Mary Lincoln was not unprecedented. One night earlier in the war, she became enraged at a tall, beautiful Connecticut woman who called on the president to discuss a claim. The visitor fell to her knees, wrapped her arms around Lincoln's legs, and was pleading her case when Mrs. Lincoln came in and "jumped at conclusions. 'Out of the room, you baggage,' she cried, and going into the hall she shouted to Edward, one of the household servants, 'Put this woman out and never admit her again.'" The president instructed Congressman Henry C. Deming of Hartford: "Send that long-legged woman back to Connecticut and keep her there."[257] In July 1861, when Lincoln attempted to aid a poor Irish widow gain a pension, he remarked that "Mrs. Lincoln is getting a little jealous."[258]

The First Lady was more than just a little jealous. Her friend Elizabeth Keckly, who thought her "extremely jealous," observed that "if a lady desired to court her displeasure, she could select no surer way to do it than to pay marked attention to the President. These little jealous freaks often were a source of perplexity to Mr. Lincoln." Mrs. Keckly recalled that one evening, as the First Couple was getting dressed for a reception, the president asked: "Well, mother, who must I talk with to-night—shall it be Mrs. D.?"

"That deceitful woman! No, you shall not listen to her flattery."

"Well, then, what do you say to Miss C.? She is too young and handsome to practise deceit."

"Young and handsome, you call her! You should not judge beauty for me. No, she is in league with Mrs. D., and you shall not talk with her."

"Well, mother, I must talk with some one. Is there any one that you do not object to?"

"I don't know as it is necessary that you should talk to anybody in particular. You know well enough, Mr. Lincoln, that I do not approve of your flirtations with silly women, just as if you were a beardless boy, fresh from school."

"But, mother, I insist that I must talk with somebody. I can't stand around like a simpleton, and say nothing. If you will not tell me who I may talk with, please tell me who I may *not* talk with."

"There is Mrs. D. and Miss C. in particular. I detest them both. Mrs. B. also will come around you, but you need not listen to her flattery. These are the ones in particular."

"Very well, mother; now that we have settled the question to your satisfaction, we will go down-stairs."[259]

Miss C. was the beautiful, accomplished Kate Chase, daughter of the treasury secretary. Mary Lincoln was especially jealous of her. In January 1864, she struck from the invitation list for a cabinet dinner the names of that belle, her father and her husband, Rhode Island Senator William Sprague. When the president learned of this, he overruled his wife, and, as Nicolay reported, "there soon arose such a rampage as the House hasn't seen for a year." Mary Lincoln's rage made White House secretary William O. Stoddard cower "at the violence of the storm." Nicolay too was buffeted by it. As he told Hay, "after having compelled Her S[atanic] Majesty to invite the Spragues I was taboo, and she made up her mind resolutely not to have me at the dinner."[260]

Mary Lincoln declined an invitation to attend Kate Chase's wedding and unsuccessfully urged her husband to boycott that event, the highlight of the social season. According to a woman who was in Washington at the time, the Lincolns argued about the matter, "and the music of her voice penetrated the utmost end of the house."[261]

White House tradition dictated that at receptions the president choose a woman to lead the promenade with him. "The custom is an absurd one," Mary Lincoln insisted. "On such occasions our guests recognize the position of the President as first of all; consequently, he takes the lead in everything; well, now, if they recognize his position they should also recognize mine. I am his wife, and should lead with him. And yet he offers his arm to any other lady in the room, making her first with him and placing me second. The custom is an absurd one, and I mean to abolish it. The dignity I owe to my position, as Mrs. President, demands that I should not hesitate any longer to act."[262]

As her conduct at City Point indicated, Mary Lincoln had few compunctions about berating her husband in the presence of others. Oregon Senator George H. Williams recalled riding in a carriage with the president and First Lady and "being treated the entire ride with upbraiding and a tirade from Mrs. Lincoln," throughout which Lincoln sat "with tired, worn, patient face, saying not a word."[263] On February 22, 1864, while attending a fair to benefit the Christian Commission, Lincoln was surprised by the crowd's demand for a speech. According to General Richard J. Oglesby, who had prevailed upon him to attend the meeting only by promising that he would not have to speak, Lincoln reluctantly delivered a few remarks. Afterward, while the First Couple and Oglesby awaited their carriage, Mrs. Lincoln said to her husband: "That was the worst speech I ever listened to in my life. How any man could get up and deliver such remarks to an audience is more than I can understand. I wanted the earth to sink and let me go through." The president made no reply. He, his wife, and the general rode back to the White House in silence.[264]

How often an enraged, jealous Mary Lincoln attacked her husband is impossible to say, but Mrs. Keckly reported that when "in one of her wayward impulsive moods, she was apt to say and do things that wounded him deeply," and she "often wounded him in unguarded moments."[265] Mrs. Lincoln herself acknowledged that during their courtship, "I doubtless trespassed, many times & oft, upon his great tenderness & amiability of character." That pattern continued throughout the marriage.[266]

On the way back to City Point from the review, Lincoln's spirits seemed to recover, evidently lifted by the magnificent appearance of the Army of the James. He had spent several hours reviewing the soldiers, who cheered him enthusiastically. Colonel Theodore Lyman of General Meade's staff reported that as Lincoln "rode down the ranks, plucking off his hat gracefully by the hinder part of the brim, the troops cheered quite loudly." The colonel unflatteringly described his commander-in-chief as "the ugliest man I ever put my eyes on," with "an expression of plebeian vulgarity in his face that is offensive (you recognize the recounter of coarse stories)." But, Lyman added, the president had "the look of sense and wonderful shrewdness, while the heavy eyelids give him a mark almost of genius," and all in all, he seemed like "a very honest and kindly man" with "no trace of low passions in his face." In sum, "he is such a mixture of all sorts, as only America brings forth" and "is as much like a highly intellectual and benevolent Satyr as anything I can think of." Lyman was "well content to have him at the head of affairs."[267] The next morning Captain Barnes as usual reported to the *River Queen*, where Lincoln received him cordially and told him that Mrs. Lincoln was unwell. The two men then visited the headquarters of Grant, who sat rather silent while Lincoln and Admiral Porter discussed news from the front.

After lunch, Robert Todd Lincoln visited the *Bat* and invited Barnes to join the First Family's excursion to the Point of Rocks on the Appomattox River. The captain accepted and returned with Robert to the *River Queen*, where Lincoln received him with customary warmth. Mrs. Lincoln, however, made it clear that she found Barnes's presence offensive, so he did not accompany the presidential party on its stroll through the woods.

That night General Sherman arrived from North Carolina, where his 80,000-man army was being resupplied. Over the next two days he along with Admiral Porter and Grant conferred with Lincoln aboard the *River Queen*. The president initially appeared worn out to Sherman, who recalled that as the discussion progressed, "he warmed up and looked more like himself." The ship's after-cabin had no tables or maps. "We merely sat at our ease in such chairs as happened to be there," Sherman wrote three years later.[268]

As the president listened anxiously, Grant explained how Sheridan's men would soon swing around Lee's flank and sever his supply lines. Grant's only concern was that before Sheridan could do so, Lee might abandon Petersburg and Richmond and try to connect with Joseph E. Johnston. If the Confederates made such a move, they would be pursued hotly. The president took great interest in this scenario. Grant assured him he could prevent Lee's breakout, for Sheridan's cavalry were just then moving on the Confederates' communications. Sherman remarked that even if the Army of Northern Virginia did break out, he could fend off both Johnston and Lee until Grant caught up and placed the Confederates in a fatal vise. When Lincoln expressed fear that in Sherman's absence Johnston might escape southward by rail, the general replied: "I have him where he cannot move without breaking up his army, which, once disbanded, can never again be got together."

In response to the president's questions about the march from Georgia to North Carolina, Sherman regaled him with amusing tales of his troops, known informally as "bummers." The president, Sherman wrote, "laughed at my former troubles with the Sanitary Commission and Christian Commission and told an apt illustration of the confusion their super philanthropy had sometimes occasioned." According to Sherman, Lincoln's "face brightened wonderfully" in "lively conversation," and he became "the very impersonation of good-humor and fellowship." But if the conversation flagged, his face "assumed a sad, and sorrowful expression." The president exclaimed more than once: "Must more blood be shed! Cannot this last bloody battle be avoided!" The generals observed that it was up to the Confederates.[269]

Shortly after the second discussion ended around noon on March 28, Lincoln encountered a journalist who had just arrived from a sojourn in Savannah and Charleston. "How do the people like being back in the Union again?" the president asked. "I think some of them are reconciled to it," came the reply, "if we may draw conclusions from the action of one planter, who, while I was there, came down the Savannah River with his whole family—wife, children, negro woman and her children, of whom he was father—and with his crop of cotton, which he was anxious to sell at the highest price." Lincoln's eyes twinkled as he remarked laughingly: "I see; patriarchal times once more; Abraham, Sarah, Isaac, Hagar and Ishmael, all in one boat! I reckon they'll accept the situation now that they can sell their cotton at a price never dreamed of before the war."[270]

Sherman returned to North Carolina that afternoon, and the following day Grant left City Point to launch his final offensive. Before departing for the front, the commanding general bade farewell to Lincoln. While doing so, he told him of the clever but impractical advice he regularly received. "The last plan proposed was to supply our men with bayonets just a foot longer than those of the enemy, and then charge them. When they met, our bayonets would go clear through the enemy, while theirs would not reach far enough to touch our men, and the war would be ended."

Lincoln with a chuckle replied: "Well, there is a good deal of terror in cold steel. I had a chance to test it once myself. When I was a young man, I was walking along a back street in Louisville one night about twelve o'clock, when a very tough-looking citizen sprang out of an alleyway, reached up to the back of his neck, pulled out a bowie-knife that seemed to my stimulated imagination about three feet long, and planted himself square across my path. For two or three minutes he flourished his weapon in front of my face, appearing to try to see just how near he could come to cutting my nose off without quite doing it. He could see in the moonlight that I was taking a good deal of interest in the proceeding, and finally he yelled out, as he steadied the knife close to my throat: 'Stranger, kin you lend me five dollars on that?' I never reached in my pocket and got out money so fast in all my life. I handed him a bank-note, and said: 'There's ten, neighbor; now put up your scythe.'"

As they strolled to the depot, Lincoln appeared to Horace Porter "more serious than at any other time since he had visited headquarters. The lines in his face seemed deeper, and the rings under his eyes were of a darker hue. It was plain that the weight of responsibility was oppressing him." He cordially shook hands with Grant and his staff and "said in a voice broken by an emotion he could ill conceal: 'Good-by, gentlemen. God bless you all! Remember, your success is my success.'"[271]

For the next few days Lincoln spent much of his time in the telegraph office, reading and sending messages. He also toured hospitals. "Time hung wearily with the President," an officer recalled, "and as he walked through the hospitals or rode amid the tents, his rueful countenance bore sad evidence of the anxiety and anguish that possessed him."[272] Sometimes he took excursions with Admiral Porter on the river and carriage rides around the countryside. He carried a detailed map of the area showing the location of all the forces and often explained to Porter how he would act if he were the commander in charge. One day they visited a deserted fort overlooking the Union army's works. After Porter described the difficulties the troops had in constructing it under enemy fire and the hardships they endured throughout the harsh winter, Lincoln remarked: "The country can never repay these men for what they have suffered and endured."[273]

On April 1, when journalist Sylvanus Cadwallader handed him Confederate battle flags captured earlier that day by Sheridan's men at the decisive engagement of Five Forks, Lincoln joyfully exclaimed: "Here is something material—something I can see, feel, and understand. This means victory. This *is* victory." With the aid of Cadwallader he updated maps into which he had stuck red-headed and black-headed pins indicating the position of both armies.[274]

The following day, Union forces broke through the Confederate lines, forcing Lee to abandon Petersburg. A jubilant Lincoln telegraphed Grant: "Allow me to tender to you, and all with you, the nation[']s grateful thanks for this additional, and magnificent success."[275] On April 3, at the general's invitation, Lincoln hastened to inspect the fallen city. En route, his train halted as thousands of Rebel prisoners crossed the tracks. They were mostly conscript youngsters in rags and lacking blankets, shoes, and headgear. Their appearance moved the president to exclaim: "Poor boys! poor boys! If they only knew what we are trying to do for them they would not have fought us, and they would not look as they do."[276]

Upon arrival, Lincoln, along with his son Tad and Admiral Porter, quickly rode down the largely deserted streets to Grant's headquarters. The president's face radiated joy as he grabbed the general's hand, which he shook for a long while as he poured from his overflowing heart profound thanks and congratulations. It was one of the happiest moments of his life. "The scene was singularly affecting, and one never to be forgotten," recalled one of Grant's aides.

Lincoln said: "Do you know, general, I had a sort of sneaking idea all along that you intended to do something like this; but I thought some time ago that you would so maneuver as to have Sherman come up and be near enough to cooperate with you."

"Yes," replied Grant, "I thought at one time that Sherman's army might advance far enough to be in supporting distance of the Eastern armies when the spring campaign against Lee opened; but I had a feeling that it would be better to let Lee's old antagonists give his army the final blow, and finish up the job. If the Western troops were even to put in an appearance against Lee's army, it might give some of our politicians a chance to stir up sectional feeling in claiming everything for the troops from their own section of the country. The Western armies have been very successful in their campaigns, and it is due to the Eastern armies to let them vanquish their old enemy single-handed."[277]

Lincoln then discussed postwar political arrangements, emphasizing as he had done with Sherman that he wished the Rebels to be treated leniently. After about an hour and a half, Grant returned to the front.

On his way back to the train station, Lincoln passed by numerous houses demolished by artillery fire. He paused before the remains of a mansion, which had been struck over 100 times, and shook his head. Blacks and soldiers had broken into warehouses and were helping themselves to the abundant tobacco. The president and Admiral Porter each strapped a bale onto their horses' backs. As they rode along, troops greeted Lincoln jocularly, shouting out, "How are you, Abe?" and "Hello, Abe!"[278] Upon returning to City Point, Lincoln was refreshed and energized, happily convinced that the war would soon end.

That evening aboard the *Malvern,* the president asked Admiral Porter: "Can't the navy do something at this particular moment to make history?"

"Not much," replied Porter; "the navy is doing its best just now holding in utter uselessness the rebel navy, consisting of four heavy ironclads. If those should get down to City Point they would commit great havoc. . . . In consequence, we filled up the river with stones so that no vessels can pass either way. It enables us to 'hold the fort' with a very small force, but quite sufficient to prevent any one from removing the obstructions. Therefore the rebels' ironclads are useless to them."

"But can't we make a noise?" asked Lincoln; "that would be refreshing."

Porter obligingly had several ships fire broadsides rapidly for an hour, lighting up the night sky. Lincoln acknowledged "that the noise was a very respectable one."

Suddenly a distant huge explosion caused the *Malvern* to rock, prompting Lincoln to leap up and exclaim: "I hope to Heaven one of them has not blown up!"

Porter assured him that no Union vessels had been harmed but rather that the Confederates were destroying their ironclads.

"Well," Lincoln remarked, "our noise has done some good; that's a cheap way of getting rid of ironclads. I am certain Richmond is being evacuated, and that Lee has surrendered, or those fellows would not blow up their ironclads." Shortly thereafter three more such explosions announced the destruction of the remaining ironclads. To clear the river, Porter ordered the immediate removal of all obstructions. By the morning that task had been accomplished, and boats began sweeping the James for mines.[279]

Visiting Richmond

April 4 was the most remarkable day of Lincoln's presidency. Learning that Union troops were entering Richmond, he exclaimed: "Thank God that I have lived to see this! It seems to me that I have been dreaming a horrid dream for four years, and now the nightmare is gone. I want to see Richmond."[280] At 9 A.M., he and Tad, along with his bodyguard (army Captain Charles B. Penrose), naval Captain A. H. Adams, and Lieutenant W. W. Clemens of the Signal Corps, set sail for the Virginia capital aboard the *River Queen,* escorted by the *Bat,* the *Malvern,* and the *Columbus,* which carried the presidential cavalry escort and carriage. The captain of the *River Queen,* fearful that his vessel might strike a mine, had Lincoln ride on the upper deck, where he was less likely to be injured in such an eventuality.

The flotilla soon shrank. The *Bat* was unable to pass the first line of remaining obstructions at Aikens's Landing and was left behind. At the second such line, by Drewry's Bluff, the *River Queen* and the *Malvern* were grounded as they approached an imposing array of mines, sunken vessels, and rock-filled crates. Lincoln, Porter, Penrose, Clemmens, and Tad transferred to the admiral's elaborate barge, propelled by twelve stalwart oarsmen. Lincoln wryly told Porter, "this brings to my mind a fellow who once came to me to ask for an appointment as minister abroad. Finding he could not get that, he came down to some more modest position. Finally he asked to be made a tide-waiter. When he saw he could not get that, he asked me for an old pair of trousers. But it is well to be humble."[281]

As the party tried to pass the U.S.S. *Perry,* which was stuck fast, Lincoln and the others nearly lost their lives. The barge headed toward a stretch of deep water between the *Perry* and the shore, but it was not wide enough for the oarsmen to row through. So it was decided to try to approach the passage rapidly and glide by the ship. As it moved forward, the barge unexpectedly encountered a strong current that sent her directly under the steamer's giant paddle wheel. At that moment, the ship's engineer began to turn the wheel, inadvertently threatening to kill everyone in the barge. Lincoln and Porter hallooed, impelling the captain to rush to the engine room and stop the wheel in the nick of time, for one more rotation would have smashed the barge. As they forged ahead, Lincoln seemed exceptionally happy, though he looked askance at the ugly mines that had been hauled to the riverbanks.

After proceeding another 7 miles, the party arrived at Richmond, landing near the notorious Libby Prison. No reception committee greeted them, even though General Godfrey Weitzel, whose black troops were among the first to enter the city, had been alerted. The presidential party arrived earlier than expected.

As Lincoln and his companions stepped ashore, the journalist Charles C. Coffin pointed them out to some nearby blacks, who shouted "Hallelujah!" and "Glory! Glory! Glory!" Dozens of them raced to the landing, yelling and screaming "Hurrah! hurrah! President Linkum hab come!" Hearing the commotion, more blacks—men, women, and children—poured into the streets, crying "Bress de Lord! Bress de Lord!" One woman with tears in her eyes exclaimed, "I thank you, dear Jesus, that I behold President Linkum!" Poor whites also flocked to see the eminent visitor. Coffin informed readers of the Boston *Journal* that "no written page or illuminated canvas can give the reality of the event—the enthusiastic bearing of the people—the blacks and poor whites who have suffered untold horrors during the war, their demonstrations of pleasure, the shouting, dancing, the thanksgiving to God, the mention of the name of Jesus—as if President Lincoln were next to the son of God in their affections—the jubilant cries, the countenances beaming with unspeakable joy, the tossing up of caps, the swinging of arms of a motley crowd—some in rags, some bare-foot, some wearing pants of Union blue, and coats of Confederate gray, ragamuffins in dress, through the hardships of war, but yet of stately bearing."[282]

As soon as Lincoln landed, some blacks cried out that the president had arrived. Others, mistakenly assuming that this was an allusion to Jefferson Davis, shouted: "Hang him!" "Hang him!" "Show him no quarter!" Upon realizing that it was Lincoln, they were overjoyed.[283] When some of them knelt before Lincoln, he said: "Don't kneel to me. That is not right. You must kneel to God only, and thank him for the liberty you will hereafter enjoy."[284]

When Lincoln asked directions to General Weitzel's headquarters, a black man offered to show the way. The presidential party was led by half a dozen sailors from the barge, armed with carbines; another six brought up the rear. Sandwiched between those two lines, Lincoln walked along holding Tad's hand. Flanking them were Porter, Adams, Penrose, Clemmens, and Coffin. Blacks surrounded the little group, frantically shouting, clapping, dancing, throwing hats into the air, waving bonnets and handkerchiefs, and applauding loudly. They stirred up great clouds of dust, which mingled with smoke from smoldering buildings set ablaze by the retreating Confederates and made the warm atmosphere quite oppressive. Lincoln, wearing a long overcoat, was perspiring freely and fanning himself to cool off.

Because of the heat, and because Tad had trouble keeping up, the little party stopped to rest. At that point, according to Coffin, "an old negro, wearing a few rags, whose white, crisp hair appeared through his crownless straw hat, lifted the hat from his head, kneeled upon the ground, clasped his hands, and said, 'May de good Lord bress and keep you safe, Massa President Linkum.'" The president raised his own hat and bowed.[285] Lincoln's gesture, Coffin thought, "upset the forms, laws, customs, and ceremonies of centuries. It was a death-shock to chivalry, and a mortal wound to caste."[286] A white woman observing this scene turned away contemptuously. Lincoln nearly teared up as he listened to the grateful blessings showered on him and the thanks offered to God and Jesus. As the procession made its way slowly up the street, it paused once again, this time at Libby Prison, where Union officers had been incarcerated in especially grim conditions. When someone suggested that it be torn down, Lincoln objected, saying it should be preserved as a monument. A white man in shirtsleeves rushed from the sidewalk toward the president and shouted, "Abraham Lincoln, God bless you! You are the poor man's friend!" Then a beautiful white teen-aged girl pushed though the crowd to hand the president a bouquet of roses with a card bearing the simple message: "From Eva to the Liberator of the slaves."[287] Eventually, word reached General Weitzel that the president had arrived, and a squad of cavalry was dispatched to escort him to headquarters, which had been established in the Confederate White House.

There Lincoln, looking pallid and fatigued, sat down in Jefferson Davis's chair and quietly requested a glass of water. Captain Barnes, who had finally caught up with the presidential party, recalled that there "was no triumph in his gesture or attitude. He lay back in the chair like a tired man whose nerves had carried him beyond his strength."[288] He wore a "look of unutterable weariness, as if his spirit, energy and animating force were wholly exhausted," Coffin reported.[289] So tired was he that when he stepped onto the balcony to acknowledge the cheering crowd in the street, he merely bowed rather than speaking.

Soon General Weitzel arrived, along with General George F. Shepley, military governor of Virginia. After congratulating them, Lincoln met privately with some Confederate leaders who had requested an interview. Among them was former Associate Justice of the U.S. Supreme Court John A. Campbell, who had served as the Confederate assistant secretary of war. He gave Lincoln a very low bow. The president received him in a dignified yet cordial manner. After explaining that he had no authorization to negotiate on behalf of the Confederacy or Virginia, the agitated Campbell, who was one of the negotiators Lincoln had met with at Hampton Roads two months earlier, recommended a lenient peace and stated that the war for all intents and purposes was over, that the Army of Northern Virginia could not be held together, and that leading Virginians would help restore the Union. Weitzel, whom the president invited to sit in on the discussion, recalled that Lincoln "insisted that he could not treat with any Rebels until they had laid down their arms and surrendered, and that if this were first done he would go as far as he possibly could to prevent the shedding of another drop of blood, and that he and the good people of the North were surfeited with this thing and wanted it to end as soon as possible."[290] Lincoln added that he would consider the matter, that he had originally planned to return to City Point but would remain overnight, and that he would like Campbell to meet with him the following day, along with any citizens who might prove useful.

After this conversation, Lincoln joined Weitzel and Shepley for a tour of Richmond in an ordinary two-seat buggy. As they rode along, hundreds of the city's blacks in a frenzy of exultation shouted out expressions of gratitude and joy, sang songs of deliverance, wept, and threw their hands in the air. A black correspondent told readers of the Philadelphia *Press* that there was "no describing the scene along the route. The colored population was wild with enthusiasm. Old men thanked God in a very boisterous manner, and old women shouted upon the pavement as high as they had ever done at religious revival."[291] One celebrant declared: "Jeff Davis did not wait to see his master but he had come at last."[292] Others exclaimed "thank God, Jesus Christ has come at last" and "God Bless Abum Linkum, bless his heart, I give him the last thing I got in the world."[293] According to Shepley, Lincoln "looked at it all attentively, with a face expressive only of a sort of pathetic wonder. Occasionally its sadness would alternate with one of his peculiar smiles, and he would remark on the great proportion of those whose color indicated a mixed lineage from the white master and the black slave; and that reminded him of some little story of his life in Kentucky, which he would smilingly tell."[294] A white woman noted that the president "seemed tired and old."[295]

At Capitol Square, Lincoln addressed a huge crowd of blacks: "My poor friends, you are free—free as air. You can cast off the name of slave and trample upon it; it will come to you no more. Liberty is your birthright. God gave it to you as he gave it to others, and it is a sin that you have been deprived of it for so many years. But you must try to deserve this priceless boon. Let the world see that you merit it, and are able to maintain it by your good works. Don't let your joy carry you into excesses. Learn the laws and obey them; obey God's commandments and thank him for giving you liberty, for to him you owe all things. There, now, let me pass on; I have but little time to spare. I want to see the capital, and must return at once to Washington to secure to you that liberty which you seem to prize so highly."[296] He toured the capitol building, which the legislators had precipitously abandoned two days earlier. Overturned desks, bundles of Confederate money, and random government documents were strewn about haphazardly. En route back to the landing site, the presidential entourage rolled past the notorious prisons, Libby and Castle Thunder, both overflowing with captured Rebels. At the wharf, as Lincoln boarded a cutter that would take him to the *Malvern,* an elderly black woman cried out: "Don't drown, Massa Abe, for God's sake!"[297]

The next morning, General Edward Hastings Ripley warned Lincoln of a plot against his life and recommended steps to guard against it. "No, General Ripley, it is impossible for me to adopt and follow your suggestions," he replied. "I deeply appreciate the feeling which has led you to urge them on me, but I must go on as I have begun in the course marked out for me; for I cannot bring myself to believe that any human being lives who would do me any harm."[298] (Soon thereafter, while describing his experiences in Richmond, Lincoln played down the chances that he could be assassinated in Washington: "I walked alone on the street, and anyone could have shot me from a second-story window.")[299]

Let 'em Up Easy: Dealing with the Defeated Rebels

The president then met again with Campbell, who brought with him an eminent Richmond attorney, Gustavus A. Myers. Lincoln began by reading a memo reiterating the three preconditions for peace that he had presented at the Hampton Roads conference. He added that it seemed futile "to be more specific with those who will not say they are ready for the indispensable terms, even on conditions to be named by themselves. If there be any who are ready for those indispensable terms, on any conditions whatever, let them say so, and state their conditions, so that such conditions can be distinctly known, and considered."

To encourage die-hards to surrender, Lincoln offered a practical inducement: "the remission of confiscations being within the executive power, if the war be now further persisted in, by those opposing the government, the making of confiscated property at the least to bear the additional cost, will be insisted on; but that confiscations (except in cases of third party intervening interests) will be remitted to the people of any State which shall now promptly, and in good faith, withdraw it's troops and other support, from further resistance to the government. What is now said as to remission of confiscations has no reference to supposed property in slaves."

According to Myers, Lincoln provided a running commentary on this document, saying that in regard "to the confiscation of property, that *that* was in his power, and he should be disposed to exercise that power in the spirit of true liberality." He also "professed himself really desirous to see an end of the struggle, and said he hoped in the Providence of God that there never would be another" and "that he was thinking over a plan by which the Virginia Legislature might be brought to hold their meeting in the Capitol in Richmond,—for the purpose of seeing whether they desired to take any action on behalf of the State in view of the existing state of affairs, and informed

Genl Weitzel that he would write to him from City point on that subject in a day or two. The outline of his plan being, that safe conduct should be given to the members to come hither, and that after a reasonable time were allowed them to deliberate, should they arrive at no conclusion, they would have safe conduct afforded them to leave Richmond."

The three men then discussed loyalty oaths. Myers remarked "that the conciliatory course pursued by the Federal forces since their arrival in Richmond, had had a powerful effect in allaying the apprehension and producing kindly feelings on the part of the Citizens" and that "the opinion that the adoption of any other course on the part of the Federal authorities would be productive of irritation and conducive to no good result." Lincoln replied "that he had never attached much importance to the oath of allegiance being required," but would defer to Weitzel. The general said he was not disposed to require it. "Other conversation occurred," Myers recorded, "in which the President declared his disposition to be lenient towards all persons, however prominent, who had taken part in the struggle, and certainly no exhibition was made by him of any feeling of vindictiveness or exultation."

Campbell had a slightly different recollection: the president "with emphasis and gesture" declared "that he had said nothing in the paper as to pains and penalties. That he supposed, that it would not be proper to offer a pardon to Mr. Davis, whom we familiarly call Jeff Davis—who says he won't have one. But that most anyone can have most anything of the kind for the asking." Lincoln added "that he had been thinking of a plan for calling the Virginia Legislature, that had been sitting in Richmond, together, and to get them [to] vote for the restoration of Virginia to the Union. That he had not arranged the matter to his satisfaction and would not decide upon it until after his return to City Point, and he would communicate with Genl. Weitzell." He deemed it of "the greatest importance that the same organization that has been casting the influence and support of the State to the rebels should bring the State back into the Union."[300] Campbell then read Lincoln a paper suggesting that Grant be authorized to establish an armistice which would lead to permanent peace; that no loyalty oaths be required; that no property be confiscated; and that modes be spelled out for negotiating with Confederate officials. Lincoln rejected the proposed armistice: "We will not negotiate with men as long as they are fighting against us. The last election established this as the deliberate determination of the country."[301] He asked for a copy of Campbell's statement and said he would take it under advisement. The interview was civil, and the participants separated in good humor.

Around noon Lincoln called at Weitzel's headquarters and told him that he would consider the issues carefully and send instructions the following day. As they discussed the best way to treat the defeated enemy, Lincoln said that he was reluctant to issue orders on the matter but did advise the general: "If I were in your place I'd let 'em up easy, let 'em up easy."[302] Then he returned to the *Malvern* and steamed back to City Point.

When General Shepley, an accomplished lawyer, heard of Lincoln's decision authorizing the members of the Virginia Legislature to reconvene, he predicted that it would be wildly unpopular in the North, that the cabinet would disapprove, and that

Weitzel might well be blamed unless he had a presidential order in writing. He explained his thinking: "By this shrewd move of Judge Campbell the rebel legislature, assembled under the new constitution recognizing the Confederacy, will covertly gain recognition as a legal and valid legislature, and creep into the Union with all its rebel legislation in force, thus preserving all the peculiar rebel institutions, including slavery; and they will get, as the price of defeat, all they hoped to achieve as the fruits of victory. The thing is monstrous."[303]

On April 6, anticipating that Weitzel might be unfairly blamed for the president's decision, Lincoln sent him a formal order confirming his earlier verbal instructions: "It has been intimated to me that the gentlemen who have acted as the Legislature of Virginia, in support of the rebellion, may now desire to assemble at Richmond, and take measures to withdraw the Virginia troops, and other support from resistance to the General government. If they attempt it, give them permission and protection, until, if at all, they attempt some action hostile to the United States, in which case you will notify them and give them reasonable time to leave; and at the end of which time, arrest any who may remain." Weitzel was to regard this document as private but could show it to Campbell.[304]

"The drafting of that order, though so short, gave me more perplexity than any other paper I ever drew up," Lincoln told Virginia Governor Francis H. Pierpont. He worked on it for hours that night, trying to make clear that the men who had been serving in the legislature were to reassemble for the sole purpose of withdrawing the army from the field. "But if I had known that General Lee would surrender so soon I would not have issued the proclamation," he added. Lincoln assured Pierpont that "your government at Alexandria was fully in my mind, and I intended to recognize the restored government, of which you were head, as the rightful government of Virginia."[305]

As Shepley predicted, Lincoln's order sparked a firestorm of protest, and the cabinet disapproved of the plan. Stanton, as he later said, "*vehemently opposed*" the scheme and held "several very earnest conversations" with the president, advising him "that any effort to reorganize the Government should be under Federal authority solely, treating the rebel organizations and government as absolutely null and void."[306] Welles, Dennison, and Speed also objected. When Senator Wade learned of Lincoln's plan, he reportedly said in furious tones "that there had been much talk about the assassination of Lincoln—that if he authorized the approval of that paper . . . by God, the sooner he was assassinated the better."[307] Fellow Radical George W. Julian said he never noticed "such force and fitness in Ben Wade's swearing."[308]

The legislators remaining in Richmond did meet and grossly overstepped the bounds Lincoln had placed on their authority. They acted as though they were the legitimate government of the commonwealth, empowered to negotiate peace terms. Lincoln was understandably indignant, and three days later revoked the order to Weitzel. When the press blamed that general for the action of the legislature and condemned him as a Rebel sympathizer, he refuted the charge by citing Lincoln's text. To the cabinet, Lincoln explained that he thought "the members of the legislature, being the prominent and influential men of their respective counties, had better come together and undo their own work" of secession. The president said he "felt assured they would do this" and believed their action would prove to be "a good one. Civil government must be reestablished as soon as possible. There must be courts and law and order, or society would be broken up, the disbanded armies would turn into robber bands and guerrillas."[309]

Endgame

Events were rapidly overtaking the peacemakers. On April 7, as Union cavalry pursued the Confederates fleeing westward, Lincoln remarked that "Sheridan seemed to be getting Virginia soldiers out of the war faster than this legislature could think."[310] He made a similar observation in a message to Grant describing his instructions to Weitzel. "I do not think it very probable that anything will come of this," he said, "but I have thought best to notify you, so that if you should see signs, you may understand them. From your recent despatches it seems that you are pretty effectually withdrawing the Virginia troops from opposition to the government. Nothing I have done, or probably shall do, is to delay, hinder, or interfere with you in your work."[311]

The Army of Northern Virginia was indeed dwindling as more and more troops deserted. The Confederate Congress in desperation had authorized the enlistment of blacks, and Jefferson Davis had reluctantly assented. When told that the Rebels might resort to such a measure, Lincoln remarked that "when they had reached that stage the cause of the war would cease and hostilities with it. The evil would cure itself."[312]

At City Point, a Confederate prisoner of war, General Rufus Barringer, asked to see Lincoln, who expressed keen interest in meeting him. "I have never seen a live rebel general in full uniform," he remarked. When the captive identified himself as a brother of Daniel Barringer, whom the president had befriended when they both served in Congress, Lincoln relaxed and joyfully reminisced about his days as a U.S. Representative. After a long conversation, he innocently asked Barringer: "Do you think I can be of any service to you?" Everyone in earshot laughed heartily at such a quaint question. Realizing how naïve he sounded, Lincoln quickly began writing a note to Stanton. As he did so, he told Barringer: "I suppose they will send you to Washington, and there I have no doubt they will put you in the old Capitol prison. I am told it isn't a nice sort of a place, and I am afraid you won't find it a very comfortable tavern; but I have a powerful friend in Washington—he's the biggest man in the country,—and I believe I have some influence with him when I don't ask too much. Now I want you to send this card of introduction to him, and if he takes the notion he may put you on your parole, or let up on you that way or some other way. Anyhow, it's worth trying." The note asked Stanton to make Barringer's "detention in Washington as comfortable as possible." Speechless at this display of presidential magnanimity, Barringer left the tent and burst into tears. He was paroled three months later.[313]

On April 6, Mary Lincoln returned to City Point and once again engaged in hysterics. She came with an entourage consisting of her confidante-cum-dressmaker Elizabeth Keckly, Senator Charles Sumner and his young French friend Charles Adolphe Pineton (the Marquis de Chambrun), James Speed, Assistant Secretary of the Interior William T. Otto, and Iowa Senator James Harlan with his wife and daughter Mary, who was the object of Robert Lincoln's affections. The First Lady, sorely disappointed that she had been unable to accompany her husband on his entry into Richmond two days earlier, was eager to tour that city. So while Lincoln attended to business, she and her friends headed up the James for the Confederate capital.

Upon her return the following day, she expressed a desire to visit Petersburg. Lincoln reluctantly agreed to join her. She put a damper on the event by behaving much as she had done two weeks earlier. Just as she had then snapped at Mrs. Grant for daring to sit next to her, she now scolded Mrs. Harlan for a similar breach of etiquette. Making matters worse, she exploded in anger at Admiral Porter for inviting his wife as well as Mrs. Harlan and other ladies to join the excursion. According to Porter, she threw herself on the ground and tore her hair. Later she upbraided him in a "very sharp letter." Porter laconically noted that Mrs. Lincoln had "an extremely jealous disposition."[314]

Some black servants aboard the *River Queen* wished to accompany the presidential party. Chambrun reported that Lincoln, who "was blinded by no prejudices against race or color" and who "had not what can be termed false dignity," invited them to sit with him and his companions.[315] In Petersburg, he got off one of his better puns. At a house which George L. Hartsuff had commandeered as his headquarters, the general explained that its owner was demanding rent. Pointing to a hole in the wall created by a Union artillery shell, Lincoln quipped, "I think our batteries have given him *rents* enough without asking for more."[316] That morning he also sent Grant a telegram which succinctly expressed the iron determination that characterized his leadership throughout the war: "Gen. Sheridan says 'If the thing is pressed I think that Lee will surrender.' Let the *thing* be pressed."[317]

As the visitors toured the town, where most houses were closed and most shops either abandoned or vandalized, blacks crowded the streets to cheer their liberator while whites hastily sought refuge to avoid having to look upon him. After consulting with General Hartsuff, Lincoln reported to his companions that "[a]nimosity in the town is abating, the inhabitants now accept accomplished facts, the final downfall of the Confederacy, and the abolition of slavery. There still remains much for us to do, but every day brings new reason for confidence in the future."[318] On the way back to City Point, he ordered the carriage to halt before a tall tree, whose beauty he analyzed. Like a botany teacher lecturing students, he pointed out its strong trunk and elaborate branches, comparing it to an oak and striving to make his fellow passengers appreciate the distinctive character of different types of trees.

Farewell to City Point: Hospital Visits

The next night Lincoln returned to Washington, where Seward had recently been injured in a carriage accident. Before departing, the president spent five hours visiting the hospitals of each corps, despite the doctors' warning that greeting thousands of men would be more than he could endure. When the physicians spoke proudly of the hospital facilities, he replied: "Gentlemen, you know better than I *how* to *conduct* these hospitals, but I came here to take by the hand the men who have achieved our glorious victories."[319] And so he began shaking hands with the wounded. Private

Wilbur Fisk noted that Lincoln "appeared to take delight in it. I believe he had almost as much pleasure in honoring the boys, as the boys did in receiving the honor from him. It was an unexpected honor, coming from the man upon whom the world is looking with so much interest, and the boys were pleased with it beyond measure. Everything passed off in a very quiet manner; there was no crowding or disorder of any kind." The patients who were not bedridden formed a line along which Lincoln passed, speaking to every one as he shook hands:

"Are you well, sir?"

"How do you do to-day?"

"How are you, sir?"

Then he entered the stockades and tents to greet those too weak to join the line. Fisk commented that "Mr. Lincoln presides over millions of people, and each individual share of his attention must necessarily be very small, and yet he wouldn't slight the humblest of them all. . . . The men not only reverence and admire Mr. Lincoln, but they love him."[320]

After shaking the hands of all the Union soldiers, he turned to enter tents housing Confederate wounded.

"Mr. President, you do not want to go in there!" exclaimed a doctor.

"Why not, my boy?" he asked.

"Why, sir, they are sick rebel prisoners."

"That is just where I do want to go," he said and shook the hands of many surprised Confederates.[321]

Nearly every soldier asked the president about the military and political situation and smiled with happiness when Lincoln said: "Success all along the line." He assured them that the war would end within six weeks.[322]

Lincoln's mood in his final days at the front oscillated between hearty bonhomie and sad introspection. Chambrun recalled that "it was rare to converse with him a while without feeling something poignant. . . . Mr. Lincoln was quite humorous, although one could always detect a bit of irony in his humor. He would relate anecdotes, seeking always to bring the point out clearly. He willingly laughed either at what was being said to him, or at what he said himself. But all of a sudden he would retire within himself; then he would close his eyes, and all his features would at once bespeak a kind of sadness as indescribable as it was deep. After a while, as though it were by an effort of his will, he would shake off this mysterious weight under which he seemed bowed; his generous and open disposition would again reappear. In one evening I happened to count over twenty of these alternations and contrasts."

In discussing peace plans, Lincoln emphasized the need to show mercy to the defeated foe. When it was suggested that Jefferson Davis be hanged, he calmly replied: "Let us judge not, that we be not judged." Told that the suffering of Union soldiers in Libby Prison should trump the claims of mercy, he repeated that biblical injunction twice. When Chambrun alluded to the possibility of war between France and the United States over Napoleon III's intervention in Mexico, Lincoln remarked: "There has been war enough. I know what the American people want, but, thank God, I count for something, and during my second term there will be no more fighting."

In the afternoon, Lincoln asked a military band to play "La Marseillaise," saying "he had a great liking for that tune." To Chambrun he noted the irony of the situation: "You must come over to America to hear it." (Napoleon III had banned that revolutionary anthem from France.) Upon learning that Chambrun was unfamiliar with the song "Dixie," he requested the band to strike it up, much to the musicians' surprise. "That tune is now Federal property; it belongs to us, and, at any rate, it is good to show the rebels that with us they will be free to hear it again."[323]

At 10 P.M., the *River Queen* weighed anchor and headed for Washington. As it pulled away, Lincoln, lost in thought, stood at the rail gazing at the distant hills. He continued to meditate long after they disappeared from view. It is hard to imagine the profound feelings that ran through his mind that night. He probably reviewed the entire course of the war, from the shelling of Fort Sumter through the capture of Richmond. He may have thought of all the blood shed by the 620,000 men killed over the past four years, including friends like Elmer Ellsworth, Ben Hardin Helm, and Edward D. Baker; all the wounded, many of whom he had spoken to that day; all the mourning widows and orphans; all the vast destruction of property, so vividly apparent amid the ruins of Petersburg and Richmond. Counterbalancing those grim reflections, he probably derived immense satisfaction recalling the joy of the liberated slaves who thronged about him in those two cities. How could justice for those people be secured while simultaneously granting mercy to their former masters?

Lincoln and Congress had both addressed the problem of Reconstruction and had reached an impasse. He had stuck by his Ten Percent plan and the Radicals had countered with the Wade–Davis bill. He had stymied them with his veto; they had thwarted him by refusing to recognize the Louisiana government and seat its congressmen and senators. His principal motive in framing Reconstruction policy had been to induce the Confederates to surrender. Now that the war was virtually over, should he move to compromise with the Radicals? If so, how far?

36

"I Feel a Presentiment That I Shall Not Outlast the Rebellion. When It Is Over, My Work Will Be Done."

The Final Days
(April 9–15, 1865)

Lincoln had no doubt that the Union would ultimately triumph, but, he said in July 1864, "I may not live to see it. I feel a presentiment that I shall not outlast the rebellion. When it is over, my work will be done."[1] To Harriet Beecher Stowe he made a similar prediction: "Whichever way it [the war] ends, I have the impression that *I* shan't last long after it's over."[2] He told his friend Owen Lovejoy that he might die even before peace came: "This war is eating my life out; I have a strong impression that I shall not live to see the end."[3]

Return to Washington

On April 9, as Lee was surrendering to Grant at Appomattox, the *River Queen* sailed up Chesapeake Bay and the Potomac River. Thomas Stackpole, a White House steward, reported that en route, the First Lady struck her husband in the face, damned him, and cursed him. At a dinner party aboard ship, Mrs. Keckly observed a young captain try to make pleasant conversation: "Mrs. Lincoln, you should have seen the President the other day, on his triumphal entry into Richmond. He was the cynosure of all eyes. The ladies kissed their hands to him, and greeted him with the waving of handkerchiefs. He is quite a hero when surrounded by pretty young ladies." The officer "suddenly paused with a look of embarrassment. Mrs. Lincoln turned to him with flashing eyes, with the remark that his familiarity was offensive to her. Quite a scene followed."[4] Mary Harlan similarly recalled how a young officer aboard the *River Queen* described an episode of the president's visit to Richmond: all doors were closed to Lincoln save one, which "was opened furtively and a fair hand extended a bunch of flowers, which he took." Mrs. Lincoln "made manifest her dislike of the story, much to the narrator's chagrin."[5]

To his shipboard companions Lincoln read for hours, mostly from Shakespeare's *Macbeth*. After reciting the thane's guilty soliloquy following the murder of his cousin, King Duncan, the president remarked "how true a description of the murderer that one was; when, the dark deed achieved, its tortured perpetrator came to envy the

799

sleep of his victim." He read that scene several times. While passing Mount Vernon, Adolphe de Chambrun predicted to Lincoln that Americans would one day revere his house in Springfield as much as they did George Washington's estate. "Springfield! How happy, four years hence, will I be to return there in peace and tranquility!" the president exclaimed.[6] A few days earlier, when John Todd Stuart had asked him if he intended to return to the Illinois capital after his presidency, Lincoln replied: "Mary does not expect ever to go back there, and don't want to go—but I do—I expect to go back and make my home in Springfield for the rest of my life."[7]

During the voyage, Lincoln did not discuss his Reconstruction policy with Charles Sumner, its chief opponent. Instead, he reminisced, observing that he could not understand why people thought Seward had been his chief advisor. "I have counseled with you twice as much as I ever did with him," he told the Massachusetts senator.[8] As they approached Washington, the First Lady said: "That city is full of our enemies." Lincoln impatiently exclaimed: "Enemies! We must never speak of that!"[9]

Last Public Speech

Lincoln rejoiced greatly at Lee's surrender. "The very day after his return from Richmond," Stanton recalled, "I passed with him some of the happiest moments of my life; our hearts beat with exultation at the victories."[10] But the president did not long indulge in celebrating, for he had to deal with the thorny issues of Reconstruction. On April 10, when Virginia Governor Francis H. Pierpont congratulated him on the fall of Richmond, he replied: "I want it distinctly understood that I claim no part nor lot in the honor of the military movements in front of Richmond[.] All the honor belongs to the military. After I went to the front, I made two or three suggestions to Gen. Grant about military movements, and he knocked the sand from under me so quickly that I concluded I knew nothing about it and offered no more advice." From Pierpont, Lincoln wanted information rather than congratulations. What should be done in Virginia now that Lee had surrendered? Elements of the disloyal state legislature had reassembled in Richmond but had overstepped their mandate. Should Pierpont, as governor of loyal Virginia (based in Alexandria) proceed to the state capital? How would people there receive him? "Will they rush forward and try to seize all the offices?" he asked. "Will they sulk and do nothing? . . . Is there any Union sentiment among the Southern people strong enough to develop itself? If so, what measures should be adopted to foster this sentiment?" Lincoln enjoined Pierpont to be "industrious, and ascertain what Union sentiment there is in Virginia, and keep me advised."[11]

Virginia was a special case, since it had a Unionist government (under Pierpont) already in place. What about the other states lately in rebellion? Of them, Louisiana was furthest along the road to restoration. Lincoln wanted to continue nurturing the Hahn government there and win congressional recognition for it. But to do so he had to overcome the resistance of Radicals in Congress, many of whom shared Andrew Johnson's view that "treason must be made odious" and "traitors must be impoverished, their social power broken." Wealthy Confederates should be arrested, tried, convicted, and hanged, the vice-president said: "We have put down these traitors in arms; let us put them down in law, in public judgment, and in the morals of the world."[12] When an abolitionist suggested disfranchisement rather than execution would be the best punishment for Rebel leaders, Johnson replied: "a very good way to disfranchise them is to break their necks!"[13]

Less punitive Radicals, concerned more about protecting former slaves than punishing their erstwhile masters, championed black suffrage. Salmon P. Chase wrote Lincoln predicting that "it will be, hereafter, counted equally a crime & a folly if the colored loyalists of the rebel states shall be left to the control of restored rebels."[14] On April 11, Lincoln moved dramatically closer to those Radicals in a carefully prepared address delivered from the White House, in which he indirectly responded to Chase.

On April 10, the president was twice serenaded by thousands of cheering Washingtonians, who clamored for a speech. To their disappointment, he replied that he would not deliver one then but would do so the next day. As a gesture to placate them, he instructed the Marine band to play "Dixie." In justifying that selection, he jocularly explained: "I have always thought 'Dixie' one of the best tunes I have ever heard. Our adversaries over the way attempted to appropriate it, but I insisted yesterday that we fairly captured it. [Applause.] I presented the question to the Attorney General, and he gave it as his legal opinion that it is our lawful prize. [Laughter and applause.] I now request the band to favor me with its performance."[15] The way for this magnanimous gesture had been paved by young Tad, who preceded his father at the window, waving a Confederate flag (the one that Elmer Ellsworth had torn down in May 1861) until a servant yanked him away, much to the amusement of the assembled multitude.

The night of April 11, Lincoln, as promised, delivered a formal speech to a crowd whose response to his appearance was unusually intense. Standing near him, Noah Brooks found "something terrible about the enthusiasm with which the beloved Chief Magistrate was received—cheers upon cheers, wave after wave of applause rolled up, the President modestly standing quiet until it was over."[16] Elizabeth Keckly wrote that she "never saw such a mass of heads before. It was like a black, gently swelling sea. The swaying motion of the crowd, in the dim uncertain light, was like the rising and falling of billows—like the ebb and flow of the tide upon the stranded shore of the ocean. Close to the house the faces were plainly discernible, but they faded into mere ghostly outlines on the outskirts of the assembly; and what added to the weird, spectral beauty of the scene, was the confused hum of voices that rose above the sea of forms, sounding like the subdued, sullen roar of an ocean storm, or the wind soughing through the dark lonely forest. It was a grand and imposing scene."[17]

When Brooks expressed surprise that the president had a manuscript from which to read, he explained: "It is true that I don't usually read a speech, but I am going to say something to-night that may be important. I am going to talk about reconstruction, and sometimes I am betrayed into saying things that other people don't like. In a little off-hand talk I made the other day I used the phrase 'Turned tail and ran.'" Senator Sumner "was very much offended by that, and I hope he won't be offended again."[18] As Lincoln read from his text, Brooks held up a candle so that he could see it. After finishing each page, the president let it fall to the floor, where Tad energetically scooped it up. (Upon completing his remarks, Lincoln quipped to Brooks: "That was a pretty fair speech, I think, but you threw some light on it.")[19]

As the president spoke from a window of the White House, his wife and Clara Harris, daughter of New York Senator Ira Harris, stood at a nearby window chatting so loudly that they nearly drowned out the president. Initially, the crowd tolerated this unbecoming behavior, but in time some people emphatically told the noisemakers to quiet down. Disconcerted by their shushing, Lincoln feared that something he said had given offense. But he soon realized that no disrespect was meant and, with "an expression of pain and mortification which came over his face as if such strokes were not new," continued reading his speech.[20]

Instead of delivering the expected triumphal paean to the conquering Union army and navy, he dwelt at length on the problems of Reconstruction, explaining how he and General Banks had labored to make Louisiana a model for the other seceded states. Frankly allowing that some Radical criticism of their handiwork was valid, he dismissed as "a merely pernicious abstraction" the question of whether the rebellious states were in or out of the Union. Some Radicals insisted that by seceding, the Confederate states had reverted to the status of territories and could therefore be governed by Congress. Lincoln resisted that line of argument, asserting that he and the Radicals "agree that the seceded States, so called, are out of their proper practical relation with the Union; and that the sole object of the government, civil and military, in regard to those States is to again get them into that proper practical relation. I believe it is not only possible, but in fact, easier, to do this, without deciding, or even considering, whether these states have even been out of the Union, than with it. Finding themselves safely at home, it would be utterly immaterial whether they had ever been abroad. Let us all join in doing the acts necessary to restoring the proper practical relations between these states and the Union; and each forever after, innocently indulge his own opinion whether, in doing the acts, he brought the States from without, into the Union, or only gave them proper assistance, they never having been out of it."

To strengthen this rhetorical appeal for Republican unity, Lincoln offered the Radicals an important substantive concession. Hitherto he had expressed support for black suffrage only in private. Now, fatefully, he made that support public: "It is also unsatisfactory to some that the elective franchise is not given to the colored man. I would myself prefer that it were now conferred on the very intelligent, and on those who serve our cause as soldiers." To be sure, he acknowledged, the Louisiana Legislature had not availed itself of the opportunity afforded it by the new state constitution to enfranchise blacks, but "the question is not whether the Louisiana government, as it stands, is quite all that is desirable. The question is 'Will it be wiser to take it as it is, and help to improve it; or to reject, and disperse it?' 'Can Louisiana be brought into proper practical relation with the Union *sooner* by *sustaining*, or by *discarding* her new State Government?'" Putting it another way, he asked: "Concede that the new government of Louisiana is only to what it should be as the egg is to the fowl, shall we sooner have the fowl by hatching the egg than by smashing it?"

Months later Frederick Douglass acknowledged that though Lincoln's call for black suffrage "seemed to mean but little" at the time, it actually "meant a great deal. It was just like Abraham Lincoln. He never shocked prejudices unnecessarily. Having learned statesmanship while splitting rails, he always used the thin edge of the wedge first—and the fact that he used it at all meant that he would if need be, use the thick as well as the thin."[21] Owen Lovejoy used this same image to describe Lincoln's approach to emancipation. In dealing with slavery, he had inserted the thin edge of the wedge in March 1862 (with the recommendation to help compensate those Border States adopting gradual emancipation), drove it in deeper in 1863 (with the Emancipation Proclamation), and fully drove home the thick part in 1865 (with the Thirteenth Amendment.) Even before March 1862, Lincoln had worked behind the scenes to persuade Delaware to emancipate its slaves. So it was with black suffrage. In 1864, Lincoln had privately urged Governor Hahn to enfranchise at least some blacks in Louisiana. In 1865, he publicly endorsed the same policy. To be sure, Louisiana was a special case, for a number of educated blacks lived in New Orleans. Possibly Lincoln did not mean to extend suffrage to uneducated blacks in other states, but that seems unlikely, for if he wanted to enfranchise only educated blacks, he would not have suggested that black soldiers, regardless of educational background, be granted voting rights.

One member of Lincoln's audience did not underestimate the importance of Lincoln's call for limited black suffrage. Upon hearing the president's words, a handsome, popular, impulsive, 26-year-old actor named John Wilkes Booth turned to a friend and declared: "That means nigger citizenship. Now, by God, I'll put him through!"[22] He added: "That is the last speech he will ever make."[23]

Clearly Lincoln was moving toward the Radical position. Now that the war was over, there was no need to inveigle Confederates into surrendering by offering them exceptionally lenient peace terms. His proclaimed support for limited black suffrage was but one sign of his willingness to meet Radical critics halfway. In March, he had signed the Freedman's Bureau Act without reservation. It established a federal agency, the Bureau of Refugees, Freedmen and Abandoned Lands, to protect the interests of the former slaves as well as white refugees. (The agency was forbidden to practice discrimination based on race; whatever benefits blacks enjoyed were to be afforded to whites equally and vice versa.) No longer would liberated blacks work under the supervision of provost marshals and treasury agents; the legislation even held out the promise, somewhat vaguely, of land redistribution. Lincoln's concern all along, according to chaplain John Eaton, "was to illustrate the capacity of these [black] people for the privileges, duties and rights of freedom."[24]

Moreover, Lincoln suggested that he was willing to compromise on Reconstruction policy. On April 10, he told Governor Pierpont "that he had no plan for reorganization, but must be guided by events."[25] Stanton testified that Lincoln at war's end had not "matured any plan."[26] While he hoped that Congress would seat Louisiana's senators and congressmen, in his April 11 speech he acknowledged that conditions varied from state to state and that "no exclusive, and inflexible plan can safely be prescribed as to details and colatterals. Such exclusive, and inflexible plan, would surely become a new entanglement. Important principles may, and must, be inflexible." As for the Louisiana government, he said that although he had promised to sustain it, "bad promises are better broken than kept" and he would "treat this as a bad promise, and break it, whenever I shall be convinced that keeping it is adverse to the public interest." He closed with a tantalizing hint: "it may be my duty to make some new announcement to the people of the South. I am considering, and shall not fail to act, when satisfied that action will be proper."[27]

What Lincoln meant in those closing remarks is not clear, but three days later at a cabinet meeting he "said he thought he had made a mistake at Richmond in sanctioning the assembling of the Virginia Legislature & had perhaps been too fast in his desires for early reconstruction."[28] He made a similar remark to House Speaker Schuyler Colfax, confessing that he was "not sure that it was wise" and that it "was a doubtful experiment at best."[29] Commenting on that cabinet meeting, pro- Radical Attorney General James Speed remarked to Salmon P. Chase that the president never "seemed so near our views."[30]

Reconstruction Policies: The Last Cabinet Meeting

Despite his ill-advised decision to let the Virginia Legislature reconvene, Lincoln shared the Radicals' desire to keep the old leadership class of the South from returning to power. In Louisiana he had worked to block reactionaries' attempts to gain positions of authority, and presumably he would do so in other states. As Frederick Douglass plausibly speculated in December 1865, if Lincoln had lived, "no rebels would hold the reins of Government in any one of the late rebellious states."[31]

Lincoln was not disposed to withdraw his support for amnesty for most Confederates. According to Gideon Welles, he "dreaded and deprecated violent and revengeful feelings, or any malevolent demonstrations toward those of our countrymen who were involved, voluntarily or involuntarily, in the rebellion."[32] But what should be done with the Confederate leaders? He told Grant that he hoped that they would slip out of the country without his knowledge. Similarly, in response to Postmaster General William Dennison's query about letting Rebel *eminenti* escape, Lincoln said: "I should not be sorry to have them out of the country; but I should be for following them up pretty close, to make sure of their going."[33] In discussing the possibility of capturing Jefferson Davis, Mrs. Lincoln allegedly exclaimed: "Don't allow him to escape the law! He must be hanged." The president replied: "Let us judge not that we be not judged."[34] When asked if he should order the arrest of Jacob Thompson, who had been a Confederate agent in Canada as well as James Buchanan's secretary of the interior, Lincoln replied: "no, I rather think not. When you have got an elephant by the hind leg, and he's trying to run away, it's best to let him run."[35]

But what if prominent Confederates did not emigrate? Lincoln told Schuyler Colfax "that he did not want their blood, but that we could not have peace or order in the South . . . while they remained there with their great influence to poison public opinion." To encourage them to flee, he suggested that military authorities "inform them that if they stay, they will be punished for their crimes, but if they leave, no attempt will be made to hinder them. Then we can be magnanimous to all the rest and have peace and quiet in the whole land."[36] Lincoln did not indicate what he would recommend if they *still* refused to take the hint.

Though the president was moving in their direction, some Radicals remained hostile to his Reconstruction policy, especially his willingness to grant amnesty.

Noah Brooks reported that "the extremists are thirsting for a general hanging, and if the President fails to gratify their desires in this direction, they will be glad, for it will afford them more pretexts for the formation of a party which shall be pledged to 'a more vigorous policy.'"[37]

The subject of amnesty came up at a cabinet meeting on April 14. According to Welles, Lincoln expressed the hope that "there would be no persecution, no bloody work, after the war was over. None need expect he would take any part in hanging or killing those men, even the worst of them. Frighten them out of the country, open the gates, let down the bars, scare them off," he said, gesturing as if he were shooing sheep. "Enough lives have been sacrificed. We must extinguish our resentments if we expect harmony and union."[38] Stanton reported that Lincoln "spoke very kindly of General Lee and others of the Confederacy" and showed "in marked degree the kindness and humanity of his disposition, and the tender and forgiving spirit that so eminently distinguished him."[39] (Lincoln habitually referred to the Confederacy's president and its leading general as "Jeffy D" and "Bobby Lee.")[40]

At the April 14 cabinet meeting, with Grant in attendance, Lincoln stressed that Reconstruction "was the great question now before us, and we must soon begin to act."[41] At his request, Stanton had drafted an executive order establishing temporary military rule in Virginia and North Carolina, restoring the authority of federal laws, to be enforced by provost marshals. (It did not deal with the sensitive issue of black suffrage, for as Stanton explained to Charles Sumner on April 16, "there were differences among our friends on that subject, and it would be unwise, in his judgment, to press it in this stage of the proceedings.")[42] When Stanton read this projet to his colleagues, Welles objected to lumping Virginia and North Carolina together in a single military district. The navy secretary noted that the administration had recognized the Pierpont regime in Virginia as the legitimate government of the Old Dominion during the struggle over West Virginia statehood. Lincoln "said the point was well taken" and "that the same thing had occurred to him and the plan required maturing and perfecting." Therefore he instructed Stanton "to take the document, separate it, adapt one plan to Virginia and her loyal government—another to North Carolina which was destitute of legal State authority and submit copies of each to each member of the Cabinet."[43] He added that the federal government "can't undertake to run State governments in all these Southern States. Their people must do that,—though I reckon at first some of them may do it badly."[44] He asked Stanton to supply copies of the modified proposal to his colleagues and suggested that the document be discussed at the next scheduled cabinet meeting. Lincoln expressed relief that Congress had adjourned until December. For several months no more filibusters led by obstructionists like Charles Sumner, in league with Border State Conservatives, could thwart the will of the congressional majority.

Turning to military matters, Lincoln predicted the imminent arrival of important news, for the previous night he had had what he called "the usual dream which he had preceding nearly every great and important event of the war. Generally the news had been favorable which succeeded this dream, and the dream itself was always the same." He explained that "he seemed to be in some singular, indescribable vessel, and that he was moving with great rapidity towards an indefinite shore; that he had this dream preceding Sumter, Bull Run, Antietam, Gettysburg, Stone River, Vicksburg, Wilmington, etc." Grant interrupted, observing emphatically that "Stone River was certainly no victory, and he knew of no great results which followed from it." Lincoln replied that "however that might be, his dream preceded that fight." He continued: "I had this strange dream again last night, and we shall, judging from the past, have great news very soon. I think it must be from Sherman," for "[m]y thoughts are in that direction, as are most of yours."[45]

The cabinet found Lincoln in exceptionally good spirits. Stanton, who thought the president seemed "very cheerful and hopeful," remarked: "That's the most satisfactory Cabinet meeting I have attended in many a long day." He asked a colleague: "Didn't our chief look grand today?"[46] He later remarked that "Lincoln was grander, graver, [and] more thoroughly up to the occasion than he had ever seen him."[47] Frederick Seward, substituting for his bedridden father, recalled that the president wore "an expression of visible relief and content."[48] Treasury Secretary Hugh McCulloch "never saw Mr. Lincoln so cheerful and happy as he was on the day of his death. The burden which had been weighing upon him for four long years, and which he had borne with heroic fortitude, had been lifted; the war had been practically ended; the Union was safe. The weary look which his face had so long worn, and which could be observed by those who knew him well, even when he was telling humorous stories, had disappeared. It was bright and cheerful."[49] To James Harlan, secretary-of-the-interior-designate, Lincoln seemed "transfigured," for his customary expression of "indescribable sadness" had abruptly become "an equally indescribable expression of serene joy, as if conscious that the great purpose of his life had been achieved."[50] Similarly, Mary Lincoln reported that her husband was "supremely cheerful" and that during their afternoon carriage ride, his "manner was even playful." She remarked to him, laughingly, "you almost startle me by your great cheerfulness." He responded: "and well I may feel so, Mary, I consider *this day* the war, has come to a close. We must *both*, be more cheerful in the future—between the war and the loss of our darling Willie—we have both, been very miserable."[51]

Decision to Attend Ford's Theatre

The previous evening, Lincoln had been too sick with a headache to take a carriage ride with his wife, who wished to see the brilliant illuminations celebrating Lee's surrender. Grant, at Lincoln's request, had agreed to accompany her. As she and the general entered their carriage, a crowd that had gathered outside the White House repeatedly shouted "Grant!" Taking offense, Mrs. Lincoln instructed the driver to let her out, but she changed her mind when the crowd also cheered for the president. This happened again and again as the carriage proceeded around town. The First Lady evidently thought it inappropriate that the general should be cheered before her husband was. The next day, Grant declined the president's invitation to join him and Mrs. Lincoln to attend a performance of *Our American Cousin,* for he feared incurring her displeasure once more. Moreover, Mrs. Grant informed her husband that she did not wish to be around the First Lady after the unpleasantness at City Point three weeks earlier. (Later, Mrs. Grant told Hamilton Fish "that she objected strenuously to accompanying Mrs. Lincoln.")[52] Grant said "we will go visit our children . . . and this will be a good excuse."[53] When the First Lady's messenger announced that the presidential carriage would call for her and her husband at 8 P.M., Julia Grant curtly informed him that they would not be in town that night. And so they were rolling along aboard a train headed toward New Jersey while the Lincolns' carriage rumbled toward Ford's Theatre.

Others also declined the president's invitation, including Colfax, Stanton, and Stanton's assistant, Thomas T. Eckert. When Mrs. Stanton heard that Mrs. Grant had declined, she said to the general-in-chief's wife that she too would refuse: "I will not sit without you in the box with Mrs. Lincoln."[54] The secretary of war had sought to discourage Lincoln from theater-going, for he worried about his safety.

After learning that the Grants would not attend the performance at Ford's Theatre, Lincoln felt inclined to follow suit, but the First Lady insisted that they go. The press had announced that he and the general would be in attendance, and the audience would be terribly disappointed if neither man appeared.

The president had no adequate security detail that night. This was not unusual, for at his request bodyguards did not accompany him to theatrical performances. John F. Parker, one of four Metropolitan Police patrolmen who had been detailed to the Interior Department to protect the White House and its furnishings, not its occupants, was part of the entourage that night, as was Charles Forbes, a White House messenger. (The Executive Mansion needed guarding, for vandals purloined from it valuable ornaments and cut souvenir swatches from rugs and curtains.) Neither Parker nor Forbes was a true bodyguard, nor were they asked to protect Lincoln. The man who had been performing that duty zealously, Ward Hill Lamon, was in Richmond on a presidential mission. When John Wilkes Booth made his fatal way to the presidential box, Parker was either at an adjacent tavern or watching the play, which Lincoln may have urged him to do. (Parker had a dismal record as a Metropolitan Police patrolman before 1865, and three years later was dismissed for neglecting his duty. He was not, however, disciplined for his conduct on April 14, 1865. A board of the Metropolitan Police conducted an investigation but took no action against him.)

Lincoln's Insouciance Regarding Security

Lincoln was notoriously indifferent about his safety, even though he had read many death threats. "Soon after I was nominated at Chicago, I began to receive letters threatening my life," he remarked to the painter Francis B. Carpenter in 1864. "The first one or two made me a little uncomfortable, but I came at length to look for a regular installment of this kind of correspondence in every week's mail, and up to inauguration day I was in constant receipt of such letters. It is no uncommon thing to receive them now; but they have ceased to give me apprehension." When Carpenter expressed surprise at such a casual disregard of serious danger, Lincoln replied: "Oh, there is nothing like getting *used* to things!"[55] He placed threatening missives in a file marked "assassination letters."

To Colonel Charles G. Halpine, who one day in 1863 asked Lincoln why he did not have his White House visitors screened as military commanders did, he explained that it "would never do for a President to have guards with drawn sabres at his door, as if he fancied he were, or were trying to be, or assuming to be, an emperor." To surround himself thus "would only be to put the idea" of assassination into the minds of adversaries and thus "lead to the very result it was intended to prevent."[56]

That same year, Lincoln told Noah Brooks: "I long ago made up my mind that if anybody wants to kill me, he will do it. If I wore a shirt of mail, and kept myself surrounded by a body-guard, it would be all the same. There are a thousand ways of getting at a man if it is desirable that he should be killed. Besides, in this case, it seems to me the man who would come after me [Hamlin] would be just as objectionable to my enemies—if I have any."[57] He thought it impossible to obtain foolproof protection. To well-wishers concerned about assassins, he commented, "I should have to lock myself up in a box" and that he simply could not "be shut up in an iron cage and guarded."[58] Because he was so good-natured himself, he found it hard to believe that anyone would do him harm. When General James H. Van Alen warned him that ill-disposed folk might attack him as he walked alone from the White House to the War Department along a tree-lined path, he trustfully replied: "Oh, they wouldn't hurt *me*."[59]

Lincoln's insouciance about his safety was widely shared. With the exception of a crazed Briton who pulled the triggers of two guns in a miraculously unsuccessful attempt to kill to Andrew Jackson, no leading American public official had been the target of a murderer. In 1862, Seward asserted that "[a]ssassination is not an American practice or habit" and inaccurately predicted that "one so vicious and so desperate cannot be engrafted into our political system. This conviction of mine has steadily gained strength since the Civil War began. Every day's experience confirms it. The President, during the heated season, occupies a country house near the Soldiers' Home, two or three miles from the city. He goes to and from that place on horseback, night and morning, unguarded. I go there unattended at all hours, by daylight and moonlight, by starlight and without any light."[60]

Starting in 1862, Lincoln did have military escorts when he rode to and from the Soldiers' Home. At first he protested, saying half in jest that he and his wife could barely hear themselves talk above the racket made by spurs and sabers, and that some of the cavalry escort appeared to be such "new hands and very awkward" that he was "more afraid of being shot by the accidental discharge of one of their carbines or revolvers, than of any attempt upon his life, or for his capture by the roving squads of Jeb Stuart's cavalry."[61] A Pennsylvania infantry company was assigned to guard the cottage where he and his family stayed, and a New York cavalry unit usually accompanied him on his daily commute. The following year, an Ohio squad replaced the New Yorkers. One August night in 1864, while Lincoln was riding alone from the White House back to the Soldiers' Home, a would-be assassin shot his hat off. Thereafter, security precautions became more stringent. Lamon, who claimed that he had good reason to be frightened about the president's safety, started to sleep at the White House. There John Hay observed him one night as he slumbered before the door to the president's bedroom in an "attitude of touching and dumb fidelity with a small arsenal of pistols & Bowie knives around him."[62]

The Final Day

Around 3 o'clock on April 14, the Lincolns visited the navy yard and toured the monitor *Montauk*. The ship's doctor reported that they "seemed very happy, and so expressed themselves."[63] Later that afternoon, Illinois Governor Richard J. Oglesby called at the White House with his state's adjutant general, Isham Nicholas Haynie of Springfield. Delighted to see old friends, the president chatted with them for a while, then read aloud from the latest book by humorist Petroleum V. Nasby (pen name for David Ross Locke). Ignoring repeated summonses to dinner, Lincoln continued to read, laughing and commenting as he went along.

After supper, Lincoln met with Speaker of the House Schuyler Colfax. Earlier in the day, when the congressman mentioned to him that he was about to visit California, the president said he wished that he could go too: "I have very large ideas of the mineral wealth of our nation. I believe it practically inexhaustible. It abounds all over the western country, from the Rocky Mountains to the Pacific, and its development has scarcely commenced. During the war, when we were adding a couple of millions of dollars every day to our national debt, I did not care about encouraging the increase in the volume of our precious metals. We had the country to save first. But, now that the rebellion is overthrown, and we know pretty nearly the amount of our national debt, the more gold and silver we mine makes the payment of that debt so much the easier. Now, I am going to encourage that in every possible way. We shall have hundreds of thousands of disbanded soldiers, and many have feared that their return home in such great numbers might paralyze industry by furnishing suddenly a greater supply of labor than there will be a demand for. I am going to try and attract them to the hidden wealth of our mountain ranges, where there is room enough for all. Immigration, which even the war has not stopped, will land upon our shores hundreds of thousands more per year from over-crowded Europe. I intend to point them to the gold and silver that waits for them in the West. Tell the miners from me that I shall promote their interests to the utmost of my ability, because their prosperity is the prosperity of the nation; and we shall prove, in a very few years, that we are, indeed, the *treasury of the world*."[64] That evening Lincoln admonished the speaker: "Don't forget, Colfax, to tell those miners that that's my speech to them, which I send by you."[65]

When Colfax told Lincoln that many people had feared for his safety while he was visiting the Virginia capital, he smilingly replied: "Why, if any one else had been President, and had gone to Richmond, I would have been alarmed too; but I was not scared about myself a bit."[66]

Around 8:30, as Lincoln prepared to leave the White House, he asked his elder son if he would like to come along. Robert declined, citing fatigue. So his parents climbed into their carriage and proceeded to pick up Major Henry R. Rathbone and his step-sister (who was also his fiancée), Clara Harris. When the Grants announced that they could not join the presidential party, Mrs. Lincoln had invited the young

couple to take their place. The First Lady called Miss Harris a "dear friend."[67] Together the two women often took carriage rides, and Miss Harris regularly attended
plays with the Lincolns. The party reached Ford's Theatre about half an hour after
the curtain had risen on Tom Taylor's light comedy, *Our American Cousin*. As they
entered, the orchestra struck up "Hail to the Chief," and the audience rose to greet
them with vociferous applause, which Lincoln acknowledged with a smile and bow.
As he moved toward the box, he looked to one observer "mournful and sad."[68]

John Wilkes Booth: Mad Racist

John Wilkes Booth had spent the day plotting to assassinate Lincoln, Vice-President
Johnson, and Secretary of State Seward. The previous autumn, Booth had begun
hatching a scheme to kidnap the president, spirit him off to Richmond, and exchange
him for Confederate prisoners of war. That enterprise fizzled in mid-March when the
conspirators planned to intercept Lincoln on his way to a hospital. With the failure of
the capture plot, some of the conspirators quit Booth's team.

Weeks later, when Lincoln toured Richmond, Booth was outraged. According to
Booth's sister, the president's "triumphant entry into the fallen city (which was not
magnanimous), breathed fresh air upon the fire which consumed him."[69] (Richmond
was the city where Booth had first won acclaim as an actor.) He had been sleeping
badly and was experiencing difficulties with his fiancée. Depressed, Booth began
drinking more heavily than usual, consuming as much as a quart of brandy in less
than two hours. When a friend offered him a drink, he said: "Yes, anything to drive
away the blues."[70] Booth's good friend Harry Langdon believed that "[w]hiskey had a
great deal to do with the murder."[71] John Deery concurred, speculating that "Booth
was as much crazed by the liquor he drank as by any motive when he shot Lincoln."[72]
He was known as "a hard drinker of the strongest brandy."[73]

Booth was even more disconsolate at the news of Lee's surrender on April 9, for
he was feeling guilty about his failure to strike a blow for the Confederacy. He had
promised his mother not to join the Confederate army. In late 1864, he wrote her saying he had started "to deem myself a coward and to despise my own existence."[74] His
loving sister Asia asked him pointedly after he declared his undying devotion to the
South: "Why not fight for her, then? Every Marylander worthy of the name is fighting her battles."[75] When he expressed to Harry C. Ford, treasurer of Ford's Theatre,
disappointment that Lee had surrendered his sword after having promised never to
do so, Ford pointedly asked what the young actor had done compared to Lee. Defensively, Booth replied that he was as brave as Lee. "Well," Ford sneered, "you have not
got three stars yet to show it."[76] With the war virtually over, what could he do to redeem himself in his own eyes? Killing Lincoln might salve his troubled conscience.
On April 14 (Good Friday), when he heard that Grant and the president would attend
Ford's Theatre that night, he impulsively decided to seize the opportunity to kill Lincoln, which three days before he had resolved to do. Earlier he had mentioned the
possibility of murdering the president, but not to his colleagues in the capture plot. At
Lincoln's inauguration, he had apparently tried to break through the line of guards
protecting the president.

Summoning the remnants of the kidnapping team (David Herold, George Atzerodt, and Lewis Powell), Booth assigned them various tasks. Powell was to kill Seward, Atzerodt was to kill Andrew Johnson, and Herold was to assist Booth escape after he shot Lincoln. The murder of Johnson and Seward might well heighten the effect of the presidential assassination, throwing the government into chaos.

Booth's motives are not entirely clear, but he was an avid white supremacist whose racist rage formed an important part of his psyche. Indignation at the proposal that blacks would become citizen-voters prompted him to act. (As already noted, Booth responded to Lincoln's call for black suffrage by vowing "That means nigger citizenship. Now by God I'll put him through!") Thus Lincoln was a martyr to black civil rights, as much as Martin Luther King and other activists who fell victim to racist violence a century later. In September 1864, Booth nearly shot a black man who entered a barber shop where he had been waiting for a haircut. When the black expressed joy at a recent Union army victory, Booth asked peremptorily: "Is that the way you talk among gentlemen, and with your hat on too?"

"When I go into a parlor among ladies, I take my hat off, but when I go into a bar-room or a barber shop or any other public place, I keep my hat on," came the reply.

Incensed, Booth reached for his gun and would have used it if another patron had not intervened.[77]

In November 1864, Booth expressed his belief in white supremacy and hatred for Republicans: "This country was formed for the *white* not for the black man," he wrote in a letter probably meant for his brother-in-law. "And looking upon *African slavery* from the same stand-point, as held by those noble framers of our Constitution, I for one, have ever considered *it,* one of the greatest blessings (both for themselves and us,) that God ever bestowed upon a favored nation." As evidence to support that conclusion, he cited the "wealth and power" of the whites and the blacks' "elevation in happiness and enlightenment above their race, elsewhere." He had lived amid slavery for most of his life and had "seen *less* harsh treatment from Master to Man than I have beheld in the north from father to son." All Republicans were traitors, he maintained, and "the entire party, deserved the fate of poor old [John] Brown."[78]

Booth spelled out his views on slavery, race, and abolitionism in a speech that he composed in December 1860 but did not deliver. Intended for an audience in Philadelphia, where he was visiting his mother, it defended slavery as "a happiness" for the slaves "and a social & political blessing" for whites. "I have been through the whole South and have marked the happiness of master & man. . . . I have seen the Black man w[h]ip[p]ed but only when he deserved much more than he received. And had an abolitionist used the lash, he would have got double." Booth condemned abolitionists in the most bloodthirsty terms: "Such men I call tra[i]tors and treason should be stamped to death and not al[l]owed to stalk abroad in any land. So deep is my hatred for such men that I could wish I had them in my grasp And I [had] the power to crush [them]. I'd grind them into dust! . . . Now that we have found the serpent that mad[d]ens us, we should crush it in its, birth. . . . I tell you Sirs when treason weighs heavy in the scale, it is time for us to throw off all gentler feelings of our natures and summon resolution, pride, justice, Ay, and revenge."[79]

Although he did not mention Lincoln in this screed, Booth came to believe that the president deserved to be stamped to death, ground into powder, and crushed, for Lincoln was not only an abolitionist like John Brown, but also a tyrant like Julius Caesar. "When Caesar had conquered the enemies of Rome and the power that was his menaced the liberties of the people, Brutus arose and slew him," Booth wrote as he planned to assassinate Lincoln.[80] In the summer of 1864, he told his sister that the president's advisors ruled him and that he was "made the tool of the North, to crush out, or try to crush out slavery, by robbery, rapine, slaughter and bought armies." Lincoln, he predicted, would become a "Bonaparte in one great move, that is, by overturning this blind Republic and making himself a king. This man's re-election . . . I tell you—will be a reign! . . . You'll see, you'll see, that reelection means succession. His kin and friends are in every place of office already." Lincoln was "a false president," a "Sectional Candidate" who had been elected by fraud and who was "yearning for a kingly succession as hotly as ever did [the Spartan monarch] Ariston."[81] Similarly, in late 1864 he told his brother Edwin "that Lincoln would be made King of America." Edwin speculated that this conviction "drove him beyond the limits of reason."[82] When George P. Kane, the former police commissioner of Baltimore, was arrested on a well-founded suspicion of treason, Booth exclaimed: "the man who could drag him from the bosom of his family for no crime whatever, but a mere suspicion that he may commit one sometime, deserves a dog's death!"[83] The men responsible for Kane's arrest and long incarceration, Booth thought, were Lincoln and Seward. Booth also blamed the president and secretary of state for the execution of his friend John Yates Beall in early 1865.

Northern Democrats and some Radical Republicans had long been condemning Lincoln as a tyrant. During the 1864 election campaign, a few Northern newspapers, as noted above, called for the president's assassination. Even before then, a New York editor had lectured the president: "Behave yourself in [the] future, boss, or we shall be obliged to make an island of your head and stick it on the end of a pole."[84] In May 1863, a speaker at Cooper Union paraphrased Patrick Henry's famous "treason" speech: "Let us also remind Lincoln that Caesar had his Brutus and Charles the First his Cromwell. Let us also remind the George the Third of the present day that he, too, may have his Cromwell or his Brutus."[85]

Southern newspapers also called for Lincoln's death. The editors of the Richmond *Dispatch* said: "Assassination in the abstract is a horrid crime . . . but to slay a tyrant is no more assassination than war is murder. Who speaks of Brutus as an assassin? What Yankee ever condemned the Roundhead crew who brought Charles I to the block, although it would be a cruel libel to compare him politically or personally to the tyrants who are now lording it over the South?"[86] The Baltimore *South* ran a poem suggesting that Lincoln be hanged:[87]

> Two posts standant;
> One beam crossant;
> One rope pendent;
> Abram on the end on't;
> Glorious! Splendent.

In late 1864, the Selma, Alabama, *Dispatch* carried an ad by a lawyer offering to act the role of assassin: "If the citizens of the Southern Confederacy will furnish me with the cash, or good securities for the sum of one million dollars, I will cause the lives of Abraham Lincoln, William H. Seward, and Andrew Johnson to be taken by the 1st of March next. This will give us peace, and satisfy the world that cruel tyrants can not live in a 'land of liberty.' If this is not accomplished, nothing will be claimed beyond the sum of fifty thousand dollars, in advance, which is supposed to be necessary to reach and slaughter the three villains."[88]

After the assassination, many Northerners blamed such violent rhetoric for creating the atmosphere that predisposed Booth to murder Lincoln. Said a California newspaper: "The deed of horror and infamy . . . is nothing more than the expression in action, of what secession politicians and journalists have been for years expressing in words. Wilkes Booth has simply carried out what the Copperhead journalists who have denounced the President as a 'tyrant,' a 'despot,' a 'usurper,' hinted at, and virtually recommended. His weapon was the pistol, theirs the pen; and though he surpassed them in ferocity, they equaled him in guilt. . . . Wilkes Booth has but acted out what Copperhead orators and the Copperhead press have been preaching for years."[89]

Booth was biased against immigrants, especially from Ireland, as well as blacks. During the 1850s he, like many other Marylanders, supported the nativist Know-Nothing Party, and in 1864 he denounced Lincoln's supporters as "false-hearted, unloyal foreigners," "bastard subjects of other countries," and "apostates" who "would glory in the downfall of the Republic." Booth also had a snobbish streak that made him reluctant to dine with the laborers on his father's farm. That snobbery also led him to condemn Lincoln's "appearance, his pedigree, his coarse low jokes and anecdotes, his vulgar similes, and his frivolity."[90]

While Booth's act resembled the racist crime of James Earl Ray, who assassinated Martin Luther King, Jr., in 1968, it was also the work of a deeply neurotic man with conflicted feelings about his parents. He seems to have identified the Confederacy with his beloved mother and the North, embodied by Lincoln, with his father. In the draft of an undelivered speech, written in 1860, he spoke extravagantly of his love of country: "Indeed *I* love her so that I oft mentally exclaim, *with Richelieu*. O my native land let me but ward this dagger from thy heart! and die upon thy bossom. Such is my love that I could be content to crawl on to old age. With all the curses, that could be heaped upon me, *to see her safe from this coming tempest!*" He asserted that "I am . . . a mear child a boy, [compared] to some I see around me. A child indeed and this union is my Mother. A Mother that I love with an unutterable affection. You are all her children, and is there no son but I to speak in its Mother's cause[?] O would that I could place my worship for her in another heart, in the heart of some great orator, who might move you all to love her, *to help her now when she is dieing*. . . . You all do love her. You all would die for her." He hoped she could be saved peacefully, but if not, "it must be done with blood. Ay with blood & justice." The South "has been wronged. Ay wronged. She has been laughed at, preayed upon and wronged. . . . She must be reconciled. How can she. Why as I said before with naught but justice. The Abolition party must throw away their principals. They must be hushed forever. Or else it must be done by the punishment of her aggressors. By justice that demands the blood of her oppressors. By the blood of *those,* who in wounding her have slain us all, with naught save blood and justice. Ay blood, in this case, should season justice." When Booth wrote thus about his exaggerated love of country, he meant the entire United States, but once war broke out, he regarded the South as his country. "My love is for the South alone," he stated toward the end of the conflict.[91] To his sister he declared: "So help me holy God! my soul, life, and possessions are for the South."[92] During the war, he had acted as a sometime Confederate courier, spy, and smuggler. To kill Lincoln would be to help the Confederacy as it was dying. Then he could perish on her bosom.

In late 1864, Booth apologized to his mother for leaving her "to do what work I can for a poor oppressed downtrodden people." Extravagantly, he declared his undying devotion: "Heaven knows how dearly I love you. . . . Darling Mother I can not write you, you will understand the deep regret, the forsaking your dear side, will make me suffer, for you have been the best, the noblest, an example for all mothers." Much as he would like to please her by staying out of harm's way, "the cause of liberty & justice" called. "I have not a *single selfish motive* to spur me on to this," he protested, "nothing save the sacred duty, I feel I *owe the cause I love,* the cause of the South." He felt compelled "to go and share the sufferings of my brave countrymen, holding an unequal strife (for every right human & divine) against the most ruthless enemy, the world has ever known."[93]

This letter tends to corroborate the statement of an actress that the "love and sympathy between him and his mother were very close, very strong. No matter how far apart they were, she seemed to know, in some mysterious way, when anything was wrong with him. If he were ill, or unfit to play, he would often receive a letter of sympathy, counsel, and warning, written when she could not possibly have received any news of him. He has told me of this, himself."[94] Two weeks before the assassination, Booth's mother wrote him saying: "I never yet doubted your love & devotion to me—in fact I always gave you praise for being the fondest of all my boys."[95] According to his brother Edwin, John was "his mother's darling."[96] When away from her, he wrote every Sunday.

By killing Lincoln, Booth also hoped, not unreasonably, that he would achieve lasting renown for doing something truly memorable. A schoolmate recalled that as an adolescent he "always said 'he would make his name remembered by succeeding generations.'"[97] "I must have fame! fame!" he reportedly exclaimed. In 1864 he declared: "What a glorious opportunity there is for a man to immortalize himself by killing Lincoln!"[98] A week before the assassination, he remarked to a friend: "What an excellent chance I had to kill the President, if I had wished, on inauguration day!"[99] When asked what good that would have done, he replied: "I could live in history."[100] To another friend who allegedly posed the same question, Booth cited a passage from Colley Cibber's adaptation of *Richard III:*

> The daring youth that fired the Ephesian dome
> Outlives in fame the pious fool that reared it.[101]

In early 1865, Booth told an acquaintance that he longed to "do something which the world would remember for all time."[102] The evening he shot Lincoln, Booth replied to someone who predicted that he would never achieve the fame his father had attained: "When I leave the stage for good, I will be the most famous man in America."[103]

In the revealing diary he kept while fleeing his pursuers after the assassination, Booth wrote: "I am abandoned, with the curse of Cain upon me. When if the world knew my heart, *that one* blow would have made me great." When the Army of Northern Virginia surrendered on April 9, he determined that "something decisive & great must be done." Mystified by the execration he was receiving in the press, he wallowed in self-pity: "For doing what Brutus was honored for, what made Tell a hero" he was now unfairly "looked upon as a common cutthroat." He boasted that he had "too great a soul to die like a criminal." Clearly, he thought by doing something "decisive & great" he would be honored just as Brutus was for killing Julius Caesar and William Tell was for killing Hermann Gessler.[104] As the fugitive Booth was chatting with the family of Richard H. Garrett, a Virginia farmer in whose tobacco barn he would die, the subject of Lincoln's assassin came up. When Garrett's daughter speculated that the villain probably had been well paid, Booth opined that "he wasn't paid a cent, but did it for notoriety's sake."[105]

Booth's famous brother Edwin considered John mentally unbalanced from boyhood. "He was a rattle-pated fellow, filled with Quixotic notions," Edwin wrote. "We regarded him as a . . . wild-brained boy, and used to laugh at his patriotic froth whenever secession was discussed. That he was insane on that one point no one who knew him can doubt."[106] A friend in Washington reported that shortly before the assassination Booth "seemed a bit crazed."[107] Once in a burst of maniacal temper he nearly strangled to death his brother-in-law for mildly criticizing Jefferson Davis.

Booth's mental instability and fondness for liquor may have been in part genetic. His alcoholic father, the celebrated English-born tragedian Junius Brutus Booth, suffered from spells of madness. In the winter of 1829, he broke character on stage and shouted as the management hustled him away: "Take me to the Lunatic Hospital!"[108] One day he was about to hang himself when his wife, the former Mary Ann Holmes, stopped him. "My God—my God! what could have come over me?" he exclaimed.[109] On other occasions, he tried to commit suicide by overdosing on laudanum and by leaping into the waters off Charleston harbor. He had homicidal as well as suicidal impulses. In 1824, he asked a fellow actor: "I must cut somebody's throat today, and whom shall I take? Shall it be Wallack, or yourself, or who?" Just then John Henry Wallack appeared, and Booth draw a long dagger and attempted to stab him. (His son John Wilkes would use a similar weapon against Major Rathbone in the assassination.) One night in 1838, for no good reason, Junius assaulted a friend and dealt him a serious blow with an andiron. In 1835, after failing to appear for a performance, he apologized, citing "a mind disordered" and "a partial derangement." At that same time, his doctor reported that Booth "has for years past kept his wife in misery, and his friends in fear by his outrageous threats & acts [and] has bothered his acquaintances by vexatious importunity, till they bolt their doors against him."[110]

When drunk, Junius Booth directed tirades against Mary Ann and may have beaten her. He certainly humiliated her and their children when it was revealed that he had earlier married and then abandoned a woman in England, Marie Christine Adelaide Delannoy. When John Wilkes was 12 years old, Adelaide sued for divorce. Her allegations about Junius and Mary Ann's "adulterous intercourse" and "the fruits of said adulterous intercourse" were extremely embarrassing, as were her screaming confrontations with her husband on the streets of Baltimore.[111] Legally, John Wilkes was a bastard. After the divorce from Adalaide was finalized, Junius wed Mary Ann on John Wilkes's thirteenth birthday. The embarrassment persisted, for the press ran lurid stories again at the time of Adelaide's death in 1858. John Wilkes probably harbored strong feelings against his father for abusing his mother and humiliating him. Those negative feelings could not be expressed openly, for Junius died in 1852. John Wilkes evidently displaced the buried rage against his father onto Republicans and their leader, Abraham Lincoln.

Booth hated Lincoln passionately, holding the president responsible for all that had gone wrong in the nation. "Our country owed all her troubles to him," he wrote in his diary.[112] A few months before the assassination, he told his friend Alfred W. Smiley that "he had a personal hatred of Lincoln." Smiley inferred from Booth's "utterances that he had a very strong hatred of Abe Lincoln." One of those utterances was particularly emphatic: "I would rather have my right arm cut off at the shoulder than see Lincoln made president again." A barber recalled that while being shaved, Booth would deliver "a tirade against Lincoln." He "would sit in the chair and call Lincoln all the vile names he could think of, 'a rail splitting this, that, and the other thing.' His enmity towards Lincoln was intense."[113] On another occasion, Booth took offense during an argument about Lincoln and reached for his gun, but was persuaded not to kill the president's defender.

By assassinating Lincoln, Booth unconsciously avenged his mother, whose troubles were the fault of Junius Brutus Booth. Immediately after shooting the president, Booth reportedly said not only "sic semper tyrannis" but also "the South is avenged" (or "Revenge for the South.")[114]

Booth's sister reported that "he wanted to be loved of the Southern people above all things." As he lay dying, he said: "Tell my mother—tell my mother that I did it for my country—that I die for my country." If in fact he unconsciously equated his mother with the South and his father with Lincoln, the killing of Lincoln would in effect be a way of proving his love for her.

Booth's willingness to die for his country also had roots in a martyr complex. He despised John Brown's abolitionist views but extravagantly admired his courage. Booth called Brown, whose execution he witnessed, "a man inspired, the grandest character of the century." His favorite literary figures were martyrs for liberty in the works of Shakespeare, Schiller, Byron, and Plutarch. Booth's sister thought his "wild ambition" had been inborn and "fed to fever-heat by the unhealthy tales of Bulwer."[115]

Assassination

Once seated in their box at Ford's Theatre, the Lincolns and their guests sat back to enjoy the show. Around 10:30, as Booth made his way toward them, he encountered

Charles Forbes outside the box and gained admission after showing him a card. (Lamon probably would not have allowed him to pass. Mrs. Lincoln ultimately held Forbes responsible for her husband's death.) After entering the anteroom, Booth barred the door behind him with an improvised jam. Through a tiny peephole he had bored earlier he could see the president. Waiting till there was but one actor on stage, he opened the inner door, stepped quickly toward the president's rocking chair, and shot him in the back of the head at point-blank range with a derringer. Rathbone struggled with the assassin, who slashed the major's arm badly with a long dagger, then leaped to the stage. (Booth liked to make sensational jumps onto the stage, especially when entering the witches' cave in *Macbeth*.) Upon landing, he shouted out "sic semper tyrannis" (thus always to tyrants), the Virginia state motto. Striding across the stage, he escaped out the back door, mounted a horse, and rode toward southern Maryland, following the route he had earlier established as part of the kidnapping scheme.

The instant Lincoln was shot he lost consciousness, never to regain it in the remaining nine hours of his life. Amid the pandemonium in Ford's Theatre, three doctors (Charles Leale, Albert King, and Charles Taft) made their way to the presidential box. They removed Lincoln from his chair, placed him on the floor, and inspected his body for wounds. Meanwhile, guards cleared the theater. Discovering the hole in the back of his head, which they realized was fatal, the physicians feared that he could not survive being transported back to the White House. So they had him carried across the street to the boardinghouse of William Petersen, where he was laid diagonally across a bed that was too short to accommodate his long body.

Mary Lincoln later told a friend that "she saw the flash and heard the report of the pistol," and "that something suddenly brushed past her . . . rubbing off her Shawl. It was *Booth* as he jumped from the Box."[116] She then screamed and fainted.

Once she recovered from her faint, Mary Lincoln crossed the street to the Petersen house, escorted by Clara Harris and the bleeding Major Rathbone. Entering that domicile, she frantically exclaimed: "Where is my husband! Where is my husband!" as she wrung her hands in extreme anguish. Upon reaching his bedside, she repeatedly kissed his head, which was slowly oozing blood and brain tissue. "How can it be so?" she asked. "Do speak to me!"[117] When he failed to respond, she suggested that Tad be sent for, saying "she knew he would speak to him because he loved him so well."[118] With his tutor, the boy had been attending a performance of "Alladin" at nearby Grover's Theater. But she had second thoughts about summoning him to the Petersen house. "O, my poor 'Taddy,'" she asked plaintively, "what *will* become of him? O do not send for him, his violent grief would disturb the House."[119]

Tad in fact had heard the dreadful news when the management of Grover's Theater announced it to the audience. He became hysterical and was taken to the White House, where he burst out to the guard Thomas F. Pendel, "O Tom Pen! Tom Pen! they have killed papa dead. They've killed papa dead!"[120] Pendel informed Tad's brother Robert, who had been socializing with John Hay. The two young men immediately rushed to Tenth Street, accompanied by Senator Sumner, who had happened to come to the Executive Mansion under the impression that the president had been taken there.

At the Petersen house, Robert spoke briefly to his mother, then entered his father's room and took a position at the head of the bed, crying audibly. Soon he composed himself, but on two occasions he sobbed loudly and leaned his head on Sumner's shoulder. He had the presence of mind to ask that his mother's good friend Elizabeth Dixon, wife of Connecticut Senator James Dixon, be notified. She came quickly to help comfort the distraught First Lady. "I held her & supported her as well as I could & twice we persuaded her to go into another room," Mrs. Dixon reported.[121] The senator's wife was accompanied by her sister, Mary Kinney, and Mrs. Kinney's daughter, Constance. Another Connecticut matron, Mary Jane Welles, wife of Gideon Welles, also rushed to help console the First Lady. Andrew Johnson called but abruptly left when Stanton, who knew that Mrs. Lincoln disliked the vice-president, advised him that his presence was unnecessary.

As the bedroom in the Petersen house filled with cabinet members, doctors, generals, and others, Mary Lincoln occupied the front parlor, attended by some friends, including Clara Harris and the family minister, Dr. Phineas T. Gurley, pastor of the New York Avenue Presbyterian Church. Miss Harris, whose dress was soaked with the blood of her fiancé, Major Rathbone, reported that "Poor Mrs. Lincoln all through that dreadful night would look at me with horror & scream, oh! my husband's blood, my dear husband's blood!"[122] In hysterics, she repeatedly asked: "Why didn't he shoot me?"[123] Mary Lincoln made frequent visits to the bedroom. On one occasion she was so taken aback by his distorted features that she fainted. Coming to, she pleaded with her dying spouse: "Love, live but for one moment to speak to me once—to speak to our children!"[124]

Lincoln's fitful breathing reminded Stanton of "an aeolian harp, now rising, now falling and almost dying away, and then reviving."[125] Around 7 A.M., as Mary Lincoln sat by the bedside, her husband's breathing grew so stertorous that she jumped up shrieking, then fell to the floor. Hearing her, Stanton, who had in effect taken charge of the government, entered from an adjoining room and loudly snapped: "Take that woman out and do not let her in again."[126] As Mrs. Dixon helped her return to the front parlor, she moaned: "Oh, my God, and have I given my husband to die?" An observer told a friend that he "never heard so much agony in so few words."[127]

At 7:22 A.M., the president finally stopped breathing. "Now he belongs to the ages," Stanton said tearfully.[128]

When Gurley broke the news to Mary Lincoln, she cried out: "O—*why* did you not let me know? *Why did* you not *tell* me?"

"Your friends thought it was not *best*," Gurley replied. "You must be resigned to the will of God. You must be calm and trust in God and in your friends."[129]

At Stanton's suggestion, Gurley delivered a prayer, then escorted Mary Lincoln back to the White House. On exiting the Petersen home, she glanced at Ford's Theatre and cried: "Oh, that *dreadful* house!"[130] Upon reaching the Executive Mansion, they were accosted by Tad, who repeatedly asked: "Where is my *Pa?* Where *is* my Pa?" Apparently, he expected that his father, though shot, would come home with Mary. "Taddy, your Pa is dead," Dr. Gurley replied. Unprepared for those shocking words, the grief-stricken lad screamed: "O what shall I do? What *shall* I do? My

Brother is dead. My Father is dead. O what shall I do? What will become of me? O what *shall* I do? O mother *you* will not die will you. O don't *you* die Ma. You *won[']t* die will you Mother? If *you* die I shall be all alone. O *don[']t* die Ma."[131]

The next day, when Gideon Welles and James Speed called at the White House, Tad asked tearfully: "Oh, Mr. Welles, who killed my father?" Neither gentleman could offer an answer or staunch their own tears. Tad's grief was so intensified by his mother's that he begged her: "Don't cry so, Mama! don't cry, or you will make me cry, too! You will break my heart. . . . I cannot sleep if you cry." The lad tried to comfort her, saying: "Papa was good and he is gone to heaven. He is happy there. He is with God and brother Willie."[132]

To a White House caller on April 16 he asked: "Do you think my father has gone to heaven ?"

"I have not a doubt of it," came the reply.

"Then," said Tad, "I am glad he has gone there, for he never was happy after he came here. This was not a good place for him!"[133]

The Funeral

On Saturday, April 15, a chilly rain fell as horrified and dumbfounded Washingtonians gathered before the White House and milled about. Among them were many blacks who, according to Welles, were "weeping and wailing their loss. This crowd did not appear to diminish through the whole of that cold, wet day; they seemed not to know what was to be their fate since their great benefactor was dead." The navy secretary confided to his diary that "their hopeless grief affected me more than almost anything else, though strong and brave men wept when I met them."[134] The abolitionist Jane Grey Swisshelm reported that "the presence of the thousands of Freed-people who regarded Abraham Lincoln as their Moses" was striking. "With tears and lamentations they lean their faces against the iron fence around the Presidential Mansion, and groan with a feeling akin to despair lest now, that their friend is gone, they shall be returned to their old masters." She heard a black woman exclaim: "My good President! My good President! I would rather have died myself! I would rather have given the babe from my bosom! Oh, Jesus! Oh, Jesus!" Mrs. Swisshelm concluded that the "mourning for President Lincoln is no mockery of woe, but the impassioned outburst of heartfelt grief; and it is touching to see, on every little negro hut in the suburbs, some respectful testimonial of sorrow. Many deprived themselves of a meal to get a yard or two of black [cloth] to hang above their poor door or window. Was ever mortal so wept by the poor?"[135]

Mary Lincoln was so grief-stricken that she did not attend the obsequies for her husband. On April 18, Lincoln's embalmed body lay in state in the East Room of the White House, where over 20,000 persons filed past the open casket to pay their last respects. Thousands of others would have done so but were deterred by the long lines and went home rather than wait hours to gain admission. Many of the teary-eyed mourners looked upon the coffin as if it contained a beloved friend or family member. Some spoke farewells to the inanimate remains. Conspicuous among them were less prosperous citizens, both white and black, who remarked: "He was the poor man's friend."

On April 19, the anniversary of the first bloodshed of both the Civil and Revolutionary Wars, Lincoln's funeral took place in that same cavernous room. Dr. Gurley delivered the sermon in which he quoted Lincoln's statement made to him and other clergy who had called at the White House in the gloomiest days of the war: "Gentlemen, my hope of success in this great and terrible struggle rests on that immutable foundation, the justice and goodness of God, and when events are very threatening and prospects very dark, I still hope that in some way which man can not see all will be well in the end."[136]

The body was then conveyed to the Capitol, where it lay in state until the following evening. The Twenty-second U.S. Colored Infantry regiment led an immense, solemn procession past grieving multitudes lining crepe-bedecked Pennsylvania Avenue. Bringing up the rear were 4,000 blacks, including leaders of the African Methodist Episcopal Church and various fraternal orders. Gideon Welles noted that there "were no truer mourners, when all were sad, than the poor colored people who crowded the streets, joined the procession, and exhibited their woe, bewailing the loss of him whom they regarded as a benefactor and father. Women as well as men, with their little children, thronged the streets, sorrow, trouble, and distress depicted on their countenances and in their bearing."[137] Another witness heard blacks sorrowfully declare that they "had lost their best friend." Blacks outside the nation's capital shared the Washingtonians' sorrow. In Charleston, South Carolina, the black population seemed stricken upon hearing of Lincoln's death. "I never saw such sad faces," a journalist wrote, "or heard such heavy hearts beatings, as here in Charleston the day the dreadful news came! The colored people—the native loyalists—were like children bereaved of an only and loved parent." One woman, "so absorbed in her grief that she noticed no one," cried loud and long. The reporter concluded that "her heart told her that he whom Heaven had sent in answer to her prayers was lying in a bloody grave, and she and her race were left—*fatherless.*"[138]

The gloom that pervaded the capital was broken only by some Radical Republicans and abolitionists, who opposed Lincoln's Reconstruction policy because of its leniency toward the defeated Confederates. At a caucus, several Radicals seemed glad that Andrew Johnson, who called for harsh punishment of the Rebels, would be in charge. "I like the radicalism of the members of this caucus," Congressman George W. Julian wrote. "Their hostility towards Lincoln's policy of conciliation and contempt for his weakness were undisguised; and the universal feeling among radical men here is that his death is a god-send." Julian wrote in his memoirs: "I spent most of the afternoon in a political caucus, held for the purpose of considering the necessity for a new Cabinet and a line of policy less conciliatory than that of Mr. Lincoln; and while everybody was shocked at his murder, the feeling was nearly universal that the accession of Johnson to the presidency would prove a godsend to the country."[139] Senator Zachariah Chandler believed that God "continued Mr. Lincoln in office as long as he was useful, and then substituted a better man to finish the work."[140] Ben Wade told that "better man," Andrew Johnson: "we have faith in you. By the gods, there will be no trouble now in running the government!"[141] He added: "Mr. Lincoln had too much of human kindness in him to deal with these infamous traitors, and I am glad that it has fallen into your hands to deal out justice to them."[142] Henry Winter Davis said the "assassination was a great crime, but the change is no calamity. I suppose God has punished us enough by his weak rule—& ended it! I spoke to no man in Washington who did not consider the change a great blessing."[143] Jane Grey Swisshelm echoed Davis: "I do *not* look upon this death as a National calamity," for she said she feared "the destruction of our Government through the leniency and magnanimity of President Lincoln." She believed that God "removed from this important place one who was totally incapable of understanding, or believing in, the wickedness, the cruelty, and barbarism of the Southern people."[144] William Lloyd Garrison, Jr., told a friend that "Mr. Lincoln's too great kindness of heart led him to a mistaken leniency, but Andy Johnson has fought the beasts of Ephesus on their own soil and has learned by bitter experience their implacable nature. 'Thorough' will be the word now. . . . The nation sails into new waters now and it may be providential that a new hand grasps the rudder."[145]

Several Christian clergymen also welcomed the ascension of Johnson to power. Within hours of learning that Lincoln had died, Henry Ward Beecher declared: "Johnson's little finger was stronger than Lincoln's loins."[146] A Presbyterian minister in Freeport, Illinois, asserted that Lincoln "had fulfilled the purpose for which God had raised him up, and he passed off the stage because some different instrument was needed for the full accomplishment of the Divine purpose in the affairs of our nation."[147] Other clergy told their flocks that God allowed the assassination because "a sharper cutting instrument" was wanted, a "man of sterner mood than the late President," to punish the Rebels. Hence the continuation of Lincoln in office "would not have been so favorable to God's plan as his removal."[148]

The events of April 19 impressed a Washington correspondent, who wrote: "In point of sad sublimity and moral grandeur, the spectacle was the most impressive ever witnessed in the national capital. The unanimity and depth of feeling, the decorum, good order, and complete success of all the arrangements, and the solemn dignity which pervaded all classes, will mark the obsequies of Abraham Lincoln as the greatest pageant ever tendered to the honored dead on this continent."[149]

In Lincoln's Springfield, the mourning was especially profound. Its residents flocked instinctively to the statehouse square to share their grief with fellow townsmen. The city council, reflecting their wishes, passed resolutions calling for the president's remains to be buried in their city. Initially, Mary Lincoln had insisted that her husband be interred in Chicago, but eventually her son Robert and David Davis persuaded her to accept Springfield, though she had been "vehemently opposed" to the Illinois capital.[150]

The Funeral Train

Stanton and other leading Republicans, fearing aftershocks from the assassination, planned to have a train convey the body back to Springfield, retracing the route taken by Lincoln in 1861. According to Illinois Congressman-elect Shelby Cullom, the country "was so wrought up no one seemed certain what was to happen; no one knew but that there would be a second and bloodier revolution, in which the Government might fall into the hands of a dictator; and it was thought the funeral trip would serve to arouse the patriotism of the people, which it did."[151] Mrs. Lincoln adamantly opposed those plans but ultimately yielded.

So on April 21, a heavily draped, nine-car train bearing the president's body, along with the remains of Willie Lincoln, departed Washington for Illinois. At the depot, the sight of grief-stricken black troops moved the assembled dignitaries to tears. Thirteen days later the train arrived in Springfield, having traveled 1,654 miles, retracing the route Lincoln took in February 1861 (with Pittsburgh and Cincinnati omitted and Chicago added).

At several cities, the coffin was displayed for public viewing. In Philadelphia, enormous crowds paid a "grand, emphatic and unmistakable tribute of affectionate devotion to the memory of our martyred chief," according to a local paper. Resembling "the multitudinous waves of the swelling sea," they "surged along our streets from every quarter of the city." Well before the train was due to arrive, people gathered at the depot and along the procession route, forming an "impenetrable mass." They were so jam-packed that many were injured, and several women fainted. And yet order prevailed, for all appreciated "the great solemnity of the occasion." Those wishing to view the remains had to wait up to five hours before being admitted to Independence Hall, where they were allowed but a brief glimpse of the open coffin.[152] Similar demonstrations of widespread, profound grief took place at Baltimore, Harrisburg, New York, Albany, Buffalo, Cleveland, Columbus, Indianapolis, Chicago, and Springfield.

As the train chugged westward, people gathered at crepe-festooned depots and wherever roads crossed the tracks. Observers demonstrated their respect in various ways: doffing hats and bonnets, weeping, slowly waving flags and handkerchiefs, singing hymns as they knelt by the grading. At night, large bonfires were lit, around which children huddled. Some parents shook their youngsters awake so they could see and remember forever the sight of Lincoln's funeral train. (In later years, the children recalled not only the passing railroad cars but also the flowing tears of the grownups, which they found deeply unsettling.) Farmers decorated their houses with flags and evergreens and paused respectfully in their fields to pay mute homage to the martyred president. Banners and arches bore touching inscriptions:

> "All joy is darkened; the mirth of the land is gone."
> "We have prayed for you; now we can only weep."
> "He has Fulfilled his Mission."
> "Mournfully and tenderly bear him to his grave."
> "Millions bless thy name."
> "Revere his Memory."
> "Weep, sweet country weep, let every section mourn; the North has lost its
>   champion, the South its truest friend."
> "He still lives in the hearts of his countrymen."
> "How we loved him."
> "Washington the Father and Lincoln the Saviour."

"A glorious career of service and devotion is crowned with a martyr's death."

"There's a great spirit gone!"

"The heart of the nation throbs heavily at the portals of the tomb."

"Servant of God, well done,/ Thy race is o'er, thy victory won."

"Too good for Earth, to Heaven, thou art fled,/ And left the Nation in tears."

"We loved him, yes, no tongue can tell/ How much we loved him, and how well."

"The Poor Man's Champion—The People Mourn Him."

"We Honor Him Dead who Honored us while Living."

"Behold how they loved him."

"We loved him much, but now we love him more."

"His death has made him immortal."

"Our guiding star has fallen; our nation mourns."

"Know ye not that a great man has fallen this day in Israel."

Quotations from Shakespeare adorned some banners:

"Good night! and flights of angels sing thee to thy rest."

"His life was gentle, and the elements/So mixed in him, that nature might stand up

And say to all the world,/This was a man."

Some inscriptions were taken from Lincoln's own public utterances:

"With malice toward none, with charity for all."

"Sooner than surrender these principles, I would rather be assassinated on the spot."

"Upon this act, I invoke the considerate judgment of mankind, and the gracious favor of Almighty God."

"Let us resolve that the martyred dead shall not have died in vain."

Among the million-plus mourners who availed themselves of the opportunity to view Lincoln's remains were many women, some of whom tried to kiss the president's lifeless face. When forbidden to do so, they protested loudly and refused to move on. To a Baltimore observer, that face seemed to preserve "the expression it bore in life, half-smiling, the whole face indicating the energy and humor which had character-ized the living man."[153] By the time the train reached New York, however, Lincoln's face had become discolored. No matter how skillfully the undertakers administered powder, rouge, and amber, it grew frightfully pitted, hollow-cheeked, and black. As time passed, the body came to resemble a mummy. The New York *Evening Post* re-ported that the eyes had sunk, the cheeks had turned dark, and the tightly compressed lips resembled "a straight sharp line." In sum, it was "not the genial, kindly face of Abraham Lincoln; it is but a ghastly shadow."[154]

Many blacks flocked to bid farewell to the president. At Baltimore they "were convulsed with a grief they could not control, and sobs, cries, and tears told how deeply they mourned their deliverer."[155] In Indianapolis, a procession marched carrying a large facsimile of the Emancipation Proclamation and banners reading "Colored Men, always Loyal," "Lincoln, Martyr of Liberty," "He lives in our Memories," and "Slavery is Dead." A different motto adorned the banner of black members of the Cleveland chapter of the Grand United Order of Odd Fellows: "We mourn for Abraham Lincoln, the True Friend of Liberty."[156] In New York, the 5,000 blacks who had planned to join the procession were shocked when the city council forbade them to participate. The *Evening Post* denounced the city council's order: "Our late President was venerated by the whole colored population with a peculiar degree of feeling; they looked upon him as the liberator of their race; and now . . . to be refused the privilege of paying respect to his remains is mortifying and humiliating. Besides, we have accepted the services of these citizens in the war, and it is disgraceful ingratitude to shut them out of our civic demonstration."[157] The eminent black clergyman and abolitionist J. Sella Martin protested that Lincoln's final public speech, in which he endorsed black suffrage, left "no doubt that had he been consulted he would have urged, as a dying request, that the representatives of the race which had come to the nation's rescue in the hour of peril, and which he had lifted by the most solemn official acts to the dignity of citizens and defenders of the Union, should be allowed the honor of following his remains to the grave."[158] The city council's action so outraged Stanton that he fired off a telegram from Washington to the New York authorities: "It is the desire of the Secretary of War that no discrimination respecting color should be exercised in admitting persons to the general procession tomorrow. In this city a black regiment formed part of the funeral escort."[159] Discouraged by the officials' action, most blacks abandoned their plans to march. Yet over 200 did join the procession, holding aloft banners inscribed: "Abraham Lincoln, Our Emancipator" and "To Millions of Bondsmen he Liberty Gave."[160] To protect them, the police chief, John Kennedy, provided an escort, which turned out to be unnecessary, for spectators cheered and waved handkerchiefs as the blacks passed by. One black woman between her sobs exclaimed, "He died for me! He was crucified for me! God bless him!"[161]

The tremendous outpouring of dignified grief led to the virtual standstill of New York's commerce and financial transactions for nearly two weeks. The editors of the New York *Times* regarded this cessation of business-as-usual as "a prompt, spontaneous and deliberate sacrifice by the industrious, the frugal, the pecuniarily responsible body of the people" which "raises the character of the whole nation far above the imputation of sordidness, of persistent and unchangeable devotion to Mammon, so falsely urged against it by outside commentators." Moreover, they concluded, "in the presence of the ready self-sacrifice which our present bereavement has illustrated, the theory that republics are ungrateful may at least bear revision."[162] In New York, copies of Lincoln's second inaugural sold briskly and appeared in many store windows, framed by black crepe or flowers. Copies of his farewell address to Springfield also found many buyers.

As the train moved westward, one of the dignitaries aboard noted that mourners seemed "more wrought up," for in the Midwest "there were not only expressions of deep sorrow, but of vengeance as well, especially toward the South."[163] In fact, anger at the South pervaded the East as well as the West. In countless funeral sermons and editorials, Northerners denounced the states lately in rebellion and demanded that Confederate leaders be executed.

At Chicago, a man observing the thousands of mourners passing through the courthouse remarked: "I have seen three deceased Kings of England lying in state, but have never witnessed a demonstration so vast in its proportions, so unanimous and spontaneous, as that which has been evoked by the arrival in the city of the remains of the fallen President."[164] The Chicago *Tribune* noted that as the coffin was conveyed through the city, "there were no downcast countenances, but none that were not sad and pitiful. There were no loud voices in the unnumbered throngs. Men expressed themselves in subdued tones, and often nothing would be heard but the indescribable murmur of ten thousand voices, modulated to a whisper, and the careful tread of countless feet on the damp pavement of the streets."[165]

Officials on the train, astounded by the intense outpouring of grief, feared that authorities in Springfield might not have made adequate preparations. (It was estimated that 5 million people saw the funeral car and casket in the various cities where it was displayed.) So at Albany, a member of the Illinois delegation was dispatched to the Prairie State capital to help with arrangements, which went smoothly.

For twenty-four hours, Springfield mourners streamed by the casket, before it was closed and placed in a receiving vault at Oak Ridge cemetery, 2 miles from the center of town on May 4. In the procession to the cemetery, immediately following the hearse was a black man, the Rev. Mr. Henry Brown, who led Lincoln's horse, Old Bob. Brown had worked for the Lincolns as a handyman. Other Springfield blacks, including Lincoln's friend and barber, William Florville, brought up the rear of the procession. Among Lincoln's black friends and acquaintances in Springfield were Spencer Donnegan, Jameson Jenkins, and Mariah Vance; they, too, may well have been in the rear guard.

At Oak Ridge, the most eminent Methodist in the country, Bishop Matthew Simpson of Evanston, delivered a eulogy, during which he mistakenly identified a passage from Lincoln's 1839 speech about banking as a condemnation of slavery. Commenting on the funeral train journey, he declared: "Among the events of history there have been great processions of mourners. There was one for the patriarch Jacob, which went up from Egypt, and the Egyptians wondered at the evidences of reverence and filial affection which came from the hearts of the Israelites. There was mourning when Moses fell upon the heights of Pisgah and was hid from human view. There have been mournings in the kingdoms of the earth when kings and princes have fallen, but never was there, in the history of man, such mourning as that which has accompanied this funeral procession, and has gathered around the mortal remains of him who was our loved one." Like many other observers, the bishop paid tribute to Lincoln's uniqueness: "he made all men feel a sense of himself—a recognition of individuality—a self-relying power. They saw in him a man whom they believed would do what is right, regardless of all consequences. It was this moral feeling which gave him the greatest hold on the people, and made his utterances almost oracular."[166]

Controversy over a Location for the Tomb and Monument

The selection of the gravesite proved controversial. Springfield's civic leaders had purchased a 6-acre lot, known as the Mather Block, near the statehouse for Lincoln's final resting place, but Mary Lincoln objected, insisting "that it was her desire to be laid by the side of her husband when she died, and that such would be out of the question in a public place of the kind."[167] (Nine years later, she gave a different reason, arguing that Lincoln wanted to be buried in a quiet place.)

On April 28, Secretary of War Stanton informed the Springfield committee, headed by Illinois Governor Richard J. Oglesby, that Mrs. Lincoln's "final and positive determination is that the remains must be placed in Oakridge Cemetery—and nowhere else." Two more peremptory messages of similar import quickly followed.[168] On May 1, Robert Todd Lincoln told Oglesby in no uncertain terms that he and his mother "demand that our wishes be consulted."[169]

Mary Lincoln's decision did not sit well. "The people are in a rage about it and all the hard stories that ever were told about her are told over again," wrote Lincoln's friend H. P. H. Bromwell from Springfield. "She has no friends here."[170] In June, a visitor echoed that judgment, observing that "I have not heard one person speak well of Mrs. Lincoln since I came here."[171] The previous month, Dr. Phineas D. Gurley, who had delivered the benediction at Lincoln's funeral, reported from the Illinois capital that everyone there "loved Mr. Lincoln, but as for Mrs. L., I cannot say as much. Hard things are said of her by all classes of people, and when I got to know how she was regarded by her old neighbors and even by her relatives in S[pringfield], I did not wonder that she had decided to make her future home in Chicago. . . . The ladies of Springfield say that Mr. Lincoln's death hurt her ambition more than her affections—a hard speech, but many people think so who do not say so."[172]

(Mary Lincoln decided to settle in Chicago in part because she had fallen out with her sisters. "I can never go back to Springfield!" she exclaimed to her closest confidante, Elizabeth Keckly.[173] She resented Frances Todd Wallace's failure to express thanks for the appointment her husband had received as paymaster. In addition, Frances seemed insufficiently pleased by Mary and Abraham's success, and had resisted Mrs. Lincoln's appeals to have her daughter stay at the White House after Willie's death. The relative who did serve that function, Elizabeth Todd Edwards, was also estranged from Mary. Evidently the sisters had quarreled over Ninian Edwards's conservative politics and misconduct in the office to which Lincoln had appointed him. Moreover, Mary Lincoln resented some unflattering comments about her in a letter by Elizabeth's daughter Julia. Like many another critic of the First Lady's regal ways, Ann Todd Smith had spoken disparagingly of "Queen Victoria's court" at Washington. When word of this criticism reached her, Mary Lincoln wrote witheringly of Ann's "malice," "*wrath*," "*vindictiveness*," and "envious feeling.")[174]

Mrs. Lincoln also clashed with the Lincoln National Monument Association, formed in May with Governor Oglesby at its head. When she learned of their plan to erect a memorial at the Mather Block, she peppered Oglesby with imperious ultimatums. On June 5, she wrote: "unless I receive within the next ten days, an Official assurance that the Monument will be erected over the Tomb in Oak Ridge Cemetery, in accordance with my oft expressed wishes, I shall yield my consent, to the request of the National Monument association in Washington & that of numerous other friends in the Eastern States & have the sacred remains deposited, in the vault, prepared for Washington, under the Dome of the National Capitol." Five days later, she reiterated her threat, insisting that her decision was "unalterable" and demanding written assurances that only she, Lincoln, their sons, and their sons' families would be buried in the tomb. The next day, she assured Oglesby that her wishes "will meet the approval of the whole civilized world." Haughtily, she added: "It is very painful to me, to be treated in this manner, by some of those I considered my friends, such conduct, will not add, very much, to the honor of our state."[175]

Although it was clearly the widow's prerogative to determine the burial site of her husband, it was not her right to dictate the location of a memorial honoring his memory. But what was the association to do? One observer of the controversy advised Oglesby that "Mrs. L is a vain woman and vanity will decide the matter tho she may think that there are other and higher motives."[176] So the board of directors of the National Lincoln Monument Association decided by a one-vote majority to acquiesce.

Indignation at Mary Lincoln might have been even greater if the public had learned that a few weeks after the assassination she sold her husband's shirts to a shady character for $84. Ward Hill Lamon sent an emissary to retrieve them. When she left the White House in late May, she took with her several dozen boxes and twenty trunks. Some journalists believed that she "stole a great deal of Government silver, spoons[,] forks[,] etc[.,] and a large quantity of linen and stuffs."[177] Early in 1866, the New York *Daily News* commented that "[n]o one would have said a word against a *few souvenirs* having been taken away. But to despoil the whole house of the best of everything; to send off by railroad more than seventy large packing-cases filled with the newest carpets, curtains, and works of art which have been provided for the adornment of the house, and not for the use of any one family; this was felt to be not exactly in good taste. It is not longer any wonder that the [White] house looks empty, dingy, and shabby."[178] At that same time, the New York *World* reported that "[f]or the $100,00 appropriated in the last four years for alleged repairs and furniture for the White House, there is now actually *nothing* to show on the premises; the Republican officer can be named who says that he furnished ninety boxes to pack up the removed traps. Another prominent Republican says that it required fifteen carts to remove the luggage from the White House; and in addition to this expenditure and these removals, it is a notorious fact that the thirty thousand dollars lately appropriated to furnish the Executive Mansion will nearly all be absorbed by the creditors for the persons who occupied the house ten months ago."[179] Republican Senator Benjamin F. Wade stated that Mary Lincoln "took a hundred boxes . . . away with her, and the Commissioner of Public Buildings swore there were fifteen other boxes that she wanted to carry off and he had to interfere to prevent her. At any rate she cleaned out the White House. I didn't know but she was going to run a big hotel with all she carried off."[180]

Mary Lincoln heatedly denied such charges, but the statement of Supreme Court Justice David Davis, a close friend of Lincoln and the executor of his estate, lends credence to the allegations. On July 3, 1873, when Orville H. Browning told Davis "that all the charges against her of having pilfered from the White House were false," the judge replied "that the proofs were too many and too strong against her to admit of doubt of her guilt; that she was a natural born thief; that stealing was a sort of insanity with her, and that she carried away, from the White House, many things that were of no value to her after she had taken them, and that she had carried them away only in obedience to her irresistable propensity to steal."[181] As noted above, Thaddeus Stevens, chairman of the House Ways and Means Committee, covered up the scandal and got Congress to pay for refurnishing the White House.

When philanthropists attempted to raise a fund for Mary Lincoln's support shortly after the assassination, she apparently wrote three letters to an agent (probably Alexander Williamson, Tad's tutor) soliciting money on her behalf in which she urged him "to secure subscriptions when the tragedy is fresh and feeling most poignant" and telling him he could "subtract 25 per cent from all moneys collected" as a fee.[182]

National Mourning for a Lost Father

The nation's enormous outpouring of grief testified to the profound love and respect that Lincoln inspired, an emotional bond like the one between a child and a nurturing, wise parent. In 1866, J. G. Holland of the Springfield, Massachusetts, *Republican* wrote that Lincoln "[m]ore than any of his predecessors was . . . regarded as the father of his people."[183] The Unitarian divine James Freeman Clarke noted in a sermon on April 16 (a day which came to be known as Black Easter) that Booth's act "was not only assassination . . . it was parricide; for Abraham Lincoln was as a father to the whole nation. The nation felt orphaned yesterday morning."[184] Another Massachusetts minister, the Congregationalist Elias Nason, likened the pain caused by Lincoln's death to the "profound personal grief we feel, as when a dear old father, a beloved mother, or a brother is torn relentlessly from breast." To Nason, the widespread grieving "is not mourning for some great national loss only." It was instead "lamentation for one who has been very near and very dear to us; for one who seemed to be of the immediate circle of our own familiar friends and acquaintances; for one who had so identified himself with our own views and feelings that he seemed to be an elementary part of our own being,—bone of our bone, blood of our blood; for one so entirely with us in sympathy, in genius, in love, in action, in aspiration, that he must ever bear the august appellation of the People's Own Beloved President. Even the little children looked upon him as their own kind-hearted ruler."[185] Yet other Bay State ministers noted that "[s]trong men have wept, and been convulsed with grief, as if they had lost a father or brother," and that "[w]e all seemed to have lost a father, a brother, a dear bosom-friend."[186] A Baptist preacher in Philadelphia lamented that the "nation's Father has been struck down in all his gentle kingliness."[187] In Illinois, a college president told his students and faculty that Lincoln "was endeared to every individual of the loyal millions of this people. . . . Each feels as if the dastardly blow . . . had been struck at a member of his own household. We mourn not merely for a public man, but for a dearly-beloved friend and brother."[188]

On April 16, a preacher in Maine told his parishioners: "Our Father . . . has fallen and we feel ourselves orphans." Three days later he remarked that it would seem strange "to one who did not know the circumstances of the case, to hear how often the word 'Father,' has fallen from trembling lips these last few days. 'I feel,' says one, and another, and another, 'as if I had lost my Father,' or, 'as I did when my Father died.' Such is the common feeling and the common word."[189]

Many other clergy echoed this paternal theme. Back in Illinois, a Presbyterian in Freeport noted that the country loved Lincoln "as it never loved another. He was the best and greatest, the greatest because the best, the most loving, the most lovable, the most brotherly, the most fatherly man of all our rulers. . . . How remarkable the affection of the people for this man!"[190] Other eulogists noted that "we have lost our noblest son, our bravest brother, our kindest father" and "a friend who was a father to the humblest in the land."[191] As a member of the Christian Commission, Theodore L. Cuyler had gotten to know Lincoln; he was so distraught by the assassination of the man he called a "dear departed father" that he could not write out a sermon. He therefore spoke extemporaneously to his New York congregation, saying that the "plain homespun kind-voiced President was so near to every one of us—so like our own relative that we were wont to call him 'Uncle Abe' and 'Father Abraham.' There was no disrespect in this; but rather a respect so deep and honest that it could afford to be familiar." Cuyler concluded that "[o]ur father died at the right time; for his mighty work was done."[192] Andrew Leete Stone predicted that generations to come "shall speak his name as our fathers spoke to us the name of Washington, and shall grow up revering and guarding the hallowed memory of this second *Father of his country*; whom History will write, also, *the Father of a race*."[193]

Many blacks did in fact regard Lincoln as a father. In Troy, New York, a black preacher mourned Lincoln as "the Father of our nation." Another black minister there elaborated: "We, as a people, feel more than all others that we are bereaved. We had learned to love Mr. Lincoln as we have never loved man before. We idolized his very name. We looked up to him as our saviour, our deliverer. His name was familiar with our children, and our prayers ascended to God in his behalf. He had taught us to love him. The interest he manifested in behalf of the oppressed, the weak and those who had none to help them, had won for him a large place in our heart. It was something so new to us to see such sentiments manifested by the chief magistrate of the United State that we could not help but love him."[194] The congregation of the Zion Baptist Church in Cincinnati heard its pastor proclaim that if Lincoln's assassin had "given us [blacks] the choice to deliver him or ourselves to death, we would have said, take me; take father or mother, sister, brother; but do not take the life of the father of this people." He noted that "[e]very freedman wept" at "the death of our father, ABRAHAM LINCOLN."[195]

The most eloquent black eulogy for Lincoln was delivered by Frederick Douglass before a large audience at Manhattan's Cooper Union on June 1, 1865, a day of national humiliation marking the end of the official mourning period for Lincoln. "No people or class of people in the country," he declared, "have a better reason for lamenting the death of Abraham Lincoln, and for desiring to honor and perpetuate his memory, than have the colored people." The record of the martyred president, when compared "with the long line of his predecessors, many of whom were merely the facile and servile instruments of the slave power," was impressive. Douglass acknowl-edged that Lincoln was "unsurpassed in his devotion to the welfare of the white race," and that "he sometimes smote" blacks "and wounded them severely"; nevertheless he was also "in a sense hitherto without example, emphatically the black man's Presi-dent: the first to show any respect for their rights as men . . . . He was the first Ameri-can President who . . . rose above the prejudice of his times, and country." If during the early stages of the Civil War the president had favored colonizing the freedmen abroad, Douglass asserted, "Lincoln soon outgrew his colonization ideas and schemes and came to look upon the Black man as an American citizen."

To illustrate this point, Douglass cited his personal experience: "It was my ex-ceeding great privilege to know Abraham Lincoln personally. I saw and conversed with him at different times during his administration." Douglass found Lincoln's willingness to receive him remarkable in itself: "He knew that he could do nothing which would call down upon him more fiercely the ribaldry of the vulgar than by showing any respect to a colored man." (In a draft of this speech, Douglass said: "Some men there are who can face death and dangers, but have not the moral courage to contradict a prejudice or face ridicule. In daring to admit, nay in daring to invite a Negro to an audience at the White house, Mr. Lincoln did that which he knew would be offensive to the crowd and excite their ribaldry. It was saying to the country, I am President of the black people as well as the white, and I mean to respect their rights and feelings as men and as citizens.")

When Douglass was admitted to the president's office, he found him easy to talk with: "He set me at perfect liberty to state where I differed from him as freely as where I agreed with him. From the first five minutes I seemed to myself to have been acquainted with [him] during all my life . . . [H]e was one of the very few white Americans who could converse with a negro without anything like condescension, and without in anywise reminding him of the unpopularity of his color."

Douglass recalled one episode in particular that demonstrated Lincoln's "kindly disposition towards colored people." While Douglass was talking with the president, a White House aide on two occasions announced that the governor of Connecticut sat in an adjacent room, eager for an interview. "Tell the Governor to wait," said the president. "I want to have a long talk with my friend Douglass." Their conversation continued for another hour. Douglass later speculated that "[t]his was probably the first time in the history of the country when the Governor of a State was required to wait for an interview, because the President of the United States was engaged in con-versation with a negro."

Douglass did not rely solely on his own experience to explain why Lincoln should be considered "emphatically the black man's President." He told the Cooper Union audience about "[o]ne of the most touching scenes connected with the funeral of our lamented President," which "occurred at the gate of the Presidential Mansion: A col-ored woman standing at the gate weeping, was asked the cause of her tears. 'Oh! Sir,' she said, 'we have lost our Moses.' 'But,' said the gentleman, 'the Lord will send you another; That may be,' said the weeping woman, 'but Ah! we had him.'" (Dozens of funeral sermons likened Lincoln to Moses.

This woman, according to Douglass, represented millions of blacks who "from first to last, and through all, whether through good or through evil report, fully believed in Abraham Lincoln." Despite his initial tardiness in attacking slavery, Douglass said, they "firmly trusted in him" with a faith that constituted "no blind trust unsupported by reason." Blacks had "early caught a glimpse of the man, and from the evidence of their senses, they believed in him. They viewed him not in the light of separate individual acts, but in the light of his mission, in his manifest relation to events and in the philosophy of his statesmanship. Viewing him thus they trusted him as men are seldom trusted. They did not care what forms of expression the President adopted, whether it were justice, expedience, or military necessity, so that they see slavery abolished and liberty established in the country."

Black people, Douglass maintained, could observe with their own eyes astounding progress: "Under Abraham Lincoln[']s beneficent rule, they saw themselves being gradually lifted to the broad plain of equal manhood; under his rule, and by measures approved by him, they saw gradually fading the handwriting of ages which was against them. Under his rule, they saw millions of their brethren proclaimed free and invested with the right to defend their freedom. Under his rule, they saw the Confederate states . . . broken to pieces, overpowered, conquered, shattered to fragments, ground to powder, and swept from the face of existence. Under his rule, they saw the Independence of Hayti and Liberia recognized, and the whole colored race steadily rising into the friendly consideration of the American people. In their broad practical common sense, they took no captious exceptions to the unpleasant incidents of their transition from slavery to freedom. All they wanted to know was that those incidents were only transitional not permanent."[196]

Many of his contemporaries ranked Lincoln second only to Washington, but Rutherford B. Hayes disagreed, privately writing that "Lincoln is overshadowing Washington. Washington is formal, statue-like, a figure for exhibition."[197] That is indeed the reason Lincoln was more warmly remembered than Washington; people admired Washington, but they loved as well as admired Lincoln. The Rev. Mr. William James Potter told his Massachusetts parishioners that while the first president "was the father of our country," Lincoln "was its savior. And in many respects he came nearer to the heart of the people than did even Washington."[198] In Wisconsin, Edward Searing, professor of Latin and French at Milton College, went even further, publicly declaring that Lincoln "was greater than Washington, as a *man,* and did a much greater work." Washington's "*main work*" was to win freedom for three million colonists, while Lincoln, as "an *incident* in *his* work," freed four million slaves. "Washington's work was great, Lincoln's gigantic." Moreover, Searing claimed, the sixteenth president outshone the first one intellectually: "I believe Lincoln to have been much superior to Washington—superior as a speaker, as a writer and as a clear-headed original thinker."[199] Another Midwestern academic, Richard Edwards, president of Illinois Normal University, reached a similar conclusion: "Lincoln the Liberator, contending for a grand, unselfish and beneficent idea, is greater in his opportunities and his position, than Washington the Patriot, fighting for the freedom of his native land."[200] A black Presbyterian minister concurred, stating that in "some things Abraham Lincoln is to be regarded as superior to Washington" and that if "the American people have reason to rejoice in the life and labors of a Washington, then the colored people of our country have a much greater reason to rejoice that Abraham Lincoln was permitted to occupy the executive chair."[201] Theodore Cuyler boldly predicted that within fifty years "the foremost name in American history will be the name that was signed to the Edict of Emancipation."[202]

Lincoln was so beloved that some preachers interpreted his assassination as God's way of thwarting idolatry. A Philadelphia Baptist asked: "Was not President Lincoln's death necessary to the nation's life? Were we not leaning on an arm of flesh forgetful of the ever loving God?"[203] Thomas M. Hopkins, a Presbyterian divine in Indiana, maintained that "God cannot tolerate idols. . . . This nation was on the point of worshipping Mr. Lincoln. . . . Ask these heavy hearts why this sadness? and they will reply . . . we loved our President and were lo[a]th to spare him. . . . We knew not how much we loved him until he was gone. This fact alone shows us that there was danger of his occupying too great a space in our hearts." Hopkins added that to "the soldiers and their families he was a friend, a loving father."[204]

Indeed, the troops reverenced Lincoln profoundly and were enraged at the assassins. "We moved away slowly to our quarters, as if each had lost a near and dear friend at home," a private reported. "I always thought that he was most loved by all the Army," he added. "What a hold Old Honest Abe had on the hearts of the soldiers of the army could only be told by the way they showed their mourning for him."[205] A Wisconsin soldier thought "[n]o man, not even Grant himself, possesses the entire love of the army as did President Lincoln. We mourn him not only as a President but as a man, for we had learned to love him as one possessed of every manly principle."[206] From Fort Stevens in Washington, one trooper wrote that "[e]veryone here looks sad, and the men all feel terribly indignant . . . . I would pitty any of them [the assassins] who fall into the hands of the army. I would like to be a private executioner of any one of them. . . . *Death to Traitors* is now the unanimous cry, particularly in the army."[207] Black troops were especially saddened.

In late 1862, soldiers had started referring to the president as "Father Abraham" and continued to do so for the remainder of his life, most notably during the 1864 election campaign. An Illinois corporal recalled that during "the last two years of the war especially, the men had come to regard Mr. Lincoln with sentiments of veneration and love. To them he really was 'Father Abraham,' with all that term implied."[208] A lieutenant in the U.S. Colored Troops told his wife, "I am getting to regard Old Abe almost as a *Father*—to almost venerate him—so earnestly do I believe in his earnestness, fidelity, honesty & Patriotism." Another lieutenant wrote: "With us of the U.S. Colored Army the death of Lincoln is indeed the loss of a friend. From him we received our commission—and toward him we have even looked as toward a Father."[209] With heartfelt emotion the troops sang, "We are coming, Father Abraham, three hundred thousand more."

Some members of Congress also felt the magnetic force of Lincoln's paternal nature. A White House secretary noted that they "became bound to him by near ties of mutual understanding and respect. A sort of family feeling grew in the hearts of many, unconsciously regarding themselves as watching the control of the common household by a man who oddly combined the functions of a father and an elder brother."[210] One of the most important elements in Lincoln's success as president was his ability to inspire in congressmen, senators, and their constituents filial trust and devotion. In part, it stemmed from the eloquence of his public utterances, which Harriet Beecher Stowe said "more resembled a father's talks to his children than a State paper." In the first inaugural address, his words to the South, in the view of a Republican congressman, contained "conciliatory promises" and "such winning arguments and admonitions only, as a tender father might employ with a wayward offspring."[211] Other literary figures echoed the theme. "So wise and good he was," George William Curtis told his friend Charles Eliot Norton. "Never had a country a father so tender and true."[212] Even Lincoln's harshest critics among the abolitionists paid their tribute. Parker Pillsbury called him as "[o]ur kind, gentle, noble hearted chief magistrate."[213]

Lincoln radiated the positive Old Man archetype, embodying the Wise Father. Many Northerners sensed this intuitively and trusted him. Without that trust, Northern morale might well have flagged, crippling the administration and the war effort. Few things contributed more to Lincoln's success as president than his ability to inspire the kind of confidence that children accord a benevolent father.

Lincoln's Greatness

Lincoln's personality was the North's secret weapon in the Civil War, the key variable that spelled the difference between victory and defeat. He was a model of psychological maturity, a fully individuated man who attained a level of consciousness unrivaled in the history of American public life. He managed to be strong-willed without being willful, righteous without being self-righteous, and moral without being moralistic. Most politicians, indeed, most people, are dominated by their own petty egos. They take things personally, try to dominate one another, waste time and energy on feuds and vendettas, project their unacceptable qualities onto others, displace anger and rage, and put the needs of their own clamorous egos above all other considerations. A dramatic exception to this pattern, Lincoln achieved a kind of balance and wholeness that led one psychologist to remark that he had more "psychological honesty" than anyone since Christ.[214] If one considers Christ as a psychological paradigm, the analogy is apt. (In 1866, John Hay stated flatly that "Lincoln with all his foibles, is the greatest character since Christ.")[215]

Lincoln's high degree of consciousness enabled him to suppress his own egotism while steadily focusing on the main goal: victory in the Civil War. As a friend observed, he "managed his politics upon a plan entirely different from any other man the country has ever produced. . . . In his conduct of the war he acted upon the theory that but one thing was necessary, and that was a united North. He had all shades of sentiments and opinions to deal with, and the consideration was always presented to his mind, How can I hold these discordant elements together?"[216] In a less conscious man, envy, jealousy, self-righteousness, false pride, vanity, and the other shortcomings of ordinary humanity would have undermined his ability to maintain Northern unity and resolve.

Strengthening that resolve was Lincoln's exceptional eloquence. The public letters—to Horace Greeley, Erastus Corning, James C. Conkling, and Albert Hodges—as well as his formal addresses and state papers—including the speech at Gettysburg, the two inaugurals, and the messages to Congress—inspired profound respect, confidence, and trust. So, too, did his character and personality, which made him loved as well as respected and trusted. Few leaders in American history combined those qualities as well as Lincoln.

Lincoln's greatness was widely acknowledged even before his death, and after it, his fame grew dramatically, spreading around the globe. In Switzerland, a leading historian of the Reformation predicted two weeks after the assassination that the "name of President Lincoln will remain one of the greatest that history has to inscribe on its annals."[217] In England, Professor Goldwin Smith declared that Lincoln would "live in the love of the nation and of mankind forever."[218] Leo Tolstoy's tribute, given during an interview in 1909, provides moving testimony to the universality of Lincoln's fame. The Russian novelist admired Lincoln's "peculiar moral power" and "the greatness of his character." Lincoln, he said, "was what Beethoven was in music, Dante in poetry, Raphael in painting, and Christ in the philosophy of life." No political leader matched Lincoln, in Tolstoy's judgment: "Of all the great national heroes and statesmen of history Lincoln is the only real giant. Alexander, Frederick the Great, Caesar, Napoleon, Gladstone and even Washington stand in greatness of character, in depth of feeling and in a certain moral power far behind Lincoln. Lincoln was a man of whom a nation has a right to be proud; he was a Christ in miniature, a saint of humanity, whose name will live thousands of years in the legends of future generations. We are still too near to his greatness, and so can hardly appreciate his divine power; but after a few centuries more our posterity will find him considerably bigger than we do. His genius is still too strong and too powerful for the common understanding, just as the sun is too hot when its light beams directly on us." Lincoln "lived and died a hero, and as a great character he will live as long as the world lives. May his life long bless humanity!"[219]

Postlude

Lincoln speaks to us not only as a champion of freedom, democracy, and national unity, but also as a source of inspiration. Few will achieve his world historical importance, but many can profit from his personal example, encouraged by the knowledge that despite a childhood of emotional malnutrition and grinding poverty, despite a lack of formal education, despite a series of career failures, despite a miserable marriage, despite a tendency to depression, despite a painful midlife crisis, despite the early death of his mother and his siblings as well as of his sweetheart and two of his four children, he became a model of psychological maturity, moral clarity, and unimpeachable integrity. His presence and his leadership inspired his contemporaries; his life story can do the same for generations to come.

ACKNOWLEDGMENTS

It is customary for authors to conclude their acknowledgments with an expression of gratitude to their spouses. I would like to bend tradition by opening with a heartfelt tribute to my better-half-to-be, the lovely and long-suffering Lois Erickson McDonald, who for the past two decades has demonstrated Lincolnian forbearance in tolerating my absences on innumerable research trips and has shown even greater forbearance when I am back in Connecticut. Without her support and love, I could not have completed this biography.

Those research binges were spent mostly in Washington, D.C., and Springfield, Illinois. In the nation's capital, my sister and brother-in-law (Sue and Edwin Coover) repeatedly put me up for weeks at a time, going far and above the call of family duty to facilitate my scholarly endeavors. In the Illinois capital, Sarah Thomas, daughter of the distinguished Lincoln biographer Benjamin P. Thomas, kindly allowed me the use of her home for several summers. In addition, Richard Hart and his wife Ann extended gracious hospitality at their Springfield home on numerous occasions, and Jim and Mary Patton permitted me to housesit for them. Sandy and Wayne C. Temple could not have been more kind to me during my sojourns in Springfield. While in Chicago, I had the pleasure of staying with my Andover classmate, attorney Wally Winter, historian manqué and good friend. In Boston, my daughter Jessica often put me up at her apartment, and my Manhattan-based brother Lloyd did the same for me again and again. Other hospitable hosts include William Lee Miller in Charlottesville, Virginia; Brett McMillan and Megan McDonald in Portland, Maine; Robert Bray in Bloomington, Illinois; and Charles Hubbard in Harrogate, Tennessee. To all, my heartiest thanks for making road trips thoroughly enjoyable as well as productive. I could not have afforded to conduct the research undergirding this book without their generosity.

Grants from the Lincoln Institute were vital in many ways, especially in enabling me to ransack repositories in locations where I had no friends or family to impose on. In those repositories I received much-appreciated help from librarians and archivists. At the Manuscript Division of the Library of Congress, which became in effect a second home, I benefited greatly from the kind assistance and warm friendship of John Sellers, Jeff Flannery, and their colleagues, including Fred Bauman, who transcribed for me many documents written in German *langschrift*. At the National Archives, the legendary Michael Musick helped me on several occasions. There the indefatigable Karen Needles has unearthed for me rare and valuable documents. I also spent a great deal of time in the John Hay Library at Brown University, where Samuel Streit, Jennifer Lee, Mary Jo Kline, J. Andrew Moul, Rosemary Cullen, Ann Dodge, Peter Harrington, and others in the Special Collections Department treated me like family. The staff at the Abraham Lincoln Presidential Library in Springfield—including Kim Bauer, Jill Blessman, Bob Cavanagh, Kathryn Harris, Mary Michals, Cheryl Pence, Cheryl Schnirring, and Thomas Schwartz—were unfailingly helpful and cordial over the years.

I extend thanks, too, to their counterparts at Allegheny College, the Lincoln Museum of Fort Wayne, Indiana, Lincoln Memorial University, the Chicago History Museum, the University of Chicago, the Newberry Library, the Huntington Library, the New York Public Library, Columbia University, the New-York Historical Society, Bowdoin College, the A. K. Smiley Library in Redlands, California, the New Hampshire Historical Society, the University of Vermont, the University of

Maine, Bowdoin College, the Maine State Archives, Dartmouth College, the Massachusetts Historical Society, the Boston Public Library, the American Antiquarian Society, the Lenox Public Library, the New York State Library, Syracuse University, Cornell University, the University of Rochester, the University of Michigan, the Detroit Public Library, the Wisconsin State Historical Society, the Historical Society of Pennsylvania, the Historical Society of Western Pennsylvania, the Hagley Museum and Library of Wilmington, Delaware, the Maryland Historical Society, the Johns Hopkins University, the Virginia Historical Society, the Library of Virginia, the University of Virginia, West Virginia University, Harvard University, Yale University, Princeton University, the Connecticut Historical Society, Bryn Mawr College, the Kentucky Historical Society, the Filson Club, the University of Kentucky, the Missouri Historical Society, the Minnesota Historical Society, the Indiana Historical Society, the Indiana State Library, the University of Indiana, the Northern Indiana Center for History, Depauw University, Vincennes University, the Evansville Public Library, the Vandalia Public Library, the Willard Library (Evansville), the University of Iowa, the State Historical Society of Iowa, the Iowa State Archives, the University of Illinois, the Illinois State Archives, the Abraham Lincoln Public Library in Springfield, Illinois, the Ohio Historical Society (Columbus), the Western Reserve Historical Society (Cleveland), and the Cincinnati Historical Society.

Librarians at my home institution, Connecticut College in New London, have been unusually helpful. Special thanks are due to the indefatigable efforts of the Interlibrary Loan officers (Helen Aitner and Emily Aylward) and to James McDonald, Beth Hansen, Lori Blados, Brian Rogers, Connie Dowell, and Carol Strang. The best student I taught in my thirty-three years at the College, Minor Myers III, helped significantly as I tried to identify Lincoln's anonymous journalism. His parents were exceptionally hospitable whenever my quest for the historical Lincoln took me to Bloomington, Illinois. The R. Francis Johnson Faculty Development Fund at Connecticut College helped defray some research expenses.

Fellow scholars have been generous in reading portions of my manuscript, sharing information with me, and allowing me to see their works-in-progress. Among them are Douglas L. Wilson and Rodney O. Davis of the Lincoln Studies Center at Knox College; Allen Guelzo and Gabor Boritt of Gettysburg College; Lewis E. Lehrman; William Hanchett of San Diego State University; Doris Kearns Goodwin of Concord, Massachusetts; Richard Wightman Fox of the University of Southern California; Herman Belz of the University of Maryland; Roger D. Bridges of Springfield; Terry Alford of Northern Virginia Community College; Ari Hoogenboom of Brooklyn College; the late John Y. Simon of Southern Illinois University; Ron Soodalter of Manhattan; the late Don E. Fehrenbacher of Stanford University; Richard Striner and Joshua Wolf Shenk of Washington College; Mark Plummer and Silvana Saddili of Illinois State University; Frank Milligan of President Lincoln's Cottage in Washington; James Oakes of the City University of New York; William Lee Miller of the University of Virginia; Mark E. Steiner of the University of Houston; William C. Harris of North Carolina State University; Thomas Turner of Bridgewater State College; Jennifer L. Weber of the University of Kansas; Lucas Morel of Washington and Lee University; Brooks Simpson of Arizona State University; the late Phillip Shaw Paludan of the University of Illinois at Springfield; Jason Emerson of Cazenovia, New York; Michael Vorenberg of Brown University; Wayne C. Temple of the Illinois State Archives; Richard Hart of Springfield; Stephen Berry of the University of Georgia; John Lupton, Daniel Stowell, and Cullom Davis of the Lincoln Legal Papers; Robert Bray of Illinois Wesleyan University; Paul Verduin of Silver Spring, Maryland; Jennifer Fleischner of Adelphi University; Kenneth Winkle of the University of Nebraska; Joan E. Cashin of Ohio State University; Gerald J. Prokopowicz of Eastern Carolina University; Guy Fraker of Bloomington, Illinois; and Russell H. Beatie of New York.

The camaraderie of many other Lincolnians makes membership in the Lincoln fraternity especially enjoyable. Among them are Richard Carwardine of Oxford University; Hans Trefousse of Brooklyn College; James McPherson of Princeton University; Joseph Fornieri of the Rochester Institute of Technology; Mike Musick, Steve Carson, Fred Martin, Scott Sandage, Don Kennon, Paul Pascal, Stephen Goldman, Michelle A. Krowl, Gordon Leidner, Jonathan Mann, Clark Evans, Rodney Ross, Bob Willard, and other members of the board of directors of the Abraham Lincoln Institute in Washington; Laurin A. Wollan of Sweet Briar, Virginia; Ronald Rietveld of California State University at Fullerton; Daniel Mark Epstein of Baltimore; Matthew Pinsker of Dickinson College; Dan Weinberg of Chicago; Daniel Pierson of Beaver Dam, Wisconsin; Roger Fisher of the University of Minnesota; Michael Bishop and James Swanson of Washington, D.C.; Steven K. Rogstad of Grand Rapids, Michigan; Richard Hart, Fred Hoffmann, Don Tracy, and other colleagues on the board of the Abraham Lincoln Association in Springfield; John Hoffmann of the University of Illinois; and Andrew Ferguson of *The Weekly Standard*.

In the 1960s it was my good fortune to have been taught by David Herbert Donald at both Princeton and Johns Hopkins Universities. He took me under his wing when I was a college freshman and made a tremendous difference in my life, for which I will be eternally grateful.

I am also grateful to my editor at the Johns Hopkins University Press, Robert J. Brugger, who helped focus and condense the manuscript. Further aiding in that process was an old friend from graduate school days, William Evitts of Baltimore, who carefully went over the manuscript of the first volume line by line. Richard Behn of the Lincoln Institute also gave the manuscript a close reading. For assistance in obtaining artwork for these volumes, I am indebted to William Furry of the Illinois State Historical Society and his counterparts at the Library of Congress, the Abraham Lincoln Presidential Library, and the Indiana Historical Society. At the Westchester Book Group, Lyndee Stalter, Susan Baker, and their colleagues exerted themselves heroically to get this biography out in time for the bicentennial of Lincoln's birth.

Thanks, thanks to all.

NOTE ON SOURCES

Because the notes to this biography had to be kept lean, they are confined mostly to identifying primary sources and do not acknowledge properly the secondary works on Lincoln and his times which I have consulted. Far more extensive and discursive notes may be found in the original unedited version of the book, which is available online at www.knox.edu/lincolnstudies. Readers curious about the enormous secondary literature on Lincoln are referred to that version.

In using primary sources, I have relied wherever possible on contemporary documents rather than reminiscences. Calvin Coolidge once remarked that many people in his hometown of Plymouth, Vermont, "remember some of the most interesting things that never happened."[1] Coolidge's quip raises a question that historians regularly face: How much credence should be given to the reminiscences of people who knew Lincoln, especially to those recalling events and words from the distant past?

James G. Randall's four-volume account of Lincoln's presidency contains an appendix, primarily the handiwork of the author's wife, Ruth Painter Randall, warning that "the vagueness of reminiscence given after many years is familiar to all careful historical students; if, in the haste of general reading, this matter is disregarded, the essence of the subject is overlooked. Huge tomes could be written to show the doubtfulness of long-delayed memories." The Randalls sensibly noted that "the historian must use reminiscence, but he must do so critically. Even close-up evidence is fallible. When it comes through the mists of many years some of it may be true, but a careful writer will check it with known facts. Contradictory reminiscences leave doubt as to what is to be believed; unsupported memories are in themselves insufficient as proof; statements induced under suggestion, or psychological stimulus . . . call especially for careful appraisal." The Randalls urged particular caution in using the reminiscences gathered by William H. Herndon, Lincoln's law partner, shortly after the Civil War. Because of J. G. Randall's prestige as a Lincoln authority (which Mrs. Randall did not enjoy), subsequent scholars have tended to shy away from the Herndon materials, regarding them as unreliable.[2]

Among the skeptics was Herndon's biographer and Randall's preeminent protégé, David Herbert Donald, who spelled out some of the problems involved in using reminiscences: "To collect historical data through oral interviews, though sometimes necessary, is always hazardous. The reminiscences of a graybearded grandfather have to be guided or they are likely to become incoherent rambling. Yet in controlling an interview, it is very difficult not to influence the informant. To ask some questions is to suggest the answers desired."[3]

The most thorough students of the Herndon collection, Douglas L. Wilson and Rodney O. Davis, have cogently argued that the Randalls' skepticism was exaggerated.[4] Since the Randalls' day (their critique of Herndon appeared in 1945), historians have come to view reminiscent materials more favorably. The rise of oral history has lent new respectability to interviews like those conducted by Herndon.[5]

Wilson noted that the Randalls treated Herndon's informants as if they were witnesses in court. Like defense attorneys, they sought to discredit everyone who asserted that Lincoln and Ann Rutledge were in love. "Historical scholarship," Wilson argues, "for whatever similarities it might bear to trying a case in a court of law, is a very different kind of enterprise and employs different methods. Observing the evidentiary safeguards of a criminal trial would, after all, bring a substantial portion of historical inquiry to a halt, for much of what we want to know about the past simply cannot be established on these terms. Abraham Lincoln's early life is a perfect example. Virtually everything we know about Lincoln as a child and as a young man—his incessant reading and self-education, his storytelling, his honesty, his interest in politics, and so forth—comes exclusively from the recollections of the people who knew him. Non-contemporary, subjective, often unable to be confirmed even by the recollections of others, to say nothing of contemporary documents, this evidence is sheer reminiscence." Wilson acknowledges that the Randalls' "caveats about such evidence and the admixture of error and bias it may contain are certainly justified," but adds that "the historian or biographer has no alternative but to find a way to work with it and, indeed, with anything that may be indicative of the truth."[6]

I make extensive use of the Herndon materials, which Wilson rightly calls "the richest source of information on Lincoln's early life." He points out that "Herndon spent a prodigious amount of time and effort pursuing and procuring information about Abraham Lincoln." The documents he collected "show that he examined and cross-examined his informants with care, that he sought information both open-endedly and on a wide variety of specific topics, that he checked up on doubtful or conflicting stories, and that he acted in accordance with his stated purpose, which was to learn and publish the truth about his great law partner."[7]

The people Herndon interviewed have also been underestimated, Wilson contends: "It is sometimes maintained by an appeal to common experience that Herndon's informants could not have been expected to summon obscure events from the distant past with anything like accuracy, much less historical reliability, and that Herndon was naive to have believed them." Such objections, Wilson says, "make it appear that Herndon asked his informants to recall . . . things they had not thought about or discussed with anyone for twenty-five or thirty years." In fact, the people whom Herndon consulted had, during the years when Lincoln's fame grew, "frequent occasion to recall their personal contacts with him and keep alive their memories of his early days."[8]

Having studied the Herndon archive closely, I concur with Wilson and Davis as well as Albert J. Beveridge, who, after examining Herndon's papers, wrote that "everywhere it is obvious that Herndon is intent on telling the truth himself and getting the truth from those who could give personal, first-hand information."[9] Beveridge told a Lincoln biographer, "I have examined the credibility of Herndon very much as if he were a hostile witness in a murder trial; and there is absolutely no doubt that the old man (he was not very old when he collected this data) was well-nigh fanatically devoted to truth. It is only when he assumes to analyze the 'souls' of other people that he is untrustworthy. . . . But I repeat, that when he states a fact as a fact, you can depend upon it that it is a fact."[10] The Herndon-Weik collection is not without its faults and must be used carefully, but it should be treated as a gold mine rather than a high-level nuclear waste dump.

I have also made extensive use of other reminiscent material, most notably that contained in the clipping collections at the Lincoln Museum in Fort Wayne, Indiana, and the Abraham Lincoln Presidential Library in Springfield. These sources, too, must be treated with caution, especially when Lincoln's words are quoted. Purists might argue that, given the vagaries of memory, all such quotations should be dismissed out of hand. But as Don E. Fehrenbacher noted, there is "a great accumulation of spoken words attributed to Lincoln that cannot be ignored." By being too "fastidious," he warned, historians might produce works "impoverished as a consequence."[11]

Fehrenbacher correctly observed that there "is no simple formula for judging the authenticity of recollected utterances" To estimate their credibility "is a complex and often inconclusive enterprise," he pointed out. "Special problems abound, such as that of recollections said to be based on contemporaneous notes. Unfortunately, these precious source materials seem never to have survived, and the list of persons assertedly using them includes some of the Munchausens of Lincoln literature. Yet not all such claims are dubious enough to be dismissed out of hand."

As Fehrenbacher noted, researchers must also ask: "how much should factual inaccuracy count against the overall credibility of a quotation?" Clearly "the nub of a recollection may be right, even though the details are wrong, but even so, erroneous statements of fact seem to indicate that verbal recall from the same source will be only roughly accurate at best." Then there is the informant "who in one or more instances proves to be, not just inaccurate, but demonstrably untruthful, perhaps even to the point of inventing conversations that never took place." Must "the rest of this person's testimony be set aside according to the rule, *falsus in uno, falsus in omnibus*, or is it more reasonable to judge each quotation separately on the principle that even habitual liars tell the truth some of the time?"

Dealing with contradictory recollections raises further problems. Fehrenbacher sensibly counseled, "it might seem that giving credence to those on one side means withholding credence from those on the other. Such is not necessarily the case, however; for there can be little doubt that Lincoln the consummate politician sometimes spoke differently on the same subject to different people."

I have tried to verify the recollections of informants by using contemporary evidence, but as Fehrenbacher noted, "satisfactory verification is impossible because the narrator was the only person present to hear what Lincoln said—or at least the only person to leave any record of what he said. The best one can do in such cases is make a judgment based on the auditor's general reputation, if that is known, plus the circumstantial and substantive verisimilitude of the quotation."

I have employed Fehrenbacher's rules when using recollected words of Lincoln. "First," he said, "it should be recognized that many a quotation has a provenance too weak and/or a substance too dubious to be incorporated in serious historical writing." In order to judge whether a quote is marred by a "substance too dubious," I have examined Lincoln's own writings closely, as well as the vast literature about him, developing over more than two decades a nose for what "smells" authentically Lincolnian. This procedure is hardly scientific, and there is room for disagreement among historians of good will. I have also tried to learn as much as possible about those reporting Lincoln's words in order to assess their veracity.

Fehrenbacher also advised that "insofar as the pace of narrative or argument will allow it, the reader should be given some measure of a quotation's authenticity." It would be tedious to clutter the text with such qualifiers as "if we can believe the recollective memory of X," and the reader should supply such a disclaimer before all recollected quotes, which are identified in the notes. While trying to avoid such clumsiness, I have sought to distinguish canonical utterances of Lincoln from "recollective testimony."[12]

I have not, however, heeded Fehrenbacher's advice to treat such testimony as indirect rather than direct discourse. To be sure, such language may not be strictly accurate, but paraphrasing Lincoln's alleged words robs them of much of their impact.

Historians have understandably relied more heavily on contemporary sources than on reminiscences, but as Donald A. Ritchie has persuasively argued, "[d]ocuments written at the time have an immediacy about them and are not influenced by subsequent events, and yet those documents can be incomplete, in error, or written to mislead. A statement is not necessarily truer if written down at the time than if recalled later in testimony. Whether written or oral, evidence must be convincing and verifiable." I have tried to follow Ritchie's sound advice: "Treat oral evidence as cautiously as any other form of evidence."[13]

NOTES

List of Abbreviations

AL MSS DLC: Abraham Lincoln Papers, Library of Congress

CSmH: Huntington Library, San Marino, California

DLC: Library of Congress

HI: Herndon's Informants

H-W MSS DLC: Herndon-Weik Papers, Library of Congress

ICHi: Chicago History Museum

IHi: Abraham Lincoln Presidential Library and Museum, Springfield

InU: Indiana University

LMF: Lincoln Museum, Fort Wayne

MHi: Massachusetts Historical Society

RPB: Brown University

Chapter 19. "The Man Does Not Live Who Is More Devoted to Peace Than I Am"

1. Garrett allegedly expressed this view in a letter to Mayor James G. Berret of Washington. Washington *Globe*, 7 Feb. 1861.

2. Springfield correspondence, 28 Jan., *Missouri Democrat* (St. Louis), 29 Jan. 1861, Michael Burlingame, ed., *Lincoln's Journalist: John Hay's Anonymous Writings for the Press, 1860–1864* (Carbondale: Southern Illinois University Press, 1998), 21.

3. Chase to Lincoln, Columbus, 28 Jan. 1861, AL MSS DLC.

4. Thurlow Weed Barnes, *Life of Thurlow Weed Including His Autobiography and a Memoir* (2 vols.; Boston: Houghton Mifflin, 1884), 1:605–606.

5. Indianapolis correspondence, 11 Feb., New York *World*, 15 Feb. 1861, Burlingame, ed., *Lincoln's Journalist*, 24.

6. Reminiscences of Henry B. Carrington, Indianapolis *News*, 11 Feb. 1908.

7. Reminiscences of William P. Wood, Washington *Sunday Gazette*, 23 Jan. 1887.

8. Rochester *Democrat*, n.d., copied in the Baltimore *Sun*, 22 Feb. 1861.

9. Indianapolis correspondence by Hay, 11 Feb., New York *World*, 15 Feb. 1861, Burlingame, ed., *Lincoln's Journalist*, 25.

10. Reminiscences of Thomas Ross in an unidentified newspaper article, [1903?], clipping collection, LMF.

11. John G. Nicolay, "Some Incidents in Lincoln's Journey from Springfield to Washington," Michael Burlingame, ed., *An Oral History of Abraham Lincoln: John G. Nicolay's Interviews and Essays* (Carbondale: Southern Illinois University Press, 1996), 117.

12. John Hay, "The Heroic Age in Washington," lecture of 1871, Michael Burlingame, ed., *At Lincoln's Side: John Hay's Civil War Correspondence and Selected Writings* (Carbondale: Southern Illinois University Press, 2000), 117.

13. Henry Villard, *Memoirs of Henry Villard, Journalist and Financier, 1835–1900* (2 vols.; Boston: Houghton Mifflin, 1904), 1:152.

14. Nicolay, "Some Incidents in Lincoln's Journey," Burlingame, ed., *Oral History of Lincoln*, 111.

15. George W. Hazzard to his wife, Buffalo, 17 Feb. 1861, AL MSS, Addendum 1, DLC.

16. Roy P. Basler et al., eds., *Collected Works of Abraham Lincoln* [hereafter *CWL*] (8 vols. plus index; New Brunswick, NJ: Rutgers University Press, 1953–1955), 4:192.

17. *The Israelite* (Cincinnati), 15 Mar. 1861, in Bertram W. Korn, *American Jewry and the Civil War* (Philadelphia: Jewish Publication Society of America, 1951), 41.

18. Charleston, South Carolina, *Courier,* 19 Feb. 1861.

19. *CWL,* 4:195–196.

20. Indianapolis correspondence, 11 Feb., New York *World,* 15 Feb. 1861, Burlingame, ed., *Lincoln's Journalist,* 26, 27.

21. New York *Herald,* 12 Feb. 1861.

22. Cincinnati correspondence, 12 Feb., Baltimore *Sun,* 14 Feb. 1861; George W. Sanders to Stephen A. Douglas, Cincinnati, 12 Feb. 1861, Douglas Papers, University of Chicago.

23. William L. Hodge to John Austin Stevens, Washington, 18, 19 Feb. 1861, Stevens Papers, New-York Historical Society.

24. Washington correspondence by Kritick, 11 Mar., Charleston *Courier,* 14 Mar. 1861; Baltimore *Exchange,* 12 Mar. 1861; Louisville *Journal,* n.d., quoted in George S. Cottman, "Lincoln in Indianapolis," *Indiana Magazine of History* 24 (1928):9.

25. New Orleans *Crescent,* 21 Feb. 1861.

26. Boston *Daily Advertiser,* 16 Feb. 1861.

27. New York *Evening Post,* 16 Feb. 1861.

28. New York *Herald,* 15 Feb. 1861.

29. *Frank Leslie's Illustrated Newspaper,* 23 Feb. 1861.

30. Clay to John A. Andrew, n.p., 18 Feb. 1861, Andrew Papers, MHi.

31. Indianapolis correspondence, 11 Feb., New York *World,* 15 Feb. 1861, Burlingame, ed., *Lincoln's Journalist,* 26.

32. Nicolay, "Some Incidents in Lincoln's Journey," Burlingame, ed., *Oral History of Lincoln,* 109–110; Ward Hill Lamon, *Recollections of Abraham Lincoln, 1847–1865,* ed. Dorothy Lamon Teillard (2nd ed.; Washington, DC: privately published, 1911), 36.

33. Cincinnati *Gazette,* n.d., copied in the Albany *Atlas and Argus,* n.d., clipping collection, LMF.

34. Cincinnati correspondence, 12 Feb., New York *World,* 15 Feb. 1861, Burlingame, ed., *Lincoln's Journalist,* 28.

35. *CWL,* 4:197.

36. Rutherford B. Hayes to Sardis Birchard, Cincinnati, 15 Feb. 1861, Charles Richard Williams, ed., *Diary and Letters of Rutherford*

Birchard Hayes (5 vols.; Columbus: Ohio State Archeological and Historical Society, 1922–1926), 2:5.

37. William Henry Smith in Francis Fisher Brown, *The Every-Day Life of Abraham Lincoln* (New York: N. D. Thompson, 1886), 382–383.

38. Cincinnati correspondence, 12 Feb., New York *World,* 15 Feb. 1861, Burlingame, ed., *Lincoln's Journalist,* 29–30.

39. Cincinnati *Gazette,* 13 Feb. 1861.

40. William T. Coggeshall, *Lincoln Memorial: The Journeys of Abraham Lincoln from Springfield to Washington, 1861, as President Elect, and from Washington to Springfield, 1865, as President Martyred, Comprising an Account of Public Ceremonies on the Entire Route, and Full Details of Both Journeys* (Columbus: Ohio State Journal, 1865), 35.

41. *CWL,* 4:199.

42. Annie U. P. Jay to J. G. Wright, Raysville, 17 Feb. 1861, Anna W. Wright Papers, Indiana State Library, Indianapolis.

43. Philadelphia *Morning Pennsylvanian,* 14 Feb. 1861.

44. *The Israelite* (Cincinnati), 15 Feb. 1861, in Korn, *American Jewry and the Civil War,* 41.

45. Cincinnati, Ohio, German Workmen to Lincoln, Feb. 1861, AL MSS DLC.

46. *CWL,* 4:202.

47. Rutherford B. Hayes to Sardis Birchard, Cincinnati, 15 Feb. 1861, Williams, ed., *Diary and Letters of Hayes,* 2:6.

48. Columbus correspondence, 13 Feb., Cincinnati *Gazette,* 14 Feb. 1861.

49. Columbus correspondence, 13 Feb., New York *World,* 18 Feb. 1861.

50. *Ohio State Journal* (Columbus), 13 Feb. 1861.

51. Cincinnati correspondence, 13 Feb., New York *Herald,* 14 Feb. 1861.

52. *CWL,* 4:204.

53. Edwin R. Reynolds *Congressional Globe,* 36th Congress, 2nd Session, Appendix, 1008 (18 Feb. 1861).

54. C. Carter to William Overton Winston, Philadelphia, 16 Feb. 1861, Winston Family Papers, Virginia Historical Society.

55. New York *Herald,* New York *Daily News,* 15 Feb. 1861.

56. Washington correspondence, 23 Feb., Chicago *Tribune,* 27 Feb. 1861.

57. A leading Columbus banker in Victor Searcher, *Lincoln's Journey to Greatness: A Factual Account of the Twelve-Day Inaugural Trip* (Philadelphia: Winston, 1960), 134.

58. Undated memo, William T. Coggeshall Papers, Ohio Historical Society.

59. Columbus correspondence, 13 Feb., New York *World,* 18 Feb. 1861; Columbus correspondence, 13 Feb., Chicago *Tribune,* 14 Feb. 1861.

60. James A. Garfield to his wife, Columbus, 17 Feb. 1861, in John Shaw, ed., *Crete and James: Personal Letters of Lucretia and James Garfield* (East Lansing: Michigan State University Press, 1994), 107; Garfield to B. A. Hinsdale, Columbus, 17 Feb. 1861, Garfield Papers, DLC.

61. William Dennison to Francis P. Blair, Columbus, 19 Feb. 1861, Blair Family Papers, DLC.

62. Columbus correspondence, 13 Feb., New York *Tribune,* 18 Feb. 1861.

63. Lamon, *Recollections of Lincoln,* 33–34.

64. This is a composite of two versions of the story, told in Indiana and later in New York. *CWL,* 4:193; Stephen Fiske, "When Lincoln Was First Inaugurated," *Ladies' Home Journal,* Mar. 1897, 7.

65. *CWL,* 4:207.

66. John M. Cook to Stephen A. Douglas, Steubenville, 15 Feb. 1861, Douglas Papers, University of Chicago.

67. *CWL,* 4:208.

68. Nicolay to Therena Bates, Pittsburgh, 15 Feb. 1861, Michael Burlingame, ed., *With Lincoln in the White House: Letters, Memoranda, and Other Writings of John G. Nicolay, 1860–1865* (Carbondale: Southern Illinois University Press, 2000), 27.

69. *CWL,* 4:208–209.

70. Ibid., 4:210–215.

71. Ibid., 4:245.

72. New York *World,* 16 Feb. 1861.

73. New York *Tribune,* 16 Feb. 1861.

74. Villard, *Memoirs,* 1:152.

75. Baltimore *Exchange,* 20 Feb. 1861; Washington *States and Union,* 16 Feb. 1861; Pittsburgh *Post,* 16 Feb. 1861.

76. Springfield (Massachusetts) *Republican,* 18 Feb. 1861.

77. Washington correspondence, 16 Feb. 1861, an unidentified clipping enclosed in John Perkins to S. S. Cox, [New York], Sunday [n.d.], Cox Papers, RPB.

78. Cleveland *Plain Dealer,* 18 Feb. 1861.

79. Cleveland correspondence, 15 Feb., Cincinnati *Gazette,* 16 Feb. 1861.

80. David Davis to his wife, Buffalo, 17 Feb. 1861, Davis Papers, IHi.

81. Nicolay to Therena Bates, Buffalo, 17 Feb. 1861, Burlingame, ed., *With Lincoln in the White House,* 28.

82. Cleveland correspondence, 15 Feb., Chicago *Tribune,* 16 Feb. 1861; *CWL,* 4:215–216.

83. Riddle in Browne, *Every-Day Life of Lincoln,* 387.

84. Nicolay, "Some Incidents in Lincoln's Journey," Burlingame, ed., *Oral History of Lincoln,* 112.

85. Rutherford B. Hayes to Laura Platt Mitchell, Cincinnati, 13 Feb. 1861, Ari Hoogenboom, *Rutherford B. Hayes: Warrior and President* (Lawrence: University Press of Kansas, 1995), 113.

86. Cleveland *Plain Dealer,* 18 Feb. 1861.

87. Buffalo correspondence by "Wilkins" (Uriah Painter), 17 Feb., Philadelphia *Inquirer,* 20 Feb. 1861.

88. "Semi-occasional" to Thurlow Weed, Erie, 20 Feb. 1861, Weed Papers, University of Rochester.

89. Erie *Weekly Gazette,* 21 Feb. 1861, in J. H. Cramer, "A President-Elect in Western Pennsylvania," *Pennsylvania Magazine of History and Biography* 71 (1947):216–217.

90. Grace Bedell to Lincoln, Westfield, New York, 18 Oct. 1860; Lincoln to Grace Bedell, Springfield, 19 Oct. 1860, *CWL,* 4:129–130.

91. Springfield correspondence, 28 Jan., New York *Evening Post,* 1 Feb. 1861.

92. Anna Ridgely diary, 6 Feb. 1861, IHi; Truman H. Bartlett to Charles W. McLellan, Chocorua, New Hampshire, 3 Nov. 1907, Lincoln Collection, RPB.

93. Grace Bedell Billings to E. B. Briggs, Delphos, Kansas, 1 Mar. 1939, Westfield, New York, *Republican,* 14 May 1939; "Lincoln's Beard," Washington *Post,* 14 Oct. 1910.

94. *CWL,* 4:220.

95. Buffalo correspondence, 16 Feb., New York *World,* 19 Feb. 1861, Burlingame, ed., *Lincoln's Journalist,* 33.

96. Buffalo correspondence, 18 Feb., New York *World,* 19 Feb. 1861, Burlingame, ed., *Lincoln's Journalist,* 34.

97. Nicolay to Therena Bates, Buffalo, 17 Feb. 1861, Burlingame, ed., *With Lincoln in the White House,* 28.

98. *CWL,* 4:220–221.

99. Benjamin Brown French to Henry Flagg French, Washington, 6 Mar. 1861, French Family Papers, DLC.

100. Washington correspondence, 19, 20 Feb., Cincinnati *Enquirer,* n.d., copied in the *Illinois State Register* (Springfield), 22, 23 Feb. 1861.

101. Washington correspondence, n.d., New York *Express,* 20 Feb. 1861.

102. Washington correspondence, 16 Feb. 1861, in an unidentified clipping enclosed in John Perkins to S. S. Cox, [New York], Sunday [n.d.], Cox Papers, RPB.

103. Washington correspondence, 14 Feb., Baltimore *American,* 15 Feb. 1861.

104. Charles Francis Adams to Richard Henry Dana, Washington, 18 Feb. 1861, Dana Family Papers, MHi.

105. Charles Francis Adams to John A. Andrew, Washington, 22 Feb. 1861, Andrew Papers, MHi; Charles Francis Adams diary, 16, 20, 21 Feb. 1861, Adams Family Papers, MHi; Charles Francis Adams, paraphrased in Charles Francis Adams, Jr., diary entry for 19 Feb. 1861, in *Charles Francis Adams, 1835–1915: An Autobiography* (Boston: Houghton Mifflin Company, 1916), 77; Charles Francis Adams, Jr.

to Richard Henry Dana, Washington, 21 Feb. [misdated Jan.] 1861, Dana Papers, MHi.

106. Samuel R. Curtis to his wife, Washington, 24 Feb. 1861, Kenneth E. Colton, ed., "'The Irrepressible Conflict of 1861': The Letters of Samuel Ryan Curtis," *Annals of Iowa,* 3rd series, 24 (1942):32–33.

107. Samuel R. Curtis, manuscript journal, 13 Feb. 1861, IHi.

108. William S. Holman to Allen Hamilton, Washington, 18 Feb. 1861, Hamilton Papers, Indiana State Library, Indianapolis.

109. Edward Everett diary, 15 Feb. 1861, Everett Papers, MHi.

110. James R. Roche to Edward Harrick, New York, 20 Feb. 1861, Harrick Papers, New-York Historical Society.

111. Samuel Bowles to Henry L. Dawes, Springfield, 26 Feb. 1861, Dawes Papers, DLC.

112. Bigelow to William Hargreaves, [New York], 21 Feb. 1861, Bigelow Papers, New York Public Library.

113. Lewis P. W. Balch to Seward, Newport, 23 Feb. 1861, Seward Papers, University of Rochester.

114. Philadelphia *Public Ledger,* 16 Feb. 1861; Philadelphia *Argus,* n.d., and the New York *Express,* n.d., copied in the Baltimore *Sun,* 18 Feb. 1861.

115. Allan Nevins and Milton Halsey Thomas, eds., *Diary of George Templeton Strong, 1835–1875* (4 vols.; New York: Macmillan, 1952), 3:100 (entry for 18 Feb. 1861).

116. New York *World,* 15 Feb. 1861.

117. Baltimore *Exchange,* 20 Feb. 1861; Baltimore *American,* 16 Feb. 1861.

118. Baltimore *Sun,* 15 Feb. 1861.

119. Kennedy to Abraham Comingo, Baltimore, 9 Mar. 1861, Civil War Papers, Maryland Historical Society.

120. Sherrard Clemens to John C. Underwood, Richmond, 18 Feb. 1861, enclosed in Underwood to Seward, Washington, 23 Feb. 1861, Seward Papers, University of Rochester.

121. Thomas S. Kennedy to John J. Crittenden, Louisville, 16 Feb. 1861, Crittenden Papers, DLC.

122. Louisville *Democrat,* 24 Feb. 1861.

123. Judd to Lyman Trumbull, Buffalo, 17 Feb. 1861, Trumbull Papers, DLC; Judd to his wife Ada, Buffalo, 18 Feb. 1861, Judd Papers, IHi.

124. Garfield to B. A. Hinsdale, Columbus, 17 Feb. 1861, Garfield Papers, DLC.

125. *Ohio State Journal* (Columbus), 16 Feb. 1861.

126. Buffalo correspondence, 17 Feb., New York *Tribune,* 19 Feb. 1861.

127. Springfield (Massachusetts) *Republican,* 18, 25 Feb. 1861.

128. Albany *Evening Journal,* 21 Feb. 1861.

129. Providence *Journal,* 15 Feb. 1861.

130. Washington correspondence, 18 Feb., Chicago *Tribune,* 21 Feb. 1861.

131. Albany correspondence, 18 Feb., New York *Tribune,* 19 Feb. 1861.

132. Buffalo correspondence, 17 Feb., New York *Tribune,* 19 Feb. 1861.

133. Nicolay, "Some Incidents in Lincoln's Journey," Burlingame, ed., *Oral History of Lincoln,* 117.

134. Albany correspondence, 18 Feb., New York *World,* 21 Feb. 1861, Burlingame, ed., *Lincoln's Journalist,* 37–38.

135. New York *Daily News,* 20 Feb. 1861.

136. Albany correspondence, 18 Feb., New York *Herald,* 19 Feb. 1861; reminiscences of Andrew J. Provost, "Lincoln as He Knew Him," New York *Times,* 12 Feb. 1922, p. 73.

137. Albany correspondence, 18 Feb., New York *Times,* 19 Feb. 1861.

138. Ibid.

139. Albany *Atlas and Argus,* 20 Feb. 1861.

140. *CWL,* 4:225–226.

141. Provost, "Lincoln as He Knew Him."

142. New York *Herald,* 20 Feb. 1861.

143. Albany correspondence, 20 Feb., New York *World,* 21 Feb. 1861.

144. The Rev. Dr. Thomas Reed Rawson to his brother, Albany, 23 Feb. 1861.

145. E. R. Tinker to Henry L. Dawes, North Adams, 24 Feb. 1861, Dawes Papers, DLC.

146. Diary of Samuel J. May, entry for 19 Feb. 1861, May Papers, Cornell University.

147. Lincoln to Washburne, Cleveland, 15 Feb. 1861, *CWL,* 4:217.

148. Washington correspondence by James E. Harvey, 18 Feb., Philadelphia *North American and United States Gazette,* 19 Feb. 1861.

149. Lamon to Washburne, Philadelphia, 21 Feb. 1861, Washburne Papers, DLC.

150. Lamon, *Recollections of Lincoln,* 35.

151. Nicolay to Therena Bates, Washington, 24 Feb. 1861, Burlingame, ed., *With Lincoln in the White House,* 28.

152. *CWL,* 4:228.

153. Stephen R. Fiske, "Lincoln's Trip to the White House," *The Metropolis,* n.d, copied in the St. Louis *Globe-Democrat,* 28 July 1891; New York *Herald,* 20 Feb. 1861.

154. James R. Roche to Edward Harrick, New York, 20 Feb. 1861, Harrick Papers, New-York Historical Society.

155. Report of M. B. [Kate Warne] for Allan Pinkerton, New York, 19 Feb. *1861,* in Norma B. Cuthbert, ed., *Lincoln and the Baltimore Plot, 1861: From Pinkerton Records and Related Papers* (San Marino, CA: Huntington Library, 1949), 41; New York *Tribune,* 20 Feb. 1861.

156. William Hayes Ward, ed., *Abraham Lincoln: Tributes from His Associates, Reminiscences of Soldiers, Statesmen and Citizens* (New York: T. Y. Crowell, 1895), 1.

157. Louisa Lee Schuyler diary, Hamilton-Schuyler Papers, William L. Clements Library, University of Michigan (entry for 19 Feb. 1861); Lavinia Goodell to her sister Maria Goodell Frost, Brooklyn, 25 Feb. 1861, Goodell Papers, Berea College, in Elizabeth S. Peck, ed., "Lincoln in New York," *Lincoln Herald* 60 (1958):129.

158. Walt Whitman, "Death of Abraham Lincoln," lecture delivered in New York, 14 Apr. 1879, Whitman, *Complete Prose Works* (Philadelphia: David McKay, 1892), 308.

159. New York *Times,* 20 Feb. 1861.

160. New York *Tribune,* 20 Feb. 1861.

161. Charles Eugene Hamlin, *The Life and Times of Hannibal Hamlin* (2 vols.; Cambridge, MA: Riverside Press, 1899), 2:387–388.

162. New York correspondence, n.d., Boston *Courier,* n.d., copied in the New York *Daily News,* 5 Mar. 1861.

163. Weed to Seward, New York, 21 Feb. 1861, Seward Papers, University of Rochester.

164. Grinnell to Seward, [New York,] 20 Feb. [1861], Seward Papers, University of Rochester.

165. John Pope, "War Reminiscences, IX," *National Tribune* (Washington), 5 Feb. 1891, in Peter Cozzens and Robert I. Girardi, eds., *The Military Memoirs of General John Pope* (Chapel Hill: University of North Carolina Press, 1998), 179–180.

166. *The American Annual Cyclopaedia and Register of Important Events for the Year 1861* (New York: D. Appleton, 1864), 415.

167. Fiske, "When Lincoln Was First Inaugurated," 7.

168. *CWL,* 4:223–233.

169. New York *Times,* 21 Feb. 1861; New York *Herald,* 22 Feb. 1861; New York correspondence by B., 24 Feb., Boston *Journal,* 26 Feb. 1861.

170. New York *Herald,* 22 Feb. 1861.

171. An unidentified weekly paper, quoted in the St. Louis *Globe-Democrat,* [19 Feb. 1911?], clipping collection, LMF.

172. New York correspondence by B., 24 Feb., Boston *Journal,* 26 Feb. 1861.

173. Bronson Murray to Ward Hill Lamon, New York, 20 Feb. 1861, in Harry E. Pratt, ed., *Concerning Mr. Lincoln, in Which Abraham Lincoln Is Pictured As He Appeared to Letter Writers of His Time* (Springfield, IL: Abraham Lincoln Association, 1944), 54.

174. George C. Shepard to Mr. and Mrs. Lucius M. Boltwood, New York, 21 Feb. 1861, in Pratt, ed., *Concerning Mr. Lincoln,* 56.

175. Philadelphia *Inquirer,* 21 Feb. 1861.

176. Horace Randal to "My dear Captain," New York, 20 Feb. 1861, Schoff Civil War Collection, William L. Clements Library, University of Michigan.

177. Philadelphia *Press,* 22 Feb. 1861.

178. *CWL,* 4:237; Philadelphia correspondence, 21 Feb., New York *World,* 25 Feb. 1861,

Burlingame, ed., *Lincoln's Journalist,* 40; Philadelphia *Press,* 22 Feb. 1861.

179. Undated clipping from the San Francisco *Chronicle,* LMF.

180. New York *Herald,* 22 Feb. 1861.

181. Philadelphia correspondence, 21 Feb., New York *World,* 25 Feb. 1861, Burlingame, ed., *Lincoln's Journalist,* 40.

182. *CWL,* 4:235–236.

183. Ibid., 4:238; Trenton correspondence, 22 Feb., New York *World,* 25 Feb. 1861.

184. Oliver Wendell Holmes, *Grandmother's Story and Other Poems* (Boston: Houghton Mifflin, 1892), 89.

185. Pinkerton to Herndon, Philadelphia, 25 Aug. 1866, *HI,* 312.

186. Memorandum by Stone, 21 Feb. 1861, AL MSS DLC.

187. Frederick Seward, *Reminiscences of a War-Time Statesman and Diplomat, 1830–1915* (New York: G. P. Putnam's Sons, 1916), 137.

188. George W. Hazzard to Lincoln, [Feb. 1861?], AL MSS DLC.

189. Thomas Cadwallerder to Lincoln, Baltimore, 31 Dec. 1860, ibid.

190. "A Lady" to Lincoln, n.p., [Feb. 1861], ibid.

191. Judd interviewed by Herndon, [Nov. 1866], *HI,* 433.

192. Isaac N. Arnold, *The History of Abraham Lincoln, and the Overthrow of Slavery* (Chicago: Clarke, 1866), 171.

193. Washington correspondence, 25 Feb., Cincinnati *Gazette,* n.d., copied in the *Illinois State Register* (Springfield), 28 Feb. 1861; Washington correspondence by Van [D. W. Bartlett], 27 Feb., Springfield (Massachusetts) *Republican,* 1 Mar. 1861.

194. *CWL,* 4:240.

195. Philadelphia *Daily Evening Bulletin,* 22 Feb. 1861; Philadelphia *Press,* 22 Feb. 1861.

196. Harrisburg correspondence, 23 Feb., New York *Times,* 25 Feb. 1861.

197. Philadelphia *Morning Pennsylvanian,* 25 Feb., 4 Mar. 1861.

198. Du Pont to William Whetten, Philadelphia, 1 Mar. 1861, John D. Hayes, ed., *Samuel Francis Du Pont: A Selection from His*

Civil War Letters (3 vols.; Ithaca, NY: Cornell University Press, 1969), 1:38–39.

199. Pinkerton to William H. Herndon, Philadelphia, 23 Aug. 1866, *HI*, 322.

200. A. K. McClure to Alonzo Rothschild, Philadelphia, 9 May 1907, Lincoln Contemporaries Collection, LMF.

201. Harrisburg correspondence, 22 Feb., New York *World*, 23 Feb. 1861, Burlingame, ed., *Lincoln's Journalist*, 41–42.

202. *CWL*, 4:243.

203. Harrisburg correspondence, 22 Feb., Philadelphia *Inquirer*, 23 Feb. 1861.

204. Judd to Pinkerton, Chicago, 3 Nov. 1867, in Allan Pinkerton, *History and Evidence of the Passage of Abraham Lincoln from Harrisburg, Pa., to Washington, D.C.* (New York: Rode & Brand, 1907), 22.

205. *HI*, 434, 286; Washburne to his wife, Sunday morning [24 Feb. 1861], Washburn Family Papers, Washburn Memorial Library, Norlands, Maine; Washburne in Allen Thorndike Rice, ed., *Reminiscences of Abraham Lincoln by Distinguished Men of His Time* (New York: North American Review, 1888), 38.

206. Pinkerton report, 23 Feb. 1861, in *HI*, 287.

207. Ibid., 292.

208. New York *Daily News*, 26, 28 Feb. 1861.

209. Harrisburg correspondence, 23 Feb., New York *Times*, 24 Feb. 1861.

210. Hale to his wife, Washington, 24 Feb. 1861, Hale Papers, New Hampshire Historical Society.

211. Samuel R. Curtis, manuscript journal, 23 Feb. 1861, IHi.

212. Dawes, "Mr. Lincoln's Arrival in Washington," undated manuscript, Dawes Papers, DLC.

213. Philadelphia correspondence by "Rittenhouse," 25 Feb., Washington *States and Union*, 27 Feb. 1861; Philadelphia *Morning Pennsylvanian*, 25 Feb. 1861.

214. Nevins and Thomas, eds., *Strong Diary*, 3:102 (entry for 23 Feb. 1861).

215. Washington correspondence, n.d., Louisville *Journal*, n.d., in the Washington *States and Union*, 4 Mar. 1861.

216. Gayle Thornbrough, ed., *The Diary of Calvin Fletcher* (7 vols.; Indianapolis: Indiana Historical Society, 1972–1981), 7:54 (entry for 25 Feb. 1861).

217. New York *World*, 25 Feb. 1861.

218. Dispatch from the train between Harrisburg and Baltimore, 23 Feb., New York *Herald*, 24 Feb. 1861.

219. Austin Blair to Zachariah Chandler, Jefferson, Ohio, 27 Feb. 1861, Chandler Papers, DLC.

220. *Illinois State Register* (Springfield), 25 Feb. 1861.

221. James Marsh to Elihu B. Washburne, Rockford, 27 Feb. 1861, Washburne Papers, DLC.

222. Washington correspondence, 25 Feb., Cincinnati *Enquirer*, n.d., copied in the *Illinois State Register* (Springfield), 28 Feb. 1861.

223. Cincinnati *Gazette*, 26 Feb. 1861.

224. John B. Dillon to Henry S. Lane, Indianapolis, 1 Mar. 1861, Lane Papers, InU.

225. Washington correspondence by Forney, 25 Feb., Philadelphia *Press*, 26 Feb. 1861.

226. Baltimore *American*, n.d., copied in the Providence *Journal*, 28 Feb. 1861.

Chapter 20. "I Am Now Going to Be Master"

1. Henry Adams, *The Education of Henry Adams: An Autobiography* (Boston: Houghton Mifflin, 1918), 99.

2. Washington correspondence by Sigma, 16 July, Cincinnati *Commercial*, 20 July 1861.

3. Washington correspondence, 24 Feb., Philadelphia *Press*, 25 Feb. 1861.

4. Ida M. Tarbell, *The Life of Abraham Lincoln* (2 vols.; New York: McClure, Phillips, 1900), 1:423.

5. Washington correspondence, 2 Mar., New York *World*, 5 Mar. 1861, Michael Burlingame, ed., *Lincoln's Journalist: John Hay's Anonymous Writings for the Press, 1860–1864* (Carbondale: Southern Illinois University Press, 1998), 51.

6. John Pope, "War Reminiscences, IX," *National Tribune* (Washington), 5 Feb. 1891, in

Peter Cozzens and Robert I. Girardi, eds., *The Military Memoirs of General John Pope* (Chapel Hill: University of North Carolina Press, 1998), 181.

7. Washington correspondence, n.d., Baltimore *Sun*, n.d., copied in the *Missouri Democrat* (St. Louis), 28 Feb. 1861.

8. Washington correspondence, 27 Feb., Cincinnati *Gazette*, 28 Feb. 1861.

9. Baltimore *Exchange*, 25 Feb. 1861.

10. Lucius E. Chittenden, *Recollections of President Lincoln and His Administration* (New York: Harper & Brothers, 1891), 71.

11. W. C. Rives to W. C. Rives, Jr., Washington, 24 Feb. 1861, Rives Papers, DLC; C. to the editor, Washington, 19 May, New York *Times*, 2 June 1862.

12. Washington correspondence, 23 Feb., New York *World*, 25 Feb. 1861

13. Washington correspondence by "our special correspondent" (Uriah Painter), n.d., Philadelphia *Inquirer*, 25 Feb. 1861.

14. Washington correspondence 24 Feb., New York *Herald*, 25 Feb. 1861.

15. Goodrich to John A. Andrew, Washington, 23 Feb. 1861, Andrew Papers, MHi.

16. Wilder Dwight to Horace Gray, Washington, 27 Feb. 1861, Gray Papers, DLC.

17. Chittenden, *Recollections of Lincoln*, 74–75.

18. Samuel F. Vinton to Robert C. Winthrop, Washington, 1 Mar. 1861, Winthrop Autograph Collection, MHi.

19. W. H. L. Wallace to Ann Wallace, Washington, 27 Feb. 1861, Wallace-Dickey Papers, IHi.

20. Palmer, *Personal Recollections of John M. Palmer: The Story of an Earnest Life* (Cincinnati: Clarke, 1901), 84.

21. Washington correspondence, 25 Feb., Philadelphia *Press*, 26 Feb. 1861.

22. George S. Boutwell, *Reminiscences of Sixty Years in Public Affairs* (2 vols.; New York: McClure, Phillips, 1902), 1:274.

23. Washington correspondence, 27 Feb., Philadelphia *Press*, 28 Feb. 1861.

24. A special dispatch, n.d., to the New York *Express*, n.d., copied in the Richmond *Enquirer*, 16 Mar. 1861.

25. Charles S. Morehead, speech delivered in Liverpool, England, on 9 Oct. 1862, Liverpool *Mercury*, 13 Oct. 1862, excerpted in David Rankin Barbee and Milledge L. Bonham, Jr., eds., "Fort Sumter Again," *Mississippi Valley Historical Review* 28 (1941):71–72; Morehead to Crittenden, Staten Island, New York, 23 Feb. 1862, in Mrs. Chapman Coleman, *The Life of John J. Crittenden* (2 vols.; Philadelphia: J. B. Lippincott, 1871), 2:337.

26. Michael Burlingame and John R. Turner Ettlinger, eds., *Inside Lincoln's White House: The Complete Civil War Diary of John Hay* (Carbondale: Southern Illinois University Press, 1997), 28 (entry for 22 Oct. 1861).

27. Washington *Evening Star*, 28 Feb. 1861.

28. Washington correspondence, 27 Feb., New York *Herald*, 28 Feb. 1861.

29. A. R. Boteler, "Mr. Lincoln and the Force Bill," *The Annals of the War Written by Leading Participants North and South*, comp. A. K. McClure (Philadelphia: Times, 1879), 223–226.

30. Henry L. Dawes, "Washington the Winter before the War," *Atlantic Monthly* 72 (1893):166.

31. Washington correspondence, 26 Feb., *Missouri Democrat* (St. Louis), 2 Mar. 1861.

32. Washington correspondence by S., 26 Feb., Chicago *Tribune*, 1 Mar. 1861.

33. Alexander Doniphan to John Doniphan, Washington, 22 Feb. 1861, in Roger D. Launius, *Alexander William Doniphan: Portrait of a Missouri Moderate* (Columbia: University of Missouri Press, 1997), 248.

34. Charles Francis Adams, Jr., undated diary entry in Charles Francis Adams, Jr., *Charles Francis Adams, 1835–1915: An Autobiography* (Boston: Houghton Mifflin, 1916), 78.

35. Orville H. Browning to Lincoln, Springfield, 17 Feb. 1861, AL MSS DLC.

36. Seward to Lincoln, [Washington], 24 Feb. 1861, Seward Papers, University of Rochester.

37. Charles Dickens, *The Personal History of David Copperfield*, ed. Trevor Blount (Harmondsworth: Penguin, 1966), 436.

38. By far the best analysis of the evolution of the first inaugural is Douglas L. Wilson's characteristically thoughtful discussion in *Lincoln's Sword: The Presidency and the Power of Words* (New York: Alfred A. Knopf, 2006), 42–70.

39. Logan, statement to a meeting of the Springfield bar, 15 Apr. 1865, quoted in Charles S. Zane, "Lincoln as I Knew Him," *Sunset: The Pacific Monthly* 29 (1912): 434.

40. Adams, "Great Secession Winter of 1860–1861," *Proceedings of the Massachusetts Historical Society* 43 (1909–1910): 683.

41. Washington correspondence, 28 Feb., New York *Tribune,* 1 Mar. 1861.

42. John A. Bingham, "Abraham Lincoln," speech delivered at Cadiz, Ohio, 15 Apr. 1886, *The Current* (Chicago), 24 Apr. 1886, 282.

43. Charles Francis Adams, Jr., to Albert L. Bacheller, Boston, 20 Jan. 1896, Wyles Collection, University of California at Santa Barbara; Adams, *Autobiography,* 96; Adams's address to the Massachusetts Historical Society, Feb. 1909, *Proceedings of the Massachusetts Historical Society* 42 (1908–1909): 147–148.

44. William H. Bailhache to his wife, Washington, 3 Mar. 1861, Lincoln Collection, InU.

45. Rock Island *Argus,* n.d., copied in the *Illinois State Register* (Springfield), 22 Mar. 1861.

46. Alexander Hagner, *A Personal Narrative of the Acquaintance of My Father and Myself with Each of the Presidents of the United States* (Washington, DC: W. F. Roberts, 1915), 46.

47. Lincoln to Curtin, Springfield, 21 Dec. 1860, Roy P. Basler et al., eds., *Collected Works of Abraham Lincoln* [hereafter *CWL*] (8 vols. plus index; New Brunswick, NJ: Rutgers University Press, 1953–1955), 4:158.

48. Henry Winter Davis to Samuel Francis Du Pont, [Washington], [Feb. or Mar. 1861], transcript, S. F. Du Pont Papers, Hagley Museum, Wilmington, Delaware.

49. Milliken to Cameron, Philadelphia, 22 Feb. 1861, Cameron Papers, DLC.

50. William M. Reynolds to Edward McPherson, Springfield, 21 Jan. 1861, McPherson Papers, DLC; William Larimer, Jr., to Cameron, Pittsburgh, 6 Feb. 1861, Cameron Papers, DLC.

51. John Covode to Lincoln, Washington, 16 Jan. 1861, AL MSS DLC.

52. Robert McKnight to Lincoln, Washington, 29 Dec. 1860, ibid.

53. Andrew G. Curtin to Alexander K. McClure, Bellefonte, 2 Jan. 1861, telegram, ibid.

54. Thaddeus Stevens to Simon Stevens, Washington, 10 Feb. 1861, Beverly Wilson Palmer, ed., *The Selected Papers of Thaddeus Stevens* (2 vols.; Pittsburgh: University of Pittsburgh Press, 1997–1998), 1:207.

55. Swett to Lincoln, Washington, 8 Jan. 1861, AL MSS DLC.

56. Washington correspondence, 26 Feb., New York *World,* 28 Feb. 1861, Burlingame, ed., *Lincoln's Journalist,* 45.

57. Stevens to Washburne, Washington, 19 Jan. 1861, AL MSS DLC; Stevens to Chase, Washington, 3 Feb. 1861, Chase Papers, Historical Society of Pennsylvania.

58. Samuel W. McCall, *Thaddeus Stevens* (Boston: Houghton Mifflin, 1899), 311–312.

59. Cameron interviewed by Nicolay, 20 Feb. 1875, Michael Burlingame, ed., *An Oral History of Abraham Lincoln: John G. Nicolay's Interviews and Essays* (Carbondale: Southern Illinois University Press, 1996), 42.

60. Jesse W. Weik, *The Real Lincoln: A Portrait,* ed. Michael Burlingame (1922; Lincoln: University of Nebraska Press, 2002), 226.

61. J. K. Moorhead, interviewed by John G. Nicolay, Washington, 12 and 13 May 1880, Burlingame, ed., *Oral History of Lincoln,* 41.

62. James C. Conkling to the editor, Springfield, 4 Oct., Chicago *Tribune*, 8 Oct. 1879.

63. Blair to Gideon Welles, Washington, 22 Jan. 1874, Lincoln Collection, Yale University.

64. Lincoln to Colfax, Washington, 8 Mar. 1861, *CWL*, 4:278.

65. Howard K. Beale and Alan W. Brownsword, eds., *Diary of Gideon Welles, Secretary of the Navy under Lincoln and Johnson* (3 vols.; New York: W.W. Norton, 1960), 1:481 (entry for Dec. 1863).

66. Frank Blair to Montgomery Blair, St. Louis, n.d. [13 Dec. 1860], Blair-Lee Family Papers, Princeton University.

67. New York *Herald*, n.d., clipping in notebook, Gideon Welles Papers, Connecticut Historical Society; Charles A. Dana, *Recollections of the Civil War: With the Leaders at Washington and in the Field in the Sixties* (New York: D. Appleton, 1898), 170; Washington correspondence by Noah Brooks, 2 May, Sacramento *Daily Union*, 27 May 1863, in Michael Burlingame, ed., *Lincoln Observed: Civil War Dispatches of Noah Brooks* (Baltimore, MD: Johns Hopkins University Press, 1998), 48.

68. Washington correspondence, 2 May, Sacramento *Daily Union*, 27 May 1863, in Burlingame, ed., *Lincoln Observed*, 49; Noah Brooks to George Witherle, Washington, 23 Dec. 1863, ibid., 97–98.

69. William H. Russell, *My Diary North and South* (Boston: T.O.H.P. Burnham, 1863), 24 (entry for 28 Mar. 1861).

70. William M. Gwin, "Gwin and Seward: A Secret Chapter in Ante-Bellum History," *Overland Monthly*, 1891, 469.

71. Goodrich to John A. Andrew, Washington, 25 Feb. 1861, Andrew Papers, MHi.

72. Greeley to Beman Brockway, New York, 12 Mar. 1861, Greeley Papers, DLC.

73. Elizabeth Keckley, *Behind the Scenes; or, Thirty Years a Slave and Four Years in the White House* (New York: G. W. Carleton, 1868), 128.

74. Washington correspondence, 28 Feb. and 3 Mar., New York *Times*, 1 and 4 Mar. 1861.

75. Washington correspondence, 3 Mar., Philadelphia *Inquirer*, 4 Mar. 1861.

76. Mark Howard to Gideon Welles, Washington, 25 Feb. 1861, Welles Papers, IHi.

77. Washington correspondence by Sigma, 4 Mar., Cincinnati *Commercial*, 6 Mar. 1861.

78. Washington correspondence by John Hay, 26 Feb., New York *World*, 28 Feb. 1861, Burlingame, ed., *Lincoln's Journalist*, 46.

79. Greeley to Beman Brockway, Washington, 28 Feb. 1861, Greeley Papers, DLC.

80. Frederick W. Seward, *William H. Seward: An Autobiography from 1801 to 1834 with a Memoir of His Life and Selections from His Letters* (3 vols.; New York: Derby and Miller, 1891), 2:511.

81. Charles Francis Adams diary, 28 Feb. 1861, Adams Family Papers, MHi.

82. Beale, ed., *Welles Diary*, 2:391–392 (entry for 3 Dec. 1865).

83. Seward to Lincoln, Washington, 2 Mar. 1861, AL MSS DLC.

84. Reply to Mayor James G. Berret at Washington, DC, 27 Feb. 1861, *CWL*, 4:246–247.

85. Norman B. Judd, interviewed by John G. Nicolay, Washington, 28 Feb. 1876, Burlingame, ed., *Oral History of Lincoln*, 47.

86. F. B. Sanborn, *Recollections of Seventy Years* (2 vols.; Boston: R. G. Badger, 1909), 1:26–27.

87. *CWL*, 4:273.

88. John Bigelow diary, 27 Mar. 1861, New York Public Library.

89. Seward to his wife, Washington, 8 Mar. 1861, Seward, *William H. Seward*, 2:518.

90. J. W. Schuckers, *The Life and Public Services of Salmon Portland Chase* (New York: D. Appleton, 1874), 207; Charles Francis Adams diary, 5 Mar. 1861, Adams Family Papers, MHi.

91. James G. Blaine, *Twenty Years of Congress: From Lincoln to Garfield* (2 vols.; Norwich, CT: Henry Bill, 1884–1886), 1:286.

92. Louisville *Journal*, n.d., copied in the *Ohio State Journal* (Columbus), 11 Mar. 1861.

93. New York *Herald*, 28 June 1858.

94. Reminiscences of George B. Loring, New York *Tribune*, 9 Aug. 1885.

95. Washington *National Intelligencer,* 5 Mar. 1861.

96. Washington correspondence, 4 Mar., *Missouri Democrat* (St. Louis), 9 Mar. 1861.

97. Hay, "The Heroic Age in Washington," in Michael Burlingame, ed., *At Lincoln's Side: John Hay's Civil War Correspondence and Selected Writings* (Carbondale: Southern Illinois University Press, 2000), 119.

98. Charles Francis Adams diary, 4 Mar. 1861, Adams Family Papers, MHi.

99. Cincinnati *Commercial,* 11 Mar. 1861.

100. Montgomery Meigs to his brother, John F. Meigs, Washington, 4 Mar. 1861, Meigs Papers, DLC.

101. John Z. Goodrich to John A. Andrew, Washington, 4 Mar. 1861, Andrew Papers, MHi.

102. Washington correspondence, 4 Mar., New York *Times,* 5 Mar. 1861; New York *Commercial* Advertiser, 7 Mar. 1861; Washington *National Intelligencer,* 5 Mar. 1861; Gustave Koerner to his daughter Sophie, Washington, 4 Mar. 1861, in Thomas J. McCormack, ed., *Memoirs of Gustave Koerner, 1809–1896* (2 vols.; Cedar Rapids, IA: Torch Press, 1909), 2:118; Washington correspondence by J. Teasdale, editor of the *Iowa State Register,* 4 Mar., *Iowa State Register* (Des Moines), 20 Mar. 1861; *The Liberator* (Boston), 8 Mar. 1861; Edwin Greble to Mrs. Susan V. Greble, Baltimore, 4 Mar. 1861, Edwin Greble Papers, DLC.

103. Dodge to his wife Annie, Washington, 4 Mar. 1861, typescript in "Data Chronologically arranged for ready reference in preparation of a Biography of Grenville Mellen Dodge," Dodge Papers, Iowa State Archives, Des Moines.

104. Manuscript reminiscences of John Caldwell Tidball, 124–127, DLC; Washington correspondence by Weed, 4 Mar., Albany *Evening Journal,* 6 Mar. 1861.

105. Washington correspondence, 6 Mar., Springfield (Massachusetts) *Republican,* 10 Mar. 1861.

106. Washington correspondence, 5 Mar., New York *Commercial Advertiser,* 7 Mar. 1861.

107. Washington *National Republican,* 5 Mar. 1861.

108. Washington correspondence, 4 Mar., New York *Times,* 5 Mar. 1861; Koerner, *Memoirs,* 2:118; Washington correspondence, 6 Mar., Springfield (Massachusetts) *Republican,* 10 Mar. 1861.

109. *Congressional Globe,* 37th Congress, Special Senate Session, 1436–1439 (6 Mar. 1861).

110. Stanton to Buchanan, Washington, 12 Mar. 1861, Buchanan Papers, Historical Society of Pennsylvania.

111. *Frank Leslie's Illustrated Newspaper,* 23 Mar. 1861; New York *Herald,* 6 Mar. 1861.

112. Fiske, "When Lincoln Was First Inaugurated," 8; [Mary Abigail Dodge], *Gail Hamilton's Life in Letters* (2 vols.; Boston: Lee and Shepard, 1901), 1:314.

113. George A. Sala, Washington correspondence, n.d., London *Telegraph,* n.d., copied in the *Ohio State Journal* (Columbus), 2 Apr. 1864.

114. Charles Francis Adams diary, 4 Mar. 1861, Adams Family Papers, MHi.

115. New York *Herald,* 6 Mar. 1861.

116. A. Oakey Hall, "The Great Lincoln Inauguration," *Frank Leslie's Popular Monthly* 43 (Mar. 1897): 259.

117. Fiske, "When Lincoln Was First Inaugurated," 8.

118. New York correspondence, 5 Mar., Washington *States and Union,* 6 Mar. 1861.

119. Isaac Sherman to Francis P. Blair, Sr., New York, 8 Mar. 1861, Blair-Lee Family Papers, Princeton University.

120. Montgomery correspondence, 7 Mar., Baltimore *American,* 12 Mar. 1861.

121. Benjamin Brown French, *Witness to the Young Republic: A Yankee's Journal, 1828–1870,* ed. Donald B. Cole and John J. McDonough (Hanover, NH: University Press of New England, 1989), 348 (entry for 6 Mar. 1861).

122. Ryland Fletcher to [Joseph] Barrett, Proctorsville, 9 Mar. 1861, Lincoln Collection, RPB.

123. Providence *Journal,* 5 Mar. 1861.

124. Justin S. Morrill to his wife, Washington, 5 Mar. 1861, Morrill Papers, DLC.

125. Albany *Evening Journal,* 5 Mar. 1861.

126. Samuel R. Curtis journal, 4 Mar. 1861, IHi.

127. New York *Tribune*, 5, 6 Mar. 1861.

128. New York *Times*, 5, 6 Mar. 1861.

129. Boston *Atlas and Bee*, 5 Mar. 1861.

130. Philadelphia correspondence, n.d., *National Anti-Slavery Standard*, (New York), 9 Mar. 1861.

131. Jersey City *American Standard*, 5 Mar. 1861, Howard Cecil Perkins, ed., *Northern Editorials on Secession* (2 vols.; New York: D. Appleton-Century, 1942), 1:625–626.

132. J. C. Welling to Charles Sumner, n.p., [5 Mar. 1861?], Sumner Papers, Harvard University.

133. Vallandigham, *The Record of Hon. C. L. Vallandigham on Abolitionism, the Union, and the Civil War* (6th ed.; Columbus, OH: J. Walter, 1863), 99.

134. Allan Nevins and Milton Halsey Thomas, eds., *Diary of George Templeton Strong, 1835–1875* (4 vols.; New York: Macmillan, 1952), 3:106 (entry for 5 Mar. 1861).

135. New York *Daily News*, 5 Mar. 1861.

136. H. D. Faulkner to Lincoln, New York, 5 Mar. 1861, AL MSS DLC.

137. *Frank Leslie's Illustrated Newspaper*, 16 Mar. 1861.

138. Charles Francis Adams, Jr., diary entry for 4 Mar. 1861, Adams Family Papers, MHi.

139. Edward Everett journal, 4 Mar. 1861, Everett Papers, MHi.

140. Washington correspondence, 5 Mar., Charleston *Mercury*, 9 Mar. 1861.

141. Charleston *Mercury*, 5 Mar. 1861.

142. Washington *States and Union*, 21 Mar. 1861.

143. Wigfall to F. W. Pickens, Washington, 4 Mar. 1861, *Official Records of the War of the Rebellion*, I, 1:261 (hereafter *OR*).

144. John A. Campbell to his mother, Washington, 6 Mar. 1861, Campbell Papers, Alabama State Archives, copy, Doubleday-Catton Collection, DLC.

145. Lucius Quinton Washington to L. Pope Walker, Washington, 5 Mar. 1861, *OR*, I, 1:263.

146. *National Anti-Slavery Standard* (New York), 9 Mar. 1861; Oliver Johnson to J. Miller McKim, [New York], 28 Mar. 1861, Samuel J. May Anti-Slavery Manuscript Collection, Cornell University.

147. *Douglass' Monthly* 3 (Apr. 1861):475.

148. Lydia Maria Child to John Greenleaf Whittier, Wayland, Massachusetts, 21 Jan. 1862, Child Papers, DLC.

149. *The Liberator* (Boston), 8 Mar. 1861; diary of Samuel J. May, 4 Mar. 1861, May Papers, Cornell University.

150. Wright to Chase, n.p., 7 Mar. 1861, Mary Scrugham, *The Peaceable Americans of 1860–1861: A Study in Public Opinion* (New York: Columbia University Press, 1921), 88.

151. Oliver Johnson to J. Miller McKim, New York, 7 Mar. 1861, Samuel J. May Anti-Slavery Manuscript Collection, Cornell University.

152. London *Times*, 19 Mar. 1861.

153. London *Punch*, 30 Mar. 1861, in Herbert Mitgang, ed., *Abraham Lincoln, A Press Portrait: His Life and Times from the Original Newspaper Documents of the Union, the Confederacy, and Europe* (Chicago: Quadrangle Books, 1971), 249.

154. Paris *La Patrie*, 29 Mar. 1861, ibid., 249.

155. George S. Converse to S. S. Cox, Columbus, 5 Mar. 1861, Cox Papers, RPB.

156. *Illinois State Register* (Springfield), 6 Mar. 1861.

157. *Congressional Globe*, 37th Congress, Special Senate Session, 1439 (6 Mar. 1861).

158. John E. Wool to Sarah Wool, Washington, 5 Mar. 1861, Wool Papers, New York State Library.

159. Washington correspondence, 4 Mar., Alexandria, Virginia, *Gazette*, 5 Mar. 1861.

160. Robert Y. Conrad to E. P. W. Conrad, Richmond, 6 Mar. 1861, "The Break-Up of a Nation: Robert Y. Conrad's Letters at the Virginia Secession Convention," *Winchester-Frederick Historical Society Journal* 8 (1994–1995):4

161. James C. Taylor to Stephen A. Douglas, Christiansburg, Virginia, 18 Mar. 1861, Douglas Papers, University of Chicago.

162. Baltimore *Sun,* 5, 6 Mar. 1861.

163. Washington correspondence by J. Teasdale, editor of the *Iowa State Register,* 4 March, *Iowa State Register* (Des Moines), 20 Mar. 1861.

164. *Missouri Republican* (St. Louis), n.d., copied in *Illinois State Journal* (Springfield), 7 Mar. 1861.

165. Baltimore correspondence, 4 Mar., Cincinnati *Gazette,* n.d., copied in the *Illinois State Journal* (Springfield), 7 Mar. 1861.

166. John Pendleton Kennedy journal, 4, 5 Mar. 1861, and Kennedy to George S. Bryan, Baltimore, 15 Mar. 1861, letterpress copy, Kennedy Papers, Enoch Pratt Free Library, Baltimore; Kennedy to [Abram] Comingo, Baltimore, 9 Mar. 1861, Civil War Papers, Maryland Historical Society.

167. Baltimore *American,* 5 Mar. 1861.

168. Baltimore *Clipper,* 9 Mar. 1861.

169. Gilmer to Stephen A. Douglas, Greensboro, 8 Mar. 1861, Douglas Papers, University of Chicago.

170. Raleigh *Standard,* 9 Mar., copied in the New York *Daily News,* 12 Mar. 1861.

171. Worth to his brother, Asheboro, 16 Mar. 1861, in Joseph Grégoire de Roulhac Hamilton, ed., *The Correspondence of Jonathan Worth* (2 vols; Raleigh: Edwards & Broughton, 1909), 1:134.

172. Nashville *Republican Banner,* 6 Mar. 1861.

173. Knoxville *Whig,* 9 Mar., copied in the *Missouri Democrat* (St. Louis), 16 Mar. 1861.

174. Washington *Daily Globe,* 6 Mar. 1861.

175. Washington correspondence by Ben: Perley Poore, 4, 5 Mar., Boston *Journal,* 5 Mar. 1861.

176. Louisville *Democrat,* 6 Mar. 1861.

177. Mobile *Register,* n.d., quoted in the Louisville *Democrat,* 12 Mar. 1861.

178. Henry Winter Davis to Samuel Francis Du Pont, [Washington], 20 Mar. 1861, transcript, S. F. Du Pont Papers, Hagley Museum, Wilmington, Delaware.

179. Washington correspondence, 4 Mar., New York *Times,* 5 Mar. 1861.

180. Thomas A. R. Nelson to W. G. Brownlow, Jonesboro, Tennessee, 13 Mar. 1861, Knoxville *Tri-Weekly Whig,* 16 Mar. 1861.

181. Message to Congress, 4 July 1861, *CWL,* 4:424.

Chapter 21. "A Man So Busy Letting Rooms in One End of His House"

1. Memorandum by John G. Nicolay, 3 July 1861, in Michael Burlingame, ed., *With Lincoln in the White House: Letters, Memoranda, and Other Writings of John G. Nicolay, 1860–1865* (Carbondale: Southern Illinois University Press, 2000), 46.

2. Henry J. Raymond, *The Life and Public Services of Abraham Lincoln* (New York: Derby and Miller, 1865), 720.

3. Francis B. Carpenter, *Six Months at the White House with Abraham Lincoln: The Story of a Picture* (New York: Hurd and Houghton, 1867), 276.

4. Robert Wilson to William H. Herndon, Sterling, Illinois, 10 Feb. 1866, Douglas L. Wilson and Rodney O. Davis, eds., *Herndon's Informants: Letters, Interviews, and Statements about Abraham Lincoln* [hereafter *HI*](Urbana: University of Illinois Press, 1998), 207.

5. Columbus *Ohio Statesman,* 8 Nov. 1860.

6. Charles E. Stuart to Jacob Thompson, Kalamazoo, 30 Apr. 1857, quoted in David Edward Meerse, "James Buchanan, the Patronage, and the Northern Democratic Party, 1857–1858" (Ph.D. dissertation, University of Illinois, 1969), 44–45.

7. Muriel Bernitt, ed., "Two Manuscripts of Gideon Welles," *New England Quarterly* 11 (1938):594.

8. Washington correspondence by Sigma, 7 Mar., Cincinnati *Commercial,* 8 Mar. 1861.

9. Hanscom quoted in Ben: Perley Poore, "Recollections of Abraham Lincoln," in James Parton, ed., *Some Noted Princes, Authors, and Statesmen of Our Time* (Norwich, CT: Henry Bill, 1886), 352.

10. Washington correspondence by Sigma, 8 Mar., Cincinnati *Commercial,* 9 Mar. 1861.

11. Seward to his wife, Washington, 16 Mar. 1861, Frederick W. Seward, *William H. Seward: An Autobiography from 1801 to 1834 with a Memoir of His Life and Selections from His Letters* (3 vols.; New York: Derby and Miller, 1891), 2:530.

12. Schuyler Colfax to his mother, Washington, n.d. [mid-Mar. 1861], O. J. Hollister, *Life of Schuyler Colfax* (New York: Funk & Wagnalls, 1886), 173.

13. *Frank Leslie's Illustrated Newspaper,* 6 Apr. 1861.

14. John Hay to William Leete Stone, Washington, 15 Mar. 1861, Michael Burlingame, ed., *At Lincoln's Side: John Hay's Civil War Correspondence and Selected Writings* (Carbondale: Southern Illinois University Press, 2000), 5.

15. Nicolay to Therena Bates, Washington, 24 Mar. 1861, Burlingame, ed., *With Lincoln in the White House,* 31.

16. "White House Sketches, No. 13," New York *Citizen,* 24 Nov. 1866, in William O. Stoddard, *Inside the White House in War-Times: Memoirs and Reports of Lincoln's Secretary,* ed. Michael Burlingame (1890; Lincoln: University of Nebraska Press, 2000), 199.

17. John Hay, "The Heroic Age in Washington," lecture of 1871, in Burlingame, ed., *At Lincoln's Side,* 126.

18. Washington correspondence by Van [D. W. Bartlett], 21 Jan., Springfield (Massachusetts) *Republican,* 24 Jan. 1863.

19. Washington correspondence, 12, 22 Mar., Cincinnati *Gazette,* 13, 25 Mar. 1861.

20. "A Disappointed Office-seeker Discourseth to his Brothers," Washington, 20 Mar., New York *Evening Post,* 26 Mar. 1861.

21. Schurz to his wife, Alton, 25 July 1860, in Frederic Bancroft, ed., *Speeches, Correspondence and Political Papers of Carl Schurz* (6 vols.; New York: G. P. Putnam's Sons, 1913), 1:120.

22. Washington correspondence, 18 Mar., New York *Tribune,* 19 Mar. 1861.

23. John Hay, "The Heroic Age in Washington," Burlingame, ed., *At Lincoln's Side,* 125.

24. Herndon, "Lincoln's Individuality," Emanuel Hertz, ed., *The Hidden Lincoln: From the Letters and Papers of William H. Herndon* (New York: Viking, 1938), 418.

25. Henry Clay Whitney, *Life on the Circuit with Lincoln,* ed. Paul M. Angle (1892; Caldwell, ID: Caxton, 1940), 438–439.

26. Washington correspondence, 18 Mar., New York *Tribune,* 19 Mar. 1861.

27. Washington correspondence by Sigma, 14 Mar., Cincinnati *Commercial,* 15 Mar. 1861.

28. Washington correspondence, 24 Mar., Philadelphia *Press,* 25 Mar. 1861.

29. Hawkins Taylor to William Butler, Washington, 22 Mar. 1861, O. M. Hatch Papers, IHi.

30. Fessenden to Elizabeth Warriner, Washington, 17 Mar. 1861, Fessenden Papers, Bowdoin College.

31. Henry Villard, *Memoirs of Henry Villard, Journalist and Financier: 1838–1900* (2 vols.; Boston: Houghton Mifflin, 1904), 1:156.

32. Helen Nicolay, *Personal Traits of Abraham Lincoln* (New York: Century, 1912), 259.

33. New York *Times,* 4 Apr. 1861.

34. Washington correspondence, 18 Mar., New York *Herald,* 19 Mar. 1861.

35. *Congressional Globe,* 37th Congress, Special Senate Session, 1496 (23 Mar. 1861).

36. Orville H. Browning to Lincoln, Quincy, Illinois, 26 Mar. 1861, AL MSS DLC.

37. William O. Stoddard, "White House Sketches, No. 2," New York *Citizen,* 25 Aug. 1866, in Stoddard, *Inside the White House,* ed. Burlingame, 151, 57; Robert Colby to Lincoln, New York, 18 May 1861, AL MSS DLC; Washington correspondence by Noah Brooks, 7 Nov., Sacramento *Daily Union,* 4 Dec. 1863, in Michael Burlingame, ed., *Lincoln Observed: Civil War Dispatches of Noah Brooks* (Baltimore, MD: Johns Hopkins University Press, 1998), 83.

38. John Russell Young, "Lincoln as He Was," Pittsburgh *Dispatch,* 23 Aug. 1891.

39. Stoddard, "White House Sketches, No. 2," New York *Citizen,* 25 Aug. 1866, in

Stoddard, *Inside the White House,* ed. Burlingame, 151, 57.

40. William H. Osborn to N. P. Banks, New York, 26 Dec. 1863, Banks Papers, DLC.

41. John W. Starr, "Lincoln and the Office Seekers," typescript dated 1936, addenda, p. 6, Lincoln files, "Patronage" folder, Lincoln Memorial University, Harrogate, Tennessee.

42. John Russell Young, "John Hay, Secretary of State," *Munsey's Magazine,* 8 Jan. 1929, 247; Young in the Philadelphia *Evening Star,* 22 Aug. 1891, p. 4, cc. 3–6, p. 4, c. 1; Young, writing in 1898, quoted in T. C. Evans, "Personal Reminiscences of John Hay," Chattanooga, Tennessee, *Sunday Times,* 30 July 1905.

43. Joseph Bucklin Bishop, "A Friendship with John Hay," *Century Magazine* 71 (Mar. 1906):778.

44. Mitchel to Hay, East Orange, New Jersey, 12 Feb. 1905, Hay Papers, RPB.

45. James T. DuBois and Gertrude S. Mathews, *Galusha A. Grow: Father of the Homestead Law* (Boston: Houghton Mifflin, 1917), 266–267.

46. Michael Burlingame, "The Authorship of the Bixby Letter," in Burlingame, ed., *At Lincoln's Side,* 169–184.

47. Hay to Garfield, Washington, 16 Feb. 1881, Hay Papers, RPB.

48. Washington correspondence, 6 Mar., New York *World,* 8 Mar. 1861, Michael Burlingame, ed., *Lincoln's Journalist: John Hay's Anonymous Writings for the Press, 1860–1864* (Carbondale: Southern Illinois University Press, 1998), 54.

49. Schuyler Colfax to [Daniel D. Pratt], Washington, 7 Dec. 1860, Pratt Papers, Indiana State Library, Indianapolis.

50. Hay, "Life in the White House in the Time of Lincoln," Burlingame, ed., *At Lincoln's Side,* 131–132.

51. Robert L. Wilson to William H. Herndon, Sterling, Illinois, 10 Feb. 1866, *HI,* 206–207.

52. Adam Gurowski, *Diary* (3 vols.; Washington: Morrison, 1862–1866), 1:16–17 (section headed March 1861).

53. Robert L. Wilson to Herndon, Sterling, Illinois, 10 Feb. 1866, *HI,* 206.

54. Charles Francis Adams diary, 10 Mar. 1861, Adams Family Papers, MHi.

55. New York *Tribune,* 4 Mar. 1861.

56. Lincoln to William Sprague, Washington, 10 May 1861, Roy P. Basler et al., eds., *Collected Works of Abraham Lincoln* [hereafter *CWL*] (8 vols. plus index; New Brunswick, NJ: Rutgers University Press, 1953–1955), 4:365.

57. William O. Stoddard, "White House Sketches, No. 5," New York *Citizen,* 15 Sept. 1866, in Stoddard, *Inside the White House,* ed. Burlingame, 161.

58. Bates to James O. Broadhead, Washington, 26 Mar. 1861, Broadhead Papers, Missouri Historical Society, in Harry J. Carman and Reinhard H. Luthin, *Lincoln and the Patronage* (New York: Columbia University Press, 1943), 54.

59. Galloway to Thurlow Weed, Columbus, 23 Mar. 1861, Weed Papers, University of Rochester; Galloway to David Davis, Columbus, 29 Mar. 1861, David Davis Papers, IHi.

60. Washington correspondence, 25 Feb., Philadelphia *Press,* 26 Feb. 1861.

61. Daniel W. Wilder to William H. Herndon, Rochester, New York, 24 Nov. 1866, *HI,* 419.

62. Lincoln to Seward, Washington, 8 Dec. 1860, *CWL,* 4:149.

63. Charles A. Dana, *Recollections of the Civil War: With the Leaders at Washington and in the Field in the Sixties* (New York: D. Appleton, 1898), 3.

64. Lincoln, memorandum on the appointment of surveyor and collector of the port of New York, [ca. 8 Apr. 1861], *CWL,* 4:325.

65. Leonard Swett to William H. Herndon, Chicago, 17 Jan. 1866, *HI,* 165.

66. Washington correspondence, n.d., Cincinnati *Commercial,* n.d., copied in the *Illinois State Register* (Springfield), 6 Mar. 1861.

67. Barney to Chase, New York, 23 July 1861, Chase Papers, Historical Society of Pennsylvania.

68. Charles A. Dana to Chase, New York, 22 Feb. 1861, Chase Papers, Historical Society of Pennsylvania.

69. John Austin Stevens, Jr., to John Austin Stevens, Sr., Washington, 9 July 1861, Stevens Papers, New-York Historical Society.

70. Lincoln to Chase, Washington, 8 May 1861, *CWL*, 4:361.

71. Bernitt, ed., "Two Manuscripts of Gideon Welles," 594.

72. *The Journal of Benjamin Moran, 1857–1865*, ed. Sarah Agnes Wallace and Frances Elma Gillespie (2 vols.; Chicago: University of Chicago Press, 1948–1949), 2:1092 (entry for 19 Nov. 1862); Charles Francis Adams diary, 1 May 1865, Adams Family Papers, MHi; Adams to Richard Henry Dana, London, 11 June 1862, Dana Papers, MHi.

73. Washington correspondence, 23 Mar., New York *Evening Post*, 23 Mar. 1861.

74. George W. Julian, *Political Recollections, 1840 to 1872* (Chicago: Jansen, McClurg, 1884), 183.

75. Springfield correspondence by Henry Villard, 3 Dec., New York *Herald*, 9 Dec. 1860.

76. Grimshaw to Lyman Trumbull, 3 Dec. 1863, quoted in Carman and Luthin, *Lincoln and the Patronage*, 118.

77. John T. Morton to Lyman Trumbull, Topeka, 16 Nov. 1863, Trumbull Papers, DLC.

78. Willard L. King, *Lincoln's Manager: David Davis* (Cambridge, MA: Harvard University Press, 1960), 179.

79. William P. Wood to the Senate Judiciary Committee, Washington, 8 July 1861, Lamon Papers, CSmH.

80. Benjamin Brown French to Henry Flagg French, Washington, 5 July 1861, French Family Papers, DLC.

81. Lavern Marshall Hamand, "Ward Hill Lamon: Lincoln's 'Particular Friend'" (Ph.D. dissertation, University of Illinois, 1949), 233–252; Jesse W. Weik, *The Real Lincoln: A Portrait*, ed. Michael Burlingame (1922; Lincoln: University of Nebraska Press, 2002), 218.

82. Michael Burlingame and John R. Turner Ettlinger, eds., *Inside Lincoln's White House: The Complete Civil War Diary of John Hay* (Carbondale: Southern Illinois University Press, 1997), 245 (entry for 8 Nov. 1864).

83. Richard C. McCormick's reminiscences, New York, 29 Apr., New York *Evening Post*, 3 May 1865.

84. White to Jesse W. Weik, Kittery Point, Maine, 12 Aug. 1894, Weik, *Real Lincoln*, ed. Burlingame, 383.

85. Jason Marsh to Lyman Trumbull, Rockford, 26 May 1862, Trumbull Papers, DLC.

86. O. C. Dake to David Davis, Washington, 7 May 1861, David Davis Papers, IHi.

87. Davis to W. W. Orme, St. Louis, 19 Jan. 1861, Morgan Papers, Illinois Historical Survey, University of Illinois, quoted in Hamand, "Ward Hill Lamon," 133.

88. Davis to Harvey Hogg, West Point, New York, 17 June 1861, Lamon Papers, CSmH, quoted in Hamand, "Ward Hill Lamon," 232.

89. O. C. Dake to David Davis, Washington, 7 May 1861, David Davis Papers, IHi.

90. George Gibbs to John Austin Stevens, Washington, 23 Oct. 1861, Stevens Papers, New-York Historical Society.

91. Washington correspondence, 31 Mar., New York *Times*, 1 Apr. 1861.

92. Washington correspondence, n.d., *Missouri Democrat* (St. Louis), 1 Apr., copied in the Portland *Oregonian*, 29 Apr. 1861.

93. George W. Julian in Allen Thorndike Rice, ed., *Reminiscences of Abraham Lincoln by Distinguished Men of His Time* (New York: North American Review, 1888), 51.

94. Washington correspondence by X Y Z, 31 Mar., Philadelphia *Press*, 1 Apr. 1861.

95. Washington correspondence by Special, 30 Mar., Cincinnati *Commercial*, 1 Apr. 1861.

96. Noah Brooks, *Abraham Lincoln and the Downfall of American Slavery* (New York: G. P. Putnam's Sons, 1894), 417.

97. Dr. Samuel Long to Lyman Trumbull, Collinsville, Illinois, 26 Nov. 1862, Trumbull Papers, DLC.

98. David L. Gregg to Lincoln, Honolulu, 24 Jan. 1863, AL MSS DLC.

99. Baker to Anson G. Henry, Washington, 9 July [1861], Henry Papers, IHi.

100. Washington correspondence, 30 Mar., New York *Herald,* 31 Mar. 1861.

101. Cameron to Leonard Swett, Washington, 10 Mar. 1861, David Davis Papers, IHi.

102. John Hay, "Heroic Age in Washington," Burlingame, ed., *At Lincoln's Side,* 125.

103. *CWL,* 6:51.

104. *Journal of Benjamin Moran,* ed. Wallace and Gillespie, 2:1166 (entry for 21 May 1863).

105. Lincoln to James Pollock, Washington, 15 Aug. 1861, *CWL,* 4:485.

106. Lincoln to William B. Thomas, Washington, 8 May 1861, ibid., 4:362.

107. Lincoln to John W. Forney, Washington, 20 July 1861, ibid., 4:456.

108. Trumbull to [O. M. Hatch], Washington, 24 Mar. 1861, Hatch Papers, IHi.

109. *CWL,* 4:321.

110. David Donald, *Lincoln's Herndon* (New York: Alfred A. Knopf, 1948), 153.

111. W. W. Orme to Leonard Swett, Washington, 14 May [1861], David Davis Papers, IHi.

112. Henry C. Whitney to Herndon, n.p., 23 June 1887, *HI,* 620; William H. L. Wallace to his wife, Washington, 9 Mar. 1861, Harry E. Pratt, ed., *Concerning Mr. Lincoln, in Which Abraham Lincoln Is Pictured As He Appeared to Letter Writers of His Time* (Springfield, IL: Abraham Lincoln Association, 1944), 71.

113. Henry Winter Davis to Samuel Francis du Pont, [Washington], 20 Mar. 1861, transcript, S. F. Du Pont Papers, Hagley Museum, Wilmington, Delaware.

114. Nicolay to Ozias M. Hatch, Washington, 7 Mar. 1861, Burlingame, ed., *With Lincoln in the White House,* 30.

115. Indianapolis correspondence by Charles A. Page, 30 Apr. 1865, in Charles A. Page, *Letters of a War Correspondent,* ed. James R. Gilmore (Boston: L. C. Page, 1899), 376.

116. Dubois to Lincoln, Springfield, 27 Mar. 1861, AL MSS DLC.

117. Lincoln to Dubois, Washington, 30 Mar. 1861, *CWL,* 4:302.

118. Dubois to Lincoln, Springfield, 6 Apr. 1861, AL MSS DLC.

119. Dubois to Henry C. Whitney, Springfield, 6 Apr. 1865, *HI,* 620.

120. Howard K. Beale and Alan W. Brownsword, eds., *Diary of Gideon Welles, Secretary of the Navy under Lincoln and Johnson* (3 vols.; New York: W.W. Norton, 1960), 1:57.

121. Swett to Herndon, Chicago, 17 Jan. 1866, *HI,* 165.

122. Maunsell B. Field, *Memories of Many Men and of Some Women: Being Personal Recollections of Emperors, Kings, Queens, Princes, Presidents, Statesmen, Authors, and Artists, at Home and Abroad, during the Last Thirty Years* (New York: Harper, 1874), 310.

123. Lamon to Richard Yates, Washington, 3 July 1864, draft, Lamon Papers, CSmH, quoted in Hamand, "Ward Hill Lamon," 348–349.

124. Hawkins Taylor to William Butler, Washington, 22 Mar. 1861, Ozias M. Hatch Papers, IHi.

125. James M. Scovel, "Personal Recollections of Abraham Lincoln," *Lippincott's Monthly Magazine* 44 (Aug. 1889): 248.

126. Knox to Lincoln, Chicago, 3 Oct. 1861, AL MSS DLC.

127. Conkling to Lyman Trumbull, Springfield, 31 May 1862, Trumbull Papers, DLC.

128. Conkling to Lyman Trumbull, Peoria, 30 June 1862, ibid.

129. Horace White to William Butler, Chicago, 11 Nov. 1862, William Butler Papers, ICHi.

130. Peck to Trumbull, Chicago, 21 Mar. 1861, Trumbull Papers, DLC

131. W. M. Dickson to Friedrich Hassaurek, Cincinnati, 15 Feb. 1864, Hassaurek Papers, Ohio Historical Society.

132. Samuel R. Curtis to his wife, Washington, 1 May 1861, Kenneth E. Colton, ed., "'The Irrepressible Conflict of 1861': The Letters of Samuel Ryan Curtis," *Annals of Iowa,* 3rd series, 24 (1942):47.

133. Grenville M. Dodge to his wife Annie, Washington, 12 Mar. 1861, typescript in "Data

Chronologically arranged for ready reference in preparation of a Biography of Grenville Mellen Dodge," Dodge Papers, Iowa State Archives, Des Moines.

134. Zachariah Chandler to Lincoln, Washington, 30 Mar. 1861, AL MSS DLC.

135. Fessenden to Elizabeth Warriner, Washington, 17 Mar. 1861, Fessenden Papers, Bowdoin College; Fessenden to James S. Pike, Portland, 8 Sept. 1861, Pike Papers, DLC.

136. Washington correspondence by "Aga," 21 Mar., Baltimore *Sun*, 22 Mar. 1861.

137. Gardiner Worthington to Lincoln, New York, 27 Mar. 1861, AL MSS DLC.

138. Egbert L. Viele, "A Trip with Lincoln, Chase and Stanton," *Scribner's Monthly* 16 (1878):818.

139. John Conness to Andrew Johnson, New York, 31 May 1865, William H. Wallace file, Letters of Application and Recommendation during the Administrations of Abraham Lincoln and Andrew Johnson, 1861–1869, Record Group 59, M 650, National Archives.

140. Charles H. Ray to John A. Andrew, Springfield, 17 Jan. 1861, Andrew Papers, MHi.

141. J. Edward Murr, "Some Pertinent Observations Concerning 'Abe Lincoln—The Hoosier,'" 17–18, unpublished typescript, Murr Papers, DePauw University, Greencastle, Indiana.

142. Charles Washburn to Elihu B. Washburne, 23 May 1861, Russell K. Nelson, "The Early Life and Congressional Career of Elihu B. Washburne" (Ph.D. dissertation, University of North Dakota, 1954), 238.

143. Halstead to Timothy C. Day, Washington, 8 June, 16 July 1861, Sarah J. Day, *The Man on a Hill Top* (Philadelphia: Ware Brothers, 1931), 243, 247.

144. Smith to Richard W. Thompson, Washington, 16 Apr. 1861, Thompson Collection, LMF.

145. Undated notes by George Harrington, Harrington Papers, Missouri Historical Society.

146. George W. Rives to Lyman Trumbull, Paris, Illinois, 12 Feb. 1862, Trumbull Papers, DLC.

147. Washington correspondence by Van [D. W. Bartlett], 12 Nov., Springfield (Massachusetts) *Republican*, 16 Nov. 1861.

148. Joseph Bucklin Bishop, *Notes and Anecdotes of Many Years* (New York: Scribner's, 1925), 65–66.

149. John B. Alley in Rice, ed., *Reminiscences of Lincoln*, 589.

150. Alexander Milton Ross, *Recollections and Experiences of an Abolitionist: From 1855 to 1865* (Toronto: Rowsell and Hutchinson, 1875), 138.

151. Statement by Whitney, [Nov. 1866?], in *HI*, 406.

152. *La Patrie* (Paris), 21 July 1861, in Herbert Mitgang, ed., *Abraham Lincoln, A Press Portrait: His Life and Times from the Original Newspaper Documents of the Union, the Confederacy, and Europe* (Chicago: Quadrangle Books, 1971), 274.

153. Titian J. Coffey in Rice, ed., *Reminiscences of Lincoln*, 240.

154. James Mitchell to Matthew Simpson, Washington, 20 Oct. 1863, Matthew Simpson Papers, DLC.

155. John Lanahan to Matthew Simpson, Washington, 27 June 1864 and [Alexandria, Virginia?], Nov. 1861 [no day indicated], ibid.

156. D. H. Whitney to Matthew Simpson, Washington, 20 May 1863, ibid.

157. Field, *Memories of Many Men and of Some Women*, 310.

158. Washington correspondence, 14 Mar., New York *World*, 15 Mar. 1861.

159. New York *Herald*, 9 Dec. 1860.

160. Lincoln to Seward, Washington, 18 Mar. 1861, *CWL*, 4:293.

161. Washington correspondence by Special, 15 Mar., Cincinnati *Commercial*, 16 Mar. 1861.

162. New York *Daily News*, 28 Mar. 1861.

163. Gustave Koerner to Lyman Trumbull, Belleville, Illinois, 1 May 1862, Trumbull

Papers, DLC; Washington correspondence, 14 Mar., New York *Herald,* 16 Mar. 1861.

164. Clay's recollections in Rice, ed., *Reminiscences of Lincoln,* 300.

165. Michael Burlingame, "The Early Life of Carl Schurz, 1829–1865" (Ph.D. dissertation, Johns Hopkins University, 1971), 320–354.

166. Albert G. Browne, Jr., to John A. Andrew, Washington, [28 Mar. 1861], Andrew Papers, MHi.

167. Koerner to [Richard Yates], Belleville, 28 May 1862, in the possession of a private collector represented by Jonathan Mann.

168. Washington correspondence by Special, 28 Mar., Cincinnati *Commercial,* 29 Mar. 1861.

169. Washington correspondence, 7 Mar., New York *Herald,* 8 Mar. 1861.

170. Thomas J. Pickett, "Reminiscences of Lincoln," Lincoln, Nebraska, *Daily State Journal,* 12 Apr. 1881.

171. Charles Francis Adams diary, 10 Mar. 1861, Adams Family Papers, MHi.

172. Albert G. Browne, Jr., to John A. Andrew, Washington, [28 Mar. 1861], Andrew Papers, MHi.

173. Washington correspondence, 29 Mar., Cincinnati *Enquirer,* n.d., copied in the *Illinois State Register* (Springfield), 2 Apr. 1861.

174. Kenneth M. Stampp, *America in 1857: A Nation on the Brink* (New York: Oxford University Press, 1990), 73.

175. Wallace and Gillespie, eds., *Journal of Moran,* 2:909 (entry for 20 Nov. 1861).

176. William James Stillman, *Autobiography of a Journalist* (2 vols.; Boston: Houghton Mifflin, 1901), 1:369.

177. Lincoln to Seward, Washington, 18 Mar. 1861, *CWL,* 4:292.

178. *The Nation,* 24 Jan. 1867.

179. Charles Francis Adams diary, 12 Mar. 1861, Adams Family Papers, MHi.

180. Henry Cabot Lodge journal, 10 June 1876, Lodge Papers, MHi; Charles Francis Adams diary, 12, 28, 31 Mar. 1861, Adams Family Papers, MHi.

181. Letter by "Sparta," n.d., Indianapolis *Daily Journal,* 5 Apr. 1861.

182. John B. Alley in Rice, ed., *Reminiscences of Lincoln,* 577–579; Edward Everett Hale, *Memories of a Hundred Years* (2 vols.; New York: Macmillan, 1904), 2:78.

183. Lincoln to John A. Gilmer, Springfield, 15 Dec. 1860, *CWL,* 4:151.

184. Washington correspondence, 18 Mar., New York *Herald,* 19 Mar. 1861.

185. Josiah M. Lucas to Hicks, Washington, 11 Jan. 1861, Hicks Papers, Maryland Historical Society.

186. Hicks to Seward, Annapolis, 28 Mar. 1861, AL MSS DLC.

187. Davis to [John Sherman], n.p., 30 May 1862, Sherman Papers, DLC.

188. Benjamin Brown French to his son Frank, Washington, 20 Mar. 1861, French Family Papers, DLC.

189. Washington correspondence by Ben: Perley Poore, 7 Mar., Boston *Journal,* 7 Mar. 1861.

190. Washington correspondence, 27 Mar., Springfield (Massachusetts) *Republican,* 30 Mar. 1861; Washington correspondence, 25 Mar., Baltimore *Sun,* 26 Mar. 1861.

191. Clemens to [W. W. Shiver of Wheeling, Virginia], Washington, 1 Mar. 1861, William P. Palmer Collection, Western Reserve Historical Society, Cleveland.

Chapter 22. "You Can Have No Conflict Without Being Yourselves the Aggressors"

1. John G. Nicolay and John Hay, *Abraham Lincoln: A History* (10 vols.; New York: Century, 1890), 3:371.

2. Charles Francis Adams, Jr., to Frederic Bancroft, n.p., 11 Oct. 1911, copy, Allan Nevins Papers, Columbia University.

3. New York *Tribune,* 27 Feb. 1861.

4. Baron Rudolph Schleiden, minister to the United States from the Republic of Bremen, dispatch to his home government, Washington, 18 Feb. 1861, copy, Carl Schurz Papers, DLC.

5. Memorandum by John A. Campbell, n.d., in Henry G. Connor, *John Archibald Campbell, Associate Justice of the United States Supreme Court, 1853–1861* (Boston: Houghton Mifflin, 1920), 116.

6. Charles S. Morehead, speech delivered in Liverpool, England, on 9 Oct. 1862, Liverpool *Mercury*, 13 Oct. 1862, excerpted in David Rankin Barbee and Milledge L. Bonham, Jr., eds., "Fort Sumter Again," *Mississippi Valley Historical Review* 28 (1941):66.

7. John Forsyth and Martin J. Crawford to Robert Toombs, dispatch no. 3, Washington, 8 Mar. 1861, copy, Confederate States of America Papers, DLC.

8. Edward Everett journal, 23 Aug. 1861, Everett Papers, MHi.

9. John D. Defrees to Jesse K. Dubois, Indianapolis, 12 Nov. 1860, AL MSS DLC.

10. Edouard de Stoeckl to Alexander Gortchakov, Washington, 9 Apr. 1861, dispatch 20, photocopy, Principal Archive of the Ministry of Foreign Affairs, Russian Reproductions, Papers of the Foreign Copying Project, DLC; Albert A. Woldman, *Lincoln and the Russians* (Cleveland: World, 1952), 49.

11. Martin Crawford, ed., *William Howard Russell's Civil War: Private Diary and Letters, 1861–1862* (Athens: University of Georgia Press, 1992), 26.

12. Scott to Seward, Washington, 3 Mar. 1861, in John Bigelow, ed., *Letters and Memorials of Samuel J. Tilden* (2 vols.; New York: Harper, 1908), 1:157.

13. Montgomery Blair to Gideon Welles, Washington, 17 May 1873, Welles Papers, DLC.

14. Howard K. Beale and Alan W. Brownsword, eds., *Diary of Gideon Welles, Secretary of the Navy under Lincoln and Johnson* [hereafter *Welles Diary*] (3 vols.; New York: W. W. Norton, 1960), 1:4. See also Gideon Welles, "Fort Sumter," *The Galaxy* 10 (Nov. 1870), Albert Mordell, comp., *Civil War and Reconstruction: Selected Essays by Gideon Welles*

(New York: Twayne Publishers, 1959), 40–42; John Niven, *Gideon Welles, Lincoln's Secretary of the Navy* (New York: Oxford University Press, 1973), 325.

15. Howard K. Beale, ed., *The Diary of Edward Bates, 1859–1866* (Annual Report of the American Historical Association for 1930, vol. 4; Washington, DC: U.S. Government Printing Office, 1933), 177 (entry for 9 Mar. 1861).

16. Lincoln to Scott, Washington, 9 March 1861, Roy P. Basler et al., eds., *Collected Works of Abraham Lincoln* [hereafter *CWL*] (8 vols. plus index; New Brunswick, NJ: Rutgers University Press, 1953–1955). 4:279. See also Nicolay for Lincoln to Scott, Washington, 9 Mar. 1861, Michael Burlingame, ed., *With Lincoln in the White House: Letters, Memoranda, and Other Writings of John G. Nicolay, 1860–1865* (Carbondale: Southern Illinois University Press, 2000), 30.

17. Scott to Lincoln, Washington, 12 Mar. 1861, AL MSS DLC.

18. Butler to Lyman Trumbull, Springfield, 20 Mar. 1861, Trumbull Papers, DLC.

19. William B. Plato to Lyman Trumbull, Geneva, Kane County, Illinois, 29 Mar. 1861, ibid.

20. Pillsbury to Francis Jackson, n.p., 13 Mar. 1861, William Lloyd Garrison Papers, Boston Public Library.

21. Francis P. Blair, Sr., to Martin Van Buren, Silver Spring, Maryland, 1 May 1861, Martin Van Buren Papers, Chadwyck-Healey microfilm edition; William Ernest Smith, *The Francis Preston Blair Family in Politics* (2 vols.; New York: Macmillan, 1933), 2:9–10; Francis P. Blair, Sr., to Montgomery Blair, Silver Spring, 12 Mar. 1861, AL MSS DLC.

22. Dexter A. Hawkins to John Sherman, New York, 23 Mar. 1861, Sherman Papers, DLC.

23. Washington correspondence by Sigma, 13 Mar., Cincinnati *Commercial*, 14 Mar. 1861.

24. Lincoln to Seward, Washington, 15 Mar. 1861, *CWL*, 4:284.

25. Seward to Lincoln, Washington, 15 Mar. 1861, AL MSS DLC.

26. Bates to Lincoln, Washington, 15 Mar. 1861, AL MSS DLC.

27. Montgomery Blair, speech at Clarksville, Maryland, 26 Aug. 1865, Chicago *Tribune*, 1 Sept. 1865.

28. E. J. Arthur to Edward DeLeon, 18 Feb. 1861, DeLeon Papers, University of South Carolina, in Allan Nevins, *The Emergence of Lincoln* (2 vols.; New York: Charles Scribner's Sons, 1950), 2:335.

29. Beale, ed., *Welles Diary*, 6.

30. Washington correspondence by F., 31 Mar., New York *Morning Express,* 2 Apr. 1861.

31. William L. Hodge to John Austin Stevens, Washington, 5 Apr. 1861, Stevens Papers, New-York Historical Society.

32. Charles Russell Lowell to his mother, Mt. Savage, 28 Mar. 1861, in Edward Waldo Emerson, *Life and Letters of Charles Russell Lowell, Captain Sixth United States Cavalry, Colonel Second Massachusetts Cavalry, Brigadier-General United States Volunteers* (Boston: Houghton Mifflin, 1907), 196.

33. Gayle Thornbrough et al., eds., *The Diary of Calvin Fletcher* (8 vols.; Indianapolis: Indiana Historical Society, 1972–1981), 7:81 (entry for 4 Apr. 1861).

34. William Jayne to Lyman Trumbull, Springfield, 4 Apr. 1861, Trumbull Family Papers, IHi.

35. Washington correspondence by Cyd, 29 Mar., *Ohio State Journal* (Columbus), 1 Apr. 1861.

36. Stanton to John A. Dix, Washington 16, 19 Mar. 1861, Dix Papers, Columbia University.

37. Washington correspondence, 1 April, *National Anti-Slavery Standard* (New York), 6 Apr. 1861.

38. Henry Winter Davis to Samuel F. Du Pont, 21 Mar. 1861, transcript, S. F. Du Pont Papers, Hagley Museum, Wilmington, Delaware.

39. Washington correspondence, 6 Apr., New York *Herald,* 7 Apr. 1861.

40. Washington *States and Union,* 21 Mar. 1861.

41. William B. Allison to Samuel J. Kirkwood, Dubuque, 7 Apr. 1861, Kirkwood Papers, Iowa Historical Society, Des Moines.

42. J. H. Jordan to Lincoln, Cincinnati, 4, 5 Apr. 1861, AL MSS DLC.

43. Mark Howard to Gideon Welles, Hartford, 28 Mar. 1861, Welles Papers, DLC.

44. Benjamin Brown French to his son Frank, Washington, 5 Apr. 1861, French Family Papers, DLC.

45. Fox to his wife Virginia, Washington, 19 Mar. 1861, Fox Papers, New-York Historical Society.

46. Hurlbut interviewed by Nicolay, 4 May 1876, Michael Burlingame, ed., *An Oral History of Abraham Lincoln: John G. Nicolay's Interviews and Essays* (Carbondale: Southern Illinois University Press, 1996), 64; Stephen A. Hurlbut to Lincoln, n.p., 27 Mar. 1861, AL MSS DLC.

47. Lamon to Seward, Charleston, 25 Mar. 1861, Seward Papers, University of Rochester.

48. Cameron interviewed by Nicolay, 20 Feb. 1875, Burlingame, ed., *Oral History of Lincoln,* 42.

49. William Gwin in *Overland Monthly* 18 (1891):469; John A. Campbell, "Facts of History," *Southern Historical Society Papers* 42 (1917):32–34.

50. Edward Younger, ed., *Inside the Confederate Government: The Diary of Robert Garlick Hill Kean* (New York: Oxford University Press, 1957), 113 (entry for 22 Oct. 1863).

51. Washington correspondence by Special, 1 Apr., Cincinnati *Commercial,* 2 Apr. 1861. Cf. Washington correspondence, 31 Mar., New York *Herald,* 1 Apr. 1861.

52. Message to Congress, 4 July 1861, *CWL*, 4:424.

53. Neal Dow to Lincoln, Portland, Maine, 13 Mar. 1861, AL MSS DLC.

54. William H. Aspinwall to Lincoln, New York, 31 Mar. 1861, ibid.

55. Washington correspondence by Sigma, 13 Mar., Cincinnati *Commercial,* 14 Mar. 1861.

56. *The War of the Rebellion: A Compilation of the Official Records of the Union and Confederate Armies* (128 vols.; Washington DC: Government Printing Office, 1880–1901) [hereafter *OR*]) I, 1:200–201.

57. Blair to Welles, Washington, 17 May 1873, in Welles, *Lincoln and Seward* (New York: Sheldon, 1874), 65; Blair to Samuel Wylie Crawford, n.p., 6 May 1882, in Crawford, *Genesis of the Civil War* (New York: Webster, 1887), 365; Sam Ward to S. L. M. Barlow, Washington, 31 Mar. 1861, Barlow Papers, CSmH.

58. Welles, opinion on Fort Sumter, 29 March 1861, AL MSS DLC.

59. Chase, opinion on Fort Sumter, 29 March 1861, AL MSS DLC.

60. Montgomery Blair to Lincoln, [Washington, 29 Mar. 1861], AL MSS DLC.

61. Bates, opinion on Fort Sumter, 29 Mar. 1861, AL MSS DLC; Beale, ed., *Bates Diary,* 180 (entry for 29 Mar. 1861).

62. Smith, opinion on Fort Sumter, 29 March 1861, AL MSS DLC.

63. Washington correspondence, 3 Apr., Springfield (Massachusetts) *Republican,* 6 Apr. 1861.

64. Joseph Blanchard to Lincoln, Elmira, Illinois, 28 Mar. 1861, AL MSS DLC.

65. W. H. West to Lincoln, Bellefontaine, Ohio, 3 Apr. 1861, ibid.

66. Montgomery Meigs diary, 31 Mar. 1861, copy, Nicolay Papers, DLC.

67. E. D. Keyes, journal entries for Mar. 29 and 31, 1861, E. D. Keyes, *Fifty Years' Observations of Men and Events, Civil and Military* (New York: Charles Scribner's Sons, 1884), 378.

68. Keyes, journal entry for 15 Oct. 1860, ibid., 370.

69. Joseph Holt and Winfield Scott to Lincoln, Washington, 5 Mar. 1861, AL MSS DLC.

70. Washington correspondence by D. W. B., 12 Mar., New York *Tribune,* 14 Mar. 1861.

71. Holt interviewed by Nicolay, Washington, 2 Apr. 1874, in Burlingame, ed., *Oral History of Lincoln,* 72.

72. Anderson to Lorenzo Thomas, Fort Sumter, 8 Apr. 1861, *OR,* I, 1:294.

73. Anderson, statement to Major Ellison Capers, Crawford, *Genesis of the Civil War,* 111.

74. Michael Burlingame and John R. Turner Ettlinger, eds., *Inside Lincoln's White House: The Complete Civil War Diary of John Hay* [hereafter *Hay Diary*] (Carbondale: Southern Illinois University Press, 1997), 21 (entry for 9 May 1861).

75. Seward, memo on Fort Sumter, 29 Mar. 1861, AL MSS DLC.

76. Meigs to the editor of the New York *Tribune,* Washington, 14 Sept. 1865, Philadelphia *Press,* 18 Sept. 1865.

77. Frederick Seward, *William H. Seward: An Autobiography from 1801 to 1834, with a Memoir of His Life, and Selections from His Letters* (3 vols.; New York: Derby and Miller, 1891), 2:534.

78. Keyes, *Fifty Years Observations,* 383.

79. Campbell, "Facts of History," 34–35.

80. Porter, *Incidents and Anecdotes of the Civil War* (New York: D. Appleton, 1885), 15; statement by Porter, 25 Mar. 1873, S. W. Crawford Papers, DLC; David D. Porter, "Journal of Occurrences during the War of the Rebellion," 1:52–68, Porter Papers, DLC. Porter's various accounts of Lincoln's words differ; I have conflated them here.

81. Welles, *Lincoln and Seward,* 55.

82. Gideon Welles, *Civil War and Reconstruction: Selected Essays,* comp. Albert Mordell (New York: Twayne, 1959), "Fort Sumter," 57–61; Beale ed., *Welles Diary,* 16–21.

83. Washington correspondence, 1 Apr., New York *Times,* New York *Herald,* 2 Apr. 1861.

84. Washington correspondence, 28 Mar., New York *Evening Post,* 28 Mar. 1861.

85. Beale, ed., *Welles Diary* 1:24–25; Welles, "Fort Sumter," Mordell, comp., *Civil War and Reconstruction,* 66–67.

86. Robert Means Thompson and Richard Wainwright, eds., *Confidential Correspondence of Gustavus Vasa Fox, Assistant Secretary of the Navy, 1861–1865* (2 vols.; New York: Printed for the Naval History Society by the De Vinne Press, 1918–1919), 1:40; Fox to his wife, Washington, 2 May 1861, Fox Papers, New-York Historical Society.

87. Welles to Montgomery Blair, Hartford, 30 Apr. 1873, Blair Family Papers, DLC.

88. "A Friend" [James E. Harvey] to A. G. Magrath, 6 Apr. 1861, *OR*, I, 1:287.

89. Seward to Weed, Washington, 25 June 1861, Weed Papers, University of Rochester.

90. Charles Francis Adams, Jr., to Frederic Bancroft, South Lincoln, Massachusetts, 26 Nov. 1912, Bancroft Papers, Columbia University.

91. Washington correspondence, 10 July, New York *World*, 12 July 1861, in Michael Burlingame, ed., *Lincoln's Journalist: John Hay's Anonymous Writings for the Press, 1860–1864* (Carbondale: Southern Illinois University Press, 1998), 75.

92. Beale, ed., *Welles Diary*, 1:25; Welles, "Fort Sumter," Mordell, comp., *Civil War and Reconstruction*, 68–69.

93. Porter, *Incidents and Anecdotes*, 283.

94. Seward, *Seward*, 2:535.

95. "A Douglas man" to Stephen A. Douglas, Petersburg, Virginia, 9 Dec. 1860, Douglas Papers, University of Chicago.

96. Ralph Haswell Lutz, "Rudolf Schleiden and the Visit to Richmond, April 25, 1861," *Annual Report of the American Historical Association for the Year 1915* (Washington, DC: Smithsonian Institution Press, 1917), 210.

97. Lord Lyons to John Russell, Washington, 4 Feb. 1861, James J. Barnes and Patience P. Barnes, eds., *Private and Confidential: Letters from British Ministers in Washington to the Foreign Secretaries in London, 1844–1867* (Selinsgrove: Susquehanna University Press, 1993), 240.

98. Lord Lyons to Lord John Russell, Washington, 26 Mar. 1861, Thomas Wodehouse

Legh (Lord Newton), *Lord Lyons: A Record of British Diplomacy* (3 vols.; New York: Longmans, Green, 1913), 1:33.

99. Lord Lyons to Lord John Russell, Washington, 7 Jan. 1861, ibid., 1:30.

100. Norman B. Ferris, *Desperate Diplomacy: William H. Seward's Foreign Policy, 1861* (Knoxville: University of Tennessee Press, 1976), 20; Lyons to Russell, Washington, 12 Feb. 1861, Barnes and Barnes, eds., *Private and Confidential*, 241.

101. Edward Everett journal, 23 Aug. 1861, Everett Papers, MHi.

102. *CWL*, 4:317.

103. David Dudley Field to Gideon Welles, New York, 20 May 1873, Welles Papers, IHi, photostatic copy, J. G. Randall Papers, DLC.

104. Frederick Seward, *Reminiscences of a War-Time Statesman and Diplomat, 1830–1915* (New York: G. P. Putnam's Sons, 1916), 147.

105. John Lothrop Motley to his wife, Woodland Hill, 23 June 1861, George William Curtis, ed., *The Correspondence of John Lothrop Motley* (2 vols.; New York: Harper & Brothers, 1889), 1:394.

106. Carl Schurz, *The Reminiscences of Carl Schurz* (3 vols.; New York: McClure, 1907–1908), 2:242–243.

107. Rudolf Schleiden's dispatch to his home government, Washington, 4 Mar. 1861, copy, Carl Schurz Papers, DLC.

108. Daniel W. Crofts, *Reluctant Confederates: Upper South Unionists in the Secession Crisis* (Chapel Hill: University of North Carolina Press, 1989), 301.

109. Allan B. Magruder, "A Piece of Secret History: President Lincoln and the Virginia Convention of 1861," *Atlantic Monthly* 35 (Apr. 1875):439; Allan B. Magruder to Jeremiah S. Black, Baltimore, 27 July 1874, Black Papers, DLC.

110. Herring to the editor, Abingdon, Illinois, 22 Oct. 1879, Chicago *Tribune*, n.d., clipping in the S. W. Crawford Papers, Virginia Historical Society.

111. John Minor Botts, *The Great Rebellion: Its Secret History, Rise, Progress, and Disastrous*

Failure (New York: Harper & Brothers, 1866), 196.

112. Washington correspondence, 13 Mar., Baltimore *American,* n.d., copied in the New York *Times,* 15 Mar. 1861.

113. Robert Y. Conrad to E. W. P. Conrad, Richmond, 6 Apr. 1861, "The Break-Up of a Nation: Robert Y. Conrad's Letters at the Virginia Secession Convention," *Winchester-Frederick Historical Society Journal* 8 (1994–1995):15–16.

114. Burlingame and Ettlinger, eds., *Hay Diary,* 28 (entry for 28 Oct. 1861).

115. George Plumer Smith to Hay, Philadelphia, 9 Jan. 1863, AL MSS DLC..

116. John Hay to George Plumer Smith, Washington, 10 Jan. 1863, Burlingame, ed., *At Lincoln's Side,* 30.

117. Memorandum by Smith, dated Philadelphia, 5 Mar. 1878, enclosed in Smith to Hay, Philadelphia, 9 Mar. 1878, Nicolay Papers, DLC.

118. New York *Times,* 16 July 1866.

119. *Congressional Globe,* 40th Congress, 2nd Session, 1207 (17 Feb. 1868); Baldwin to S. W. Crawford, Staunton, 1 Aug. 1869, S. W. Crawford Papers, Library of Virginia, Richmond.

120. Washington correspondence, 5 Apr., Philadelphia *Inquirer,* 6 Apr. 1861.

121. Washington correspondence, 7 Apr., New York *Herald,* 8 Apr. 1861.

122. Memo enclosed in Fox to Benson J. Lossing, Washington, 7 Sept. 1864, in an unidentified clipping, LMF.

123. Adams to Welles, on board the *Sabine* off Pensacola, 1 Apr. 1861, Welles Papers, DLC.

124. New York *Tribune,* 27 Mar. 1861.

125. *CWL,* 4:437.

126. Simon Cameron to Robert S. Chew, Washington, 6 Apr. 1861, ibid., 4:323.

127. Theodore Calvin Pease and James G. Randall, eds., *The Diary of Orville Hickman Browning* (2 vols.; Springfield: Illinois State Historical Library, 1925–1933), 1:563 (24 July 1862).

128. "Fort Sumpter," undated memorandum by George Harrington, Harrington Papers, Missouri Historical Society.

129. Campbell, "Facts of History," 35–36.

130. Campbell to Seward, Washington, 13 Apr. 1861, ibid., 38–41.

131. Washington correspondence by Special, 11 Apr., Cincinnati *Commercial,* 12 Apr. 1861.

132. Nicolay and Hay, *Lincoln,* 4:62.

133. Cleveland *Plain Dealer,* 9 Apr. 1861, quoted in John Thomas Hubbell, "The Northern Democracy and the Crisis of Disunion, 1860–1861" (Ph.D. dissertation, University of Illinois, 1969), 179; John L. O'Sullivan to Samuel J. Tilden, Lisbon, [Portugal], 1 Aug. 1861, Tilden Papers, New York Public Library.

134. Washington correspondence by B., 5 Apr., New York *Evening Post,* 6 Apr. 1861

135. Virginia Fox diary, 5 Feb. 1861, Levi Woodbury Papers, DLC.

136. George P. Bissell to Gideon Welles, Hartford, 9 Apr. 1861, Welles Papers, CSmH.

137. Anonymous to Lincoln, New York, 10 Apr. 1861, AL MSS DLC.

138. Washington correspondence, 11 Apr., Cincinnati *Gazette,* 12 Apr. 1861.

139. Washington correspondence, 9 Apr., Philadelphia *Inquirer,* 10 Apr. 1861; William Sprague to Lincoln, Providence, 11 Apr. 1861; Levin Tilmon to Lincoln, New York, 8 Apr. 1861, AL MSS DLC.

140. Winfield Scott to Lincoln, Washington, 9 Apr. 1861, AL MSS DLC; Washington correspondence, 11 Apr., New York *Times,* 12 Apr. 1861.

141. Lincoln to Curtin, Washington, 8 Apr. 1861, *CWL,* 4:324.

142. Washington correspondence, 10 Apr., New York *Herald,* 11 Apr. 1861.

143. Washington correspondence by Special, 10 Apr., Cincinnati *Commercial,* 11 Apr. 1861.

144. Washington correspondence by Special, 11 Apr., Cincinnati *Commercial* and New York *Herald,* 12 Apr. 1861.

145. John A. Bingham, "Abraham Lincoln," *The Current* (Chicago), 24 Apr. 1886, 282.

146. J. L. Pugh to William Porcher Miles, 24 Jan. 1861, quoted in William Barney, *The Road to Secession: A New Perspective on the Old South* (New York: Praeger, 1972), 196.

147. New York *Tribune*, n.d., quoted in Mrs. Roger A. Pryor, *My Day: Reminiscences of a Long Life* (New York: Macmillan, 1909), 158–159.

148. Indianapolis *Journal*, 11 Apr. 1861.

149. Memphis *Bulletin*, 8 Mar. 1861.

150. Washington correspondence, 7 Apr., New York *Times*, 8 Apr. 1861.

151. Joseph Holt, *Letter from the Hon. Joseph Holt, Upon the Policy of the General Government, the Pending Revolution, Its Objects, Its Probable Results If Successful, and the Duty of Kentucky in the Crisis* (Washington, DC: Henry Polkinhorn, 1861), 5.

152. Washington correspondence, 8 May, London *Times*, 22 May 1861.

153. Robert Y. Conrad to his wife, Richmond, 13 Apr. 1861, "Conrad's Letters at the Virginia Secession Convention," 18.

154. Davis to Bragg, Montgomery, 3 Apr. 1861, Haskell M. Monroe, Jr., and James T. McIntosh, eds., *The Papers of Jefferson Davis* (11 vols.; Baton Rouge: Louisiana State University Press, 1991–2003), 7:85

155. Edward McPherson, *The Political History of the United States During the Great Rebellion* (Washington, DC: Philp & Solomons, 1864), 112.

156. Jeremiah Clemens, speech in Huntsville, Alabama, 13 Mar. 1864, ibid., 113.

157. Wigfall to Jefferson Davis, Charleston, 10 Apr. 1861, in Louise Wigfall Wright, *A Southern Girl in '61: The War-Time Memories of a Confederate Senator's Daughter* (New York: Doubleday and Page, 1905), 36.

158. Pleasant A. Stovall, *Robert Toombs: Statesman, Speaker, Soldier, Sage* (New York: Cassell, 1892), 226; Crawford, *Genesis of the Civil War*, 421.

159. Crawford and Roman to Toombs, Washington, 1 Apr. 1861, copy of a telegram, Confederate States of America Papers, DLC.

160. Lathers, "Address delivered to Jefferson Davis at Montgomery, 1861, one week before the firing on Fort Sumter," Richard Lathers Papers, DLC.

161. Simon Bolivar Buckner to Beriah Magoffin, 8 Mar. 1861, quoted in Charles Royster, "Fort Sumter: At Last the War," in Gabor S. Boritt, ed., *Why the Civil War Came* (New York: Oxford University Press, 1996), 210.

162. Davis to F. W. Pickens, Washington, 20 Jan. 1861, in Rowland Dunbar, ed., *Jefferson Davis, Constitutionalist: His Letters, Papers and Speeches* (10 vols.; Jackson: Mississippi Department of Archives and History, 1923), 5:40.

163. Fox to Montgomery Blair, at sea, 17 Apr. 1861, Thompson and Wainwright, eds., *Correspondence of Fox*, 1:34–35.

164. *CWL*, 4:351.

165. AL MSS DLC.

166. Seward to his wife, Washington, 5 June 1861, Seward, *Seward*, 2:590.

167. Boston *Transcript*, n.d., copied in the *Home Journal*, n.d., copied in the *Missouri Democrat* (St. Louis), 23 Sept. 1861.

168. Seward to Weed, Washington, 1 Apr. 1862, Weed Papers, University of Rochester; Allan Nevins and Milton Halsey Thomas, eds., *Diary of George Templeton Strong, 1835–1875* (4 vols.; New York: Macmillan, 1952), 3:292 (entry for 28 Jan. 1863); Henry W. Bellows to his wife, Washington, 23 Apr. 1863, Bellows Papers, MHi.

169. Seward's remarks paraphrased by John Hay, Burlingame and Ettlinger, eds., *Hay Diary*, 211–212 (entry for 24 June 1864).

170. Second inaugural address, *CWL*, 8:332.

171. Pease and Randall, eds., *Browning Diary*, 1:453 (entry for 9 Feb. 1861).

Chapter 23. "I Intend to Give Blows"

1. This is a conflation of two versions of these remarks, one from the Perryville correspondence, 28 Apr., New York *World*, 29 Apr. 1861, and the other from the New York *Tribune*, 1 May 1861, reproduced in Roy P. Basler et al., eds., *Collected Works of Abraham Lincoln* [hereafter *CWL*] (8 vols. plus index;

New Brunswick, NJ: Rutgers University Press, 1953–1955), 4:345.

2. Stanton to John A. Dix, Washington, 8 Apr. 1861, Dix Papers, Columbia University.

3. Lincoln to Erastus Corning and others, Washington, 12 June 1863, *CWL,* 6:263.

4. Lincoln to John M. Clayton, Springfield, 28 July 1849, ibid., 2:60.

5. Eulogy on Henry Clay, 6 July 1852, ibid., 2:125.

6. Annual message to Congress, 1 Dec. 1862, ibid., 5:537.

7. Washington correspondence, 12 Apr., New York *World,* 13 Apr. 1861; Washington correspondence, 12 Apr., Cincinnati *Gazette,* n.d, copied in the *Illinois State Register* (Springfield), 16 Apr. 1861.

8. Washington correspondence, 12 Apr., New York *World,* 13 Apr. 1861.

9. Benjamin Brown French to his son Frank, Washington, 14 Apr. 1861, French Family Papers, DLC.

10. Washington correspondence, 14 Apr., Cincinnati *Commercial,* n.d., copied in the *Illinois State Register* (Springfield), 17 Apr. 1861; Washington correspondence, 14 Apr., New York *Tribune,* 15 Apr. 1861.

11. A. H. H. Stuart to F. S. Wood, Staunton, Virginia, 22 June 1875, photocopy, Stuart Papers, Virginia State Library, Richmond.

12. Reply to a Virginia delegation, 13 Apr. 1861, *CWL,* 4:331.

13. Alexander K. McClure, *Abraham Lincoln and Men of War-Times* (Philadelphia: Times, 1892), 69.

14. Philadelphia *Press,* n.d., in the New York *Evening Post,* 18 Aug. 1863.

15. George Alfred Townsend, *Washington Outside and Inside* (Hartford, CT: Betts, 1874), 714–715.

16. Albert G. Browne, Jr., to John A. Andrew, Washington, [28 Mar. 1861], Andrew Papers, MHi.

17. Washington correspondence, 3 Apr., Springfield (Massachusetts) *Republican,* 6 Apr. 1861.

18. Washington correspondence, 24 June, New York *Examiner,* 27 June 1861, in Michael

Burlingame, ed., *Dispatches from Lincoln's White House: The Anonymous Civil War Journalism of Presidential Secretary William O. Stoddard* (Lincoln: University of Nebraska Press, 2002), 12.

19. Washington *States and Union,* 15 Apr. 1861.

20. John G. Nicolay and John Hay, *Abraham Lincoln: A History* (10 vols.; New York: Century, 1890), 4:79.

21. Draft of proclamation, 15 Apr. 1861, AL MSS DLC; *CWL,* 4:332.

22. John Pendleton Kennedy journal, 15 Apr. 1861, Kennedy Papers, Enoch Pratt Free Library, Baltimore.

23. John Pendleton Kennedy to Robert C. Winthrop, Baltimore, 25 Apr. 1861, Winthrop Family Papers, MHi.

24. Louisville *Journal,* n.d., copied in the New York *Times,* 18 Apr. 1861.

25. Lincoln to Harris, Washington, [1?] May 1861, *CWL,* 4:351; Michael Burlingame and John R. Turner Ettlinger, eds., *Inside Lincoln's White House: The Complete Civil War Diary of John Hay* [hereafter *Hay Diary*] (Carbondale: Southern Illinois University Press, 1997), 17 (entry for 3 May 1861).

26. Worth to C. W. Woolen, Asheboro, 17 May 1861, in J. G. de Roulhac Hamilton, ed., *The Correspondence of Jonathan Worth* (2 vols.; Raleigh: Edwards & Broughton, 1909), 1:147.

27. John Minor Botts, *The Great Rebellion: Its Secret History, Rise, Progress, and Disastrous Failure* (New York: Harper & Brothers, 1866), 205; Rives to Robert C. Winthrop, Castle Hill, 19 Apr. 1861, Winthrop Family Papers, MHi.

28. Nicholson to "Dear Green," 5 May 1861, in Daniel W. Crofts, *Reluctant Confederates: Upper South Unionists in the Secession Crisis* (Chapel Hill: University of North Carolina Press, 1989), 351.

29. George William Brown, *Baltimore and the Nineteenth of April, 1861: A Study of the War* (Baltimore, MD: Johns Hopkins University Press, 1887), 74.

30. S. Teackle Wallis to James Alfred Pearce, Baltimore, 18 July 1861, in Bernard C.

Steiner, "James Alfred Pearce," *Maryland Historical Magazine* 19 (1924):26.

31. Lincoln to Johnson, Washington, 24 Apr. 1861, *CWL,* 4:343.

32. George Ashmun to Isaac N. Arnold, Springfield, Massachusetts, 15 Oct. 1864, Springfield, Massachusetts, *Republican,* 26 Oct. 1864; Washington correspondence, 14 Apr., 15 May, New York *Tribune,* 15 Apr., 16 May 1861; Simon P. Hanscom in the Washington *National Republican,* 16 Sept. 1866; Nicolay and Hay, *Lincoln,* 4:80; J. G. Holland, *Life of Abraham Lincoln* (Springfield, MA: G. Bill, 1866), 300–303; F. Lauriston Bullard, "Abraham Lincoln and George Ashmun," *New England Quarterly* 19 (1946): 198–200; Robert W. Johannsen, *Stephen A. Douglas* (New York: Oxford University Press, 1973), 859–860; Robert W. Johannsen, "The Douglas Democracy and the Crisis of Disunion," *Civil War History* 9 (1963): 229–230, 243.

33. Isaac Miller Short, *Abraham Lincoln: Early Days in Illinois* (Kansas City, MO: Simpson, 1927), 249, 860.

34. "Lincoln and Douglas: Their Last Interview," undated memorandum written by Illinois Congressman Philip B. Fouke for Ward Hill Lamon, Jeremiah S. Black Papers, DLC.

35. *CWL,* 4:426.

36. Edward Kirkwood to Gideon Welles, Brattleboro, Vermont, 16 Apr. 1861, Welles Papers, DLC.

37. James R. Doolittle to Lyman Trumbull, Racine, 24 Apr. 1861, Trumbull Papers, DLC.

38. Washington correspondence by John Hay, 16 Apr., *Illinois State Journal* (Springfield), 23 Apr. 1861, in Michael Burlingame, ed., *Lincoln's Journalist: John Hay's Anonymous Writings for the Press, 1860–1864* (Carbondale: Southern Illinois University Press, 1998), 57–58.

39. Washington correspondence, 17 Apr., New York *Times,* 18 Apr. 1861.

40. James H. Campbell to his wife, Juliet Lewis Campbell, Washington, 24 Apr. 1861, Campbell Papers, Schoff Civil War Collection, William L. Clements Library, University of Michigan.

41. Diary of Clifford Arrick, 20 Apr. 1861, Frontier Guard Records, DLC.

42. Henry Villard, *Memoirs of Henry Villard, Journalist and Financier: 1838–1900* (2 vols.; Boston: Houghton Mifflin, 1904), 1:169–170.

43. Philadelphia correspondence, 23 Apr., New York *Herald,* 24 Apr. 1861.

44. Nicolay and Hay, *Lincoln,* 4:152.

45. Harriet Beecher Stowe, *Men of Our Times; or, Leading Patriots of the Day* (Hartford, CT: Hartford Publishing Company, 1868), 473.

46. Magruder's reminiscences, taken from an unpublished memoir, edited by his brother, Allan B. Magruder, Philadelphia *Weekly Times,* 28 Dec. 1878; Samuel D. Sturgis to the editor of the Philadelphia *Evening Telegraph,* 12 June 1870, draft, Sturgis Papers, in *Recollected Words of Abraham Lincoln,* compiled and edited by Don E. Fehrenbacher and Virginia Fehrenbacher (Stanford, CA: Stanford University Press, 1996), 431–432; Magruder to an unidentified resident of Philadelphia, Galveston, 8 May 1870, Philadelphia *Evening Telegraph,* n.d., copied in the New York *Times,* 23 May 1870.

47. Francis P. Blair, Sr., to William Cullen Bryant, 5 Aug. 1866, draft, Blair Family Papers, DLC; Montgomery Blair in the New York *Evening Post,* 30 Sept. 1865.

48. Lincoln, 4 July 1861 message to Congress, first draft, AL MSS DLC.

49. Burlingame and Ettlinger, eds., *Hay Diary,* 8 (entry for 22 Apr. 1861).

50. Nicolay and Hay, *Lincoln,* 4:106–107.

51. *Kansas State Journal* (Lawrence), 9 May 1861, in Edgar Langsdorf, "Jim Lane and the Frontier Guard," *Kansas Historical Quarterly* 9 (1940):16–17.

52. Ward Hill Lamon, Washington *Evening Star,* 24 May 1890.

53. Oliver C. Bosbyshell, "When and Where I Saw Lincoln," Michael A. Cavanaugh, comp., *Military Essays and Recollections of the Pennsylvania Commandery of the Military Order of the Loyal Legion of the United States, 1904–1933* (2 vols.; Wilmington, NC: Broadfoot Publishing Company, 1995), 2:17–18;

Heber Thompson, *The First Defenders* (n.p., 1910), 151.

54. Washington correspondence by Bayard Taylor, 19 Apr., New York *Tribune*, 23 Apr. 1861.

55. Burlingame and Ettlinger, eds., *Hay Diary*, 2–3 (entry for 19 Apr. 1861).

56. Robert M. McLane, speech to a secessionist meeting in Baltimore, 1 Feb. 1861, quoted in a letter to the editor of the Baltimore *Clipper* by C. N., Fort Warren, 3 Feb. 1862, copy, John Sherman Papers, DLC.

57. Burlingame and Ettlinger, eds., *Hay Diary*, 3 (entry for 19 Apr. 1861).

58. Philadelphia *Press,* 22 Apr., copied in the New York *Times*, 23 Apr. 1861.

59. George W. Brown and Thomas H. Hicks to Lincoln, Baltimore, 18 Apr. 1861; telegram from George W. Brown and Thomas H. Hicks to Lincoln, Baltimore, 19 Apr. 1861, AL MSS DLC.

60. Speech by B. F. Watson, who was the major of the regiment, given in Lowell, Massachusetts, 19 Apr. 1886, quoted in an article by John Towle, Boston *Evening Journal*, 16 Apr. 1911; Thomas E. Ballard to Truman H. Bartlett, Boston, 1 Aug. 1907, Bartlett Papers, Boston University; Edward F. Jones to Daniel Butterfield, Binghamton, New York, 19 Apr. 1901, in Julia Lorrilard Butterfield, *A Biographical Memorial of General Daniel Butterfield* (New York: Grafton, 1904), 29.

61. Nicolay, memorandum of events, 21 Apr. 1861, in Michael Burlingame, ed., *With Lincoln in the White House: Letters, Memoranda, and Other Writings of John G. Nicolay, 1860–1865* (Carbondale: Southern Illinois University Press, 2000), 37.

62. Nicolay, memorandum of events, 20 Apr. 1861, ibid., 36.

63. Baltimore *Exchange,* n.d., copied in the Cincinnati *Commercial,* 30 Apr. 1861.

64. Washington correspondence by [George W.] S[imonton], 1 May, New York *Times*, 4 May 1861; Brown, *Baltimore and 19th of April,* 71–74; George M. Brown's statement, dated Baltimore, 7:30 P.M., 21 Apr., Washington

National Intelligencer, 22 Apr. 1861; Nicolay, memorandum of events, 21 Apr. 1861, Burlingame, ed., *With Lincoln in the White House,* 37; George T. M. Davis to Prosper M. Wetmore, New York, 1 May 1861, in John Austin Stevens, *The Union Defence Committee of the City of New York: Minutes, Reports, and Correspondence* (New York: Union Defence Committee, 1885), 153–156; Washington correspondence, 28 Apr., New York *Times,* 1 May 1861.

65. William Faxon to Mark Howard, Washington, 12 May [1862], Mark Howard Papers, Connecticut Historical Society, Hartford.

66. Burlingame and Ettlinger, eds., *Hay Diary,* 8 (entry for 23 Apr. 1861).

67. Andrew H. Reeder to Simon Cameron, Philadelphia, 24 Apr. 1861, AL MSS DLC.

68. Villard to Joseph Medill and Charles Henry Ray, Havre-de-Grace, Maryland, 29 Apr. 1861, Ray Papers, CSmH.

69. New York *Tribune,* 25 Apr. 1861; New York *Times,* 24, 26, 27 Apr. 1861; New York *Daily News,* 25 Apr. 1861; New York *World,* 10 May 1861.

70. New York *Evening Post,* n.d., copied in the *Ohio State Journal* (Columbus), 27 Apr. 1861.

71. John Bigelow, *Retrospections of an Active Life* (5 vols.; New York: Baker & Taylor, 1909–1913), 1:366–367.

72. John Bigelow diary, New York Public Library (entry for 8 May 1861).

73. George Gibbs to John Austin Stevens, Washington, 26 Apr. 1861, Stevens Papers, New-York Historical Society.

74. Barney to Chase, New York, 23 Apr. 1861, Chase Papers, Historical Society of Pennsylvania.

75. Henry W. Bellows to his son, New York, 25 Apr. 1861, Henry W. Bellows Papers, MHi.

76. Manton Marble to Martin Anderson, New York, 11 June 1861, Anderson Papers, University of Rochester.

77. George Hoadly to Chase, Cincinnati, 19 Sept. 1861, Chase Papers, DLC.

78. Washington correspondence, 1 May, New York *Tribune*, 2 May 1861.

79. Washington correspondence by Van [D. W. Bartlett], 18 Sept., Springfield (Massachusetts) *Republican*, 21 Sept. 1861.

80. Burlingame and Ettlinger, eds., *Hay Diary*, 5, 6 (entries for 21, 22 Apr. 1861).

81. This is a conflation of the following sources: *CWL*, 4:341–342, which reproduces what Nicolay and Hay gave in their biography of Lincoln; an account in the Baltimore *Sun*, 23 Apr. 1861, evidently based on what Richard Fuller told someone; Washington correspondence, 24 Apr., New York *Times*, 27 Apr. 1861; and William Cullen Bryant's dispatch dated New York, 24 Apr., New York *Evening Post*, 24 Apr. 1861. "Haggle" in this case means to cut clumsily or to hack.

82. Fuller to Chase, Baltimore, 23 Apr. 1861, Chase Papers, DLC.

83. Washington correspondence, n.d., Philadelphia *Gazette*, n.d., copied in the Chicago *Tribune*, 28 Sept. 1861.

84. Robert Livingston Stanton, "Reminiscences of President Lincoln," written ca. 1883, Robert Brewster Stanton Papers, New York Public Library.

85. Seward to Hicks, Washington, 22 Apr. 1861, *Abraham Lincoln: Complete Works, Comprising His Speeches, Letters, State Papers, and Miscellaneous Writings*, ed. John G. Nicolay and John Hay (2 vols.; New York: Century, 1902), 2:37. The inclusion of this letter in Nicolay and Hay's edition of Lincoln's writings suggests that Lincoln may have drafted it for Seward's signature.

86. George P. Bissell to Gideon Welles, Hartford, 24 Apr. 1861, Welles Papers, CSmH.

87. Charles R. Miller to Salmon P. Chase, New York, 24 Apr. 1861, Chase Papers, DLC; E. Seeley to Gideon Welles, New York, 25 Apr. 1861, Welles Papers, DLC.

88. John Pendleton Kennedy journal, 21 Apr. 1861, Kennedy Papers, Enoch Pratt Free Library, Baltimore.

89. Washington correspondence by G. W. A., 29 Apr., Cincinnati *Gazette*, 3 May 1861.

90. Granville Moody to Chase, Cincinnati, 30 Apr. 1861, Chase Papers, DLC.

91. Andrew H. Reeder to Simon Cameron, Philadelphia, 24 Apr. 1861, AL MSS DLC.

92. Indianapolis *Journal*, 1 May 1861.

93. George T. M. Davis to Prosper M. Wetmore, New York, 1 May 1861, in Stevens, *Union Defence Committee*, 154.

94. Reply to a delegation of Baltimore citizens, 15 Nov. 1861, *CWL*, 5:24.

95. Burlingame and Ettlinger, eds., *Hay Diary*, 11 (entry for 24 Apr. 1861).

96. Seward to Weed, Washington, 26 Apr. 1861, Weed Papers, University of Rochester.

97. James H. Campbell to Juliet Lewis Campbell, Washington, 27 Apr. 1861, Campbell Papers, Schoff Civil War Collection, William L. Clements Library, University of Michigan.

98. Washington correspondence, 28 Apr., New York *Times*, 1 May 1861; reminiscences of E. A. Spring, unidentified clipping with date "1898" penciled in, LMF; Washington correspondence, 25 Apr., New York *Tribune*, 26 Apr. 1861; Washington correspondence, 25 Apr., New York *World*, 30 Apr. 1861; Washington correspondence, 1 May, Cincinnati *Commercial*, 2 May 1861; Washington correspondence, 15 May, Springfield (Massachusetts) *Republican*, 17 May 1861.

99. *National Anti-Slavery Standard* (New York), 4 May 1861.

100. Burlingame and Ettlinger, eds., *Hay Diary*, 12 (entry for 25 Apr. 1861); *CWL*, 4:344.

101. Washington correspondence, 5 May, Chicago *Tribune*, 7 May 1861; report of the commissioners (Otho Scott, Robert McLane, and William J. Ross), contained in the Baltimore correspondence, 6 May, New York *Tribune*, 8 May 1861; *CWL*, 4:356.

102. Statement regarding suspension of habeas corpus in Maryland, [ca. 15 Sept. 1861], *CWL*, 4:523.

103. Dix to Silas M. Stillwell, Baltimore, 6 Nov. 1861, draft, Dix Papers, Columbia University.

104. McClellan to Dix, 20 Aug. 1861, *Official Records of the War of the Rebellion* [hereafter *OR*], I, 2, 1:589; Randolph B. Marcy to Dix, 11 Oct. 1861, and A. V. Colburn to Dix, 18 Sept. 1861, Dix Papers, in Martin Lichterman, "John Adams Dix: 1798–1879" (Ph.D. dissertation, Columbia University, 1952), 458.

105. Dix to Samuel J. Tilden, Baltimore, 3 Dec. 1861, Tilden Papers, New York Public Library.

106. Message to Congress, 26 May 1862, *CWL*, 5:241–242.

107. Gideon Welles, *Lincoln and Seward* (New York: Sheldon, 1874), 122–124; Howard K. Beale and Alan W. Brownsword, eds., *Diary of Gideon Welles, Secretary of the Navy under Lincoln and Johnson* (3 vols.; New York: W. W. Norton, 1960), 1:174 (entry for 15 Oct. 1862), 414 (22 Aug. 1863); Seward in conversation with Henry W. Bellows, 22 Apr. 1863, described in Bellows to his wife, Washington, 23 Apr. 1863, Bellows Papers, MHi; Bates to Francis Lieber, Washington, 12 Nov. 1862, Lincoln Cabinet Collection, LMF.

108. Theodore Calvin Pease and James G. Randall, eds., *The Diary of Orville Hickman Browning* (2 vols.; Springfield: Illinois State Historical Library, 1925–1933), 1:489 (entry for 28 July 1861).

109. Lyman Trumbull to his wife Julia, Washington, 2 July 1861, Trumbull Family Papers, IHi.

110. Henry W. Bellows to his son, New York, 2 May 1861, and to his wife, Washington, 20 May 1861, Henry W. Bellows Papers, MHi.

111. Philadelphia correspondence, 23 Apr., New York *Tribune*, 24 Apr. 1861; Francis B. Carpenter, "A Day with Governor Seward at Auburn," July 1870, Seward Papers, University of Rochester.

112. Memorandum, [ca. 17 May 1861], *CWL*, 4:372.

113. Henry Steele Commager, ed., *Documents of American History* (5th ed.; New York: Appleton-Century-Crofts, 1949), 401.

114. Henry Winter Davis to Sophie Du Pont, Baltimore, 5 May 1861, transcript, S. F. Du Pont Papers, Hagley Museum, Wilmington, Delaware.

115. AL MSS DLC.

116. Joel Parker, "Habeas Corpus and Martial Law," *North American Review* 93 (Oct. 1861):498.

117. Binney, *The Privilege of the Writ of Habeas Corpus under the Constitution* (Philadelphia: C. Sherman & Sons, 1862), 36.

118. Wilbourn E. Benton, ed., *1787: Drafting the U.S. Constitution* (2 vols.; College Station: Texas A & M University Press, 1986), 1:976, 991.

119. Bates to Lincoln, Washington, 5 July 1861, *OR*, II, 2:28.

120. *U.S. Statutes at Large*, 12:326.

121. Washington correspondence, 16 May, New York *Tribune*, 17 May 1861.

122. George Lunt to Caleb Cushing, Newburyport, Massachusetts, 11 July 1861, Caleb Cushing Papers, DLC.

123. Lincoln to Browning, Washington, 22 Sept. 1861, *CWL*, 4:532.

124. Dr. Henry Howard Furness, paraphrasing Lincoln, in Henry C. Whitney, *Life on the Circuit with Lincoln*, ed. Paul M. Angle (Caldwell, ID: Caxton, 1940), 332.

125. Garrett Davis to George D. Prentice, Baltimore, 28 Apr. 1861, Louisville *Journal*, 2 May, copied in the New York *Tribune*, 5 May 1861.

126. Washington correspondence by John W. Forney, 11 Sept., Philadelphia *Press*, 12 Sept. 1861.

127. Reminiscences of John W. Forney in a lecture delivered in November 1865 before the Ladies' Soldiers' Aid Society of Weldon, Pennsylvania, New York *Evening Post*, 30 Nov. 1865.

128. W. L. Underwood to an unidentified correspondent in St. Louis, n.p., n.d., New York *Times*, 11 May 1861.

129. Philadelphia *Evening Bulletin*, 2 Jan. 1890.

130. Burlingame and Ettlinger, eds., *Hay Diary*, 19 (entry for 6 May 1861).

131. *CWL*, 4:428.

132. Buckner, public letter dated 12 September 1861, in the Clarksville *Jeffersonian*, 13 Sept. 1861, quoted in Robert McNutt McElroy, *Kentucky in the Nation's History* (New York: Moffat, Yard, 1909), 536; Lincoln to Buckner, Washington, 10 July 1861, *CWL*, 4:444.

133. Joshua F. Speed to Lincoln, Louisville, 2 June 1861, Robert Anderson Papers, DLC.

134. Speed to Holt, Louisville, 7 Sept. 1861, Holt Papers, DLC.

135. McClellan to Lincoln, Cincinnati, 30 May 1861, Stephen W. Sears, ed., *The Civil War Papers of George B. McClellan: Selected Correspondence, 1860–1865* (New York: Ticknor & Fields, 1989), 28.

136. R. W. Johnson, *A Soldier's Reminiscences in Peace and War* (Philadelphia: J. B. Lippincott, 1886), 172–173.

137. Lincoln to Magoffin, Washington, 24 Aug. 1861, *CWL*, 4:497.

138. Jackson to Simon Cameron, Jefferson City, Missouri, 17 Apr. 1861, *OR*, III, 1:83.

139. Cameron to Lyon, 30 Apr. 1861, *OR*, I, 1:675

140. Charles Gibson to "My dear Sir," Washington, 13 May 1861, Gibson Papers, Missouri Historical Society.

141. Lorenzo Thomas to Harney, Washington, 27 May 1861, *CWL*, 4:387.

142. Lincoln to Blair, Washington, 18 May 1861, ibid., 4:372.

143. Various reminiscences of Francis Pierpont, typescripts, Pierpont Papers, West Virginia University.

144. *OR*, I, 2, 1:723.

145. Herbert Clifford Francis Bell, *Lord Palmerston* (2 vols.; London: Longmans, Green, 1936), 2:275.

146. Charles Sumner quoting Seward, Edward Everett journal, 23 Aug. 1861, Everett Papers, MHi.

147. Seward to Weed, 23 Nov. 1837, in Thurlow Weed Barnes, *Life of Thurlow Weed Including His Autobiography and a Memoir* (2 vols.; Boston: Houghton Mifflin, 1883–1884), 1:62.

148. Edouard de Stoeckl to Alexander Gortchakov, Washington, 6 May 1861, dispatch 30, photocopy, Principal Archive of the Ministry of Foreign Affairs, Russian Reproductions, Papers of the Foreign Copying Project, DLC; Albert A. Woldman, *Lincoln and the Russians* (Cleveland: World, 1952), 62.

149. Paul Revere Frothingham, *Edward Everett: Orator and Statesman* (Boston: Houghton Mifflin, 1925), 433.

150. John D. Defrees to Josiah G. Holland, Washington, 8 Aug. 1865, in Allen C. Guelzo, ed., "Holland's Informants: The Construction of Josiah Holland's 'Life of Abraham Lincoln'," *Journal of the Abraham Lincoln Association* 23 (2002):46.

151. William H. Seward to Charles F. Adams, 21 May 1861, draft, AL MSS DLC.

152. Charles Francis Adams diary, 10 June 1861, MHi.

153. J. C. Levenson, ed., *The Letters of Henry Adams* (6 vols.; Cambridge, MA: Belknap Press of Harvard University Press, 1982–1988), 1:239.

154. Sumner to Richard Henry Dana, Washington, 30 June 1861, Beverly Wilson Palmer, ed., *The Selected Letters of Charles Sumner* (2 vols.; Boston: Northeastern University Press, 1990), 2:73

155. Benjamin Perley Poore in Rice, ed., *Reminiscences of Abraham Lincoln*, 223; Schurz, *Reminiscences*, 2:240–241.

156. William B. Wilson, *A Few Acts and Actors in the Tragedy of the Civil War in the United States* (Philadelphia: by the author, 1892), 111.

157. Lincoln to Oliver P. Morton, Washington, 29 Sept. 1861, *CWL*, 4:541.

158. Blair to Cameron, 2 June 1861, in David W. Miller, *Second Only to Grant: Quartermaster General Montgomery C. Meigs, A Biography* (Shippensburg, PA: White Mane Books, 2000), 95.

159. Lincoln to Scott, Washington, 5 June 1861, *CWL*, 4:394.

160. Scott to Lincoln, Washington, 5 June 1861, AL MSS DLC.

161. Meigs diary, 29 July 1861, copy, Nicolay Papers, DLC.

162. Gibbs to John Austin Stevens, Washington, 25, 29 July [1861], and "Memoranda," [Aug. 1861], John Austin Stevens Papers, New-York Historical Society.

163. Washington correspondence, 18 April, Philadelphia *Inquirer,* 19 Apr. 1861.

164. Washington correspondence, 13 May, New York *Tribune,* 14 May 1861.

165. Browning to John C. Bagby, Washington, 26 Feb. 1862, Bagby Papers, IHi.

166. Washington correspondence, 16 May, New York *Herald,* 17 May 1861; New York *Tribune,* 16 May 1861; Washington correspondence, 15, 17 May, New York *Times,* 16, 18 May 1861.

167. Lincoln to E. D. Morgan, Washington, 20 May 1861, *CWL,* 4:375.

168. Rush Hawkins's reminiscences, Margaret B. Stillwell, ed., "Hawkins of the *Hawkins Zouaves,*" in Deoch Fulton, ed., *Bookmen's Holiday, Notes and Studies Written in Tribute to Harry Miller Lydenberg* (New York: New York Public Library, 1943), 96.

169. Washington correspondence by "Leo," 19 August, New York *Times,* 21 Aug. 1861.

170. Schurz, *Reminiscences,* 2:242.

171. Burlingame and Ettlinger, eds., *Hay Diary,* 20 (entry for 7 May 1861).

172. Washington correspondence, 30 May, New York *Tribune,* 31 May 1861.

173. Washington correspondence by "Indiana" [John D. Defrees], 9 July, *Cincinnati Commercial,* 12 July 1861; Defrees in Francis B. Carpenter, *The Inner Life of Abraham Lincoln: Six Months at the White House* (New York: Hurd and Houghton, 1867), 126–127.

174. Washington correspondence, 4 July, Philadelphia *Press,* 5 July 1861.

175. Washington correspondence, 6 July, *Ohio State Journal* (Columbus), 10 July 1861.

176. Washington correspondence by "Au Revoir," 20 July, *Missouri Democrat* (St. Louis), 25 July 1861.

177. Burlingame and Ettlinger, eds., *Hay Diary,* 20 (entry for 7 May 1861).

178. *CWL,* 4:360.

179. Ibid., 4:421–441.

180. Washington correspondence, 10 July, Chicago *Evening Journal,* 13 July 1861.

181. Washington correspondence, 5 July, New York *World,* 8 July 1861.

182. Washington correspondence by Sigma, 6 July, Cincinnati *Commercial,* 11 July 1861.

183. Henry Winter Davis to Samuel Francis Du Pont, [Washington], [ca. 5 July 1861], transcript, S. F. Du Pont Papers, Hagley Museum, Wilmington, Delaware; James H. Campbell to his wife, Washington, 5 and 6 July 1861, Campbell Papers, Schoff Civil War Collection, William L. Clements Library, University of Michigan.

184. Washington correspondence, 12 July, London *Times,* 29 July 1861.

185. Washington correspondence, 9 July, Cincinnati *Commercial,* n.d., copied in the Chicago *Tribune,* 15 July 1861.

186. New York *Tribune,* 6 July 1861.

187. Providence *Journal,* 6 July 1861.

188. Benjamin Brown French to Henry Flagg French, Washington, 5 July 1861, French Family Papers, DLC.

189. Curtis to John J. Pinkerton, North Shore, New York, 9 July 1861, Edward Cary, *George William Curtis* (Boston: Houghton Mifflin, 1894), 147.

190. *Harper's Weekly,* 20 July 1861.

191. Nicholas B. Wainwright, ed., *A Philadelphia Perspective: The Diary of Sidney George Fisher Covering the Years, 1834–1871* (Philadelphia: Historical Society of Pennsylvania, 1967), 396, 410–411 (entries for 6 July, 5 Dec. 1861).

192. Motley to his wife, Woodland Hill, 23 June 1861, George William Curtis, ed., *The Correspondence of John Lothrop Motley* (2 vols.; New York: Harper & Brothers, 1889), 1:395.

193. Motley to the duchess of Argyll, Vienna, 27 May 1865, Curtis, ed., *Correspondence of John Lothrop Motley,* 2:77.

194. New York *World,* 6 July 1861.

195. *Ohio State Journal* (Columbus), 6 July 1861.

196. *Frank Leslie's Illustrated Newspaper,* 13 July 1861.

197. London *Spectator,* 20 July 1861, copied in *The Living Age* (Boston), 24 Aug. 1861, 496; London *Times,* n.d., copied in the Boston *Journal,* 2 Aug. 1861.

198. *Illinois State Journal* (Springfield), 9 July 1861; *Douglass' Monthly* 4 (Aug. 1861): 497.

199. Dubuque, Iowa, *Herald,* 10 July 1861, quoted in John Thomas Hubbell, "The Northern Democracy and the Crisis of Disunion, 1860–1861" (Ph.D. dissertation, University of Illinois, 1969), 242.

200. *Congressional Globe,* 37th Congress, 1st Session, 68 (11 July 1861).

201. William Parr to S. S. Cox, Linville, Ohio, 9 July 1861, Cox Papers, RPB.

202. New Orleans *Bulletin,* 8 July 1861, copied in the Providence *Journal,* 17 July 1861.

203. Philadelphia *Daily News,* New York *Times,* 6 July 1861.

204. Howe to Horace Rublee, Washington, 3 July 1861, Howe Papers, Wisconsin Historical Society.

205. Lyman Trumbull to his wife Julia, Washington, 14 July 1861, Trumbull Family Papers, IHi.

206. James W. Grimes to William P. Fessenden, Washington, [day not indicated] May 1861, copy, Fessenden Papers, Bowdoin College.

207. New York *Daily News,* 12 July 1864.

208. Higginson to Louisa Higginson, 23 Aug. 1861, Mary Thacher Higginson, ed., *Letters and Journals of Thomas Wentworth Higginson, 1846–1906* (Boston: Houghton Mifflin, 1921), 157–158.

209. Springfield (Massachusetts) *Republican,* 16 Oct. 1861.

210. Washington correspondence by Rolla, n.d., Cleveland *Plain Dealer,* 29 Nov. 1861.

211. Washington correspondence by Edward Dicey, n.d., London *Spectator,* n.d., quoted in *Frank Leslie's Illustrated Newspaper,* 17 May 1862.

212. Washington correspondence, 6 Jan., *Missouri Republican* (St. Louis), 10 Jan. 1862, in Burlingame, ed., *Lincoln's Journalist,* 188.

213. Washington correspondence by Van [D. W. Bartlett], 5 Feb., Springfield (Massachusetts) *Republican,* 8 Feb. 1862.

214. Henry L. Dawes to his wife, Washington, 17 Jan. 1862, Dawes Papers, DLC.

215. *Frank Leslie's Illustrated Newspaper,* 1 Feb. 1862; Manton Marble to Martin B. Anderson, New York, 11 June 1861, Anderson Papers, University of Rochester.

216. Manton Marble to Martin B. Anderson, New York, 1 Aug. 1861, Anderson Papers, University of Rochester.

217. William M. Dickson to Friedrich Hassaurek, Cincinnati, 25 Dec. 1861, Hassaurek Papers, Ohio Historical Society.

218. A. Mann, Jr., to E. B. Washburne, New York, 1 May 1862, Washburne Papers, DLC; A. Mann, Jr., to Lyman Trumbull, New York, 18 Jan. 1862, Trumbull Papers, DLC.

219. John P. Crawford to Lincoln, New York, 10 Aug. 1861, AL MSS DLC.

220. Washington correspondence, 26 Aug., *National Anti-Slavery Standard* (New York), 31 Aug. 1861.

221. Charles Eliot Norton to Henry W. Bellows, Newport, 25 Aug. 1861, Bellows Papers, MHi

222. James A. Hamilton, *Reminiscences of James A. Hamilton; or, Men and Events, At Home and Abroad, during Three Quarters of a Century* (New York: C. Scribner, 1869), 477.

223. New York *Evening Post,* 29 Apr. 1861.

224. Burlingame and Ettlinger, eds., *Hay Diary,* 11 (entry for 25 Apr. 1861).

225. Message to Congress, 4 July 1861, *CWL,* 4:427.

226. Frank E. Brownell, "Ellsworth's Career," Philadelphia *Weekly Times,* 18 June 1881.

227. W. W. Orme to David Davis, Washington, 11 May 1861, David Davis Papers, IHi.

228. Washington correspondence, 24 May, New York *Tribune* and New York *Herald,* 25 May 1861.

229. "Stories of Lincoln," New York *Mail and Express,* 11 Feb. 1899, p. 11.

230. John A. Kasson in Rice, ed., *Reminiscences of Abraham Lincoln,* 378.

231. Frank Brownell, quoted in Frank G. Carpenter, "Col. Ellsworth," Washington correspondence, 25 May, Los Angeles *Times*, 4 June 1887; St. Louis *Post-Dispatch*, 24 May 1901.

232. [Hay], "Ellsworth," *Atlantic Monthly*, July 1861, 124.

233. Lincoln to Ephraim and Phoebe Ellsworth, Washington, 25 May 1861, *CWL*, 4:385–386.

234. *Harper's Weekly*, 4 May 1861.

235. Burlingame and Ettlinger, eds., *Hay Diary*, 16 (entry for 1 May 1861).

236. Alexander K. Randall to Lincoln, Madison, Wisconsin, 6 May 1861, *OR*, III, 1:168–169.

237. Henry L. Dawes to his wife, Washington, 15 July 1861, Dawes Papers, DLC; Chase to Alphonso Taft, Washington, 28 Apr. 1861, John Niven, ed., *The Salmon P. Chase Papers* (5 vols.; Kent, OH: Kent State University Press, 1993–1998), 3:63.

238. Halstead to Timothy C. Day, Washington, 11 June 1861, in Sarah J. Day, *The Man on a Hill Top* (Philadelphia: Ware Brothers, 1931), 245.

239. Timothy C. Day to Murat Halstead, Cincinnati, 13 June 1861, Halstead Papers, Cincinnati Historical Society.

240. Henry L. Dawes to his wife, Washington, 15 July 1861, Dawes Papers, DLC.

241. Edouard de Stoeckl to Alexander Gortchakov, Washington, 6 May 1861, dispatch 30, photocopy, Principal Archive of the Ministry of Foreign Affairs, Russian Reproductions, Papers of the Foreign Copying Project, DLC; Woldman, *Lincoln and the Russians*, 61.

242. William P. Fessenden to J. S. Pike, Portland, 8 Sept. 1861, Pike Papers, DLC.

243. New York *Times*, 18, 20, 21, 22 Apr. 1861.

244. Indianapolis *Journal*, 1 May 1861.

245. New York *Tribune*, 26 June 1861.

246. William A. Croffut, *An American Procession, 1855–1914: A Personal Chronicle of Famous Men* (Boston: Little, Brown, 1931), 123.

247. George T. M. Davis to Prosper M. Wetmore, New York, 1 May 1861, in Stevens, *Union Defence Committee*, 153–155.

248. John L. Motley to his wife, Washington, 20 June 1861, Curtis, ed., *Correspondence of Motley*, 1:382.

249. Scott to McClellan, Washington, 3 May 1861, *OR*, I, 51, 1:369–370.

250. Colfax to Greeley, South Bend, Indiana, [14?] June 1861, Greeley Papers, DLC.

251. Edouard de Stoeckl to Alexander Gortchakov, Washington, 3 July 1861, dispatch 46, photocopy, Principal Archive of the Ministry of Foreign Affairs, Russian Reproductions, Papers of the Foreign Copying Project, DLC.

252. Meigs to Seward, 13 May 1861, in Miller, *Second Only to Grant*, 93.

253. Adam Gurowski, *Diary* (3 vols.; Boston: Lee and Shepard, 1862–1866), 1:47 (entry for May 1861).

254. United States Congress, *Report of the Joint Committee on the Conduct of the War* (3 vols.; Washington, DC, 1863), 2:38.

255. Meigs diary, 29 June 1861, copy, Nicolay Papers, DLC.

256. John Bigelow diary, New York Public Library (entry for 3 July 1861).

257. Reminiscences of Gary W. Hazleton, Edward S. Bragg Papers, Palmer Collection, Western Reserve Historical Society, copy, Nevins Papers, Columbia University.

258. Nicolay to Therena Bates, Washington, 21 July 1861, Burlingame, ed., *With Lincoln in the White House*, 51.

259. Dahlgren diary, copy, Nicolay Papers, DLC (entry for 21 July 1861).

260. Mendell to Lorenzo Thomas, Centreville, 4 P.M.., 21 July 1861, *OR*, I, 2:747.

261. Nicolay to Therena Bates, Washington, 21 July 1861, Burlingame, ed., *With Lincoln in the White House*, 52.

262. Bill Arp, *Bill Arp, So Called: A Side Show of the Southern Side of the War* (New York: Metropolitan Record, 1866), 93.

263. B. S. Alexander to ?, 21 July 1861, *OR*, I, 2:747.

264. McDowell to E. D. Townsend, Fairfax Court House, 21 July 1861, *OR*, I, 2:316.

265. E. B. Washburne to his wife, Washington, 22 July 1861, Washburn Family Papers,

Washburn Memorial Library, Norlands, Maine.

266. Robert L. Wilson to William H. Herndon, Sterling, Illinois, 10 Feb. 1866, in Douglas L. Wilson and Rodney O. Davis, eds., *Herndon's Informants: Letters, Interviews, and Statements about Abraham Lincoln* (Urbana: University of Illinois Press, 1998), 207.

267. Washington correspondence by John Hay, 22 July, New York *World,* 24 July 1861, in Burlingame, ed., *Lincoln's Journalist,* 78.

268. Pease and Randall, eds., *Browning Diary,* 1:485 (entry for 22 July 1861).

269. William A. Richardson, remarks in the House of Representatives, 24 July and 1 August 1861, *Congressional Globe,* 37th Congress, 1st Session, 246, 387. Washburne told a similar story to his wife. Washburne to his wife, Washington, 22 July 1861, Washburn Family Papers, Washburn Memorial Library, Norlands, Maine.

270. Henry Winter Davis to Sophie Du Pont, Baltimore, 4 Aug. 1861, and to S. F. Du Pont, Long Branch, NJ, 21 Aug. 1861, transcripts, S. F. Du Pont Papers, Hagley Museum, Wilmington, Delaware.

271. Manton Marble to Martin B. Anderson, New York, 1 Aug. 1861, Martin B. Anderson Papers, University of Rochester.

272. New York *Herald,* 22 July 1861; Chicago *Evening Journal,* 20 Aug. 1861.

273. Stanton to Buchanan, 26 July 1861, in George C. Gorham, *Life and Public Services of Edwin M. Stanton* (2 vols.; Boston: Houghton Mifflin, 1899), 1:223.

274. Leonard Swett to his wife Laura, Washington, 6 August 1861, David Davis Papers, IHi.

275. Lyman Trumbull to James R. Doolittle, Lakeside, Connecticut, 31 Aug. 1861, typescript, Doolittle Papers, Wisconsin State Historical Society.

276. Lyman Trumbull to his wife Julia, Washington, 28 July 1861, Trumbull Family Papers, IHi.

277. Charles Capen McLaughlin et al., eds., *The Papers of Frederick Law Olmsted* (6 vols.;

Baltimore, MD: Johns Hopkins University Press, 1977–1992), 4:138.

278. I[srael] D. Andrews to Samuel J. Tilden, Washington, 18 Aug. 1861, Tilden Papers, New York Public Library.

279. Bellows to Charles Eliot Norton, Walpole, New Hampshire, 21 Aug. 1861, Charles Eliot Norton Papers, Harvard University.

280. E. Peshine Smith to Henry C. Carey, Rochester, 17 Aug. 1861, Henry C. Carey Papers in the Edward Carey Gardiner Collection, Historical Society of Pennsylvania.

281. Usher to Samuel J. Tilden, Terre Haute, 17 Aug. 1861, Tilden Papers, New York Public Library.

282. Greeley to Moncure D. Conway, New York, 17 Aug. 1861, Conway Papers, Columbia University.

283. New York *Tribune,* 23 July 1861.

284. Greeley to Moncure D. Conway, New York, 17 Aug. 1861, Conway Papers, Columbia University.

285. Greeley to Lincoln, New York, 29 July 1861, AL MSS DLC.

286. Burlingame and Ettlinger, eds., *Hay Diary,* 193 (entry for 30 Apr. 1864).

287. Washington correspondence, 29 Aug. New York *Tribune,* 30 Aug. 1861.

288. Washington correspondence, n.d., Philadelphia *Gazette,* n.d., copied in the Chicago *Tribune,* 28 Sept. 1861.

289. Washington correspondence, 10 Sept., Philadelphia *Press,* 11 Sept. 1861; Philadelphia *Daily News,* 13 Sept. 1861.

290. Washington correspondence, [28 Aug.], New York *Times,* 29 Aug. 1861.

291. Providence *Journal,* 27 July 1861.

292. George William Curtis to Charles Eliot Norton, North Shore, New York, 29 July, 19 Aug. 1861, Curtis Papers, Harvard University.

293. George P. Goff to Nicolay, Washington, 9 Feb. 1889, Nicolay Papers, DLC.

294. John Hay, "The Heroic Age in Washington," 1871 lecture, in Michael Burlingame, ed., *At Lincoln's Side: John Hay's Civil War Correspondence and Selected Writings*

(Carbondale: Southern Illinois University Press, 2000), 126.

295. James T. Du Bois and Gertrude S. Mathews, *Galusha A. Grow, Father of the Homestead Law* (Boston: Houghton Mifflin, 1917), 250.

296. Washington correspondence, 5 Aug., *National Anti-Slavery Standard* (New York), 10 Aug. 1861.

297. Thompson "Abraham Lincoln," manuscript, Thompson Papers, LMF, in Charles Roll, *Colonel Dick Thompson: The Persistent Whig* (Indianapolis: Indiana Historical Bureau, 1948), 174.

298. Walt Whitman, *Specimen Days,* in Whitman, *Complete Prose Works* (Philadelphia: David McKay, 1892), 24–25.

299. William T. Sherman, *Memoirs of Gen. William T. Sherman* (2 vols.; New York: C. L. Webster, 1892), 1:217–219.

300. William Todd, *The Seventy-Ninth Highlanders: New York Volunteers in the War of Rebellion, 1861–1865* (Albany, NY: Brandow, Barton, 1886), 53–54.

301. *CWL,* 4:457–458.

302. John Littlefield, "Personal Recollections of Abraham Lincoln," lecture delivered in Brooklyn on 2 Dec. 1875, Brooklyn *Daily Eagle,* 3 Dec. 1875, p. 4.

303. Hamilton, "A True Story of President Lincoln," the New York *Sun,* n.d., reprinted in an unidentified newspaper clipping, LMF.

304. Pease and Randall, eds., *Browning Diary,* 1:537 (entry for 2 Apr. 1862).

305. James Taussig to members of a committee of Missouri Radicals, *Missouri Democrat* (St. Louis), 9 June 1863; William Howard Russell, *My Diary North and South* (New York: Harper and Brothers, 1863), 188 (entry for 26 Aug. 1861).

306. Robert Patterson, *A Narrative of the Campaign in the Valley of the Shenandoah in 1861* (Philadelphia: Sherman, 1865), 18–19.

307. Washington correspondence, 29 July, New York *Examiner,* 1 Aug. 1861, Burlingame, ed., *Dispatches from Lincoln's White House,* 16.

Chapter 24. Sitzkrieg

1. Richard Smith to Joseph H. Barrett, Cincinnati, 7 Aug. 1861, Lincoln Miscellaneous Collection, University of Chicago.

2. Benjamin Brown French to his son Frank, Washington, 8 Dec. 1861, French Family Papers, DLC.

3. Washington correspondence by John W. Forney, 1 Sept., Philadelphia *Press,* 12 Sept. 1861.

4. William B. Wilson, *A Few Acts and Actors in the Tragedy of the Civil War in the United States* (Philadelphia: self-published, 1892), 111.

5. McClellan to his wife, Washington, 27, 30 July, 9[10] Aug. 1861, in Stephen W. Sears, ed., *The Civil War Papers of George B. McClellan: Selected Correspondence, 1860–1865* (New York: Ticknor and Fields, 1989), 70, 71, 82.

6. *OR,* I, 2:197.

7. McClellan to Lincoln, Washington, 2 Aug. 1861; McClellan to his wife, Washington, 2 Aug. 1861, in Sears, ed., *Papers of McClellan,* 74–75.

8. Stephen W. Sears, *George B. McClellan: The Young Napoleon* (New York: Ticknor & Fields, 1988), 111, 70.

9. Nicolay to Therena Bates, Washington, 7 July 1861, in Michael Burlingame, ed., *With Lincoln in the White House: Letters, Memoranda, and Other Writings of John G. Nicolay, 1860–1865* (Carbondale: Southern Illinois University Press, 2000), 47; Washington correspondence, 5 July, New York *Tribune,* 6 July 1861.

10. John D. Hayes, ed., *Samuel Francis Du Pont: A Selection from his Civil War Letters* (3 vols.; Ithaca, NY: Cornell University Press, 1969), 1:94.

11. Washington correspondence, 16 June, New York *Times,* 18 June 1861.

12. McClellan to his wife, Washington, 11 Sept. 1861, Sears, ed., *Papers of McClellan,* 98.

13. Nicolay memorandum, 20 Nov. 1861; Nicolay to Therena Bates, Washington, 21 November 1861, in Burlingame, ed., *With Lincoln in the White House,* 62.

14. Washington correspondence, 21 Nov., New York *World*, 23 Nov. 1861.

15. Stephen W. Sears, ed., *For Country, Cause & Leader: The Civil War Journal of Charles B. Haydon* (New York: Ticknor & Fields, 1993), 130 (entry for 21 Nov. 1861).

16. McClellan to Scott, Beverly, VA, 18 July 1861, Sears, ed., *Papers of McClellan*, 60.

17. McClellan to his wife, Washington, 8 Aug. 1861, Sears, ed., *Papers of McClellan*, 81.

18. McClellan to his wife, Washington, 13 Oct. 1861, ibid., 107.

19. Scott to Cameron, Washington, 12 August 1861, *OR*, I, 11, 3:6.

20. Howard K. Beale and Alan W. Brownsword, eds., *Diary of Gideon Welles, Secretary of the Navy under Lincoln and Johnson* [hereafter *Welles Diary*] (3 vols.; New York: W. W. Norton, 1960), 1:241–242 (entry for 25 Feb. 1863).

21. Gideon Welles, undated typed memo, Welles Papers, CSmH.

22. McClellan to his wife, Washington, 27 Sept. 1861, Sears, ed., *Papers of McClellan*, 103–104.

23. Edward Everett journal, entry for 25 Sept. 1862, MHi.

24. Chandler to his wife, Washington, 27 Oct. 1861, and St. Louis, 12 Oct. 1861, Chandler Papers, DLC.

25. Michael Burlingame and John R. Turner Ettlinger, eds., *Inside Lincoln's White House: The Complete Civil War Diary of John Hay* (Carbondale: Southern Illinois University Press, 1997), 29 (entry for 26 Oct. 1861).

26. Ibid., 28 (entry for 26 Oct. 1861).

27. Order dated 1 Nov. 1861, Roy P. Basler et al., eds., *Collected Works of Abraham Lincoln* [hereafter *CWL*] (8 vols. plus index; New Brunswick, NJ: Rutgers University Press, 1953–1955), 5:10.

28. Burlingame and Ettlinger, eds., *Hay Diary*, 30 (entry for [Nov. 1861]).

29. Washington correspondence by John Hay, 26 October, *Missouri Republican* (St. Louis), 31 Oct. 1861, in Michael Burlingame, ed., *Lincoln's Journalist: John Hay's Anonymous*

Writings for the Press, 1860–1864 (Carbondale: Southern Illinois University Press, 1998), 126.

30. Henry M. Smith of the Chicago *Tribune* to "Bro. G.", Washington, Friday [ca. 31 Oct. 1861], Charles Henry Ray Papers, CSmH.

31. Washington correspondence by Van [D. W. Bartlett], 5 Nov., Springfield, Massachusetts, *Republican*, 8 Nov. 1861.

32. Washington correspondence by Van [D. W. Bartlett], 31 Oct., Springfield, Massachusetts, *Republican*, 1 Nov. 1861; Washington correspondence, 28 Oct., New York *World*, 29 Oct. 1861; Washington correspondence by Ben: Perley Poore, 30 Oct., Boston *Evening Journal*, 1 Nov. 1861.

33. Herndon to Lyman Trumbull, Springfield, 20 Nov. 1861, Trumbull Papers, DLC.

34. John J. Bagby to Zachariah Chandler, Detroit, 6 Dec. 1861, Chandler Papers, DLC.

35. Michael Burlingame, *The Inner World of Abraham Lincoln* (Urbana: University of Illinois Press, 1994), 182.

36. Burlingame and Ettlinger, eds., *Hay Diary*, 32 (entry for 13 Nov. 1861).

37. William H. Russell, *My Diary North and South* (Boston: T.O.H.P. Burnham, 1863), 552 (entry for 9 Oct. 1861).

38. Comte de Paris diary, entry for 28 Sept. 1861, in Russel H. Beatie, *The Army of the Potomac* (3 vols.; Cambridge, MA: Da Capo Press, 2002–2007), 1:489.

39. David Dixon Porter, "Journal of Occurrences during the War of the Rebellion," vol. 1, 173–174, Porter Papers, DLC.

40. Memorandum by C. C. Buel, New York, 23 Nov. 1885 (recalling the words uttered the previous evening by Horace Porter), Richard Watson Gilder Papers, New York Public Library.

41. F. A. Mitchel to John Hay, East Orange, New Jersey, 3 Jan. 1889, Nicolay-Hay Papers, IHi.

42. In 1869, Burnside told this story at a dinner party in London. Manuscript diary of Benjamin Moran, DLC (entry for 11 Dec. 1869).

43. Bancroft to his wife, Washington, 16 Dec. 1861, Bancroft Papers, Cornell University.

44. Sears, *McClellan*, 59.

45. Nicholas B. Wainwright, ed., *A Philadelphia Perspective: The Diary of Sidney George Fisher Covering the Years, 1834–1871* (Philadelphia: Historical Society of Pennsylvania, 1967), 443 (entry for 9 Dec. 1862).

46. McClellan to his wife, Washington, [ca. 11 Oct. 1861], Sears, ed., *Papers of McClellan*, 106–107.

47. Albert E. H. Johnson. "Reminiscences of the Hon. Edwin M. Stanton," *Columbia Historical Society Records* 13 (1910):73.

48. Sears, *McClellan*, 116–117.

49. McClellan to S. L. M. Barlow, Washington, 8 Nov. 1861, Sears, ed., *Papers of McClellan*, 128.

50. McClellan to his wife, Washington, 29 Sept. 1861, ibid., 104.

51. *OR*, I, 5, 1:9–11.

52. Sears, *McClellan*, 123.

53. Joseph E. Johnston to W. H. C. Whiting, Manassas, 12 Sept. 1861, *OR*, I, 5:848.

54. Washington correspondence by John Hay, 22 Oct., *Missouri Republican* (St. Louis), 27 October 1861, in Burlingame, ed., *Lincoln's Journalist*, 122.

55. James Roman Ward to his father, Baltimore, 24 Oct. 1861, photostatic copy, Civil War Papers, Maryland Historical Society.

56. Stoddard, "White House Sketches No. 6," New York *Citizen*, 22 Sept. 1866, in William O. Stoddard, *Inside the White House in War-Times: Memoirs and Reports of Lincoln's Secretary*, ed. Michael Burlingame (1890; Lincoln: University of Nebraska Press, 2000), 166–167.

57. Rush C. Hawkins, *Hawkins of the Hawkins Zouaves*, ed. Margaret Bingham Stillwell, in *Bookman's Holiday: Notes and Studies Written and Gathered in Tribute to Harry Miller Lydenberg* (New York: New York Public Library, 1943), 96.

58. George Gibbs to John Austin Stevens, Washington, 25 Oct. 1861, Stevens Papers, New-York Historical Society.

59. Noah Brooks, "Personal Recollections of Lincoln," in Michael Burlingame, ed., *Lincoln Observed: Civil War Dispatches of Noah Brooks* (Baltimore, MD: Johns Hopkins University Press, 1998), 215.

60. Weed to Seward, Albany, 27 Oct. 1861, AL MSS DLC.

61. Benjamin Welch, Jr., to George G. Fogg, New York, 22 Oct. 1861, Fogg Papers, New Hampshire Historical Society.

62. Stanton to John A. Dix, Washington, 26 Oct. 1861, Dix Papers, Columbia University.

63. Washington correspondence, 7 Oct., New York *Examiner*, 10 Oct. 1861, in Michael Burlingame, ed., *Dispatches from Lincoln's White House: The Anonymous Civil War Journalism of Presidential Secretary William O. Stoddard* (Lincoln: University of Nebraska Press, 2002), 32.

64. Washington correspondence, 12 Sept., Chicago *Evening Journal*, 16 Sept. 1861.

65. Washington correspondence by Stoddard, 14 Oct., New York *Examiner*, 17 Oct. 1861, Burlingame, ed., *Dispatches from Lincoln's White House*, 36.

66. Washington correspondence, 3 Nov., Chicago *Evening Journal*, 6 Nov. 1861.

67. Nicolay, memorandum, 2 Oct. 1861, in Burlingame, ed., *With Lincoln in the White House*, 59.

68. Burlingame and Ettlinger, eds., *Hay Diary*, 123 (entry for 9 Dec. 1863).

69. Pope to Valentine B. Horton, St. Louis, 22 Aug. 1861, Pope Papers, New-York Historical Society.

70. Reminiscences of Emil Preetorius, in Ida M. Tarbell, *The Life of Abraham Lincoln* (2 vols.; New York: McClure, Phillips, 1900), 2:61–62n.

71. George Wilkes to the editor, Washington, 18 Aug., New York *Times*, 20 Aug. 1861.

72. Scott to Frémont, Washington, 23 Sept. 1861, *OR*, I, 3:185.

73. Louisville *Courier*, n.d., copied in the Cincinnati *Commercial*, 3 Sept. 1861.

74. Speed to Lincoln, Cincinnati, 1 Sept. 1861, and Louisville, 3 Sept. 1861, AL MSS DLC.

75. Speed to Joseph Holt, Louisville, 7 Sept. 1861, Holt Papers, DLC.

76. Robert Anderson to Lincoln, Louisville, 13 Sept. 1861, AL MSS DLC.

77. London *Economist*, n.d., copied in *The Liberator* (Boston), 18 Nov. 1861.

78. Blair to Sumner, 16 Oct. 1861, in James Ford Rhodes, *History of the United States from the Compromise of 1850* (4 vols.; New York: Harper & Brothers, 1893–1899), 3:478.

79. Lincoln to Frémont, Washington, 2 Sept. 1861, *CWL*, 4:506.

80. Frémont to Lincoln, [St. Louis], 8 Sept. 1861, AL MSS DLC.

81. John Russell to Lyman Trumbull, Bluefield, Illinois, 17 Dec. 1861, Trumbull Papers, DLC.

82. Washington correspondence, 11 Sept., Chicago *Tribune*, 12 Sept. 1861.

83. Auburn *Northern Independent*, n.d., copied in the *Illinois State Register* (Springfield), 18 Oct. 1861.

84. *Douglass's Monthly* 4 (Oct. 1861): 531.

85. *The Liberator* (Boston), 20 Sept. 1861.

86. *National Anti-Slavery Standard* (New York), 28 Sept. 1861.

87. Lowell to Jane Norton, Cambridge, MA, 28 Sept. 1861, Charles Eliot Norton, ed., *Letters of James Russell Lowell* (2 vols.; New York: Harper & Brothers, 1894), 1:314.

88. Horace Elisha Scudder, *James Russell Lowell: A Biography* (2 vols.; Boston: Houghton Mifflin, 1901), 2:29.

89. B. Rush Plumly to Chase, St. Louis, 15 Sept. 1861, Chase Papers, DLC.

90. Fessenden to James W. Grimes, Portland, 26 Sept. 1861, Fessenden Papers, Bowdoin College.

91. Fessenden to J. S. Pike, Portland, 8 Sept. 1861, Pike Papers, DLC.

92. Wade to Zachariah Chandler, Jefferson, Ohio, 23 Sept. 1861, Chandler Papers, DLC.

93. Gerrit Smith, speech at Peterboro, New Hampshire, 22 Sept. 1861, New York *Tribune*, 28 Sept., copied in *The Liberator* (Boston), 11 Oct. 1861.

94. Sumner to Francis Lieber, Boston, 17 Sept. 1861, Beverly Wilson Palmer, ed., *The Selected Letters of Charles Sumner* (2 vols.; Boston: Northeastern University Press, 1990), 2:79.

95. Lydia Maria Child to John Greenleaf Whittier, Wayland, Massachusetts, 21 Jan. 1862 and 22 Sept. 1861, Child Papers, Microfiche edition, ed., Milton Meltzer and Patricia G. Holland.

96. Bancroft to his wife, [New York], 14 Sept. 1861, Bancroft Papers, Cornell University.

97. Medill to Chase, Chicago, 15 Sept. 1861, John Niven, ed., *The Salmon P. Chase Papers* (5 vols.; Kent, Ohio: Kent State University Press, 1993–1998), 3:97–98.

98. Chicago *Tribune*, 16 Sept., copied in the *Missouri Democrat* (St. Louis), 17 Sept. 1861.

99. J. H. Cooper to John F. Potter, Burlington, Wisconsin, 17 Sept. 1861, Potter Papers, Wisconsin State Historical Society.

100. Saint Cloud (Minnesota) *Democrat*, 19 Sept. 1861, in Sylvia D. Hoffert, *Jane Grey Swisshelm: An Unconventional Life, 1815–1884* (Chapel Hill: University of North Carolina Press, 2004), 126.

101. Ashtabula *Sentinel*, n.d., copied in *The Liberator* (Boston), 11 Oct. 1861.

102. George Hoadly to Chase, Cincinnati, 18, 19 Sept. 1861, Chase Papers, DLC.

103. Jacob Brinkerhoff to Chase, Warren, Ohio, 18 Sept. 1861, ibid.

104. New York *Herald*, n.d., and Buffalo *Courier*, n.d., both copied in *The Liberator* (Boston), 27 Sept., 4 Oct. 1861.

105. Thomas Ewing to Hugh Ewing, Lancaster, Ohio, 2 Nov. 1861, typescript, Ewing Family Papers, DLC.

106. Springfield (Massachusetts) *Republican*, 17 Sept. 1861.

107. Thomas Starr King to Henry W. Bellows, San Francisco, 18 Mar. 1862, Bellows Papers, MHi.

108. Burlingame and Ettlinger, eds., *Hay Diary*, 123 (entry for 9 Dec. 1863).

109. Josiah B. Grinnell, *Men and Events of Forty Years: Autobiographical Reminiscences of an*

Active Career from 1850 to 1890 (Boston: D. Lothrop, 1891), 174.

110. Jessie B. Frémont to Thomas Starr King, Nahant, 16 Oct. 1863, *The Letters of Jessie Benton Frémont*, ed. Pamela Herr and Mary Lee Spence (Urbana: University of Illinois Press, 1993), 356.

111. Elizabeth Blair Lee to Samuel Phillips Lee, Bethlehem, 17 Sept. 1861, *Wartime Washington: The Civil War Letters of Elizabeth Blair Lee*, ed. Virginia Jeans Laas (Urbana: University of Illinois Press, 1991), 79.

112. Cincinnati *Press*, n.d., copied in the New York *Evening Express*, 6 Jan. 1862.

113. Lincoln to Jessie Frémont, Washington, 12 Sept. 1861, *CWL*, 4:519.

114. Excerpt from Jessie Benton Frémont's "Great Events," 1891, in Herr and Spence, eds., *Letters of Jessie Benton Frémont*, 265–266.

115. Orville H. Browning to Lincoln, Quincy, 30 Apr. 1861, AL MSS DLC.

116. Browning to Lincoln, Quincy, 17 Sept. 1861, ibid.

117. Lincoln to Browning, Washington, 22 Sept. 1861, *CWL*, 4:531–532.

118. Lincoln said this to Charles Edwards Lester. Lester, *Life and Public Services of Charles Sumner* (New York: United States Publishing Company, 1874), 359–360.

119. Washington correspondence, 8 Sept., *National Anti-Slavery Standard* (New York), 14 Sept. 1861.

120. George William Curtis to Charles Eliot Norton, n.p., [late Aug. 1861], quoted in Norton to Henry W. Bellows, Newport, 25 Aug. 1861, Bellows Papers, MHi.

121. Lincoln to David Hunter, Washington, 9 Sept. 1861, *CWL*, 4:513.

122. Montgomery Blair to Lincoln, St. Louis, 14 Sept. 1861, AL MSS DLC.

123. Elizabeth Blair Lee to Samuel Phillips Lee, Silver Spring, 22 Oct. 1861, in Laas, ed., *Wartime Washington*, 90n2.

124. Meigs diary, 18 Sept. 1861, copy, Nicolay Papers, DLC.

125. This is William P. Fessenden's summary of a letter he received from a friend. Fessenden to James W. Grimes, Portland, 26 Sept. 1861, Fessenden Papers, Bowdoin College.

126. Frémont to Edward D. Townsend, St. Louis, 16 Sept. 1861, AL MSS DLC.

127. Thomas Ewing to Lincoln, Lancaster, Ohio, 17 Sept. 1861, ibid.

128. Thomas Ewing to Hugh Ewing, Lancaster, Ohio, 2 Nov. 1861, typescript, Ewing Papers, DLC.

129. Elizabeth Blair Lee to Samuel Phillips Lee, Philadelphia, 7 Oct. 1861, Laas, ed., *Wartime Washington*, 84.

130. Thomas Wentworth Higginson to his mother, n.p., 1 Nov. 1861, in Mary Thatcher Higginson, ed., *Letters and Journals of Thomas Wentworth Higginson, 1846–1906* (Boston: Houghton Mifflin, 1921), 160.

131. Yates to Gustave Koerner, [Springfield], ca. 23 Oct. 1861, Thomas J. McCormack, ed., *Memoirs of Gustave Koerner, 1809–1896* (2 vols.; Cedar Rapids, IA: Torch Press, 1909), 2:188.

132. Chase to Cameron, Washington, 7 Oct. 1861, in Niven, ed., *Chase Papers*, 3:100.

133. Curtis to Lincoln, Benton Barracks (near St. Louis), 12 Oct. 1861, AL MSS DLC.

134. "Report of Lorenzo Thomas, 21 October 1861," in *Report of the Joint Committee on the Conduct of the War*, 37th Congress, 3rd Session, House Reports (3 vols.; Washington, DC: Government Printing Office, 1863), 3:8.

135. Trumbull to Lincoln, Alton, 1 Oct. 1861, AL MSS DLC.

136. Wool to Sarah Wool, Fort Monroe, 7, 9, 10, 21 Oct. 1861, Wool Papers, New York State Library, Albany.

137. Howard K. Beale, ed., *The Diary of Edward Bates, 1859–1866* (Annual Report of the American Historical Association for 1930, vol. 4; Washington, DC: U.S. Government Printing Office, 1933), 198 (entry for 18 Oct. 1861).

138. Bates to James Broadhead, in William E. Parish, *Turbulent Partnership: Missouri and the Union, 1861–1865* (Columbia: University of Missouri Press, 1963), 73.

139. Washington correspondence by Van [D. W. Bartlett], 29 Oct., Springfield, Massachusetts, *Republican*, 1 Nov. 1861.

140. *CWL*, 5:1.

141. Burlingame and Ettlinger, eds., *Hay Diary*, 123 (entry for 9 Dec. 1863).

142. Moncure Conway, *Autobiography: Memories and Experiences of Moncure Daniel Conway* (2 vols.; London: Cassell, 1904), 1:380.

143. Nicolay to John Hay, Springfield, 21 Oct. 1861, in Burlingame, ed., *With Lincoln in the White House*, 61.

144. Bates to Chase, St. Louis, 11 Sept. 1861, Chase Papers, Historical Society of Pennsylvania.

145. Richard Smith to Chase, Cincinnati, 7 Nov. 1861, Chase Papers, DLC

146. Washington correspondence by Van [D. W. Bartlett], 5 Nov., Springfield, Massachusetts, *Republican*, 8 Nov. 1861.

147. Cincinnati *Press,* n.d, copied in the *Illinois State Register* (Springfield), 13 Nov. 1861.

148. Thaddeus Stevens to Simon Stevens, Washington, 5 Nov. 1861, Stevens Papers, DLC.

149. *The Liberator* (Boston), 20 Sept. 1861.

150. Garrison to Oliver Johnson, Boston, 7 Oct. 1861, Walter M. Merrill, ed., *The Letters of William Lloyd Garrison* (6 vols.; Cambridge, MA: Harvard University Press, 1971–1981), 5:37.

151. Speech at Albany, 7 Feb. 1862, *National Anti-Slavery Standard* (New York), 22 Feb. 1862.

152. Julian in Allen Thorndike Rice, ed., *Reminiscences of Abraham Lincoln by Distinguished Men of His Time* (New York: North American Review, 1888), 55.

153. Henry D. Bacon to S. L. M. Barlow, n.p., 20 Jan. 1862, Barlow Papers, CSmH, copy, Allan Nevins Papers, Columbia University.

154. W. A. Croffut, *An American Procession, 1855–1914: A Personal Chronicle of Famous Men* (Boston: Little, Brown, 1931), 73.

155. Washington correspondence, 27 Nov., Philadelphia *Inquirer,* 28 Nov. 1861.

156. Henry Winter Davis to Samuel Francis Du Pont, [Baltimore], 18 Dec. 1861, transcript, S. F. Du Pont Papers, Hagley Museum, Wilmington, Delaware.

157. *Official Records of the Union and Confederate Navies in the War of the Rebellion* [hereafter *ORN*], I, 17:19.

158. Benjamin Butler, *Autobiography and Personal Reminiscences of Major-General Benj. F. Butler: Butler's Book* (Boston: A. M. Thayer, 1892), 287–288.

159. *CWL,* 4:528.

160. Samuel F. Du Pont to Henry Winter Davis, New York, 8 Oct. 1861, in John D. Hayes, ed., *Samuel Francis Du Pont: A Selection from His Civil War Letters* (3 vols.; Ithaca, NY: Published for the Eleutherian Mills Historical Library by the Cornell University Press, 1969), 1:163.

161. Diary of William T. Coggeshall, 25 Nov. 1861, in Freda Postle Koch, *Colonel Coggeshall: The Man Who Saved Lincoln* (Columbus, Ohio: Poko Press, 1985), 61.

162. Sherman to Lincoln, 17 Oct. 1861, AL MSS DLC; Burlingame and Ettlinger, eds., *Hay Diary*, 27 (entries for 17, 18 Oct. 1861).

163. David Homer Bates, *Lincoln Stories Told by Him in the Military Office in the War Department during the Civil War, Recorded by One of the Listeners* (New York: W. E. Rudge, 1926), 24.

164. New York *Evening Post,* 1 Nov. 1864.

165. Mark Howard to Gideon Welles, Hartford, 14 Nov. 1861; Fanny Eames to Welles, New York, 14 Nov. 1861, Welles Papers, DLC.

166. *ORN,* 12:291.

167. Ron Soodalter, *Hanging Captain Gordon: The Life and Trial of an American Slave Trader* (New York: Atria Books, 2006), 153.

168. John G. Barnard, remarks made at a dinner in 1871, as recalled by "S.S.," New York *Tribune,* 21 Oct. 1885.

169. Dawes to his wife, Washington, 11 Dec. 1861, Dawes Papers, DLC.

170. Adam Gurowski, *Diary* (3 vols.; Boston: Lee and Shepard, 1862–1866), 1:136 (entry for Dec. 1861).

171. McClellan to Lincoln, Washington, 10 Dec. 1861, AL MSS DLC.

172. John A. Bingham to Joshua Giddings, Washington, 19 Dec. 1861, Giddings Papers, Ohio Historical Society.

173. Chandler to his wife, Washington, 27 Oct. 1861, Chandler Papers, DLC.

174. Dawes to his wife, Washington, 6 Jan. 1862, Dawes Papers, DLC.

175. Wade to Zachariah Chandler, Jefferson, Ohio, 8 Oct. 1861, Chandler Papers, DLC.

176. Conway to George Luther Stearns, Washington, 1 Nov. 1861, in Frank Preston Stearns, *The Life and Public Services of George Luther Stearns* (Philadelphia: J. B. Lippincott, 1907), 257; Conway to James Freeman Clarke, Washington, 27 Jan. 1862, Clarke Papers, MHi.

177. Charles F. Mitchell to John Sherman, Flemingsburg, Kentucky, 21 Dec. 1861, 1 Feb. 1862, Sherman Papers, DLC.

178. John Y. Simon, "Truman Smith and Lincoln," *Lincoln Herald* 67 (1965):127.

179. Charles E. Pike to James S. Pike, Oskosh, 2 Oct. (continuation of a letter begun on 15 Sept.) 1861, Pike Papers, University of Maine.

180. Mrs. L. B. Farnum to George Bancroft, n.p., 5 Jan. 1862, Bancroft Papers, MHi.

181. [F. M. Finch?] to Julian, Franklin, 26 Jan. 1862, Giddings-Julian Papers, DLC.

182. Henry Winter Davis to Sophie Du Pont, [n.p.], 4 Dec. 1862, transcript, S. F. Du Pont Papers, Hagley Museum, Wilmington, Delaware.

183. Charles Eliot Norton to George Perkins Marsh, Cambridge, 9 Nov. 1861, Marsh Papers, University of Vermont; George Gibbs to John Austin Stevens, Washington, 12 Sept. 1861, Stevens Papers, New-York Historical Society.

184. P. P. Enos to Lyman Trumbull, Springfield, 7 Jan. 1862, Trumbull Papers, DLC.

185. Gustave Koerner to Lyman Trumbull, Belleville, 26 and 2 Jan. 1862, ibid.

186. J. F. Amkeny to Washburne, Freeport, 23 Dec. 1861, Washburne Papers, DLC.

187. J. W. Shaffer to Washburne, Fort Leavenworth, Kansas, 24 Dec. 1861, ibid.

188. W. C. Dunning to Washburne, Byron, Illinois, 10 Jan. 1862; A. J. Betts to Washburne, Durand, Illinois, 29 Jan. 1862, ibid.

189. Wait Talcott to Lyman Trumbull, Rockford, 18 January 1862, Lyman Trumbull Papers, DLC.

190. J. H. Jordan to John Sherman, Cincinnati, 22 Dec. 1861, John Sherman Papers, DLC.

191. Timothy C. Day to John Sherman, Cincinnati, 18 Jan. 1862, ibid.

192. E. B. Talcott to Elihu B. Washburne, Chicago, 28 Dec. 1861, Washburne Papers, DLC.

193. John A. Dahlgren diary, copy, Nicolay Papers, DLC (entry for 2 Jan. 1862).

194. Hans L. Trefousse, *The Radical Republicans: Lincoln's Vanguard for Racial Justice* (New York: Alfred A. Knopf, 1968), 184.

195. *CWL*, 5:88.

196. Isaac N. Arnold, *The Life of Abraham Lincoln* (Chicago: Jansen, McClurg, 1885), 297.

197. William O. Stoddard, "White House Sketches No. 6," New York *Citizen*, 22 Sept. 1866, in Stoddard, *Inside the White House*, ed. Burlingame, 167.

198. Fessenden to his family, Washington, 14 Jan. 1862, in Francis Fessenden, *Life and Public Services of William Pitt Fessenden* (2 vols.; Boston: Houghton Mifflin, 1907), 1:259–260.

199. William S. Holman to Allen Hamilton, Washington, 17 Jan. 1862, Richard W. Thompson Papers, LMF.

200. Weed to William Evarts, 20 Feb. 1862, Brainerd Dyer, *The Public Career of William M. Evarts* (Berkeley: University of California Press, 1933), 52.

201. W. M. Dickson to Friedrich Hassaurek, Cincinnati, 27 Sept. 1861, Hassaurek Papers, Ohio Historical Society.

202. Lincoln to McClernard, Washington, 10 Nov. 1861, *CWL*, 5:20.

203. Lawrence Beaumont Stringer, "From the Sangamon to the Potomac: More Light on Abraham Lincoln," typescript of an unpublished manuscript, p. 94, Edgar Dewitt Jones Papers, Detroit Public Library.

204. Buell to Lincoln, Louisville, 5 Jan. 1862, AL MSS DLC.

205. Halleck to McClellan, St. Louis, 28 Nov. 1861, *OR,* I, 8:389.

206. Lincoln to Hunter, Washington, 31 Dec. 1861, *CWL,* 5:84–85.

207. Lincoln to Buell, Washington, 6 Jan. 1862, ibid., 5:90–91.

208. Lincoln to Buell, Washington, 7 Jan. 1862, ibid., 5:91–92.

209. Lincoln to Cameron, Washington, 10 Jan. 1862, ibid., 5:95.

210. John A. Dahlgren diary, copy, Nicolay Papers, DLC (entry for 2 Jan. 1862).

211. Meigs to his father, Washington, 2 Mar. 1862, Meigs Papers, DLC.

212. M. C. Meigs, "The Relations of President Lincoln and Secretary Stanton to the Military Commanders in the Civil War," an article written in 1888, *American Historical Review* 26 (1921):292.

213. McDowell memorandum, 13 Jan. 1862, in Henry J. Raymond, *The Life and Public Services of Abraham Lincoln* (New York: Derby and Miller, 1865), 773.

214. McDowell memorandum, 13 Jan. 1862, in Raymond, *Lincoln,* 776; Meigs, "Relations of Lincoln and Stanton to the Military Commanders," 292–293, 295.

215. William B. Franklin, "The First Great Crime of the War," in Alexander K. McClure, ed., *The Annals of the War Written by Leading Participants North and South* (Philadelphia: Times Publishing Company, 1879), 79.

216. McDowell memorandum, 13 Jan. 1862, in Raymond, *Lincoln,* 777; Meigs, "Relations of President Lincoln and Secretary Stanton to the Military Commanders," 293.

217. Malcolm Ives to James G. Bennett, Washington, 15 Jan. 1862 [misdated 1861], Bennett Papers, DLC.

218. Beale, ed., *Bates Diary,* 223 (entry for 10 Jan. 1862).

219. New York *Times,* 17 Nov. 1861.

220. Benson J. Lossing, *Pictorial History of the Civil War in the United States of America* (2 vols.; Hartford: Belknap, 1868), 2:156.

221. Washington correspondence by Van [D. W. Bartlett], 19 Nov., Springfield, Massachusetts, *Republican,* 23 Nov. 1861.

222. Gideon Welles, "Capture and Release of Mason and Slidell," in Albert Mordell, compiler, *Civil War and Reconstruction: Selected Essays by Gideon Welles* (New York: Twayne, 1959), 270.

223. Titian J. Coffee in Rice, ed., *Reminiscences of Abraham Lincoln,* 245.

224. Stoeckl to Gortchakoff, n.d., in Albert A. Woldman, *Lincoln and the Russians* (Cleveland: World, 1952), 92.

225. Gideon Welles, *Lincoln and Seward* (New York: Sheldon, 1874), 185–187; Welles, "Capture and Release of Mason and Slidell," 276; "Suppressed dispatch," Washington correspondence, 29 Dec., New York *Tribune,* 31 Dec. 1861.

226. Weed to Archbishop John J. Hughes, London, 7, 22 Dec. 1861, photostatic copies, Weed Papers, University of Rochester.

227. Russell, *Diary,* 126 (entry for 4 July 1861).

228. Lossing, *Pictorial History of the Civil War,* 2:162.

229. David Donald, *Charles Sumner and the Rights of Man* (New York: Alfred A. Knopf, 1970), 35.

230. Theodore Calvin Pease and James G. Randall, eds., *The Diary of Orville Hickman Browning* (2 vols.; Springfield: Illinois State Historical Library, 1925–1933), 1:514 (entry for 10 Dec. 1861).

231. Ibid., 1:515 (entry for 15 Dec. 1861).

232. Anson S. Miller to E. B. Washburne, Rockford, 25 Dec. 1861, Washburne Papers, DLC.

233. Richard J. Corwine to John Sherman, Cincinnati, 29 Dec. 1861, John Sherman Papers, DLC.

234. Russell, *Diary,* 217 (entry for 16 Dec. 1861).

235. Charles Cowley, *Leaves from a Lawyer's Life, Afloat and Ashore* (Boston: Lee & Shepard, 1879), 192.

236. John A. Dahlgren diary, copy, Nicolay Papers, DLC (entry for 18 Dec. 1861).

237. Washington correspondence, by "Occasional," 18 Dec., Philadelphia *Press,* 19 Dec. 1861.

238. *Forney's Progress,* 4 Sept. 1884, typed copy, David Rankin Barbee Papers, Georgetown University.

239. Pease and Randall, eds., *Browning Diary,* 1:516 (entry for 21 Dec. 1861).

240. Sumner to Bright, Washington, 30 Dec. 1861, Edward L. Pierce, *Memoir and Letters of Charles Sumner* (4 vols.; Boston: Roberts Brothers, 1877–1893), 4:59.

241. James R. Doolittle to Lincoln, Washington, 19 Dec. 1861, AL MSS DLC.

242. *CWL,* 5:63.

243. Pease and Randall, eds., *Browning Diary,* 1:516 (entry for 21 Dec. 1861).

244. Sumner to Bright, Washington, 23 Dec. 1861, Palmer, ed., *Sumner Letters,* 2:87; Edward Waldo Emerson, ed., *Journals of Ralph Waldo Emerson, 1856–1863* (Boston: Houghton Mifflin, 1913), 380 (entry for 31 Jan. 1862).

245. Beale, ed., *Bates Diary,* 216 (entry for 25 Dec. 1861).

246. John Niven, ed., *The Salmon P. Chase Papers* (5 vols.; Kent, Ohio: Kent State University Press, 1993–1998), 1:319–320 (diary entry for 25 Dec. 1861).

247. Frederick Seward, *Reminiscences of a War-Time Statesman and Diplomat, 1830–1915* (New York: G. P. Putnam's Sons, 1916), 189–190.

248. Horace Porter, *Campaigning with Grant* (New York: Century, 1897), 408–409.

249. Washington correspondence by Agate [Whitelaw Reid], 19 Apr. 1863, Cincinnati *Gazette,* n.d., clipping in scrapbook, Reid Family Papers, DLC.

250. Sumner to Richard Cobden, Washington, 31 Dec. 1861, in Palmer, ed., *Sumner Letters,* 2:92.

251. Alexander T. Galt, memorandum, Washington, 5 Dec. 1861, in Oscar Douglas Skelton, *The Life and Times of Sir Alexander Tilloch Galt* (Toronto: Oxford University Press, 1920), 315.

252. Boston correspondence, 30 Dec. 1861, New York *Herald,* 1 Jan. 1862

253. Joseph Gillespie to William Kellogg, Edwardsville, Illinois, 28 Dec. 1861, Gillespie Papers, ICHi.

254. Henry Winter Davis to Samuel Francis Du Pont, [Baltimore], [late Dec. 1861], transcript, S. F. Du Pont Papers, Hagley Museum, Wilmington, Delaware.

255. *Frank Leslie's Illustrated Newspaper,* 11 Jan. 1862.

256. John A. Logan to his wife, Washington, 27 Dec. 1861, John A. Logan Papers, DLC.

257. Washington correspondence, 1 Jan., Philadelphia *Press,* 2 Jan. 1862.

258. Washington correspondence, 3 Jan., Indianapolis *Journal,* 11 Jan. 1862; Washington correspondence, 23 Dec., Chicago *Evening Journal,* 27 Dec. 1861.

259. Lynn Marshall Case and Warren F. Spencer, *The United States and France: Civil War Diplomacy* (Philadelphia: University of Pennsylvania Press, 1970), 193–194.

260. Memo by Slidell, Paris, 25 July 1862, *ORN,* II, 3:484.

261. John Eaton, *Grant, Lincoln and the Freedmen: Reminiscences of the Civil War* (New York: Longmans, Green, 1907), 178.

262. Welles to an unidentified correspondent, Hartford, 19 Mar. 1874, Lincoln Cabinet Collection, LMF.

263. Sumner, conversation with Edward Everett Hale, Washington, 26 Apr. 1862, Hale, *Memories of One Hundred Years* (2 vols.; New York: Macmillan, 1902), 2:192.

264. Bancroft to his wife, [Washington], 16 Dec. 1861, Bancroft Papers, Cornell University.

265. This is based on Fisher's unpublished essay, "The Trial of John H. Surratt for the Murder of President Lincoln," typescript, pp. 3–3½, George P. Fisher Papers, DLC; J. Thomas Scharf, *History of Delaware, 1609–1888* (2 vols.; Philadelphia: L. J. Richards, 1888), 1:345n-346n, which indicates no source; and on the reminiscences of Burrton's son, in H. Clay Reed, "Lincoln's Compensated Emancipation Plan and its Relations to Delaware," *Delaware Notes* 7 (1931): 38.

266. Pease and Randall, eds., *Browning Diary*, 1:512 (entry for 1 Dec. 1861); David Davis to Leonard Swett, 26 Nov. 1862, David Davis Papers, IHi.

267. Bancroft to his wife, [Washington], 16 Dec. 1861, Bancroft Papers, Cornell University.

268. George W. Smalley told this to George Luther Stearns. Stearns to his wife, Washington, 25 Jan. 1864, Stearns, *Life and Public Services of Stearns*, 327.

269. *CWL*, 5:48–49.

270. Snethen to Wendell Phillips, Baltimore, 25 Aug. 1864, Phillips Papers, Harvard University.

271. John A. Logan to his wife, Washington, 12 Jan. 1862, Logan Papers, DLC.

272. *House Journal*, 1862, quoted in Harold Bell Hancock, *Delaware during the Civil War: A Political History* (Wilmington: Historical Society of Delaware, 1961), 110.

273. *Congressional Globe*, 3 April 1862, in Patience Essah, *A House Divided: Slavery and Emancipation in Delaware, 1638–1865* (Charlottesville: University Press of Virginia, 1996), 170.

274. *Congressional Globe*, 37th Congress, 2nd Session, 1923–1924 (6 May 1862).

275. Dover *Delawarean* and Samuel Townsend, quoted in William H. Williams, *Slavery and Freedom in Delaware, 1639–1865* (Wilmington, DE: SR Books, 1996), 175.

276. Essah, *House Divided*, 171.

277. E. Darwin Smith to Thurlow Weed, Rochester, 13 Nov. 1861, Weed Papers, University of Rochester.

278. *CWL*, 5:35–53.

279. New York *World*, Philadelphia *Inquirer*, 4 Dec. 1861; *Missouri Democrat* (St. Louis), 5 Dec. 1861.

280. *Congressional Globe*, 37th Congress, 2nd Session, 83 (12 Dec. 1861).

281. Washington correspondence, 11 Dec., Chicago *Times*, n.d., copied in the *Illinois State Register* (Springfield), 16 Dec. 1861.

282. Cincinnati *Commercial*, 4 Dec. 1861. See also Springfield, Massachusetts, *Republican*, 4 Dec. 1861.

283. New York *Evening Post*, 4 Dec., copied in the New York *World*, 5 Dec. 1861.

284. Charles H. Brown, *William Cullen Bryant* (New York: Scribner, 1971), 435.

285. Norton to George William Curtis, Cambridge, MA, 5 Dec. 1861, Sara Norton and M. A. De Wolfe Howe, eds., *Letters of Charles Eliot Norton* (2 vols.; Boston: Houghton Mifflin, 1913), 1:246.

286. Washington correspondence by Van [D. W. Bartlett], 27 Nov., Springfield, Massachusetts, *Republican*, 29 Nov. 1861.

287. Washington correspondence, 4 Nov., *National Anti-slavery Standard* (New York), 9 Nov. 1861.

288. Giles Badger Stebbins's speech at the 29th annual meeting of the Massachusetts Antislavery Society, New York *Evening Express*, 27 Jan. 1862.

289. Helen Nicolay, *Personal Traits of Abraham Lincoln* (New York: Century, 1912), 32.

290. Washington correspondence by James Brooks, 31 Jan., New York *Evening Express*, 1 Feb. 1862.

291. Lydia Maria Child to Mary Stearns, Wayland, Massachusetts, 15 Dec. 1861, 30 Jan. 1862, *Lydia Maria Child: Selected Letters, 1817–1880*, ed. Milton Meltzer and Patricia G. Holland (Amherst: University of Massachusetts Press, 1982), 399–400, 405.

292. Owen Lovejoy, *His Brother's Blood: Speeches and Writings, 1838–64*, ed. William F. Moore and Jane Ann Moore (Urbana: University of Illinois Press, 2004), 277.

293. Lincoln to Bancroft, Washington, 18 Nov. 1861, *CWL*, 5:26.

294. Washington correspondence by Sigma, 3 Dec., Cincinnati *Commercial*, 9 Dec. 1861.

295. *National Anti-Slavery Standard* (New York), 14 Dec. 1861.

296. Mott to Martha Coffin Wright, Philadelphia, 5 Dec. 1861, in Beverly Wilson Palmer, ed., *Selected Letters of Lucretia Coffin Mott* (Urbana: University of Illinois Press, 2002), 317–318.

297. Elizabeth Cady Stanton to Gerrit Smith, Seneca Falls, NY, 16 Dec. 1861, in Ann D. Gordon, ed., *The Selected Papers of Elizabeth Cady Stanton and Susan B. Anthony* (4 vols.; New Brunswick, NJ: Rutgers University Press, 1997–2006), 1:470.

298. Child to Mary Stearns, Wayland, Massachusetts, 15 Dec. 1861, 30 Jan. 1862, *Lydia Maria Child: Selected Letters,* ed. Meltzer and Holland, 399–400, 405.

299. William P. Fessenden to his son Frank, Washington, 6 Dec. 1861, Fessenden Papers, Bowdoin College.

300. Fessenden to his son William, Washington, 15 Dec. 1861; Fessenden to Elizabeth Warriner, Washington, 4, 19 Jan. 1862, Fessenden Papers, Bowdoin College.

301. Henry L. Dawes to his wife Electa, Washington, 4, 5 Dec. 1861, Dawes Papers, DLC.

302. James H. Paige to John F. Potter, Milwaukee, 1 Jan. 1862, Potter Papers, Wisconsin State Historical Society.

303. Conkling to Lyman Trumbull, Springfield, 16 Dec. 1861, Trumbull Papers, DLC.

304. Shubal York to Lyman Trumbull, Paris, Illinois, 5 Dec. 1861, ibid.

305. Dr. P. A. Allaire to Lyman Trumbull, Aurora, Illinois, 10 Dec. 1861, ibid.

306. John Russell to Lyman Trumbull, Bluffdale, Illinois, 17 Dec. 1861, 4 Feb. 1862, ibid.

307. New York *Independent,* n.d., copied in New York *World,* 7 Dec. 1861; Worthington G. Snethen to Lyman Trumbull, Baltimore, 8 Dec. 1861, Trumbull Papers, DLC; Worthington G. Snethen to George W. Julian, Baltimore, 20 Jan. 1862, Giddings-Julian Papers, DLC.

308. Garrison to Oliver Johnson, Boston, 6 Dec. 1861, Merrill, ed., *Letters of Garrison,* 5:47; Garrison to Sumner, Boston, 20 Dec. 1861, ibid., 5:53; *The Liberator* (Boston), 6 Dec. 1861.

309. New York *Tribune,* 27 May 1862.

310. New York *Herald,* 17 April 1862.

311. *Weekly Anglo-African* (New York), 7 Dec. 1861.

312. Benjamin Quarles, *The Negro in the Civil War* (Boston: Little, Brown, 1953), 149.

313. Douglass to Gerrit Smith, Rochester, 22 Dec. 1861, Smith Papers, Syracuse University; *Douglass's Monthly,* Jan. 1862, p. 577.

314. "Emigration to Hayti," *Douglass's Monthly,* Jan. and May 1861, 386, 450; John W. Blassingame et al., eds., *The Frederick Douglass Papers, Series 1: Speeches, Debates, and Interviews* (5 vols.; New Haven, CT: Yale University Press, 1979–1991), 4:437–438 (speech of 11 May 1853).

315. Gerrit Smith to Thaddeus Stevens, 6 Dec. 1861, *The Liberator* (Boston), 20 Dec. 1861.

316. Chicago *Tribune,* n.d., copied in the *Missouri Democrat* (St. Louis), 6 Dec. 1861.

317. Washington correspondence, 4 Dec., Boston *Journal,* 6 Dec. 1861.

318. Lincoln quoted Senator Davis's remark to Kansas Senator Samuel C. Pomeroy. Adams S. Hill to Sydney Howard Gay, Washington, 25 Aug. 1862, Gay Papers, Columbia University.

319. *Congressional Globe,* 37th Congress, 2nd Session, 1633 (11 Apr. 1862).

320. Ibid., 2504–2505 (2 June 1862).

321. Charles N. Schaeffer to Edward McPherson, Gettysburg, 16 Dec. 1861, McPherson Papers, DLC.

322. James M. McPherson, ed., *The Negro's Civil War: How American Negroes Felt and Acted during the War for the Union* (New York: Pantheon Books, 1965), 77.

323. Eli Nichols to John Sherman, New Castle, Ohio, 20 Jan. 1862, John Sherman Papers, DLC.

324. William Davis Gallagher to Chase, St. Louis, 12 Feb. 1862, Chase Papers, Historical Society of Pennysylvania; Richard S. West, *Lincoln's Scapegoat General: A Life of Benjamin F. Butler, 1818–1893* (Boston: Houghton Mifflin, 1965), 83–85.

325. *Douglass's Monthly,* Mar. 1861, p. 420.

326. *National Anti-Slavery Standard* (New York), 15 Feb. 1862, and *Once a Week: An Illustrated Miscellany of Art, Science, and Popular Information,* 1 Feb. 1862, in Harriet Martineau, *Writings on Slavery and the American Civil War,*

ed. Deborah Anna Logan (DeKalb: Northern Illinois University Press, 2002), 161, 183–184.

327. Sears, ed., *Papers of McClellan,* 26.

328. Washington correspondence, 9 Dec., New York *Herald,* 10 Dec. 1861.

329. Washington correspondence, 14 Nov., New York *Tribune,* 15 Nov. 1861.

330. Ibid.

331. Washington correspondence, 20 Nov., Cincinnati *Gazette* 21 Nov. 1861; Smith to S. L. M. Barlow, 22 Nov. 1861, Barlow Papers, in Richard J. Thomas, "Caleb Blood Smith: Whig Orator and Politician—Lincoln's Secretary of Interior" (Ph.D. dissertation, University of Indiana, 1969), 205.

332. Barlow to Stanton, New York, 21 Nov. 1861, in Frank A. Flower, *Edwin McMasters Stanton: The Autocrat of Rebellion, Emancipation, and Reconstruction* (New York: Western W. Wilson, 1905), 122.

333. John G. Nicolay and John Hay, *Abraham Lincoln: A History* (10 vols.; New York: Century, 1890), 5:125–126.

334. Francis B. Carpenter, *The Inner Life of Abraham Lincoln: Six Months at the White House* (New York: Hurd and Houghton, 1867), 136.

335. Washington *Sunday Chronicle,* 29 Dec. 1861.

336. James Smart, ed., *A Radical View: The "Agate" Dispatches of Whitelaw Reid, 1861–1865* (2 vols.; Memphis: Memphis State University Press, 1976), 1:83–84 (dispatch from Frankfort, Kentucky, 17 Dec. 1861).

337. Washington correspondence, 4 Dec., Philadelphia *Inquirer,* 5 Dec. 1861.

338. Washington correspondence, 4 Dec., Philadelphia *Inquirer,* 5 Dec. 1861; *OR,* III, 1:708.

339. C. H. Ray to Elihu B. Washburne, Chicago, 5 Dec. 1861, Elihu B. Washburne Papers, DLC; C. H. Ray to Lyman Trumbull, Chicago, 6 Dec. 1861, Trumbull Papers, DLC.

340. John H. Bryant to Lyman Trumbull, Princeton, Illinois, 8 Dec. 1861, Trumbull Papers, DLC.

341. Speech of Phillips in Boston, 7 Jan. 1862, Boston *Post,* n.d., copied in the New York *Evening Express,* 9 Jan. 1862.

342. Speech at the Massachusetts Antislavery Society in Boston, New York *Evening Express,* 27 Jan. 1862.

343. W. W. Orme to Leonard Swett, Washington, 14 May [1861], David Davis Papers, IHi.

344. Nicolay memorandum, 2 Oct. 1861, in Burlingame, ed., *With Lincoln in the White House,* 59.

345. Reminiscences of Edward Jay Allen in E. J. Edwards, "New Chronicles," Pittsburgh *Gazette-Times,* [6 Nov.?] 1913, clipping, C. L. Goodwin Papers, Indiana State Library, Indianapolis.

346. [James G. Blaine] to Gen. John L. Hodsdon, Washington, 13 May 1861, Records of the Adjutant General, Congressional Delegation Correspondence, Maine State Archives, Augusta.

347. Grimes to William P. Fessenden, Washington, 13 Nov. 1861, copy, Fessenden Papers, Bowdoin College.

348. Henry Winter Davis to Samuel Francis Du Pont, [Baltimore], 18 Dec. 1861, transcript, S. F. Du Pont Papers, Hagley Museum, Wilmington, Delaware.

349. Barnett to S. L. M. Barlow, Washington, 14 June 1861, Barlow Papers, CSmH.

350. New York *Times,* 28 Aug. 1861; Simeon Nash to S. P. Chase, Gallipolis, Ohio, 27 Aug. 1861, Chase Papers, DLC; John B. Alley to Henry L. Dawes, Lynn, Massachusetts, 19 Aug. 1861, Dawes Papers, ibid.; Washington correspondence by "Rhode Island," 12 Sept., Providence *Journal,* 16 Sept. 1861.

351. Jacob W. Schuckers to Whitelaw Reid, Philadelphia, 3 Oct. 1872, Reid Family Papers, DLC.

352. New York *Times,* 25 July 1861.

353. Boston *Transcript,* 19 Aug., copied in the Cincinnati *Commercial,* 24 Aug. 1861.

354. Hitchcock to Mary Mann, St. Louis, 22 Feb. 1862, Hitchcock Papers, DLC.

355. Beale, ed., *Welles Diary,* 1:127 (entry for 12 Sept. 1862).

356. Albert G. Riddle, *Recollections of War Times: Reminiscences of Men and Events in Washington, 1860–1865* (New York: G. P. Putnam's Sons, 1895), 180.

357. *CWL*, 5:96.

358. Henry Winter Davis to Samuel Francis Du Pont, [Baltimore], 8 Feb. 1862, transcript, S. F. Du Pont Papers, Hagley Museum, Wilmington, Delaware.

359. Niven, ed., *Chase Papers*, 1:325 (diary entry for 12 Jan. 1862).

360. Alexander K. McClure, *Abraham Lincoln and Men of War-Times* (Philadelphia: Times, 1892), 150; Fessenden to his father, Washington, 20 Jan. 1862, Fessenden Papers, Bowdoin College.

361. Beale, ed., *Welles Diary*, 1:57.

362. Washington correspondence by Sigma, 19 Jan., Cincinnati *Commercial*, 23 Jan. 1862; Boston *Advertiser*, 10 Feb., copied in the Cincinnati *Commercial*, 14 Feb. 1862.

363. Washington correspondence, 14 Jan., Philadelphia *Inquirer*, 15 Jan. 1862.

364. Israel D. Andrews to David Davis, Washington, 28 Jan. [1862], David Davis Papers, IHi.

365. Washington correspondence by "Observer," 31 Jan., *Iowa State Register* (Des Moines), 5 Feb. 1862.

366. Boston *Transcript*, 19 Aug., copied in the Cincinnati *Commercial*, 24 Aug. 1861.

367. Carpenter, *Six Months at the White House*, 138–139.

368. Samuel Galloway to Henry L. Dawes, Columbus, 9 June 1862, Henry L. Dawes Papers, DLC.

369. Washington correspondence by Van [D. W. Bartlett], 1 Oct., Springfield, Massachusetts, *Republican*, 5 Oct. 1861.

370. Niven, ed., *Chase Papers*, 1:325 (diary entry for 12 Jan. 1862).

371. William B. H. Dowse to Albert J. Beveridge, Boston, 10 Oct. 1925, Albert J. Beveridge Papers, DLC.

372. Albert E. H. Johnson, "Reminiscences of the Hon. Edwin M. Stanton, Secretary of War," *Records of the Columbia Historical Society* 13(1910): 71.

373. Charles F. Benjamin to Horace White, 1 June 1914, White Papers, IHi.

374. Dawes, "Recollections of Stanton under Lincoln," *Atlantic Monthly*, Feb. 1894, 163; Dawes, "Some Sayings of Mr. Lincoln," undated typescript, Dawes Papers, DLC.

375. Dawes to Julius Rockwell, Washington, 25 Jan. 1862, Rockwell Family Papers, Lenox Public Library, Lenox, Massachusetts.

376. Washington correspondence by Van [D. W. Bartlett], 15 Jan., Springfield, Massachusetts, *Republican*, 18 Jan. 1862.

377. Fessenden to Elizabeth Warriner, Washington, 19 Jan. 1862, Fessenden Papers, Bowdoin College.

378. Portland *Oregonian*, 20 May 1862.

379. Washington correspondence, 19 Jan., Philadelphia *Inquirer*, 20 Jan. 1862.

380. Washington correspondence by James Brooks, 16 Jan., New York *Evening Express*, 17 Jan. 1862.

381. Fernando Wood to Lincoln, New York, 15 Jan. 1862, AL MSS DLC.

382. Cincinnati *Enquirer*, 16 Jan. 1862.

383. *The Military Memoirs of General John Pope*, ed. Peter Cozzens and Robert I. Girardi (Chapel Hill: University of North Carolina Press, 1998), 115.

384. Lately Thomas, *Between Two Empires: The Life Story of California's First Senator, William McKendree Gwin* (Boston: Houghton Mifflin, 1969), 274.

385. Allan Nevins and Milton Halsey, eds., *Diary of George Templeton Strong, 1835–1875* (4 vols.; New York: Macmillan, 1952), 2:203 (entry for 29 Jan. 1862).

386. Washington correspondence by Van [D. W. Bartlett], 15 Jan., Springfield, Massachusetts, *Republican*, 18 Jan. 1862.

387. New York *Herald*, 15 Jan. 1862.

388. Fessenden to Elizabeth Warriner, Washington, 19 Jan. 1862, Fessenden Papers, Bowdoin College.

389. Holt to Lincoln, St. Louis, 15 Jan. 1862, AL MSS DLC.

390. Edwards Pierrepont to Lincoln, New York, 19 Jan. 1862, AL MSS DLC.

391. New York *Tribune,* in Tarbell, *Lincoln,* 2:80.

392. Stanton to Dana, Washington, 24 Jan. 1862, Dana Papers, DLC.

393. Bernard A. Weisberger, *Reporters for the Union* (Boston: Little, Brown, 1953), 223.

394. Washington correspondence by John Hay, 15 Jan., *Missouri Republican* (St. Louis), 19 Jan. 1862, in Burlingame, ed., *Lincoln's Journalist,* 196–197.

395. Beale, ed., *Welles Diary,* 1:57.

396. *McClellan's Own Story: The War for the Union* (New York: C. L. Webster, 1887), 152.

397. Beale, ed., *Welles Diary,* 1:67–68.

398. Joshua F. Speed to Joseph Holt, Washington, 4 Feb. 1862, Holt Papers, DLC.

399. Washington correspondence, 27 Jan., Philadelphia *Inquirer,* 28 Jan. 1862.

400. Chicago *Tribune,* 26 Mar. 1864.

401. *Memoirs of Pope,* ed. Cozzens and Girardi, 115.

402. Russell, *Diary,* 372 (entry for 9 Oct. 1861).

403. *CWL,* 5:98–99.

Chapter 25. "This Damned Old House"

1. John Hay, "Life in the White House in the Time of Lincoln," in Michael Burlingame, ed., *At Lincoln's Side: John Hay's Civil War Correspondence and Selected Writings* (Carbondale: Southern Illinois University Press, 2000), 134.

2. William O. Stoddard, *Inside the White House in War Times: Memoirs and Reports of Lincoln's Secretary,* ed. Michael Burlingame (1890; Lincoln: University of Nebraska Press, 2000), 41; Helen Nicolay, *Lincoln's Secretary: A Biography of John G. Nicolay* (New York: Longmans, Green, 1949), 227.

3. Edward Dicey, *Six Months in the Federal States* (London: Macmillan, 1863), 98.

4. Theodore Ledyard Cuyler, *Recollections of a Long Life: An Autobiography* (New York: Baker & Taylor, 1902), 143.

5. Stoddard, *Inside the White House,* ed. Burlingame, 5.

6. Ibid., 155.

7. Ibid., 11, 145.

8. Ibid., 145, 26.

9. "Report of the Commissioner of Public Buildings," in *Annual Report of the Secretary of the Interior* (Washington, DC: U.S. Government Printing Office, 1864), 661.

10. Dicey, *Six Months,* 15.

11. Nicolay to Therena Bates, Washington, 20 July 1862, in Michael Burlingame, ed., *With Lincoln in the White House: Letters, Memoranda, and Other Writings of John G. Nicolay, 1860–1865* (Carbondale: Southern Illinois University Press, 2000), 86.

12. Mary Lincoln to Mrs. Charles Eames, Washington, 26 July 1862, Justin G. Turner and Linda Levitt Turner, eds., *Mary Todd Lincoln: Her Life and Letters* (New York: Alfred A. Knopf, 1972), 130.

13. Lincoln to Welles, Washington, 16 Mar. 1861, Roy P. Basler et al., eds., *Collected Works of Abraham Lincoln* [hereafter *CWL*] (8 vols. plus index; New Brunswick, NJ: Rutgers University Press, 1953–1955), 4:288.

14. William O. Stoddard, *Abraham Lincoln: The True Story of a Great Life* (New York: Fords, Howard, & Hulbert, 1884), 403.

15. Anson G. Henry to his wife, Washington, n.d., fragment of a letter, Henry Papers. IHi.

16. Hay, "Life in the White House," Burlingame, ed., *At Lincoln's Side,* 134.

17. Albany *Evening Journal,* in Burlingame, ed., *With Lincoln in the White House,* xix.

18. Hay to William H. Herndon, Paris, 5 Sept. 1866, Burlingame, ed., *At Lincoln's Side,* 109; Washington correspondence, 17 Mar., New York *Times,* 18 Mar. 1861.

19. Washington correspondence, 6 Apr., New York *Examiner,* 9 Apr. 1863, Michael Burlingame, ed., *Dispatches from Lincoln's White House: The Anonymous Civil War Journalism of Presidential Secretary William O. Stoddard* (Lincoln: University of Nebraska Press, 2002), 145.

20. J. G. Holland, *Life of Abraham Lincoln* (Springfield, MA: G. Bill, 1866), 429.

21. Hay, "Life in the White House," Burlingame, ed., *At Lincoln's Side,* 133.

22. Washington correspondence, 19 Oct., New York *Evening Post,* 21 Oct. 1865.

23. William Bender Wilson, *A Few Acts and Actors in the Tragedy of the Civil War in the United States* (Philadelphia: By the author, 1892), 110.

24. "Reminiscences of President Lincoln," by the editor of the Lowell *Citizen,* in Frank Moore, ed., *Anecdotes, Poetry and Incidents of the Civil War: North and South, 1861–1865* (New York: printed for subscribers, 1866), 483.

25. F. B. Carpenter, *Six Months at the White House with Abraham Lincoln: The Story of a Picture* (New York: Hurd and Houghton, 1867), 279.

26. Frazer Kirkland, *Reminiscences of the Blue and Gray, '61–'65* (Chicago: Preston, 1895), 641.

27. Stoddard, "White House Sketches No. 10," *New York Citizen,* 20 Oct. 1866, Stoddard, *Inside the White House,* ed. Burlingame, 188.

28. Carpenter, *Six Months at the White House,* 251–252.

29. New York *Evening Post,* 1 Nov. 1864.

30. Cuyler, *Recollections,* 144–145.

31. Stoddard, "White House Sketches No. 2," New York *Citizen,* 25 Aug. 1866, Stoddard, *Inside the White House,* ed. Burlingame, 149.

32. Hay, "Life in the White House," Burlingame, ed., *At Lincoln's Side,* 134.

33. Washington *Post,* 13 Mar. 1893.

34. Betty John Libby, *The Sketches, Letters & Journal of Libby Beaman, Recorded in the Pribilof Islands, 1879–1880* (Tulsa, OK: Council Oak Books, 1987), 23; Edouard de Stoeckl to Alexander Gortchakov, Washington, 12 Mar. 1861, dispatch 15, photocopy, Principal Archive of the Ministry of Foreign Affairs, Russian Reproductions, Papers of the Foreign Copying Project, DLC.

35. William H. Russell, *My Diary North and South* (New York: Harper and Brothers, 1863), 22 (entry for 27 Mar. 1861).

36. Henry W. Bellows to his son, Washington, 17 Oct. 1861, Bellows Papers, MHi.

37. Olmsted to Mary Perkins Olmsted, Washington, 2 July 1861, Charles Capen McLaughlin et al., eds., *The Papers of Frederick Law Olmsted* (6 vols.; Baltimore, MD: Johns Hopkins University Press, 1977–1992), 4:126.

38. Allan Nevins and Milton Halsey Thomas, eds., *Diary of George Templeton Strong, 1835–1875* (4 vols.; New York: Macmillan, 1952), 3:188, 204 (entries for 23 Oct. 1861 and 29 Jan. 1862).

39. Ernest d'Hauterive, ed., "Voyage du Prince Napoleon aux Etats-Unis, 1861," *Revue de Paris* 40 (1933):256.

40. Dana diary, entries for 7, 4 Jan. 1862; Dana to his wife, Washington, 4 May 1864, Dana Papers, MHi.

41. Russell, *Diary,* 22 (entry for 27 Mar. 1861).

42. Howard K. Beale, ed., *The Diary of Edward Bates, 1859–1866* (Annual Report of the American Historical Association for the Year 1930, vol. IV; Washington, DC: U.S. Government Printing Office, 1933), 177 (entry for 8 Mar. 1861).

43. Washington correspondence by Ben: Perely Poore, 9 Mar., Boston *Evening Journal,* 12 Mar. 1861.

44. Charles Francis Adams diary, 8 Mar. 1861, Adams Family Papers, MHi.

45. Washington correspondence by "A looker on," 10 Mar., Philadelphia *Press,* 11 Mar. 1861; Washington *Star,* 9 Mar. 1861.

46. Charles Francis Adams diary, 8 Mar. 1861, Adams Family Papers, MHi; diary of Benjamin Moran, secretary of the American legation in London, 16 Aug. 1865, DLC.

47. Nicolay to Therena Bates, Washington, 10 Mar. 1861, Burlingame, ed., *With Lincoln in the White House,* 30.

48. William O. Stoddard, "White House Sketches," nos. 2 and 8, New York *Citizen,* 25 Aug., 6 Oct. 1866, Stoddard, *Inside the White House,* ed. Burlingame, 150, 179.

49. Washington correspondence, 18 July, Baltimore *Patriot,* n.d. copied in the *Missouri Democrat* (St. Louis), 21 July 1861.

50. Washington correspondence by Mary Clemmer Ames, 8 Jan., Springfield (Massachusetts) *Republican*, 11 Jan. 1862.

51. Charles Henry Davis journal, 9 Mar. 1861, in Charles H. Davis, *Life of Charles Henry Davis, Rear Admiral, 1807–1877* (Boston: Houghton Mifflin, 1899), 115.

52. David D. Porter, "Journal of Occurrences during the War of the Rebellion," vol. 1, pp. 56–58, Porter Papers, DLC.

53. Herman Melville to Elizabeth Shaw Melville, Washington, 24–25 Mar. 1861, Merrell R. Davis and William H. Gilman, eds., *The Letters of Herman Melville* (New Haven, CT: Yale University Press, 1960), 210.

54. Washington correspondence by "Occasional," 24 Mar., Philadelphia *Press*, 27 Mar. 1861.

55. Fox to his wife, Washington, 27 Mar. 1861, Robert Means Thompson and Richard Wainwright, eds., *Confidential Correspondence of Gustavus Vasa Fox, Assistant Secretary of the Navy, 1861–1865* (2 vols.; New York: Printed for the Naval History Society by the De Vinne Press, 1918–1919), 1:11.

56. George Bancroft to his wife, Washington, 15, 18 Dec. 1861, Bancroft Papers, Cornell University.

57. Motley to his wife, Washington, 20 June 1861, George William Curtis, ed., *The Correspondence of John Lothrop Motley* (2 vols.; New York: Harper & Brothers, 1889), 1:387.

58. Dana diary, entries for 7, 14 Jan. 1862; Dana to his wife, Washington, 4 May 1864, Dana Papers, MHi.

59. Letter from Charles Strong to George Templeton Strong, paraphrased in Nevins and Thomas, eds., *Strong Diary*, 3:104 (entry for 27 Feb. 1861); entry for 11 Sept. 1862, ibid., 3:255.

60. John Bigelow diary, New York Public Library (entry for 9 July 1861).

61. Hay, "Life in the White House," Burlingame, ed., *At Lincoln's Side*, 135.

62. Washington correspondence, 3 Jan., Sacramento *Daily Union*, 29 Jan. 1863, in Michael Burlingame, ed., *Lincoln Observed:*

Civil War Dispatches of Noah Brooks (Baltimore, MD: Johns Hopkins University Press, 1998), 17.

63. Unidentified reminiscence, Rochester *Daily Democrat*, 19 Apr. 1865.

64. Benjamin Brown French, *Witness to the Young Republic: A Yankee's Journal, 1828–1870*, ed. Donald B. Cole and John J. McDonough (Hanover, NH: University Press of New England, 1989), 418, 383, 463 (entries for 3 Mar. 1863, 18 Dec. 1861, 22 Jan. 1865).

65. Francis B. Carpenter interviewed by Harrydele Hallmark, Los Angeles *Times*, 17 Feb. 1895.

66. Mary Lincoln to John Hay, Washington, 22 May 1862, Hay Papers, DLC.

67. Hay, "Life in the White House," Burlingame, ed., *At Lincoln's Side*, 135–136.

68. "Howard Glyndon," penname of Laura Catherine Redden Searing, "The Truth about Mrs. Lincoln," *The Independent* (New York), 10 Aug. 1882, 4–5.

69. John Hay, "Tad Lincoln," New York *Tribune*, 19 July 1871, in Burlingame, ed., *At Lincoln's Side*, 112.

70. Elizabeth Keckley, *Behind the Scenes; or, Thirty Years a Slave and Four Years in the White House* (New York: G. W. Carleton, 1868), 180.

71. *CWL*, 7:320.

72. Reminiscences of Mary Miner Hill, 1923, SC 1985, IHi.

73. John Hay, "Death of 'Tad' Lincoln," unidentified clipping, scrapbook, Hay Papers, RPB.

74. *CWL*, 6:256.

75. Elizabeth L. Comstock to Mary Todd Lincoln, Baltimore, 26 Nov. 1864, AL MSS DLC.

76. Browning, interview with Nicolay, Springfield, 17 June 1875, Michael Burlingame, ed., *An Oral History of Abraham Lincoln: John G. Nicolay Interviews and Essays* (Carbondale: Southern Illinois University, 1996), 3; David Davis to his wife, St. Louis, 15 Dec. 1861, Davis Papers, IHi.

77. Herndon to Jesse W. Weik, Springfield, 5 Feb. 1891, H-W MSS DLC.

78. Halstead to Timothy C. Day, Washington, 11, 8 June 1861, Sarah J. Day, *The Man on a Hill Top* (Philadelphia: Ware Brothers, 1931), 245, 243.

79. Mary Todd Lincoln to James Gordon Bennett, Washington, 4 Oct. 1862, Turner and Turner, eds., *Mary Todd Lincoln*, 138.

80. Mary Todd Lincoln to David Davis, New York, 17 Jan. 1861, ibid., 71; summary of a letter from William Butler, who had spoken with Lincoln, to Judd, n.p., n.d., in Judd to Lyman Trumbull, Chicago, 3 Jan. 1861, Trumbull Papers, DLC.

81. Henry B. Stanton, *Random Recollections* (New York: Harper and Brothers, 1887), 221.

82. Herman Kreismann to Charles Henry Ray, Washington, 16 Jan. 1861, Ray Papers, CSmH.

83. George B. Lincoln to Gideon Welles, Riverdale, NJ, 25 Apr. 1874, in "New Light on the Seward-Welles-Lincoln Controversy," *Lincoln Lore* no. 1718 (Apr. 1981):2–3.

84. Donn Piatt, *Memories of the Men Who Saved the Union* (New York: Belford, Clarke, 1887), 31.

85. Keckley, *Behind the Scenes*, 131.

86. Elizabeth Blair Lee to her husband, Silver Spring, MD, 14 Jan. [1863], Virginia Jeans Laas, ed., *Wartime Washington: The Civil War Letters of Elizabeth Blair Lee* (Urbana: University of Illinois Press, 1991), 231.

87. Washington correspondence by Van [D. W. Bartlett], 8 Oct., Springfield (Massachusetts) *Republican*, 11 Oct. 1861.

88. Gayle Thornbrough et al., eds., *The Diary of Calvin Fletcher* (7 vols.; Indianapolis: Indiana Historical Society, 1972–1981), 7:388 (entry for 2 Apr. 1862).

89. Washington correspondence by I. C., Feb. 1862 (no day of the month indicated), Springfield (Massachusetts) *Republican*, 22 Feb. 1862.

90. Villard, *Memoirs*, 1:147–148.

91. Thomas D. Jones to William Linn McMillen, Springfield, 11 Feb. 1861, Lincoln Collection, Lilly Library, InU. See also J. W. Shaffer to E. B. Washburne, Freeport, 29 Jan. 1861, Washburne Papers, DLC.

92. This story is related in several sources cited in Burlingame, ed., *At Lincoln's Side*, 272 note 18.

93. Ellery Sedgwick, *The Happy Profession* (Boston: Little, Brown, 1946), 161–162.

94. Wayne C. Temple, "Mary Todd Lincoln's Travels," *Journal of the Illinois State Historical Society* 52 (1959):185–186.

95. Lincoln to Irwin, Washington, 20 Mar. 1861, *CWL*, 4:296. To Lincoln, Irwin had made a special plea for his friend: "Enclosed find George Opdycke's letter, endorsing my friend Denison This with the letters already in your hands will certainly satisfy you of his good moral character and capacity for the situation asked for—And now my friend I ask you for his appointment as the only one I have any interest in—I have been a consistent and warm political friend of yours from your first to your last race, and have at all times been for you against all others—Socially I shall not speak of—I ask this as a Republican, and for a working Republican, nor do I think you can have an applicant who will be more strongly recommended. I have arranged for the clerkship for Goudy, if Mr Denison is appointed—of which I will certainly not doubt." Irwin to Lincoln, Springfield, 27 Feb, 1861, AL MSS DLC. Among the contestants for the post was Philip Dorsheimer, a prominent German leader. Francis P. Blair to Chase, Silver Spring, 26 Mar. 1861, Chase Papers, Historical Society of Pennsylvania. Denison was born in 1822 in Greenfield, Massachusetts. Marston was born in Deerfield, New Hampshire, in 1832; at the age of 19 he began working for a New York bank, Belknap & James, and in 1854 became a partner in F. P. James & Co. In 1853, he had helped set up banks in Wisconsin and Illinois. He remained in the Midwest on and off for the next eight years. He was introduced to Springfield society in 1855. In 1862, he established a Wall Street firm, William H. Marston & Co. According to a biographical sketch of Marston, he was "recognized as the leader in the Stock Market and as one of the boldest and most successful

operators that Wall Street had known at that period. During Mr. Marston's residence in the West, his headquarters were at Springfield, Illinois, and Abraham Lincoln was his lawyer and friend. He was also intimate with General John A. Logan." Biographical sketch of Marston, typescript marked "Will appear in the History of Prominent Families of New York, which will be published in Nov.", Bunn Family Papers, Sangamon Valley Collection, Lincoln Public Library, Springfield; Mrs. John M. Palmer, "Remembrances of Two Springfield Weddings of the Olden Time," *Journal of the Illinois State Historical Society* 3 (1910):40. I am grateful to Linda Garvert for calling these items to my attention.

96. Chase to Lincoln, Washington, 16 May 1861, AL MSS DLC; Lincoln to Chase, Washington, 18 May 1861, *CWL*, 4:373.

97. James A. Briggs to Salmon P. Chase, Eaton, Ohio, 30 Sept. 1863, Chase Papers, DLC.

98. Annotation by Briggs to an article from the Painesville *Press and Advertiser*, 13 Feb. 1861, in James A. Briggs Scrapbooks, vol. 1, p. 56, Western Reserve Historical Society.

99. New York *Daily News*, 5 Apr. 1861; Oran Follett to Salmon P. Chase, Sandusky, Ohio, 12 Nov. 1862, Chase Papers, DLC; agreement between Marston and Denison, 15 Feb. 1861, Denison Papers, IHi. Follett's informant was James A. Briggs.

100. Arthur Harry Rice, "Henry B. Stanton as a Political Abolitionist" (E.D. dissertation, Columbia University Teachers College, 1968), 453–459.

101. Samuel Hotaling to William P. Fessenden, New York, 4 July 1864, Fessenden Papers, Western Reserve Historical Society.

102. Burlingame, "Mary Todd Lincoln's Unethical Conduct as First Lady," in Burlingame, ed., *At Lincoln's Side*, 185–203.

103. Diary of Charles Francis Adams, Jr., entry for 10 Mar. 1861, Adams Family Papers, MHi; Charles Francis Adams, Jr., *Charles Francis Adams, 1835–1915: An Autobiography* (Boston: Houghton Mifflin, 1916), 103.

104. Franklin Brooks, "The Lincoln Years in the Papers of Amos and Edward Tuck," *Dartmouth College Library Bulletin* 21 (1981): 64–69; Benjamin Brown French to Henry Flagg French, Washington, 14 Mar. 1861, French Family Papers, DLC.

105. Mary Lincoln to Seward, Washington, 22 Mar. [1861], Turner and Turner, eds., *Mary Todd Lincoln*, 81.

106. Manuscript diary of Orville H. Browning, 29 July 1861, IHi; Burlingame, ed., *At Lincoln's Side*, 186.

107. Hartford *Courant*, 8 Mar. 1861.

108. Mary Lincoln to Ward Hill Lamon, [11] Apr. [1861], Turner and Turner, eds., *Mary Todd Lincoln*, 83.

109. Davis to Ward Hill Lamon, Bloomington, Illinois, 6 May 1861, and Clinton, Illinois, 31 May 1861, Lamon Papers, CSmH.

110. "Union" to Lincoln, Washington, 26 June 1861, typed copy, IHi. A notation indicates that the original is in the Nicolay Papers, DLC. It was not there in 2008, though a card file in the Manuscript Division of the Library of Congress, cataloguing all items in the Nicolay Papers, indicates that it once was.

111. Colfax to John G. Nicolay, South Bend, Indiana, 17 July 1875, Nicolay Papers, DLC.

112. The source of this story was Lincoln King, who claimed that he knew Mrs. Lincoln's paramour "intimately" in New York in the late nineteenth century. *The Sky Rocket* (Primghar, Iowa), 15 Mar. 1929; King to William E. Barton, Primghar, Iowa, 9 Aug. 1930, Barton Papers, University of Chicago.

113. Benjamin Brown French to his son Frank, Washington, 3 Sept. 1861, French Family Papers, DLC.

114. James R. Doolittle to his wife Mary, Washington, 16 Feb. 1862, Doolittle Papers, State Historical Society of Wisconsin.

115. George W. Adams to [David Goodman] Croly, Washington, 7 Oct. 1867, Manton Marble Papers, DLC; New York *Tribune*, 17 Oct. 1867.

116. Z. Young to Lincoln, Washington, 9 Nov. 1864, AL MSS DLC.

896 Notes to Pages 267–268

117. Oswald Garrison Villard to Isaac Markens, New York, 26 Mar. 1927, Lincoln Collection, RPB.

118. Letter to Wakeman seen by Wakeman's daughter, who described it to her own daughter, Elizabeth M. Alexanderson, of Englewood, New Jersey. Newark, NJ, *Star,* 3 Mar. 1951.

119. *Congressional Globe,* 41st Congress, 2nd Session, 5397 (9 July 1870).

120. Mary Lincoln to Abram Wakeman, n.p., 20 Feb. 1865, Turner and Turner, eds., *Mary Todd Lincoln,* 202.

121. Martin Crawford, ed., *William Howard Russell's Civil War: Private Diary and Letters, 1861–1862* (Athens: University of Georgia Press, 1992), 162 (entry for 3 Nov. 1861).

122. On Watt, see Burlingame, ed., *At Lincoln's Side,* 192–198.

123. George Bancroft to his wife, [Washington], 12 Dec. 1861, Bancroft Papers, Cornell University; William P. Fessenden to Elizabeth Warriner, Washington, 8 Dec. 1861, Lincoln Collection, Western Reserve Historical Society.

124. *Government Contracts,* House Report No. 2, 37th Congress, 2nd Session, vol. 1 (serial no. 1142), 72–73, 501–505. The exact chronology of this story is confused. On August 8, it was reported that the president would remove Wood and name Benjamin Brown French in his stead. Lincoln told French that he would appoint him commissioner of public buildings on September 1. In fact, the appointment was made on September 6. French, *Witness to the Young Republic,* ed. Cole and McDonough, 370–374. Mary Todd Lincoln claimed that her husband, "to save his [Wood's] family from disgrace—When the Senate *would not* confirm him, [re]nominated him until the 1st of Sep. with a promise from him, he would resign." Mary Todd Lincoln to John F. Potter, Washington, 13 September 1861, Turner and Turner, eds., *Mary Todd Lincoln,* 104. B. B. French explained that Lincoln appointed him without consulting him, but before the document was signed the president decided that it was his duty to reappoint Wood. So, French told his son, "I was sent for to go to the

President's, and had an interview with both him and Mrs. Lincoln. I have the vanity to believe that Mrs. L. and I rather cottoned to each other. The President explained that when he ordered my appointment he thought that Mr. Wood had been rejected by the Senate, but finding that he had not been—only laid over—and being very strong pressed by Mr. W. & his friends to give Mr. Wood an opportunity to resign! he had concluded to appoint him until the 1st of Sept. when he is to resign and I am to be appointed." B. B. French to his son Frank, Washington, 20 Aug. 1861, French Family Papers, DLC.

125. Mary Todd Lincoln to John F. Potter, Washington, 13 Sept. 1861, Turner and Turner, eds., *Mary Todd Lincoln,* 104.

126. Crawford, ed., *Russell's Civil War,* 162 (diary entry for 3 Nov. 1861).

127. Anson G. Henry to Isaac Newton, Olympia, Washington Territory, 21 Apr. 1864, AL MSS DLC.

128. Greeley to Beman Brockway, Washington, 12 Mar. 1861, Greeley Papers, DLC.

129. Wendell Phillips told this to the journalist Samuel Wilkeson. Wilkeson to Sydney Howard Gay, [Washington], n.d., Gay Papers, Columbia University.

130. Ralph Y. McGinnis and Calvin N. Smith, eds., *Abraham Lincoln and the Western Territories* (Chicago: Nelson-Hall, 1993), 150–155; James W. Nesmith to James Harlan, Cincinnati, 23 Oct. 1865, Lyon file, Letters of Application and Recommendation During the Administrations of Abraham Lincoln and Andrew Johnson, 1861–1869, Record Group 59, M 650, National Archives; Deren Kellogg, "Lincoln Administration and the Southwestern Territories" (Ph.D. dissertation, University of Illinois, 2000) 217.

131. Mary Lincoln to Elizabeth Todd Grimsley, Washington, 29 Sept. 1861, Turner and Turner, eds., *Mary Todd Lincoln,* 105.

132. Lincoln to John Todd Stuart, Washington, 30 Mar. 1861, *CWL,* 4:303.

133. Herndon's account in Caroline Dall, "Journal of a tour through Illinois, Wisconsin

and Ohio, Oct. & Nov. 1866," entry for 29 Oct. 1866, Dall Papers, Bryn Mawr College.

134. Lincoln to Baker, Washington, 15 June 1863, *CWL*, 6:275–276. Bailhache held a position in the quartermaster's department throughout the war. William H. Bailhache, "History of Service," undated memo, Lincoln Collection, RPB.

135. John T. Stuart to Lincoln, Springfield, 3 Apr. 1861, AL MSS DLC.

136. Washington correspondence, 12 Feb., St. Louis *Globe-Democrat*, 14 Feb. 1895, 23.

137. Elizabeth J. Grimsley to Lincoln, Springfield, 22 Nov. 1864, AL MSS DLC.

138. Mary Lincoln, interview with William H. Herndon, [Sept. 1866], Douglas L. Wilson and Rodney O. Davis, eds., *Herndon's Informants: Letters, Interviews, and Statements about Abraham Lincoln* [hereafter *HI*] (Urbana: University of Illinois Press, 1998), 359.

139. Keckley, *Behind the Scenes*, 129.

140. "The Late Secretary Stanton," *Army and Navy Journal*, 1 Jan. 1870.

141. Peck to Lyman Trumbull, Chicago, 27 Aug. 1861, Trumbull Papers, DLC.

142. William Jayne to Lyman Trumbull, Yankton, Dakota Territory, 13 Oct. 1861, ibid.

143. Lincoln to John Todd Stuart, Washington, 30 Mar. 1861, *CWL*, 4:303.

144. Henry S. Huidekoper, "Lincoln as I Knew Him," Philadelphia *Ledger*, 7 Feb. 1915.

145. John T. Hanks to Lincoln, Canyon Village, Oregon, 25 Feb. 1864, AL MSS DLC.

146. Henry C. Whitney, *Life on the Circuit with Lincoln*, ed., Paul M. Angle (1892; Caldwell, ID: Caxton, 1940), 419.

147. Mary Clemmer Ames, *Ten Years in Washington: Life and Scenes in the National Capital, as a Woman Sees Them* (Hartford, CT: A. D. Worthington, 1875), 239.

148. Adams, *Charles Francis Adams, Jr.*, 103 (diary entry for 11 Mar. 1861).

149. Comments of Mrs. Owen Lovejoy, paraphrased in the Reverend Mr. David Todd to the Reverend Mr. John Todd, Providence, Illinois, 11 June 1862, copy, J. G. Randall Papers, DLC.

150. *Mary Chesnut's Civil War*, ed. C. Vann Woodward (New Haven, CT: Yale University Press, 1983), 21 (diary entry for 10 Mar. 1861).

151. Washington *Post*, 12 Mar. 1893, 2.

152. Crawford, ed., *Russell's Civil War*, 162 (diary entry for 3 Nov. 1861).

153. A. K. McClure to Alonzo Rothschild, Philadelphia, 9 May 1907, Lincoln Contemporaries Collection, LMF.

154. Keckley, *Behind the Scenes*, 101.

155. Clipping from the New York *Commercial Gazette*, 9 Jan. 1887, J. G. Randall Papers, DLC; Washington correspondence by Vidette, 11 Dec. 1861, New York *Commercial Advertiser*, 13 Dec. 1861; reminiscences of John Palmer Usher, unidentified clipping, Otto Eisenschiml Papers, University of Iowa.

156. Ernest d'Hauterive, ed., "Voyage du Prince Napoleon aux Etats-Unis, 1861," *Revue de Paris* 40 (1933): 259 (diary entry for 6 Aug. 1861).

157. Crawford, ed., *Russell's Civil War*, 185 (diary entry for 23 Nov. 1861).

158. Russell to John T. Delane, Quebec, 11 Feb. 1862, ibid., 222.

159. James W. Nesmith to his wife, Washington, 5 Feb. 1862, photocopy, J. G. Randall Papers, DLC.

160. E. S. Denison to Dudley C. Denison, Washington, 15 Feb. 1864, George S. Denison Papers, DLC.

161. An unidentified New York paper copied in the *Illinois State Register* (Springfield), 30 Oct. 1864.

162. Edward Atkinson to his wife, Washington, [26 Feb. 1865], Atkinson Papers, MHi.

163. Washington correspondence by Mary Clemmer Ames, 8 Jan., Springfield, Massachusetts, *Republican*, 11 Jan. 1862.

164. Washington correspondence by E. H. Arr., 9 Feb., Springfield, Massachusetts, *Republican*, 20 Feb. 1864.

165. Mrs. James A. Mulligan told this to Maria Lydig Daly. Daly, *Diary of a Union Lady, 1861–1865*, ed. Harold Earl Hammond (New York: Funk & Wagnalls, 1962), 87 (entry for 20 Dec. 1861).

166. Elizabeth Blair Lee to Samuel Phillips Lee, Washington, 1 Mar. 1862, in Laas, ed., *Wartime Washington*, 104.

167. Lydia Maria Child to Mary Elizabeth Preston Stearns, Wayland, Massachusetts 15 Dec. 1861, *Lydia Maria Child: Selected Letters, 1817–1880*, ed. Milton Meltzer and Patricia G. Holland (Amherst: University of Massachusetts Press, 1982), 400; Child to John Greenleaf Whittier, Wayland, Massachusetts, 22 Sept. 1861, Child Papers, Microfiche edition, ed., Patricia G. Holland and Milton Meltzer.

168. Lydia Maria Child to Lucy Searle, Wayland, Massachusetts 11 Oct. 1861, Lydia Maria Child Letters, Samuel J. May Antislavery Collection, Cornell University.

169. A. Oakey Hall to Thurlow Weed, New York, 17 Aug. 1861, Weed Papers, University of Rochester.

170. Robert C. Winthrop, Jr., to P. P. Ellis, Boston, 10 Oct. 1861, Winthrop Family Papers, MHi.

171. Henry W. Bellows to Joseph Bellows, New York, 1 Feb. 1862, Henry W. Bellows Papers, MHi.

172. Hannah Matthews to Mrs. A. H. Pidge, Washington, 31 Jan. 1864, Schuyler Colfax Papers, Northern Indiana Center for History, South Bend.

173. Julia Taft Bayne, *Tad Lincoln's Father* (1924; Lincoln: University of Nebraska Press, 2001), 3.

174. James H. Campbell to his wife, Juliet Lewis Campbell, Washington, 28 Jan. 1863, Campbell Papers, Schoff Civil War Collection, William L. Clements Library, University of Michigan.

175. Julia Trumbull to Lyman Trumbull, Kingston, NY, 26 Sept. 1861, Trumbull Family Papers, William L. Clements Library, University of Michigan.

176. Fanny Seward diary, entry for 9 Sept. 1861, in Patricia Carley Johnson, ed., "Sensitivity and Civil War: The Selected Diaries and Papers, 1858–1868, of Frances Adeline Seward" (Ph.D. dissertation, University of Rochester, 1963), 360–361.

177. Diary of William T. Coggeshall, 7 Dec. 1861, in Freda Postle Koch, *Colonel Coggeshall: The Man Who Saved Lincoln* (Columbus, Ohio: Poko Press, 1985), 61; A. H[omer] B[yington] to Sydney [Howard Gay], Washington, 23 Mar. [1864], Gay Papers, Columbia University.

178. Undated, unsigned manuscript in the hand of John Hay, J. W. Schuckers Papers, DLC.

179. Wikoff gave the information to Simon P. Hanscom, who filed the story which appeared on December 3.

180. Washington correspondence, 14 Feb., New York *Tribune*, 15 Feb. 1862; Wikoff's narrative of events, dated 20 Feb., New York *Herald*, 3 Mar. 1862.

181. Orville H. Browning manuscript diary, IHi, 3 Mar. 1862; Washington correspondence, 14, 15 Feb., Chicago *Tribune*, 15 and 20 Feb. 1862; Washington correspondence, 13 Feb., New York *Tribune*, New York *Herald*, 14 Feb. 1862.

182. A. K. McClure to Alonzo Rothschild, Philadelphia, 9 May 1907, Lincoln Contemporaries Collection, LMF.

183. Frank Maloy Anderson, *The Mystery of "A Public Man": A Historical Detective Story* (Minneapolis: University of Minnesota Press, 1948), 126–128.

184. Forney, *Anecdotes of Public Men* (New York: Harper and Brothers, 1873), 366.

185. George Gibbs to John Austin Stevens, Washington, 3, 16 Oct. 1861, Stevens Papers, New-York Historical Society.

186. Davis to his wife Sarah, St. Louis, 15 Dec. 1861, Davis Family Papers, IHi.

187. Henry Smith to Charles Henry Ray and Joseph Medill, [Washington], 4 Nov. 1861, Ray Papers, CSmH. See also Adam Gurowski to Horace Greeley, Washington, 1 Oct. 1861, Greeley Papers, New York Public Library.

188. Hawley to Charles Dudley Warner, n.p., n.d., in Arthur L. Shipman, ed., "Letters of Joseph R. Hawley," typescript dated 1929, p. 387, Connecticut Historical Society, Hartford.

189. Washington correspondence, 21 Oct. 1861, Missouri *Republican* (St. Louis), 25 Oct. 1861, Michael Burlingame, ed., *Lincoln's*

Journalist: John Hay's Anonymous Writings for the Press, 1860–1864 (Carbondale: Southern Illinois University Press, 1998), 120.

190. Olmsted to Mary Perkins Olmsted, Washington, 28 Sept. 1861, McLaughlin et al., eds., *Papers of Olmsted*, 4:207.

191. Wool to his wife, Baltimore, 28 Sept. 1862, Wool Papers, New York State Library, Albany.

192. A. Mann, Jr., to E. B. Washburne, New York, 1 May 1862, Washburne Papers, DLC.

193. Daly, *Diary of a Union Lady*, 86 (entry for 19 Dec. 1861).

194. Fessenden to Elizabeth Warriner, Washington, 1 Dec. 1861, Fessenden Papers, Bowdoin College.

195. Philo S. Shelton to Thurlow Weed, Boston, 7 Feb. 1862, Weed Papers, University of Rochester.

196. Matthew Hale Smith, *Sunshine and Shadow in New York* (Hartford, CT: Burr, 1868), 285–289; C. A. Dana to J. S. Pike, New York, 4 Jan. 1862, Pike Papers, University of Maine; Washington correspondence, 11 Feb., New York *World*, 12 Feb. 1862.

197. T. J. Barnett to S. L. M. Barlow, Washington, 27 Oct. 1862, Barlow Papers, CSmH.

198. Washington correspondence, 2 Mar., Philadelphia *Inquirer*, 3 Mar. 1862.

199. George Gibbs to John Austin Stevens, Washington, 16 Oct. 1861, Stevens Papers, New-York Historical Society.

200. U.S. Senate, 59th Congress, 2nd Session, Report 69 (1903); Watt, "Declaration for Invalid Pension," 25 Aug. 1890, and Jane M. Watt, "Dependent Widow's Declaration for Pension," 29 Jan. 1892, Pension Records, National Archives; Watt to General [name indecipherable], Washington, 16 Jan. 1861; Watt to Lorenzo Thomas, 10 Sept. and 3 Dec. 1861, Records of the Adjutant General's Office, Letters Received, Main Series, Record Group 94, ibid.; Watt's service record, ibid.

201. John B. Blake, commissioner, to John Watt, Washington, 10 June 1858, copy, enclosing "a copy of the decision of the Secretary of the Interior upon the charges preferred against you by Mr. John Saunders," and Blake to Watt, Washington, 5 July 1859, copy, Records of the Commissioner of Public Buildings, letters sent, vols. 13 and 14, Record Group 42, Microcopy 371, reel 7, National Archives.

202. New York *Tribune*, 28 Jan. 1862.

203. Washington correspondence, 14 Oct., *National Anti-Slavery Standard* (New York), 19 Oct. 1861; Mary Todd Lincoln to John F. Potter, Washington, 13 Sept. 1861, in Turner and Turner, eds., *Mary Todd Lincoln*, 104; Potter, journal entry for 15 Sept. 1861, Potter Papers, Wisconsin State Historical Society.

204. C. A. Dana to J. S. Pike, New York, 8 Nov. 1861, Pike Papers, University of Maine.

205. Washington correspondence, 6 Oct., *National Anti-Slavery Standard* (New York), 12 Oct. 1861.

206. Washington correspondence by Van [D. W. Bartlett], 2 Sept., Springfield (Massachusetts) *Republican*, 7 Sept. 1861.

207. Orville H. Browning, manuscript diary, IHi, 3 Mar. 1862.

208. C. A. Dana to J. S. Pike, New York, 8 Nov. 1861, Pike Papers, University of Maine.

209. New York *Commercial Advertiser*, 4 Oct. 1867.

210. Upperman to Caleb B. Smith, Washington, 21 Oct. 1861, copy, Records of the U.S. Senate, Committee on Public Buildings and Grounds, 37th Congress, Record Group 46, National Archives; Financial Records of the Office of Public Buildings and Grounds, Record Group 42, entry 19, box 13, ibid.; records of the Commissioner of Public Buildings, letters sent, vols. 13 and 14, Record Group 42, Microcopy 371, reel 7, ibid.

211. Caleb B. Smith to W. H. Seward, Washington, 27 Oct. 1861, Seward Papers, University of Rochester.

212. Memo by Smith, Washington, 11 Dec. 1861, Records of the Commissioner of Public Buildings, Letters Received, Record Group 42, volume 37, microcopy 371, reel 7, National Archives.

213. Upperman to Foot, Washington, 6 Dec. 1861, Records of the U.S. Senate, Committee on Public Buildings and Grounds, 37th Congress, Record Group 46, National Archives.

214. New York *Commercial Advertiser,* 4 Oct. 1867.

215. Pennsylvania Congressman Benjamin Boyer, a member of the House Ways and Means Committee, told this story to Maryland journalist William Glenn. Bayly Ellen Marks and Mark Norton Schatz, eds., *Between North and South: A Maryland Journalist Views the Civil War, the Narrative of William Wilkins Glenn, 1861–1869* (Rutherford, NJ: Fairleigh Dickinson University Press, 1976), 175–176, 296 (entries for 16 Mar. 1865 and 4 Oct. 1867).

216. Benjamin B. French to Lincoln, Washington, 1 Apr. 1864, AL MSS DLC.

217. Lincoln to Whittlesey, Washington, 11 Mar. 1862, *Journal of the Abraham Lincoln Association* 17 (1996):52.

218. Undated, unsigned manuscript in the hand of John Hay, J. W. Schuckers Papers, DLC.

219. John Hay diary, 13 Feb. 1867, RPB.

220. Washington correspondence, 16 Oct., New York *Tribune,* 17 Oct. 1867.

221. George W. Adams to [David Goodman] Croly, Washington, 7 Oct. 1867, Manton Marble Papers, DLC.

222. Orville H. Browning diary, 3 July 1873 IHi; John Hay diary, 13 Feb. 1867, RPB.

223. D. P. Holloway to John Watt, Washington, 14 Mar. 1862, copy, AL MSS DLC.

224. Orville H. Browning diary, 3 Mar. 1862 IHi. In the Ward Hill Lamon Papers at the Henry E. Huntington Library is the following document, dated on its folder [Feb. 1] 1863:

"His Excellency
Abraham Lincoln
Due to John Watt
1863
To Commissary stores for the use of the President[']s House $361.00
the items and vouchers for this sum of money are in the hand [of] Genl Simm Draper

To Cash sent to Mrs Lincoln from this city [Washington?] to Mrs L by a draft at her request $350.00
the authority to send the same to Mrs Lincoln to New York is also in the hand of Mr Draper
To Cash paid Mrs Lincoln Hotel bill in Boston, receipt in Mr Lincoln[']s hand 15.00
To Cash handed Mrs Lincoln NY 10[.00]
$736.00
Mr. Watts presents this account with reluctance & never intended to present it for payment and departs from his purpose originally intended as the wishes of the Hon Secretary Smith has [*sic*] not been carried out by Mr Newton the head of the Agriculture bureau in not compensation [compensating] him for time and services in his visit to Europe for that Bureau, as that has not been done Mr Watts feels bound to present the above bill for payment as he cannot afford now to lose it. Mr Watts parted with the vouchers refer[re]d to with the understanding that the account would be promptly paid."

225. Watt to Cameron, n.p., n.d., Turner and Turner, eds., *Mary Todd Lincoln,* 103n.

226. Davis to his wife, St. Louis, 19, 23 February 1862, David Davis Papers, IHi.

227. Washington correspondence by "Iowa," 4 Feb. 1862, Burlington, Iowa, *Hawk-Eye,* 8 Feb. 1862, p. 2, c. 3; Marks and Schatz, eds., *Narrative of William Watkins Glenn,* 176 (4 Oct. 1867).

228. New York correspondence by "Metropolitan," 9 Oct. 1867, Boston *Post,* 11 Oct. 1867.

229. Marks and Schatz, eds., *Narrative of William Wilkins Glenn,* 176 (4 Oct. 1867).

230. C. A. Dana to J. S. Pike, New York, 8 Nov. 1861, Pike Papers, University of Maine.

231. Harry E. Pratt and Earnest E. East, "Mrs. Lincoln Refurbishes the White House," *Lincoln Herald* 47 (1945): 13–22.

232. Bill for $6,858 from William H. Carryl & Bro., 31 July 1861, First Auditor's Records, Miscellaneous Records, Treasury Department, Record Group 217, no. 143610, National Archives.

233. I have conflated two of French's accounts of this conversation. Burlingame,

Inner World of Lincoln, 299–300, and French, *Witness to the Young Republic,* ed. Cole and McDonough, 382.

234. James R. Doolittle to his wife Mary, Washington, 16 Feb. 1862, Doolittle Papers, State Historical Society of Wisconsin.

235. B. B. French to his son Frank, Washington, 13 Apr. 1862, French Family Papers, DLC.

236. Washington correspondence, 7 Feb., New York *Tribune,* 8 Feb. 1862.

237. James R. Doolittle to his wife Mary, Washington, 16 Feb. 1862, Doolittle Papers, State Historical Society of Wisconsin.

238. Russell, *Diary,* 28 (entry for 30 Mar. 1861).

239. Indianapolis *Journal,* 12 Feb. 1862.

240. An unidentified New York paper copied in the *Illinois State Register* (Springfield), 30 Oct. 1864; Davis to his wife Sarah, Washington, 25 Dec. 1862, Davis Papers, IHi.

241. Allen Peskin, "Putting the 'Baboon' to Rest: Observations of a Radical Republican on Lincoln's Funeral Train," *Lincoln Herald* 27 (1979):77.

242. Jean Baker, *Mary Todd Lincoln: A Biography* (New York: W.W. Norton, 1987), 192.

243. Letter by "Polly P. Perkins," Observatory Hill, East District, 1 Oct., Springfield, Massachusetts, *Republican,* 19 Oct. 1861.

244. E. Miller to Amanda Hanna, Crawfordsville, Indiana, 2 Mar. 1862, Robert B. Hanna Family Papers, Indiana Historical Society.

245. B. B. French to his son Frank, Washington, 9 July 1865, 3 Jan. 1866, French Family Papers, DLC.

246. French, *Witness to the Young Republic,* ed. Cole and McDonough, 479 (entry for 24 May 1865).

247. Washington correspondence, 2 Feb., New York *Herald,* 3 Feb. 1862.

248. Washington correspondence by Ben: Perley Poore, 6 Feb., Boston *Evening Journal,* 8 Feb. 1862; Washington correspondence, 4 Feb., Philadelphia *Inquirer,* 5 Feb. 1862.

249. Washington correspondence n.d. [ca. 2 Feb.], New York *Evening Express,* 3 Feb. 1862.

250. William O. Stoddard, "Recollections of a Checkered Lifetime," typescript, Stoddard Papers, Detroit Public Library, 2 vols., 2:346–348, 366.

251. B. B. French to his son Frank, Washington, 2 Feb., 13 Mar. 1862, French Family Papers, DLC.

252. Washington correspondence by Ben: Perley Poore, 6 Feb., Boston *Evening Journal,* 8 Feb. 1862.

253. New York *Herald,* 5 Feb. 1862.

254. Mrs. Henry A. Wise to her father, Edward Everett, Washington, 2 Mar. 1862, Everett Papers, MHi.

255. Washington correspondence by Miriam [Mrs. John A. Kasson], 26 June, *Iowa State Register* (Des Moines), 8 July 1862.

256. Washington correspondence, 10 Mar., *National Anti-Slavery Standard* (New York), 15 Mar. 1862.

257. Washington correspondence, 26 Aug., *National Anti-Slavery Standard* (New York), 31 Aug. 1861.

258. Henry L. Dawes to his wife, Washington, 29 Jan. 1862, Dawes Papers, DLC.

259. Washington correspondence by Van [D. W. Bartlett], 5 Feb., Springfield (Massachusetts) *Republican,* 8 Feb. 1862; Washington correspondence by Ben: Perely Poore, 2 Feb., Boston *Evening Journal,* 4 Feb. 1862; Hans L. Trefousse, *Benjamin Franklin Wade, Radical Republican from Ohio* (New York: Twayne, 1963), 167.

260. Philadelphia *Sunday Dispatch,* 9 Feb. 1862.

261. Cincinnati *Commercial,* 10 Feb. 1862.

262. Cincinnati *Gazette,* n.d., copied in the New York *Evening Express,* 11 Feb. 1862.

263. Washington correspondence by Mary Clemmer Ames, 25 Feb., Springfield (Massachusetts) *Republican,* 1 Mar. 1862.

264. Indianapolis *Journal,* 8 Feb. 1862.

265. Wendell Phillips, speech in Hartford, 21 Feb. 1862, Chicago *Times,* 28 Feb. 1862.

266. A. K. McClure to Alonzo Rothschild, Philadelphia, 9 May 1907, Lincoln Contemporaries Collection, LMF.

Chapter 26. "I Expect to Maintain
This Contest Until Successful, or
Till I Die"

1. William O. Stoddard, "White House
Sketches No. 6," New York *Citizen*, 22 Sept.
1866, in Stoddard, *Inside the White House in War
Times: Memoirs and Reports of Lincoln's Secretary*,
ed. Michael Burlingame (1890; Lincoln:
University of Nebraska Press, 2000), 166.

2. New York *World*, 15 Jan., 13 Mar. 1862.

3. Allan Nevins and Milton Halsey
Thomas, eds., *The Diary of George Templeton
Strong, 1835–1875* (4 vols.; New York: Macmillan,
1952), 3:188, 204 (entries for 23 Oct. 1861 and
29 Jan. 1862).

4. John Pendleton Kennedy to Robert C.
Winthrop, Baltimore, 16 Feb. 1862, Winthrop
Family Papers, MHi.

5. Howard K. Beale, ed., *The Diary of
Edward Bates, 1859–1866* (Annual Report of
the American Historical Association for the
Year 1930, vol. IV; Washington, DC: U.S.
Government Printing Office, 1933), 218 (entry
for 31 Dec. 1861).

6. Trumbull to Yates, Washington, 6 Feb.
1862, L. U. Reavis Papers, ICHi.

7. Yates to Trumbull, Springfield, 14 Feb.
1862, Lyman Trumbull Papers, DLC.

8. Washington correspondence by Van
[D. W. Bartlett], 22 Jan., Springfield, Massachusetts, *Republican*, 24 Jan. 1862.

9. Washington correspondence by
Ben: Perley Poore, 1 Jan., Boston *Journal*,
3 Jan. 1862.

10. "Notes at Washington" by S[amuel]
B[owles], Springfield, Massachusetts,
Republican, 27 Mar. 1862.

11. Philadelphia *Press*, 21 Apr. 1862.

12. Providence *Journal*, 13 Mar. 1862.

13. Maria Lydig Daly, *Diary of a Union
Lady, 1861–1865*, ed. Harold Earl Hammond
(New York: Funk & Wagnalls, 1962), 135–136
(entry for 22 May 1862).

14. Washington correspondence by Ben:
Perley Poore, 1 Jan., Boston *Journal*, 3 Jan. 1862.

15. Washington correspondence, 27 Jan.,
New York *Commercial Advertiser*, 28 Jan. 1862.

16. Smith to Henry Shelton Sanford, 19
Feb. 1862, Sanford Papers, in John Y. Simon,
"Lincoln and Truman Smith," *Lincoln Herald*
67 (1965): 127.

17. E. P. Norton to S. S. Cox, New York,
31 Jan. 1862, Cox Papers, RPB.

18. Washington correspondence, 9 Feb.,
New York *Evening Post*, 10 Feb. 1862.

19. William Kellogg to Joseph Gillespie,
Washington, 9 Feb. 1862, Joseph Gillespie
Papers, ICHi.

20. Wendell Phillips, speech in Boston,
17 Apr., in *The Liberator* (Boston), 25 Apr. 1862;
Noyes W. Miner to John Y. Scammon et al.,
Belvidere, Illinois, 1 Aug. 1871, Quincy,
Illinois, *Whig*, 16 Mar. 1872, copied in the New
York *Times*, 23 Mar. 1872.

21. McClellan to Lincoln, Camp Scott,
20 Apr. 1862, AL MSS DLC.

22. New York *Tribune*, 18 Jan. 1862;
Washington correspondence, 21 Jan., New
York *Evening Post*, 22 Jan. 1862.

23. George W. Rives to Lyman Trumbull,
Paris, Illinois, 12 Feb. 1862, Lyman Trumbull
Papers, DLC.

24. John Hay to Herndon, Paris, 5 Sept.
1866, Douglas L. Wilson and Rodney O.
Davis, eds., *Herndon's Informants: Letters,
Interviews, and Statements about Abraham
Lincoln* [hereafter *HI*] (Urbana: University of
Illinois Press, 1998), 332.

25. Nicolay to the Chicago *Tribune*,
Washington, 19 June 1863, in Michael
Burlingame, ed., *With Lincoln in the White
House: Letters, Memoranda, and Other Writings
of John G. Nicolay, 1860–1865* (Carbondale:
Southern Illinois University Press, 2000), 116.

26. Stoddard, "White House Sketches No.
2," New York *Citizen*, 25 Aug. 1866, in
Stoddard, *Inside the White House in War Times*,
ed., Burlingame, 148.

27. Francis B. Carpenter, *The Inner Life of
Abraham Lincoln: Six Months at the White House*
(New York: Hurd and Houghton, 1867),
258–259.

28. Public address, 11 Apr. 1865, in Roy P.
Basler et al., eds., *Collected Works of Abraham*

Lincoln [hereafter *CWL*] (8 vols. plus index; New Brunswick, NJ: Rutgers University Press, 1953–1955), 8:401.

29. Mary Todd Lincoln, interview with Herndon, [Sept. 1886], *HI*, 358.

30. Paxton Hibben, *Henry Ward Beecher: An American Portrait* (New York: G.H. Doran, 1927), 156.

31. Carpenter, *Inner Life of Lincoln*, 230.

32. Isabella Beecher Hooker to John Hooker, 19 Nov. 1862, in Debby Applegate, *The Most Famous Man in America: The Biography of Henry Ward Beecher* (New York: Doubleday, 2006), 341; Thomas Beecher to Henry Ward Beecher, 10 Aug. 1862, Beecher Papers, Yale University.

33. Ward Hill Lamon, *Recollections of Abraham Lincoln, 1847–1865*, ed. Dorothy Lamon Teillard (2nd ed.; Washington, DC: The Editor, 1911), 261.

34. Gay told to this to Josephine Shaw Lowell. William Rhinelander Stewart, *The Philanthropic Work of Josephine Shaw Lowell* (New York: Macmillan, 1911), 23 (diary entry for 3 Apr. 1862).

35. Carpenter, *Inner Life of Lincoln*, 281–282.

36. Endorsement dated 23 Dec. 1862 on a letter from Henry P. Tappan to Lincoln, University of Michigan, 22 Nov. 1862, AL MSS DLC.

37. Stoddard, "White House Sketches No. 4," New York *Citizen*, 8 Sept. 1866, Stoddard, *Inside the White House*, ed. Burlingame, 157–158.

38. Carpenter, *Inner Life of Lincoln*, 253–254.

39. Washington correspondence, 19 Oct., New York *Evening Post*, 21 Oct. 1865.

40. Marie Caroline Post, *The Life and Memoirs of Comte Régis de Trobriand, Major-General in the Army of the United States* (New York: E. P. Dutton, 1909), 252.

41. Washington correspondence by Van [D. W. Bartlett], 1 Jan., Springfield, Massachusetts, *Republican*, 4 Jan. 1862.

42. Letter by Congressman A. S. Diven, Columbia, Missouri, *Statesman*, 14 Feb. 1862, copy, Allan Nevins Papers, Columbia University.

43. This comment was made on 17 Jan. 1862 to Moncure Conway, editor of the Boston *Commonwealth*, and William Henry Channing. Boston *Commonwealth*, 6 Sept. 1862.

44. Washington correspondence, 6 Feb., New York *Tribune*, 7 Feb. 1862.

45. Speed to Joseph Holt, Washington, 4 Feb. 1862, Holt Papers, DLC.

46. Theodore Calvin Pease and James G. Randall, eds., *The Diary of Orville Hickman Browning* (2 vols.; Springfield: Illinois State Historical Library, 1925–1933), 1:595 (entry for 12 Dec. 1862).

47. Washington correspondence by Whitelaw Reid, 10 Mar. 1863, Cincinnati *Gazette*, n.d., scrapbook, Reid Family Papers, DLC.

48. Washington correspondence by "Miriam" (Mrs. John A. Kasson), 20 Feb., *Iowa State Register* (Des Moines), 1 Mar. 1862.

49. Major J. G. Benton to James Watson Webb, Washington, 28 Feb. 1862, James Watson Webb Papers, Sterling Library, Yale University.

50. Dillard C. Donnohue, interview with Jesse W. Weik, 13 Feb. 1887, *HI*, 602.

51. Nicolay, journal entry for 17 Feb. 1862, in Burlingame, ed., *With Lincoln in the White House*, 69.

52. Henry A. Wise to A. H. Foote, Washington, 23 Jan. 1862, in *CWL*, 5:108.

53. Henry A. Wise to A. H. Foote, Washington, 31 Jan. 1862, William P. Palmer Collection, Western Reserve Historical Society.

54. Robert V. Bruce, *Lincoln and the Tools of War* (Indianapolis: Bobbs-Merrill, 1956), 162.

55. Virginia Fox diary, [26?] Jan. 1862, Levi Woodbury Papers, DLC.

56. Michael Burlingame and John R. Turner Ettlinger, eds., *Inside Lincoln's White House: The Complete Civil War Diary of John Hay* (Carbondale: Southern Illinois University Press, 1997), 28–29 (entry for 26 Oct. 1861).

57. Stoddard, *Inside the White House*, ed. Burlingame, 21–23, 163; Washington correspondence, 22 Sept. 1862, New York *World*, 23 Sept. 1861; Washington correspondence, 20 Sept., Philadelphia *Press*, 21 Sept. 1861.

58. Stanton to Charles A. Dana, Washington, 24 Jan. 1862, Dana Papers, DLC.

59. Washington correspondence by "Linkensale," 14 Jan., *Iowa State Register* (Des Moines), 21 Jan. 1862.

60. G. W. Gans to John Sherman, Eaton, Ohio, 23 Feb. 1862, John Sherman Papers, DLC.

61. Fanny Garrison to Theodore Tilton, Boston, 6 Apr. 1862, Tilton Papers, New-York Historical Society.

62. Stanton to Herman Dyer, Washington, 18 May 1862, Stanton Papers, DLC.

63. Burlingame and Ettlinger, eds., *Hay Diary*, 35 (entry for [Mar. 1862]).

64. Cincinnati *Gazette*, 3 Mar., quoted in the Cincinnati *Commercial*, 14 Mar. 1862.

65. Washington correspondence, 5 Feb., New York *Tribune*, 6 Feb. 1862.

66. McClellan to Stanton, Washington, 31 Jan. [3 Feb.] 1862, AL MSS DLC.

67. Lincoln to McClellan, Washington, 3 Feb. 1862, *CWL*, 5:119.

68. Henry Wilson interviewed by Nicolay, 16 Nov. 1875, in Michael Burlingame, ed., *An Oral History of Abraham Lincoln: John G. Nicolay's Interviews and Essays* (Carbondale: Southern Illinois University Press, 1996), 84.

69. Washington correspondence, 12 Mar., New York *Evening Post*, 13 Mar. 1862.

70. Sumner to John A. Andrew, Washington, 27 Apr. 1862, Beverly Wilson Palmer, ed., *The Selected Letters of Charles Sumner* (2 vols.; Boston: Northeastern University Press, 1990), 2:112.

71. Stanton to Lander, Washington, 17 Feb. 1862, Stanton Papers, DLC.

72. Horace White to Joseph Medill, Washington, 3 Mar. 1862, Charles Henry Ray Papers, CSmH.

73. Unidentified newspaper clipping, "Anecdotes of Abraham Lincoln," Lincoln Shrine, A. K. Smiley Library, Redlands, California; William O. Stoddard, *Abraham Lincoln: The True Story of a Great Life* (New York: Fords, Howard, & Hulbert, 1884), 285.

74. Nicolay memorandum, 27 Feb. 1862, in Burlingame, ed., *With Lincoln in the White House*, 72.

75. Virginia Fox diary, entry for 7 Mar. 1862, Levi Woodbury Papers, DLC.

76. Washington correspondence, 20 Feb., New York *Tribune*, 22 Feb. 1862.

77. Washington correspondence by "Linkensale," 4 Mar., *Iowa State Register* (Des Moines), 12 Mar. 1862.

78. Washington correspondence by Van [D. W. Bartlett], 22 Jan., Springfield, Massachusetts, *Republican*, 24 Jan. 1862.

79. Washington correspondence, 12 Mar., New York *Commercial Advertiser*, 13 Mar. 1862.

80. James H. Campbell to his wife, Juliet Lewis Campbell, Washington, 4 Mar. 1862, Campbell Papers, Schoff Civil War Collection, William L. Clements Library, University of Michigan.

81. Owen Lovejoy to his children, Washington, 23 Feb. 1862, Lovejoy Papers, William L. Clements Library, University of Michigan.

82. William Florville to Lincoln, Springfield, 27 Dec. 1863, AL MSS DLC.

83. Nathaniel P. Willis in Elizabeth Keckley, *Behind the Scenes; or, Thirty Years a Slave and Four Years in the White House* (New York: G. W. Carleton, 1868), 106–107; Washington correspondence, 21 Feb., Philadelphia *Inquirer*, 22 Feb. 1862; Washington correspondence, 24 Feb., New York *Herald*, 26 Feb. 1862.

84. Horatio Nelson Taft diary, DLC (entries for 13 Jan., 20 Feb. 1862).

85. Julia Taft Bayne, *Tad Lincoln's Father* (Boston: Little, Brown, 1931), 8.

86. Diary of Fanny Seward, 5 Feb. 1863, in Patricia Carley Johnson, ed., "Sensitivity and Civil War: The Selected Diaries and Papers, 1858–1868, of Frances Adeline Seward" (Ph.D. dissertation, University of Rochester, 1963), 647.

87. New York *World*, weekly edition, 8 Mar. 1862.

88. William O. Stoddard, "White House Sketches No. 1," New York *Citizen*, 18 Aug. 1866, in Stoddard, *Inside the White House in War Times*, ed. Burlingame, 145.

89. Beale, ed., *Bates Diary*, 233 (entry for 18 Feb. 1862).

90. Nicolay, journal entry for 20 Feb. 1862, in Burlingame, ed., *With Lincoln in the White House*, 71.

91. Washington correspondence, 20 Feb., Philadelphia *Inquirer*, 21 Feb. 1862.

92. Elihu Washburne to his wife, [Washington], 21 Feb. [1862], Washburn Family Papers, Washburn Memorial Library, Norlands, Maine.

93. Keckley, *Behind the Scenes*, 103.

94. Anna L. Boyden, *Echoes from Hospital and White House: A Record of Mrs. Rebecca R. Pomroy's Experience in War* (Boston: D. Lothrop, 1884), 56.

95. Mrs. Henry A. Wise (née Charlotte Everett) to her father, Edward Everett, Washington, 2 Mar. 1862, Everett Papers, MHi.

96. Washington correspondence by Van [D. W. Bartlett], 26 Feb., Springfield, Massachusetts, *Republican*, 28 Feb. 1862; Washington correspondence, 27 Feb., New York *Evening Post*, 28 Feb. 1862.

97. "Washington as It Appeared in March, 1862," Brooklyn *Daily Eagle*, 23 Jan. 1887.

98. Francis B. Fox to Ida Tarbell, New York, 13 Nov. 1939, Tarbell Papers, Allegheny College.

99. Boyden, *Echoes from Hospital*, 62.

100. Lincoln to Stanton, Washington, 15 July 1862, *CWL*, 5:326.

101. Washington correspondence, 24 Mar., New York *Examiner*, 27 Mar. 1862, Michael Burlingame, ed., *Dispatches from Lincoln's White House: The Anonymous Civil War Journalism of Presidential Secretary William O. Stoddard* (Lincoln: University of Nebraska Press, 2002), 66.

102. LeGrande Cannon, *Personal Reminiscences of the Rebellion, 1861–1866* (New York: Burr Printing House, 1895), 173–174; LeGrande Cannon to Herndon, near Burlington, Vermont, 7 Oct. [1889], *HI*, 679. The quoted passage appears in *King John*, act 3, scene 4, lines 79–81.

103. Matthew Simpson's funeral oration in David B. Chesebrough, *No Sorrow Like Our Sorrow: Northern Protestant Ministers and the*

Assassination of Lincoln (Kent, Ohio: Kent State University Press, 1994), 135.

104. Mary Todd Lincoln to Francis B. Carpenter, Chicago, 15 Nov. [1865], in Justin G. Turner and Linda Levitt Turner, eds., *Mary Todd Lincoln: Her Life and Letters* (New York: Knopf, 1972), 285.

105. Washburne to his wife, [Washington,] Tuesday [20 May 1862], Washburn Family Papers, Washburn Memorial Library, Norlands, Maine.

106. Mary Lincoln to Julia Ann Sprigg, Washington, 29 May 1862, in Turner and Turner, eds., *Mary Todd Lincoln*, 127.

107. Keckley, *Behind the Scenes*, 104–105.

108. Elizabeth Todd Edwards, interviewed by Herndon, [1865–1866], *HI*, 444–445.

109. Elizabeth Edwards to Julia Edwards, Washington, 2 Mar. 1862, in Ruth Painter Randall, *Mary Todd Lincoln: Biography of a Marriage* (Boston: Little, Brown, 1953), 287.

110. Ibid., 289.

111. David Davis to W. W. Orme, [St. Louis], 23 Feb. 1862, Orme Papers, IHi.

112. Alexander Williamson, interviewed in the New York *Press*, 14 Apr. 1889; Keckley, *Behind the Scenes*, 107.

113. Josiah Kent, *Illinois State Journal* (Springfield), 9 Jan. 1909.

114. Elizabeth Todd Grimsley, "Six Months in the White House," *Journal of the Illinois State Historical Society* 19 (1926–1927): 53–54.

115. Stoddard, *Inside the White House in War Times*, ed. Burlingame, 66.

116. Bayne, *Tad Lincoln's Father*, 8.

117. Helen Nicolay, *Lincoln's Secretary: A Biography of John G. Nicolay* (New York: Longmans, Green, 1949), 133.

118. Noah Brooks, *Washington in Lincoln's Time* (New York: Century, 1895), 281.

119. Margarita Spalding Gerry, ed., *Through Five Administrations: Reminiscences of Colonel William H. Crook, Body-Guard to President Lincoln* (New York: Harper and Brothers, 1910), 23.

120. Davis to his wife Sarah, St. Louis, 23 Feb. 1862, Davis Papers, IHi.

121. George Brinton McClellan, *McClellan's Own Story: The War for the Union* (New York: C. L. Webster, 1887), 195–196.

122. Burlingame and Ettlinger, eds., *Hay Diary*, 35 (entry for [Mar. 1862]).

123. McDowell, speech at San Francisco, 21 Oct. 1864, New York *Herald*, 4 Dec. 1864.

124. Stephen W. Sears, *To the Gates of Richmond: The Peninsula Campaign* (Boston: Houghton Mifflin, 1992), 7.

125. *CWL*, 5: 149–150.

126. Samuel P. Heintzelman journal, entry for 8 Mar. 1862, Heintzelman Papers, DLC.

127. Lincoln to McClellan, Washington, 9 May 1862, *CWL*, 5:208.

128. John G. Nicolay and John Hay, *Abraham Lincoln: A History* (10 vols.; New York: Century, 1890), 5:221, citing an interview by Nicolay with Gustavus Fox.

129. Burlingame and Ettlinger, eds., *Hay Diary*, 36 (entry for [Mar. 1862]).

130. Beale, ed., *Bates Diary*, 239 (entry for 11 Mar. 1862).

131. Burlingame and Ettlinger, eds., *Hay Diary*, 36 (entry for [Mar. 1862]).

132. "Notes at Washington," by S[amuel] B[owles], n.d., Springfield, Massachusetts, *Republican*, 27 Mar. 1862.

133. Washington correspondence, 12 Mar., New York *Evening Post*, 13 Mar. 1862.

134. Josiah G. Holland to George William Curtis, New York, 18 Apr. 1862, Curtis Papers, Staten Island Institute of Arts and Sciences.

135. Blair to Frémont, 24 Aug. 1861, New York *Herald*, 8 Mar. 1862; Washington correspondence, 6 Apr., New York *Tribune*, 7 Apr. 1862.

136. Elizabeth Blair Lee to Samuel P. Lee, Silver Spring, Maryland, 6 Mar. 1862 in Virginia Jeans Laas, ed., *Wartime Washington: The Civil War Letters of Elizabeth Blair Lee* (Urbana: University of Illinois Press, 1991), 106–107.

137. Burlingame and Ettlinger, eds., *Hay Diary*, 36 (entry for [Mar. 1862]).

138. Noah Brooks, "Personal Recollections of Abraham Lincoln," *Harper's New Monthly Magazine* 31 (July 1865): 225.

139. Ulysses S. Grant, *Personal Memoirs of U. S. Grant* (2 vols.; New York: C. L. Webster, 1885–1886), 2:122.

140. McClellan, *McClellan's Own Story*, 165.

141. New York *Herald*, 6 Apr. 1862.

142. Burlingame and Ettlinger, eds., *Hay Diary*, 35 (entry for [Mar. 1862]).

143. Fessenden to Elizabeth Warriner, Washington, 15 Mar. 1862, Fessenden Papers, Bowdoin College.

144. Spinner to Timothy C. Day, Washington, [ca. 15 Mar.] 1862, in Sarah J. Day, *The Man on a Hill Top* (Philadelphia: Ware Brothers, 1931), 260.

145. Adams S. Hill to Henry W. Bellows, [Washington], 2 Apr. [1862], Bellows Papers, MHi.

146. Gurowski to Zachariah Chandler, Washington, 12 Mar. 1862, Chandler Papers, DLC.

147. Fessenden to Elizabeth Warriner, Washington, 15 Mar. 1862, Fessenden Papers, Bowdoin College.

148. New York *Herald*, 18 Mar. 1862.

149. Washington correspondence by Van [D. W. Bartlett], 12 Mar., Springfield, Massachusetts, *Republican*, 14 Mar. 1862.

150. Thomas Ewing to Lincoln, Lancaster, Ohio, 9 Apr. 1862, AL MSS DLC.

151. Washington correspondence by Van [D. W. Bartlett], 11 Mar., Springfield, Massachusetts, *Republican*, 15 Mar. 1862.

152. George W. Julian in Rice, ed., *Reminiscences of Lincoln*, 53.

153. Hitchcock diary, entry for 15 Mar. 1862, copy, William A. Croffut Papers, DLC.

154. John A. Dahlgren diary, copy, Nicolay Papers, DLC (entry for 9 Mar. 1862).

155. Meigs to his father, Washington, 9 Mar. 1862, Meigs Papers, DLC.

156. Benjamin P. Thomas and Harold M. Hyman, *Stanton: The Life and Times of Lincoln's Secretary of War* (New York: Alfred A. Knopf, 1962), 181.

157. Howard K. Beale and Alan W. Brownsword, eds., *Diary of Gideon Welles, Secretary of the Navy under Lincoln and Johnson*

[hereafter *Welles Diary*] (3 vols.; New York: W. W. Norton, 1960), 1:67.

158. Cornelius S. Bushnell to Welles, n.p., n.d. [received 16 Mar. 1877], Welles Papers, CSmH.

159. Letter by Henry A. Wise, published in the Boston *Daily Advertiser*, n.d, copied in the Boston *Journal*, 20 Mar. 1862; Worden's narrative, Worden Papers, Lincoln Memorial University, Harrogate, Tennessee; Washington correspondence, 10, 11 Mar., New York *Tribune*, 11, 12 Mar. 1862; Washington correspondence, 10, 11 Mar., New York *Tribune*, 10 Mar., Philadelphia *Inquirer*, 11 Mar. 1862.

160. William F. Keeler to his wife Anna, aboard the *Monitor*, 7 May 1862, Robert W. Daly, ed., *Aboard the USS Monitor, 1862: The Letters of Acting Paymaster William Frederick Keeler, U.S. Navy, to His Wife, Anna* (Annapolis: U.S. Naval Institute, 1964), 106–107.

161. McClellan to S. L. M. Barlow, Washington, 16 Mar. 1862, Sears, ed., *McClellan Papers*, 213.

162. Pease and Randall, eds., *Browning Diary*, 1:537–538 (entry for 2 Apr. 1862).

163. Johnston to Lee, Lee's Farm, 22 Apr. 1862, *OR*, I, 11, 3:456.

164. Beale, ed., *Welles Diary*, 1:124 (entry for 12 Sept. 1862).

165. McClellan to his wife, near Yorktown, 6 Apr. 1862, Sears, ed., *McClellan Papers*, 230.

166. McClellan to Lincoln, near Yorktown, 5 Apr. 1862, AL MSS DLC.

167. McClellan to his wife, before Yorktown, 11 Apr. 1862, Sears, ed., *McClellan Papers*, 235.

168. Washington correspondence by Van [D. W. Bartlett], 6 June [misdated 22 May], Springfield, Massachusetts, *Republican*, 9 June 1862.

169. Lincoln to McClellan, Washington, 6 Apr. 1862, *CWL*, 5:182.

170. Lincoln to McClellan, Washington, 9 Apr. 1862, ibid., 5:184–185.

171. Ibid., 5:203.

172. Richard C. McCormick's reminiscences, New York, 29 Apr. 1865, New York *Evening Post*, 5 May 1865, semi-weekly edition.

173. Stanton to Herman Dyer, Washington, 18 May 1862, Stanton Papers, DLC.

174. Henry Winter Davis to Samuel Francis Du Pont, Baltimore, 6 April 1862, transcript, S. F. Du Pont Papers, Hagley Museum, Wilmington, Delaware.

175. Daly, *Diary of a Union Lady*, 140 (entry for 5 June 1862).

176. Israel Washburn to Hannibal Hamlin, Augusta, 23 May 1862, Israel Washburn Papers, DLC.

177. Barney to Chase, New York, 30 June 1862, Chase Papers, Historical Society of Pennsylvania.

178. Henry W. Bellows to Joseph Bellows, New York, 1 Feb. 1862, Bellows Papers, MHi.

179. C. A. Dana to J. S. Pike, New York, 28 May 1862, Pike Papers, University of Maine.

180. Washington correspondence, 21 Apr., New York *Examiner*, 24 Apr. 1862, Burlingame, ed., *Dispatches from Lincoln's White House*, 74.

181. McClure to Ellen McClellan, Philadelphia, 13 Jan. 1892, McClellan Papers, DLC.

182. McClellan to his wife, before Yorktown, 8 Apr. 1862, Sears, ed., *McClellan Papers*, 234.

183. New York *Tribune*, 13 May 1862; Norfolk correspondence, 11 May, New York *Herald*, 13 May 1862.

184. Fort Monroe correspondence, 9 May, New York *Herald*, 12 May 1862; "Captain F. A. Rowe's Reminiscences," New York, Mar. 1905, in Philip Corell, ed., *History of the Naval Brigade, 99th N.Y. Volunteers, Union Coast Guard, 1861–65* (New York: Regimental Veteran Association, 1905), unpaginated.

185. Fortress Monroe correspondence, 9 May, New York *Tribune*, 12 May 1862; Fort Monroe correspondence, 9 May, New York *Herald*, 12 May 1862; Fortress Monroe correspondence, 9 May, Baltimore *American*, n.d., copied in the Washington *Star*, 12 May 1862.

186. Joseph B. Carr, "Operations of 1861 around Fort Monroe," Robert Underwood Johnson, Clarence Clough, eds., *Battles and*

Leaders of the Civil War (4 vols.; New York: Century, [1887–88]), 2:152

187. Capt. Wilson Barstow to Elizabeth Barstow Stoddard, Baltimore, 12 May 1862, Barstow Papers, DLC.

188. Washington correspondence by Van [D. W. Bartlett], 13 May, Springfield, Massachusetts, *Republican*, 17 May 1862.

189. Stanton to Wool, Washington, 16 May 1862, Wool Papers, New York State Library.

190. Ari Hoogenboom, *Fox of the Union Navy* (Baltimore, MD: Johns Hopkins University Press, forthcoming).

191. Capt. Wilson Barstow to Elizabeth Barstow Stoddard, Baltimore, 12 May 1862, Barstow Papers, DLC.

192. Garrison's Station, New York, correspondence, 25 June, New York *Herald*, 26 June 1862.

193. Willoughby point correspondence, 10 May, New York *Herald*, 12 May 1862.

194. William F. Keeler to his wife Anna, aboard the *Monitor*, 9 May 1862, Daly, ed., *Aboard the USS Monitor*, 115; Wilson Barstow to Elizabeth Barstow Stoddard, Baltimore, 12 May 1862, Barstow Papers, DLC.

195. Washington *Evening Star*, 12 May 1862.

196. Chase to his daughter Janet, steamer "Baltimore," 11 May 1862, Niven, ed., *Chase Papers*, 3:197.

197. Nevins and Thomas, eds., *Strong Diary*, 3:210 (entry for 16 Mar. 1862).

198. Washington correspondence, 28 Apr., New York *Evening Post*, 29 Apr. 1862.

199. *Iowa State Register* (Des Moines), 25 May 1862.

200. Trumbull to John A. McClernand, Washington, 24 May 1862, McClernand Papers, IHi.

201. Washington correspondence by D. W. Bartlett, 18 July, New York *Independent*, 23 July 1862.

202. Lincoln to McClellan, Fort Monroe, 9 May 1862, *CWL*, 5:208–209.

203. Adams S. Hill to Sydney Howard Gay, Washington, [7 or 8 or 9] June [1862], Sydney Howard Gay Papers, Columbia University.

204. Herman Haupt, *Reminiscences of General Herman Haupt* (Milwaukee: Wright & Joys, 1901), 50.

205. Washington correspondence, 9 July, New York *Evening Post*, 10 July 1862.

206. Sumner to Richard Henry Dana, Washington, 26 May 1862, Richard Henry Dana Papers, MHi.

207. George William Curtis to Charles Eliot Norton, n.p., 26 May 1862, George William Curtis Papers, Harvard University.

208. Nicolay to Therena Bates, Washington, 25 May 1862, in Burlingame, ed., *With Lincoln in the White House*, 78–79.

209. Washington correspondence, 26 May, Chicago *Tribune*, 31 May 1862; Washington correspondence by Van [D. W. Bartlett], 28 May, Springfield, Massachusetts, *Republican*, 30 May 1862.

210. Memo by Col. John P. C. Shanks, "Conversation between President Lincoln & Col. Zagonyi, Written out by Col. Shanks who was present at the interview," recounting a conversation with Lincoln on 15 June 1862, Sydney Howard Gay Papers, Columbia University.

211. Lincoln to McDowell, Washington, 24 May 1862, *CWL*, 5:233.

212. Madeleine Vinton Dahlgren, ed., *Memoir of John A. Dahlgren* (Boston: Osgood, 1882), 375 (diary entry for 24 May 1862).

213. Lincoln to Frémont, Washington, 24 May 1862, *CWL*, 5:231.

214. Yates to Trumbull, Springfield, 14 Feb. 1862, Lyman Trumbull Papers, DLC.

215. *CWL*, 5:231.

216. McDowell to C. A. Hecksher, 17 June 1862, Barlow Papers, in Allan Nevins, *The War for the Union* (4 vols.; New York: Charles Scribner's Sons, 1959–1971), 2:128; *CWL*, 5:233.

217. Lincoln to Chase, Washington, 25 May 1862, *CWL*, 5:235.

218. Lincoln to Frémont, Washington, 15 June 1862, *CWL*, 5:271.

219. Lincoln to McClellan, Washington, 25 May 1862, *CWL*, 5:236, 237.

220. Henry Winter Davis to Samuel Francis Du Pont, Baltimore, [no day indicated] June 1862, transcript, S. F. Du Pont Papers, Hagley Museum, Wilmington, Delaware.

221. Memo by Col. John P. C. Shanks, "Conversation between President Lincoln & Col. Zagonyi, Written out by Col. Shanks who was present at the interview," recounting a conversation with Lincoln on 15 June 1862, Sydney Howard Gay Papers, Columbia University.

222. *CWL,* 5:246.

223. Washington correspondence by Van [D. W. Bartlett], 3 June, Springfield, Massachusetts, *Republican,* 7 June 1862.

224. Memo by Col. John P. C. Shanks, "Conversation between President Lincoln & Col. Zagonyi, Written out by Col. Shanks who was present at the interview," recounting a conversation with Lincoln on 15 June 1862, Gay Papers, Columbia University.

225. Washington correspondence, 2 June, Cincinnati *Commercial,* 3 June 1862.

226. McClellan to his wife, Camp Lincoln, 22 June 1862, Sears, ed., *McClellan Papers,* 305.

227. *CWL,* 5:272.

228. Nicolay to Therena Bates, Washington, 5 June 1862, Burlingame, ed., *With Lincoln in the White House,* 80.

229. Washington correspondence by Van [D. W. Bartlett], 17 June, Springfield, Massachusetts, *Republican,* 20 June 1862; Washington correspondence, 16 June, Cincinnati *Commercial,* 17 June 1862.

230. *CWL,* 5:276.

231. New York correspondence, 25 June, New York *Herald,* 26 June 1862.

232. Peter Cozzens and Robert I. Girardi, eds., *The Military Memoirs of General John Pope* (Chapel Hill: University of North Carolina Press, 1998), 121.

233. Henry T. Cheever to his sister Elizabeth, Worcester, 3 July 1862, Cheever Papers, American Antiquarian Society.

234. General Augustus L. Chetlain, "Recollections of General U. S. Grant," *Military Essays and Recollections: Papers Read Before the Commandery of the State of Illinois, Military Order of the Loyal Legion of the United States* (4 vols.; Chicago: McClurg, 1891) 1:30.

235. Thomas J. McCormack, ed., *Memoir of Gustave Koerner, 1809–1896* (2 vols.; Cedar Rapids, IA: Torch Press, 1909), 2:216.

236. Washburne to Grant, Washington, 24 Jan. 1864, John Y. Simon, ed., *Grant Papers,* 9:522–523.

237. Beale, ed., *Welles Diary,* 1:126 (entry for 12 Sept. 1862).

238. McClellan to Stanton, Camp Lincoln, 25 June 1862, Sears, ed., *McClellan Papers,* 309–310.

239. *CWL,* 5:286.

240. Washington correspondence by Van [D. W. Bartlett], 22 July, Springfield, Massachusetts, *Republican,* 24 July 1862.

241. McClellan to Stanton, Savage Station, 28 June 1862, Sears, ed., *McClellan Papers,* 323.

242. Pease and Randall, eds., *Browning Diary,* 1:559 (entry for 14 July 1862).

243. Lincoln to McClellan, Washington, 28 June 1862, *CWL,* 5:289–290.

244. Lincoln to McClellan, Washington, 1 July 1862, *CWL,* 5:298.

245. Lincoln to McClellan, Washington, 2 July 1862, *CWL,* 5:301.

246. McClellan to Stanton, Harrison's Bar, 3 July 1862, Sears, ed., *McClellan Papers,* 333.

247. *CWL,* 5:305–306.

248. *CWL,* 5:307.

249. Cincinnati *Commercial,* 12 Sept. 1862.

250. Washington correspondence, 28 Nov., New York *Independent,* 3 Dec. 1863.

251. Washington correspondence by Van [D. W. Bartlett], 17 Dec., Springfield, Massachusetts, *Republican,* 19 Dec. 1862.

252. Henry C. Deming, *Eulogy of Abraham Lincoln* (Hartford, CT: A. N. Clark, 1865), 40.

253. New York *Evening Post,* 28 July 1862.

254. W. H. Smith in "Lincoln as the Loneliest Man," clipping from the Drayter (?) Gleaner, 2 Nov. 1937, clipping collection, LMF.

255. Theodore Burton, address given in 1909, in *Addresses Delivered at the Lincoln Dinners of the Republican Club of New York in*

Response to the Toast Abraham Lincoln,
1887–1909 (New York: Republican Club of
New York, 1909), 307–308.

256. Washington correspondence by
B. M. F., 29 July, Cincinnati *Gazette*, 1 Aug. 1862.

257. Hilon Parker to his father, Fort [Meigs?],
2 Aug. 1863, Hilon Parker Papers, Williams L.
Clements Library, University of Michigan.

258. Dawes to his wife Electa, Washington,
3 July 1862, Dawes Papers, DLC.

259. Fessenden to Elizabeth Warriner,
Washington, 6 July 1862, Fessenden Family
Papers, Bowdoin College.

260. N. C. McFarland to John Sherman,
Hamilton, 8 July 1862, John Sherman Papers,
DLC.

261. New York *Evening Post*, 7 July 1862.

262. Phillips to Charles Sumner, n.p., 29
June 1862, Sumner Papers, Harvard University.

263. Samuel J. May, Jr., to "Dear Charles,"
Leicester, Mass., 17 July 1862, May Papers,
Boston Public Library.

264. Lincoln to Seward, Washington,
28 June 1862, *CWL*, 5:292.

265. Pease and Randall, eds., *Browning
Diary*, 1:559 (entry for 14 July 1862).

266. Medill to Lyman Trumbull, Chicago,
4 July 1862, Lyman Trumbull Papers, DLC.

267. Henry L. Dawes to his wife, Washington, 5 July 1862, Dawes Papers, DLC.

268. Harrison G. O. Blake to Lincoln,
Medina, Ohio, 28 July 1862, AL MSS DLC.

269. Nathaniel S. Berry, et al. to Lincoln,
Concord, 30 July 1862, ibid.

270. Nevins and Thomas, eds., *Strong
Diary*, 3:244 (entry for 26 July 1862).

271. Cincinnati *Commercial*, 9 July 1862.

272. Lincoln to Agenor-Etienne de Gas-
parin, Washington, 4 Aug. 1862, *CWL*, 5:355.

273. Edgar F. Brown to "Dear Hannah,"
Washington, 27 July 1862, Edgar F. Brown
Papers, DLC.

274. *CWL*, 5:367.

275. Meigs pocket diary, entry for 5 July
1862, DLC.

276. Burlingame and Ettlinger, eds., *Hay
Diary*, 191 (entry for 28 Apr. 1864).

277. Washington correspondence by Agate
[Whitelaw Reid], 10 July, Cincinnati *Gazette*,
14 July 1862.

278. McClellan to his wife, Berkeley, 17 July
1862, Sears, ed., *McClellan Papers*, 362.

279. Sears, *George B. McClellan*, 227.

280. William C. Davis, *Lincoln's Men: How
President Lincoln Became Father to an Army and
a Nation* (New York: Free Press, 1999), 68,
citing Charles A. Fuller, "Personal Recollections," 46.

281. Harrison's Landing correspondence,
9 July, New York *Herald*, 11 July 1862.

282. Washington correspondence, 11 July,
New York *Evening Post*, 12 July 1862

283. David Herbert Donald, *Lincoln* (New
York: Simon and Schuster, 1995), 359, citing
Charles N. Walker and Rosemary Walker,
eds., "Diary of War of Robert S. Robertson,"
Old Fort News, 28 (Jan.-Mar. 1965), 42.

284. William F. Keeler to his wife Anna,
aboard the *Monitor*, 23 July 1862, Daly, ed.,
Aboard the USS Monitor, 189.

285. New York *Evening Post* and New York
Herald, 14 July 1862.

286. Joseph Hopkins Twichell to his father,
near Harrison's Landing, 9 July 1862, Peter
Messent and Steve Courtney, eds., *The Civil
War Letters of Joseph Hopkins Twichell: A
Chaplain's Story* (Athens: University of
Georgia Press, 2006), 165–166.

287. Davis, *Lincoln's Men*, 69.

288. McClellan to Lincoln, Camp near Harrison's Landing, 7 July 1862, AL MSS DLC.

289. Carl Sandburg note, source unidentified, Sandburg-Barrett Papers, Newberry
Library, Chicago.

290. Welles, "History of Emancipation," in
Albert Mordell, comp. *Selected Essays of Gideon
Welles: Civil War and Reconstruction* (New
York: Twayne, 1959), 235–236.

291. McClellan to his wife, Berkeley, 9, 10
July 1862, Sears, ed., *McClellan Papers*, 348.

292. Ibid., 370.

293. Nicolay to Therena Bates, Washington
13 July 1862, Burlingame, ed., *With Lincoln in
the White House*, 85.

294. Lincoln to McClellan, Washington, 13 July 1862, *CWL,* 5:322.

295. McClellan to his wife, Berkeley, 15 July 1862, Sears, ed., *McClellan Papers,* 358.

296. Pease and Randall, eds., *Browning Diary* 1:563 (entry for 25 July 1862).

297. Welles, *Lincoln and Seward* (New York: Sheldon, 1874), 197.

298. Washington correspondence by Sigma, 13 July, Cincinnati *Commercial,* 18 July 1862; Washington correspondence by Agate [Whitelaw Reid], 13 July, Cincinnati *Gazette,* 16 July 1862; Adams S. Hill to Sydney Howard Gay, Washington, 12 July 1862, Gay Papers, Columbia University.

299. Chandler to his wife, Washington 6, 11 July 1862, Chandler Papers, DLC.

300. Edward Everett Hale to Henry W. Bellows, Brookline, Massachusetts, 8 July 1862, Bellows Papers, MHi.

301. Benjamin Brown French, *Witness to the Young Republic: A Yankee's Journal, 1828–1870,* ed. Donald B. Cole and John J. McDonough (Hanover, NH: University Press of New England, 1989), 405.

302. *CWL,* 5:358-359.

303. Speech by Leonard Swett, 26 Apr. 1880, Chicago *Times,* 27 Apr. 1880.

304. Washington correspondence, 6 Aug., New York *Tribune,* 7 Aug. 1862; Washington correspondence by Agate [Whitelaw Reid], 7 Aug., Cincinnati *Gazette,* 11 Aug. 1862.

305. Washington correspondence, 6 Aug., Chicago *Tribune,* 7 Aug. 1862; Washington correspondence, 6 Aug., Cincinnati *Gazette,* 7 Aug. 1862.

306. Providence *Journal,* 12 August 1862; Washington correspondence by [E]rastus B[rooks], 12 July, New York *Evening Express,* 14 July 1862.

Chapter 27. "The Hour Comes for Dealing with Slavery"

1. Francis B. Carpenter, *The Inner Life of Abraham Lincoln: Six Months at the White House* (New York: Hurd and Houghton, 1867), 20–21.

2. Maria Lydig Daly, *Diary of a Union Lady, 1861–1865,* ed. Harold Earl Hammond (New York: Funk & Wagnalls, 1962), 179 (entry for 28 Sept. 1862).

3. Robert C. Winthrop, Jr., *A Memoir of Robert C. Winthrop* (Boston: Little, Brown, 1897), 229 (entry for 31 July 1863).

4. Carl Schurz, *The Reminiscences of Carl Schurz* (3 vols.; New York: McClure, 1907–1908), 2:309–310.

5. Moncure D. Conway, *Autobiography: Memories and Experiences* (2 vols.; Boston: Houghton Mifflin, 1904), 1:161.

6. Carpenter, *Inner Life of Abraham Lincoln,* 77.

7. Allan Nevins and Milton Halsey Thomas, eds., *Diary of George Templeton Strong, 1835–1875* (4 vols.; New York: Macmillan, 1952), 3:204–205 (entry for 29 Jan. 1862).

8. Cincinnati *Gazette,* 25 July 1862.

9. Cheever to Gerrit Smith, New York, 6 Mar. 1861, Smith Papers, Syracuse University.

10. Memorandum, Washington, 26 Apr. 1862, of a conversation with Sumner in December 1861, Edward Everett Hale, *Memories of One Hundred Years* (2 vols.; New York: Macmillan, 1902), 2:191; Sumner to John A. Andrew, Washington, 27 Dec. 1861, Andrew Papers, MHi.

11. Frank Abial Flower, *Edwin McMasters Stanton: The Autocrat of Rebellion, Emancipation, and Reconstruction* (Akron, OH: Saalfield, 1905), 183.

12. *CWL,* 5:146; Hale, *Memories of One Hundred Years,* 2:194–195.

13. Howe to Frank Bird, Washington, 5 Mar. 1862, in Laura E. Richards, ed., *Letters and Journals of Samuel Gridley Howe* (2 vols.; Boston: D. Estes, 1906–1909), 2:500–501.

14. Roy P. Basler et al., eds., *Collected Works of Abraham Lincoln* [hereafter *CWL*] (8 vols. plus index; New Brunswick, NJ: Rutgers University Press, 1953–1955), 5:144–145.

15. William F. Moore and Jane Ann Moore, eds., *His Brother's Blood: Speeches and Writings of Owen Lovejoy, 1838–1864* (Urbana: University of Illinois Press, 2004), 320.

16. Child to Horace Greeley, Wayland, Massachusetts, 9 Mar. 1862, *Lydia Maria Child: Selected Letters, 1817–1880,* ed. Milton Meltzer and Patricia G. Holland (Amherst: University of Massachusetts Press, 1982), 407.

17. Moncure D. Conway to his wife Ellen, [Boston], 8 Mar. [1862], Conway Papers, Columbia University.

18. Phillips's lecture at the Smithsonian Institution, Washington, 14 Mar., New York *Tribune,* 18 Mar. 1862; Washington *Evening Star,* 15 Mar. 1862.

19. Moncure D. Conway to his wife Ellen, [Boston], 8 Mar. [1862], Conway Papers, Columbia University.

20. Wendell Phillips's speech in Boston, 18 Apr., New York *Tribune,* 19 Apr. 1862; Phillips to his wife Ann, en route from Milwaukee to Madison, Wisconsin, 31 Mar. 1862, Phillips Papers, Harvard University.

21. Wendell Phillips Garrison et al., *William Lloyd Garrison, 1805–1879: The Story of His Life Told by His Children* (4 vols.; New York: Century, 1885–1889), 4:49; *American Annual Cyclopedia and Register of Important Events of the Year 1862,* 789; *The Liberator* (Boston), 14 Mar. 1862.

22. Potter, journal entries for 12, 29 Mar. 1862, Potter Papers, Wisconsin State Historical Society.

23. Maria Weston Chapman to Mary Estlin, 18 Mar. 1862, in McPherson, *Struggle for Equality,* 96.

24. New York *Tribune,* 7, 8, 11, 24 Mar. 1862.

25. Sumner to an abolitionist friend, Boston, 5 June 1862, Boston *Evening Journal,* n.d., copied in the New York *Tribune,* 16 June 1862; Emerson, "American Civilization," *The Atlantic Monthly,* Apr. 1862, 511.

26. George W. Curtis to Charles Eliot Norton, North Shore, New York, 6 Mar., 18 June 1862, Curtis Papers, Harvard University.

27. Washington correspondence, 6 Mar., Chicago *Tribune,* 10 Mar. 1862.

28. Chicago *Tribune,* 20 Mar. 1862.

29. Springfield, Massachusetts, *Republican,* 8 Mar. 1862.

30. Elihu Burritt to Lincoln, New Britain, Connecticut, 2 June 1862, AL MSS DLC.

31. Holt to David Davis, Washington, 3 May 1863, Davis Papers, IHi.

32. Cincinnati *Commercial,* 11 Mar. 1862.

33. Washington correspondence, 7 Mar., New York *World,* 8 Mar. 1862.

34. Henry W. Bellows to his wife, Washington, 6 Mar. 1862, Bellows Papers, MHi.

35. Providence *Journal,* 8 Mar. 1862.

36. S. A. Raymond to John Sherman, Toledo, 10 Mar. 1862, John Sherman Papers, DLC.

37. Isaac N. Arnold, *The History of Abraham Lincoln and the Overthrow of Slavery* (Chicago: Clarke, 1866), 275.

38. Boston *Courier,* n.d., copied in the Boston *Evening Journal,* 11 Mar. 1862.

39. New York *Herald,* 8 Mar. 1862.

40. Thomas H. Hicks to Lincoln, Cambridge, Maryland, 18 Mar. 1862, AL MSS DLC.

41. Baltimore *American,* n.d., copied in the Cincinnati *Commercial,* 21 Mar. 1862.

42. Stoddard to Martin B. Anderson, Washington, 11 Mar. 1862, Martin B. Anderson Papers, University of Rochester.

43. J. Dille to John Sherman, Newark, 3 July 1862, John Sherman Papers, DLC.

44. Charles Eliot Norton to George Perkins Marsh, Cambridge, Massachusetts, 27 Apr. 1862, Marsh Papers, University of Vermont; Norton to George William Curtis, Cambridge, 8 Mar. 1862, Sara Norton and M. A. De Wolfe Howe, eds., *Letters of Charles Eliot Norton* (2 vols.; Boston: Houghton Mifflin, 1913), 1:252–253.

45. Washington correspondence, 10 Mar., *National Anti-Slavery Standard* (New York), 15 Mar. 1862.

46. *Frank Leslie's Illustrated Newspaper,* 22 Mar. 1862.

47. Cincinnati *Commercial,* 14 Mar. 1862.

48. Schuyler Colfax to Lincoln, South Bend, Indiana, 18 Oct. 1862, AL MSS DLC.

49. David McCulloch to "Dr. Manning," Peoria, 12 Mar. 1862, Earnest E. East Papers, IHi.

50. Washington correspondence by John W. Forney, 14 Mar., Philadelphia *Press,* 15 Mar. 1862.

51. Lincoln to Raymond, Washington, 9 Mar. 1862, *CWL,* 5:153.

52. Raymond to Lincoln, Albany, 15 Mar. 1862, AL MSS DLC.

53. New York *Times,* 8 Mar. 1862.

54. Liverpool *Post,* 20 Mar., copied in the Chicago *Tribune,* 5 Apr. 1862; London *Star and Dial,* n.d., copied in the Philadelphia *Press,* 13 Apr. 1862.

55. *Congressional Globe,* 37th Congress, 2nd Session, 1154 (10 Mar. 1862).

56. W. M. Dickson to Friedrich Hassaurek, Cincinnati, 10 Apr., 9 June 1862, Hassaurek Papers, Ohio Historical Society.

57. Michael Burlingame, ed., *With Lincoln in the White House: Letters, Memoranda, and Other Writings of John G. Nicolay, 1860–1865* (Carbondale: Southern Illinois University Press, 2000), 73 (journal entry for 9 Mar. 1862).

58. Memo by Crisfield, 10 Mar. 1862, Louisville *Democrat,* 26 Oct. 1862, copied in the New York *Herald,* 31 Oct. 1862; Adams S. Hill to Sydney Howard Gay, [Washington], n.d., Gay Papers, Columbia University.

59. Lincoln to James A. McDougall, Washington, 14 Mar. 1862, *CWL,* 5:160–161.

60. Schurz, *Reminiscences,* 2:328–329.

61. Hugh Campbell to Joseph Holt, Philadelphia, 24 July 1862, Holt Papers, DLC.

62. Washington correspondence by Van [D. W. Bartlett], 11 Mar., Springfield, Massachusetts, *Republican,* 15 Mar. 1862.

63. Washington correspondence by Forney, 12 Mar., Philadelphia *Press,* 13 Mar. 1862.

64. Washington correspondence, 12 Mar., Chicago *Tribune,* 15 Mar. 1862.

65. New York *Tribune,* 24 Mar. 1862.

66. Lincoln to Greeley, Washington, 24 Mar. 1862, *CWL,* 5:169.

67. Jacob Brinkerhoff to John Sherman, Columbus, 23 Feb. 1862, John Sherman Papers, DLC.

68. Baltimore *American,* n.d., copied in the Chicago *Times,* 18 Apr. 1862.

69. Crisfield to his wife, Washington, 25 Apr. 1862, Crisfield Papers, Maryland Historical Society.

70. Theodore Calvin Pease and James G. Randall, eds., *The Diary of Orville Hickman Browning* (2 vols.; Springfield: Illinois State Historical Library, 1925–1933), 1:541 (entry for 14 Apr. 1862).

71. Washington correspondence, 10 Mar., *National Anti-Slavery Standard* (New York), 15 Mar. 1862.

72. *CWL,* 5:192.

73. Francis F. Browne, *The Every-Day Life of Abraham Lincoln* (New York: N. D. Thompson, 1887), 533.

74. Speech at Freeport, Illinois, 27 Aug. 1858, *CWL,* 3:42.

75. Martin B. Pasternak, *Rise Now and Fly to Arms: The Life of Henry Highland Garnet* (New York: Garland, 1995), 105.

76. James M. McPherson, ed., *The Negro's Civil War: How American Negroes Felt and Acted during the War for the Union* (New York: Pantheon Books, 1965), 45; *Weekly Anglo-African,* 22 Mar. 1862.

77. Beecher, *Freedom and War: Discourses on Topics Suggested by the Times* (Boston: Ticknor and Fields, 1863), 264.

78. Child to Robert Wallcut, Wayland, Massachusetts, 20 Apr. 1862, Garrison Papers, Boston Public Library; Child to Lucy Osgood, Wayland, Massachusetts, 20 Apr. 1862, *Child Letters,* ed. Meltzer and Holland, 410.

79. *National Anti-Slavery Standard* (New York), 26 Apr. 1862.

80. Washington correspondence, 7 Apr., *National Anti-Slavery Standard* (New York), 12 Apr. 1862.

81. Julian to William Lloyd Garrison, Washington, 16 Apr. 1862, Garrison Papers, Boston Public Library.

82. Charles Eliot Norton to George Perkins Marsh, Cambridge, 27 Apr. 1862, Marsh Papers, University of Vermont.

83. Moore and Moore, eds., *Lovejoy Speeches,* 345.

84. Harriet Martineau, *National Anti-Slavery Standard* (New York), 24 Mar. 1859; Samuel May, Jr., to Elizabeth Buffum Chace, Boston, 22 Apr. 1862, in Lillie Buffam Wyman and Arthur Crawford Wyman, *Elizabeth Buffam Chace, 1806–1899: Her Life and Environment* (2 vols.; Boston: W. B. Clarke, 1914), 1:236.

85. Arnold, *Lincoln,* 229; Moore and Moore, eds., *Lovejoy Speeches,* 345.

86. F. D. Parish to John Sherman, Sandusky, 18 Apr. 1862, John Sherman Papers, DLC.

87. G. O. Pond to Lyman Trumbull, Griggsville, 14 Apr. 1862, Lyman Trumbull Papers, DLC.

88. London *Times,* n.d., copied in the New York *Times,* 22 May 1862.

89. Nevins and Thomas, eds., *Strong Diary,* 3:217 (entry for 16 Apr. 1862).

90. Washington correspondence, 17 Apr., New York *Evening Express,* 18 Apr. 1862.

91. Chicago *Times,* 8 Apr. 1862.

92. Chicago *Times,* n.d., quoted in the Baltimore *Republican,* 21 May 1862.

93. George W. Smalley to Sydney Howard Gay, Strasburg [Virginia], 21 June 1862, Gay Papers, Columbia University.

94. Horatio King to James Buchanan, Washington, 27 Apr. 1862, draft, King Papers, DLC.

95. Peter Sturtevant to Lincoln, New York, 16 May 1862, AL MSS DLC.

96. Reverdy Johnson to Lincoln, New York, 16 May 1862, AL MSS DLC.

97. Henry Winter Davis to Samuel Francis Du Pont, [Baltimore], [no day indicated] July 1862, transcript, S. F. Du Pont Papers, Hagley Museum, Wilmington, Delaware.

98. Washington correspondence, 9 June, *National Anti-Slavery Standard* (New York), 14 June 1862.

99. Salmon P. Chase to Lincoln, Washington, 16 May 1862, AL MSS DLC.

100. Washington correspondence, 16, 18 May, New York *Herald,* 17, 19 May 1862; Lincoln to Chase, Washington, [17 May 1862], *CWL,* 5:219.

101. Washington correspondence, 16 May, Cincinnati *Commercial,* 17 May 1862; Washing-ton correspondence, 17 May, New York *Times,* 18 May 1862.

102. Edward Atkinson to "Dear Ned," Boston, 10 June 1862, Atkinson Papers, MHi.

103. George W. Smalley to Sydney Howard Gay, Strasburg [Virginia], 21 June 1862, Gay Papers, Columbia University.

104. Adams S. Hill to Sydney Howard Gay, [Washington, 20 May 1862], Gay Papers, Columbia University.

105. Proclamation of 19 May 1862, *CWL,* 5:222–223.

106. Israel Washburn to Hannibal Hamlin, Augusta, 23 May 1862, Israel Washburn Papers, DLC.

107. George Gorden Meade to his wife, camp opposite Fredericksburg, 23 May 1862, in George Meade, *The Life and Letters of George Gordon Meade* (2 vols.; New York: Charles Scribner's Sons, 1913), 1:267.

108. J. Dille to John Sherman, Newark, Ohio, 24 May 1862, John Sherman Papers, DLC.

109. Henry Winter Davis to Sophie Du Pont, Louviers [near Wilmington], 2 Sept. 1862, and [Baltimore], 20 May 1862, transcript, S. F. Du Pont Papers, Hagley Museum, Wilmington, Delaware.

110. Providence *Journal,* 21 May 1862; *Frank Leslie's Illustrated Newspaper,* 7 June 1862.

111. Alexander T. Stewart to Lincoln, New York, 21 May 1862, AL MSS DLC.

112. New York *Herald,* 20, 21 May 1862.

113. Medill to Chase, Chicago, 30 May 1862, Niven, ed., *Chase Papers,* 3:207.

114. Chase to Greeley, Washington, 21 May 1862, ibid. 3:203.

115. Hans L. Trefousse, *The Radical Republicans: Lincoln's Vanguard for Racial Justice* (New York: Alfred A. Knopf, 1969) 218; Adam Gurowski, *Diary* (Boston: Lee and Shepard, 1863), 210 (entry for May 1862).

116. Lydia Maria Child to Jessie Fremont, n.d., *The Liberator* (Boston), 11 Oct. 1862.

117. Garrison to Charles B. Sedgwick, Boston, 20 May 1862, Walter M. Merrill, ed., *The Letters of William Lloyd Garrison* (6 vols.;

Cambridge, MA: Harvard University Press, 1971–1981), 5:93.

118. Samuel J. May, Jr., to Richard Webb, Boston, 27 May 1862, May Papers, Boston Public Library; George B. Cheever in the New York *Herald*, 22 May 1862.

119. Victor B. Howard, *Religion and the Radical Republican Movement, 1860–1870* (Lexington: University Press of Kentucky, 1986), 28.

120. *Congressional Globe*, 37th Congress, 2nd Session, 3125 (5 July 1862).

121. Thaddeus Stevens to Dr. Joseph Gibbons, n.p., 17 Apr. 1862, photocopy, Schoff Collection, William L. Clements Library, University of Michigan.

122. Philip A. Bell in the *Pacific Appeal*, 14 June 1862, in C. Peter Ripley, ed., *The Black Abolitionist Papers* (5 vols.; Chapel Hill: University of North Carolina Press, 1985–1992), 5:143–145.

123. Andrew to Stanton, Boston, 19 May 1862, Henry Greenleaf Pearson, *The Life of John A. Andrew, Governor of Massachusetts, 1861–1865* (2 vols.; Boston: Houghton Mifflin, 1904), 2:12–13.

124. Pierce to Chase, Port Royal, SC, 13 May 1862, Niven, ed., *Chase Papers*, 3:199.

125. New York *Tribune*, 20 May 1862.

126. New York *Independent*, 22 May 1862.

127. Samuel J. May, Jr., to Richard Webb, Boston, 27 May 1862, May Papers, Boston Public Library.

128. *National Anti-Slavery Standard* (New York), 24 May 1862.

129. Washington correspondence, 26 May, *National Anti-Slavery Standard* (New York), 31 May 1862.

130. Schurz to Lincoln, Philadelphia, 19 May 1862, AL MSS DLC.

131. George W. Curtis to Charles Eliot Norton, North Shore, New York, 6 Mar. 1862, Curtis Papers, Harvard University.

132. Washington correspondence, 14 Apr., New York *Tribune*, 15 Apr. 1862.

133. Washington correspondence by Van [D. W. Bartlett], 29 Apr., Springfield, Massachusetts, *Republican*, 1 May 1862.

134. Pease and Randall, eds., *Browning Diary*, 1:555 (entry for 1 July 1862).

135. *The War of the Rebellion: A Compilation of the Official Records of the Union and Confederate Armies* (128 vols.; Washington: Government Printing Office, 1880–1901) [hereafter *OR*], III, 2:200; New York *Herald*, 11 July 1862.

136. Washington correspondence by Van [D. W. Bartlett], 24 June, Springfield, Massachusetts, *Republican*, 27 June 1862.

137. Ethan Allen, "Lincoln and the Slave Trader Gordon," in William Hayes Ward, ed., *Abraham Lincoln, Tributes of His Associates: Reminiscences of Soldiers, Statesmen, and Citizens* (New York: Thomas Y. Crowell, 1895), 168.

138. Hamilton R. Gamble to Lincoln, St. Louis, 2 May 1863, AL MSS DLC.

139. Lincoln told this to Dr. Stone, who told it to Gordon's father, who in turn told it to the author of a letter dated Wednesday (probably written in January or February 1862 but misfiled August 1851) signed "H." and addressed to "Dear Sir" (probably John W. Garrett), Garrett Family Papers, DLC.

140. Denver *Tribune*, 18 May 1879.

141. New York *World*, 6 Feb. 1862.

142. Sumner to Orestes Brownson, Washington, 2 Feb. 1862, Beverly Wilson Palmer, ed., *The Selected Letters of Charles Sumner* (2 vols.; Boston: Northeastern University Press, 1990), 2:100.

143. New York *World*, 29 January 1862.

144. Sarah Forbes Hughes, ed., *Letters and Recollections of John Murray Forbes* (2 vols.; Boston: Houghton Mifflin, 1899), 1:285.

145. Robert Murray, "The Slaver Erie, or the Career of Gordon, the Slaver Captain," typescript of an 1866 unpublished MS, in the possession of Ron Soodalter, 43, 46 (courtesy of Ron Soodalter); New York *Tribune*, 6 Feb. 1862; New York *World*, 29 Jan. 1862.

146. Howard K. Beale, ed., *The Diary of Edward Bates, 1859–1866* (Annual Report of the American Historical Association for the Year 1930, vol. IV; Washington, DC: U.S. Government Printing Office, 1933), 233 (entry for 18 Feb. 1862).

147. *CWL*, 5:128.

148. Nevins and Thomas, eds., *Strong Diary*, 3:209 (entry for 22 Feb. 1862).

149. *Frank Leslie's Illustrated Newspaper*, 15 Mar. 1862.

150. Undated letter by "Pynchon," a resident of Hampden County, Massachusetts, to the editor, Springfield, Massachusetts, *Republican*, 8 July 1862.

151. London *Daily News*, 8 Mar. 1862, in Ron Soodalter, *Hanging Captain Gordon: The Life and Trial of an American Slave Trader* (New York: Atria, 2006), 226–227.

152. Erastus Wright to E. B. Washburne, Springfield, 11 Apr. 1864, Washburne Papers, DLC.

153. John B. Alley in Allen Thorndike Rice, ed., *Reminiscences of Abraham Lincoln by Distinguished Men of His Time* (New York: North American Review, 1888), 583.

154. J. P. Thompson, "A Talk with President Lincoln," *The Congregationalist and Boston Recorder*, 30 Mar. 1866, 50.

155. Sumner to an unidentified personal friend, Washington, 5 June 1862, *The Liberator* (Boston), 20 June 1862.

156. Moncure D. Conway to his wife Ellen, n.p., 17 Mar. [1862], Conway Papers, Columbia University.

157. Ida M. Tarbell, *The Life of Abraham Lincoln* (4 vols.; New York: Lincoln History Society, 1902), 3:73.

158. Child to Sumner, Wayland, Massachusetts, 22 June 1862, *Child Letters*, ed. Meltzer and Holland, 412.

159. *Principia*, 10 April 1862, in M. Leon Perkal, "William Goodell: A Life of Reform" (Ph.D. dissertation, City University of New York, 1972), 304.

160. *Christian Recorder*, 12 Sept. 1863.

161. Stearns to Sumner, Boston, 10 Feb. 1862, Sumner Papers, Harvard University.

162. *CWL*, 5:317–319.

163. Frederick Pike to J. S. Pike, Washington, 13 July 1862, Pike Papers, University of Maine.

164. Adams S. Hill to Sydney Howard Gay, Washington, 14 July 1862, Gay Papers,

Columbia University; Washington correspondence, 15 July, New York *Evening Post*, 16 July 1862; Washington correspondence by Van [D. W. Bartlett], 15 July, Springfield, Massachusetts, *Republican*, 19 July 1862.

165. Pease and Randall, eds., *Browning Diary*, 1:559–560 (entry for 15 July 1862).

166. Isaac N. Arnold, *The Life of Abraham Lincoln* (Chicago: Jansen, McClurg, 1885), 251.

167. Frank E. Foster to John Sherman, Columbus, 10 May 1862, John Sherman Papers, DLC.

168. Henry Winter Davis to Samuel Francis Du Pont, [Baltimore], [no day indicated] July 1862, transcript, S. F. Du Pont Papers, Hagley Museum, Wilmington, Delaware.

169. Trumbull to his wife, Washington, 12 July 1862, Trumbull Family Papers, IHi.

170. Henry Winter Davis to Samuel Francis Du Pont, [Baltimore], [no day indicated] July 1862, transcript, S. F. Du Pont Papers, Hagley Museum, Wilmington, Delaware.

171. Pease and Randall, eds., *Browning Diary*, 1:558 (entry for 14 July 1862).

172. Lincoln to Solomon Foot, Washington, 15 July 1862, *CWL*, 5:326.

173. Ibid., 5:328–331.

174. Washington correspondence by Agate [Whitelaw Reid], 16 July, Cincinnati *Gazette*, 19 July 1862.

175. Trumbull to his wife, Washington, 16 July 1862, Trumbull Family Papers, IHi.

176. Fessenden to Hamilton Fish, Washington, 15 July 1862, Fish Papers, DLC.

177. George W. Julian in Rice, ed., *Reminiscences of Lincoln*, 58.

178. Smith to George Thompson, 25 Jan. 1862, printed letter, in Ralph Volney Harlow, *Gerrit Smith, Philanthropist and Reformer* (New York: H. Holt, 1939), 431–432.

179. W. M. Dickson to Friedrich Hassaurek, Cincinnati, 9 June 1862, Hassaurek Papers, Ohio Historical Society.

180. Duke Frederick, "The Second Confiscation Act: A Chapter in Civil War Politics" (Ph.D. dissertation, University of Chicago, 1966), 211–214.

181. Julian in Rice, ed., *Reminiscences of Lincoln*, 238.

182. Adams S. Hill to Sydney Howard Gay, Washington, 17 July 1862, Gay Papers, Columbia University.

183. *Congressional Globe,* 37th Congress, 2nd Session, 3382 (16 July 1862).

184. Washington correspondence, 17 July, New York *Herald,* 18 July 1862.

185. Adams S. Hill to Sydney Howard Gay, Washington, 17 July 1862, Gay Papers, Columbia University; Washington correspondence by Hill, 17 July, New York *Tribune,* 18 July 1862.

186. George W. Julian, *Political Recollections, 1840 to 1872* (Chicago: Jansen, McClurg, 1884), 220.

187. Adams S. Hill to Sydney Howard Gay, Washington, 18 July 1862, Gay Papers, Columbia University.

188. Washington correspondence, 18 July, New York *Evening Post,* 19 July 1862.

189. New York *Evening Post,* 19 July 1862.

190. *CWL,* 5:341.

191. John Sherman, *John Sherman's Recollections of Forty Years in the House, Senate and Cabinet: An Autobiography* (2 vols.; Chicago: Werner, 1895), 1:316.

192. Beale, ed., *Welles Diary,* 1:70–71.

193. Adams's speech, 14 Apr. 1842, John T. Morse, *John Quincy Adams* (Boston: Houghton Mifflin, 1887), 264–265.

194. William Whiting, *The War Powers of the President, and the Legislative Powers of Congress in Relation to Rebellion, Treason and Slavery* (Boston: Shorey, 1862), 58.

195. Hay to Mary Jay, Washington, 20 July 1862, in Michael Burlingame, ed., *At Lincoln's Side: John Hay's Civil War Correspondence and Selected Writings* (Carbondale: Southern Illinois University Press, 2000), 23.

196. Niven, ed., *Chase Papers,* 1:348 (diary entry for 21 July 1862); *CWL,* 5:336–337.

197. Carpenter, *Inner Life of Abraham Lincoln,* 21.

198. Niven, ed., *Chase Papers,* 1:351 (diary entry for 22 July 1862).

199. Stanton memo, 22 Sept. 1862, Stanton Papers, DLC.

200. Benjamin Moran diary, 15 Sept. 1873, DLC.

201. John Palmer Usher, *President Lincoln's Cabinet* (Omaha: n.p., 1925), 17.

202. Stanton memo, 22 Sept. 1862, Stanton Papers, DLC.

203. Washington correspondence by Van [D. W. Bartlett], 23 Sept., Springfield, Massachusetts, *Republican,* 27 Sept. 1862.

204. Carpenter, *Inner Life of Abraham Lincoln,* 21–22.

205. Norton to George William Curtis, Cambridge, 31 July 1862, Norton and Howe, eds., *Letters of Charles Eliot Norton,* 1:255.

Chapter 28. "Would You Prosecute the War with Elder-Stalk Squirts, Charged with Rose Water?"

1. James B. Newcomer to Henry S. Lane, Reading, Pennsylvania, 11 July [1862], typed copy, Lane Papers, InU.

2. Washington correspondence by Sigma, 4 July, Cincinnati *Gazette,* 7 July 1862.

3. David Davis to W. W. Orme, Lincoln, Illinois, 15 Oct. 1862, Orme Papers, IHi.

4. Frederick Pike to J. S. Pike, Calais, 3 Aug. 1862, Pike Papers, University of Maine.

5. Henry W. Bellows to Cyrus Augustus Bartol, Walpole, N. H., 18 Aug. 1862, Bellows Papers, MHi.

6. Mahlon D. Ogden to James R. Doolittle, Chicago, 6 Aug. 1862, typescript, Doolittle Papers, State Historical Society of Wisconsin.

7. Allan Nevins and Milton Halsey Thomas, eds., *Diary of George Templeton Strong, 1835–1875* (4 vols.; New York: Macmillan, 1952), 3:244 (entry for 26 July 1862).

8. Sherman Blocker to John Sherman, Wadsworth, Ohio, 23 Apr. 1862; Dr. J. H. Jordan to John Sherman, Cincinnati, 1 Jan. 1862, John Sherman Papers, DLC.

9. Yates to Lincoln, Springfield, 11 July 1862, AL MSS DLC.

10. Edward Lillie Pierce to N. P. Banks, Boston, 15 Sept. 1862, Banks Papers, DLC.

11. George W. Bell to John Sherman, Lawrence, Kansas, 23 July 1862, John Sherman Papers, DLC.

12. William P. Fessenden to J. S. Pike, Portland, 2 Aug. 1862, Pike Papers, University of Maine.

13. Washington correspondence by Van [D. W. Bartlett], 22 July, Springfield, Massachusetts, *Republican*, 24 July 1862; Washington correspondence, 21 July, Cincinnati *Gazette*, 22 July 1862; Washington correspondence, 22 July, New York *Evening Post*, 23 July 1862.

14. Lincoln to Cuthbert Bullitt, Washington, 28 July 1862, Roy P. Basler et al., eds., *Collected Works of Abraham Lincoln* [hereafter *CWL*] (8 vols. plus index; New Brunswick, NJ: Rutgers University Press, 1953–1955), 5:346.

15. Washington correspondence, n.d., New York *Tribune*, 5 Aug., copied in the New York *Times*, 6 Aug. 1862.

16. T. J. Barnett to S. L. M. Barlow, Friday [25 Sept. 1862], Barlow Papers, CSmH.

17. Washington *Chronicle*, 12 Nov. 1862, in Michael Burlingame, ed., *With Lincoln in the White House: Letters, Memoranda, and Other Writings of John G. Nicolay, 1860–1865* (Carbondale: Southern Illinois University Press, 2000), 91.

18. Henry W. Halleck to Horatio Wright, Washington, 25 Aug., 18 Nov. 1862, *OR*, I, 16:421; I, 20, 2: 67–68.

19. Washington correspondence, 4 Aug., New York *Herald*, 5 Aug. 1862.

20. Frederick Law Olmsted to Lincoln, Chesapeake Bay, 6 July 1862, AL MSS DLC.

21. New York correspondence, n.d., London *Times*, n.d., copied in the Chicago *Tribune*, 3 July 1862.

22. Orville H. Browning to Lincoln, Quincy, Illinois, 11 Aug. 1862, AL MSS DLC.

23. New York *Commercial Advertiser*, n.d., copied in the Providence *Journal*, 17 July 1862.

24. Nevins and Thomas, eds., *Strong Diary*, 3:244–245, 246, 253 (entries for 4, 16 Aug., 4 Sept. 1862).

25. John C. Henshaw to David Davis, Washington, 28 July 1862, David Davis Papers, IHi.

26. J. B. Bond to James Watson Webb, New York, 6 Aug. 1862, Webb Papers, Sterling Library, Yale University; Henry W. Bellows to Edward Everett Hale, New York, 5 July 1862, Bellows Papers, MHi.

27. John Appleton to W. P. Fessenden, Bangor, Maine, 22 Aug., 14 Dec. 1862, Fessenden Papers, Western Reserve Historical Society, Cleveland.

28. [A. Finch?] to Zachariah Chandler, Milwaukee, 10 Sept. 1862, Chandler Papers, DLC.

29. Israel Washburn to W. P. Fessenden, Augusta, Maine, 12 Sept. 1862, Fessenden Papers, Western Reserve Historical Society, Cleveland.

30. Israel D. Andrews to David Davis, Washington, 16 July [1862], David Davis Papers, IHi.

31. Diary of William T. Coggeshall, 26 Nov. 1863, in Freda Postle Koch, *Colonel Coggeshall: The Man Who Saved Lincoln* (Columbus, OH: Poko Press, 1985), 61.

32. Theodore Calvin Pease and James G. Randall, eds., *The Diary of Orville Hickman Browning* (2 vols.; Springfield: Illinois State Historical Library, 1925–1933), 1:589 (entry for 29 Nov. 1862).

33. Peter Cozzens and Robert I. Girardi, eds., *The Military Memoirs of General John Pope* (Chapel Hill: University of North Carolina Press, 1998), 124.

34. Halleck to McClellan, St. Louis, 17 Feb. 1862, *OR*, I, 7:628.

35. Washington correspondence, probably by Moncure Conway, 24 Jan., Boston *Commonwealth*, 31 Jan. 1863.

36. Halleck to Lincoln, Corinth, 2 July 1862, *OR*, I, 16, 2:89.

37. Halleck to Lincoln, Corinth, Mississippi, 10 July 1862, AL MSS DLC.

38. Asa Mahan, *A Critical History of the Late American War* (New York: A. S. Barnes, 1877), 144–145.

39. Lincoln to Halleck, Washington, 14 July 1862, *CWL*, 5:323.

40. Halleck to McClellan, Washington, 30 July 1862, *OR*, I, 11, 3:343.

41. McClellan to S.L.M. Barlow, Berkeley, 23 July 1862; McClellan to his wife Mary Ellen, 20 July 1862, Stephen W. Sears, ed., *The Civil War Papers of George B. McClellan: Selected Correspondence, 1860–1865* (New York: Ticknor and Fields, 1989), 369, 368.

42. *McClellan's Own Story: The War for the Union* (New York: C. L. Webster, 1887), 137.

43. Trumbull to his wife, Washington, 12 July 1862, Trumbull Family Papers, IHi.

44. Washington correspondence, 27 July, *Missouri Republican* (St. Louis), n.d., clipping in scrapbook, Hay Papers, DLC, in Michael Burlingame, ed., *Lincoln's Journalist: John Hay's Anonymous Writings for the Press, 1860–1864* (Carbondale: Southern Illinois University Press, 1998), 288; Jonathan Birch in Jesse W. Weik, *The Real Lincoln: A Portrait*, ed. Michael Burlingame (1922; Lincoln: University of Nebraska Press, 2002), 134.

45. Dennis Hanks, interview with William H. Herndon, Paris, Illinois, 26 Mar. 1888, in Douglas L. Wilson and Rodney O. Davis, eds., *Herndon's Informants: Letters, Interviews, and Statements about Abraham Lincoln* (Urbana: University of Illinois Press, 1998), 654.

46. William Thompson Lusk to his mother, Headquarters of Stevens' Division, 28 July 1862, in William Thompson Lusk, *War Letters of William Thompson Lusk, Captain, Assistant Adjutant-General, United States Volunteers 1861–1863* (New York: Privately printed, 1911), 170.

47. *Harper's Weekly*, 9 Aug. 1862.

48. Burlingame, ed., *Lincoln's Journalist*, 288.

49. Grant to E. B. Washburne, 22 July 1862, John Y. Simon, ed., *The Papers of Ulysses S. Grant* (31 vols. to date; Carbondale: Southern Illinois University Press, 1967–), 5:226; Bates to Hamilton Gamble, 24 July 1862, in John F. Marszelek, *Commander of All Lincoln's Armies: A Life of Henry W. Halleck* (Cambridge, MA: Harvard University Press, 2004), 135.

50. Marszelek, *Halleck*, 135.

51. Washington correspondence, 29 Oct., Sacramento *Daily Union*, 26 Nov. 1863, in Michael Burlingame, ed., *Lincoln Observed: Civil War Dispatches of Noah Brooks* (Baltimore, MD: Johns Hopkins University Press, 1998), 75.

52. Howard K. Beale and Alan W. Brownsword, eds., *Diary of Gideon Welles, Secretary of the Navy under Lincoln and Johnson* (3 vols.; New York: W. W. Norton, 1960), 1:107, 320, 444 (entries for 3 Sept. 1862, 2 June and 26 Sept. 1863).

53. Chase to his daughter Kate, Washington, 13 July 1862, John Niven, ed., *The Salmon P. Chase Papers* (5 vols.; Kent, OH: Kent State University Press, 1993–1998), 3:227.

54. Pease and Randall, eds., *Browning Diary*, 1:563 (entry for 25 July 1862).

55. Halleck to Elizabeth Hamilton Halleck, Washington, 9 Aug. 1862, Schoff Civil War Collection, William L. Clements Library, University of Michigan.

56. Washington correspondence, n.d., Springfield, Massachusetts, *Republican*, n.d., copied in the Providence *Journal*, 11 Aug. 1862.

57. Halleck to Elizabeth Hamilton Halleck, Washington, 9 Aug. 1862, Schoff Civil War Collection, William L. Clements Library, University of Michigan.

58. Nevins and Thomas, eds., *Strong Diary*, 3:246 (entry for 16 Aug. 1862).

59. Swett to his wife, Washington, [31?] July 1862, David Davis Papers, IHi.

60. Memorandum of Interviews between Lincoln and Officers of the Army of the Potomac, 8–9 July 1862, *CWL*, 5:309–311.

61. Madeleine Vinton Dahlgren, *Memoir of John A. Dahlgren, Rear-Admiral United States Navy* (Boston: J. R. Osgood, 1882), 379.

62. Niven, ed., *Chase Papers*, 1:366 (diary entry for 19 Aug. 1862).

63. Halleck to Elizabeth Hamilton Halleck, Washington, 9 Aug. 1862, Schoff Civil War Collection, William L. Clements Library, University of Michigan.

64. Address of 14 July 1862, *OR*, I, 12, 3:474.

65. Haupt to his wife, Washington, 17 and 18 July 1862, typed copies, Lewis Haupt Papers, DLC.

66. James M. McPherson, *Battle Cry of Freedom: The Civil War Era* (New York: Oxford University Press, 1988), 501.

67. Washington correspondence, 12 Aug., New York *Tribune*, 13 Aug. 1862.

68. Henry Winter Davis to Samuel Francis Du Pont, [Baltimore], 20 Nov. 1862, transcript, S. F. Du Pont Papers, Hagley Museum, Wilmington, Delaware.

69. Edwin B. [Munger?] to [Israel] Washburn, [Anna?], 11 Sept. 1862, Israel Washburn Papers, DLC.

70. John G. Nicolay and John Hay, *Abraham Lincoln: A History* (10 vols.; New York: Century, 1890), 6:15n.

71. Hugh Ewing to his father, Thomas Ewing, Camp at Upton's Hill, Virginia, 5 Sept. 1862, Ewing Family Papers, DLC.

72. McClellan to his wife, Alexandria, 29 Aug. 1862, Sears, ed., *McClellan Papers*, 419.

73. McClellan to Lincoln, near Alexandria, 20 Aug. 1862, ibid., 416.

74. McClellan to his wife, Alexandria, 29 Aug. 1862, ibid., 417.

75. *CWL*, 5:399.

76. Michael Burlingame and John R. Turner Ettlinger, eds., *Inside Lincoln's White House: The Complete Civil War Diary of John Hay* (Carbondale: Southern Illinois University Press, 1997), 37 (entry for 1 Sept. 1862).

77. Adams S. Hill to Sydney Howard Gay, n.p., n.d., Gay Papers, Columbia University.

78. Halleck to McClellan, Washington, 31 Aug. 1862, *Army of the Potomac: Report of Maj.-Gen. George B. McClellan, Aug. 4, 1863* (New York: Sheldon, 1864), 346.

79. McClellan to Halleck, near Alexandria, 31 Aug. 1862, Sears, ed., *McClellan Papers*, 426.

80. Burlingame and Ettlinger, eds., *Hay Diary*, 37-38 (entry for 1 Sept. 1862).

81. Beale, ed., *Welles Diary*, 1:113, 116 (entries for 7, 8 Sept. 1862).

82. Pease and Randall, eds., *Browning Diary*, 1:589 (entry for 29 Nov. 1862).

83. Washington correspondence by Horace White, 23 Jan., Chicago *Tribune*, 28 Jan. 1863.

84. [Porter] to Manton Marble, n.p, 10 Aug. 1862, Manton Marble Papers, DLC.

85. McClellan to his wife, Berkeley, 10 Aug. 1862, Sears, ed., *McClellan Papers*, 389.

86. Washington correspondence, 26 Jan., *National Anti-Slavery Standard* (New York), 31 Jan. 1863.

87. Washington correspondence by Van [D. W. Bartlett], 28 Jan., Springfield, Massachusetts, *Republican*, 30 Jan. 1863.

88. Washington correspondence, 4 Sept., Chicago *Tribune*, 9 Sept. 1862; Adams S. Hill to Sydney Howard Gay, Washington, 4 Sept. 1862, Gay Papers, Columbia University; Washington correspondence, 8 Sept., *National Anti-Slavery Standard* (New York), 13 Sept. 1862.

89. Adams S. Hill to Sydney Howard Gay, Washington, 8, 12 Sept. 1862, Gay Papers, Columbia University.

90. Burlingame and Ettlinger, eds., *Hay Diary*, 40 (entry for [mid-Sept. 1862?]).

91. Sears, *McClellan*, 254-255.

92. A photographic reproduction of that document appears in Frank Abial Flower, *Edwin McMasters Stanton: The Autocrat of Rebellion, Emancipation, and Reconstruction* (New York: W. W. Wilson, 1905), between pages 190 and 191.

93. Pope to Halleck, Centreville, 1 Sept. 1862, *OR*, I, 12 3:83.

94. Nevins and Thomas, eds., *Strong Diary*, 3:259 (entry for 24 Sept. 1862).

95. Bates memo, added to a copy of the memo about McClellan to Lincoln from Edwin M. Stanton, Salmon P. Chase, Caleb B. Smith, and Edward Bates, [2 Sept. 1862], AL MSS DLC.

96. Niven, ed., *Chase Papers*, 1:368–369 (diary entry for 2 Sept. 1862); Beale, ed., *Welles Diary*, 1:105 (entry for 2 Sept. 1862).

97. Ibid.

98. Bates memo, added to a copy of the memo about McClellan to Lincoln from

Edwin M. Stanton, Salmon P. Chase, Caleb B. Smith, and Edward Bates, [2 Sept. 1862], AL MSS DLC.

99. Burlingame and Ettlinger, eds., *Hay Diary*, 38, 39 (entry for 5 Sept. 1862).

100. Jacob D. Cox, *Military Reminiscences of the Civil War* (2 vols.; New York: C. Scribner's Sons, 1900), 1:209.

101. Washington correspondence, 8 Sept., *National Anti-Slavery Standard* (New York), 13 Sept. 1862.

102. James G. Smart, ed., *A Radical View: The "Agate" Dispatches of Whitelaw Reid, 1861–1865* (2 vols.; Memphis, TN: Memphis State University Press, 1976), 1:227 (Washington correspondence, 10 Sept. 1862, Cincinnati *Gazette*).

103. Zachariah Chandler to Lyman Trumbull, Detroit, 10 Sept. 1862, Trumbull Papers, DLC.

104. Lincoln to Key, Washington, 26 Sept. 1862, *CWL*, 5:442.

105. Burlingame and Ettlinger, eds., *Hay Diary*, 41 (entry for 26 Sept. 1862).

106. Washington correspondence by John Hay, 1 Oct., *Missouri Republican* (St. Louis), 6 Oct. 1862, in Michael Burlingame, ed., *Lincoln's Journalist: John Hay's Anonymous Writings for the Press, 1860–1864* (Carbondale: Southern Illinois University Press, 1998), 317; Burlingame and Ettlinger, eds., *Hay Diary*, 232 (entry for 25 Sept. 1864).

107. Gideon Welles, *Lincoln and Seward* (New York: Sheldon, 1874), 197.

108. William D. Kelley, *Lincoln and Stanton: A Study of the War Administration of 1861 and 1862* (New York: G. P. Putnam's Sons, 1885), 74–75.

109. Burlingame and Ettlinger, eds., *Hay Diary*, 41 (entry for 26 Sept. 1862).

110. On September 8 Chase told this to Adams Hill. Hill to Sydney Howard Gay, Washington, 8 Sept. 1862, Gay Papers, Columbia University.

111. Garrison to Oliver Johnson, Boston, 9 Sept. 1862, Walter M. Merrill, ed., *Letters of William Lloyd Garrison* (6 vols.; Cambridge, MA: Belknap Press of Harvard University Press, 1971–1981), 5:112.

112. Gurley to Thaddeus Stevens, Cincinnati, 22 Aug. 1862, Beverly Wilson Palmer, ed., *The Selected Papers of Thaddeus Stevens* (2 vols.; Pittsburgh: University of Pittsburgh Press, 1997–1998), 1:319.

113. Washington correspondence by Agate [Whitelaw Reid], 8 Sept., Cincinnati *Gazette*, 11 Sept. 1862.

114. Niven, ed., *Chase Papers*, 1:370 (diary entry for 3 Sept. 1862); Beale, ed., *Welles Diary*, 109–110, 116 (entries for 4, 8 Sept. 1862).

115. John Pope to Valentine B. Horton, St. Paul, 1 Nov. 1862, Pope Papers, New-York Historical Society.

116. Pope to Valentine B. Horton, Milwaukee, 9, 25 Mar. 1863, ibid.

117. Adams S. Hill to Sydney Howard Gay, Washington, 8, 12 Sept. 1862, Gay Papers, Columbia University; Zachariah Chandler to Lyman Trumbull, Detroit, 10 Sept. 1862, Trumbull Papers, DLC.

118. Adams S. Hill to Sydney Howard Gay Papers, n.p., n.d. [Washington, early September 1862], Gay Papers, Columbia University.

119. Adams S. Hill to Sydney Howard Gay, Washington, 8, 12 Sept. 1862, ibid.

120. Henry W. Bellows to his wife, Washington, 3, 16 Sept. 1862, Bellows Papers, MHi.

121. *The Independent* (New York), 11 Sept. 1862, in Paxton Hibben, *Henry Ward Beecher: An American Portrait* (New York: G. H. Doran, 1927), 159.

122. New York *Evening Post*, 15 Sept. 1862.

123. John S. Davis to Henry Lane, New Albany, Indiana, 26 Oct. 1862, typescript, Lane Papers, InU.

124. Frederick Law Olmsted to Henry Whitney Bellows, Washington, 22 Sept. 1862, Jane Turner Censer, ed., *The Papers of Frederick Law Olmsted, Vol. 4: Defending the Union, The Civil War and the U. S. Sanitary Commission, 1861–1863* (Baltimore, MD: Johns Hopkins University Press, 1986), 426.

125. Washington correspondence, 4 Aug., New York *Evening Post*, 5 Aug. 1862; Washington correspondence, Boston *Transcript*, n.d., copied in the Portland *Oregonian*, 25 Sept. 1862.

126. Burlingame and Ettlinger, eds., *Hay Diary*, 191–192, 183 (entries for 28 Apr., 24 Mar. 1864).

127. Halleck to Elizabeth Hamilton Halleck, Washington, 5, 9 Sept. 1862, Schoff Civil War Collection, William L. Clements Library, University of Michigan.

128. Noah Brooks, *Washington in Lincoln's Time* (New York: Century, 1895), 37.

129. Charles A. Dana, *Recollections of the Civil War: With the Leaders at Washington and in the Field in the Sixties* (New York: D. Appleton, 1898), 187.

130. Nevins and Thomas, eds., *Strong Diary*, 3:258 (entry for 24 Sept. 1862).

131. Halleck to W. T. Sherman, Washington, 16 Feb. 1864, *OR*, I, 32, 2:408.

132. Cox, *Reminiscences*, 1:151.

133. Adams S. Hill to Sydney Howard Gay, n.p., n.d. [Washington, ca. late Aug. 1862], Gay Papers, Columbia University; Gustavus V. Fox to his wife Virginia, Washington, 29 Aug. 1862, Fox Papers, New-York Historical Society.

134. Wool to Harriette Hart, Baltimore, 24 Sept. 1862, Wool Papers, New York State Library, Albany.

135. Sears, *McClellan*, 265.

136. Sears, ed., *McClellan Papers*, 435.

137. Burlingame and Ettlinger, eds., *Hay Diary*, 38–39 (entry for 5 Sept. 1862).

138. Beale, ed., *Welles Diary*, 1:117 (entry for 8 Sept. 1862).

139. McClellan to his wife, Washington, 7 Sept. 1862, Sears, ed., *McClellan Papers*, 438.

140. Ward Hill Lamon, *Recollections of Abraham Lincoln, 1847–1865*, ed. Dorothy Lamon Teillard (Washington, DC: the editor, 1911), 289.

141. Washington correspondence by Agate [Whitelaw Reid], 6 Aug., Cincinnati *Gazette*, 11 Aug. 1862.

142. Beale, ed., *Welles Diary*, 1:116 (entry for 8 Sept. 1862).

143. Ibid., 1:118, 129 (entries for 8, 12 Sept. 1862).

144. Ibid., 1:124 (entry for 12 Sept. 1862).

145. Lincoln to McClellan, Washington, 11 Sept. 1862, *CWL*, 5:415.

146. Lincoln to McClellan, Washington, 12 Sept. 1862, *CWL*, 5:418.

147. Lincoln to Curtin, Washington, 12 Sept. 1862, *CWL*, 5:417.

148. Lincoln to Alexander Henry, Washington, 12 Sept. 1862, *CWL*, 5:418.

149. Sears, ed., *McClellan Papers*, 462.

150. Lincoln to McClellan, Washington, 15 Sept. 1862, *CWL*, 5:426.

151. Lincoln to J. K. Dubois, Washington, 15 Sept. 1862, *CWL*, 5:425–426.

152. Pease and Randall, eds., *Browning Diary*, 1:590 (entry for 29 Nov. 1862).

153. Sears, *McClellan*, 270.

154. Washington correspondence, 22 Sept. 1862, Smart, ed., *"Agate" Dispatches*, 1:232.

155. Edward Everett diary, entry for 25 Sept. 1862, MHi.

156. W. W. Orme to David Davis, Springfield, Missouri, 19 Oct. 1862, David Davis Papers, IHi.

157. Gustavus V. Fox to his wife Virginia, Washington, 23 Sept. [1862], Fox Papers, New-York Historical Society.

158. Adams S. Hill to Sydney Howard Gay, Washington, 25 Aug. 1862, Gay Papers, Columbia University.

159. Usher to Lincoln, Washington, 2 Aug. 1862, AL MSS DLC.

160. W. D. Gallagher to Salmon P. Chase, St. Louis, 12 Feb. 1862, Chase Papers, Historical Society of Pennsylvania.

161. Professor F. W. Newman to the editor of the *English Leader*, 1 Sept. 1864, copied in the *National Anti-Slavery Standard* (New York), 8 Oct. 1864.

162. James Mitchell to Lincoln, Washington, 1 July 1862, AL MSS DLC.

163. *Congressional Globe*, 37th Congress, 2nd Session, 1632 (11 Apr. 1862).

164. Ibid., appendix, 99 (11 Apr. 1862).

165. "Report of the Select Committee on Emancipation and Colonization," House Reports no. 148, 37th Congress, 2nd Session,

issued 16 July 1862 (Washington, DC: U.S. Government Printing Office, 1862), 14–16.

166. *CWL*, 5:370–375; W. W. McLain to R. R. Gurley of Haddenfield, NJ, Washington, DC, 26 Aug. 1862, American Colonization Society Papers, Manuscript Division, DLC (microfilm copy).

167. Washington correspondence, 18 Jan., New York *Times*, 19 Jan. 1862; Joseph Enoch Williams et al. to the Honorable the Senate and House of Representatives, [Apr. 1862], 37A-G21.4, Select Committee on Emancipation, Petitions & Memorials, ser. 467, 37th Congress, RG 233 [D-83], in Leon F. Litwack, *North of Slavery: The Negro in the Free States, 1790–1860* (Chicago: University of Chicago Press, 1961), 262.

168. Alton, Illinois, *Telegraph*, 15 Jan. 1855.

169. Washington correspondence, by B. F. M., 15 Aug., Cincinnati *Gazette*, 20 Aug. 1862.

170. Henry Highland Garnet to Thomas Hamilton, 11 Oct. 1862, in the *Pacific Appeal*, Oct.-Nov. 1862.

171. Purvis to Samuel C. Pomeroy, Philadelphia, 28 Aug. 1862, New York *Tribune*, 30 Sept. 1862.

172. *Christian Recorder*, 23 Aug. 1862.

173. J. C. Davis and several others to Lincoln, Aug. 1862, in *An Appeal from the Colored Men of Philadelphia to the President of the United States*, in Herbert Aptheker, ed., *A Documentary History of the Negro People in the United States* (New York: Citadel Press, 1969), 473–474.

174. C. Peter Ripley, ed., *The Black Abolitionist Papers* (5 vols.; Chapel Hill: University of North Carolina Press, 1985–1992), 5:152.

175. *Douglass's Monthly*, Sept. 1862, 707–708.

176. Douglass to Gerrit Smith, Rochester, 8 Sept. 1862, Smith Papers, Syracuse University; *Douglass's Monthly*, Jan. 1862, 577.

177. Niven, ed., *Chase Papers*, 1:362 (diary entry for 15 Aug. 1862).

178. *The Liberator* (Boston), 22 Aug. 1862.

179. Beriah Green to Gerrit Smith, Whitesboro, NY, 12 Sept. 1862, Smith Papers, Syracuse University.

180. Chicago *Tribune*, 26 Sept. 1862.

181. New York *Times*, 1 Oct. 1862.

182. New York *Evening Express*, 23 Sept. 1862.

183. British and Foreign Anti-Slavery Society, *The Anti-Slavery Reporter and Aborigines' Friend*, 222.

184. Blair to Lincoln, Silver Spring, Maryland, 16 Nov. 1861, AL MSS DLC.

185. Chase to Lincoln, Washington, 12 Nov. 1861, AL MSS DLC.

186. Thompson to Francis P. Blair, Sr., Washington, 15 Nov. 1861, Blair-Lee Papers, Princeton University.

187. Lincoln to Chase, Washington, 27 Nov. 1861, Roy P. Basler, ed., *Collected Works of Abraham Lincoln, First Supplement* (Westport, CT: Greenwood Press, 1974), 112.

188. Usher to Richard W. Thompson, Washington, 26 Dec. 1861, Richard W. Thompson Papers, LMF.

189. Beale, ed., *Welles Diary*, 1:150–151 (entry for 26 Sept. 1862).

190. Thaddeus Stevens to [Salmon] P. Chase, Lancaster, 25 Aug. 1862, in Palmer, ed., *Stevens Papers*, 1:319–320.

191. Adams S. Hill to Sydney Howard Gay, Washington, 25 Aug. 1862, Gay Papers, Columbia University.

192. New York *Tribune*, 30 Jan. 1873.

193. *Pomeroy Investigation; Reports of the Joint Committee Appointed by the Legislature of Kansas, 1873, to Investigate Charges of Corruption and Bribery Against Hon. S. C. Pomeroy, and Members of the Legislature* (Topeka, KS, 1873), 4.

194. Pomeroy to James R. Doolittle, Washington, 20 Oct. 1862, typescript, Doolittle Papers, State Historical Society of Wisconsin.

195. Usher to Richard W. Thompson, Washington, 17 Sept. 1862, Richard W. Thompson Papers, LMF.

196. Washington correspondence, 11, 12 Sept., New York *Tribune*, 12, 13 Sept. 1862.

197. Albany *Evening Journal*, n.d., copied in the New York *Times*, 4 Oct. 1862.

198. Ambrose W. Thompson to Richard W. Thompson, New York, 6 Oct. 1862, copy, Ambrose W. Thompson Papers, DLC.

199. New York *Tribune*, 17 Oct. 1862.

200. Washington correspondence, 2 Nov., New York *Tribune*, 3 Nov. 1862.

201. Diary of Donald McLeod, 23 Oct. 1862, McLeod Family Papers, Virginia Historical Society.

202. Beale, ed., *Welles Diary*, 1:152 (entry for 26 Sept. 1862).

203. Washington *Chronicle*, 6 Jan. 1863; Noah Brooks, "Personal Recollections of Abraham Lincoln," (July 1865) in Michael Burlingame, ed., *Lincoln Observed: Civil War Dispatches of Noah Brooks* (Baltimore, MD: Johns Hopkins University Press, 1998), 205; Washington correspondence, 7 Sept., New York *Tribune*, 8 Sept. 1862.

204. Charles K. Tuckerman, "Personal Recollections of Abraham Lincoln," *The Magazine of American History with Notes and Queries*, May 1888, 412–413.

205. Washington correspondence, 25 July, New York *Evening Post* and New York *Herald*, 26 July 1862.

206. Lincoln to Chase, Washington, 8 Aug. 1862, *CWL*, 5:362.

207. Henry T. Cheever to his sister Elizabeth, Worcester, 10 July 1862, Cheever Family Papers, American Antiquarian Society; Wright to Chase, Boston, 6 July 1862, in Philip G. Wright and Elizabeth Q. Wright, *Elizur Wright: The Father of Life Insurance* (Chicago: University of Chicago Press, 1937), 217.

208. Speech of 4 July 1862, in Philip S. Foner and Yuval Taylor, eds., *Frederick Douglass: Selected Speeches and Writings* (Chicago: Lawrence Hill Books, 1999), 505; *Douglass's Monthly*, August 1862.

209. Speech of 1 Aug. 1862, Wendell Phillips, *Speeches, Lectures, and Letters* (Boston: J. Redpath, 1863), 448, 456, 454, 452, 455, 459–460, 453.

210. Washington correspondence, 18 Aug., New York *Examiner*, 21 Aug. 1862, Michael Burlingame, ed., *Dispatches from Lincoln's White House: The Anonymous Civil War Journalism of Presidential Secretary William O. Stoddard* (Lincoln: University of Nebraska Press, 2002), 95; John Eaton, *Grant, Lincoln, and the Freedmen: Reminiscences of the Civil War with Special Reference to the Work for the Contrabands and Freedmen of the Mississippi Valley* (New York: Longmans, Green, 1907), 184.

211. New York *Herald*, 11 Dec. 1862.

212. *The Independent* (New York), 14 Aug. 1862, in William C. Beecher and Samuel Scoville, *A Biography of Rev. Henry Ward Beecher* (New York: C. L. Webster, 1888), 332–333.

213. *The Independent* (New York), 17 July 1862, in Allan Nevins, *The War for the Union* (4 vols.; New York: Scribner, 1959–1971), 2:301.

214. *The Liberator* (Boston), 25 July 1862.

215. Andrew J. Graham to Gerrit Smith, 11 Aug. 1862, in Ralph Volney Harlow, *Gerrit Smith, Philanthropist and Reformer* (New York: H. Holt, 1939), 435.

216. Beriah Green to Gerrit Smith, Whitesboro, NY, 21 Aug. 1862, Smith Papers, Syracuse University.

217. Harlan to George B. Cheever, Mt. Pleasant, Iowa, 4 Sept. 1862, Cheever Family Papers, American Antiquarian Society.

218. Frederick Pike to J. S. Pike, Calais, 3 Aug. 1862, Pike Papers, University of Maine.

219. Stevens to Simon Stevens, Lancaster, 10 Aug. 1862, Palmer, ed., *Stevens Papers*, 1:318.

220. "Enquirer" to the editor of the New York *Tribune*, Auburn, New York, 28 July 1862, enclosed in Sydney Howard Gay to Lincoln, New York, 30 July [1862], Gay Papers, Columbia University.

221. Rossiter Johnson in the New York *Tribune*, n.d., copied in the *Staten Islander*, 29 Apr. 1891.

222. H. L. Stevens to Sydney Howard Gay, 7 Sept. 1862, Gay Papers, Columbia University; George William Curtis to "My darling girl," Staten Island, 17 Aug. 1862, Curtis Papers, Staten Island Institute of Arts and Sciences.

223. Adams Hill to Sydney Howard Gay, [Washington, 9 July 1862], Gay Papers, Columbia University.

224. Sumner to Elizabeth, Duchess of Argyll, 11 Aug. 1862, Edward Lillie Pierce, *Memoir and Letters of Charles Sumner* (4 vols.; Boston: Roberts Brothers, 1877–1893), 4:84.

225. Henderson quoted in Adlai E. Stevenson, *Something of Men I Have Known, with Some Papers of a General Nature, Political, Historical, and Retrospective* (Chicago: A. C. McClurg, 1909), 352–353.

226. Moncure Daniel Conway, "A Southern Abolitionist's Memories of Mr. Lincoln," London *Fortnightly Review*, 15 May 1865, in Rufus Rockwell Wilson, ed., *Intimate Memories of Lincoln* (Elmira, NY: Primavera Press, 1945), 182.

227. Remarks made on 20 June 1862, *CWL*, 5:278–279; William D. Kelley to the editor of the New York *Tribune*, Philadelphia, 23 Sept. 1885, in Kelley, *Lincoln and Stanton*, 83–85.

228. Samuel G. Buckingham, *The Life of William A. Buckingham, the War Governor of Connecticut* (Springfield, MA: W. F. Adams, 1894), 262.

229. Schuyler Colfax in Rice, ed., *Reminiscences of Lincoln*, 335.

230. Albany *Evening Journal*, 30 June 1862.

231. William Harlan Hale, *Horace Greeley: Voice of the People* (New York: Harper & Brothers, 1950), 269.

232. New York *Tribune*, 20 Aug. 1862.

233. Wendell Phillips to Sydney Howard Gay, n.p., 2 Sept. 1862, Gay Papers, Columbia University.

234. Cincinnati *Commercial*, 25 Aug. 1862; Washington *National Intelligencer*, n.d, quoted in the Washington correspondence, 23 Aug., New York *Times*, 24 Aug. 1862.

235. Philadelphia *Ledger*, n.d., copied in the Washington *Evening Star*, 27 Aug. 1862.

236. Indianapolis *Journal*, 25 Aug. 1862.

237. Lincoln to Greeley, Washington, 22 Aug. 1862, *CWL*, 5:388–389; Rice, ed., *Reminiscences of Lincoln*, 525n.

238. Washington correspondence, 24 Aug., Cincinnati *Gazette*, 25 Aug. 1862.

239. Washington correspondence, New York *Times*, 24 Aug. 1862.

240. George Ashmun to Lincoln, Springfield, Massachusetts, 25 Aug. 1862, AL MSS DLC.

241. James W. White to Horace Greeley, Washington, 23 Aug. 1862, Greeley Papers, DLC.

242. John B. Henderson to Lincoln, Louisiana, Missouri, 3 Sept. 1862, AL MSS DLC.

243. New York *Times* in Harlan Hoyt Horner, *Lincoln and Greeley* (Urbana: University of Illinois Press, 1953), 275.

244. Thurlow Weed to William H. Seward, Albany, 23 Aug. 1862, AL MSS DLC.

245. Howe to Lincoln, Green Bay, 25 Aug. 1862, AL MSS DLC.

246. Indianapolis *Journal*, 25 Aug. 1862.

247. Horace Greeley to George W. Wright, 27 Aug. 1862, Greeley Papers, DLC; Allen C. Guelzo, *Lincoln's Emancipation Proclamation: The End of Slavery in America* (New York: Simon & Schuster, 2004), 135.

248. Sydney H. Gay to Lincoln, [New York, Aug. 1862], AL MSS DLC.

249. Adams S. Hill to Sydney Howard Gay, Washington, 1 Sept. 1862, Gay Papers, Columbia University.

250. Guelzo, *Emancipation Proclamation*, 151–152.

251. Sanford E. Church to Thurlow Weed, Albion, New York, 24 Aug. 1862, Weed Papers, University of Rochester.

252. Gerrit Smith to Lincoln, Peterboro, New York, 9 Oct. 1862, AL MSS DLC; speech of Lovejoy at Peoria, 13 Sept., Cincinnati *Commercial*, 22 Sept. 1862.

253. Wendell Phillips to Sydney H. Gay, n.p., 2 Sept. 1862, Gay Papers, Columbia University.

254. "J. S." to William Lloyd Garrison, 1 Sept. 1862, *The Liberator* (Boston), 5 Sept. 1862, in James M. McPherson, *The Struggle for Equality: Abolitionists and the Negro in the Civil War and Reconstruction* (Princeton, NJ: Princeton University Press, 1964), 117.

255. Beriah Green to Gerrit Smith, Whitesboro, New York, 14 Oct. 1862, Smith Papers, Syracuse University.

256. Robert C. Winthrop, Jr., to Robert C. Winthrop, Sr., Baden Baden, 11 Sept. 1862, Winthrop Family Papers, MHi.

257. Washington correspondence, 24 Aug., New York *Tribune,* 25 Aug. 1862.

258. Douglass to Gerrit Smith, Rochester, New York, 7 Mar. 1863, Smith Papers, Syracuse University.

259. *National Anti-Slavery Standard* (New York), 30 Aug. 1862.

260. Washington correspondence, n.d., Springfield, Massachusetts, *Republican,* n.d., copied in the Providence *Journal,* 11 Aug. 1862.

261. Reid's dispatch of 24 Aug. 1862 in Smart, ed., *"Agate" Dispatches,* 1:215.

262. Washington correspondence, 24 Aug., New York *Tribune*, 25 Aug. 1862.

263. Brownson to Samuel G. Howe, Elizabeth, New Jersey, 13 Sept. 1862, Schoff Civil War Collection, William L. Clements Library, University of Michigan.

264. Washington correspondence, 3 November, New York *Tribune,* 9 Nov. 1862.

265. Reply to Chicago clergymen, 13 September 1862, *CWL,* 5:420–425.

266. William W. Patton, *President Lincoln and the Chicago Memorial on Emancipation: A Paper Read Before the Maryland Historical Society December 12th, 1887* (Baltimore, MD: J. Murphy, 1888), 32.

267. Leonard Swett to his wife Laura, New York, 10 Aug. 1862, David Davis Family Papers, IHi.

268. Speech by Swett, 26 Apr. 1880, Chicago *Times,* 27 Apr. 1880.

269. Garrison to Oliver Johnson, 9 Sept. 1862, Merrill, ed., *Garrison Letters,* 5:112.

270. Douglass to Gerrit Smith, 8 Sept. 1862, in McPherson, *Struggle for Equality,* 117.

271. Thaddeus Stevens to Simon Stevens, Lancaster, 5 Sept. 1862, Palmer, ed., *Stevens Papers,* 1:323.

272. Northampton *Free Press,* n.d., copied in the Boston *Commonwealth,* 20 Sept. 1862.

273. Henry Winter Davis to Samuel Francis Du Pont, [Baltimore], 11 July 1862, transcript, S. F. Du Pont Papers, Hagley Museum, Wilmington, Delaware.

274. Jacob Barker to Lincoln, New Orleans, 16 July 1862, AL MSS DLC.

275. Lincoln to Cuthbert Bullitt, Washington, 28 July 1862, *CWL,* 5:344–346.

276. Beale, ed., *Welles Diary,* 1:143 (entry for 22 Sept. 1862).

277. George S. Boutwell in Rice, ed., *Reminiscences of Lincoln,* 126.

278. Niven, ed., *Chase Papers,* 1:393–394 (diary entry for 22 Sept. 1862).

279. Josiah Blackburn in the London, Ontario, *Free Press,* [19?] July 1864, copied in the New York *Times,* 1 Aug. 1864.

280. Montgomery Blair, "The Republican Party As It Was and Is," *North American Review* 131 (1880): 426.

281. Welles, "History of Emancipation," *The Galaxy* 14 (1872): 847; Niven, ed., *Chase Papers,* 1:394–395 (diary entry for 22 Sept. 1862).

282. Blair to Lincoln, 23 Sept. 1862, draft, Blair Papers, DLC.

283. Hezekiah S. Bundy to Chase, Reeds Mill, 3 Oct. 1862, Chase Papers, DLC.

284. Theodore Tilton to William Lloyd Garrison, New York, 24 Sept. 1862, Garrison Papers, Boston Public Library.

285. Sallie Holley to Abby Kelley, 30 Sept. 1862, in Dorothy Sterling, *Ahead of Her Time: Abby Kelley and the Politics of Anti-Slavery* (New York: W. W. Norton, 1991), 336.

286. Adam Gurowski, *Diary* (Boston: Lee and Shepard, 1862), 280, 278 (entries for 24, 23 Sept. 1862).

287. *Douglass's Monthly,* Jan. 1863.

288. Beriah Green to Gerrit Smith, Whitesboro, New York, 14 Oct. 1862, Smith Papers, Syracuse University.

289. Parker Pillsbury to Theodore Tilton, Boston, 12 Dec. 1862, Miscellaneous Manuscripts, New-York Historical Society.

290. Lydia Child to Sarah Shaw, Wayland, 30 Oct. 1862, *Lydia Maria Child: Selected Letters, 1817–1880,* ed. Milton Meltzer and

Patricia G. Holland (Amherst: University of Massachusetts Press, 1982), 419.

291. Washington correspondence, 29 Dec., New York *Tribune*, 30 Dec. 1862.

292. John M. Forbes to Charles Sumner, Boston, 27 Dec. 1862, AL MSS DLC.

293. *The Liberator* (Boston), 26 Sept. 1862, copied in the Cincinnati *Commercial*, 3 Oct. 1862.

294. Garrison to Fanny Garrison, Boston, 25 Sept. 1862, Merrill, ed., *Garrison Letters*, 5:114–115.

295. New York *Herald*, 6 Oct. 1862.

296. George B. Cheever to his sister Elizabeth Washburn, New York, 29 Sept. 1862, Cheever Family Papers, American Antiquarian Society.

297. Andrew to Albert G. Browne, Jr., 23 Sept. 1862, in Henry Greenleaf Pearson, *The Life of John A. Andrew, Governor of Massachusetts, 1861–1865* (2 vols.; Boston: Houghton Mifflin, 1904), 2:51.

298. May to Richard Webb, 23 Sept. 1862, in McPherson, *Struggle for Equality*, 119.

299. *National Anti-Slavery Standard* (New York), 27 Sept. 1862.

300. Thodore Tilton to Garrison, New York, 24 Sept. 1862, Garrison Papers, Boston Public Library.

301. *Douglass's Monthly*, Oct. 1862, 721.

302. *Weekly Anglo-African* (New York), n.d., copied in the Springfield, Massachusetts, *Republican*, 9 Oct. 1862, and in the *National Anti-Slavery Standard* (New York), 4 Oct. 1862.

303. Boston *Commonwealth*, 4 Oct. 1862.

304. *The Works of Charles Sumner* (15 vols.; Boston: Lee and Shepard, 1870–1883), 7:199.

305. Hannibal Hamlin to Lincoln, Bangor, Maine, 25 Sept. 1862, AL MSS DLC.

306. New York *Tribune*, 24 Sept. 1862.

307. Washington correspondence by Forney, 23 Sept., Philadelphia *Press*, 24 Sept. 1862.

308. Pittsburgh *Gazette*, 24 Sept. 1862.

309. New York *Evening Post*, n.d., copied in Springfield, Massachusetts, *Republican*, 24 Sept. 1862; Allan Nevins, *The Evening Post: A Century of Journalism* (New York: Boni and Liveright, 1922), 295.

310. New York *Times*, 28 Sept. 1862.

311. *Illinois State Journal* (Springfield), 24 Sept. 1862.

312. Springfield, Massachusetts, *Republican*, 24 Sept. 1862.

313. Emerson, "The President's Proclamation," *The Atlantic Monthly*, November 1862, 639–640.

314. William Henry Furness, "A Word of Consolation for the Kindred of Those Who Have Fallen in Battle, A Discourse of September 28, 1862" (n.d., n.p.), 7, 13, quoted in George M. Fredrickson, *The Inner Civil War: Northern Intellectuals and the Crisis of the Union* (New York: Harper Torchbooks, 1965), 118.

315. Charles Eliot Norton to George W. Curtis, Cambridge, Massachusetts, 23 Sept. 1862, Sara Norton and M. A. DeWolfe Howe, eds., *Letters of Charles Eliot Norton* (2 vols.; Boston: Houghton Mifflin, 1913), 1:256.

316. *Harper's Weekly*, 4 October 1862.

317. McClure, *Lincoln and Men of War-Times*, 269.

318. Andrew to Adam Gurowski, [Boston], 6 Sept. 1862, letterpress copy, Andrew Papers, MHi.

319. Trumbull to Yates, Beardstown, Illinois, 19 Sept. 1862, L. U. Reavis Papers, ICHi.

320. Dan Elbert Clark, *Samuel Jordan Kirkwood* (Iowa City: State Historical Society of Iowa, 1917), 249.

321. Reply to loyal governors, 26 Sept. 1862, *CWL*, 5:441.

322. Washington correspondence, 26 Sept. 1862, Philadelphia *Inquirer*, 27 Sept. 1862; Samuel J. Kirkwood, "The Loyal Governors at Altoona in 1862," *Iowa Historical Record* 7–9 (1891–1893), 213–214.

323. Boutwell in Rice, ed., *Reminiscences of Lincoln*, 400.

324. Washington correspondence by Agate, 25 Sept. 1862, Smart, ed., *"Agate" Dispatches*, 1:234–236; *CWL*, 5:438.

325. Washington correspondence, 26 Sept., New York *Evening Express*, 27 Sept. 1862; New

York *Evening Express,* n.d., copied in the Cincinnati *Commercial,* 30 Sept. 1862.

326. Nevins and Thomas, eds., *Strong Diary,* 3:262 (entry for 27 Sept. 1862).

327. Washington *National Intelligencer,* 23 Sept. 1862.

328. New York *Herald,* 24, 27, 29 Sept. 1862.

329. Lord John Russell, memorandum of 13 Oct. 1862, in Spencer Walpole, *The Life of Lord John Russell* (2 vols.; London: Longmans, Green, 1889), 2:351; Lynn M. Case and Warren F. Spencer, *The United States and France: Civil War Diplomacy* (Philadelphia: University of Pennsylvania Press, 1970), 359; Howard Jones, *Abraham Lincoln and a New Birth of Freedom: The Union and Slavery in the Diplomacy of the Civil War* (Lincoln: University of Nebraska Press, 1999), 117, 122.

330. Chicago *Times,* 24 Sept. 1862; Boston *Post,* n.d., copied in the Springfield, Massachusetts, *Republican,* 24 Sept. 1862.

331. New York *Evening Express,* 23 Sept. 1862.

332. E. T. Bainbridge to Joseph Holt, Louisville, 29 Sept. 1862, Holt Papers, DLC.

333. Louisville *Democrat,* 24 Sept. 1862, copied in the New York *Herald,* 29 Sept. 1862; Louisville *Democrat,* n.d., copied in the Cincinnati *Commercial,* 27 Sept. 1862.

334. Louisville *Journal,* n.d., copied in Springfield, Massachusetts, *Republican,* 2 Oct. 1862.

335. Hamilton Gray to Lincoln, Maysville, Kentucky, 7 Jan. 1863, AL MSS DLC.

336. St. Louis correspondence, 23 Sept., New York *Herald,* 27 Sept. 1862.

337. Hugh Campbell to Joseph Holt, St. Louis, 26 Sept. 1862, Holt Papers, DLC.

338. Wheeling *Press,* n.d., copied in the Springfield, Massachusetts, *Republican,* 2 Oct. 1862.

339. Canton, Ohio, *Starke County Democrat,* 24 Sept. 1864, in Frank L. Klement, *Lincoln's Critics: The Copperheads of the North,* ed. Steven K. Rogstad (Shippensburg, PA: White Mane, 1999), 114.

340. Charles Mason, former chief justice of Iowa, diary entry, 23 Sept. 1862, in Hubert H.

Wubben, *Civil War Iowa and the Copperhead Movement* (Ames: Iowa State University Press, 1980), 84.

341. Ibid., 116

342. Halstead to Chase, Cincinati, 19 Feb. 1863, Cincinnati *Enquirer,* 28 Sept. 1885.

343. Burlingame and Ettlinger, eds., *Hay Diary,* 41 (entry for 24 Sept. 1862).

344. Adams S. Hill to Sydney Howard Gay, n.p., n.d. [Washington, 18 Sept. 1862], Gay Papers, Columbia University.

345. Washington correspondence by H., 24 Sept., New York *Evening Express,* 25 Sept. 1862.

346. Klement, *Lincoln's Critics,* 116.

347. Dunbar Rowland, ed., *Jefferson Davis, Constitutionalist: His Letters, Papers, and Speeches* (10 vols.; Jackson: Printed for the Mississippi Dept. of Archives and History, 1923), 5:409.

348. Washington correspondence by Erastus Brooks, 7 Dec., New York *Evening Express,* 8 Dec. 1862.

349. Richmond *Enquirer,* 1 Oct., copied in the New York *Herald,* 4 Oct. 1862.

350. New York *Herald,* 22 Oct. 1862.

351. London *Times,* 7 Oct. 1862, in Herbert Mitgang, ed., *Abraham Lincoln: A Press Portrait* (Chicago: Quadrangle Books, 1971), 320.

352. London *Morning Post,* n.d, quoted in Charles C. Coffin's lecture on the Emancipation Proclamation, Coffin Papers, New England Genealogical Society Library, Boston.

353. Dana to Seward, New York, 23 Sept. 1862, AL MSS DLC.

354. Guelzo, *Emancipation Proclamation,* 178.

355. [Porter] to Manton Marble, n.p., 30 Sept. 1862, Marble Papers, DLC.

356. John Gregory Smith to Lincoln, St. Albans, Vermont, 30 Dec. 1864, University of Vermont, Burlington.

357. McPherson, *Political History of the United States,* 227.

358. Boston *Journal,* n.d., copied in the New York *Tribune,* 30 Sept. 1862.

359. Annotation by Thompson on a letter he wrote to Lincoln but did not send, Wash-

ington, 26 Jan. 1863, typescript, Thompson Collection, Indiana State Library, Indianapolis; R. W. Thompson, "Abraham Lincoln," undated manuscript, R. W. Thompson Papers, IHi.

360. Lincoln to Hamlin, Washington, 28 Sept. 1862, *CWL*, 5:444.

Chapter 29. "I Am Not a Bold Man, But I Have the Knack of Sticking to My Promises!"

1. David Davis to W. W. Orme, Bloomington, 20 Oct. 1862, Orme Papers, IHi.

2. W. W. Orme to David Davis, Springfield, Missouri, 24 Oct. 1862, David Davis Papers, IHi.

3. Fessenden to James W. Grimes, Portland, 19 Oct. 1862, Fessenden Papers, Bowdoin College.

4. Frederick Pike to J. S. Pike, Calais, 22 Oct. 1862, Pike Papers, University of Maine.

5. John Pope to Valentine B. Horton, St. Paul, 1 Nov. 1862, Pope Papers, New-York Historical Society.

6. New York *Tribune*, 16 Oct. 1862.

7. Allan Nevins, *The War for the Union* (4 vols.; New York: Scribner, 1959–1971), 2:319.

8. *The Crisis* (Columbus), 5 Mar. 1862; Cincinnati *Enquirer*, 4 Aug. 1862.

9. Reginald Charles McGrane, *William Allen: A Study in Western Democracy* (Columbus: Ohio State Archaeological and Historical Society, 1925), 157–158.

10. Speech of 15 Dec. 1862, in Samuel Sullivan Cox, *Eight Years in Congress, from 1857 to 1865: Memoir and Speeches* (New York: D. Appleton, 1865), 264.

11. Hezekiah S. Bundy to Chase, Reed's Mill, 18 Oct. 1862, Chase Papers, DLC.

12. *The Crisis* (Columbus), 29 Oct. 1862, in Reed W. Smith, *Samuel Medary & The Crisis: Testing the Limits of Press Freedom* (Columbus: Ohio State University Press, 1995), 102.

13. Nicolay to Therena Bates, Washington, 16 Oct. 1862, in Michael Burlingame, ed., *With Lincoln in the White House: Letters, Memoranda, and Other Writings of John G. Nicolay, 1860–1865*

(Carbondale: Southern Illinois University Press, 2000), 89.

14. Washington correspondence by Van [D. W. Bartlett], 21 Oct., Springfield, Massachusetts, *Republican*, 25 Oct. 1862.

15. John A. Jones to David Davis, Georgetown, DC, 27 Oct. 1862, Davis Papers, IHi.

16. George W. Towner to Albert G. Myrick, Nyack, New York, 9 Nov. 1862, Myrick Papers, William L. Clements Library, University of Michigan.

17. New York *World*, 18 Nov. 1862, in Forrest G. Wood, *Black Scare: The Racist Response to Emancipation and Reconstruction* (Berkeley: University of California Press, 1968), 20.

18. Allan Nevins and Milton Halsey Thomas, eds., *Diary of George Templeton Strong, 1835–1875* (4 vols.; New York: Macmillan, 1952), 3:272 (entry for 5 Nov, 1862).

19. Washington correspondence, 6 Nov., New York *Times,* 7 Nov. 1862.

20. Boston *Evening Journal,* 3 Nov. 1862.

21. Lawrence Weldon to W. W. Orme, Springfield, 24 Nov. 1862, in Harry E. Pratt, "The Repudiation of Lincoln's War Policy in 1862: The Stuart-Swett Congressional Campaign," *Journal of the Illinois State Historical Society* 24 (1931):140.

22. Swett to Orme, Bloomington, 18 Nov. 1862, Orme Papers, IHi.

23. Trumbull to Zachariah Chandler, Springfield, 9 Nov. 1862, Chandler Papers, DLC.

24. Virginia Jeans Laas, ed., *Wartime Washington: The Civil War Letters of Elizabeth Blair Lee* (Urbana: University of Illinois Press, 1991), 202, 204, 209.

25. Hay-Stoddard memorandum of a meeting Lincoln had on 30 Sept. 1863, Nicolay-Hay Papers, IHi.

26. Lincoln to A. G. Hodges, Washington, 4 Apr. 1864, Roy P. Basler et al., eds., *Collected Works of Abraham Lincoln* [hereafter *CWL*] (8 vols. plus index; New Brunswick, NJ: Rutgers University Press, 1953–1955), 7:282.

27. John McClintock, sermon of 16 Apr. 1865, in *Our Martyred President: Voices from the*

Pulpit of New York and Brooklyn (New York: Tibbals and Whiting, 1865), 136.

28. Louisville correspondence by Agate [Whitelaw Reid], 25 Oct. 1862, in James G. Smart, ed., *A Radical View: The "Agate" Dispatches of Whitelaw Reid, 1861–1865* (2 vols.; Memphis: Memphis State University Press, 1976), 1:91.

29. Julian in Allen Thorndike Rice, ed., *Reminiscences of Abraham Lincoln by Distinguished Men of His Time* (New York: North American Review, 1888), 55–56.

30. Theodore Tilton to Wendell Phillips, Brooklyn, [6 Nov. 1862], Phillips Papers, Harvard University.

31. Washington correspondence by Van [D. W. Bartlett], 24 Nov., Springfield, Massachusetts, *Republican,* 28 Nov. 1862.

32. Washington correspondence, 21 Nov., New York *Tribune,* 22 Nov. 1862.

33. Lincoln to George Robertson, Washington, 20 Nov. 1862, *CWL,* 5:502.

34. Washington correspondence, 23 Nov., New York *Tribune,* 24 Nov. 1862.

35. Washington correspondence, 4 Nov., New York *Evening Post,* 5 Nov. 1862.

36. George S. Boutwell, *Speeches and Papers Relating to the Rebellion and the Overthrow of Slavery* (Boston: Little, Brown, 1867), 362.

37. Washington correspondence, 19 Dec., New York *Times,* 20 Dec. 1862.

38. Theodore Calvin Pease and James G. Randall, eds., *The Diary of Orville Hickman Browning* (2 vols.; Springfield: Illinois State Historical Library, 1925–1933), 1:607 (entry for 30 Dec. 1862).

39. Washington correspondence, 25 Dec., Cincinnati *Gazette,* 27 Dec. 1862; Washington correspondence, 25 Dec., New York *Tribune,* 26 Dec. 1862.

40. Washington correspondence, 30 Dec., New York *Evening Post,* 31 Dec. 1862.

41. T. J. Barnett to S. L. M. Barlow, Washington, 30 Nov. 1862, Barlow Papers, CSmH.

42. Horace White to Lincoln, Chicago, 22 Oct. 1862, AL MSS DLC.

43. Medill to Ozias M. Hatch, Chicago, 13 Oct. 1862, Hatch Papers, IHi.

44. W. M. Dickson to Friedrich Hassaurek, Cincinnati, 10 Apr. 1862, Hassaurek Papers, Ohio Historical Society.

45. Francis Springer to Hawkins Taylor, Burlington, Iowa, 19 Oct. 1862, AL MSS DLC.

46. Letter from an unidentified correspondent to B. F. M., n.p., n.d., Washington correspondence by B. F. M., 25 Oct., Cincinnati *Gazette,* 30 Oct. 1862.

47. William Cullen Bryant to Lincoln, New York, 22 Oct. 1862, AL MSS DLC.

48. Washington correspondence, 9 Dec. 1862, Sacramento *Daily Union,* 5 Jan. 1863, in Michael Burlingame, ed., *Lincoln Observed: Civil War Dispatches of Noah Brooks* (Baltimore, MD: Johns Hopkins University Press, 1998), 14.

49. Lydia Child to Sarah Shaw, Wayland, Massachusetts, 11 Nov. 1862, in *Lydia Maria Child: Selected Letters, 1817–1880,* ed. Milton Meltzer and Patricia G. Holland (Amherst: University of Massachusetts Press, 1982), 420.

50. Michael Burlingame and John R. Turner Ettlinger, eds., *Inside Lincoln's White House: The Complete Civil War Diary of John Hay* (Carbondale: Southern Illinois University Press, 1997), 62 (entry for 14 July 1863).

51. Smith to John F. Potter, Washington, 4 Oct. 1862, Potter Papers, Wisconsin State Historical Society.

52. O. M. Hatch interviewed by Nicolay, Springfield, June 1875, in Michael Burlingame, ed., *An Oral History of Abraham Lincoln: John G. Nicolay's Interviews and Essays* (Carbondale: Southern Illinois University Press, 1996), 16.

53. T. J. Barnett to S. L. M. Barlow, Washington, 23 Sept. 1862, Barlow Papers, CSmH.

54. W. M. Dickson to Friedrich Hassaurek, Cincinnati, 27 Sept. 1862, Hassaurek Papers, Ohio Historical Society.

55. Pope to Richard Yates, St. Paul, 21 Sept. 1862, copy, Samuel Kirkwood Papers, Iowa State Archives, Des Moines.

56. William M. Dickson "A Leaf from the Unwritten History of the Rebellion," draft,

Dickson Papers, William L. Clements Library, University of Michigan.

57. Washington correspondence by W., 7 Oct., Cincinnati *Commercial*, 8 Oct. 1862.

58. General S. S. Sumner, "General Sumner and Lincoln," *The Magazine of History with Notes and Queries*, Extra number, no. 153 (1924), *Rare Lincolniana* no. 37, p. 38.

59. Headquarters of the Army of the Potomac correspondence, 4 Oct., New York *Herald*, 7 Oct. 1862.

60. Washington correspondence, 6 Oct., Philadelphia *Inquirer*, 7 Oct. 1862.

61. John L. Parker, *Henry Wilson's Regiment* (Boston: Rand Avery, 1887), 205.

62. William C. Davis, *Lincoln's Men: How President Lincoln Became Father to an Army and a Nation* (New York: Free Press, 1999), 81.

63. Allan Nevins, ed., *A Diary of Battle: The Personal Journals of Colonel Charles S. Wainwright, 1861–1865* (New York: Harcourt, Brace & World, 1962), 109 (entry for 2 Oct. 1862).

64. Flavius J. Bellamy to his parents, Sharpsburg, 4 Oct. 1862, Flavius J. Bellamy Papers, Indiana State Library.

65. Thomas H. Mann to his family, 7 Oct. 1862, in John J. Hennessy, ed., *Fighting with the Eighteenth Massachusetts: The Civil War Memoir of Thomas H. Mann* (Baton Rouge: Louisiana State University Press, 2000), 106.

66. Walter and Bob Carter to an unidentified correspondent, opposite Shepardstown, 3 Oct. 1862, in Robert Goldthwaite Carter, *Four Brothers in Blue; or, Sunshine and Shadows of the War of the Rebellion, A Story of the Great Civil War from Bull Run to Appomattox* (Washington, DC: Gibson Brothers, 1913), 137.

67. Headquarters of the Army of the Potomac correspondence, 2 Oct., New York *Herald*, 7 Oct. 1862.

68. Stephen W. Sears, ed., *The Civil War Papers of George B. McClellan* (New York: Ticknor and Fields, 1989), 490.

69. Washington correspondence by Van [D. W. Bartlett], 7 Oct., Springfield, Massachusetts, *Republican*, 11 Oct. 1862.

70. David Davis to Leonard Swett, Washington, 26 Nov. 1862, David Davis Papers, IHi.

71. *Spirit of the Times* (New York), n.d., copied in the Cincinnati *Commercial*, 24 Oct. 1862.

72. McClellan to his wife, Sharpsburg, 2 Oct. 1862, Sears, ed., *McClellan Papers*, 488.

73. O. M. Hatch interviewed by Nicolay, Springfield, June 1875, in Burlingame, ed., *Oral History of Lincoln*, 16.

74. Sharpsburg correspondence, 8 Oct., New York *Times*, 12 Oct. 1862.

75. Du Pont to his wife, Washington, 16 Oct. 1862, and at sea aboard the *Keystone*, 10 21 Oct. 1862; and to Henry Winter Davis, 25 Oct. 1862, in John D. Hayes, ed., *Samuel Francis Du Pont: A Selection from His Civil War Letters* (3 vols.; Ithaca, NY: Published for the Eleutherian Mills Historical Library by the Cornell University Press, 1969), 2:245–247, 251–253.

76. Benjamin Brown French, *Witness to the Young Republic: A Yankee's Journal, 1828–1870*, ed. Donald B. Cole and John J. McDonough (Hanover, NH: University Press of New England, 1989), 405 (entry for 3 August. 1862).

77. Washington correspondence by Van [D. W. Bartlett], 17 Dec., Springfield, Massachusetts, *Republican*, 19 Dec. 1862.

78. Lincoln quoted by Frederick Law Olmsted in Nevins and Thomas, eds., *Strong Diary*, 3:278 (entry for 13 Dec. 1862); Horace Furness to his wife, Washington, 24 Nov. 1862, H. H. F. Joyce, ed., *The Letters of Horace Furness* (2 vols.; Boston: Houghton Mifflin 1922), 1:125–127.

79. Washington correspondence, 18 Nov., New York *Times*, 19 Nov. 1862.

80. Halleck to McClellan, Washington, 6 Oct. 1862, *The War of the Rebellion: A Compilation of the Official Records of the Union and Confederate Armies* (128 vols.; Washington, DC: U.S. Government Printing Office, 1880–1891) [hereafter *OR*], I, 19:72.

81. Halleck to Elizabeth Hamilton Halleck, Washington, 7 Oct. 1862, Schoff Civil War Collection, William L. Clements Library, University of Michigan.

82. Halleck to McClellan, Washington, 14 Oct. 1862, *OR*, I, 19, 2:421.

83. Lincoln to McClellan, Washington, 25 Oct. 1862, *CWL*, 5:474.

84. Stephen W. Sears, *George B. McClellan: The Young Napoleon* (New York: Ticknor & Fields, 1988), 334.

85. Lincoln to McClellan, Washington, 27 Oct. 1862, *CWL*, 5:479.

86. Nicolay to Therena Bates, Washington, 13 Oct. 1862, in Burlingame, ed., *With Lincoln in the White House*, 89.

87. Lincoln to McClellan, Washington, 26 Oct. 1862, *CWL*, 5:477.

88. Smith to Thurlow Weed, Washington, 29 Sept. 1862, Weed Papers, University of Rochester.

89. Chandler to his wife, Washington, 10 Dec. 1862, Chandler Papers, DLC.

90. Willet Raynor to Zachariah Chandler, Burr Oak, Michigan, 4 Dec. 1862, ibid.

91. Lincoln to McClellan, Washington, 13 Oct. 1862, *CWL*, 5:460–461.

92. Adams S. Hill to Sydney Howard Gay, Washington, 13 Oct. 1862, in Louis Morris Starr, *Bohemian Brigade: Civil War Newsmen in Action* (New York: Alfred A. Knopf, 1954), 152.

93. *OR*, I, 19, 1:81.

94. Washington correspondence, 3 Nov., *National Anti-Slavery Standard* (New York), 8 Nov. 1862.

95. Cooke, "Interview with Lincoln," reminiscences written in 1890, *American History Illustrated* 7 (1972):10–11.

96. Diary of William T. Coggeshall, 23 Oct. 1862, in Freda Postle Koch, *Colonel Coggeshall: The Man Who Saved Lincoln* (Columbus, Ohio: Poko Press, 1985), 69.

97. Nicolay to Hay, Washington, 26 Oct. 1862, in Burlingame, ed., *With Lincoln in the White House*, 90.

98. Sears, ed., *McClellan Papers*, 515.

99. John A. Jones to David Davis, Georgetown, DC, 27 Oct. 1862, Davis Papers, IHi.

100. Washington correspondence, 3 Nov., New York *Tribune*, 9 Nov. 1862.

101. Nicolay to Therena Bates, Washington, 9 Nov. 1862, in Burlingame, ed., *With Lincoln in the White House*, 90–91.

102. Joseph L. Maguire to N. P. Banks, New York, 11 Nov. 1862, Banks Papers, DLC; Chase to Timothy C. Day, Washington, 24 Feb. 1862, in Sarah J. Day, *The Man on a Hill Top* (Philadelphia: Ware Brothers, 1931), 259; Victor Faide to John A. Andrew, New York, 28 Aug. 1864, Andrew Papers, MHi.

103. Francis P. Blair, Sr. to Francis P. Blair, Jr., 7 Nov. 1862, Blair Family Papers, DLC; Francis P. Blair, Sr., to Montgomery Blair, 2 Mar. 1863, ibid.

104. Pease and Randall, eds., *Browning Diary*, 1:590 (entry for 29 Nov. 1862).

105. Burlingame and Ettlinger, eds., *Hay Diary*, 232 (entry for 25 Sept. 1864).

106. Henry to his wife, Washington, 12 Apr. 1863, Henry Papers, IHi.

107. Horace Porter, *Campaigning with Grant* (New York: Century, 1897), 415.

108. J. G. Barnard to [John Sherman], Washington, 6 Jan. 1863 [misdated 1862], John Sherman Papers, DLC.

109. Halleck letter of 9 Nov. 1862 quoted in Murray M. Horowitz, "That Presidential Grub: Lincoln versus His Generals," *Lincoln Herald* 79 (1977):160.

110. Sears, *McClellan*, xii.

111. Washington correspondence, 9, 16 Nov., *National Anti-Slavery Standard* (New York), 15, 22 Nov. 1862.

112. Washington correspondence, 14 Nov., New York *Evening Post*, 15 Nov. 1862.

113. Trumbull to Butler, Washington, 26 Nov. 1862, Butler Papers, ICHi.

114. Trumbull to M. Carey Lea, Washington, 5 Nov. 1861, Horace White, *The Life of Lyman Trumbull* (Boston: Houghton Mifflin, 1913), 171.

115. Trumbull to his son Walter, n.p., n.d., ibid., 430.

116. *Congressional Globe*, 37th Congress, 3rd Session, 2973 (27 June 1862).

117. Wright to Chase, Boston, 13 Nov. 1862, in Philip G. Wright and Elizabeth Q. Wright, *Elizur Wright: The Father of Life Insurance*

(Chicago: University of Chicago Press, 1937), 217; Morton to Richard Yates, Indianapolis, 13 Nov. 1862, L. U. Reavis Papers, ICHi.

118. Horace White to William Butler, Chicago, 11 Nov. 1862, Butler Papers, ICHi.

119. Reminiscences of John Palmer Usher, unidentified clipping, scrapbook no. 1, Otto Eisenschiml Papers, University of Iowa.

120. Adams S. Hill to Sydney Howard Gay, [Washington, late Sept. or early Oct. 1862], Gay Papers, Columbia University; Washington correspondence, 9 Oct., New York *Tribune*, 10 Oct. 1862.

121. Nicolay to Therena Bates, Washington, 16 Oct. 1862, in Burlingame, ed., *With Lincoln in the White House*, 89.

122. John Niven, ed., *The Salmon P. Chase Papers* (5 vols.; Kent, OH: Kent State University Press, 1993–1998), 3:294–295.

123. Halleck to Buell, Washington, 19 Oct. 1862, *OR*, I, 16, 2:626–627.

124. John A. Jones to David Davis, Georgetown, DC, 27 Oct. 1862, Davis Papers, IHi.

125. Halleck to Rosecrans, Washington, 24 Oct. 1862, *OR*, I, 16, 2:641.

126. Halleck to Rosecrans, Washington, 5 Dec. 1862, *OR*, I, 20, 2:123.

127. Halleck to Rosecrans, Washington, 4 Dec. 1862, *OR*, I, 20, 2:118.

128. David Dixon Porter, "The Opening of the Lower Mississippi," *Century Magazine* 29 (1884–1885): 924; Porter, *Incidents and Anecdotes of the Civil War* (New York: D. Appleton, 1885), 96.

129. David Dixon Porter, "Journal of Occurrences during the War of the Rebellion," 1:389–392, 416, Porter Papers, DLC.

130. Niven, ed., *Chase Papers*, 1:404 (entry for 27 Sept. 1862).

131. Washington correspondence, 10 Dec., Cincinnati *Gazette*, 11 Dec. 1862.

132. Henry Lee, Jr., to John A. Andrew, Washington, 5 Nov. 1861, George Bancroft Papers, MHi.

133. Frank E. Howe to John A. Andrew, Washington, 23 Jan. 1862, Andrew Papers, MHi.

134. David Edward Cronin, *The Evolution of a Life* (New York: S. W. Green's Son, 1884), 232.

135. Lincoln to Isaac N. Arnold, Washington, 26 May 1863, *CWL*, 6:231.

136. Washington correspondence by Van [D. W. Bartlett], 11 Feb., Springfield, Massachusetts, *Republican*, 13 Feb. 1863.

137. Col. John Wesley Turner to Adam Badeau, New York, 12 Mar. 1863, Schoff Civil War Collection, William L. Clements Library, University of Michigan.

138. Halleck to Banks, Washington, 8 Nov. 1862, Banks Papers, DLC.

139. Halleck to Banks, Washington, 11 May 1863, *OR*, I, 15:726.

140. Morton to Lincoln, Indianapolis, 27 Oct. 1862, W. H. H. Terrell, *Indiana in the War of the Rebellion: Report of the Adjutant General* (Indianapolis: Douglass and Conner, 1869), 26.

141. John F. Marszalek, *Commander of All Lincoln's Armies: A Life of General Henry W. Halleck* (Cambridge, MA: Harvard University Press, 2004), 170.

142. Forney to Chase, Philadelphia, 26 Sept. 1862, Chase Papers, Historical Society of Pennsylvania.

143. Henry Winter Davis to Sophie Du Pont, [Baltimore], 24 Sept. 1862, transcript, S. F. Du Pont Papers, Hagley Museum, Wilmington, Delaware.

144. Washington correspondence, 20 Oct., *National Anti-Slavery Standard* (New York), 25 Oct. 1862.

145. New York *Times*, 7 Nov. 1862.

146. Bancroft to Francis Lieber, 29 Oct. 1862, Lieber Papers, in Victor B. Howard, *Religion and the Radical Republican Movement, 1860–1870* (Lexington: University Press of Kentucky, 1990), 46.

147. *Frank Leslie's Illustrated Newspaper*, 22 Nov. 1862.

148. Schurz to Lincoln, New Baltimore, Virginia, 8 Nov. 1862, AL MSS DLC.

149. Lincoln to Schurz, Washington, 10 Nov. 1862, *CWL*, 5:494–495.

150. Schurz to Lincoln, Centreville, Virginia, 20 Nov. 1862, AL MSS DLC.

151. Lincoln to Schurz, Washington, 24 Nov. 1862, *CWL*, 5:509–510.

152. C. H. Kettler to Lyman Trumbull, Waterloo, Illinois, 22 Dec. 1861, Lyman Trumbull Papers, DLC.

153. Carl Schurz, *The Reminiscences of Carl Schurz* (3 vols.; New York: McClure, 1907–1908), 2:396.

154. Cincinnati *Gazette,* 17 Oct. 1862.

155. William H. West to Lincoln, Bellefontaine, Ohio, 20 Oct. 1862, AL MSS DLC.

156. Washington *Daily Morning Chronicle,* 12 Nov. 1862, in Burlingame, ed., *With Lincoln in the White House,* 91–92.

157. Dawes to his wife, Washington, 10 Dec. 1862, Dawes Papers, DLC.

158. *CWL,* 5:518-537.

159. New York *Tribune,* 4, 3 Dec. 1862.

160. Providence *Journal,* 3 Dec. 1862.

161. New York *Times,* 2 Dec. 1862.

162. Pease and Randall, eds., *Browning Diary,* 1:591 (entry for 1 Dec. 1862).

163. Allan G. Bogue, ed., "William Parker Cutler's Congressional Diary of 1862–1863," *Civil War History* 33 (1987):320.

164. Dawes to his wife, Washington, 2 Dec. 1862, Dawes Papers, DLC.

165. James A. Garfield to Burke Hinsdale, Washington, 1 Dec. 1862, Frederick D. Williams, ed., *The Wild Life of the Army: Civil War Letters of James A. Garfield* (East Lansing: Michigan State University Press, 1964), 185.

166. Boston *Commonwealth,* 6 Dec. 1862.

167. Paxton Hibben, *Henry Ward Beecher: An American Portrait* (New York: G. H. Doran, 1927), 160.

168. Quoted in the New York *Herald,* 3 Dec. 1862.

169. Ashley to George B. Cheever, Washington, 23 Dec. 1862, Cheever Family Papers, American Antiquarian Society.

170. Henry Winter Davis to Mrs. S. F. Du Pont, n.p., 2 Jan. 1863, transcript, S. F. Du Pont Papers, Hagley Museum, Wilmington, Delaware.

171. Elizabeth Blair Lee to her husband, Silver Spring, Maryland, 2 Dec. 1862, Laas, ed., *Wartime Washington,* 211.

172. Boston *Commonwealth,* 6 Dec. 1862.

173. *The Liberator* (Boston), 26 Dec. 1862.

174. *National Anti-Slavery Standard* (New York), 27 Dec. 1862.

175. Washington correspondence, 21 Dec., ibid., 27 Dec. 1862.

176. *CWL,* 5:536, 530.

177. New York *Evening Express,* 2 Dec. 1862.

178. Charles Ray Wilson, "The Cincinnati Daily Enquirer and Civil War Politics: A Study of Copperhead Opinion" (Ph.D. dissertation, University of Chicago, 1934), 186.

179. David Davis to Leonard Swett, Lenox, Massachusetts, 26 Nov. 1862, David Davis Papers, IHi.

180. Pease and Randall, eds., *Browning Diary,* 1:611–612 (entry for 9 Jan. 1863).

181. Lincoln to Curtis, Washington, 10 Jan. 1863, *CWL,* 6:52; Hendersons's reminiscences in Walter B. Stevens, "Lincoln and Missouri," *Missouri Historical Review* 10 (1915–1916):84.

182. James Taussig to members of a committee of Missouri Radicals, *Missouri Democrat* (St. Louis), 9 June 1863.

183. Beale, ed., *Welles Diary,* 1:180 (entry for 4 Nov. 1862).

184. United States Congress, *Report of the Joint Committee on the Conduct of the War* (3 vols.; Washington, DC: U.S. Government Printing Office, 1863), 1:650.

185. William P. Fessenden to James W. Grimes, Portland, 19 Oct. 1862, Fessenden Papers, Bowdoin College.

186. Kelley in Rice, ed., *Reminiscences of Lincoln,* 278.

187. Chicago *Tribune,* 5 Feb. 1863; Mason Brayman to "My Darling Ditty," Boise City, Idaho, 22 Apr. 1877, Lincoln Associates Collection, LMF.

188. Curtis to Charles Eliot Norton, North Shore, New York, 11 Nov. 1862, Curtis Papers, Harvard University.

189. Lincoln to Halleck, Steamer Baltimore off Aquia Creek, 27 Nov. 1862, *CWL,* 5:514-515.

190. Washington correspondence, 12 Dec., New York *Times,* 13 Dec. 1862.

191. Haupt, "The Railroad Brigade," Philadelphia *Weekly Times,* 22 Sept. 1884, in

Peter Cozzens, ed., *Battles and Leaders of the Civil War, Volume 6* (Urbana: University of Illinois Press, 2002), 470.

192. Haupt to his wife, Washington, 15, 18 Dec. 1862, typescripts, Lewis Haupt Papers, DLC.

193. Henry Villard, *Memoirs of Henry Villard, Journalist and Financier: 1835–1900* (2 vols.; Boston: Houghton Mifflin, 1904), 1:391.

194. Baltimore *American*, 26 Mar. 1864, in J. T. Dorris, "President Lincoln's Clemency," *Lincoln Herald* 55 (1953):6.

195. William Henry Wadsworth to S. L. M. Barlow, Washington, 16 Dec. 1862, Barlow Papers, CSmH.

196. William O. Stoddard, "White House Sketches No. VII," New York *Citizen*, 29 Sept. 1866, in Stoddard, *Inside the White House in War Times: Memoirs and Reports of Lincoln's Secretary*, ed. Michael Burlingame (1890; Lincoln: University of Nebraska Press, 2000), 171; J. E. Gallaher, *Best Lincoln Stories Tersely Told* (Chicago: M. A. Donohue, 1898), 81.

197. Henry Winter Davis to S. F. Du Pont, n.p., 2 Jan. 1863, transcript, S. F. Du Pont Papers, Hagley Museum, Wilmington, Delaware.

198. Peoria *Transcript*, 27 Dec. 1862.

199. Herman Haupt to his wife, Washington, 18 Dec. 1862, typescript, Lewis Haupt Papers, DLC.

200. Reminiscences of Edward Rosewater in Victor Rosewater, "Lincoln in Emancipation Days," *St. Nicholas* 65 (Feb. 1937):13.

201. Washington correspondence, 4 Dec., Sacramento *Daily Union*, 30 Dec. 1862, in Burlingame, ed., *Lincoln Observed*, 13.

202. Washington correspondence by Murat Halstead, 1 Dec., Cincinnati *Commercial*, 4 Dec. 1862.

203. T. S. Bell to Joseph Holt, Louisville, 22 Dec. 1862, Holt Papers, DLC.

204. David Davis to Leonard Swett, Lenox, Massachusetts, 26 Nov. 1862, Davis to Laura Swett, Washington, 21 Dec. 1862, Davis to W. W. Orme, Washington, 9 Dec. 1862, Davis Papers, IHi.

205. Willard L. King, *Lincoln's Manager: David Davis* (Cambridge, MA: Harvard University Press, 1960), 207.

206. Hilon Parker to his brother, Cairo, Illinois, 29 Dec. 1862, Parker Papers, William L. Clements Library, University of Michigan.

207. Sam [Wilkeson] to Sydney Howard Gay, Washington, 15 Aug. 1862 and [ca. late Dec. 1862], Gay Papers, Columbia University.

208. New York *Times*, 10 May 1885.

209. Washington correspondence by Van [D. W. Bartlett], 28 Apr., Springfield, Massachusetts, *Republican*, 2 May 1863.

210. Message to the Army of the Potomac, 22 Dec. 1862, *CWL*, 6:13.

211. Wainwright, *A Diary of Battle*, ed. Nevins, 149–150 (entry for 25 Dec. 1862).

212. Stoddard, *Inside the White House*, ed. Burlingame, 101.

213. W. K. Strong to Samuel R. Curtis, New York, 23 Dec. 1862, Curtis Papers, Yale University.

214. Julia Lorrilard Butterfield, ed., *A Biographical Memorial of General Daniel Butterfield* (New York: Grafton Press, 1904), 159.

215. Washington correspondence, 25 Dec., New York *Times*, 26 Dec. 1862.

216. "Excerpts from the Journal of Henry J. Raymond," *Scribner's Monthly* 19 (Jan. 1880):424.

217. *OR*, I, 21:67.

218. Washington correspondence by Agate [Whitelaw Reid], 19 Dec., Cincinnati *Gazette*, 22 Dec. 1862.

219. Washington correspondence, 16 Jan., Boston *Commonwealth*, 24 Jan. 1863.

220. W. M. Dickson to Friedrich Hassaurek, Cincinnati, 31 Dec. 1862, Hassaurek Papers, Ohio Historical Society.

221. *Harper's Weekly*, 27 Dec. 1862.

222. French, *Witness to the Young Republic*, ed. Cole and McDonough, 415 (entry for 21 Dec. 1862).

223. W. K. Strong to Samuel R. Curtis, New York, 23 Dec. 1862, Curtis Papers, Yale University.

224. Nevins and Thomas, eds., *Strong Diary*, 3:281–282 (entry for 18 Dec. 1862).

225. Norton to George W. Curtis, Cambridge, 12 Nov. 1862, in Sara Norton and M. A. De Wolfe Howe, eds., *Letters of Charles Eliot Norton* (2 vols.; Boston: Houghton Mifflin, 1913), 1:258.

226. James [Hill?] to Edward McPherson, Chambersburg, Pennsylvania, 19 Dec. 1862; [R. G. McCreary?] to Edward McPherson, Gettysburg, Pennsylvania, 17 Dec. 1862, Edward McPherson Papers, DLC.

227. Brownson to Charles Sumner, Elizabeth, New Jersey, 26 Dec. 1862, Sumner Papers, Harvard University.

228. New York *World,* 5 Jan. 1863.

229. New York *Evening Post,* 18 Dec. 1862.

230. Washington correspondence, 24 Jan., Boston *Commonwealth,* 31 Jan. 1863.

231. Thomas C. Slaughter to Henry S. Lane, Corydon, Indiana, 24 Dec. 1862, typescript, Lane Papers, InU.

232. George F. Williams to Sumner, Boston 17 Dec. 1862, Sumner Papers, Harvard University.

233. Kelley in Rice, ed., *Reminiscences of Lincoln,* 276.

234. Chandler to Lyman Trumbull, Detroit, 10 Sept. 1862, Trumbull Papers, DLC; Chandler to his wife, Washington, 18 Dec. 1862, Chandler Papers, DLC.

235. W. M. Dickson to Friedrich Hassaurek, Cincinnati, 31 Dec. 1862, Hassaurek Papers, Ohio Historical Society.

236. Fessenden to Elizabeth Warriner, Washington, 10, 18 Jan. 1863, Fessenden Papers, Bowdoin College.

237. Jay to Sumner, New York, 18 Dec. 1862, Sumner Papers, Harvard University.

238. Thomas C. Slaughter to Henry S. Lane, Corydon, Indiana, 24 Dec. 1862, typescript, Lane Papers, InU.

239. Chandler to his wife, Washington 10, 18 Dec. 1862, Chandler Papers, DLC.

240. Lydia Maria Child to John Greenleaf Whittier, Wayland, Massachusetts, 22 Sept. 1861, Child Papers, DLC; Medill to Schuyler Colfax, n.p., n.d., O. J. Hollister, *Life of Schuyler Colfax* (New York: Funk & Wagnalls, 1886), 200.

241. Sam Wilkeson to Sydney Howard Gay, [Washington, ca. 19 Feb. 1863], Gay Papers, Columbia University.

242. James A. Hamilton to Hamilton Fish, Nevis, New York, 20 Sept. 1861, Fish Papers, DLC.

243. James A. Hamilton, *Reminiscences of James A. Hamilton; or, Men and Events, At Home and Abroad, During Three Quarters of a Century* (New York: C. Scribner, 1869), 530.

244. Stevens to Simon Stevens, Lancaster, 17 Nov. 1862, Beverly Wilson Palmer, ed., *The Selected Papers of Thaddeus Stevens* (2 vols.; Pittsburgh: University of Pittsburgh Press, 1997–1998), 1:328.

245. Pease and Randall, eds., *Browning Diary,* 1:597 (entry for 16 Dec. 1862); Fessenden, manuscript account of the 1862 cabinet crisis, Fessenden Papers, Bowdoin College.

246. Beale, ed., *Welles Diary,* 1:203, 205 (entries for 20, 23 Dec. 1862).

247. Fessenden, manuscript account of the 1862 cabinet crisis, Fessenden Papers, Bowdoin College; Chase to Zachariah Chandler, Washington, 20 Sept. 1862, Niven, ed., *Chase Papers,* 3:276.

248. Pease and Randall, eds., *Browning Diary,* 1:602 (entry for 19 Dec. 1862).

249. Frank Blair to his father, n.d., Blair-Lee Papers, Princeton University, in Nevins, *War for the Union,* 2:336.

250. Fessenden, manuscript account of the 1862 cabinet crisis, Fessenden Papers, Bowdoin College.

251. Seward, *Seward,* 3: 146–147; Sam Wilkeson to Sydney Howard Gay, [Washington, 19 Dec. 1862], Gay Papers, Columbia University; Washington correspondence, 20 Dec., New York *Times,* 22 Dec. 1862.

252. Pease and Randall, eds., *Browning Diary,* 1:600–601, 604 (entries for 18 and 22 Dec. 1862).

253. The second point of the document contained this sentence: "The theory of our government, and the early and uniform practical construction thereof, is, that the President should be aided by a Cabinet Council, agreeing with him in political

principles and general policy, and that all important public measures and appointments should be the result of their combined wisdom and deliberation." Fessenden, manuscript account of the 1862 cabinet crisis, Fessenden Papers, Bowdoin College.

254. Beale, ed., *Welles Diary*, 1:195 (entry for 20 Dec. 1862); Fessenden, manuscript account of the 1862 cabinet crisis, Fessenden Papers, Bowdoin College; Washington correspondence, 21 Dec., New York *Tribune*, 22 Dec. 1862.

255. Washington correspondence by [Henry J.] R[aymond], 20 Dec., New York *Times*, 22 Dec. 1862.

256. Fessenden, manuscript account of the 1862 cabinet crisis, Fessenden Papers, Bowdoin College.

257. Philo S. Shelton to Thurlow Weed, Boston, 24 Dec. 1862, Weed Papers, University of Rochester.

258. Samuel Wilkeson to Sidney Howard Gay, [Washington, late Dec. 1862], Gay Papers, Columbia University.

259. Howard K. Beale, ed., *The Diary of Edward Bates, 1859–1866* (Annual Report of the American Historical Association for the Year 1930, vol. IV; Washington: U.S. Government Printing Office, 1933), 269 (entry for 19 Dec. 1862).

260. Fessenden, manuscript account of the 1862 cabinet crisis, Fessenden Papers, Bowdoin College.

261. Beale, ed., *Welles Diary*, 1:196 (entry for 20 Dec. 1802).

262. Fessenden, manuscript account of the 1862 cabinet crisis, Fessenden Papers, Bowdoin College.

263. Francis Fessenden, *Life and Public Services of William Pitt Fessenden* (2 vols.; Boston: Houghton Mifflin, 1907), 2:244; Beale, ed., *Welles Diary*, 1:196 (entry for 20 Dec. 1862).

264. Washington correspondence, 21 Dec., New York *Herald*, 22 Dec. 1862; Fessenden, manuscript account of the 1862 cabinet crisis, Fessenden Papers, Bowdoin College; Beale, ed., *Welles Diary*, 197 (entry for 20 Dec. 1862).

265. Beale, ed., *Welles Diary*, 1:196–198 (entry for 20 Dec. 1862); Fessenden, manuscript account of the 1862 cabinet crisis, Fessenden Papers, Bowdoin College.

266. Fessenden, manuscript account of the 1862 cabinet crisis, Fessenden Papers, Bowdoin College.

267. Beale, ed., *Welles Diary*, 1:201–202 (entry for 20 Dec. 1862).

268. Fredrick W. Seward interviewed by Nicolay, 9 Jan. 1879, in Burlingame, ed., *Oral History of Lincoln*, 87.

269. Washington correspondence by Agate [Whitelaw Reid], 22 Dec., Cincinnati *Gazette*, 25 Dec. 1862.

270. Madeleine Vinton Dahlgren, *Memoir of John A. Dahlgren, Rear-Admiral United States Navy* (Boston: J. R. Osgood, 1882), 383 (diary entry for 22 Dec. 1862).

271. Washington correspondence by Agate [Whitelaw Reid], 26 Mar. 1863, Cincinnati *Gazette*, scrapbook, Reid Family Papers, DLC.

272. Washington correspondence, 22 Dec. 1862, Smart, ed., *"Agate" Dispatches*, 1:253.

273. Lincoln to Seward and Chase, Washington, 20 Dec. 1862, *CWL*, 6:12.

274. Washington correspondence, 21 Dec., New York *Herald*, 22 Dec. 1862.

275. Fessenden to Elizabeth Warriner, Washington, 20–21 Dec. 1861; Fessenden to his father, Washington, 20 Dec. 1862, Fessenden Papers, Bowdoin College.

276. Pease and Randall, eds., *Browning Diary*, 1:603 (entry for 22 Dec. 1862).

277. Fessenden, manuscript account of the 1862 cabinet crisis, Fessenden Papers, Bowdoin College.

278. Beale, ed., *Bates Diary*, 291 (entry for 10 May 1863).

279. John Eaton, *Grant, Lincoln, and the Freedmen* (New York: Longmans, Green, 1907), 178.

280. Hay to Nicolay, Washington, 7 Aug. 1863, in Michael Burlingame, ed., *At Lincoln's Side: John Hay's Civil War Correspondence and Selected Writings* (Carbondale: Southern Illinois University Press, 2000), 49.

281. Burlingame and Ettlinger, eds., *Hay Diary,* 104 (entry for 30 Oct. 1863).

282. Seward to Richard M. Blatchford, Washington, 22 Dec. [1862], Lincoln Collection, Yale University.

283. Dahlgren, *Memoir,* 383–384.

284. Column by "Occasional" (John W. Forney), Washington *Sunday Chronicle,* 3 Dec. 1865.

285. Washington correspondence by Van [D. W. Bartlett], 23 Dec., Springfield, Massachusetts, *Republican,* 25 Dec. 1862.

286. Hamlin to Israel Washburn, Washington, 24 Dec. 1862, Washburn Family Papers, Washburn Memorial Library, Norlands, Maine.

287. William P. Fessenden to his son William, Washington, 21 Dec. 1862; Fessenden to his father, Washington, 20 Dec. 1862, Fessenden Papers, Bowdoin College; Fessenden to James Shepherd Pike, Portland, 5 Apr. 1863, Pike Papers, DLC.

288. Chandler to Austin Blair, Washington, 22 Dec. 1862, Blair Papers, Detroit Public Library.

289. Chandler to his wife, Washington, 10 Feb. 1863, Chandler Papers, DLC.

290. Samuel Wilkeson to Sidney Howard Gay, [Washington, ca. 21 Feb. 1863], Gay Papers, Columbia University.

291. New York *Tribune,* 27 Jan. 1863.

292. Samuel Wilkeson to Sidney Howard Gay, [Washington, ca. 21 Feb. 1863], Gay Papers, Columbia University.

293. Elizabeth Blair Lee to Samuel Phillips Lee, Silver Spring, Maryland, 14 Jan. 1863, Laas, ed., *Wartime Washington,* 231.

294. Chandler to his wife, Washington, 17 Feb. 1865, Chandler Papers, DLC.

295. Col. John Wesley Turner to Adam Badeau, New York, 12 Mar. 1863, Schoff Civil War Collection, William L. Clements Library, University of Michigan.

296. Burlingame and Ettlinger, eds., *Hay Diary,* 105 (entry for 30 Oct. 1863).

297. Washington correspondence, 18 Jan., New York *Times,* 19 Jan. 1863.

298. Washington correspondence, 20 May, Sacramento *Daily Union,* 12 June 1863, in Burlingame, ed., *Lincoln Observed,* 53.

299. Caleb B. Smith to Thurlow Weed, Washington, 29 Sept. 1862, Weed Papers, University of Rochester.

300. Davis to Swett, 26 Nov. 1862 in King, *Davis,* 204.

301. Usher to R. W. Thompson, Washington, 25 July 1862, Thompson Papers, Indiana State Library, Indianapolis.

302. Beale, ed., *Welles Diary,* 1:191 (entry for 12 Dec. 1862).

303. Washington correspondence, 18 Dec., New York *Evening Post,* 18 Dec. 1862.

304. Waitman Willey and Jacob B. Blair to Francis H. Pierpont, telegram, Washington, 27 Dec. 1862, Pierpont Papers, West Virginia University.

305. J. B. Blair to Pierpont, telegram, Washington, 29 Dec. 1862, ibid.

306. Pierpont to Jacob B. Blair, Wheeling, 20 Dec. 1862, AL MSS DLC.

307. From Pierpont's reminiscences, Fairmont, West Virginia, correspondence, 17 Mar. [1876], Wheeling *Intelligencer,* clipping pasted into Pierpont's scrapbook number 2, Pierpont Papers, West Virginia University.

308. *CWL,* 6:27–28.

309. Blair's account given in the Washington correspondence by Lan, 26 Jan. [1876], Pittsburgh *Dispatch,* n.d., clipping in scrapbook number 1, Francis H. Pierpont Papers, West Virginia University; Blair's account given to Granville Parker, paraphrased in Granville Parker, *The Formation of the State of West Virginia* (Wellsburg: Glass & Son, 1875), 185–186; Waitman T. Willey, "The Final Crisis in Our Struggle for Statehood," *West Virginia Historical Magazine* 1 (1901):20–24.

310. Pierpont's reminiscences, Fairmont, West Virginia, correspondence, 17 Mar. [no year indicated], Wheeling *Intelligencer,* clipping pasted into scrapbook number 2, Pierpont Papers, West Virginia University.

311. David Davis to Laura Swett, Washington, 21 Dec. 1862; Laura R. Swett to David

Davis, Bloomington, 13 Dec. 1862, David Davis Papers, IHi.

312. David Davis to Swett, Washington, 16 Dec. 1862, ibid; Lincoln to Fanny Mc-Cullough, Washington, 23 Dec. 1862, *CWL*, 6:16–17.

313. W. W. Orme to David Davis, Bloomington, 2 Jan. 1863, David Davis Papers, IHi.

314. Francis B. Carpenter, *The Inner Life of Abraham Lincoln: Six Months at the White House* (New York: Hurd and Houghton, 1867), 84.

315. Montgomery Blair, Memorandum on Draft of Final Emancipation Proclamation, 31 Dec. 1862, AL MSS DLC.

316. Boston *Commonwealth*, 10 Jan. 1863.

317. Sermon of 26 Sept. 1862, in Edward Everett Hale, ed., *James Freeman Clarke: Autobiography, Diary and Correspondence* (Boston: Houghton Mifflin, 1899), 243.

318. Pease and Randall, eds., *Browning Diary*, 1:555 (entry for 1 July 1862). This was part of a hastily drafted paper Lincoln said he would read to the cabinet.

319. Niven, ed., *Chase Papers*, 1:349, 360 (diary entries for 31 July, 2 Aug. 1862).

320. Samuel R. Curtis to Lyman Trumbull, St. Louis, 19 Dec. 1861, Trumbull Papers, DLC.

321. W. W. Orme to David Davis, Bloomington, 7 Feb. 1863, David Davis Papers, IHi.

322. Representative Chilton A. White in V. Jacque Voegeli, *Free but Not Equal: The Midwest and the Negro during the Civil War* (Chicago: University of Chicago Press, 1967), 99.

323. John Mercer Langston, *From the Virginia Plantation to the National Capitol; or, The First and Only Negro Representative in Congress from the Old Dominion* (Hartford, CT: American Publishing, 1894), 206.

324. *U.S. Statutes at Large*, 12:599.

325. Justin Hamilton to John Sherman, Mendon, Ohio, 24 May 1862, John Sherman Papers, DLC.

326. Simeon Nash to Chase, Gallipolis, Ohio, 2 May 1862, Chase Papers, DLC.

327. Samuel J. Kirkwood to [Halleck], Des Moines, 5 Aug. 1862, letterpress copy, Kirk-

wood Papers, State Historical Society of Iowa, Iowa City.

328. Washington correspondence, 15 Sept., New York *Tribune*, 17 Sept. 1862.

329. Washington correspondence, 5 Aug., Chicago *Tribune*, 6 Aug. 1862; Washington correspondence, 4 Aug., 15 Sept., New York *Tribune*, 5 Aug., 17 Sept. 1862; Washington correspondence, 4 Aug., New York *Herald* and Cincinnati *Gazette*, 5 Aug. 1862; Chicago *Morning Post*, 7 Aug. 1862, copy, Allan Nevins Papers, Columbia University.

330. Swett to his wife Laura, New York, 10 Aug. 1862, David Davis Family Papers, IHi.

331. Washington correspondence by Jane Grey Swisshelm, 10 Feb., St. Cloud *Democrat*, 26 Feb. 1863, in Arthur J. Larsen, ed., *Crusader and Feminist: Letters of Jane Grey Swisshelm, 1858–1865* (Saint Paul: Minnesota Historical Society, 1934), 172.

332. Browning to Lincoln, Quincy, Illinois, 11 Aug. 1862, AL MSS DLC.

333. Washington correspondence by Agate [Whitelaw Reid], 25 July, Cincinnati *Gazette*, 29 July 1862.

334. Ibid.

335. Washington correspondence, 28 Jan., New York *World*, 29 Jan. 1862; Washington correspondence, 6 Feb., Philadelphia *Inquirer*, 7 Feb. 1862.

336. Robert Harryman to S. S. Cox, Newark, Ohio, 26 Jan. 1862, Cox Papers, RPB.

337. Israel Washburn to Hannibal Hamlin, Augusta, 17 and 20 Dec. 1862, Israel Washburn Papers, DLC.

338. Kirkwood to [Halleck], Des Moines, 5 Aug. 1862, letterpress copy, Kirkwood Papers, State Historical Society of Iowa, Iowa City.

339. Kirkwood to Mrs. Harriet N. Kellogg, [Des Moines], 28 Mar. [1863], letterpress copy, ibid.

340. Pease and Randall, eds., *Browning Diary*, 1:562 (entry for 24 July 1862).

341. Lincoln to John A. Dix, Washington, 14 Jan. 1863, *CWL*, 6:56.

342. Lincoln to Andrew Johnson, Washington, 26 Mar. 1863, *CWL*, 149–150.

343. Lincoln to Banks, Washington, 29 Mar. 1863, *CWL*, 6:154.

344. Lincoln to Grant, Washington, 9 Aug. 1863, *CWL*, 6:374.

345. Conversation with a committee from the Puritan Church of New York, headed by the Rev. Dr. George B. Cheever, 30 May 1863, New York *World*, 12 June 1863.

346. Washington correspondence by Van [D. W. Bartlett], 22 Apr., Springfield, Massachusetts, *Republican*, 24 Apr. 1863.

347. New York *Evening Post*, 7 Feb. 1863.

348. George Alfred Townsend, *Washington, Outside and Inside* (Cincinnati: Betts, 1874), 715.

349. Browning interviewed by Nicolay, Springfield, 17 June 1875, in Burlingame, ed., *Oral History of Lincoln*, 5.

350. N. Worth Brown and Randolph C. Downes, eds., "A Conference with Abraham Lincoln: From the Diary of Reverend Nathan Brown," *Northwest Ohio Quarterly* 22 (1949–1950):61–62.

351. *Principia*, 8 Jan. 1863, in M. Leon Perkal, "William Goodell: A Life of Reform" (Ph.D. dissertation, City University of New York, 1972), 377.

352. Mrs. Florence Weston Stanley to Dwight C. Sturges, [Needham, Massachusetts?], 7 Feb. 1935, *Christian Science Monitor*, 12 Feb. 1935.

353. Washington correspondence, 3 Jan., Sacramento *Daily Union*, 29 Jan. 1863, in Burlingame, ed., *Lincoln Observed*, 15.

354. Isaac N. Arnold, *The History of Abraham Lincoln and the Overthrow of Slavery* (Chicago: Clarke, 1866), 304.

355. Seward, *Seward*, 2:151; W. R. Livermore, "The Emancipation Pen," *Massachusetts Historical Society Proceedings* 44(1911):595–596.

356. "Emancipation Pen," 595–596; Summer, *Complete Works*, 9:435.

357. Schurz, *Reminiscences*, 2:317.

358. Alexander K. McClure, *Abraham Lincoln and Men of War-Times* (Philadelphia: Times, 1892), 284.

359. Speed to William H. Herndon, Louisville, 7 Feb. 1866, Douglas L. Wilson and Rodney O. Davis, eds., *Herndon's Informants:*

Letters, Interviews, and Statements about Abraham Lincoln (Urbana: University of Illinois Press, 1998), 197.

360. Wade to George W. Julian, Ashtabula, 29 Sept. 1862, Giddings-Julian Papers, DLC.

361. Fawn M. Brodie, *Thaddeus Stevens, Scourge of the South* (New York: W. W. Norton, 1959), 159.

362. *The Liberator* (Boston), 2 January 1863, in Wendell Garrison et al., *William Lloyd Garrison, 1805–1879: The Story of His Life Told by His Children* (4 vols.; New York: Century, 1885–1889), 4:70.

363. Tyler to his wife, Boston, 1 Jan. 1863, Jessica T. Austen, ed., *Moses Coit Tyler, 1835–1900: Selections from His Letters and Diaries* (Garden City, NY.: Doubleday, Page, 1911), 19.

364. Donald Yacovone, *Samuel Joseph May and the Dilemmas of the Liberal Persuasion, 1797–1871* (Philadelphia: Temple University Press, 1991), 173–174.

365. Maria Weston Chapman to Abby Hopper Gibbons, n.p., 5 Jan. 1863, in Sarah Hopper Emerson, ed., *Life of Abby Hopper Gibbons* (2 vols.; New York: G.P. Putnam's Sons, 1897), 1:384.

366. Tilton to Susan B. Anthony, 11 Jan. 1863, in Ida Husted Harper, *The Life and Work of Susan B. Anthony* (2 vols.; Indianapolis, IN: Hollenbeck, 1898), 1:225–226; Tilton to Garrison, New York, 9 Jan. 1863, Garrison Papers, Boston Public Library.

367. *Weekly Anglo-African* (New York), 10 Jan. 1863; Martin B. Pasternak, *Rise Now and Fly to Arms: The Life of Henry Highland Garnet* (New York: Garland, 1995), 107.

368. Douglass, speech of 6 Feb. 1863, in John W. Blassingame et al., eds., *The Frederick Douglass Papers, Series One: Speeches, Debates, and Interviews* (5 vols.; New Haven, CT: Yale University Press, 1979–1992), 3:568.

369. Ibid.

370. H. Ford Douglas to Fredrick Douglass, Colliersville, Tennessee, 8 Jan. 1863, C. Peter Ripley, ed., *The Black Abolitionist Papers* (5 vols.; Chapel Hill: University of North Carolina Press, 1985–1992), 5:166.

371. Benjamin Rush Plumly to Lincoln, Philadelphia, 1 Jan. 1863, AL MSS DLC.

372. Lucy N. Colman, letter of 1 Nov., Rochester *Express,* 10 Nov. 1864; Sojourner Truth to Oliver Johnson, 17 Nov. 1864, *National Anti-Slavery Standard* (New York), 17 Dec. 1864.

373. New York *Tribune,* 3 Jan. 1863.

374. Child to William Lloyd Garrison Haskins, Wayland, Massachusetts, 28 Dec. 1862, *Child Letters,* ed. Meltzer and Holland, 423.

375. Parker, speech of 7 May 1856, in Mason Lowance, ed., *Against Slavery: An Abolitionist Reader* (New York: Penguin Books, 2000), 288.

376. Diary of Archbishop Martin J. Spalding, 1 Jan. 1863, in Kenneth J. Zanca, "Baltimore's Catholics and the Funeral of Abraham Lincoln," *Maryland Historical Magazine* 98 (2003): 94.

377. Cincinnati *Enquirer,* 4 Jan. 1863.

378. Chicago *Times,* 3 Jan. 1863; Columbus *Crisis,* 14 Jan. 1863.

379. New York *Metropolitan Record,* n.d., copied in the New York *Evening Express,* 9 Jan. 1863.

380. New York *Journal of Commerce,* n.d., copied ibid., 3 Jan. 1863.

381. New York *Evening Express,* 9 Jan. 1863.

382. *OR,* II, 5:807–808.

383. Richmond *Enquirer,* n.d,, copied in the New York *Evening Post,* 7 Jan. 1863.

384. Caleb Cushing to Edward Everett, Newburyport, 26 Sept. 1862, draft, Cushing Papers, DLC.

385. Curtis, *Executive Power* (Boston: Little, Brown, 1862), 13.

386. Lincoln to Kirkland, Washington, 7 Dec. 1862, *CWL,* 5:544.

387. Charles P. Kirkland, *A Letter to the Hon. Benjamin R. Curtis* (New York: Latimer Bros. & Seymour, 1862), 13.

388. *Frank Leslie's Illustrated Newspaper,* 25 Oct. 1862.

389. Benjamin Moran diary, 11 Dec. 1869, DLC.

390. Washington correspondence, 3 Oct., Cincinnati *Commercial,* 4 Oct. 1862.

391. Carpenter, *Inner Life of Abraham Lincoln,* 87.

392. Edward Everett Hale, *Memories of a Hundred Years* (2 vols.; New York: Macmillan, 1904), 2:193; Carpenter, *Inner Life of Abraham Lincoln,* 90.

393. Moncure D. Conway, *Autobiography: Memories and Experiences* (2 vols.; Boston: Houghton Mifflin, 1904), 1:381.

Chapter 30. "Go Forward, and Give Us Victories"

1. Benjamin Brown French, *Witness to the Young Republic: A Yankee's Journal, 1828–1870,* ed. Donald B. Cole and John J. McDonough (Hanover, NH: University Press of New England, 1989), 417 (entry for 18 Feb. 1863).

2. George William Curtis to Charles Eliot Norton [North Shore, New York], 28 Dec. 1862, George William Curtis Papers, Harvard University; Washington correspondence, 31 Dec. 1862, Boston *Evening Journal,* 2 Jan. 1863.

3. Montgomery Meigs to Ambrose E. Burnside, Washington, 30 Dec. 1862, *The War of the Rebellion: A Compilation of the Official Records of the Union and Confederate Armies* (128 vols.; Washington: Government Printing Office, 1880–1901) [hereafter *OR*], I, 21:917.

4. Frederick Pike to J. S. Pike, Machias, 11 Oct. 1863, Pike Papers, University of Maine.

5. Henry B. Stanton to Gerrit Smith, New York, 23 Jan. 1863, May Anti-Slavery Manuscript Collection, Cornell University; Stanton to Susan B. Anthony, 16 Jan. 1863, in Ida Husted Harper, *The Life and Work of Susan B. Anthony* (2 vols.; Indianapolis: Bowen-Merrill, 1899), 1:226.

6. Washington correspondence, 16 Feb., New York *Examiner,* 19 Feb. 1863, in Michael Burlingame, ed., *Dispatches from Lincoln's White House: The Anonymous Civil War Journalism of Presidential Secretary William O. Stoddard* (Lincoln: University of Nebraska Press, 2002), 137.

7. William O. Stoddard, "White House Sketches No. 12," New York *Citizen,* 3 November 1866, in Stoddard, *Inside the White*

House in War Times: Memoirs and Reports of Lincoln's Secretary, ed. Michael Burlingame (1890; Lincoln: University of Nebraska Press, 2000), 194.

8. Washington correspondence by Van [D. W. Bartlett], 11 Mar., Springfield, Massachusetts, *Republican,* 16 Mar. 1863.

9. David Davis to W. W. Orme, Washington, 16 Feb. 1863, Orme Papers, IHi.

10. Dana to [J. K. Schubert?], Washington, 23 Feb. 1863, Dana Papers, MHi.

11. John Pendleton Kennedy to Robert C. Winthrop, Baltimore, 4 Jan. 1863, Winthrop Family Papers, IHi.

12. Hawkins Taylor to Lyman Trumbull, Washington, 26 Jan. 1863, Trumbull Papers, DLC.

13. Daniel Hamilton to Sherman, Milan, Ohio, 25 Dec. 1862, and S. S. L'Hommedieu to Sherman, Cincinnati, 18 Jan. 1863, John Sherman Papers, DLC.

14. Davis Chambers to John Sherman, Zanesville, 15 Nov. 1862, ibid.

15. Lewis D. Campbell to William B. Campbell, 20 Jan. 1863, Campbell Family Papers, Duke University, in William C. Harris, "Conservative Unionists in 1864," *Civil War History* 38 (1992):303.

16. Halstead to Chase, Cincinnati, 19 Feb. 1863, in the Cincinnati *Enquirer,* 28 Sept. 1885.

17. Halstead to John Sherman, Cincinnati, 8 Feb. 1863, Sherman Papers, DLC.

18. George S. Denison to James Denison, New Orleans, 3 Jan. 1863, 6 Sept. 1864, George S. Denison Papers, DLC.

19. Weed to John Bigelow, Albany, 16 Jan. 1863, John Bigelow, *Retrospections of an Active Life* (5 vols.; New York: Baker & Taylor, 1909–1913), 1:596.

20. Washington correspondence, 10 Feb., St. Cloud *Democrat,* 26 Feb. 1863, in Arthur J. Larsen, ed., *Crusader and Feminist: Letters of Jane Grey Swisshelm, 1858–1865* (Saint Paul: Minnesota Historical Society, 1934), 173.

21. Medill to Elihu B. Washburne, Chicago, 14 Jan. 1863, Elihu B. Washburne Papers, DLC.

22. Jackson Grimshaw to Ozias M. Hatch, Quincy, 12 Feb. 1863, Hatch Papers, IHi.

23. Cutler diary, entry for 26 Jan. 1863, in Julia Perkins Cutler, *Life and Times of Ephraim Cutler* (Cincinnati: R. Clarke, 1890), 300.

24. Dawes to his wife, Washington, 1, 12 Feb. 1863, Dawes Papers, DLC.

25. Washington correspondence, 4 Feb., Sacramento *Daily Union,* 3 Mar. 1863, in Michael Burlingame, ed., *Lincoln Observed: Civil War Dispatches of Noah Brooks* (Baltimore, MD: Johns Hopkins University Press, 1998), 22.

26. Charles Gibson to Hamilton Gamble, Washington, 4 Jan. 1863, Gamble Papers, Missouri Historical Society.

27. John W. Crisfield to his wife, Washington, 23 Jan. 1863, Crisfield Papers, Maryland Historical Society.

28. Boston *Evening Journal,* 2 Feb. 1863.

29. William Pitt Fessenden to his family, Washington, 24, 10 Jan. 1863, Francis Fessenden, *Life and Public Services of William Pitt Fessenden* (2 vols.; Boston: Houghton Mifflin, 1907), 1:265.

30. William Pitt Fessenden to William Cullen Bryant, Washington, 17 Jan. 1863, Bryant-Godwin Papers, New York Public Library.

31. John Sherman to William T. Sherman, Mansfield, Ohio, 7 May 1863, William T. Sherman Papers, DLC.

32. Washington correspondence, 5 Feb., Boston *Evening Journal,* 9 Feb. 1863.

33. Usher to Allen Hamilton, Washington, 4 Feb. 1863, copy, Richard W. Thompson Papers, LMF.

34. Moncure D. Conway, *Autobiography: Memories and Experiences* (2 vols.; Boston: Houghton Mifflin, 1904), 1:379.

35. Conway journal, 5 Feb. 1863, in John d'Entremont, *Southern Emancipator: Moncure Conway, the American Years, 1832–1865* (New York: Oxford University Press, 1987), 91–92.

36. Victor B. Howard, *Religion and the Radical Republican Movement, 1860–1870*

(Lexington: University Press of Kentucky, 1990), 57.

37. Frank Preston Stearns, *The Life and Public Services of George Luther Stearns* (Philadelphia: J. B. Lippincott, 1907), 280.

38. John Sherman to William T. Sherman, 18 May 1863, in V. Jacque Voegeli, *Free but Not Equal: The Midwest and the Negro during the Civil War* (Chicago: University of Chicago Press, 1967), 82.

39. Murat Halstead to John Sherman, Cincinnati, 8 Feb. 1863, John Sherman Papers, DLC.

40. Theodore Calvin Pease and James G. Randall, eds., *The Diary of Orville Hickman Browning* (2 vols.; Springfield: Illinois State Historical Library, 1925–1933), 1: 613 (entry for 12 Jan. 1863).

41. This statement was made on 9 January 1863. Ibid., 1:612 (entry for 10 January 1863).

42. Henry W. Bellows to his wife, Washington, 23 Apr. 1863, Bellows Papers, MHi.

43. Pease and Randall, eds., *Browning Diary*, 1:616 (entry for 19 Jan. 1863).

44. William D. Kelley, speech in New York, n.d., in Washington correspondence by Agate [Whitelaw Reid], 26 Nov., Cincinnati *Gazette*, 30 Nov. 1863.

45. New York *Evening Post*, 27 Aug. 1863.

46. Josephine Shaw Lowell diary, entry for 20 May 1863, copy, Allan Nevins Papers, Columbia University.

47. Sumner to Francis Lieber, Washington, 17 Jan. 1863, Edward Lillie Pierce, *Memoir and Letters of Charles Sumner* (4 vols.; Boston: Roberts Brothers, 1877–1893), 4:114.

48. Ward Hill Lamon, drafts and anecdotes, folder 6, Lamon Papers, CSmH.

49. David Davis to Leonard Swett, Washington, 23 Jan. 1863, David Davis Papers, IHi.

50. Washington correspondence by Noah Brooks, 22 July, Sacramento *Daily Union*, 13 Aug. 1863, in Burlingame, ed., *Lincoln Observed*, 60.

51. Lincoln to Halleck, Washington, 15 Jan. 1862, Roy P. Basler et al., eds., *Collected Works of Abraham Lincoln* [hereafter *CWL*] (8 vols.

plus index; New Brunswick, NJ: Rutgers University Press, 1953–1955), 5:100.

52. Curtis to Halleck, Pea Ridge, 10 Mar. 1862, Curtis Papers, State Historical Society of Iowa, Des Moines.

53. Colonel George G. Lyon to Sigel, Fairfax Courthouse, [Virginia], 10 Oct. 1862, Sigel Papers, New-York Historical Society.

54. Caspar Butz to Sigel, Chicago, 25 Dec. 1862, ibid.

55. Lincoln to Sigel, Washington, 5 Feb. 1863, *CWL*, 6:93.

56. Washington correspondence by Noah Brooks, 12 Apr., Sacramento *Daily Union*, 8 May 1863, in Burlingame, ed., *Lincoln Observed*, 44.

57. James B. Fry in Allen Thorndike Rice, ed., *Reminiscences of Abraham Lincoln by Distinguished Men of His Time* (New York: North American, 1886), 392.

58. Lincoln to Burnside, Washington, 27 July 1863, *CWL*, 6:350; Albert D. Richardson, *A Personal History of Ulysses S. Grant* (Hartford, CT: American Publishing Company, 1868), 336–337.

59. Washington correspondence, 20 Jan., Boston *Evening Journal*, 22 Jan. 1863.

60. Pope to Henry H. Sibley, St. Paul, 28 Sept. 1862, *OR*, I, 13:686.

61. Pope to Halleck, St. Paul, 23 Sept. 1863, ibid., 13:663–664.

62. Lincoln to Stanton, Washington, 20 Sept. 1862, *CWL*, 5:432.

63. Lincoln to Halleck, Headquarters, Army of the Potomac, 3 Oct. 1862, *CWL*, 5:449.

64. David A. Nichols, *Lincoln and the Indians: Civil War Policy and Politics* (Columbia: University of Missouri Press, 1978), 95, 98.

65. Ibid., 96.

66. Washington *Daily Morning Chronicle*, 12 Nov. 1862.

67. *CWL*, 5:493.

68. John Pope to Lincoln, St. Paul, 11 Nov. 1862, AL MSS DLC.

69. Ramsey to Lincoln, St. Paul, 10 Nov. 1862, *OR*, I, 13:787.

70. Jane Grey Swisshelm, *Half a Century* (Chicago: J. G. Swisshelm, 1880), 223.

71. Washington correspondence, 28 Nov., New York *Tribune,* 29 Nov. 1862.

72. Unidentified Minnesota newspaper copied in the Washington correspondence, 22 Nov., New York *Times,* 23 Nov. 1862.

73. Stephen R. Riggs to Lincoln, Saint Anthony, 17 Nov. 1862, AL MSS DLC.

74. Thaddeus Williams to Lincoln, St. Paul, 22 Nov. 1862, ibid.

75. Washington correspondence, 5 Dec., New York *Tribune,* 6 Dec. 1862.

76. Lincoln to the Senate, 11 Dec. 1862, *CWL,* 5:551.

77. Ramsey diary, 23 Nov. 1864, in Don E. Fehrenbacher and Virginia Fehrenbacher, eds., *Recollected Words of Abraham Lincoln* (Stanford, CA: Stanford University Press, 1996), 372.

78. Washington correspondence, 23 Feb., St. Cloud *Democrat,* 5 Mar. 1863, Larsen, ed., *Crusader and Feminist,* 184.

79. Washington correspondence by Jane Grey Swisshelm, 1 May, St. Cloud *Democrat,* 14 May 1863, ibid., 225; Swisshelm, *Half a Century,* 234.

80. Cyrus Aldrich, Morton S. Wilkinson, and William Windom to Lincoln, Washington, 3 Dec. 1862, Washington *Evening Star,* 5 Dec. 1862; Nichols, *Lincoln and the Indians,* 104.

81. Dole to Caleb B. Smith, Washington, 10 Nov. 1862, New York *Tribune,* 8 Dec. 1862.

82. Henry B. Whipple, *Light and Shadows of a Long Episcopate: Being Reminiscences and Recollections of the Right Reverend Henry Benjamin Whipple* (New York: Macmillan, 1899), 136–137.

83. Hiram M. Chittenden, *History of Early Steamboat Navigation on the Missouri River: Life and Adventures of Joseph La Barge* (New York: F. P. Harper, 1903), 342.

84. John Beason to Henry W. Bellows, Philadelphia, [1862], Bellows Papers, MHi.

85. Nichols, *Lincoln and the Indians,* 145.

86. Washington correspondence by Van [D. W. Bartlett], 14 Jan., Springfield, Massachusetts, *Republican,* 16 Jan. 1863.

87. Nicolay to Therena Bates, Washington, 4 Jan. 1863, in Michael Burlingame, ed., *With Lincoln in the White House: Letters, Memoranda, and Other Writings of John G. Nicolay, 1860–1865* (Carbondale: Southern Illinois University Press, 2000), 102.

88. Howard K. Beale and Alan W. Brownsword, eds., *Diary of Gideon Welles, Secretary of the Navy under Lincoln and Johnson* (3 vols.; New York: W. W. Norton, 1960), 2:280 (entry for 14 Apr. 1865).

89. Lincoln to Rosecrans, Washington, 5 Jan., 31 Aug. 1863, *CWL,* 6:39, 424–425.

90. Garfield to Rosecrans, 18 Dec. 1863, in Allan Nevins, *The War for the Union* (4 vols.; New York: Scribner, 1959–1971), 3:203.

91. Lincoln to Burnside, Washington, 30 Dec. 1862, *CWL,* 6:22.

92. Lincoln to Halleck, Washington, 1 Jan. 1863, *CWL,* 6:31.

93. Halleck to Burnside, Washington, 7 Jan. 1863 [misdated 1862], Schoff Civil War Collection, William L. Clements Library, University of Michigan.

94. Lincoln to Burnside, Washington, 8 Jan. 1863, *CWL,* 6:46.

95. Fessenden to his son William, Washington, 10 Jan. 1863, Fessenden Papers, Bowdoin College.

96. Charles Francis Adams, Jr., *Charles Francis Adams, 1835–1915: An Autobiography* (Boston: Houghton Mifflin, 1916), 161.

97. "Excerpts from the Journal of Henry J. Raymond," *Scribner's Monthly* 19 (Mar. 1880): 705.

98. W. B. Franklin to Richard Henry Dana, York, Pennsylvania, 3 June 1863, Dana Papers, MHi.

99. James G. Blaine to E. B. Washburne, Auburn, Maine, 6 May 1863, Elihu B. Washburne Papers, DLC.

100. Noah Brooks, *Washington in Lincoln's Time* (New York: Century, 1895), 52.

101. Carl Schurz, *The Reminiscences of Carl Schurz* (3 vols.; New York: McClure, 1907–1908), 2:403.

102. Lincoln to Hooker, Washington, 26 Jan. 1863, *CWL*, 6:78–79.

103. Brooks, *Washington in Lincoln's Time*, 53.

104. Nicolay to Robert Todd Lincoln, 1878 [no day or month indicated], in Helen Nicolay, *Lincoln's Secretary: A Biography of John G. Nicolay* (New York: Longmans, Green, 1949), 278.

105. Noah Brooks, *Abraham Lincoln and the Downfall of American Slavery* (New York: G. P. Putnam's Sons, 1894), 356–357.

106. Henry to his wife, Washington, 12 Apr. 1863, Henry Papers, IHi.

107. Nicolay to Therena Bates, Washington, 8 Feb. 1863, in Burlingame, ed., *With Lincoln in the White House*, 104.

108. Nicolay to Therena Bates, Washington, 8 Mar. 1863, ibid., 105.

109. Nicolay to Therena Bates, Washington, 5 Apr. 1863, ibid., 108.

110. Colfax, *Life and Principles of Abraham Lincoln: Address Delivered at the Court House Square, at South Bend, April 24, 1865* (Philadelphia: J. B. Rodgers, 1865), 14.

111. Washington correspondence by Whitelaw Reid, ca. 7 Mar. 1863, Cincinnati *Gazette*, n.d., scrapbook, Reid Family Papers, DLC.

112. Fox to Du Pont, Washington, 6 Sept. 1862, 16 Feb. 1863, in Robert Means Thompson and Richard Wainwright, eds., *Confidential Correspondence of Gustavus Vasa Fox, Assistant Secretary of the Navy, 1861–1865* (2 vols.; New York: Printed for the Naval History Society by the De Vinne Press, 1918–1919), 1:154–155, 180.

113. Fox to Du Pont, Washington, 16, 20 Feb. 1863, John D. Hayes, ed., *Samuel Francis Du Pont: A Selection from His Civil War Letters* (3 vols.; Ithaca, NY: Published for the Eleutherian Mills Historical Library by the Cornell University Press, 1969), 2:450.

114. A. D. Richardson to Sydney Howard Gay, Washington, 20 Mar. 1863, Gay Papers, Columbia University.

115. Madeleine Vinton Dahlgren, *Memoir of John A. Dahlgren, Rear-Admiral United States Navy* (Boston: J. R. Osgood, 1882), 389 (diary entry for 29 Mar. 1863).

116. James M. Merrill, *The Making of an Admiral: A Biography of Samuel Francis Du Pont* (New York: Dodd, Mead, 1986), 289.

117. Du Pont to his wife, Port Royal, 27 Mar. 1863, *Du Pont Correspondence*, ed. Hayes, 2:516–517.

118. Fox to Du Pont, Washington, 12 Feb. 1863, Thompson and Wainwright, eds., *Confidential Correspondence of Fox*, 1:178.

119. Gideon Welles, *Lincoln and Seward* (New York: Sheldon, 1874), 200.

120. Beale, ed., *Welles Diary*, 2:236 (entry for 16 Feb. 1863).

121. Noah Brooks, "Personal Recollections of Abraham Lincoln," in Burlingame, ed., *Lincoln Observed*, 212-213.

122. Dahlgren, *Memoir of Dahlgren*, 390 (diary entry for 26 Apr. 1863).

123. Adams S. Hill to Sydney Howard Gay, Washington, 14 Apr. 1863, Gay Papers, Columbia University.

124. "President Lincoln's Notion for Harbor Defense," unidentified clipping, [1885], Nicolay Papers, DLC.

125. Nicolay to Therena Bates, Washington, 16 Apr. 1863, Burlingame, ed., *With Lincoln in the White House*, 109.

126. Washington correspondence, 1 Jan., Sacramento *Daily Union*, 4 Feb. 1864, in Burlingame, ed., *Lincoln Observed*, 100–101.

127. T. J. Barnett to S. L. M. Barlow, Washington, 12, 27 Oct. 1862, Barlow Papers, CSmH.

128. Lincoln to Hunter and Du Pont, Washington, 14 Apr. 1863, *CWL*, 6:174.

129. Henry Winter Davis to Du Pont, 2 May 1863, *Du Pont Correspondence*, ed. Hayes, 3: 80–82.

130. Welles to his son Edgar, Washington, 13 Dec. 1863, Welles Papers, DLC.

131. David Davis to William H. Hanna, Washington, 8 Feb. 1863, David Davis Papers, IHi.

132. Letter by Walter Carter, 27 Apr. 1863, Robert Goldthwaite Carter, *Four Brothers in Blue; or, Sunshine and Shadows of the War of the Rebellion, A Story of the Great Civil War from*

Bull Run to Appomattox (Washington, DC: Gibson Brothers, 1913), 235.

133. Stephen Minot Weld, *War Diary and Letters of Stephen Minot Weld* (Cambridge, MA: Riverside Press, 1912), 170 (diary entry for 5 Apr. 1863).

134. Undated letter in Carter, *Four Brothers in Blue*, 237.

135. Richard S. Skidmore, ed., *The Civil War Journal of Billy Davis: From Hopewell, Indiana to Port Republic, Virginia* (Greencastle, IN: Nugget Publishers, 1989), 134, in William C. Davis, *Lincoln's Men: How President Lincoln Became Father to an Army and a Nation* (New York: Free Press, 1999), 65.

136. Darius N. Couch in *Battles and Leaders of the Civil War*, ed. Robert Underwood Johnson and Clarence Clough Buel (4 vols.; New York: Century, 1887–1888), 3:120.

137. Brooks, *Washington in Lincoln's Time*, 50–51.

138. Washington correspondence, 12 Apr., Sacramento *Daily Union*, 8 May 1863, in Burlingame, ed., *Lincoln Observed*, 42.

139. Washington correspondence by C., 9 Sept., Chicago *Tribune*, 14 Sept. 1861.

140. G. G. Benedict, *Vermont in the Civil War* (2 vols.; Burlington, VT: Free Press, 1886), 1:133.

141. Washington *Sunday Morning Chronicle* in Carl Sandburg, *Abraham Lincoln: The War Years* (4 vols.; New York: Harcourt, Brace, 1939), 1:531.

142. Paschal P. Ripley to Lincoln, Montpelier, Vermont, 9 Jan. 1865, AL MSS DLC.

143. Dawes, "A Study of Abraham Lincoln," typescript, pp. 53–57, Dawes Papers, DLC.

144. Michael Burlingame and John R. Turner Ettlinger, eds., *Inside Lincoln's White House: The Complete Civil War Diary of John Hay* (Carbondale: Southern Illinois University Press, 1997), 64 (entry for 18 July 1863).

145. William O. Stoddard, "White House Sketches No. 7," New York *Citizen*, 29 Sept. 1866, in Stoddard, *Inside the White House in War Times*, ed. Burlingame, 171.

146. General George Stoneman, statement dated 1881, in Osborn H. Oldroyd, ed., *The Lincoln Memorial: Album-Immortelles* (New York: G. W. Carleton, 1883), 221.

147. Holt, interview with Nicolay, Washington, 29 Oct. 1875, in Michael Burlingame, ed., *An Oral History of Abraham Lincoln: John G. Nicolay's Interviews and Essays* (Carbondale: Southern Illinois University Press, 1996), 69.

148. Jonathan T. Dorris, "President Lincoln's Clemency," *Lincoln Herald*, 55 (1953):2–12; P. S. Ruckman, Jr., David Kincaid, "Inside Lincoln's Clemency Decision Making," *Presidential Studies Quarterly* 29 (1999): 84–99.

149. Colfax, *Life and Principles of Lincoln*, 17.

150. Reminiscences of J. H. Van Alen in Van Alen to the editors of the New York *Evening Post*, New York, 22 Apr., New York *Evening Post*, 11 May 1865.

151. Holt interviewed by Nicolay, Washington, 29 Oct. 1875, in Burlingame, ed., *Oral History of Lincoln*, 69-70.

152. Burlingame and Ettlinger, eds., *Hay Diary*, 64 (entry for 18 July 1863).

153. Mary A. Livermore, *My Story of the War* (Hartford, CT: A. D. Worthington, 1890), 568.

154. John D. Paxton, Lynchburg, VA., "Abraham Lincoln at Bay," manuscript in the J. G. Randall Papers, DLC.

155. Dawes, "A Study of Abraham Lincoln," typescript, pp. 53–57, Dawes Papers, DLC.

156. Washington correspondence by Ben: Perley Poore, 2 Feb., Boston *Evening Journal*, 4 Feb. 1863; Washington *Sunday Chronicle*, 15 June 1862.

157. Julia Lorrilard Butterfield, ed., *A Biographical Memorial of General Daniel Butterfield* (New York: Grafton Press, 1904), 161–162.

158. Washington correspondence, 12 Apr., Sacramento *Daily Union*, 8 May 1863, in Burlingame, ed., *Lincoln Observed*, 43.

159. Egbert L. Viele, "Lincoln as a Story-Teller," in William Hayes Ward, ed., *Abraham Lincoln: Tributes from His Associates* (New York: T. Y. Crowell, 1895), 124.

160. Memorandum on Hooker's campaign against Richmond, [ca. 6–10 Apr. 1863], *CWL*, 6:164–165.

161. Henry to his wife, Washington, 12 Apr. 1863, Henry Papers, IHi.

162. Henry W. Bellows to his wife and daughter, Washington, 19 Apr. 1863, Bellows Papers, MHi.

163. Marszalek, *Halleck*, 171.

164. Brooks, *Washington in Lincoln's Time*, 52.

165. Brooks, *Lincoln and the Overthrow of American Slavery*, 357.

166. "A Word about Hooker," Chicago *Tribune*, 5 February 1863; Washington correspondence, 28 January 1863, ibid.

167. T. Harry Williams, *Lincoln and His Generals* (New York: Alfred A. Knopf, 1952), 232.

168. Couch in *Battles and Leaders of the Civil War*, ed. Johnson and Buel, 3:155.

169. Army correspondence by A. R. W., near Falmouth, 9 May, Boston *Evening Journal*, 12 May 1863.

170. Lincoln to Hooker, Washington, 15 Apr. 1863, *CWL*, 6:175.

171. Memorandum, 28 Apr. 1863, *CWL*, 6:190–191.

172. E. A. S. Clarke to W. P. Palmer, New York, 3 Apr. 1914, Palmer Collection, Western Reserve Historical Society.

173. Washington correspondence, 2 May, Sacramento *Daily Union*, 27 May 1863, in Burlingame, ed., *Lincoln Observed*, 49.

174. Lincoln to Hooker, Washington, 28 Apr. 1863, *CWL*, 6:189–190.

175. Robert C. Winthrop, Sr., to Robert C. Winthrop, Jr., New York, 27 Apr. 1863, Winthrop Family Papers, MHi.

176. Washington correspondence by Van [D. W. Bartlett], 11 Mar., Springfield, Massachusetts, *Republican*, 14 Mar. 1863.

177. Beale, ed., *Welles Diary*, 1:291 (entry for 4 May 1863).

178. *CWL*, 6:196; Daniel Butterfield to Lincoln, Head Quarters, Army of the Potomac, 3 May 1863, AL MSS DLC.

179. Lincoln to Daniel Butterfield, Washington, 3 May 1863, Roy P. Basler, ed.,

Collected Works of Abraham Lincoln, First Supplement (Westport, CT: Greenwood Press, 1974), 186–187.

180. Nicolay to Therena Bates, Washington, 3 May 1863, in Burlingame, ed., *With Lincoln in the White House*, 110–111.

181. Reminiscences of John W. Forney in a lecture delivered in Nov. 1865 before the Ladies' Soldiers' Aid Society of Weldon, Pennsylvania, New York *Evening Post*, 30 Nov. 1865.

182. Washington correspondence, 8 May, Sacramento *Daily Union*, 5 June 1863, in Burlingame, ed., *Lincoln Observed*, 50; Brooks, *Washington in Lincoln's Time*, 58.

183. John Sherman to William T. Sherman, Mansfield, Ohio, 7 May 1863, William T. Sherman Papers, DLC.

184. "Lincoln as the Loneliest Man," clipping from the Drayter [?] *Gleaner*, 2 Nov. 1937, LMF.

185. Wendell Phillips, *Speeches, Lectures, and Letters* (Boston: Walker, Wise, 1864), 549.

186. Boston *Traveller*, n.d., copied in the New York *World*, 29 May 1863.

187. Bellows to Mrs. Schuyler, New York, 3 Feb. 1863, Bellows Papers, MHi.

188. Medill to Nicolay, Niagara Falls, 17 Aug. 1863, Nicolay Papers, DLC.

189. Washington correspondence by Agate [Whitelaw Reid], 29 Oct., Cincinnati *Gazette*, 3 Nov. 1863.

190. Beale, ed., *Welles Diary*, 1:336 (entry for 20 June 1863).

191. Meade to his wife, 8 May 1863, in George Gordon Meade, ed., *The Life and Letters of George Gordon Meade* (2 vols.; New York: Charles Scribner's Sons, 1913), 1:372.

192. Lincoln to Hooker, Headquarters, Army of the Potomac, 7 May 1863, *CWL*, 201.

193. Washington correspondence, 8 May, Sacramento *Daily Union*, 5 June 1863, in Burlingame, ed., *Lincoln Observed*, 51.

194. Lincoln to Hooker, Washington, 14 May 1863, *CWL*, 6:217.

195. Meade, *Meade*, 1:385.

196. Washington correspondence by Whitelaw Reid, 25 May 1863, Cincinnati *Gazette*, n.d., scrapbook, Reid Family Papers, DLC.

197. Leander Jay S. Turnkey to Matthew Simpson, Olympia, 23 Feb. 1863, Simpson Papers, DLC.

198. James [Hill?] to Edward McPherson, Chambersburg, Pennsylvania, 19 Dec. 1862, Edward McPherson Papers, DLC.

199. Washington correspondence, 5 June, Boston *Commonwealth*, 12 June 1863.

200. Washington correspondence, 4 July, Sacramento *Daily Union*, 28 July 1863, in Burlingame, ed., *Lincoln Observed*, 56.

201. Lincoln to Hooker, Washington, 5 June 1863, *CWL*, 6:249.

202. Marszalek, *Halleck*, 175.

203. Lincoln to Hooker, Washington, 10 June 1863, *CWL*, 6:257.

204. Beale, ed., *Welles Diary*, 1:328–329 (entry for 14 June 1863).

205. Garfield to J. Harrison Rhodes, Washington, 22 Sept. 1862, in Frederick D. Williams, ed., *The Wild Life of the Army: Civil War Letters of James A. Garfield* (East Lansing: Michigan State University Press, 1964), 138–139.

206. Lincoln to Schenck, Washington, 14 June 1863, *CWL*, 6:274.

207. Lincoln to Hooker, Washington, 14 June 1863, *CWL*, 6:273.

208. Elizabeth Blair Lee to Samuel Phillips Lee, Silver Spring, Maryland, 23 June 1863, Virginia Jeans Laas, ed., *Wartime Washington: The Civil War Letters of Elizabeth Blair Lee* (Urbana: University of Illinois Press, 1991), 276.

209. Joseph Hooker to Lincoln, Fairfax Station, 16 June 1863, AL MSS DLC.

210. Lincoln to Hooker, Washington, 16 June 1863, *CWL*, 6:282.

211. Ibid., 6:281.

212. Beale, ed., *Welles Diary*, 1:340 (entry for 23 June 1863).

213. Ibid., 1:344 (entry for 26 June 1863).

214. George S. Boutwell in Rice, ed., *Reminiscences of Lincoln*, 128.

215. Nevins, *War for the Union*, 3:95.

216. Brooks, *Washington in Lincoln's Time*, 59–60.

217. Lincoln to Meade, Washington, 27 July 1863, *CWL*, 6:350.

218. Brooks, *Washington in Lincoln's Time*, 18–19.

219. Horace White, *The Life of Lyman Trumbull* (Boston: Houghton Mifflin, 1913), 203.

220. Card by Vallandigham, Cincinnati *Enquirer*, 10 Nov. 1860, in *The Record of Hon. C. L. Vallandigham on Abolition, the Union and the Civil War* (Columbus: J. Walter, 1863), 91.

221. *Congressional Globe*, 37th Congress, 2nd Session, Appendix 52–60.

222. *OR*, I, 23, 2:237.

223. James Madison Cutts, Jr., to Lincoln, Cincinnati, 20, 26 July 1863, AL MSS DLC.

224. *OR*, II, 5:636, 641.

225. *American Annual Cyclopædia and Register of Important Events of the Year 1863* (New York: D. Appleton, 1864), 689.

226. Ibid., 799.

227. New York *Herald*, 19 May 1863.

228. *National Anti-Slavery Standard* (New York), and New York *Independent*, n.d., quoted in *The Crisis* (Columbus), 27 May 1863.

229. Nathaniel P. Tallmadge to William H. Seward, Fond du Lac, Wisconsin, 24 May 1863, AL MSS DLC.

230. *Harper's Weekly*, 30 May 1863.

231. *American Annual Cyclopedia, 1863*, 474.

232. Ibid., 481.

233. Stanton to Burnside, Washington, 8 May 1863, Burnside Papers, Generals Papers and Books, Record Group 94, National Archives.

234. Lincoln to Burnside, Washington, 29 May 1863, *CWL*, 6:237.

235. Edward McPherson, *The Political History of the United States of America during the Great Rebellion* (Washington, DC: Philp & Solomons, 1865), 162.

236. Chicago *Times*, 28 Feb. 1863, in Craig D. Tenney, "Major General A. E. Burnside and the First Amendment: A Case Study of Civil War Freedom of Expression" (Ph.D. dissertation, Indiana University, 1977), 70.

237. Grant to Hurlbut, Lake Providence, Louisiana, 13 Feb. 1863, *OR*, I, 24, 3:50.

238. Stanton to Burnside, Washington, 1 June 1863, *OR*, II, 5:724.

239. Isaac N. Arnold and Lyman Trumbull to Lincoln, Chicago, 3 June 1863, forwarding F. C. Sherman and several others to Lincoln, Chicago, 3 June 1863, AL MSS DLC.

240. Illinois Legislature, Resolutions, 4 June 1863, Springfield, AL MSS DLC.

241. Lincoln to Erastus Corning & others, Washington [12 June] 1863, *CWL*, 6:260–269.

242. New York *World*, 16 June 1863.

243. George William Curtis to Charles Eliot Norton, [North Shore, New York], 19 June 1863, Curtis Papers, Harvard University.

244. John G. Nicolay and John Hay, *Abraham Lincoln: A History* (10 vols.; New York: Century, 1890), 7:349.

245. Barney to Chase, New York, 16 June 1863, Chase Papers, Historical Society of Pennsylvania.

246. *American Annual Cyclopædia for 1863,* 803.

247. *CWL*, 6:302.

248. Alexander K. McClure to Lincoln, Philadelphia, 30 June 1863, AL MSS DLC.

249. Lincoln to McClure, Washington, 30 June 1863, *CWL*, 6:311.

250. Statement of John Harper in George C. Gorham, *Life and Public Services of Edwin M. Stanton* (2 vols.; Boston: Houghton Mifflin, 1899), 2:99.

251. Horace Porter, *Campaigning with Grant* (New York: Century, 1897), 248.

252. Marszalek, *Halleck,* 175–176.

253. Reminiscences of Tannatt, typescript dated 1913, F. F. Browne Papers, Newberry Library, Chicago.

254. James B. Fry in Rice, ed., *Reminiscences of Lincoln,* 402.

255. Burlingame and Ettlinger, eds., *Hay Diary,* 62 (entry for 14 July 1863).

256. Lincoln to Halleck, Washington, 6 July 1863, *CWL*, 6:318.

257. Fehrenbacher and Fehrenbacher, eds., *Recollected Words of Lincoln,* 480.

258. Halleck to Meade, Washington, 8 July 1863, *OR*, I, 27, 1:85.

259. Marszalek, *Halleck,* 179.

260. *OR*, I, 27, 1:84.

261. Elizabeth Blair Lee to Samuel Phillips Lee, Washington, 4 July 1863, Laas, ed., *Wartime Washington,* 283.

262. Tarbell, *Life of Lincoln,* 3:141–142.

263. Beale, ed., *Welles Diary,* 1:363–364 (entry for 7 July 1863).

264. Robert Todd Lincoln, memo sent to Nicolay, 5 Jan. 1885, in Burlingame, ed., *Oral History of Lincoln,* 88-89.

265. *OR*, I, 27, 1:92.

266. Burlingame and Ettlinger, eds., *Hay Diary,* 62, 63 (entries for 14, 15 July 1863).

267. *OR*, I, 27, 1:92.

268. Ibid., 93–94.

269. Lincoln to Meade, Washington, 14 July 1863, *CWL*, 6:327–328.

270. William Swinton, *Campaigns of the Army of the Potomac* (New York: C.B. Richardson, 1866), 371n.

271. Lincoln to O. O. Howard, Washington, 21 July 1863, *CWL*, 6:341.

272. Burlingame and Ettlinger, eds., *Hay Diary,* 64–65 (entry for 19 July 1863).

273. Beale, ed., *Welles Diary,* 1:370-371 (entry for 14 July 1863).

274. Ibid., 1:383 (entry for 24 July 1863).

275. Ibid., 1:439 (entry for 21 Sept. 1863).

276. Dana to James Shepherd Pike, 29 July 1863, in Benjamin P. Thomas and Harold M. Hyman, *Stanton: The Life and Times of Lincoln's Secretary of War* (New York: Alfred A. Knopf, 1962), 275.

277. Washington correspondence, 17 July 1863, Cincinnati *Gazette,* n.d., Reid Family Papers, scrapbook, DLC; David Davis to Julius Rockwell, Bloomington, Illinois, 19 Aug. 1863, Davis Papers, DLC.

278. Verses on Lee's invasion of the North, [19 July 1863], Basler, ed., *Collected Works of Lincoln, First Supplement,* 194.

279. Peter Cozzens, ed., *Battles and Leaders of the Civil War,* vol. 6 (Urbana: University of Illinois Press, 2004), 264.

280. *OR,* IV, 2:687.

281. Grant to Halleck, before Vicksburg, 7 March 1863, *OR*, I, 24, 1:19.

282. Dahlgren, *Memoir,* 389 (diary entry for 29 Mar. 1863); Albert D. Richardson to Sydney Howard Gay, Washington, 20 Mar. 1863, Gay Papers, Columbia University; Albert D. Richardson, *The Secret Service: The Field, the Dungeon, and the Escape* (Hartford, CT: American Publishing, 1865), 324–325.

283. Anson G. Henry to his wife, Washington, 12 Apr. 1863, Henry Papers, IHi.

284. Fox to D. G. Farragut, Washington, 2 Apr. 1863, in Thompson and Wainwright, eds., *Correspondence of Fox,* 1:331.

285. Thomas and Hyman, *Stanton,* 269.

286. Lincoln to McClernand, Washington, 22 Jan. 1863, *CWL,* 6:70.

287. Washington correspondence by D. W. Bartlett, 6 June, New York *Independent,* 11 June 1863.

288. Washington correspondence, 25 May 1863, Philadelphia *Inquirer,* copied in the Chicago *Tribune,* 29 May 1863, in Fehrenbacher and Fehrenbacher, eds., *Recollected Words of Lincoln,* 11.

289. Albert B. Chandler in Ward, ed., *Lincoln: Tributes from His Associates,* 220.

290. Brooks, "Personal Recollections of Lincoln," in Burlingame, ed., *Lincoln Observed,* 217.

291. Beale, ed., *Welles Diary,* 1:364–365 (entry for 7 July 1863).

292. Response to a serenade, 7 July 1863, *CWL,* 6:319–320.

293. Charles Ray Wilson, "The Cincinnati Daily Enquirer and Civil War Politics: A Study of Copperhead Opinion" (Ph.D. dissertation, University of Chicago, 1934), 224.

294. G. Dean to S. S. Cox, n.p., 10 July 1863, Cox Papers, RPB.

295. Brooks, "Personal Reminiscences of Lincoln," *Scribner's Monthly* 15 (1877–1878): 567.

296. Lincoln to Grant, Washington, 13 July 1863, *CWL,* 6:326.

297. Chicago *Republican,* n.d., copied in the New York *Evening Post,* 14 June 1865.

298. Meigs to Halleck, Washington, 22 Nov. 1862, Banks Papers, DLC.

299. Lincoln to Banks, Washington, 22 Nov. 1862, *CWL,* 5:505–506.

300. Washington correspondence by Whitelaw Reid, ca. 7 Mar. 1863, Cincinnati *Gazette,* n.d., clipping in scrapbook, Reid Family Papers, DLC.

301. Conway journal, 5 Feb. 1863, in d'Entremont, *Southern Emancipator,* 91–92.

302. Halleck to Banks, Washington, 23 May 1863, *OR*, I, 26, 1:500.

303. *CWL,* 6:409.

304. Lincoln to Banks, Washington, 5 Aug. 1863, *CWL,* 6:364.

305. George William Curtis to Charles Eliot Norton, North Shore, New York, 12 July 1863, Curtis Papers, Harvard University.

306. Sumner to John Murray Forbes, Washington, 25 Dec. 1862, in Sarah Forbes Hughes, ed., *Letters and Recollections of John Murray Forbes* (2 vols.; Boston: Houghton Mifflin, 1899), 1:349.

307. Washington correspondence, 24, 25 Dec., New York *Tribune,* 25, 26 Dec. 1862.

308. *OR,* I, 26, 1:45.

309. New York *Times,* 11 June 1863.

310. Dana, *Recollections,* 86.

311. Benjamin Quarles, *The Negro in the Civil War* (Boston: Little, Brown, 1953), 224.

312. New York *Tribune,* 8 Sept. 1865.

313. Grant to Lincoln, Cairo, Illinois, 23 Aug. 1863, AL MSS DLC.

314. Lincoln to James C. Conkling, Washington, 26 Aug. 1863, *CWL,* 6:408–410.

315. Charles Russell Lowell to John Murray Forbes, Centreville, 13 Sept. 1863, and to Josephine Lowell, Washington, 3 Aug. [1863], Edward W. Emerson, *Life and Letters of Charles Russell Lowell, Captain, Sixth United States Cavalry, Colonel Second Massachusetts Cavalry, Brigadier-General United States Volunteers* (Boston: Houghton Mifflin, 1907), 296, 290.

316. Washington correspondence, 20 Mar., New York *World,* 21 Mar. 1863.

317. Order of retaliation, 30 July 1863, *CWL,* 6:357.

318. *Weekly Anglo-African*, 17 Aug. 1863, in Donald Yacovone, "The Pay Crisis and the 'Lincoln Despotism,'" in Martin H. Blatt, Thomas J. Brown, and Donald Yacovone, eds., *Hope & Glory: Essays on the Legacy of the Fifty-Fourth Massachusetts Regiment* (Amherst: University of Massachusetts in association with Massachusetts Historical Society, 2001), 45.

319. This account relies most heavily on Douglass to George Luther Stearns, Philadelphia, 12 Aug. 1863, copy, Records of the Free Military School for Command of Colored Regiments, Historical Society of Pennsylvania, and Douglass's speech of 4 Dec. 1863, in John W. Blassingame et al., eds., *The Frederick Douglass Papers, Series One: Speeches, Debates, and Interviews* (5 vols.; New Haven, CT: Yale University Press, 1979–1992), 3:606–608.

320. Douglass's speech of 4 Dec. 1863, in Blassingame et al., eds., *Douglass Papers*, 3:606.

321. Address at Sanitary Fair, Baltimore, 18 Apr. 1864; Lincoln to Stanton, Washington, 17 May 1864, *CWL*, 7:302–303, 345.

322. Frederick Douglass, *Life and Times of Frederick Douglass* (Hartford, CT: Park, 1881), 423–424.

323. Lincoln to Stanton, Washington, 17 May 1864, *CWL*, 7:346.

324. Douglass, *Life and Times of Douglass*, 423.

325. New York *World*, 11 Dec. 1863.

326. Bates to Chase, St. Louis, 19 July 1863, Chase Papers, Historical Society of Pennsylvania.

327. Bates to Welles, Washington, 6 June 1863, Lincoln Collection, Yale University.

Chapter 31. "The Signs Look Better"

1. Fell to Lyman Trumbull, Cincinnati, 11 Aug. 1863, Trumbull Papers, DLC.

2. George D. Morgan to George G. Fogg, Irvington, 24 Nov. 1863, Fogg Papers, New Hampshire Historical Society.

3. Franklin B. Sanborn to Moncure D. Conway, n.p., 2 Nov. [1863, misfiled 1864], Conway Papers, Columbia University.

4. Washington correspondence, 5 July, New York *Examiner*, 9 July 1863, in Michael

Burlingame, ed., *Dispatches from Lincoln's White House: The Anonymous Civil War Journalism of Presidential Secretary William O. Stoddard* (Lincoln: University of Nebraska Press, 2002), 162–163.

5. Hay to Nicolay, Washington, 7 Aug., 11 Sept. 1863, Michael Burlingame, ed., *At Lincoln's Side: John Hay's Civil War Correspondence and Selected Writings* (Carbondale: Southern Illinois University Press, 2000), 49, 54.

6. Diary of Joseph T. Mills, 19 Aug. 1864, in Roy P. Basler et al., eds., *Collected Works of Abraham Lincoln* [hereafter *CWL*] (8 vols. plus index; New Brunswick, NJ: Rutgers University Press, 1953–1955), 7:507.

7. Amos Tuck to William E. Chandler, Boston, 12 Dec. 1864, Chandler Papers, New Hampshire Historical Society.

8. B. Rush Plumly to N. P. Banks, New Orleans, 20 Oct. 1864, Banks Papers, DLC.

9. John F. Marszalek, *Commander of All Lincoln's Armies: A Life of General Henry W. Halleck* (Cambridge, MA: Belknap Press of Harvard University Press, 2004), 183.

10. "The House Top: A Night Piece (July, 1863)," *Selected Poems of Herman Melville*, ed. Hennig Cohen (New York: Fordham University Press, 1991), 34.

11. Washington correspondence, 25 July, New York *Independent*, 30 July 1863.

12. New York *Tribune*, 15 July 1863.

13. Seymour to Samuel J. Tilden, Albany, 6 Aug. 1863, Tilden Papers, New York Public Library.

14. Thurlow Weed in the Albany *Evening Journal*, ca. 15 Apr. 1863, in Stewart Mitchell, *Horatio Seymour of New York* (Cambridge, MA: Harvard University Press, 1938), 274n.

15. John F. Seymour to his brother, Washington, 19 Jan. 1863, manuscript biography of Horatio Seymour by the governor's nephew, Horatio Seymour, in Alexander J. Wall, *A Sketch of the Life of Horatio Seymour, 1810–1886* (New York: privately printed, 1929), 29–30.

16. Horace Greeley, *The American Conflict* (2 vols.; Hartford, CT: O. D. Case, 1867), 2:502, 500.

17. Mitchell, *Horatio Seymour*, 305.

18. Philo Shelton to Thurlow Weed, Bolton, Massachusetts, 16 July 1863, Weed Papers, University of Rochester; Washington correspondence 15, 16 July, New York *Tribune*, 16, 17 July 1863.

19. Michael Burlingame and John R. Turner Ettlinger, eds., *Inside Lincoln's White House: The Complete Civil War Diary of John Hay* (Carbondale: Southern Illinois University Press, 1997), 70 (entry for 6 Aug. 1863); Lincoln to Seymour, Washington, 7 Aug. 1863, *CWL*, 6:369.

20. Lincoln to Seymour, Washington, 16 Aug. 1863, *CWL*, 6:391.

21. Seymour to Belmont, Albany, 12 Aug. 1863, in Allan Nevins, *The War for the Union* (4 vols.; New York: Scribner, 1959–1971), 3:170 (original in privately-owned Belmont Papers).

22. Marszalek, *Halleck*, 183.

23. Burlingame and Ettlinger, eds., *Hay Diary*, 74 (entry for 14 Aug. 1863).

24. Ibid., 67 (entry for 25 July 1863).

25. James R. Gilmore, *Personal Recollections of Abraham Lincoln and the Civil War* (Boston: L.C. Page, 1898), 199.

26. Burlingame and Ettlinger, eds., *Hay Diary*, 73 (entry for 13 Aug. 1863).

27. Seymour to Samuel J. Tilden, Albany, 6 Aug. 1863, Tilden Papers, New York Public Library.

28. Barnett to Barlow, Washington, 2 and 7 July 1863, Barlow Papers, CSmH.

29. Chandler to Trumbull, Detroit, 6 Aug. 1863, Trumbull Papers, DLC.

30. Ida M. Tarbell, *The Life of Abraham Lincoln* (2 vols.; New York: Lincoln Memorial Association, 1900), 2:149.

31. Reminiscences of Austin Brown, manuscript memo with penciled date of 1866 added within brackets, Austin Brown Papers, Indiana State Library.

32. *Frank Leslie's Illustrated Newspaper*, 13 Sept. 1863.

33. Howard K. Beale, ed., *The Diary of Edward Bates, 1859–1866* (Annual Report of the American Historical Association for 1930, vol.

4; Washington, DC: U.S. Government Printing Office, 1933), 306 (entry for 14 Sept. 1863).

34. Howard K. Beale and Alan W. Brownsword, eds., *Diary of Gideon Welles, Secretary of the Navy under Lincoln and Johnson* (3 vols.; New York: W. W. Norton, 1960), 1:432 (entry for 14 Sept. 1863).

35. Statement by the son of Robert B. Carnahan, U. S. district attorney for the western district of Pennsylvania, Pittsburgh, May 1896, Tarbell Papers, Allegheny College.

36. John Niven, ed., *The Salmon P. Chase Papers* (5 vols.; Kent, Ohio: Kent State University Press, 1993–1998), 1:441–442 (diary entry for 14 Sept. 1863); Beale, ed., *Welles Diary*, 1:434 (entry for 15 Sept. 1863).

37. Andrew G. Curtin to Lincoln, Harrisburg, 18 Sept. 1863, AL MSS DLC.

38. Opinion on the draft, [14 Sept.?] 1863, *CWL*, 6:448.

39. Ibid., 447–449.

40. Thomas F. Pendel, *Thirty-Six Years in the White House* (Washington, DC: Neale, 1902), 17–18.

41. *CWL*, 5:515–516; 6:8.

42. Lincoln to Curtis, Washington, 2 Jan. 1863, *CWL*, 6:34.

43. Lincoln to O. D. Filley, Washington, 22 Dec. 1863, *CWL*, 7:86.

44. Lincoln to Curtis, Washington, 5 Jan. 1863, *CWL*, 6:36–37.

45. Brown to Lincoln, Jefferson City, 7 Jan. 1863, AL MSS DLC.

46. Lincoln to Brown, Washington, 7 Jan. 1863, *CWL*, 6:42.

47. James Taussig to members of a committee of Missouri Radicals, *Missouri Democrat* (St. Louis), 9 June 1863.

48. Beale, ed., *Bates Diary*, 294 (entry for 30 May 1863).

49. James Taussig in the *Missouri Democrat* (St. Louis), 9 June 1863; Washington correspondence, 13 Nov., New York *Evening Post*, 14 Nov. 1863.

50. Henry T. Blow to Lincoln, St. Louis, Mar. 22, 1863, AL MSS DLC.

51. Lincoln to Schofield, Washington, 27 May 1863, *CWL*, 6:234.

52. Lincoln to Schofield, Washington, 13 July 1863, *CWL*, 6:326.

53. Lincoln to Henry T. Blow, Washington, 13 July 1863, *CWL*, 6:325.

54. Burlingame and Ettlinger, eds., *Hay Diary*, 66 (entry for 23 July 1863).

55. Hamilton R. Gamble to Lincoln, St. Louis, 13 July 1863, AL MSS DLC.

56. Lincoln to H. R. Gamble, Washington, 23 July 1863, *CWL*, 6:344.

57. Lincoln endorsement, [ca. 11 Apr. 1863], ibid., 6:167.

58. Noah Brooks, "Personal Recollections of Abraham Lincoln," in Michael Burlingame, ed., *Lincoln Observed: Civil War Dispatches of Noah Brooks* (Baltimore, MD: Johns Hopkins University Press, 1998), 208.

59. Curtis, manuscript journal, 27 Mar. 1864, Curtis Papers, Iowa State Archives, Des Moines.

60. Lincoln to Curtis, Washington, 8 June 1863, *CWL*, 6:253.

61. Gamble to Bates, 10 Aug. 1863, Bates Papers, Missouri Historical Society.

62. Medill to Nicolay, Niagara Falls, 17 Aug. 1863, Nicolay Papers, DLC.

63. Quoted in Albert Castel, "Order No. 11 and the Civil War on the Border," *Missouri Historical Review* 57 (1963):364.

64. Mark E. Neely, "'Unbeknownst to Lincoln': A Note on Radical Pacification in Missouri during the Civil War," *Civil War History* 44 (1998):214.

65. Lincoln to Schofield, Washington, 1 Oct. 1863, *CWL*, 6:492–493.

66. *The War of the Rebellion: A Compilation of the Official Records of the Union and Confederate Armies* (128 vols.; Washington: Government Printing Office, 1880–1901), I, 22, 1:574.

67. Shelby allegedly made this remark in 1897. Lt. Col. R. H. Hunt, *General Order No. 11* (Topeka: Kansas Commandery of the Military Order of the Loyal Legion of the United States, 1908), 6, quoted in Donald B. Connelly, *John M. Schofield and the Politics of Generalship* (Chapel Hill: University of North Carolina Press, 2006), 77.

68. Ewing to John Sherman, Kansas City, Missouri, 12 Jan. 1864, Sherman Papers, DLC.

69. Lincoln to Fletcher, Washington, 20 Feb. 1865, *CWL*, 8:308.

70. Lincoln to Schofield, Washington, 22 June 1863, *CWL*, 6:291.

71. Burlingame and Ettlinger, eds., *Hay Diary*, 88 (entry for 29 Sept. 1863).

72. Ibid., 89 (entry for 29 Sept. 1863).

73. Horace White to William P. Fessenden, Washington, 7 Nov. 1863, Fessenden Papers, DLC.

74. Beale, ed., *Bates Diary*, 308 (entry for 30 Sept. 1863).

75. Edward Bates to Lincoln, Washington, 22 Oct. 1863, AL MSS DLC.

76. Halleck to Schofield, Washington, 26 Sept. 1863, *OR*, I, 22, 2:574–575.

77. Burlingame and Ettlinger, eds., *Hay Diary*, 87 (entry for 28 Sept. 1863).

78. Walter B. Stevens, *A Reporter's Lincoln*, ed. Michael Burlingame (1916; Lincoln: University of Nebraska Press, 1998), 145–147.

79. Enos Clarke, interview with J. McCan Davis, 2 Dec. 1898, Ida M. Tarbell Papers, Allegheny College.

80. The following account of the meeting is based on a detailed memorandum by John Hay and William O. Stoddard. Michael Burlingame, ed., *At Lincoln's Side: John Hay's Civil War Correspondence and Selected Writings* (Carbondale: Southern Illinois University Press, 2000), 57–64.

81. Stevens, *A Reporter's Lincoln*, ed. Burlingame, 148–149.

82. Lane told this to Major Champion Vaughn, former editor of the Leavenworth *Times,* who told Schofield. Schofield diary, 13 Oct. 1863, in John McAllister Schofield, *Forty-Six Years in the Army* (New York: Century, 1897), 99.

83. Charles Philip Johnson, in Tarbell, *Life of Lincoln*, 2:177.

84. Burlingame and Ettlinger, eds., *Hay Diary*, 125 (entry for 10 Dec. 1863).

85. Beale, ed., *Bates Diary*, 308 (entry for 30 Sept. 1863).

86. Burlingame, ed., *At Lincoln's Side*, 64.

87. Burlingame and Ettlinger, eds., *Hay Diary*, 89–90 (entry for 30 Sept. 1863).

88. Washington correspondence by Agate [Whitelaw Reid], 5 Oct., Cincinnati *Gazette*, 8 Oct. 1863; Washington correspondence, 5 Oct., New York *Evening Post*, 6 Oct. 1863.

89. Burlingame and Ettlinger, eds., *Hay Diary*, 101 (entry for 28 Oct. 1863).

90. Ibid., 125 (entry for 10 Dec. 1863).

91. William D. Kelley, *Lincoln and Stanton* (New York: Putnam's, 1885), 86.

92. Lincoln to Drake et al., Washington, 5 Oct. 1863, *CWL*, 6:499–504.

93. Burlingame and Ettlinger, eds., *Hay Diary*, 93–94 (entry for 18 Oct. 1863).

94. Hart to Chase, St. Louis, 24 Oct. 1863, Chase Papers, DLC.

95. New York *Independent*, 29 Oct. 1863.

96. Nicolay, memorandum of 8 Dec. 1863, Michael Burlingame, ed., *With Lincoln in the White House: Letters, Memoranda, and Other Writings of John G. Nicolay, 1860–1865* (Carbondale: Southern Illinois University Press, 2000), 121.

97. New York *Commercial Advertiser*, reprinted in the St. Joseph *Morning Herald*, 31 Oct. 1863, in David DeArmond March, "The Life and Times of Charles D. Drake" (Ph.D. dissertation, University of Missouri, 1949), 249–250.

98. New York *Times*, 3 Oct. 1863.

99. Washington *Chronicle*, reprinted in the St. Joseph *Morning Herald*, 1 Nov. 1863, in March, "Drake," 250.

100. New York *Evening Post*, 3 Oct. 1863.

101. Washington correspondence by Van [D. W. Bartlett], 7 Oct., Springfield, Massachusetts, *Republican*, 9 Oct. 1863.

102. Lincoln to Schofield, Washington, 1 Oct. 1863, *CWL*, 6:492; Gamble to Lincoln, 30 Sept. 1863, draft, Gamble Papers, Missouri Historical Society.

103. Gamble to Lincoln, Saint Louis, 1 Oct. 1863, AL MSS DLC.

104. Beale, ed., *Bates Diary*, 310 (entry for 16 Oct. 1863).

105. Ralph S. Hart to Chase, St. Louis, 30 Oct. 1863, Chase Papers, DLC; Burlingame and Ettlinger, eds., *Hay Diary*, 111 (entry for 18 Nov. 1863).

106. Bates to Edwards, 2 Nov., New York *Times*, 16 Nov. 1863.

107. Brown to N. B. Judd, Washington, 11 Dec. 1863, Lincoln Collection, RPB.

108. Burlingame and Ettlinger, eds., *Hay Diary*, 127 (entry for 13 Dec. 1863).

109. Schofield, *Forty-Six Years in the Army*, 108–109.

110. *CWL*, 7:78.

111. Burlingame and Ettlinger, eds., *Hay Diary*, 129 (entry for 23 Dec. 1863).

112. Morton S. Wilkinson, interviewed by Nicolay, 22 May 1876, in Michael Burlingame, ed., *An Oral History of Abraham Lincoln: John G. Nicolay's Interviews and Essays* (Carbondale: Southern Illinois University Press, 1996), 60.

113. Washington correspondence, 26 Dec., *Ohio State Journal* (Columbus), 29 Dec. 1863.

114. Burlingame and Ettlinger, eds., *Hay Diary*, 85 (entry for 27 Sept. 1863).

115. Washington correspondence, 26 Sept., New York *Independent*, 1 Oct. 1863).

116. Hay, "Life in the White House in the Time of Lincoln," in Burlingame, ed., *At Lincoln's Side*, 133.

117. Washington *Sunday Herald*, 5 Dec. 1886, in Stephen Berry, *House of Abraham: Lincoln and the Todds, A Family Divided by War* (Boston: Houghton Mifflin, 2007), 147.

118. Katherine Helm, *The True Story of Mary, Wife of Lincoln* (New York: Harper, 1928), 188.

119. Ibid., 233.

120. Ibid., 231.

121. Emily Todd Helm to Lincoln, Lexington, 30 Oct. 1864, AL MSS DLC.

122. Burlingame, ed., *With Lincoln in the White House*, 243.

123. Burlingame and Ettlinger, eds., *Hay Diary*, 85 (entry for 27 Sept. 1863).

124. Albert B. Chandler in William Hayes Ward, ed., *Abraham Lincoln, Tributes from His Associates: Reminiscences of Soldiers, Statesmen and Citizens* (New York: T. Y. Crowell, 1895), 222; Lincoln to Burnside, Washington, 25 Sept. 1863, *CWL*, 6:480.

125. Lincoln to Rosecrans, Washington, 21 Sept. 1863, *CWL*, 6:472–473.

126. Niven, ed., *Chase Papers*, 1:453–454 (diary entry for 24 Sept. 1863).

127. Burlingame and Ettlinger, eds., *Hay Diary*, 87 (entry for 27 Sept. 1863).

128. Ibid., 99 (entry for 24 Oct. 1863).

129. Charles A. Dana, *Recollections of the Civil War: With the Leaders at Washington and in the Field in the Sixties* (New York: D. Appleton, 1898), 127, 123.

130. Lincoln to Robert A. Maxwell, Washington, 23 Sept. 1863, *CWL*, 6:475.

131. Gilmore, "Why Rosecrans Was Removed," Atlanta *Constitution*, 22 Dec. 1895.

132. Garfield to Rosecrans, 18 Dec. 1863, Nevins, *War for the Union*, 3:203.

133. New York *Tribune*, 3 Oct. 1863.

134. Greeley to Salmon P. Chase, New York, 27 Aug. 1863, Chase Papers, Historical Society of Pennsylvania.

135. Barnett to S. L. M. Barlow, Washington, 14 Sept., 10 June 1863, Barlow Papers, CSmH.

136. Lyman Trumbull to Zachariah Chandler, 4 Aug. 1863, Chandler Papers, DLC.

137. William O. Stoddard, *Inside the White House in War Times: Memoirs and Reports of Lincoln's Secretary*, ed. Michael Burlingame (1890; Lincoln: University of Nebraska Press, 2000), 73.

138. Chicago *Times*, 31 Dec. 1862.

139. T. J. Barnett to S.L.M. Barlow, Washington, 2, 6, 9, 10 July 1863, Barlow Papers, CSmH.

140. Morse to William M. Goodrich, 9 July 1863, in Nevins, *War for the Union*, 3:170–171.

141. Lincoln to Mary Todd Lincoln, Washington, 8 Aug. 1863, *CWL*, 6:372.

142. Grimshaw to Ozias M. Hatch, 8 Sept. 1862, 12 Feb. 1863, Hatch Papers, IHi.

143. *CWL*, 6:406–411.

144. Conkling to Lincoln, Springfield, 4 Sept. 1863, AL MSS DLC.

145. James A. Briggs to Salmon P. Chase, New York, 5 Sept. 1863, Chase Papers, DLC.

146. F. B. Sanborn to Moncure D. Conway, Concord, Massachusetts, 3 Sept. 1863, Conway Papers, Columbia University; *National Anti-Slavery Standard* (New York), 12 Sept. 1863.

147. Charles Sumner to Lincoln, Boston, 7 Sept. 1863, AL MSS DLC.

148. Josiah Quincy to Lincoln, Quincy, Massachusetts, 7 Sept. 1863, AL MSS DLC.

149. Allen C. Guelzo, "Defending Emancipation: Abraham Lincoln and the Conkling Letter, 1863," *Civil War History* 48 (2002): 313–337.

150. New York *Times*, 3 Sept. 1863.

151. New York *Evening Post*, 3 Sept. 1863.

152. Allan Nevins and Milton Halsey, eds., *Diary of George Templeton Strong, 1835–1875* (4 vols.); New York: Macmillan, 1952), 355 (entry for 3 Sept. 1863); *North American Review* 98 (Jan. 1864):244.

153. *Illinois State Register* (Springfield) 8 Sept. 1863.

154. F. B. Sanborn to Moncure D. Conway, Concord, Massachusetts, 3 Sept. 1863, Conway Papers, Columbia University.

155. Norton to George William Curtis, Cambridge, 3 Sept. 1863, Sara Norton and M. A. De Wolfe Howe, eds., *Letters of Charles Eliot Norton* (2 vols.; Boston: Houghton Mifflin, 1913), 1:263.

156. Hay to Nicolay, Washington, 11 Sept. 1863, in Burlingame, ed., *At Lincoln's Side*, 54.

157. Louis A. Warren, *Lincoln's Gettysburg Declaration: "A New Birth of Freedom"* (Fort Wayne, IN: Lincoln National Life Foundation, 1964), xv, 51.

158. Cairnes to George William Curtis, n.p., n.d., quoted in George William Curtis to Charles Eliot Norton, North Shore, New York, 5 Nov. 1863, Curtis Papers, Harvard University.

159. Frank L. Klement, *The Limits of Dissent: Clement L. Vallandigham & the Civil War* (Lexington: University Press of Kentucky, 1970), 240.

160. Halstead to Chase, Cincinnati, 28 Aug. 1863, Chase Papers, DLC.

161. V. Jacque Voegeli, *Free but Not Equal: The Midwest and the Negro during the Civil War* (Chicago: University of Chicago Press, 1967), 126; Klement, *Limits of Dissent*, 243–248.

162. W. F. Lyons, *Brigadier-General Thomas F. Meagher* (1870; Danbury, CT: Archer Editions Press, 1975), 182.

163. Beale, ed., *Welles Diary*, 1:470 (entry for 14 Oct. 1863).

164. Washington correspondence, 27 Nov., New Haven *Palladium*, 30 Nov. 1863.

165. Chase to Jay Cooke, Washington, 4 Sept. 1863, Chase Papers, DLC.

166. Andrew G. Curtin to Lincoln, Harrisburg, 4 Sept. 1863, AL MSS DLC.

167. Curtin to E. D. Morgan, Harrisburg, 1 Oct. 1863, Morgan Papers, New York State Library.

168. Stephen W. Sears, *George B. McClellan: The Young Napoleon* (New York: Ticknor and Fields, 1988), 357.

169. Alexander K. McClure, *Abraham Lincoln and Men of War-Times* (Philadelphia: Times, 1892), 265.

170. George William Curtis to Charles Eliot Norton, New York, 15 Oct. 1863, Curtis Papers, Harvard University.

171. Speech of October 3, New York *World*, 7 Oct. 1863.

172. Burlingame and Ettlinger, eds., *Hay Diary*, 105–106 (entry for 1 Nov. 1863).

173. James A. Briggs to Chase, New York, 2 Nov. 1863, Chase Papers, DLC.

174. Thaddeus Stevens to Chase, Lancaster, 8 Oct. 1863, Beverly Wilson Palmer, ed., *The Selected Papers of Thaddeus Stevens* (2 vols.; Pittsburgh: University of Pittsburgh Press, 1997–1998), 1:413–414.

175. Henry Winter Davis to Samuel F. Du Pont, n.p., 5 Dec. 1863, transcript, S. F.

Du Pont Papers, Hagley Museum, Wilmington, Delaware.

176. Washington correspondence by Agate [Whitelaw Reid], 28 Oct., Cincinnati *Gazette*, 2 Nov. 1863; James A. Briggs to Chase, New York, 2 Nov. 1863, Chase Papers, DLC.

177. Washington correspondence, 2 Nov., *National Anti-Slavery Standard* (New York), 7 Nov. 1863.

178. Baltimore *American*, 29 Oct. 1863.

179. Washington correspondence, 21 Oct., New York *Tribune*, 22 Oct. 1863.

180. *OR*, III, 3:861.

181. Burlingame and Ettlinger, eds., *Hay Diary*, 97 (entry for 22 Oct. 1863).

182. Donn Piatt, *Memories of the Men Who Saved the Union* (New York: Belford, Clarke, 1887), 45.

183. Lincoln to Augustus W. Bradford, Washington, 2 Nov. 1863, *CWL*, 6:556–557.

184. Washington correspondence, 9 Nov., *National Anti-Slavery Standard* (New York), 14 Nov. 1863.

185. Augustus W. Bradford to George Vickers, Annapolis, 27 Oct. 1863, Bradford Papers, Maryland Historical Society.

186. John W. Crisfield to Augustus W. Bradford, Princess Anne, Maryland, 14 Nov. 1863, Crisfield Papers, Maryland Historical Society.

187. Israel Washburn Jr. to Lincoln, Orono, Maine, 15 Sept. 1863, AL MSS DLC.

188. Lincoln to Zachariah Chandler, Washington, 20 Nov. 1863, *CWL*, 7:24.

189. Washington correspondence, 4 Nov., New York *Evening Post*, 5 Nov. 1863.

190. Response to a serenade, 7 July 1863, *CWL*, 6:319–320.

191. John Murray Forbes to Lincoln, Boston, 8 Sept. 1863, AL MSS DLC.

192. Burlingame and Ettlinger, eds., *Hay Diary*, 20 (entry for 7 May 1861).

193. *Congressional Globe*, 37th Congress, 1st Session, 4 (4 July 1861).

194. *Long Remembered: Facsimiles of the Five Versions of the Gettysburg Address in the Handwriting of Abraham Lincoln* (Washington, DC:

Library of Congress, 1963), 3; *Collier's,* 7 Feb. 1925.

195. Washington correspondence, 14 Nov., Boston *Evening Journal,* 17 Nov. 1863.

196. Washington correspondence, 18 November, ibid., 20 November 1863.

197. *CWL,* 7:17.

198. Mary Todd Lincoln to Lincoln, Washington, 18 Nov. 1863, Justin G. Turner, Linda Levitt Turner, eds., *Mary Todd Lincoln: Her Life and Letters* (New York: Alfred A. Knopf, 1972), 158.

199. Nevins, *War for the Union,* 3:446–447.

200. Washington *Daily Morning Chronicle,* 21 Nov. 1863.

201. Pittsburgh *Daily Commercial,* 23 Nov. 1863.

202. Boston *Evening Journal,* 23 Nov. 1863.

203. Philadelphia *Press,* 20 Nov. 1863.

204. Benjamin Brown French, *Witness to the Young Republic: A Yankee's Journal, 1828–1870,* ed. Donald B. Cole and John J. McDonough (Hanover, NH: University Press of New England, 1989), 435–436.

205. Josephine Forney Roedel, diary entry for 19 Nov. 1863, DLC.

206. Burlingame and Ettlinger, eds., *Hay Diary,* 113 (entry for 19 Nov. 1863).

207. Warren, *Lincoln's Gettysburg Declaration,* 79.

208. Cincinnati *Commercial,* 23 Nov. 1863.

209. Sam Wood to Bradford R. Wood, n.p., n.d., quoted in Bradford Wood to George G. Fogg, Copenhagen, Denmark, 20 Oct. 1863, Fogg Papers, New Hampshire Historical Society; Washington correspondence, 15 Aug., 13 Oct., New York *Evening Post,* 17 Aug., 14 Oct. 1863.

210. Burlingame and Ettlinger, eds., *Hay Diary,* 113 (entry for 19 Nov. 1863).

211. Philadelphia *Daily Age,* 21 Nov. 1863.

212. *Harper's Weekly,* 5 Dec. 1863.

213. Henry C. Robinson to George B. McClellan, 17 July 1864, McClellan Papers, DLC.

214. Milwaukee *Sentinel,* 26 Nov. 1863.

215. New York *Herald,* 21 Nov. 1863.

216. New York *World,* 20 Nov. 1863.

217. Boston *Evening Journal,* 23 Nov. 1863.

218. Washington *Chronicle,* 21 Nov, 1861.

219. Sophronia E. Bucklin, *In Hospital and Camp: A Woman's Record of Thrilling Incidents among the Wounded in the Late War* (Philadelphia: J. E. Potter, 1869), 195.

220. Gettysburg correspondence, 19 Nov. 1863, New York *Times,* in *Lincoln in the Times: The Life of Abraham Lincoln as Originally Reported in the New York Times,* ed. David Herbert Donald and Harold Holzer (New York: St. Martin's Press, 2005), 190.

221. Burlingame and Ettlinger, eds., *Hay Diary,* 113 (entry for 19 Nov. 1863).

222. *CWL,* 7:17–23. The manuscript which Lincoln read from is not extant. Unlike the version published by Joseph L. Gilbert, a surviving early version of the speech—the so-called Nicolay copy—does not contain "under God."

223. Columbus *Ohio State Journal,* 23 Nov. 1863.

224. Everett to Mrs. Hamilton Fish, Boston, 18 Mar. 1864, Fish Papers, DLC.

225. Cincinnati *Gazette,* 23 Nov. 1863.

226. *Ohio State Journal* (Columbus), 4 Apr. 1864.

227. Philadelphia *Press,* 21, 25 Nov. 1863.

228. Chicago *Tribune,* 20 Nov. 1863.

229. Washington *Daily Morning Chronicle,* 21 Nov. 1863.

230. Philadelphia *Evening Bulletin,* 20 Nov. 1863.

231. Springfield, Massachusetts, *Republican,* 21 Nov. 1863.

232. Providence *Daily Journal,* 20 Nov. 1863.

233. *Harper's Weekly,* 5 and 12 Dec. 1863.

234. Judith Kennedy Johnson, ed., *The Journals of Charles King Newcomb* (Providence, RI: Brown University Press, 1946), 194, 196, (entries for 21 Aug. and 23 Nov. 1863).

235. Charles Francis Adams, Jr., to Charles Francis Adams, Newport, Rhode Island, 7 Mar. 1865, in Worthington Chauncey Ford, ed., *A Cycle of Adams Letters, 1861–1865* (2 vols.; Boston: Houghton Mifflin, 1920), 2:257.

236. Everett to Lincoln, Washington, 20 Nov. 1863, AL MSS DLC.

237. Statement of James Speed in Joseph H. Barrett, *Abraham Lincoln and His Presidency* (2 vols.; New York: D. Appleton, 1924), 2:208.

238. Lincoln to Everett, Washington, 20 Nov. 1863, *CWL*, 7:24.

239. Brooks, "Personal Reminiscences of Lincoln," *Scribner's Monthly Magazine* 15 (March 1878):678.

240. Edward Dicey, *Six Months in the Federal States* (2 vols.; London: Macmillan, 1863), 1:227.

241. Columbus *Crisis*, 2 Dec. 1863.

242. Chicago *Times*, 23 Nov. 1863.

243. Gettysburg *Weekly Patriot and Union*, 26 Nov. 1863.

244. Chicago *Times*, 25 Nov. 1863.

245. Ibid., 23 Nov. 1863.

246. New York *World*, 27 November 1863.

247. *Cheshire Republican* (New Hampshire), 2 Dec. 1863.

248. New York *World*, 27 Nov. 1863.

249. Boston *Daily Courier*, 1 Dec. 1863

250. New York correspondence, 20 Nov., London *Times*, 4 Dec. 1863.

251. Warren, *Lincoln's Gettysburg Declaration*, 170.

252. Philadelphia *Evening Bulletin*, 10 Nov. 1863; Washington *Daily Morning Chronicle*, 21 Nov. 1863.

253. "Abraham Lincoln: Remarks at the Funeral Services Held in Concord, April 19, 1863," in Emerson, *Miscellanies* (Boston: Houghton Mifflin, 1884), 311.

254. Washington correspondence by "Zeta," 3 Dec., Chicago *Tribune*, 8 Dec. 1863.

255. Washington correspondence, 14 Dec., Chicago *Tribune*, 15 Dec. 1863.

256. Gustavus V. Fox to his wife Virginia, Washington, 6 Dec. 1863, Fox Papers, New-York Historical Society.

257. Washington correspondence, 14 Jan., Chicago *Tribune*, 19 Jan. 1864.

258. Samuel Wilkeson, "How Mr. Lincoln Indorsed the Negro," unidentified clipping, Redlands Shrine, A.K. Smiley Library, Redlands, California.

259. Washington correspondence, 22 Nov., New York *Times*, 23 Nov. 1863.

260. John Hay, "The Heroic Age in Washington," 1871, in Michael Burlingame, ed., *At Lincoln's Side: John Hay's Civil War Correspondence and Selected Writings* (Carbondale: Southern Illinois University Press, 2000), 128.

261. Nicolay memorandum, 7 December 1863, Burlingame, ed., *With Lincoln in the White House*, 121.

262. *CWL*, 6:457.

263. Ibid., 6:518.

Chapter 32. "I Hope to Stand Firm Enough to Not Go Backward"

1. John Savage, *The Life and Public Services of Andrew Johnson* (New York: Derby & Miller, 1866), 260.

2. Lincoln to Johnson, Washington, 3 July 1862, Roy P. Basler et al., eds., *Collected Works of Abraham Lincoln* [hereafter *CWL*] (8 vols. plus index; New Brunswick, NJ: Rutgers University Press, 1953–1955), 5:303.

3. Lincoln to Johnson, Washington, 11 July 1862, *CWL*, 5:313.

4. Lincoln to Halleck, Washington, 11 July 1862, *CWL*, 5:313.

5. Lincoln to John M. Fleming and Robert Morrow, Washington, 9 Aug. 1863, *CWL*, 6:373.

6. Lincoln to Johnson, Washington, 11 Sept. 1863, *CWL*, 6:440.

7. Lincoln to Rosecrans, Washington, 4 Oct. 1863, *CWL*, 6:498.

8. Charles Francis Adams, ed., *Memoirs of John Quincy Adams: Comprising Portions of His Diary from 1795 to 1848* (12 vols.; Philadelphia: J. B. Lippincott, 1874–1877), 11:19 (entry for 16 Sept. 1841).

9. David L. Swain to Nicholas Woodfin, 11 May 1862, in Norman D. Brown, *Edward Stanly: Whiggery's Tarheel "Conqueror"* (University: University of Alabama Press, 1974), 206.

10. William E. Doubleday to Zachariah Chandler, New York, 3 June 1862, Chandler Papers, DLC.

11. Sumner to an unidentified correspondent, 5 June 1862, *The Liberator* (Boston), 20 June 1862.

12. Moncure Conway, *Autobiography: Memories and Experiences* (2 vols.; New York: Cassell, 1904), 1:380, 383.

13. Henry W. Bellows to his son, Washington, 7 June 1862, Bellows Papers, MHi.

14. George B. Cheever to his sister Elizabeth Washburn, n.p., 3 June 1862, Cheever Family Papers, American Antiquarian Society.

15. New York *Tribune,* semiweekly ed., 20 June 1862.

16. James C. Welling diary, entry for 27 Sept. 1862, in Allen Thorndike Rice, ed., *Reminiscences of Abraham Lincoln by Distinguished Men of His Time* (New York: North American, 1886), 533.

17. *CWL,* 5:445; Stanly to Lincoln, 15 Jan. 1862, in Congressional Committee Reports, 40th Congress, 1st Session, House report 7, 331–332, in J. G. de Roulhac Hamilton, *Reconstruction in North Carolina* (Raleigh, NC: Edwards and Broughton, 1906), 89.

18. Boutwell to N. P. Banks, Washington, 26 May 1863, Banks Papers, DLC.

19. Lincoln to Reverdy Johnson, Washington, 26 July 1862, *CWL,* 5:342–343.

20. Lincoln to Cuthbert Bullitt, Washington, 28 July 1862, *CWL,* 5:344–346.

21. Lincoln to August Belmont, Washington, 31 July 1862, *CWL,* 5:350.

22. Lincoln to Butler, Washington, 14 Oct. 1862, *CWL,* 5:462–463.

23. Lincoln to Shepley, Washington, 21 Nov. 1862, *CWL,* 5:504–505.

24. John P. Usher interviewed by Nicolay, 8 Oct. 1878, in Michael Burlingame, ed., *An Oral History of Abraham Lincoln: John G. Nicolay's Interviews and Essays* (Carbondale: Southern Illinois University Press, 1996), 67.

25. Benjamin F. Flanders to Lincoln, New Orleans, 16 Jan. 1864, AL MSS DLC.

26. Lincoln to Thomas Cottman, Washington, 15 Dec. 1863, *CWL,* 7:66–67.

27. Boutwell to Banks, Washington, 5 Aug. 1863, Banks Papers, DLC.

28. Lincoln to Banks, Washington, 5 Nov. 1863, *CWL,* 7:1.

29. Flanders to Chase, New Orleans, 12 Dec. 1863, Chase Papers, Historical Society of Pennsylvania.

30. Chase to Greeley, Washington, 9 Oct. 1863, John Niven, ed., *The Salmon P. Chase Papers* (5 vols.; Kent, Ohio: Kent State University Press, 1993–1998), 4:151.

31. Lincoln to Banks, Washington, 5 Nov. 1863, *CWL,* 7:1–2.

32. Lincoln to McClernand, Washington, 8 Jan. 1863, *CWL,* 6:49.

33. Lincoln to Hurlbut, Washington, [c. Aug. 15?] 186[3], draft, *CWL,* 6:387.

34. William C. Harris, *With Charity for All: Lincoln and the Restoration of the Union* (Lexington: University Press of Kentucky, 1997), 114.

35. Lincoln to Hurlbut, Washington, 31 July 1863, *CWL,* 6:358.

36. Washington correspondence by Van [D. W. Bartlett], 24 Nov., Springfield, Massachusetts, *Republican,* 28 Nov. 1863.

37. Etheridge to Richard W. Thompson, Washington, 23 Mar. 1863, Thompson Papers, LMF.

38. Dawes to his wife Electa, Washington, 8 Dec. 1863, Dawes Papers, DLC.

39. Nicolay, memorandum, 6 Dec. 1863, in Burlingame, ed., *With Lincoln in the White House,* 121.

40. Michael Burlingame and John R. Turner Ettlinger, eds., *Inside Lincoln's White House: The Complete Civil War Diary of John Hay* (Carbondale: Southern Illinois University Press, 1997), 121 (entry for 9 Dec. 1863).

41. Washington correspondence, 7 Dec., Cincinnati *Commercial,* 10 Dec. 1863.

42. Reid to John Hay, n.d., in Royal Cortissoz, *The Life of Whitelaw Reid* (2 vols.; New York: C. Scribner's Sons, 1921), 2:130.

43. Howard K. Beale and Alan W. Brownsword, eds., *Diary of Gideon Welles, Secretary of the Navy under Lincoln and Johnson* (3 vols.; New York: W. W. Norton, 1960), 1:481

(entry for Dec. 1863—no day of the month indicated).

44. Lincoln to Montgomery Blair, Washington, 2 Nov. 1863, *CWL*, 6:555.

45. Whitelaw Reid to Horace Greeley, Washington, 2 Nov. 1863, Cortissoz, *Reid*, 1:107.

46. Chandler to Lincoln, Detroit, 15 Nov. 1863, AL MSS DLC.

47. Lincoln to Chandler, Washington, 20 Nov. 1863, *CWL*, 7:24.

48. Nashville *Press*, n.d., copied in the Philadelphia *Inquirer*, 5 Jan. 1864; John S. Brien to William H. Seward, Nashville, 21 July 1863, AL MSS DLC.

49. Lincoln to Rosecrans, Washington, 4 Oct. 1863, *CWL*, 6:498.

50. Burlingame and Ettlinger, eds., *Hay Diary*, 71 (entry for 9 Aug. 1863).

51. Lincoln to Banks, Washington, 31 Jan. 1864, *CWL*, 7:162.

52. Annual message to Congress and Proclamation of Amnesty and Reconstruction, 8 Dec. 1863, *CWL*, 7:50–55.

53. Washington correspondence, 10 Dec., Cincinnati *Commercial*, 11 Dec. 1863.

54. Washington correspondence, 12 Dec. 1863, Sacramento *Daily Union*, 18 Jan. 1864, in Michael Burlingame, ed., *Lincoln Observed: Civil War Dispatches of Noah Brooks* (Baltimore, MD: Johns Hopkins University Press, 1998), 94; Noah Brooks to George Witherle, Washington, 23 Dec. 1863, ibid., 97.

55. William Dennison to Lincoln, Columbus, 10 Dec. 1863, AL MSS DLC.

56. Washington correspondence, 12 Dec. 1863, Sacramento *Daily Union*, 18 Jan. 1864, in Burlingame, ed., *Lincoln Observed*, 94.

57. Chicago *Tribune*, 14 and 30 Dec. 1863.

58. *Congressional Globe*, 38th Congress, 1st Session, 289 (13 June 1864).

59. New York *Herald*, 11 Dec. 1863.

60. Burlingame and Ettlinger, eds., *Hay Diary*, 121–122 (entry for 9 Dec. 1863).

61. Washington correspondence by "Occasional" (John W. Forney), 9 Dec., Philadelphia *Press*, 10 Dec. 1863.

62. Samuel Galloway to Lincoln, Columbus, 19 Dec. 1863, AL MSS DLC.

63. Allan Nevins and Milton Halsey, eds., *Diary of George Templeton Strong, 1835–1875* (4 vols.; New York: Macmillan, 1952), 3:379 (entry for 11 Dec. 1863).

64. Norton to G. W. Curtis, Cambridge, 10 Dec. 1863, Sara Norton and M. A. De Wolfe Howe, eds., *Letters of Charles Eliot Norton* (2 vols.; Boston: Houghton Mifflin, 1913), 1:266.

65. *Watchman and Reflector*, n.d., copied in *Little's Living Age*, 6 Feb. 1864, 283.

66. Everett diary, 10 Dec. 1863, Everett Papers, MHi.

67. Washington correspondence, 10 Dec., Cincinnati *Commercial*, 14 Dec. 1863.

68. Charles Upson to Austin Blair, Washington, 4 Jan. 1864 [misdated 1863], 9 Dec. 1863, Blair Papers, Detroit Public Library.

69. Chicago *Tribune*, 14 Dec. 1863.

70. Boston *Commonwealth*, 18 and 11 Dec. 1863.

71. New York *Independent*, 17 Dec. 1863.

72. Henry Winter Davis to Samuel F. Du Pont, n.p., 11 Dec. 1863, transcript, S. F. Du Pont Papers, Hagley Museum, Wilmington, Delaware.

73. Burlingame and Ettlinger, eds., *Hay Diary*, 125 (entry for 10 Dec. 1863).

74. Usher's recollections in *Humorous and Pathetic Stories of Abraham Lincoln* (5th ed., 2nd series; Fort Wayne, IN: Lincoln Publishing Co., 1900), 16.

75. John P. Usher to Richard W. Thompson, Washington, 14 Aug. 1864, R. W. Thompson Papers, LMF; Chase to Lincoln, Washington, 12 Apr. 1865, AL MSS DLC.

76. Speech by Swett, 22 Oct. 1887, Chicago *Times*, 23 Oct. 1887.

77. Lincoln to Thomas Cottman, Washington, 15 Dec. 1863, *CWL* 7:66.

78. New York *Times*, 11 Dec. 1863; *Harper's Weekly*, 19 Dec. 1863.

79. The Rev. Mr. John G. Fee to Wendell Phillips, *Liberator*, 18 Mar. 1864; Whitelaw Reid to Anna E. Dickinson, Washington, 3 Apr. 1864, Dickinson Papers, DLC.

80. New York *Evening Post,* 10, 15 Dec. 1863.

81. New York *World,* 10 Dec. 1863.

82. Charles Ray Wilson, "The Cincinnati Daily Enquirer and Civil War Politics: A Study of Copperhead Opinion" (Ph.D. dissertation, University of Chicago, 1934), 245–246.

83. Dubuque *Herald,* 20 December 1863, in Hubert H. Wubben, *Civil War Iowa and the Copperhead Movement* (Ames: Iowa State University Press, 1980), 107.

84. Washington correspondence, 9 Dec., Chicago *Tribune,* 10 Dec. 1863.

85. Fessenden to his family, Washington, 19 Dec. 1862, Francis Fessenden, *Life and Public Services of William Pitt Fessenden* (2 vols.; Boston: Houghton Mifflin, 1907), 1:266–267.

86. Butler to Wendell Phillips, Fort Monroe, 11 Dec. 1862, Jessie Ames Marshall, ed., *Private and Official Correspondence of Gen. Benjamin F. Butler, During the Period of the Civil War* (5 vols.; Norwood, MA: Plimpton Press, 1917), 3:204.

87. Phillips to Butler, Boston, 13 Dec. 1862, ibid., 207.

88. Phillips's speech, 22 Dec. 1863, *National Anti-Slavery Standard* (New York), 9 Jan. 1864, in Andrew Kull, *The Color-Blind Constitution* (Cambridge: Harvard University Press, 1992), 246.

89. Douglass to an English correspondent, [July 1864], *The Liberator* (Boston), 16 Sept. 1864.

90. John Russell Young quoted in T. C. Evans, "Personal Reminiscences of John Hay," Chattanooga, Tennessee, *Sunday Times,* 30 July 1905.

91. Washington correspondence by "Norman," 31 Dec. 1863, *Ohio State Journal* (Columbus), 2 Jan. 1864.

92. Hay to Nicolay, at sea off the coast of Florida, 8 Feb. 1864, in Michael Burlingame ed., *At Lincoln's Side: John Hay's Civil War Correspondence and Selected Writings* (Carbondale: Southern Illinois University Press, 2000), 75.

93. Hay to Lincoln, mouth of the St. John's River, 8 Feb. 1864, ibid., 75–76.

94. Hawley to Charles Dudley Warner, Jacksonville, Florida, 4 Mar. 1864, Arthur L.

Shipman, "Letters of Joseph R. Hawley," typescript dated 1929, 199, Connecticut Historical Society.

95. Hay to N. P. Banks, Key West, 7 Mar. 1864, in Burlingame, ed., *At Lincoln's Side,* 78–79.

96. New York *Herald,* 23 Feb. 1864.

97. *Washington National Republican*, in the New York *Times,* 7 Mar. 1864.

98. Banks to Lincoln, New Orleans, 30 Dec. 1863, AL MSS DLC.

99. Boutwell to Banks, Washington, 21 Dec. 1863, Banks Papers, DLC; Boutwell to Banks, Washington, 11 Jan. 1864, W. P. Palmer Collection, Western Reserve Historical Society.

100. Lincoln to Banks, Washington, 24 Dec. 1864, *CWL,* 7:89-90.

101. Lincoln to Banks, Washington, 13 Jan. 1864, *CWL,* 7:123-124.

102. Lincoln to Hahn, Washington, 13 Mar. 1864, *CWL,* 7:243.

103. Springfield, Massachusetts, *Republican,* weekly ed., 2 Jan. 1864.

104. Chase to Durant, Washington, 28 Dec. 1863, Niven, ed., *Chase Papers,* 4:230.

105. Chase to Stickney, Washington, 29 Dec. 1863, in LaWanda Cox, *Lincoln and Black Freedom: A Study in Presidential Leadership* (Columbia: University of South Carolina Press, 1981), 80.

106. Lincoln's December 16 endorsement on John L. Riddell to Lincoln, 15 Dec. 1863, *CWL,* 7:71.

107. Durant to Chase, New Orleans, 16 Jan., 21 Feb. 1864, Niven, ed., *Chase Papers,* 4:258, 301.

108. Flanders to Chase, New Orleans, 14 Jan. 1864, Chase Papers, Historical Society of Pennsylvania.

109. Durant to Chase, New Orleans, 21 Feb. 1864, in Niven, ed., *Chase Papers,* 4:302.

110. Lincoln to Hahn, Washington, 13 Mar. 1864, *CWL,* 7:243.

111. Petition dated 10 Mar. 1864, *The Liberator* (Boston), 1 Apr. 1864.

112. Reminiscences of John W. Forney in a lecture delivered in November 1865 before the

Ladies' Soldiers' Aid Society of Weldon, Pennsylvania, New York *Evening Post*, 30 Nov. 1865.

113. Washington correspondence, 5 Mar., *Ohio State Journal* (Columbus), 9 Mar. 1864.

114. New York *Evening Post*, 4 Mar. 1864.

115. Chase to Durant, Washington, 28 Dec. 1863, Niven, ed., *Chase Papers*, 4:230.

116. George S. Denison to Chase, New Orleans, 8 Oct. 1864, Chase Papers, DLC.

117. New York *Times*, 23 June 1865.

118. Lincoln to Banks, Washington, 9 Aug. 1864, *CWL*, 7:486.

119. Wayne McVeagh in Burlingame and Ettlinger, eds., *Hay Diary*, 120 (entry for 28 Nov. 1863).

120. Howard K. Beale, ed., *The Diary of Edward Bates, 1859–1866* (Annual Report of the American Historical Association for the Year 1930, vol. IV; Washington, DC: U.S. Government Printing Office, 1933), 310 (entry for 17 Oct. 1863).

121. Henry Winter Davis to Samuel F. Du Pont, n.p., [9?] Jan. 1864, transcript, S. F. Du Pont Papers, Hagley Museum, Wilmington, Delaware.

122. Trumbull to N. P. Banks, Washington, 18 Feb. 1864, Banks Papers, IHi.

123. Lyman Trumbull to H. G. McPike, Washington, 6 Feb. 1864, draft, Trumbull Papers, DLC.

124. W. W. Orme to David Davis, Chicago, 3 Apr. 1864, David Davis Papers, IHi.

125. W. M. Dickson to Friedrich Hassaurek, Cincinnati, 15 Feb. 1864, Hassaurek Papers, Ohio Historical Society.

126. C. H. Spahr to John Sherman, Jamestown, Ohio, 6 May 1864, Sherman Papers, DLC.

127. Beecher to Chase, Brooklyn, 28 Dec. 1863, Niven, ed., *Chase Papers*, 4:231; Stearns to William Lloyd Garrison, 12 Sept., Boston *Commonwealth*, 23 Sept. 1864.

128. Charles Scheffer to Ignatius Donnelly, 1 Feb. 1864, in Martin Ridge, *Ignatius*

Donnelly: The Portrait of a Politician (Chicago: University of Chicago Press, 1962), 83.

129. August Wattles to Horace Greeley, 6 Feb. 1864, Greeley Papers, New York Public Library.

130. Richard Henry Dana, Jr., to his father, Richard Henry Dana, Sr., Washington, 4 May 1864, and Lakeville, Connecticut, 6 Aug. 1864, Richard Henry Dana Papers, MHi.

131. Child to Gerrit Smith, Wayland, Massachusetts, 22 Apr. 1864, Smith Papers, Syracuse University.

132. Sumner to Richard Cobden, 18 Sept. 1864, Edward L. Pierce, *Memoir and Letters of Charles Sumner* (4 vols.; Boston: Roberts Brothers, 1877–1893), 4:199–200.

133. A. G. Riddle, *Recollections of War Times: Reminiscences of Men and Events in Washington, 1860–1865* (New York: G. P. Putnam's Sons, 1895), 267.

134. Fessenden to his son William, Washington, 7 Feb. 1864; Fessenden to his son Frank, Washington, 23 Mar. 1864; Fessenden to Elizabeth Warriner, Washington, 27 Feb, 1864; Fessenden to Thomas Amory Deblois, Washington, [1?] Mar. 1864, Fessenden Papers, Bowdoin College.

135. Grimes to William P. Fessenden, Burlington, Iowa, [6?] Aug. 1864, copy, ibid.

136. Timothy O. Howe to John F. Potter, Washington, 20 Jan. 1864, Potter Papers, Wisconsin State Historical Society.

137. Hoar to John Murray Forbes, 4 May 1864, in Moorfield Storey, *Ebenezer Rockwood Hoar: A Memoir* (Boston: Houghton Mifflin, 1911), 140–141.

138. Forbes to George William Curtis, draft, Boston, 28 Apr. 1864, in Sarah Forbes Hughes, ed., *Letters and Recollections of John Murray Forbes* (2 vols.; Boston: Houghton Mifflin, 1899), 2:89.

139. Springfield, Massachusetts, *Republican*, 13 Feb. 1864.

140. Mullet to Chase, Washington, Washington, 16 May 1864, Chase Papers, DLC.

141. Bradford Wood to Chase, Copenhagen, 19 May 1863, ibid.

142. Morgan to Thurlow Weed, Washington, 6 Mar. 1864, Weed Papers, University of Rochester.

143. Henry Winter Davis to Samuel F. Du Pont, n.p., 29 Feb. 1864, transcript, S. F. Du Pont Papers, Hagley Museum, Wilmington, Delaware.

144. Beale, ed., *Bates Diary*, 333 (entry for 13 Feb. 1864).

145. Shelby M. Cullom, *Fifty Years of Public Service: Personal Recollections* (Chicago: A. C. McClurg, 1911), 98.

146. Chase to William Sprague, Washington, 26 Nov. 1863, Niven, ed., *Chase Papers*, 4:204.

147. Diary of William T. Coggeshall, 26 Nov. 1863, in Freda Postle Koch, *Colonel Coggeshall: The Man Who Saved Lincoln* (Columbus, Ohio: Poko Press, 1985), 63.

148. Chase to Levitt, Washington, 24 Jan. 1864, Niven, ed., *Chase Papers*, 4:262.

149. Chase to Eli A. Spencer, Washington, 14 Dec. 1863, ibid., 4:217.

150. [John D. Defrees] to Josiah G. Holland, Washington, 8 Aug. 1865, J. G. Holland Papers, New York Public Library in Allen Guelzo, ed., "Holland's Informants: The Construction of Josiah Holland's 'Life of Abraham Lincoln,'" *Journal of the Abraham Lincoln Association* 23 (2002): 44; Thurlow Weed to John Bigelow, Albany, 12 Dec. 1863, in John Bigelow, *Retrospections of an Active Life* (5 vols.; New York: Baker & Taylor, 1909–1913), 2:110; Burlingame and Ettlinger, eds., *Hay Diary*, 103 (entry for 29 Oct. 1863).

151. John B. Alley in Rice, ed., *Reminiscences of Lincoln*, 582.

152. Burlingame and Ettlinger, eds., *Hay Diary*, 103, 93, 78 (entries for 29 and 18 Oct. 1863 and for [July–Aug. 1863]).

153. Cullom, *Fifty Years of Public Service*, 94.

154. Beale, ed., *Bates Diary*, 333 (entry for 13 Feb. 1864).

155. Medill to Lincoln, Chicago, 17 Feb. 1864, AL MSS DLC.

156. Mark Delahay to Samuel Curtis, Washington, 12 Jan. 1864, Curtis Papers, Iowa State Archives, Des Moines.

157. David Davis to W. W. Orme, Washington, 29 and 30 Mar. 1864, Davis Papers, IHi.

158. Sam Wilkeson to Sydney Howard Gay, [Washington, ca. Feb. 1864], Gay Papers, Columbia University.

159. Chase to James C. Hall, Washington, 18 Jan. 1864, *Ohio State Journal* (Columbus), 11 Mar. 1864.

160. Halpine to J. G. Bennett, Brattleboro, Vermont, 30 Mar. 1864, Lincoln Collection, ICHi.

161. Charles R. Wilson, ed., "The Original Chase Organization Meeting and the Next Presidential Election," *Mississippi Valley Historical Review* 23 (1936): 76.

162. *The American Annual Cyclopedia of Important Events of the Year 1864* (New York: D. Appleton, 1869), 784.

163. J. M. Winchell to the editor of the New York *Times*, Hyde Park, New York, 14 August, New York *Times*, 15 Sept. 1874.

164. Richard C. Parsons to Chase, Cleveland, 9 Dec. 1863, Chase Papers, DLC.

165. Isaac Welsh to Sherman, Armstrongs Mills, Ohio, 25 Feb. 1864, Sherman Papers, DLC.

166. G. W. Gordon to Sherman, Springfield, Ohio, 26 Feb. 1864, ibid.

167. Speech at Hillsboro, Ohio, in Aug. 1863, New York *Evening Post*, 15 Aug. 1863.

168. Samuel Galloway to Lincoln, Columbus, Ohio, 25 Feb. 1864, AL MSS DLC.

169. Burlingame and Ettlinger, eds., *Hay Diary*, 105 (entry for 30 Oct. 1863).

170. John Palmer Usher to Richard W. Thompson, Washington, 17, 25 Feb. 1864, R. W. Thompson Papers, LMF.

171. John P. Usher, *President Lincoln's Cabinet* (Omaha: n.p., 1925), 14.

172. Washington correspondence, 26 Feb., *Ohio State Journal* (Columbus), 1 Mar. 1864.

173. David Davis to Julius Rockwell, Washington, 25 Feb. 1864, Davis Papers, DLC.

174. John Palmer Usher to R. W. Thompson, Washington, 25 Feb. 1864, R. W. Thompson Papers, LMF.

175. Swayne to Samuel J. Tilden, Washington, 19 Feb. 1864, Tilden Papers, New York Public Library.

176. Medill to Joseph K. C. Forrest, Chicago, 17 Dec. 1863, AL MSS DLC.

177. David Davis to Julius Rockwell, Washington, 24 Jan. [1864], Davis Papers, DLC.

178. Elihu B. Washburne to Thomas Gregg, Washington, 2 Jan. 1864, W. P. Palmer Collection, Western Reserve Historical Society.

179. Homer Byington to Sydney Howard Gay, Washington, 5 Mar. 1864, Gay Papers, Columbia University.

180. New York *Times,* 29 Feb. 1864; Springfield, Massachusetts, *Republican,* 7 Jan. 1864.

181. Washington correspondence by Van [D. W. Bartlett], 24 Nov., Springfield, Massachusetts, *Republican,* 28 Nov. 1863.

182. Foster to his wife, Washington, 31 May 1864, Foster Papers, MHi.

183. Washington *Chronicle,* 14 Jan. 1864.

184. David Davis to Julius Rockwell, Washington, 25 Feb. 1864, Davis Papers, DLC.

185. New York *Times,* 15 Jan. 1864.

186. Thomas Brown to Chase, San Francisco, 4 Jan. 1864, Chase Papers, DLC.

187. Charles Eliot Norton to Marsh, Cambridge, 22 Feb., 19 Apr. 1864, Marsh Papers, University of Vermont.

188. William H. Kent to Sydney Howard Gay, n.p., 25 Feb. 1864, Gay Papers, Columbia University.

189. John Sherman to Timothy C. Day, 28 Mar. 1864, quoted in Day to Sherman, Cincinnati, 4 Apr. 1864, Sherman Papers, DLC.

190. W. D. Bickham to John Sherman, Dayton, 1 Mar. 1864, ibid.

191. James A. Briggs to Salmon P. Chase, New York, 5 Sept. 1863, 8 June 1864, Chase Papers, DLC.

192. Clarke to Chase, Boston, 26 Feb. 1864, ibid.

193. Colfax to Sydney Howard Gay, Washington, 6 Feb. 1864, Gay Papers, Columbia University.

194. Washington correspondence, n.d., Boston *Watchtower,* n.d., quoted in Victor B. Howard, *Religion and the Radical Republican Movement, 1860–1870* (Lexington: University Press of Kentucky, 1990), 71.

195. Cameron interview, New York *Times,* 3 June 1878; Washington correspondence, 10 Jan., New York *Times,* 11 Jan. 1864. The text of the letter appears in the New York *Times,* 17 Jan. 1864.

196. Burlingame and Ettlinger, eds., *Hay Diary,* 141 (entry for 9 Jan. 1864).

197. Chandler to Amos Tuck, Philadelphia, 15 Dec. 1864, draft, William E. Chandler Papers, New Hampshire Historical Society.

198. Copy of a letter given to Chandler by Tuck on January 6, 1864, about twenty minutes before he introduced the resolution to the convention, ibid.

199. Memorandum of a statement Chandler made to James F. Colby on 6 Nov. 1911, ibid.

200. Fessenden to his son William, Washington, 7 Feb. 1864, Fessenden Papers, Bowdoin College.

201. Fessenden to Elizabeth Warriner, Washington, 27 Dec. 1863, ibid.

202. W. M. Dickson to Friedrich Hassaurek, Cincinnati, 15 Feb. 1864, Hassaurek Papers, Ohio Historical Society.

203. *Ohio State Journal* (Columbus), 27 Feb. 1864.

204. David Davis to W. W. Orme, Washington, 29 Feb. 1864, typescript, Davis Papers, ICHi.

205. Burlingame and Ettlinger, eds., *Hay Diary,* 141 (entry for 8 Jan. 1864).

206. Beale, ed., *Bates Diary,* 345 (entry for 9 Mar. 1864).

207. Davis to Thurlow Weed, Washington, 14 Mar. 1864, Weed Papers, University of Rochester.

208. Franklin B. Sanborn to Moncure D. Conway, Worcester, Massachusetts, 3 May 1864, Conway Papers, Columbia University.

209. Davis to Julius Rockwell, Washington, 13 Mar. 1864, Davis Papers, DLC.

210. *Congressional Globe*, 38th Congress, 1st Session, Appendix, 50 (27 Feb. 1864).

211. Riddle, *Recollections*, 274–275; Elizabeth Blair Lee to Samuel Phillips Lee, Washington, 18 Jan. 1864, Virginia Jeans Laas, ed., *Wartime Washington: The Civil War Letters of Elizabeth Blair Lee* (Urbana: University of Illinois Press, 1991), 393.

212. Riddle, *Recollections*, 273–276; Riddle, "Interview with Prest. Lincoln," 12 Dec. [no year indicated], manuscript in the Riddle Papers, Western Reserve Historical Society.

213. Elizabeth Blair Lee to Samuel Phillips Lee, Washington, 24 Apr. 1864, Laas, ed., *Letters of Elizabeth Blair Lee*, 371.

214. Noah Brooks, *Washington, D. C., in Lincoln's Time*, ed. Herbert Mitgang (1895; Chicago: Quadrangle Books, 1971), 113; Washington correspondence, 21 Mar., Sacramento *Daily Union*, 17 Apr. 1863, in Burlingame, ed., *Lincoln Observed*, 26–27.

215. Murat Halstead to Ida Tarbell, Cincinnati, 2 July 1900, Tarbell Papers, Allegheny College.

216. Washington correspondence, 18 Mar., Sacramento *Daily Union*, 14 Apr. 1863, in Burlingame, ed., *Lincoln Observed*, 26.

217. Briggs to Chase, New York, 30 Sept. 1863, Chase Papers, DLC.

218. Nicolay to Lincoln, New York, 30 March 1864, Michael Burlingame, ed., *With Lincoln in the White House: Letters, Memoranda, and Other Writings of John G. Nicolay, 1860–1865* (Carbondale: Southern Illinois University Press, 2000), 132–133.

219. Weed to David Davis, Albany, 9 Feb. 1864, David Davis Papers, IHi.

220. Lincoln to Chase, Washington, 12 Feb. 1864, *CWL*, 7:181.

221. Nicolay to Lincoln, New York, 30 Mar. 1864, Burlingame, ed., *With Lincoln in the White House*, 133.

222. Morgan to Weed, Washington, 6 Mar. 1864, Weed Papers, University of Rochester.

223. John Conness in Rice, ed., *Reminiscences of Lincoln*, 564.

224. Washington correspondence, 27 April, Boston *Evening Traveler*, 29 Apr. 1865.

225. Lincoln to Chase, Washington, 28 June 1864, *CWL*, 7:412–413 (two items of the same date).

226. Burlingame and Ettlinger, eds., *Hay Diary*, 213 (entry for 30 June 1864).

227. Lucius E. Chittenden, *Recollections of President Lincoln and His Administration* (New York: Harper & Brothers, 1891), 379.

228. William Henry Smith, "Private Memoranda—War Times," 12 July 1864, photocopy, J. G. Randall Papers, DLC.

229. Hay to William H. Herndon, Paris, 5 Sept. 1866, in Burlingame, ed., *At Lincoln's Side*, 110.

230. William D. Kelley, *Lincoln and Stanton* (New York: Putnam's, 1885), 86; Burlingame and Ettlinger, eds., *Hay Diary*, 216 (entry for 1 July 1864).

231. Charles Richard Williams, ed., *Diary and Letters of Rutherford Birchard Hayes* (5 vols.; Columbus: Ohio State Archeological and Historical Society, 1922–1926), 3:243 (diary entry for 18 May 1873).

232. Lewis D. Campbell to Thurlow Weed, Hamilton, Ohio, 23 Nov. 1864, Weed Papers, University of Rochester.

233. B. Rush Plumly to N. P. Banks, New Orleans, 20 Oct. 1864, Banks Papers, DLC.

234. Burlingame and Ettlinger, eds., *Hay Diary*, 212–214 (entry for 30 June 1864); New York *Daily News*, 1 July 1864; Washington correspondence, 1 July, Cincinnati *Commercial*, n.d., copied in the New York *Daily News*, 12 July 1864; John Sherman, *John Sherman's Recollections of Forty Years in the House, Senate and Cabinet: An Autobiography* (2 vols.; Chicago: Werner, 1896), 1:337; William Henry Smith, private memoranda, in Burlingame and Ettlinger, eds., *Hay Diary*, 354; James W. White to Horace Greeley, Washington, 3 July 1864, Sydney Howard Gay Papers, Columbia University; Franklin B. Sanborn to Moncure

D. Conway, Florence, Massachusetts, 10 July 1864, Conway Papers, Columbia University.

235. Washington correspondence, n.d. Springfield, Massachusetts, *Republican*, n.d., copied in the St. Paul *Press*, 22 July 1864.

236. Usher to Richard W. Thompson, Washington, 5 July 1864, R. W. Thompson Papers, LMF.

237. Burlingame and Ettlinger, eds., *Hay Diary*, 215, 216 (entries for 30 June, 1 July 1864).

238. Fessenden to Elizabeth Warriner, Washington, 3 July 1864; Fessenden to Edward [Fan?], Washington, 3 July 1864; Fessenden to his son William, Washington, 8 July 1864, Fessenden Papers, Bowdoin College; Fessenden to John Searle Tenney of Maine, n.p., n.d., in Fessenden, *Fessenden*, 1:316–318.

239. Burlingame and Ettlinger, eds., *Hay Diary*, 216 (entry for 1 July 1864).

240. Charles A. Jellison, *Fessenden of Maine, Civil War Senator* (Syracuse, NY: Syracuse University Press, 1962), 182–183.

241. New York *Daily News*, 2 July 1864.

242. Fessenden to Elizabeth Warriner, Washington, 4 Sept. 1864, Fessenden Papers, Bowdoin College.

243. Alexander K. McClure, *Abraham Lincoln and Men of War-Times* (Philadelphia: Times, 1892), 136.

244. James B. Fry in Rice, ed., *Reminiscences of Lincoln*, 390.

245. Herndon, "Analysis of the Character of Lincoln," *Abraham Lincoln Quarterly* 1 (1941):406–407.

246. Lincoln to Hooker, Washington, 26 Jan. 1863, *CWL*, 6:78.

247. Noah Brooks, "Personal Recollections of Abraham Lincoln," in Burlingame, ed., *Lincoln Observed*, 216.

248. Lincoln to Washburne, Washington, 26 Oct. 1863, *CWL*, 6:540.

249. New York *Commercial Advertiser*, n.d., copied in an unidentified clipping, J. G. Randall Papers, DLC.

250. Swett to Herndon, Chicago, 17 Jan. 1866, in Douglas L. Wilson and Rodney O. Davis,

eds., *Herndon's Informants: Letters, Interviews, and Statements about Abraham Lincoln* (Urbana: University of Illinois Press, 1998), 164.

251. Nicolay and Hay, *Lincoln*, 9:59.

252. Interview between Stevens and Lincoln as related by R. M. Hoe, Burlingame, ed., *Oral History of Lincoln*, 78.

253. Robert Livingston Stanton, "Reminiscences of President Lincoln," (ca. 1883), 8, Robert Brewster Stanton Papers, New York Public Library.

254. Noah Brooks, *Abraham Lincoln and the Downfall of American Slavery* (New York: G. P. Putnam's Sons, 1894), 385.

255. Washburne to Grant, Washington, 24 January 1864, John Y. Simon, ed., *The Papers of Ulysses S. Grant* (Carbondale: Southern Illinois University Press, 1967–), 9:522–523.

256. Chicago *Republican*, n.d., copied in the New York *Evening Post*, 14 June 1865.

257. Washburne's letter is quoted in Jones to Grant, 14 Jan. 1864, Simon, ed., *Grant Papers*, 9:542.

258. Albert D. Richardson, *A Personal History of Ulysses S. Grant* (Hartford, CT: American Publishing Company, 1868), 413.

259. Jones's statement in Tarbell, *Lincoln*, 2:188.

260. Simon, ed., *Grant Papers*, 10:166–167.

261. Rawlins to James H. Wilson, 3 Mar. 1864, ibid., 9:544.

262. James F. Rusling, *Men and Things I Saw in Civil War Days* (New York: Eaton & Mains, 1899), 16.

263. *The War of the Rebellion: A Compilation of the Official Records of the Union and Confederate Armies* (128 vols.; Washington: Government Printing Office, 1880–1901) [hereafter *OR*], I, 17, 2:424, 432.

264. Cincinnati *Enquirer*, 4 Jan. 1863.

265. Isaac Markens, *Abraham Lincoln and the Jews* (New York: the author, 1909), 12.

266. Washington correspondence, 8 Jan., by Isaac M. Wise, *The Israelite* (Cincinnati), 16 Jan. 1863 (vol. 9, # 28); "The Last of General Grant's Order," ibid., 23 Jan. 1863; Washington correspondence, 7 Jan., New York *Tribune*, 8 Jan. 1863.

267. Halleck to Grant, Washington, 21 Jan. 1863, *OR*, I, 24, 1:9.

268. Nicolay memorandum, Washington, 8 Mar. 1864, in Burlingame, ed., *With Lincoln in the White House*, 129.

269. Washington correspondence, 8 Mar., New York *Tribune*, 9 Mar. 1864; Washington correspondence, 9 Mar., Sacramento *Daily Union*, 9 Apr. 1864, in Burlingame, ed., *Lincoln Observed*, 104.

270. Nicolay memorandum, Washington, 8 Mar. 1864, in Burlingame, ed., *With Lincoln in the White House*, 130.

271. Brooks, *Lincoln and the Downfall of American Slavery*, 387.

272. *CWL*, 7:234.

273. *The American Annual Cyclopedia and Register of Important Events for the Year 1864* (New York: D. Appleton, 1865), 67.

274. Washington correspondence, 14 Mar., New York *Examiner*, 17 Mar. 1864, Michael Burlingame, ed., *Dispatches from Lincoln's White House: The Anonymous Civil War Journalism of Presidential Secretary William O. Stoddard* (Lincoln: University of Nebraska Press, 2002), 217–218.

275. John Russell Young quoted in the Chicago *Tribune*, 1 Sept. 1885.

276. Horace Porter, "Lincoln and Grant" in Peter Cozzens, ed., *Battles and Leaders of the Civil War*, vol. 6 (Urbana: University of Illinois Press, 2004), 79.

277. James Taussig to members of a committee of Missouri Radicals, *Missouri Democrat* (St. Louis), 9 June 1863.

278. Finney to Smith, 29 Jan. 1864, in Ralph Volney Harlow, *Gerrit Smith: Philanthropist and Reformer* (New York: H. Holt, 1939), 439–440.

279. Fessenden to his son Frank, Washington, 23 Mar. 1864, Fessenden Papers, Bowdoin College; Fessenden to J. S. Pike, Washington, 9 Mar. 1864, Pike Papers, DLC.

280. Horace White to William P. Fessenden, Washington, 7 Nov. 1863, Fessenden Papers, DLC.

281. Marshall, ed., *Correspondence of Butler*, 4:66; 3:675–676; E. D. Webster to Seward, 3, 9,

14 Mar. 1864, Seward Papers, University of Rochester.

282. Burlingame and Ettlinger, eds., *Hay Diary*, 197–198 (entry for 22 May 1864).

283. Carl Wittke, *Against the Current: The Life of Karl Heinzen* (Chicago: University of Chicago Press, 1945), 189, 196.

284. Sinclair Tousey to Gerrit Smith, New York, 25 Mar. 1864, Smith Papers, Syracuse University.

285. Benjamin P. Thomas, *Abraham Lincoln: A Biography* (New York: Alfred A. Knopf, 1952), 424.

286. John D. Defrees to Richard W. Thompson, Washington, 16 Apr. 1864, Thompson Papers, LMF.

287. New York *Tribune*, 20 Mar. 1864.

288. Harlan Hoyt Horner, *Lincoln and Greeley* (Urbana: University of Illinois Press, 1953), 341–342.

289. David Davis to W. W. Orme, 29 Mar. 1864, David Davis Papers, IHi.

290. Carl Sandburg's notes of an interview with Joseph Fifer, [1923], Sandburg-Barrett Collection, Newberry Library, Chicago. Swett was Fifer's informant.

291. Elizabeth Cady Stanton to Lydia Maria Child, New York, [ca. 22 Apr. 1864] in Ann D. Gordon, ed., *The Selected Papers of Elizabeth Cady Stanton and Susan B. Anthony* (4 vols.; New Brunswick, NJ: Rutgers University Press, 1997–2006), 1:514.

292. James M. McPherson, *The Struggle for Equality: Abolitionists and the Negro in the Civil War and Reconstruction* (Princeton, NJ: Princeton University Press, 1964), 108; Dickinson to [Elizabeth Cady Stanton], Philadelphia, 12 July 1864, CSmH, quoted in J. Matthew Gallman, *America's Joan of Arc: The Life of Anna Elizabeth Dickinson* (New York: Oxford University Press, 2006), 40–41.

293. Boston *Daily Courier*, 28 Apr. 1864.

294. Gallman, *Dickinson*, 39.

295. McKim to Samuel J. May, Jr., Philadelphia, 6 May 1863, Samuel J. May Anti-Slavery Manuscript Collection, Cornell University; McKim to William Lloyd

Garrison, Washington, [9?] May [1864], and Kelley to McKim, Washington, 1 May 1864, copy enclosed in McKim to Garrison, Philadelphia, 3 May 1864, Garrison Papers, Boston Public Library.

296. Whitelaw Reid to Anna E. Dickinson, Washington, 3 Apr. 1864, Dickinson Papers, DLC.

297. George W. Smalley to Wendell Phillips, New York, 15 Mar. 1864, Phillips Papers, Harvard University, in Irving H. Bartlett, ed., *Wendell and Ann Phillips: The Community of Reform, 1840–1880* (New York: W. W. Norton, 1979), 188–191.

298. Phillips to Moncure D. Conway, n.p., 16 Mar. 1864, Conway Papers, Columbia University.

299. Wendell Phillips's speech in Cooper Union, 22 Dec. 1863, New York *Times,* 23 Dec. 1863; *Ohio State Journal* (Columbus), 31 Dec. 1863.

300. Carl Wittke, *Refugees of Revolution: The German Forty-Eighters in America* (Philadelphia: University of Pennsylvania Press, 1952), 246.

301. Andrew to John Murray Forbes, n.p., n.d., in Hughes, ed., *Forbes Letters,* 2:122.

302. Frederick Douglass to E. Gilbert, Rochester, 23 May 1864, New York *Times,* 27 May 1864.

303. William Cheek and Aimee Lee Cheek, *John Mercer Langston and the Fight for Black Freedom, 1829–65* (Urbana: University of Illinois Press, 1989), 424.

304. Francis B. Carpenter, *The Inner Life of Abraham Lincoln: Six Months at the White House* (New York: Hurd and Houghton, 1867), 220–221.

305. Letter dated Boston, 27 May 1864, in Edward McPherson, *The Political History of the United States of America During the Great Rebellion* (Washington: Philp & Solomons, 1865), 412.

306. Stebbins to Garrison, 22 July 1864, *The Liberator* (Boston), in Howard, *Religion and the Radical Republican Movement,* 78.

307. *National Anti-Slavery Standard* (New York), 18 June 1864.

308. Washington correspondence, 30 May, New York *Daily News,* 2 June 1864.

309. Oliver Johnson to Henry T. Cheever, Philadelphia, 16 June 1864, Cheever Family Papers, American Antiquarian Society.

310. Henry C. Wright to William L. Garrison, Valley Falls, 8 May 1864, Garrison Papers, Boston Public Library.

311. Child to Gerrit Smith, Wayland, Massachusetts, 23 July 1864, *Lydia Maria Child: Selected Letters, 1817–1880,* ed. Milton Meltzer and Patricia G. Holland (Amherst: University of Massachusetts Press, 1982), 445; Child to Whittier, n.p., n.d., in Helene Gilbert Baer, *The Heart Is Like Heaven: The Life of Lydia Maria Child* (Philadelphia: University of Pennsylvania Press, 1964), 280.

312. Frémont to Worthington G. Snethen et al., New York, 4 June 1864, New York *Daily News,* 6 June 1864.

313. Simeon Nash to Chase, Gallipolis, Ohio, 10 June 1864, Chase Papers, DLC; Curtis to Daniel Ricketson, North Shore, New York, 30 June 1864, Curtis Papers, Harvard University.

314. Franklin B. Sanborn to Moncure D. Conway, Pepperell, Massachusetts, 20 June 1864, Conway Family Papers, Dickinson College.

315. Samuel May, Jr., to William Lloyd Garrison, Lexington, Massachusetts, [27?] June 1864, Garrison Papers, Boston Public Library.

316. Amasa J. Parker to Samuel J. Tilden, Albany, 7 July 1864, Tilden Papers, New York Public Library.

317. Henry Mayer, *All on Fire: William Lloyd Garrison and the Abolition of Slavery* (New York: St. Martin's, 1998), 562, 563.

318. Walter M. Merrill, ed., *The Letters of William Lloyd Garrison* (6 vols.; Cambridge, MA: Harvard University Press, 1971-1981), 5:181.

319. McPherson, *Struggle for Equality,* 260–261.

320. Auguste Laugel, *The United States During the War* (New York: Bailliere Brothers, 1866), 299 (diary entry for 13 Sept. 1864).

321. *The Liberator* (Boston), 18 Mar. 1864.

322. Garrison to Francis W. Newman, n.d., in Wendell Phillips Garrison et al., *William Lloyd Garrison, 1805–1879: The Story of His Life Told by His Children* (4 vols.; New York: Century, 1885–1889), 4:119–120.

323. Laugel, *United States During the War*, 302 (diary entry for 24 Sept. 1864).

324. William Lloyd Garrison to Lincoln, Boston, 13 Feb. 1865, AL MSS DLC.

325. *The Liberator* (Boston), n.d., copied in the *National Anti-Slavery Standard* (New York), 3 Sept. 1864.

326. *The Liberator* (Boston), n.d., copied in the *National Anti-Slavery Standard* (New York), 8 Oct. 1864.

327. Philadelphia *Press,* 17 Mar. 1864.

328. Lovejoy to Garrison, 22 Feb. 1864, *The Liberator* (Boston), n.d., copied in the *Ohio State Journal* (Columbus), 8 Apr. 1864.

329. Owen Lovejoy, *His Brother's Blood: Speeches and Writings, 1838–1864,* ed. William F. Moore and Jane Ann Moore (Urbana: University of Illinois Press, 2004), 380.

330. Ibid., 389.

331. Carpenter, *Inner Life of Abraham Lincoln,* 47–48.

332. Washington correspondence, 19 Oct. 1863, *National Anti-Slavery Standard* (New York), 23 Oct. 1863.

333. Child to Gerrit Smith, Wayland, Massachusetts, 23 July 1864, *Letters of Child,* ed. Meltzer and Holland, 445; Child to Whittier, n.p., n.d., in Baer, *The Heart is Like Heaven,* 280.

334. Lucy Stone to Susan B. Anthony, 12 July 1864, Blackwell Papers, DLC, in Wendy Hamand Venet, *Neither Ballots Nor Bullets: Women Abolitionists and the Civil War* (Charlottesville: University Press of Virginia, 1991), 140–141.

335. Elizabeth Buffum Chace to Garrison, Valley Falls, 5 May 1864, Garrison Papers, Boston Public Library.

336. Mott to Martha Coffin Wright et al., Philadelphia, 25 Jan. 1864, in Beverly Wilson Palmer, ed., *Selected Letters of Lucretia Coffin Mott* (Urbana: University of Illinois Press, 2002), 338.

337. Journal of Abby Hooper Gibbons, 20 July 1862, in Sarah Hopper Emerson, ed., *Life of Abby Hopper Gibbons, Told Chiefly Through Her Correspondence* (2 vols.; New York: G.P. Putnam's Sons, 1896–1897), 1:348.

338. Maria Weston Chapman to Lizzie Chapman Laugel, Weymouth, Massachusetts, 23 Feb. 1864, Weston Sisters Papers, Boston Public Library.

339. *The Independent* (New York), 29 June 1864; Tilton to Garrison, New York, 30 June 1864, Garrison Papers, Boston Public Library.

340. Simeon Nash to Chase, Gallipolis, Ohio, 10 June 1864, Chase Papers, DLC; Nash to John Sherman, Gallipolis, Ohio, 17 June 1864, Sherman Papers, DLC.

341. Oliver Johnson to Garrison, New York, 23 June 1864, Garrison Papers, Boston Public Library.

342. Child to Whittier, Wayland, Massachusetts, 19 June 1864, in John Albree, ed., *Whittier Correspondence from the Oak Knoll Collections, 1830–1892* (Salem, MA: Essex Book and Print Club, 1911), 147.

343. Maria Weston Chapman to Lizzie Chapman Laugel, Weymouth, Massachusetts, 23 Feb. 1864, Weston Sisters Papers, Boston Public Library.

344. Brooks, *Washington in Lincoln's Time,* ed. Mitgang, 142.

345. U. F. Murphy, *Presidential Election, 1864: Proceedings of the National Union Convention Baltimore, Md., June 7th and 8th 1864* (New York: Baker & Godwin, 1864), 4.

346. *The American Annual Cyclopedia and Register of Important Events of the Year 1864* (New York: D. Appleton, 1865), 788.

347. Ibid.

348. Undated memo by Nicolay, [1891?], enclosed in Nicolay to Charles Eugene Hamlin, Washington, 24 Feb. 1896, in C. E. Hamlin, *The Life and Times of Hannibal Hamlin* (Cambridge: Riverside Press, 1899), 593–594.

349. Nicolay to John Hay, Baltimore, 6 June 1864, Burlingame, ed., *With Lincoln in the White House,* 145.

350. Endorsement, [6 June 1864], *CWL,* 7:376.

351. Nicolay to Hay, Baltimore, 5 June 1864, in Burlingame, ed., *With Lincoln in the White House*, 144.

352. George Luther Stearns to Andrew Johnson, Boston, 9 June 1864, LeRoy P. Graf and Ralph W. Haskins, eds., *The Papers of Andrew Johnson* (16 vols.; Knoxville: University of Tennessee Press, 1967–2000), 6:721.

353. A. E. Johnston quoted in Margarita Spalding Gerry, ed., *Through Five Administrations: Reminiscences of Colonel William H. Crook, Body-Guard to President Lincoln* (New York: Harper & Brothers, 1910), 45.

354. Brooks, *Washington in Lincoln's Time*, ed. Mitgang, 148, 142.

355. Nicolay to Hay, Baltimore, 6 June 1864, in Burlingame, ed., *With Lincoln in the White House*, 145.

356. New York *Journal of Commerce*, n.d., copied in the New York *Evening Express*, 9 June 1864.

357. Burlingame and Ettlinger, eds., *Hay Diary*, 199 (entry for 5 June 1864).

358. Reply to serenade, 9 June 1864, *CWL*, 7:384.

359. Garrison to Helen E. Garrison, Philadelphia, 11 June 1864, Merrill, ed., *Garrison Letters*, 5:212.

360. William Garrison to his wife, 27 June 1864, Garrison Family Papers, Smith College, in Harriet Hyman Alonso, *Growing Up Abolitionist: The Story of the Garrison Children* (Amherst: University of Massachusetts Press, 2002), 218.

361. Pennington to the editor of the *Weekly Anglo-African*, New York, 9 June 1864, issue of 25 June 1864.

362. Franklin B. Sanborn to Moncure D. Conway, Pepperell, Massachusetts, 20 June 1864, Conway Family Papers, Dickinson College; Franklin B. Sanborn to Moncure D. Conway, Florence, Massachusetts, 10 July 1864, Conway Papers, Columbia University.

363. New York *Evening Post*, 9 June 1864.

364. Ibid., 1 June 1864.

365. Lincoln to William Cullen Bryant, Washington, 27 June 1864, *CWL*, 7:410.

366. *Round Table* (New York), n.d., copied in the New York *Evening Express*, 9 June 1864.

367. *CWL*, 7:380.

368. Ibid., 7:383–384.

369. Committee of the National Union Convention to Lincoln, 14 June 1864, AL MSS DLC.

370. A. K. McClure, *Our Presidents and How We Make Them* (New York: Harper & Brothers, 1900), 184.

371. New York *World*, n.d., copied in the New York *Evening Express*, 9 June 1864.

372. Butler to his wife, Fort Monroe, 11 June 1864, Marshall, ed., *Correspondence of Butler*, 4:337.

373. Theodore Tilton to Wendell Phillips, New York, 31 May 1864, Phillips Papers, Harvard University.

Chapter 33. "Hold on with a Bulldog Grip and Chew and Choke as Much as Possible"

1. Lieber to Charles Sumner, New York, 31 Aug. 1864, Sumner Papers, Harvard University.

2. Response to a serenade, 10 Nov. 1864, Roy P. Basler et al., eds., *Collected Works of Abraham Lincoln* [hereafter *CWL*] (8 vols. plus index; New Brunswick, NJ: Rutgers University Press, 1953–1955), 8:101.

3. Michael Burlingame and John R. Turner Ettlinger, eds., *Inside Lincoln's White House: The Complete Civil War Diary of John Hay* (Carbondale: Southern Illinois University Press, 1997), 193–194 (entry for 30 Apr. 1864).

4. Brooks Simpson, *Ulysses S. Grant: Triumph over Adversity, 1822–1865* (Boston: Houghton Mifflin, 2000), 278.

5. William Conant Church, *Ulysses S. Grant and the Period of National Preservation and Reconstruction* (New York: G. P. Putnam's Sons, 1897), 248–249.

6. Howard K. Beale and Alan W. Brownsword, eds., *Diary of Gideon Welles, Secretary of the Navy under Lincoln and Johnson* (3 vols.; New York: W. W. Norton, 1960), 2:26 (entry for 9 May 1864).

7. Lincoln to Grant, Washington, 30 Apr. 1864, *CWL*, 7:324.

8. Grant to Lincoln, Culpepper Court House, Virginia, 1 May 1864, in John Y. Simon, ed., *The Papers of Ulysses S. Grant* (Carbondale: Southern Illinois University Press, 1967–), 10:380.

9. William O. Stoddard, "White House Sketches No. 7," New York *Citizen*, 29 Sept. 1866, in Stoddard, *Inside the White House in War Times: Memoirs and Reports of Lincoln's Secretary*, ed. Michael Burlingame (1890; Lincoln: University of Nebraska Press, 2000), 173.

10. A. G. Riddle, *Recollections of War Times: Reminiscences of Men and Events in Washington, 1860–1865* (New York: G. P. Putnam's Sons, 1895), 266.

11. Lincoln to W. C. Bryant, Washington, 27 June 1864, *CWL*, 7:410.

12. Allan Nevins and Milton Halsey Thomas, eds., *Diary of George Templeton Strong, 1835–1875* (4 vols.; New York: Macmillan, 1952), 3:449 (entry for 20 May 1864).

13. Henry E. Wing, *When Lincoln Kissed Me: A Story of the Wilderness Campaign* (New York: Eaton & Mains, 1913), 38.

14. Burlingame and Ettlinger, eds., *Hay Diary*, 195 (entry for 9 May 1864).

15. Response to a serenade, 9 May 1864, *CWL*, 7:334.

16. Colfax in Allen Thorndike Rice, ed., *Reminiscences of Abraham Lincoln by Distinguished Men of His Time* (New York: North American, 1886), 337.

17. Isaac N. Arnold, *The Life of Abraham Lincoln* (Chicago: Jansen, McClurg, 1885), 375.

18. Burlingame and Ettlinger, eds., *Hay Diary*, 196 (entry for 14 May 1864).

19. Colfax in Rice, ed., *Reminiscences of Lincoln*, 338.

20. Nicolay to Therena Bates, Washington, 15 May 1864, in Michael Burlingame, ed., *With Lincoln in the White House: Letters, Memoranda, and Other Writings of John G. Nicolay, 1860–1865* (Carbondale: Southern Illinois University Press, 2000), 141.

21. Washington correspondence, 18 Apr., New York *Examiner*, 21 Apr. 1864, in Michael Burlingame, ed., *Dispatches from Lincoln's White House: The Anonymous Civil War Journalism of Presidential Secretary William O. Stoddard* (Lincoln: University of Nebraska Press, 2002), 222.

22. John A. Dix to Stanton, New York, 18 May 1864, Lincoln Collection, ICHi.

23. James R. Gilmore to Sydney Howard Gay, Washington, 18 May 1864, Gay Papers, Columbia University.

24. J. G. Randall and Richard N. Current, *Lincoln the President: Last Full Measure* (New York: Dodd, Mead, 1955), 156, quoting Frank A. Flower to C. F. Gunther, 14 Feb. 1904, Gunther Papers, ICHi.

25. Lincoln to Dix, Washington, 18 May 1864, *CWL*, 7:348.

26. Stanton to Dix, Washington, 20 May 1864, *OR*, III, 4:394–395.

27. Henry E. Bowen interviewed in New York *Times*, 30 May 1875.

28. New York *World*, 23 May 1864.

29. Reed W. Smith, *Samuel Medary and The Crisis: Testing the Limits of Press Freedom* (Columbus: Ohio State University Press, 1995), 140.

30. Beale, ed., *Welles Diary*, 2:38 (entry for 23 May 1864).

31. James R. Gilmore to Sydney Howard Gay, Washington, 18 May 1864, Gay Papers, Columbia University.

32. Colfax, *Life and Principles of Abraham Lincoln: Address Delivered at the Court House Square, at South Bend, April 24, 1865* (Philadelphia: J. B. Rodgers, 1865), 12.

33. John G. Nicolay and John Hay, *Abraham Lincoln: A History* (10 vols.; New York: Century, 1890), 9:364.

34. Washington correspondence by R. S. B., 20 Aug., Philadelphia *Inquirer*, 22 Aug. 1864.

35. Ida M. Tarbell, *The Life of Abraham Lincoln* (2 vols.; New York: McClure, Phillips, 1900), 2:195.

36. Columbus, Ohio, *Crisis*, 3 Aug. 1864, in Smith, *Medary*, 91.

37. Lincoln to Grant, Washington, 15 June 1864, *CWL*, 7:393.

38. Speech, 19 May 1864, *CWL*, 7:395.

39. Noah Brooks, *Washington, D. C., in Lincoln's Time*, ed. Herbert Mitgang (1895; Chicago: Quadrangle Books, 1971), 138.

40. Horace Porter to his wife, City Point, 24 June 1864, Porter Papers, DLC.

41. Horace Porter, *Campaigning with Grant* (New York: Century, 1897), 218–219.

42. Sylvanus Cadwallader, *Three Years with Grant*, ed. Benjamin P. Thomas (New York: Knopf, 1955), 233.

43. Horace Porter to his wife, City Point, 24 June 1864, Porter Papers, DLC; Porter, *Campaigning with Grant*, 219–220.

44. Porter, *Campaigning with Grant*, 223.

45. Theodore Calvin Pease and James G. Randall, eds., *The Diary of Orville Hickman Browning* (2 vols.; Springfield: Illinois State Historical Library, 1925–1933), 1:673 (entry for 26 June 1864).

46. Porter, *Campaigning with Grant*, 223.

47. Beale, ed., *Welles Diary*, 2:58 (entry for 24 June 1864).

48. Howard K. Beale, ed., *The Diary of Edward Bates, 1859–1866* (Annual Report of the American Historical Association for the Year 1930, vol. IV; Washington, DC: U.S. Government Printing Office, 1933), 378 (entry for 25 June 1864).

49. Alvin C. Voris of the 67th Ohio Infantry to J. H. Chamberlin, Bermuda Hundred, Virginia, 4 July 1864, typescript, Voris Papers, Virginia Historical Society.

50. Francis B. Carpenter, *The Inner Life of Abraham Lincoln: Six Months at the White House* (New York: Hurd and Houghton, 1867), 283.

51. Church, *Grant*, 231–232.

52. Nicolay memorandum, n.d., Nicolay-Hay Papers, IHi.

53. F. B. Sanborn to Moncure D. Conway, Worcester, 13 July 1864, Conway Family Papers, Dickinson College.

54. Willard Cutter to Elizabeth Cutter, 11 July 1864, in Matthew Pinsker, *Lincoln's Sanctuary: Abraham Lincoln and the Soldiers'*

Home (New York: Oxford University Press, 2003), 136.

55. Lincoln to Grant, Washington, 10 July 1864, *CWL*, 7:437.

56. Burlingame and Ettlinger, eds., *Hay Diary*, 221 (entry for 11 July 1864).

57. Ibid., 222, 223 (entries for 13, 14 July 1864); Beale, ed., *Welles Diary*, 2:88 (entry for 26 July 1864).

58. Brooks, *Washington, D.C., in Lincoln's Time*, ed. Mitgang, 162.

59. Burlingame and Ettlinger, eds., *Hay Diary*, 219 (entry for 4 July 1864).

60. Brooks, *Washington, D. C., in Lincoln's Time*, ed. Mitgang, 162.

61. Lincoln to Stanton, Washington, 14 July 1864, *CWL*, 7:439–440.

62. Memo read to cabinet, [14? July] 186[4], *CWL*, 7:439.

63. Carpenter, *Inner Life of Abraham Lincoln*, 302.

64. J. W. Schuckers to Chase, Washington, 15 July 1864, Chase Papers, DLC; Britton A. Hill to Thomas Ewing, Washington, 14 July 1864, Ewing Family Papers, DLC.

65. B. B. French to his son Frank, Washington, 17 July 1864, French Family Papers, DLC.

66. Curtis to Charles Eliot Norton, North Shore, New York, 12 July 1864, Curtis Papers, Harvard University.

67. Britton A. Hill to Thomas Ewing, Washington, 29 July 1864, Ewing Family Papers, DLC.

68. George Harrington to William P. Fessenden, Washington, 1 Aug. 1864, Lincoln Collection, Yale University; Simpson, *Grant*, 367; David S. Sparks, ed., *Inside Lincoln's Army: The Diary of Marsena Rudolph Patrick, Provost Marshall General, Army of the Potomac* (New York: Thomas Yoseloff, 1964), 409–410 (entry for 5 Aug. 1864); George R. Agassiz, ed., *Meade's Headquarters, 1863–1865: Letters of Colonel Theodore Lyman from the Wilderness to Appomattox* (Boston: Atlantic Monthly Press, 1922), 204 (journal entry for 1 Aug. 1864).

69. Grant to Halleck, City Point, Virginia, 1 Aug. 1864, Simon, ed., *Grant Papers*, 11:358.

70. Lincoln to Grant, Washington, 3 Aug. 1864, *CWL*, 7:476.

71. Lincoln to Grant, Washington, 17 Aug. 1864, *CWL*, 7:499.

72. J. K. Herbert to Benjamin Butler, Washington, 11 Aug. 1864, in Jessie Ames Marshall, ed., *Private and Official Correspondence of Gen. Benjamin F. Butler, During the Period of the Civil War* (5 vols.; Norwood, MA: Plimpton Press, 1917), 5:35.

73. Lincoln to Stanton, Washington, 5 Feb. 1864, *CWL*, 7:169.

74. *Congressional Globe*, 38th Congress, 1st Session, 3449 (1 July 1864).

75. Hale to his wife, 29 May 1864, in Richard H. Sewell, *John P. Hale and the Politics of Abolition* (Cambridge, MA: Harvard University Press, 1965), 210.

76. Burlingame and Ettlinger, eds., *Hay Diary*, 217–218 (entry for 4 July 1864).

77. Washington correspondence, 28 February, Chicago *Tribune*, 3 Mar. 1864; Worthington G. Snethen to Wendell Phillips, Baltimore, 25 Aug. 1864, Phillips Papers, Harvard University.

78. Gerald S. Henig, *Henry Winter Davis: Antebellum and Civil War Congressman from Maryland* (New York: Twayne, 1973), 9; Davis to S. F. Dupont, 20 Dec. 1859, 26 Apr. 1863; n.d. 1860; June 1862; 11 Nov. 1859, S. F. Dupont Papers, Hagley Museum.

79. Burlingame and Ettlinger, eds., *Hay Diary*, 245 (entry for 8 Nov. 1864).

80. Washington correspondence, 28 Feb., Chicago *Tribune*, 3 Mar. 1864.

81. Montgomery Blair to Augustus W. Bradford, 26 Jan. 1864, Bradford Papers, Maryland Historical Society; Henig, *Davis*, 196–197; Davis to S. F. Dupont, n.p., 28 Jan. 1864, transcript, S. F. Dupont Papers, Hagley Museum.

82. Buffalo *Morning Express*, 24 Aug. 1864.

83. Henig, *Davis*, 167, 174.

84. Davis to S. F. Dupont, 11 July 1862; July 1862; 20 Mar. 1861, S. F. Dupont Papers, Hagley Museum.

85. Proclamation, 8 July 1864, *CWL*, 7:433–434.

86. Stevens to Edward McPherson, [Lancaster?], 10 July 1864, in Beverly Wilson Palmer, ed., *The Selected Papers of Thaddeus Stevens* (2 vols.; Pittsburgh: University of Pittsburgh Press, 1997–1998), 1:500.

87. *The American Annual Cyclopedia and Register of Important Events of the Year 1864* (New York: D. Appleton, 1865), 308–310.

88. New York *World*, in Randall and Current, *Last Full Measure*, 209.

89. Beale, ed., *Welles Diary*, 2:98 (entry for 8 Aug. 1864).

90. Carpenter, *Inner Life of Abraham Lincoln*, 145.

91. Mary Todd Lincoln interviewed by Herndon, [Sept. 1866], Douglas L. Wilson and Rodney O. Davis, eds., *Herndon's Informants: Letters, Interviews, and Statements about Abraham Lincoln* [hereafter *HI*] (Urbana: University of Illinois Press, 1998), 358.

92. J. K. Herbert to Benjamin F. Butler, Washington, 6 Aug. 1864, *Correspondence of Butler*, ed. Marshall, 5:8.

93. Plumly to N. P. Banks, Washington, 9 Aug. 1864, Banks Papers, DLC.

94. Brooks, *Washington, D.C., in Lincoln's Time*, ed. Mitgang, 156.

95. James G. Blaine, *Twenty Years of Congress: From Lincoln to Garfield* (2 vols.; Norwich, CT: Henry Bill, 1884-1886), 2:44.

96. New York *Times*, 12 Aug. 1864.

97. Ashtabula *Sentinel*, 17 Aug. 1864, and New York *Times*, 26 Aug. 1864, in Hans L. Trefousse, *Benjamin Franklin Wade, Radical Republican from Ohio* (New York: Twayne, 1963), 227, 228.

98. Washington correspondence, 1 July, Sacramento *Daily Union*, 26 July 1864, in Michael Burlingame, ed., *Lincoln Observed: Civil War Dispatches of Noah Brooks* (Baltimore, MD: Johns Hopkins University Press, 1998), 120.

99. Usher to R. W. Thompson, Washington, 14 Aug. 1864, R. W. Thompson Papers, LMF.

100. John D. Defrees to Benjamin F. Wade, Washington, 7 Aug. 1864, copy, AL MSS DLC.

101. Browning to Thomas Ewing, Washington, 4 Oct. 1864, Ewing Family Papers, DLC.

102. *Congressional Globe,* 38th Congress, 1st Session, 2038 (2 May 1864).

103. New York *World,* 15 Aug. 1864.

104. E. A. Stansbury to Charles Sumner, New York, 10 Aug. 1864, Sumner Papers, Harvard University.

105. E. A. Stansbury to Lincoln, New York, 9 Aug. 1864, AL MSS DLC.

106. Henry Winter Davis to Samuel F. Du Pont, n.p., 18 Aug. 1864, transcript, S. F. Du Pont Papers, Hagley Museum, Wilmington, Delaware.

107. Henry Winter Davis to Henry Cheever, Baltimore, 21 July 1864, Cheever Family Papers, American Antiquarian Society.

108. Chase to his daughter Kate, Washington, 17 Sept. 1864, John Niven, ed., *The Salmon P. Chase Papers* (5 vols.; Kent, Ohio: Kent State University Press, 1993–1998), 4:432.

109. Sumner to John Bright, 27 Sept. 1864, Beverly Wilson Palmer, ed., *The Selected Letters of Charles Sumner* (2 vols.; Boston: Northeastern University Press, 1990), 2:253.

110. Cincinnati *Commercial,* 8 Aug., copied in the New York *World,* 10 Aug. 1864.

111. Yates to Greeley et al., Springfield, 6 Sept. 1864, Theodore Tilton Papers, New-York Historical Society.

112. Andrew to Greeley et al., Boston, 3 Sept. 1864; Joseph A. Gilmore to Theodore Tilton, Concord, 5 Sept. 1864; Buckingham to Theodore Tilton et al., Norwich, 3 Sept. 1864; Thomas Carney to Theodore Tilton et al., Leavenworth, 12 Sept, 1864; William M. Stone to Tilton et al., Des Moines, 9 Sept. 1864; Andrew G. Curtin to Tilton et al., Saratoga Springs, 8 Sept. 1864, ibid.

113. Davis to S. F. Du Pont, n.p., 18 Aug. 1864, John D. Hayes, ed., *Samuel Francis Du Pont: A Selection from His Civil War Letters* (3 vols.; Ithaca, NY: Published for the Eleutherian Mills Historical Library by the Cornell University Press, 1969), 3:370.

114. New York *Sun,* 30 June 1889.

115. Lewis D. Campbell to John A. Andrew, Hamilton, Ohio, 27 Aug. 1864, Andrew Papers, MHi; Lewis D. Campbell to Thurlow Weed, Hamilton, Ohio, 12 Nov. 1864, Weed Papers, University of Rochester.

116. Albany, New York, *Statesman, n.d.,* copied in the Bridgeport, Connecticut, *Farmer, n.d.,* copied in the La Crosse, Wisconsin, *Daily Democrat,* 30 Aug. 1864.

117. Alexander K. McClure, *Abraham Lincoln and Men of War-Times* (Philadelphia: Times, 1892), 126.

118. George Luther Stearns to Wendell Phillips, Boston, 26 Aug. 1864, Wendell Phillips Papers, Harvard University.

119. Schurz, *The Reminiscences of Carl Schurz* (3 vols.; New York: McClure, 1907–1908), 3:103–104.

120. Boston *Evening Journal, n.d.,* copied in the Springfield, Massachusetts, *Republican,* 18 Apr. 1865.

121. Davis to Julius Rockwell, Bloomington, 4 Aug. 1864, Davis Papers, DLC.

122. Erasmus Peshine Smith to Henry C. Carey, Pittsfield, 21 Sept. 1864, Henry C. Carey Papers in the Edward Carey Gardiner Collection, Historical Society of Pennsylvania.

123. *Suffolk Herald* (New York), n.d., copied in the La Crosse, Wisconsin, *Daily Democrat,* 17 Aug., 1 Sept. 1864.

124. Concord, New Hampshire, *Monitor, n.d.,* copied ibid., 23 Aug. 1864.

125. Weed to Seward, New York, 22 August 1864, AL MSS DLC.

126. J. W. Shaffer to Benjamin Butler, New York, 17 Aug. 1864, in *Correspondence of Butler,* ed. Marshall, 5:68.

127. Swett to his wife, New York, n.d., and Washington, 8 Sept. 1864, in Tarbell, *Lincoln,* 2:201–202.

128. Swett interviewed by Nicolay, Washington, 16 Oct. 1878, in Michael Burlingame, ed., *An Oral History of Abraham Lincoln: John G.*

Nicolay's Interviews and Essays (Carbondale: Southern Illinois University Press, 1996), 58.

129. Bross, *Biographical Sketch of the Late B. J. Sweet* (Chicago: Jansen, McClurg, 1878), 16.

130. Carpenter, *Inner Life of Lincoln*, 275.

131. Undated memo by Francis Pierpont, Pierpont Papers, West Virginia University.

132. Raymond to Lincoln, New York, 22 Aug. 1864, AL MSS DLC.

133. New York *World*, 18 Aug. 1864.

134. Weed to Seward, New York, 22 Aug. 1864, AL MSS DLC.

135. Beale, ed., *Bates Diary*, 388 (entry for 22 July 1864); Hay to Jewett, Washington, 18 July 1864, Michael Burlingame ed., *At Lincoln's Side: John Hay's Civil War Correspondence and Selected Writings* (Carbondale: Southern Illinois University Press, 2000), 88.

136. Greeley to Lincoln, New York, 7 July 1864, AL MSS DLC.

137. Porter, *Campaigning with Grant*, 179.

138. Chauncey M. Depew, *My Memories of Eighty Years* (New York: C. Scribner's Sons, 1922), 62.

139. Lincoln to Greeley, Washington, 9, 15 July 1864, *CWL*, 7:435, 442.

140. Ashley, *Address of Hon. J. M. Ashley, at the Fourth Annual Banquet of the Ohio Republican League* (New York: New York Evening Post, 1891), 13.

141. Shelby M. Cullom, *Fifty Years of Public Service: Personal Recollections* (Chicago: McClurg, 1911), 101.

142. Burlingame and Ettlinger, eds., *Hay Diary*, 224 (entry for ca. 21 July 1864).

143. Lincoln to "whom it may concern," Washington, [1]8 July 1864, *CWL*, 8:63.

144. New York *Daily News*, 22 July 1864.

145. Beale, ed., *Welles Diary*, 2:112 (entry for 19 Aug. 1864).

146. Joseph E. McDonald, interview in the Pittsburgh *Commercial*, n.d, copied in the New York *Times*, 28 Dec. 1882.

147. Jacob M. Manning in the *Christian Advocate and Journal*, 4 Aug. 1864, in Victor B. Howard, *Religion and the Radical Republican Movement, 1860–1870* (Lexington: University Press of Kentucky, 1990), 80.

148. Boston *Daily Journal*, 5 Aug. 1864.

149. Philadelphia *Bulletin*, n.d., copied in the New York *World*, 29 July 1864.

150. Mark W. Delahay to Lincoln, Leavenworth, 8 August 1864, AL MSS DLC.

151. Cincinnati *Enquirer*, 25 July 1864.

152. Detroit *Free Press*, n.d., copied in the New York *World*, 29 July 1864.

153. Nevins and Thomas, eds., *Strong Diary*, 3:474 (entry for 19 Aug. 1864).

154. *Speech of Hon. Reverdy Johnson, of Maryland, Delivered before the Brooklyn McClellan Central Association, October 21, 1864* (Brooklyn: Brooklyn McClellan Association, 1864), 7, quoted in Michael Vorenberg, *Final Freedom: The Civil War, the Abolition of Slavery, and the Thirteenth Amendment* (Cambridge: Cambridge University Press, 2002), 150.

155. Arnold M. Shankman, *The Pennsylvania Antiwar Movement, 1861–1865* (Rutherford, NJ: Fairleigh Dickinson University Press, 1980), 180.

156. Noah Brooks, *Abraham Lincoln and the Downfall of American Slavery* (New York: G. P. Putnam's Sons, 1894), 402.

157. Joseph E. McDonald, interview in the Pittsburgh *Commercial*, n.d, copied in the New York *Times*, 28 Dec. 1882.

158. Baltimore correspondence, 17 Aug., New York *Daily News*, n.d., copied in the *National Anti-Slavery Standard* (New York), 24 Sept. 1864.

159. Edmund Kirke [James R. Gilmore], *Down in Tennessee, and Back by Way of Richmond* (New York: Carleton, 1864), 282; James R. Gilmore, *Personal Recollections of Abraham Lincoln and the Civil War* (Boston: L.C. Page, 1898), 289.

160. Burlingame and Ettlinger, eds., *Hay Diary*, 230 (entry for 23 Sept. 1864).

161. Swett to Herndon, Chicago, 17 Jan. 1866, *HI*, 164.

162. Lincoln to Wakeman, Washington, 25 July 1864, *CWL*, 7:461.

163. Wakeman to Lincoln, New York, 12 Aug. 1864, AL MSS DLC.

164. New York *Herald*, 1 Feb. 1864.

165. Burlingame and Ettlinger, eds., *Hay Diary*, 229 (entry for 23 Sept. 1864).

166. Greeley to W. O. Bartlett, New York, 30 Aug. 1864, Greeley Papers, New York Public Library.

167. Oliver Carlson, *The Man Who Made News: James Gordon Bennett* (New York: Duell, Sloan and Pearce, 1942), 370.

168. Burlingame and Ettlinger, eds., *Hay Diary*, 230 (entry for 23 Sept. 1864).

169. Beale, ed., *Welles Diary*, 2:259 (entry for 16 Mar. 1865).

170. Memorandum, 23 Aug. 1864, *CWL*, 7:514.

171. Interview with Alexander W. Randall and Joseph T. Mills, 19 Aug. 1864, *CWL*, 7:506–507.

172. Burlingame and Ettlinger, eds., *Hay Diary*, 248 (entry for 11 Nov. 1864).

173. Lincoln to Charles D. Robinson, Washington, 17 Aug. 1864, draft, *CWL*, 7:499–501.

174. Douglass to Theodore Tilton, Rochester, 15 Oct. 1864, in Philip S. Foner, ed., *The Life and Writings of Frederick Douglass* (5 vols.; New York: International Publishers, 1950), 3:423.

175. New York *World*, 15, 19 Aug. 1864.

176. Douglass, speech at Rochester, 18 Apr. 1865, Washington *Daily Morning Chronicle*, 27 Apr. 1865.

177. Douglass, *Life and Times*, 435.

178. John Eaton, *Grant, Lincoln, and the Freedmen: Reminiscences of the Civil War with Special Reference to the Work for the Contrabands and Freedmen of the Mississippi Valley* (New York: Longmans, Green, 1907), 175–176.

179. Raymond to Lincoln, New York, 22 Aug. 1864, AL MSS DLC.

180. Charles Eliot Norton to George William Curtis, Ashfield, Massachusetts, 24 July 1864, Sara Norton and M. A. De Wolfe Howe, eds., *Letters of Charles Eliot Norton* (2 vols.; Boston: Houghton Mifflin, 1913), 1:274.

181. Dana to Raymond, Washington, 26 July 1864, George Jones Papers, New York Public Library.

182. Nicolay to John Hay, Washington, 25 Aug. 1864; Nicolay to Therena Bates, Washington, 28 Aug. 1864, Burlingame, ed., *With Lincoln in the White House*, 152–154; H. A. Tilden to [Samuel J. Tilden], Wash[ington], 26 Aug. 1864, Tilden Papers, New York Public Library; Washington correspondence, 26 Aug., New York *World*, 27 Aug. 1864.

183. Lincoln to Raymond, Washington, 24 Aug. 1864, *CWL*, 7:517.

184. Forbes to Gustavus V. Fox, Yacht Azela, bound to New Bedford, 6 Sept. 1864, in Hughes, ed., *Letters of Forbes*, 2:102–103.

185. John Murray Forbes to John A. Andrew, New Bedford, 3 Sept. 1864, and Naushon, 5 September 1864, Andrew Papers, MHi.

186. New York *World*, 29, 30 July, 25 Aug. 1864.

187. Burlingame and Ettlinger, eds., *Hay Diary*, 238 (entry for 11 Oct. 1864).

188. Memorandum by Fox, Washington, 29 Mar. 1883, in Hughes, ed., *Letters of Forbes*, 2:105.

189. Forbes to Charles Eliot Norton, Naushon, 25 Aug. 1864, Norton Papers, Harvard University.

Chapter 34. "The Wisest Radical of All"

1. Noah Brooks, *Washington, D.C., in Lincoln's Time*, ed. Herbert Mitgang (1895; Chicago: Quadrangle Books, 1971), 164.

2. Joseph P. Thompson, "A Talk with President Lincoln," *The Congregationalist and Boston Recorder*, 30 Mar. 1866, p. 50.

3. Joseph Hooker to Dr. B. M. Stevens, Watertown, New York, 1 Sept. 1864, Schoff Civil War Collection, William L. Clements Library, University of Michigan.

4. J. W. Rathbone to Manton Marble, Albany, 4 Nov. 1864, Manton Marble Papers, DLC.

5. Solomon Newton Pettis, interview, Washington *Post*, 16 Aug. 1891.

6. John H. Clifford to Robert C. Winthrop, New Bedford, 13, 25 Sept., 18 Nov. 1864, Winthrop Family Papers, MHi.

7. John Pendleton Kennedy to Robert C. Winthrop, Newport, 6 Sept. 1864, ibid.

8. Allan Nevins and Milton Halsey Thomas, eds., *Diary of George Templeton Strong, 1835–1875* (4 vols.; New York: Macmillan, 1952), 3:481 (entry for 5 Sept. 1864).

9. Tilton to Anna E. Dickinson, New York, 13 July, 3, 5 Sept. 1864, Dickinson Papers, DLC.

10. Dickinson to "My Dear Friend," Philadelphia, 3 Sept. 1864, *National Anti-Slavery Standard* (New York), 10 Sept. 1864.

11. New York *Tribune,* 6 Sept. 1864.

12. Nicolay to Lincoln, New York, 30 Aug. 1864, in Michael Burlingame, ed., *With Lincoln in the White House: Letters, Memoranda, and Other Writings of John G. Nicolay, 1860–1865* (Carbondale: Southern Illinois University Press, 2000), 155.

13. Lillie B. Chace to Anna E. Dickinson, Valley Falls, 19 Sept. 1864, Dickinson Papers, DLC; Sumner to John A. Stevens, Boston, 1, 17 Sept. 1864, Stevens Papers, New-York Historical Society.

14. Sumner to Francis Lieber, 3 Sept. 1864, in Edward Lillie Pierce, *Memoir and Letters of Charles Sumner* (4 vols.; Boston: Roberts, 1877–1893), 4:198.

15. Sumner, speech at Fanueil Hall, 28 Sept., Boston *Daily Advertiser,* 29 Sept. 1864.

16. Butler to Simon Cameron, n.d., Cincinnati Gazette, 5 Oct. 1864; Beverly Wilson Palmer, ed., *The Selected Papers of Thaddeus Stevens* (2 vols.; Pittsburgh: University of Pittsburgh Press, 1997–1998), 1:502.

17. Frederick Douglass to Theodore Tilton, Rochester, 15 Oct. 1864, Philip S. Foner, ed., *The Life and Writings of Frederick Douglass* (5 vols.; New York: International Publishers, 1950), 3:424; Douglass to Garrison, Rochester, 17 Sept. 1864, *The Liberator* (Boston), 23 Sept. 1864, ibid., 407.

18. Weekly *Anglo-African* (New York), 24 Sept. 1864.

19. Speech at Syracuse, N.Y., 6 Oct. 1864, in C. Peter Ripley, ed., *The Black Abolitionist*

Papers (5 vols.; Chapel Hill: University of North Carolina Press, 1985–1992), 5:306.

20. *Weekly Pacific Appeal* (San Francisco), 9 Jan. 1864.

21. *The Liberator* (Boston), 20 May 1864.

22. Ibid., 22 July 1864.

23. Reply to the loyal colored people of Baltimore, 7 Sept. 1864, Roy P. Basler et al., eds., *Collected Works of Abraham Lincoln* [hereafter *CWL*] (8 vols. plus index; New Brunswick, NJ: Rutgers University Press, 1953–1955), 7:542.

24. Sojourner Truth to Oliver Johnson, 17 November 1864, *National Anti-Slavery Standard* (New York), 17 Dec. 1864.

25. Pillsbury to Theodore Tilton, Concord, New Hampshire, 22 May 1864, and Henniker, New Hampshire, 10 July 1864, Miscellaneous Manuscripts, New-York Historical Society; Pillsbury to Wendell Phillips, Concord, 27 Aug. 1864, Wendell Phillips Papers, Harvard University.

26. Elizabeth Cady Stanton to Wendell Phillips, New York, 6 June 1863 [1864], Wendell Phillips Papers, Harvard University; Elizabeth Cady Stanton to Susan B. Anthony, New York City, 25 Sept. 1864, Theodore Stanton and Harriot Stanton Blatch, eds., *Elizabeth Cady Stanton as Revealed in Her Letters, Diary and Reminiscences* (2 vols.; New York: Harper & Brothers, 1922), 2:101.

27. Wendy Hamand Venet, *Neither Ballots Nor Bullets: Women Abolitionists and the Civil War* (Charlottesville: University Press of Virginia, 1991), 138.

28. Smith to Stanton, 3 Oct. 1864, Stanton Papers, DLC.

29. Venet, *Neither Ballots Nor Bullets,* 138; diary entry, 12 February 1901, Stanton and Blatch, eds., *Elizabeth Cady Stanton,* 2:355.

30. Conway to Oliver Johnson, Brighton, England, 26 July 1864, *National Anti-Slavery Standard* (New York), 27 Aug. 1864.

31. *National Anti-Slavery Standard* (New York), 23 July 1864.

32. Wright to Gerrit Smith, 19 Aug. 1864, in Arthur Harry Rice, "Henry B. Stanton as a

Political Abolitionist" (Ph.D. dissertation, Columbia University, 1968), 405.

33. Phillips to Elizabeth Cady Stanton, n.p., 27 Sept. 1864, Ann D. Gordon, ed., *The Selected Papers of Elizabeth Cady Stanton and Susan B. Anthony* (4 vols.; New Brunswick, NJ: Rutgers University Press, 1997–2006), 1:531.

34. Speech of October 20 at Boston, in Henry Wilson, *History of the Rise and Fall of the Slave Power in America* (3 vols.; Boston: Osgood, 1872–1877), 3:547.

35. Maria Weston Chapman to Lizzie Chapman Laugel, Weymouth, Massachusetts, 23 Feb. 1864, Weston Sisters Papers, Boston Public Library.

36. Speech of Phillips, Oct. 26, New York *Daily News*, 27 Oct. 1864.

37. Frederick William Seward, *William H. Seward: An Autobiography from 1801 to 1834, with a Memoir of his Life and Selections from His Letters* (3 vols.; New York: Derby and Miller, 1891), 3:215.

38. *The Liberator* (Boston), 28 Oct. 1864.

39. Elizabeth Cady Stanton to Susan B. Anthony, New York, 22 Aug. 1864, Stanton and Blatch, eds., *Elizabeth Cady Stanton*, 2:101; Oliver Johnson to Anna E. Dickinson, New York, 22 Sept. 1864, Dickinson Papers, DLC.

40. McKim to Caroline Weston, Philadelphia, 2 June 18[64], Weston Sisters Papers, Boston Public Library.

41. Maria Weston Chapman to Lizzie Chapman Laugel, Weymouth, Massachusetts, 23 Feb. 1864, Weston Sisters Papers, Boston Public Library.

42. May to Phillips, Philadelphia, 30 Sept. 1864, draft, May Papers, Boston Public Library.

43. May to Richard Webb, Boston, 2 Jan. 1865, ibid.

44. Theodore Tilton to Anna E. Dickinson, New York, 30 June 1864, Dickinson Papers, DLC.

45. Theodore Tilton to Judge [Hugh L.?] Bond, New York, 30 June [1864], Tilton Papers, New-York Historical Society.

46. R. S. Matthews to Theodore Tilton, Baltimore, 6 July 1864, ibid.

47. Kelley to J. Miller McKim, Washington, 1 May 1864, copy, Garrison Papers, Boston Public Library.

48. James T. Pratt to [Rufus L.] Baker, South Glastonbury, 16 Nov. 1864, Schoff Civil War Collection, William L. Clements Library, University of Michigan.

49. Wendell Garrison to Ellie Garrison, 12 July 1864, Harriet Hyman Alonso, *Growing Up Abolitionist: The Story of the Garrison Children* (Amherst: University of Massachusetts Press, 2002), 218–219.

50. Parker Pillsbury to Wendell Phillips, Concord, New Hampshire, 27 Aug. 1864, Phillips Papers, Harvard University.

51. Elizabeth Cady Stanton to Susan B. Anthony, New York, 25 Sept. 1864, Stanton and Blatch, eds., *Elizabeth Cady Stanton*, 2:100.

52. Henry A. Tilden to [Samuel J. Tilden], Wash[ington], 26 Aug. 1864, Tilden Papers, New York Public Library.

53. Nevins and Thomas, eds., *Strong Diary*, 3:480–481.

54. Nicolay to Theodore Tilton, Washington, 6 Sept. 1864, Burlingame, ed., *With Lincoln in the White House*, 158.

55. Nicolay to Therena Bates, Washington, 11 Sept. 1864, ibid.

56. Howard K. Beale and Alan W. Brownsword, eds., *Diary of Gideon Welles, Secretary of the Navy under Lincoln and Johnson* (3 vols.; New York: W.W. Norton, 1960), 1:440–441 (21 Sept. 1863).

57. Charles B. Sedgwick to John Murray Forbes, Syracuse, 5 Sept. 1864, in Sarah Forbes Hughes, ed., *Letters and Recollections of John Murray Forbes* (2 vols.; Boston: Houghton Mifflin, 1899), 2:101, 107.

58. Curtis to Charles Eliot Norton, [North Shore, New York], 24 Sept. 1864, Curtis Papers, Harvard University.

59. Annie Wittenmyer, *Under the Guns: A Woman's Reminiscences of the Civil War* (Boston: E. B. Stillings, 1895), 240.

60. George Forrester Williams in *The Independent* 53:2398, in Fehrenbacher and

Fehrenbacher, eds., *Recollected Words of Lincoln*, 498.

61. Grant to Washburne, City Point, Virginia, 16 Aug. 1864, John Y. Simon, ed., *The Papers of Ulysses S. Grant* (Carbondale: Southern Illinois University Press, 1967–), 12:16–17.

62. Thompson, "A Talk with President Lincoln," 50; Thompson's sermon in New York, 30 Apr. 1865, in *Our Martyr President, Abraham Lincoln: Voices from the Pulpit of New York and Brooklyn* (New York: Tibbals and Whiting, 1865), 191.

63. George B. Cheever to Theodore Tilton, Newport, Rhode Island, n.d., Tilton Papers, New-York Historical Society; George B. Cheever to his wife Elizabeth, New York, 22 Sept., 1 Nov. 1864, Cheever Family Papers, American Antiquarian Society.

64. Lucius Fairchild to Lincoln, Madison, Wisconsin, 13 Sept. 1864, AL MSS DLC.

65. Weed to Seward, New York, 10 Sept. [1864], ibid.

66. New York *Evening Post*, 20 Sept. 1864, in Allan Nevins, *The Evening Post: A Century of Journalism* (New York: Boni and Liveright, 1922), 313.

67. John Sherman to William T. Sherman, 4 Sept. 1864, John Sherman Papers, DLC.

68. Sherman, speech in Sandusky, New York *Tribune*, 7 Oct. 1864.

69. Letter from Washington by Charles Moore, n.d., who spoke with Jerome, *Century Magazine*, July 1895, 476–477.

70. Wilson to Lincoln, Natick, Massachusetts, 5 Sept. 1864, AL MSS DLC.

71. Chicago *Tribune*, 1 Sept. 1864.

72. Interview between Thaddeus Stevens and Lincoln as recounted by R. M. Hoe, n.d., in Michael Burlingame, ed., *An Oral History of Abraham Lincoln: John G. Nicolay's Interviews and Essays* (Carbondale: Southern Illinois University Press, 1996), 78.

73. Elizabeth Blair Lee to Samuel Phillips Lee, Silver Spring, [Maryland], 24 Sept. [1864], Virginia Jeans Laas, ed., *Wartime Washington: The Civil War Letters of Elizabeth Blair Lee*

(Urbana: University of Illinois Press, 1991), 433.

74. Chandler to his wife, New York, 8 Sept. 1864, Chandler Papers, DLC.

75. Sawyer to Frémont, Pittsburgh, 13 Sept. 1864, in Allan Nevins, *Frémont: Pathmarker of the West* (New York: D. Appleton-Century Company, 1939), 579.

76. Letter by Jessie Frémont, Nov. 1889, Samuel T. Pickard, *Life and Letters of John Greenleaf Whittier* (2 vols.; Cambridge, MA: Riverside Press, 1894), 2:487.

77. Frémont to George L. Stearns, et al., Nahant, 17 Sept. 1864, Boston *Daily Advertiser*, 23 Sept. 1864.

78. This account is based primarily on Henry Winter Davis to S. F. Dupont, n.p., 28 or 29 Sept. 1864, in John D. Hayes, ed., *Samuel Francis Du Pont: A Selection from His Civil War Letters* (3 vols.; Ithaca, NY: Published for the Eleutherian Mills Historical Library by the Cornell University Press, 1969), 3:393–394; Hans L. Trefousse, "Zachariah Chandler and the Withdrawal of Frémont in 1864," *Lincoln Herald* 70 (1968):181–188.

79. Lincoln to Montgomery Blair, Washington, 23 Sept. 1864, *CWL*, 8:18.

80. Beale, ed., *Welles Diary*, 2:156–157 (entry for 23 Sept. 1864).

81. William Ernest Smith, *The Francis Preston Blair Family in Politics* (2 vols.; New York: Macmillan, 1933), 2:288.

82. Gustavus V. Fox to his wife Virginia, Washington, 23 Sept. 1864, Fox Papers, New-York Historical Society.

83. Blair to Lincoln, Washington, 23 Sept. 1864, AL MSS DLC.

84. David Davis to Lincoln, Bloomington, 4 Oct. 1864, ibid.

85. Davis to S.F. Du Pont, [28 or 29 Sept.] 1864, in Hayes, ed., *Du Pont Letters*, 3:393.

86. Henry Winter Davis to S. F. Du Pont, 28 Sept. 1864, ibid., 3:395.

87. Beale, ed., *Welles Diary*, 2:158n (undated footnote).

88. Howard K. Beale, ed., *The Diary of Edward Bates, 1859–1866* (Annual Report of

the American Historical Association for the Year 1930, vol. IV; Washington, DC: U.S. Government Printing Office, 1933), 291 (entry for 10 May 1864).

89. Blair to Frémont, Washington, 24 Aug. 1861, in John G. Nicolay and John Hay, *Abraham Lincoln: A History* (10 vols.; New York: Century, 1890), 9:334.

90. Washington correspondence by Van [D. W. Bartlett], 25 Mar., Springfield, Massachusetts, *Republican,* 27 Mar. 1863.

91. J. K. Herbert to Benjamin Butler, Washington, 26 Sept. 1864, in Jessie Ames Marshall, ed., *Private and Official Correspondence of Gen. Benjamin F. Butler, during the Period of the Civil War* (5 vols.; Norwood, MA: Plimpton Press, 1917), 5:168.

92. Chandler to Austin Blair, Detroit, 29 Sept. 1864, Blair Papers, Detroit Public Library.

93. Michael Burlingame and John R. Turner Ettlinger, eds., *Inside Lincoln's White House: The Complete Civil War Diary of John Hay* (Carbondale: Southern Illinois University Press, 1997), 254 (entry for 18 Dec. 1864).

94. Smith, *Blair Family,* 2:292.

95. Francis P. Blair, Sr., to Frank Blair, 23 Sept. 1864, copied in Elizabeth Blair Lee to Samuel Phillips Lee, Silver Spring, [Maryland], 24 Sept. [1864], Laas, ed., *Letters of Elizabeth Blair Lee,* 433.

96. Beale, ed., *Bates Diary,* 413 (entry for 23 Sept. 1864).

97. Burlingame and Ettlinger, eds., *Hay Diary,* 230 (entry for 24 Sept. 1864).

98. St. Louis *Anzeiger des Westens,* n.d., copied in the La Crosse, Wisconsin, *Daily Democrat,* 17 Aug. 1864.

99. Thomas J. McCormack, ed., *Memoirs of Gustave Koerner, 1809–1896* (2 vols.; Cedar Rapids, IA: Torch Press, 1909), 2:432.

100. George B. Lincoln to Andrew Johnson, Brooklyn, 11 June 1864, Graf and Haskins, eds., *Johnson Papers,* 6:732.

101. Hugh McCulloch to his wife, Washington, 25 Sept. 1864, Hugh McCulloch Papers, InU.

102. Wade to Chandler, Jefferson, Ohio, 2 Oct. 1864, Chandler Papers, DLC.

103. Chandler to his wife, Washington, 2 Sept. 1864, ibid.

104. J. K. Herbert to Benjamin F. Butler, Washington, 26 Sept. 1864, in *Correspondence of Butler,* ed. Marshall, 5:167.

105. Smith, *Blair Family,* 2:285.

106. Davis to S. F. Dupont, n. p., 25 Sept. 1864, transcript, S. F. Du Pont Papers, Hagley Museum, Wilmington, Delaware.

107. Peter G. Sauerwine to Edward McPherson, Baltimore, 8 Oct. 1864, McPherson Papers, DLC.

108. George B. Cheever to Theodore Tilton, Newport, Rhode Island, n.d., Tilton Papers, New-York Historical Society; George B. Cheever to his wife Elizabeth, New York, 22 Sept., 1 Nov. 1864, Cheever Family Papers, American Antiquarian Society.

109. "Old-Time Facts and Fancies" by "An Old-Timer," clipping marked "Chicago News, 2-29-1896," LMF.

110. Peoria correspondence, 4 Aug., New York *Daily News,* 12 Aug. 1864.

111. Proceedings of the peace convention, Cincinnati *Commercial,* 20 Oct. 1864, copied in the New York *Daily News,* 24 Oct. 1864; article by Matthew Page Andrews, New York *Times,* 12 Feb. 1928.

112. Cincinnati *Enquirer,* 29 Mar. 1864, Charles Ray Wilson, "The Cincinnati Daily Enquirer and Civil War Politics: A Study of Copperhead Opinion" (Ph.D. dissertation, University of Chicago, 1934), 253–254.

113. La Crosse, Wisconsin, *Daily Democrat,* 16 Aug. 1864.

114. Sidney Kaplan, "The Miscegenation Issue in the Election of 1864," *Journal of Negro History* 34 (1949) 274–343; Michael Vorenberg, *Final Freedom: The Civil War, the Abolition of Slavery, and the Thirteenth Amendment* (Cambridge: Cambridge University Press, 2001), 141.

115. Cyrus [Bearenderfer?] to Daniel Musser, 20 Feb. 1864, Musser Papers, Pennsylvania Historical and Museum Commission, in Arnold

M. Shankman, *The Pennsylvania Antiwar Movement, 1861–1865* (Rutherford, NJ: Fairleigh Dickinson University Press, 1980), 196.

116. Interview with Alexander W. Randall and Joseph T. Mills, 19 Aug. 1864, *CWL*, 7:508.

117. Simeon Nash to John Sherman, Gallipolis, Ohio, 17 June 1864, Sherman Papers, DLC.

118. John McMahon to Lincoln, Harmbrook, Pennsylvania, 5 Aug. 1864, Nicolay Papers, DLC; "Nicolay" to McMahon, Washington, 6 Aug. 1864, *CWL*, 7:483.

119. Cleveland *Plain Dealer* in Donnal V. Smith, "Chase and Civil War Politics," *Ohio Archaeological and Historical Quarterly* (1931): 134.

120. Columbus *Crisis*, 3 Aug. 1864, in David Lindsey, *"Sunset" Cox: Irrepressible Democrat* (Detroit: Wayne State University Press, 1959), 84.

121. Kenneth Silverman, *Lightning Man: The Accursed Life of Samuel F. B. Morse* (New York: Alfred A. Knopf, 2003), 410–411.

122. Bridgeport, Connecticut, *Farmer*, n.d., copied in the La Crosse, Wisconsin, *Daily Democrat*, 30 Aug. 1864; Cincinnati Enquirer, n.d., Wilson, "Cincinnati Enquirer," 294.

123. Elizabeth F. Yager, "The Presidential Campaign of 1864 in Ohio," *Ohio Archaeological and Historical Quarterly* 34 (1925): 572-573; "Campaign of 1864 in Ohio," 572–573; Cincinnati *Enquirer*, 23, 24 Sept. 1864.

124. James J. Farran to Alexander Long, Cincinnati, 26 June 1864, Long Papers, Cincinnati Historical Society.

125. Columbus *Crisis*, 27 Jan. 1864, in Reed W. Smith, *Samuel Medary and The Crisis: Testing the Limits of Press Freedom* (Columbus: Ohio State University Press, 1995), 130.

126. *The Old Guard: A Monthly Journal Devoted to the Principles of 1776 and 1787* (New York), Oct. 1864, 224.

127. New York *Daily News*, 27 July, 12, 14 Sept. 1864.

128. La Crosse *Daily Democrat*, 25 Aug. 1864.

129. Hans L. Trefousse, *First Among Equals: Abraham Lincoln's Reputation during His Administration* (New York: Fordham University Press, 2005), 112.

130. Chicago *Times*, 7 June 1864.

131. Greensburg, Pennsylvania, *Argus*, 10, 17 Aug. 1864, in Shankman, *Antiwar Movement in Pennsylvania*, 177, 192.

132. New York *Daily News*, 12 Sept. 1864.

133. Reginald C. McGrane, *William Allen: A Study in Western Democracy* (Columbus: Ohio State Archaeological and Historical Society, 1925), 168.

134. New York *World*, 9 Sept. 1864.

135. Ward Hill Lamon, *Recollections of Abraham Lincoln, 1847–1865*, ed. Dorothy Lamon Teillard (Washington, DC: the editor, 1911), 143.

136. Lamon, drafts and anecdotes (ca. 1887), folder 1, Lamon Papers, CSmH, in Don E. Fehrenbacher and Virginia Fehrenbacher, eds., *Recollected Words of Abraham Lincoln* (Stanford, CA: Stanford University Press, 1996), 290.

137. Lamon, *Recollections of Lincoln*, 149.

138. Washington correspondence, 16 Oct., New York *Tribune*, 17 Oct. 1864.

139. Johnson speech in Brooklyn, in Bernard Christian Steiner, *Life of Reverdy Johnson* (New York: Russell & Russell, 1970), 64-65.

140. Browning to Edgar Cowan, Quincy, Illinois, 6 Sept. 1864, photostatic copy, J. G. Randall Papers, DLC.

141. New York *World*, 26 Sept. 1864; E. V. Haughwout & Co. to Marble, New York, 26, 27, and 28 Sept. 1864; [Marble] to Col. Frank E. Howe, New York, 26 Sept. 1864; and Marble to [E. V. Haughwout & Co.], "Wednesday 2 AM", filed at the end of September 1864, and [3 Oct. 1864], draft, Marble Papers, DLC.

142. Maria Lydig Daly, *Diary of a Union Lady, 1861–1865*, ed. Harold Earl Hammond (New York: Funk & Wagnalls, 1962), 305 (entry for 25 Sept. 1864).

143. George W. Adams to [David Goodman] Croly, Washington, 7 Oct. 1867, Manton Marble Papers, DLC. In 1862, Congress passed a supplemental appropriation of $2,613 to cover expenses involved in plating gas fittings at the

White House. Elisha Whittlesey to George Harrington, Washington, 6 Mar. 1862, Letters Received, vol. 27, Records of the Commissioner of Public Buildings, microfilm edition, Record Group 42, microcopy 371, National Archives. On July 30, 1862, Haughwout received $2,343 from the Commissioner of Public Buildings for plating White House cutlery. Financial Records of the Commissioner of Public Buildings, entry 19, box 13, ibid.

144. Bayly Ellen Marks and Mark Norton Schatz, eds., *Between North and South: A Maryland Journalist Views the Civil War, The Narrative of William Wilkins Glenn* (Rutherford, NJ: Farleigh Dickinson University Press, 1976), 296 (4 Oct. 1867).

145. New York *World,* 30 Sept. and 1 Oct. 1864.

146. Unidentified New York newspaper copied in the *Illinois State Register,* (Springfield) 30 Oct. 1864.

147. New York correspondence by "Metropolitan," 9 Oct. 1867, Boston *Post,* 11 Oct. 1867.

148. Columbus *Crisis,* 20 July 1864.

149. A. H[omer] B[yington] to [Sydney Howard] Gay, Washington, 23 Mar. [1864]; Sam Wilkeson to Sydney Howard Gay, [Washington, ca. 23 March 1864], Gay Papers, Columbia University.

150. Mary Edwards Raymond, ed., *Some Incidents in the Life of Mrs. Benjamin S. Edwards* (privately printed, 1909), 11–12, 16; Elizabeth Keckley, *Behind the Scenes* (New York: G. W. Carleton, 1868), 149–150.

151. Julia Taft Bayne, *Tad Lincoln's Father* (Boston: Little, Brown, 1931), 49.

152. Keckly, *Behind the Scenes,* 145.

153. James H. Linsley to Miss Conant, Bermuda Hundred, Virginia, 16 June 1864, typescript, Schoff Civil War Collection, William L. Clements Library, University of Michigan.

154. Edward McPherson, *The Political History of the United States of America During the Great Rebellion* (Washington, DC: Philp & Solomons, 1865), 364.

155. Thomas Clark, *Reminiscences* (New York: T. Whittaker, 1895), 142.

156. Washington correspondence by "Rhode Island," 18 Oct., Providence *Journal,* 21 Oct. 1861.

157. Stanton to Benjamin Butler, Washington, 17 Nov. 1863, *OR,* II, 6:528.

158. W.A. Croffut, ed., *Fifty Years in Camp and Field: The Diary of Major-General Ethan Allen Hitchcock, U.S.A.* (New York: G. P. Putnam's Sons, 1909), 458.

159. Nicolay memorandum, 14 Dec. 1863, Burlingame, ed., *With Lincoln in the White House,* 122.

160. Burlingame and Ettlinger, eds., *Hay Diary,* 207–208 (entry for 17 June 1864).

161. John Sherman, *Recollections of Forty Years in the House, Senate and Cabinet: An Autobiography* (2 vols.; Chicago: Werner, 1895), 1:324.

162. Lincoln to John Brough and Samuel P. Heintzelman, Washington, 20 June 1864, *CWL,* 7:402.

163. Speech of Congressman Robert Mallory at Lexington, n.d., *Illinois State Register,* Springfield 4 Nov. 1864.

164. Curtis to Charles Eliot Norton, North Shore, New York, 1 Sept. 1864, Curtis Papers, Harvard University.

165. Fenton in Allen Thorndike Rice, ed., *Reminiscences of Abraham Lincoln by Distinguished Men of His Time* (New York: North American, 1886), 69.

166. Lincoln to Chase, Washington, 28 June 1864, *CWL,* 7:414.

167. Weed to Lincoln, Albany, 18 Oct. 1863, AL MSS DLC.

168. Lincoln to Weed, Washington, 14 Oct. 1864, *CWL,* 6:513–514.

169. Weed to David Davis, New York, 29 Mar. 1864, David Davis Papers, IHi.

170. Ibid.

171. Weed to David Davis, Albany, 15 Mar. [1864], ibid.

172. Weed to David Davis, Albany, 24 Mar. [1864], ibid.

173. David Davis to Weed, Washington, 21 Mar. 1864, Weed Papers, University of

Notes to Pages 706–715

983

Rochester; same to same, Washington, 4 Apr. 1864, Davis Papers, IHi.

174. Lincoln to Weed, Washington, 25 Mar. 1864, *CWL*, 7:268.

175. Nicolay to Lincoln, New York, 30 Mar. 1864, in Burlingame, ed., *With Lincoln in the White House*, 132–133.

176. Barney to Chase, New York, 5 Sept. 1864, Chase Papers, Historical Society of Pennsylvania; Barney to Fessenden, New York, 31 Aug. 1864, Fessenden Papers, Western Reserve Historical Society.

177. John Murray Forbes to John A. Andrew, New Bedford, 3 Sept. 1864, Andrew Papers, MHi.

178. Beale, ed., *Welles Diary*, 2:138 (entry for 5 Sept. 1864).

179. Charles Jones to Raymond, 2 Aug. 1864, Raymond Papers, New York Public Library.

180. Beale, ed., *Welles Diary*, 2:176 (entry for 13 Oct. 1864).

181. Speech by Swett, 22 Oct., Chicago *Times*, 23 Oct. 1880.

182. E. W. Andrews in Rice, ed., *Reminiscences of Lincoln*, 304.

183. Noah Brooks, "Personal Recollections of Abraham Lincoln," in Michael Burlingame, ed., *Lincoln Observed: Civil War Dispatches of Noah Brooks* (Baltimore, MD: Johns Hopkins University Press, 1998), 217.

184. Bryant to John Murray Forbes, n.p., n.d., in Hughes, ed., *Letters and Recollections of Forbes*, 2:101.

185. Ward Hunt to Lincoln, Utica, 9 Aug. 1864, AL MSS DLC; Lincoln to Hunt, Washington, 16 Aug. 1864, *CWL*, 7:498.

186. Julian in Rice, ed., *Reminiscences of Lincoln*, 232.

187. Memorandum of a conversation, 20 June 1864, *CWL*, 7:402.

188. Lincoln to Morton McMichael, Washington, 5 Aug. 1864, *CWL*, 7:481.

189. Swett to Herndon, 1887, Douglas L. Wilson and Rodney O. Davis, eds., *Herndon's Informants: Letters, Interviews, and Statements about Abraham Lincoln* [hereafter *HI*] (Urbana: University of Illinois Press, 1998), 165n.

190. John Hay to James C. Welling, Washington, 25 July 1864, *CWL*, 7:462.

191. W. D. Gallagher to Salmon P. Chase, Louisville, 11 June 1863, Chase Papers, Historical Society of Pennsylvania.

192. Lincoln to Albert G. Hodges, Washington, 4 Apr. 1864, *CWL*, 7:281–282.

193. Lincoln to Eliza Gurney, Washington, 4 Sept. 1864, *CWL*, 7:535.

194. Undated memo known as the "Meditation on the Divine Will," probably written in 1864, *CWL*, 5:403–404.

195. Lincoln to Isaac M. Schemerhorn, Washington, 12 Sept. 1864, *CWL*, 8:1–2.

196. Speech to the 164th Ohio Regiment, 18 Aug. 1864, *CWL*, 7:504–505.

197. Speech to the 166th Ohio Regiment, 22 Aug. 1864, *CWL*, 7:512.

198. Lincoln to John A. J. Creswell, Washington, 17 Mar. 1864, *CWL*, 7:251.

199. Lincoln to Creswell, Washington, 7 Mar. 1864, *CWL*, 7:226–227.

200. Lew Wallace, *Lew Wallace: An Autobiography* (2 vols.; New York: Harper, 1906), 2:670, 672, 684–685; Wallace to his wife, Washington, 13 Mar. 1864, Baltimore, 1 Apr. 1864, Wallace Papers, Indiana Historical Society; Wallace to Benson J. Lossing, Crawfordsville, Indiana, 26 Jan. 1864, ibid.

201. Henry Winter Davis to Samuel F. Du Pont, n.p., 29 Feb. 1864, transcript, S. F. Du Pont Papers, Hagley Museum, Wilmington, Delaware.

202. Speech in Baltimore, 18 Apr. 1864, *CWL*, 7:301–302.

203. William L. W. Seabrook, *Maryland's Great Part in Saving the Union* (Westminster, MD.: American Sentinel, 1913), 55–56.

204. Lincoln to Henry W. Hoffman, Washington, 10 Oct. 1864, *CWL*, 8:41

205. Burlingame and Ettlinger, eds., *Hay Diary*, 230 (entry for 24 Sept. 1864).

206. Child to Eliza Scudder, Wayland, Massachusetts, 14 Nov. 1864, Samuel J. May Collection of Antislavery Papers, Cornell University.

207. Philbrick to Nicolay, Washington, 28 Oct. 1864, Nicolay Papers, DLC.

208. Washington correspondence, 19 Oct., Sacramento *Daily Union*, 25 Nov. 1864, in Burlingame, ed., *Lincoln Observed*, 138.

209. Washington correspondence, 2 Nov., Sacramento *Daily Union*, 2 Dec. 1864, ibid., 142.

210. James J. Faran to Alexander Long, Cincinnati, 26 June 1864, Long Papers, Cincinnati Historical Society.

211. *CWL*, 8:52–53.

212. *The American Annual Cyclopedia, 1864*, 769.

213. New York Society for the Diffusion of Political Knowledge, *Hand-book of the Democracy for 1863 & '64* (New York, 1863), 2.

214. *The American Annual Cyclopedia and Register of Important Events of the Year 1864* (New York: D. Appleton, 1865), 766.

215. New York *Daily News*, 18, 25 Oct. 1864.

216. Stoddard, "White House Sketches, No. 11," New York *Citizen*, 27 Oct. 1866, in William O. Stoddard, *Inside the White House in War Times: Memoirs and Reports of Lincoln's Secretary*, ed. Michael Burlingame (1890; Lincoln: University of Nebraska Press, 2000), 190.

217. Brooks, "Personal Recollections of Abraham Lincoln," in Burlingame, ed., *Lincoln Observed*, 211; Mary Lincoln, interview with William H. Herndon, Sept. 1866, *HI*, 361.

218. E. S. Nadel, "Some Impressions of Lincoln," *Scribner's Magazine* 39 (Mar. 1906):370.

219. New York *Evening Post*, 1 Nov. 1864.

220. William O. Stoddard, *Inside the White House in War Times* (New York: C. L. Webster, 1890), 55.

221. Lincoln to William T. Sherman, Washington, 19 Sept. 1864, *CWL*, 8:11.

222. William T. Sherman to John Sherman, 7 July 1863, Sherman Family Papers, DLC.

223. Lincoln to Schurz, Washington, 13 Mar. 1864, *CWL*. 7:243–244.

224. Carl Schurz to Theodore Petrasch, Bethlehem, Pennsylvania, 12 Oct. 1864, Joseph Schafer, ed., *Intimate Letters of Carl Schurz,*

1841–1869 (Madison: State Historical Society of Wisconsin, 1928), 306–309.

225. Schurz, *The Reminiscences of Carl Schurz* (3 vols.; New York: McClure, 1907–1908), 3:104–105.

226. Response to a serenade, 19 Oct. 1864, *CWL*, 8:53.

227. Henry W. Bellows to his son, 2 Nov. 1864, Bellows Papers, MHi.

228. Israel Washburn to Elihu B. Washburne, Portland, 27 July 1864, Washburn Family Papers, Washburn Memorial Library, Norlands, Maine.

229. Nicolay to Therena Bates, Washington, 18 Sept. 1864, in Burlingame, ed., *With Lincoln in the White House*, 160.

230. George W. Adams to Manton Marble, Washington, 20 Sept. 1864, Marble Papers, DLC; Cameron to William P. Fessenden, Washington, 10 Sept. 1864, Lincoln Collection, Yale University.

231. William D. Kelley to Lincoln, Philadelphia, 30 Sept. 1864, AL MSS DLC.

232. George Boker to Bayard Taylor, 13 Oct. 1864, in Edward Sculley Bradley, *George Henry Boker: Poet and Patriot* (Philadelphia: University of Pennsylvania Press, 1927), 224.

233. James T. Hale to Gideon Welles, Bellefonte, 17 Oct. 1864, Welles Papers, DLC.

234. Charles Sumner, in David Ross Locke, *The Struggles (Social, Financial, and Political) of Petroleum V. Nasby* (Boston: Richards, 1872), 15.

235. Benjamin P. Thomas and Harold M. Hyman, *Stanton: The Life and Times of Lincoln's Secretary of War* (New York: Alfred A. Knopf, 1962), 330.

236. Burlingame and Ettlinger, eds., *Hay Diary*, 240–241 (entry for 11 Oct. 1864).

237. Alexander K. McClure, *Abraham Lincoln and Men of War-Times* (Philadelphia: Times, 1892), 202.

238. Peck to Singleton, Washington, 14 Oct. 1864, in Harry E. Pratt, ed., *Concerning Mr. Lincoln: In Which Abraham Lincoln Is Pictured as He Appeared to Letter Writers of His Time*

(Springfield, IL: Abraham Lincoln Association, 1944), 113.

239. Burlingame and Ettlinger, eds., *Hay Diary,* 243 (entry for 8 Nov. 1864).

240. Washington correspondence by Noah Brooks, 17 May, Sacramento *Daily Union,* 14 June 1865, in Burlingame, ed., *Lincoln Observed,* 198–199.

241. Washington correspondence, 11 Nov., Sacramento *Daily Union,* 10 Dec. 1864, ibid., 142–143; Burlingame and Ettlinger, eds., *Hay Diary,* 244 (entry for 8 Nov. 1864).

242. Washington *Post,* 24 Sept. 1889.

243. Burlingame and Ettlinger, eds., *Hay Diary,* 245 (entry for 8 Nov. 1864).

244. Washington correspondence, 11 Nov., Sacramento *Daily Union,* 10 Dec. 1864, in Burlingame, ed., *Lincoln Observed,* 143.

245. Burlingame and Ettlinger, eds., *Hay Diary,* 244 (entry for 8 Nov. 1864).

246. Washington correspondence, 11 Nov. Sacramento *Daily Union,* 10 Dec. 1864, in Burlingame, ed., *Lincoln Observed,* 143–144.

247. Burlingame and Ettlinger, eds., *Hay Diary,* 246 (entry for 8 Nov. 1864).

248. Washington correspondence, 11 Nov., Sacramento *Daily Union,* 10 Dec. 1864, in Burlingame, ed., *Lincoln Observed,* 144.

249. *CWL,* 8:96.

250. Burlingame and Ettlinger, eds., *Hay Diary,* 246 (entry for 8 Nov. 1864).

251. Strasburg, Virginia, dispatch of 8 Nov. 1864, in the *Green Mountain Freeman* (Montpelier, Vermont), in Emil Rosenblatt, ed., *Anti-Rebel: The Civil War Letters of Wilbur Fisk* (Croton-on-Hudson: E. Rosenblatt, 1983), 276.

252. Charles Russell Lowell to his wife, near Smithfield, 1 Sept. 1864, in Edward W. Emerson, *Life and Letters of Charles Russell Lowell, Captain Sixth United States Cavalry, Colonel Second Massachusetts Cavalry, Brigadier-General United States Volunteers* (Boston: Houghton Mifflin, 1907), 333.

253. James M. McPherson, *For Cause and Comrades: Why Men Fought in the Civil War* (New York: Oxford University Press, 1997), 176-177.

254. John Walter Lee to his father, 6 Sept. 1864, in Joseph Allan Frank, *With Ballot and Bayonet: The Political Socialization of American Civil War Soldiers* (Athens: University of Georgia Press, 1998), 95.

255. Major Thaddeus H. Capron of 59th Illinois Infantry, "War Diary of Thaddeus H. Capron, 1861–65," *Journal of the Illinois State Society* (1919) 12:395 (letter dated East Point, 1 Oct. 1864).

256. Joseph P. Thompson, sermon delivered in New York, 30 Apr. 1865, in *Our Martyr President,* 191.

257. Washington correspondence, 12 Nov., *National Anti-Slavery Standard* (New York), 19 Nov. 1864.

258. Washington correspondence, 11 Nov., Sacramento *Daily Union,* 10 Dec. 1864, in Burlingame, ed., *Lincoln Observed,* 145.

259. *CWL,* 8:100–101.

260. Burlingame and Ettlinger, eds., *Hay Diary,* 248 (entry for 11 Nov. 1864).

261. Nicolay and Hay, *Lincoln,* 9:379; Washington correspondence, 11 Nov., London *Times,* n.d., copied in the New York *Daily News,* 20 Dec. 1864.

262. Child to Eliza Scudder, Wayland, Massachusetts, 14 Nov. 1864, Samuel J. May Antislavery Papers Collection, Cornell University.

263. Reply to Maryland Union Committee, 17 Nov. 1864, *CWL,* 8:113.

264. Washington correspondence, 21 Nov., *National Anti-Slavery Standard* (New York), 26 Nov. 1864.

265. *CWL,* 8:149–150.

266. *Harper's Weekly,* 19 Nov. 1864.

267. J. W. Geary to his wife, near Savannah, no day of the month indicated, December 1864, in William Alan Blair, ed., *A Politician Goes to War: The Civil War Letters of John White Geary* (University Park: Pennsylvania State University Press, 1995), 217.

268. Norton to George Perkins Marsh, Cambridge, 29 Dec. 1864, Marsh Papers, University of Vermont.

269. Chauncey B. Welton to his parents, 13 Oct. 1864, in Christine Dee, ed., *Ohio's War: The Civil War in Documents* (Athens, OH: Ohio University Press, 2006), 181.

270. Edward Younger, ed., *Inside the Confederate Government: The Diary of Robert Garlick Hill Kean, Head of the Bureau of War* (New York: Oxford University Press, 1957), 177 (entry for 20 Nov. 1864).

271. Sarah Woolfolk Wiggins, ed., *The Journals of Josiah Gorgas, 1857–1878* (Tuscaloosa: University of Alabama Press, 1995), 139 (entry for 17 Nov. 1864).

272. J. W. Geary to his wife, Atlanta, 24 Nov. 1864, in Blair, ed., *A Politician Goes to War,* 211.

273. Brooks, *Washington, D.C., in Lincoln's Time,* ed. Mitgang, 198.

274. James M. Winchell, "Three Interviews with President Lincoln," *The Galaxy* 16 (1873): 40.

275. *CWL,* 8:113.

276. Brooks, *Washington, D.C., in Lincoln's Time,* ed. Mitgang, 200.

277. Noah Brooks, *Abraham Lincoln: The Nation's Leader in the Great Struggle through which was Maintained the Existence of the United States* (Washington, DC: National Tribune, 1909), 403.

278. Dispatch dated 10 September, London *Daily News,* 27 Sept. 1864, in Allan Nevins, *The War for the Union* (4 vols.; New York: Scribner, 1959–1971), 4:103, 141–142.

279. Washington correspondence, 2 Nov. 1863, 21 July 1862, New York *Examiner,* 5 Nov. 1863, 24 July 1862, in Michael Burlingame, ed., *Dispatches from Lincoln's White House: The Anonymous Civil War Journalism of Presidential Secretary William O. Stoddard* (Lincoln: University of Nebraska Press, 2002), 185, 88.

280. Stowe in *Littell's Living Age,* 6 Feb. 1864, 284.

281. Phillips to Elizabeth Cady Stanton, 23 Apr. 1865, Ida Husted Harper Collection, CSmH.

282. Smith to Lydia Maria Child, 21 Nov. 1864, in Ralph Volney Harlow, *Gerrit Smith, Philanthropist and Reformer* (New York: H. Holt, 1939), 441.

283. Stone to an unidentified friend, 12 Dec. 1864, in Elinor Rice Hays, *Morning Star: A Biography of Lucy Stone, 1818–1893* (New York: Harcourt, Brace & World, 1961), 183.

284. Curtis to Charles Eliot Norton, New York, 9 Nov. 1864, Curtis Papers, Harvard University.

285. Child to Eliza Scudder, Wayland, Massachusetts, 14 Nov. 1864, Samuel J. May Antislavery Papers Collection, Cornell University.

286. Bradford Wood to Chase, Copenhagen, 29 Dec. 1864, Chase Papers, DLC.

287. Davis to S. F. Du Pont, 28 or 29 Sept. 1864, in Hayes, ed., *Du Pont Letters,* 3:392.

288. Conway's article, *Fraser's Magazine,* Jan. 1865, in Mary Elizabeth Burtis, *Moncure Conway, 1832–1907* (New Brunswick, NJ: Rutgers University Press, 1952), 116.

289. G. S. Hillard to J. F. Fisher, Boston, 21 Feb. 1865, Francis F. Hart Collection, Historical Society of Pennsylvania; C. H. Brainard to William Lloyd Garrison, Boston, 25 July 1864, Garrison Papers, Boston Public Library.

290. Grant to Stanton, City Point, 10 Nov. 1864, *OR,* I, 42, 3:581.

291. *CWL,* 8:326.

292. Thurlow Weed to Lincoln, New York, 4 Mar. 1865, AL MSS DLC.

293. Brooks, "Personal Recollections of Abraham Lincoln," in Burlingame, ed., *Lincoln Observed,* 205–206.

Chapter 35. "Let the *Thing* Be Pressed"

1. Michael Burlingame and John R. Turner Ettlinger, eds., *Inside Lincoln's White House: The Complete Civil War Diary of John Hay* (Carbondale: Southern Illinois University Press, 1997), 76–77, 241 (entries for [July–Aug. 1863], 13 Oct. 1864).

2. John Jay to Chase, New York, 23 Nov. 1864, Chase Papers, DLC.

3. Benjamin P. Thomas and Harold M. Hyman, *Stanton: The Life and Times of Lincoln's Secretary of War* (New York: Alfred A. Knopf, 1962), 337.

4. Undated memo by Ebenezer Rockwood Hoar enclosed in Hoar to James Ford Rhodes, Concord, 9 Feb. 1894, Rhodes Papers, MHi.

5. Howard K. Beale and Alan W. Brownsword, eds., *Diary of Gideon Welles, Secretary of the Navy under Lincoln and Johnson* (3 vols.; New York: W. W. Norton, 1960), 2:182 (entry for 26 Nov. 1864).

6. Blair to John A. Andrew, Silver Spring, 19 Nov. 1864, Andrew Papers, MHi.

7. Montgomery Blair to E. D. Morgan, 20 Nov. 1864, Morgan Papers, New-York Historical Society, in Allan Nevins, *The War for the Union* (4 vols.; New York: Scribner, 1959–1971), 4:118; Charles A. Dana to James Shepherd Pike, Washington, 12 Dec. 1864, Pike Papers, University of Maine.

8. Howard K. Beale, ed., *The Diary of Edward Bates, 1859–1866* (Annual Report of the American Historical Association for the Year 1930, vol. IV; Washington, DC: U.S. Government Printing Office, 1933), 427–428 (entry for 22 Nov. 1864).

9. Coffey in Allen Thorndike Rice, ed., *Reminiscences of Abraham Lincoln by Distinguished Men of His Time* (New York: North American Publishing Company, 1886), 197.

10. John G. Nicolay and John Hay, *Abraham Lincoln: A History* (10 vols.; New York: Century, 1890), 9:392.

11. Sumner to Lincoln, Boston, 20 Nov. 1864, AL MSS DLC.

12. Colfax to Lincoln, South Bend, Indiana, 23 Oct. 1864, AL MSS DLC.

13. Colfax to Chase, Washington, 5 Dec. 1864, Chase Papers, Historical Society of Pennsylvania.

14. Albert Smith to Lincoln, Boston, 29 Nov. 1864, AL MSS DLC.

15. Beale ed., *Welles Diary*, 2:193 (entry for 6 Dec. 1864).

16. Ewing to Lincoln, Washington, 3 Dec. 1864, AL MSS DLC.

17. Henry Wilson interviewed by John G. Nicolay, Washington, 1 Apr. 1874, in Michael Burlingame, ed., *An Oral History of Abraham Lincoln: John G. Nicolay's Interviews and Essays*

(Carbondale: Southern Illinois University Press, 1996), 85.

18. Lafayette Foster interviewed by John G. Nicolay, 23 October 1878, ibid., 53.

19. George Sewall Boutwell, *Reminiscences of Sixty Years in Public Affairs* (2 vols.; New York: McClure, Phillips, 1902), 2:29

20. Josiah Bushnell Grinnell, *Men and Events of Forty Years: Autobiographical Reminiscences of an Active Career from 1850 to 1890* (Boston: D. Lothrop, 1891), 173.

21. Edwards Pierrepont to Lincoln, New York, 24 Nov. 1864, AL MSS DLC.

22. Colfax to Chase, Washington, 5 Dec. 1864, Chase Papers, Historical Society of Pennsylvania.

23. Washington correspondence, New York *Independent*, n.d., copied in the *National Anti-Slavery Standard*, 17 Dec. 1864.

24. John B. Alley in Rice, ed., *Reminiscences of Lincoln*, 582; Henry Wilson, conversation with John G. Nicolay, Washington, 1 Apr. 1874, in Burlingame, ed., *Oral History of Lincoln*, 85.

25. J. W. Schuckers, *The Life and Public Services of Salmon Portland Chase* (New York: Appleton, 1874), 487.

26. Francis B. Carpenter, *The Inner Life of Abraham Lincoln: Six Months at the White House* (New York: Hurd and Houghton, 1867), 219.

27. Noah Brooks, *Statesmen* (New York: Charles Scribner's Sons, 1893), 170; Brooks, *Abraham Lincoln and the Downfall of American Slavery* (New York: G. P. Putnam's Sons, 1895), 439.

28. John D. Defrees to Josiah G. Holland, Washington, 8 Aug. 1865, in Allen C. Guelzo, "Holland's Informants: The Construction of Josiah Holland's 'Life of Abraham Lincoln,'" *Journal of the Abraham Lincoln Association* 23 (2002):46–47.

29. Beale, ed., *Welles Diary*, 2:181 (entry for 26 Nov. 1864).

30. Undated memo by Ebenezer Rockwood Hoar enclosed in Hoar to James Ford Rhodes, Concord, 9 Feb. 1894, Rhodes Papers, MHi.

31. J. W. Schuckers to Evarts, 11 June 1875, in Brainerd Dyer, *The Public Career of William*

M. Evarts (Berkeley: University of California Press, 1933), 157n; Boutwell, *Reminiscences,* 2:29.

32. Baltimore *American and Commercial Advertiser,* 9 Dec. 1864, in Don E. Fehrenbacher and Virginia Fehrenbacher, eds., *Recollected Words of Abraham Lincoln* (Stanford, CA: Stanford University Press, 1996), 15.

33. Boutwell, *Reminiscences,* 2:29.

34. Burlingame and Ettlinger, eds., *Hay Diary,* 217 (entry for 1 July 1864).

35. Fessenden to Chase, 20 Oct. 1864, in Schuckers, *Chase,* 510.

36. New York *Tribune,* 7 Dec. 1864; George Wood to Chase, Washington, 21 Nov. 1864, Chase Papers, DLC.

37. Truman Woodruff to Chase, St. Louis, 7 Dec. 1864, Chase Papers, DLC.

38. R. D. Musser to Chase, Nashville, Tennessee, 8 Dec. 1864, ibid.

39. Richard Smith told this to Enoch T. Carson. Carson to Chase, Cincinnati, 7 Dec. 1864, ibid.

40. Nicolay to Therena Bates, Washington, 8 Dec. 1864, Michael Burlingame, ed., *With Lincoln in the White House: Letters, Memoranda, and Other Writings of John G. Nicolay, 1860–1865* (Carbondale: Southern Illinois University Press, 2000), 166.

41. Beale, ed., *Welles Diary,* 2:196 (entry for 15 Dec. 1864); Virginia Fox diary, 10 Dec. 1864, Levi Woodbury Papers, DLC.

42. Blair to Samuel J. Tilden, Washington, 5 June 1868, in John Bigelow, ed., *Letters and Literary Memorials of Samuel J. Tilden* (2 vols.; New York: Harper, 1908), 1:233; Dana to James Shepherd Pike, Washington, 12 Dec. 1864, Pike Papers, University of Maine.

43. Chase to Lincoln, Washington, 6 Dec. 1864, AL MSS DLC.

44. Hay to [Charles S.] Spencer, Washington, 25 Nov. [1864], in Michael Burlingame, ed., *At Lincoln's Side: John Hay's Civil War Correspondence and Selected Writings* (Carbondale: Southern Illinois University Press, 2000), 101.

45. Lincoln to Mrs. Bixby, Washington, 21 Nov. 1864, Roy P. Basler et al., eds., *Collected Works of Abraham Lincoln* [hereafter *CWL*] (8 vols. plus index; New Brunswick, NJ: Rutgers University Press, 1953–1955), 8:116–117; Michael Burlingame, "The Authorship of the Bixby Letter," in Burlingame, ed., *At Lincoln's Side,* 169–184.

46. Randall and Current, *Last Full Measure,* 48.

47. Sandburg, *Abraham Lincoln: The War Years* (4 vols.; New York: Harcourt, Brace, 1939), 3:669; Sandburg, *Abraham Lincoln: The Prairie Years and the War Years* (New York: Harcourt, Brace, 1954), 640.

48. David A. Anderson, ed., *The Literary Works of Abraham Lincoln* (Columbus, Ohio: Charles E. Merrill Publishing Company, 1970), vi.

49. Herbert Joseph Edwards and John Erskine Hankins, *Lincoln the Writer: The Development of His Literary Style* (University of Maine Studies, second series, no. 76; Orono: University of Maine, 1962), 90, 92.

50. Daniel Kilham Dodge, "The Emotional and Intellectual Side of Lincoln," typescript enclosed in Dodge to David Kinley, Urbana, Illinois, 17 Feb. 1924, Dodge Papers, Lincoln Shrine, A. K. Smiley Public Library, Redlands, California.

51. Burlingame, "The Authorship of the Bixby Letter," 171.

52. Philadelphia *Age,* n.d., copied in the Columbus, Ohio, *Crisis,* 16 Dec. 1864.

53. Elizabeth Keckley, *Behind the Scenes* (New York: G. W. Carleton, 1868), 121–122.

54. Katherine Helm, *The True Story of Mary, Wife of Lincoln* (New York: Harper, 1928), 227, 229–230.

55. Lincoln to Grant, Washington, 19 Jan. 1865, *CWL,* 8:223.

56. Grant to Lincoln, Annapolis Junction, Maryland, 21 Jan. 1865, AL MSS DLC.

57. Pease and Randall, eds., *Browning Diary,* 1:693 (entry for 14 Nov. 1864).

58. H. P. H. Bromwell's reminiscences in the Denver *Tribune,* 18 May 1879.

59. Dix to Lincoln, New York, 14 Feb. 1865, AL MSS DLC.

60. New York *Times*, 16 Dece. 1864.

61. *CWL*, 8:141.

62. Isaac N. Arnold, "Abraham Lincoln: A Paper Read Before the Royal Historical Society, London, June 16th, 1881" (pamphlet; Chicago: Fergus Printing Company, 1881), 28.

63. Charles Francis Adams to his son, London, 24 Mar. 1865, Adams Papers, MHi.

64. Burlingame and Ettlinger, eds., *Hay Diary*, 211 (entry for 24 June 1864).

65. Boston *Commonwealth*, 24 Dec. 1864.

66. New York *Times*, 20 Dec. 1864.

67. *CWL*, 8:151–152.

68. New York *Independent*, 8 Dec. 1864.

69. Reuben D. Mussey to Lincoln, Nashville, 9 Dec. 1864, AL MSS DLC.

70. Oliver Johnson to Lincoln, New York, 7 Dec. 1864, AL MSS DLC.

71. Stanton to Grant, 3 Mar. 1865, John Y. Simon, ed., *The Papers of Ulysses S. Grant* (Carbondale: Southern Illinois University Press, 1967–), 14:91.

72. *CWL*, 8:152.

73. Elizabeth Cady Stanton to Susan B. Anthony, New York, 8 Dec. 1864, Theodore Stanton and Harriot Stanton Blatch, eds., *Elizabeth Cady Stanton as Revealed in Her Letters, Diary and Reminiscences* (2 vols.; New York: Harper and Brothers, 1922), 2:103.

74. Julius Rockwell to David Davis, Pittsfield, 7 Dec. 1864; Samuel F. Miller to David Davis, Washington, 21 Dec. 1864, David Davis Papers, IHi.

75. Washington correspondence, 7 Dec. 1864, Sacramento *Daily Union*, 11 Jan. 1865, in Michael Burlingame, ed., *Lincoln Observed: Civil War Dispatches of Noah Brooks* (Baltimore, MD: Johns Hopkins University Press, 1998), 150–151; Brooks to George Witherle, Washington, 10 Dec. 1864, ibid., 155.

76. Washington correspondence by Noah Brooks, 10 Jan., Sacramento *Daily Union*, 22 Feb. 1865, ibid., 157.

77. James Grant Wilson, "Recollections of Lincoln," *Putnam's Magazine*, Feb. 1909:529.

78. Washington correspondence by Noah Brooks, 22 Mar., Sacramento *Daily Union*,

19 Apr. 1865, in Burlingame, ed., *Lincoln Observed*, 175–176.

79. Henry B. Anthony to Lincoln, Providence, 24 Aug. 1863, AL MSS DLC.

80. Lincoln to Hackett, Washington, 2 Nov. 1863, *CWL*, 6:558–559.

81. Hay, "Life in the White House in the Time of Lincoln," Burlingame, ed., *At Lincoln's Side*, 136.

82. Henry to his wife, Washington, 13 Mar. 1865, Henry Papers, IHi.

83. Carpenter, *Inner Life of Abraham Lincoln*, 276.

84. Forbes to Henry W. Bellows, Boston, 13 Dec. 1861, Bellows Papers, MHi

85. Samuel Hooper to Chase, Washington, 10 Mar. 1865, Chase Papers, Historical Society of Pennsylvania.

86. Burlingame and Ettlinger, eds., *Hay Diary*, 249 (entry for 11 Nov. 1864).

87. Hugh McCulloch to his wife, Washington, 2 Oct. 1864, Hugh McCulloch Papers, InU.

88. Hugh McCulloch, *Men and Measures of Half a Century: Sketches and Comments* (New York: C. Scribner's Sons, 1888), 193.

89. *CWL*, 8:149; Rollins in Osborn H. Oldroyd, ed., *The Lincoln Memorial: Album-Immortelles* (New York: G. W. Carleton, 1882), 492–493.

90. Corbin to Lincoln, Washington, 8 Dec. 1864, AL MSS DLC.

91. Elizabeth Blair Lee to Samuel Phillips Lee, Washington, 2 Feb. 1865, Virginia Jeans Laas, ed., *Wartime Washington: The Civil War Letters of Elizabeth Blair Lee* (Urbana: University of Illinois Press, 1991), 472.

92. David Lindsey, *"Sunset" Cox: Irrepressible Democrat* (Detroit: Wayne State University Press, 1959), 93.

93. Samuel S. Cox, *Union-Disunion-Reunion: Three Decades of Federal Legislation, 1855–1885* (Washington, DC: J. M. Stoddart, 1885), 310.

94. John Jay Janney, "Talking with the President: Four Interviews with Abraham Lincoln," *Civil War Times Illustrated* 26 (Sept. 1987): 34.

95. Samuel S. Cox, *Eight Years in Congress: From 1857 to 1865* (New York: Appleton, 1865), 398.

96. Seward, "The Situation and the Duty: Speech of William H. Seward at Auburn, N.Y., 31 October 1868" (pamphlet; Washington, DC: Philp and Solomons, 1868), 23.

97. Ashley to Lincoln, Washington, 25 Dec. 1864, AL MSS DLC.

98. *Congressional Globe*, 38th Congress, 2nd Session, 180 (9 Jan. 1865).

99. Isaac N. Arnold, *The History of Abraham Lincoln and the Overthrow of Slavery* (Chicago: Clarke, 1866), 469.

100. Herrick to Seward, New York, 8 Aug. 1865, Seward Papers, University of Rochester.

101. Nicolay, memorandum, 18 Jan. 1865, in Burlingame, ed., *With Lincoln in the White House*, 171.

102. *Congressional Globe*, 38th Congress, 2nd Session, 530 (31 Jan. 1865).

103. George H. Yeaman to Lincoln, Owensboro, Kentucky, 13 Jan. 1862, AL MSS DLC.

104. Robert W. Latham to Seward, Washington, 9 Jan. 1865, Seward Papers, University of Rochester.

105. Blair to Andrew Johnson, 16 June 1865, LeRoy P. Graf and Ralph W. Haskins, eds., *The Papers of Andrew Johnson* (16 vols.; Knoxville: University of Tennessee Press, 1967–2000), 8:247.

106. Lincoln to Ashley, Washington, 31 Jan. 1865, *CWL*, 8:248.

107. Elizabeth Peabody to Horace Mann, Jr., [mid Feb. 1865], in Arlin Turner, ed., "Elizabeth Peabody Visits Lincoln, February 1865," *New England Quarterly* 48 (Mar. 1975):119–120.

108. Cornelius Cole to his wife, Washington, 31 Jan. 1865, in *Memoirs of Cornelius Cole, Ex-Senator of the United States from California* (New York: McLoughlin Brothers, 1908), 220.

109. Schurz to his wife, Washington, 1 Feb. 1865, in Joseph Schafer, ed., *Intimate Letters of Carl Schurz, 1841–1869* (Madison: State Historical Society of Wisconsin, 1928), 314–315.

110. Martin B. Pasternak, *Rise Now and Fly to Arms: The Life of Henry Highland Garnet* (New York: Garland, 1995), 120.

111. Isaac N. Arnold, *The Life of Abraham Lincoln* (Chicago: Jansen, McClurg, 1885), 366.

112. Garrison to Lincoln, Boston, 13 Feb. 1865, AL MSS DLC.

113. *The Liberator* (Boston), 10 Feb. 1865.

114. Chamberlain letter to the editor, New York, 22 Sept. 1883, New York *Tribune*, 4 Nov. 1883.

115. John Murray Forbes to Garrison, Boston, 18 Jan. 1865, Garrison Papers, Boston Public Library.

116. *CWL*, 8:254–255.

117. William Ernest Smith, *The Francis Preston Blair Family in Politics* (2 vols.; New York: Macmillan, 1933), 2:303; Blair to Greeley, Silver Spring, [20?] December 1864, Greeley Papers, New York Public Library; Lincoln to Blair, Washington, 18 Jan. 1865, *CWL*, 8:220–221.

118. Carl Sandburg's notes of an interview with Joseph Fifer, [1923], Sandburg-Barrett Collection, Newberry Library, Chicago.

119. Thomas E. Schott, *Alexander H. Stephens of Georgia: A Biography* (Baton Rouge: Louisiana State University Press, 1988), 442.

120. Chandler to his wife, Washington, 25 Jan. 1865, Chandler Papers, DLC.

121. Washington correspondence, 8 Feb., Springfield, Massachusetts, *Republican*, n.d., copied in the New York *World*, 11 Feb. 1865.

122. Joseph Medill to Lincoln, Washington, 15 Jan. 1865, AL MSS DLC.

123. Henry Ward Beecher in Rice, ed., *Reminiscences of Lincoln*, 249–250.

124. Henry Ward Beecher to Lincoln, Brooklyn, 4 Feb. 1865, AL MSS DLC.

125. Beale, ed., *Welles Diary*, 2:231–232 (entry for 30 Jan. 1865).

126. New York *Herald*, 23 Jan. 1865.

127. Lincoln to Seward, Washington, 31 Jan. 1865, *CWL*, 8:250–251.

128. Lincoln to Grant, Washington, 1 Feb. 1865, *CWL*, 8:252.

129. Grant to Lincoln, City Point, 1 Feb. 1865, AL MSS DLC.

130. [Singleton] to [Beverly Tucker?], [11?] Sept. 1864, Clement C. Clay Correspondence, Record Group 109, National Archives, in Ludwell Johnson, "Lincoln's Solution to the Problem of Peace Terms, 1864–1865," *Journal of Southern History* 34 (1968):579.

131. Pease and Randall, eds., *Browning Diary,* 1:694, 695 (entries for 24 and 26 Nov. 1864).

132. Singleton interviewed by John E. Wilkie, Chicago *Times,* 26 Dec. 1885.

133. New York *Times,* 12 Feb. 1928.

134. Alexander Long to Greeley, Washington, 11 Jan. 1865, Greeley Papers, New York Public Library.

135. Washington correspondence, 1 Feb., New York *Tribune,* 2 Feb. 1865; Jewett to the editor of the New York *Tribune,* Washington, 4 Feb., New York *Tribune,* 6 Feb. 1865.

136. Washington correspondence, 1 Feb., Cincinnati *Gazette,* 2 Feb. 1865.

137. Reminiscences of Stephens given to Evan P. Howell in 1882, in Howell to Henry Watterson, n.p., n.d., in the Louisville *Courier-Journal,* n.d., copied in an unidentified clipping, LMF.

138. Washington correspondence, 22 Feb., by Van [D. W. Bartlett], Springfield, Massachusetts, *Republican,* 25 Feb. 1865.

139. Reminiscences of Stephens given to Evan P. Howell in 1882, in Howell to Henry Watterson, n.p., n.d, in the Louisville *Courier-Journal,* n.d., copied in an unidentified clipping, LMF.

140. Stephens's account of the conference, given shortly after its conclusion, to the editor of a newspaper in his hometown, Augusta *Chronicle and Sentinel,* 7 June 1865.

141. Alexander H. Stephens, *A Constitutional View of the Late War between the States: Its Causes, Character, Conduct and Results, Presented in a Series of Colloquies at Liberty Hall* (2 vols.; Philadelphia: National Publishing Company, 1868–1870), 2:600, 601, 608.

142. John A. Campbell, *Reminiscences and Documents Relating to the Civil War during the Year 1865* (Baltimore, MD: John Murphy, 1887), 12–13.

143. Augusta *Chronicle and Sentinel,* 7 June 1865.

144. Stephens, *Constitutional View,* 2:612.

145. Augusta *Chronicle and Sentinel,* 7 June 1865.

146. Washington correspondence, 22 Feb. by Van [D. W. Bartlett], Springfield, Massachusetts, *Republican,* 25 Feb. 1865.

147. Stephens, *Constitutional View,* 2:617.

148. John Eaton, *Grant, Lincoln, and the Freedmen: Reminiscences of the Civil War with Special Reference to the Work for the Contrabands and Freedmen of the Mississippi Valley* (New York: Longmans, Green, 1907), 89.

149. William J. Cooper, *Jefferson Davis, American* (New York: Alfred A. Knopf, 2000), 513.

150. Richmond *Dispatch,* 7 Feb. 1865, in Edward McPherson, *The Political History of the United States of America During the Great Rebellion* (Washington: Philp and Solomons, 1865), 572.

151. John A. Campbell to Benjamin R. Curtis, Fort Pulaski, Georgia, 20 July 1865, *Century Magazine,* Oct. 1889, 952.

152. Singleton interviewed by John E. Wilkie, Chicago *Times,* 26 Dec. 1885.

153. Chandler to his wife, Washington, 6, 10 Feb. 1865, Chandler Papers, DLC.

154. Message to Congress, [5 Feb. 1865], *CWL,* 8:261.

155. John Palmer Usher interviewed by John G. Nicolay, Washington, 11 Oct. 1877, Burlingame, ed., *Oral History of Lincoln,* 66.

156. Beale, ed., *Welles Diary,* 2:237 (entry for 6 Feb. 1865).

157. John Palmer Usher interviewed by John G. Nicolay, Washington, 11 Oct. 1877, Burlingame, ed., *Oral History of Lincoln,* 66.

158. Memo by Fessenden on a summons to a cabinet meeting dated Washington, 5 Feb. 1865, Fessenden Papers, Bowdoin College.

159. Message to the House of Representatives, 10 Feb. 1865, *CWL,* 8:284–285.

160. Washington correspondence, 12 February, Sacramento *Daily Union*, 22 Mar. 1865, in Burlingame, ed., *Lincoln Observed*, 163.

161. *Congressional Globe*, 38th Congress, 2nd Session, 733 (10 Feb. 1865).

162. Franklin B. Sanborn to Moncure D. Conway, Concord, Massachusetts, 19 Feb. 1865, Conway Papers, Columbia University.

163. George L. Stearns to Moncure D. Conway, Boston, 13 Mar. 1865, ibid.

164. May to Richard Webb, Boston, 2 Jan. 1865, May Papers, Boston Public Library.

165. Richmond *Sentinel,* 6 Feb. 1865, in George C. Rable, *The Confederate Republic: A Revolution against Politics* (Chapel Hill: University of North Carolina Press, 1994), 292.

166. Gideon Welles, "Lincoln and Johnson: Their Plan of Reconstruction and the Resumption of National Authority," *Galaxy* 13 (Apr. 1872), 522.

167. Sara Pryor, *My Day: Reminiscences of a Long Life* (New York: Macmillan, 1909), 251.

168. Weldon in Rice, ed., *Reminiscences of Lincoln,* 212–213.

169. Edward Atkinson to his wife, Washington, 5 July 1864, Atkinson Papers, MHi; Beale, ed., *Welles Diary,* 2:66 (entry for 5 July 1864).

170. Lincoln to Canby, Washington, 12 Dec. 1864, *CWL,* 8:164.

171. John Murray Forbes to Edward Atkinson, Washington, 8 Mar. 1865, Atkinson Papers, MHi.

172. Morgan to Thurlow Weed, Washington, 29 May 1864, Weed Papers, Rochester University.

173. C. A. Dana to J. S. Pike, Washington, 10 May 1865, Pike Papers, University of Maine.

174. Pease and Randall, eds., *Browning Diary,* 2:5 (entry for 1 Feb. 1865).

175. Lincoln to Grant, Washington, 7 Feb. 1865, *CWL,* 8:267.

176. Grant to Stanton, City Point, 8 Mar. 1865, in Simon, ed., *Grant Papers,* 14:113.

177. Browning manuscript diary, entry for 3 July 1873, IHi; John Hay diary, entry for 13 Feb. 1867, Brown University.

178. James A. Briggs to Chase, New York, 15 Feb. 1864, Chase Papers, DLC; Draper to Fessenden, New York, 25, 30 Sept. 1864; Draper to Fessenden, Savannah, 23 Jan. 1865; Draper to Fessenden, New York, 16 Nov. 1864, Fessenden Papers, Western Reserve Historical Society.

179. Beale, ed., *Welles Diary,* 2:220 (entry for 3 Jan. 1865).

180. Leonard Swett to his son, Washington, n.d., David Davis Papers, IHi; Washington correspondence, 12 March, Sacramento *Daily Union*, 11 April 1865, in Burlingame, ed., *Lincoln Observed*, 172–174; New York *World*, 10 March 1865; Rochester, New York, *Union*, 11 March 1865.

181. Sally Emerson to Abby Gibbons, 8 Mar. 1865, in Margaret Hope Bacon, *Abby Hopper Gibbons: Prison Reformer and Social Activist* (Albany: State University of New York Press, 2000), 127.

182. Beale, ed., *Welles Diary,* 2:251 (entry for 4 Mar. 1865).

183. Washington correspondence, 4 Mar., New York *Times*, 5 Mar. 1865; Washington correspondence, 12 Mar., Sacramento *Daily Union*, 10 Apr. 1865, Burlingame, ed., *Lincoln Observed*, 166–167; Charles Adolphe de Pineton, Marquis de Chambrun, *Impressions of Lincoln and the Civil War: A Foreigner's Account* (New York: Random House, 1952), 37; John W. Forney, *Anecdotes of Public Men* (New York: Harper and Brothers, 1873), 177.

184. Beale, ed., *Welles Diary,* 2:252 (entry for 4 Mar. 1865).

185. Diary of William T. Coggeshall, 4 Mar. 1865, in Freda Postle Koch, *Colonel Coggeshall: The Man who Saved Lincoln* (Columbus, Ohio: Poko Press, 1985), 72.

186. Chandler to his wife, Washington, 6 Mar. 1865, Chandler Papers, DLC.

187. New York *World*, 6, 7 March 1865, in Hans L. Trefousse, *Andrew Johnson: A Biography* (New York: W. W. Norton, 1989), 190.

188. Ervin Chapman, *Latest Light on Abraham Lincoln* (New York: Fleming H. Revell, 1917), 294.

189. John W. Defrees to Richard W. Thompson, Washington, 20 Apr. 1865, Thompson Papers, LMF.

190. David D. Porter, *Incidents and Anecdotes of the Civil War* (New York: D. Appleton, 1885), 287; "Lincoln's Religion: Answer of William H. Herndon to Mrs. Lincoln," Springfield, 12 January 1874, *Illinois State Register* (Springfield), 14 Jan. 1874.

191. Brooks, *Washington, D.C., in Lincoln's Time*, ed. Mitgang, 74.

192. Story written for Noah Brooks, [6 Dec. 1864], *CWL*, 8:155.

193. Ibid., 8:332–333.

194. Washington correspondence, 4 Mar., New York *Herald*, 5 Mar. 1865.

195. Washington correspondence, 12 Mar., Sacramento *Daily Union*, 10 Apr. 1865, in Burlingame, ed., *Lincoln Observed*, 168.

196. Washington *Chronicle*, 2 Feb. 1864; *Missouri Republican* (St. Louis), n.d., copied in the *Illinois State Register* (Springfield), 8 Jan. 1865.

197. Frederick Douglass, *Life and Times of Frederick Douglass* (Hartford, CT: Park, 1881), 444; Rice, ed., *Reminiscences of Lincoln*, 192–193.

198. Keckley, *Behind the Scenes*, 160.

199. James Shepherd Pike, undated entry, notebook number 17, covering the period 4 Feb. to 30 May 1865, Pike Papers, University of Maine.

200. Halleck to Francis Lieber, Washington, 5 Mar. 1865, Lieber Papers, CSmH.

201. Carpenter, *Inner Life of Abraham Lincoln*, 234.

202. J. P. Thompson, sermon delivered in New York, 30 Apr. 1865, in *Our Martyr President, Abraham Lincoln: Voices from the Pulpit of New York and Brooklyn* (New York: Tibbals and Whiting, 1865), 202.

203. Lincoln to Weed, Washington, 15 Mar. 1865, *CWL*, 8:356.

204. A. B. Bradford to Simon Cameron, Enon Valley, Lawrence County, Pennsylvania, 8 Mar. 1865, Cameron Papers, DLC.

205. Journal of Richard Harvey Phelps in Kenneth H. Bernard, "Lincoln and the Civil War as Viewed by a Dissenting Yankee of Connecticut," *Lincoln Herald* 76 (1974):213.

206. New York *Herald* in Ronald C. White, *Lincoln's Greatest Speech: The Second Inaugural* (New York: Simon and Schuster, 2002), 190.

207. Chicago *Times*, 6 Mar. 1865.

208. White, *Lincoln's Greatest Speech*, 194, 191.

209. New York *World*, 6 Mar. 1865.

210. New York *Times*, 6 Mar. 1865.

211. Nevins, *War for the Union*, 4:218–219.

212. Charles Francis Adams, Jr., to Charles Francis Adams, Newport, Rhode Island, 7 Mar. 1865, in Worthington C. Ford, ed., *A Cycle of Adams Letters, 1861–1865* (2 vols.; Boston: Houghton Mifflin, 1920), 2:257–258.

213. James R. Doolittle to his brother, 4 Mar. 1865, James R. Doolittle Papers, State Historical Society of Wisconsin.

214. Duke of Argyll to Sumner, 5 Apr. 1865, Massachusetts Historical Society, *Proceedings*, 47 (1913):87.

215. London *Saturday Review*, in *Little's Living Age*, 85 (April–June 1865), 87.

216. London *Spectator*, 25 Mar. 1865.

217. James Grant Wilson, "Recollections of Lincoln," *Putnam's Monthly* 5 (Feb. 1909): 675.

218. *The Liberator* (Boston), 13 Jan. 1865.

219. Ibid., 22 July 1864.

220. Burlingame and Ettlinger, eds., *Hay Diary*, 253–254 (entry for 18 Dec. 1864).

221. Elizabeth Cady Stanton to Susan B. Anthony, New York, 29 Dec. 1864, in *Elizabeth Cady Stanton as Revealed in Her Letters, Diary and Reminiscences*, ed. Theodore Stanton and Harriot Stanton Blatch (2 vols.; New York: Harper and Brothers, 1922), 2:104.

222. Herman Belz, *Reconstructing the Union: Theory and Policy during the Civil War* (Ithaca, NY: Cornell University Press, 1969), 257.

223. Washington correspondence, 12 Apr., Sacramento *Daily Union*, 8 May 1865, in Burlingame, ed., *Lincoln Observed*, 184.

224. *Congressional Globe*, 38th Congress, 2nd Session, 300 (17 Jan. 1865).

225. Washington correspondence, 12 Apr., Sacramento *Daily Union*, 8 May 1865, in Burlingame, ed., *Lincoln Observed*, 184.

226. Ashley to the Boston *Commonwealth*, issue of 4 Mar. 1865.

227. Lincoln to Trumbull, Washington, 9 Jan. 1865, *CWL*, 8:207.

228. Belz, *Reconstructing the Union*, 270.

229. *Congressional Globe*, 38th Congress, 2nd Session, 1129 (27 Feb. 1865).

230. Dana to Charles Francis Adams, Cambridge, 3 Mar. 1865, Adams Papers, MHi.

231. Springfield, Massachusetts, *Republican*, quoted in the Boston *Commonwealth*, 18 Mar. 1865.

232. Samuel Bowles to Maria Whitney, Springfield, 12 Mar. 1865, in George S. Merriam, *The Life and Times of Samuel Bowles* (2 vols.; New York: Century, 1885), 1:419.

233. Nicolay, memorandum, 18 Jan. 1865, in Burlingame, ed., *With Lincoln in the White House*, 171.

234. Crook, "Lincoln as I Knew Him," *Harper's Magazine*, 115 (June 1907):45.

235. Lincoln to Hurlbut, Washington, 14 Nov. 1864, *CWL*, 8:106–107.

236. Hurlbut to Lincoln, New Orleans, 29 Nov. 1864, AL MSS DLC.

237. LaWanda Cox, *Lincoln and Black Freedom: A Study in Presidential Leadership* (Columbia: University of South Carolina Press, 1981), 117.

238. Kelley to S.N.T., n.p., n.d., *New Orleans Tribune*, 23 May 1865, ibid., 118.

239. Brown to the editor of the *Missouri Democrat*, 22 Dec. 1864, ibid., 129.

240. *Congressional Globe*, 38th Congress, 2nd Session, 300 (17 Jan. 1865).

241. James M. McPherson, *The Struggle for Equality: Abolitionists and the Negro in the Civil War and Reconstruction* (Princeton, NJ: Princeton University Press, 1964), 310–311.

242. Chicago *Tribune*, 22 Mar. 1865.

243. Beale, ed., *Welles Diary*, 2:264 (entry for 23 Mar. 1865).

244. New York *Evening Express*, 12 Jan. 1863.

245. John S. Barnes, "With Lincoln from Washington to Richmond in 1865," *Appleton's Magazine* 9 (May 1907): 517.

246. Ibid., 517, 520.

247. Adam Badeau, *Grant in Peace, from Appomattox to Mount McGregor: A Personal Memoir* (Hartford, CT: S. S. Scranton, 1887), 362.

248. Ibid., 360.

249. Sylvanus Cadwallader, *Three Years with Grant*, ed. Benjamin P. Thomas (New York: Alfred A. Knopf, 1955), 282.

250. Septima Collis, *A Woman's War Record, 1861–1865* (New York: G. P. Putnam's Sons, 1889), 60.

251. Barnes, "With Lincoln," 522.

252. Horace Porter, *Campaigning with Grant* (New York: Century, 1897), 407–408, 410.

253. Badeau, *Grant in Peace*, 358–360; Barnes, "With Lincoln," 524.

254. Schurz, manuscript of *Reminiscences*, Schurz Papers, DLC. This passage does not appear in the published version of the memoirs.

255. Ellery Sedgwick, *The Happy Profession* (Boston: Little, Brown, 1946), 163.

256. Carl Schurz, interview with Ida Tarbell, 6 Nov. 1897, Tarbell Papers, Allegheny College.

257. Reminiscences of Congressman Augustus Brandagee in the New London, Connecticut, *Day*, 8 Feb. 1894.

258. Reminiscences of Schuyler Hamilton, New York *Tribune*, 24 Mar. 1889.

259. Keckley, *Behind the Scenes*, 124–126.

260. Nicolay to Hay, Washington, 18, 29 Jan. 1864, Burlingame, ed., *At Lincoln's Side*, 124, 125.

261. "Presidential Domestic Squabbles," Washington correspondence, n.d., Rochester *Union*, n.d., unidentified clipping, Lincoln scrapbooks, 5:44, Judd Stewart Papers, CSmH.

262. Keckley, *Behind the Scenes*, 144–145.

263. Multonomah, Oregon, Bar Association, *In Memoriam: The Honorable George H. Williams, 1823–1910* (Portland: Multonomah Bar Association, 1910), 23.

264. Carl Sandburg and Paul M. Angle, *Mary Lincoln: Wife and Widow* (New York: Harcourt, Brace, 1932), 112.

265. Keckley, *Behind the Scenes*, 146, 147.

266. Mary Lincoln to Josiah G. Holland, Chicago, 4 Dec. 1865, in Justin G. Turner and Linda Levitt Turner, eds., *Mary Todd Lincoln: Her Life and Letters* (New York: Alfred A. Knopf, 1972), 293.

267. Lyman to his wife, 26 Mar. 1865, in George R. Agassiz, ed., *Meade's Headquarters, 1863–1865: Letters of Colonel Theodore Lyman from the Wilderness to Appomattox* (Boston: Atlantic Monthly Press, 1922), 325.

268. Sherman to G. P. A. Healey, Washington, 13 Jan. 1868, West Point Library (courtesy of Susan Lintelmann, curator of manuscripts).

269. Porter, *Campaigning with Grant*, 423–424; Sherman to G. P. A. Healey, Washington, 13 Jan. 1868, West Point Library (courtesy of Susan Lintelmann, curator of manuscripts); Sherman to Isaac Arnold, 28 Nov. 1872, Arnold Papers, ICHi; Sherman to John W. Draper, St. Louis, 27 Nov. 1868, Draper Papers, DLC; "Admiral Porter's Account of the Interview with Mr. Lincoln," 1866, in William T. Sherman, *Memoirs of Gen. W. T. Sherman* (2 vols.; New York: C. L. Webster, 1891–1892), 2:325–327.

270. Charles Carleton Coffin in Rice, *Reminiscences of Lincoln*, 176–177; Coffin, *Abraham Lincoln* (New York: Harper & Brothers, 1893), 193.

271. Porter, *Campaigning with Grant*, 424–426.

272. Collis, *A Woman's War Record*, 61–62.

273. Frank Rauscher, *Music on the March, 1826–'65: With the Army of the Potomac* (Philadelphia: W. F. Fell, 1892), 226.

274. Cadwallader, *Three Years with Grant*, 307.

275. *CWL*, 8:383.

276. William Burnett Wright, article in the *Congregationalist* 40, no. 22, in Coffin, *Lincoln*, 501.

277. Porter, *Campaigning with Grant*, 450–451.

278. Porter, "Journal of Occurrences during the War of the Rebellion," 2:48, Porter Papers, DLC.

279. Porter, *Incidents and Anecdotes*, 292–293.

280. Ibid., 294.

281. Ibid., 294–295.

282. Charles Carleton Coffin, *The Boys of '61, or Four Years of Fighting* (Boston: Estes and Lauriat, 1886), 511; Coffin, "Late Scenes in Richmond," *Atlantic Monthly*, June 1865, 754; Coffin, *Lincoln*, 193; Coffin in the Boston *Journal*, Herbert Mitgang, ed., *Abraham Lincoln: A Press Portrait* (Chicago: Quadrangle Press, 1971), 453–454.

283. Dispatch datelined Richmond, 6 Apr. 1865, in R. J. M. Blackett, ed., *Thomas Morris Chester, Black Civil War Correspondent: His Dispatches from the Virginia Front* (Baton Rouge: Louisiana State University Press, 1989), 294.

284. Porter, *Incidents and Anecdotes*, 295.

285. Coffin in Rice, ed., *Reminiscences of Lincoln*, 182.

286. Coffin, "Late Scenes in Richmond," *Atlantic Monthly*, June 1865, 755.

287. Porter, *Incidents and Anecdotes*, 300–301.

288. Barnes, "With Lincoln," 749.

289. Coffin in Rice, ed., *Reminiscences of Lincoln*, 183.

290. Weitzel, "The Fall of Richmond," Philadelphia *Times*, in Peter Cozzens and Robert I. Girardi, eds., *New Annals of the Civil War* (Mechanicsburg, PA.: Stackpole Books, 2004), 519.

291. Dispatch datelined Richmond, 6 Apr. 1865, in Blackett, ed., *Thomas Morris Chester*, 295.

292. Diary of Mrs. Thomas Walker Doswell (Mrs. Francis Anne Sutton), entry for 4 Apr. 1865, library.thinkquest.org/J0113361/diary.htm.

293. Samuel Henry Roberts to Harvey Robert, Headquarters of the 3rd brigade, 2nd division, 24th Army Corps, Richmond, 16 Apr. 1865, photocopy in the S. H. Roberts Papers, Virginia Historical Society.

294. Shepley, "Incidents of the Capture of Richmond," *Atlantic Monthly*, July 1880, 28.

295. Sara Agnes Pryor, letter of 5 Apr. 1865, in Pryor, *Reminiscences*, 357.

296. Porter, *Incidents and Anecdotes*, 297–298. Some sources suggest that he did not address the

crowd, but Lelian Cook, a 17-year-old girl living at the home of the Rev. Mr. Moses D. Hoge, recorded in her diary for 4 Apr. 1865 that after visiting Jefferson Davis's residence, "Lincoln appeared on the square, accompanied by an escort of colored troops. He was in a carriage-and-four. I heard he made an address to the colored people, telling them they were free, and had no master now but God." Richmond *News Leader,* 3 Apr. 1935, p. 2. Porter's version sounds like Lincoln's address to blacks who called at the White House in November 1864.

297. Blackett, ed., *Thomas Morris Chester,* 297.

298. Otto Eisenschiml, ed., *Vermont General: The Unusual War Experiences of Edward Hastings Ripley, 1862–1865* (New York: Devin-Adair, 1960), 307–308.

299. Chapman, *Latest Light on Lincoln,* 2:500.

300. *CWL,* 8:386–387; Myers, manuscript memoranda, Virginia Historical Society; Campbell to James S. Speed, 31 Aug. 1865, *Southern Historical Society Papers,* new series, 4:68–69; Richmond correspondence, n.d., New York *Herald,* n.d., copied in the Chicago *Tribune,* 12 July 1865.

301. Washington correspondence, 20 Apr., New York *Tribune,* n.d., copied in the Chicago *Tribune,* 26 Apr. 1865.

302. Thomas Thatcher Graves in *Battles and Leaders of the Civil War,* ed. Robert Underwood Johnson and Clarence Clough Buel (4 vols.; New York: Century, 1887–1888), 4:728.

303. Shepley, "Incidents of the Capture of Richmond," 27.

304. *CWL,* 8:389.

305. Charles H. Ambler, *Francis H. Pierpont: Union War Governor of Virginia and Father of West Virginia* (Chapel Hill: University of North Carolina Press, 1937), 256–257.

306. Frank Abial Flower, *Edwin McMasters Stanton: The Autocrat of Rebellion, Emancipation, and Reconstruction* (New York: W. W. Wilson, 1905), 271.

307. Hans L. Trefousse, *Benjamin Franklin Wade: Radical Republican from Ohio* (New York: Twayne, 1963), 246.

308. Ibid.

309. Beale, ed., *Welles Diary,* 2:279–280 (entry for 13 Apr. 1865).

310. Dana to Stanton, Richmond, 7 Apr. 1865, *OR,* I, 46, 3:619.

311. *CWL,* 8:388.

312. Beale, ed., *Welles Diary,* 2:222 (entry for 6 Jan. 1865).

313. Collis, *A Woman's War Record,* 62–69.

314. Benson Lossing, diary fragment, 25 Apr. 1865, University of Virginia.

315. Chambrun, "Personal Recollections of Mr. Lincoln," *Scribner's Magazine,* Jan. 1893: 28.

316. Benson Lossing, diary fragment, 25 Apr. 1865, University of Virginia.

317. *CWL,* 8:392.

318. Chambrun, "Personal Recollections of Mr. Lincoln," 29.

319. Nellie Hancock to Cornelia Hancock, [City Point], 11 Apr. 1865, in Henrietta Stratton Jaquette, ed., *South after Gettysburg: Letters of Cornelia Hancock from the Army of the Potomac, 1863–1865* (Philadelphia: University of Pennsylvania Press, 1937), 170.

320. Emil and Ruth Rosenblatt, eds., *Hard Marching Every Day: The Civil War Letters of Private Wilbur Fisk, 1861–1865* (Lawrence: University Press of Kansas, 1992), 322–323 (dispatches dated 6th Corps Hospital, City Point, 9, 20 Apr. 1865).

321. Adelaide W. Smith, *Reminiscences of an Army Nurse during the Civil War* (New York: Greaves, 1911), 224.

322. Nellie Hancock to Cornelia Hancock, [City Point], 11 Apr. 1865, in Jaquette, ed., *South after Gettysburg,* 170.

323. Chambrun, "Personal Recollections of Mr. Lincoln," 32–34.

Chapter 36. "I Feel a Presentiment That I Shall Not Outlast the Rebellion"

1. Boston *Evening Journal,* n.d., copied in the Springfield, Massachusetts, *Republican,* 18 Apr. 1865.

2. Stowe, *Men of Our Times* (Hartford, CT: Hartford Publishing Co., 1868), 73.

3. Francis B. Carpenter, *The Inner Life of Abraham Lincoln: Six Months at the White House* (New York: Hurd and Houghton, 1867), 17.

4. Elizabeth Keckley, *Behind the Scenes* (New York: G. W. Carleton, 1868), 166–167.

5. Evidently a summary of a letter by Mary Harlan Lincoln, in William H. Slade, "Abraham Lincoln's Shakespeare," typescript, J. G. Randall Papers, Library of Congress.

6. Chambrun, "Personal Recollections of Mr. Lincoln," *Scribner's Magazine*, January 1893, 35.

7. Stuart interviewed by Nicolay, Springfield, 24 June 1875, in Michael Burlingame, ed., *An Oral History of Abraham Lincoln: John G. Nicolay's Interviews and Essays* (Carbondale: Southern Illinois University Press, 1996), 14.

8. Sumner to Frank Bird, 16 April 1871, in Beverly Wilson Palmer, ed., *The Selected Letters of Charles Sumner* (2 vols.; Boston: Northeastern University Press, 1990), 2:549.

9. Chambrun, "Personal Recollections of Mr. Lincoln," 35.

10. B. F. Morris, comp., *Memorial Record of the Nation's Tribute to Abraham Lincoln* (Washington, DC: W. H. & O. H. Morrison, 1865), 13.

11. Recollections of Pierpont, typescript, Pierpont Papers, West Virginia University.

12. Washington *Daily Morning Chronicle*, 4 Apr. 1865.

13. Washington correspondence, 25 Apr., St. Cloud *Democrat*, 4 May 1865, in Arthur J. Larsen, ed., *Crusader and Feminist: Letters of Jane Grey Swisshelm, 1858–1865* (Saint Paul: Minnesota Historical Society, 1934), 292.

14. Chase to Lincoln, Washington, 4 Apr. 1865, AL MSS DLC.

15. Roy P. Basler et al., eds., *Collected Works of Abraham Lincoln* [hereafter *CWL*] (8 vols. plus index; New Brunswick, NJ: Rutgers University Press, 1953–1955), 8:393.

16. Noah Brooks, *Statesmen* (New York: C. Scribner's Sons, 1893), 214.

17. Keckley, *Behind the Scenes*, 176.

18. Brooks, *Statesmen* 214.

19. Brooks, "Some Reminiscences of Abraham Lincoln," *Scribner's Monthly* 15 (1878): 567.

20. Boston *Daily Advertiser*, 7 Oct. 1867.

21. Manuscript of a speech, [ca. Dec. 1865], Douglass Papers, DLC.

22. Michael W. Kauffman, *American Brutus: John Wilkes Booth and the Lincoln Conspiracies* (New York: Random House, 2004), 210.

23. Lewis Powell told this to Thomas T. Eckert. "Impeachment of the President," House Report no. 7, 40th Congress, 1st Session (1867): 674.

24. Eaton to Lincoln, 13 June 1864, in LaWanda Cox, *Lincoln and Black Freedom: A Study in Presidential Leadership* (Columbia: University of South Carolina Press, 1981), 29.

25. Charles H. Ambler, *Francis H. Pierpont: Union War Governor of Virginia and Father of West Virginia* (Chapel Hill: University of North Carolina Press, 1937), 254–258.

26. "Impeachment of the President," 401, 403–404.

27. *CWL*, 8:399–405.

28. John Niven, ed., *The Salmon P. Chase Papers* (5 vols.; Kent, OH: Kent State University Press, 1993–1998), 1:530 (diary entry for 15 Apr. 1865); Howard K. Beale and Alan W. Brownsword, eds., *Diary of Gideon Welles, Secretary of the Navy under Lincoln and Johnson* (3 vols.; New York: W. W. Norton, 1960), 2:279–280 (entry for 13 Apr. 1865).

29. Colfax to Isaac Arnold, 1 May 1867, in Fehrenbacher and Fehrenbacher, eds., *Recollected Words of Lincoln*, 114.

30. Niven, ed., *Chase Papers*, 1:530 (diary entry for 15 Apr. 1865).

31. Douglass, draft of a speech, ca. Dec. 1865, Douglass Papers, DLC.

32. Welles, "Lincoln and Johnson: Their Plan of Reconstruction and the Resumption of National Authority," *Galaxy* 13 (Apr. 1872): 522.

33. Frederick W. Seward, *Reminiscences of a War-Time Statesman and Diplomat, 1830–1915* (New York: G. P. Putnam's Sons, 1916), 255.

34. Chambrun. "Personal Recollections," 33; Lloyd Lewis, *Myths after Lincoln* (New York: Harcourt, Brace, 1929), 38–39.

35. Charles A. Dana, *Recollections of the Civil War: With the Leaders at Washington and*

in the Field in the Sixties (New York: D. Appleton, 1898), 274.

36. Colfax to Isaac Arnold, 1 May 1867, in Fehrenbacher and Fehrenbacher, eds., *Recollected Words of Lincoln,* 114.

37. Washington correspondence, 12 Apr., Sacramento *Daily Union,* 8 May 1865, Michael Burlingame, ed., *Lincoln Observed: Civil War Dispatches of Noah Brooks* (Baltimore, MD: Johns Hopkins University Press, 1998), 185.

38. Welles, "Lincoln and Johnson," 526.

39. Stanton to John A. Dix, Washington, 15 Apr. 1865, and Stanton to Charles Francis Adams, Washington, 15 Apr. 1865, *OR,* I, 46, 3:780, 785.

40. David Homer Bates, "Lincoln and Charles A. Dana," in William Hayes Ward, ed., *Abraham Lincoln: Tributes from his Associates* (New York: T. Y. Crowell, 1895), 229.

41. Beale, ed., *Welles Diary,* 2:281 (entry for 14 Apr. 1865).

42. Welles quoted in *The Works of Charles Sumner* (15 vols.; Boston: Lee and Shepard, 1870–1883), 9:479.

43. Beale, ed., *Welles Diary,* 2:282 (entry for 14 Apr. 1865); Welles to Andrew Johnson, Hartford, 27 July 1869, Johnson Papers, DLC.

44. Seward, *Reminiscences of a War-Time Statesman,* 256.

45. Beale, ed., *Welles Diary,* 2:282–283 (entry for 14 Apr. 1865).

46. Stanton to John A. Dix, Washington, 15 Apr. 1865, *OR,* I, 46, 3:780; W. Emerson Reck, *A. Lincoln, His Last 24 Hours* (Jefferson, NC: McFarland, 1987), 40.

47. Stanton's reminiscences in a memorandum by Moorfield Storey, 2 Feb. 1868, in Storey, "Dickens, Stanton, Sumner, and Storey," *Atlantic Monthly* 145 (1930):464.

48. Seward, *Reminiscences of a War-Time Statesman,* 254.

49. Hugh McCulloch, *Men and Measures of Half of a Century: Sketches and Comments* (New York: Charles Scribner's Sons, 1888), 222.

50. Ida M. Tarbell, *The Life of Abraham Lincoln* (2 vols.; New York: McClure, Phillips, 1900), 2:232.

51. Mary Lincoln to Francis B. Carpenter, Chicago, 15 Nov. 1865, in Turner and Turner, eds., *Mary Todd Lincoln,* 284–285.

52. Hamilton Fish diary, entry for 12 Nov. 1869, Fish Papers, DLC.

53. Reminiscences of Susan Man McCulloch, privately owned, in Benjamin P. Thomas and Harold M. Hyman, *Stanton: The Life and Times of Lincoln's Secretary of War* (New York: Alfred A. Knopf, 1962), 395.

54. Adam Badeau, *Grant in Peace, from Appomattox to Mount McGregor: A Personal Memoir* (Hartford: S. S. Scranton, 1887), 362.

55. Carpenter, *Inner Life of Lincoln,* 62–63.

56. Ibid., 65–67.

57. Brooks, *Washington, in Lincoln's Time,* 38.

58. Nicolay interview, Chicago *Herald,* 4 Dec. 1887; Leonard Swett, "Conspiracies of the Rebellion," *North American Review* (Feb. 1887):187.

59. J. H. Van Alen to the editors of the New York *Evening Post,* New York, 22 Apr., New York *Evening Post,* 11 May 1865.

60. Seward to John Bigelow, Washington, 15 July 1862, in Bigelow, *Retrospections of an Active Life* (5 vols.; New York: Baker & Taylor, 1909–1913), 2:548.

61. Carpenter, *Inner Life of Lincoln,* 67.

62. Michael Burlingame and John R. Turner Ettlinger, eds., *Inside Lincoln's White House: The Complete Civil War Diary of John Hay* (Carbondale: Southern Illinois University Press, 1997), 246 (entry for 8 Nov. 1864).

63. Dr. G. B. Todd to his brother, 30 Apr. 1865, in Timothy S. Good, ed., *We Saw Lincoln Shot: One Hundred Eyewitness Accounts* (Jackson: University Press of Mississippi, 1995), 71.

64. Osborn H. Oldroyd, ed, *Lincoln Memorial: Album-Immortelles* (New York; Carleton, 1882), 374–375.

65. Reck, *A. Lincoln: His Last 24 Hours,* 57.

66. Colfax, *Life and Principles of Abraham Lincoln: Address Delivered at the Court House Square, at South Bend, April 24, 1865* (Philadelphia: J. B. Rodgers, 1865), 10.

67. Mary Lincoln to J. B. Gould, Avignon, France, 22 Apr. 1880, in Justin G. Turner and Linda Levitt Turner, eds., *Mary Todd Lincoln: Her Life and Letters* (New York: Alfred A. Knopf, 1972), 697.

68. Dr. Charles A. Leale to Benjamin Butler, 20 July 1867, in Good, ed., *We Saw Lincoln Shot*, 60.

69. Asia Booth Clarke, *The Unlocked Book: A Memoir of John Wilkes Booth by His Sister* (New York: G. P. Putnam's Sons, 1938), 139.

70. James Tanner to Henry F. Walch, Washington, 17 Apr. 1865, William L. Clements Library, University of Michigan.

71. Langdon interview with George Alfred Townsend, 1883, in Terry Alford, "Why Booth Shot Lincoln," in Charles M. Hubbard, ed., *Lincoln and His Contemporaries* (Macon, GA: Mercer University Press, 1999), 133.

72. John Deery, co-proprietor of a billiard parlor frequented by Booth, New York *Sunday Telegraph*, 23 May 1909.

73. Alfred W. Smiley in an interview with Louis J. Mackey, 1894, in Ernest C. Mitchell, *John Wilkes Booth in the Pennsylvania Oil Region* (Meadville, PA: Crawford County Historical Society, 1987), 72.

74. Booth to Mary Ann Holmes Booth, [Philadelphia, Nov. 1864], in John Rhodehamel, ed., *Right or Wrong, God Judge Me: The Writings of John Wilkes Booth* (Urbana: University of Illinois Press, 1997), 130.

75. Clarke, *Unlocked Book*, 115.

76. Harry Ford in Kauffman, *American Brutus*, 218.

77. James Lawson, the barber, interviewed in 1894 by Louis J. Mackey, in Miller, *Booth in the Pennsylvania Oil Region*, 70.

78. Rhodehamel, ed., *Right or Wrong, God Judge Me*, 125.

79. Ibid., 62–64, 56–58.

80. Booth to the editors of the Washington *National Intelligencer*, Washington, 14 Apr. 1865, ibid., 149.

81. Clarke, *Unlocked Book*, 124–125.

82. Edwin Booth to Nahum Capen, Windsor Hotel, 28 July 1881, ibid., 202–203.

83. Kauffman, *American Brutus*, 124.

84. New York *Copperhead*, 11 July 1863, in George S. Bryan, *Great American Myth* (New York: Carrick & Evans, 1940), 39.

85. New York *Herald*, 19 May 1863, in Kauffman, *American Brutus*, 200.

86. Ibid., 121.

87. Baltimore *South*, 7 June 1861, in Bryan, *Great American Myth*, 391.

88. Cheesebrough, *No Sorrow Like Our Sorrow*, 42–43.

89. San Francisco *Daily Dramatic Chronicle*, 17 Apr. 1865, in Kauffman, *American Brutus*, 80.

90. Clarke, *Unlocked Book*, 124–125, 63–65, 124.

91. Draft of an undelivered speech, Philadelphia, late Dec. 1860; Booth "to whom it may concern," [Philadelphia, Nov. 1864], Rhodehamel, ed., *Right or Wrong, God Judge Me*, 59–60, 126.

92. Clarke, *Unlocked Book*, 115.

93. Rhodehamel, ed., *Right or Wrong, God Judge Me*, 130–131.

94. Ann Hartley Gilbert, *The Stage Reminiscences of Mrs. Gilbert*, ed. Charlotte M. Martin (New York: Charles Scribner's Sons, 1901), 57–58.

95. Letter of 28 Mar. 1865 in Kauffman, *American Brutus*, 199.

96. Edwin Booth to Nahum Capen, Windsor Hotel, 28 July 1881, in Clarke, *Unlocked Book*, 203.

97. Clarke, *Unlocked Book*, 152, 155–158.

98. Stanley Kimmel, *The Mad Booths of Maryland* (Indianapolis, IN: Bobbs-Merrill, 1940), 150, 175.

99. Samuel Knapp Chester testimony, 12 May 1865, Benn Pitman, comp., *The Assassination of President Lincoln and the Trial of the Conspirators David E. Herold, Mary E. Surratt, Lewis Payne, George A. Atzerodt, Edward Spangler, Samuel A. Mudd, Samuel Arnold, Michael O'Laughlin* (Cincinnati: Moore, Wilstach & Baldwin, 1865), 45.

100. Kaufmann, *American Brutus*, 205.

101. *Richard III*, act 3, scene 1; New York *World*, 25 Apr. 1865, in Kaufmann, *American Brutus*, 245.

102. New York *Clipper*, 29 Apr. 1865, in Alford, "Why Booth Shot Lincoln," 132.

103. Kimmel, *The Mad Booths*, 219.

104. Booth's diary, Rhodehamel, *Right or Wrong, God Judge Me*, 154–155.

105. Kimmel, *Mad Booths*, 249.

106. Edwin Booth to Nahum Capen, Windsor Hotel, 28 July 1881, in Clarke, *Unlocked Book*, 202–203.

107. John Deery, co-proprietor of a billiard parlor frequented by Booth, New York *Sunday Telegraph*, 23 May 1909.

108. Stephen M. Archer, *Junius Brutus Booth: Theatrical Prometheus* (Carbondale: Southern Illinois University Press, 1992), 114.

109. Kauffman, *American Brutus*, 84.

110. Archer, *Junius Brutus Booth*, 137, 136.

111. Ibid., 323.

112. Rhodehamel, ed., *Right or Wrong, God Judge Me*, 154.

113. Alfred W. Smiley in an interview with Louis J. Mackey, 1894; James Lawson in an interview with Louis J. Mackey, 1894, in Mitchell, *Booth in the Pennsylvania Oil Region*, 72–73, 70.

114. Good, ed., *We Saw Lincoln*, 21.

115. Clarke, *Unlocked Book*, 107–108, 140, 124, 59–60.

116. Horatio Nelson Taft diary, 30 Apr. 1865, DLC.

117. George Francis to his niece Josephine, Washington, 5 May 1865, Lincoln Collection, ICHi.

118. John Palmer Usher to his wife, Washington, 15 Apr. 1865, copy, Usher Papers, DLC.

119. Horatio Nelson Taft diary, 30 Apr. 1865, DLC.

120. Thomas F. Pendel, *Thirty-Six Years in the White House* (Washington, DC: Neale Publishing Company, 1902), 44.

121. Reck, *A. Lincoln: His Last 24 Hours*, 139.

122. Clara Harris to "My dear Mary," 25 Apr. 1865, Ira Harris Papers, New-York Historical Society, in Kauffman, *American Brutus*, 37–38.

123. Maunsell B. Field, *Memories of Many Men and of Some Women: Being Personal Recollections of Emperors, Kings, Queens, Princes, Presidents, Statesmen, Authors, and Artists, at Home and Abroad, during the Last Thirty Years* (New York: Harper, 1874), 322.

124. Charles S. Taft, "Abraham Lincoln's Last Hours," *Century Magazine*, Feb. 1893, 635.

125. Stanton's reminiscences in a memorandum by Moorfield Storey, 2 Feb. 1868, in Storey, "Dickens, Stanton, Sumner, and Storey," 463.

126. Charles A. Leale, "Lincoln's Last Hours" (pamphlet New York: n. p., 1909), 11.

127. James Tanner to Henry F. Walch, Washington, 17 Apr. 1865, William L. Clements Library, University of Michigan.

128. There are variations on this wording, but Stanton said either this or something very similar according to people present, including John Hay, James Tanner, and Charles Taft. Bryan, *Great American Myth*, 189.

129. Horatio Nelson Taft diary, 30 Apr. 1865, DLC.

130. Field, *Memories of Many Men*, 326.

131. Horatio Nelson Taft diary, 30 Apr. 1865, DLC.

132. Beale, ed., *Welles Diary*, 2:290 (entry for 15 Apr. 1865); Keckley, *Behind the Scenes*, 192, 196.

133. Carpenter, *Inner Life of Lincoln*, 293.

134. Beale, ed., *Welles Diary*, 2:290 (entry for 15 Apr. 1865).

135. Washington correspondence, 17 Apr., St. Cloud *Democrat*, 27 Apr. 1865, Larsen, ed., *Crusader and Feminist*, 287–288.

136. William T. Coggeshall, *Lincoln Memorial: The Journeys of Abraham Lincoln from Springfield to Washington, 1861, as President Elect, and from Washington to Springfield, 1865, as President Martyred* (Columbus: Ohio State Journal, 1865), 127.

137. Beale, ed., *Welles Diary*, 2:293 (entry for 19 Apr. 1865).

138. B.F. Winslow to his grandfather, Washington, 18 Apr. 1865, S. Griswold Flagg Collection, Yale University; Carpenter, *Inner Life of Lincoln*, 207–208.

139. George W. Julian, "George W. Julian's Journal—The Assassination of Lincoln,"

Indiana Magazine of History 11 (1915):335; George W. Julian, *Political Recollections, 1840 to 1872* (Chicago: Jansen, McClurg, 1884), 255.

140. Chandler to his wife, Washington, 23 Apr. 1865, Chandler Papers, DLC.

141. Julian, *Political Recollections*, 257.

142. Undated manuscript in the Henry L. Dawes Papers, "The Reconstruction Period, 1865–1869," in William C. Harris, *Lincoln's Last Months* (Cambridge, MA: Belknap Press of Harvard University Press, 2004), 227.

143. Davis to Samuel F. Du Pont, n.p., 22 Apr. 1865, transcript, S. F. Du Pont Papers, Hagley Museum, Wilmington, Delaware.

144. Washington correspondence, 17, 25 Apr., St. Cloud *Democrat*, 27 Apr., 4 May 1865, Larsen, ed., *Crusader and Feminist*, 288, 290.

145. William Lloyd Garrison, Jr., to Martha Wright, 16 Apr. 1865, Garrison Papers, Smith College, in James M. McPherson, *The Struggle for Equality: Abolitionists and the Negro in the Civil War and Reconstruction* (Princeton, NJ: Princeton University Press, 1964), 314.

146. Debby Applegate, *The Most Famous Man in America: The Biography of Henry Ward Beecher* (New York: Doubleday, 2006), 357.

147. David B. Chesebrough, *No Sorrow Like Our Sorrow: Northern Protestant Ministers and the Assassination of Lincoln* (Kent, OH: Kent State University Press, 1994), 69.

148. T. H. Barr, *A Discourse, Delivered by the Rev. T. H. Barr, at Canaan Center, April 19, 1865, on the Occasion of the Funeral Obsequies of Our Late President, Abraham Lincoln* (Wooster, Ohio: Republican Steam Power Press, 1865), 10; Francis Le Baron Robbins, *A Discourse on the Death of Abraham Lincoln* (Philadelphia: H. B. Ashmead, 1865), 13; Gordon Hall, *President Lincoln's Death: Its Voice to the People* (Northampton, MA: Trumbull & Gere, 1865), 10.

149. Coggeshall, *Lincoln Memorial*, 133.

150. Theodore Calvin Pease and James G. Randall, eds., *The Diary of Orville Hickman Browning* (2 vols.; Springfield: Illinois State Historical Library, 1925–1933), 2:22 (entry for 17 Apr. 1865).

151. Shelby M. Cullom, *Fifty Years of Public Service: Personal Recollections* (Chicago: McClurg, 1911), 107.

152. Philadelphia *Inquirer*, 24 April 1865, in Coggeshall, *Lincoln Memorial*, 149–150, 156.

153. Baltimore *Sun*, 22 April 1865, in Victor Searcher, *Farewell to Lincoln* (New York: Abingdon Press, 1965), 99.

154. New York *Evening Post*, 26 Apr. 1865.

155. Isaac N. Arnold, *The Life of Abraham Lincoln* (Chicago: Jansen, McClurg, 1885), 437.

156. Coggeshall, *Lincoln Memorial*, 265, 222.

157. New York *Evening Post*, 24 Apr. 1865.

158. J. Sella Martin to the editors of the New York *Evening Post*, New York, 24 Apr., New York *Evening Post*, 24 Apr. 1865.

159. Searcher, *Farewell to Lincoln*, 139.

160. Ibid., 140.

161. New York *Tribune*, 25 Apr. 1865.

162. Coggeshall, *Lincoln Memorial*, 199.

163. Cullom, *Fifty Years of Public Service*, 107.

164. John Carroll Power, *Abraham Lincoln* (Springfield, IL: E. A. Wilson, 1875), 197–198.

165. Chicago *Tribune*, 3 May 1865.

166. *Our Martyr President*, 394, 401.

167. Keckley, *Behind the Scenes*, 199.

168. Mark A. Plummer, *Lincoln's Rail-Splitter: Governor Richard J. Oglesby* (Urbana: University of Illinois Press, 2001), 110.

169. Robert Todd Lincoln to Oglesby, Washington, 1 May 1865, Robert Todd Lincoln Papers, IHi (courtesy of Jason Emerson).

170. H. P. H. Bromwell to his parents, Springfield, 30 Apr. 1865, in Harry E. Pratt, ed., *Concerning Mr. Lincoln: In Which Abraham Lincoln Is Pictured as He Appeared to Letter Writers of His Time* (Springfield, IL: Abraham Lincoln Association, 1944), 129.

171. Sarah Sleeper to her mother, Springfield, June, 1865 (no day of the month indicated), Sleeper Papers, Small Collection 1405, IHi.

172. Gurley to E. Darwin Brooks, Washington, 22 May 1865, Gurley Papers, DLC.

173. Keckley, *Behind the Scenes*, 200.

174. Mary Lincoln to Elizabeth Todd Grimsley, Washington, 29 Sept. 1861, Turner and Turner, eds., *Mary Todd Lincoln*, 105.

175. Ibid., 241–245.

176. Plummer, *Oglesby*, 112.

177. Bayly Ellen Marks and Mark Norton Schatz, eds., *Between North and South: A Maryland Journalist Views the Civil War: The Narrative of William Wilkins Glenn, 1861–1869* (Rutherford, NJ: Fairleigh Dickinson University Press, 1976), 296 (entry for 4 Oct. 1867).

178. Washington correspondence, 7 Jan., New York *Daily News*, 9 Jan. 1866.

179. Ibid.

180. Jefferson, Ohio, correspondence, Cincinnati *Commercial*, 2 Nov. 1867.

181. David Davis statement in the Orville Hickman Browning diary, 3 July 1873, IHi.

182. Ellery Sedgwick saw three such letters in the possession of W. K. Bixby of St. Louis, who refused to have them published. Ellery Sedgwick, *The Happy Profession* (Boston: Little, Brown, 1946), 163.

183. J. G. Holland, *Life of Abraham Lincoln* (Springfield, MA: G. Bill, 1866), 429.

184. *Sermons Preached in Boston on the Death of Abraham Lincoln, together with the Funeral Services in the East Room of the Executive Mansion at Washington* (Boston: J. E. Tilton, 1865), 96.

185. Elias Nason, *Eulogy on Abraham Lincoln, Late President of the United States: Delivered before the New England Historic-Genealogical Society, Boston, May 3, 1865* (Boston: W.V. Spencer, 1865), in Chesebrough, *No Sorrow Like Our Sorrow*, 6.

186. John E. Todd and Warren H. Cudworth in *Sermons Preached in Boston on the Death of Lincoln*, 82, 200.

187. George Dana Boardman, *Addresses, Delivered in the Meeting-House of the First Baptist Church of Philadelphia, April 14th, 16th, and 19th, 1865* (Philadelphia: Sherman, 1865), 52.

188. Richard Edwards, *The Life and Character of Abraham Lincoln: An Address Delivered at the Hall of the Normal University, April 19th, 1865* (Peoria, IL: N. C. Nason, 1865), 3.

189. Charles Carroll Everett, *A Sermon in Commeration of the Death of Abraham Lincoln, Late President of the United States* (Bangor: Benjamin A. Burr, 1865), 5, 21–22.

190. Isaac Eddy Carey, *Abraham Lincoln: The Value to the Nation of his Exalted Character, Rev. Mr. Carey's Fast Day Sermon, Preached June 1, 1865, in the First Presbyterian Church of Freeport, Ill.* ([Freeport? IL]: n.p., 1865), in Chesebrough, *No Sorrow Like Our Sorrow*, 7.

191. Unidentified clipping in Ford's Theatre archive, in Thomas Goodrich, *The Darkest Dawn: Lincoln, Booth, and the Great American Tragedy* (Bloomington: Indiana University Press, 2005), 237; sermon by William Ives Buddington, in *Our Martyr President, Abraham Lincoln: Voices from the Pulpit of New York and Brooklyn* (New York: Tibbals and Whiting, 1865), 111.

192. Sermon by Cuyler in *Our Martyr President*, 168, 171.

193. *Sermons Preached in Boston*, 348.

194. *A Tribute of Respect by the Citizens of Troy, to the Memory of Abraham Lincoln* (Troy, NY: Young & Benson, 1865), 154, 44–45.

195. Wallace Shelton, *Discourse upon the Death of Abraham Lincoln* (Newport, KY: W. S. Bailey, 1865), 4, in Chesebrough, *No Sorrow Like Our Sorrow*, 4, and Charles Joseph Stewart, "A Rhetorical Study of the Reaction of the Protestant Pulpit in the North to Lincoln's Assassination" (Ph.D. dissertation, University of Illinois, 1963), 112.

196. Douglass Papers, DLC.

197. Charles Richard Williams, *Diary and Letters of Rutherford Birchard Hayes* (5 vols.; Columbus, OH: Ohio State Archelogical and Historical Society, 1922–1926), 1:23.

198. William J. Potter, *The National Tragedy: Four Sermons Delivered before the First Congregational Society, New Bedford, on the Life and Death of Abraham Lincoln* (New Bedford, MA: A. Taber & Brother, 1865), 16.

199. Edward Searing, *President Lincoln in History: An Address Delivered in the Congregational Church, Milton, Wisconsin, on Fast Day,*

June 1st, 1865 (Janesville WI: Veeder & Devereux, 1865), 18–19.

200. Edwards, *Life and Character of Lincoln*, 19.

201. Joseph A. Prime, "Sermon Preached in the Liberty Street Presbyterian Church (Colored)," *A Tribute of Respect*, 154, 156.

202. Cuyler in *Our Martyr President*, 165.

203. Boardman in *Addresses Delivered in the Meeting-House of the First Baptist Church of Philadelphia*, 39.

204. Thomas M. Hopkins, *A Discourse on the Death of Abraham Lincoln, Delivered in the 1st Presbyterian Church in Bloomington, Indiana, April 19th, 1865* ([Bloomington?]: n.p., 1865), 5–6.

205. William C. Davis, *Lincoln's Men: How President Lincoln Became Father to an Army and a Nation* (New York: Free Press, 1999), 238–239.

206. James K. Newton to his parents, near Montgomery, Alabama, 7 May 1865, in Stephen E. Ambrose, ed., *A Wisconsin Boy in Dixie: The Selected Letters of James K. Newton* (Madison: University of Wisconsin Press, 1961), 152.

207. Captain John Henry Wilson, captain of the 1st Massachusetts Infantry, to his wife, Washington, 16 Apr. 1865, in Frederick C. Drake, "A Letter on the Death of Lincoln," *Lincoln Herald* 84 (1982):237.

208. Davis, *Lincoln's Men*, 226.

209. Charles Augustus Hill to his wife, 12 Dec. 1863; Lt. Warren Goodale to his children, 15 Apr. 1865, both in Joseph T. Glaathaar, *Forged in Battle: The Civil War Alliance of Black Soldiers and White Officers* (New York: Meridian, 1990), 208–209.

210. William O. Stoddard, *Abraham Lincoln: The True Story of a Great Life* (New York: Fords, Howard, & Hulbert, 1884), 359.

211. Stowe, *Men of Our Times*, 60; Henry C. Deming, *Eulogy of Abraham Lincoln* (Hartford: A. N. Clark, 1865), 25.

212. Curtis to Charles Eliot Norton, n.p., 15 Apr. 1865, Curtis Papers, Harvard University.

213. Parker Pillsbury to George B. Cheever, Concord, New Hampshire, 27 Apr. 1865,

Cheever Family Papers, American Antiquarian Society.

214. Morton Prince to Albert J. Beveridge, Nahant, Massachusetts, 13 Oct. 1925, Beveridge Papers, DLC.

215. Hay to William H. Herndon, Paris, 5 Sept. 1866, in Michael Burlingame, ed., *At Lincoln's Side: John Hay's Civil War Correspondence and Selected Writings* (Carbondale: Southern Illinois University Press, 2000), 111.

216. Leonard Swett to William Herndon, Chicago, 17 Jan. 1866, in Douglas L. Wilson and Rodney O. Davis, eds., *Herndon's Informants: Letters, Interviews, and Statements about Abraham Lincoln* (Urbana: University of Illinois Press, 1998), 165.

217. Merle d'Aubigne to George G. Fogg, Geneva, 27 Apr. 1865, New York *Evening Post*, 29 July 1865.

218. Goldwin Smith, *Macmillan's Magazine*, June 1865, copied in the New York *Evening Post*, 15 June 1865.

219. New York *World*, 7 Feb. 1909.

Note on Sources

1. William Allen White, *A Puritan in Babylon: The Story of Calvin Coolidge* (New York: Macmillan, 1938), vii.

2. [Ruth Painter Randall], "Sifting the Ann Rutledge Evidence," in J. G. Randall, *Lincoln the President: Springfield to Gettysburg* (2 vols.; New York: Dodd, Mead, 1945), 2:324–325. J. G. Randall told a friend that his wife "helped me handsomely with the Ann Rutledge chapter. It is very largely her work." Randall to Francis S. Ronalds, n.p., 3 February 1945, copy, Randall Papers, Library of Congress.

3. David Donald, *Lincoln's Herndon* (New York: Alfred A. Knopf, 1948), 195.

4. Douglas L. Wilson and Rodney O. Davis, eds., *Herndon's Informants: Letters, Interviews, and Statements about Abraham Lincoln* (Urbana: University of Illinois Press, 1998), 21–24.

5. See Rebecca Sharpless, "The History of Oral History," in Thomas L. Charlton, Lois E.

Myers, and Rebecca Sharpless, eds., *Handbook of Oral History* (Lanham, MD: Altamira Press, 2006), 19–42.

6. Douglas L. Wilson, *Lincoln before Washington: New Perspectives on the Illinois Years* (Urbana: University of Illinois Press, 1997), 91–92.

7. Ibid., x, 28.

8. Ibid., 32.

9. Albert J. Beveridge, "Lincoln as His Partner Knew Him," *Literary Digest International Book Review* 1 (September 1923): 33.

10. Beveridge to Nathaniel Wright Stephenson, Beverly Farms, Massachuestts, 18 December 1925, copy, Beveridge Papers, Library of Congress.

11. Don E. Fehrenbacher, *Lincoln in Text and Context: Collected Essays* (Stanford, CA: Stanford University Press, 1987), 277–278.

12. Ibid., 277–278, 281; Don E. Fehrenbacher and Virginia Fehrenbacher, eds., *Recollected Words of Abraham Lincoln* (Stanford, CA: Stanford University Press, 1996), xlvii–liv.

13. Donald A. Ritchie, *Doing Oral History* (New York: Twayne, 1995), 92.

INDEX

Entries for newspapers may appear under the newspaper's title or the place of publication.